AMERICAN and BRITISH POETRY

A Guide to the Criticism
1925–1978

compiled by

Harriet Semmes Alexander

SWALLOW PRESS
Athens, Ohio • London • Chicago

Swallow Press books are published by
Ohio University Press, Athens, Ohio 45701

Library of Congress Cataloging in Publication Data

Alexander, Harriet Semmes, 1949–
    American and British poetry.

1. American poetry—History and criticism—Bibliography.
2. English poetry—History and criticism—Bibliography.
I. Title
Z1231.P7A44   1984   [PS303]   821'.008   83-24114
ISBN 0-8040-0848-5

CONTENTS

Note

This bibliography was compiled to provide a listing of criticism not collected elsewhere, and to permit the user to see at a glance a survey of the criticism on a particular work over an extended period.

Because of the volume of publication in this area, the compiler set the following limitations in considering sources for inclusion.

1. Only criticism of poems of a thousand lines or less has been included.

2. Only criticism or explanations of the entire work was considered, except in cases where little information was available on a given poem or the criticism was particularly noteworthy. In these cases the designation (P) following the citation indicates partial explanation.

3. No criticism of less than four sentences has been included.

4. Because books on specific poets are readily accessible through other bibliographic tools, they were not included in the sources.

Each of the journals and books consulted was examined from cover to cover (with the exception of journal book reviews), and each article and book scanned for content. Fortunately, most of the material was available at the Memphis Public Library and at the Memphis State University Library, where my colleagues, particularly in the reference department, have assisted through their interest, encouragement and understanding. Three who have earned special gratitude — Janell Rudolph, Deborah Blackstone, and Angela Cody — helped by typing, filing, proofreading and checking citations.

I wish to thank George Hendrick and Donna Gerstenberger, who offered encouragement and suggestions for organizing this work. They helped to make this first effort as painless as such a major work can be.

I also wish to thank my family and friends for their understanding and support, and particularly my mother, who helped so much in the last few weeks of preparation of the final copy of the manuscript.

A

ABBE, GEORGE

"The Book"
> GEORGE ABBE. *You and Contemporary Poetry*, 1965 ed., pp. 123-29.

"The Garage"
> GEORGE ABBE. *You and Contemporary Poetry*, 1965 ed., pp. 117-19.

"Horizon Thing"
> GEORGE ABBE. *You and Contemporary Poetry*, 1965 ed., pp. 110-13.

"Traffic Quince"
> GEORGE ABBE. *You and Contemporary Poetry*, 1965 ed., pp. 72-73; pp. 97-98.

ABERCROMBIE, LASCELLES

"Sale of St. Thomas"
> "Henry Newbolt, 'Poetry and Drama,'" in *Georgian Poetry*, p. 95.

ACCONCI, VITO HANNIBAL

"RE"
> PETER D. HERTZ. "Minimal Poetry," *Western Humanities Review* 24(1), Winter 1970, 37-38.

ADAMS, HENRY

"As a musician who, in absent thought"
> STEPHEN MOONEY. "The Education of Henry Adams (Poet)," *Tennessee Studies in Literature* 6 (1961), 29-30.

"Buddha and Brahma"
> JOHN W. CROWLEY. "The Suicide of the Artist: Henry Adams' *Life of George Cabot Lodge*," *New England Quarterly* 46(2), June 1973, 199-200.
> STEPHEN MOONEY. "The Education of Henry Adams (Poet)," *Tennessee Studies in Literature* 6 (1961), 28-29.

"Here was the eagles' nest"
> STEPHEN MOONEY. "The Education of Henry Adams (Poet)," *Tennessee Studies in Literature* 6 (1961), 30.

"Prayer to the Virgin of Chartres"
> STEPHEN MOONEY. "The Education of Henry Adams (Poet)," *Tennessee Studies in Literature* 6 (1961), 26-28.

ADAMS, LEONIE

"Bird and Bosom — Apocalyptic"
> BABETTE DEUTSCH. *Poetry in Our Time*, pp. 237-38; second ed., pp. 263-64.

ADCOCK, FLEUR

"For Andrew"
> MARGARET BYERS. "Cautious Vision: Recent British Poetry by Women," in *British Poetry Since 1960*, p. 76.

"Unexpected Visit"
> MARGARET BYERS. "Cautious Vision: Recent British Poetry by Women," in *British Poetry Since 1960*, pp. 76-77.

ADDISON, JOSEPH

"Letter from Italy, to the Right Honourable Charles Lord Halifax"
> JAY ARNOLD LEVINE. "The Status of the Verse Epistle Before Pope," *Studies in Philology* 59(4), October 1962, 680-82.

AGEE, JAMES

"Pygmalion"
> VICTOR A. KRAMER. "Agee's Early Poem 'Pygmalion' and His Aesthetic," *Mississippi Quarterly* 29(2), Spring 1976, 191-96.

"Sunday: Outskirts of Knoxville, Tennessee"
> ELIZABETH DREW. *Poetry*, pp. 211-13.
> ELIZABETH DREW and JOHN L. SWEENEY. *Directions in Modern Poetry*, pp. 243-47.
> JAMES A. FREEMAN. "Agee's 'Sunday' Meditation," *Concerning Poetry* 3(2), Fall 1970, 37-39.

AIKEN, CONRAD

"The Crystal"
> JAMES DICKEY. *Babel to Byzantium*, pp. 86-89.
> JAMES DICKEY. "A Gold-Mine of Consciousness," *Poetry* 94(1), April 1959, 42-43.
> ROY HARVEY PEARCE. *The Continuity of American Poetry*, pp. 357-58.

"Dead Leaf in May"
> JAMES ZIGERELL. *Explicator* 25(1), September 1966, Item 5.

AIKEN, CONRAD *(Cont.)*

"Hallowe'en"

> ROY HARVEY PEARCE. *The Continuity of American Poetry*, pp. 356-57.

"Morning Song" (Senlin)

> HARRY BROWN and JOHN MILSTEAD. *What the Poem Means*, p. 1.
>
> JAMES M. REID. *100 American Poems of the Twentieth Century*, pp. 141-44.

"South End"

> JAMES M. REID. *100 American Poems of the Twentieth Century*, pp. 144-45.

"Sursum Corda"

> DONALD A. STAUFFER. "Genesis, or the Poet as Maker," in *Poets at Work*, pp. 72-76. Reprinted in: *Reading Modern Poetry*, first ed., pp. 240-41.

"Tetélestai"

> CALVIN S. BROWN. "The Achievement of Conrad Aiken," *Georgia Review* 27(4), Winter 1973, 486-87.
>
> REUEL DENNEY. "Conrad Aiken," in *Six American Poets from Emily Dickinson to the Present*, p. 156.

AKENSIDE, MARK

"Ode on the Winter Solstice"

> WILLIAM FROST. *English Masterpieces*, edited by William Frost, Maynard Mack, and Leonard Dean, vol. 6: *Romantic and Victorian Poetry*, pp. 3-4.

"Ode to the Evening Star"

> KARL KROEBER. *Romantic Narrative Art*, pp. 59-60.

ALDINGTON, RICHARD

"Daybreak"

> L. S. DEMBO. *Conceptions of Reality in Modern American Poetry*, pp. 20-21.

"The Walk"

> NORMAN T. GATES. "Richard Aldington and F. S. Flint: Poets' Dialogue," *Papers on Language and Literature* 8(1), Winter 1972, 63-69.

ALLING, KENNETH

"Dead Wasp"

> GEORGE ABBE. *You and Contemporary Poetry*, pp. 30-31; second ed., pp. 40-41.

ALLISON, DRUMMOND

"We Shall Have Company"

> IAN HAMILTON. "The Forties," in *A Poetry Chronicle*, pp. 76-77.

ALURISTA

"Address"

> CARLOTA CARDENAS DE DWYER. "Address by Alurista," *English Journal* 65(1), January 1976, 65-66.

AMES, RICHARD

"The Folly of Love"

> FELICITY NUSSBAUM. "Juvenal, Swift, and *The Folly of Love*," *Eighteenth Century Studies* 9(4), Summer 1976, 546-49.

AMIS, KINGSLEY

"A Dream of Fair Women"

> DAVID HOLBROOK. *Llareggub Revisited*, pp. 27-32.

"Masters"

> R. J. KAUFMANN. "A Poetry for Sisyphus," *Prairie Schooner* 40(1), Spring 1966, 26-27. (P)

"Nocturne"

> DAVID HOLBROOK. *Llareggub Revisited*, pp. 32-33.

"St. Asaphs"

> DAVID HOLBROOK. *Lost Bearings in English Poetry*, pp. 185-86.

AMMONS, A. R.

"The Arc Inside and Out"

> HAROLD BLOOM. "The New Transcendentalism: The Visionary Strain in Merwin, Ashbery, and Ammons," *Chicago Review* 24(2), 1972, 42-43. Reprinted in: Harold Bloom. *Figures of Capable Imagination*, pp. 147-49.

"The Constant"

> LAURENCE LIEBERMAN. *Unassigned Frequencies*, p. 67.

"Corson's Inlet"

> FREDERICK BUELL. " 'To Be Quiet in the Hands of the Marvelous': The Poetry of A. R. Ammons," *Iowa Review* 8(1), Winter 1977, 73-75.
>
> JOHN ROMANO. "The New Laureates," *Commentary* 60(4), October 1975, 56.
>
> GUY ROTELLA. " 'Ghostlier Demarcations, Keener Sounds': A. R. Ammons' 'Corson's Inlet,' " *Concerning Poetry* 10(2), Fall 1977, 25-33.

"Essay on Poetics"

> HAROLD BLOOM. "The New Transcendentalism: The Visionary Strain in Merwin, Ashbery, and Ammons," *Chicago Review* 24(3), 1972, 36-39.
>
> FREDERICK BUELL. " 'To Be Quiet in the Hands of the Marvelous': The Poetry of A. R. Ammons," *Iowa Review* 8(1), Winter 1977, 80-84.

"Guide"

> HAROLD BLOOM. *Figures of Capable Imagination*, pp. 215-18.

"I went to the summit" (*Sphere*)

> HAROLD BLOOM. *A Map of Misreading*, pp. 200-3.

"Motion"

> ROBERT PINSKY. *The Situation of Poetry*, pp. 147-49.

"Peak"

> HAROLD BLOOM. *Figures of Capable Imagination*, pp. 226-28.
>
> LAURENCE LIEBERMAN. *Unassigned Frequencies*, p. 64.

"Periphery"

> HAROLD BLOOM. *Figures of Capable Imagination*, p. 163.

"Play"

> LAWRENCE KRAMER. "The Wodwo Watches the Water Clock: Language in Postmodern British and American Poetry," *Contemporary Literature* 18(3), Summer 1977, 329-31.

"Plunder"

> HAROLD BLOOM. *Figures of Capable Imagination*, pp. 225-26.
>
> ROBERT PINSKY. *The Situation of Poetry*, pp. 153-54.

"Raft"

HYATT H. WAGGONER. "The Poetry of A. R. Ammons: Some Notes and Reflections," *Salmagundi* 22-23 (Spring-Summer 1973), 286-87. Reprinted in: *Contemporary Poetry in America*, p. 331.

"So I Said I Am Ezra"

FREDERICK BUELL. " 'To Be Quiet in the Hands of the Marvelous': The Poetry of A. R. Ammons," *Iowa Review* 8(1), Winter 1977, 67-68. (P)

"Uh, Philosophy"

LAURENCE LIEBERMAN. *Unassigned Frequencies,* pp. 62-63.

ANDERSON, JOHN

"Refusals"

MERLE E. BROWN. "Dodecaphonic Scales," *Iowa Review* 4(4), Fall 1973, 125-26.

ANDERSON, LEE

"Prevailing Winds"

ROY P. BASLER. "The Poet as Composer — Lee Anderson," *Sewanee Review* 80(1), Winter 1972, 156.

ANDERSON, PATRICK

"Drinker"

BABETTE DEUTSCH. *Poetry in Our Time,* p. 117; second ed., pp. 127-28.

ANDREWS, BRUCE

"Bananas are an example"

ROBERT PINSKY. *The Situation of Poetry,* pp. 87-9.

ANONYMOUS

"Adam Lay Y-bounden"

EDMUND REISS. *The Art of the Middle English Lyric,* pp. 139-42.

D. S. SAVAGE. *The Personal Principle,* pp. 48-49.

SARAH STANBURY SMITH. " 'Adam Lay I-Bowndyn' and the *Vinculum Amoris,*" *English Language Notes* 15(2), December 1977, 98-101.

"Advice to a Painter to Draw the Duke by"

GEORGE DE FOREST LORD. "Satire and Sedition: The Life and Work of John Ayloffe," *Huntington Library Quarterly* 29(3), May 1966, 266-68.

"Almsgiving"

CARL T. BERKHOUT. "Some Notes on the Old English 'Almsgiving,' " *English Language Notes* 10(2), December 1972, 81-85.

"Alysoun"

ARTHUR K. MOORE. *The Secular Lyric in Middle English,* pp. 68-69.

EDMUND REISS. *The Art of the Middle English Lyric,* pp. 59-65.

THEO STEMMLER. "An Interpretation of *Alysoun,*" in *Chaucer and Middle English Studies in Honor of Rossell Hope Robbins,* pp. 111-18.

"Annot and John"

DANIEL J. RANSOM. " 'Annot and John' and the Ploys of Parody," *Studies in Philology* 75(2), April 1978, 121-41.

"The Annunciation" ("Gabriel, from Hevene-King")

SARAH APPLETON WEBER. *Theology and Poetry in the Middle English Lyric,* pp. 32-46.

"Aristocracy"

CHARLES E. MODLIN. "Aristocracy in the Early Republic," *Early American Literature* 6(3), Winter 1971-72, 252-57.

"As I lay upon a night"

SARAH APPLETON WEBER. *Theology and Poetry in the Middle English Lyric,* pp. 69-86.

"Assembly of Ladies"

JOHN STEPHENS. "The Questioning of Love in the *Assembly of Ladies,*" *Review of English Studies,* n.s., 24(94), May 1973, 129-40.

"At a sprynge-wel under a thorn"

PETER DRONKE. *The Medieval Lyric,* pp. 69-70.

"Auld Maitland"

GARDNER B. TAPLIN. "Andrew Lang as a Student of the Traditional Narrative Ballad," *Tulane Studies in English* 14 (1965), 67.

"The Awntyrs off Arthure"

RALPH HANNA III. "*The Awntyrs off Arthure*: An Interpretation," *Modern Language Quarterly* 31(3), September 1970, 275-97.

THORLAC TURVILLE-PETRE. " 'Summer Sunday,' 'De Tribus Regibus Mortuis,' and 'The Awntyrs off Arthure': Three Poems in the Thirteen-Line Stanza," *Review of English Studies,* n.s., 25(97), February 1974, 9-11.

"Balow my Babe"

MARGARET B. McDOWELL. "Folk lullabies: Songs of anger, love, and fear," *Women's Studies* 5(2), 1977, 211.

"Barbara Allen"

EDWARD A. BLOOM, CHARLES H. PHILBRICK, and ELMER M. BLISTEIN. *The Order of Poetry,* pp. 73-75.

"The Bargain of Judas"

J. D. W. CROWTHER. " 'The Bargain of Judas,' " *English Language Notes* 13(4), June 1976, 245-49.

"The Battle of Brunanburh"

FRANCES RANDALL LIPP. "Contrast and Point of View in *The Battle of Brunanburh,*" *Philological Quarterly* 48(2), April 1969, 166-77.

"The Battle of Maldon"

J. B. BESSINGER. "*Maldon* and the *Óláfsdrápa*: An Historical Caveat," *Comparative Literature* 14(1), Winter 1962, 23-35. Reprinted in: *Old English Literature,* pp. 237-52.

N. F. BLAKE. "The genesis of *The Battle of Maldon,*" *Anglo Saxon England* 7 (1978), 119-29.

W. F. BOLTON. "Byrhtnoð in the Wilderness," *Modern Language Review* 64(3), July 1969, 481-90.

DAVID G. HALE. "Structure and Theme in 'The Battle of Maldon,' " *Notes & Queries,* n.s., 15(7), July 1968, 242-43.

EDWARD B. IRVING, JR. "The Heroic Style in *The Battle of Maldon,*" *Studies in Philology* 58(3), July 1961, 457-67.

WARREN A. SAMOUCE. "General Byrhtnoth," *Journal of English and Germanic Philology* 62(1), January 1963, 129-35.

MICHAEL J. SWANTON. "*The Battle of Maldon*: A Literary Caveat," *Journal of English and Germanic Philology* 67(3), July 1968, 441-50.

ANONYMOUS *(Cont.)*

"The Battle of Otterburn"

> JOHN W. CLARK. "Popular Ballads: The Heroic and Tragic Voice of the Common Man," *Minnesota Review* 6(3), 1966, 223-24.

"A Betrayed Maiden's Lament"

> JANE L. CURRY. "Waking the Well," *English Language Notes* 2(1), September 1964, 1-4.

"Binnorie: or, The Two Sisters"

> EDWARD A. BLOOM, CHARLES H. PHILBRICK, and ELMER M. BLISTEIN. *The Order of Poetry*, pp. 75-78.

"The Bird with Four Feathers"

> A. KENT HIEATT and CONSTANCE HIEATT. " 'The Bird with Four Feathers': Numerical Analysis of a Fourteenth Century Poem," *Papers on Language and Literature* 6(1), Winter 1970, 18-38.

"The Bitter Withy"

> MARK W. BOOTH. "The Ballad and the Brain," *Georgia Review* 32(2), Summer 1978, 371-86.

"Bless me you stars!"

> JOHN H. O'NEILL. "An Unpublished 'Imperfect Enjoyment' Poem," *Papers on Language and Literature* 13(2), Spring 1977, 197-202.

"Blodles & bonles, blod has nou bon"

> STEPHEN MANNING. *Wisdom and Number*, p. 145.

"Blow, Northern Wind"

> ARTHUR K. MOORE. *The Secular Lyric in Middle English*, pp. 65-68.

"The Bury New Loom"

> MARTHA VICINUS. "The Study of Nineteenth Century British Working Poetry," *College English* 32(5), February 1971, 550-52.

"Carmen de situ Dunelmi"

> H. S. OFFLER. "The Date of Durham (*Carmen de Situ Dunelmi*)," *Journal of English and Germanic Philology* 61(3), July 1962, 591-94.

"The Cherry-Tree Carol"

> SHERWYN T. CARR. "The Middle English Nativity Cherry Tree: The Dissemination of a Popular Motif," *Modern Language Quarterly* 36(2), June 1975, 142-44.

"Chevy Chase"

> JOHN W. CLARK. "Popular Ballads: The Heroic and Tragic Voice of the Common Man," *Minnesota Review* 6(3), 1966, 223-25.

"Christ and Satan"

> THOMAS D. HILL. "The Fall of Satan in the Old English *Christ and Satan*," *Journal of English and Germanic Philology* 76(3), July 1977, 315-25.

"Christis Kirk on the Green"

> ALLAN H. MACLAINE. "The *Christis Kirk* Tradition: Its Evolution in Scots Poetry to Burns," *Studies in Scottish Literature* 2(1), July 1964, 11-14.

"Christ's Coming" ("Conquering and to Conquer")

> STEPHEN MANNING. *Wisdom and Number*, pp. 19-21.

> EDMUND REISS. *The Art of the Middle English Lyric*, pp. 117-22.

"Clerk Saunders"

> LAURENCE LERNER. *An Introduction to English Poetry*, pp. 1-16.

"The Coal-owner and the Pitman's Wife"

> LAURENCE LERNER. *An Introduction to English Poetry*, pp. 175-76.

"Come, Little Babe, come Silly Soul"

> MARGARET B. MCDOWELL. "Folk lullabies: Songs of anger, love, and fear," *Women's Studies* 5(2), 1977, 211-12.

"The Coming of Christ"

> see "Christ's Coming"

"Complaint of a lover, that defied love, and was by love after the more tormented"

> ALAN T. BRADFORD. "Mirrors of Mutability: Winter Landscapes in Tudor Poetry," *English Literary Renaissance* (4)1, Winter 1974, 6-7.

"Conquering and to Conquer"

> see "Christ's Coming"

"Corpus Christi Carol" ("He bare him up, he bare him down")

> FRANCIS BERRY. "A Medieval Poem and its Secularized Derivative," *Essays in Criticism* 5(4), October 1955, 299-314.

> STEPHEN MANNING. *Wisdom and Number*, pp. 115-17.

"Crist made to man a fair present"

> see "Divine Love"

"Cronica"

> ROSSELL HOPE ROBBINS. "Victory at Whitby, A. D. 1451," *Studies in Philology* 67(4), October 1970, 495-504.

"Cristes milde moder, seynte marie"

> STEPHEN MANNING. *Wisdom and Number*, pp. 94-96.

"Daniel"

> HARRY JAY SOLO. "The Twice-Told Tale: A Reconsideration of the Syntax and Style of the Old English *Daniel*, 245-429," *Papers on Language and Literature* 9(4), Fall 1973, 347-64. (P)

"A Danish Tale"

> BURTON R. POLLIN. "Southey's 'Battle of Blenheim' Parodied in the *Morning Chronicle* — A Whig Attack on the Battle of Copenhagen," *Bulletin of the New York Public Library* 72(8), October 1968, 507-17.

"De Clerico et Puella"

> ARTHUR K. MOORE. *The Secular Lyric in Middle English*, pp. 70-72.

"De Tribus Regibus Mortuis"

> THORLAC TURVILLE-PETRE. " 'Summer Sunday,' 'De Tribus Regibus Mortuis,' and 'The Awntyrs off Arthure': Three Poems in the Thirteen-Line Stanza," *Review of English Studies*, n.s., 25(97), February 1974, 7-9.

"Death and Life"

> A. C. SPEARING. *Medieval Dream-Poetry*, pp. 166-70.

"The Death of Edgar"

> NEIL D. ISAACS. " 'The Death of Edgar' (And Others)," *American Notes & Queries*, n.s., 4(4), December 1965, 52-55.

"The Demon Lover"

> GÉMINO H. ABAD. *A Formal Approach to Lyric Poetry*, pp. 212-14, 347.

"Deor"

> MORTON W. BLOOMFIELD. "The Form of *Deor*," in *Old English Literature*, pp. 212-28.

> JAMES L. BOREN. "The Design of the Old English *Deor*," in *Anglo-Saxon Poetry*, pp. 264-76.

> NORMAN E. ELIASON. "Two Old English Scop Poems," *PMLA* 81(3), June 1966, 185-92.

JEROME MANDEL. "Contrast in Old English Poetry," *Chaucer Review* 6(1), Summer 1971, 10-11.

MURRAY F. MARKLAND. "*Deor*: Paes Ofereode; Pisses Swa Maeg," *American Notes & Queries*, n.s., 11(3), November 1972, 35-36.

THOMAS T. TUGGLE. "The Structure of *Deor*," *Studies in Philology* 74(3), July 1977, 229-42.

"The Descent into Hell"

THOMAS D. HILL. "Cosmic Stasis and the Birth of Christ: The Old English *Descent into Hell*, Lines 99-106," *Journal of English and Germanic Philology* 71(3), July 1972, 382-89.

"A Dialogue betweene the Soule and the Body"

ROSALIE OSMOND. "Body and Soul Dialogues in the Seventeenth Century," *English Literary Renaissance* 4(3), Autumn 1974, 385-87.

"Divine Love" ("Christ made to man a fair present")

STEPHEN MANNING. *Wisdom and Number*, pp. 146-50.

"The Dream of the Rood"

ROBERT B. BURLIN. "The Ruthwell Cross, *The Dream of the Rood* and the Vita Contemplativa," *Studies in Philology* 65(1), January 1968, 23-43.

J. A. BURROW. "An Approach to *The Dream of the Rood*," in *Old English Literature*, pp. 253-67.

JOHN CANUTESON. "The Crucifixion and the Second Coming in *The Dream of the Rood*," *Modern Philology* 66(4), May 1969, 293-97.

ROBERT R. EDWARDS. "Narrative Technique and Distance in the *Dream of the Rood*," *Papers on Language and Literature* 6(3), Summer 1970, 291-301.

ALVIN A. LEE. "Toward a Critique of *The Dream of the Rood*," in *Anglo-Saxon Poetry*, pp. 163-91.

JEROME MANDEL. "Contrast in Old English Poetry," *Chaucer Review* 6(1), Summer 1971, 9-10.

THOMAS J. NAPIERKOWSKI. "A Dream of the Cross," *Concerning Poetry* 11(1), Spring 1978, 3-12.

RICHARD C. PAYNE. "Convention and Originality in the Vision Framework of *The Dream of the Rood*," *Modern Philology* 73(4, pt. 1), May 1976, 329-41.

"The Dying Maiden's Complaint"

ROSAMOND TUVE. "Sacred 'Parody' of Love Poetry and Herbert," *Studies in the Renaissance* 8 (1961), 263-67.

"Eadwacer"

KEMP MALONE. "Two English *Frauenlieder*," *Comparative Literature* 14(1), Winter 1962, 106-11.

"Earth plant"

FRANCHOT BALLINGER. "The Response Center: Man and Nature in Pueblo and Navaho Ritual Songs and Prayers," *American Quarterly* 30(1), Spring 1978, 100-1.

"Edward"

GÉMINO H. ABAD. *A Formal Approach to Lyric Poetry*, pp. 75-78.

GÉMINO H. ABAD. *In Another Light*, pp. 115-26.

JEROME BEATY and WILLIAM H. MATCHETT. *Poetry From Statement to Meaning*, pp. 145-49.

CLEANTH BROOKS, JOHN THIBAUT PURSER, and ROBERT PENN WARREN. *An Approach to Literature*, pp. 435-37; second ed., pp. 435-37; third ed., pp. 288-90; fourth ed., pp. 289-92; fifth ed., pp. 341-44.

JOHN W. CLARK. "Popular Ballads: The Heroic and Tragic Voice of the Common Man," *Minnesota Review* 6(3), 1966, 228-29.

EARL DANIELS. *The Art of Reading Poetry*, pp. 151-54.

FRED B. MILLETT, ARTHUR W. HOFFMAN and DAVID R. CLARK. *Reading Poetry*, second ed., pp. 10-11.

"Edy be thou, Heavene-Quene" see "Queen of Heaven"

"Erthe toc of erthe, erthe wyth woh"

EDMUND REISS. *The Art of the Middle English Lyric*, pp. 51-56.

"Exemplum de beata virgine & gaudius eius"

SARAH APPLETON WEBER. *Theology and Poetry in the Middle English Lyric*, pp. 48-55.

"Exodus"

ROBERT T. FARRELL. "A Reading of OE. *Exodus*," *Review of English Studies*, n.s., 20(80), November 1969, 401-17.

PETER J. LUCAS. "An Interpretation of 'Exodus' 46-53," *Notes & Queries*, n.s., 16(10), October 1969, 364-66. (P)

JOHN F. VICKREY. "*Exodus* and the treasure of Pharaoh," *Anglo-Saxon England* 1 (1972), 159-65. (P)

"The Fates of Men"

NEIL D. ISAACS. "Up a Tree: To See *The Fates of Men*," in *Anglo-Saxon Poetry*, pp. 363-75. (P)

"Fine Flowers in the Valley"

AGNES STEIN. *The Uses of Poetry*, p. 35.

"The Five Joys" ("Hail be thou, Mary, maiden bright")

STEPHEN MANNING. *Wisdom and Number*, pp. 75-77.

SARAH APPLETON WEBER. *Theology and Poetry in the Middle English Lyric*, pp. 182-86.

"For ou Pat is so feir ant brist"

STEPHEN MANNING. *Wisdom and Number*, pp. 126-31.

"Fowles in the Frith"

DAVID DAICHES. *A Study of Literature*, pp. 151-52.

DAVID LUISI. *Explicator* 25(6), February 1967, Item 47.

STEPHEN MANNING. "Game and Earnest in the Middle English and Provencal Love Lyrics," *Comparative Literature* 18(3), Summer 1966, 239-40.

EDMUND REISS. *The Art of the Middle English Lyric*, pp. 19-22.

EDMUND REISS. "A Critical Approach to the Middle English Lyric," *College English* 27(5), February 1966, 366-67.

"The Fox and the Wolf"

SACVAN BERCOVITCH. "Clerical Satire in Pe Vox and Pe Wolf," *Journal of English and Germanic Philology* 65(2), April 1966, 287-94.

NICOLAI VON KREISLER. "Satire in *The Vox and the Wolf*," *Journal of English and Germanic Philology* 69(4), October 1970, 650-58.

"Frankie and Johnny"

CLEANTH BROOKS, JOHN THIBAUT PURSER, and ROBERT PENN WARREN. *An Approach to Literature*, pp. 431-32; second ed., pp. 431-32; third ed., pp. 285-86; fourth ed., pp. 286-88; fifth ed., pp. 336-38.

"The Freiris of Berwik"

EVERETT C. JOHNSTON. "The Transmutation of Fraire Johine in 'The Freiris of Berwik,'" *Studies in Scottish Literature* 5(1), July 1967, 57-59.

ANONYMOUS *(Cont.)*

"The French Primero"

    STEVEN W. MAY. " 'The French Primero': A Study in Renaissance Textual Transmission and Taste," *English Language Notes* 9(2), December 1971, 102-8.

"From the pond in the white valley"

    FRANCHOT BALLINGER. "The Response Center: Man and Nature in Pueblo and Navaho Ritual Songs and Prayers," *American Quarterly* 30(1), Spring 1978, 96-97.

"From where you stay quietly"

    FRANCHOT BALLINGER. "The Response Center: Man and Nature in Pueblo and Navaho Ritual Songs and Prayers," *American Quarterly* 30(1), Spring 1978, 103.

"Ful feir flour is Pe lilie"

    STEPHEN MANNING. *Wisdom and Number*, pp. 113-14.

"Gabriel, from Hevene-King"

    see "The Annunciation"

"Genesis B"

    MICHAEL D. CHERNISS. "Heroic Ideals and the Moral Climate of *Genesis B*," *Modern Language Quarterly* 30(4), December 1969, 479-97.

    J. R. HALL. "*Geongordom* and *Hyldo* in Genesis B: Serving the Lord for the Lord's Favor," *Papers on Language and Literature* 11(3), Summer 1975, 302-16.

    THOMAS D. HILL. "The Fall of Angels and Man in the Old English *Genesis B*," in *Anglo-Saxon Poetry*, pp. 279-90.

"Gifts of Men"

    DOUGLAS D. SHORT. "The Old English *Gifts of Men*, Line 13," *Modern Philology* 71(4), May 1974, 388-89. (P)

"Glade Us Maiden, Moder Milde"

    SARAH APPLETON WEBER. *Theology and Poetry in the Middle English Lyric*, pp. 156-64.

"Gold and al this werdis wyn"

    EDMUND REISS. *The Art of the Middle English Lyric*, pp. 133-36.

"Grievous is my sorrow"

    ROSAMOND TUVE. "Sacred 'Parody' of Love Poetry and Herbert," *Studies in the Renaissance* 8 (1961), 263-67.

"Hail be thou, Mary, maiden bright"

    see "The Five Joys"

"The Hangman's Tree"

    M. L. ROSENTHAL and A. J. M. SMITH. *Exploring Poetry*, pp. 308-9; second ed., p. 142.

"He bare him up, he bare him down"

    see "Corpus Christi Carol"

"He yaf himself as good felowe"

    STEPHEN MANNING. *Wisdom and Number*, pp. 121-22.

"Helen of Kirconnell"

    GÉMINO H. ABAD. *A Formal Approach to Lyric Poetry*, pp. 295-96.

"The Herone flewe eist, the Herone flewe weste"

    FRANCIS BERRY. "A Medieval Poem and its Secularized Derivative," *Essays in Criticism* 5(4), October 1955, 299-314.

"Heʒe Louerd, Pou here my bone"

    STEPHEN MANNING. *Wisdom and Number*, pp. 51-55.

"Hostis Herodis impie"

    STEPHEN MANNING. *Wisdom and Number*, pp. 118-20.

"The Hunting of the Cheviot"

    JOHN W. CLARK. "Popular Ballads: The Heroic and Tragic Voice of the Common Man," *Minnesota Review* 6(3), 1966, 223-24.

"The Husband's Message"

    RALPH W. V. ELLIOTT. "Form and Image in the Old English Lyrics," *Essays in Criticism* 11(1), January 1961, pp. 6-8.

    MARGARET E. GOLDSMITH. "The Enigma of *The Husband's Message*," in *Anglo-Saxon Poetry*, pp. 242-63.

"I am a fool, I can no good"

    see "Love"

"I am Iesu, That Cum to Fith"

    JOHN E. HALLWAS. *Explicator* 32(7), March 1974, Item 51.

"I am on the way"

    FRANCHOT BALLINGER. "The Response Center: Man and Nature in Pueblo and Navaho Ritual Songs and Prayers," *American Quarterly* 30(1), Spring 1978, 104-5.

"I haue laborede sore and suffered deyʒth"

    STEPHEN MANNING. *Wisdom and Number*, p. 46.

"I Have Lived After My Lust"

    LEONARD NATHAN. "Gascoigne's 'Lullabie' and Structures in the Tudor Lyric," in *The Rhetoric of Renaissance Poetry*, pp. 59-61.

"I sayh him with fless al bisprad"

    see "Christ's Coming"

"I Sing of a Maiden"

    DAVID G. HALLIBURTON. "The Myden Makeles," *Papers on Language and Literature* 4(2), Spring 1968, 115-20.

    THOMAS JEMIELITY. " 'I Sing of a Maiden': God's Courting of Mary," *Concerning Poetry* 2(1), Spring 1969, 53-59.

    STEPHEN MANNING. *Wisdom and Number*, pp. 159-67.

    BARBARA C. RAW. " 'As Dew in Aprille,' " *Modern Language Review* 55(3), July 1960, pp. 411-14.

    EDMUND REISS. *The Art of the Middle English Lyric*, pp. 159-64.

    LEO SPITZER. *Essays on English and American Literature*, pp. 233-46.

    SARAH APPLETON WEBER. *Theology and Poetry in the Middle English Lyric*, pp. 55-60.

"I Went to Death"

    EDMUND REISS. *The Art of the Middle English Lyric*, pp. 153-56.

"Ich Am of Irlaunde"

    NORMAN HOLLAND. *Explicator* 15(9), June 1957, Item 55.

"Ichót a burde in bowre bright"

    See "Blow, Northern Wind"

"Iesu cristes milde moder"

    SARAH APPLETON WEBER. *Theology and Poetry in the Middle English Lyric*, pp. 137-45.

"Iesu Dulcis Memoria"

    STEPHEN MANNING. *Wisdom and Number*, pp. 39-40.

"Ihesu for thy holy name"
John C. Hirsh. "A Fifteenth-Century Commentary on 'Ihesu for Thy Holy Name,' " *Notes & Queries*, n.s., 17(2), February 1970, 44-45.

"Ihesu, suete sone dere"
see "The Virgin's Song"

"In that blisful bearnes buirde"
Peter Dronke. *The Medieval Lyric*, p. 67.

"In the vaile of restless mind"
see "Quia Amore Langueo"

"It is my hogan where, from the back corners beauty radiates . . ."
Franchot Ballinger. "The Response Center: Man and Nature in Pueblo and Navaho Ritual Songs and Prayers," *American Quarterly* 30(1), Spring 1978, 93.

"It Wern Fowre Letterys of Purposy"
Marie Borroff. " 'It Wern Fowre Letterys of Purposy': A New Interpretation," *Notes & Queries*, n.s., 23(7), July 1976, 294-95.

"Jacob and Joseph"
Oscar Sherwin. "Art's Spring-Birth: The Ballad of *Iacob and Iosep*," *Studies in Philology* 42(1), January 1945, 1-18.

"Jesse James"
Cleanth Brooks and Robert Penn Warren. *Understanding Poetry*, 4th ed., pp. 22-23.

"Johnie Armstrong"
Cleanth Brooks and Robert Penn Warren. *Understanding Poetry*, pp. 35-39; rev. ed., pp. 9-13; third ed., pp. 31-35.

"Jone O'Grinfilt, Jr."
Martha Vicinus. "The Study of Nineteenth Century British Working Poetry," *College English* 32(5), February 1971, 556-58.

"Judas"
Peter Dronke. *The Medieval Lyric*, pp. 67-69.

"Judgment Day II"
Richard L. Hoffman. "The Theme of *Judgment Day II*," *English Language Notes* 6(3), March 1969, pp. 161-64.

"Judith"
David Chamberlain. "*Judith*: A Fragmentary and Political Poem," in *Anglo-Saxon Poetry*, pp. 135-59.
John P. Hermann. "The Theme of Spiritual Warfare in the Old English *Judith*," *Philological Quarterly* 55(1), Winter 1976, 1-9.
Burton Raffel. "*Judith*: Hypermetricity and Rhetoric," in *Anglo-Saxon Poetry*, pp. 124-34.

"The Knight Stained from Battle"
see "What is he, this lordling, that cometh from the fight"

"The Laily Worm and the Mackrel of the Sea"
Gémino H. Abad. *A Formal Approach to Lyric Poetry*, pp. 212-14, 347.

"The Lamentation of Glumdalclitch, for the Loss of Grildrig. A Pastoral"
Patricia Koster. "Notes Upon Notes: Gulliver And The Pepper-Water-Worms," *Scriblerian* 2(1), Autumn 1969, 29-30. (P)
Alan T. McKenzie. " 'The Lamentation of Glumdalclitch for the Loss of Grildrig. A Pastoral': What We Have Been Missing," *Texas Studies in Literature and Language,* 12(4), Winter 1971, pp. 583-94.

Alan T. McKenzie. "Lemuel Gulliver and Pepper-Water-Worms," *Scriblerian* 1(1), Autumn 1968, 31-32. (P)

"Land of Cokaygne"
Clifford Davidson. "The Sins of the Flesh in the Fourteenth-Century Middle English 'Land of Cokaygne,' " *Ball State University Forum* 11(4), Autumn 1970, 21-26.
Thomas D. Hill. "Parody and Theme in the Middle English 'Land of Cokaygne,' " *Notes & Queries*, n.s., 22(2), February 1975, pp. 55-59.

"Lenten is come with love to towne"
see "Spring"

"Leuede sainte marie, moder and maide"
Stephen Manning. *Wisdom and Number*, p. 42.

"Leuedy, for Pare Blisse/Pat Pu Heddest at Pe Frume"
Sarah Appleton Weber. *Theology and Poetry in the Middle English Lyric*, pp. 167-74, 186-91.

"London Lickpenny"
Arthur K. Moore. *The Secular Lyric in Middle English*, pp. 164-65.
Denys Thompson. *The Uses of Poetry*, pp. 148-49.

"Lord Randal"
Gémino H. Abad. *A Formal Approach to Lyric Poetry*, pp. 73-77.
Cleanth Brooks and Robert Penn Warren. *Understanding Poetry*, pp. 122-25; rev. ed., pp. 48-51; third ed., pp. 47-49.
John W. Clark. "Popular Ballads: The Heroic and Tragic Voice of the Common Man," *Minnesota Review* 6(3), 1966, 225-28.

"Louerd, Pu clepedest me"
Stephen Manning. *Wisdom and Number*, pp. 36-38.
Robert D. Stevick. "The Criticism of Middle English Lyrics," *Modern Philology* 64(2), November 1966, 105-10.

"Love"
John E. Hallwas. "The Identity of the Speaker in 'I am a fol, i can no god,' " *Papers on Language and Literature* 10(4), Fall 1974, 415-17.

"Lovely Tear from Lovely Eye"
John E. Hallwas. *Explicator* 35(3), Spring 1977, 12-13.

"A Lyke-Wake Dirge"
Vincent Buckley. *Poetry and the Sacred*, p. 27.

"Magnolia, Philomel"
Winifred Nowottny. *The Language Poets Use*, pp. 163-66.

"Maiden in the mor lay"
Peter Dronke. *The Medieval Lyric*, pp. 195-96.
Edmund Reiss. *The Art of the Middle English Lyric*, pp. 99-106.
D. W. Robertson, Jr. "Historical Criticism," *English Institute Essays*, 1950, pp. 26-27.

"The maidens came/When I was in my mother's bower"
Archibald MacLeish. *Poetry and Experience*, pp. 30-33.

"The Man in the Moon"
Arthur K. Moore. *The Secular Lyric in Middle English*, pp. 95-97.

ANONYMOUS *(Cont.)*

"The Man of Double Deed"

    SHARON CAMERON. "'A Loaded Gun': Dickinson and the Dialectic of Rage," *PMLA* 93(3), May 1978, pp. 427-29.

"The Marriage of Sir Gawain"

    RALPH HANNA III. "*The Awntyrs off Arthure*: An Interpretation," *Modern Language Quarterly* 31(3), September 1970, 280.

"Maxims II"

    STANLEY B. GREENFIELD and RICHARD EVERT. "*Maxims II*: Gnome and Poem," in *Anglo-Saxon Poetry*, pp. 337-54.

"Me Ðingkit"

    JOHN C. HIRSH. *Explicator* 35(3), Spring 1977, 11.

"Mery it is while sumer y-last"

    EDMUND REISS. *The Art of the Middle English Lyric*, pp. 3-6.

"Metrical Epilogue to the *Pastoral Care*"

    NEIL D. ISAACS. "Still Waters Run *Undíop*," *Philological Quarterly* 44(4), October 1965, 545-49.

"Middelerd For Mon Wes Mad"

    RALPH HANNA. "A Note on a Harley Lyric," *English Language Notes* 7(4), June 1970, 243-46. (P)

    CELIA TOWNSEND WELLS. "Line 21 of 'Middelerd for Mon Wes Mad,'" *English Language Notes* 10(3), March 1973, 167-69.

"Pe milde Lomb isprad o rode"

    SARAH APPLETON WEBER. *Theology and Poetry in the Middle English Lyric*, pp. 94-109.

"Phe minde of Phi passiun"

    STEPHEN MANNING. *Wisdom and Number*, pp. 13-14.

"Mum and the Sothsegger"

    DAN EMBREE. "'Richard the Redeless' and 'Mum and the Sothsegger': A Case of Mistaken Identity," *Notes & Queries*, n.s., 22(1), January 1975, 4-12.

"Naueth my saule bute fur and ys"

    EDMUND REISS. *The Art of the Middle English Lyric*, pp. 25-28.

"Nou Goth Sonne Under Wod" ("Sunset on Calvary")

    JOHN L. CUTLER. *Explicator* 4(1), October 1945, Item 7. Reprinted in: *Readings for Liberal Education*, first ed., II: 506-7.

    STEPHEN MANNING. "Nou goth Sonne vnder wod," *Modern Language Notes* 74(7), November 1959, 578-81.

    STEPHEN MANNING. *Wisdom and Number*, pp. 80-84.

    EDMUND REISS. *The Art of the Middle English Lyric*, pp. 15-17.

    EDMUND REISS. "A Critical Approach to the Middle English Lyric," *College English* 27(5), February 1966, 375-76.

    C. G. THAYER. *Explicator* 11(4), February 1953, Item 25.

"Now as I am the child of White Shell Woman . . ."

    FRANCHOT BALLINGER. "The Response Center: Man and Nature in Pueblo and Navaho Ritual Songs and Prayers," *American Quarterly* 30(1), Spring 1978, 97-99.

"Now ich see blostme springe"

    STEPHEN MANNING. *Wisdom and Number*, pp. 22-23.

"Now Shrinketh Rose and Lily-Flower"

    STEPHEN MANNING. *Wisdom and Number*, pp. 100-5.

"Now Sprinkes the Spray"

    EDMUND REISS. *The Art of the Middle English Lyric*, pp. 45-49.

"Now this is the day"

    FRANCHOT BALLINGER. "The Response Center: Man and Nature in Pueblo and Navaho Ritual Songs and Prayers," *American Quarterly* 30(1), Spring 1978, 105-7.

"The numbre of droppes of Blode"

    JOHN C. HIRSH. "Two English Devotional Poems of the Fifteenth Century," *Notes & Queries*, n.s., 15(1), January 1968, 4-11.

"The Nutbrowne Maide"

    KARL KROEBER. *Romantic Narrative Art*, pp. 13-19.

    ARTHUR K. MOORE. *The Secular Lyric in Middle English*, pp. 182-88.

"O glorius God, redemer of mankynde"

    JOHN C. HIRSH. "Two English Devotional Poems of the Fifteenth Century," *Notes & Queries*, n.s., 15(1), January 1968, 4-11.

"O our Mother the Earth, O our Father the Sky"

    FRANCHOT BALLINGER. "The Response Center: Man and Nature in Pueblo and Navaho Ritual Songs and Prayers," *American Quarterly* 30(1), Spring 1978, 102.

"O Waly Waly"

    DAVID HOLBROOK. *Llareggub Revisited*, pp. 53-54.

"Of a rose, a lovely rose"

    LEO SPITZER. *Essays on English and American Literature*, pp. 216-33.

"Of Alphus"

    CHARLES LAMAR THOMPSON and CHARLES WEINER. "An Approach to Poetry Through Transformational Processes," *English Journal* 61(3), March 1972, 373.

"Of Jesu Christ I Sing"

    see "Now ich see blostme springe"

"Of the troubled common welth restored to quiet by the mighty power of god"

    DOUGLAS L. PETERSON. *The English Lyric from Wyatt to Donne*, pp. 82-83.

"An Old Song of an Old Cavalier and a New"

    DAVID FARLEY-HILLS. *The Benevolence of Laughter*, pp. 43-44.

"The Oldham Weaver"

    LAURENCE LERNER. *An Introduction to English Poetry*, pp. 173-74.

"On Cristes day, I vnderstond"

    STEPHEN MANNING. *Wisdom and Number*, pp. 112-13. (P)

"On the Passion"

    see "Whenne ich see on roode"

"The Parliament of the Three Ages"

    CONSTANCE HIEATT. "*Winner and Waster* and the *Parliament of the Three Ages*," *American Notes & Queries*, n.s., 4(7), March 1966, 100-102.

    DAVID E. LAMPE. "The Poetic Strategy of the *Parlement of the Three Ages*," *Chaucer Review* 7(3), Winter 1973, 173-83.

    RUSSELL A. PECK. "The Careful Hunter in *The Parlement of the Thre Ages*," *ELH* 39(3), September 1972, 333-41.

    A. C. SPEARING. *Medieval Dream-Poetry*, pp. 134-37.

John Speirs. "'Wynnere and Wastoure' and 'The Parlement of the Thre Ages,'" *Scrutiny* 17(3), Autumn 1950, 228-41.

"Patience"

J. J. Anderson. "The Prologue of *Patience*," *Modern Philology* 63(4), May 1966, 283-87.

Malcolm Andrew. "Jonah and Christ in *Patience*," *Modern Philology* 70(3), February 1973, 230-33.

D. S. Brewer. "The *Gawain*-Poet; A General Appreciation of Four Poems," *Essays in Criticism* 17(2), April 1967, 130-42.

Ordelle G. Hill. "The Audience of *Patience*," *Modern Philology* 66(2), November 1968, 103-9.

Charles Moorman. "The Role of the Narrator in *Patience*," *Modern Philology* 61(2), November 1963, 90-95.

David Williams. "The Point of *Patience*," *Modern Philology* 68(2), November 1970, 127-36.

"Peblis to the Play"

Allan H. MacLaine. "The *Christis Kirk* Tradition: Its Evolution in Scots Poetry to Burns," *Studies in Scottish Literature* 2(1), July 1964, 7-11.

"The Phoenix"

N. F. Blake. "The Form of *The Phoenix*," in *Old English Literature*, pp. 268-78.

Daniel G. Calder. "The vision of paradise: a symbolic reading of the Old English *Phoenix*," *Anglo Saxon England* 1 (1972), 167-81.

Joanne Spencer Kantrowitz. "The Anglo-Saxon *Phoenix* and Tradition," *Philological Quarterly* 43(1), January 1964, 1-13.

"Queen of Heaven" ("Edy be thou, Heavene-Quene")

Stephen Manning. *Wisdom and Number*, pp. 97-100.

"Quia Amore Langueo"

Stephen Manning. *Wisdom and Number*, pp. 59-62.

James I. Wimsatt. "The Canticle of Canticles, Two Latin Poems, and 'In a valey of Pis restles mynde,'" *Modern Philology* 75(4), May 1978, 327-45.

"Resignation"

Alan Bliss and Allen J. Frantzen. "The Integrity of *Resignation*," *Review of English Studies*, n.s., 27(108), November 1976, 390-402.

"Rhyming Poem"

J. E. Cross. "Aspects of Microcosm And Macrocosm in Old English Literature," *Comparative Literature* 14(1), Winter 1962, 11-15.

Ruth P. M. Lehmann. "The Old English *Riming Poem*: Interpretation, Text, and Translation," *Journal of English and Germanic Philology* 69(3), July 1970, 437-49.

"Richard the Redeless"

Dan Embree. "'Richard the Redeless' and 'Mum and the Sothsegger': A Case of Mistaken Identity," *Notes & Queries*, n.s., 22(1), January 1975, 4-12.

"Riddle 20"

Donald Kay. "Riddle 20: A Revaluation," *Tennessee Studies in Literature* 13 (1968), 133-39.

"Riddle 29"

Frank Walters. "Language Structure and the Meanings of the *Exeter Book* Riddles," *Ball State University Forum* 19(3), Summer 1978, 49-53.

"Riddle 39"

Christopher B. Kennedy. "Old English Riddle No. 39," *English Language Notes* 13(2), December 1975, 81-85.

"Riddle 44"

Frank Walters. "Language Structure and the Meanings of the *Exeter Book* Riddles," *Ball State University Forum* 19(3), Summer 1978, 48-49.

"Riddle 45"

William M. Ryan. "Let the Riddles Be Your Key," *New Letters* 45(1), September 1978, 109-10.

"Riddle 47"

Fred C. Robinson. "Artful Ambiguities in the Old English 'Book-Moth' Riddle," in *Anglo-Saxon Poetry*, pp. 355-62.

Geoffrey Russom. "Exeter Riddle 47: A Moth Laid Waste to Fame," *Philological Quarterly* 56(1), Winter 1977, 129-36.

Frank Walters. "Language Structure and the Meanings of the *Exeter Book* Riddles," *Ball State University Forum* 19(3), Summer 1978, 53-55.

"Riddle 60"

Margaret E. Goldsmith. "The Enigma of *The Husband's Message*," in *Anglo-Saxon Poetry*, pp. 242-63.

Roy F. Leslie. "The Integrity of Riddle 60," *Journal of English and Germanic Philology* 67(3), July 1968, 451-57.

F. H. Whitman. "Riddle 60 and Its Source," *Philological Quarterly* 50(1), January 1971, 108-15.

"Riddle 74"

K. S. Kiernan. "The Mysteries of the Sea-eagle in Exeter Riddle 74," *Philological Quarterly* 54(2), Spring 1975, 518-22.

"Riddle 95"

K. S. Kiernan. "*Cwene*: The Old Profession of Exeter Riddle 95," *Modern Philology* 72(4), May 1975, 384-89.

"The Ruin"

James F. Doubleday. "*The Ruin*: Structure and Theme," *Journal of English and Germanic Philology* 71(3), July 1972, 369-81.

Hugh T. Keenan. "The Ruin as Babylon," *Tennessee Studies in Literature* 11(1966), 109-17.

Arnold V. Talentino. "Moral Irony in *The Ruin*," *Papers on Language and Literature* 14(1), Winter 1978, 3-10.

"St. Erkenwald"

T. McAlindon. "Hagiography into Art: a Study of *St. Erkenwald*," *Studies in Philology* 67(4), October 1970, 472-94.

Vincent F. Petronella. "*St. Erkenwald*: Style as the Vehicle for Meaning," *Journal of English and Germanic Philology* 66(4), October 1967, 532-40.

Mary-Ann Stouck. "'Mournynge and Myrthe' in the Alliterative *St. Erkenwald*," *Chaucer Review* 10(3), Winter 1976, 243-54.

"Satire Against the Blacksmiths"

Arthur K. Moore. *The Secular Lyric in Middle English*, pp. 98-99.

ANONYMOUS *(Cont.)*

"The Seafarer"

ROBERT BUX BOSSE. "Aural Aesthetic and the Unity of *The Seafarer*," *Papers on Language and Literature* 9(1), Winter 1973, 3-14.

J. E. CROSS. "Aspects of Microcosm And Macrocosm in Old English Literature," *Comparative Literature* 14(1), Winter 1962, 15-22.

W. A. DAVENPORT. "The Modern Reader and the Old English *Seafarer*," *Papers on Language and Literature* 10(3), Summer 1974, 227-40.

I. L. GORDON. "Traditional Themes in *The Wanderer* and *The Seafarer*," *Review of English Studies*, n.s., 5(17), January 1954, 1-13.

MARTIN GREEN. "Man, Time, and Apocalypse in *The Wanderer, The Seafarer*, and *Beowulf*," *Journal of English and Germanic Philology* 74(4), October 1975, 506-12.

W. F. KLEIN. "Purpose and the 'Poetics' of *The Wanderer* and *The Seafarer*," in *Anglo-Saxon Poetry*, pp. 218-23.

R. F. LESLIE. "Analysis of Stylistic Devices and Effects in Anglo-Saxon Literature," in *Old English Literature*, pp. 78-79.

JOHN C. POPE. "Dramatic Voices in *The Wanderer* and *The Seafarer*," in *Old English Literature*, pp. 163-97.

RAYMOND P. TRIPP, JR. "The Narrator as Revenant: A Reconsideration of Three Old English Elegies," *Papers on Language and Literature* 8(4), Fall 1972, 352-56.

DOROTHY WHITELOCK. "The Interpretation of *The Seafarer*," in *Old English Literature*, pp. 198-211.

ROSEMARY WOOLF. "*The Wanderer, The Seafarer*, and the Genre of *Planctus*," in *Anglo-Saxon Poetry*, pp. 202-7.

"Second Advice to a Painter"

WARREN L. CHERNAIK. "The Heroic Occasional Poem: Panegyric and Satire in the Restoration," *Modern Language Quarterly* 26(4), December 1965, 530-32.

"See Much, Say Little, and Learn to Suffer in Time"

DOUGLAS L. PETERSON. *The English Lyric from Wyatt to Donne*, pp. 11-12.

"Shoot Falce Loue I Care Not"

MACDONALD EMSLIE. *Explicator* 13(7), May 1955, Item 44.

"Sir Cleges"

SHERWIN T. CARR. "The Middle English Nativity Cherry Tree: The Dissemination of a Popular Motif," *Modern Language Quarterly* 36(2), June 1975, 144-47. (P)

"Sir Gowther"

SHIRLEY MARCHALONIS. "*Sir Gowther*: The Process of a Romance," *Chaucer Review* 6(1), Summer 1971, 14-29.

"Sir Orfeo"

MICHAEL D. BRISTOL. "The Structure of the Middle English *Sir Orfeo*," *Papers on Language and Literature* 6(4), Fall 1970, 339-47.

EDWARD E. FOSTER. "Fantasy and Reality in *Sir Orfeo*," *Ball State University Forum* 14(4), Autumn 1973, 22-29.

KENNETH R. R. GROS LOUIS. "The Significance of Sir Orfeo's Self-Exile," *Review of English Studies*, n.s., 18(71), August 1967, 245-52.

JAMES F. KNAPP. "The Meaning of *Sir Orfeo*," *Modern Language Quarterly* 29(3), September 1968, 263-73.

"Sir Patrick Spens"

GÉMINO H. ABAD. *A Formal Approach to Lyric Poetry*, pp. 103-7.

CLEANTH BROOKS, JOHN THIBAUT PURSER, and ROBERT PENN WARREN. *An Approach to Literature*, pp. 429-31; second ed., pp. 429-31; third ed., pp. 283-84; fourth ed., pp. 284-86; fifth ed., pp. 334-36.

CLEANTH BROOKS and ROBERT PENN WARREN. *Understanding Poetry*, 4th ed., pp. 25-26.

EARL DANIELS. *The Art of Reading Poetry*, pp. 137-41.

LLOYD FRANKENBERG. *Invitation to Poetry*, pp. 111-13.

WILLIAM H. MATCHETT. "The Integrity of 'Sir Patrick Spence,'" *Modern Philology* 68(1), August 1970, 25-31.

ARTHUR K. MOORE. "The Literary Status of the English Popular Ballad," *Comparative Literature* 10(1), Winter 1958, 11-13.

MARK VAN DOREN. *Introduction to Poetry*, pp. 125-29. Reprinted in: *Readings for Liberal Education*, revised ed., II: 6-9; third ed., II: 6-8; fourth and fifth eds., II: 8-10.

"Sodenly Afraide"

EDMUND REISS. *The Art of the Middle English Lyric*, pp. 146-50.

"Somer is comen and winter gon"

PETER DRONKE. "Two Thirteenth-Century Religious Lyrics," in *Chaucer and Middle English Studies in Honor of Rossell Hope Robbins*, pp. 398-403.

STEPHEN MANNING. *Wisdom and Number*, pp. 114-15.

"Song of the Husbandman"

ARTHUR K. MOORE. *The Secular Lyric in Middle English*, pp. 85-87.

"Soul's Address to the Body"

MARY HEYWARD FERGUSON. "The Structure of the *Soul's Address to the Body* in Old English," *Journal of English and Germanic Philology* 69(1), January 1970, 72-80.

"Spring"

STEPHEN MANNING. "Game and Earnest in the Middle English and Provencal Love Lyrics," *Comparative Literature* 18(3), Summer 1966, 231-33.

EDMUND REISS. *The Art of the Middle English Lyric*, pp. 67-73.

"Stabat iuxta Christi crucem"

STEPHEN MANNING. *Wisdom and Number*, pp. 150-54.

"Staie, Passenger"

STANLEY STEWART. *The Enclosed Garden*, pp. 99-100.

"Step on a crack: Break your mother's back"

FREDERICK VON ENDE. "Child's Play, You Say?" *CEA Critic* 35(2), January 1973, 34.

"Stond wel, moder, vnder rode"

STEPHEN MANNING. *Wisdom and Number*, pp. 77-80.

SARAH APPLETON WEBER. *Theology and Poetry in the Middle English Lyric*, pp. 125-45.

"Suete Sone, Reu on Me, & Brest Out of Pi Bondis"

SARAH APPLETON WEBER. *Theology and Poetry in the Middle English Lyric*, pp. 117-21.

"Sumer is comen and winter gon"
see "Somer is comen and winter gon"

"Sumer Is Icumen In"

HUNTINGTON BROWN. *Explicator* 3(4), February 1945, Item 34.

JEFFREY A. HELTERMAN. "The Antagonistic Voices of 'Sumer Is Icumen In,'" *Tennessee Studies in Literature* 18 (1973), 13-17.

THEODORE C. HOEPFNER. *Explicator* 3(3), December 1944, Item 18.

STEPHEN MANNING. *Explicator* 18(1), October 1959, Item 2.

ARTHUR K. MOORE. *The Secular Lyric in Middle English*, pp. 50-52.

EDMUND REISS. *The Art of the Middle English Lyric*, pp. 9-12.

"Summer Sunday"

THORLAC TURVILLE-PETRE. "'Summer Sunday,' 'De Tribus Regibus Mortuis,' and 'The Awntyrs off Arthure': Three Poems in the Thirteen-Line Stanza," *Review of English Studies*, n.s., 25(97), February 1974, 4-6.

"Sunset on Calvary"

see "Nou Goth Sonne Under Wod"

"Swarte smekeyd smethes, smateryd wyth smoke"

EDMUND REISS. *The Art of the Middle English Lyric*, pp. 167-70.

"Symmie and his Bruder"

ALLAN H. MACLAINE. "The *Christis Kirk* Tradition: Its Evolution in Scots Poetry to Burns," *Studies in Scottish Literature* 2(1), July 1964, 15-16.

"Tam Lin"

E. B. LYLE. "The Ballad *Tam Lin* and Traditional Tales of Recovery from the Fairy Troop," *Studies in Scottish Literature* 6(3), January 1969, 175-85.

JOHN D. NILES. "*Tam Lin*: Form and Meaning in a Traditional Ballad," *Modern Language Quarterly* 38(4), December 1977, 336-47.

"Tale of Gamelyn"

EDWARD Z. MENKIN. "Comic Irony and the Sense of Two Audiences in the *Tale of Gamelyn*," *Thoth* 10(1), Winter 1969, 41-53.

"The ten comauwndementis I have broke"

STEPHEN MANNING. *Wisdom and Number*, pp. 40-41.

"That lovely lady sat and song"

STEPHEN MANNING. *Wisdom and Number*, pp. 49-50.

"Ther is no rose of swych vertu"

STEPHEN MANNING. *Wisdom and Number*, pp. 155-58.

"Think Before You Speak"

DOUGLAS L. PETERSON. *The English Lyric from Wyatt to Donne*, pp. 17-18.

"Thirty Days Hath September"

THEODORE SPENCER. "How to Criticize a Poem (In the Manner of Certain Contemporary Critics)," *New Republic* 109(23), 6 December 1943, 816-18. Reprinted in: *The Creative Reader*, pp. 847-49; second ed., pp. 899-901. Also: *Readings for Liberal Education*, II: 340-42; second ed., II: 12-14.

"Thomas Rhymer"

EARL DANIELS. *The Art of Reading Poetry*, pp. 141-47.

C. DAY-LEWIS. *The Lyric Impulse*, pp. 68-69.

"Three Lessons to Make Ready for Death"

DOUGLAS L. PETERSON. *The English Lyric from Wyatt to Donne*, pp. 13-15.

"The Three Ravens"

CLEANTH BROOKS and ROBERT PENN WARREN. *Understanding Poetry*, pp. 118-21; rev. ed., pp. 45-48; third ed., pp. 44-46.

EARL DANIELS. *The Art of Reading Poetry*, pp. 131-37. Reprinted in: *Readings for Liberal Education*, II: 363-66; revised ed., II: 6-9.

TYRUS HILLWAY. *Explicator* 5(5), March 1947, Item 36.

SEYMOUR LAINOFF. *Explicator* 17(8), May 1959, Item 55.

LOUIS G. LOCKE. *Explicator* 4(8), June 1946, Item 54.

M. L. ROSENTHAL and A. J. M. SMITH. *Exploring Poetry*, pp. 311-14; second ed., pp. 145-47.

"To-morrow shall be my dancing day"

VINCENT BUCKLEY. *Poetry and the Sacred*, p. 27.

"The Twa Corbies"

EARL DANIELS. *The Art of Reading Poetry*, 132-37. Reprinted in: *Readings for Liberal Education*, II: 363-66; revised ed., II: 6-9.

ELIZABETH DREW. *Poetry*, pp. 93-94.

T. R. HENN. *The Apple and the Spectroscope*, pp. 15-20.

ARTHUR K. MOORE. "The Literary Status of the English Popular Ballad," *Comparative Literature* 10(1), Winter 1958, 15-16.

"Undo the dore, my spuse dere"

STEPHEN MANNING. *Wisdom and Number*, pp. 125-26.

EDMUND REISS. *The Art of the Middle English Lyric*, pp. 125-30.

"An Unwilling Minstrel"

RICHARD LEIGHTON GREENE. "'If I Sing, Tie Up Your Cows,'" *Notes & Queries*, n.s., 11(3), March 1964, 88-89.

"Vaine is the fleting welth"

DOUGLAS L. PETERSON. *The English Lyric from Wyatt to Donne*, pp. 85-86.

"The Virgin's Song"

STEPHEN MANNING. *Wisdom and Number*, pp. 48-49.

"Wae's me, wae's me"

EDWIN MUIR. *The Estate of Poetry*, pp. 17-18.

"Wait a Little"

see "Louerd, Þu clepedst me"

"The Wanderer"

I. L. GORDON. "Traditional Themes in *The Wanderer* and *The Seafarer*," *Review of English Studies*, n.s., 5(17), January 1954, 1-13.

MARTIN GREEN. "Man, Time, and Apocalypse in *The Wanderer, The Seafarer*, and *Beowulf*," *Journal of English and Germanic Philology* 74(4), October 1975, 506-12.

STANLEY B. GREENFIELD. "*The Wanderer*: A Reconsideration of Theme and Structure," *Journal of English and Germanic Philology* 50(4), October 1951, 451-65.

BERNARD F. HUPPÉ. "*The Wanderer*: Theme and Structure," *Journal of English and Germanic Philology* 42(4), October 1943, 516-38.

W. F. KLEIN. "Purpose and the 'Poetics' of *The Wanderer* and *The Seafarer*," in *Anglo-Saxon Poetry*, pp. 212-18.

R. F. LESLIE. "*The Wanderer*: Theme and Structure," in *Old English Literature*, pp. 139-62.

JOHN C. POPE. "Dramatic Voices in *The Wanderer* and *The Seafarer*," in *Old English Literature*, pp. 163-76.

ANONYMOUS *(Cont.)*

"The Wanderer" *(cont.)*

> D. W. ROBERTSON, JR. "Historical Criticism," *English Institute Essays*, 1950, pp. 18-23.
>
> THOMAS C. RUMBLE. "From *Eardstapa* to *Snottor On Mode*: The Structural Principle of 'The Wanderer,'" *Modern Language Quarterly* 19(3), September 1958, 225-30.
>
> RAYMOND P. TRIPP, JR. "The Narrator as Revenant: A Reconsideration of Three Old English Elegies," *Papers on Language and Literature* 8(4), Fall 1972, 345-52.
>
> SUSIE I. TUCKER. "Return to *The Wanderer*," *Essays in Criticism* 8(3), July 1958, 229-37.
>
> ROSEMARY WOOLF. "*The Wanderer, The Seafarer*, and the Genre of *Planctus*," in *Anglo-Saxon Poetry*, pp. 197-202.

"Wanne i thenke thinges thre"

> EDMUND REISS. *The Art of the Middle English Lyric*, p. 75.

"Wanne mine eyhnen misten"

> STEPHEN MANNING. *Wisdom and Number*, pp. 15-17.
>
> EDMUND REISS. *The Art of the Middle English Lyric*, pp. 89-92.

"A Wayle Whyte as Whalles Bon"

> ARTHUR K. MOORE. *The Secular Lyric in Middle English*, pp. 64-65.

"The Weddynge of Sir Gawen and Dame Ragnell"

> RALPH HANNA III. "*The Awntyrs off Arthure*: An Interpretation," *Modern Language Quarterly* 31(3), September 1970, 281.

"Weep You No More, Sad Fountains"

> LAURENCE PERRINE. *Explicator* 34(8), April 1976, Item 61.

"Wel, qwa sal thir hornes blau"

> EDMUND REISS. *The Art of the Middle English Lyric*, pp. 95-97.
>
> EDMUND REISS. "A Critical Approach to the Middle English Lyric," *College English* 27(5), February 1966, 377-79.
>
> ROSSELL HOPE ROBBINS. "A Highly Critical Approach to the Middle English Lyric," *College English* 30(1), October 1968, 74-75.

"Weping hauep myn wonges wet"

> E. G. STANLEY. "Richard Hyrd (?) 'Rote of Resoun Ryht' in Ms. Harley 2253," *Notes & Queries*, n.s., 22(4), April 1975, 155-57.

"Wen the Turuf Is Thi Tuur"

> EDMUND REISS. *The Art of the Middle English Lyric*, pp. 83-87.

"Western Wind, When Wilt Thou Blow"

> GÉMINO H. ABAD. *A Formal Approach to Lyric Poetry*, pp. 363-64.
>
> GÉMINO H. ABAD. *In Another Light*, pp. 127-33.
>
> F. W. BATESON. *English Poetry*, p. 81. Reprinted in: *The Case for Poetry*, p. 13; second ed., p. 10.
>
> CLEANTH BROOKS and ROBERT PENN WARREN. *Understanding Poetry*, revised ed., pp. 177-78; 3rd ed., pp. 245-46; 4th ed., pp. 138-39.
>
> JEROME BEATY and WILLIAM H. MATCHETT. *Poetry From Statement to Meaning*, pp. 170-71.
>
> JOHN CIARDI. *How Does a Poem Mean?* pp. 996-98; rev. ed., pp. 361-68.
>
> STANLEY E. CLAYES and JOHN GERRIETTS. *Ways to Poetry*, pp. 163-64.

> ROBERTS W. FRENCH. "'Western Wind' and the Complexity of Poetry," *English Journal* 60(2), February 1971, 212-14.
>
> CHARLES FREY. "Interpreting 'Western Wind,'" *ELH* 43(3), Fall 1976, 259-78.
>
> WALTER GIERASCH. *Explicator* 14(7), April 1956, Item 43.
>
> RICHARD R. GRIFFITH. *Explicator* 21(9), May 1963, Item 69. Abridged in: *The Case for Poetry*, second ed., pp. 10-11.
>
> NAT HENRY. *Explicator* 16(1), October 1957, Item 5.
>
> ARTHUR O. LEWIS, JR. *Explicator* 15(5), February 1957, Item 28.
>
> ARCHIBALD MACLEISH. *Poetry and Experience*, pp. 62-63, 66-67.
>
> JOHN FREDERICK NIMS. *Western Wind*, p. 5.
>
> DOUGLAS D. SHORT and PORTER WILLIAMS, JR. "'Westron Wynde': A Problem in Syntax and Interpretation," *Papers on Language and Literature* 13(2), Spring 1977, 187-92.
>
> PATRIC M. SWEENEY. *Explicator* 14(1), October 1955, Item 6.
>
> LEONARD UNGER and WILLIAM VAN O'CONNOR. *Poems for Study*, pp. 12-13.
>
> ROBERT PENN WARREN. "Pure and Impure Poetry," *Kenyon Review* 5(2), Spring 1943, 233-35. Reprinted in: *Criticism*, p. 369. Also: *Critiques and Essays in Criticism*, pp. 89-90. Also: *Essays in Modern Literary Criticism*, pp. 250-51. Also: *The Kenyon Critics*, pp. 22-24. Abridged in: *The Case for Poetry*, p. 13; second ed., pp. 9-10.

"What is he, this lordling, that cometh from the fight"

> EDMUND REISS. *The Art of the Middle English Lyric*, pp. 109-14.

"When Favour's golden hook is baited"

> STANLEY JONES. "Regency Newspaper Verse: An Anonymous Squib on Wordsworth," *Keats-Shelley Journal* 27(1978), 87-107.

"When Pi hed whaketh"

> STEPHEN MANNING. *Wisdom and Number*, pp. 17-19.

"Whenne ich see on roode" ("On the Passion")

> EDMUND REISS. *The Art of the Middle English Lyric*, pp. 31-36.

"White was the sheet"

> I. A. RICHARDS. *Poetries: Their Media and Ends*, pp. 59-61.

"Who is This that Cometh from Edom?"

> see "What is he, this lordling, that cometh from the fight"

"Widsith"

> ROBERT P. CREED. "Widsith's Journey Through Germanic Tradition," in *Anglo-Saxon Poetry*, pp. 376-87.
>
> NORMAN E. ELIASON. "Two Old English Scop Poems," *PMLA* 81(3), June 1966, 185-92.

"The Wife of Usher's Well"

> GÉMINO H. ABAD. *A Formal Approach to Lyric Poetry*, pp. 108-9.
>
> CLEANTH BROOKS and ROBERT PENN WARREN. *Understanding Poetry*, pp. 42-45; rev. ed., pp. 16-20; third ed., pp. 38-41.
>
> C. DAY-LEWIS. *The Lyric Impulse*, pp. 66-67.
>
> DANIEL MCDONALD. "The Baleful Wife of Usher's Well," *Ball State Teachers College Forum* 5(2), Spring 1964, 39-42.

ARTHUR K. MOORE. "The Literary Status of the English Popular Ballad," *Comparative Literature* 10(1), Winter 1958, 13-14.

FRANCIS LEE UTLEY. "Oral Genres as Bridge to Written Literature," *Genre* 2(2), June 1969, 95-102.

"The Wife's Lament"

RUDOLPH C. BAMBAS. "Another View of the Old English Wife's Lament," *Journal of English and Germanic Philology* 62(2), April 1963, 303-9. Reprinted in: *Old English Literature*, pp. 229-36.

ROBERT P. FITZGERALD. "*The Wife's Lament* and 'The Search for the Lost Husband,' " *Journal of English and Germanic Philology* 62(4), October 1963, 769-77.

KEMP MALONE. "Two English *Frauenlieder*," *Comparative Literature* 14(1), Winter 1962, 111-17.

ALAIN RENOIR. "A Reading Context for *The Wife's Lament*," in *Anglo-Saxon Poetry*, pp. 236-41.

RAYMOND P. TRIPP, JR. "The Narrator as Revenant: A Reconsideration of Three Old English Elegies," *Papers on Language and Literature* 8(4), Fall 1972, 356-60.

J. A. WARD. "*The Wife's Lament*: An Interpretation," *Journal of English and Germanic Philology* 59(1), January 1960, 26-33.

"Winner and Waster"
see "Wynnere and Wastoure"

"Wið Faerstice"

MINNA DOSKOW. "Poetic Structure and the Problem of the Smiths in 'Wið Faerstice,' " *Papers on Language and Literature* 12(3), Summer 1976, 321-26.

DONALD K. FRY. "*Wulf and Eadwacer*: A Wen Charm," *Chaucer Review* 5(4), Spring 1971, 247-63.

STANLEY R. HAUER. "Structure and Unity in the Old English Charm *Wið Faerstice*," *English Language Notes* 15(4), June 1978, 250-57.

"Wip Wennum"

DONALD K. FRY. "*Wulf and Eadwacer*: A Wen Charm," *Chaucer Review* 5(4), Spring 1971, 247-63.

"Withe heavye hert I call to thee"

CAROLYN R. S. LENZ. "An Earlier Version of a Religious Lyric by Thomas Tallis," *Review of English Studies*, n.s., 24(95), August 1973, 301-4.

"Worldes blisse, have good day"

EDMUND REISS. *The Art of the Middle English Lyric*, pp. 39-42.

"Wulf and Eadwacer"

JOHN F. ADAMS. " 'Wulf and Eadwacer': An Interpretation," *Modern Language Notes* 73(1), January 1958, 1-5.

PETER DRONKE. *The Medieval Lyric*, pp. 91-92.

RALPH W. V. ELLIOTT. "Form and Image in the Old English Lyrics," *Essays in Criticism* 11(1), January 1961, 2-4.

DONALD K. FRY. "*Wulf and Eadwacer*: A Wen Charm," *Chaucer Review* 5(4), Spring 1971, 247-63.

RUTH P. M. LEHMANN. "The Metrics and Structure of 'Wulf and Eadwacer,' " *Philological Quarterly* 48(2), April 1969, 151-65.

"Wy Haue ʒe No Reuthe on My Child?"

SARAH APPLETON WEBER. *Theology and Poetry in the Middle English Lyric*, pp. 111-17.

"Wynnere and Wastoure"

CONSTANCE HIEATT. "*Winner and Waster* and the *Parliament of the Three Ages*," *American Notes & Queries*, n.s., 4(7), March 1966, 102-4.

JERRY D. JAMES. "The Undercutting of Conventions in *Wynnere and Wastoure*," *Modern Language Quarterly* 25(3), September 1964, 243-58.

A. C. SPEARING. *Medieval Dream-Poetry*, pp. 129-34.

JOHN SPEIRS. " 'Wynnere and Wastoure' and 'The Parlement of the Thre Ages,' " *Scrutiny* 17(3), Autumn 1950, 241-50.

"Wynter Wakeneth Al My Care"

LEWIS H. MILLTER, JR. "Two Poems of Winter," *College English* 28(4), January 1967, 316-17.

EDMUND REISS. *The Art of the Middle English Lyric*, pp. 75-81.

"Young Waters"

JOHN EDWARD HARDY. *The Curious Frame*, pp. 1-21.

ANSEN, ALAN

"An Occupational Hazard"

NORMAN FRIEDMAN. "The Wesleyan Poets — IV," *Chicago Review* 19(3), June 1967, 66-67.

ARENSBERG, WALTER

"Voyage A L'Infini"

KENNETH FIELDS. "Past Masters: Walter Conrad Arensberg And Donald Evans," *Southern Review*, n.s., 6(2), Spring 1970, 322-24.

ARNOLD, MATTHEW

"Bacchanalia"

CHARLES MAHAN. "Matthew Arnold's Concept of History," *Studies in the Humanities* 1(2), Winter 1969-1970, 29.

"The Buried Life"

PATRICIA M. BALL. *The Central Self*, pp. 190-91.

PATRICIA M. BALL. *The Heart's Events*, pp. 2-3.

JAMES BENZIGER. *Images of Eternity*, pp. 217-18.

PAUL G. BLOUNT. "Matthew Arnold on Wordsworth," *Studies in the Literary Imagination* 1(1), April 1968, 9-10.

HARRY BROWN and JOHN MILSTEAD. *What the Poem Means*, p. 4.

JANE F. EARLY. "Matthew Arnold's Troublesome 'Dramatic' Monologues," *Genre* 8(4), December 1975, 313-14.

R. A. FORSYTH. " 'The Buried Life' — The Contrasting Views of Arnold and Clough in the Context of Dr. Arnold's Historiography," *ELH* 35(2), June 1968, 234-41.

E. D. H. JOHNSON. *The Alien Vision of Victorian Poetry*, pp. 149-50.

WENDELL STACY JOHNSON. *Sex and Marriage in Victorian Poetry*, pp. 69-70.

ALICE N. STITELMAN. "Lyrical Process in Three Poems by Matthew Arnold," *Victorian Poetry* 15(2), Summer 1977, 134-39.

DAVID TROTTER. "Hidden Ground Within: Matthew Arnold's Lyric and Elegiac Poetry," *ELH* 44(3), Fall 1977, 549-52.

"Dover Beach"

GÉMINO H. ABAD. *In Another Light*, pp. 250-52.

MELVIN W. ASKEW. "Form and Process in Lyric Poetry," *Sewanee Review* 72(2), Spring 1964, 293.

WILLIAM CADBURY. "Coming to Terms with 'Dover Beach,' " *Criticism* 8(2), Spring 1966, 126-38.

ARNOLD, MATTHEW *(Cont.)*
"Dover Beach" *(cont.)*

GALE H. CARRITHERS, JR. "Missing Persons on Dover Beach?" *Modern Language Quarterly* 26(2), June 1965, 264-66.

DAVID DAICHES and WILLIAM CHARVAT. *Poems in English*, p. 723.

PAUL DEAN and JACQUELINE JOHNSON. " 'Wandering between Two Worlds': Matthew Arnold in Limbo," *Durham University Journal*, n.s., 40(1), December 1978, 67.

RODNEY DELASANTA. *Explicator* 18(1), October 1959, Item 7.

JAMES DICKEY. "Arnold: Dover Beach," in *Master Poems of the English Language,* pp. 713-15.

JAMES DICKEY. *Babel to Byzantium,* pp. 235-38.

ELIZABETH DREW. *Poetry,* pp. 221-23.

JANE F. EARLY. "Matthew Arnold's Troublesome 'Dramatic' Monologues," *Genre* 8(4), December 1975, 315-16.

R. A. FORSYTH. "The Myth of Nature and the Victorian Compromise of the Imagination," *ELH* 31(2), June 1964, 233-37.

GERHARD FRIEDRICH. "A Teaching Approach to Poetry," *English Journal* 49(2), February 1960, 79-81.

ELISABETH G. GITTER. "Undermined Metaphors in Arnold's Poetry," *Victorian Poetry* 16(3), Autumn 1978, 278-79.

FREDERICK L. GWYNN. *Explicator* 8(6), April 1950, Item 46.

JAMES L. HILL. "The Frame for the Mind: Landscape in 'Lines Composed a Few Miles Above Tintern Abbey,' 'Dover Beach,' and 'Sunday Morning,' " *Centennial Review* 18(1), Winter 1974, 39-43.

NORMAN N. HOLLAND. "Psychological Depths and 'Dover Beach,' " *Victorian Studies* 9(Suppl.), September 1965, 5-28.

GERHARD JOSEPH. "Victorian Frames: The Windows and Mirrors of Browning, Arnold, and Tennyson," *Victorian Poetry* 16(1-2), Spring-Summer 1978, 81-82.

J. P. KIRBY. *Explicator* 1(6), April 1943, Item 42. Reprinted in: *Readings for Liberal Education,* II: 524-25; revised ed., II: 162-63.

MURRAY KRIEGER. " 'Dover Beach' and the Tragic Sense of Eternal Recurrence," *University of Kansas City Review* 23(1), Autumn 1956, 73-79.

LOIS T. MILLER. "The Eternal Note of Sadness: An Analysis of Matthew Arnold's 'Dover Beach,' " *English Journal* 54(5), May 1965, 447-48.

GENE MONTAGUE. *Explicator* 18(2), November 1959, Item 15.

THEODORE MORRISON. "Dover Beach Revisited: A New Fable for Critics," *Harper's Magazine* 180(3), February 1940, 235-44. Reprinted in: *The Creative Reader,* pp. 862-73; second ed., pp. 912-23.

D. S. NEFF. "Love and Strife in 'Dover Beach,' " *Victorian Newsletter* 53 (Spring 1978), 28-30.

JOHN S. PHILLIPSON. " 'Dover Beachhead,' " *CEA Critic* 24(2), February 1962, 4.

RUTH PITMAN. "On Dover Beach," *Essays in Criticism* 23(2), April 1973, 109-36.

FREDERICK A. POTTLE. *Explicator* 2(6), April 1944, Item 45.

M. L. ROSENTHAL and A. J. M. SMITH. *Exploring Poetry,* pp. 180-81; second ed., pp. 482-83.

NORMAN C. STAGEBERG. *Explicator* 9(5), March 1951, Item 34. Reprinted in: Norman C. Stageberg and Wallace L. Anderson. *Poetry as Experience,* p. 492.

AGNES STEIN. *The Uses of Poetry,* pp. 349-51.

ALICE N. STITELMAN. "Lyrical Process in Three Poems by Matthew Arnold," *Victorian Poetry* 15(2), Summer 1977, 139-42.

M. G. SUNDELL. "Arnold's Dramatic Meditations," *Victorian Newsletter* 32 (Fall 1967), 1-2.

WILLIAM I. THOMPSON. "Collapsed Universe and Structured Poem: An Essay in Whiteheadian Criticism," *College English* 28(1), October 1966, 34-35.

WILLIAM B. TOOLE, III. "Arnold's 'Dover Beach,' " *CEA Critic* 30(9), June 1968, 8-9.

"A Dream"

R. A. FORSYTH. " 'The Buried Life' — The Contrasting Views of Arnold and Clough in the Context of Dr. Arnold's Historiography," *ELH* 35(2), June 1968, 239-44.

"Empedocles on Etna"

CHARLES ALTIERI. "Arnold and Tennyson: The Plight of Victorian Lyricism as Context of Modernism," *Criticism* 20(3), Summer 1978, 282-88.

JAMES BENZIGER. *Images of Eternity,* pp. 201-7.

CHARLES BERRYMAN. "Matthew Arnold's *Empedocles on Etna,*" *Victorian Newsletter* 29 (Spring 1966), 5-9.

DEREK COLVILLE. *Victorian Poetry and the Romantic Religion,* pp. 97-103.

BARBARA T. GATES. "Arnold's *Empedocles* and the *Book of Common Prayer,*" *Renascence* 28(4), Summer 1976, 215-22.

JUNE STEFFENSEN HAGEN. "Arnold's 'Empedocles on Etna' in its Own Terms," *Arnold Newsletter* 2(1), Spring 1974, 3-7.

E. D. H. JOHNSON. *The Alien Vision of Victorian Poetry,* pp. 173-78.

WENDELL STACY JOHNSON. "Matthew Arnold's Dialogue," *University of Kansas City Review* 27(2), Winter 1960, 115.

FRED KAPLAN. *Miracles of Rare Device,* pp. 124-42.

FRANK KERMODE. *Romantic Image,* pp. 12-18.

ALBERT J. LUBELL. "Matthew Arnold: Between Two Worlds," *Modern Language Quarterly* 22(3), September 1961, 254-56.

S. NAGARAJAN. "Arnold and the *Bhagavad Gita*: A Reinterpretation of *Empedocles on Etna,*" *Comparative Literature* 12(4), Fall 1960, 335-47.

GABRIEL PEARSON. "The Importance of Arnold's *Merope,*" in *The Major Victorian Poets,* pp. 232-35.

MEREDITH B. RAYMOND. "Apollo and Arnold's 'Empedocles on Etna,' " *Review of English Literature* 8(3), July 1967, 22-32.

MARY W. SCHNEIDER. "Orpheus in Three Poems by Matthew Arnold," *Victorian Poetry* 10(1), Spring 1972, 32-39.

"Epilogue to Lessing's Laocoön"

JANE F. EARLY. "Matthew Arnold's Troublesome 'Dramatic' Monologues," *Genre* 8(4), December 1975, 310.

"A Farewell"
see "Switzerland"

"The Forsaken Merman"

DEREK COLVILLE. *Victorian Poetry and the Romantic Religion,* pp. 78-83.

JANE F. EARLY. "Matthew Arnold's Troublesome 'Dramatic' Monologues," *Genre* 8(4), December 1975, 308-14.

NORMAN FRIEDMAN. "The Young Matthew Arnold 1847-1849: 'The Strayed Reveller' and 'The Forsaken Merman,'" *Victorian Poetry* 9(4), Winter 1971, 421-28.

HOWARD W. FULWEILER. "Matthew Arnold: The Metamorphosis of a Merman," *Victorian Poetry* 1(3), August 1963, 208-12.

FRANK R. GIORDANO, JR. "In Defense of Margaret: Another Look at Arnold's 'The Forsaken Merman,'" *Victorian Newsletter* 54 (Fall 1978), 23-28.

WENDELL STACY JOHNSON. *Sex and Marriage in Victorian Poetry*, pp. 58-59.

"Growing Old"

WENDELL STACY JOHNSON. "Youth and Age in Arnold's Poetry," *Arnoldian* 4(1), Fall 1976, 11-12.

"Haworth Churchyard"

PAUL DEAN and JACQUELINE JOHNSON. "'Wandering between Two Worlds': Matthew Arnold in Limbo," *Durham University Journal*, n.s., 40(1), December 1978, 69-70.

MARJORIE PERLOFF. "Yeats and the Occasional Poem: 'Easter 1916,'" *Papers on Language and Literature* 4(3), Summer 1968, 314-18.

KATHLEEN TILLOTSON. "'Haworth Churchyard': The Making of Arnold's Elegy," *Brontë Society Transactions* 15(2), 1967, 105-22.

"Heine's Grave"

PAUL DEAN and JACQUELINE JOHNSON. "'Wandering between Two Worlds': Matthew Arnold in Limbo," *Durham University Journal*, n.s., 40(1), December 1978, 70.

M. G. SUNDELL. "Arnold's Dramatic Meditations," *Victorian Newsletter* 32(Fall 1967), 2-4.

"Human Life"

GEORGE FORBES. "Arnold's 'Oracles,'" *Essays in Criticism* 23(1), January 1973, 52-53.

"In Harmony with Nature"

GEORGE FORBES. "Arnold's 'Oracles,'" *Essays in Criticism* 23(1), January 1973, 45-47.

ALBERT VAN AVER. "Disharmony in Matthew Arnold's 'In Harmony with Nature,'" *Personalist* 48(4), Autumn 1967, 573-78.

"In Utrumque Paratus"

GEORGE FORBES. "Arnold's 'Oracles,'" *Essays in Criticism* 23(1), January 1973, 42-45.

JAN B. GORDON. "Disenchantment with Intimations: A Reading of Arnold's 'In Utrumque Paratus,'" *Victorian Poetry* 3(3), Summer 1965, 192-96.

E. D. H. JOHNSON. *The Alien Vision of Victorian Poetry*, p. 160.

W. STACY JOHNSON. *Explicator* 10(7), May 1952, Item 46.

"Isolation"

see also "Switzerland"

ELIZABETH DREW. *Poetry*, pp. 145-47.

DONALD STAUFFER. *The Nature of Poetry*, pp. 232-35.

"The Last Word"

EDWARD A. BLOOM, CHARLES H. PHILBRICK and ELMER M. BLISTEIN. *The Order of Poetry*, pp. 82-84.

EARL DANIELS. *The Art of Reading Poetry*, p. 273.

"Lines Written in Kensington Gardens"

DAVID TROTTER. "Hidden Ground Within: Matthew Arnold's Lyric and Elegiac Poetry," *ELH* 44(3), Fall 1977, 530-31.

"Memorial Verses"

F. W. BATESON. *English Poetry and the English Language*, pp. 106-8. (P)

JAMES BENZIGER. *Images of Eternity*, pp. 5-6.

PAUL G. BLOUNT. "Matthew Arnold on Wordsworth," *Studies in the Literary Imagination* 1(1), April 1968, 4.

"A Modern Sappho"

ALLAN BRICK. "Equilibrium in the Poetry of Matthew Arnold," *University of Toronto Quarterly* 30(1), October 1960, 50-61. Reprinted in: *British Victorian Literature*, pp. 137-38.

JANE F. EARLY. "Matthew Arnold's Troublesome 'Dramatic' Monologues," *Genre* 8(4), December 1975, 308-9.

"Morality"

JAMES BENZIGER. *Images of Eternity*, pp. 207-9.

GEORGE FORBES. "Arnold's 'Oracles,'" *Essays in Criticism* 23(1), January 1973, 50-52.

"Mycerinus"

JAMES BENZIGER. *Images of Eternity*, pp. 200-1.

JANE F. EARLY. "Matthew Arnold's Troublesome 'Dramatic' Monologues," *Genre* 8(4), December 1975, 306-8, 311-13.

ELLEN S. GAHTAN. "'Nor help for pain': Matthew Arnold and Sophocles' *Philoctetes*," *Victorian Newsletter* 48 (Fall 1975), 23-24.

"The Neckan"

HOWARD W. FULWEILER. "Matthew Arnold: The Metamorphosis of a Merman," *Victorian Poetry* 1(3), August 1963, 212-15.

HOWARD W. FULWEILER. "The Real Issues in Arnold's 'The Neckan,'" *Victorian Poetry* 2(3), Summer 1964, 205-8.

"The New Sirens"

E. D. H. JOHNSON. *The Alien Vision of Victorian Poetry*, pp. 164-65.

"Obermann Once More"

PAUL DEAN and JACQUELINE JOHNSON. "'Wandering between Two Worlds': Matthew Arnold in Limbo," *Durham University Journal*, n.s., 40(1), December 1978, 70-71.

E. D. H. JOHNSON. *The Alien Vision of Victorian Poetry*, pp. 206-7.

CHARLES MAHAN. "Matthew Arnold's Concept of History," *Studies in the Humanities* 1(2), Winter 1969-1970, 29-30.

RUTH apROBERTS. "The Theme of Vocation: Matthew Arnold," *Victorian Poetry* 16(1-2), Spring-Summer 1978, 56-57.

"Palladium"

E. D. H. JOHNSON. *The Alien Vision of Victorian Poetry*, p. 158.

ALICE N. STITELMAN. "Lyrical Process in Three Poems by Matthew Arnold," *Victorian Poetry* 15(2), Summer 1977, 142-46.

"Parting"

see also "Switzerland"

GERHARD JOSEPH. "Victorian Frames: The Windows and Mirrors of Browning, Arnold, and Tennyson," *Victorian Poetry* 16(1-2), Spring-Summer 1978, 79-80.

ARNOLD, MATTHEW *(Cont.)*

"Philomela"

JEROME BEATY and WILLIAM H. MATCHETT. *Poetry From Statement to Meaning,* pp. 109-12.

CLEANTH BROOKS and ROBERT PENN WARREN. *Understanding Poetry,* 4th ed., pp. 349-50.

"Quiet Work"

GEORGE FORBES. "Arnold's 'Oracles,'" *Essays in Criticism* 23(1), January 1973, 48-49.

"Religious Isolation"

G. THOMAS FAIRCLOUGH. "The Sestet of Arnold's 'Religious Isolation,'" *Notes & Queries,* n.s., 9(8), August 1962, 302-3. (P)

GEORGE FORBES. "Arnold's 'Oracles,'" *Essays in Criticism* 23(1), January 1973, 47-48.

"Requiescat"

JAMES R. KREUZER. *Elements of Poetry,* pp. 219-20.

WRIGHT THOMAS and STUART GERRY BROWN. *Reading Poems: An Introduction to Critical Study,* p. 639.

LEONARD UNGER and WILLIAM VAN O'CONNOR. *Poems for Study,* pp. 16-17.

"Resignation"

GEORGE FORBES. "The Reluctant Lover and the World: Structure and Meaning in Arnold's 'Resignation' and 'Stanzas in Memory of the Author of "Obermann"'," *Studies in English Literature 1500-1900* 16(4), Autumn 1976, 662-70.

E. D. H. JOHNSON. *The Alien Vision of Victorian Poetry,* pp. 168-71.

JONATHAN MIDDLEBROOK. "'Resignation,' 'Rugby Chapel,' and Thomas Arnold," *Victorian Poetry* 8(4), Winter 1970, 291-97.

M. G. SUNDELL. "'Tintern Abbey' and 'Resignation,'" *Victorian Poetry* 5(4), Winter 1967, 255-64.

"Revolutions"

CHARLES MAHAN. "Matthew Arnold's Concept of History," *Studies in the Humanities* 1(2), Winter 1969-1970, 21-22.

"Rugby Chapel"

JAMES BENZIGER. *Images of Eternity,* pp. 216-17.

CURTIS DAHL. "The Victorian Wasteland," in *Victorian Literature,* p. 36.

PAUL DEAN and JACQUELINE JOHNSON. "'Wandering between Two Worlds': Matthew Arnold in Limbo," *Durham University Journal,* n.s., 40(1), December 1978, 70.

WENDELL STACY JOHNSON. "'Rugby Chapel': Arnold as a Filial Poet," *University Review* 34(2), Winter 1967, 107-13.

HARVEY KERPNECK. "The Road to Rugby Chapel," *University of Toronto Quarterly* 34(2), January 1965, 188-96.

JONATHAN MIDDLEBROOK. "'Resignation,' 'Rugby Chapel' and Thomas Arnold," *Victorian Poetry* 8(4), Winter 1970, 291-97.

WILLIAM S. PETERSON. "The Landscapes of 'Rugby Chapel,'" *Victorian Newsletter* 25 (Spring 1964), 22-23.

JOHN O. WALLER. "Doctor Arnold's Sermons and Matthew Arnold's 'Rugby Chapel,'" *Studies in English Literature 1500-1900* 9(4), Autumn 1969, 633-46.

"The Scholar-Gipsy"

CLEANTH BROOKS and ROBERT PENN WARREN. *Understanding Poetry,* pp. 545-49; rev. ed., 416-20.

HARRY BROWN and JOHN MILSTEAD. *What the Poem Means,* p. 5.

DAVID R. CARROLL. "Arnold's Tyrian Trader and Grecian Coaster," *Modern Language Review* 64(1), January 1969, 27-33.

DEREK COLVILLE. *Victorian Poetry and the Romantic Religion,* pp. 90-97.

PAUL DEAN and JACQUELINE JOHNSON. "'Wandering between Two Worlds': Matthew Arnold in Limbo," *Durham University Journal,* n.s., 40(1), December 1978, 68.

WALLACE DOUGLAS, ROY LAMSON, and HALLETT SMITH. *The Critical Reader,* pp. 46-49.

PHILIP DREW. "Matthew Arnold and the Passage of Time: A Study of *The Scholar-Gipsy* and *Thyrsis,*" in *The Major Victorian Poets,* pp. 199-224.

A. E. DYSON. "The Last Enchantments," *Review of English Studies,* n.s., 8(31), August 1957, 257-65. Reprinted in: A. E. Dyson. *Between Two Worlds,* pp. 41-52.

PAUL EDWARDS. "Hebraism, Hellenism, and 'The Scholar-Gipsy,'" *Durham University Journal,* n.s., 23(3), June 1962, 121-27.

DAVID L. EGGENSCHWILER. "Arnold's Passive Questers," *Victorian Poetry* 5(1), Spring 1967, 1-9.

ANDREW FARMER. "Arnold's Gipsy Reconsidered," *Essays in Criticism* 22(1), January 1972, 64-73.

NEIL H. HERTZ. "Poetry in an Age of Prose: Arnold and Gray," in *In Defense of Reading,* pp. 57-75.

E. D. H. JOHNSON. *The Alien Vision of Victorian Poetry,* pp. 199-202.

G. WILSON KNIGHT. "*The Scholar Gypsy*: An Interpretation," *Review of English Studies,* n.s., 6(21), January 1955, 53-62. Reprinted in: G. Wilson Knight. *Neglected Powers,* pp. 231-42.

LAURENCE LERNER. *The Uses of Nostalgia,* pp. 228-32.

ARTHUR MIZENER. "Arnold: The Scholar-Gipsy," in *Master Poems of the English Language,* pp. 722-27.

GENE MONTAGUE. *Explicator* 18(2), November 1959, Item 15.

GABRIEL PEARSON. "The Importance of Arnold's *Merope,*" in *The Major Victorian Poets,* pp. 237-41.

LAURENCE PERRINE. *Explicator* 15(5), February 1957, Item 33.

GEORG ROPPEN and RICHARD SOMMER. *Strangers and Pilgrims,* pp. 318-36.

MICHAEL G. SUNDELL. "Life, Imagination, and Art in Arnold's Oxford Elegies," *Criticism* 15(4), Fall 1963, 310-16.

ROGER B. WILKENFELD. "The Argument of 'The Scholar-Gipsy,'" *Victorian Poetry* 7(2), Summer 1969, 117-28.

"Self-Dependence"

GEORGE FORBES. "Arnold's 'Oracles,'" *Essays in Criticism* 23(1), January 1973, 49-50.

FRANK GIORDANO, JR. "Rhythm and Rhyme in 'Self-Dependence,'" *English Language Notes* 13(1), September 1975, 29-35.

ELISABETH G. GITTER. "Undermined Metaphors in Arnold's Poetry," *Victorian Poetry* 16(3), Autumn 1978, 277-78.

"Shakespeare"

FRED A. DUDLEY. *Explicator* 4(8), June 1946, Item 57.

ROBERT A. GREENBERG. "Patterns of Imagery: Arnold's 'Shakespeare,'" *Studies in English Literature 1500-1900* 5(4), Autumn 1965, 723-33.

E. M. HALLIDAY. *Explicator* 6(1), October 1947, Item 4.

F. R. LEAVIS. *Education and the University*, pp. 73-76.

TOM T. TRUSS, JR. *Explicator* 19(8), May 1961, Item 56.

"The Sick King in Bokhara"

ALLAN BRICK. "Equilibrium in the Poetry of Matthew Arnold," *University of Toronto Quarterly* 30(1), October 1960, 52. Reprinted in: *British Victorian Literature*, pp. 139-40.

"Sohrab and Rustum"

ALLAN BRICK. "Equilibrium in the Poetry of Matthew Arnold," in *British Victorian Literature*, pp. 142-44.

DEREK COLVILLE. *Victorian Poetry and the Romantic Religion*, pp. 103-11.

HERBERT R. COURSEN, JR. " 'The Moon Lies Fair': The Poetry of Matthew Arnold," *Studies in English Literature 1500-1900* 4(4), Autumn 1964, 574-75.

E. D. H. JOHNSON. *The Alien Vision of Victorian Poetry*, pp. 190-91.

WENDELL STACY JOHNSON. " 'Rugby Chapel': Arnold as a Filial Poet," *University Review* 34(2), Winter 1967, 108-9.

GABRIEL PEARSON. "The Importance of Arnold's *Merope*," in *The Major Victorian Poets*, pp. 235-37.

MARK SIEGCHRIST. "Accurate Construction in Arnold's *Sohrab and Rustum*," *Papers on Language and Literature* 14(1), Winter 1978, 51-60.

"Stanzas from the Grande Chartreuse"

CHARLES ALTIERI. "Arnold and Tennyson: The Plight of Victorian Lyricism as Context of Modernism," *Criticism* 20(3), Summer 1978, 288-89.

CHRISTOPHER CLAUSEN. "Tintern Abbey to Little Gidding: The Past Recaptured," *Sewanee Review* 84(3), Summer 1976, 411-13.

PAUL DEAN and JACQUELINE JOHNSON. " 'Wandering Between Two Worlds': Matthew Arnold in Limbo," *Durham University Journal*, n.s., 40(1), December 1978, 67-68.

E. D. H. JOHNSON. *The Alien Vision of Victorian Poetry*, pp. 198-99.

HARVEY KERPNECK. "The Road to Rugby Chapel," *University of Toronto Quarterly* 34(2), January 1965, 190-91.

M. G. SUNDELL. "Arnold's Dramatic Meditations," *Victorian Newsletter* 32 (Fall 1967), 4-5.

DAVID TROTTER. "Hidden Ground Within: Matthew Arnold's Lyric and Elegiac Poetry," *ELH* 44(3), Fall 1977, 542-45.

"Stanzas in Memory of the Author of 'Obermann' "

PAUL G. BLOUNT. "Matthew Arnold on Wordsworth," *Studies in the Literary Imagination* 1(1), April 1968, 7-8.

GEORGE FORBES. "The Reluctant Lover and the World: Structure and Meaning in Arnold's 'Resignation' and 'Stanzas in Memory of the Author of "Obermann" '," *Studies in English Literature 1500-1900* 16(4), Autumn 1976, 671.

E. D. H. JOHNSON. *The Alien Vision of Victorian Poetry*, pp. 171-72.

"The Strayed Reveller"

PATRICIA M. BALL. *The Central Self*, pp. 195-96.

NORMAN FRIEDMAN. "The Young Matthew Arnold 1847-1849: 'The Strayed Reveller' and 'The Forsaken Merman,' " *Victorian Poetry* 9(4), Winter 1971, 406-21.

LEON A. GOTTFRIED. "Matthew Arnold's 'The Strayed Reveller,' " *Review of English Studies*, n.s., 11(44), November 1960, 403-9.

E. D. H. JOHNSON. *The Alien Vision of Victorian Poetry*, pp. 167-68.

DOROTHY M. MERMIN. "The Two Worlds in Arnold's 'The Strayed Reveller,' " *Studies in English Literature 1500-1900* 12(4), Autumn 1972, 735-43.

M. G. SUNDELL. "Story and Context in 'The Strayed Reveller,' " *Victorian Poetry* 3(3), Summer 1965, 161-70.

"A Summer Night"

JAMES BENZIGER. *Images of Eternity*, pp. 210-11.

DEREK COLVILLE. *Victorian Poetry and the Romantic Religion*, pp. 83-85.

HERBERT R. COURSEN, JR. " 'The Moon Lies Fair': The Poetry of Matthew Arnold," *Studies in English Literature 1500-1900* 4(4), Autumn 1964, 571-72.

DAVID TROTTER. "Hidden Ground Within: Matthew Arnold's Lyric and Elegiac Poetry," *ELH* 44(3), Fall 1977, 537-59.

"Switzerland"

PATRICIA M. BALL. *The Heart's Events*, pp. 33-47.

RONALD E. BECHT. "Matthew Arnold's 'Switzerland': The Drama of Choice," *Victorian Poetry* 13(1), Spring 1975, 35-45.

WENDELL STACY JOHNSON. *Sex and Marriage in Victorian Poetry*, pp. 59-63.

"Thyrsis"

JAMES BENZIGER. *Images of Eternity*, pp. 212-14.

HARRY BROWN and JOHN MILSTEAD. *What the Poem Means*, pp. 5-6.

DEREK COLVILLE. *Victorian Poetry and the Romantic Religion*, pp. 85-88.

PAUL DEAN and JACQUELINE JOHNSON. " 'Wandering between Two Worlds': Matthew Arnold in Limbo," *Durham University Journal*, n.s., 40(1), December 1978, 68-69.

PHILIP DREW. "Matthew Arnold and the Passage of Time: A Study of *The Scholar-Gipsy* and *Thyrsis*," in *The Major Victorian Poets*, pp. 199-224.

DAVID L. EGGENSCHWILER. "Arnold's Passive Questers," *Victorian Poetry* 5(1), Spring 1967, 9-11.

RICHARD GIANNONE. "The Quest Motif in 'Thyrsis,' " *Victorian Poetry* 3(2), Spring 1965, 71-80.

E. D. H. JOHNSON. *The Alien Vision of Victorian Poetry*, pp. 202-4.

HARVEY KERPNECK. "The Road to Rugby Chapel," *University of Toronto Quarterly* 34(2), January 1965, 191-92.

LAURENCE LERNER. *The Uses of Nostalgia*, pp. 233-38.

MICHAEL G. SUNDELL. "Life, Imagination, and Art in Arnold's Oxford Elegies," *Criticism* 15(4), Fall 1963, 316-21.

"To a Gipsy Child by the Sea-Shore"

E. D. H. JOHNSON. *The Alien Vision of Victorian Poetry*, pp. 148-49.

WENDELL STACY JOHNSON. "Youth and Age in Arnold's Poetry," *Arnoldian* 4(1), Fall 1976, 10. (P)

"To a Republican Friend, 1848"

ALLAN BRICK. "Equilibrium in the Poetry of Matthew Arnold," *University of Toronto Quarterly* 30(1), October 1960, 48-49.

DAVID J. DELAURA. "Matthew Arnold and the Nightmare of History," in *Victorian Poetry*, pp. 46-47.

ARNOLD, MATTHEW *(Cont.)*

"To Marguerite"

KATHLEEN TILLOTSON. " 'Yes: in the Sea of Life,' " *Review of English Studies,* n.s., 3(12), October 1952, 346-64.

"To Marguerite — Continued"
see also "Switzerland"

ELISABETH G. GITTER. "Undermined Metaphors in Arnold's Poetry," *Victorian Poetry* 16(3), Autumn 1978, 275-77.

E. D. H. JOHNSON. *The Alien Vision of Victorian Poetry,* p. 151.

"Tristram and Iseult"

ALLAN BRICK. "Equilibrium in the Poetry of Matthew Arnold," *University of Toronto Quarterly* 30(1), October 1960, 51-52. Reprinted in: *British Victorian Literature,* pp. 138-39.

ARTHUR HUGH CLOUGH. "Arnold — The Strayed Reveller and Other Poems — 1849; Empedocles on Etna and Other Poems — 1852; Alexander Smith — Poems — 1853; William Sydney Walker — The Poetical Remains — 1852; William Allingham — Poems — 1850," in *Victorian Scrutinies,* pp. 160-63.

JOHN P. FARRELL. "Matthew Arnold and the Middle Ages: The Uses of the Past," *Victorian Studies* 13(3), March 1970, 335-38.

ROBERT A. GREENBERG. "Matthew Arnold's Refuge of Art: 'Tristram and Iseult,' " *Victorian Newsletter* 25 (Spring 1964), 1-4.

E. D. H. JOHNSON. *The Alien Vision of Victorian Poetry,* pp. 188-90.

WENDELL STACY JOHNSON. "Matthew Arnold's Dialogue," *University of Kansas City Review* 27(2), Winter 1960, 113-15.

WENDELL STACY JOHNSON. *Sex and Marriage in Victorian Poetry,* pp. 65-68.

MASAO MIYOSHI. "Narrative Sequence and the Moral System: Three Tristram Poems," *Victorian Newsletter* 35 (Spring 1969), 7-9.

M. G. SUNDELL. "The Intellectual Background and Structure of Arnold's *Tristram and Iseult,*" *Victorian Poetry* 1(4), November 1963, 272-83.

"Westminster Abbey"

PAUL DEAN and JACQUELINE JOHNSON. " 'Wandering between Two Worlds': Matthew Arnold in Limbo," *Durham University Journal,* n.s., 40(1), December 1978, 71.

"The World and the Quietist"

GEORGE FORBES. "Arnold's 'The World and the Quietist' and The *Bhagavad Gita,*" *Comparative Literature* 25(2), Spring 1973, 153-60.

ROBERT A. GREENBERG. "Matthew Arnold's Mournful Rhymes: A Study of 'The World and the Quietist,' " *Victorian Poetry* 1(4), November 1963, 284-90.

"Youth of Nature"

PAUL G. BLOUNT. "Matthew Arnold on Wordsworth," *Studies in the Literary Imagination* 1(1), April 1968, 6-7.

ASHBERY, JOHN

"All and Some"

LAWRENCE KRAMER. "The Wodwo Watches the Water Clock: Language in Postmodern British and American Poetry," *Contemporary Literature* 18(3), Summer 1977, 337-42. (P)

"As You Came from the Holy Land"

HAROLD BLOOM. *A Map of Misreading,* pp. 203-6.

"Clepsydra"

HAROLD BLOOM. *Figures of Capable Imagination,* pp. 178-80.

HAROLD BLOOM. "John Ashbery: The Charity of The Hard Moments," *Salmagundi* 22-23 (Spring-Summer 1973), 110-11. Reprinted in: *Contemporary Poetry in America,* pp. 117-18.

"Clouds"

HAROLD BLOOM. "The New Transcendentalism: The Visionary Strain in Merwin, Ashbery, and Ammons," *Chicago Review* 24(3), 1972, 34.

"Definition of Blue"

DAVID KALSTONE. *Five Temperaments,* pp. 173-75.

"The Double Dream of Spring"

FRED MORAMARCO. "John Ashbery and Frank O'Hara: The Painterly Poets," *Journal of Modern Literature* 5(3), September 1976, 458-59.

"Evening in the Country"

HAROLD BLOOM. *Figures of Capable Imagination,* pp. 187-89.

HAROLD BLOOM. "John Ashbery: The Charity of The Hard Moments," *Salmagundi* 22-23 (Spring-Summer 1973), 116-18. Reprinted in: *Contemporary Poetry in America,* pp. 123-25.

"Farm Implements and Rutabagas in a Landscape"

DONALD REVELL. "John Ashbery's Tangram," *Notes on Modern American Literature* 1(2), Spring 1977, Item 12.

"Fragment"

HAROLD BLOOM. *Figures of Capable Imagination,* pp. 192-200.

HAROLD BLOOM. "John Ashbery: The Charity of The Hard Moments," *Salmagundi* 22-23 (Spring-Summer 1973), 120-25. Reprinted in: *Contemporary Poetry in America,* pp. 127-32.

"Grand Galop"

DAVID KALSTONE. *Five Temperaments,* pp. 194-95.

"The Instruction Manual"

FRED MORAMARCO. "John Ashbery and Frank O'Hara: The Painterly Poets," *Journal of Modern Literature* 5(3), September 1976, 448-49.

"A Last World"

HAROLD BLOOM. *Figures of Capable Imagination,* pp. 174-77.

HAROLD BLOOM. "John Ashbery: The Charity of The Hard Moments," *Salmagundi* 22-23 (Spring-Summer 1973), 107-8. Reprinted in: *Contemporary Poetry in America,* pp. 114-15.

"Leaving the Atocha Station"

PAUL CARROLL. *The Poem In Its Skin,* pp. 6-25.

FRED MORAMARCO. "John Ashbery and Frank O'Hara: The Painterly Poets," *Journal of Modern Literature* 5(3), September 1976, 452-53.

"Mixed Feelings"

DAVID KALSTONE. *Five Temperaments,* p. 197.

"The New Spirit"

HAROLD BLOOM. *Figures of Capable Imagination,* pp. 201-4.

HAROLD BLOOM. "John Ashbery: The Charity of The Hard Moments," *Salmagundi* 22-23 (Spring-Summer 1973), 125-28. Reprinted in: *Contemporary Poetry in America*, pp. 132-35.

"No Way Of Knowing"

CHARLES ALTIERI. "Motives In Metaphor: John Ashbery and the Modernist Long Poem," *Genre* 11(4), Winter 1978, 662-68.

"The Painter"

FRED MORAMARCO. "John Ashbery and Frank O'Hara: The Painterly Poets," *Journal of Modern Literature* 5(3), September 1976, 449-50.

"Parergon"

HAROLD BLOOM. *Figures of Capable Imagination*, pp. 191-92.

HAROLD BLOOM. "John Ashbery: The Charity of The Hard Moments," *Salmagundi* 22-23 (Spring-Summer 1973), 119-20. Reprinted in: *Contemporary Poetry in America*, pp. 126-27.

"The Recital"

HAROLD BLOOM. *Figures of Capable Imagination*, pp. 207-8. (P)

HAROLD BLOOM. "John Ashbery: The Charity of The Hard Moments," *Salmagundi* 22-23 (Spring-Summer 1973), 131. (P) Reprinted in: *Contemporary Poetry in America*, p. 138.

"Self-Portrait in a Convex Mirror"

CHARLES ALTIERI. "Motives In Metaphor: John Ashbery and the Modernist Long Poem," *Genre* 11(4), Winter 1978, 676-87.

BERNARD F. ENGEL. "On John Ashbery's 'Self-Portrait in a Convex Mirror,' " *Notes on Modern American Literature* 2(1), Winter 1977, Item 4.

DAVID KALSTONE. *Five Temperaments*, pp. 175-85.

LAURENCE LIEBERMAN. *Unassigned Frequencies*, pp. 3-61.

FRED MORAMARCO. "John Ashbery and Frank O'Hara: The Painterly Poets," *Journal of Modern Literature* 5(3), September 1976, 461-62.

"The Skaters"

HAROLD BLOOM. *Figures of Capable Imagination*, pp. 180-82.

HAROLD BLOOM. "John Ashbery: The Charity of The Hard Moments," *Salmagundi* 22-23 (Spring-Summer 1973), 111-13. Reprinted in: *Contemporary Poetry in America*, pp. 118-20.

MICHAEL DAVIDSON. "Languages of Post-Modernism," *Chicago Review* 27(1), Summer 1975, 17-18.

FRED MORAMARCO. "John Ashbery and Frank O'Hara: The Painterly Poets," *Journal of Modern Literature* 5(3), September 1976, 453-55.

"Soonest Mended"

HAROLD BLOOM. *Figures of Capable Imagination*, pp. 185-87.

HAROLD BLOOM. "John Ashbery: The Charity of The Hard Moments," *Salmagundi* 22-23 (Spring-Summer 1973), 115-16. Reprinted in: *Contemporary Poetry in America*, pp. 122-23.

DAVID KALSTONE. *Five Temperaments*, pp. 192-93.

"Sunrise in Suburbia"

HAROLD BLOOM. *Figures of Capable Imagination*, pp. 189-91.

HAROLD BLOOM. "John Ashbery: The Charity of The Hard Moments," *Salmagundi* 22-23 (Spring-Summer 1973), 118-19. Reprinted in: *Contemporary Poetry in America*, pp. 125-26.

"The System"

HAROLD BLOOM. "John Ashbery: The Charity of The Hard Moments," *Salmagundi* 22-23 (Spring-Summer 1973), 128-31. Reprinted in: *Contemporary Poetry in America*, pp. 135-38.

ASHLEY, LEONARD R. N.

"The Game"

LEONARD R. N. ASHLEY. "The Rules of the Game," *Concerning Poetry* 1(1), Spring 1968, 37-44.

ATWOOD, MARGARET

"Astral Traveller"

ELI MANDEL. "Modern Canadian Poetry," *Twentieth Century Literature* 16(3), July 1970, 177.

"Book of Ancestors"

MAUREEN DILLIOTT. "Emerging from the Cold: Margaret Atwood's 'You Are Happy,' " *Modern Poetry Studies* 8(1), Spring 1977, 88-90.

"Circe/Mud Poems"

MAUREEN DILLIOTT. "Emerging from the Cold: Margaret Atwood's 'You Are Happy,' " *Modern Poetry Studies* 8(1), Spring 1977, 81-83.

"Four Evasions"

MAUREEN DILLIOTT. "Emerging from the Cold: Margaret Atwood's 'You Are Happy,' " *Modern Poetry Studies* 8(1), Spring 1977, 85-86.

"Newsreel: Man and Firing Squad"

MAUREEN DILLIOTT. "Emerging from the Cold: Margaret Atwood's 'You Are Happy,' " *Modern Poetry Studies* 8(1), Spring 1977, 75-76.

"Siren Song"

MAUREEN DILLIOTT. "Emerging from the Cold: Margaret Atwood's 'You Are Happy,' " *Modern Poetry Studies* 8(1), Spring 1977, 81.

"Spring Poem"

MAUREEN DILLIOTT. "Emerging from the Cold: Margaret Atwood's 'You Are Happy,' " *Modern Poetry Studies* 8(1), Spring 1977, 78.

"Tricks with Mirrors"

MAUREEN DILLIOTT. "Emerging from the Cold: Margaret Atwood's 'You Are Happy,' " *Modern Poetry Studies* 8(1), Spring 1977, 78-79.

"You Are Happy"

MAUREEN DILLIOTT. "Emerging from the Cold: Margaret Atwood's 'You Are Happy,' " *Modern Poetry Studies* 8(1), Spring 1977, 79-80.

AUDEN, W. H.

"Adolescence"

LILLIAN FEDER. *Ancient Myth in Modern Poetry*, pp. 324-25.

EDWARD MENDELSON. "The Coherence of Auden's *The Orators*," *ELH* 35(1), March 1968, 131-32.

"Advent"

MONROE K. SPEARS. "Auden's Longer Poems," in *Modern Poetry*, pp. 360-61.

"The Aliens"

EVELYN A. FLORY. "Auden and Eiseley: The Development of a Poem," *Concerning Poetry* 8(1), Spring 1975, 67-73.

H. M. WAIDSON. "Auden and German Literature," *Modern Language Review* 70(2), April 1975, 362-63.

AUDEN, W. H. *(Cont.)*

"And the age ended, and the last deliverer died"
see also "In Time of War"

"And the age ended, and the last deliverer died" (In Time of War, 12)
GILBERT HIGHET. *The Powers of Poetry,* pp. 194-95.

"Another Time"
JOOST DAALDER. "W. H. Auden's 'Another Time,'"
Concerning Poetry 5(1), Spring 1972, 65-66.

"As He Is"
GEORGE T. WRIGHT. "A General View of Auden's
Poetry," *Tennessee Studies in Literature* 10 (1965),
48-50.

"As I Walked Out One Evening"
CLEANTH BROOKS and ROBERT PENN WARREN. *Under-
standing Poetry,* third ed., pp. 332-35.
HARRY BROWN and JOHN MILSTEAD. *What the Poem
Means,* p. 7.
BABETTE DEUTSCH. *Poetry in Our Time,* pp. 387-90;
second ed., pp. 433-35.
MICHAEL HENNESSY. "'The Country of Considera-
tion': Auden's Search for Place," *Thoth* 15(3), Fall
1975, 18.
EDWARD C. MCALEER. "As Auden Walked Out,"
College English 18(5), February 1957, 271-72.
ELLSWORTH MASON. *Explicator* 12(7), May 1954, Item
43.

"As it is, plenty"
see "His Excellency"

"As Well As Can Be Expected"
see "Taller To-day"

"August for the people and their favourite islands"
JOSEPH WARREN BEACH. *Obsessive Images,* pp. 125-26.
ELTON EDWARD SMITH. *The Angry Young Men of the
Thirties,* p. 121.

"Better Not"
see "No Change of Place"

"The Birth of Architecture"
RICHARD A. JOHNSON. "Auden's Architecture of
Humanism," *Virginia Quarterly Review* 48(1), Winter
1972, 97-99.

"Birthday Poem"
GILBERT HIGHET. *The Powers of Poetry,* p. 31. (P)

"A Bride in the 30's"
CHRISTOPHER GILLIE. *Movements in English Litera-
ture,* pp. 128-30.
BARBARA HARDY. "W. H. Auden, Thirties to Sixties: A
Face and a Map," *Southern Review,* n.s., 5(3),
Summer 1969, 666-68. Reprinted in: Barbara Hardy.
The Advantage of Lyric, pp. 105-6.

"Brussels in Winter"
ROBIN SKELTON. *The Poetic Pattern,* pp. 62-63.

"Bucolics"
see also "Streams," "Winds," "Woods"
LILLIAN FEDER. *Ancient Myth in Modern Poetry,* pp.
261-62.
MICHAEL HENNESSY. "'The Country of Consideration': Auden's Search for Place," *Thoth* 15(3), Fall
1975, 21-23.

"Casino"
LILLIAN FEDER. *Ancient Myth in Modern Poetry,* pp.
146, 247-48.

"The Cave of Making"
RICHARD A. JOHNSON. "Auden's Architecture of
Humanism," *Virginia Quarterly Review* 48(1), Winter
1972, 103-4.
H. M. WAIDSON. "Auden and German Literature,"
Modern Language Review 70(2), April 1975, 359-60.

"The Cave of Nakedness"
RICHARD A. JOHNSON. "Auden's Architecture of
Humanism," *Virginia Quarterly Review* 48(1), Winter
1972, 114-15.

"Certainly our city with its byres of poverty down"
ELTON EDWARD SMITH. *The Angry Young Men of the
Thirties,* pp. 121-22.

"A Change of Air"
GEORGE P. ELLIOTT, KARL SHAPIRO, STEPHEN SPEN-
DER and W. H. AUDEN. "On W. H. Auden's 'A
Change of Air,'" in *The Contemporary Poet as Artist
and Critic,* pp. 168-87.
ANTHONY OSTROFF, EDITOR. "A Symposium on W. H.
Auden's 'A Change of Air,'" *Kenyon Review* 26(1),
Winter 1964, pp. 190-208.

"City Without Walls"
LILLIAN FEDER. *Ancient Myth in Modern Poetry,* pp.
340-43.
LAURENCE LERNER. *An Introduction to English Poetry,*
pp. 199-215.

"The Climbers" ("Two Climbs," "Fleeing from short-haired
mad executives")
JOSEPH WARREN BEACH. *Obsessive Images,* p. 108.
GEOFFREY THURLEY. *The Ironic Harvest,* pp. 85-87.

"The Common Life"
RICHARD A. JOHNSON. "Auden's Architecture of
Humanism," *Virginia Quarterly Review* 48(1), Winter
1972, 115-16.
PATRICIA MEYER SPACKS. "Pope's Satiric Use of
Nature," *Studies in the Literary Imagination* 5(2),
October 1972, 50-51.

"A Communist to Others"
D. E. S. MAXWELL. *The Poets of the Thirties,* pp. 41,
131-32, 135.

"Consider"
LILLIAN FEDER. *Ancient Myth in Modern Poetry,* pp.
323-24.
RICHARD JOHNSON. "Auden and the Art of Clarifica-
tion," *Yale Review* 61(4), June 1972, 498-503.
D. E. S. MAXWELL. *The Poets of the Thirties,* pp.
147-48.
ELTON EDWARD SMITH. *The Angry Young Men of the
Thirties,* pp. 101-2.
CHAD and EVA T. WALSH. *Twice Ten,* pp. 248-53.

"Crisis"
HAROLD MORLAND. *Explicator* 5(2), November 1946,
Item 17.
F. A. PHILBRICK. *Explicator* 5(6), April 1947, Item 45.

"Dame Kind"
ROBERT BLOOM. "W. H. Auden's Bestiary of the
Human," *Virginia Quarterly Review* 42(2), Spring
1966, 228-31.
LILLIAN FEDER. *Ancient Myth in Modern Poetry,* pp.
266-67.
MONROE K. SPEARS. "Auden in the Fifties: Rites of
Homage," *Sewanee Review* 69(3), Summer 1961,
391-92.

"Dear, though the night is gone"
LLOYD FRANKENBERG. *Invitation to Poetry,* p. 172.

"Death's Echo"
HELEN E. HAWORTH. "Man's Tragic Dilemma in Auden and Sophocles," *Queen's Quarterly* 77(4), Winter 1970, 566-75.

"The Decoys"
EDWARD MENDELSON. "The Coherence of Auden's *The Orators,*" *ELH* 35(1), March 1968, 127.
M. L. ROSENTHAL. *The Modern Poets,* pp. 189-91.

"Detective Story"
MICHAEL HENNESSY. "'The Country of Consideration': Auden's Search for Place," *Thoth* 15(3), Fall 1975, 19. (P)

"The Diaspora"
ROBERT E. KNOLL. "The Style of Contemporary Poetry," *Prairie Schooner* 29(2), Summer 1955, 122-24.

"Dichtung and Wahrheit"
ROBERT BLOOM. "W. H. Auden's Bestiary of the Human," *Virginia Quarterly Review* 42(2), Spring 1966, 228-29.

"The Dirge" (*Age of Anxiety,* IV)
LILLIAN FEDER. *Ancient Myth in Modern Poetry,* pp. 167-68.

"Doom Is Dark and Deeper Than Any Sea-Dingle"
MORTON W. BLOOMFIELD. "'Doom Is Dark and Deeper Than Any Sea-Dingle': W. H. Auden and *Sawles Warde,*" *Modern Language Notes* 63(8), December 1948, 548-52.
HARRY BROWN and JOHN MILSTEAD. *What the Poem Means,* p. 7.
LILLIAN FEDER. *Ancient Myth in Modern Poetry,* pp. 321-22.
CLIVE JAMES. "Auden's Achievement," *Commentary* 56(6), December 1973, 54.
DUNCAN ROBERTSON. *Explicator* 28(8), April 1970, Item 70.

"Encomium Balnei"
RICHARD A. JOHNSON. "Auden's Architecture of Humanism," *Virginia Quarterly Review* 48(1), Winter 1972, 106-7.

"The Epigoni"
LILLIAN FEDER. *Ancient Myth in Modern Poetry,* p. 340.

"Epilogue" (*Age of Anxiety,* IV)
LILLIAN FEDER. *Ancient Myth in Modern Poetry,* pp. 169-70.

"Et in Arcadia Ego"
LILLIAN FEDER. *Ancient Myth in Modern Poetry,* pp. 176-77.

"The Exiles" ("Ode: To Edward Upward," "Ode II" from *The Orators*)
JOSEPH WARREN BEACH. *Obsessive Images,* pp. 146-47.

"The Fall of Rome"
LILLIAN FEDER. *Ancient Myth in Modern Poetry,* p. 334.

"Family Ghosts"
CLEANTH BROOKS. *Modern Poetry and the Tradition,* pp. 126-29.
SISTER M. CLEOPHAS. *Explicator* 7(1), October 1948, Item 1. Reprinted in: *Reading Modern Poetry,* first ed., pp. 294-95.

"First Things First"
A. KINGSLEY WEATHERHEAD. "The Good Place in the Latest Poems of W. H. Auden," *Twentieth Century Literature* 10(3), October 1964, 103.

"Fish in the unruffled lakes"
RUTH H. BAUERLE. *Explicator* 26(7), March 1968, Item 57.

"Fleeing from short-haired mad executives"
see "The Climbers"

"For Friends Only"
RICHARD A. JOHNSON. "Auden's Architecture of Humanism," *Virginia Quarterly Review* 48(1), Winter 1972, 111-12.

"Foxtrot from a Play"
WILLIAM POWER. *Explicator* 16(6), March 1958, Item 32.

"From scars where kestrels hover"
see "Missing"

"Fugal-Chorus"
WILLIAM FROST. *Explicator* 11(3), December 1952, Item 21.
FREDERICK A. POTTLE. *Explicator* 11(6), April 1953, Item 40.

"The Geography of the House"
RICHARD A. JOHNSON. "Auden's Architecture of Humanism," *Virginia Quarterly Review* 48(1), Winter 1972, 105-6.

"Get there if you can and see the land you once were proud to own"
D. E. S. MAXWELL. *The Poets of the Thirties,* pp. 143-44.
D. S. SAVAGE. *The Personal Principle,* pp. 161-62.
ELTON EDWARD SMITH. *The Angry Young Men of the Thirties,* pp. 100-1.

"Grub First, Then Ethics" ("On Installing an American Kitchen in Lower Austria")
RICHARD A. JOHNSON. "Auden's Architecture of Humanism," *Virginia Quarterly Review* 48(1), Winter 1972, 107-10.
JUSTIN REPLOGLE. "Auden's Homage to Thalia," *Bucknell Review* 11(2), March 1963, 113-14. (P)

"Hammerfest"
A. KINGSLEY WEATHERHEAD. "The Good Place in the Latest Poems of W. H. Auden," *Twentieth Century Literature* 10(3), October 1964, 103-4.

"A Happy New Year" ("Not All the Candidates Pass")
D. E. S. MAXWELL. *The Poets of the Thirties,* pp. 128-31.
JOHN WAIN. *Professing Poetry,* pp. 87-90.

"Have a Good Time"
PAUL CUMMINS. "The Sestina in the 20th Century," *Concerning Poetry* 11(1), Spring 1978, 18-20.
EDWARD MENDELSON. "The Coherence of Auden's *The Orators,*" *ELH* 35(1), March 1968, 127.
F. A. PHILBRICK. *Explicator* 4(3), December 1945, Item 21.

"A Healthy Spot"
J. N. SATTERWHITE. *Explicator* 21(7), March 1963, Item 57.

"Hegel and the Schoolchildren"
see "Schoolchildren"

AUDEN, W. H. *(Cont.)*

"Here on the cropped grass" ("Two Worlds")

LILLIAN FEDER. *Ancient Myth in Modern Poetry*, p. 145, 328-29.

BARBARA HARDY. "W. H. Auden, Thirties to Sixties: A Face and a Map," *Southern Review*, n.s., 5(3), Summer 1969, 664-65. Reprinted in: Barbara Hardy. *The Advantage of Lyric*, p. 103.

"Herman Melville"

ELTON EDWARD SMITH. *The Angry Young Men of the Thirties*, p. 127.

"His Excellency" ("As it is, plenty")

JOSEPH WARREN BEACH. *Obsessive Images*, pp. 301-2.

"Homage to Clio"

ROBERT BLOOM. "W. H. Auden's Bestiary of the Human," *Virginia Quarterly Review* 42(2), Spring 1966, 222-25.

LILLIAN FEDER. *Ancient Myth in Modern Poetry*, pp. 265-66.

BARBARA HARDY. "W. H. Auden, Thirties to Sixties: A Face and a Map," *Southern Review*, n.s., 5(3), Summer 1969, 671-72. Reprinted in: Barbara Hardy. *The Advantage of Lyric*, pp. 109-10.

"Horae Canonicae"

see also "Nones," "Prime"

ROBERT M. ADAMS. *Strains of Discord*, pp. 125-27.

LILLIAN FEDER. *Ancient Myth in Modern Poetry*, pp. 263-64.

FREDERICK P. W. MCDOWELL. " 'Subtle, Various, Ornamental, Clever': Auden in His Recent Poetry," *Wisconsin Studies in Contemporary Literature* 3(3), Fall 1962, 29-44.

HOWARD NEMEROV. *Poetry and Fiction*, pp. 131-33.

"In Father's Footsteps"

see "Our Hunting Fathers"

"In Memory of Sigmund Freud"

LILLIAN FEDER. *Ancient Myth in Modern Poetry*, p. 147.

"In Memory of W. B. Yeats"

GÉMINO H. ABAD. *A Formal Approach to Lyric Poetry*, pp. 59-64.

ELIZABETH DREW. *Poetry*, pp. 267-70.

EDWARD CALLAN. "W. H. Auden: The Farming of a Verse," *Southern Review*, n.s., 3(2), Spring 1967, 346-50.

LILLIAN FEDER. *Ancient Myth in Modern Poetry*, pp. 248-49.

G. S. FRASER. "Auden: In Memory of W. B. Yeats," in *Master Poems of the English Language*, pp. 1017-21.

LUCY S. MCDIARMID. "Poetry's Landscape in Auden's Elegy for Yeats," *Modern Language Quarterly* 38(2), June 1977, 167-77.

EDWARD W. ROSENHEIM, JR. "The Elegiac Act: Auden's 'In Memory of W. B. Yeats,' " *College English* 27(5), February 1966, 422-25.

ROBERT ROTH. "The Sophistication of W. H. Auden: A Sketch in Longinian Method," *Modern Philology* 48(3), February 1951, 198-202.

CHAD and EVAN T. WALSH. *Twice Ten*, pp. 253-56.

"In Praise of Limestone"

MICHAEL HENNESSY. " 'The Country of Consideration': Auden's Search for Place," *Thoth* 15(3), Fall 1975, 20-21.

RICHARD JOHNSON. "Auden and the Art of Clarification," *Yale Review* 61(4), June 1972, 509-13.

REBECCA PRICE PARKIN. "The Facsimile of Immediacy in W. H. Auden's 'In Praise of Limestone,' " *Texas Studies in Literature and Language* 7(3), Autumn 1965, 295-304.

"In Sickness and in Health"

LILLIAN FEDER. *Ancient Myth in Modern Poetry*, pp. 160-61, 257-59.

BARBARA HARDY. "W. H. Auden, Thirties to Sixties: A Face and a Map," *Southern Review*, n.s. 5(3), Summer 1969, 668-69. Reprinted in: Barbara Hardy. *The Advantage of Lyric*, pp. 107-8.

"In Time of War"

see also "And the age ended, and the last deliverer died"

ROBERT BLOOM. "W. H. Auden's Bestiary of the Human," *Virginia Quarterly Review* 42(2), Spring 1966, 215-18.

ELTON EDWARD SMITH. *The Angry Young Men of the Thirties*, pp. 124-26.

"Ischia"

JUSTIN REPLOGLE. "Auden's Homage to Thalia," *Bucknell Review* 11(2), March 1963, 107-8.

"It was Easter as I walked in the public gardens"

see also "1929"

ROBERT BLOOM. "W. H. Auden's Bestiary of the Human," *Virginia Quarterly Review* 42(2), Spring 1966, 210-11.

LILLIAN FEDER. *Ancient Myth in Modern Poetry*, pp. 322-23.

ELTON EDWARD SMITH. *The Angry Young Men of the Thirties*, p. 103.

D. E. S. MAXWELL. *The Poets of the Thirties*, pp. 148-49.

"It's No Use Raising a Shout"

GEORGE MCFADDEN. *Explicator* 15(2), November 1956, Item 12.

J. H. NATTERSTAD. "Auden's 'It's No Use Raising a Shout': A New Perspective," *Concerning Poetry* 3(1), Spring 1970, 17-20.

MARK ROWAN. *Explicator* 15(2), November 1956, Item 12.

JOHN H. SUTHERLAND. *Explicator* 15(2), November 1956, Item 12.

"January 1, 1931"

TREVOR DAVISON. "The Method of Auden's 'The Orators,' " *Durham University Journal*, n.s., 32(3), June 1971, 176.

EDWARD MENDELSON. "The Coherence of Auden's *The Orators*," *ELH* 35(1), March 1968, 128-29.

"Journey to Iceland"

JOSEPH WARREN BEACH. *Obsessive Images*, pp. 121-22.

"Kairos and Logos"

JOSEPH WARREN BEACH. *Obsessive Images*, pp. 355-56.

LILLIAN FEDER. *Ancient Myth in Modern Poetry*, pp. 154-55.

"Law Like Love"

LEONARD UNGER and WILLIAM VAN O'CONNOR. *Poems for Study*, pp. 647-49.

"Lay your sleeping head, my love"

see "Lullaby"

"A Letter to Christopher Isherwood, Esq."
see "Journey to Iceland"

"Look, stranger, on this island now"
see "On This Island"

"Lullaby"

JEROME BEATY and WILLIAM H. MATCHETT. *Poetry From Statement to Meaning*, pp. 35-45.

CLEANTH BROOKS, JOHN THIBAUT PURSER, and ROBERT PENN WARREN. *An Approach to Literature*, 5th edition, pp. 396-97.

CLEANTH BROOKS and ROBERT PENN WARREN. *Understanding Poetry*, 4th ed., pp. 143-44.

ROBERT W. CASWELL. *Explicator* 26(5), January 1968, Item 44.

ELIZABETH JONES. "Auden's 'Lullaby,' " *Notes and Queries*, n.s., 25(4), August 1978, 339.

STEPHEN SPENDER. "W. H. Auden and His Poetry," *Atlantic Monthly* 192(1), July 1953, 79.

"Makers of History"

LILLIAN FEDER. *Ancient Myth in Modern Poetry*, pp. 338-39.

"The Malverns"

BARBARA HARDY. "W. H. Auden, Thirties to Sixties: A Face and a Map," *Southern Review*, n.s., 5(3), Summer 1969, 665-66. Reprinted in: Barbara Hardy. *The Advantage of Lyric*, pp. 104-5.

D. E. S. MAXWELL. *The Poets of the Thirties*, pp. 132-33.

"The Managers"

LILLIAN FEDER. *Ancient Myth in Modern Poetry*, p. 172.

"The Masque" (*Age of Anxiety*, V)

LILLIAN FEDER. *Ancient Myth in Modern Poetry*, pp. 168-69.

"Meiosis"

GLADYS GARNER LEITHAUSER. "W. H. Auden's 'Meiosis,' " *English Language Notes* 8(2), December 1970, 120-26.

"Memorial for the City"

LILLIAN FEDER. *Ancient Myth in Modern Poetry*, pp. 334-36.

BARBARA HARDY. "W. H. Auden, Thirties to Sixties: A Face and a Map," *Southern Review*, n.s., 5(3), Summer 1969, 670-71. Reprinted in: Barbara Hardy. *The Advantage of Lyric*, pp. 108-9.

RICHARD JOHNSON. "Auden and the Art of Clarification," *Yale Review* 61(4), June 1972, 507-9.

FREDERICK P. W. MCDOWELL. " 'Subtle, Various, Ornamental, Clever': Auden in His Recent Poetry," *Wisconsin Studies in Contemporary Literature* 3(3), Fall 1962, 34-35.

MONROE K. SPEARS. "The Dominant Symbols of Auden's Poetry," *Sewanee Review* 59(3), Summer 1951, 416-17.

"Miss Gee"

JOHN T. IRWIN. "MacNeice, Auden, and the Art Ballad," *Contemporary Literature* 11(1), Winter 1970, 75-76.

"Missing" ("From stars where kestrels hover")

JOSEPH WARREN BEACH. *Obsessive Images*, pp. 219-20.

"Mundus et Infans"

GILBERT HIGHET. *The Powers of Poetry*, pp. 167-73.

THOMAS THORNBURG. *Explicator* 27(5), January 1969, Item 33.

"Musée des Beaux Arts"

GÉMINO H. ABAD. *In Another Light*, pp. 175-94.

HARRY BROWN and JOHN MILSTEAD. *What the Poem Means*, p. 8.

ARTHUR F. KINNEY. "Auden, Bruegel, and 'Musée des Beaux Arts,' " *College English* 24(7), April 1963, 529-31.

JOHN F. LYNEN. "Forms of Time in Modern Poetry," *Queen's Quarterly* 82(3), Autumn 1975, 352.

JOHN CLARK PRATT. *The Meaning of Modern Poetry*, pp. 111, 104-5, 120-21, 128-30.

NANCY SULLIVAN. "Perspective and the Poetic Process," *Wisconsin Studies in Contemporary Literature* 6(1), Winter-Spring 1965, 129-31.

"1929"

see also "It was Easter as I walked in the public gardens"

BARBARA HARDY. "W. H. Auden, Thirties to Sixties: A Face and a Map," *Southern Review*, n.s., 5(3), Summer 1969, 657-62. Reprinted in: Barbara Hardy. *The Advantage of Lyric*, pp. 97-101.

M. L. ROSENTHAL. *The Modern Poets*, pp. 183-87.

"No Change of Place"

MICHAEL HENNESSY. " 'The Country of Consideration': Auden's Search for Place," *Thoth* 15(3), Fall 1975, 15-17.

"Nones"

see also "Horae Canonicae"

ROBERT BLOOM. "W. H. Auden's Bestiary of the Human," *Virginia Quarterly Review* 42(2), Spring 1966, 220-22.

LILLIAN FEDER. *Ancient Myth in Modern Poetry*, p. 173.

"Not All The Candidates Pass"
see "A Happy New Year"

"Now from my window-sill I watch the night"
see "A Happy New Year"

"O love, the interest itself in thoughtless Heaven" (*Look! Stranger*, I)

D. E. S. MAXWELL. *The Poets of the Thirties*, pp. 127-28.

ELTON EDWARD SMITH. *The Angry Young Men of the Thirties*, p. 119.

"O What Is That Sound?"

ECKOE M. AHERN. "There May Be Many Answers," *English Journal* 51(9), December 1962, 657-58.

LAURENCE PERRINE and JANE JOHNSTON. *Explicator* 30(5), January 1972, Item 41.

AGNES STEIN. *The Uses of Poetry*, pp. 13-14.

"O Where Are You Going?"

M. L. ROSENTHAL. *The Modern Poets*, p. 189.

CHAD and EVA T. WALSH. *Twice Ten*, p. 246-48.

"O Who Can Ever Gaze His Fill"
see "Death's Echo"

"Ode II" (*The Orators*)
see "The Exiles"

"Ode: To Edward Upward"
see "The Exiles"

"Ode to Gaea"

LILLIAN FEDER. *Ancient Myth in Modern Poetry*, pp. 174-76.

AUDEN, W. H. *(Cont.)*

"Ode to My Pupils"
see "Which Side Am I Supposed to Be On?"

"Ode to Terminus"
LILLIAN FEDER. *Ancient Myth in Modern Poetry*, pp. 268-69.

"On Installing an American Kitchen in Lower Austria"
see "Grub First, Then Ethics"

"On This Island"
RICHARD JOHNSON. "Auden and the Art of Clarification," *Yale Review* 61(4), June 1972, 503-7.

"Our Hunting Fathers" ("In Father's Footsteps")
DAVID DAICHES and WILLIAM CHARVAT. *Poems in English*, p. 743.
LILLIAN FEDER. *Ancient Myth in Modern Poetry*, p. 327.

"Oxford"
LILLIAN FEDER. *Ancient Myth in Modern Poetry*, pp. 149-50.

"Palais des Beaux Arts"
see "Musée des Beaux Arts"

"Pascal" *(Another Time)*
ELTON EDWARD SMITH. *The Angry Young Men of the Thirties*, pp. 127-28.

"Paysage Moralisé"
JOSEPH WARREN BEACH. *Obsessive Images*, pp. 104-13, 223-24.
PAUL CUMMINS. "The Sestina in the 20th Century," *Concerning Poetry* 11(1), Spring 1978, 17-18.
LILLIAN FEDER. *Ancient Myth in Modern Poetry*, p. 328.
VIRGINIA M. HYDE. "The Pastoral Formula of W. H. Auden and Piero di Cosimo," *Contemporary Literature* 14(3), Summer 1973, 339-41.
ELTON EDWARD SMITH. *The Angry Young Men of the Thirties*, p. 120.

"Petition"
see "Sir, No Man's Enemy, Forgiving All"

"Prime"
see also "Horae Canonicae"
LILLIAN FEDER. *Ancient Myth in Modern Poetry*, pp. 170-71.
LUCY S. MCDIARMID. "Auden and the Redeemed City: Three Allusions," *Criticism* 13(4), Fall 1971, 340-50.

"Prologue" *(The Orators)*
see "Adolescence"

"The Prophets"
BARBARA HARDY. *The Advantage of Lyric*, pp. 85-86.

"The Quest"
LILLIAN FEDER. *Ancient Myth in Modern Poetry*, pp. 252-55.

"The Questioner Who Sits So Sly"
SEYMOUR CHATMAN. *Explicator* 28(3), November 1969, Item 21.
LILLIAN FEDER. *Ancient Myth in Modern Poetry*, pp. 244-45.
M. L. ROSENTHAL. *The Modern Poets*, pp. 187-89.
ELTON EDWARD SMITH. *The Angry Young Men of the Thirties*, pp. 98-100.

"Reflections in a Forest"
ROBERT BLOOM. "W. H. Auden's Bestiary of the Human," *Virginia Quarterly Review* 42(2), Spring 1966, 226-27.

"The Sabbath"
ROBERT BLOOM. "W. H. Auden's Bestiary of the Human," *Virginia Quarterly Review* 42(2), Spring 1966, 227-28.

"Schoolchildren" ("Hegel and the Schoolchildren")
ROBERT BLOOM. "W. H. Auden's Bestiary of the Human," *Virginia Quarterly Review* 42(2), Spring 1966, 215.
RICHARD A. LONG. *Explicator* 7(4), February 1949, Item 32.

"Secondary Epic"
LILLIAN FEDER. *Ancient Myth in Modern Poetry*, pp. 339-40.

"Secrets"
ROBERT BLOOM. "W. H. Auden's Bestiary of the Human," *Virginia Quarterly Review* 42(2), Spring 1966, 219-20.

"September 1, 1939"
DAPHNE NICHOLSON BENNETT. "Auden's 'September 1, 1939': An Interpreter's Analysis," *Quarterly Journal of Speech* 42(1), February 1956, 1-13.
THOMAS R. EDWARDS. *Imagination and Power*, pp. 203-10.
LILLIAN FEDER. *Ancient Myth in Modern Poetry*, pp. 147-49.
M. L. ROSENTHAL. *The Modern Poets*, pp. 193-95.
MARK SCHORER. "Auden: September 1, 1939," in *Master Poems of the English Language*, pp. 1025-28.

"Serenade"
BARBARA HARDY. *The Advantage of Lyric*, pp. 92-93.

"The Seven Ages" *(Age of Anxiety*, II)
LILLIAN FEDER. *Ancient Myth in Modern Poetry*, pp. 163-66.

"The Shield of Achilles"
ELIZABETH DREW. *Poetry*, p. 167.
LILLIAN FEDER. *Ancient Myth in Modern Poetry*, pp. 336-37.
LAURENCE LERNER. "Reading Modern Poetry," in *English Poetry*, edited by Alan Sinfield, pp. 154-60.
JOHN F. LYNEN. "Forms of Time in Modern Poetry," *Queen's Quarterly* 82(3), Autumn 1975, 350-52.
FREDERICK P. W. MCDOWELL. " 'Subtle, Various, Ornamental, Clever': Auden in His Recent Poetry," *Wisconsin Studies in Contemporary Literature* 3(3), Fall 1962, 36-37.
M. L. ROSENTHAL. *Poetry and the Common Life*, pp. 100-101.
MONROE K. SPEARS. "Auden in the Fifties: Rites of Homage," *Sewanee Review* 69(3), Summer 1961, 384.
CHAD and EVA T. WALSH. *Twice Ten*, pp. 260-62.

"A Shock"
EDWARD H. COHEN. "Auden's 'A Shock,' " *Notes on Contemporary Literature* 4(4), September 1974, 7-8.

"Sir, No Man's Enemy, Forgiving All"
CLEANTH BROOKS. *Modern Poetry and the Tradition*, pp. 1-2.
WALLACE CABLE BROWN. *Explicator* 3(5), March 1945, Item 38.

BABETTE DEUTSCH. *Poetry in Our Time,* pp. 381-82; second ed., pp. 426-28.

LILLIAN FEDER. *Ancient Myth in Modern Poetry,* pp. 245-46.

D. A. ROBERTSON, JR., W. K. WIMSATT, JR., and HALLET SMITH. *Explicator* 3(7), May 1945, Item 51.

GEOFFREY THURLEY. *The Ironic Harvest,* pp. 57-59.

MELVIN G. WILLIAMS. "Auden's 'Petition': A Synthesis of Criticism," *Personalist* 46(2), Spring 1965, 222-32.

"Something Is Bound to Happen"
see "Doom Is Dark and Deeper Than Any Sea-Dingle"

"Song for St. Cecilia's Day"
BABETTE DEUTSCH. *Poetry in Our Time,* pp. 390-31; second ed., pp. 435-37.

INGEBORG HOUGH. *Explicator* 18(6), March 1960, Item 35.

"Spain 1937"
JOSEPH WARREN BEACH. *Obsessive Images,* pp. 226-27.

C. B. COX and A. E. DYSON. *Modern Poetry,* pp. 90-97.

STANLEY G. ESKIN. "The Literature of the Spanish Civil War: Observations on the Political Genre," *Genre* 4(1), March 1971, 88-99.

LILLIAN FEDER. *Ancient Myth in Modern Poetry,* pp. 330-32.

CHRISTOPHER GILLIE. *Movements in English Literature,* pp. 131-32.

M. L. ROSENTHAL. *The Modern Poets,* pp. 191-93.

DELMORE SCHWARTZ. "The Two Audens," *Kenyon Review* 1(1), Winter 1939, 43-44.

JOHN WAIN. *Professing Poetry,* pp. 83-84.

"Streams"
see also "Bucolics"
JUSTIN REPLOGLE. "Auden's Homage to Thalia," *Bucknell Review* 11(2), March 1963, 108.

"A Summer Night"
BARBARA HARDY. "W. H. Auden, Thirties to Sixties: A Face and a Map," *Southern Review,* n.s., 5(3), Summer 1969, 662-64. Reprinted in: Barbara Hardy. *The Advantage of Lyric,* pp. 102-3.

GEOFFREY THURLEY. *The Ironic Harvest,* pp. 65-68.

"Taller To-day" ("As Well As Can Be Expected")
D. E. S. MAXWELL. *The Poets of the Thirties,* p. 145.

"Thanksgiving for a Habitat"
RICHARD A. JOHNSON. "Auden's Architecture of Humanism," *Virginia Quarterly Review* 48(1), Winter 1972, 99-103.

"Their Lonely Betters"
ROBERT BLOOM. "W. H. Auden's Bestiary of the Human," *Virginia Quarterly Review* 42(2), Spring 1966, 218-19.

CLEANTH BROOKS. "The Modern Writer and the Burden of History," *Tulane Studies in English* 22 (1977), 161-62.

BARBARA HARDY. *The Advantage of Lyric,* pp. 93-94.

RICHARD WILBUR. *Responses,* pp. 178-79.

"There are some birds in these valleys"
see "The Decoys"

"This Loved One" (*Poems,* XVIII)
JOSEPH WARREN BEACH. *Obsessive Images,* pp. 199-200.

"Through the Looking-Glass"
D. E. S. MAXWELL. *The Poets of the Thirties,* pp. 167-68.

A. E. RODWAY and F. W. COOK. "An Altered Auden," *Essays in Criticism* 8(3), July 1958, 312-16.

"To T. S. Eliot On His Sixtieth Birthday"
DENNIS A. WENTRAUB. *Explicator* 31(9), May 1973, Item 75.

"Tonight at Seven-Thirty"
RICHARD A. JOHNSON. "Auden's Architecture of Humanism," *Virginia Quarterly Review* 48(1), Winter 1972, 112-14.

"The Truest Poetry Is the Most Feigning"
JOHN WAIN. *Professing Poetry,* pp. 100-102.

"Two Climbs"
see "The Climbers"

"Two Worlds"
see "Here on the cropped grass"

"Under boughs between our tentative endearments how should we hear" (*Poems,* 1930, XXVIII)
D. E. S. MAXWELL. *The Poets of the Thirties,* pp. 145-46.

"The Unknown Citizen"
CLEANTH BROOKS and ROBERT PENN WARREN. *Understanding Poetry,* 4th ed., pp. 290-91.

"Venus Will Now Say a Few Words"
JOSEPH WARREN BEACH. *Obsessive Images,* pp. 198-99.

BABETTE DEUTSCH. *Poetry in Our Time,* pp. 380-81; second ed., pp. 425-26.

"Victor"
JOHN T. IRWIN. "MacNeice, Auden, and the Art Ballad," *Contemporary Literature* 11(1), Winter 1970, 76-78.

"The Wanderer"
see "Doom Is Dark And Deeper Than Any Sea-Dingle"

"The Watchers"
see "A Happy New Year"

"Watching in three planes from a room overlooking the courtyard"
see "January 1, 1931"

"The Watershed"
CHRISTOPHER GILLIE. *Movements in English Literature,* pp. 126-27.

"We have brought you, they said, a map of the country"
see "Have a Good Time"

"Which Side Am I Supposed to Be On?" ("Ode to My Pupils")
CALVIN B. LECOMPTE, JR. *Explicator* 8(3), December 1949, Item 21.

RICHARD A. LONG. *Explicator* 6(6), April 1948, Item 39.

EDWARD MENDELSON. "The Coherence of Auden's *The Orators,*" *ELH* 35(1), March 1968, 129-30.

"Whitsunday in Kirchstetten"
LILLIAN FEDER. *Ancient Myth in Modern Poetry,* pp. 267-68.

MONROE K. SPEARS. "In Memoriam W. H. Auden," *Sewanee Review* 82(4), Fall 1974, 676-78.

A. KINGSLEY WEATHERHEAD. "The Good Place in the Latest Poems of W. H. Auden," *Twentieth Century Literature* 10(3), October 1964, 106.

"The Willow-Wren and the Stare"

    JUSTIN REPLOGLE. "Auden's Homage to Thalia," *Bucknell Review* 11(2), March 1963, 114-17.

"Winds"

    see also "Bucolics"

    LILLIAN FEDER. *Ancient Myth in Modern Poetry,* pp. 174, 261.

    MONROE K. SPEARS. "Auden in the Fifties: Rites of Homage," *Sewanee Review,* 69(3), Summer 1961, 381-82.

"Woods"

    see also "Bucolics"

    VIRGINIA M. HYDE. "The Pastoral Formula of W. H. Auden and Piero di Cosimo," *Contemporary Literature* 14(3), Summer 1973, 333-37.

AYLOFFE, JOHN

"Oceana and Britannia"

    GEORGE DE FOREST LORD. "Satire and Sedition: The Life and Work of John Ayloffe," *Huntington Library Quarterly* 29(3), May 1966, 270-72.

B

BAILEY, PHILLIP JAMES

"Life's More Than Breath and the Quick Round of Blood" (*Festus*)

    I. A. RICHARDS. *Practical Criticism,* pp. 21-30.

BALE, JOHN

"The resurreccion of the masse"

    RAINER PINEAS. "John Bale's Nondramatic Works of Religious Controversy," *Studies in the Renaissance* 9 (1962), 229-31.

BARAKA, IMAMU AMIRI

"An Agony. As Now"

    NATHANIEL MACKEY. "The Changing Same: Black Music in the Poetry of Amiri Baraka," *Boundary 2* 6(2), Winter 1978, 379-80.

    WERNER SOLLORS. "Does Axel's Castle Have a Street Address, or, What's New? Tendencies in the Poetry of Amiri Baraka (LeRoi Jones)," *Boundary 2* 6(2), Winter 1978, 400-1.

"Axel's Castle"

    WERNER SOLLORS. "Does Axel's Castle Have a Street Address, or, What's New? Tendencies in the Poetry of Amiri Baraka (LeRoi Jones)," *Boundary 2* 6(2), Winter 1978, 389-91.

"Betancourt"

    WILLIAM C. FISCHER. "The Pre-Revolutionary Writings of Imamu Amiri Baraka," *Massachusetts Review* 14(2), Spring 1973, 271-74.

    WERNER SOLLORS. "Does Axel's Castle Have a Street Address, or, What's New? Tendencies in the Poetry of Amiri Baraka (LeRoi Jones)," *Boundary 2* 6(2), Winter 1978, 396-97.

"Black Art"

    M. L. ROSENTHAL. *Poetry and the Common Life,* pp. 108-10.

    WERNER SOLLORS. "Does Axel's Castle Have a Street Address, or, What's New? Tendencies in the Poetry of Amiri Baraka (LeRoi Jones)," *Boundary 2* 6(2), Winter 1978, 407-8.

"Black Bourgeoisie"

    WERNER SOLLORS. "Does Axel's Castle Have a Street Address, or, What's New? Tendencies in the Poetry of Amiri Baraka (LeRoi Jones)," *Boundary 2* 6(2), Winter 1978, 392-93.

"BLACK DADA NIHILISMUS"

    WILLIAM C. FISCHER. "The Pre-Revolutionary Writings of Imamu Amiri Baraka," *Massachusetts Review* 14(2), Spring 1973, 291-93.

    LEE A. JACOBUS. "Imamu Amiri Baraka: The Quest for Moral Order," in *Modern Black Poets,* pp. 118-19.

"Black People!"

    LEE A. JACOBUS. "Imamu Amiri Baraka: The Quest for Moral Order," in *Modern Black Poets,* pp. 123-24.

"The Bridge"

    NATHANIEL MACKEY. "The Changing Same: Black Music in the Poetry of Amiri Baraka," *Boundary 2* 6(2), Winter 1978, 371-72.

"Consider This"

    WERNER SOLLORS. "Does Axel's Castle Have a Street Address, or, What's New? Tendencies in the Poetry of Amiri Baraka (LeRoi Jones)," *Boundary 2* 6(2), Winter 1978, 391.

"A contract . . ."

    WERNER SOLLORS. "Does Axel's Castle Have a Street Address, or, What's New? Tendencies in the Poetry of Amiri Baraka (LeRoi Jones)," *Boundary 2* 6(2), Winter 1978, 402-3.

"The Dead Lady Canonized"

    KIMBERLY W. BENSTON. "Ellison, Baraka, and the Faces of Tradition," *Boundary 2* 6(2), Winter 1978, 346-47.

"The Disguise"

    WERNER SOLLORS. "Does Axel's Castle Have a Street Address, or, What's New? Tendencies in the Poetry of Amiri Baraka (LeRoi Jones)," *Boundary 2* 6(2), Winter 1978, 397-98.

"From an Almanac"

    LEE A. JACOBUS. "Imamu Amiri Baraka: The Quest for Moral Order," in *Modern Black Poets,* pp. 113-16.

" 'Green Lantern's Solo' "

    LEE A. JACOBUS. "Imamu Amiri Baraka: The Quest for Moral Order," in *Modern Black Poets,* pp. 119-20.

"Human to Spirit, Humanism to Animals"

    LEE A. JACOBUS. "Imamu Amiri Baraka: The Quest for Moral Order," in *Modern Black Poets,* pp. 124-25.

"Hymn for Lanie Poo"

    WILLIAM C. FISCHER. "The Pre-Revolutionary Writings of Imamu Amiri Baraka," *Massachusetts Review* 14(2), Spring 1973, 266-67.

BARAKA, IMAMU AMIRI *(Cont.)*

"Hymn for Lanie Poo" *(cont.)*

JAY WRIGHT. "Love's Emblem Lost: LeRoi Jones's 'Hymn for Lanie Poo,'" *Boundary 2* 6(2), Winter 1978, 415-34.

"In Memory of Radio"

JOHN HAKAC. "Baraka's 'In Memory of Radio,'" *Concerning Poetry* 10(1), Spring 1977, 85.

"It's Nation Time"

WERNER SOLLORS. "Does Axel's Castle Have a Street Address, or, What's New? Tendencies in the Poetry of Amiri Baraka (LeRoi Jones)," *Boundary 2* 6(2), Winter 1978, 408-9.

"LOOK FOR YOU YESTERDAY/HERE YOU COME TODAY"

WILLIAM C. FISCHER. "The Pre-Revolutionary Writings of Imamu Amiri Baraka," *Massachusetts Review* 14(2), Spring 1973, 264-65.

"The Measure of Memory (The Navigator)"

NATHANIEL MACKEY. "The Changing Same: Black Music in the Poetry of Amiri Baraka," *Boundary 2* 6(2), Winter 1978, 373-75.

"Parthenos"

WERNER SOLLORS. "Does Axel's Castle Have a Street Address, or, What's New? Tendencies in the Poetry of Amiri Baraka (LeRoi Jones)," *Boundary 2* 6(2), Winter 1978, 394-95.

"A Poem for Democracy"

LEE A. JACOBUS. "Imamu Amiri Baraka: The Quest for Moral Order," in *Modern Black Poets*, p. 117.

"A Poem for Willie Best"

WILLIAM C. FISCHER. "The Pre-Revolutionary Writings of Imamu Amiri Baraka," *Massachusetts Review* 14(2), Spring 1973, 282-83.

"Rhythm & Blues"

WILLIAM C. FISCHER. "The Pre-Revolutionary Writings of Imamu Amiri Baraka," *Massachusetts Review* 14(2), Spring 1973, 283-84.

NATHANIEL MACKEY. "The Changing Same: Black Music in the Poetry of Amiri Baraka," *Boundary 2* 6(2), Winter 1978, 363-65.

"Tele/vision"

AGNES STEIN. *The Uses of Poetry*, pp. 108-9.

"Trespass Into Spirit"

WERNER SOLLORS. "Does Axel's Castle Have a Street Address, or, What's New? Tendencies in the Poetry of Amiri Baraka (LeRoi Jones)," *Boundary 2* 6(2), Winter 1978, 406-7.

BARKER, GEORGE

"Allegory of the Adolescent and the Adult"

ROBIN SKELTON. "Barker: Allegory of the Adolescent and the Adult," in *Master Poems of the English Language*, pp. 1039-41.

"Elegy on Spain"

LILLIAN FEDER. *Ancient Myth in Modern Poetry*, p. 380.

"Goodman Jacksin and the Angel"

LILLIAN FEDER. *Ancient Myth in Modern Poetry*, pp. 382-83.

"Memorial (For Two Young Seamen Lost Overboard in a Storm in Mid-Pacific, January, 1940)"

C. DAY LEWIS. *The Poetic Image*, pp. 128-30. Reprinted in: *Reading Modern Poetry*, pp. 248-49.

"Sacred Elegies"

LILLIAN FEDER. *Ancient Myth in Modern Poetry*, pp. 381-82.

"Secular Elegies"

LILLIAN FEDER. *Ancient Myth in Modern Poetry*, pp. 380-81.

"Sonnet to My Mother"

GÉMINO H. ABAD. *A Formal Approach to Lyric Poetry*, pp. 349-56, 388-89.

JANET A. EMIG. "Teaching a Modern Sonnet," *English Journal* 51(3), March 1962, 220-21.

M. L. ROSENTHAL. *Poetry and the Common Life*, pp. 114-16.

"Summer Song"

C. DAY-LEWIS. *The Lyric Impulse*, pp. 140-42.

"Three Memorial Sonnets"

MARTHA FODASKI. "Barker: Three Memorial Sonnets," in *Master Poems of the English Language*, pp. 1032-36.

"To Father Gerard Manley Hopkins, S.J."

MICHAEL ROUTH. *Explicator* 33(8), April 1975, Item 65.

BARLOW, JOEL

"Advice to a Raven in Russia"

JAMES T. F. TANNER. "The 'Triple Ban' in Joel Barlow's 'Advice to a Raven in Russia,'" *Early American Literature* 12(3), Winter 1977/78, 294-95. (P)

"Canal"

KENNETH R. BALL. "Joel Barlow's 'Canal' and Natural Religion," *Eighteenth Century Studies* 2(3), Spring 1969, 225-39.

"The Hasty Pudding"

ROBERT D. ARNER. "The Smooth and Emblematic Song: Joel Barlow's *The Hasty Pudding*," *Early American Literature* 7(1), Spring 1972, 76-91.

BARNES, WILLIAM

"My Orchard in Linden Lee"

R. A. FORSYTH. "The Conserving Myth of William Barnes," *Victorian Studies* 6(4), June 1963, 352-53.

BARNFIELD, RICHARD

"The Complaint of Chastitie"

HARRY MORRIS. "Richard Barnfield: *The Affectionate Shepheard*," *Tulane Studies in English* 10 (1960), 35.

"Helens Rape"

HARRY MORRIS. "Richard Barnfield: *The Affectionate Shepheard*," *Tulane Studies in English* 10 (1960), 35-37.

"The Shepheards Content"

HARRY MORRIS. "Richard Barnfield: *The Affectionate Shepheard*," *Tulane Studies in English* 10 (1960), 13-38.

"The Teares of an affectionate Shepheard sicke for Love"

HARRY MORRIS. "Richard Barnfield: *The Affectionate Shepheard*," *Tulane Studies in English* 10 (1960), 13-38.

BAYLY, THOMAS HAYNES

"She wore a wreath of roses"

> JAMES REEVES and MARTIN SEYMOUR-SMITH. *Inside Poetry,* pp. 55-58.

BEATTIE, JAMES

"The Hermit"

> E. H. KING. "James Beattie's *Retirement* and *The Hermit*: Two Early Romantic Poems," *South Atlantic Quarterly* 72(4), Autumn 1973, 580-83.

"The Minstrel"

> E. H. KING. "James Beattie's *The Minstrel* (1771, 1774): Its Influence on Wordsworth," *Studies in Scottish Literature* 8(1), July 1970, 3-29.

"Retirement"

> E. H. KING. "James Beattie's *Retirement* and *The Hermit*: Two Early Romantic Poems," *South Atlantic Quarterly* 72(4), Autumn 1973, 576-80.

"Verses Occasioned by the Death of the Rev^d Mr. Charles Churchill"

> E. H. KING. "James Beattie's 'Verses occasioned by the Death of the Rev^d Mr. Charles Churchill' (1765) and the Demise of Augustan Satire," *Studies in Scottish Literature* 12(4), April 1975, 234-49.

BEAUMONT, FRANCIS

"An Elegy on the Lady Markham"

> PHILIP J. FINKELPEARL. " 'Wit' in Francis Beaumont's Poems," *Modern Language Quarterly* 28(1), March 1967, 34-37.

"Mermaid Club"

> PHILIP J. FINKELPEARL. "Beaumont, Fletcher, and 'Beaumont & Fletcher': Some Distinctions," *English Literary Renaissance* 1(2), Spring 1971, 148-49.

> PHILIP J. FINKELPEARL. " 'Wit' in Francis Beaumont's Poems," *Modern Language Quarterly* 28(1), March 1967, 38-42.

BEAUMONT, JOSEPH

"The Love-Knott"

> STANLEY STEWART. *The Enclosed Garden,* pp. 21-22.

BECKETT, SAMUEL

"Whoroscope"

> PATRICIA CONNORS. "Samuel Beckett's *Whoroscope* as a Dramatic Monologue," *Ball State University Forum* 19(2), Spring 1978, 26-32.

> WILLIAM BYSSHE STEIN. "Beckett's 'Whoroscope': Turdy Ooscopy," *ELH* 42(1), Spring 1975, 125-55.

BEDE

"Death-Song"

> HOWELL D. CHICKERING, JR. "Some Contexts for Bede's *Death-Song*," *PMLA* 91(1), January 1976, 91-100.

BELITT, BEN

"Charwoman"

> JOHN HUTTON LANDIS. "A 'Wild Severity': Towards A Reading of Ben Belitt," *Salmagundi* 22-23 (Spring-Summer 1973), 188-89. Reprinted in: *Contemporary Poetry in America,* p. 222.

> RICHARD VINE. "Death and the Eye," *Modern Poetry Studies* 7(1), Spring 1976, 66-67.

"Chipmunks"

> ROBERT BOYERS. "To Confront Nullity: The Poetry of Ben Belitt," *Sewanee Review* 81(4), Autumn 1973, 764-65. Reprinted in: Robert Boyers. *Excursions,* pp. 184-85.

"Contemporary Suite: 1934"

> EDNA LOU WALTON. *Trial Balances,* pp. 11-13.

"Cricket Hill: Vermont"

> WILLARD SPIEGELMAN. " 'In the Mask of the Upper and Nether': Ben Belitt's Places," *Modern Poetry Studies* 7(1), Spring 1976, 32.

"Double Poem of the World's Burning"

> ROBERT WEISBERG. "Ben Belitt: Speaking Words Against the Word," *Modern Poetry Studies* 7(1), Spring 1976, 52-55.

"Fat Tuesday"

> ROBERT BOYERS. "To Confront Nullity: The Poetry of Ben Belitt," *Sewanee Review* 81(4), Autumn 1973, 766-72. Reprinted in: Robert Boyers. *Excursions,* pp. 186-91.

"Full Moon: The Gorge"

> ROBERT WEISBERG. "Ben Belitt: Speaking Words Against the Word," *Modern Poetry Studies* 7(1), Spring 1976, 57-59.

"Gayosso Ambulance Service: Emergency"
see also "The Gorge"

> JOHN HUTTON LANDIS. "A 'Wild Severity': Towards A Reading of Ben Belitt," *Salmagundi* 22-23 (Spring-Summer 1973), 195-96. Reprinted in: *Contemporary Poetry in America,* pp. 229-30.

"The Gorge"
see also "Gayosso Ambulance Service: Emergency"

> JEROME MAZZARO. "Some Versions of Self: The Poetry of Ben Belitt," *Modern Poetry Studies* 7(1), Spring 1976, 22-24.

> WILLARD SPIEGELMAN. " 'In the Mask of the Upper and Nether': Ben Belitt's Places," *Modern Poetry Studies* 7(1), Spring 1976, 34-39.

> RICHARD VINE. "Death and the Eye," *Modern Poetry Studies* 7(1), Spring 1976, 78-80.

"The Guanajuato Mummies"

> ROBERT WEISBERG. "Ben Belitt: Speaking Words Against the Word," *Modern Poetry Studies* 7(1), Spring 1976, 55-57.

"The Hornet's House"

> HOWARD NEMEROV. *Reflexions on Poetry and Poetics,* p. 80.

"John Keats: Surgeon"

> JOHN HUTTON LANDIS. "A 'Wild Severity': Towards A Reading of Ben Belitt," *Salmagundi* 22-23 (Spring-Summer 1973), 189-91. Reprinted in: *Contemporary Poetry in America,* pp. 223-25.

"Karamazov"

> JEROME MAZZARO. "Some Versions of Self: The Poetry of Ben Belitt," *Modern Poetry Studies* 7(1), Spring 1976, 11-12.

"The Lightning Rod Man"

> JOHN HUTTON LANDIS. "A 'Wild Severity': Towards A Reading of Ben Belitt," *Salmagundi* 22-23 (Spring-Summer 1973), 193-94. Reprinted in: *Contemporary Poetry in America,* pp. 227-28.

BELITT, BEN *(Cont.)*

"The Loco-Bird"

ROBERT BOYERS. "To Confront Nullity: The Poetry of Ben Belitt," *Sewanee Review* 81(4), Autumn 1973, 763-64. Reprinted in: Robert Boyers. *Excursions*, pp. 183-84.

"The Orange Tree"

ROBERT BOYERS. "To Confront Nullity: The Poetry of Ben Belitt," *Sewanee Review* 81(4), Autumn 1973, 755-62. Reprinted in: Robert Boyers. *Excursions*, pp. 178-83.

JOHN HUTTON LANDIS. "A 'Wild Severity': Towards A Reading of Ben Belitt," *Salmagundi* 22-23 (Spring-Summer 1973), 197-99. Reprinted in: *Contemporary Poetry in America*, pp. 231-33.

"The Orphaning"

ROBERT BOYERS. "To Confront Nullity: The Poetry of Ben Belitt," *Sewanee Review* 81(4), Autumn 1973, 772-73. Reprinted in: Robert Boyers. *Excursions*, pp. 191-92.

JOHN HUTTON LANDIS. "A 'Wild Severity': Towards A Reading of Ben Belitt," *Salmagundi* 22-23 (Spring-Summer 1973), 196-97. Reprinted in: *Contemporary Poetry in America*, pp. 230-31.

JEROME MAZZARO. "Some Versions of Self: The Poetry of Ben Belitt," *Modern Poetry Studies* 7(1), Spring 1976, 18-19.

"The Repellant"

ROBERT WEISBERG. "Ben Belitt: Speaking Words Against the Word," *Modern Poetry Studies* 7(1), Spring 1976, 51-52.

"Siesta: Mexico/Vermont"

JOHN HUTTON LANDIS. "A 'Wild Severity': Towards A Reading of Ben Belitt," *Salmagundi* 22-23 (Spring-Summer 1973), 192. Reprinted in: *Contemporary Poetry in America*, p. 226.

"Smerdyakov with a Guitar"

JOHN HUTTON LANDIS. "A 'Wild Severity': Towards A Reading of Ben Belitt," *Salmagundi* 22-23 (Spring-Summer 1973), 189. Reprinted in: *Contemporary Poetry in America*, p. 223.

"Song of the King's Huntsmen"

EDNA LOU WALTON. *Trial Balances*, p. 11.

"Soundings: Block Island"

JOHN HUTTON LANDIS. "A 'Wild Severity': Towards A Reading of Ben Belitt," *Salmagundi* 22-23 (Spring-Summer 1973), 199-205. Reprinted in: *Contemporary Poetry in America*, pp. 233-38.

"Swan Lake"

ROBERT WEISBERG. "Ben Belitt: Speaking Words Against the Word," *Modern Poetry Studies* 7(1), Spring 1976, 50-51.

"This Scribe, My Hand"

ROBERT WEISBERG. "Ben Belitt: Speaking Words Against the Word," *Modern Poetry Studies* 7(1), Spring 1976, 59-60.

"Xerox"

ROBERT WEISBERG. "Ben Belitt: Speaking Words Against the Word," *Modern Poetry Studies* 7(1), Spring 1976, 48-49.

BENEDIKT, MICHAEL

"Project for Metaphor Sculpture"

LOUIS GALLO. "A Note on Mole's Notes: Michael Benedikt and The Idea of Transformation," *Modern Poetry Studies* 8(1), Spring 1977, 25-26.

BENÉT, STEPHEN VINCENT

"John Brown's Body"

PETER J. SHEEHAN. "Benét's *John Brown's Body* — For Study," *English Journal* 58(2), February 1969, 219-25.

"Ode to Walt Whitman"

MORTON D. ZABEL. "The American Grain," *Poetry* 48(5), August 1936, 279-81.

BENTLEY, BETH

"The Lesson"

JOHN W. HUGHES. "Humanism and the Orphic Voice," *Saturday Review* 54(21), 22 May 1971, 33.

BERRY, FRANCIS

"In Honour of London Town"

G. WILSON KNIGHT. *Neglected Powers*, pp. 474-75.

"Photograph"

FRANCIS BERRY. "Poetic Vision by Francis Berry — an Experience," in G. Wilson Knight, *Neglected Powers*, pp. 477-78.

G. WILSON KNIGHT. *Neglected Powers*, pp. 444-45.

"Poor Old Hudders"

G. WILSON KNIGHT. *Neglected Powers*, p. 476.

"Spain, 1939: from Devon"

G. WILSON KNIGHT. *Neglected Powers*, pp. 452-53.

BERRY, WENDELL

"An Anniversary"

SPEER MORGAN. "Wendell Berry: A Fatal Singing," *Southern Review*, n.s., 10(4), Autumn 1974, 874-77.

"The Apple Tree"

JOHN DITSKY. "Wendell Berry: Homage to the Apple Tree," *Modern Poetry Studies* 2(1), 1971, 9-10.

"Canticle"

JOHN DITSKY. "Wendell Berry: Homage to the Apple Tree," *Modern Poetry Studies* 2(1), 1971, 10-11.

"Dark with Power"

LOUIS UNTERMEYER. *50 Modern American & British Poets*, p. 345.

"The House"

ROBERT HASS. "Wendell Berry: Finding the Land," *Modern Poetry Studies* 2(1), 1971, 30-32.

"The Return"

ROBERT HASS. "Wendell Berry: Finding the Land," *Modern Poetry Studies* 2(1), 1971, 16-28.

"The Supplanting"

SPEER MORGAN. "Wendell Berry: A Fatal Singing," *Southern Review*, n.s., 10(4), Autumn 1974, 871.

"Window Poems"

ROBERT HASS. "Wendell Berry: Finding the Land," *Modern Poetry Studies* 2(1), 1971, 28-30.

BERRYMAN, JOHN

"Ah when you drift hover before you kiss" (*Berryman's Sonnets*, 4)

J. M. LINEBARGER. "A Commentary on *Berryman's Sonnets*," *John Berryman Studies* 1(1), January 1975, 14.

"And now I've sent"

ARTHUR OBERG. *Modern American Lyric*, p. 64.

"The Animal Trainer"

IAN HAMILTON. *A Poetry Chronicle*, p. 115.

GABRIEL PEARSON. "John Berryman," in *The Modern Poet*, edited by Ian Hamilton, pp. 115-16.

"Anomalous I linger, and ignore" (*Berryman's Sonnets*, 88)

J. M. LINEBARGER. "A Commentary on *Berryman's Sonnets*," *John Berryman Studies* 1(1), January 1975, 21.

"An apple arc'd"

MARTIN DODSWORTH. "John Berryman: An Introduction," in *The Survival of Poetry*, pp. 102-5.

"At Chinese Checkers"

JOSEPH WARREN BEACH. *Obsessive Images*, pp. 86-87, 177-78.

"Audacities and fetes of the drunken weeks!" (*Berryman's Sonnets*, 33)

J. M. LINEBARGER. "A Commentary on *Berryman's Sonnets*," *John Berryman Studies* 1(1), January 1975, 17.

"The Ball Poem"

MARTIN DODSWORTH. "John Berryman: An Introduction," in *The Survival of Poetry*, pp. 106-10.

"Beethoven Triumphant"

JOEL CONARROE. "After Mr. Bones: John Berryman's Last Poems," *Hollins Critic* 13(4), October 1976, 10-12.

"Began with swirling, blind, unstilled oh still" (*Berryman's Sonnets*, 106)

J. M. LINEBARGER. "*Berryman's Sonnets*: Tradition and the Individual Talent," *Concerning Poetry* 6(1), Spring 1973, 19-20.

J. M. LINEBARGER. "A Commentary on *Berryman's Sonnets*," *John Berryman Studies* 1(1), January 1975, 23.

"Bell to sore knees vestigial crowds, let crush" (*Berryman's Sonnets*, 44)

J. M. LINEBARGER. "A Commentary on *Berryman's Sonnets*," *John Berryman Studies* 1(1), January 1975, 17.

"Big Buttons, Cornets: the Advance"

WILLIAM WASSERSTROM. "Cagey John: Berryman as Medicine Man," *Centennial Review* 12(3), Summer 1968, 339-44.

"Boston Common"

STEVEN AXELROD. "Colonel Shaw in American Poetry: 'For the Union Dead' and its Precursors," *American Quarterly* 24(4), October 1972, 534.

JOSEPH WARREN BEACH. *Obsessive Images*, p. 236.

"Certainty Before Lunch"

JOHN HAFFENDEN. "Berryman's 'Certainty Before Lunch,'" *John Berryman Studies* 1(3), July 1975, 15-16.

"Christian to Try: 'I am so coxed in it'" (*Berryman's Sonnets*, 111)

J. M. LINEBARGER. "A Commentary on *Berryman's Sonnets*," *John Berryman Studies* 1(1), January 1975, 23.

"The clots of age, grovel and palsy, crave" (*Berryman's Sonnets*, 42)

J. M. LINEBARGER. "A Commentary on *Berryman's Sonnets*," *John Berryman Studies* 1(1), January 1975, 17.

"The cold rewards trail in, when the man is blind" (*Berryman's Sonnets*, 29)

J. M. LINEBARGER. "A Commentary on *Berryman's Sonnets*," *John Berryman Studies* 1(1), January 1975, 16.

"Crouched on a low ridge sloping to where you pour" (*Berryman's Sonnets*, 26)

J. M. LINEBARGER. "A Commentary on *Berryman's Sonnets*," *John Berryman Studies* 1(1), January 1975, 16.

"The Dangerous Year"

JOSEPH WARREN BEACH. *Obsessive Images*, pp. 83-84, 204.

"Desires of Men and Women"

RICHARD WILBUR. "Poetry's Debt to Poetry," *Hudson Review* 26(2), Summer 1973, 291-92. Reprinted in: Richard Wilbur. *Responses*, 180-82.

"Despair"

ARTHUR OBERG. *Modern American Lyric*, pp. 82-84.

"The Disciple"

ROBERT FITZGERALD. "Poetry and Perfection," *Sewanee Review* 56(4), Autumn 1948, 690-91. (P)

IAN HAMILTON. *A Poetry Chronicle*, pp. 111-13.

"The Elder Presences" (*Dream Songs*, 72)

SUSAN G. BERNDT. "Rock-a-Bye Baby in the Tree Top," *John Berryman Studies* 3(1-2), Winter-Spring 1977, 52-59.

"Eleven Addresses to the Lord"

ROBERT PHILLIPS. *The Confessional Poets*, pp. 102-3.

ERNEST C. STEFANIK. "A Cursing Glory: John Berryman's *Love & Fame*," *Renascence* 25(3), Spring 1973, 123-26.

"Fall and rise of her midriff bells. I watch." (*Berryman's Sonnets*, 77)

J. M. LINEBARGER. "A Commentary on *Berryman's Sonnets*," *John Berryman Studies* 1(1), January 1975, 20.

"For you am I collared O to quit my dear" (*Berryman's Sonnets*, 69)

J. M. LINEBARGER. "A Commentary on *Berryman's Sonnets*," *John Berryman Studies* 1(1), January 1975, 19.

"For you an idyl, was it not, so far" (*Berryman's Sonnets*, 90)

J. M. LINEBARGER. "A Commentary on *Berryman's Sonnets*," *John Berryman Studies* 1(1), January 1975, 21.

"Four oval shadows, paired, ringed each by sun" (*Berryman's Sonnets*, 81)

J. M. LINEBARGER. "A Commentary on *Berryman's Sonnets*," *John Berryman Studies* 1(1), January 1975, 20.

BERRYMAN, JOHN *(Cont.)*

"Great citadels whereon the gold sun falls" *(Berryman's Sonnets,* 9)

>   WILLIAM J. MARTZ. "John Berryman," in *Seven American Poets from MacLeish to Nemerov,* pp. 188-89.

"Henry's Confession"

>   WILLIAM J. MARTZ. "John Berryman," in *Seven American Poets from MacLeish to Nemerov,* pp. 204-5.

"Her & It"

>   J. D. McCLATCHY. "John Berryman: The Impediments to Salvation," *Modern Poetry Studies* 6(3), Winter 1975, 268.

>   ROBERT PHILLIPS. *The Confessional Poets,* pp. 101-2.

>   ERNEST C. STEFANIK. "A Cursing Glory: John Berryman's *Love & Fame,*" *Renascence* 25(3), Spring 1973, 118-19.

"Homage to Mistress Bradstreet"

>   GARY Q. ARPIN. "Mistress Bradstreet's Discontents," *John Berryman Studies* 1(3), July 1975, 2-7.

>   JOHN BERRYMAN. *The Freedom of the Poet,* pp. 327-29.

>   IAN HAMILTON. *A Poetry Chronicle,* pp. 13, 115-19.

>   ALAN HOLDER. "Anne Bradstreet Resurrected," *Concerning Poetry* 2(1), Spring 1969, 11-18.

>   WILLIAM J. MARTZ. "John Berryman," in *Seven American Poets from MacLeish to Nemerov,* pp. 191-98.

>   GABRIEL PEARSON. "John Berryman," in *The Modern Poet,* edited by Ian Hamilton, pp. 112-14, 118-19.

>   PETER STITT. " 'Bitter Sister, Victim! I Miss You': John Berryman's *Homage to Mistress Bradstreet,*" *John Berryman Studies* 1(2), April 1975, 2-11.

>   LARRY VONALT. "Henry as Mistress Bradstreet," *John Berryman Studies* 3(3), Summer 1977, 17-33.

"The Home Ballad"

>   ERNEST C. STEFANIK. "A Cursing Glory: John Berryman's *Love & Fame,*" *Renascence* 25(3), Spring 1973, 123.

"How can I sing, western & dry & thin *(Berryman's Sonnets,* 32)

>   J. M. LINEBARGER. "A Commentary on *Berryman's Sonnets,*" *John Berryman Studies* 1(1), January 1975, 16-17.

"How far upon these songs with my strict wrist *(Berryman's Sonnets,* 47)

>   J. M. LINEBARGER. "A Commentary on *Berryman's Sonnets,*" *John Berryman Studies* 1(1), January 1975, 18.

"Huffy Henry hid the day"

>   GARY Q. ARPIN. "Forward to the End: Berryman's First Dream Song," *John Berryman Studies* 1(4), Fall 1975, 7-11.

>   JO BRANS. "Bones Bound, Henry Hero: A Reading of Berryman's First Dream Song," *John Berryman Studies* 1(4), Fall 1975, 12-16.

>   CHARLES MOLESWORTH. "Shining the Start: Some Gloss on Berryman's First Dream Song," *John Berryman Studies* 1(4), Fall 1975, 17-22.

>   ERNEST C. STEFANIK, JR. "Knowing Henry: A Reading of Dream Song 1," *John Berryman Studies* 1(4), Fall 1975, 23-29.

>   LARRY VONALT. "Dream Songs First and Last," *John Berryman Studies* 1(4), Fall 1975, 30-35.

" 'I couldn't leave you' you confessed next day" *(Berryman's Sonnets,* 34)

>   J. M. LINEBARGER. "A Commentary on *Berryman's Sonnets,*" *John Berryman Studies* 1(1), January 1975, 17.

"I lift — lift you five states away your glass" *(Berryman's Sonnets,* 13)

>   J. M. LINEBARGER. "A Commentary on *Berryman's Sonnets,*" *John Berryman Studies* 1(1), January 1975, 14-15.

"I wished, all the mild days of middle March" *(Berryman's Sonnets,* 1)

>   J. M. LINEBARGER. "*Berryman's Sonnets:* Tradition and the Individual Talent," *Concerning Poetry* 6(1), Spring 1973, 19-21.

>   J. M. LINEBARGER. "A Commentary on *Berryman's Sonnets,*" *John Berryman Studies* 1(1), January 1975, 13.

" 'If long enough I sit here, she, she'll pass' " *(Berryman's Sonnets,* 89)

>   J. M. LINEBARGER. "A Commentary on *Berryman's Sonnets,*" *John Berryman Studies* 1(1), January 1975, 21.

"If not white shorts-then in a princess gown" *(Berryman's Sonnets,* 22)

>   J. M. LINEBARGER. "A Commentary on *Berryman's Sonnets,*" *John Berryman Studies* 1(1), January 1975, 15-16.

"If we sang in the wood"

>   MARTIN DODSWORTH. "John Berryman: An Introduction," in *The Survival of Poetry,* pp. 118-19.

"I'm cross with god who has wrecked this generation" *(Dream Songs,* 153)

>   SHOZO TOKUNAGA. "Private Voice, Public Voice — John Berryman and Robert Lowell," *John Berryman Studies* 1(2), April 1975, 18-20.

"In a poem made by Cummings, long since, his" *(Berryman's Sonnets,* 27)

>   J. M. LINEBARGER. "A Commentary on *Berryman's Sonnets,*" *John Berryman Studies* 1(1), January 1975, 16.

"Infallible symbolist! — Tanker driven ashore" *(Berryman's Sonnets,* 80)

>   J. M. LINEBARGER. "A Commentary on *Berryman's Sonnets,*" *John Berryman Studies* 1(1), January 1975, 20.

"Love & Fame"

>   ERNEST C. STEFANIK. "A Cursing Glory: John Berryman's *Love & Fame,*" *Renascence* 25(3), Spring 1973, 115-27.

"The man who made her let me climbed the derrick" *(Berryman's Sonnets,* 93)

>   J. M. LINEBARGER. "A Commentary on *Berryman's Sonnets,*" *John Berryman Studies* 1(1), January 1975, 21-22.

"Marble nor monuments whereof then we spoke" *(Berryman's Sonnets,* 40)

>   J. M. LINEBARGER. "A Commentary on *Berryman's Sonnets,*" *John Berryman Studies* 1(1), January 1975, 17.

"The marker slants"

>   MARTIN DODSWORTH. "John Berryman: An Introduction," in *The Survival of Poetry,* pp. 126-27.

"Moths white as ghosts among these hundreds cling" (*Berryman's Sonnets*, 14)

> J. M. LINEBARGER. "A Commentary on *Berryman's Sonnets*," *John Berryman Studies* 1(1), January 1975, 15.

"Musculatures and skulls. Later some throng" (*Berryman's Sonnets*, 38)

> J. M. LINEBARGER. "A Commentary on *Berryman's Sonnets*," *John Berryman Studies* 1(1), January 1975, 17.

"My daughter's heavier"

> A. J. ALBERTI. "Sam Johnson Meets The Oklahoma Kid On The Road to Heaven: A Reading Of The Last Dream Song," *John Berryman Studies* 3(1-2), Winter-Spring 1977, 84-92.
>
> GARY ARPIN. "Anabasis," *John Berryman Studies* 3(1-2), Winter-Spring 1977, 5-7.
>
> JACK V. BARBERA. "Book 7, Henry's Women, His Daughter," *John Berryman Studies* 3(1-2), Winter-Spring 1977, 93-114.
>
> JACK V. BARBERA. "'Into the Dusk-Charged Air,'" *John Berryman Studies* 3(1-2), Winter-Spring 1977, 140-45.
>
> SUSAN G. BERNDT. "Jack Barbera's Prognosis," *John Berryman Studies* 3(1-2), Winter-Spring 1977, 119-21.
>
> SUSAN G. BERNDT. "The Last Word," *John Berryman Studies* 3(1-2), Winter-Spring 1977, 75-83.
>
> SUSAN G. BERNDT. "Poet as Self-Critic," *John Berryman Studies* 3(1-2), Winter-Spring 1977, 25-27.
>
> SUSAN G. BERNDT. "Rock-a-Bye Baby in the Tree Top," *John Berryman Studies* 3(1-2), Winter-Spring 1977, 51-60.
>
> KATHE DAVIS FINNEY. "Barbera: Henry Scolding," *John Berryman Studies* 3(1-2), Winter-Spring 1977, 115-18.
>
> KATHE DAVIS FINNEY. "'A Dying Fall Beneath the Music,'" *John Berryman Studies* 3(1-2), Winter-Spring 1977, 61-71.
>
> PETER STITT. "On Unextended Wings: The Last Dream Song," *John Berryman Studies* 3(1-2), Winter-Spring 1977, 122-27.
>
> CHARLES THORNBURY. "Henry's Last Heavy Daughter," *John Berryman Studies* 3(1-2), Winter-Spring 1977, 28-50.
>
> CHARLES THORNBURY. "Response: A Postscript To Henry's Daughters," *John Berryman Studies* 3(1-2), Winter-Spring 1977, 128-36.
>
> LARRY VONALT. "Dream Songs First and Last," *John Berryman Studies* 1(4), Fall 1975, 30-35.
>
> ANNE B. WARNER. "Dream Song 385: A Summing Up," *John Berryman Studies* 3(1-2), Winter-Spring 1977, 8-24.

"The Nervous Songs"

> GABRIEL PEARSON. "John Berryman," in *The Modern Poet*, edited by Ian Hamilton, p. 121.

"Of 1826"

> JOHN FREDERICK NIMS. *Western Wind*, pp. 338-39.

" — Oh, I suffer from a strike"

> CHARLES MOLESWORTH. "'With Your Own Face On': The Origins and Consequences of Confessional Poetry," *Twentieth Century Literature* 22(2), May 1976, 170-71.

"The Old Boys' blazers like a Mardi-Gras" (*Berryman's Sonnets*, 17)

> J. M. LINEBARGER. "A Commentary on *Berryman's Sonnets*," *John Berryman Studies* 1(1), January 1975, 15.

"Once when they found me, some refrain '*Quoi faire?*'" (*Berryman's Sonnets*, 65)

> J. M. LINEBARGER. "A Commentary on *Berryman's Sonnets*," *John Berryman Studies* 1(1), January 1975, 19.

"Our lives before bitterly our mistake" (*Berryman's Sonnets*, 86)

> J. M. LINEBARGER. "A Commentary on *Berryman's Sonnets*," *John Berryman Studies* 1(1), January 1975, 21.

"Our Sunday morning when dawn-priests were applying" (*Berryman's Sonnets*, 71)

> WILLIAM J. MARTZ. "John Berryman," in *Seven American Poets from MacLeish to Nemerov*, pp. 187-88. (P)

"A penny, pity, for the runaway ass" (*Berryman's Sonnets*, 102)

> J. M. LINEBARGER. "A Commentary on *Berryman's Sonnets*," *John Berryman Studies* 1(1), January 1975, 22.

"The poet hunched, so, whom the worlds admire" (*Berryman's Sonnets*, 5)

> J. M. LINEBARGER. "A Commentary on *Berryman's Sonnets*," *John Berryman Studies* 1(1), January 1975, 14.

"A Point of Age"

> JOSEPH WARREN BEACH. *Obsessive Images*, pp. 84-85.

"The Possessed"

> AGNES STEIN. *The Uses of Poetry*, p. 270.

"Rackman and victim grind: sound all these weeks" (*Berryman's Sonnets*, 6)

> J. M. LINEBARGER. "A Commentary on *Berryman's Sonnets*," *John Berryman Studies* 1(1), January 1975, 14.

"'Ring us up when you want to see us . . .' — 'Sure'" (*Berryman's Sonnets*, 110)

> J. M. LINEBARGER. "*Berryman's Sonnets*: Tradition and the Individual Talent," *Concerning Poetry* 6(1), Spring 1973, 23.
>
> J. M. LINEBARGER. "A Commentary on *Berryman's Sonnets*," *John Berryman Studies* 1(1), January 1975, 23.

"The Search"

> ERNEST C. STEFANIK. "A Cursing Glory: John Berryman's *Love & Fame*," *Renascence* 25(3), Spring 1973, 120-21.

"Snow Line"

> ARTHUR OBERG. *Modern American Lyric*, pp. 50-52.

"Sometimes the night echoes to prideless wailing" (*Berryman's Sonnets*, 25)

> J. M. LINEBARGER. "A Commentary on *Berryman's Sonnets*," *John Berryman Studies* 1(1), January 1975, 16.

"A spot of poontang on a five-foot piece" (*Berryman's Sonnets*, 104)

> J. M. LINEBARGER. "A Commentary on *Berryman's Sonnets*," *John Berryman Studies* 1(1), January 1975, 22-23.

BERRYMAN, JOHN *(Cont.)*

"A Strut for Roethke"

> Jo Porterfield. *Explicator* 32(4), December 1973, Item 25.

"Sunderings and luxations, *luxe,* and grief-" *(Berryman's Sonnets,* 56)

> J. M. Linebarger. "A Commentary on *Berryman's Sonnets,*" *John Berryman Studies* 1(1), January 1975, 18.

"They come too thick, hail-hard, and all beside" *(Berryman's Sonnets,* 50)

> J. M. Linebarger. "A Commentary on *Berryman's Sonnets,*" *John Berryman Studies* 1(1), January 1975, 18.

"They may suppose, because I would not cloy your ear" *(Berryman's Sonnets,* 23)

> J. M. Linebarger. "A Commentary on *Berryman's Sonnets,*" *John Berryman Studies* 1(1), January 1975, 16.

"This fellow keeps on sticking at his drum" *(Dream Songs,* 270)

> Jack V. Barbera. "Book 7, Henry's Women, His Daughter," *John Berryman Studies* 3(1-2), Winter-Spring 1977, 105-6.

"Three, almost, now into the ass's years" *(Berryman's Sonnets,* 105)

> J. M. Linebarger. "A Commentary on *Berryman's Sonnets,*" *John Berryman Studies* 1(1), January 1975, 23.

"Thrice, or I moved to sack, I saw you: how" *(Berryman's Sonnets,* 16)

> J. M. Linebarger. "A Commentary on *Berryman's Sonnets,*" *John Berryman Studies* 1(1), January 1975, 15.

"Today is it? Is it today? I shudder" *(Berryman's Sonnets,* 60)

> Louis Untermeyer. *50 Modern American & British Poets,* p. 292.

"A tongue there is wags, down in the dark wood O" *(Berryman's Sonnets,* 51)

> J. M. Linebarger. "A Commentary on *Berryman's Sonnets,*" *John Berryman Studies* 1(1), January 1975, 18.

"The Translator — I & II" *(Dream Songs)*

> William Wasserstrom. "Cagey John Berryman as Medicine Man," *Centennial Review* 12(3), Summer 1968, 353-54.

"Trophy"

> Gary Q. Arpin. "Establishing a Tradition: JB's Student Verse," *John Berryman Studies* 3(4), Fall 1977, 15.

"Troubling are masks . . . the faces of friends, my face" *(Berryman's Sonnets,* 31)

> J. M. Linebarger. "A Commentary on *Berryman's Sonnets,*" *John Berryman Studies* 1(1), January 1975, 16.

"The two plantations Great grandmother brought" *(Berryman's Sonnets,* 76)

> J. M. Linebarger. "A Commentary on *Berryman's Sonnets,*" *John Berryman Studies* 1(1), January 1975, 20.

"Under the scorpion both, back in the Sooner State" *(Berryman's Sonnets,* 70)

> J. M. Linebarger. "A Commentary on *Berryman's Sonnets,*" *John Berryman Studies* 1(1), January 1975, 19.

"A wasp skims nearby up the bright warm air" *(Berryman's Sonnets,* 28)

> J. M. Linebarger. "A Commentary on *Berryman's Sonnets,*" *John Berryman Studies* 1(1), January 1975, 16.

"What can to you this music wakes my years" *(Berryman's Sonnets,* 92)

> J. M. Linebarger. "A Commentary on *Berryman's Sonnets,*" *John Berryman Studies* 1(1), January 1975, 21.

"When I recall I could believe you'd go" *(Berryman's Sonnets,* 55)

> J. M. Linebarger. "A Commentary on *Berryman's Sonnets,*" *John Berryman Studies* 1(1), January 1975, 18.

"Who for those ages ever without some blood" *(Berryman's Sonnets,* 3)

> J. M. Linebarger. "A Commentary on *Berryman's Sonnets,*" *John Berryman Studies* 1(1), January 1975, 14.

"Whom undone David into the dire van sent" *(Berryman's Sonnets,* 21)

> J. M. Linebarger. "A Commentary on *Berryman's Sonnets,*" *John Berryman Studies* 1(1), January 1975, 15.

"Winter Landscape"

> John Berryman. "One Answer to a Question: Changes," in *The Freedom of the Poet,* pp. 324-26.
>
> Arthur and Catherine Evans. "Pieter Bruegel and John Berryman: Two Winter Landscapes," *Texas Studies in Literature and Language* 5(3), Autumn 1963, 309-18.

"World's Fair"

> Margaret M. McBride. *Explicator* 34(3), November 1975, Item 22.

"You in your stone home where the sycamore" *(Berryman's Sonnets,* 10)

> J. M. Linebarger. "A Commentary on *Berryman's Sonnets,*" *John Berryman Studies* 1(1), January 1975, 14.

"You, Lise, contrite I never thought to see" *(Berryman's Sonnets,* 18)

> J. M. Linebarger. "A Commentary on *Berryman's Sonnets,*" *John Berryman Studies* 1(1), January 1975, 15.

"You sailed in sky-high, with your speech askew" *(Berryman's Sonnets,* 19)

> J. M. Linebarger. "A Commentary on *Berryman's Sonnets,*" *John Berryman Studies* 1(1), January 1975, 15.

"Your shining — where? — rays my wide room with gold" *(Berryman's Sonnets,* 2)

> J. M. Linebarger. "A Commentary on *Berryman's Sonnets,*" *John Berryman Studies* 1(1), January 1975, 13-14.

BEST, CHARLES

"A Sonnet of the Moon"

LAURENCE PERRINE. "The Importance of Tone in the Interpretation of Literature," *College English* 24(5), February 1963, 390-91.

BETJEMAN, JOHN

"Beside the Sea"

R. E. WIEHE. "Summoned by Nostalgia: John Betjeman's Poetry," *Arizona Quarterly* 19(1), Spring 1963, 38.

"A Child Ill"

R. E. WIEHE. "Summoned by Nostalgia: John Betjeman's Poetry," *Arizona Quarterly* 19(1), Spring 1963, 43.

"Holy Trinity"

R. E. WIEHE. "Summoned by Nostalgia: John Betjeman's Poetry," *Arizona Quarterly* 19(1), Spring 1963, 40-41.

"How to Get On in Society"

R. E. WIEHE. "Summoned by Nostalgia: John Betjeman's Poetry," *Arizona Quarterly* 19(1), Spring 1963, 37-38.

"In a Bath Teashop"

ROBIN SKELTON. *Poetry*, pp. 118-19.

"In Westminster Abbey"

ELIZABETH DREW. *Poetry*, p. 155.

"In Willesden Churchyard"

PETER THOMAS. "John Bull Speaks: Reflections on the Collected Poems of John Betjeman," *Western Humanities Review* 27(3), Summer 1973, 292-93.

"A Lincolnshire Church"

R. E. WIEHE. "Summoned by Nostalgia: John Betjeman's Poetry," *Arizona Quarterly* 19(1), Spring 1963, 39-40.

"Middlesex"

LAURENCE LERNER. *An Introduction to English Poetry*, pp. 210-14.

"N. W. 5 and N. 6"

R. E. WIEHE. "Summoned by Nostalgia: John Betjeman's Poetry," *Arizona Quarterly* 19(1), Spring 1963, 41-42.

"The Old Liberals"

R. E. WIEHE. "Summoned by Nostalgia: John Betjeman's Poetry," *Arizona Quarterly* 19(1), Spring 1963, 41.

BIDART, FRANK

"Golden State"

ROBERT PINSKY. *The Situation of Poetry*, pp. 140-44. (P)

ROBERT PINSKY. "Two Examples of Poetic Discursiveness," *Chicago Review* 27(1), Summer 1975, 138-41. (P)

BINYON, LAURENCE

"The Supper"

JAMES GRANVILLE SOUTHWORTH. "Laurence Binyon," *Sewanee Review* 43(3), July-September 1935, 343-46.

BIRKENHEAD, JOHN

"Among Rose buds slept a Bee"

CHARLES CLAY DOYLE. "An Unhonored English Anacreon: John Birkenhead," *Studies in Philology* 71(2), April 1974, 201-4.

"The Lute"

CHARLES CLAY DOYLE. "An Unhonored English Anacreon: John Birkenhead," *Studies in Philology* 71(2), April 1974, 198-201.

"Of Himself"

CHARLES CLAY DOYLE. "An Unhonored English Anacreon: John Birkenhead," *Studies in Philology* 71(2), April 1974, 195-98.

BISHOP, ELIZABETH

"Argument"

JAN B. GORDON. "Days and Distances: The Cartographic Imagination of Elizabeth Bishop," *Salmagundi* 22-23 (Spring-Summer 1973), 303-5. Reprinted in: *Contemporary Poetry in America*, pp. 357-59.

"The Armadillo"

FRANK MACSHANE. "The New Poetry," *American Scholar* 37(4), Autumn 1968, 643-44. (P)

"Arrival at Santos"

CRALE D. HOPKINS. "Inspiration as Theme: Art and Nature in the Poetry of Elizabeth Bishop," *Arizona Quarterly* 32(3), Autumn 1976, 205.

"At the Fishhouses"

SYBIL ESTESS. "Shelters for 'What is Within': Meditation and Epiphany in the Poetry of Elizabeth Bishop," *Modern Poetry Studies* 8(1), Spring 1977, 53-59.

CRALE D. HOPKINS. "Inspiration as Theme: Art and Nature in the Poetry of Elizabeth Bishop," *Arizona Quarterly* 32(3), Autumn 1976, 204-5.

DAVID KALSTONE. *Five Temperaments*, pp. 18-21.

NANCY L. MCNALLY. "Elizabeth Bishop: The Discipline of Description," *Twentieth Century Literature* 11(4), January 1966, 197-200.

WILLARD SPIEGELMAN. "Landscape and Knowledge: The Poetry of Elizabeth Bishop," *Modern Poetry Studies* 6(3), Winter 1975, 204-8.

"The Bight"

SYBIL P. ESTESS. "Elizabeth Bishop: The Delicate Art of Map Making," *Southern Review*, n.s., 13(4), Autumn 1977, 717-18.

DAVID KALSTONE. *Five Temperaments*, p. 23.

WILLARD SPIEGELMAN. "Landscape and Knowledge: The Poetry of Elizabeth Bishop," *Modern Poetry Studies* 6(3), Winter 1975, 209-11.

"Brazil, January 1, 1502"

CRALE D. HOPKINS. "Inspiration as Theme: Art and Nature in the Poetry of Elizabeth Bishop," *Arizona Quarterly* 32(3), Autumn 1976, 205-6.

DAVID KALSTONE. *Five Temperaments*, pp. 28-30.

WILLARD SPIEGELMAN. "Landscape and Knowledge: The Poetry of Elizabeth Bishop," *Modern Poetry Studies* 6(3), Winter 1975, 217-18.

"Cape Breton"

SYBIL ESTESS. "Shelters for 'What is Within': Meditation and Epiphany in the Poetry of Elizabeth Bishop," *Modern Poetry Studies* 8(1), Spring 1977, 50-53.

BISHOP, ELIZABETH *(Cont.)*

"Cape Breton" *(cont.)*

MARJORIE PERLOFF. "Elizabeth Bishop: The Course of a Particular," *Modern Poetry Studies* 8(3), Winter 1977, 188-90.

WILLARD SPIEGELMAN. "Elizabeth Bishop's 'Natural Heroism,'" *Centennial Review* 22(1), Winter 1978, 35-37.

"Casabianca"

NANCY SULLIVAN. "Perspective and the Poetic Process," *Wisconsin Studies in Contemporary Literature* 6(1), Winter-Spring 1965, 128-29.

"A Cold Spring"

JAN B. GORDON. "Days and Distances: The Cartographic Imagination of Elizabeth Bishop," *Salmagundi* 22-23 (Spring-Summer 1973), 302-3. Reprinted in: *Contemporary Poetry in America*, pp. 356-57.

"The Colder the Air"

KARL F. THOMPSON. *Explicator* 12(5), March 1954, Item 33.

"Crusoe in England"

DAVID KALSTONE. *Five Temperaments*, pp. 35-36.

JEROME MAZZARO. "The Recent Poems of Elizabeth Bishop," *South Carolina Review* 10(1), November 1977, 99-115.

WILLIAM JAY SMITH. "Geographical Questions: The Recent Poetry of Elizabeth Bishop," *Hollins Critic* 14(1), February 1977, 4-5.

"The End of March, Duxbury"

JEROME MAZZARO. "The Recent Poems of Elizabeth Bishop," *South Carolina Review* 10(1), November 1977, 111.

"Faustina, or Rock Roses"

WILLARD SPIEGELMAN. "Elizabeth Bishop's 'Natural Heroism,'" *Centennial Review* 22(1), Winter 1978, 41-42.

"Filling Station"

MARJORIE PERLOFF. "Elizabeth Bishop: The Course of a Particular," *Modern Poetry Studies* 8(3), Winter 1977, 190-91.

"The Fish"

GEORGE ABBE. *You and Contemporary Poetry*, pp. 78-80; 1965 ed., pp. 103-5.

SYBIL P. ESTESS. "Elizabeth Bishop: The Delicate Art of Map Making," *Southern Review*, n.s., 13(4), Autumn 1977, 713-17.

CRALE D. HOPKINS. "Inspiration as Theme: Art and Nature in the Poetry of Elizabeth Bishop," *Arizona Quarterly* 32(3), Autumn 1976, 200-2.

NANCY L. MCNALLY. "Elizabeth Bishop: The Discipline of Description," *Twentieth Century Literature* 11(4), January 1966, 192-94.

JAMES M. REID. *100 American Poems of the Twentieth Century* pp. 210-13.

WILLARD SPIEGELMAN. "Elizabeth Bishop's 'Natural Heroism,'" *Centennial Review* 22(1), Winter 1978, 42-44.

"Five Flights Up"

SYBIL P. ESTESS. "History as Geography," *Southern Review*, n.s., 13(4), Autumn 1977, 856.

"Florida"

DAVID KALSTONE. *Five Temperaments*, pp. 16-18.

WILLARD SPIEGELMAN. "Landscape and Knowledge: The Poetry of Elizabeth Bishop," *Modern Poetry Studies* 6(3), Winter 1975, 208-9.

"The Imaginary Iceberg"

HARRY BROWN and JOHN MILSTEAD. *What the Poem Means*, p. 11.

WILLARD SPIEGELMAN. "Landscape and Knowledge: The Poetry of Elizabeth Bishop," *Modern Poetry Studies* 6(3), Winter 1975, 215-16.

"In the Waiting Room"

DAVID KALSTONE. *Five Temperaments*, pp. 32-34.

WILLIAM JAY SMITH. "Geographical Questions: The Recent Poetry of Elizabeth Bishop," *Hollins Critic* 14(1), February 1977, 6-9.

WILLARD SPIEGELMAN. "Elizabeth Bishop's 'Natural Heroism,'" *Centennial Review* 22(1), Winter 1978, 38-39.

"Jeronimo's House"

JANET A. EMIG. "The Poem as Puzzle," *English Journal* 52(3), March 1963, 222-24.

"Large Bad Picture"

JAN B. GORDON. "Days and Distances: The Cartographic Imagination of Elizabeth Bishop," *Salmagundi* 22-23 (Spring-Summer 1973), 298-300. Reprinted in: *Contemporary Poetry in America*, pp. 352-54.

"Little Exercise"

CRALE D. HOPKINS. "Inspiration as Theme: Art and Nature in the Poetry of Elizabeth Bishop," *Arizona Quarterly* 32(3), Autumn 1976, 199-200.

"The Man-Moth"

BERNARD DUFFEY. *Poetry in America*, pp. 255-56.

RALPH J. MILLS, JR. *Contemporary American Poetry*, pp. 78-81.

JAMES M. REID. *100 American Poems of the Twentieth Century*, pp. 213-15.

"Manuelzinho"

WILLARD SPIEGELMAN. "Elizabeth Bishop's 'Natural Heroism,'" *Centennial Review* 22(1), Winter 1978, 40-41.

"The Map"

SYBIL P. ESTESS. "Elizabeth Bishop: The Delicate Art of Map Making," *Southern Review*, n.s., 13(4), Autumn 1977, 708-13.

LLOYD FRANKENBERG. *Pleasure Dome*, pp. 331-33. Reprinted in: *Reading Modern Poetry*, pp. 228-29; revised ed., pp. 212-13.

JAN B. GORDON. "Days and Distances: The Cartographic Imagination of Elizabeth Bishop," *Salmagundi* 22-23 (Spring-Summer 1973), 297-98. Reprinted in: *Contemporary Poetry in America*, pp. 351-52.

"The Monument"

NANCY L. MCNALLY. "Elizabeth Bishop: The Discipline of Description," *Twentieth Century Literature* 11(4), January 1966, 194-97.

MARJORIE PERLOFF. "Elizabeth Bishop: The Course of a Particular," *Modern Poetry Studies* 8(3), Winter 1977, 185-87.

"The Moose"

DAVID KALSTONE. *Five Temperaments*, pp. 38-39.

WILLIAM JAY SMITH. "Geographical Questions: The Recent Poetry of Elizabeth Bishop," *Hollins Critic* 14(1), February 1977, 9-11.

WILLARD SPIEGELMAN. "Elizabeth Bishop's 'Natural Heroism,'" *Centennial Review* 22(1), Winter 1978, 37-38.

"The Mountain"

CRALE D. HOPKINS. "Inspiration as Theme: Art and Nature in the Poetry of Elizabeth Bishop," *Arizona Quarterly* 32(3), Autumn 1976, 203-4.

"One Art"

SYBIL P. ESTESS. "History as Geography," *Southern Review,* n.s., 13(4), Autumn 1977, 854-55.

DAVID KALSTONE. *Five Temperaments,* pp. 39-40.

"Over 2000 Illustrations and a Complete Concordance"

DAVID KALSTONE. *Five Temperaments,* pp. 27-28.

WILLARD SPIEGELMAN. "Landscape and Knowledge: The Poetry of Elizabeth Bishop," *Modern Poetry Studies* 6(3), Winter 1975, 213-15.

"Poem" (*Geography III*)

SYBIL P. ESTESS. "Elizabeth Bishop: The Delicate Art of Map Making," *Southern Review,* n.s., 13(4), Autumn 1977, 721-25.

WILLARD SPIEGELMAN. "Landscape and Knowledge: The Poetry of Elizabeth Bishop," *Modern Poetry Studies* 6(3), Winter 1975, 221-22.

"Quai d'Orleans"

RALPH J. MILLS, JR. *Contemporary American Poetry,* pp. 72-83, *passim.*

"Questions of Travel"

ASHLEY BROWN. "Elizabeth Bishop in Brazil," *Southern Review,* n.s., 13(4), Autumn 1977, 695-96.

CRALE D. HOPKINS. "Inspiration as Theme: Art and Nature in the Poetry of Elizabeth Bishop," *Arizona Quarterly* 32(3), Autumn 1976, 208-12.

DAVID KALSTONE. *Five Temperaments,* pp. 30-32.

WILLARD SPIEGELMAN. "Landscape and Knowledge: The Poetry of Elizabeth Bishop," *Modern Poetry Studies* 6(3), Winter 1975, 218-20.

"Roosters"

WILLARD SPIEGELMAN. "Elizabeth Bishop's 'Natural Heroism,'" *Centennial Review* 22(1), Winter 1978, 30-32.

"Sandpiper"

SYBIL P. ESTESS. "Elizabeth Bishop: The Delicate Art of Map Making," *Southern Review,* n.s., 13(4), Autumn 1977, 719-21.

SYBIL P. ESTESS. "Shelters for 'What is Within': Meditation and Epiphany in the Poetry of Elizabeth Bishop," *Modern Poetry Studies* 8(1), Spring 1977, 50-51.

DAVID KALSTONE. *Five Temperaments,* pp. 21-22.

"Wading at Wellfleet"

WILLARD SPIEGELMAN. "Elizabeth Bishop's 'Natural Heroism,'" *Centennial Review* 22(1), Winter 1978, 32-34.

BISHOP, JOAN

"Profile"

GEORGE ABBE. *You and Contemporary Poetry,* 1957 ed., p. 16; rev. ed., pp. 18-19.

BISHOP, JOHN PEALE

"Ballet"

S. C. MOORE. *Explicator* 23(2), October 1964, Item 12.

"Behavior of the Sun"

ROBERT WOOSTER STALLMAN. *Explicator* 5(1), October 1946, Item 6.

ROBERT WOOSTER STALLMAN. "The Poetry of John Peale Bishop," *Western Review* 11(1), Autumn 1946, 15-16.

"Divine Nativity"

JOSEPH FRANK. "Force and Form: A Study of John Peale Bishop," *Sewanee Review* 55(1), Winter 1947, 97-98.

"No More the Senator"

ROBERT F. FLEISSNER. "Bishop's 'No More the Senator' Once More," *Notes on Contemporary Literature* 2(1), January 1972, 11-14.

"O Let Not Virtue Seek"

JOSEPH FRANK. "Force and Form: A Study of John Peale Bishop," *Sewanee Review* 55(1), Winter 1947, 91-93.

"Perspectives are Precipices"

ROBERT WOOSTER STALLMAN. *Explicator* 5(2), November 1946, Item 8.

ROBERT WOOSTER STALLMAN. "An Interpretation of John Peale Bishop's 'Perspectives are Precipices,'" in *The Creative Reader,* second ed., pp. 944-45.

ROBERT WOOSTER STALLMAN. "The Poetry of John Peale Bishop," *Western Review* 11(1), Autumn 1946, 17-19.

ALLEN TATE. "A Note on Bishop's Poetry," *Southern Review* 1(2), Autumn 1935, 362-63.

"A Recollection"

R. W. STALLMAN. *Explicator* 19(7), April 1961, Item 43.

"The Return"

ALLEN TATE. *Reactionary Essays on Poetry and Ideas,* pp. 58-60. Reprinted in: Allen Tate. *On the Limits of Poetry,* pp. 243-44. Also: Allen Tate. *Essays of Four Decades,* pp. 353-54.

ALLEN TATE. "A Note on Bishop's Poetry," *Southern Review* 1(2), Autumn 1935, 361-62.

"The Saints"

JOSEPH FRANK. "Force and Form: A Study of John Peale Bishop," *Sewanee Review* 55(1), Winter 1947, 95-96.

"Southern Pines"

ROBERT WOOSTER STALLMAN. *Explicator* 4(6), April 1946, Item 46.

ROBERT WOOSTER STALLMAN. "The Poetry of John Peale Bishop," *Western Review* 11(1), Autumn 1946, 10-12.

"Speaking of Poetry"

BABETTE DEUTSCH. *Poetry in Our Time,* pp. 191-93; second ed., pp. 208-10.

JOSEPH FRANK. "Force and Form: A Study of John Peale Bishop," *Sewanee Review* 55(1), Winter 1947, 83-86.

"A Subject of Sea Change"

JOSEPH FRANK. "The Achievement of John Peale Bishop," *Minnesota Review* 2(3), Spring 1962, 343-44.

"The Tree"

JOSEPH FRANK. "Force and Form: A Study of John Peale Bishop," *Sewanee Review* 55(1), Winter 1947, 98-99.

BLACKBURN, PAUL
"The Once-Over"
> M. L. ROSENTHAL. *Poetry and the Common Life*, pp. 40-43.

BLACKMUR, RICHARD PALMER
"The Dead Ride Fast"
> KIMON FRIAR and JOHN MALCOLM BRINNIN. *Modern Poetry*, p. 446.

"Judas, Not Pilate, Had a Wakened Mind" ("Judas Priest," III)
> ALLEN TATE. *Reason in Madness*, pp. 175-79.

"Missa Vocis"
> DONALD A. STAUFFER. "Genesis, of the Poet As Maker," in *Poets at Work*, pp. 43-52.
> DONALD A. STAUFFER. "Genesis, or the Poet as Maker," in John Holmes, *Writing Poetry*, pp. 131-40.

"One grey and foaming day"
> ALLEN TATE. *Reason in Madness*, pp. 180-81.

"The Spear"
> ALLEN TATE. *Reason in Madness*, pp. 174-75.

BLAIR, ROBERT
"The Grave"
> JAMES MEANS. "A Reading of *The Grave*," *Studies in Scottish Literature* 12(4), April 1975, 270-81.

BLAKE, WILLIAM
"Ah! Sun-Flower"
> FREDERICK L. BEATY. *Light from Heaven*, pp. 123-24.
> HAROLD BLOOM. *The Visionary Company*, pp. 41-42.
> C. M. BOWRA. *The Romantic Imagination*, p. 45. Reprinted in: *The Dimensions of Poetry*, p. 347.
> THOMAS R. EDWARDS. *Imagination and Power*, pp. 152-54.
> JOHN E. GRANT. "The Fate of Blake's Sun-Flower: A Forecast and Some Conclusions," *Blake Studies* 5(2), Spring 1973, 7-50.
> HILTON LANDRY. "The Symbolism of Blake's Sunflower," *New York Public Library Bulletin* 66(9), November 1962, 613-16.
> WOLF MANKOWITZ. "William Blake: (2) The Songs of Experience," *Politics and Letters* 1 (Winter-Spring 1947), 20.
> M. L. ROSENTHAL. *The Modern Poets*, p. 15.
> JOAN O. SIMMONS. "Teaching Symbolism in Poetry," *College English* 23(4), January 1962, 301-2.

"Ahania"
> H. M. MARGOLIOUTH. "Notes on Blake," *Review of English Studies* 24(96), October 1948, 304. (P)
> MORTON D. PALEY. "Method and Meaning in Blake's *Book of Ahania*," *Bulletin of the New York Public Library* 70(1), January 1966, 27-33.

"America: A Prophecy"
> H. M. MARGOLIOUTH. "Notes on Blake," *Review of English Studies* 24(96), October 1948, 303-4. (P)
> HAROLD SPICER. "Biblical Sources of William Blake's *America*," *Ball State University Forum* 8(3), Summer 1967, 23-29.

"And did those feet in ancient time"
> F. W. BATESON. *English Poetry*, pp. 7-9.
> NANCY M. GOSLEE. " 'In Englands green & pleasant Land': The Building of Vision in Blake's Stanzas from *Milton*," *Studies in Romanticism* 13(2), Spring 1974, 105-25.
> L. G. LOCKE. *Explicator* 1(5), March 1943, Item 38.

"The Angel"
> WOLF MANKOWITZ. "William Blake: (2) The Songs of Experience," *Politics and Letters* 1 (Winter-Spring 1947), 19-20.
> ROBIN SKELTON. *The Poetic Pattern*, pp. 112-13.

"Auguries of Innocence"
> T. R. BARNES. *English Verse*, pp. 159-63.
> JOHN E. GRANT. "Apocalypse in Blake's 'Auguries of Innocence,' " *Texas Studies in Literature and Language* 5(4), Winter 1964, 489-503.
> KATHLEEN RAINE. "Blake: Auguries of Innocence," in *Master Poems of the English Language*, pp. 364-72.
> LEONARD UNGER and WILLIAM VAN O'CONNOR. *Poems for Study*, pp. 341-43.

"The Blossom"
> WARREN U. OBER. " 'Poor Robin' & Blake's 'The Blossom,' " *Blake Newsletter* 9(2), Fall 1975, 42-43.
> A. M. WILKINSON. "Illuminated — or Not? A Note on Blake's *Songs of Innocence and of Experience*," *Modern Language Review* 57(3), July 1962, 388-90.

"The Book of Thel"
> FREDERICK L. BEATY. *Light from Heaven*, pp. 118-19.
> HAROLD BLOOM. *The Visionary Company*, pp. 45-49.
> ROLAND A. DUERKSEN. "The Life-in-Death Theme in *The Book of Thel*," *Blake Studies* 2(2), Spring 1970, 15-22.
> ROBERT F. GLECKNER. "Blake's *Thel* and the Bible," *Bulletin of the New York Public Library* 64(11), November 1960, 573-80.
> ANNE KOSTELANETZ MELLOR. "Blake's Designs for *The Book of Thel*: An Affirmation of Innocence," *Philological Quarterly* 50(2), April 1971, 193-207.
> DONALD R. PEARCE. "Natural Religion and the Plight of Thel," *Blake Studies* 8(1), 1978, 23-35.
> RODGER L. TARR. " 'The Eagle' Versus 'The Mole': The Wisdom of Virginity in *Comus* and *The Book of Thel*," *Blake Studies* 3(2), Spring 1971, 187-94.

"The Book of Urizen"
> HAROLD BLOOM. *The Visionary Company*, pp. 66-75.
> MOLLYANNE MARKS. "Structure and Irony in Blake's 'The Book of Urizen,' " *Studies in English Literature 1500-1900* 15(4), Autumn 1975, 579-90.
> W. J. T. MITCHELL. "Poetic and Pictorial Imagination in Blake's *The Book of Urizen*," *Eighteenth Century Studies* 3(1), Fall 1969, 83-107.
> MARTIN PRICE. "The Standard of Energy," in *Romanticism and Consciousness*, pp. 255-58.
> LESLIE TANNENBAUM. "Blake's Art of Crypsis: *The Book of Urizen* and Genesis," *Blake Studies* 5(1), Fall 1972, 141-64.

"The Chimney Sweeper" (*Songs of Experience*)
> T. R. BARNES. *English Verse*, p. 155.
> HARRY BROWN and JOHN MILSTEAD. *What the Poem Means*, p. 14.
> RONALD PRIMEAU. "Blake's Chimney Sweeper as Afro-American Minstrel," *New York Public Library Bulletin* 78(4), Summer 1975, 418-30.

BRIAN WILKIE. "Blake's *Innocence and Experience*: An Approach," *Blake Studies* 6(2), 1975, 123-25.

"The Chimney Sweeper" (*Songs of Innocence*)

GÉMINO H. ABAD. *A Formal Approach to Lyric Poetry*, pp. 223-25.

T. R. BARNES. *English Verse*, pp. 154-55.

WALTON BEACHAM. *The Meaning of Poetry*, pp. 118-20.

DONALD A. DIKE. "The Difficult Innocence: Blake's Songs and Pastoral," *ELH* 28(4), December 1961, 371-73.

WALLACE JACKSON. "William Blake in 1789: Unorganized *Innocence*," *Modern Language Quarterly* 33(4), December 1972, 398-99.

PAUL D. MCGLYNN. *Explicator* 27(3), November 1968, Item 20.

MARTIN K. NURMI. "Fact and Symbol in 'The Chimney Sweeper' of Blake's *Songs of Innocence*," *New York Public Library Bulletin* 68(4), April 1964, 249-56.

RONALD PRIMEAU. "Blake's Chimney Sweeper as Afro-American Minstrel," *New York Public Library Bulletin* 78(4), Summer 1975, 418-30.

MICHELE LEISS STEPTO. "Mothers and Fathers in Blake's *Songs of Innocence*," *Yale Review* 67(3), Spring 1978, 364-65.

HAROLD E. TOLIVER. *Pastoral Forms and Attitudes*, pp. 218-19.

"The Clod and the Pebble"

GÉMINO H. ABAD. *A Formal Approach to Lyric Poetry*, pp. 302-4.

FREDERICK L. BEATY. *Light from Heaven*, pp. 122-23.

ARTHUR DICKSON. *Explicator* 2(2), November 1943, Item 12.

THOMAS R. EDWARDS. *Imagination and Power*, pp. 154-56.

JEAN H. HAGSTRUM. "William Blake's 'The Clod & the Pebble,'" in *Restoration and Eighteenth-Century Literature*, pp. 381-88.

WOLF MANKOWITZ. "William Blake: (2) The Songs of Experience," *Politics and Letters* 1 (Winter-Spring 1947), 18-19.

"Olybrius," *Explicator* 1(4), February 1943, Item 32.

MAX F. SCHULZ. "Point of View in Blake's 'The Clod and the Pebble,'" *Papers on Language and Literature* 2(3), Summer 1966, 217-24.

BRIAN WILKIE. "Blake's *Innocence and Experience*: An Approach," *Blake Studies* 6(2), 1975, 129-30.

"A Cradle Song"

DONALD A. DIKE. "The Difficult Innocence: Blake's Songs and Pastoral," *ELH* 28(4), December 1961, 368-39.

"The Crystal Cabinet"

JOHN ADLARD. "Blake's Crystal Cabinet," *Modern Language Review* 62(1), January 1967, 28-30.

HAROLD BLOOM. *The Visionary Company*, pp. 52-54.

NORTHROP FRYE. "The Keys to the Gates," in *Romanticism and Consciousness*, p. 248.

JOHN SUTHERLAND. "Blake: A Crisis of Love and Jealousy," *PMLA* 87(3), May 1972, 429-30.

HAROLD E. TOLIVER. *Pastoral Forms and Attitudes*, pp. 219-20.

"The Divine Image"

HAROLD BLOOM. *The Visionary Company*, pp. 38-39.

ROBERT F. GLECKNER. "William Blake and the Human Abstract," *PMLA* 76(4), September 1961, 373-79.

JOHN HOWARD. "Swendenborg's *Heaven and Hell* and Blake's *Songs of Innocence*," *Papers on Language and Literature* 4(4), Fall 1968, 395.

DAVID J. SMITH. *Explicator* 25(8), April 1967, Item 69.

"A Dream"

DONALD A. DIKE. "The Difficult Innocence: Blake's Songs and Pastoral," *ELH* 28(4), December 1961, 361-62.

"Earth's Answer"

D. W. HARDING. *Experience Into Words*, pp. 41-44.

WOLF MANKOWITZ. "William Blake: (2) The Songs of Experience," *Politics and Letters* 1 (Winter-Spring 1947), 16-17.

CHAD and EVA T. WALSH. *Twice Ten*, pp. 43-44.

"The Echoing Green"

CLEANTH BROOKS and ROBERT PENN WARREN. *Understanding Poetry*, fourth ed., pp. 30-31.

MICHELE LEISS STEPTO. "Mothers and Fathers in Blake's *Songs of Innocence*," *Yale Review* 67(3), Spring 1978, 359-60.

E. M. W. TILLYARD. *Poetry Direct and Oblique*, pp. 9-12; revised ed., pp. 12-15. Reprinted in: *Criticism*, pp. 286-88.

"Enion's Protest" (*The Four Zoas*)

AGNES STEIN. *The Uses of Poetry*, pp. 102-4.

"Europe"

DAVID V. ERDMAN. "Blake: the Historical Approach," in *Explication as Criticism*, pp. 154-59.

CAROL P. KOWLE. "Plate III and the Meaning of *Europe*," *Blake Studies* 8(1), 1978, 89-99.

AILEEN WARD. "The forging of Orc: Blake and the idea of revolution," in *Literature in Revolution*, pp. 214-15.

"The Everlasting Gospel"

DAVID V. ERDMAN. "'Terrible Blake in His Pride': An Essay on *The Everlasting Gospel*," in *From Sensibility to Romanticism*, pp. 331-56.

JEAN HALL. "Blake's *Everlasting Gospel*," *Blake Studies* 4(1), Fall 1971, 61-72.

MICHAEL A. TOLLEY. "William Blake's Use of the Bible in a Section of 'The Everlasting Gospel,'" *Notes & Queries*, n.s., 9(5), May 1962, 171-76.

"The Fly"

ROBERT F. GLECKNER. "Blake, Gray, and the Illustrations," *Criticism* 19(2), Spring 1977, 118-40.

JOHN E. GRANT. "Interpreting Blake's 'The Fly,'" *New York Public Library Bulletin* 67(9), November 1963, 593-615.

LEO KIRSCHBAUM. "Blake's 'The Fly,'" *Essays in Criticism* 11(2), April 1961, 154-63.

C. N. MANLOVE. "Engineered Innocence: Blake's 'The Little Black Boy' and 'The Fly,'" *Essays in Criticism* 27(2), April 1977, 117-19.

ROBERT MIKKELSEN. "William Blake's Revisions of the *Songs Of Innocence* and *Of Experience*," *Concerning Poetry* 2(2), Fall 1969, 63-64.

WARREN STEVENSON. "Artful Irony in Blake's 'The Fly,'" *Texas Studies in Literature and Language* 10(1), Spring 1968, 77-82.

"The French Revolution"

WILLIAM F. HALLORAN. "William Blake's *The French Revolution*: A Note on the Text and a Possible Emendation," *The New York Public Library Bulletin* 72(1), January 1968, 3-18. (P)

BLAKE, WILLIAM *(Cont.)*

"The Gates of Paradise"

NORTHROP FRYE. "The Keys to the Gates," in *Romanticism and Consciousness*, pp. 248-51.

GAIL KMETZ. "A Reading of Blake's *The Gates of Paradise*," *Blake Studies* 3(2), Spring 1971, 171-85.

"Holy Thursday" *(Songs of Experience)*

JOHN TODHUNTER. "John Todhunter's Lectures on Blake 1872-1874," ed. by Ian Fletcher, *Blake Newsletter* 8(1-2), Summer-Fall 1974, 9.

"Holy Thursday" *(Songs of Innocence)*

HAROLD BLOOM. *The Visionary Company*, pp. 37-38.

DONALD A. DIKE. "The Difficult Innocence: Blake's Songs and Pastoral," *ELH* 28(4), December 1961, 373-74.

ROBERT F. GLECKNER. "Point of View and Context in Blake's Songs," *New York Public Library Bulletin* 61(11), November 1957, 534-35. Reprinted in: *English Romantic Poets*, p. 72.

JUSTUS GEORGE LAWLER. *The Christian Image*, pp. 81-82.

"How sweet I roam'd from field to field"

HAROLD BLOOM. *The Visionary Company*, pp. 13-14.

L. C. KNIGHTS. "Early Blake," *Sewanee Review* 79(3), Summer 1971, 380-82.

"The Human Abstract"

HAROLD BLOOM. *The Visionary Company*, pp. 38-39.

THOMAS R. EDWARDS. *Imagination and Power*, pp. 145-49.

ROBERT F. GLECKNER. "William Blake and the Human Abstract," *PMLA* 76(4), September 1961, 373-79.

JOHN TODHUNTER. "John Todhunter's Lectures on Blake 1872-1874," ed. by Ian Fletcher, *Blake Newsletter* 8(1-2), Summer-Fall 1974, 10.

"I Asked a Thief"

M. L. ROSENTHAL and A. J. M. SMITH. *Exploring Poetry*, pp. 455-58; second ed., pp. 333-35.

"I Saw a Chapel All of Gold"

GÉMINO H. ABAD. *A Formal Approach to Lyric Poetry*, pp. 306-7.

ROBERT ARTHUR. "Irony and Paradox in William Blake's 'I Saw a Chapel All of Gold'," in Walton Beacham, *The Meaning of Poetry*, pp. 294-96.

FREDERICK L. BEATY. *Light from Heaven*, pp. 124-25.

ALLAN RODWAY. *The Romantic Conflict*, pp. 135-36.

"Imitation of Pope: A Compliment to the Ladies"

M. E. BACON. *Explicator* 28(9), May 1970, Item 79.

"Infant Sorrow"

FREDERICK L. BEATY. *Light from Heaven*, pp. 125-26.

VINCENT BUCKLEY. *Poetry and the Sacred*, pp. 129-31.

ROBERT F. GLECKNER. " 'The Lamb' and 'The Tyger' — How Far With Blake?" *English Journal* 51(8), November 1962, 539-40.

WOLF MANKOWITZ. "William Blake: (2) The Songs of Experience," *Politics and Letters* 1 (Winter-Spring 1947), 21-22.

NORMAN NATHAN. "Blake's Infant Sorrow," *Notes & Queries*, n.s., 7(3), March 1960, 99-100.

BRIAN WILKIE. "Blake's *Innocence and Experience*: An Approach," *Blake Studies* 6(2), 1975, 126-27.

"Introduction" *(Songs of Experience)*

F. W. BATESON. *English Poetry*, pp. 37-39.

MAUD BODKIN. *Archetypal Patterns in Poetry*, pp. 317-21.

NORTHROP FRYE. "Blake's Introduction to Experience," *Huntington Library Quarterly* 21(1), November 1957, 57-67.

ROBERT F. GLECKNER. "Point of View and Context in Blake's Songs," *New York Public Library Bulletin* 61(11), November 1957, 535-37.

D. W. HARDING. *Experience Into Words*, pp. 41-44.

WOLF MANKOWITZ. "William Blake: (2) The Songs of Experience," *Politics and Letters* 1 (Winter-Spring 1947), 15-16.

JOHN TODHUNTER. "John Todhunter's Lectures on Blake 1872-1874," ed. by Ian Fletcher, *Blake Newsletter* 8(1-2), Summer-Fall 1974, 8-9.

RENE WELLEK. "Literary Criticism and Philosophy," *Scrutiny* 5(4), March 1937, 377-78. Reprinted in: *The Importance of Scrutiny*, pp. 24-25.

"Introduction" *(Songs of Innocence)*

WILLIAM R, BOWDEN. *Explicator* 11(6), April 1953, Item 41.

LLOYD FRANKENBERG. *Invitation to Poetry*, pp. 63-65.

MARGARET GIOVANNINI. *Explicator* 8(1), October 1949, Item 5.

JOHN HOWARD. "Swedenborg's *Heaven and Hell* and Blake's *Songs of Innocence*," *Papers on Language and Literature* 4(4), Fall 1968, 395-96.

HOWARD JUSTIN. *Explicator* 11(1), October 1952, Item 1.

FRANK D. MCCONNELL. "Romanticism, Language, Waste: A Reflection on Poetics and Disaster," *Bucknell Review* 20(3), Winter 1972, 135-39.

MICHELE LEISS STEPTO. "Mothers and Fathers in Blake's *Songs of Innocence*," *Yale Review* 67(3), Spring 1978, 357-58.

CHAD and EVA T. WALSH. *Twice Ten*, p. 42.

ARTHUR WORMHOUDT. *Explicator* 7(7), May 1949, Item 55.

"The Lamb"

HAROLD BLOOM. *The Visionary Company*, pp. 34-35.

JIM S. BORCK. "Blake's 'The Lamb': The Punctuation of Innocence," *Tennessee Studies in Literature* 19(1974), 163-75.

MICHELE LEISS STEPTO. "Mothers and Fathers in Blake's *Songs of Innocence*," *Yale Review* 67(3), Spring 1978, 370.

CHAD and EVA T. WALSH. *Twice Ten*, p. 45.

"The Lily"

MARY LYNN JOHNSON. "Emblem and Symbol in Blake," *Huntington Library Quarterly* 37(2), February 1974, 166-69.

WOLF MANKOWITZ. "William Blake: (2) The Songs of Experience," *Politics and Letters* 1 (Winter-Spring 1947), 20.

BRIAN WILKIE. "Blake's *Innocence and Experience*: An Approach," *Blake Studies* 6(2), 1975, 122-23.

"The Little Black Boy"

JACOB H. ADLER. "Symbol and Meaning in 'The Little Black Boy,'" *Modern Language Notes* 72(6), June 1957, 412-15.

HAROLD BLOOM. *The Visionary Company*, pp. 35-37.

C. B. COX and A. E. DYSON. *The Practical Criticism of Poetry*, pp. 65-70.

DONALD A. DIKE. "The Difficult Innocence: Blake's Songs and Pastoral," *ELH* 28(4), December 1961, 367.

A. E. DYSON. "The Little Black Boy: Blake's Song of Innocence," *Critical Quarterly* 1(1), Spring 1959, 44-47.

RALPH D. EBERLY. *Explicator* 15(7), April 1957, Item 42.

HOWARD H. HINKEL. "From Pivotal Idea to Poetic Ideal: Blake's Theory of Contraries and 'The Little Black Boy,'" *Papers on Language and Literature* 11(1), Winter 1975, 39-45.

JOHN HOWARD. "Swedenborg's *Heaven and Hell* and Blake's *Songs of Innocence*," *Papers on Language and Literature* 4(4), Fall 1968, 392-95.

LLOYD N. JEFFREY. *Explicator* 17(4), January 1959, Item 27.

C. N. MANLOVE. "Engineered Innocence: Blake's 'The Little Black Boy' and 'The Fly,'" *Essays in Criticism* 27(2), April 1977, 112-17.

MICHELE LEISS STEPTO. "Mothers and Fathers in Blake's *Songs of Innocence*," *Yale Review* 67(3), Spring 1978, 365-67.

MARK VAN DOREN. *Introduction to Poetry*, pp. 110-15.

J. E. WHITESELL. *Explicator* 5(6), April 1947, Item 42.

"Little Boy Found" (*Songs of Innocence*)

THOMAS E. CONNOLLY and GEORGE R. LEVINE. "Pictorial and Poetic Design in Two Songs of Innocence," *PMLA* 82(2), May 1967, 257-64.

J. G. KEOGH, THOMAS E. CONNOLLY, and GEORGE R. LEVINE. "Two Songs of Innocence," *PMLA* 84(1), January 1969, 137-40.

"Little Boy Lost" (*Songs of Innocence*)

DONALD A. DIKE. "The Difficult Innocence: Blake's Songs and Pastoral," *ELH* 28(4), December 1961, 363-64.

THOMAS E. CONNOLLY and GEORGE R. LEVINE. "Pictorial and Poetic Design in Two Songs of Innocence," *PMLA* 82(2), May 1967, 257-64.

J. G. KEOGH, THOMAS E. CONNOLLLY, and GEORGE R. LEVINE. "Two Songs of Innocence," *PMLA* 84(1), January 1969, 137-40.

MICHELE LEISS STEPTO. "Mothers and Fathers in Blake's *Songs of Innocence*," *Yale Review* 67(3), Spring 1978, 363-64.

"Little Girl Found"

IRENE H. CHAYES. "Blake and Tradition: 'The Little Girl Lost' and 'The Little Girl Found,'" *Blake Newsletter* 4(1), Summer 1970, 25-28.

IRENE H. CHAYES. "Little Girls Lost: Problems of a Romantic Archetype," *Bulletin of the New York Public Library* 67(9), November 1963, 579-92.

STUART PETERFREUND. "The Name of Blake's Lyca Re-examined," *American Notes & Queries*, n.s., 13(9), May 1975, 133-36.

A. M. WILKINSON. "Illuminated — or Not? A Note on Blake's *Songs of Innocence and of Experience*," *Modern Language Review* 57(3), July 1962, 390-91.

"Little Girl Lost"

VINCENT BUCKLEY. *Poetry and the Sacred*, pp. 138-42.

IRENE H. CHAYES. "Blake and Tradition: 'The Little Girl Lost' and 'The Little Girl Found,'" *Blake Newsletter* 4(1), Summer 1970, 25-28.

IRENE H. CHAYES. "Little Girls Lost: Problems of a Romantic Archetype," *Bulletin of the New York Public Library* 67(9), November 1963, 579-92.

DONALD A. DIKE. "The Difficult Innocence: Blake's Songs and Pastoral," *ELH* 28(4), December 1961, 363-64.

CONSTANCE M. DRAKE. "An Approach to Blake," *College English* 29(7), April 1968, 543-45.

STUART PETERFREUND. "The Name of Blake's Lyca Re-examined," *American Notes & Queries*, n.s., 13(9), May 1975, 133-36.

A. M. WILKINSON. "Illuminated — or Not? A Note on Blake's *Songs of Innocence and of Experience*," *Modern Language Review* 57(3), July 1962, 390-91.

"London"

F. W. BATESON. "The Proof of a Pudding," in W. K. Wimsatt, Jr., *What to Say About a Poem*, pp. 20-21.

WALTON BEACHAM. *The Meaning of Poetry*, pp. 6-10.

MARIUS BEWLEY. *Masks & Mirrors*, pp. 77-103.

WILLIAM BLISSETT. "Poetic Wave and Poetic Particle," *University of Toronto Quarterly* 24(1), October 1954, 5-6.

EDWARD A. BLOOM, CHARLES H. PHILBRICK, and ELMER M. BLISTEIN. *The Order of Poetry*, pp. 88-92.

HAROLD BLOOM. *Poetry and Repression*, pp. 34-44.

HAROLD BLOOM. *The Visionary Company*, pp. 42-43.

C. M. BOWRA. *The Romantic Imagination*, pp. 42-43.

CLEANTH BROOKS, JOHN THIBAUT PURSER, and ROBERT PENN WARREN. *An Approach to Literature*, pp. 496-98; second ed., pp. 496-98; third ed., pp. 387-90; fourth ed., pp. 383-85; fifth ed., pp. 376-78.

VINCENT BUCKLEY. *Poetry and the Sacred*, pp. 132-37.

JONATHAN CULLER. "Structuralism and Literature," in *Contemporary Approaches to English Studies*, pp. 72-75.

V. DOYNO. "Blake's Revision of 'London,'" *Essays in Criticism* 22(1), January 1972, 58-63.

ELIZABETH DREW. *Poetry*, pp. 166-67.

THOMAS R. EDWARDS. *Imagination and Power*, pp. 141-45.

ARCHIBALD A. HILL. "Imagery and Meaning: A Passage from Milton, and from Blake," *Texas Studies in Literature and Language* 11(3), Fall 1969, 1095-1105. Reprinted in: Archibald A. Hill. *Constituent and Pattern in Poetry*, pp. 73-82.

KARL KIRALIS. "'London' in the Light of *Jerusalem*," *Blake Studies* 1(1), Fall 1968, 5-15.

WOLF MANKOWITZ. "William Blake: (2) The Songs of Experience," *Politics and Letters* 1 (Winter-Spring 1947), 21.

M. L. ROSENTHAL. *Poetry and the Common Life*, pp. 83-86.

M. L. ROSENTHAL and A. J. M. SMITH. *Exploring Poetry*, pp. 693-95; second ed., p. 489. Reprinted in: *Readings for Liberal Education*, third ed., II: 77; fourth ed., II: 73-74; fifth ed., II: 71-72.

GRANT C. ROTI and DONALD L. KENT. "The Last Stanza of Blake's London," *Blake: An Illustrated Quarterly* 11(1), Summer 1977, 19-21.

HELEN WATSON-WILLIAMS. "The Blackened Wall: Notes on Blake's *London* and Eliot's *The Waste Land*," *English* 10(59), Summer 1955, 181-84.

W. K. WIMSATT, JR. *What to Say About a Poem*, pp. 12-16.

"Long John Brown & Little Mary Bell"

FREDERICK L. BEATY. *Light from Heaven*, p. 123.

BLAKE, WILLIAM *(Cont.)*

"Mad Song"

> HAROLD BLOOM. *The Visionary Company*, pp. 14-15.
>
> L. C. KNIGHTS. "Early Blake," *Sewanee Review* 79(3), Summer 1971, 387-89.

"Memory"

> L. C. KNIGHTS. "Early Blake," *Sewanee Review* 79(3), Summer 1971, 385-87.
>
> LEONE VIVANTE. *English Poetry*, p. 91.

"The Mental Traveller"

> HAROLD BLOOM. *The Visionary Company*, pp. 54-60.
>
> IZAK BOUWER and PAUL MCNALLY. "'The Mental Traveller': Man's Eternal Journey," *Blake: An Illustrated Quarterly* 12(3), Winter 1978-79, 184-92.
>
> GERALD E. ENSCOE. "The Content of Vision: Blake's 'Mental Traveller,'" *Papers on Language and Literature* 4(4), Fall 1968, 400-413.
>
> NORTHROP FRYE. "Blake's 'The Mental Traveller,'" in *The Dimensions of Poetry*, pp. 350-51. Reprinted in: *Master Poems of the English Language*, pp. 380-81.
>
> NORTHROP FRYE. "The Keys to the Gates," in *Romanticism and Consciousness*, pp. 247-48.
>
> KARL KROEBER. *Romantic Narrative Art*, pp. 74-76.
>
> GIORGIO MELCHIORI. "Cups of Gold for The Sacred Fount: Aspects of James's Symbolism," *Critical Quarterly* 7(4), Winter 1965, 309-11.
>
> MARTIN K. MURMI. "Joy, Love, and Innocence in Blake's 'The Mental Traveller,'" *Studies in Romanticism* 3(2), Winter 1964, 109-17.
>
> MORTON D. PALEY. "The Female Babe and 'The Mental Traveller,'" *Studies in Romanticism* 1(2), Winter 1962, 97-104.
>
> KATHLEEN RAINE. *Defending Ancient Springs*, pp. 80-81.
>
> JOHN H. SUTHERLAND. "Blake's 'Mental Traveller,'" *Journal of English Literary History* 22(2), June 1955, 136-47.
>
> JAMES BENTLEY TAYLOR. "The Case of William Blake: Creation, Regression and Pathology," *Psychoanalytic Review* 50(3), Fall 1963, 139-54.
>
> CHAD and EVA T. WALSH. *Twice Ten*, pp. 50-54.

"My Pretty Rose Tree"

> ROBERT F. GLECKNER. *Explicator* 13(7), May 1955, Item 43.
>
> ROBERT F. GLECKNER. "Point of View and Context in Blake's Songs," *New York Public Library Bulletin* 61(11), November 1957, 531-32. Reprinted in: *English Romantic Poets*, pp. 68-70.

"My Silks and Fine Array"

> CLEANTH BROOKS. "Current Critical Theory and the Period Course," *CEA Critic* 12(7), October 1950, 1, 5-6.
>
> CLEANTH BROOKS and ROBERT PENN WARREN. *Understanding Poetry*, fourth ed., pp. 326-27.

"My Spectre Around Me Night & Day"

> FREDERICK L. BEATY. *Light from Heaven*, pp. 127-29.
>
> JOHN SUTHERLAND. "Blake: A Crisis of Love and Jealousy," *PMLA* 87(3), May 1972, 427-29.

"Never Pain to Tell Thy Love"

> G. J. FINCH. "'Never Pain to Tell Thy Love' — Blake's Problem Poem," *Blake Studies* 4(1), Fall 1971, 73-79.
>
> D. W. HARDING. *Experience Into Words*, pp. 39-41.

"Night"

> DONALD A. DIKE. "The Difficult Innocence: Blake's Songs and Pastoral," *ELH* 28(4), December 1961, 369-70.

"Nurse's Song" *(Songs of Experience)*

> VINCENT BUCKLEY. *Poetry and the Sacred*, p. 123.

"Nurse's Song" *(Songs of Innocence)*

> HARRY BROWN and JOHN MILSTEAD. *What the Poem Means*, p. 14.
>
> VINCENT BUCKLEY. *Poetry and the Sacred*, pp. 121-22.

"On Another's Sorrow"

> DONALD A. DIKE. "The Difficult Innocence: Blake's Songs and Pastoral," *ELH* 28(4), December 1961, 369.

"A Poison Tree"

> T. R. BARNES. *English Verse*, pp. 158-59.
>
> PHILIP J. GALLAGHER. "The Word Made Flesh: Blake's 'A Poison Tree' and the Book of Genesis," *Studies in Romanticism* 16(2), Spring 1977, 237-49.
>
> EDWARD C. SAMPSON. *Explicator* 6(3), December 1947, Item 19.
>
> BARBARA F. LEFCOWITZ. "Omnipotence of Thought and the Poetic Imagination: Blake, Coleridge, and Rilke," *Psychoanalytic Review* 59(3), Fall 1972, 418-21.
>
> WINIFRED NOWOTTNY. *The Language Poets Use*, pp. 180-83.

"A Pretty Epigram for the Entertainment of Those Who Paid Great Sums in the Venetian and Flemish Ooze"

> M. E. BACON. *Explicator* 28(9), May 1970, Item 79.

"The Scoffers"

> CLEANTH BROOKS and ROBERT PENN WARREN. *Understanding Poetry*, pp. 579-82; revised ed., pp. 423-27; third ed., p. 381; fourth ed., pp. 329-30.

"The Shepherd"

> DONALD A. DIKE. "The Difficult Innocence: Blake's Songs and Pastoral," *ELH* 28(4), December 1961, 359-61.
>
> A. E. DYSON and JULIAN LOVELOCK. *Masterful Images*, pp. 131-33.

"The Sick Rose"

> H. L. ANSHUTZ and D. W. CUMMINGS. *Explicator* 29(4), December 1970, Item 32.
>
> HAROLD BLOOM. *The Visionary Company*, pp. 40-41.
>
> C. M. BOWRA. *The Romantic Imagination*, p. 44. Reprinted in: *The Case for Poetry*, p. 25; second ed., p. 24. Also: *The Dimensions of Poetry*, pp. 346-47.
>
> REUBEN ARTHUR BROWER. *The Fields of Light*, pp. 6-11.
>
> VINCENT BUCKLEY. *Poetry and the Sacred*, pp. 125-26.
>
> STANLEY E. CLAYES and JOHN GERRIETTS. *Ways to Poetry*, pp. 42-43.
>
> CONSTANCE M. DRAKE. "An Approach to Blake," *College English* 29(7), April 1968, 547.
>
> ELIZABETH DREW. *Poetry*, p. 63.
>
> A. E. DYSON and JULIAN LOVELOCK. *Masterful Images*, pp. 134-35.
>
> THOMAS R. EDWARDS. *Imagination and Power*, pp. 156-58.
>
> T. R. HENN. *The Apple and the Spectroscope*, pp. 38-41.
>
> F. R. LEAVIS. "'Thought' and Emotional Quality: Notes in the Analysis of Poetry," *Scrutiny* 13(1), Spring 1945, 69-70.

WOLF MANKOWITZ. "William Blake: (2) The Songs of Experience," *Politics and Letters* 1 (Winter-Spring 1947), 17-18.

LAURENCE PERRINE. "The Nature of Proof in the Interpretation of Poetry," *English Journal* 51(6), September 1962, 398. Abridged in: *The Case for Poetry*, second ed., pp. 24-25.

EDGAR SMITH ROSE. "The Anatomy of Imagination," *College English* 27(5), February 1966, 350-52.

M. L. ROSENTHAL and A. J. M. SMITH. *Exploring Poetry*, pp. 501-2; second ed., p. 355.

E. M. W. TILLYARD. *Poetry Direct and Oblique*, pp. 168-70; revised ed., pp. 64-65. Reprinted in: *The Case for Poetry*, p. 25; second ed., p. 24.

BRIAN WILKIE. "Blake's *Innocence and Experience*: An Approach," *Blake Studies* 6(2), 1975, 130-34.

"Soft Snow"

ALLAN RODWAY. *The Romantic Conflict*, p. 137.

"Tiriel"

WILLIAM F. HALLORAN. "Blake's *Tiriel*: Snakes, Curses, and a Blessing," *South Atlantic Quarterly* 70(2), Spring 1971, 161-79.

D. W. HARDING. *Experience Into Words*, pp. 47-48.

KARL KROEBER. *Romantic Narrative Art*, pp. 71-74.

"To Autumn"

IRENE H. CHAYES. "Blake and the Seasons of the Poet," *Studies in Romanticism* 11(3), Summer 1972, 225-40.

ROBERT F. GLECKNER. "Blake's Seasons," *Studies in English Literature 1500-1900* 5(3), Summer 1965, 539-51.

GEOFFREY H. HARTMAN. *Beyond Formalism*, pp. 200-201.

"To Butts, 22 November 1802"

RANDEL HELMS. "Blake at Felpham: A Study in the Psychology of Vision," *Literature and Psychology* 22(2), 1972, 59-60.

"To Flaxman, 12 September 1800"

RANDEL HELMS. "Blake at Felpham: A Study in the Psychology of Vision," *Literature and Psychology* 22(2), 1972, 58-59.

"To Spring"

IRENE H. CHAYES. "Blake and the Seasons of the Poet," *Studies in Romanticism* 11(3), Summer 1972, 225-40.

ROBERT F. GLECKNER. "Blake's Seasons," *Studies in English Literature 1500-1900* 5(3), Summer 1965, 539-51.

GEOFFREY H. HARTMAN. *Beyond Formalism*, pp. 195-200.

LEONE VIVANTE. *English Poetry*, pp. 89-90.

W. K. WIMSATT, JR. "The Structure of Romantic Nature Imagery," in *The Age of Johnson*, pp. 300-301. Reprinted in: W. K. Wimsatt, Jr. *The Verbal Icon*, pp. 112-13. Also: *English Romantic Poets*, pp. 32-33.

"To Summer"

IRENE H. CHAYES. "Blake and the Seasons of the Poet," *Studies in Romanticism* 11(3), Summer 1972, 225-40.

ROBERT F. GLECKNER. "Blake's Seasons," *Studies in English Literature 1500-1900* 5(3), Summer 1965, 539-51.

"To the Muses"

T. R. BARNES. *English Verse*, pp. 151-52.

LEONE VIVANTE. *English Poetry*, p. 92.

"To Tirzah"

FREDERICK L. BEATY. *Light from Heaven*, p. 122.

HAROLD BLOOM. *The Visionary Company*, pp. 43-44.

"To Winter"

IRENE H. CHAYES. "Blake and the Seasons of the Poet," *Studies in Romanticism* 11(3), Summer 1972, 225-40.

ROBERT F. GLECKNER. "Blake's Seasons," *Studies in English Literature 1500-1900* 5(3), Summer 1965, 539-51.

GEOFFREY H. HARTMAN. *Beyond Formalism*, pp. 201-4.

"The Tyger"

HAZARD ADAMS. "Reading Blake's Lyrics: 'The Tyger,'" *Texas Studies in Literature and Language* 2(1), Spring 1960, 18-37.

MARY R. and RODNEY M. BAINE. "Blake's Other Tigers and 'The Tyger,'" *Studies in English Literature 1500-1900* 15(4), Autumn 1975, 563-78.

RODNEY M. BAINE. "Blake's 'Tyger': The Nature of the Beast," *Philological Quarterly* 46(4), October 1967, 488-98.

ROY P. BASLER. *Sex, Symbolism, and Psychology in Literature*, pp. 19-24. Reprinted in: *The Dimensions of Poetry*, pp. 347-50. Also: *Master Poems of the English Language*, pp. 374-76.

JEROME BEATY and WILLIAM H. MATCHETT. *Poetry From Statement to Meaning*, pp. 242-44.

HAROLD BLOOM. *Poetry and Repression*, pp. 45-51.

HAROLD BLOOM. *The Visionary Company*, pp. 31-34.

C. M. BOWRA. *The Romantic Imagination*, pp. 47-49. Reprinted in: *Readings for Liberal Education*, revised ed., II: 84.

JOSEPH X. BRENNAN. "The Symbolic Framework of Blake's 'The Tyger,'" *College English* 22(6), March 1961, 406-7.

WILLIAM S. DOXEY. "William Blake and William Herschel: The Poet, The Astronomer, and 'The Tyger,'" *Blake Studies* 2(2), Spring 1970, 5-13.

CONSTANCE M. DRAKE. "An Approach to Blake," *College English* 29(7), April 1968, 545-46.

ELIZABETH DREW. *Discovering Poetry*, p. 160.

JOHN E. GRANT. "The Art and Argument of 'The Tyger,'" *Texas Studies in Literature and Language* 2(1), Spring 1960, 38-54.

D. W. HARDING. *Experience Into Words*, pp. 32-35.

JAMES HAZEN. "Blake's Tyger and Milton's Beasts," *Blake Studies* 3(2), Spring 1971, 163-70.

FRED KAPLAN. "'The Tyger' and Its Maker: Blake's Vision of Art and the Artist," *Studies in English Literature 1500-1900* 7(4), Autumn 1967, 617-27. Reprinted in: Fred Kaplan. *Miracles of Rare Device*, pp. 17-28.

CHRISTOPHER KEANE. "Blake and O'Neill: A Prophecy," *Blake Studies* 2(2), Spring 1970, 23-34.

WOLF MANKOWITZ. "William Blake: (2) The Songs of Experience," *Politics and Letters* 1 (Winter-Spring 1947), 22-23.

ROBERT MIKKELSEN. "William Blake's Revisions of the *Songs Of Innocence* and *Of Experience*," *Concerning Poetry* 2(2), Fall 1969, 64-69.

BLAKE, WILLIAM (*Cont.*)

"The Tyger" (*cont.*)

PAUL MINER. " 'The Tyger': Genesis & Evolution in the Poetry of William Blake," *Criticism* 4(1), Winter 1962, 59-73.

ELIZABETH NITCHIE. *Explicator* 1(4), February 1943, Item 34.

MARTIN K. NURMI. "Blake's Revisions of *The Tyger*," *PMLA* 71(4), September 1956, 669-83.

COLEMAN O. PARSONS. "Tygers Before Blake," *Studies in English Literature 1500-1900* 8(4), Autumn 1968, 573-92.

ELI PFEFFERKORN. "The Question of the Leviathan and the Tiger," *Blake Studies* 3(1), Fall 1970, 53-60.

FREDERICK A. POTTLE. *Explicator* 8(5), March 1950, Item 39.

M. L. ROSENTHAL and A. J. M. SMITH. *Exploring Poetry*, pp. 185-87; second ed., pp. 486-88.

WARREN STEVENSON. " 'The Tyger' as Artefact," *Blake Studies* 2(1), Fall 1969, 5-19.

GEORGE WINCHESTER STONE, JR. *Explicator* 1(3), December 1942, Item 19.

L. J. SWINGLE. "Answers to Blake's 'Tyger': A Matter of Reason or of Choice?" *Concerning Poetry* 2(1), Spring 1969, 61-71.

MICHAEL J. TOLLEY. "Remarks on 'The Tyger,' " *Blake Newsletter* 1(2), Fall 1967, 10-13.

CHAD and EVA T. WALSH. *Twice Ten*, pp. 45-50.

AILEEN WARD. "The forging of Orc: Blake and the idea of revolution," in *Literature in Revolution*, pp. 220-21.

HARRY WILLIAMS. "The Tyger and the Lamb," *Concerning Poetry* 5(1), Spring 1972, 49-56.

"Visions of the Daughters of Albion"

FREDERICK L. BEATY. *Light from Heaven*, pp. 129-31.

HAROLD BLOOM. *The Visionary Company*, pp. 49-52.

JANE E. PETERSON. "The *Visions of the Daughters of Albion*: A Problem in Perception," *Philological Quarterly* 52(2), April 1973, 252-64.

HENRY H. WASSER. "Notes on the *Visions of the Daughters of Albion*," *Modern Language Quarterly* 9(3), September 1948, 292-97.

"When early morn walks forth in sober gray"

L. C. KNIGHTS. "Early Blake," *Sewanee Review* 79(3), Summer 1971, 390-91.

"William Bond"

JOHN SUTHERLAND. "Blake: A Crisis of Love and Jealousy," *PMLA* 87(3), May 1972, 426-27.

BLAKELY, HENRY

"My Daddy"

GEORGE E. KENT. "Notes on the 1974 Black Literary Scene," *Phylon* 36(2), June 1975, 194-95.

BLUNDEN, EDMUND

"A. G. A. V."

JON SILKIN. *Out of Battle*, pp. 116-17.

"A Country God"

PHILIP GARDNER. "Edmund Blunden: War Poet," *University of Toronto Quarterly* 42(3), Spring 1973, 223.

"In Festubert"

PHILIP GARDNER. "Edmund Blunden: War Poet," *University of Toronto Quarterly* 42(3), Spring 1973, 222-23.

"The Memorial, 1914-1918"

PHILIP GARDNER. "Edmund Blunden: War Poet," *University of Toronto Quarterly* 42(3), Spring 1973, 234.

"The Midnight Skaters"

JON SILKIN. *Out of Battle*, pp. 118-19.

"1916 Seen from 1921"

JON SILKIN. *Out of Battle*, pp. 115-16.

"The Pike"

JON SILKIN. *Out of Battle*, p. 118.

"Preparations for Victory"

JON SILKIN. *Out of Battle*, pp. 108-9.

"Report on Experience"

JAMES REEVES and MARTIN SEYMOUR-SMITH. *Inside Poetry*, pp. 46-48.

JON SILKIN. *Out of Battle*, pp. 119-20.

"Return of the Native"

JON SILKIN. *Out of Battle*, pp. 117-18.

"Third Battle of Ypres"

PHILIP GARDNER. "Edmund Blunden: War Poet," *University of Toronto Quarterly* 42(3), Spring 1973, 225-27.

JON SILKIN. *Out of Battle*, pp. 112-15.

"Thomasine"

"Menander's Mirror: Mr. Blunden's 'Thomasine,' " *Times Literary Supplement*, 20 January 1945, p. 27.

"The Veteran"

PHILIP GARDNER. "Edmund Blunden: War Poet," *University of Toronto Quarterly* 42(3), Spring 1973, 224-25.

"Vlamertinghe: Passing the Chateau, July 1917"

JON SILKIN. *Out of Battle*, pp. 110-11.

"Zero"

JON SILKIN. *Out of Battle*, p. 109.

BLY, ROBERT

"Afternoon Sleep"

GEORGE S. LENSING and RONALD MORAN. *Four Poets and the Emotive Imagination*, pp. 75-77.

"Awakening"

AGNES STEIN. *The Uses of Poetry*, pp. 356-58.

"The Busy Man Speaks"

PAUL A. LACEY. *The Inner War*, p. 45.

"Counting Small-Boned Bodies"

GEORGE S. LENSING and RONALD MORAN. *Four Poets and the Emotive Imagination*, p. 79.

"Driving Toward the Lac Qui Parle River"

PAUL A. LACEY. *The Inner War*, pp. 39-41.

"Evolution from the Fish"

ANTHONY LIBBY. "Fire and Light, Four Poets to the End and Beyond," *Iowa Review* 4(2), Spring 1973, 113-14.

ANTHONY LIBBY. "Robert Bly Alive in Darkness," *Iowa Review* 3(3), Summer 1972, 84-85.

"Hatred of Men With Black Hair"

R. P. DICKEY. "The New Genteel Tradition in American Poetry," *Sewanee Review* 82(4), Fall 1974, 737.

"Like the New Moon I Will Live My Life"

GEORGE S. LENSING and RONALD MORAN. *Four Poets and the Emotive Imagination*, pp. 80-81.

"A Man Writes to a Part of Himself"

PAUL A. LACEY. *The Inner War*, pp. 42-43.

"Poem Against the Rich"

JAMES G. KENNEDY. "The Two European Cultures and the Necessary New Sense of Literature," *College English* 31(6), March 1970, 580-82.

"Sleepers Joining Hands"

MICHAEL ATKINSON. "Robert Bly's *Sleepers Joining Hands*: Shadow and Self," *Iowa Review* 7(4), Fall 1976, 135-53.

DONALD HALL. "Notes on Robert Bly and *Sleepers Joining Hands*," *Ohio Review* 15(1), Fall 1973, 92-93.

"Surprised by Evening"

ALAN D. PERLIS. "Science, Mysticism, and Contemporary Poetry," *Western Humanities Review* 29(3), Summer 1975, 217.

"Watering the Horse"

PAUL A. LACEY. *The Inner War*, pp. 38-39.

"Where We Must Look For Help"

PAUL A. LACEY. *The Inner War*, pp. 41-42.

GEORGE S. LENSING and RONALD MORAN. *Four Poets and the Emotive Imagination*, pp. 72-73.

BOGAN, LOUISE

"The Alchemist"

PAUL RAMSEY. "Louise Bogan," *Iowa Review* 1(3), Summer 1970, 118-19.

"Betrothed"

ELIZABETH P. PERLMUTTER. "A Doll's Heart: The Girl in the Poetry of Edna St. Vincent Millay and Louise Bogan," *Twentieth Century Literature* 23(2), May 1977, 170-71.

"Chanson Un Peu Naive"

ELIZABETH P. PERLMUTTER. "A Doll's Heart: The Girl in the Poetry of Edna St. Vincent Millay and Louise Bogan," *Twentieth Century Literature* 23(2), May 1977, 173.

"Come Sleep .."

JACQUELINE RIDGEWAY. "The necessity of form to the poetry of Louise Bogan," *Women's Studies* 5(2), 1977, 145-47.

"The Dream"

HARRY BROWN and JOHN MILSTEAD. *What the Poem Means*, p. 16.

JAMES M. REID. *100 American Poems of the Twentieth Century*, pp. 146-47.

"Fifteenth Farewell"

JACQUELINE RIDGEWAY. "The necessity of form to the poetry of Louise Bogan," *Women's Studies* 5(2), 1977, 143-45.

"Girl's Song"

ELIZABETH P. PERLMUTTER. "A Doll's Heart: The Girl in the Poetry of Edna St. Vincent Millay and Louise Bogan," *Twentieth Century Literature* 23(2), May 1977, 174-75.

"Henceforth, From the Mind"

PAUL RAMSEY. "Louise Bogan," *Iowa Review* 1(3), Summer 1970, 119-20.

"Medusa"

PAUL RAMSEY. "Louise Bogan," *Iowa Review* 1(3), Summer 1970, 121.

"Men Loved Wholly Beyond Wisdom"

PAUL RAMSEY. "Louise Bogan," *Iowa Review* 1(3), Summer 1970, 117-18.

"My Voice Not Being Proud"

ELIZABETH P. PERLMUTTER. "A Doll's Heart: The Girl in the Poetry of Edna St. Vincent Millay and Louise Bogan," *Twentieth Century Literature* 23(2), May 1977, 172.

"Old Countryside"

PAUL RAMSEY. "Louise Bogan," *Iowa Review* 1(3), Summer 1970, 121-22.

"Second Song"

PAUL RAMSEY. "Louise Bogan," *Iowa Review* 1(3), Summer 1970, 120. (P)

"Simple Autumnal"

ROBERT PINSKY. *The Situation of Poetry*, pp. 97-99.

"Solitary Observations Brought Back From a Short Sojourn in Hell"

EARL DANIELS. *The Art of Reading Poetry*, pp. 199-200.

"Song" ("Love me because I am lost")

JACQUELINE RIDGEWAY. "The necessity of form to the poetry of Louise Bogan," *Women's Studies* 5(2), 1977, 143.

"Song for the Last Act"

PAUL RAMSEY. "Louise Bogan," *Iowa Review* 1(3), Summer 1970, 122-23.

"Sonnet" ("Since you would claim the sources of my thought")

JACQUELINE RIDGEWAY. "The necessity of form to the poetry of Louise Bogan," *Women's Studies* 5(2), 1977, 145.

"A Tale"

JACQUELINE RIDGEWAY. "The necessity of form to the poetry of Louise Bogan," *Women's Studies* 5(2), 1977, 141-42.

"To Wine"

PAUL RAMSEY. "Louise Bogan," *Iowa Review* 1(3), Summer 1970, 120.

"Words for Departure"

ELIZABETH P. PERLMUTTER. "A Doll's Heart: The Girl in the Poetry of Edna St. Vincent Millay and Louise Bogan," *Twentieth Century Literature* 23(2), May 1977, 167-69.

BOLTON, EDMUND

"London, King Charles His Augusta, or City Royal"

THOMAS H. BLACKBURN. "Edmund Bolton's *London, King Charles His Augusta, or City Royal*," *Huntington Library Quarterly* 25(4), August 1962, 315-23.

BOOTH, PHILIP

"Letter from a Distant Land"

ROBERT F. STOWELL. "Twentieth Century Poetry About Thoreau," *Thoreau Society Bulletin* 116 (Summer 1971), 2.

BOTTRALL, RONALD

"Natural Order"

RONALD BOTTRALL. "Ronald Bottrall," in *The Poet Speaks*, pp. 43-44.

BOWERS, EDGAR

"Adam's Song to Heaven"

HELEN P. TRIMPI. "Context for 'Being,' 'Divinity,' and 'Self' in Valéry and Edgar Bowers," *Southern Review*, n.s., 13(1), Winter 1977, 65-66.

"Autumn Shade"

HELEN P. TRIMPI. "Context for 'Being,' 'Divinity,' and 'Self' in Valéry and Edgar Bowers," *Southern Review*, n.s., 13(1), Winter 1977, 72-80.

"Dark Earth and Summer"

RICHARD G. STERN. "The Poetry of Edgar Bowers," *Chicago Review* 11(3), Autumn 1957, 73-75.

HELEN P. TRIMPI. "The Theme of Loss in the Earlier Poems of Catherine Davis and Edgar Bowers," *Southern Review*, n.s., 9(3), Summer 1973, 613-14.

"From J. Haydn to Constanze Mozart (1791)"

HELEN P. TRIMPI. "The Theme of Loss in the Earlier Poems of Catherine Davis And Edgar Bowers," *Southern Review*, n.s., 9(3), Summer 1973, 615.

"Grove and Building"

HELEN P. TRIMPI. "Context for 'Being,' 'Divinity,' and 'Self' in Valéry and Edgar Bowers," *Southern Review*, n.s., 13(1), Winter 1977, 49-50.

"Late Winter Night"

HELEN P. TRIMPI. "The Theme of Loss in the Earlier Poems of Catherine Davis And Edgar Bowers," *Southern Review*, n.s., 9(3), Summer 1973, 614-15.

"The Mountain Cemetery"

HELEN P. TRIMPI. "The Theme of Loss in the Earlier Poems of Catherine Davis And Edgar Bowers," *Southern Review*, n.s., 9(3), Summer 1973, 612.

"Oedipus at Colonus"

HELEN P. TRIMPI. "Context for 'Being,' 'Divinity,' and 'Self' in Valéry and Edgar Bowers," *Southern Review*, n.s., 13(1), Winter 1977, 50-51.

"The Prince"

HELEN P. TRIMPI. "The Theme of Loss in the Earlier Poems of Catherine Davis And Edgar Bowers," *Southern Review*, n.s., 9(3), Summer 1973, 611.

"A Song for Rising"

HELEN P. TRIMPI. "Context for 'Being,' 'Divinity,' and 'Self' in Valéry and Edgar Bowers," *Southern Review*, n.s., 13(1), Winter 1977, 81-82.

"The Virgin Mary"

JOHN CLARK PRATT. *The Meaning of Modern Poetry*, pp. 293, 280, 294-95, 297, 291, 307, 305-6, 309.

BOWKER, JAMES

"Hard Times, or the Weaver Speaks to His Wife"

MARTHA VICINUS. "The Study of Nineteenth Century British Working Poetry," *College English* 32(5), February 1971, 559-61.

BOWLES, WILLIAM LISLE

"To the River Itchin"

W. K. WIMSATT, JR. "The Structure of Romantic Nature Imagery," in *The Age of Johnson*, p. 294. Reprinted in: *English Romantic Poets*, pp. 27-28.

BOYD, MARK ALEXANDER

"Sonet" ("Fra banc to banc fra vod to vod I rin")

IAN ROSS. "Sonneteering in Sixteenth-Century Scotland," *Texas Studies in Literature and Language* 6(2), Summer 1964, 266-68.

BRACKENRIDGE, HUGH HENRY

"Poem on Divine Revelation"

THOMAS P. HAVILAND. "The Miltonic Quality of Brackenridge's *Poem on Divine Revelation*," *PMLA* 56(2), June 1941, 588-92.

BRADSTREET, ANNE

"Another Letter to My Husband"

ROSEMARY M. LAUGHLIN. "Anne Bradstreet: Poet in Search of Form," *American Literature* 42(1), March 1970, 9-10.

" 'As loving Hind' "

KENNETH A. REQUA. "Anne Bradstreet's Poetic Voices," *Early American Literature* 9(1), Spring 1974, 13.

" 'As weary pilgrim, now at rest' "

KENNETH A. REQUA. "Anne Bradstreet's Poetic Voices," *Early American Literature* 9(1), Spring 1974, 16.

"Before the Birth of one of her Children"

ANN STANFORD. "Anne Bradstreet: Dogmatist and Rebel," *New England Quarterly* 39(3), September 1966, 379-80. (P)

"Contemplations"

ROBERT DALY. *God's Altar*, pp. 117-26.

JANE DONAHUE EBERWEIN. "The 'Unrefined Ore' of Anne Bradstreet's Quarternions," *Early American Literature* 9(1), Spring 1974, 23.

ANNE HILDEBRAND. "Anne Bradstreet's Quarternions and 'Contemplations,' " *Early American Literature* 8(2), Fall 1973, 117-25.

WILLIAM J. IRVIN. "Allegory and Typology 'Imbrace and Greet': Anne Bradstreet's 'Contemplations,' " *Early American Literature* 10(1), Spring 1975, 30-46.

ROSEMARY M. LAUGHLIN. "Anne Bradstreet: Poet in Search of Form," *American Literature* 42(1), March 1970, 10-12.

ROBERT D. RICHARDSON, JR. "The Puritan Poetry of Anne Bradstreet," *Texas Studies in Literature and Language* 9(3), Autumn 1967, 323-31.

ALVIN H. ROSENFELD. "Anne Bradstreet's 'Contemplations': Patterns of Form and Meaning," *New England Quarterly* 43(1), March 1970, 79-96.

"A Dialogue between Old England and New; concerning their present Troubles, Anno, 1642"

KENNETH A. REQUA. "Anne Bradstreet's Poetic Voices," *Early American Literature* 9(1), Spring 1974, 8-9.

"Elegie upon that Honourable and renowned Knight, Sir Philip Sidney, who was untimely slaine at the Seige of Zutphen, Anno, 1586"

KENNETH A. REQUA. "Anne Bradstreet's Poetic Voices," *Early American Literature* 9(1), Spring 1974, 3-6.

ANN STANFORD. "Anne Bradstreet's Portrait of Sir Philip Sidney," *Early American Literature Newsletter* 1(3), Winter 1966-1967, 11-13.

"The Flesh and the Spirit"

ROBERT D. RICHARDSON, JR. "The Puritan Poetry of Anne Bradstreet," *Texas Studies in Literature and Language*, 9(3), Autumn 1967, 321.

"In memory of my dear grandchild Elizabeth Bradstreet, who deceased August, 1665 being a year and a half old"

ROBERT DALY. *God's Altar*, pp. 110-12.

JANE DONAHUE EBERWEIN. "The 'Unrefined Ore' of Anne Bradstreet's Quarternions," *Early American Literature* 9(1), Spring 1974, 22-23.

ANN STANFORD. "Anne Bradstreet: Dogmatist and Rebel," *New England Quarterly* 39(3), September 1966, 385-86.

"In reference to her Children, 23 June, 1656"

KENNETH A. REQUA. "Anne Bradstreet's Poetic Voices," *Early American Literature* 9(1), Spring 1974, 13.

"A Letter to her Husband, absent upon Publick employment"

ROBERT DALY. *God's Altar*, pp. 106-8.

JANE DONAHUE EBERWEIN. "The 'Unrefined Ore' of Anne Bradstreet's Quarternions," *Early American Literature* 9(1), Spring 1974, 24-25.

ROSAMUND R. ROSENMEIER. " 'Divine Translation': A Contribution to the Study of Anne Bradstreet's Method in the Marriage Poems," *Early American Literature* 12(2), Fall 1977, 125-27.

"On my dear Grand-child Simon Bradstreet, who dyed on 16 November 1669 being but a month and one day old"

ROBERT DALY. *God's Altar*, pp. 115-16.

"A Pilgrim"

ANN STANFORD. "Anne Bradstreet: Dogmatist and Rebel," *New England Quarterly* 39(3), September 1966, 387-88.

"To Her Father with some verses"

KENNETH A. REQUA. "Anne Bradstreet's Poetic Voices," *Early American Literature* 9(1), Spring 1974, 12.

"To My Dear and loving Husband"

ROBERT DALY. *God's Altar*, pp. 104-6.

"Upon a Fit of Sickness, Anno. 1632 Aetatis suae"

ROBERT D. RICHARDSON, JR. "The Puritan Poetry of Anne Bradstreet," *Texas Studies in Literature and Language* 9(3), Autumn 1967, 318-19.

"Upon my Son Samuel his goeing for England, November 6, 1657"

KENNETH A. REQUA. "Anne Bradstreet's Poetic Voices," *Early American Literature* 9(1), Spring 1974, 14.

"Upon the burning of our house, July 10th, 1666"

ROSEMARY M. LAUGHLIN. "Anne Bradstreet: Poet in Search of Form," *American Literature* 42(1), March 1970, 12-13.

KENNETH A. REQUA. "Anne Bradstreet's Poetic Voices," *Early American Literature* 9(1), Spring 1974, 16-17.

ROBERT D. RICHARDSON, JR. "The Puritan Poetry of Anne Bradstreet," *Texas Studies in Literature and Language* 9(3), Autumn 1967, 321-22.

ROSAMUND R. ROSENMEIER. " 'Divine Translation': A Contribution to the Study of Anne Bradstreet's Method in the Marriage Poems," *Early American Literature* 12(2), Fall 1977, 131-33.

ANN STANFORD. "Anne Bradstreet: Dogmatist and Rebel," *New England Quarterly* 39(3), September 1966, 383-85.

HYATT H. WAGGONER. *American Poets*, p. 10.

"The Vanity of all worldly things"

ROBERT DALY. *God's Altar*, pp. 96-99.

ROBERT D. RICHARDSON, JR. "The Puritan Poetry of Anne Bradstreet," *Texas Studies in Literature and Language* 9(3), Autumn 1967, 320.

BRAUN, RICHARD EMIL

"Against Nature"

JEROME MAZZARO. "Putting It Together: The Poetry of Richard Emil Braun," *Modern Poetry Studies* 5(3), Winter 1974, 256-57.

"Da Nuces"

JEROME MAZZARO. "Putting It Together: The Poetry of Richard Emil Braun," *Modern Poetry Studies* 5(3), Winter 1974, 263.

"The Lilies"

JEROME MAZZARO. "Putting It Together: The Poetry of Richard Emil Braun," *Modern Poetry Studies* 5(3), Winter 1974, 260-61.

"Listening"

JEROME MAZZARO. "Putting It Together: The Poetry of Richard Emil Braun," *Modern Poetry Studies* 5(3), Winter 1974, 258-59.

BRAUTIGAN, RICHARD

"Haiku Ambulance"

ROBERT KERN. "Williams, Brautigan, and the Poetics of Primitivism," *Chicago Review* 27(1), Summer 1975, 52-53.

"Xerox Candybar"

ROBERT KERN. "Williams, Brautigan, and the Poetics of Primitivism," *Chicago Review* 27(1), Summer 1975, 55-56.

BRENNAN, J. KEIRN

"Let the Rest of the World Go By"

CLEANTH BROOKS and ROBERT PENN WARREN. *Understanding Poetry*, fourth ed., pp. 130-33.

BRETON, NICHOLAS

"In the merry month of May"

LAURENCE LERNER. "What Pastoral Is," in his *The Uses of Nostalgia*, pp. 32-33.

"A Report Song"

LAURENCE LERNER. *The Uses of Nostalgia*, p. 34.

BRETT, ARTHUR

"Patientia victrix"

JOHN J. TEUNISSEN. "The Book of Job and Stuart Politics," *University of Toronto Quarterly* 43(1), Fall 1973, 26-29.

BRIDGES, ROBERT

"The College Garden"

DONALD E. STANFORD. "Robert Bridges and the Free Verse Rebellion," *Journal of Modern Literature* 2(1), September 1971, 28.

"Come se quando"

DONALD E. STANFORD. "Robert Bridges and the Free Verse Rebellion," *Journal of Modern Literature* 2(1), September 1971, 23-25.

"Eros"

M. L. ROSENTHAL and A. J. M. SMITH. *Exploring Poetry*, pp. 183-85; second ed., pp. 485-86.

"Kate's Mother"

DONALD E. STANFORD. "Robert Bridges and the Free Verse Rebellion," *Journal of Modern Literature* 2(1), September 1971, 29-30.

BRIDGES, ROBERT *(Cont.)*

"London Snow"

> JEROME BEATY and WILLIAM H. MATCHETT. *Poetry From Statement to Meaning*, pp. 246-48.

"Low Barometer"

> YVOR WINTERS. "The Poetry of Gerard Manley Hopkins (I)," *Hudson Review* 1(4), Winter 1949, 458-60. Reprinted in: Yvor Winters. *The Function of Criticism*, pp. 105-7.

"Nightingales"

> JEROME BEATY and WILLIAM H. MATCHETT. *Poetry From Statement to Meaning*, pp. 21-27.

> CLEANTH BROOKS and ROBERT PENN WARREN. *Understanding Poetry*, pp. 198-200; revised ed., pp. 95-97; third ed., pp. 100-102; fourth ed., p. 366.

> FRANK DOGGETT. "Romanticism's Singing Bird," *Studies in English Literature 1500-1900* 14(4), Autumn 1974, 558-60.

"Ode to Music"

> ANDREW J. GREEN. "Bridges' Odes for Music," *Sewanee Review* 49(1), January-March 1941, 30-38.

"Poor Poll"

> KIMON FRIAR and JOHN MALCOLM BRINNIN. *Modern Poetry*, pp. 560-61.

> DONALD E. STANFORD. "Robert Bridges and the Free Verse Rebellion," *Journal of Modern Literature* 2(1), September 1971, 25-27.

"The Psalm"

> DONALD E. STANFORD. "Robert Bridges and the Free Verse Rebellion," *Journal of Modern Literature* 2(1), September 1971, 28-29.

"The Tapestry"

> DONALD E. STANFORD. "Robert Bridges and the Free Verse Rebellion," *Journal of Modern Literature* 2(1), September 1971, 27.

BRINNIN, JOHN MALCOLM

"The Alps"

> DAVID DAICHES. "Some Notes on Contemporary American Poetry," in *Modern American Poetry*, edited by B. Rajan, pp. 113-14. (P)

"The Ascent"

> JOSEPH WARREN BEACH. *Obsessive Images*, p. 99.

"Dachau"

> PHILIP L. GERBER, ED. "A Kind of Exorcism: A Conversation with John Malcolm Brinnin," *Prairie Schooner* 48(3), Fall 1974, 219-21.

"The Fortunate Isles"

> JOSEPH WARREN BEACH. *Obsessive Images*, pp. 136-38, 167-68.

"Goodnight, When the Door Swings"

> DAVID DAICHES. "Some Notes on Contemporary American Poetry," in *Modern American Poetry*, edited by B. Rajan, p. 114. (P)

"Islands: A Song"

> JOSEPH WARREN BEACH. *Obsessive Images*, pp. 135-36.

"Mardi Gras"

> JOSEPH WARREN BEACH. *Obsessive Images*, p. 350.

"Meditation on Tombs"

> JOSEPH WARREN BEACH. *Obsessive Images*, pp. 233-34, 347.

"New Year's Eve"

> JOSEPH WARREN BEACH. *Obsessive Images*, pp. 138-39, 331-32.

"Pretense Employs Us Innocence Must Lie"

> JOSEPH WARREN BEACH. *Obsessive Images*, p. 334.

"A Sail"

> JOSEPH WARREN BEACH. *Obsessive Images*, pp. 166-67.

"Second Sight"

> JOSEPH WARREN BEACH. *Obsessive Images*, pp. 168-69.

"Skin Diving in the Virgins"

> JAMES M. REID. *100 American Poems of the Twentieth Century*, pp. 238-39.

"This Voyaging"

> JOSEPH WARREN BEACH. *Obsessive Images*, p. 139.

"Views of the Favorite Colleges"

> SISTER MARY HUMILIATA. *Explicator* 14(4), January 1956, Item 20.

"The World Is a Wedding"

> JOSEPH WARREN BEACH. *Obsessive Images*, p. 82.

"The Worm in the Whirling Cross"

> KIMON FRIAR and JOHN MALCOLM BRINNIN. *Modern Poetry*, pp. 447-49. (Quoting J. F. Nims)

> JOHN THEOBALD. "The World in a Cross Word," *Poetry* 71(2), November 1947, 82-90.

BRONTË, ANNE

"The Three Guides"

> EDWARD CHITHAM. "Almost Like Twins," *Brontë Society Transactions* 16(5), 1975, 370.

BRONTË, EMILY

"Cold in the Earth"

> F. R. LEAVIS. "Reality and Sincerity: Notes in the Analysis of Poetry," *Scrutiny* 19(2), Winter 1952-3, 90-94.

"Fall leaves, fall; die, flowers, away"

> D. R. BEETON. "Emily Brontë and Jan Christian Smuts," *Brontë Society Transactions* 15(3), 1968, 219-20.

"I am the only being whose doom"

> JAMES REEVES and MARTIN SEYMOUR-SMITH. *Inside Poetry*, pp. 34-36.

"I'll walk where my own nature would be leading"

> D. R. BEETON. "Emily Brontë and Jan Christian Smuts," *Brontë Society Transactions* 15(3), 1968, 218.

"No Coward Soul Is Mine"

> LAWRENCE J. STARZYK. "The Faith of Emily Brontë's Immortality Creed," *Victorian Poetry* 11(4), Winter 1973, 295-305.

"Remembrance"

> REED WHITTMORE. "Brontë: Remembrance," in *Master Poems of the English Language*, pp. 684-86.

"Why ask to know the date — the clime"

> JONATHAN WORDSWORTH. "Wordsworth and the Poetry of Emily Brontë," *Brontë Society Transactions* 16(2), 1972, 85-89.

BROOKE, RUPERT

"Dust"

> G. WILSON KNIGHT. *Neglected Powers*, pp. 299-300.

"The Old Vicarage, Grantchester"

> G. WILSON KNIGHT. *Neglected Powers*, p. 301.

"The Soldier"
BERNARD BERGONZI. *Heroes' Twilight*, pp. 43-44.
EARL DANIELS. *The Art of Reading Poetry*, pp. 270-72.
"Tiare Tahiti"
G. WILSON KNIGHT. *Neglected Powers*, p. 301.

BROOKS, GWENDOLYN

"The Anniad"
ARTHUR P. DAVIS. "The Black-and-Tan Motif in the Poetry of Gwendolyn Brooks," *CLA Journal* 6(2), December 1962, 93-94.
"the ballad of chocolate Mabbie"
ARTHUR P. DAVIS. "The Black-and-Tan Motif in the Poetry of Gwendolyn Brooks," *CLA Journal* 6(2), December 1962, 92.
"Ballad of Pearl May Lee"
ARTHUR P. DAVIS. "The Black-and-Tan Motif in the Poetry of Gwendolyn Brooks," *CLA Journal* 6(2), December 1962, 92-93.
"The Ballad of Rudolph Reed"
DELOIS GARRETT. "Dream Motif in Contemporary Negro Poetry," *English Journal* 59(6), September 1970, 768.
CLENORA F. HUDSON. "Racial Themes in the Poetry of Gwendolyn Brooks," *CLA Journal* 17(1), September 1973, 18.
"Big Bessie Throws Her Son into the Street"
WILLIAM H. HANSELL. "The Poet-Militant and Foreshadowings of a Black Mystique: Poems in the Second Period of Gwendolyn Brooks," *Concerning Poetry* 10(2), Fall 1977, 38-39.
"Boys. Black"
WILLIAM H. HANSELL. "Essences, Unifyings, and Black Militancy: Major Themes in Gwendolyn Brooks' *Family Pictures* and *Beckonings*," *Black American Literature Forum* 11(2), Summer 1977, 65-66.
"A Bronzeville Mother Loiters in Mississippi./Meanwhile a Mississippi Mother Burns Bacon"
ARTHUR P. DAVIS. "Gwendolyn Brooks: Poet of the Unheroic," *CLA Journal* 7(2), December 1963, 122.
"Bronzeville Woman in a Red Hat"
ARTHUR P. DAVIS. "The Black-and-Tan Motif in the Poetry of Gwendolyn Brooks," *CLA Journal* 6(2), December 1962, 95.
"The *Chicago Defender* Sends a Man to Little Rock"
ARTHUR P. DAVIS. "Gwendolyn Brooks: Poet of the Unheroic," *CLA Journal* 7(2), December 1963, 122-23.
CLENORA F. HUDSON. "Racial Themes in the Poetry of Gwendolyn Brooks," *CLA Journal* 17(1), September 1973, 18.
SUE S. PARK. "A Study in Tension: Gwendolyn Brooks's 'The *Chicago Defender* Sends a Man to Little Rock,'" *Black American Literature Forum* 11(1), Spring 1977, 32-34.
"The Chicago Picasso"
WILLIAM H. HANSELL. "Aestheticism Versus Political Militancy in Gwendolyn Brooks's 'The Chicago Picasso' and 'The Wall,'" *CLA Journal* 17(1), September 1973, 11-13.
"An Interview with Gwendolyn Brooks," *Contemporary Literature* 11(1), Winter 1970, 1-2.

"First fight. Then fiddle. Ply the slipping String"
JAMES A. EMANUEL. "A Note on the Future of Negro Poetry," *Negro American Literature Forum* 1(1), Fall 1967, [2-3].
CLENORA F. HUDSON. "Racial Themes in the Poetry of Gwendolyn Brooks," *CLA Journal* 17(1), September 1973, 20.
"Horses Graze"
WILLIAM H. HANSELL. "Essences, Unifyings, and Black Militancy: Major Themes in Gwendolyn Brooks' *Family Pictures* and *Beckonings*," *Black American Literature Forum* 11(2), Summer 1977, 64.
"In the Mecca"
MARVA RILEY FURMAN. "Gwendolyn Brooks: the 'Unconditioned' Poet," *CLA Journal* 17(1), September 1973, 2-3.
WILLIAM HANSELL. "Gwendolyn Brooks's 'In the Mecca': A Rebirth into Blackness," *Negro American Literature Forum* 8(2), Summer 1974, 199-207.
"In the Time of Detachment, in the Time of Cold"
WILLIAM HANSELL. "The Poet-Militant and Foreshadowings of a Black Mystique: Poems in the Second Period of Gwendolyn Brooks," *Concerning Poetry* 10(2), Fall 1977, 43-44.
"Jessie Mitchell's Mother"
ARTHUR P. DAVIS. "The Black-and-Tan Motif in the Poetry of Gwendolyn Brooks," *CLA Journal* 6(2), December 1962, 94-95.
"kitchenette building"
EDWARD CLARK. "Studying and Teaching Afro-American Literature," *CLA Journal* 16(1), September 1972, 101-3.
"The Life of Lincoln West"
WILLIAM H. HANSELL. "Essences, Unifyings, and Black Militancy: Major Themes in Gwendolyn Brooks': *Family Pictures* and *Beckonings*," *Black American Literature Forum* 11(2), Summer 1977, 64-65.
"the mother"
SUZANNE JUHASZ. *Naked and Fiery Forms*, pp. 152-53.
"My dreams, my works, must wait till after hell"
CLENORA F. HUDSON. "Racial Themes in the Poetry of Gwendolyn Brooks," *CLA Journal* 17(1), September 1973, 19.
"Negro Hero"
CLENORA F. HUDSON. "Racial Themes in the Poetry of Gwendolyn Brooks," *CLA Journal* 17(1), September 1973, 19-20.
"of De Witt Williams on his way to Lincoln Cemetery"
CLENORA F. HUDSON. "Racial Themes in the Poetry of Gwendolyn Brooks," *CLA Journal* 17(1), September 1973, 17.
"Old People Working"
WILLIAM H. HANSELL. "The Poet-Militant and Foreshadowings of a Black Mystique: Poems in the Second Period of Gwendolyn Brooks," *Concerning Poetry* 10(2), Fall 1977, 37-38.
"Open my rooms, let in the light and air"
ARTHUR P. DAVIS. "Gwendolyn Brooks: Poet of the Unheroic," *CLA Journal* 7(2), December 1963, 120-21.
"Piano After War"
ALAN C. LUPACK. *Explicator* 36(4), Summer 1978, 2-3.

BROOKS, GWENDOLYN *(Cont.)*

"The Preacher Ruminates Behind the Sermon"

WILLIAM H. HANSELL. "Essences, Unifyings, and Black Militancy: Major Themes in Gwendolyn Brooks' *Family Pictures* and *Beckonings*," *Black American Literature Forum* 11(2), Summer 1977, 63.

"Riders to the Blood-Red Wrath"

WILLIAM H. HANSELL. "The Poet-Militant and Fore-shadowings of a Black Mystique: Poems in the Second Period of Gwendolyn Brooks," *Concerning Poetry* 10(2), Fall 1977, 39-41.

"Riot"

MARVA RILEY FURMAN. "Gwendolyn Brooks: The 'Unconditioned' Poet," *CLA Journal* 17(1), September 1973, 6-7.

"The Sight of the Horizon"

WILLIAM H. HANSELL. "The Poet-Militant and Fore-shadowings of a Black Mystique: Poems in the Second Period of Gwendolyn Brooks," *Concerning Poetry* 10(2), Fall 1977, 42-43.

"Spaulding and Francois"

WILLIAM H. HANSELL. "The Poet-Militant and Fore-shadowings of a Black Mystique: Poems in the Second Period of Gwendolyn Brooks," *Concerning Poetry* 10(2), Fall 1977, 38.

"The Sundays of Satin-Legs Smith"

ARTHUR P. DAVIS. "Gwendolyn Brooks: Poet of the Unheroic," *CLA Journal* 7(2), December 1963, 119-20.

"To Don at Salaam"

WILLIAM H. HANSELL. "Essences, Unifyings, and Black Militancy: Major Themes in Gwendolyn Brooks' *Family Pictures* and *Beckonings*," *Black American Literature Forum* 11(2), Summer 1977, 64.

"To Keorapetse Kgositsile (Willie)"

MARVA RILEY FURMAN. "Gwendolyn Brooks: The 'Unconditioned' Poet," *CLA Journal* 17(1), September 1973, 8.

WILLIAM H. HANSELL. "Essences, Unifyings, and Black Militancy: Major Themes in Gwendolyn Brooks' *Family Pictures* and *Beckonings*," *Black American Literature Forum* 11(2), Summer 1977, 64.

"The Wall"

WILLIAM H. HANSELL. "Aestheticism Versus Political Militancy in Gwendolyn Brooks' 'The Chicago Picasso' and 'The Wall,' " *CLA Journal* 17(1), September 1973, 13-15.

"Way-Out Morgan"

MARVA RILEY FURMAN. "Gwendolyn Brooks: the 'Unconditioned' Poet," *CLA Journal* 17(1), September 1973, 5.

"We Real Cool"

BARBARA B. SIMS. *Explicator* 34(8), April 1976, Item 58.

BROWN, HARRY

"Fourth Elegy: The Poet Compared to an Unsuccessful General"

HAYDEN CARRUTH. "The Poet with Wounds," *Poetry* 71(4), January 1948, 217-21.

BROWN, STERLING A.

"The Ballad of Joe Meek"

CHARLES H. ROWELL. "Sterling A. Brown and the Afro-American Folk Tradition," *Studies in the Literary Imagination* 7(2), Fall 1974, 149-51.

"Frankie and Johnny"

CHARLES H. ROWELL. "Sterling A. Brown and the Afro-American Folk Tradition," *Studies in the Literary Imagination* 7(2), Fall 1974, 148-49.

"Ma Rainey"

CHARLES H. ROWELL. "Sterling A. Brown and the Afro-American Folk Tradition," *Studies in the Literary Imagination* 7(2), Fall 1974, 140-42.

"Memphis Blues"

CHARLES H. ROWELL. "Sterling A. Brown and the Afro-American Folk Tradition," *Studies in the Literary Imagination* 7(2), Fall 1974, 145-47.

"New St. Louis Blues"

CHARLES H. ROWELL. "Sterling A. Brown and the Afro-American Folk Tradition," *Studies in the Literary Imagination* 7(2), Fall 1974, 139-40.

"The Odyssey of Big Boy"

EUGENIA W. COLLIER. "I Do Not Marvel, Countee Cullen," in *Modern Black Poets*, pp. 75-76.

"Old Lem"

CHARLES H. ROWELL. "Sterling A. Brown and the Afro-American Folk Tradition," *Studies in the Literary Imagination* 7(2), Fall 1974, 144. (P)

"Southern Road"

CHARLES H. ROWELL. "Sterling A. Brown and the Afro-American Folk Tradition," *Studies in the Literary Imagination* 7(2), Fall 1974, 137-39.

BROWN, THOMAS EDWARD

"My Garden"

EARL DANIELS. *The Art of Reading Poetry*, pp. 260-61.

LEONARD UNGER and WILLIAM VAN O'CONNOR. *Poems for Study*, p. 33.

BROWNE, WILLIAM

"Epitaph on the Countess Dowager of Pembroke"

GÉMINO H. ABAD. *A Formal Approach to Lyric Poetry*, pp. 42-43.

WINIFRED NOWOTTNY. *The Language Poets Use*, pp. 108-11.

ALLEN TATE. "Understanding Modern Poetry," *College English* 1(7), April 1940, 570. Reprinted in: Allen Tate. *On the Limits of Poetry*, p. 125. Also: Allen Tate. *Reason in Madness*, pp. 95-96. Also: Allen Tate. *Essays of Four Decades*, pp. 165-66.

BROWNING, ELIZABETH BARRETT

"The Cry of the Children"

C. C. CUNNINGHAM. *Literature as a Fine Art*, pp. 135-42.

"The Development of Genius"

M. RAYMOND. "Elizabeth Barrett's Early Poetics: The 1820s 'The Bird Pecks Through the Shell,' " *Browning Society Notes* 8(3), December 1978, 4-5.

"Go from me. Yet I feel that I shall stand" (*Sonnets from the Portuguese*, VI)

CAROL MCGINNIS KAY. "An Analysis of Sonnet 6 in *Sonnets from the Portuguese*," *Concerning Poetry* 4(1), Spring 1971, 17-21.

"How do I love thee?" (*Sonnets from the Portuguese*, XLIII)

WILLIAM T. GOING. *Explicator* 11(8), June 1953, Item 58.

ROBERT B. HEILMAN. *Explicator* 4(1), October 1945, Item 3. Reprinted in: *Readings for Liberal Education,* II: 213-14; revised ed., II: 120-21.

JOHN S. PHILLIPSON. " 'How Do I Love Thee?' — an Echo of St. Paul," *Victorian Newsletter* 22 (Fall 1962), 22.

"Lord Walter's Wife"

ALETHEA HAYTER. " 'These Men Over-Nice': Elizabeth Barrett Browning's 'Lord Walter's Wife,' " *Browning Society Notes* 8(2), August 1978, 5-7.

"A Musical Instrument"

PATRICIA MERIVALE. "The Pan Figure in Victorian Poetry: Landor to Meredith," *Philological Quarterly* 44(2), April 1965, 264-65.

"The Poet's Enchiridion"

M. RAYMOND. "Elizabeth Barrett's Early Poetics: The 1820s 'The Bird Pecks Through the Shell,' " *Browning Society Notes* 8(3), December 1978, 5-6.

"To George Sand, A Desire"

SANDRA M. DONALDSON. "Elizabeth Barrett's Two Sonnets to George Sand," *Studies in Browning and His Circle* 5(1), Spring 1977, 19-20.

"To George Sand, A Recognition"

SANDRA M. DONALDSON. "Elizabeth Barrett's Two Sonnets to George Sand," *Studies in Browning and His Circle* 5(1), Spring 1977, 21-22.

BROWNING, ROBERT

"Abt Vogler"

JAMES BENZIGER. *Images of Eternity,* pp. 183-86.

ALAN BISHOP and JOHN FERNS. " 'Art in obedience to laws': Form and Meaning in Browning's 'Abt Vogler,' " *Victorian Poetry* 12(1), Spring 1974, 25-32.

HAROLD BLOOM. *Poetry and Repression,* pp. 186-91.

STEPHEN BROWN. "Browning and Music," *Browning Society Notes* 6(3), December 1976, 3-4, 7.

DEREK COLVILLE. *Victorian Poetry and the Romantic Religion,* pp. 146-51.

G. WILSON KNIGHT. *Neglected Powers,* pp. 252-54.

SHIV K. KUMAR. "The Moment in the Dramatic Monologues of Robert Browning," in *British Victorian Literature,* p. 95.

ROBERT LANGBAUM. *The Poetry of Experience,* pp. 140-43.

CHAD and EVA T. WALSH. *Twice Ten,* pp. 73-78.

"Along the Beach"
see "James Lee's Wife"

"Among the Rocks"
see "James Lee's Wife"

"Amphibian"

WILLIAM WHITLA. "Sources for Browning in Byron, Blake, and Poe," *Studies in Browning and His Circle* 2(1), Spring 1974, 9-14.

"Andrea del Sarto"

GÉMINO H. ABAD. *A Formal Approach to Lyric Poetry,* pp. 116-19.

RICHARD BENVENUTO. "Lippo and Andrea: The Pro and Contra of Browning's Realism," *Studies in English Literature 1500-1900* 13(4), Autumn 1973, 643-52.

ELIZABETH BIEMAN. "An Eros *Manque*: Browning's 'Andrea del Sarto,' " *Studies in English Literature 1500-1900* 10(4), Autumn 1970, 651-68.

HAROLD BLOOM. *Poetry and Repression,* pp. 191-94.

STEPHEN C. BRENNAN. "Andrea's Twilight Piece: Structure and Meaning in 'Andrea del Sarto,' " *Studies in Browning and His Circle* 5(1), Spring 1977, 34-50.

HARRY BROWN and JOHN MILSTEAD. *What the Poem Means,* pp. 20-21.

PAUL A. CUNDIFF. " 'Andrea del Sarto,' " *Tennessee Studies in Literature* 13(1968), 27-38.

DAVID DAICHES and WILLIAM CHARVAT. *Poems in English,* pp. 717-18.

MARIO L. D'AVANZO. "King Francis, Lucrezia, and the Figurative Language of 'Andrea del Sarto,' " *Texas Studies in Literature and Language* 9(4), Winter 1968, 523-36.

VINCENT C. DE BAUN. "Browning: Art Is Life Is Thought," *CLA Journal* 14(4), June 1971, 398-401.

ROBERT F. GARRATT. "Browning's Dramatic Monologue: the Strategy of the Double Mask," *Victorian Poetry* 11(2), Summer 1973, 115-16, 118-20.

E. D. H. JOHNSON. *The Alien Vision of Victorian Poetry,* pp. 111-12.

WENDELL STACY JOHNSON. *Sex and Marriage in Victorian Poetry,* pp. 213-15.

A. R. JONES. "Robert Browning and the Dramatic Monologue: The Impersonal Art," *Critical Quarterly* 9(4), Winter 1967, 321-22.

GERHARD JOSEPH. "Victorian Frames: The Windows and Mirrors of Browning, Arnold, and Tennyson," *Victorian Poetry* 16(1-2), Spring-Summer 1978, 75-76.

FRED KAPLAN. *Miracles of Rare Device,* pp. 94-108.

ROBERT LANGBAUM. *The Poetry of Experience,* pp. 148-55.

SYDNEY MENDEL. *Explicator* 22(9), May 1964, Item 77.

DOROTHY M. MERMIN. "Speaker and Auditor in Browning's Dramatic Monologues," *University of Toronto Quarterly* 45(2), Winter 1976, 145-46.

CHAD and EVA T. WALSH. *Twice Ten,* p. 80.

"Any Wife to Any Husband"

WENDELL STACY JOHNSON. *Sex and Marriage in Victorian Poetry,* pp. 207-8.

RICHARD KELLY. "The Dramatic Relationship Between 'By the Fire-Side' and 'Any Wife to Any Husband,' " *Victorian Newsletter* 39 (Spring 1971), 20-21.

"Apollo and the Fates"

ROBERT R. COLUMBUS and CLAUDETTE KEMPER. "Browning's Fuddling Apollo or the Perils of Parleying," *Tennessee Studies in Literature* 12 (1967), 85-95.

MARK SIEGCHRIST. "Type Needs Antitype: The Structure of Browning's *Parleyings,*" *Victorian Newsletter* 50(Fall 1976), 3-4.

"Apparent Failure"

JOHN LUCAS. "Apparent Failure," *Browning Society Notes* 6(1), March 1976, 17-23.

"Bad Dreams"

HAROLD BLOOM. *Poetry and Repression,* pp. 196-98.

DONALD S. HAIR. "Exploring *Asolando,*" *Browning Society Notes* 8(1), April 1978, 3-4.

"Bad Dreams, III"

CHAD and EVA T. WALSH. *Twice Ten,* pp. 72-73.

"Beatrice Signorini"

BARBARA ARNETT MELCHIORI. " 'Beatrice Signorini,' " *Browning Society Notes* 7(3), December 1977, 81-87.

BROWNING, ROBERT (*Cont.*)

"Beatrice Signorini" (*cont.*)

JOHN G. RUDY. "Browning's 'Beatrice Signorini' and the Problems of Aesthetic Aspiration," *Browning Society Notes* 7(3), December 1977, 87-94.

"Beside the Drawing Board"

see also "James Lee's Wife"

G. ROBERT STANGE. *Explicator* 17(5), February 1959, Item 32.

"Bishop Blougram's Apology"

SUSAN HARDY AIKEN. "Bishop Blougram and Carlyle," *Victorian Poetry* 16(4), Winter 1978, 323-40.

ISOBEL ARMSTRONG. "Browning and the 'Grotesque' Style," in *The Major Victorian Poets*, pp. 116-18.

R. G. COLLINS. "Browning's Practical Prelate: The Lesson of *Bishop Blougram's Apology*," *Victorian Poetry* 13(1), Spring 1975, 1-20.

DAVID R. EWBANK. "Bishop Blougram's Argument," *Victorian Poetry* 10(3), Autumn 1972, 257-63.

WILLIAM IRVINE. "Four Monologues in Browning's *Men and Women*," *Victorian Poetry* 2(3), Summer 1964, 158-60.

E. D. H. JOHNSON. *The Alien Vision of Victorian Poetry*, pp. 98-99.

CAREY H. KIRK. "Checkmating Bishop Blougram," *Victorian Poetry* 10(3), Autumn 1972, 265-71.

ROBERT G. LAIRD. " 'He did not Sit Five Minutes': The Conversion of Gigadibs," *University of Toronto Quarterly* 45(4), Summer 1976, 295-313.

ROBERT LANGBAUM. *The Poetry of Experience*, pp. 100-2.

JULIA MARKUS. "Bishop Blougram and the Literary Men," *Victorian Studies* 21(2), Winter 1978, 171-95.

DOROTHY M. MERMIN. "Speaker and Auditor in Browning's Dramatic Monologues," *University of Toronto Quarterly* 45(2), Winter 1976, 148-53.

RUPERT E. PALMER, JR. "The Uses of Character in 'Bishop Blougram's Apology,' " *Modern Philology* 58(2), November 1960, 108-18.

WILLIAM O. RAYMOND. "Browning's Casuists," *Studies in Philology* 37(4), October 1940, 648-53.

ARNOLD SHAPIRO. "A New (Old) Reading of Bishop Blougram's Apology: The Problem of the Dramatic Monologue," *Victorian Poetry* 10(3), Autumn 1972, 243-56.

ELLEN F. SHIELDS. "Bishop Blougram and the Cardinals," *Victorian Newsletter* 37 (Spring 1970), 21-24.

C. E. TANZY. "Browning, Emerson, and Bishop Blougram," *Victorian Studies* 1(3), March 1958, 255-66.

C. N. WENGER. "The Masquerade in Browning's Dramatic Monologues," *College English* 3(3), December 1941, 228-29.

"The Bishop Orders His Tomb"

GÉMINO H. ABAD. *A Formal Approach to Lyric Poetry*, pp. 78-80.

FRANCIS W. BONNER. *Explicator* 22(7), March 1964, Item 57.

HARRY BROWN and JOHN MILSTEAD. *What the Poem Means*, pp. 27-28.

EARL DANIELS. *The Art of Reading Poetry*, pp. 99-101.

VINCENT C. DE BAUN. "Browning: Art Is Life Is Thought," *CLA Journal* 14(4), June 1971, 396-97.

ERNEST L. FONTANA. "Browning's St. Praxed's Bishop: A Naturalistic View," *Victorian Poetry* 10(3), Autumn 1972, 278-82.

ROBERT F. GARRATT. "Browning's Dramatic Monologue: the Strategy of the Double Mask," *Victorian Poetry* 11(2), Summer 1973, 115-16, 120-22.

ROBERT A. GREENBERG. "Ruskin, Pugin, and the Contemporary Context of 'The Bishop Orders His Tomb,' " *PMLA* 84(6), October 1966, 1588-94.

NATHANIEL I. HART. *Explicator* 29(5), January 1971, Item 36.

A. R. JONES. "Robert Browning and the Dramatic Monologue: The Impersonal Art," *Critical Quarterly* 9(4), Winter 1967, 325-27.

G. MALCOLM LAWS, JR. "Death and Browning's Dying Bishop," in *Romantic and Victorian*, pp. 318-28.

BARBARA MELCHIORI. "Where the Bishop Ordered his Tomb," *Review of English Literature* 5(3), July 1964, 7-26.

DOROTHY M. MERMIN. "Speaker and Auditor in Browning's Dramatic Monologues," *University of Toronto Quarterly* 45(2), Winter 1976, 143.

VINCENT M. MILOSEVICH. *Explicator* 27(9), May 1969, Item 67.

GEORGE MONTEIRO. "The Apostasy and Death of St. Praxed's Bishop," *Victorian Poetry* 8(3), Autumn 1970, 209-18.

LAURENCE PERRINE. *Explicator* 24(2), October 1965, Item 12.

CHARLES T. PHIPPS. "The Bishop as Bishop: Clerical Motif and Meaning in 'The Bishop Orders His Tomb At St. Praxed's Church,' " *Victorian Poetry* 8(3), Autumn 1970, 199-208.

LAWRENCE POSTON, III. "Ritual in 'The Bishop Orders His Tomb,' " *Victorian Newsletter* 17 (Spring 1960), 27-28.

LIONEL STEVENSON. "The Pertinacious Victorian Poets," in *Victorian Literature*, pp. 25-26.

"By the Fireside"

see also "James Lee's Wife"

ISOBEL ARMSTRONG. "Browning and the 'Grotesque' Style," in *The Major Victorian Poets*, pp. 105-11.

WENDELL STACY JOHNSON. *Sex and Marriage in Victorian Poetry*, pp. 199-201.

RICHARD KELLY. "The Dramatic Relationship Between 'By the Fire-Side' and 'Any Wife to Any Husband,' " *Victorian Newsletter* 39 (Spring 1971), 20-21.

JACOB KORG. "Browning's Art and 'By the Fire-Side,' " *Victorian Poetry* 15(2), Summer 1977, 147-58.

V. S. SETURAMAN. "Browning's 'By the Fireside': 'The Path Grey Heads Abhor,' " *Notes & Queries*, n.s., 9(8), August 1962, 297-98.

LIONEL STEVENSON. "The Death of Love: A Touchstone of Poetic Realism," *Western Humanities Review* 14(4), Autumn 1960, 371-72.

"Caliban upon Setebos"

PATRICIA M. BALL. *The Central Self*, p. 218.

E. K. BROWN. "The First Person in 'Caliban Upon Setebos,' " *Modern Language Notes* 66(6), June 1951, 392-95.

HARRY BROWN and JOHN MILSTEAD. *What the Poem Means*, pp. 21-22.

WENDELL V. HARRIS. "Browning's Caliban, Plato's Cosmogony, and Bentham on Natural Religion," *Studies in Browning and His Circle* 3(2), Fall 1975, 95-103.

JOHN HOWARD. "Caliban's Mind," *Victorian Poetry* 1(4), November 1963, 249-57.

LAURENCE PERRINE. "Browning's 'Caliban Upon Setebos': A Reply," *Victorian Poetry* 2(2), Spring 1964, 124-27.

ARNOLD SHAPIRO. "Browning's Psalm of Hate: 'Caliban upon Setebos', Psalm 50, and *The Tempest*," *Papers on Language and Literature* 8(1), Winter 1972, 53-62.

MICHAEL TIMKO. "Browning Upon Butler; or, Natural Theology in the English Isle," *Criticism* 7(2), Spring 1965, 141-50.

ROBERT W. WITT. "Caliban Upon Plato," *Victorian Poetry* 13(2), Summer 1975, 136.

THOMAS P. WOLFE. "Browning's Comic Magician: Caliban's Psychology and the Reader's," *Studies in Browning and His Circle* 6(2), Fall 1978, 7-24.

"Childe Roland to the Dark Tower Came"

SUSAN HARDY AIKEN. "Structural Imagery in 'Childe Roland To the Dark Tower Came,'" *Browning Institute Studies* 5(1977), 23-36.

GEORGE ARMS. "'Childe Roland' and 'Sir Galahad,'" *College English* 6(5), February 1945, 258-62.

THOMAS J. ASSAD. "Browning's 'Childe Roland to the Dark Tower Came,'" *Tulane Studies in English* 21(1974), 67-76.

HAROLD BLOOM. "How to Read a Poem: Browning's *Childe Roland*," *Georgia Review* 28(3), Fall 1974, 404-18.

HAROLD BLOOM. *A Map of Misreading*, pp. 106-22.

HAROLD BLOOM. *Poetry and Repression*, pp. 198-204.

WILLIAM CADBURY. "Lyric and Anti-Lyric Forms: A Method for Judging Browning," *University of Toronto Quarterly* 34(1), October 1964, 55-58.

C. C. CLARKE. "Humor and Wit in 'Childe Roland,'" *Modern Language Quarterly* 23(4), December 1962, 323-36.

CURTIS DAHL. "The Victorian Wasteland," in *Victorian Literature*, pp. 34-36.

MARIO L. D'AVANZO. "'Childe Roland to the Dark Tower Came': The Shelleyan and Shakespearean Context," *Studies in English Literature 1500-1900* 17(4), Autumn 1977, 695-708.

PHILIP DREW. "'Childe Roland' and the Urban Wilderness," *Browning Society Notes* 8(3), December 1978, 19-22.

DAVID V. ERDMAN. "Browning's Industrial Nightmare," *Philological Quarterly* 36(4), October 1957, 427-35.

ROBERT F. GARRATT. "Browning's Dramatic Monologue: the Strategy of the Double Mask," *Victorian Poetry* 11(2), Summer 1973, 115-16, 124-25.

VICTOR HOAR. "A Note on Browning's 'Childe Roland to the Dark Tower Came,'" *Victorian Newsletter* 27 (Spring 1965), 26-28.

R. E. HUGHES. "Browning's *Child Roland* and the Broken Taboo," *Literature and Psychology* 9(2), Spring 1959, 18-19.

EUGENE R. KINTGEN. "Childe Roland and the Perversity of the Mind," *Victorian Poetry* 4(4), Autumn 1966, 253-58.

ROBERT LANGBAUM. *The Poetry of Experience*, pp. 192-200.

JOHN KING McCOMB. "Beyond the Dark Tower: Childe Roland's Painful Memories," *ELH* 42(3), Fall 1975, 460-70.

JOYCE S. MEYERS. "'Childe Roland to the Dark Tower Came': A Nightmare Confrontation With Death," *Victorian Poetry* 8(4), Winter 1970, 335-39.

PHILIP RAISOR. "The Failure of Browning's Childe Roland," *Tennessee Studies in Literature* 17(1972), 99-110.

GEORG ROPPEN and RICHARD SOMMER. *Strangers and Pilgrims*, pp. 304-17.

ARNOLD SHAPIRO. "'Childe Roland,' *Lear*, and the Ability to See," *Papers on Language and Literature* 11(1), Winter 1975, 88-94.

LIONEL STEVENSON. "The Pertinacious Victorian Poets," in *Victorian Literature*, pp. 23-24.

LESLIE M. THOMPSON. "Biblical Influence in 'Childe Roland to the Dark Tower Came,'" *Papers on Language and Literature* 3(4), Fall 1967, 339-53.

JUDITH WEISSMAN. "Browning's Politics of Hell: 'Childe Roland to the Dark Tower Came' and 'The Statue and the Bust,'" *Concerning Poetry* 10(2), Fall 1977, 13-20.

JOHN W. WILLOUGHBY. "Browning's 'Childe Roland to the Dark Tower Came,'" *Victorian Poetry* 1(4), November 1963, 291-99.

"Cleon"

WILFRED L. GUERIN. "Browning's 'Cleon': A Teilhardian View," *Victorian Poetry* 12(1), Spring 1974, 13-23.

WILLIAM IRVINE. "Four Monologues in Browning's *Men and Women*," *Victorian Poetry* 2(3), Summer 1964, 162-63.

ROMA A. KING, JR. "Browning: 'Mage' and 'Maker' — A Study in Poetic Purpose and Method," *Victorian Newsletter* 20 (Fall 1961), 21-25.

G. WILSON KNIGHT. *Neglected Powers*, pp. 248-50.

YOUNG G. LEE. "The Human Condition: Browning's 'Cleon,'" *Victorian Poetry* 7(1), Spring 1969, 56-62.

EDWARD C. McALEER. "Browning's 'Cleon' and Auguste Comte," *Comparative Literature* 8(2), Spring 1956, 142-45.

ADRIENNE MUNICH. "Emblems of Temporality In Browning's 'Cleon,'" *Browning Institute Studies* 6(1978), 117-36.

NANCY B. RICH. "New Perspective on the Companion Poems of Robert Browning," *Victorian Newsletter* 36 (Fall 1969), 7-8.

G. W. SPENCE. "Browning's Cleon and St. Paul," *Studies in Browning and His Circle* 6(2), Fall 1978, 25-31.

"Clive"

ROBERT FELGAR. "Browning's Narrative Technique in 'Clive,'" *Browning Society Notes* 4(3), December 1974, 10-16.

MARK SIEGCHRIST. "Narrative Obtuseness in Browning's 'Clive,'" *Studies in Browning and His Circle* 3(1), Spring 1975, 53-60.

HAYDEN WARD. "Moral Irony in Browning's 'Clive,'" *Browning Society Notes* 4(3), December 1974, 16-24.

"Count Gismond"

JOHN V. HAGOPIAN. "The Mask of Browning's Countess Gismond," *Philological Quarterly* 40(1), January 1961, 153-55.

SISTER MARCELLA M. HOLLOWAY. "A Further Reading of 'Count Gismond,'" *Studies in Philology* 60(3), July 1963, 549-53.

DOROTHY M. MERMIN. "Speaker and Auditor in Browning's Dramatic Monologues," *University of Toronto Quarterly* 45(2), Winter 1976, 141-42.

JOHN J. ROBERTS. "The Rebirth Archetype in 'Count Gismond,'" *Browning Society Notes* 6(2), July 1976, 17-18.

BROWNING, ROBERT *(Cont.)*

"Count Gismond" *(cont.)*

> INA BETH SESSIONS. "The Dramatic Monologue," *PMLA* 62(2), June 1947, 510-11.

> JOHN W. TILTON and R. DALE TUTTLE. "A New Reading of 'Count Gismond,'" *Studies in Philology* 59(1), January 1962, 83-95.

> MICHAEL TIMKO. "Ah, Did You Once See Browning Plain?" *Studies in English Literature 1500-1900* 6(4), Autumn 1966, 731-42.

"Cristina"

> DEREK COLVILLE. *Victorian Poetry and the Romantic Religion*, pp. 152-53.

> CLYDE S. KILBY. *Explicator* 2(2), November 1943, Item 16.

"De Gustibus — "

> NANCY B. RICH. "New Perspective on the Companion Poems of Robert Browning," *Victorian Newsletter* 36 (Fall 1969), 8-9.

"A Death in the Desert"

> FRANK COVENTRY. "Browning's Orthodoxy," *Browning Society Notes* 5(3), December 1975, 23-25.

> VIRGINIA M. HYDE. "The Fallible Parchment: Structure in Robert Browning's *A Death in the Desert*," *Victorian Poetry* 12(2), Summer 1974, 125-35.

> ELINOR SHAFFER. "Browning's St. John: The Casuistry of the Higher Criticism," *Victorian Studies* 16(2), December 1972, 205-21.

> A. S. P. WOODHOUSE. *The Poet and His Faith*, pp. 233-34.

"Dîs Aliter Visum"

> WENDELL STACY JOHNSON. *Sex and Marriage in Victorian Poetry*, pp. 223-24.

> FRED KAPLAN. *Miracles of Rare Device*, pp. 115-23.

"An Epistle Containing the Strange Medical Experience of Karshish, the Arab Physician"

> JAMES R. BENNETT. "Lazarus in Browning's 'Karshish,'" *Victorian Poetry* 3(3), Summer 1965, 189-91.

> DEREK COLVILLE. *Victorian Poetry and the Romantic Religion*, p. 144.

> CURTIS DAHL. "Browning and the Historical Novel of Antiquity," *Studies in Browning and His Circle* 1(1), Spring 1973, 13-15.

> WILFRED L. GUERIN. "Irony and Tension in Browning's 'Karshish,'" *Victorian Poetry* 1(2), April 1963, 132-39.

> WILLIAM IRVINE. "Four Monologues in Browning's *Men and Women*," *Victorian Poetry* 2(3), Summer 1964, 160-62.

> ROMA A. KING, JR. "Karshish Encounters Himself: An Interpretation of Browning's 'Epistle,'" *Concerning Poetry* 1(1), Spring 1968, 23-33.

> SHIV K. KUMAR. "The Moment in the Dramatic Monologues of Robert Browning," in *British Victorian Literature*, pp. 100-1.

> MARY K. MISHLER. "God Versus God: The Tension in 'Karshish,'" *English Language Notes* 13(2), December 1975, 132-37.

> NANCY B. RICH. "New Perspective on the Companion Poems of Robert Browning," *Victorian Newsletter* 36 (Fall 1969), 7-8.

"Evelyn Hope"

> GEORGE O. MARSHALL, JR. "Evelyn Hope's Lover," *Victorian Poetry* 4(1), Winter 1966, 32-34.

> SUSAN G. RADNER. "Love and the Lover in Browning's 'Evelyn Hope,'" *Literature and Psychology* 16(2), Spring 1966, 115-16.

> CHAD and EVA T. WALSH. *Twice Ten*, pp. 66-68.

"The Flight of the Duchess"

> PETER N. HEYDON. "Whatever Became of the *Pauline* Poet?" *Browning Society Notes* 3(1), March 1973, 14-20.

> WENDELL STACY JOHNSON. *Sex and Marriage in Victorian Poetry*, pp. 194-96.

"Flute-Music, With an Accompaniment"

> C. CASTAN. "Browning's 'Flute-Music, With an Accompaniment' as a Love Drama," *Browning Society Notes* 7(1), March 1977, 4-11.

> DONALD S. HAIR. "Exploring *Asolando*," *Browning Society Notes* 8(1), April 1978, 4-5.

"A Forgiveness"

> ROBERT FELGAR. "Browning's Narrative Art," *Studies in Browning and His Circle* 3(2), Fall 1975, 83-84.

"Fra Lippo Lippi"

> SUSAN HARDY AIKEN. "Patterns of Imagery in 'Fra Lippo Lippi,'" *Studies in Browning and His Circle* 3(1), Spring 1975, 61-75.

> ISOBEL ARMSTRONG. "Browning and the 'Grotesque' Style," in *The Major Victorian Poets*, p. 118.

> RICHARD BENVENUTO. "Lippo and Andrea: The Pro and Contra of Browning's Realism," *Studies in English Literature 1500-1900* 13(4), Autumn 1973, 643-52.

> HARRY BROWN and JOHN MILSTEAD. *What the Poem Means*, pp. 23-24.

> VINCENT C. DE BAUN. "Browning: Art Is Life Is Thought," *CLA Journal* 14(4), June 1971, 392-95.

> ROBERT F. GARRATT. "Browning's Dramatic Monologue: The Strategy of the Double Mask," *Victorian Poetry* 11(2), Summer 1973, 115-16, 122-24.

> SUSAN HACKETT and JOHN FERNS. "A Portrait of the Artist as a Young Monk: The Degree of Irony in Browning's 'Fra Lippo Lippi,'" *Studies in Browning and His Circle* 4(2), Fall 1976, 105-18.

> PHILIP HOBSBAUM. "The Rise of the Dramatic Monologue," *Hudson Review* 28(2), Summer 1975, 235-37.

> CHARLES M. HUDSON, JR. and EDWARD H. WEATHERLY. "The Survey Course at the University of Missouri," *College English* 8(6), March 1947, 323-27.

> WILLIAM IRVINE. "Four Monologues in Browning's *Men and Women*," *Victorian Poetry* 2(3), Summer 1964, 156-58.

> E. D. H. JOHNSON. *The Alien Vision of Victorian Poetry*, pp. 116-18.

> A. R. JONES. "Robert Browning and the Dramatic Monologue: The Impersonal Art," *Critical Quarterly* 9(4), Winter 1967, 322-25.

> J. L. KENDALL. "Lippo's Vision," *Victorian Newsletter* 18 (Fall 1960), 18-21.

> WALTRAUD LEISGANG. "*Fra Lippo Lippi*: A Picture-Poem," *Browning Society Notes* 3(3), December 1973, 20-32.

> PAUL A. MAKURATH, JR. "Fra Lippo's Theory of Art," *Studies in Browning and His Circle* 4(2), Fall 1976, 95-104.

> R. G. MALBONE. *Explicator* 25(3), November 1966, Item 20.

DOROTHY M. MERMIN. "Speaker and Auditor in Browning's Dramatic Monologues," *University of Toronto Quarterly* 45(2), Winter 1976, 146-48.

GLEN OMANS. "Browning's 'Fra Lippo Lippi,' A Transcendentalist Monk," *Victorian Poetry* 7(2), Summer 1969, 129-45.

LAURENCE PERRINE. *Explicator* 16(3), December 1957, Item 18.

W. DAVID SHAW. "Character and Philosophy in 'Fra Lippo Lippi,'" *Victorian Poetry* 2(2), Spring 1964, 127-32.

MARK SIEGCHRIST. "The Puritan St. Jerome in Browning's 'Fra Lippo Lippi,'" *Studies in Browning and His Circle* 1(2), Fall 1973, 26-27.

DAVID SONSTROEM. "On Resisting Brother Lippo," *Texas Studies in Literature and Language* 15(4), Winter 1974, 721-34.

"Fust and His Friends"

ROBERT R. COLUMBUS and CLAUDETTE KEMPER. "Browning's Fuddling Apollo or the Perils of Parleying," *Tennessee Studies in Literature* 12(1967), 95-99.

MARK SIEGCHRIST. "Type Needs Antitype: The Structure of Browning's *Parleyings*," *Victorian Newsletter* 50 (Fall 1976), 18.

"The Glove"

LOUISE SCHUTZ BOAS. *Explicator* 2(2), November 1943, Item 13.

LOUIS S. FRIEDLAND. *Explicator* 1(7), May 1943, Item 54.

LOUIS S. FRIEDLAND. *Explicator* 2(4), February 1944, Item 30.

NEIL D. ISAACS and RICHARD M. KELLY. "Dramatic Tension and Irony in Browning's 'The Glove,'" *Victorian Poetry* 8(2), Summer 1970, 157-59.

E. D. H. JOHNSON. *The Alien Vision of Victorian Poetry*, p. 106.

WENDELL STACY JOHNSON. *Sex and Marriage in Victorian Poetry*, pp. 196-97.

DAVID SONSTROEM. "'Fine Speeches Like Gold' in Browning's 'The Glove,'" *Victorian Poetry* 15(1), Spring 1977, 85-90.

BENNETT WEAVER. "A Primer Study in Browning's Satire," *College English* 14(2), November 1952, 80.

R. W. WHIDDEN. *Explicator* 2(3), December 1943, Item 23.

"Good, to forgive"

CORY BIEMAN DAVIES. "From Knowledge to Belief in *La Saisiaz: The Two Poets of Croisic*," *Studies in Browning and His Circle* 6(1), Spring 1978, 14.

"A Grammarian's Funeral"

RICHARD D. ALTICK. "'A Grammarian's Funeral': Browning's Praise of Folly?" *Studies in English Literature 1500-1900* 3(4), Autumn 1963, 449-60.

HARRY BROWN and JOHN MILSTEAD. *What the Poem Means*, pp. 19-20.

WILLIAM CADBURY. "Lyric and Anti-Lyric Forms: A Method for Judging Browning," *University of Toronto Quarterly* 34(1), October 1964, 54-55.

C. C. CLARKE. "Humor and Wit in 'Childe Roland,'" *Modern Language Quarterly* 23(4), December 1962, 324-25.

DAVID DAICHES and WILLIAM CHARVAT. *Poems in English*, p. 717.

NIGEL FOXELL. *Ten Poems Analyzed*, pp. 185-201.

ROBERT L. KELLY. "Dactyls and Curlews: Satire in 'A Grammarian's Funeral,'" *Victorian Poetry* 5(1), Spring 1967, 105-12.

GEORGE MONTEIRO. "A Proposal for Settling the Grammarian's Estate," *Victorian Poetry* 3(4), Autumn 1965, 266-70.

J. MITCHELL MORSE. "Browning's Grammarian, Warts and All," *CEA Critic* 20(1), January 1958, 1, 5.

MARY W. SCHNEIDER. "Browning's Grammarian," *Studies in Browning and His Circle* 6(1), Spring 1978, 57-65.

ROBERT C. SCHWEIK. "The Structure of 'A Grammarian's Funeral,'" *College English* 22(6), March 1961, 411-12.

MARTIN J. SVAGLIC. "Browning's Grammarian: Apparent Failure or Real?" *Victorian Poetry* 5(2), Summer 1967, 93-104.

"Halbert and Hob"

WOLFGANG FRANKE. "'Halbert and Hob': Browning at Wuthering Heights," *Browning Society Notes* 5(3), December 1975, 3-8.

"Holy-Cross Day"

BARBARA MELCHIORI. "Browning and the Bible: an Examination of 'Holy Cross Day,'" *Review of English Literature* 7(2), April 1966, 20-42.

BENNETT WEAVER. "A Primer Study in Browning's Satire," *College English* 14(2), November 1952, 79-80.

"Home Thoughts from Abroad"

GÉMINO H. ABAD. *A Formal Approach to Lyric Poetry*, pp. 188-89, 191-92.

"Home-Thoughts, from the Sea"

FREDERICK L. GWYNN. *Explicator* 12(2), November 1953, Item 12. Reprinted in: *Readings for Liberal Education*, third ed., II: 131-32; fourth ed., II: 130-31.

"How It Strikes a Contemporary"

SUSAN HARDY AIKEN. "On Clothes and Heroes: Carlyle and 'How It Strikes a Contemporary,'" *Victorian Poetry* 13(2), Summer 1975, 99-109.

CHARLINE R. KVAPIL. "'How It Strikes a Contemporary': A Dramatic Monologue," *Victorian Poetry* 4(4), Autumn 1966, 279-83.

RAYMOND F. MCQUADE. "'How It Strikes a Contemporary': Browning's Split-Level View," *Studies in Browning and His Circle* 4(2), Fall 1976, 72-76.

"In a Balcony"

E. D. H. JOHNSON. *The Alien Vision of Victorian Poetry*, pp. 104-6.

WENDELL STACY JOHNSON. *Sex and Marriage in Victorian Poetry*, pp. 202-4.

P. G. MUDFORD. "The Artistic Consistency of Browning's *In a Balcony*," *Victorian Poetry* 7(1), Spring 1969, 31-40.

ELMER EDGAR STOLL. "Browning's *In a Balcony*," *Modern Language Quarterly* 3(3), September 1942, 407-15.

"In a Gondola"

ISOBEL ARMSTRONG. "Browning and the 'Grotesque' Style," in *The Major Victorian Poets*, pp. 115-16.

"In the Doorway"
see "James Lee's Wife"

"Incident of the French Camp"

ISAAC ASIMOV. *Familiar Poems, Annotated*, pp. 158-62.

BROWNING, ROBERT (*Cont.*)

"The Italian in England"

BERNADINE BROWN. "Robert Browning's 'The Italian in England,'" *Victorian Poetry* 6(2), Summer 1968, 179-83.

"Ivàn Ivànovitch"

PHILIP DREW. "'The Raw Material of Moral Sentiment': Another View of 'Ivàn Ivànovitch,'" *Browning Society Notes* 5(2), July 1975, 3-6.

E. WARWICK SLINN. "The Judgement of Instinct in 'Ivàn Ivànovitch,'" *Browning Society Notes* 4(1), March 1974, 3-9.

"James Lee's Wife"

see also "Beside the Drawing Board" and "By the Fireside"

PATRICIA M. BALL. *The Heart's Events*, pp. 145-65.

WENDELL STACY JOHNSON. *Sex and Marriage in Victorian Poetry*, pp. 219-23.

FRANCINE GOMBERG RUSSO. "Browning's 'James Lee's Wife': A Study in Neurotic Love," *Victorian Poetry* 12(3), Autumn 1974, 219-34.

GLENN SANDSTROM. "'James Lee's Wife' — and Browning's," *Victorian Poetry* 4(4), Autumn 1966, 259-70.

"Johannes Agricola in Meditation"

J. W. HARPER. "'Eternity our Due': Time in the Poetry of Robert Browning," in *Victorian Poetry*, pp. 60-62.

LAURENCE LERNER. *An Introduction to English Poetry*, pp. 157-63.

NANCY B. RICH. "New Perspective on the Companion Poems of Robert Browning," *Victorian Newsletter* 36 (Fall 1969), 6-7.

GEORGE WASSERMAN. *Explicator* 24(7), March 1966, Item 59.

JOHN W. WILLOUGHBY. *Explicator* 21(1), September 1962, Item 5.

"The King"

JOHN GRUBE. "Browning's 'The King,'" *University of Toronto Quarterly* 37(1), October 1967, 69-74.

"The Laboratory"

GÉMINO H. ABAD. *A Formal Approach to Lyric Poetry*, pp. 198-99.

EARL DANIELS. *The Art of Reading Poetry*, pp. 92-95.

DOROTHY M. MERMIN. "Speaker and Auditor in Browning's Dramatic Monologues," *University of Toronto Quarterly* 45(2), Winter 1976, 142-43.

LIONEL STEVENSON. "The Pertinacious Victorian Poets," *University of Toronto Quarterly* 21(3), April 1952, 243-44. Reprinted in: *Victorian Literature*, pp. 27-29.

"The Last Ride Together"

RICHARD D. ALTICK. "Memo to the Next Annotator of Browning," *Victorian Poetry* 1(1), January 1963, 64.

RUSSELL M. GOLDFARB. "Sexual Meaning in 'The Last Ride Together,'" *Victorian Poetry* 3(4), Autumn 1965, 255-61. Revised in: Russell M. Goldfarb. *Sexual Repression and Victorian Literature*, pp. 66-81.

WENDELL STACY JOHNSON. *Sex and Marriage in Victorian Poetry*, p. 202.

SHIV K. KUMAR. "The Moment in the Dramatic Monologues of Robert Browning," in *British Victorian Literature*, p. 94.

"A Light Woman"

GEORGE MONTEIRO. "Henry James and the Lessons of Sordello," *Western Humanities Review* 31(1), Winter 1977, 69-73.

"Love Among the Ruins"

FRANK ALLEN. "Sex and the Dreaming Egotist: A Reading of 'Love Among the Ruins,'" *Browning Society Notes* 5(1), March 1975, 8-14.

WILLIAM CADBURY. "Lyric and Anti-Lyric Forms: A Method for Judging Browning," *University of Toronto Quarterly* 34(1), October 1964, 58-66.

DEREK COLVILLE. *Victorian Poetry and the Romantic Religion*, pp. 153-55.

DAVID V. ERDMAN. "Browning's Industrial Nightmare," *Philological Quarterly* 36(4), October 1957, 425-26.

"Martin Relph"

DANIEL R. SCHWARZ. "Rituals and Ceremonies of 'A Strange Old Man': A Reading of 'Martin Relph,'" *Browning Society Notes* 5(1), March 1975, 17-25.

"Master Hughes of Saxe-Gotha"

RICHARD D. ALTICK. "The Symbolism of Browning's 'Master Hughes of Saxe-Gotha,'" *Victorian Poetry* 3(1), Winter 1965, 1-7.

HAROLD BLOOM. *Poetry and Repression*, pp. 178-81.

MARGARET WALKER DILLING. "Robert Browning's 'Master Hughes of Saxe-Gotha,'" *Studies in Browning and His Circle* 1(2), Fall 1973, 37-43.

ROBERT LANGBAUM. *The Poetry of Experience*, pp. 144-46.

BENNETT WEAVER. "A Primer Study in Browning's Satire," *College English* 14(2), November 1952, 78-79.

"Meeting at Night"

GÉMINO H. ABAD. *A Formal Approach to Lyric Poetry*, pp. 44-47.

EDWARD A. BLOOM, CHARLES H. PHILBRICK, and ELMER M. BLISTEIN. *The Order of Poetry*, pp. 79-82.

JOHN D. BOYD. "Browning's 'Meeting at Night' and 'Parting at Morning,'" *Browning Society Notes* 5(3), December 1975, 14-20.

RALPH W. CONDEE. *Explicator* 12(4), February 1954, Item 23.

CHARLES W. COOPER and JOHN HOLMES. *Preface to Poetry*, pp. 182-83.

KARL KROEBER. "Touchstones for Browning's Victorian Complexity," *Victorian Poetry* 3(2), Spring 1965, 101-7.

F. R. LEAVIS. "Imagery and Movement: Notes in the Analysis of Poetry," *Scrutiny* 13(2), September 1945, 130-31.

LAURENCE PERRINE. *Sound and Sense*, pp. 41-42; second ed., pp. 46-47; third ed., pp. 55-56; fourth ed., pp. 50-51.

L. J. SWINGLE. "Browning's 'Meeting at Night' and 'Parting at Morning': Complexities Within the Romantic Quest," *Browning Society Notes* 5(3), December 1975, 8-14.

"Memorabilia"

YAO SHEN. "A Note on Browning's 'Eagle-Feather,'" *Studies in Browning and His Circle* 5(2), Fall 1977, 7-16.

"My Last Duchess"

JOSHUA ADLER. "Structure and Meaning in Browning's 'My Last Duchess,' " *Victorian Poetry* 15(3), Autumn 1977, 219-27.

THOMAS J. ASSAD. "Browning's 'My Last Duchess,' " *Tulane Studies in English* 10(1960), 117-28.

JEROME BEATY and WILLIAM H. MATCHETT. *Poetry From Statement to Meaning*, pp. 85-90.

CLEANTH BROOKS, JOHN THIBAUT PURSER, and ROBERT PENN WARREN. *An Approach to Literature*, pp. 437-39; second ed., pp. 437-39; third ed., pp. 291-93; fourth ed., pp. 294-96; fifth ed., pp. 349-51.

OLLIE COX. "The 'Spot of Joy' in 'My Last Duchess,' " *CLA Journal* 12(1), September 1968, 70-76.

R. F. FLEISSNER. "Browning's Last Lost Duchess: A Purview," *Victorian Poetry* 5(3), Autumn 1967, 217-19.

LOUIS S. FRIEDLAND. "Ferrara and *My Last Duchess*," *Studies in Philology* 33(4), October 1936, 656-84.

ROBERT F. GARRATT. "Browning's Dramatic Monologue: the Strategy of the Double Mask," *Victorian Poetry* 11(2), Summer 1973, 115-18.

ROBERT A. GREENBERG. "Ruskin, Pugin, and the Contemporary Context of 'The Bishop Orders His Tomb,' " *PMLA* 84(6), October 1966, 1593-94.

ROBERT HAWKINS. *Preface to Poetry*, p. 86.

GILBERT HIGHET. *The Powers of Poetry*, pp. 308-12.

EDWIN HONIG. "Browning: My Last Duchess," in *Master Poems of the English Language*, pp. 679-81.

B. R. JERMAN. "Browning's Witless Duke," *PMLA* 72(3), June 1957, 488-93.

A. R. JONES. "Robert Browning and the Dramatic Monologue: The Impersonal Art," *Critical Quarterly* 9(4), Winter 1967, 318-20.

RICHARD RAY KIRK and ROGER PHILIP McCUTCHEON. *An Introduction to the Study of Poetry*, pp. 17-24.

ROBERT LANGBAUM. *The Poetry of Experience*, pp. 82-85. Reprinted in: *Poems and Critics*, pp. 204-8.

DOROTHY M. MERMIN. "Speaker and Auditor in Browning's Dramatic Monologues," *University of Toronto Quarterly* 45(2), Winter 1976, 140-41.

STANTON MILLET. "Art and Reality in 'My Last Duchess,' " *Victorian Newsletter* 17 (Spring 1960), 25-27.

GEORGE MONTEIRO. "Browning's 'My Last Duchess,' " *Victorian Poetry* 1(3), August 1963, 234-37.

SISTER MARY DE LOURDES MUENCH. "Taking the Duchess off the Wall," *English Journal* 57(2), February 1968, 203-5.

LEONARD NATHANSON. *Explicator* 19(9), June 1961, Item 68.

LAURENCE PERRINE. "Browning's Shrewd Duke," *PMLA* 74(1), March 1959, 157-59.

JOHN OLIVER PERRY. *The Experience of Poems*, pp. 56-59.

SANFORD PINSKER. " 'As If She Were Alive': Rhetorical Anguish in 'My Last Duchess,' " *Concerning Poetry* 9(2), Fall 1976, 71-73.

JOHN D. REA. " 'My Last Duchess,' " *Studies in Philology* 29(1), January 1932, 120-22. Reprinted in: *The Dimensions of Poetry*, pp. 530-32.

INA BETH SESSIONS. "The Dramatic Monologue," *PMLA* 62(2), June 1947, 508-10.

W. DAVID SHAW. "Browning's Duke as Theatrical Producer," *Victorian Newsletter* 29 (Spring 1966), 18-22.

LIONEL STEVENSON. "The Pertinacious Victorian Poets," *University of Toronto Quarterly* 21(3), April 1952, 240-42. Reprinted in: *Victorian Literature*, pp. 25-27.

MICHAEL TIMKO. "Ah, Did You Once See Browning Plain?" *Studies in English Literature 1500-1900* 6(4), Autumn 1966, 736-37.

"My Star"

JAMES F. LOUCKS. "New Light on 'My Star,' " *Browning Society Notes* 4(2), July 1974, 25-27.

LAURENCE PERRINE. *Sound and Sense*, p. 66; second ed., pp. 71-72; third ed., pp. 86-87; fourth ed., pp. 81-82.

"Nationality in Drinks"

EDWARD C. McALEER. *Explicator* 20(4), December 1961, Item 34. (P)

"Ned Bratts"

ROBERT FELGAR. "Browning as a Scholarly Interpreter," *Studies in Browning and His Circle* 1(2), Fall 1973, 74-76.

ROY E. GRIDLEY. " 'Ned Bratts': A Commentary," *Browning Society Notes* 6(1), March 1976, 10-16.

"Never the Time and the Place"

FRED KAPLAN. "Death and Lovely Song: Browning's 'Never the Time and the Place,' " *Browning Society Notes* 5(2), July 1975, 17-21.

"Numpholeptos"

J. W. HARPER. " 'Eternity our Due': Time in the Poetry of Robert Browning," in *Victorian Poetry*, pp. 79-80.

ROBERT LANGBAUM. "Browning and the Question of Myth," in *The Modern Spirit*, pp. 98-100.

WILLIAM O. RAYMOND. " 'The Jewelled Bow': A Study in Browning's Imagery and Humanism," in *British Victorian Literature*, pp. 83-85.

"Old Pictures in Florence"

JULIA MARKUS. " 'Old Pictures in Florence' Through Casa Guidi Windows," *Browning Institute Studies* 6(1978), 43-61. (P)

"On Deck"

see "James Lee's Wife"

"On the Cliff"

see "James Lee's Wife"

"One Word More"

RICHARD BENVENUTO. "Lippo and Andrea: The Pro and Contra of Browning's Realism," *Studies in English Literature 1500-1900* 13(4), Autumn 1973, 645-46.

WILLIAM T. GOING. "Browning and the Sonnet," *Tennessee Studies in Literature* 17(1972), 90.

A. R. JONES. "Robert Browning and the Dramatic Monologue: The Impersonal Art," *Critical Quarterly* 9(4), Winter 1967, 314-15.

"Pan and Luna"

DONALD S. HAIR. "Browning's 'Pan and Luna': An Experiment in Idyl," *Browning Society Notes* 4(2), July 1974, 3-8.

W. DAVID SHAW. "Mystification and Mystery: Browning's 'Pan and Luna,' " *Browning Society Notes* 4(2), July 1974, 9-12.

MARK SIEGCHRIST. "Thematic Coherence in Browning's *Dramatic Idyls*," *Victorian Poetry* 15(3), Autumn 1977, 237-39.

BROWNING, ROBERT *(Cont.)*

"Parleying With Bernard de Mandeville"

    DEREK COLVILLE. *Victorian Poetry and the Romantic Religion*, pp. 137-39.

    MARK SIEGCHRIST. "Type Needs Antitype: The Structure of Browning's *Parleyings*," *Victorian Newsletter* 50 (Fall 1976), 4.

"Parleying with Charles Avison"

    J. W. HARPER. " 'Eternity our Due': Time in the Poetry of Robert Browning," in *Victorian Poetry*, pp. 81-82.

    MARK SIEGCHRIST. "Type Needs Antitype: The Structure of Browning's *Parleyings*," *Victorian Newsletter* 50 (Fall 1976), 8.

"Parleying with Christopher Smart"

    ROBERT LANGBAUM. "Browning and the Question of Myth," in *The Modern Spirit*, p. 91.

    MARK SIEGCHRIST. "Type Needs Antitype: The Structure of Browning's *Parleyings*," *Victorian Newsletter* 50 (Fall 1976), 5.

"Parleying With Daniel Bartoli"

    MARK SIEGCHRIST. "Type Needs Antitype: The Structure of Browning's *Parleyings*," *Victorian Newsletter* 50 (Fall 1976), 4-5.

"Parleying with Francis Furini"

    ROBERT LANGBAUM. "Browning and the Question of Myth," in *The Modern Spirit*, pp. 92-94.

    MARK SIEGCHRIST. "Type Needs Antitype: The Structure of Browning's *Parleyings*," *Victorian Newsletter* 50 (Fall 1976), 6-7.

"Parleying with George Bubb Doddington"

    MARK SIEGCHRIST. "Type Needs Antitype: The Structure of Browning's *Parleyings*," *Victorian Newsletter* 50 (Fall 1976), 5-6.

"Parleying With Gerard de Lairesse"

    MARK SIEGCHRIST. "Type Needs Antitype: The Structure of Browning's *Parleyings*," *Victorian Newsletter* 50 (Fall 1976), 7-8.

"The Patriot"

    DAVID J. DE LAURA. "The Religious Imagery in Browning's 'The Patriot,' " *Victorian Newsletter* 21 (Spring 1962), 16-18.

"Parting at Morning"

    GÉMINO H. ABAD. *A Formal Approach to Lyric Poetry*, pp. 45-47.

    JOHN D. BOYD. "Browning's 'Meeting at Night' and 'Parting at Morning,' " *Browning Society Notes* 5(3), December 1975, 14-20.

    RALPH W. CONDEE. *Explicator* 12(4), February 1954, Item 23.

    CHARLES W. COOPER and JOHN HOLMES. *Preface to Poetry*, pp. 182-83.

    KARL KROEBER. "Touchstones for Browning's Victorian Complexity," *Victorian Poetry* 3(2), Spring 1965, 101-7.

    L. J. SWINGLE. "Browning's 'Meeting at Night' and 'Parting at Morning': Complexities Within the Romantic Quest," *Browning Society Notes* 5(3), December 1975, 8-14.

"Pictor Ignotus"

    MICHAEL H. BRIGHT. "Browning's 'Pictor Ignotus': An Interpretation," *Studies in Browning and His Circle* 4(1), Spring 1976, 53-61.

    J. B. BULLEN. "Browning's 'Pictor Ignotus' and Vasari's 'Life of Fra Bartolommeo Di San Marco,' " *Review of English Studies*, n.s., 23(91), August 1972, 313-19.

    PAUL F. JAMIESON. *Explicator* 11(2), November 1952, Item 8.

    E. D. H. JOHNSON. *The Alien Vision of Victorian Poetry*, pp. 110-11.

    FRED KAPLAN. *Miracles of Rare Device*, pp. 109-15.

"The Pied Piper of Hamelin"

    ISAAC ASIMOV. *Familiar Poems, Annotated*, pp. 55-73.

    WOLFGANG FRANKE. "Browning's 'Pied Piper of Hamelin': Two Levels of Meaning," *Ariel* 2(4), October 1971, 90-97.

"Pietro of Abano"

    EDWARD L. WOLFE. "Rationalization: Method and Theme in 'Pietro of Abano,' " *Browning Society Notes* 6(3), December 1976, 7-12.

"Pippa's Song"

    CLEANTH BROOKS and ROBERT PENN WARREN. *Understanding Poetry*, third ed., p. 79; fourth ed., pp. 76-77.

    ARCHIBALD A. HILL. *Constituent and Pattern in Poetry*, pp. 23-27.

    JOHN CROWE RANSOM. "The Concrete Universal: Observations on the Study of Poetry II," *Kenyon Review* 17(3), Summer 1955, 395.

"Popularity"

    RICHARD D. ALTICK. "Memo to the Next Annotator of Browning," *Victorian Poetry* 1(1), January 1963, 65-66.

    BENNETT WEAVER. "A Primer Study in Browning's Satire," *College English* 14(2), November 1952, 78. (P)

"Porphyria's Lover"

    CLEANTH BROOKS, JOHN THIBAUT PURSER, and ROBERT PENN WARREN. *An Approach to Literature*, pp. 4-7; second ed., pp. 4-7; third ed., 4-8; fourth ed., pp. 4-8.

    ALICE CHANDLER. " 'The Eve of St. Agnes' and 'Porphyria's Lover,' " *Victorian Poetry* 3(4), Autumn 1965, 273-74.

    DAVID EGGENSCHWILER. "Psychological Complexity in 'Porphyria's Lover,' " *Victorian Poetry* 8(1), Spring 1970, 39-48.

    J. W. HARPER. " 'Eternity our Due': Time in the Poetry of Robert Browning," in *Victorian Poetry*, pp. 60-61.

    EDWARD E. KELLY. "Porphyria's Lover: Fantasizer, Not Speaker," *Studies in Browning and His Circle* 3(2), Fall 1975, 126-28.

    LAURENCE LERNER. *An Introduction to English Poetry*, pp. 167-70.

    BARBARA MELCHIORI. "Some Victorian Assumptions Behind 'Porphyria's Lover,' " *Browning Society Notes* 5(1), March 1975, 3-8.

    JOHN OLIVER PERRY. *The Experience of Poems*, pp. 36-38.

    NANCY B. RICH. "New Perspective on the Companion Poems of Robert Browning," *Victorian Newsletter* 36 (Fall 1969), 6-7.

    MAX KEITH SUTTON. "Language as Defense in 'Porphyria's Lover,' " *College English* 31(3), December 1969, 280-89.

    CHAD and EVA T. WALSH. *Twice Ten*, pp. 69-71.

"Prologue" (*Asolando*)

DONALD S. HAIR. "Exploring *Asolando*," *Browning Society Notes* 8(1), April 1978, 5-6.

W. DAVID SHAW. "Browning's 'Intimations' Ode: The *Prologue* to *Asolando*," *Browning Society Notes* 8(1), April 1978, 9-10.

"Prospice"

GEORGE ARMS. *Explicator* 2(7), May 1944, Item 53.

HARRY M. CAMPBELL. *Explicator* 3(1), October 1944, Item 2.

"Rabbi Ben Ezra"

ROY P. BASLER. "Browning: Rabbi Ben Ezra," in *Master Poems of the English Language*, pp. 673-76.

HARRY BROWN and JOHN MILSTEAD. *What the Poem Means*, pp. 25-26.

DEREK COLVILLE. *Victorian Poetry and the Romantic Religion*, pp. 145-46.

MARIO L. D'AVANZO. " 'Rather I Prize the Doubt': Browning's Heroic Rabbi," *Studies in Browning and His Circle* 6(2), Fall 1978, 56-60.

DAVID FLEISHER. " 'Rabbi Ben Ezra,' 49-72: A New Key to an Old Crux," *Victorian Poetry* 1(1), January 1963, 46-52.

PHILIP DARRAUGH ORTEGO. "Robert Browning's 'Rabbi Ben Ezra,' " *CEA Critic* 30(6), March 1968, 6-7.

ROGER L. SLAKEY. "A Note on Browning's 'Rabbi Ben Ezra,' " *Victorian Poetry* 5(4), Winter 1967, 291-94.

"Reading a Book, Under the Cliff"
see "James Lee's Wife"

"Respectability"

LAURENCE PERRINE. "Browning's 'Respectability,' " *College English* 14(6), March 1953, 347-48.

"St. Martin's Summer"

KENNETH LESLIE KNICKERBOCKER. "An Echo from Browning's Second Courtship," *Studies in Philology* 32(1), January 1935, 120-24.

"La Saisiaz"

DEREK COLVILLE. *Victorian Poetry and the Romantic Religion*, pp. 135-36.

CORY BIEMAN DAVIES. "From Knowledge to Belief in *La Saisiaz: The Two Poets of Croisic*," *Studies in Browning and His Circle* 6(1), Spring 1978, 7-24.

ROMA A. KING, JR. "The Necessary Surmise: The Shaping Spirit of Robert Browning's Poetry," in *Romantic and Victorian*, pp. 351-60.

F. E. L. PRIESTLEY. "A Reading of La Saisiaz," *University of Toronto Quarterly* 25(1), October 1955, 47-59.

"Saul"

RICHARD BENVENUTO. "Lippo and Andrea: The Pro and Contra of Browning's Realism," *Studies in English Literature 1500-1900* 13(4), Autumn 1973, 644-45.

JAMES BENZIGER. *Images of Eternity*, pp. 183-89.

ELIZABETH BIEMAN. "The Ongoing Testament in Browning's 'Saul,' " *University of Toronto Quarterly* 43(2), Winter 1974, 151-68.

HARRY BROWN and JOHN MILSTEAD. *What the Poem Means*, pp. 26-27.

VINETA COLBY. "Browning's 'Saul': The Exorcism of Romantic Melancholy," *Victorian Poetry* 16(1-2), Spring-Summer 1978, 88-99.

CURTIS DAHL and JENNIFER L. BREWER. "Browning's 'Saul' and the Fourfold Vision: A Neoplatonic-Hermetic Approach," *Browning Institute Studies* 3(1975), 101-18.

WARD HELLSTROM. "Time and Type in Browning's *Saul*," *ELH* 33(3), September 1966, 370-89.

FRED KAPLAN. *Miracles of Rare Device*, pp. 143-55.

J. H. McCLATCHEY. "Browning's 'Saul' as a Davidic Psalm of the Praise of God: The Poetics of Prophecy," *Studies in Browning and His Circle* 4(1), Spring 1976, 62-83.

W. DAVID SHAW. "The Analogical Argument of Browning's 'Saul,' " *Victorian Poetry* 2(4), Autumn 1964, 277-82.

D. DOUGLAS WATERS. "Mysticism, Meaning, and Structure in Browning's 'Saul,' " *Browning Institute Studies* 5(1977), 75-86.

A. S. P. WOODHOUSE. *The Poet and His Faith*, pp. 230-32.

"A Serenade at the Villa"

ARTHUR DICKSON. *Explicator* 9(8), June 1951, Item 57.

WALTER GIERASCH. *Explicator* 8(5), March 1950, Item 37.

T. O. MABBOTT. *Explicator* 8(3), December 1949, Q6.

JOHN MAYNARD. " 'Can't One Even Die In Peace?': Browning's 'A Serenade at the Villa,' " *Browning Society Notes* 6(1), March 1976, 3-10.

"Sibrandus Schafnaburgensis"

BENNETT WEAVER. "A Primer Study in Browning's Satire," *College English* 14(2), November 1952, 77-78.

"Soliloquy of the Spanish Cloister"

HARRY BROWN and JOHN MILSTEAD. *What the Poem Means*, p. 27.

DAVID DAICHES and WILLIAM CHARVAT. *Poems in English*, pp. 714-15.

THOMAS C. KISHLER. "A Note on Browning's 'Soliloquy of the Spanish Cloister,' " *Victorian Poetry* 1(1), January 1963, 70-71.

INA BETH SESSIONS. "The Dramatic Monologue," *PMLA* 62(2), June 1947, 512.

ROGER L. SLAKEY. *Explicator* 21(5), January 1963, Item 42.

DAVID SONDSTROEM. "Animal and Vegetable in the Spanish Cloister," *Victorian Poetry* 6(1), Spring 1968, 70-73.

MIRIAM K. STARKMAN. "The Manichee in the Cloister: A Reading of Browning's 'Soliloquy of the Spanish Cloister,' " *Modern Language Notes* 75(5), May 1960, 399-405.

RICHARD WEAR. "Further Thoughts on Browning's Spanish Cloister," *Victorian Poetry* 12(1), Spring 1974, 67-70.

"The Statue and the Bust"

E. D. H. JOHNSON. *The Alien Vision of Victorian Poetry*, pp. 107-9.

WENDELL STACY JOHNSON. *Sex and Marriage in Victorian Poetry*, pp. 208-11.

W. O. RAYMOND. "Browning's 'The Statue and the Bust,' " *University of Toronto Quarterly* 28(3), April 1959, 233-49.

CHAD and EVA T. WALSH. *Twice Ten*, pp. 86-87.

JUDITH WEISSMAN. "Browning's Politics of Hell: 'Childe Roland to the Dark Tower Came' and 'The Statue and the Bust,' " *Concerning Poetry* 10(2), Fall 1977, 11-13.

BROWNING, ROBERT *(Cont.)*

"Such a starved bank of moss"

CORY BIEMAN DAVIES. "From Knowledge to Belief in *La Saisiaz: The Two Poets of Croisic*," *Studies in Browning and His Circle* 6(1), Spring 1978, 15.

"A Toccata of Galuppi's"

HAROLD BLOOM. *Poetry and Repression*, pp. 181-86.

HARRY BROWN and JOHN MILSTEAD. *What the Poem Means*, p. 20.

STEPHEN BROWN. "Browning and Music," *Browning Society Notes* 6(3), December 1976, 4-7.

DAVID DAICHES and WILLIAM CHARVAT. *Poems in English*, pp. 716-17.

ARTHUR DICKSON. *Explicator* 3(2), November 1944, Item 15.

EDGAR H. DUNCAN. *Explicator* 5(1), October 1946, Item 5.

WILLIAM FROST. *English Masterpieces*, edited by William Frost, Maynard Mack, and Leonard Dean, vol. 6: *Romantic and Victorian Poetry*, pp. 13-14.

EDGAR F. HARDEN. "A New Reading of Browning's 'A Toccata of Galuppi's,'" *Victorian Poetry* 11(4), Winter 1973, 330-36.

CHARLES W. JOHNSON. "Lost 'Chord,' Wrong '-Chord,' and Other Musical Anomalies in 'A Toccata of Galuppi's,'" *Studies in Browning and His Circle* 4(1), Spring 1976, 30-40.

DONALD STAUFFER. *The Nature of Poetry*, p. 178.

WILLIAM D. TEMPLEMAN and FREDERICK A. POTTLE. *Explicator* 2(4), February 1944, Item 25.

BENNETT WEAVER. "A Primer Study in Browning's Satire," *College English* 14(2), November 1952, 80-81.

"Too Late"

JAMES F. LOUCKS. "On Two Late Interpretations of 'Too Late,'" *Browning Society Notes* 4(3), December 1974, 24-26.

LAURENCE PERRINE. "Browning's 'Too Late': A Re-Interpretation," *Victorian Poetry* 7(4), Winter 1969, 339-45.

"Transcendentalism"

RICHARD D. ALTICK. "Browning's 'Transcendentalism': A Poem in Twelve Books," *Journal of English and Germanic Philology* 58(1), January 1959, 24-28.

"Two in the Campagna"

DEREK COLVILLE. *Victorian Poetry and the Romantic Religion*, pp. 155-57.

C. DAY LEWIS. *The Poetic Image*, pp. 78-80.

WENDELL V. HARRIS. "Where Late the Sweet Birds Sang: Looking Back at the Victorians Looking Back at the Romantics Looking Back . . .," *Victorian Poetry* 16(1-2), Spring-Summer 1978, 169-70.

"The Two Poets of Croisic"

CORY BIEMAN DAVIES. "From Knowledge to Belief in *La Saisiaz: The Two Poets of Croisic*," *Studies in Browning and His Circle* 6(1), Spring 1978, 7-24.

"Up at a Villa — Down in the City"

RICHARD FLECK. "Browning's 'Up at a Villa — Down in the City' as Satire," *Victorian Poetry* 7(4), Winter 1969, 345-49.

NANCY B. RICH. "New Perspective on the Companion Poems of Robert Browning," *Victorian Newsletter* 36 (Fall 1969), 8-9.

"Waring"

JOHN F. MCCARTHY. "Browning's 'Waring': The Real Subject of the 'Fancy Portrait,'" *Victorian Poetry* 9(4), Winter 1971, 371-82.

"A Woman's Last Word"

MAURICE BROWNING CRAMER. "'A Woman's Last Word': Paradise Lost or Paradise Retained?" *Browning Society Notes* 6(2), July 1976, 3-17.

MARY ROSE SULLIVAN. "Irony in 'A Woman's Last Word,'" *Browning Society Notes* 5(2), July 1975, 14-17.

"Women and Roses"

WENDELL STACY JOHNSON. *Sex and Marriage in Victorian Poetry*, pp. 212-13.

LAWRENCE POSTON, III. "'A Novel Grace and a Beauty Strange': Browning's 'Women and Roses,'" *Browning Society Notes* 5(1), March 1975, 15-17.

"The year's at the spring"
see "Pippa's Song"

BRYANT, WILLIAM CULLEN

"The Death of the Flowers"

HYATT H. WAGGONER. *American Poets*, pp. 35-36.

"The Evening Wind"

GEORGE ARMS. "American Literature Re-Examined: William Cullen Bryant," *University of Kansas City Review* 15(3), Spring 1949, 222-23. Reprinted in: George Arms. *The Fields Were Green*, p. 18.

"A Forest Hymn"

MARIUS BEWLEY. *Masks & Mirrors*, p. 253.

"Green River"

GEORGE ARMS. "American Literature Re-Examined: William Cullen Bryant," *University of Kansas City Review* 15(3), Spring 1949, 219. Reprinted in: George Arms. *The Fields Were Green*, p. 13.

ROY HARVEY PEARCE. *The Continuity of American Poetry*, pp. 208-9.

"Hymn to Death"

GEORGE ARMS. "American Literature Re-Examined: William Cullen Bryant," *University of Kansas City Review* 15(3), Spring 1949, 220-21. Reprinted in: George Arms. *The Fields Were Green*, pp. 15-16.

HYATT H. WAGGONER. *American Poets*, pp. 36-38.

"Inscription for the Entrance to a Wood"

WALTER GIERASCH. *Explicator* 4(6), April 1946, Item 40.

G. GIOVANNI. *Explicator* 4(6), April 1946, Item 40.

"The Journey of Life"

HYATT H. WAGGONER. *American Poets*, pp. 34-35.

"The Prairies"

GEORGE ARMS. "American Literature Re-Examined: William Cullen Bryant," *University of Kansas City Review* 15(3), Spring 1949, 221. Reprinted in: George Arms. *The Fields Were Green*, p. 16.

DAVID DAICHES and WILLIAM CHARVAT. *Poems in English*, pp. 708-9.

RALPH N. MILLER. "Nationalism in Bryant's 'The Prairies,'" *American Literature* 21(2), May 1949, 227-32.

"Thanatopsis"

HARRY BROWN and JOHN MILSTEAD. *What the Poem Means*, p. 29.

E. MILLER BUDICK. "'Visible' Images and the 'Still Voice': Transcendental Vision in Bryant's 'Thanatopsis,'" *ESQ* 22(2), Second Quarter 1976, 71-77.

DENIS DONOGHUE. *Connoisseurs of Chaos*, pp. 9-11.

ALBERT F. McLEAN, JR. "Bryant's 'Thanatopsis': A Sermon in Stone," *American Literature* 31(4), January 1960, 474-79.

HYATT H. WAGGONER. *American Poets*, pp. 38-41.

"To a Waterfowl"

GEORGE ARMS. "American Literature Re-Examined: William Cullen Bryant," *University of Kansas City Review* 15(3), Spring 1949, 221-22. Reprinted in: George Arms. *The Fields Were Green*, pp. 17-18.

E. MILLER BUDICK. "The Disappearing Image in William Cullen Bryant's 'To a Waterfowl,'" *Concerning Poetry* 11(2), Fall 1978, 13-16.

DONALD DAVIE. "William Cullen Bryant: To a Waterfowl," in *Interpretations*, pp. 129-37.

ALBERT GELPI. *The Tenth Muse*, pp. 66-67.

M. L. ROSENTHAL and A. J. M. SMITH. *Exploring Poetry*, first ed., pp. 541-42.

HYATT H. WAGGONER. *American Poets*, p. 41.

BUCHANAN, ROBERT

"The Ballad of Judas Iscariot"

C. C. CUNNINGHAM. *Literature as a Fine Art: Analysis and Interpretation*, pp. 98-99.

"City Without God"

R. A. FORSYTH. "Robert Buchanan and the Dilemma of the Brave New Victorian World," *Studies in English Literature 1500-1900* 9(4), Autumn 1969, 650-54.

BULKELEY, PETER

"Elegy on Thomas Hooker"

ROBERT DALY. *God's Altar*, pp. 148-49.

BUNTING, BASIL

"Chomei at Toyama"

ANTHONY SUTER. "Basil Bunting, Poet of Modern Times," *Ariel* 3(4), October 1972, 30.

"The Spoils"

ANTHONY SUTER. "Basil Bunting, Poet of Modern Times," *Ariel* 3(4), October 1972, 31-32.

BURKE, KENNETH

"Three Seasons of Love"

JOHN CIARDI. "The Critic in Love," *Nation* 181(15), 8 October 1955, 307. (P)

BURKE, THOMAS

"From the East"

J. A. LEO LEMAY. "Robert Bolling and the Bailment of Colonel Chiswell," *Early American Literature* 6(2), Fall 1971, 114.

BURNS, ROBERT

"Address to the Deil"

DAVID DAICHES and WILLIAM CHARVAT. *Poems in English*, pp. 688-90.

"Address to the Unco' Guid or the Rigidly Righteous"

HARRY BROWN and JOHN MILSTEAD. *What the Poem Means*, pp. 30-31.

"Bonnie Doon"

RICHARD RAY KIRK and ROGER PHILIP McCUTCHEON. *An Introduction to the Study of Poetry*, pp. 16-17.

DONALD STAUFFER. *The Nature of Poetry*, pp. 164-66. Reprinted in: *Readings for Liberal Education*, revised ed., II: 92-94; third ed., II: 79-80.

"Bruce to His Men at Bannockburn"

ISAAC ASIMOV. *Familiar Poems, Annotated*, pp. 74-79.

"The Cotter's Saturday Night"

FREDERICK L. BEATY. *Light from Heaven*, pp. 64-65.

"Death and Dr. Hornbook"

WILLIAM FROST. *English Masterpieces*, edited by William Frost, Maynard Mack, and Leonard Dean, vol. 6: *Romantic and Victorian Poetry*, pp. 13-14.

"Duncan Gray"

FREDERICK L. BEATY. *Light from Heaven*, p. 14.

"Epistle to J. Lapraik"

RAYMOND BENTMAN. "Robert Burns's Use of Scottish Diction," in *From Sensibility to Romanticism*, pp. 246-48.

"Epistle to J. R******"

FREDERICK L. BEATY. *Light from Heaven*, pp. 10-11.

"Extempore — to Mr. Gavin Hamilton"

FREDERICK L. BEATY. *Light from Heaven*, p. 13.

"Go Fetch to Me a Pint o'Wine"

DAVID DAICHES and WILLIAM CHARVAT. *Poems in English*, pp. 692-93.

"Had I the wyte"

FREDERICK L. BEATY. *Light from Heaven*, pp. 8-9.

"Hallowe'en"

ALLAN H. MacLAINE. "The *Christis Kirk* Tradition: Its Evolution In Scots Poetry to Burns," *Studies in Scottish Literature* 2(4), April 1965, 239-41.

"The Holy Fair"

FREDERICK L. BEATY. *Light from Heaven*, pp. 16-17.

JAMES KINSLEY. "The Rustic Inmates of the Hamlet," *Review of English Literature* 1(1), January 1960, 21-25.

"Holy Willie's Prayer"

HARRY BROWN and JOHN MILSTEAD. *What the Poem Means*, p. 31.

DAVID DAICHES and WILLIAM CHARVAT. *Poems in English*, pp. 687-88.

"John Anderson My Jo, John"

CLYDE S. KILBY. *Poetry and Life*, pp. 19-25.

"The Jolly Beggars"

FREDERICK L. BEATY. *Light from Heaven*, pp. 17-19.

ALLAN H. MacLAINE. "Radicalism and Conservatism in Burns' *The Jolly Beggars*," *Studies in Scottish Literature* 13(1978), 125-43.

"A Man's a Man for A' That"

HARRY BROWN and JOHN MILSTEAD. *What the Poem Means*, p. 30.

PAUL GOODMAN. "Burns: A Man's a Man For A' That," in *Master Poems of the English Language*, pp. 385-87.

"Mary Morison"

MARK VAN DOREN. *Introduction to Poetry*, pp. 9-12.

BURNS, ROBERT *(Cont.)*

"The Ordination"

ALLAN H. MACLAINE. "The *Christis Kirk* Tradition: Its Evolution in Scots Poetry To Burns," *Studies in Scottish Literature* 2(4), April 1965, 237-38.

"Poor Mailie's Elegy"

JOHN C. WESTON, JR. "An Example of Burns' Contribution to the Scottish Vernacular Tradition," *Studies in Philology* 57(4), October 1960, 640-47.

"A Red, Red Rose"

CLEANTH BROOKS, JOHN THIBAUT PURSER, and ROBERT PENN WARREN. *An Approach to Literature*, fifth edition, p. 390.

JAMES E. MILLER, JR. and BERNICE SLOTE. "The Nature of a Poem," in *The Dimensions of Poetry*, pp. 3-4.

RICHARD WILBUR. "Explaining the Obvious," in *Responses*, pp. 139-45.

"Robert Burns' Answer"

FREDERICK L. BEATY. *Light from Heaven*, p. 10.

"Tam O'Shanter"

FREDERICK L. BEATY. *Light from Heaven*, p. 17.

C. C. CUNNINGHAM. *Literature as a Fine Art*, pp. 147-51.

DAVID DAICHES and WILLIAM CHARVAT. *Poems in English*, pp. 690-92.

KARL KROEBER. *Romantic Narrative Art*, pp. 4-11.

M. L. MACKENZIE. "A New Dimension for 'Tam O'Shanter,'" *Studies in Scottish Literature* 1(2), October 1963, 87-92.

ALLAN H. MACLAINE. "Burns's Use of Parody in 'Tam O'Shanter,'" *Criticism* 1(4), Fall 1959, 308-16.

RICHARD MORTON. "Narrative Irony in Robert Burns's *Tam O'Shanter*," *Modern Language Quarterly* 22(1), March 1961, 12-20.

JAMES W. TUTTLETON. "The Devil and John Barleycorn: Comic Diablerie in Scott and Burns," *Studies in Scottish Literature* 1(4), April 1964, 259-64.

JOHN C. WESTON. "The Narrator of Tam O'Shanter," *Studies in English Literature 1500-1900* 8(3), Summer 1968, 537-50.

"To a Louse"

GILBERT HIGHET. *The Powers of Poetry*, pp. 74-80.

"To a Mouse"

CLEANTH BROOKS and ROBERT B. HEILMAN. *Understanding Drama*, pp. 19-22.

HARRY BROWN and JOHN MILSTEAD. *What the Poem Means*, p. 31.

GILBERT HIGHET. *The Powers of Poetry*, pp. 74-81.

BUTLER, SAMUEL

"The Elephant in the Moon"

GEORGE R. WASSERMAN. "Samuel Butler and the Problem of Unnatural Man," *Modern Language Quarterly* 31(2), June 1970, 186-88.

"To the Happy Memory of the Most Renown'd Du-Val"

EARL MINER. *The Restoration Mode from Milton to Dryden*, pp. 407-9.

"Upon Critics Who Judge of Modern Plays Precisely by the Rules of the Ancients"

GEORGE R. WASSERMAN. "Samuel Butler and the Problem of Unnatural Man," *Modern Language Quarterly* 31(2), June 1970, 190-91.

BYNNER, WITTER

"Eden Tree"

R. P. BLACKMUR. "Versions of Solitude," *Poetry* 39(4), January 1932, 217-21.

BYRON, GEORGE GORDON, LORD

"Beppo"

FREDERICK L. BEATY. *Light from Heaven*, pp. 29-33.

HAROLD BLOOM. *The Visionary Company*, pp. 249-50.

J. PHILIP EGGERS. "Byron and the Devil's Scripture: The Poet as Historian," *Clio* 4(3), June 1975, 369-70.

"The Bride of Abydos"

FREDERICK L. BEATY. *Light from Heaven*, pp. 147-48.

"Darkness"

KARL KROEBER. *Romantic Narrative Art*, p. 55.

"The Destruction of Sennacherib"

ISAAC ASIMOV. *Familiar Poems, Annotated*, pp. 5-11.

"The Dream"

PATRICIA M. BALL. *The Heart's Events*, pp. 26-27.

"Epistle to Augusta"

PATRICIA M. BALL. *The Heart's Events*, pp. 25-26.

ROBERT R. HARSON. "Byron's 'Tintern Abbey,'" *Keats-Shelley Journal* 20 (1971), 113-21.

"Fare Thee Well"

PATRICIA M. BALL. *The Heart's Events*, pp. 21-23.

"Lines on Hearing that Lady Byron was Ill"

PATRICIA M. BALL. *The Heart's Events*, pp. 23-24.

"Mazeppa"

KARL KROEBER. *Romantic Narrative Art*, p. 145.

"On This Day I Complete My Thirty-Sixth Year"

ARTHUR DICKSON. *Explicator* 5(2), November 1946, Item 15. (P)

FREDERICK L. JONES. "Byron's Last Poem," *Studies in Philology* 31(3), July 1934, 487-89.

T. O. MABBOTT. *Explicator* 4(5), March 1946, Item 36.

"Parisina"

FREDERICK L. BEATY. *Light from Heaven*, pp. 135-36.

WILLIAM H. MARSHALL. "Byron's *Parisina* and the Function of Psychoanalytic Criticism," *The Personalist* 42(2), Spring 1961, 213-23.

"The Prisoner of Chillon"

HARRY BROWN and JOHN MILSTEAD. *What the Poem Means*, pp. 33-34.

"Prometheus"

HAROLD BLOOM. *The Visionary Company*, pp. 239-42.

"The Prophecy of Dante"

WILFRED S. DOWDEN. "The Consistency in Byron's Social Doctrine," in *British Romantic Poets*, pp. 149-50.

ALLAN RODWAY. *The Romantic Conflict*, pp. 205-7. (P)

"She walks in beauty like the night"

JEROME BEATY and WILLIAM H. MATCHETT. *Poetry From Statement to Meaning*, pp. 113-15.

"The Siege of Corinth"

J. PHILIP EGGERS. "Byron and the Devil's Scripture: The Poet as Historian," *Clio* 4(3), June 1975, 366-67.

"Stanzas to Augusta"

PATRICIA M. BALL. *The Heart's Events*, pp. 24-25.

"Stanzas to the Po"
>HAROLD BLOOM. *The Visionary Company*, pp. 269-71.

"The Vision of Belshazzar"
>ISAAC ASIMOV. *Familiar Poems, Annotated*, pp. 12-18.

"The Vision of Judgment"
>HAROLD BLOOM. *The Visionary Company*, pp. 265-69.

EDWARD E. BOSTETTER. *The Romantic Ventriloquists*, pp. 289-91.

WILFRED S. DOWDEN. "The Consistency in Byron's Social Doctrine," in *British Romantic Poets*, p. 153.

F. R. LEAVIS. *Revaluation*, pp. 148-53.

PETER QUENNELL. "Byron: The Vision of Judgment," in *Master Poems of the English Language*, pp. 521-26.

C

CAEDMON

"Hymn"

MORTON W. BLOOMFIELD. "Patristics and Old English Literature: Notes on Some Poems," *Comparative Literature* 14(1), Winter 1962, 41-43.

BERNARD F. HUPPÉ. "Caedmon's *Hymn*," in *Old English Literature*, pp. 117-38.

CALDER, ANGUS

"Crab"

LAWRENCE R. RIES. *Wolf Masks*, p. 12.

CALLANAN, J. J.

"The Outlaw of Loch Lene"

B. S. LEE. "Callanan's 'The Outlaw of Loch Lene,'" *Ariel* 1(3), July 1970, 89-100.

CAMERON, NORMAN

"Black Takes White"

VERNON SCANNELL. *Not Without Glory*, pp. 162-63.

"The Compassionate Fool"

JAMES REEVES and MARTIN SEYMOUR-SMITH. *Inside Poetry*, pp. 59-61.

CAMPBELL, JOSEPH

"The Dancer"

DAVID RIDGLEY CLARK. *Lyric Resonance*, pp. 85-90.

CAMPBELL, ROY

"The Flaming Terrapin"

ROWLAND SMITH. "Roy Campbell and His French Sources," *Comparative Literature* 22(1), Winter 1970, 2-6.

"The Gum Trees"

ROWLAND SMITH. "Roy Campbell and His French Sources," *Comparative Literature* 22(1), Winter 1970, 12-18.

"Veld Eclogue: The Pioneers"

JOHN F. POVEY. "A Lyre of Savage Thunder: A Study of the Poetry of Roy Campbell," *Wisconsin Studies in Contemporary Literature* 7(1), Winter-Spring 1966, 89-90.

CAMPION, THOMAS

"Follow Thy Fair Sun"

CLEANTH BROOKS and ROBERT PENN WARREN. *Understanding Poetry*, third ed., pp. 286-87; fourth ed., pp. 215-17.

"My Sweetest Lesbia"

LAURENCE PERRINE. "Lesbia and Love: Comment on 'A Woman's Map of Lyric Poetry' by Elizabeth Hampsten," *College English* 35(4), January 1974, 490.

"Now winter nights enlarge"

JOHN T. IRWIN. "Thomas Campion and the Musical Emblem," *Studies in English Literature 1500-1900* 10(1), Winter 1970, 121-41.

"Of Corinna Singing"

see "When to Her Lute Corinna Sings"

"There Is a Garden in Her Face"

JEROME BEATY and WILLIAM H. MATCHETT. *Poetry From Statement to Meaning*, pp. 200-201.

LAURENCE PERRINE. "Four Forms of Metaphor," *College English* 33(2), November 1971, 133-34.

"When Thou Must Home to Shades of Under Ground"

ROSEMOND TUVE. *Elizabethan and Metaphysical Imagery*, p. 16.

"When to Her Lute Corinna Sings"

ROSEMOND TUVE. *Elizabethan and Metaphysical Imagery*, pp. 15-16. Reprinted in: *Readings for Liberal Education*, revised ed., II: 27-28.

CANE, MELVILLE

"All I Knew"

JEFFREY ROBINSON. "Celebration: The Lyric Poetry of Melville Cane," *American Scholar* 38(2), Spring 1969, 290-91.

"April Flurry"

MELVILLE CANE. "Snow: Theme with Variations," *American Scholar* 22(1), Winter 1952-53, 101-2.

"Deep in Wagon-Ruts"

MELVILLE CANE. "Snow: Theme with Variations," *American Scholar* 22(1), Winter 1952-53, 97.

"The Fly"

MELVILLE CANE. "'The Fly' and Its Problems," *University of Kansas City Review* 19(3), Spring 1953, 156-62.

JEFFREY ROBINSON. "Celebration: The Lyric Poetry of Melville Cane," *American Scholar* 38(2), Spring 1969, 295.

"Hither and Thither"

MELVILLE CANE. "Snow: Theme with Variations," *American Scholar* 22(1), Winter 1952-53, 99-101.

"Hokinson"

MELVILLE CANE. "Concerning 'Hokinson,'" *University of Kansas City Review* 17(4), Summer 1951, 288-93.

"January Garden"

MELVILLE CANE. "Snow: Theme with Variations," *American Scholar* 22(1), Winter 1952-53, 97-98.

JEFFREY ROBINSON. "Celebration: The Lyric Poetry of Melville Cane," *American Scholar* 38(2), Spring 1969, 287-88.

"Last Night It Snowed"

MELVILLE CANE. "Snow: Theme with Variations," *American Scholar* 22(1), Winter 1952-53, 98-99.

"Presence of Snow"

MELVILLE CANE. "Snow: Theme with Variations," *American Scholar* 22(1), Winter 1952-53, 104-5.

"Snow in April"

MELVILLE CANE. "Snow: Theme with Variations," *American Scholar* 22(1), Winter 1952-53, 102-4.

"Snow Toward Evening"

JEFFREY ROBINSON. "Celebration: The Lyric Poetry of Melville Cane," *American Scholar* 38(2), Spring 1969, 289.

"Somewhere Hid in the Wild"

JEFFREY ROBINSON. "Celebration: The Lyric Poetry of Melville Cane," *American Scholar* 38(2), Spring 1969, 287.

"Summer Thunder"

JEFFREY ROBINSON. "Celebration: The Lyric Poetry of Melville Cane," *American Scholar* 38(2), Spring 1969, 288.

CAR, THOMAS

"Anagramme"

GEORGE WILLIAMSON. *Six Metaphysical Poets*, pp. 124-25.

CAREW, THOMAS

"Ask Me No More Where Jove Bestows"

see "Song: Ask Me No More Where Jove Bestows"

"Celia Singing"

D. F. RAUBER. "Carew Redivivus," *Texas Studies in Literature and Language* 13(1), Spring 1971, 26-28.

"The Complement"

JOHN T. SHAWCROSS. "The Poet as Orator: One Phase of His Judicial Pose," in *The Rhetoric of Renaissance Poetry*, pp. 22-23.

"A Deposition from Love"

B. KING. "The Strategy of Carew's Wit," *Review of English Literature* 5(3), July 1964, 44-46.

"Disdain Returned"

DONALD C. BAKER. *Explicator* 11(8), June 1953, Item 54.

MACDONALD EMSLIE. *Explicator* 12(1), October 1953, Item 4.

ADA LONG and HUGH MACLEAN. "'Deare *Ben*,' 'Great DONNE,' and 'my *Celia*': The Wit of Carew's Poetry," *Studies in English Literature 1500-1900* 18(1), Winter 1978, 80.

"A Divine Mistress"

JOSEPHINE MILES. *The Primary Language of Poetry in the 1640s*, pp. 4-6.

G. A. E. PARFITT. "The Poetry of Thomas Carew," in Keast, *Seventeenth Century English Poetry*, rev. ed., pp. 286-87.

"An Elegie upon the Death of the Deane of Pauls, Dr. John Donne"

T. R. BARNES. *English Verse*, pp. 58-59.

ADA LONG and HUGH MACLEAN. "'Deare *Ben*,' 'Great DONNE,' and 'my *Celia*': The Wit of Carew's Poetry," *Studies in English Literature 1500-1900* 18(1), Winter 1978, 84-88.

LOUIS L. MARTZ. *The Wit of Love*, pp. 97-100.

MICHAEL MURRIN. "Poetry as Literary Criticism," *Modern Philology* 65(3), February 1968, 203-5.

"Elegy upon the Author"

GEORGE WILLIAMSON. *Six Metaphysical Poets*, pp. 16-17.

"In answer of an Elegiacall Letter upon the Death of the King of Sweden from Aurelian Townsend, inviting me to write on that subject"

LOUIS L. MARTZ. *The Wit of Love*, pp. 74-90.

EARL MINER. *The Cavalier Mode from Jonson to Cotton*, pp. 83-84.

"Ingrateful beauty threatened"

LLOYD FRANKENBERG. *Invitation to Poetry*, pp. 52-53.

B. KING. "The Strategy of Carew's Wit," *Review of English Literature* 5(3), July 1964, 43-44.

ADA LONG and HUGH MACLEAN. "'Deare *Ben*,' 'Great DONNE,' and 'my *Celia*': The Wit of Carew's Poetry," *Studies in English Literature 1500-1900* 18(1), Winter 1978, 80-81.

A. J. SMITH. "The Failure of Love: Love Lyrics after Donne," in *Metaphysical Poetry*, edited by Malcolm Bradbury and David Palmer, pp. 56-57.

"Mediocrity in Love Rejected"

D. F. RAUBER. "Carew Redivivus," *Texas Studies in Literature and Language* 13(1), Spring 1971, 25-26.

"Obsequies to the Lady Anne Hay"

ADA LONG and HUGH MACLEAN. "'Deare *Ben*,' 'Great DONNE,' and 'my *Celia*': The Wit of Carew's Poetry," *Studies in English Literature 1500-1900* 18(1), Winter 1978, 93.

"Persuasions to Enjoy"

D. F. RAUBER. "Carew Redivivus," *Texas Studies in Literature and Language* 13(1), Spring 1971, 23-25.

"A Rapture"

PAULA JOHNSON. "Carew's 'A Rapture': The Dynamics of Fantasy," *Studies in English Literature 1500-1900* 16(1), Winter 1976, 145-55.

LAURENCE LERNER. "Sex in Arcadia," in his *The Uses of Nostalgia*, pp. 95-98.

ADA LONG and HUGH MACLEAN. "'Deare *Ben*,' 'Great DONNE,' and 'my *Celia*': The Wit of Carew's Poetry," *Studies in English Literature 1500-1900* 18(1), Winter 1978, 88-93.

EARL MINER. *The Cavalier Mode from Jonson to Cotton*, pp. 80-82.

CAREW, THOMAS *(Cont.)*

"Song: Ask Me No More Where Jove Bestows"
> CLEANTH BROOKS. *Modern Poetry and the Tradition*, pp. 21-22.
> CLEANTH BROOKS, JOHN THIBAUT PURSER, and ROBERT PENN WARREN. *An Approach to Literature*, pp. 486-88; second ed., pp. 486-88; third ed., pp. 362-63; fourth ed., pp. 354-56.
> EARL DANIELS. *The Art of Reading Poetry*, pp. 364-66.
> EARL MINER. *The Cavalier Mode from Jonson to Cotton*, pp. 135-37.
> A. J. SMITH. "The Failure of Love: Love Lyrics after Donne," in *Metaphysical Poetry*, edited by Malcolm Bradbury and David Palmer, pp. 46-47.
> MARK VAN DOREN. *Introduction to Poetry*, pp. 3-8. Reprinted in: *The Creative Reader*, pp. 853-56; second ed., pp. 907-10. Also: *Master Poems of the English Language*, pp. 154-58.

"Song: Persuasions to Enjoy"
see "Persuasions to Enjoy"

"Song: To My Inconstant Mistress"
see "To My Inconstant Mistress"

"The Spring"
> ROBERT E. JUNGMAN. "The Ending of Thomas Carew's 'The Spring,'" *Concerning Poetry* 8(2), Fall 1975, 49-50.
> G. A. E. PARFITT. "The Poetry of Thomas Carew," in *Seventeenth Century English Poetry*, revised ed., pp. 283-86.

"To A. L.: Persuasions to Love"
> EARL MINER. *The Cavalier Mode from Jonson to Cotton*, pp. 127-28.
> G. A. E. PARFITT. "The Poetry of Thomas Carew," in *Seventeenth Century English Poetry*, revised ed., pp. 288-89.
> D. F. RAUBER. "Carew Redivivus," *Texas Studies in Literature and Language* 13(1), Spring 1971, 20-23.
> ROSEMOND TUVE. *Elizabethan and Metaphysical Imagery*, p. 260. (P)

"To a Lady that desired I would love her"
> B. KING. "The Strategy of Carew's Wit," *Review of English Literature* 5(3), July 1964, 47-48.

"To Ben Jonson"
> ADA LONG and HUGH MACLEAN. "'Deare Ben,' 'Great DONNE,' and 'my Celia': The Wit of Carew's Poetry," *Studies in English Literature 1500-1900* 18(1), Winter 1978, 82-84.
> LOUIS L. MARTZ. *The Wit of Love*, pp. 95-97.
> MICHAEL MURRIN. "Poetry as Literary Criticism," *Modern Philology* 65(3), February 1968, 203-5.
> G. A. E. PARFITT. "The Poetry of Thomas Carew," in *Seventeenth Century English Poetry*, revised ed., pp. 281-82.

"To my Friend, G. N., from Wrest"
> LOUIS L. MARTZ. *The Wit of Love*, pp. 62-64.

"To My Inconstant Mistress"
> F. W. BATESON. *English Poetry and the English Language*, pp. 60-62.
> EARL DANIELS. *The Art of Reading Poetry*, pp. 349-51.
> PAULA JOHNSON. "Getting Acquainted with a Poem," *College English* 37(4), December 1975, 363-65.
> B. KING. "The Strategy of Carew's Wit," *Review of English Literature* 5(3), July 1964, 48-49.

> LOUIS L. MARTZ. *The Poem of the Mind*, p. 47.
> A. J. SMITH. "The Failure of Love: Love Lyrics after Donne," in *Metaphysical Poetry*, edited by Malcolm Bradbury and David Palmer, p. 56.

"To my worthy Friend, Master George Sandys, on his Translation of the Psalms"
> ADA LONG and HUGH MACLEAN. "'Deare Ben,' 'Great DONNE,' and 'my Celia': The Wit of Carew's Poetry," *Studies in English Literature 1500-1900* 18(1), Winter 1978, 93-94.
> G. A. E. PARFITT. "The Poetry of Thomas Carew," in *Seventeenth Century English Poetry*, revised ed., pp. 280-81. (P)
> H. R. SWARDSON. *Poetry and the Fountain of Light*, pp. 14-23.

"To Saxham"
> G. A. E. PARFITT. "The Poetry of Thomas Carew," in *Seventeenth Century English Poetry*, revised ed., pp. 282-83.

"Upon a Mole in Celia's Bosom"
> C. F. WILLIAMSON. "Two Notes on the Poems of Richard Lovelace," *Modern Language Review* 52(2), April 1957, 229.

"Upon the King's Sickness"
> ELSIE DUNCAN-JONES. *Explicator* 13(3), December 1954, Item 19. (P)

CARROLL, LEWIS, see DODGSON, CHARLES

CARTWRIGHT, WILLIAM

"To Chloe who wish'd herself young enough for me"
> PATRICIA BEER. *An Introduction to the Metaphysical Poets*, pp. 20-21.

CARY, ALICE

"Make Believe"
> CHARLES W. COOPER and JOHN HOLMES. *Preface to Poetry*, pp. 211-13.

CASSIANI, jun

"The Voice from the Side of Etna: or The Mad Monk: An Ode, in Mrs. Ratliff's manner"
> STEPHEN M. PARRISH and DAVID V. ERDMAN. "Who Wrote The Mad Monk? A Debate," *New York Public Library Bulletin* 64(4), April 1960, 231-36.

CASSIDY, JOHN

"An Attitude of Mind"
> JOHN DREW. "John Drew on John Cassidy," *Iowa Review* 6(3-4), Summer-Fall 1975, 192.

"The Dancing Man"
> JOHN DREW. "John Drew on John Cassidy," *Iowa Review* 6(3-4), Summer-Fall 1975, 190.

CAUDWELL, CHRISTOPHER

"The Art of Dying"
> D. E. S. MAXWELL. "The 'Poems' of Christopher Caudwell," *Ariel* 1(1), January 1970, 81-82.
> D. E. S. MAXWELL. *The Poets of the Thirties*, pp. 80-82.

"Classic Encounter"
> D. E. S. MAXWELL. *The Poets of the Thirties*, p. 79.

"Essay on Freewill"

D. E. S. MAXWELL. "The 'Poems' of Christopher Caudwell," *Ariel* 1(1), January 1970, 79.

D. E. S. MAXWELL. *The Poets of the Thirties*, pp. 74-75.

"The Hair"

D. E. S. MAXWELL. *The Poets of the Thirties*, p. 75.

"Heil Baldwin!"

D. E. S. MAXWELL. "The 'Poems' of Christopher Caudwell," *Ariel* 1(1), January 1970, 76.

"Hymn to Philosophy"

D. E. S. MAXWELL. *The Poets of the Thirties*, p. 74.

"Kensington Rime"

D. E. S. MAXWELL. *The Poets of the Thirties*, p. 69.

"Once I Did Think"

D. E. S. MAXWELL. "The 'Poems' of Christopher Caudwell," *Ariel* 1(1), January 1970, 74-75.

"The Requiem"

D. E. S. MAXWELL. "The 'Poems' of Christopher Caudwell," *Ariel* 1(1), January 1970, 77-78.

D. E. S. MAXWELL. *The Poets of the Thirties*, pp. 70-72.

"The Stones of Ruskin"

D. E. S. MAXWELL. "The 'Poems' of Christopher Caudwell," *Ariel* 1(1), January 1970, 80.

D. E. S. MAXWELL. *The Poets of the Thirties*, p. 78.

"Tierra del Fuego"

D. E. S. MAXWELL. "The 'Poems' of Christopher Caudwell," *Ariel* 1(1), January 1970, 78-79.

D. E. S. MAXWELL. *The Poets of the Thirties*, pp. 78-79.

"Twenty Sonnets of Wm. Smith"

D. E. S. MAXWELL. "The 'Poems' of Christopher Caudwell," *Ariel* 1(1), January 1970, 80-81.

D. E. S. MAXWELL. *The Poets of the Thirties*, pp. 76-78.

"Was It?"

D. E. S. MAXWELL. "The 'Poems' of Christopher Caudwell," *Ariel* 1(1), January 1970, 80.

CHANNING, ELLERY

"Boat Song"

LAWRENCE BUELL. *Literary Transcendentalism*, pp. 243-46.

"Near Home"

LAWRENCE BUELL. *Literary Transcendentalism*, pp. 255-58.

"Wachusett"

LAWRENCE BUELL. *Literary Transcendentalism*, pp. 253-55.

"The Wanderer"

LAWRENCE BUELL. *Literary Transcendentalism*, pp. 258-60.

CHAPMAN, GEORGE

"Hero and Leander"

JOHN HUNTINGTON. "Condemnation and Pity in Chapman's *Hero and Leander*," *English Literary Renaissance* 7(3), Autumn 1977, 307-23.

JOHN HUNTINGTON. "The Serious Trifle: Aphorisms in Chapman's *Hero and Leander*," *Studies in the Literary Imagination* 11(1), Spring 1978, 107-13.

ALBERT C. LABRIOLA. "Perspective and Illusion in *Hero and Leander*," *English Language Notes* 16(1), September 1978, 14-18.

C. S. LEWIS. "Hero and Leander," in *Elizabethan Poetry*, edited by Paul J. Alpers, pp. 239-50.

"Hymnus in Noctem"

CHARLES KENDRICK CANNON. "Chapman on the Unity of Style and Meaning," *Journal of English and Germanic Philology* 68(2), April 1969, 254-62.

"Ovid's Banquet of Sence"

JOHN HUNTINGTON. "Philosophical Seduction in Chapman, Davies, and Donne," *ELH* 44(1), Spring 1977, 40-51.

JERALD D. JAHN. "Chapman's *Enargia* and the Popular Perspective on *Ovid's Banquet of Sence*," *Tennessee Studies in Literature* 23 (1978), 15-30.

FRANK KERMODE. *Shakespeare, Spenser, Donne*, pp. 99-115.

JAMES PHARES MYERS, JR. " 'This Curious Frame': Chapman's *Ovid's Banquet of Sence*," *Studies in Philology* 65(2), April 1968, 192-206.

RHODA M. RIBNER. "The Compasse of This Curious Frame: Chapman's *Ovid's Banquet of Sence* and the Emblematic Tradition," *Studies in the Renaissance* 17(1970), 233-58.

GERALD SNARE. "Chapman's Ovid," *Studies in Philology* 75(4), October 1978, 430-50.

"The Shadow of Night"

ROY BATTENHOUSE. "Chapman's *The Shadow of Night*: An Interpretation," *Studies in Philology* 38(4), October 1941, 584-608.

CHATTERTON, THOMAS

"The Death of Nicou"

DONALD S. TAYLOR. "Chatterton: Insult and Gifts to the Rev. Mr. Catcott," *Literature and Psychology* 22(1), 1972, 42-43.

"The Exhibition"

DONALD S. TAYLOR. "Chatterton: Insult and Gifts to the Rev. Mr. Catcott," *Literature and Psychology* 22(1), 1972, 41.

CHAUCER, GEOFFREY

"ABC"

EDMUND REISS. "Dusting Off the Cobwebs: A Look at Chaucer's Lyrics," *Chaucer Review* 1(1), Summer 1966, 57-62.

"Anelida and Arcite"

MICHAEL D. CHERNISS. "Chaucer's *Anelida and Arcite*: Some Conjectures," *Chaucer Review* 5(1), Summer 1970, 9-21.

"The Complaint of Mars"

NANCY DEAN. "Chaucer's *Complaint*, A Genre Descended From the *Heroides*," *Comparative Literature* 19(1), Winter 1967, 19-26.

CHARLES A. OWEN, JR. "The Problem of Free Will in Chaucer's Narratives," *Philological Quarterly* 46(4), October 1967, 434-35.

MELVIN STORM. "The Mythological Tradition in Chaucer's *Complaint of Mars*," *Philological Quarterly* 57(3), Summer 1978, 323-35.

GEORGE WILLIAMS. "What is the Meaning of Chaucer's *Complaint of Mars*?" *Journal of English and Germanic Philology* 57(2), April 1958, 167-76.

CHAUCER, GEOFFREY *(Cont.)*

"Complaint to His Purse"

ANDREW J. FINNEL. "The Poet as Sunday Man: 'The Complaint of Chaucer to His Purse,'" *Chaucer Review* 8(2), Fall 1973, 147-58.

CHAS. D. LUDLUM. "Heavenly Word-Play in Chaucer's 'Complaint to His Purse,'" *Notes & Queries*, n.s., 23(9), September 1976, 391-92.

"The Complaint Unto Pity"

MALCOLM PITTOCK. "Chaucer: The Complaint Unto Pity," *Criticism* 1(2), Spring 1959, 160-68.

"Envoy to Scogan"

ALFRED DAVID. "Chaucer's Good Counsel to Scogan," *Chaucer Review* 3(4), Spring 1969, 265-74.

WALTER H. FRENCH. "The Meaning of Chaucer's *Envoy to Scogan*," *PMLA* 48(1), March 1933, 289-92.

R. T. LENAGHAN. "Chaucer's *Envoy to Scogan*: The Uses of Literary Conventions," *Chaucer Review* 10(1), Summer 1975, 46-61.

MARION L. POLZELLA. "'The Craft so Long to Lerne': Poet and Lover in Chaucer's 'Envoy to Scogan' and *Parliament of Fowls*," *Chaucer Review* 10(4), Spring 1976, 279-86.

"The Former Age"

A. V. C. SCHMIDT. "Chaucer and the Golden Age," *Essays in Criticism* 26(2), April 1976, 99-115.

"Fortune: Balades de Visage Sanz Peinture"

MARGARET GALWAY. "Chaucer Among Thieves," *Times Literary Supplement*, 20 April 1946, p. 187.

EDNA RIDEOUT. "Chaucer's 'Beste Frend,'" *Times Literary Supplement*, 8 February 1947, p. 79.

"The Parliament of Fowls"

DAVID CHAMBERLAIN. "The Music of the Spheres and *The Parlement of Foules*," *Chaucer Review* 5(1), Summer 1970, 32-56.

CECILY CLARK, D. S. BREWER, and MACDONALD EMSLIE. "Natural Love in *The Parlement of Foules*," *Essays in Criticism* 5(4), October 1955, 405-18.

BRUCE KENT COWGILL. "The *Parlement of Foules* and the Body Politic," *Journal of English and Germanic Philology* 74(3), July 1975, 315-35.

KATHLEEN E. DUBS and STODDARD MALARKEY. "The Frame of Chaucer's *Parlement*," *Chaucer Review* 13(1), Summer 1978, 16-24.

MACDONALD EMSLIE. "Codes of Love and Class Distinctions," *Essays in Criticism* 5(1), January 1955, 1-17.

H. M. LEICESTER, JR. "The Harmony of Chaucer's *Parlement*: A Dissonant Voice," *Chaucer Review* 9(1), Summer 1974, 15-34.

JOHN P. McCALL. "The Harmony of Chaucer's *Parliament*," *Chaucer Review* 5(1), Summer 1970, 22-31.

CHARLES A. OWEN, JR. "The Role of the Narrator in the 'Parlement of Foules,'" *College English* 14(5), February 1953, 264-69.

MARION L. POLZELLA. "'The Craft so Long to Lerne': Poet and Lover in Chaucer's 'Envoy to Scogan' and *Parliament of Fowls*," *Chaucer Review* 10(4), Spring 1976, 279-86.

FRANCIS J. SMITH. "Mirth and Marriage in *The Parlement of Foules*," *Ball State University Forum* 14(1), Winter 1973, 15-22.

A. C. SPEARING. *Medieval Dream-Poetry*, pp. 89-101.

JAMES J. WILHELM. "The Narrator and His Narrative in Chaucer's *Parlement*," *Chaucer Review* 1(4), Spring 1967, 201-6.

"Prologue" (*The Legend of Good Women*)

A. C. SPEARING. *Medieval Dream-Poetry*, pp. 101-10.

"Rime of Sir Thopas"

WALKER SCHEPS. "Sir Thopas: The Bourgeois Knight, the Minstrel and the Critics," *Tennessee Studies in Literature* 11 (1966), 35-43.

"To Rosemounde"

ARTHUR K. MOORE. *The Secular Lyric in Middle English*, pp. 132-33.

EDMUND REISS. "Dusting Off the Cobwebs: A Look at Chaucer's Lyrics," *Chaucer Review* 1(1), Summer 1966, 63-65.

ROSSELL HOPE ROBBINS. "Chaucer's 'To Rosemounde,'" *Studies in the Literary Imagination* 4(2), October 1971, 73-81.

"Womanly Noblesse"

ARTHUR K. MOORE. *The Secular Lyric in Middle English*, pp. 131-32.

CHESTER, ROBERT

"Love's Martyr"

WALTER OAKESHOTT. "*Loves Martyr*," *Huntington Library Quarterly* 39(1), November 1975, 29-49.

CHESTERTON, G. K.

"The Donkey"

DONALD STAUFFER. *The Nature of Poetry*, p. 77.

"Lepanto"

ISAAC ASIMOV. *Familiar Poems, Annotated*, pp. 80-101.

"The Rolling English Road"

DUNCAN WILLIAMS and JACK R. BROWN. *Explicator* 34(6), February 1976, Item 45.

CHILDE, WILFRED ROWLAND

"Solemn and Gray, the Immense Clouds of Even" (*Ivory Palaces*)

I. A. RICHARDS. *Practical Criticism*, pp. 155-61.

CHISHOLM, HUGH

"Lament of the Lovers"

LEONARD UNGER. "Seven Poets," *Sewanee Review* 56(1), Winter 1948, 169. (P)

"Notes on Progress"

JOSEPH WARREN BEACH. *Obsessive Images*, pp. 272-73.

CHURCHILL, CHARLES

"The Apology"

MORRIS GOLDEN. "Sterility and Eminence in the Poetry of Charles Churchill," *Journal of English and Germanic Philology* 66(3), July 1967, 335-36.

"The Candidate"

MORRIS GOLDEN. "Sterility and Eminence in the Poetry of Charles Churchill," *Journal of English and Germanic Philology* 66(3), July 1967, 342-43.

"Epistle to William Hogarth"

MORRIS GOLDEN. "Sterility and Eminence in the Poetry of Charles Churchill," *Journal of English and Germanic Philology* 66(3), July 1967, 340.

"The Farewell"

MORRIS GOLDEN. "Sterility and Eminence in the Poetry of Charles Churchill," *Journal of English and Germanic Philology* 66(3), July 1967, 343.

"Fragment of a Dedication to Dr. W. Warburton"

WALLACE C. BROWN. "Dramatic Tension in Neoclassic Satire," *College English* 6(5), February 1945, 268.

ALAN S. FISHER. "The Stretching of Augustan Satire: Charles Churchill's 'Dedication' to Warburton," *Journal of English and Germanic Philology* 72(3), July 1973, 360-77.

MORRIS GOLDEN. "Sterility and Eminence in the Poetry of Charles Churchill," *Journal of English and Germanic Philology* 66(3), July 1967, 344-45.

"Independence"

MORRIS GOLDEN. "Sterility and Eminence in the Poetry of Charles Churchill," *Journal of English and Germanic Philology* 66(3), July 1967, 344.

"Night"

MORRIS GOLDEN. "Sterility and Eminence in the Poetry of Charles Churchill," *Journal of English and Germanic Philology* 66(3), July 1967, 336.

"The Prophecy of Famine"

MORRIS GOLDEN. "Sterility and Eminence in the Poetry of Charles Churchill," *Journal of English and Germanic Philology* 66(3), July 1967, 339-40.

"The Times"

MORRIS GOLDEN. "Sterility and Eminence in the Poetry of Charles Churchill," *Journal of English and Germanic Philology* 66(3), July 1967, 343-44.

CIARDI, JOHN

"The Deaths About You, Etc."

JAMES G. SOUTHWORTH. "The Poetry of John Ciardi," *English Journal* 50(9), December 1961, 588.

"The Graph"

JOHN W. HUGHES. "Humanism and the Orphic Voice," *Saturday Review* 54(21), 22 May 1971, 31-32.

"Letter to Virginia Johnson"

HARVEY CURTIS WEBSTER. "Humanism as the Father Face (A Critical Preview)," *Poetry* 70(3), June 1947, 146-50.

"Most Like an Arch This Marriage"

JAMES G. SOUTHWORTH. "The Poetry of John Ciardi," *English Journal* 50(9), December 1961, 588-89.

"The Size of Song"

EDWARD CIFELLI. "The Size of John Ciardi's Song," *CEA Critic* 36(1), November 1973, 21-27.

"Take-Off Over Kansas"

DAN JAFFE. "Poets in the Inferno: Civilians, C.O.'s and Combatants," in *The Forties*, p. 57.

"Tenzone"

EDWARD J. GALLAGHER. *Explicator* 27(4), December 1968, Item 28. (P)

LAURENCE PERRINE. *Explicator* 28(9), May 1970, Item 82.

"To Judith Asleep"

JAMES G. SOUTHWORTH. "The Poetry of John Ciardi," *English Journal* 50(9), December 1961, 588.

CLANVOWE, JOHN

"The Cuckoo and the Nightingale"

A. C. SPEARING. *Medieval Dream-Poetry*, pp. 176-81.

CLARE, JOHN

"Autumn"

THOMAS R. FROSCH. "The Descriptive Style of John Clare," *Studies in Romanticism* 10(2), Spring 1971, 147-49.

"Badger"

GÉMINO H. ABAD. *A Formal Approach to Lyric Poetry*, pp. 263-65.

ROBERT PINSKY. *The Situation of Poetry*, pp. 120-24, 126-29.

M. L. ROSENTHAL and A. J. M. SMITH. *Exploring Poetry*, pp. 284-85; second ed., pp. 138-39.

JANET M. TODD. " 'Very copys of nature': John Clare's Descriptive Poetry," *Philological Quarterly* 53(1), January 1974, 96.

"Birds' Nests"

THOMAS R. FROSCH. "The Descriptive Style of John Clare," *Studies in Romanticism* 10(2), Spring 1971, 138-39.

"Country Letter"

JAMES REEVES and MARTIN SEYMOUR-SMITH. *Inside Poetry*, pp. 13-16.

"The Hedgehog"

JANET M. TODD. " 'Very copys of nature': John Clare's Descriptive Poetry," *Philological Quarterly* 53(1), January 1974, 97-98.

"I am: yet what I am who cares or knows?"

LLOYD FRANKENBERG. *Invitation to Poetry*, pp. 344-45.

"I hid my love when young till I"

HAROLD BLOOM. *The Visionary Company*, pp. 435-36.

"The Lark's Nest"

THOMAS R. FROSCH. "The Descriptive Style of John Clare," *Studies in Romanticism* 10(2), Spring 1971, 137-39.

"Little Trotty Wagtail"

CLEANTH BROOKS and ROBERT PENN WARREN. *Understanding Poetry*, fourth ed., pp. 347-48.

"Love and Beauty"

MARK STOREY. *Explicator* 28(7), March 1970, Item 60.

"Mouse's Nest"

JANET M. TODD. " 'Very copys of nature': John Clare's Descriptive Poetry," *Philological Quarterly* 53(1), January 1974, 97.

"The Nightingale's Nest"

JANET M. TODD. " 'Very copys of nature': John Clare's Descriptive Poetry," *Philological Quarterly* 53(1), January 1974, 88-90.

"Sand Martin"

JANET M. TODD. " 'Very copys of nature': John Clare's Descriptive Poetry," *Philological Quarterly* 53(1), January 1974, 91-92.

"Schoolboys in Winter"

LLOYD FRANKENBERG. *Invitation to Poetry*, p. 235.

"The Skylark"

L. J. SWINGLE. "Stalking the Essential John Clare: Clare in Relation to His Romantic Contemporaries," *Studies in Romanticism* 14(3), Summer 1975, 277-78.

JANET M. TODD. " 'Very copys of nature': John Clare's Descriptive Poetry," *Philological Quarterly* 53(1), January 1974, 92-94.

CLARE, JOHN *(Cont.)*

"The Sorrows of Love"

IAN GREGOR. "The Last Augustan: Some Observations on the Poetry of George Crabbe (1755-1832)," *Dublin Review* 229 (First Quarter 1955), 47.

"Summer Moods"

JAMES REEVES. "John Clare," in *Commitment to Poetry,* pp. 145-46.

"A Vision"

HAROLD BLOOM. *The Visionary Company,* pp. 444-45.

"Wilt thou go with me, sweet maid"

HAROLD BLOOM. *The Visionary Company,* pp. 441-43.

"The Wind Waves o'er the Meadows Green"

THOMAS R. FROSCH. "The Descriptive Style of John Clare," *Studies in Romanticism* 10(2), Spring 1971, 145-46.

"The Woodman"

L. J. SWINGLE. "Stalking the Essential John Clare: Clare in Relation to His Romantic Contemporaries," *Studies in Romanticism* 14(3), Summer 1975, 282-83.

CLARK, DAVID R.

"The Bee Space"

DAVID RIDGLEY CLARK. *Lyric Resonance,* pp. 210-11.

"Mountain Ash"

DAVID RIDGLEY CLARK. *Lyric Resonance,* pp. 211-15.

"Pinnacle"

DAVID RIDGLEY CLARK. *Lyric Resonance,* pp. 206-7.

"Robin"

DAVID RIDGLEY CLARK. *Lyric Resonance,* p. 204-6.

"Tree"

DAVID RIDGLEY CLARK. *Lyric Resonance,* pp. 207-10.

CLARKE, AUSTIN

"Vanishing Irish"

DONALD T. TORCHIANA. "Contemporary Irish Poetry," *Chicago Review* 17(2-3), 1964, 157-58.

CLEMO, JACK

"A Calvinist in Love"

GEOFFREY THURLEY. *The Ironic Harvest,* pp. 171-72.

"Clay-Land Moods"

GEOFFREY THURLEY. *The Ironic Harvest,* pp. 169-70.

CLEVELAND, JOHN

"A Fair Nymph Scorning a Black Boy Courting Her"

ELLIOT H. TOKSON. "The Image of the Negro in Four Seventeenth-Century Love Poems," *Modern Language Quarterly* 30(4), December 1969, 510-22.

"The Hecatomb to his Mistress"

PAUL J. KORSHIN. "The Evolution of Neoclassical Poetics: Cleveland, Denham, and Waller as Poetic Theorists," *Eighteenth Century Studies* 2(2), December 1968, 108-10.

H. M. RICHMOND. "The Intangible Mistress," *Modern Philology* 56(4), May 1959, 221.

"Square-Cap"

MARGARET FOREY. "Cleveland's 'Square-Cap': Some Questions of Structure and Date," *Durham University Journal,* n.s., 36(2), June 1975, 170-79.

"To Mrs. K. T. who askt him why he was dumb"

DAVID FARLEY-HILLS. *The Benevolence of Laughter,* pp. 28-30.

"To P. Rupert"

PAUL J. KORSHIN. "The Evolution of Neoclassical Poetics: Cleveland, Denham, and Waller as Poetic Theorists," *Eighteenth Century Studies* 2(2), December 1969, 111-12. (P)

CLIFTON, LUCILLE

"For deLawd"

SHERLEY A. WILLIAMS. "The Blues Roots of Contemporary Afro-American Poetry," *Massachusetts Review* 18(3), Autumn 1977, 552-53. (P)

"in the inner city"

SHERLEY A. WILLIAMS. "The Blues Roots of Contemporary Afro-American Poetry," *Massachusetts Review* 18(3), Autumn 1977, 551-52.

"Robert"

SHERLEY A. WILLIAMS. "The Blues Roots of Contemporary Afro-American Poetry," *Massachusetts Review* 18(3), Autumn 1977, 553-54.

CLOUGH, ARTHUR HUGH

"Duty — That's to say complying"

MICHAEL TIMKO. "The Satiric Poetry of Arthur Hugh Clough," *Victorian Poetry* 1(2), April 1963, 109-12.

"Easter Day"

DORIS N. DALGLISH. "Arthur Hugh Clough: The Shorter Poems," *Essays in Criticism* 2(1), January 1952, 40-44.

"Epi-Strauss-ium"

R. A. FORSYTH. "Herbert, Clough, and their Church-Windows," *Victorian Poetry* 7(1), Spring 1969, 17-30.

"Epithalamium"

CONSTANTINE CASTAN. "The Marriage of Epithalamium and Elegy in a Poem by Clough," *Victorian Poetry* 10(2), Summer 1972, 145-59.

"In Stratis Viarum"

BRUCE BERLIND. "A Curious Accomplishment," *Poetry* 82(1), April 1953, 28-30.

"The Judgement of Brutus"

EVELYN BARISH GREENBERGER. "Clough's 'The Judgement of Brutus': A Newly Found Poem," *Victorian Poetry* 8(2), Summer 1970, 129-50.

"Love and Reason"

FREDERICK MULHAUSER, JR. "Clough's 'Love and Reason,'" *Modern Philology* 42(3), February 1945, 174-86.

"Natura Naturans"

WENDELL STACY JOHNSON. *Sex and Marriage in Victorian Poetry,* pp. 80-81.

"Qua Cursum Ventus"

HARRY BROWN and JOHN MILSTEAD. *What the Poem Means,* p. 36.

"Sa Majesté très Chrètienne"

MASAS MIYOSHI. "Clough's Poems of Self-Irony," *Studies in English Literature 1500-1900* 5(4), Autumn 1965, 695-96.

MICHAEL TIMKO. "The Satiric Poetry of Arthur Hugh Clough," *Victorian Poetry* 1(2), April 1963, 112-14.

"Salsette and Elephanta"

EVELYN BARISH GREENBERGER. " 'Salsette and Elephanta': An Unpublished Poem by Clough," *Review of English Studies*, n.s., 20(79), August 1969, 284-305.

"Say Not the Struggle Naught Availeth"

CHARLES W. COOPER and JOHN HOLMES. *Preface to Poetry*, pp. 177-81.

ELIZABETH DREW. *Poetry*, pp. 223-24.

WILLIAM HOWARD. *Explicator* 15(6), March 1957, Item 39.

FRED B. MILLET. *Reading Poetry*, pp. 17-18; second ed., pp. 15-16.

"To the Great Metropolis"

MICHAEL TIMKO. "The Satiric Poetry of Arthur Hugh Clough," *Victorian Poetry* 1(2), April 1963, 108-9.

"Why should I say I see the things I see not?"

R. A. FORSYTH. " 'The Buried Life' — The Contrasting Views of Arnold and Clough in the Context of Dr. Arnold's Historiography," *ELH* 35(2), June 1968, 247-53.

BARBARA HARDY. "Clough's Self-Consciousness," in *The Major Victorian Poets*, pp. 257-59. Reprinted in: Barbara Hardy. *The Advantage of Lyric*, pp. 37-39.

COHEN, LEONARD

"Go by brooks, love"

DON GUTTERIDGE. "The Affective Fallacy and the Student's Response to Poetry," *English Journal* 61(2), February 1972, 217-21.

"Suzanne Takes You Down"

RUSSELL M. BROWN. " 'Suzanne' in the Classroom," *CEA Critic* 40(3), March 1978, 19-23.

COLERIDGE, HARTLEY

" 'Tis strange to me, who long have seen no face"

JAMES REEVES and MARTIN SEYMOUR-SMITH. *Inside Poetry*, pp. 7-9.

COLERIDGE, SAMUEL TAYLOR

"Anthem for the Children of Christ's Hospital"

DAVID B. EAKIN. "Coleridge's Early Poetry: Toward an Articulation in 'The Eolian Harp,' " *Concerning Poetry* 11(2), Fall 1978, 84.

"The Ballad of the Dark Ladié"

HEATHER DUBROW OUSBY. *Explicator* 35(1), Fall 1976, 21-22. (P)

"Christabel"

DOUGLAS ANGUS. "The Theme of Love and Guilt in Coleridge's Three Major Poems," *Journal of English and Germanic Philology* 59(4), October 1960, 655-63.

PATRICIA M. BALL. *The Central Self*, pp. 98-100.

ROY P. BASLER. "Christabel," *Sewanee Review* 51(1), Winter 1943, 73-95.

ROY P. BASLER. *Sex, Symbolism, and Psychology in Literature*, pp. 25-51.

LAWRENCE D. BERKOBEN. "*Christabel*: A Variety of Evil Experience," *Modern Language Quarterly* 25(4), December 1964, 400-11.

HAROLD BLOOM. *The Visionary Company*, pp. 206-11.

EDWARD E. BOSTETTER. *The Romantic Ventriloquists*, pp. 118-32.

ELIZABETH CHADWICK. "Coleridge's Headlong Horsemen: Insinuating the Supernatural," *Wordsworth Circle* 8(1), Winter 1977, 47-55.

MACDONALD EMSLIE and PAUL EDWARDS. "The Limitations of Langdale: A Reading of *Christabel*," *Essays in Criticism* 20(1), January 1970, 57-70.

WENDY STALLARD FLORY. "Fathers and Daughters: Coleridge and 'Christabel,' " *Women & Literature* 3(1), Spring 1975, 5-15.

MICHAEL E. HOLSTEIN. "Coleridge's *Christabel* as Psychodrama; Five Perspectives on the Intruder," *Wordsworth Circle* 7(2), Spring 1976, 119-28.

HUMPHRY HOUSE. " 'Kubla Khan', *Christabel* and 'Dejection,' " in *British Romantic Poets*, pp. 126-33. Reprinted in: *Romanticism and Consciousness*, pp. 311-18.

GERALD B. KAUVAR. "The Psychological Structure of English Romantic Poetry," *Psychoanalytic Review* 64(1), Spring 1977, 34-37.

G. WILSON KNIGHT. *The Starlit Dome*, pp. 83-84. Reprinted in: *English Romantic Poets*, pp. 158-59.

KARL KROEBER. *Romantic Narrative Art*, pp. 64-68.

ROSEMARIE MAIER. "The Bitch and the Bloodhound: Generic Similarity in 'Christabel' and 'The Eve of St. Agnes,' " *Journal of English and Germanic Philology* 70(1), January 1971, 62-75.

ARTHUR H. NETHERCOT. "Coleridge's 'Christabel' and LeFanu's 'Carmilla,' " *Modern Philology* 47(1), August 1949, 32-38.

TERRY OTTEN. "Christabel, Beatrice, and the Encounter With Evil," *Bucknell Review* 17(2), May 1969, 19-31.

H. W. PIPER. "The Disunity of *Christabel* and the Fall of Nature," *Essays in Criticism* 28(3), July 1978, 216-27.

THOMAS R. PRESTON. "*Christabel* and the Mystical Tradition," in *Essays and Studies in Language and Literature*, pp. 138-57.

VIRGINIA L. RADLEY. "*Christabel*: Directions Old and New," *Studies in English Literature 1500-1900* 4(4), Autumn 1964, 531-41.

RAYMOND SMITH. "Christabel and Geraldine: The Marriage of Life and Death," *Bucknell Review* 13(1), March 1965, 63-71.

JONAS SPATZ. "The Mystery of Eros: Sexual Initiation in Coleridge's 'Christabel'," *PMLA* 90(1), January 1975, 107-16.

EDWARD STRICKLAND. "Metamorphoses of the Muse in Romantic Poesis: *Christabel*," *ELH* 44(4), Winter 1977, 641-58.

CHARLES TOMLINSON. "S. T. Coleridge: Christabel," in *Interpretations*, pp. 103-12.

JAMES TWITCHELL. " 'Desire with Loathing Strangely Mixed': The Dream Work of *Christabel*," *Psychoanalytic Review* 61(1), Spring 1974, 33-44.

J. GARTH WARE. "Coleridge's Great Poems Reflecting the Mother Imago," *American Imago* 18(4), Winter 1961, 334-47.

CARL WOODRING. "Christabel of Cumberland," *Review of English Literature* 7(1), January 1966, 43-52.

ARTHUR WORMHOUDT. *The Demon Lover*, pp. 17-29, 42-47.

"The Complaint of Ninathoma"

LUCYLE WERKMEISTER & P. M. ZALL. "Coleridge's 'The Complaint of Ninathoma,' " *Notes & Queries*, n.s., 16(11), November 1969, 412-14.

"Constancy to an Ideal Object"

FREDERICK L. BEATY. *Light from Heaven*, p. 95.

A. J. HARTLEY. "Frederick Denison Maurice, Disciple and Interpreter of Coleridge: 'Constancy to an Ideal Object,' " *Ariel* 3(2), April 1972, 15-16.

COLERIDGE, SAMUEL TAYLOR *(Cont.)*

"Constancy to an Ideal Object" *(cont.)*

G. WILSON KNIGHT. *The Starlit Dome*, p. 120.

JOHN L. MAHONEY. " 'The Reptile's Lot': Theme and Image in Coleridge's Later Poetry," *Wordsworth Circle* 8(4), Autumn 1977, 359.

GEORGE M. RIDENOUR. "Source and Allusion in Some Poems of Coleridge," *Studies in Philology* 60(1), January 1963, 84-85. (P)

"Dejection: an Ode"

M. H. ABRAMS. "The Correspondent Breeze: A Romantic Metaphor," in *English Romantic Poets*, pp. 38-39.

M. H. ABRAMS. "Structure and Style In the Greater Romantic Lyric," in *From Sensibility to Romanticism*, p. 551. Reprinted in: *Romanticism and Consciousness*, p. 223.

PATRICIA M. BALL. *The Central Self*, pp. 91-93.

EUGENE MARIUS BEWLEY. "The Poetry of Coleridge," *Scrutiny* 8(4), March 1940, 415-20.

ELIZABETH BIEMAN. "Devil's Yule and Mountain Birth: Miltonic Echoes in Coleridge's *Dejection Ode*," *Milton and the Romantics* 2 (December 1976), 16-22.

HAROLD BLOOM. *The Visionary Company*, pp. 216-23.

EDWARD E. BOSTETTER. *The Romantic Ventriloquists*, pp. 132-33.

CHARLES S. BOUSLOG. "Structure and Theme in Coleridge's 'Dejection: An Ode,' " *Modern Language Quarterly* 24(1), March 1963, 42-52.

C. M. BOWRA. *The Romantic Imagination*, pp. 85-93, *passim*.

PANTHEA REID BROUGHTON. "The Modifying Metaphor in 'Dejection: An Ode,' " *Wordsworth Circle* 4(4), Autumn 1973, 241-49.

DAVID DAICHES and WILLIAM CHARVAT. *Poems in English*, pp. 700-1.

W. PAUL ELLEDGE. "Fountains Within: Motivation in Coleridge's 'Dejection: An Ode,' " *Papers on Language and Literature* 7(3), Summer 1971, 304-8.

RICHARD HARTER FOGLE. "The Dejection of Coleridge's Ode," *Journal of English Literary History* 17(1), March 1950, 71-77.

GEOFFREY GRIGSON. *The Harp of Aeolus*, pp. 35-40.

GEORGE MCLEAN HARPER. "Coleridge's Conversation Poems," in *English Romantic Poets*, pp. 154-55.

DAVID HOLBROOK. *Lost Bearings in English Poetry*, pp. 236-41.

HUMPHRY HOUSE. " 'Kubla Khan,' *Christabel* and 'Dejection,' " in *British Romantic Poets*, pp. 133-39. Reprinted in: *Romanticism and Consciousness*, pp. 320-26.

G. WILSON KNIGHT. *The Starlit Dome*, pp. 105-7, *passim*.

BARBARA F. LEFCOWITZ. "Omnipotence of Thought and the Poetic Imagination: Blake, Coleridge, and Rilke," *Psychoanalytic Review* 59(3), Fall 1972, 421-27.

MARY JANE LUPTON. "The Dark Dream of 'Dejection,' " *Literature and Psychology* 18(1), 1968, 39-47.

ABBIE FINDLAY POTTS. *The Elegaic Mode*, pp. 257-59.

SIR HERBERT READ. "Coleridge: Dejection: an Ode," in *Master Poems of the English Language*, pp. 493-98.

I. A. RICHARDS. *Poetries: Their Media and Ends*, pp. 116-19.

ALLAN RODWAY. *The Romantic Conflict*, pp. 164-65, 174-75.

J. L. SIMMONS. "Coleridge's 'Dejection: an Ode': A Poet's Regeneration," *University Review* 33(3), Spring 1967, 212-18.

NEWTON PHELPS STALLKNECHT. "The Doctrine of Coleridge's *Dejection* and Its Relation to Wordsworth's Philosophy," *PMLA* 49(1), March 1934, 196-207.

DONALD R. SWANSON. "The Growth of a Poem: Coleridge's *Dejection*," *Ball State University Forum* 12(4), Autumn 1971, 53-57.

WILLIAM I. THOMPSON. "Collapsed Universe and Structured Poem: An Essay in Whiteheadian Criticism," *College English* 28(1), October 1966, 27-29.

RONALD C. WENDLING. "Dramatic Reconciliation in Coleridge's Conversation Poems," *Papers on Language and Literature* 9(2), Spring 1973, 145-60.

"The Destiny of Nations"

PATRICIA M. BALL. *The Central Self*, pp. 82-83. (P)

G. WILSON KNIGHT. *The Starlit Dome*, pp. 136-43.

"Dura Navis"

DAVID B. EAKIN. "Coleridge's Early Poetry: Toward an Articulation in 'The Eolian Harp,' " *Concerning Poetry* 11(2), Fall 1978, 82-83.

"Duty Surviving Self-Love"

MAX F. SCHULZ. "S. T. Coleridge and the Poem as Improvisation," *Tulane Studies in English* 10 (1960), 91-92.

"The Eolian Harp"

PATRICIA M. BALL. *The Central Self*, pp. 85-86.

FREDERICK L. BEATY. *Light from Heaven*, pp. 86-87.

HAROLD BLOOM. *The Visionary Company*, pp. 194-96.

JAMES D. BOULGER. "Imagination and Speculation in Coleridge's Conversation Poems," *Journal of English and Germanic Philology* 64(4), October 1965, 693-99.

MARSHALL BROWN. "Toward an Archeology Of English Romanticism: Coleridge and Sarbiewski," *Comparative Literature* 30(4), Fall 1978, 313-37.

KENNETH BURKE. *The Philosophy of Literary Form*, pp. 93-98.

DEREK COLVILLE. *Victorian Poetry and the Romantic Religion*, pp. 6-8.

A. HARRIS FAIRBANKS. "The Form of Coleridge's Dejection Ode," *PMLA* 90(5), October 1975, 876-77.

RICHARD HARTER FOGLE. "Coleridge's Conversation Poems," *Tulane Studies in English* 5 (1955), 108-9.

FREDERICK GARBER. "The Hedging Consciousness in Coleridge's Conversation Poems," *Wordsworth Circle* 4(2), Spring 1973, 125-29.

ALBERT GÉRARD. "Counterfeiting Infinity: *The Eolian Harp* and the Growth of Coleridge's Mind," *Journal of English and Germanic Philology* 60(3), July 1961, 411-22.

ALBERT GÉRARD. "The Systolic Rythm: The Structure of Coleridge's Conversation Poems," *Essays in Criticism* 10(3), July 1960, 307-19.

GEORGE H. GILPIN. "Coleridge and the Spiral of Poetic Thought," *Studies in English Literature 1500-1900* 12(4), Autumn 1972, 648-51.

GEORGE MCLEAN HARPER. "Coleridge's Conversation Poems," in *English Romantic Poets*, pp. 147-48.

PAUL A. MAGNUSON. "The Dead Calm in the Conversation Poems," *Wordsworth Circle* 3(2), Spring 1972, 54-56.

WILLIAM H. MARSHALL. "The Structure of Coleridge's 'The Eolian Harp,' " *Modern Language Notes* 76(3), March 1961, 229-32.

C. G. Martin. "Coleridge and Cudworth: A Source for 'The Eolian Harp,'" *Notes & Queries*, n.s., 13(5), May 1966, 173-76.

E. San Juan, Jr. "Coleridge's 'The Eolian Harp' as Lyric Paradigm," *Personalist* 48(1), Winter 1967, 77-88.

William H. Scheuerle. "A Reexamination of Coleridge's 'The Eolian Harp,'" *Studies in English Literature 1500-1900* 15(4), Autumn 1975, 591-99.

Ronald C. Wendling. "Coleridge and the Consistency of 'The Eolian Harp,'" *Studies in Romanticism* 8(1), Autumn 1968, 26-42.

Joseph Whitehill. "Samuel Taylor Coleridge: Prisoner and Prophet of System," *American Scholar* 37(1), Winter 1967/68, 148-49.

Douglas Brownlow Wilson. "Two Modes of Apprehending Nature: A Gloss on the Coleridgean Symbol," *PMLA* 87(1), January 1972, 42-52.

"Fears in Solitude"

George McLean Harper. "Coleridge's Conversation Poems," in *English Romantic Poets*, pp. 151-52.

G. Wilson Knight. *The Starlit Dome*, pp. 130-31, *passim*.

Karl Kroeber. "Coleridge's 'Fears': Problems in Patriotic Poetry," *Clio* 7(3), Spring 1978, 359-73.

Jon Silkin. *Out of Battle*, pp. 6-8.

"France: an Ode"

Harold Bloom. *The Visionary Company*, pp. 215-16.

G. Wilson Knight. *The Starlit Dome*, p. 103.

Jon Silkin. *Out of Battle*, pp. 4-6.

"Frost at Midnight"

M. H. Abrams. "Structure and Style In the Greater Romantic Lyric," in *From Sensibility to Romanticism*, pp. 531-32.

Ronald A. Audet. "'Frost at Midnight': The Other Coleridge," *English Journal* 59(8), November 1970, 1080-85.

Patricia M. Ball. *The Central Self*, pp. 90-91.

Harold Bloom. *The Visionary Company*, pp. 196-99.

James D. Boulger. "Imagination and Speculation in Coleridge's Conversation Poems," *Journal of English and Germanic Philology* 64(4), October 1965, 705-11.

Derek Colville. *Victorian Poetry and the Romantic Religion*, pp. 11-12.

Frederick Garber. "The Hedging Consciousness in Coleridge's Conversation Poems," *Wordsworth Circle* 4(2), Spring 1973, 129-32.

Fred Kaplan. *Miracles of Rare Device*, pp. 44-61.

Robert Langbaum. *The Poetry of Experience*, pp. 45-46.

Paul A. Magnuson. "The Dead Calm in the Conversation Poems," *Wordsworth Circle* 3(2), Spring 1972, 58-60.

Marjorie Perloff. "Yeats and the Occasional Poem: 'Easter 1916,'" *Papers on Language and Literature* 4(3), Summer 1968, 310-11.

Michael G. Sundell. "The Theme of Self-Realization in 'Frost at Midnight,'" *Studies in Romanticism* 7(1), Autumn 1967, 34-39.

Ronald C. Wendling. "Dramatic Reconciliation in Coleridge's Conversation Poems," *Papers on Language and Literature* 9(2), Spring 1973, 145-60.

"The Garden of Boccaccio"

G. Wilson Knight. *The Starlit Dome*, pp. 117-19.

John L. Mahoney. "'The Reptile's Lot': Theme and Image in Coleridge's Later Poetry," *Wordsworth Circle* 8(4), Autumn 1977, 352-53.

George M. Ridenour. "Source and Allusion in Some Poems of Coleridge," *Studies in Philology* 60(1), January 1963, 82-83.

"Hymn Before Sunrise, in the Vale of Chamouni"

L. D. Berkoben. "The Composition of Coleridge's 'Hymn Before Sunrise': Some Mitigating Circumstances," *English Language Notes* 4(1), September 1966, 32-37.

Edward E. Bostetter. *The Romantic Ventriloquists*, pp. 134-35.

G. Wilson Knight. *The Starlit Dome*, pp. 107-9.

Elizabeth Sewell. "Coleridge: The Method and the Poetry," in *The Poet as Critic*, pp. 38-39.

"The Improvisatore"

Max F. Schulz. "S. T. Coleridge and the Poem as Improvisation," *Tulane Studies in English* 10 (1960), 92-99.

"Kubla Khan"

Douglas Angus. "The Theme of Love and Guilt in Coleridge's Three Major Poems," *Journal of English and Germanic Philology* 59(4), October 1960, 655-68.

Patricia M. Ball. *The Central Self*, pp. 100-2.

Raymond Benoit. *Single Nature's Double Name*, pp. 29-40.

James Benziger. *Images of Eternity*, pp. 26-29.

Eugene Marius Bewley. "Revaluations (XII): The Poetry of Coleridge," *Scrutiny* 8(4), March 1940, 411-14. Reprinted in: *Poems and Critics*, pp. 151-54.

Harold Bloom. *The Visionary Company*, pp. 212-15.

Maud Bodkin. *Archetypal Patterns in Poetry*, pp. 90-115.

Edward E. Bostetter. *The Romantic Ventriloquists*, pp. 84-91.

Bernard R. Breyer. "Towards an Interpretation of *Kubla Khan*," in *English Studies in Honor of James Southall Wilson*, pp. 277-90.

Leslie Brisman. "Coleridge and the Ancestral Voices," *Georgia Review* 29(2), Summer 1975, 472-83.

Leslie Brisman. *Romantic Origins*, pp. 25-33.

Cleanth Brooks, John Thibaut Purser, and Robert Penn Warren. *An Approach to Literature*, third ed., pp. 376-78; fourth ed., pp. 369-72; fifth ed., pp. 462-65.

Cleanth Brooks and Robert Penn Warren. *Understanding Poetry*, third ed., pp. 413-17.

Kenneth Burke. "Coleridge: Kubla Khan: or, A Vision in a Dream," in *Master Poems of the English Language*, pp. 439-64.

Irene H. Chayes. "'Kubla Khan' and the Creative Process," *Studies in Romanticism* 6(1), Autumn 1966, 1-21.

Michael G. Cooke. *The Romantic Will*, pp. 77-78.

A. B. England. "'Kubla Khan' Again: the Ocean, the Caverns, and the Ancestral Voices," *Ariel* 4(4), October 1973, 63-72.

Gerald E. Enscoe. "Ambivalence in 'Kubla Khan': The Cavern and the Dome," *Bucknell Review* 12(1), March 1964, 29-36.

Robert F. Fleissner. "'Kubla Khan' As An Integrationist Poem," *Negro American Literature Forum* 8(3), Fall 1974, 254-56.

COLERIDGE, SAMUEL TAYLOR *(Cont.)*
"Kubla Khan" *(cont.)*

RICHARD HARTER FOGLE. "The Romantic Unity of 'Kubla Khan,'" *College English* 13(1), October 1951, 13-18. Reprinted in: *College English* 22(2), November 1960, 112-16. Also: *The Dimensions of Poetry,* pp. 422-30.

LLOYD FRANKENBERG. *Invitation to Poetry,* pp. 43-48.

A. L. FRENCH. "Purposive Imitation: A Skirmish with Literary Theory," *Essays in Criticism* 22(2), April 1972, 126-28.

NEAL L. GOLDSTIEN. "Coleridge's 'Kubla Khan': Mythic Unity and an Analogue in Folklore and Legend," *Queen's Quarterly* 75(4), Winter 1968, 642-50.

S. K. HENINGER, JR. "A Jungian Reading of 'Kubla Khan,'" *Journal of Aesthetics and Art Criticism* 18(3), March 1960, 358-67.

HUMPHRY HOUSE. "'Kubla Khan,' *Christabel* and 'Dejection,'" in *British Romantic Poets,* pp. 119-26. Reprinted in: *Romanticism and Consciousness,* pp. 305-11.

GERALD B. KAUVAR. "The Psychological Structure of English Romantic Poetry," *Psychoanalytic Review* 64(1), Spring 1977, 31-33.

G. W. KNIGHT. "Coleridge's Divine Comedy," in *English Romantic Poets,* pp. 164-66.

G. W. KNIGHT. *The Starlit Dome,* pp. 90-97, *passim.*

JOHN LIVINGSTON LOWES. "The Sleeping Images," in Walker Gibson, *Poems in the Making,* pp. 95-139.

ALICIA MARTINEZ. "Coleridge, 'Kubla Khan,' and the Contingent," *Concerning Poetry* 10(1), Spring 1977, 59-61.

DOROTHY F. MERCER. "The Symbolism of 'Kubla Khan,'" *Journal of Aesthetics and Art Criticism* 12(1), September 1953, 44-66.

H. W. PIPER. "The Two Paradises in *Kubla Khan,*" *Review of English Studies,* n.s., 27(106), May 1976, 148-58.

ALAN C. PURVES. "Formal Structure in 'Kubla Khan,'" *Studies in Romanticism* 1(3), Spring 1962, 187-91.

KATHLEEN RAINE. "Traditional Symbolism in *Kubla Khan,*" *Sewanee Review* 72(4), Autumn 1964, 626-42. Reprinted in: Kathleen Raine. *Defending Ancient Springs,* pp. 88-104.

ALLAN RODWAY. *The Romantic Conflict,* pp. 172-73.

RICHARD M. ROTHMAN. "A Re-examination of Kubla Khan," *English Journal* 55(2), February 1966, 169-71.

DUANE B. SCHNEIDER. "The Structure of *Kubla Khan,*" *American Notes & Queries,* n.s., 1(5), January 1963, 68-70.

ELISABETH SCHNEIDER. "The 'Dream' of *Kubla Khan,*" *PMLA* 60(3), September 1945, 784-801.

JOHN SHELTON. "The Autograph Manuscript of 'Kubla Khan' and an Interpretation," *Review of English Literature* 7(1), January 1966, 32-42.

EUGENE H. SLOANE. "Coleridge's *Kubla Khan:* The Living Catacombs of the Mind," *American Imago* 29(2), Summer 1972, 97-122.

NATHAN COMFORT STARR. "Coleridge's Sacred River," *Papers on Language and Literature* 2(2), Spring 1966, 117-25.

AGNES STEIN. *The Uses of Poetry,* pp. 255-60.

WARREN STEVENSON. "'Kubla Khan' as Symbol," *Texas Studies in Literature and Language* 14(4), Winter 1973, 605-30.

M. A. TAYLOR. "'Kubla Khan': The Well Ordered Fragment," *CEA Critic* 37(3), March 1975, 8-9.

GEORGE WATSON. "The Meaning of 'Kubla Khan,'" *Review of English Literature* 2(1), January 1961, 21-29.

CARL R. WOODRING. "Coleridge and the Khan," *Essays in Criticism* 9(4), October 1959, 361-68.

"A Letter to — "

FREDERICK L. BEATY. *Light from Heaven,* pp. 89-91.

"Lewti: or the Circassian's Love-Chart"

G. LOUIS JOUGHIN. "Coleridge's *Lewti:* The Biography of a Poem," *Texas Studies in English,* 1943, pp. 66-93.

"Limbo"

HAROLD BLOOM. *The Visionary Company,* pp. 227-30.

DANIEL P. DENEAU. "Coleridge's 'Limbo': A 'Riddling Tale'?" *Wordsworth Circle* 3(2), Spring 1972, 97-105.

"Lines Composed in a Concert Room"

LUCYLE WERKMEISTER. "Some Whys and Wherefores of Coleridge's 'Lines Composed in a Concert Room,'" *Modern Philology* 60(3), February 1963, 201-5.

"Lines to a Young Friend"
see "To a Young Friend"

"Love"

FREDERICK L. BEATY. *Light from Heaven,* p. 89.

"Monody on the Death of Chatterton"

I. A. GORDON. "The Case-History of Coleridge's *Monody on the Death of Chatterton,*" *Review of English Studies* 18(69), January 1942, 49-71.

"Ne Plus Ultra"

HAROLD BLOOM. *The Visionary Company,* pp. 230-31.

JAMES D. BOULGER. "Coleridge: The Marginalia, Myth-Making, and the Later Poetry," *Studies in Romanticism* 11(4), Fall 1972, 304-10.

GEORGE M. RIDENOUR. "Source and Allusion in Some Poems of Coleridge," *Studies in Philology* 60(1), January 1963, 91-94.

"The Nightingale"

PATRICIA M. BALL. *The Central Self,* p. 90.

HAROLD BLOOM. *The Visionary Company,* pp. 199-201.

"Ode on the Departing Year"

LOUISE SHUTZ BOAS. *Explicator* 9(2), November 1950, Item 15. (P)

ARTHUR DICKSON. *Explicator* 9(2), November 1950, Item 15. (P)

WALTER GIERASCH. *Explicator* 8(5), March 1950, Item 34.

G. WILSON KNIGHT. *The Starlit Dome,* pp. 129-30.

GEORGE M. RIDENOUR. "Source and Allusion in Some Poems of Coleridge," *Studies in Philology* 60(1), January 1963, 85-87.

MAX F. SCHULZ. "Coleridge's 'Ode on the Departing Year' and the Sacred Theory of Earth: A Case for Analogical Criticism," *Concerning Poetry* 1(1), Spring 1968, 45-54.

"On Donne's Poetry"

LLOYD FRANKENBERG. *Invitation to Poetry,* pp. 87-88.

"The Pains of Sleep"

LAURENCE LERNER. *An Introduction to English Poetry,* pp. 152-55.

JAMES TWITCHELL. " 'Desire with Loathing Strangely Mixed': The Dream Work of *Christabel*," *Psychoanalytic Review* 61(1), Spring 1974, 35-36.

"The Pang More Sharp than All"

G. WILSON KNIGHT. *The Starlit Dome*, pp. 120-21.

"The Picture"

G. WILSON KNIGHT. *The Starlit Dome*, pp. 116-17, *passim.*

"Quae Nocent Docent"

DAVID B. EAKIN. "Coleridge's Early Poetry: Toward an Articulation in 'The Eolian Harp,' " *Concerning Poetry* 11(2), Fall 1978, 84.

"The Raven"

EDWARD E. BOSTETTER. *The Romantic Ventriloquists*, pp. 108-9.

"Reflections on Having Left a Place of Retirement"

FREDERICK L. BEATY. *Light from Heaven*, p. 87.

ALBERT GERARD. "Clevedon Revisited: Further Reflections on Coleridge's 'Reflections on Having Left a Place of Retirement,' " *Notes & Queries*, n.s., 7(3), March 1960, 101-2.

G. WILSON KNIGHT. *The Starlit Dome*, p. 105.

C. G. MARTIN. "Coleridge and William Crowe's 'Lewesdon Hill,' " *Modern Language Review* 62(3), July 1967, 400-6.

"Religious Musings"

M. H. ABRAMS. "English Romanticism: The Spirit of the Age," in *Romanticism and Consciousness*, p. 105.

EDWARD E. BOSTETTER. *The Romantic Ventriloquists*, pp. 94-96.

G. WILSON KNIGHT. *The Starlit Dome*, pp. 131-36.

A. S. P. WOODHOUSE. *The Poet and His Faith*, pp. 169-70.

"The Rime of the Ancient Mariner"

DOUGLAS ANGUS. "The Theme of Love and Guilt in Coleridge's Three Major Poems," *Journal of English and Germanic Philology* 59(4), October 1960, 655-61.

PATRICIA M. BALL. *The Central Self*, pp. 96-98.

JOSEPH WARREN BEACH. *A Romantic View of Poetry*, pp. 15-22.

FREDERICK L. BEATY. *Light from Heaven*, pp. 250-57.

GEORGE BELLIS. "The Fixed Crime of *The Ancient Mariner*," *Essays in Criticism* 24(3), July 1974, 243-60.

RAYMOND BENOIT. *Single Nature's Double Name*, pp. 23-29.

EUGENE MARIUS BEWLEY. "Revaluations (XII): The Poetry of Coleridge," *Scrutiny* 8(4), March 1940, 406-11. Reprinted in: *The Importance of Scrutiny*, pp. 169-74.

HAROLD BLOOM. *The Visionary Company*, pp. 201-6.

LOUISE SCHUTZ BOAS. *Explicator* 2(7), May 1944, Item 52.

MAUD BODKIN. *Archetypal Patterns in Poetry*, pp. 26-89. Reprinted in: *The Modern Critical Spectrum*, pp. 275-305.

EDWARD E. BOSTETTER. "The Nightmare World of *The Ancient Mariner*," *Studies in Romanticism* 1(4), Summer 1962, 241-54.

EDWARD E. BOSTETTER. *The Romantic Ventriloquists*, pp. 109-18.

JAMES D. BOULGER. "Christian Skepticism In *The Rime of the Ancient Mariner*," in *From Sensibility to Romanticism*, pp. 439-52.

C. M. BOWRA. *The Romantic Imagination*, pp. 51-75. Abridged in: *The Case for Poetry*, pp. 63, 65; second ed., pp. 70-71.

R. L. BRETT. *Reason and Imagination*, pp. 87-107.

LESLIE BRISMAN. "Coleridge and the Ancestral Voices," *Georgia Review* 29(2), Summer 1975, 483-97.

LESLIE BRISMAN. *Romantic Origins*, pp. 33-53.

HARRY BROWN and JOHN MILSTEAD. *What the Poem Means*, pp. 37-38.

A. M. BUCHAN. "The Sad Wisdom of the Mariner," *Studies in Philology* 61(4), October 1964, 669-88.

ALICE CHANDLER. "Structure and Symbol in 'The Rime of the Ancient Mariner,' " *Modern Language Quarterly* 26(3), September 1965, 401-13.

IRENE H. CHAYES. "A Coleridgean Reading of 'The Ancient Mariner,' " *Studies in Romanticism* 4(2), Winter 1965, 81-103.

JOHN CIARDI. *How Does a Poem Mean?* pp. 721-22; second ed., p. 55.

MICHAEL G. COOKE. *The Romantic Will*, pp. 30-39.

HOWARD CREED. " 'The Rime of the Ancient Mariner': A Rereading," *English Journal* 49(4), April 1960, 217-22.

C. C. CUNNINGHAM. *Literature as a Fine Art*, pp. 153-56.

ABE DELSON. "The Symbolism of the Sun and Moon in *The Rime of the Ancient Mariner*," *Texas Studies in Literature and Language* 15(4), Winter 1974, 707-20.

SARAH DYCK. "Perspective in 'The Rime of the Ancient Mariner,' " *Studies in English Literature 1500-1900* 13(4), Autumn 1973, 591-604.

A. E. DYSON and JULIAN LOVELOCK. *Masterful Images*, pp. 175-92.

J. R. EBBATSON. "Coleridge's Mariner and the Rights of Man," *Studies in Romanticism* 11(3), Summer 1972, 171-206.

WILLIAM EMPSON. "The Ancient Mariner," *Critical Quarterly* 6(4), Winter 1964, 298-319.

FRANCES FERGUSON. "Coleridge and the Deluded Reader: 'The Rime of the Ancient Mariner,' " *Georgia Review* 31(3), Fall 1977, 617-35.

LORNE J. FORSTNER. "Coleridge's 'The Ancient Mariner' and the Case for Justifiable 'Mythocide': An Argument on Psychological, Epistemological and Formal Grounds," *Criticism* 18(3), Summer 1976, 211-29.

O. BRYAN FULMER. "The Ancient Mariner and the Wandering Jew," *Studies in Philology* 66(5), October 1969, 797-815.

EDWARD E. GIBBONS. "Point of View and Moral in 'The Rime of the Ancient Mariner,' " *University Review* 35(4), Summer 1969, 257-61.

D. W. HARDING. "The Theme of 'The Ancient Mariner,' " *Scrutiny* 9(4), March 1941, 334-42. Reprinted in: *The Importance of Scrutiny*, pp. 174-81. Also: *Experience Into Words*, pp. 53-71. Abridged in: *The Case for Poetry*, second ed., pp. 71-72.

LYNN H. HARRIS. *Explicator* 6(5), March 1948, Item 32.

HUMPHRY HOUSE. "The Ancient Mariner," in *English Romantic Poets*, pp. 170-95.

LLOYD N. JEFFREY. " 'Human Interest and a Semblance of Truth' in the Slaying of Coleridge's Albatross," *CEA Critic* 30(5), February 1968, 3-5.

GERALD B. KAUVAR. "The Psychological Structure of English Romantic Poetry," *Psychoanalytic Review* 64(1), Spring 1977, 33-34.

COLERIDGE, SAMUEL TAYLOR *(Cont.)*
"The Rime of the Ancient Mariner" *(cont.)*

G. W. KNIGHT. "Coleridge's Divine Comedy," in *English Romantic Poets*, pp. 159-64.

G. W. KNIGHT. *The Starlit Dome*, pp. 84-90.

CHARLES R. LARSON. "Coleridge's Ancient Mariner and the Skinner Box," *CEA Critic* 37(1), November 1974, 21-22.

MARK LITTMANN. "*The Ancient Mariner* and Initiation Rites," *Papers on Language and Literature* 4(4), Fall 1968, 370-89.

MARY JANE LUPTON. "'The Rime of the Ancient Mariner': The Agony of Thirst," *American Imago* 27(2), Summer 1970, 140-59.

DANIEL MCDONALD. "Too Much Reality: A Discussion of 'The Rime of the Ancient Mariner,'" *Studies in English Literature 1500-1900* 4(4), Autumn 1964, 543-54.

B. R. MCELDERRY, JR. "Coleridge's Revision of 'The Ancient Mariner,'" *Studies in Philology* 29(1), January 1932, 68-94.

FLORENCE MARSH. "The Ocean-Desert: *The Ancient Mariner* and *The Waste Land*," *Essays in Criticism* 9(2), April 1959, 126-33.

WILLIAM H. MARSHALL. "Coleridge, The Mariner, and Dramatic Irony," *The Personalist* 42(4), Autumn 1961, 524-32.

CHARLES E. MAY. "Objectifying the Nightmare: Cain and the Mariner," *Ball State University Forum* 14(4), Autumn 1973, 45-48.

RAIMONDA MODIANO. "Words and 'Languageless' Meanings: Limits of Expression in *The Rime of the Ancient Mariner*," *Modern Language Quarterly* 38(1), March 1977, 40-61.

ELIZABETH NITCHIE. "The Moral of the *Ancient Mariner* Reconsidered," *PMLA* 48(3), September 1933, 867-76.

ELDER OLSON. "A Symbolic Reading of the *Ancient Mariner*," in *Critics and Criticism*, pp. 138-44. Abridged in: *The Case for Poetry*, first ed., p. 67.

CHARLES A. OWEN, JR. "Structure in *The Ancient Mariner*," *College English* 23(4), January 1962, 261-67. Abridged in: *The Case for Poetry*, second ed., pp. 73-74.

WARD PAFFORD. "Coleridge's Wedding-Guest," *Studies in Philology* 60(4), October 1963, 618-26.

MORSE PECKHAM. "Toward a Theory of Romanticism," in *British Romantic Poets*, pp. 16-17.

J. W. R. PURSER. "Interpretation of *The Ancient Mariner*," *Review of English Studies*, n.s., 8(31), August 1957, 249-56.

ALLAN RODWAY. *The Romantic Conflict*, pp. 167-72.

GEORG ROPPEN and RICHARD SOMMER. *Strangers and Pilgrims*, pp. 172-208.

MAREN-SOFIE RØSTVIG. "'The Rime of the Ancient Mariner' and the Cosmic System of Robert Fludd," *Tennessee Studies in Literature* 12 (1967), 69-81.

CHARLES RICHARD SANDERS. "The *Ancient Mariner* and Coleridge's Theory of Poetic Art," in *Romantic and Victorian*, pp. 110-28.

ELIZABETH SEWELL. *The Structure of Poetry*, pp. 178-82.

GAYLE S. SMITH. "A Reappraisal of the Moral Stanzas in *The Rime of the Ancient Mariner*," *Studies in Romanticism* 3(1), Autumn 1963, 42-52.

LIONEL STEVENSON. "'The Ancient Mariner' as a Dramatic Monologue," *Personalist* 30(1), Winter 1949, 34-44. Abridged in: *The Case for Poetry*, pp. 67, 69; second ed., pp. 72-73.

ELMER EDGAR STOLL. "Symbolism in Coleridge," *PMLA* 63(1), March 1948, 214-29. Reprinted in: *English Romantic Poets*, pp. 102-18.

MILTON TEICHMAN. "The Marriage Metaphor in the *Rime of the Ancient Mariner*," *New York Public Library Bulletin* 73(1), January 1969, 40-48.

E. M. W. TILLYARD. "Coleridge: The Rime of the Ancient Mariner," in *Master Poems of the English Language*, pp. 483-88.

E. M. W. TILLYARD. *Five Poems, 1470-1870*, pp. 66-86. Reprinted in: *The Dimensions of Poetry*, pp. 416-22.

JAMES TWITCHELL. "The World above the Ancient Mariner," *Texas Studies in Literature and Language* 17(1), Spring 1975, 103-17.

LEON WALDOFF. "The Quest for Father and Identity in 'The Rime of the Ancient Mariner,'" *Psychoanalytic Review* 58(3), 1971, 439-53.

J. GARTH WARE. "Coleridge's Great Poems Reflecting the Mother Imago," *American Imago* 18(4), Winter 1961, 348-51.

MALCOLM WARE. "*The Rime of the Ancient Mariner*: A Discourse on Prayer?" *Review of English Studies*, n.s., 11(43), August 1960, 303-4.

ROBERT PENN WARREN. "A Poem of Pure Imagination (Reconsiderations VI)," *Kenyon Review* 8(3), Summer 1946, 391-427. Abridged in: *The Case for Poetry*, pp. 65, 67.

GEORGE WHALLEY. "The Mariner and the Albatross," *University of Toronto Quarterly* 16(4), July 1947, 381-98.

STEWART C. WILCOX. "The Water Imagery of the Ancient Mariner," *Personalist* 35(3), Summer 1954, 285-92.

CARL WOODRING. "The Mariner's Return," *Studies in Romanticism* 11(4), Fall 1972, 375-80.

ARTHUR WORMHOUDT. *The Demon Lover*, pp. 29-42.

"The Snow-Drop"

G. WILSON KNIGHT. *The Starlit Dome*, pp. 114-15.

LYNA LEE MONTGOMERY. "The Phoenix: Its Use as a Literary Device in English from the Seventeenth Century to the Twentieth Century," *D. H. Lawrence Review* 5(3), Fall 1972, 296-97.

"Sonnet to the Autumn Moon"

DAVID B. EAKIN. "Coleridge's Early Poetry: Toward an Articulation in 'The Eolian Harp,'" *Concerning Poetry* 11(2), Fall 1978, 83-84.

"A Stranger Minstrel"

G. WILSON KNIGHT. *The Starlit Dome*, p. 114.

"This Lime-Tree Bower My Prison"

JAMES D. BOULGER. "Imagination and Speculation in Coleridge's Conversation Poems," *Journal of English and Germanic Philology* 64(4), October 1965, 699-705.

DEREK COLVILLE. *Victorian Poetry and the Romantic Religion*, pp. 8-10.

R. A. DURR. "'This Lime-Tree Bower My Prison' and a Recurrent Action in Coleridge," *Journal of English Literary History* 26(4), December 1959, 515-30.

FREDERICK GARBER. "The Hedging Consciousness in Coleridge's Conversation Poems," *Wordsworth Circle* 4(2), Spring 1973, 133-36.

A. Gérard. "The Systolic Rhythm: The Structure of Coleridge's Conversation Poems," *Essays in Criticism* 10(3), July 1960, 316-17.

George H. Gilpin. "Coleridge and the Spiral of Poetic Thought," *Studies in English Literature 1500-1900* 12(4), Autumn 1972, 647-48.

George McLean Harper. "Coleridge's Conversation Poems," in *English Romantic Poets*, pp. 149-50.

Paul A. Magnuson. "The Dead Calm in the Conversation Poems," *Wordsworth Circle* 3(2), Spring 1972, 56-58.

Ronald C. Wendling. "Dramatic Reconciliation in Coleridge's Conversation Poems," *Papers on Language and Literature* 9(2), Spring 1973, 145-60.

"The Three Graves"

Edward E. Bostetter. *The Romantic Ventriloquists*, pp. 104-8.

"Time, Real and Imaginary"

John R. Byers, Jr. *Explicator* 19(7), April 1961, Item 46.

F. H. Heidbrink. *Explicator* 3(1), October 1944, Item 4.

A. A. Raven. *Explicator* 3(4), February 1945, Item 33.

"To a Young Ass"

Patricia M. Ball. *The Central Self*, pp. 83-84.

Frederick L. Beaty. *Light from Heaven*, pp. 245-46.

Leah Sinanglou Marcus. "Vaughan, Wordsworth, Coleridge and the *Encomium Asini*," *ELH* 42(2), Summer 1975, 231-34.

"To a Young Friend"

Patricia M. Ball. *The Central Self*, pp. 89-90.

G. Wilson Knight. *The Starlit Dome*, pp. 104-5.

"To the Author of Poems"

G. Wilson Knight. *The Starlit Dome*, p. 104.

"To the River Otter"

W. K. Wimsatt, Jr. "The Structure of Romantic Nature Imagery," in *The Age of Johnson*, pp. 296-98. Reprinted in: W. K. Wimsatt. *The Verbal Icon*, pp. 108-10. Also: *English Romantic Poets*, pp. 29-30. Also: *Romanticism and Consciousness*, pp. 81-83.

"To W. L. Bowles"

Frederick L. Beaty. *Light from Heaven*, pp. 244-45.

"To William Wordsworth"

Harold Bloom. *The Visionary Company*, pp. 223-27.

A. Reeve Parker. "Wordsworth's Whelming Tide: Coleridge and the Art of Analogy," in *Forms of Lyric*, pp. 75-102.

"Work Without Hope"

John L. Mahoney. "'The Reptile's Lot': Theme and Image in Coleridge's Later Poetry," *Wordsworth Circle* 8(4), Autumn 1977, 357-58.

COLLINS, ANNE

"The Winter of my infancy being over-past"

Stanley Stewart. *The Enclosed Garden*, pp. 106-8.

COLLINS, WILLIAM

"Epistle to Hanmer"

Ricardo Quintana. "The Scheme of Collins's *Odes on Several . . . Subjects*," in *Restoration and Eighteenth-Century Literature*, pp. 373-74.

"Ode on the Death of Mr. Thomson"

Martha Collins. "The Self-Conscious Poet: The Case of William Collins," *ELH* 42(3), Fall 1975, 366.

E. M. W. Tillyard. "William Collins's 'Ode on the Death of Thomson,'" *Review of English Literature* 1(3), July 1960, 30-38. Reprinted in: E. M. W. Tillyard. *Essays, Literary & Educational*, pp. 89-98.

"Ode on the Poetical Character"

Harold Bloom. *The Visionary Company*, pp. 3-10.

Martha Collins. "The Self-Conscious Poet: The Case of William Collins," *ELH* 42(3), Fall 1975, 363-66.

John E. Sitter. "Mother, Memory, Muse and Poetry after Pope," *ELH* 44(2), Summer 1977, 324-26.

Patricia Meyer Spacks. "Collins' Imagery," *Studies in Philology* 62(5), October 1965, 719-28.

Patricia Meyer Spacks. *The Poetry of Vision*, pp. 66-74, 210-11.

Leonard Unger and William Van O'Connor. *Poems for Study*, pp. 325-29.

Earl R. Wasserman. "Collins' 'Ode on the Poetical Character,'" *ELH* 34(1), March 1967, 92-115.

A. S. P. Woodhouse. "The Poetry of Collins Reconsidered," in *From Sensibility to Romanticism*, pp. 100-4.

"Ode on the Popular Superstitions of the Highlands of Scotland"

Ricardo Quintana. "The Scheme of Collins's *Odes on Several . . . Subjects*," in *Restoration and Eighteenth-Century Literature*, pp. 374-75.

Patricia Meyer Spacks. "Collins' Imagery," *Studies in Philology* 62(5), October 1965, 731-36.

Patricia Meyer Spacks. *The Poetry of Vision*, pp. 78-82, 211-12.

A. S. P. Woodhouse. "The Poetry of Collins Reconsidered," in *From Sensibility to Romanticism*, p. 123-26.

"Ode to Evening"

Melvin W. Askew. "Form and Process in Lyric Poetry," *Sewanee Review* 72(2), Spring 1964, 288-91.

Harry Brown and John Milstead. *What the Poem Means*, pp. 38-39.

Merle E. Brown. "On William Collins' 'Ode to Evening,'" *Essays in Criticism* 11(2), April 1961, 136-53.

Martha Collins. "The Self-Conscious Poet: The Case of William Collins," *ELH* 42(3), Fall 1975, 362-377, *passim*.

David Daiches. "Collins: Ode to Evening," in *Master Poems of the English Language*, pp. 326-29.

Earl Daniels. *The Art of Reading Poetry*, pp. 360-64.

William Frost. *English Masterpieces*, edited by William Frost, Maynard Mack, and Leonard Dean, vol. 6: *Romantic and Victorian Poetry*, p. 4.

Geoffrey H. Hartman. *Beyond Formalism*, pp. 321-23.

Peter A. Stitt. "William Collins' 'Ode to Evening,'" *Concerning Poetry* 5(1), Spring 1972, 27-33.

"Ode to Fear"

Martha Collins. "The Self-Conscious Poet: The Case of William Collins," *ELH* 42(3), Fall 1975, 362-77, *passim*.

John R. Crider. "Structure and Effect in Collins' Progress Poems," *Studies in Philology* 60(1), January 1963, 58-62.

Patricia Meyer Spacks. "Collins' Imagery," *Studies in Philology* 62(5), October 1965, 729-31.

COLLINS, WILLIAM *(Cont.)*
"Ode to Fear" *(cont.)*
> PATRICIA MEYER SPACKS. *The Poetry of Vision*, pp. 75-78, 209-10.
> A. S. P. WOODHOUSE. "The Poetry of Collins Reconsidered," in *From Sensibility to Romanticism*, pp. 111-12.

"Ode to Liberty"
> JOHN R. CRIDER. "Structure and Effect in Collins' Progress Poems," *Studies in Philology* 60(1), January 1963, 69-72.
> A. S. P. WOODHOUSE. "The Poetry of Collins Reconsidered," in *From Sensibility to Romanticism*, pp. 119-22.

"Ode to Pity"
> MARTHA COLLINS. "The Self-Conscious Poet: The Case of William Collins," *ELH* 42(3), Fall 1975, 362-77, *passim.*
> JOHN R. CRIDER. "Structure and Effect in Collins' Progress Poems," *Studies in Philology* 60(1), January 1963, 58-62.
> PATRICIA MEYER SPACKS. *The Poetry of Vision*, pp. 74-75, 208.

"Ode to Simplicity"
> JOHN R. CRIDER. "Structure and Effect in Collins' Progress Poems," *Studies in Philology* 60(1), January 1963, 62-69.
> PATRICIA MEYER SPACKS. *The Poetry of Vision*, p. 210.
> A. S. P. WOODHOUSE. "The Poetry of Collins Reconsidered," in *From Sensibility to Romanticism*, pp. 108-10.

"Ode, Written in the Beginning of the Year 1746"
> PATRICIA MEYER SPACKS. "Eighteenth-Century Poetry: The Teacher's Dilemma," *College English* 23(8), May 1962, 642-45.

"The Passions"
> MARTHA COLLINS. "The Self-Conscious Poet: The Case of William Collins," *ELH* 42(3), Fall 1975, 362-77, *passim.*

"Verses Humbly Address'd to Sir Thomas Hanmer on His Edition of Shakespear's Works"
> JOHN R. CRIDER. "Structure and Effect in Collins' Progress Poems," *Studies in Philology* 60(1), January 1963, 57-58.

COLONY, HORATIO
"The Flight and Fall of Icarus"
> G. WILSON KNIGHT. *Neglected Powers*, pp. 73-74.

CONGREVE, WILLIAM
"Doris"
> JOHN HAYMAN. "Raillery in Restoration Satire," *Huntington Library Quarterly* 31(2), February 1968, 118-19.

"Song: False though she be to me and love"
> F. W. BATESON. *English Poetry and the English Language*, p. 62.

COOKE, EBENEZER
"An Elegy (on) the Death of the Honourable Nicholas Lowe, Esq."
> EDWARD H. COHEN. "The Elegies of Ebenezer Cooke," *Early American Literature* 4(2), 1969, 52-55.

"The Sot-Weed Factor"
> ROBERT D. ARNER. "The Blackness of Darkness: Satire, Romance, and Ebenezer Cooke's *The Sot-Weed Factor*," *Tennessee Studies in Literature* 21 (1976), 1-10.

CORBET, RICHARD
"The Fairies' Farewell"
> M. E. BRADFORD. "The Prescience of Richard Corbet: Observations on 'The Fairies' Farewell,'" *Sewanee Review* 81(2), Spring 1973, 309-17.
> CLEANTH BROOKS. "The New Criticism and Scholarship," *Twentieth Century English*, 1946, pp. 373-83.

"A Proper New Ballad"
> DAVID DAICHES and WILLIAM CHARVAT. *Poems in English*, p. 656.

CORNFORD, JOHN
"All this half-felt sorrow"
> D. E. S. MAXWELL. *The Poets of the Thirties*, pp. 57-58.

"As Our Might Lessens"
> D. E. S. MAXWELL. *The Poets of the Thirties*, pp. 59-60.

"Heart of the heartless world"
> G. S. FRASER. *Vision and Rhetoric*, pp. 260-61.

"Sad Poem"
> D. E. S. MAXWELL. *The Poets of the Thirties*, pp. 58-59.

"Unaware"
> D. E. S. MAXWELL. *The Poets of the Thirties*, p. 62.

CORSO, GREGORY
"Birthplace Revisited"
> GERALD J. DULLEA. "Ginsberg and Corso: Image and Imagination," *Thoth* 11(2), Winter 1971, 25.

"Marriage"
> GERALD J. DULLEA. "Ginsberg and Corso: Image and Imagination," *Thoth* 11(2), Winter 1971, 25-26.

COTTON, CHARLES
"Bacon's Epitaph, Made by His Man"
> ROY P. BASLER. *Explicator* 2(3), December 1943, Item 20.

"Evening Quatrains"
> M. L. ROSENTHAL and A. J. M. SMITH. *Exploring Poetry*, pp. 636-38; second ed., pp. 458-59.

"To Chloris. Stanzes Irreguliers"
> EARL MINER. *The Cavalier Mode from Jonson to Cotton*, pp. 7-11.

"To my dear and most worthy Friend, Mr. Isaac Walton"
> EARL MINER. *The Cavalier Mode from Jonson to Cotton*, pp. 298-99.

"Winter"
> EARL MINER. *The Cavalier Mode from Jonson to Cotton*, pp. 185-86, 296.

COWLEY, ABRAHAM
"Against Hope"
> GEORGE WILLIAMSON. *Six Metaphysical Poets*, pp. 131-33.

"Bathing in the River"

PRISCILLA HEATH BARNUM. "The Two Angels of Cowley's *The Mistress*," *Thoth* 7(1), Winter 1966, 9-10.

"Clad all in White"

PRISCILLA HEATH BARNUM. "The Two Angels of Cowley's *The Mistress*," *Thoth* 7(1), Winter 1966, 8-9.

GEORGE WILLIAMSON. *Six Metaphysical Poets*, pp. 160-61.

"The Complaint"

GEORGE WILLIAMSON. *Six Metaphysical Poets*, pp. 153-54.

"Destinie"

WILLIAM D. MCGAW. "The Civil War in Cowley's *Destinie*," *English Language Notes* 14(4), June 1977, 268-70. (P)

"For Hope"

GEORGE WILLIAMSON. *Six Metaphysical Poets*, pp. 165-66.

"The Given Love"

GEORGE WILLIAMSON. *Six Metaphysical Poets*, p. 156.

"Hymn: to Light"

MAREN-SOFIE RØSTVIG. "Elaborate song: Conceptual Structure in Milton's 'On the Morning of Christ's Nativity,' " in *Fair Forms*, pp. 77-80.

ALLEN TATE. "Tension in Poetry," *Southern Review* 4(1), Summer 1938, 105-8. Reprinted in: *Critiques and Essays in Criticism*, pp. 57-60. Also: *Essays in Modern Literary Criticism*, pp. 270-72. Also: Allen Tate. *On the Limits of Poetry*, pp. 79-81. Also: Allen Tate. *Reason in Madness*, pp. 67-71. Also: Allen Tate. *Essays of Four Decades*, pp. 60-63. Also: *Poets on Poetry*, pp. 352-55. Also: *The Modern Critical Spectrum*, pp. 85-87.

"Love and Life"

GEORGE WILLIAMSON. *Six Metaphysical Poets*, pp. 159-60.

"The Motto"

GEORGE WILLIAMSON. *Six Metaphysical Poets*, p. 147.

"My Fate"

GEORGE WILLIAMSON. *Six Metaphysical Poets*, pp. 167-68.

"Ode: Here's to Thee Dick"

GEORGE WILLIAMSON. *Six Metaphysical Poets*, pp. 154-55.

"Ode. Of Wit"

PAUL J. KORSHIN. "The Theoretical Bases of Cowley's Later Poetry," *Studies in Philology* 66(5), October 1969, 767-78.

MICHAEL MURRIN. "Poetry as Literary Criticism," *Modern Philology* 65(3), February 1968, 206-7.

"Ode to Brutus"

JAMES G. KEOGH. "Cowley's Brutus Ode: Historical Precepts and the Politics of Defeat," *Texas Studies in Literature and Language* 19(3), Fall 1977, 382-91.

RUTH NEVO. *The Dial of Virtue*, pp. 119-22.

"On Hope"

CLARENCE H. MILLER. "The Order of Stanzas in Cowley and Crashaw's 'On Hope,' " *Studies in Philology* 61(1), January 1964, 64-73.

"On the Death of Mr. Crashaw"

GEORGE WILLIAMSON. *Six Metaphysical Poets*, pp. 170-72.

"On the Death of Mr. William Hervey"

PAUL J. KORSHIN. "The Theoretical Bases of Cowley's Later Poetry," *Studies in Philology* 66(5), October 1969, 759-60.

GEORGE WILLIAMSON. *Six Metaphysical Poets*, pp. 148-49.

"Poem on the Late Civil War"

RUTH NEVO. *The Dial of Virtue*, pp. 37-41.

"The Request"

PRISCILLA HEATH BARNUM. "The Two Angels of Cowley's *The Mistress*," *Thoth* 7(1), Winter 1966, 3-4.

JOSEPHINE MILES. *The Primary Language of Poetry in the 1640's*, pp. 46-48.

"The Rich Rival"

GEORGE WILLIAMSON. *Six Metaphysical Poets*, pp. 164-65.

"The Soul"

GEORGE WILLIAMSON. *Six Metaphysical Poets*, pp. 163-64.

"The Spring"

PRISCILLA HEATH BARNUM. "The Two Angels of Cowley's *The Mistress*," *Thoth* 7(1), Winter 1966, 5-6.

GEORGE WILLIAMSON. *Six Metaphysical Poets*, pp. 157-59.

"The Thief"

GEORGE WILLIAMSON. *Six Metaphysical Poets*, pp. 162-63.

"The Thraldome"

PRISCILLA HEATH BARNUM. "The Two Angels of Cowley's *The Mistress*," *Thoth* 7(1), Winter 1966, 4-5.

"To Mr. Hobs"

PAUL J. KORSHIN. "The Theoretical Bases of Cowley's Later Poetry," *Studies in Philology* 66(5), October 1969, 765-67.

"To Sir William Davenant"

PAUL J. KORSHIN. "The Theoretical Bases of Cowley's Later Poetry," *Studies in Philology* 66(5), October 1969, 760-61.

"To the Royal Society"

PAUL J. KORSHIN. "The Theoretical Bases of Cowley's Later Poetry," *Studies in Philology* 66(5), October 1969, 770-73.

"Upon Liberty"

RUTH NEVO. *The Dial of Virtue*, pp. 125-27.

"The Vain Love"

PRISCILLA HEATH BARNUM. "The Two Angels of Cowley's *The Mistress*," *Thoth* 7(1), Winter 1966, 8.

"A Vote"

GEORGE WILLIAMSON. *Six Metaphysical Poets*, pp. 150-51.

"When God (the Cause to Me and Men Unknown)"

CHARLES LARSON. "The Somerset House Poems of Cowley and Waller," *Papers on Language and Literature* 10(2), Spring 1974, 127-31.

COWLEY, ABRAHAM *(Cont.)*

"The Wish"

ROBERT B. HINMAN. "The Apotheosis of Faust: Poetry and New Philosophy in the Seventeenth Century," in *Metaphysical Poetry*, edited by Malcolm Bradbury and David Palmer, p. 173.

GEORGE WILLIAMSON. *Six Metaphysical Poets*, pp. 161-62.

COWLEY, MALCOLM

"The Long Voyage"

LAURENCE PERRINE. *100 American Poems of the Twentieth Century*, pp. 171-72.

COWPER, WILLIAM

"Boadicea"

ISAAC ASIMOV. *Familiar Poems, Annotated*, pp. 48-54.

"The Castaway"

D. W. HARDING. *Experience Into Words*, pp. 74-76.

LODWICK HARTLEY. *Explicator* 5(3), December 1946, Item 21.

"The Contrite Heart"

PATRICIA MEYER SPACKS. *The Poetry of Vision*, pp. 166-67.

"The Flatting Mill"

THOMAS A. REISNER. *Explicator* 32(3), November 1973, Item 22.

"The Garden"

DAVID BOYD. "Satire and Pastoral in *The Task*," *Papers on Language and Literature* 10(4), Fall 1974, 373-77.

HARRY P. KROITOR. "Cowper, Deism, and the Divinization of Nature," *Journal of the History of Ideas* 21(4), Oct.-Dec. 1960, 516-19. (P)

"Jehovah Our Righteousness"

PATRICIA MEYER SPACKS. *The Poetry of Vision*, pp. 168-69.

"Morning"

RUPIN W. DESAI. "William Cowper and the Visual Arts," *New York Public Library Bulletin* 72(6), June 1968, 360-62.

"On the Receipt of My Mother's Picture"

ALLAN RODWAY. *The Romantic Conflict*, pp. 109-10.

"The Poet, the Oyster, and Sensitive Plant"

ROBERT M. MANIQUIS. "The Puzzling *Mimosa*: Sensitivity and Plant Symbols in Romanticism," *Studies in Romanticism* 8(3), Spring 1969, 142-44.

"The Progress of Error"

HARRY P. KROITOR. "Cowper, Diesm, and the Divinization of Nature," *Journal of the History of Ideas* 21(4), Oct.-Dec. 1960, 524-26. (P)

"The Sofa"

DAVID BOYD. "Satire and Pastoral in *The Task*," *Papers on Language and Literature* 10(4), Fall 1974, 368-71.

"The Time-Piece"

DAVID BOYD. "Satire and Pastoral in *The Task*," *Papers on Language and Literature* 10(4), Fall 1974, 371-73.

"To Mary Unwin"

CLYDE S. KILBY. *Poetry and Life*, pp. 19-25.

"Yardley Oak"

C. N. MANLOVE. *Literature and Reality*, pp. 193-201.

CRABBE, GEORGE

"Abel Keene"

IAN GREGOR. "The Last Augustan: Some Observations on the Poetry of George Crabbe (1755-1832)," *Dublin Review* 229 (First Quarter 1955), 43-46.

"The Natural Death of Love"

LIONEL STEVENSON. "The Death of Love: A Touchstone of Poetic Realism," *Western Humanities Review* 14(4), Autumn 1960, 368-70.

"Peter Grimes"

GAVIN EDWARDS. "The Grimeses," *Essays in Criticism* 27(2), April 1977, 122-40.

LAURENCE LERNER. *An Introduction to English Poetry*, pp. 106-21.

"Procrastination"

IAN GREGOR. "The Last Augustan: Some Observations on the Poetry of George Crabbe (1755-1832)," *Dublin Review* 229 (First Quarter 1955), 49.

"Silford Hall"

CAROLE T. DIFFEY. "Journey to Experience: Crabbe's 'Silford Hall,'" *Durham University Journal*, n.s., 30(3), June 1969, 129-34.

D. N. GALLON. "'Silford Hall or the Happy Day,'" *Modern Language Review* 61(3), July 1966, 384-94.

"The Village"

DAVID DAICHES and WILLIAM CHARVAT. *Poems in English*, pp. 693-94.

IAN GREGOR. "The Last Augustan: Some Observations on the Poetry of George Crabbe (1755-1832)," *Dublin Review* 229 (First Quarter 1955), 38-42.

RONALD B. HATCH. "George Crabbe and the Tenth Muse," *Eighteenth Century Studies* 7(3), Spring 1974, 274-94.

KARL KROEBER. *Romantic Narrative Art*, pp. 115-17.

C. N. MANLOVE. *Literature and Reality*, pp. 180-92.

W. K. THOMAS. "Crabbe's Workhouse," *Huntington Library Quarterly* 32(2), February 1969, 149-61.

CRANCH, CHRISTOPHER

"Ralph Waldo Emerson"

HAZEN C. CARPENTER. "Emerson and Christopher Pearse Cranch," *New England Quarterly* 37(1), March 1964, 37-39.

CRANE, HART

"At Melville's Tomb"

CLEANTH BROOKS and ROBERT PENN WARREN. *Understanding Poetry*, pp. 477-82; revised ed., pp. 333-36; third ed., pp. 320-23; fourth ed., pp. 233-35.

DAVID RIDGLEY CLARK. *Lyric Resonance*, pp. 152-58.

MAX EASTMAN. *The Literary Mind*, pp. 94-97.

PHILIP FURIA. *Explicator* 33(9), May 1975, Item 73.

R. W. B. LEWIS. "Crane's Visionary Lyric: The Way to *The Bridge*," *Massachusetts Review* 7(2), Spring 1966, 239-48.

HARRIET MONROE and HART CRANE. "A Discussion with Hart Crane," *Poetry* 29(1), October 1926, 34-41. (P) Reprinted in: *Readings for Liberal Education*, revised ed., II: 243-48; third ed., II: 229-34; fourth ed., II: 231-36; fifth ed., II: 214-19.

PETER J. SHEEHAN. "Hart Crane and the Contemporary Search," *English Journal* 60(9), December 1971, 1212.

RICHARD STRIER. "The Poetics of Surrender: An Exposition and Critique of New Critical Poetics," *Critical Inquiry* 2(1), Autumn 1975, 182-86.

"Atlantis"

HARRY BROWN and JOHN MILSTEAD. *What the Poem Means*, pp. 46-47.

GLAUCO CAMBON. *The Inclusive Flame*, pp. 164-65.

BABETTE DEUTSCH. *Poetry in Our Time*, pp. 322-24; second ed., pp. 360-61.

KIMON FRIAR and JOHN MALCOLM BRINNIN. *Modern Poetry*, pp. 453-55.

HILTON LANDRY. "Of Prayer and Praise: The Poetry of Hart Crane," in *The Twenties*, edited by Richard E. Langford and William E. Taylor, pp. 22-24.

EUGENE PAUL NASSAR. *The Rape of Cinderella*, pp. 183-89.

SISTER M. BERNETTA QUINN. *The Metamorphic Tradition*, pp. 155-57.

ERIC J. SUNDQUIST. "Bringing Home the Word: Magic, Lies, and Silence in Hart Crane," *ELH* 44(2), Summer 1977, 392-93.

THOMAS A. VOGLER. "A New View of Hart Crane's Bridge," *Sewanee Review* 73(3), Summer 1965, 405-8.

HYATT H. WAGGONER. *American Poets*, p. 506.

HYATT HOWE WAGGONER. *The Heel of Elohim*, pp. 187-90.

YVOR WINTERS. *In Defense of Reason*, p. 597.

"Ave Maria"

HARRY BROWN and JOHN MILSTEAD. *What the Poem Means*, p. 41.

GLAUCO CAMBON. *The Inclusive Flame*, pp. 135-44.

KIMON FRIAR and JOHN MALCOLM BRINNIN. *Modern Poetry*, pp. 451-52.

FREDERICK J. HOFFMAN. *The Twenties*, pp. 230-31; revised ed., pp. 265-66.

EUGENE PAUL NASSAR. *The Rape of Cinderella*, pp. 153-57.

DONALD PEASE. "*The Bridge*: Emotional Dynamics of an Epic of Consciousness," in *The Twenties*, edited by Warren French, pp. 390-91.

SISTER M. BERNETTA QUINN. *The Metamorphic Tradition*, pp. 150-51.

BERNICE SLOTE. "The Structure of Hart Crane's *The Bridge*," *University of Kansas City Review* 24(3), Spring 1958, 234-35.

JOHN UNTERECKER. "The Architecture of *The Bridge*," *Wisconsin Studies in Contemporary Literature* 3(2), Spring-Summer 1962, 11-12.

THOMAS A. VOGLER. "A New View of Hart Crane's Bridge," *Sewanee Review* 73(3), Summer 1965, 383-85.

HYATT HOWE WAGGONER. *The Heel of Elohim*, pp. 174-75.

"Belle Isle"

EVELYN J. HINZ. "Hart Crane's 'Voyages' Reconsidered," *Contemporary Literature* 13(3), Summer 1972, 325-33.

"Black Tambourine"

L. S. DEMBO. "Hart Crane's Early Poetry," *University of Kansas City Review* 27(3), Spring 1961, 183-84.

EDWARD KESSLER. *Explicator* 29(1), September 1970, Item 4.

VICTOR A. KRAMER. " 'The Mid-Kingdom' of Crane's 'Black Tambourine' and Toomer's *Cane*," *CLA Journal* 17(4), June 1974, 486-97.

JAMES L. KUGEL. *The Techniques of Strangeness in Symbolist Poetry*, pp. 101-4.

PETER J. SHEEHAN. "Hart Crane and the Contemporary Search," *English Journal* 60(9), December 1971, 1210-11.

MONROE K. SPEARS. "Hart Crane," in *Six American Poets from Emily Dickinson to the Present*, pp. 205-6.

"The Bottom of the Sea"
    see "Poster"

"The Bridge of Estador"

MAURICE KRAMER. "Hart Crane's 'Reflexes,' " *Twentieth Century Literature* 13(3), October 1967, 134-35.

"The Broken Tower"

MARIUS BEWLEY. "Hart Crane's Last Poem," *Accent* 19(2), Spring 1959, 75-85. Reprinted in: Marius Bewley. *Masks & Mirrors*, pp. 324-38.

KIMON FRIAR and JOHN MALCOLM BRINNIN. *Modern Poetry*, p. 449.

JOSEPH N. RIDDEL. "Hart Crane's Poetics of Failure," in *Modern American Poetry*, edited by Jerome Mazzaro, pp. 272-73.

JOEL SALZBERG. "The Artist Manqué: Tower Symbolism in Melville and Crane," *American Transcendental Quarterly* 29(2), Winter 1976, 55-61.

MONROE K. SPEARS. "Hart Crane," in *Six American Poets from Emily Dickinson to the Present*, pp. 229-30.

ERIC J. SUNDQUIST. "Bringing Home the Word: Magic, Lies, and Silence in Hart Crane," *ELH* 44(2), Summer 1977, 395-96.

M. D. UROFF. "The Imagery of Violence in Hart Crane's Poetry," *American Literature* 43(2), May 1971, 211-13.

HYATT H. WAGGONER. *American Poets*, pp. 497-99.

"C33"

MAURICE KRAMER. "Hart Crane's 'Reflexes,' " *Twentieth Century Literature* 13(3), October 1967, 134.

"Cape Hatteras"

HARRY BROWN and JOHN MILSTEAD. *What the Poem Means*, p. 44.

GLAUCO CAMBON. *The Inclusive Flame*, pp. 151-56.

L. S. DEMBO. "Hart Crane's 'Verticalist' Poem," *American Literature* 40(1), March 1968, 77-81.

LAWRENCE DEMBO. "The Unfractioned Idiom of Hart Crane's *Bridge*," *American Literature* 27(2), May 1955, 207-14.

BREWSTER GHISELIN. "Bridge into the Sea," *Partisan Review* 16(7), July 1949, 683-84.

FREDERICK J. HOFFMAN. *The Twenties*, pp. 235-36; revised ed., pp. 269-71.

HOWARD MOSS. "Disorder as Myth: Hart Crane's *The Bridge*," *Poetry* 62(1), April 1943, 34-41.

EUGENE PAUL NASSAR. *The Rape of Cinderella*, pp. 167-74.

ALBERT VAN NOSTRAND. " 'The Bridge' and Hart Crane's 'Span of Consciousness,' " in *Aspects of American Poetry*, pp. 194-99. Reprinted in: A. D. Van Nostrand. *Everyman His Own Poet*, pp. 75-79.

DONALD PEASE. "*The Bridge*: Emotional Dynamics of an Epic of Consciousness," in *The Twenties*, edited by Warren French, pp. 396-98.

KARL SHAPIRO. "The Meaning of the Discarded Poem," in *Poets at Work*, pp. 111-18.

CRANE, HART *(Cont.)*

"Cape Hatteras" *(cont.)*

BERNICE SLOTE. "The Structure of Hart Crane's *The Bridge*," *University of Kansas City Review* 24(3), Spring 1958, 236.

BERNICE SLOTE. "Views of *The Bridge*," in *Start with the Sun*, pp. 151-54.

F. RICHARD THOMAS. "Hart Crane, Alfred Stieglitz, and Camera Photography," *Centennial Review* 21(3), Summer 1977, 299-300.

THOMAS A. VOGLER. "A New View of Hart Crane's Bridge," *Sewanee Review* 73(3), Summer 1965, 393-95.

HYATT H. WAGGONER. *American Poets*, pp. 502-5.

HYATT HOWE WAGGONER. *The Heel of Elohim*, pp. 177-84.

"Chaplinesque"

BABETTE DEUTSCH. *Poetry in Our Time*, pp. 317-18; second ed., pp. 354-55.

R. W. B. LEWIS. "Hart Crane and the Clown Tradition," *Massachusetts Review* 4(4), Summer 1963, 745-51.

ROBERT L. PERRY. "Critical Problems in Hart Crane's 'Chaplinesque,'" *Concerning Poetry* 8(2), Fall 1975, 23-27.

FRANK PORTER. "'Chaplinesque': An Explication," *English Journal* 57(2), February 1968, 191-92, 195.

PETER J. SHEEHAN. "Hart Crane and the Contemporary Search," *English Journal* 60(9), December 1971, 1211-12.

"Cutty Sark"

GLAUCO CAMBON. *The Inclusive Flame*, pp. 149-51.

BABETTE DEUTSCH. *Poetry in Our Time*, p. 324; second ed., pp. 361-62.

FREDERICK J. HOFFMAN. *The Twenties*, pp. 234-35; revised ed., p. 269.

EUGENE PAUL NASSAR. *The Rape of Cinderella*, pp. 165-67.

DONALD PEASE. "*The Bridge*: Emotional Dynamics of an Epic of Consciousness," in *The Twenties*, edited by Warren French, pp. 395-96.

BERNICE SLOTE. "The Structure of Hart Crane's *The Bridge*," *University of Kansas City Review* 24(3), Spring 1958, 235.

THOMAS A. VOGLER. "A New View of Hart Crane's Bridge," *Sewanee Review* 73(3), Summer 1965, 391-92.

"The Dance"

GLAUCO CAMBON. *The Inclusive Flame*, pp. 147-48.

DAVID RIDGLEY CLARK. *Lyric Resonance*, pp. 174-84.

FREDERICK J. HOFFMAN. *The Twenties*, pp. 233-34; revised ed., pp. 268-69.

JAMES MCMICHAEL. "Hart Crane," *Southern Review*, n.s., 8(2), Spring 1972, 300-9.

HOWARD MOSS. "Disorder as Myth: Hart Crane's *The Bridge*," *Poetry* 62(1), April 1943, 34-35.

EUGENE PAUL NASSAR. *The Rape of Cinderella*, pp. 162-64.

SISTER M. BERNETTA QUINN. *The Metamorphic Tradition*, pp. 158-62.

ERIC J. SUNDQUIST. "Bringing Home the Word: Magic, Lies, and Silence in Hart Crane," *ELH* 44(2), Summer 1977, 383-86.

THOMAS A. VOGLER. "A New View of Hart Crane's Bridge," *Sewanee Review* 73(3), Summer 1965, 389-90.

HYATT HOWE WAGGONER. *The Heel of Elohim*, pp. 175-76.

YVOR WINTERS. *Primitivism and Decadence*, pp. 30-32. Reprinted in: *Criticism*, pp. 298-99. Also: Yvor Winters. *In Defense of Reason*, pp. 44-45.

YVOR WINTERS. "The Significance of *The Bridge*, by Hart Crane or What Are We To Think of Professor X?" in *Modern Poetry*, pp. 233-34.

"Emblems of Conduct"

L. S. DEMBO. "Hart Crane and Samuel Greenberg: What Is Plagiarism?" *American Literature* 32(3), November 1960, 319-21.

"Episode of Hands"

F. RICHARD THOMAS. "Hart Crane, Alfred Stieglitz, and Camera Photography," *Centennial Review* 21(3), Summer 1977, 297-98.

"Eternity"

M. D. UROFF. "The Imagery of Violence in Hart Crane's Poetry," *American Literature* 43(2) May 1971, 209-10.

"The Fernery"

NAT HENRY. *Explicator* 36(4), Summer 1978, 7-9.

ROBERT L. PERRY. "Critical Problems in Hart Crane's 'The Fernery,'" *Explicator* 35(1), Fall 1976, 3-5.

"For the Marriage of Faustus and Helen"

BRUCE BASSOFF. "Rhetorical Pressures in 'For the Marriage of Faustus and Helen,'" *Concerning Poetry* 5(2), Fall 1972, 40-48.

DAVID RIDGLEY CLARK. *Lyric Resonance*, pp. 159-73.

L. S. DEMBO. *Conceptions of Reality in Modern American Poetry*, pp. 136-42.

JOSEPH FRANK. "Hart Crane: American Poet," *Sewanee Review* 57(1), Winter 1949, 155-56.

WILL C. JUMPER. *Explicator* 17(1), October 1958, Item 8.

MAURICE KRAMER. "Hart Crane's 'Reflexes,'" *Twentieth Century Literature* 13(3), October 1967, 134-35.

ROBERT K. MARTIN. "Hart Crane's 'For the Marriage of Faustus and Helen': Myth and Alchemy," *Concerning Poetry* 9(1), Spring 1976, 59-62.

MONROE K. SPEARS. "Hart Crane," in *Six American Poets from Emily Dickinson to the Present*, pp. 219-20.

PHILIP R. YANNELLA. "'Inventive Dust': The Metamorphoses of 'For the Marriage of Faustus and Helen,'" *Contemporary Literature* 15(1), Winter 1974, 102-22.

"Garden Abstract"

SISTER M. BERNETTA QUINN. *The Metamorphic Tradition*, pp. 160-61.

F. RICHARD THOMAS. "Hart Crane, Alfred Stieglitz, and Camera Photography," *Centennial Review* 21(3), Summer 1977, 302.

"The Harbor Dawn"

EDWARD BRUNNER. "'Your Hands Within My Hands Are Deeds': Poems of Love in *The Bridge*," *Iowa Review* 4(1), Winter 1973, 112-18.

KIMON FRIAR and JOHN MALCOLM BRINNIN. *Modern Poetry*, pp. 452-53.

FREDERICK J. HOFFMAN. *The Twenties*, p. 232; revised ed., p. 266.

EUGENE PAUL NASSAR. *The Rape of Cinderella*, pp. 158-59.

JAMES M. REID. *100 American Poems of the Twentieth Century*, pp. 178-80.

ERIC J. SUNDQUIST. "Bringing Home the Word: Magic, Lies, and Silence in Hart Crane," *ELH* 44(2), Summer 1977, 382-83.

THOMAS A. VOGLER. "A New View of Hart Crane's *Bridge*," *Sewanee Review* 73(3), Summer 1965, 385-86.

"The Idiot"

MONROE K. SPEARS. "Hart Crane," in *Six American Poets from Emily Dickinson to the Present*, pp. 228-29.

"In Shadow"

L. S. DEMBO. "Hart Crane's Early Poetry," *University of Kansas City Review* 27(3), Spring 1961, 181-82.

"Indiana"

HARRY BROWN and JOHN MILSTEAD. *What the Poem Means*, p. 43.

EUGENE PAUL NASSAR. *The Rape of Cinderella*, pp. 164-65.

ROY HARVEY PEARCE. *The Continuity of American Poetry*, p. 106.

DONALD PEASE. "*The Bridge*: Emotional Dynamics of an Epic of Consciousness," in *The Twenties*, edited by Warren French, pp. 394-95.

THOMAS A. VOGLER. "A New View of Hart Crane's *Bridge*," *Sewanee Review* 73(3), Summer 1965, 390-91.

"Key West"

KINGSLEY WIDMER. *Explicator* 18(3), December 1959, Item 17.

"Lachrymae Christi"

GLAUCO CAMBON. *The Inclusive Flame*, pp. 170-71.

BARBARA HERMAN. "The Language of Hart Crane," *Sewanee Review* 58(1), Winter 1950, 62-65.

JOSEPH RIDDEL. "Hart Crane's Poetics of Failure," *ELH* 33(4), December 1966, 487-92. Reprinted in: *Modern American Poetry*, edited by Jerome Mazzaro, pp. 288-93.

MARTIN STAPLES SHOCKLEY. "Hart Crane's 'Lachrymae Christi,' " in *Reading Modern Poetry*, pp. 321-28; revised ed., pp. 320-27.

MARTIN STAPLES SHOCKLEY. "Hart Crane's 'Lachrymae Christi,' " *University of Kansas City Review* 16(1), Autumn 1949, 31-36.

M. D. UROFF. "The Imagery of Violence in Hart Crane's Poetry," *American Literature* 43(2), May 1971, 206-7.

PHILIP R. YANNELLA. "Toward Apotheosis: Hart Crane's Visionary Lyrics," *Criticism*, 10(4), Fall 1968, 317-20.

"Legend"

MAURICE KRAMER. "Hart Crane's 'Reflexes,' " *Twentieth Century Literature* 13(3), October 1967, 133-34.

M. D. UROFF. "The Imagery of Violence in Hart Crane's Poetry," *American Literature* 43(2), May 1971, 203-4.

PHILIP R. YANNELLA. "Toward Apotheosis: Hart Crane's Visionary Lyrics," *Criticism* 10(4), Fall 1968, 313-15.

"The Mango Tree"

BERNIE LEGGETT. *Explicator* 32(3), November 1973, Item 18.

MELVIN E. LYON. *Explicator* 25(6), February 1967, Item 48.

"Moment Fugue"

PETER J. SHEEHAN. *Explicator* 31(9), May 1973, Item 78.

F. RICHARD THOMAS. "Hart Crane, Alfred Stieglitz, and Camera Photography," *Centennial Review* 21(3), Summer 1977, 301-2.

"My Grandmother's Love Letters"

L. S. DEMBO. "Hart Crane's Early Poetry," *University of Kansas City Review* 27(3), Spring 1961, 182-83.

"National Winter Garden"
see "Three Songs"

"O Carib Isle!"

KIMON FRIAR and JOHN MALCOLM BRINNIN. *Modern Poetry*, pp. 449-50.

MONROE K. SPEARS. "Hart Crane," in *Six American Poets from Emily Dickinson to the Present*, pp. 227-28.

ERIC J. SUNDQUIST. "Bringing Home the Word: Magic, Lies, and Silence in Hart Crane," *ELH* 44(2), Summer 1977, 393-94.

"Paraphrase"

BEN W. GRIFFITH, JR. *Explicator* 13(1), October 1954, Item 5.

MONROE K. SPEARS. "Hart Crane," in *Six American Poets from Emily Dickinson to the Present*, pp. 212-13.

"Passage"

GENE KORETZ. *Explicator* 13(8), June 1955, Item 47.

MAURICE KRAMER. "Hart Crane's 'Reflexes,' " *Twentieth Century Literature* 13(3), October 1967, 136-38.

R. W. B. LEWIS. "Crane's Visionary Lyric: The Way to *The Bridge*," *Massachusetts Review* 7(2), Spring 1966, 227-32.

M. L. ROSENTHAL. *The Modern Poets*, pp. 177-78.

M. L. ROSENTHAL and A. J. M. SMITH. *Exploring Poetry*, p. 458; second ed., p. 335.

MONROE K. SPEARS. "Hart Crane," in *Six American Poets from Emily Dickinson to the Present*, pp. 211-12.

M. D. UROFF. "The Imagery of Violence in Hart Crane's Poetry," *American Literature* 43(2), May 1971, 208-9.

JOHN R. WILLINGHAM and VIRGINIA MOSELEY. *Explicator* 13(8), June 1955, Item 47.

"Pastorale"

L. S. DEMBO. "Hart Crane's Early Poetry," *University of Kansas City Review* 27(3), Spring 1961, 184-85.

"Possessions"

GLAUCO CAMBON. *The Inclusive Flame*, pp. 169-70.

MONROE K. SPEARS. "Hart Crane," in *Six American Poets from Emily Dickinson to the Present*, pp. 213-15.

ALAN SWALLOW. "Hart Crane," *University of Kansas City Review* 16(2), Winter 1949, 113. (P)

M. D. UROFF. "The Imagery of Violence in Hart Crane's Poetry," *American Literature* 43(2), May 1971, 205-6.

"Poster"

EVELYN J. HINZ. "Hart Crane's 'Voyages' Reconsidered," *Contemporary Literature* 13(3), Summer 1972, 320-23.

CRANE, HART *(Cont.)*

"Praise for an Urn"

L. S. DEMBO. "Hart Crane's Early Poetry," *University of Kansas City Review* 27(3), Spring 1961, 185-86.

MONROE K. SPEARS. "Hart Crane," in *Six American Poets from Emily Dickinson to the Present*, pp. 206-7.

ALAN SWALLOW. "Hart Crane," *University of Kansas City Review* 16(2), Winter 1949, 115. (P)

MARK VAN DOREN. *Introduction to Poetry*, pp. 102-7.

"Proem: To Brooklyn Bridge"

JOSEPH J. ARPAD. "Hart Crane's Platonic Myth: The Brooklyn Bridge," *American Literature* 39(1), March 1967, 80-85.

HARRY BROWN and JOHN MILSTEAD. *What the Poem Means*, pp. 40-41.

EDWARD BRUNNER. " 'Your Hands Within My Hands Are Deeds': Poems of Love in *The Bridge*," *Iowa Review* 4(1), Winter 1973, 105-26.

GLAUCO CAMBON. *The Inclusive Flame*, pp. 132-35.

KIMON FRIAR and JOHN MALCOLM BRINNIN. *Modern Poetry*, pp. 427-28, 450-51.

FREDERICK J. HOFFMAN. *The Twenties*, pp. 229-30; revised ed., pp. 263-65.

HILTON LANDRY. "Of Prayer and Praise: The Poetry of Hart Crane," in *The Twenties*, edited by Richard E. Langford and William E. Taylor, pp. 21-22.

EUGENE PAUL NASSAR. *The Rape of Cinderella*, pp. 146-53.

ROY HARVEY PEARCE. *The Continuity of American Poetry*, p. 104.

SISTER M. BERNETTA QUINN. *The Metamorphic Tradition*, pp. 147-49.

M. L. ROSENTHAL. *The Modern Poets*, pp. 170-73.

ERIC J. SUNDQUIST. "Bringing Home the Word: Magic, Lies, and Silence in Hart Crane," *ELH* 44(2), Summer 1977, 379-80.

JOHN UNTERECKER. "The Architecture of *The Bridge*," *Wisconsin Studies in Contemporary Literature* 3(2), Spring-Summer 1962, 10-11.

THOMAS A. VOGLER. "A New View of Hart Crane's Bridge," *Sewanee Review* 73(3), Summer 1965, 382-83.

HYATT H. WAGGONER. *American Poets*, pp. 501, 505-6.

HYATT HOWE WAGGONER. *The Heel of Elohim*, pp. 171-73.

"Quaker Hill"

GLAUCO CAMBON. *The Inclusive Flame*, pp. 160-61.

FREDERICK J. HOFFMAN. *The Twenties*, p. 237; revised ed., pp. 271-72.

DAVID BULWER LUTYENS. *The Creative Encounter*, pp. 122-23.

EUGENE PAUL NASSAR. *The Rape of Cinderella*, pp. 177-79.

THOMAS A. VOGLER. "A New View of Hart Crane's Bridge," *Sewanee Review* 73(3), Summer 1965, 399-401.

"Recitative"

MAURICE KRAMER. "Hart Crane's 'Reflexes,' " *Twentieth Century Literature* 13(3), October 1967, 135-36.

MONROE K. SPEARS. "Hart Crane," in *Six American Poets from Emily Dickinson to the Present*, pp. 210-11.

M. D. UROFF. "Hart Crane's 'Recitative,' " *Concerning Poetry* 3(1), Spring 1970, 22-27.

M. D. UROFF. "The Imagery of Violence in Hart Crane's Poetry," *American Literature* 43(2), May 1971, 205.

PHILIP A. YANNELLA. "Toward Apotheosis: Hart Crane's Visionary Lyrics," *Criticism* 10(4), Fall 1968, 322-24.

"Repose of Rivers"

DAVID RIDGLEY CLARK. *Lyric Resonance*, pp. 148-51.

R. W. B. LEWIS. "Crane's Visionary Lyric: The Way to *The Bridge*," *Massachusetts Review* 7(2), Spring 1966, 249-53.

EDWARD W. ROSENHEIM, JR. *What Happens in Literature*, pp. 145-58.

M. L. ROSENTHAL. *The Modern Poets*, p. 178.

M. D. UROFF. "The Imagery of Violence in Hart Crane's Poetry," *American Literature* 43(2), May 1971, 214-15.

"The Return"

THOMAS E. SANDERS. *Explicator* 10(3), December 1951, Item 20.

"The River"

JOHN BAKER. "Commercial Sources for Hart Crane's *The River*," *Wisconsin Studies in Contemporary Literature* 6(1), Winter-Spring 1965, 45-55.

GLAUCO CAMBON. *The Inclusive Flame*, pp. 145-47.

FREDERICK J. HOFFMAN. *The Twenties*, pp. 232-33; revised ed., pp. 267-68.

HOWARD MOSS. "Disorder as Myth: Hart Crane's *The Bridge*," *Poetry* 62(1), April 1943, 34.

EUGENE PAUL NASSAR. *The Rape of Cinderella*, pp. 160-62.

DONALD PEASE. "*The Bridge*: Emotional Dynamics of an Epic of Consciousness," in *The Twenties*, edited by Warren French, pp. 393-94.

JAMES M. REID. *100 American Poems of the Twentieth Century*, pp. 173-78.

THOMAS A. VOGLER. "A New View of Hart Crane's Bridge," *Sewanee Review* 73(3), Summer 1965, 388-89.

"Royal Palm"

Z. ZATKIN DRESNER. "Levels of Meaning in Hart Crane's 'Royal Palm,' " *Thoth* 15(1), Winter 1974-75, 29-37.

"The Sad Indian"

JOHN R. SCARLETT. *Explicator* 29(8), April 1971, Item 69.

"Southern Cross"

see also "Three Songs"

SISTER M. BERNETTA QUINN. *The Metamorphic Tradition*, pp. 163-64.

"Sunday Morning Apples"

L. S. DEMBO. "Hart Crane's Early Poetry," *University of Kansas City Review* 27(3), Spring 1961, 186-87.

F. RICHARD THOMAS. "Hart Crane, Alfred Stieglitz, and Camera Photography," *Centennial Review* 21(3), Summer 1977, 304-5.

"Three Songs"

EDWARD BRUNNER. " 'Your Hands Within My Hands Are Deeds': Poems of Love in *The Bridge*," *Iowa Review* 4(1), Winter 1973, 118-26.

GLAUCO CAMBON. *The Inclusive Flame*, pp. 158-60.

LAWRENCE DEMBO. "The Unfractioned Idiom of Hart Crane's *Bridge*," *American Literature* 27(2), May 1955, 214-21.

FREDERICK J. HOFFMAN. *The Twenties*, p. 236; revised ed., p. 271.

HOWARD MOSS. "Disorder as Myth: Hart Crane's *The Bridge*," *Poetry* 62(1), April 1943, 41-42.

EUGENE PAUL NASSAR. *The Rape of Cinderella* pp. 174-77.

DONALD PEASE. "*The Bridge*: Emotional Dynamics of an Epic of Consciousness," in *The Twenties*, edited by Warren French, pp. 398-400.

BERNICE SLOTE. "The Structure of Hart Crane's *The Bridge*," *University of Kansas City Review* 24(3), Spring 1958, 237.

BERNICE SLOTE. "Views of *The Bridge*," in *Start with the Sun*, pp. 158-63.

THOMAS A. VOGLER. "A New View of Hart Crane's Bridge," *Sewanee Review* 73(3), Summer 1965, 395-99.

JOHN R. WILLINGHAM. " 'Three Songs' of Hart Crane's *The Bridge*: A Reconsideration," *American Literature* 27(1), March 1955, 62-68.

"The Tunnel"

HARRY BROWN and JOHN MILSTEAD. *What the Poem Means*, p. 46.

GLAUCO CAMBON. *The Inclusive Flame*, pp. 161-64.

LAWRENCE DEMBO. "The Unfractioned Idiom of Hart Crane's *Bridge*," *American Literature* 27(2), May 1955, 221-24.

BABETTE DEUTSCH. *Poetry in Our Time*, pp. 325-26; second ed., pp. 362-64.

DAVID BULWER LUTYENS. *The Creative Encounter*, pp. 123-24.

EUGENE PAUL NASSAR. *The Rape of Cinderella*, pp. 179-83.

DONALD PEASE. "*The Bridge*: Emotional Dynamics of an Epic of Consciousness," in *The Twenties*, edited by Warren French, pp. 401-3.

SISTER M. BERNETTA QUINN. *The Metamorphic Tradition*, p. 155.

THOMAS A. VOGLER. "A New View of Hart Crane's Bridge," *Sewanee Review* 73(3), Summer 1965, 401-5.

HYATT HOWE WAGGONER. *The Heel of Elohim*, pp. 185-88.

YVOR WINTERS. *In Defense of Reason*, pp. 596-97.

YVOR WINTERS. "The Significance of *The Bridge*, by Hart Crane or What Are We To Think of Professor X?" in *Modern Poetry*, pp. 236-37.

"Van Winkle"

HARRY BROWN and JOHN MILSTEAD. *What the Poem Means*, p. 42.

EUGENE PAUL NASSAR. *The Rape of Cinderella*, pp. 159-60.

SISTER M. BERNETTA QUINN. *The Metamorphic Tradition*, p. 152.

ERIC J. SUNDQUIST. "Bringing Home the Word: Magic, Lies, and Silence in Hart Crane," *ELH* 44(2), Summer 1977, 382-83.

THOMAS A. VOGLER. "A New View of Hart Crane's Bridge," *Sewanee Review* 73(3), Summer 1965, 386-88.

"Virginia"

see "Three Songs"

"Voyages"

HARRY BROWN and JOHN MILSTEAD. *What the Poem Means*, pp. 47-49.

BERNARD DUFFEY. *Poetry in America*, pp. 312-14.

KIMON FRIAR and JOHN MALCOLM BRINNIN. *Modern Poetry*, pp. 455-56.

EVELYN J. HINZ. "Hart Crane's 'Voyages' Reconsidered," *Contemporary Literature* 13(3), Summer 1972, 315-33.

JOHN T. IRWIN. "Naming Names: Hart Crane's 'Logic of Metaphor,' " *Southern Review*, n.s., 11(2), Spring 1975, 284-93.

MAURICE KRAMER. "Six Voyages of a Derelict Seer," *Sewanee Review* 73(3), Summer 1965, 410-23.

H. C. MORRIS. "Crane's 'Voyages' as a Single Poem," *Accent* 14(4), Autumn 1954, 291-99.

M. L. ROSENTHAL. *The Modern Poets*, pp. 179-82.

MONROE K. SPEARS. "Hart Crane," in *Six American Poets from Emily Dickinson to the Present*, pp. 215-19.

PHILIP R. YANNELLA. "Toward Apotheosis: Hart Crane's Visionary Lyrics," *Criticism* 10(4), Fall 1968, 324-33.

"Voyages II"

ROBERT A. DAY. "Image and Idea in 'Voyages II,' " *Criticism* 7(3), Summer 1965, 224-34.

BABETTE DEUTSCH. *Poetry in Our Time*, pp. 319-21; second ed., pp. 357-59.

ELIZABETH DREW and JOHN L. SWEENEY. *Directions in Modern Poetry*, pp. 212-17.

JUDITH S. FRIEDMAN and RUTH PERLMUTTER. *Explicator* 19(1), October 1960, Item 4.

WILLIAM VAN O'CONNOR. *Sense and Sensibility in Modern Poetry*, pp. 73-75.

A. POULIN, JR. *Explicator* 28(2), October 1969, Item 15.

SIDNEY RICHMAN. "Hart Crane's 'Voyages II': An Experiment in Redemption," *Wisconsin Studies in Contemporary Literature* 3(2), Spring-Summer 1962, 65-78.

LEONARD UNGER and WILLIAM VAN O'CONNOR. *Poems for Study*, pp. 637-41.

JAMES ZIGERELL. *Explicator* 13(2), November 1954, Item 7.

"Voyages VI"

LYNA LEE MONTGOMERY. "The Phoenix: Its Use as a Literary Device in English From the Seventeenth Century to the Twentieth Century," *D. H. Lawrence Review* 5(3), Fall 1972, 310-12.

HYATT H. WAGGONER. *American Poets*, pp. 500-1.

CHARLES C. WALCUTT. *Explicator* 4(7), May 1946, Item 53.

"The Wine Menagerie"

GLAUCO CAMBON. *The Inclusive Flame*, pp. 173-75.

R. W. B. LEWIS. "Crane's Visionary Lyric: The Way to *The Bridge*," *Massachusetts Review* 7(2), Spring 1966, 232-39.

JOSEPH RIDDEL. "Hart Crane's Poetics of Failure," *ELH* 33(4), December 1966, 483-87. Reprinted in: *Modern American Poetry*, edited by Jerome Mazzaro, pp. 283-88.

MONROE K. SPEARS. "Hart Crane," in *Six American Poets from Emily Dickinson to the Present*, pp. 208-9.

PHILIP R. YANNELLA. "Toward Apotheosis: Hart Crane's Visionary Lyrics," *Criticism* 10(4), Fall 1968, 320-22.

CRANE, STEPHEN

"Charity, thou art a lie"

GEORGE MONTEIRO. "Stephen Crane and the Antinomies of Christian Charity," *Centennial Review* 16(1), Winter 1972, 95-97.

"I explain the silvered passing of a ship at night"

RUTH MILLER. "Regions of Snow: The Poetic Style of Stephen Crane," *New York Public Library Bulletin* 72(5), May 1968, 335-36.

"I looked here"

RUTH MILLER. "Regions of Snow: The Poetic Style of Stephen Crane," *New York Public Library Bulletin* 72(5), May 1968, 333.

"I saw a man pursuing the horizon"

JOHN CLARK PRATT. *The Meaning of Modern Poetry*, pp. 312, 322, 325, 313.

MAX WESTBROOK. "Stephen Crane's Poetry: Perspective and Arrogance," *Bucknell Review* 11(4), December 1963, 28.

"I was in the darkness"

CLARENCE O. JOHNSON. *Explicator* 34(1), September 1975, Item 6.

"The livid lightnings flashed in the clouds"

RUTH MILLER. "Regions of Snow: The Poetic Style of Stephen Crane," *New York Public Library Bulletin* 72(5), May 1968, 347-48.

MAX WESTBROOK. "Stephen Crane's Poetry: Perspective and Arrogance," *Bucknell Review* 11(4), December 1963, 29-30.

"A man said to the universe"

CHRISTOF WEGELIN. *Explicator* 20(1), September 1961, Item 9.

"A man saw a ball of gold in the sky"

RUTH MILLER. "Regions of Snow: The Poetic Style of Stephen Crane," *New York Public Library Bulletin* 72(5), May 1968, 348-49.

MAX WESTBROOK. "Stephen Crane's Poetry: Perspective and Arrogance," *Bucknell Review* 11(4), December 1963, 28-29.

"A spirit sped"

HYATT H. WAGGONER. *American Poets*, pp. 247-48.

"There was crimson clash of war"

RUTH MILLER. "Regions of Snow: The Poetic Style of Stephen Crane," *New York Public Library Bulletin* 72(5), May 1968, 332.

"Thou art my love"

RUTH MILLER. "Regions of Snow: The Poetic Style of Stephen Crane," *New York Public Library Bulletin* 72(5), May 1968, 346-47.

" 'Truth,' said a traveller"

RUTH MILLER. "Regions of Snow: The Poetic Style of Stephen Crane," *New York Public Library Bulletin* 72(5), May 1968, 337-38.

MAX WESTBROOK. "Stephen Crane's Poetry: Perspective and Arrogance," *Bucknell Review* 11(4), December 1963, 26-28.

"Unwind my riddle"

NEAL J. OSBORN. "The Riddle in 'The Clan': A Key to Crane's Major Fiction," *New York Public Library Bulletin* 69(4), April 1965, 247-58.

" 'What says the sea, little shell?' "

RUTH MILLER. "Regions of Snow: The Poetic Style of Stephen Crane," *New York Public Library Bulletin* 72(5), May 1968, 345-46.

CRAPSEY, ADELAIDE

"Triad"

EARL DANIELS. *The Art of Reading Poetry*, p. 53.

CRASHAW, RICHARD

"Apologie for the precedent Hymne"

A. F. ALLISON. "Crashaw and St. Francois de Sales," *Review of English Studies* 24(96), October 1948, 296-300. (P)

ANTHONY LOW. *Love's Architecture*, p. 149.

"Blessed be the paps which Thou hast sucked"

ROBERT M. ADAMS. *Strains of Discord*, p. 136.

ROBERT MARTIN ADAMS. "Taste and Bad Taste in Metaphysical Poetry: Richard Crashaw and Dylan Thomas," *Hudson Review* 8(1), Spring 1955, 68-69. Reprinted in: *Seventeenth Century English Poetry*, p. 271.

WILLIAM EMPSON. *Seven Types of Ambiguity*, p. 280.

RUSSELL M. GOLDFARB. *Explicator* 19(6), March 1961, Item 35.

HAMISH SWANSTON. "The Second 'Temple,' " *Durham University Journal*, n.s., 25(1), December 1963, 19-20.

"Charitas Nimia, or the Dear Bargain"

GEORGE WILLIAMSON. *Six Metaphysical Poets*, pp. 143-44.

"Death's Lecture at the Funeral of a Young Gentleman"

GEORGE WILLIAMSON. *Six Metaphysical Poets*, pp. 128-29.

"Epiphany Hymn"

see "In the Glorious Epiphany of Our Lord God"

"Epithalamium"

JOHN TYTELL. "Sexual Imagery In The Secular And Sacred Poems of Richard Crashaw," *Literature and Psychology* 21(1), 1971, 22-23.

"The Flaming Heart"

HARRY BROWN and JOHN MILSTEAD. *What the Poem Means*, p. 49.

RICHARD GEHA, JR. "Richard Crashaw: (1613?-1650?) The Ego's Soft Fall," *American Imago* 23(2), Summer 1966, 165-68.

ANTHONY LOW. *Love's Architecture*, pp. 149-52.

MICHAEL MCCANLES. "The Rhetoric of the Sublime in Crashaw's Poetry," in *The Rhetoric of Renaissance Poetry*, pp. 208-10.

LOUIS L. MARTZ. *The Wit of Love*, pp. 124-31.

JOHN TYTELL. "Sexual Imagery in the Secular and Sacred Poems of Richard Crashaw," *Literature and Psychology* 21(1), 1971, 25-26.

"An Hymne for the Circumcision day of our Lord"

ANTHONY LOW. *Love's Architecture*, p. 127.

"A Hymn of the Nativity, sung by the Shepheards"

A. R. CIRILLO. "Crashaw's 'Epiphany Hymn': The Dawn of Christian Time," *Studies in Philology* 67(1), January 1970, 72-73.

MICHAEL MCCANLES. "The Rhetoric of the Sublime in Crashaw's Poetry," in *The Rhetoric of Renaissance Poetry*, pp. 189-98.

LOUIS L. MARTZ. *The Poetry of Meditation*, revised ed., pp. 165-67.

LOUIS L. MARTZ. *The Wit of Love*, pp. 142-47.

EARL MINER. "Wit: Definition and Dialectic," in *Seventeenth Century English Poetry*, revised ed., p. 60.

LYNA LEE MONTGOMERY. "The Phoenix: Its Use as a Literary Device in English From the Seventeenth Century to the Twentieth Century," *D. H. Lawrence Review* 5(3), Fall 1972, 274-76.

KERBY NEILL. "Structure and Symbol in Crashaw's *Hymn in the Nativity*," *PMLA* 63(1), March 1948, 101-13.

GEORGE WILLIAMSON. *Six Metaphysical Poets*, pp. 133-36.

"Hymn to the Name Above Every Name"
see "To the Name Above Every Name, the Name of Jesus"

"A Hymn to the Name and Honor of the Admirable Sainte Teresa"

ROBERT G. COLLMER. "Crashaw's 'Death More Misticall and High,'" *Journal of English and Germanic Philology* 55(3), July 1956, 373-80.

WILLIAM EMPSON. *Seven Types of Ambiguity*, pp. 276-79.

RICHARD GEHA, JR. "Richard Crashaw: (1613?-1650?) The Ego's Soft Fall," *American Imago* 23(2), Summer 1966, 163-65.

ANTHONY LOW. *Love's Architecture*, pp. 146-49.

LOUIS L. MARTZ. *The Wit of Love*, pp. 131-35.

THOMAS R. PRESTON. "*Christabel* and the Mystical Tradition," in *Essays and Studies in Language and Literature*, pp. 141-42.

JOHN TYTELL. "Sexual Imagery in the Secular and Sacred Poems of Richard Crashaw," *Literature and Psychology* 21(1), 1971, 25.

LEONARD UNGER and WILLIAM VAN O'CONNOR. *Poems for Study*, pp. 171-75.

GEORGE WILLIAMSON. *Six Metaphysical Poets*, pp. 138-41.

"In memory of the Vertuous and Learned Lady Madre de Teresa"
see "A Hymn to the Name and Honor of the Admirable Sainte Teresa"

"In the Glorious Epiphanie of Our Lord God"

A. R. CIRILLO. "Crashaw's 'Epiphany Hymn': The Dawn of Christian Time," *Studies in Philology* 67(1), January 1970, 67-88.

ANTHONY LOW. *Love's Architecture*, pp. 120-22.

MICHAEL MCCANLES. "The Rhetoric of the Sublime in Crashaw's Poetry," in *The Rhetoric of Renaissance Poetry*, pp. 189-95, 198-202.

LOUIS L. MARTZ. *The Wit of Love*, p. 142.

GEORGE WILLIAMSON. *Six Metaphysical Poets*, pp. 136-37.

"In the Holy Nativity of Our Lord God"
see "A Hymn of the Nativity, sung by the Shepheards"

"A Letter from Mr. Crashaw to the Countess of Denbigh"

EARL MINER. *The Metaphysical Mode from Donne to Cowley*, pp. 97-98.

RICHARD STRIER. "Crashaw's Other Voice," *Studies in English Literature 1500-1900* 9(1), Winter 1969, 136-48.

GEORGE WILLIAMSON. *Six Metaphysical Poets*, pp. 144-45.

"Love's Horoscope"

GEORGE WILLIAMSON. *Six Metaphysical Poets*, pp. 126-27.

"The Mother of Sorrows"

A. F. ALLISON. "Crashaw and St. Francois de Sales," *Review of English Studies* 24(96), October 1948, 301-2.

"On a prayer booke sent to Mrs. M. R."
see "Prayer. An Ode which was Praefixed to a little Prayer-book given to a Young Gentle-Woman"

"On a Treatise of Charity"
see "Upon the ensuing Treatises"

"On Hope"

CLARENCE H. MILLER. "The Order of Stanzas in Cowley and Crashaw's 'On Hope,'" *Studies in Philology* 61(1), January 1964, 64-73.

GEORGE WILLIAMSON. *Six Metaphysical Poets*, pp. 131-33.

"On the Assumption"

LOUIS L. MARTZ. "The Action of the Self: Devotional Poetry in the Seventeenth Century," in *Metaphysical Poetry*, edited by Malcolm Bradbury and David Palmer, pp. 117-21.

"On the bleeding wounds of our crucified Lord"

ROBERT M. ADAMS. *Strains of Discord*, pp. 134-35. Reprinted in: *Seventeenth Century English Poetry*, pp. 270-71.

FRANK J. FABRY. "Crashaw's 'On the Wounds of Our Crucified Lord,'" *Concerning Poetry* 10(1), Spring 1977, 51-58.

ANTHONY LOW. *Love's Architecture*, pp. 124-27.

"Prayer, An Ode, which was Praefixed to a little Prayer-book given to a Young Gentle-Woman"

ANTHONY LOW. *Love's Architecture*, pp. 153-56.

MICHAEL MCCANLES. "The Rhetoric of the Sublime in Crashaw's Poetry," in *The Rhetoric of Renaissance Poetry*, pp. 189-95, 202-6.

LOUIS L. MARTZ. *The Wit of Love*, pp. 137-39.

MARTIN TURNELL. "Richard Crashaw After Three Hundred Years," *Nineteenth Century and After* 146(870), August 1949, 104-6.

GEORGE WILLIAMSON. *Six Metaphysical Poets*, pp. 141-43.

"Sainte Mary Magdalene"
see "The Weeper"

"Sancta Maria Dolorum"
see "The Mother of Sorrows"

"The Teare"

DUDLEY FITTS. "Crashaw: The Teare," in *Master Poems of the English Language*, pp. 198-200.

"To the Name Above Every Name, the Name of Jesus"

A. R. CIRILLO. "Crashaw's 'Epiphany Hymn': The Dawn of Christian Time," *Studies in Philology* 67(1), January 1970, 69-72.

ANTHONY LOW. *Love's Architecture*, pp. 122-24.

LOUIS L. MARTZ. *The Poetry of Meditation*, pp. 62-64, 331-52.

RICHARD STRIER. "Crashaw's Other Voice," *Studies in English Literature 1500-1900* 9(1), Winter 1969, 148-50.

GEORGE WILLIAMSON. *Six Metaphysical Poets*, pp. 137-38.

CRASHAW, RICHARD *(Cont.)*

"To the Noblest and Best of Ladies, the Countess of Denbigh"

    see "A Letter from Mr. Crashaw to the Countess of Denbigh"

"To the Same Party Council Concerning Her Choise"

    MICHAEL MCCANLES. "The Rhetoric of the Sublime in Crashaw's Poetry," in *The Rhetoric of Renaissance Poetry,* pp. 206-8.

"Upon Mr. Staninough's Death"

    see "Death's Lecture at the Funeral of a Young Gentleman"

"Upon the Bleeding Crucifix"

    see "On the bleeding wounds of our crucified Lord"

"Upon the Body of our Blessed Lord, Naked & Bloody"

    ROBERT M. ADAMS. *Strains of Discord,* pp. 133-34.

    ROBERT MARTIN ADAMS. "Taste and Bad Taste in Metaphysical Poetry: Richard Crashaw and Dylan Thomas," *Hudson Review* 8(1), Spring 1955, 67. Reprinted in: *Seventeenth Century English Poetry,* first ed., pp. 269-70.

    A. ALVAREZ. *The School of Donne,* English ed., pp. 100-2; American ed., pp. 108-10.

    LEE A. JACOBUS. "Richard Crashaw as Mannerist," *Bucknell Review* 18(3), Winter 1970, 84-85.

    ANTHONY LOW. *Love's Architecture,* pp. 127-28.

"Upon the Death of a Gentleman"

    GEORGE WILLIAMSON. *Six Metaphysical Poets,* p. 128.

"Upon the ensuing Treatises"

    GEORGE WILLIAMSON. *Six Metaphysical Poets,* pp. 120-22.

"Upon two green Apricots sent to Cowley by Sir Crashaw"

    GEORGE WILLIAMSON. *Six Metaphysical Poets,* pp. 129-31.

"The Weeper"

    MARC BERTONASCO. "A New Look at Crashaw and 'The Weeper,'" *Texas Studies in Literature and Language* 10(2), Summer 1968, 177-88.

    LELAND CHAMBERS. "In Defense of 'The Weeper,'" *Papers on Language and Literature* 3(2), Spring 1967, 111-21.

    LEE A. JACOBUS. "Richard Crashaw as Mannerist," *Bucknell Review* 18(3), Winter 1970, 81-84.

    ANTHONY LOW. *Love's Architecture,* pp. 133-45.

    STEPHEN MANNING. "The Meaning of 'The Weeper,'" *Journal of English Literary History* 22(1), March 1955, 34-47.

    PAUL A. PARRISH. "Crashaw's Two Weepers," *Concerning Poetry* 10(2), Fall 1977, 47-59.

    JOHN PETER. "Crashaw and 'The Weeper,'" *Scrutiny* 19(4), October 1953, 259-73.

    JOHN TYTELL. "Sexual Imagery in the Secular and Sacred Poems of Richard Crashaw," *Literature and Psychology* 21(1), 1971, 23-24.

    GEORGE WILLIAMS. *Six Metaphysical Poets,* pp. 122-23.

    YVOR WINTERS. *The Anatomy of Nonsense,* pp. 209-10. Reprinted in: Yvor Winters. *In Defense of Reason,* pp. 538-40.

"Wishes. To his (supposed) Mistresse"

    GEORGE WILLIAMSON. *Six Metaphysical Poets,* p. 126.

CREELEY, ROBERT

"After Lorca"

    ROBERT VON HALLBERG. "Robert Creeley and the Pleasures of System," *Boundary 2* 6(3)-7(1), Spring/Fall 1978, 366-67.

"All That Is Lovely in Men"

    SAMUEL MOON. "The Springs of Action: A Psychological Portrait of Robert Creeley (Part 1: *The Whip*)," *Boundary 2* 6(3)-7(1), Spring/Fall 1978, 257-58.

"Anger"

    CYNTHIA DUBIN EDELBERG. "Robert Creeley's *Words*: The Comedy of the Intellect," *Boundary 2* 6(3)-7(1), Spring/Fall 1978, 275-78.

"A Birthday"

    LING CHUNG. "Predicaments in Robert Creeley's *Words," Concerning Poetry* 2(2), Fall 1969, 35.

    CYNTHIA DUBIN EDELBERG. "Robert Creeley's *Words*: The Comedy of the Intellect," *Boundary 2* 6(3)-7(1), Spring/Fall 1978, 269.

"The Business"

    ROBERT VON HALLBERG. "Robert Creeley and the Pleasures of System," *Boundary 2* 6(3)-7(1), Spring/Fall 1978, 368.

"The Conspiracy"

    SAMUEL MOON. "The Springs of Action: A Psychological Portrait of Robert Creeley (Part 1: *The Whip*)," *Boundary 2* 6(3)-7(1), Spring/Fall 1978, 255-56.

"The Crow"

    SAMUEL MOON. "The Springs of Action: A Psychological Portrait of Robert Creeley (Part 1: *The Whip*)," *Boundary 2* 6(3)-7(1), Spring/Fall 1978, 256-57.

"The Dishonest Mailman"

    CHARLES ALTIERI. "The Unsure Egoist: Robert Creeley and the Theme of Nothingness," *Contemporary Literature* 13(2), Spring 1972, 169-70.

"The End"

    ALLEN BARRY CAMERON. " 'Love Comes Quietly': The Poetry of Robert Creeley," *Chicago Review* 19(2), 1967, 95-96.

    SAMUEL MOON. "The Springs of Action: A Psychological Portrait of Robert Creeley (Part 1: *The Whip*)," *Boundary 2* 6(3)-7(1), Spring/Fall 1978, 259.

"Enough"

    CYNTHIA DUBIN EDELBERG. "Robert Creeley's *Words*: The Comedy of the Intellect," *Boundary 2* 6(3)-7(1), Spring/Fall 1978, 280-84.

"The Eye"

    SAMUEL CHARTERS. *Some Poems/Poets,* pp. 93-94.

"The Finger"

    JOHN VERNON. "The Cry of Its Occasion: Robert Creeley," *Boundary 2* 6(3)-7(1), Spring/Fall 1978, 318-27.

"The Flower"

    CHARLES ALTIERI. "The Unsure Egoist: Robert Creeley and the Theme of Nothingness," *Contemporary Literature* 13(2), Spring 1972, 167-68.

    TERRY R. BACON. "Closure in Robert Creeley's Poetry," *Modern Poetry Studies* 8(3), Winter 1977, 234.

    JOHN VERNON. "The Cry of Its Occasion: Robert Creeley," *Boundary 2* 6(3)-7(1), Spring/Fall 1978, 311.

"For Rainer Gerhardt"

SAMUEL MOON. "The Springs of Action: A Psychological Portrait of Robert Creeley (Part 1: *The Whip*)," *Boundary 2* 6(3)-7(1), Spring/Fall 1978, 255.

"For W. C. W."

CHARLES ALTIERI. "The Unsure Egoist: Robert Creeley and the Theme of Nothingness," *Contemporary Literature* 13(2), Spring 1972, 174-75.

CYNTHIA DUBIN EDELBERG. "Robert Creeley's *Words*: The Comedy of the Intellect," *Boundary 2* 6(3)-7(1), Spring/Fall 1978, 285-86.

ROBERT KERN. "Composition as Recognition: Robert Creeley and Postmodern Poetics," *Boundary 2* 6(3)-7(1), Spring/Fall 1978, 225-27.

ARTHUR OBERG. "Robert Creeley: And the Power to Tell *Is* Glory," *Ohio Review* 18(1), Winter 1977, 85-86.

"Hart Crane"

SAMUEL MOON. "The Springs of Action: A Psychological Portrait of Robert Creeley (Part 1: *The Whip*)," *Boundary 2* 6(3)-7(1), Spring/Fall 1978, 259-60.

"I Keep to Myself Such Measures . . ."

CYNTHIA DUBIN EDELBERG. "Robert Creeley's *Words*: The Comedy of the Intellect," *Boundary 2* 6(3)-7(1), Spring/Fall 1978, 269-70.

"I Know a Man"

CHARLES ALTIERI. "The Unsure Egoist: Robert Creeley and the Theme of Nothingness," *Contemporary Literature* 13(2), Spring 1972, 163-64.

SAMUEL MOON. "The Springs of Action: A Psychological Portrait of Robert Creeley (Part 1: *The Whip*)," *Boundary 2* 6(3)-7(1), Spring/Fall 1978, 259.

"The Immoral Proposition"

SAMUEL MOON. "The Springs of Action: A Psychological Portrait of Robert Creeley (Part 1: *The Whip*)," *Boundary 2* 6(3)-7(1), Spring/Fall 1978, 257.

"The Innocence"

ALLEN BARRY CAMERON. " 'Love Comes Quietly': The Poetry of Robert Creeley," *Chicago Review* 19(2), 1967, 97.

"Joy"

CHARLES ALTIERI. "The Unsure Egoist: Robert Creeley and the Theme of Nothingness," *Contemporary Literature* 13(2), Spring 1972, 176.

"The Kind of Act Of"

CID CORMAN. "A Requisite Commitment," *Poetry* 83(6), March 1954, 340-42.

"The Language"

CHARLES ALTIERI. "The Unsure Egoist: Robert Creeley and the Theme of Nothingness," *Contemporary Literature* 13(2), Spring 1972, 176-77.

CYNTHIA DUBIN EDELBERG. "Robert Creeley's *Words*: The Comedy of the Intellect," *Boundary 2* 6(3)-7(1), Spring/Fall 1978, 287-89.

JOHN VERNON. "The Cry of Its Occasion: Robert Creeley," *Boundary 2* 6(3)-7(1), Spring/Fall 1978, 316-18.

"Le Fou"

ROBERT VON HALLBERG. "Robert Creeley and the Pleasures of System," *Boundary 2* 6(3)-7(1), Spring/Fall 1978, 375-76.

"The Lover"

PETER QUARTERMAIN. "Robert Creeley: What Counts," *Boundary 2* 6(3)-7(1), Spring/Fall 1978, 329-30.

"The Operation"

ROBERT VON HALLBERG. "Robert Creeley and the Pleasures of System," *Boundary 2* 6(3)-7(1), Spring/Fall 1978, 377-78.

"The Pattern"

JOHN VERNON. "The Cry of Its Occasion: Robert Creeley," *Boundary 2* 6(3)-7(1), Spring/Fall 1978, 312.

"A Piece"

CYNTHIA DUBIN EDELBERG. "Robert Creeley's *Words*: The Comedy of the Intellect," *Boundary 2* 6(3)-7(1), Spring/Fall 1978, 274-75.

"The Rain"

ARTHUR OBERG. "Robert Creeley: And the Power to Tell *Is* Glory," *Ohio Review* 18(1), Winter 1977, 94-95.

"Return"

ROBERT VON HALLBERG. "Robert Creeley and the Pleasures of the System," *Boundary 2* 6(3)-7(1), Spring/Fall 1978, 371-72.

"The Rhyme"

CHARLES ALTIERI. "The Unsure Egoist: Robert Creeley and the Theme of Nothingness," *Contemporary Literature* 13(2), Spring 1972, 164-65.

"Riddle"

ROBERT F. KAUFMAN. "The Poetry of Robert Creeley," *Thoth* 11(2), Winter 1971, 32-33.

"The Riddle"

SAMUEL MOON. "The Springs of Action: A Psychological Portrait of Robert Creeley (Part 1: *The Whip*)," *Boundary 2* 6(3)-7(1), Spring/Fall 1978, 253.

"The Rocks"

ROBERT F. KAUFMAN. "The Poetry of Robert Creeley," *Thoth* 11(2), Winter 1971, 33-36.

"Some Place"

CYNTHIA DUBIN EDELBERG. "Robert Creeley's *Words*: The Comedy of the Intellect," *Boundary 2* 6(3)-7(1), Spring/Fall 1978, 267-69.

"Something"

ROBERT VON HALLBERG. "Robert Creeley and the Pleasures of System," *Boundary 2* 6(3)-7(1), Spring/Fall 1978, 369-70.

"A Song" ("I had wanted a quiet testament")

ROBERT VON HALLBERG. "Robert Creeley and the Pleasures of System," *Boundary 2* 6(3)-7(1), Spring/Fall 1978, 376-77.

"Stomping with Catullus"

WILLIAM SYLVESTER. "Robert Creeley's Poetics: I know that I hear you," *Boundary 2* 6(3)-7(1), Spring/Fall 1978, 194.

"They"

CHARLES ALTIERI. "The Unsure Egoist: Robert Creeley and the Theme of Nothingness," *Contemporary Literature* 13(2), Spring 1972, 184-85.

"Thinking"

CHARLES ALTIERI. "Placing Creeley's Recent Work: A Poetics of Conjecture," *Boundary 2* 6(3)-7(1), Spring/Fall 1978, 514-19.

"Variations"

CYNTHIA DUBIN EDELBERG. "Robert Creeley's *Words*: The Comedy of the Intellect," *Boundary 2* 6(3)-7(1), Spring/Fall 1978, 270-74.

CREELEY, ROBERT *(Cont.)*

"Waiting"

    SAMUEL CHARTERS. *Some Poems/Poets,* pp. 86-87.

    CYNTHIA DUBIN EDELBERG. "Robert Creeley's *Words:* The Comedy of the Intellect," *Boundary 2* 6(3)-7(1), Spring/Fall 1978, 286-87.

"Walking"

    LING CHUNG. "Predicaments in Robert Creeley's *Words,*" *Concerning Poetry* 2(2), Fall 1969, 32-33.

    CYNTHIA DUBIN EDELBERG. "Robert Creeley's *Words:* The Comedy of the Intellect," *Boundary 2* 6(3)-7(1), Spring/Fall 1978, 267.

"The Way"

    MICHAEL DAVIDSON. "The Presence of the Present: Morality and the Problem of Value in Robert Creeley's Recent Prose," *Boundary 2* 6(3)-7(1), Spring/Fall 1978, 547-48.

"The Whip"

    SAMUEL MOON. "The Springs of Action: A Psychological Portrait of Robert Creeley (Part 1: *The Whip*)," *Boundary 2* 6(3)-7(1), Spring/Fall 1978, 258.

"The Wicker Basket"

    PAUL CARROLL. *The Poem In Its Skin,* pp. 31-38.

"The Window"

    ARTHUR OBERG. "Robert Creeley: And the Power to Tell *Is* Glory," *Ohio Review* 18(1), Winter 1977, 95-96.

"The World"

    SAMUEL CHARTERS. *Some Poems/Poets,* pp. 88-91.

"Words"

    CYNTHIA DUBIN EDELBERG. "Robert Creeley's *Words:* The Comedy of the Intellect," *Boundary 2* 6(3)-7(1), Spring/Fall 1978, 289-91.

"Zero"

    CHARLES ALTIERI. "The Unsure Egoist: Robert Creeley and the Theme of Nothingness," *Contemporary Literature* 13(2), Spring 1972, 182-83.

CROSBY, HARRY

"Sthhe fous on ssu eod"

    VICTOR REED. "Reading a 'Sound Poem' by Harry Crosby," *English Language Notes* 6(3), March 1969, 192-96.

CROSS, JOHN

"Hietaniemi (Heroes' Cemetery — Helsinki)"

    CHAD WELSH. *Doors into Poetry,* pp. 135-37. (Quoting John Cross)

CROWE, WILLIAM

"Lewesdon Hill"

    C. G. MARTIN. "Coleridge and William Crowe's 'Lewesdon Hill,'" *Modern Language Review* 62(3), July 1967, 400-6.

CULLEN, COUNTEE

"After a Visit"

    DAVID F. DORSEY, JR. "Countee Cullen's Use of Greek Mythology," *CLA Journal* 13(1), September 1969, 75-76. (P)

"The Black Christ"

    DAVID F. DORSEY, JR. "Countee Cullen's Use of Greek Mythology," *CLA Journal* 13(1), September 1969, 72-75.

"From the Dark Tower"

    EUGENIA W. COLLIER. "I Do Not Marvel, Countee Cullen," *CLA Journal* 11(1), September 1967, 76-78. Reprinted in: *Modern Black Poets,* pp. 72-74.

    RICHARD LEDERER. "The Didactic and the Literary in Four Harlem Renaissance Sonnets," *English Journal* 62(2), February 1973, 222.

"Gods"

    NICHOLAS CANADAY, JR. "Major Themes in the Poetry of Countee Cullen," in *The Harlem Renaissance Remembered,* p. 107.

"Harlem Wine"

    NICHOLAS CANADAY, JR. "Major Themes in the Poetry of Countee Cullen," in *The Harlem Renaissance Remembered,* pp. 120-21.

"Heritage"

    NICHOLAS CANADAY, JR. "Major Themes in the Poetry of Countee Cullen," in *The Harlem Renaissance Remembered,* pp. 121-25.

    NORMA RAMSAY JONES. "Africa, As Imaged by Cullen & Co.," *Negro American Literature Forum* 8(4), Winter 1974, 264.

    MICHAEL L. LOMAX. "Countee Cullen: A Key to the Puzzle," *Studies in the Literary Imagination* 7(2), Fall 1974, 41-42.

    RONALD PRIMEAU. "Countee Cullen and Keats's 'Vale of Soul-Making,'" *Papers on Language and Literature* 12(1), Winter 1976, 85-86.

"Icarian Wings"

    DAVID F. DORSEY, JR. "Countee Cullen's Use of Greek Mythology," *CLA Journal* 13(1), September 1969, 68-69.

"The Incident"

    NICHOLAS CANADY, JR. "Major Themes in the Poetry of Countee Cullen," in *The Harlem Renaissance Remembered,* pp. 115-16.

    LAURENCE PERRINE. *100 American Poems of the Twentieth Century,* pp. 190-91.

"One Day We Played a Game"

    DAVID F. DORSEY, JR. "Countee Cullen's Use of Greek Mythology," *CLA Journal* 13(1), September 1969, 70.

"The Shroud of Color"

    DAVID F. DORSEY, JR. "Countee Cullen's Use of Greek Mythology," *CLA Journal* 13(1), September 1969, 69-70. (P)

    RONALD PRIMEAU. "Countee Cullen and Keats's 'Vale of Soul-Making,'" *Papers on Language and Literature* 12(1), Winter 1976, 78-80.

"A Thorn Forever in the Breast"

    NICHOLAS CANADAY, JR. "Major Themes in the Poetry of Countee Cullen," in *The Harlem Renaissance Remembered,* pp. 104-5.

"To a Brown Boy"

    NICHOLAS CANADAY, JR. "Major Themes in the Poetry of Countee Cullen," in *The Harlem Renaissance Remembered,* p. 109.

"To Endymion"

    DAVID F. DORSEY, JR. "Countee Cullen's Use of Greek Mythology," *CLA Journal* 13(1), September 1969, 71.

"To John Keats, Poet at Spring Time"

    RONALD PRIMEAU. "Countee Cullen and Keats's 'Vale of Soul-Making,'" *Papers on Language and Literature* 12(1), Winter 1976, 76-77.

"To the Three for Whom the Book"
  DAVID F. DORSEY, JR. "Countee Cullen's Use of Greek Mythology," *CLA Journal* 13(1), September 1969, 71-72.
"Two Poets"
  DAVID F. DORSEY, JR. "Countee Cullen's Use of Greek Mythology," *CLA Journal* 13(1), September 1969, 72.
"The Wise"
  NICHOLAS CANADAY, JR. "Major Themes in the Poetry of Countee Cullen," in *The Harlem Renaissance Remembered*, pp. 111-12.
"Uncle Jim"
  NICHOLAS CANADAY, JR. "Major Themes in the Poetry of Countee Cullen," in *The Harlem Renaissance Remembered*, pp. 116-17.
"Yet Do I Marvel"
  NICHOLAS CANADAY, JR. "Major Themes in the Poetry of Countee Cullen," in *The Harlem Renaissance Remembered*, pp. 114-15.
  DAVID F. DORSEY, JR. "Countee Cullen's Use of Greek Mythology," *CLA Journal* 13(1), September 1969, 70.
  RICHARD LEDERER. "The Didactic and the Literary in Four Harlem Renaissance Sonnets," *English Journal* 62(2), February 1973, 222.

CUMMINGS, E. E.

"all ignorance toboggans into know"
  JOHN F. LYNEN. "Forms of Time in Modern Poetry," *Queen's Quarterly* 82(3), Autumn 1975, 357-59.
"All in green went my love riding"
  WILLIAM V. DAVIS. "Cummings' 'All in Green Went My Love Riding,'" *Concerning Poetry* 3(2), Fall 1970, 65-67.
  WILL C. JUMPER. *Explicator* 26(1), September 1967, Item 6.
  CORA ROBEY. *Explicator* 27(1), September 1968, Item 2.
  BARRY SANDERS. *Explicator* 25(3), November 1966, Item 23.
"among these red pieces of"
  MAX EASTMAN. *The Literary Mind*, pp. 60-62.
  LAURA RIDING and ROBERT GRAVES. *A Survey of Modernist Poetry*, pp. 84-89.
"& sun &"
  PATRICK B. MULLEN. "E. E. Cummings and Popular Culture," *Journal of Popular Culture* 5(3), Winter 1971, 512-13.
"anyone lived in a pretty how town"
  HERBERT C. BARROWS, JR., and WILLIAM R. STEINHOFF. *Explicator* 9(1), October 1950, Item 1. Abridged in: *The Case for Poetry*, p. 95; second ed., pp. 79-80.
  HARRY BROWN and JOHN MILSTEAD. *What the Poem Means*, p. 50.
  ARTHUR CARR. *Explicator* 11(3), November 1952, Item 6. Abridged in: *The Case for Poetry*, first ed., pp. 95-96.
  DAVID R. CLARK. "Cummings' 'anyone' and 'noone,'" *Arizona Quarterly* 25(1), Spring 1969, 36-43. Reprinted in: David Ridgely Clark. *Lyric Resonance*, pp. 187-94.
  JAMES P. DOUGHERTY. "Language as a Reality in E. E. Cummings," *Bucknell Review* 16(2), May 1968, 112-22.

LAURENCE PERRINE. *100 American Poems of the Twentieth Century*, pp. 152-55.
CHARLES L. SQUIER. *Explicator* 25(4), December 1966, Item 37.
R. W. STALLMAN and R. E. WATTERS. "An Interpretation of E. E. Cummings' 'Anyone Lived in a Pretty How Town,'" in *The Creative Reader*, pp. 885-887; second ed., pp. 942-44.
THEO STEINMANN. "The Semantic Rhythm in 'Anyone Lived in a Pretty How Town,'" *Concerning Poetry* 11(2), Fall 1978, 71-79.
EVE TRIEM. "E. E. Cummings," in *Six American Poets from Emily Dickinson to the Present*, pp. 183-84.
ROBERT C. WALSH. *Explicator* 22(9), May 1964, Item 72.
DENNIS WELLAND. "Criticism in Action in the Examination Room," in *Criticism in Action*, pp. 178-87.
"applaws"
  KARL SHAPIRO. "Prosody as the Meaning," *Poetry* 73(6), March 1949, 338-40.
"as if as"
  EVE TRIEM. "E. E. Cummings," in *Six American Poets from Emily Dickinson to the Present*, p. 164.
"(b eLl s? bE"
  JOHN W. CROWLEY. "Visual-Aural Poetry: The Typography of E. E. Cummings," *Concerning Poetry* 5(2), Fall 1972, 52-53.
"because you go away i give roses"
  LAURA RIDING and ROBERT GRAVES. *A Survey of Modernist Poetry*, pp. 60-64.
"The Bigness of Canon"
  see "earth like a tipsy"
"! blac"
  S. V. BAUM. "E. E. Cummings: The Technique of Immediacy," *South Atlantic Quarterly* 53(1), January 1954, 86-88.
"brIght"
  RUSHWORTH M. KIDDER. "'Twin Obsessions': The Poetry and Paintings of E. E. Cummings," *Georgia Review* 32(2), Summer 1978, 365-68.
  ROBERT M. MCILVAINE. *Explicator* 30(1), September 1971, Item 6.
"Buffalo Bill's defunct"
  ADAM BERKLEY and EARL J. DIAS. "Letters to the Editor: Rebuttal and Response," *CEA Critic* 29(6), March 1967, 13-14.
  CLEANTH BROOKS and ROBERT PENN WARREN. *Understanding Poetry*, pp. 296-98; revised ed., pp. 158-60; third ed., pp. 185-87.
  LOUIS J. BUDD. *Explicator* 11(8), June 1953, Item 55.
  EARL J. DIAS. "e.e. cummings And Buffalo Bill," *CEA Critic* 29(3), December 1966, 6-7.
  JAY GURIAN. "The possibility of a Western poetics," *Colorado Quarterly* 15(1), Summer 1966, 75-76.
  JOHN CLARK PRATT. *The Meaning of Modern Poetry*, pp. 158, 161, 167-68, 176-77.
  DAVID RAY. "The Irony of E. E. Cummings," *College English* 23(4), January 1962, 282-90.
  M. L. ROSENTHAL. *The Modern Poets*, p. 148.
"the Cambridge ladies who live in furnished souls"
  WALTER SUTTON. *American Free Verse*, pp. 98-99.

CUMMINGS, E. E. (*Cont.*)

"curtains part)"
>PATRICK B. MULLEN. "E. E. Cummings and Popular Culture," *Journal of Popular Culture* 5(3), Winter 1971, 505-6.

"darling! because my blood can sing"
>LLOYD FRANKENBERG. *Invitation to Poetry*, pp. 280-82.

"death is more than certain"
>NORMAN FRIEDMAN. "Diction, Voice, and Tone: The Poetic Language of E. E. Cummings," *PMLA* 72(5), December 1957, 1057-58.
>LAURA RIDING and ROBERT GRAVES. *A Survey of Modernist Poetry*, pp. 244-47.

"earth like a tipsy"
>WILLIAM R. OSBORNE. *Explicator* 24(3), November 1965, Item 28.

"except in your"
>WILLIAM V. DAVIS. "E. E. Cummings 'Except in Your,'" *English Language Notes* 11(4), June 1974, 294-96.

"f/ebble a blu"
>SISTER MARY DAVID BABCOCK. "Cummings' Typography: An Ideogrammatic Style," *Renascence* 15(3), Spring 1963, 116-17.

"5/derbies-with-men-in-them"
>EVE TRIEM. "E. E. Cummings," in *Six American Poets from Emily Dickinson to the Present*, pp. 184-85.

"floatfloafloflf"
>RICHARD CROWDER. *Explicator* 16(7), April 1958, Item 41.

"goodbye Betty, don't remember me"
>M. L. ROSENTHAL. *The Modern Poets*, pp. 150-51.

"go (perpe) go"
>NAT HENRY. *Explicator* 20(8), April 1962, Item 63.
>EVE TRIEM. "E. E. Cummings," in *Six American Poets from Emily Dickinson to the Present*, p. 165.

"the greedy the people"
>LAURENCE PERRINE. *100 American Poems of the Twentieth Century*, pp. 155-57.

"La Guerre I"
>see "earth like a tipsy"

"the hours rise up putting off stars"
>HARRY BROWN and JOHN MILSTEAD. *What the Poem Means*, p. 53.

"i sing of Olaf glad and big"
>MICHAEL J. COLLINS. "Formal Allusion in Modern Poetry," *Concerning Poetry* 9(1), Spring 1976, 8-9.

"i thank You God for most this amazing"
>HARRY BROWN and JOHN MILSTEAD. *What the Poem Means*, p. 51.

"i will be"
>RICHARD GID POWERS. *Explicator* 28(6), February 1970, Item 54.

"if up's the word; and a world grows greener"
>LAURENCE PERRINE. *100 American Poems of the Twentieth Century*, pp. 150-52.

"If you can't eat you got to"
>JERRALD RANTA. "Palindromes, Poems and Geometric Form," *College English* 36(2), October 1974, 166.

"(im)c-a-t(mo)"
>VINCENT L. HENRICHS. *Explicator* 27(8), April 1969, Item 59.
>JOHN FREDERICK NIMS. *Western Wind*, pp. 431-33.

"in Just-"
>MARVIN FELHEIM. *Explicator* 14(2), November 1955, Item 11.
>C. STEVEN TURNER. *Explicator* 24(2), October 1965, Item 18.

"it's"
>DAVID R. CLARK. *Explicator* 22(6), February 1964, Item 48.
>DAVID RIDGLEY CLARK. *Lyric Resonance*, pp. 195-99.

"Jehovah buried, Satan dead"
>LAURENCE PERRINE. *100 American Poems of the Twentieth Century*, pp. 147-50.

"Jimmie's got a goil/goil/goil/Jimmie"
>PATRICK B. MULLEN. "E. E. Cummings and Popular Culture," *Journal of Popular Culture* 5(3), Winter 1971, 514-15.

"a kike is the most dangerous"
>M. L. ROSENTHAL. "Cummings and Hayes: Mr. Joy and Mr. Gloom," *New Republic* 123(12), 18 September 1950, 18.

"kind)"
>PAUL O. WILLIAMS. *Explicator* 23(1), September 1964, Item 4.

"l(a"
>JAMES DICKEY. *Babel to Byzantium*, p. 103.
>RUSHWORTH M. KIDDER. "An Introduction to the Study of Poetry: Five Assignments," *College English* 34(6), March 1973, 778-79.
>EVE TRIEM. "E. E. Cummings," in *Six American Poets from Emily Dickinson to the Present*, pp. 171-73.
>HYATT H. WAGGONER. *American Poets*, pp. 523-24.
>JAMES E. WHITE. *Explicator* 21(1), September 1962, Item 4.

"let's from some loud unworld's most rightful wrong"
>MARY S. MATTFIELD. *Explicator* 26(4), December 1967, Item 32.

"life boosts herself rapidly at me"
>FRED E. H. SCHROEDER. "Obscenity and Its Function in the Poetry of E. E. Cummings," *Sewanee Review* 73(3), Summer 1965, 474.

"listen my children and you"
>J. HAULE. "E. E. Cummings as Comic Poet: The Economy of the Expenditure of Freud," *Literature and Psychology* 25(4), 1975, 177-80.

"l oo k — pigeons fly ingand"
>THEODORE SPENCER. "Technique as Joy: Observations on the Poetry of E. E. Cummings," *Harvard Wake* 5 (Spring 1946), 26. Reprinted in: *Modern American Poetry*, edited by B. Rajan, pp. 119-20.

"love's function is to fabricate unknowness"
>GERALD LEVIN. *Explicator* 17(3), December 1958, Item 18.

"lucky means finding"
>EDWARD A. LEVENSTON. *Explicator* 34(5), January 1976, Item 36.

"a man who had fallen among thieves"
>GEORGE ABBE. *You and Contemporary Poetry*, revised ed., pp. 95-97.

WALTON BEACHAM. *The Meaning of Poetry*, pp. 281-84.

EDWARD A. BLOOM, CHARLES H. PHILBRICK, and ELMER M. BLISTEIN. *The Order of Poetry*, pp. 96-98.

"may i feel said he"

FRED E. H. SCHROEDER. "Obscenity and Its Function in the Poetry of E. E. Cummings," *Sewanee Review* 73(3), Summer 1965, 476-77.

"MEMORABILIA"

CYNTHIA BARTON. *Explicator* 22(4), December 1963, Item 26.

H. SETH FINN. *Explicator* 29(5), January 1971, Item 42.

CLYDE S. KILBY. *Explicator* 12(2), November 1953, Item 15.

"The Mind's ("

NAT HENRY. *Explicator* 20(6), February 1962, Item 49.

"mr youse needn't be so spry"

PATRICK B. MULLEN. "E. E. Cummings and Popular Culture," *Journal of Popular Culture* 5(3), Winter 1971, 510-11.

"mortals)"

GEORGE HAINES IV. ":: 2 : 1 — The World and E. E. Cummings," *Sewanee Review* 59(2), Spring 1951, 218-21.

EVE TRIEM. "E. E. Cummings," in *Six American Poets from Emily Dickinson to the Present*, pp. 186-88.

"my father moved through dooms of love"

JAMES P. DOUGHERTY. "Language as a Reality in E. E. Cummings," *Bucknell Review* 16(2), May 1968, 114-19.

GEORGE HAINES IV. ":: 2 : 1 — The World and E. E. Cummings," *Sewanee Review* 59(2), Spring 1951, 215-16.

"my sweet old etcetera"

FRED E. H. SCHROEDER. "Obscenity and Its Function in the Poetry of E. E. Cummings," *Sewanee Review* 73(3), Summer 1965, 472-73.

"no man, if men are gods"

LLOYD FRANKENBERG. *Invitation to Poetry*, pp. 73-74.

"no time ago"

NORMAN FRIEDMAN. "Diction, Voice, and Tone: The Poetic Language of E. E. Cummings," *PMLA* 72(5), December 1957, 1058.

"nobody loses all the time"

PATRICK B. MULLEN. "E. E. Cummings and Popular Culture," *Journal of Popular Culture* 5(3), Winter 1971, 517-19.

"nonsun blob a"

ARCHIBALD A. HILL. *Constituent and Pattern in Poetry*, p. 118.

EVE TRIEM. "E. E. Cummings," in *Six American Poets from Emily Dickinson to the Present*, pp. 175-77.

"nor woman"

NAT HENRY. *Explicator* 22(1), September 1963, Item 2.

"the Noster was a ship of swank"

LUTHER S. LUEDTKE. *Explicator* 26(7), March 1968, Item 59.

"o pr"

SHERIDAN BAKER. "Cummings and Catullus," *Modern Language Notes* 74(3), March 1959, 231-34.

"(one!)"

GEORGE C. BRAUER, JR. *Explicator* 16(3), December 1957, Item 14.

LOUIS C. RUS. *Explicator* 15(6), March 1957, Item 40.

"1x1"

JACK STEINBERG. *Explicator* 8(3), December 1949, Item 17.

"one's not half two"

NORMAN FRIEDMAN. "Diction, Voice, and Tone: The Poetic Language of E. E. Cummings," *PMLA* 72(5), December 1957, 1040-41.

"Paris; this April sunset completely utters"

RUSHWORTH M. KIDDER. " 'Twin Obsessions': The Poetry and Paintings of E. E. Cummings," *Georgia Review* 32(2), Summer 1978, 355-57.

"pity this busy monster, manunkind"

JOHN BRITTON. *Explicator* 18(1), October 1959, Item 5.

HARRY BROWN and JOHN MILSTEAD. *What the Poem Means*, p. 52.

JAMES P. DOUGHERTY. "Language as a Reality in E. E. Cummings," *Bucknell Review* 16(2), May 1968, 112-22.

JAMES W. GARGANO. *Explicator* 20(3), November 1961, Item 21.

NAT HENRY. *Explicator* 27(9), May 1969, Item 68.

"Poem, or Beauty Hurts Mr. Vinal"

JOHN OLIVER PERRY. *The Experience of Poems*, pp. 219-21.

"Portrait VIII"

see "Buffalo Bill's defunct"

"r-p-o-p-h-e-s-s-a-g-r"

SAM HYNES. *Explicator* 10(2), November 1951, Item 9.

M. L. ROSENTHAL. *The Modern Poets*, pp. 147-48.

EVE TRIEM. "E. E. Cummings," in *Six American Poets from Emily Dickinson to the Present*, p. 173.

"s.ti:rst;hiso,nce;ma:n"

SISTER MARY DAVID BABCOCK. "Cummings' Typography: An Ideogrammatic Style," *Renascence* 15(3), Spring 1963, 122-23.

"sh estiffl"

NAT HENRY. *Explicator* 21(9), May 1963, Item 72.

PATRICK B. MULLEN. "E. E. Cummings and Popular Culture," *Journal of Popular Culture* 5(3), Winter 1971, 508-9.

"she being Brand"

FRED E. H. SCHROEDER. "Obscenity and Its Function in the Poetry of E. E. Cummings," *Sewanee Review* 73(3), Summer 1965, 475-76.

"silence/.is"

M. L. ROSENTHAL. *The Modern Poets*, pp. 146-47.

"the sky was"

JOHN ARTHOS. "The Poetry of E. E. Cummings," *American Literature* 14(4), January 1943, 383-85.

"so little he is"

LLOYD FRANKENBERG. *Pleasure Dome*, pp. 176-77.

RUSHWORTH M. KIDDER. " 'Twin Obsessions': The Poetry and Paintings of E. E. Cummings," *Georgia Review* 32(2), Summer 1978, 357-59.

"sonnet entitled how to run the world)"

GARY LANE. *Explicator* 31(1), September 1972, Item 7.

MICHAEL L. LASSER. *Explicator* 24(5), January 1966, Item 44.

EVE TRIEM. "E. E. Cummings," in *Six American Poets from Emily Dickinson to the Present*, pp. 185-86.

CUMMINGS, E. E. *(Cont.)*

"Space being(don't forget to remember)Curved"

RICHARD B. VOWLES. *Explicator* 9(1), October 1950, Item 3.

"structure, miraculous challenge, devout am"

WALTER SUTTON. *American Free Verse,* pp. 94-95.

"sunset)edges become swiftly"

LAURA RIDING and ROBERT GRAVES. *A Survey of Modernist Poetry,* pp. 12-34.

"ta"

S. V. BAUM. "E. E. Cummings: The Technique of Immediacy," *South Atlantic Quarterly* 53(1), January 1954, 83-84.

G. R. WILSON, JR. *Explicator* 31(3), November 1972, Item 17.

"that melancholy"

JOHN LOGAN. "The Organ Grinder and the Cockatoo: An Introduction to E. E. Cummings," *Critic* 20(2), Oct.-Nov. 1961, 39-43. Reprinted in: *Modern American Poetry,* edited by Jerome Mazzaro, pp. 249-68.

"that which we who're alive in spite of mirrors"

EDITH A. EVERSON. *Explicator* 32(7), March 1974, Item 55.

"there are 6 doors"

EVE TRIEM. "E. E. Cummings," in *Six American Poets from Emily Dickinson to the Present,* p. 186.

"these children singing in stone a"

NAT HENRY. *Explicator* 13(8), June 1955, Item 51.

EDWIN M. MOSELEY. *Explicator* 9(1), October 1950, Item 2.

"this is the garden: colours come and go"

WALTER SUTTON. *American Free Verse,* p. 94.

"this little bride&groom are"

PATRICK B. MULLEN. "E. E. Cummings and Popular Culture," *Journal of Popular Culture* 5(3), Winter 1971, 516-17.

"a thrown a"

S. V. BAUM. "E. E. Cummings: The Technique of Immediacy," *South Atlantic Quarterly* 53(1), January 1954, 84-86.

"un"

WILLIAM V. DAVIS. " 'Remembrance of Miracles': e. e. cummings' 'un/der fog,' " *Notes on Modern American Literature* 1(4), Fall 1977, Item 30.

GILBERT HIGHET. *The Powers of Poetry,* pp. 143-45.

"the way to hump a cow is not"

FRED E. H. SCHROEDER. "Obscenity and Its Function in the Poetry of E. E. Cummings," *Sewanee Review* 73(3), Summer 1965, 473.

"what a proud dreamhorse pulling"

LLOYD FRANKENBERG. *Invitation to Poetry,* pp. 257-60.

EVE TRIEM. "E. E. Cummings," in *Six American Poets from Emily Dickinson to the Present,* pp. 174-75.

"what if a much of a which of a wind"

JOHN CIARDI. "Cummings: What If a Much of a Which of a Wind," in *Master Poems of the English Language,* pp. 1004-6.

MARY FRANCES CLAGGETT. " 'Glory, Jest, and Riddle,' " *English Journal* 55(3), March 1966, 353-54.

LAUREL MAUREEN O'NEAL. *Explicator* 32(1), September 1973, Item 6.

STEPHEN E. WHICHER. *Explicator* 12(2), November 1953, Item 14.

"when faces called flowers float out of the ground"

ALAN M. NADEL. *Explicator* 32(6), February 1974, Item 47.

"when god lets my body be"

HARRY BROWN and JOHN MILSTEAD. *What the Poem Means,* p. 53.

DORIS DUNDAS. *Explicator* 29(9), May 1971, Item 79.

"when you are silent, shining host by guest"

G. J. WEINBERGER. "E. E. Cummings's Benevolent God: A Reading of 'when you are silent, shining host by guest,' " *Papers on Language and Literature* 10(1), Winter 1974, 70-75.

"who are these (wraith a clinging with a wraith)"

NORMAN FRIEDMAN. "Diction, Voice, and Tone: The Poetic Language of E. E. Cummings," *PMLA* 72(5), December 1957, 1046-47.

"who knows if the moon's"

AGNES STEIN. *The Uses of Poetry,* pp. 76-79.

"who's most afraid of death? thou"

M. L. ROSENTHAL. *The Modern Poets,* pp. 148-49.

"a wind has blown the rain away"

HARRY BROWN and JOHN MILSTEAD. *What the Poem Means,* p. 50.

JOHN CLENDENNING. "Cummings, comedy, and criticism," *Colorado Quarterly* 12(1), Summer 1963, 50-53.

"yes is a pleasant country"

GARY LANE. *Explicator* 31(2), October 1972, Item 11.

CUNNINGHAM, J. V.

"The Beacon"

DENIS DONOGHUE. *Connoisseurs of Chaos,* pp. 143-44.

"The Dog-Days"

GROSVENOR E. POWELL. "The Poetry of J. V. Cunningham," in *Poets in Progress,* pp. 151-52.

"Hang up your weaponed wit" (*The Judge is Fury,* Epigram 35)

YVOR WINTERS. "The Poetry of J. V. Cunningham," *Twentieth Century Literature* 6(4), January 1961, 164.

"The Helmsman"

PAT LAMORTE. "The 'Ancient Rules' — A Vanishing Species?" *Georgia Review* 27(4), Winter 1973, 495-96.

"In the thirtieth year of life"

ROBERT PINSKY. *The Situation of Poetry,* pp. 136-39.

ROBERT PINSKY. "Two Examples of Poetic Discursiveness," *Chicago Review* 27(1), Summer 1975, 135-37.

"Meditation on Statistical Method"

YVOR WINTERS. "The Poetry of J. V. Cunningham," *Twentieth Century Literature* 6(4), January 1961, 163.

"Passion"

JOHN WILLIAMS. "J. V. Cunningham: The Major and the Minor," *Arizona Quarterly* 6(2), Summer 1950, 142-44.

"The Quest of the Opal"

YVOR WINTERS. "The Poetry of J. V. Cunningham," *Twentieth Century Literature* 6(4), January 1961, 161.

"Timor Dei"

> GROSVENOR E. POWELL. "The Poetry of J. V. Cunningham," in *Poets in Progress,* p. 142.

> JOHN WILLIAMS. "J. V. Cunningham: The Major and the Minor," *Arizona Quarterly* 6(2), Summer 1950, 137-39.

CYNEWULF

"The Fates of the Apostles"

> CONSTANCE B. HIEATT. "*The Fates of the Apostles*: Imagery, Structure, and Meaning," *Papers on Language and Literature* 10(2), Spring 1974, 115-25.

> ROBERT C. RICE. "The penitential motif in Cynewulf's *Fates of the Apostles* and in his epilogues," *Anglo Saxon England* 6 (1977), 105-13.

"Juliana"

> DANIEL G. CALDER. "The Art of Cynewulf's *Juliana,*" *Modern Language Quarterly* 34(4), December 1973, 355-71.

> CLAUDE SCHNEIDER. "Cynewulf's devaluation of heroic tradition in *Juliana,*" *Anglo Saxon England* 7 (1978), 107-18.

> JOSEPH WITTIG. "Figural narrative in Cynewulf's *Juliana,*" *Anglo Saxon England* 4 (1975), 37-55.

D

DAMON, FOSTER

"Seelig's Confession"

    DONALD E. STANFORD. "Foster Damon's Dream Frontiers," *Southern Review*, n.s., 7(1), Winter 1970, xvii.

DANDO, JOHN

"Maroccus Extaticus"

    EJNER J. JENSON. "The Wit of Renaissance Satire," *Philological Quarterly* 51(2), April 1972, 400-1.

DANFORTH, SAMUEL

"Ad Librum"

    ROBERT DALY. *God's Altar*, pp. 32-34.

DANIEL, GEORGE

"To the Memorie of the Excellent Dramatique English Poets: Mr. Fra: Beaumont and Mr. Jo: Fletcher upon the Impression of their Severall Comedies Tragedies & c."

    AVON JACK MURPHY. "The Critical Elegy of Earlier Seventeenth-Century England," *Genre* 5(1), March 1972, 83-84.

DANIEL, SAMUEL

"Are They Shadows That We See?"

    LLOYD FRANKENBERG. *Invitation to Poetry*, p. 378.

"Beautie, sweet love, is like the morning dewe" (*Delia*, 42)

    C. F. WILLIAMSON. "The Design of Daniel's Delia," *Review of English Studies*, n.s., 19(75), August 1968, 256-57.

"Care-charmer sleep, son of the sable night" (*Delia*, XLV)

    ROSEMOND TUVE. *Elizabethan and Metaphysical Imagery*, pp. 167-68.

"The Complaint of Rosamond"

    RONALD PRIMEAU. "Daniel and the *Mirror* Tradition: Dramatic Irony in *The Complaint of Rosamond*," *Studies in English Literature 1500-1900* 15(1), Winter 1975, 21-36.

"Delia! these eyes that so admireth thine" (*Delia*, XL)

    THEODORE C. HOEPFNER. *Explicator* 10(6), April 1952, Item 38. (P)

"Epistle to Henry Wriothesly"

    JAY ARNOLD LEVINE. "The Status of the Verse Epistle Before Pope," *Studies in Philology* 59(4), October 1962, 673-74.

"Epistle to the Ladie Lucie, Countesse of Bedford"

    ANTHONY LaBRANCHE. "Samuel Daniel: A Voice of Thoughtfulness," in *The Rhetoric of Renaissance Poetry*, pp. 130-31, 134-36.

"Faire and lovely maide, looke from the shore" (*Delia*, 38)

    C. F. WILLIAMSON. "The Design of Daniel's *Delia*," *Review of English Studies*, n.s., 19(75), August 1968, 255.

"O why dooth *Delia* credite so her glasse" (*Delia*, 29)

    ANTHONY LaBRANCHE. "Imitation: Getting in Touch," *Modern Language Quarterly* 31(3), September 1970, 319-20.

"A Pastoral"

    RONALD PRIMEAU. "Daniel and the *Mirror* Tradition: Dramatic Irony in *The Complaint of Rosamond*," *Studies in English Literature 1500-1900* 15(1), Winter 1975, 34-36.

"Teares, vowes, and prayers win the hardest hart" (*Delia*, 11)

    JOHN T. SHAWCROSS. "The Poet as Orator: One Phase of His Judicial Pose," in *The Rhetoric of Renaissance Poetry*, pp. 17-18.

"To the Lady Margaret"

    CECIL C. SERONSY. "Well-Languaged Daniel: A Reconsideration," *Modern Language Review* 52(4), October 1957, 494-95.

"Ulysses and the Siren"

    WRIGHT THOMAS and STUART GERRY BROWN. *Reading Poems: An Introduction to Critical Study*, p. 674.

DARLEY, GEORGE

"Browse on, my gentle flock!"

    LESLIE BRISMAN. *Romantic Origins*, pp. 203-7.

"It Is Not Beauty I Demand"

    HAROLD BLOOM. *The Visionary Company*, pp. 448-49.

DARWIN, ERASMUS

"The Temple of Nature"

    JAMES HARRISON. "Erasmus Darwin's View of Evolution," *Journal of the History of Ideas* 32(2), April-June 1971, 247-64.

DAVENANT, WILLIAM

"O thou that sleep'st like pig in straw"

    LLOYD FRANKENBERG. *Invitation to Poetry*, pp. 174-75.

"Song" ("The lark now leaves his watry nest")
 JAMES R. KREUZER. *Elements of Poetry,* pp. 92-93.

"To the Queen, entertained at Night by the Countess of Anglesey"
 WILLIAM N. FISHER. "*Occupatio* in Sixteenth- and Seventeenth-Century Verse," *Texas Studies in Literature and Language* 14(2), Summer 1972, 209-10.

DAVIDSON, DONALD

"Aunt Maria and the Gourds"
 LOUIS COWAN. "The Communal World of Southern Literature," *Georgia Review* 14(3), Fall 1960, 255-56.

"The Faring"
 WARD ALLEN. "Donald Davidson," *Sewanee Review* 78(2), Spring 1970, 399-400.

"The Last Charge"
 DAVID A. HALLMAN. "Donald Davidson, Allen Tate and All Those Falling Leaves," *Georgia Review* 27(4), Winter 1973, 555-58.

"Lee in the Mountains"
 M. E. BRADFORD. "A Durable Fire: Donald Davidson And the Profession of Letters," *Southern Review,* n.s., 3(3), Summer 1967, 727-32.
 CHRISTOPHER CLAUSEN. "Grecian Thoughts in the Home Fields: Reflections on Southern Poetry," *Georgia Review* 32(2), Summer 1978, 296-98.

"The Ninth Part of Speech: A Verse Letter: To Louis Zahner"
 LAWRENCE DESSOMMES. "The Epistemological Implications in 'The Ninth Part of Speech,'" *Mississippi Quarterly* 27(1), Winter 1973-74, 21-32.
 CHARLES EDWARD EATON. "Donald Davidson and the Dynamics of Nostalgia," *Georgia Review* 20(3), Fall 1966, 264-66.

"On a Replica of the Parthenon"
 WARD ALLEN. "Donald Davidson," *Sewanee Review* 78(2), Spring 1970, 394-95.
 M. E. BRADFORD. "A Comment On The Poetry Of Davidson," *Mississippi Quarterly* 19(1), Winter 1965-66, 41-43.

"The Tall Men"
 CHARLES EDWARD EATON. "Donald Davidson and the Dynamics of Nostalgia," *Georgia Review* 20(3), Fall 1966, 267-69.
 LOUIS D. RUBIN, JR. "The Concept of Nature in Modern Southern Poetry," *American Quarterly* 9(1), Spring 1957, 65-66.

"A Touch of Snow"
 M. E. BRADFORD. "Meaning and Metaphor in Donald Davidson's 'A Touch of Snow,'" *Southern Review,* n.s., 2(3), Summer 1966, 516-23.

"Twilight on Union Street"
 M. E. BRADFORD. "A Comment on the Poetry Of Davidson," *Mississippi Quarterly* 19(1), Winter 1965-66, 41-43.

DAVIE, DONALD

"After an Accident"
 CALVIN BEDIENT. *Eight Contemporary Poets,* p. 47.
 CALVIN BEDIENT. "On Donald Davie," *Iowa Review* 2(2), Spring 1971, 85-86.

"Creon's Mouse"
 CALVIN BEDIENT. *Eight Contemporary Poets,* pp. 35-37.

CALVIN BEDIENT. "On Donald Davie," *Iowa Review* 2(2), Spring 1971, 76-77.

"Dream Forest"
 BARRY ALPERT. "Introduction," to *The Poet in the Imaginary Museum,* pp. x-xi.

"England"
 MICHAEL SCHMIDT. "The Poetry of Donald Davie," *Critical Quarterly* 15(1), Spring 1973, 83-84.

"Epistles to Eva Hesse"
 MICHAEL SCHMIDT. "The Poetry of Donald Davie," *Critical Quarterly* 15(1), Spring 1973, 84-85.

"Ezra Pound in Pisa"
 CALVIN BEDIENT. *Eight Contemporary Poets,* pp. 40-41.

"For an Age of Plastics"
 BARRY ALPERT. "Introduction," to *The Poet in the Imaginary Museum,* pp. xvi-xvii.

"The Fountain"
 PATRICK SWINDEN. "Old Lines, New Lines: The Movement Ten Years After," *Critical Quarterly* 9(4), Winter 1967, 353-55.

"Heigh-ho on a Winter Afternoon"
 CALVIN BEDIENT. *Eight Contemporary Poets,* p. 42.
 JOHN R. REED. "Reflexive Poetry: The Winter Talent of Donald Davie," *Western Humanities Review* 19(1), Winter 1965, 52-54.

"Hornet"
 JOHN LUCAS. "Donald Davie," in *Criticism in Action,* pp. 137-39.

"Hypochondriac Logic"
 JOHN R. REED. "Reflexive Poetry: The Winter Talent of Donald Davie," *Western Humanities Review* 19(1), Winter 1965, 48-49.

"Limited Achievement"
 JOHN R. REED. "Reflexive Poetry: The Winter Talent of Donald Davie," *Western Humanities Review* 19(1), Winter 1965, 54.

"Low Lands"
 JOHN LUCAS. "Donald Davie," in *Criticism in Action,* pp. 139-41.

"A Meeting of Cultures"
 CALVIN BEDIENT. *Eight Contemporary Poets,* pp. 44-45.

"Portrait of the Artist as a Farmyard Fowl"
 CALVIN BEDIENT. *Eight Contemporary Poets,* pp. 28-29.

"Remembering the Thirties"
 JOHN LUCAS. "Donald Davie," in *Criticism in Action,* pp. 130-37.
 JOHN PRESS. "English Verse Since 1945," *Essays by Divers Hands,* 3rd series, 31(1962), 146-47.

"To a Brother in the Mystery"
 JOHN R. REED. "Reflexive Poetry: The Winter Talent of Donald Davie," *Western Humanities Review* 19(1), Winter 1965, 50-51.

"Viper-Man"
 CALVIN BEDIENT. *Eight Contemporary Poets,* pp. 47-48.
 CALVIN BEDIENT. "On Donald Davie," *Iowa Review* 2(2), Spring 1971, 86.

DAVIE, DONALD (Cont.)

"A Winter Talent"

JOHN R. REED. "Reflexive Poetry: The Winter Talent of Donald Davie," *Western Humanities Review* 19(1), Winter 1965, 46-48.

"Woodpigeons at Raheny"

CALVIN BEDIENT. *Eight Contemporary Poets*, pp. 48-49.

CALVIN BEDIENT. "On Donald Davie," *Iowa Review* 2(2), Spring 1971, 86-88.

JOHN R. REED. "Reflexive Poetry: The Winter Talent of Donald Davie," *Western Humanities Review* 19(1), Winter 1965, 45-46.

DAVIES, JOHN

"Orchestra"

JOHN HUNTINGTON. "Philosophical Seduction in Chapman, Davies, and Donne," *ELH* 44(1), Spring 1977, 51-54.

IAN SOWTON. "Hidden Persuaders as a Means of Literary Grace: Sixteenth Century Poetics and Rhetoric in England," *University of Toronto Quarterly* 32(1), October 1962, 65-68.

E. M. W. TILLYARD. *Five Poems, 1470-1870*, pp. 30-48.

DAVIES, W. H.

"The Example"

LAURENCE PERRINE. "The Importance of Tone in the Interpretation of Literature," *College English* 24(5), February 1963, 389-90.

"The Moon"

DAVID DAICHES. *Poetry and the Modern World*, pp. 53-55.

"The Villain"

LAURENCE PERRINE. *Sound and Sense*, p. 126; second ed., p. 138; third ed., p. 165; fourth ed., p. 155.

DAVIS, CATHERINE

"After a Time"

HELEN P. TRIMPI. "The Theme of Loss in the Earlier Poems of Catherine Davis And Edgar Bowers," *Southern Review*, n.s., 9(3), Summer 1973, 601-4.

"Beware, old scrounger"

HELEN P. TRIMPI. "The Theme of Loss in the Earlier Poems of Catherine Davis And Edgar Bowers," *Southern Review*, n.s., 9(3), Summer 1973, 601-3.

"Comforting hope"

HELEN P. TRIMPI. "The Theme of Loss in the Earlier Poems of Catherine Davis And Edgar Bowers," *Southern Review*, n.s., 9(3), Summer 1973, 601-3.

"Indolence"

HELEN P. TRIMPI. "The Theme of Loss in the Earlier Poems of Catherine Davis And Edgar Bowers," *Southern Review*, n.s., 9(3), Summer 1973, 596-97.

"The Last Step"

HELEN P. TRIMPI. "The Theme of Loss in the Earlier Poems of Catherine Davis And Edgar Bowers," *Southern Review*, n.s., 9(3), Summer 1973, 606-9.

"The Leaves"

HELEN P. TRIMPI. "The Theme of Loss in the Earlier Poems of Catherine Davis And Edgar Bowers," *Southern Review*, n.s., 9(3), Summer 1973, 597-98.

"The Narrow House"

HELEN P. TRIMPI. "The Theme of Loss in the Earlier Poems of Catherine Davis And Edgar Bowers," *Southern Review*, n.s., 9(3), Summer 1973, 609-11.

"Under This Lintel"

HELEN P. TRIMPI. "The Theme of Loss in the Earlier Poems of Catherine Davis And Edgar Bowers," *Southern Review*, n.s., 9(3), Summer 1973, 604-6.

DAVIS, FRANK

"Moses Mitchell"

WILLIAM J. REEVES. "The Significance of Audience in Black Poetry," *Negro American Literature Forum* 9(1), Spring 1975, 30-31.

DAY LEWIS, CECIL

"Children look down upon the morning-grey"

NORMAN C. STAGEBERG and WALLACE L. ANDERSON. *Poetry as Experience*, pp. 86-87.

"Come Live With Me and Be My Love"

ROBERT STALLMAN. *Explicator* 2(6), April 1944, Item 46.

"The Committee"

PAT LAMORTE. "The 'Ancient Rules' — A Vanishing Species?" *Georgia Review* 27(4), Winter 1973, 496-98.

"The Conflict"

HARRY BROWN and JOHN MILSTEAD. *What the Poem Means*, p. 133.

ELTON EDWARD SMITH. *The Angry Young Men of the Thirties*, p. 24.

"Cornet Solo"

RAYMOND TSCHUMI. *Thought in Twentieth-Century English Poetry*, p. 236.

"Departure in the Dark"

RAYMOND TSCHUMI. *Thought in Twentieth-Century English Poetry*, pp. 235-36.

"Do Not Expect Again a Phoenix Hour"

LYNA LEE MONTGOMERY. "The Phoenix: Its Use as a Literary Device in English from the Seventeenth Century to the Twentieth Century," *D. H. Lawrence Review* 5(3), Fall 1972, 312.

"The Image"

RAYMOND TSCHUMI. *Thought in Twentieth-Century English Poetry*, pp. 238-39.

"It Is the True Star"

ELTON EDWARD SMITH. *The Angry Young Men of the Thirties*, pp. 4-5.

"Johnny-Head-in-Air"

D. E. S. MAXWELL. *The Poets of the Thirties*, p. 118.

ELTON EDWARD SMITH. *The Angry Young Men of the Thirties*, pp. 22-24.

"The Lighted House"

RAYMOND TSCHUMI. *Thought in Twentieth-Century English Poetry*, p. 235.

"Losers"

ELTON EDWARD SMITH. *The Angry Young Men of the Thirties*, p. 21.

"Moving In"

ELTON EDWARD SMITH. *The Angry Young Men of the Thirties*, p. 21.

"The Nabara"
> D. E. S. MAXWELL. *The Poets of the Thirties*, pp. 122-24.

"Nearing Again the Legendary Isle"
> HARRY BROWN and JOHN MILSTEAD. *What the Poem Means*, p. 133.

"Newsreel"
> ELTON EDWARD SMITH. *The Angry Young Men of the Thirties*, p. 31.

"O Dreams, O Destinations"
> C. B. COX and A. E. DYSON. *Modern Poetry*, pp. 98-108.
> RAYMOND TSCHUMI. *Thought in Twentieth-Century English Poetry*, p. 236.

"O World of Many Worlds"
> DOMINIC HIBBERD. "Images of Darkness in the Poems of Wilfred Owen," *Durham University Journal*, n.s., 35(2), March 1974, 158.

"Overtures to Death"
> D. E. S. MAXWELL. *The Poets of the Thirties*, pp. 121-22.
> ELTON EDWARD SMITH. *The Angry Young Men of the Thirties*, pp. 31-32.

"The Perverse"
> ELTON EDWARD SMITH. *The Angry Young Men of the Thirties*, p. 5.

"Rest From Loving and Be Living"
> WILLIAM ELTON. *Explicator* 6(3), December 1947, Item 16.
> WILLIAM ELTON. *Explicator* 7(3), December 1948, Item 25.
> WALTER GIERASCH. *Explicator* 6(5), March 1948, Item 34.
> DAVID C. SHELDON. *Explicator* 6(5), March 1948, Item 34.

"The Schoolmaster Speaks"
> D. E. S. MAXWELL. *The Poets of the Thirties*, pp. 113-14.

"Second Defendant Speaks"
> D. E. S. MAXWELL. *The Poets of the Thirties*, pp. 113-14.

"The Sitting"
> RAYMOND TSCHUMI. *Thought in Twentieth-Century English Poetry*, pp. 240-41.

"A Time to Dance"
> DAVID DAICHES. *Poetry and the Modern World*, pp. 206-9.
> ELTON EDWARD SMITH. *The Angry Young Men of the Thirties*, p. 25.

"A Warning to Those Who Live on Mountains"
> ELTON EDWARD SMITH. *The Angry Young Men of the Thirties*, pp. 21-22.

"Word Over All"
> ELTON EDWARD SMITH. *The Angry Young Men of the Thirties*, pp. 32-33.
> RAYMOND TSCHUMI. *Thought in Twentieth-Century English Poetry*, pp. 236-38.

DE LA MARE, WALTER

"The Children of Stare"
> JAMES REEVES and MARTIN SEYMOUR-SMITH. *Inside Poetry*, pp. 71-73.

"The Ghost"
> F. R. LEAVIS. *New Bearings in English Poetry*, pp. 53-54.

"The Horseman"
> LAURENCE PERRINE. "Sinners in the Hands of an Angry Critic: 'But Deliver Us From Evil,'" *CEA Critic* 30(3), December 1967, 4.

"The Listeners"
> C. B. COX and A. E. DYSON. *Modern Poetry*, pp. 41-47.
> A. E. DYSON. "Walter de la Mare's 'The Listeners,'" *Critical Quarterly* 2(2), Summer 1960, 150-54.
> LLOYD FRANKENBERG. *Invitation to Poetry*, p. 139.
> FREDERICK L. GWYNN and RALPH W. CONDEE. *Explicator* 12(4), February 1954, Item 26. Abridged in: *The Case for Poetry*, pp. 99-100; second ed., pp. 85-86.
> GLEN A. LOVE. "Frost's 'The Census-Taker' and de la Mare's 'The Listeners,'" *Papers on Language and Literature* 4(2), Spring 1968, 198-200.
> J. M. PURCELL. *Explicator* 3(5), March 1945, Item 42. Abridged in: *The Case for Poetry*, p. 99; second ed., p. 85.

"Märchen"
> ELISABETH SCHNEIDER. *Explicator* 4(4), February 1946, Item 29. Reprinted in: *Readings for Liberal Education*, II: 526; third ed., II: 178.

"The Mocking Fairy"
> EARL DANIELS. *The Art of Reading Poetry*, pp. 57-59.

"Nostalgia"
> E. K. BROWN. "The Epilogue to Mr. de la Mare's Poetry," *Poetry* 68(2), May 1946, 90-92.

"The Scribe"
> T. R. HENN. *The Apple and the Spectroscope*, pp. 92-97.

DEKKER, THOMAS

"The Happy Heart"
> CLEANTH BROOKS and ROBERT PENN WARREN. *Understanding Poetry*, fourth ed., pp. 284-85.

DENHAM, JOHN

"Cooper's Hill"
> M. H. ABRAMS. "Structure and Style In the Greater Romantic Lyric," in *From Sensibility to Romanticism*, pp. 535-36. Reprinted in: *Romanticism and Consciousness*, pp. 208-9.
> JOHN WILSON FOSTER. "The Measure of Paradise: Topography in Eighteenth-Century Poetry," *Eighteenth Century Studies* 9(2), Winter 1975/76, 235-44.
> PAUL J. KORSHIN. "The Evolution of Neoclassical Poetics: Cleveland, Denham, and Waller as Poetic Theorists," *Eighteenth Century Studies* 2(2), December 1968, 115-25.
> EARL MINER. *The Cavalier Mode from Jonson to Cotton*, pp. 166-68.
> JOHN M. WALLACE. "*Coopers Hill*: The Manifesto of Parliamentary Royalism, 1641," *ELH* 41(4), Winter 1974, 494-540.
> EARL R. WASSERMAN. *The Subtler Language*, pp. 45-88.

DERWOOD, GENE

"Elegy on Gordon Barber"
> DAVID MADDEN. "Gene Derwood: Cassandra Sane," in *The Poetic Image in 6 Genres*, pp. 164-73.

DEVLIN, DENIS

"Liffey Bridge"

> FRANK L. KERSNOWSKI. "The Fabulous Reality of Denis Devlin," *Sewanee Review* 81(1), Winter 1973, 116.

"Lough Derg"

> BABETTE DEUTSCH. *Poetry in Our Time,* p. 218; second ed., p. 239.

"The Tomb of Michael Collins"

> FRANK L. KERSNOWSKI. "The Fabulous Reality of Denis Devlin," *Sewanee Review* 81(1), Winter 1973, 122.

DICKEY, JAMES

"Adultery"

> JOHN WILLIAM CORRINGTON. "James Dickey's Poems: 1957-1967: A Personal Appraisal," *Georgia Review* 22(1), Spring 1968, 13-15.
>
> JOYCE CAROL OATES. "Out of Stone into Flesh: The Imagination of James Dickey," *Modern Poetry Studies* 5(2), Autumn 1974, 125-26.
>
> CONSTANCE PIERCE. "Dickey's 'Adultery': A Ritual of Renewal," *Concerning Poetry* 9(2), Fall 1976, 67-69.

"Approaching Prayer"

> RAYMOND SMITH. "The Poetic Faith of James Dickey," *Modern Poetry Studies* 2(6), 1972, 264.
>
> H. L. WEATHERBY. "The Way of Exchange in James Dickey's Poetry," *Sewanee Review* 74(3), Summer 1966, 672-73.

"Armor"

> DAVID C. BERRY. "Harmony with the Dead: James Dickey's Descent into the Underworld," *Southern Quarterly* 12(3), April 1974, 238-39.

"Blood"

> RONALD BAUGHMAN. "James Dickey's *The Eye-Beaters*: 'An Agonizing New Life,'" *South Carolina Review* 10(2), April 1978, 85.

"Butterflies"

> see "Messages: Butterflies"

"Chenille"

> H. L. WEATHERBY. "The Way of Exchange in James Dickey's Poetry," *Sewanee Review* 74(3), Summer 1966, 674.

"Cherrylog Road"

> JOYCE CAROL OATES. "Out of Stone into Flesh: The Imagination of James Dickey," *Modern Poetry Studies* 5(2), Autumn 1974, 110-11.
>
> H. L. WEATHERBY. "The Way of Exchange in James Dickey's Poetry," *Sewanee Review* 74(3), Summer 1966, 674-75.

"Diabetes"

> JOYCE CAROL OATES. "Out of Stone into Flesh: The Imagination of James Dickey," *Modern Poetry Studies* 5(2), Autumn 1974, 132-33.

"A Dog Sleeping on My Feet"

> H. L. WEATHERBY. "The Way of Exchange in James Dickey's Poetry," *Sewanee Review* 74(3), Summer 1966, 669-72.

"Dover: Believing in Kings"

> RICHARD HOWARD. "On James Dickey," *Partisan Review* 33(3), Summer 1966, 421-22.

"Drinking from a Helmet"

> DAVID C. BERRY. "Harmony with the Dead: James Dickey's Descent into the Underworld," *Southern Quarterly* 12(3), April 1974, 242-43.
>
> LAURENCE LIEBERMAN. *Unassigned Frequencies,* pp. 85-87.
>
> JOYCE CAROL OATES. "Out of Stone into Flesh: The Imagination of James Dickey," *Modern Poetry Studies* 5(2), Autumn 1974, 111-13.
>
> H. L. WEATHERBY. "The Way of Exchange in James Dickey's Poetry," *Sewanee Review* 74(3), Summer 1966, 675-76.

"The Driver"

> DAVID C. BERRY. "Harmony with the Dead: James Dickey's Descent into the Underworld," *Southern Quarterly* 12(3), April 1974, 243.
>
> ROBERT ELY. "Rising and Overcoming: James Dickey's 'The Driver,'" *Notes on Modern American Literature* 2(2), Spring 1978, Item 12.
>
> CHARLES C. TUCKER. "Knowledge Up, Down, and Beyond: Dickey's 'The Driver' and 'Falling,'" *CEA Critic* 38(4), May 1976, 4-7.
>
> H. L. WEATHERBY. "The Way of Exchange in James Dickey's Poetry," *Sewanee Review* 74(3), Summer 1966, 675.

"Dust"

> LAURENCE LIEBERMAN. *Unassigned Frequencies,* pp. 102-3.

"Encounter in the Cage Country"

> LAURENCE LIEBERMAN. *Unassigned Frequencies,* pp. 99-101, 105-6.

"The Eye-Beaters"

> RONALD BAUGHMAN. "James Dickey's *The Eye-Beaters*: 'An Agonizing New Life,'" *South Carolina Review* 10(2), April 1978, 85.
>
> JOYCE CAROL OATES. "Out of Stone into Flesh: The Imagination of James Dickey," *Modern Poetry Studies* 5(2), Autumn 1974, 136-37.
>
> RAYMOND SMITH. "The Poetic Faith of James Dickey," *Modern Poetry Studies* 2(6), 1972, 269-72.

"Falling"

> RICHARD CALHOUN. "James Dickey: The Expansive Imagination," in *Modern American Poetry,* ed. by Guy Owen, p. 251.
>
> JOHN WILLIAM CORRINGTON. "James Dickey's Poems: 1957-1967: A Personal Appraisal," *Georgia Review* 22(1), Spring 1968, 22-23.
>
> LAURENCE LIEBERMAN. *Unassigned Frequencies,* pp. 80-82.
>
> CHARLES C. TUCKER. "Knowledge Up, Down, and Beyond: Dickey's 'The Driver' and 'Falling,'" *CEA Critic* 38(4), May 1976, 7-10.
>
> JOHN VERNON. *The Garden and the Map,* pp. 134-41.

"False Youth II"

> LAURENCE LIEBERMAN. *Unassigned Frequencies,* pp. 78-79.

"Fence Wire"

> JOYCE CAROL OATES. "Out of Stone into Flesh: The Imagination of James Dickey," *Modern Poetry Studies* 5(2), Autumn 1974, 108-9.

"The Fiend"

> JOAN BOBBITT. "Unnatural Order in the Poetry of James Dickey," *Concerning Poetry* 11(1), Spring 1978, 42-44.

LAURENCE LIEBERMAN. *Unassigned Frequencies*, pp. 79-80.

JOYCE CAROL OATES. "Out of Stone into Flesh: The Imagination of James Dickey," *Modern Poetry Studies* 5(2), Autumn 1974, 124.

H. L. WEATHERBY. "The Way of Exchange in James Dickey's Poetry," *Sewanee Review* 74(3), Summer 1966, 677-78.

"The Firebombing"

DAVID C. BERRY. "Harmony with the Dead: James Dickey's Descent into the Underworld," *Southern Quarterly* 12(3), April 1974, 243-44.

RICHARD HOWARD. "On James Dickey," *Partisan Review* 33(3), Summer 1966, 483-84.

ANTHONY LIBBY. "Fire and Light, Four Poets to the End and Beyond," *Iowa Review* 4(2), Spring 1973, 121-22.

LAURENCE LIEBERMAN. *Unassigned Frequencies*, pp. 87-89.

JOYCE CAROL OATES. "Out of Stone into Flesh: The Imagination of James Dickey," *Modern Poetry Studies* 5(2), Autumn 1974, 113-18.

LOUIS UNTERMEYER. *50 Modern American & British Poets*, p. 314.

H. L. WEATHERBY. "The Way of Exchange in James Dickey's Poetry," *Sewanee Review* 74(3), Summer 1966, 677.

"A Folk-Singer of the Thirties"

JOHN WILLIAM CORRINGTON. "James Dickey's Poems: 1957-1967: A Personal Appraisal," *Georgia Review* 22(1), Spring 1968, 19-22.

"For the Last Wolverine"

JOYCE CAROL OATES. "Out of Stone into Flesh: The Imagination of James Dickey," *Modern Poetry Studies* 5(2), Autumn 1974, 126-28.

"Giving a Son to the Sea"
see "Messages: Giving a Son to the Sea"

"The Heaven of Animals"

PAUL CARROLL. *The Poem In Its Skin*, pp. 43-49.

LAURENCE LIEBERMAN. *Unassigned Frequencies*, p. 96.

NORMAN SILVERSTEIN. "James Dickey's Muscular Eschatology," *Salmagundi* 22-23 (Spring-Summer 1973), 263-64. Reprinted in: *Contemporary Poetry in America*, pp. 308-9.

RAYMOND SMITH. "The Poetic Faith of James Dickey," *Modern Poetry Studies* 2(6), 1972, 260-61.

"Horses and Prisoners"

DAVID C. BERRY. "Harmony with the Dead: James Dickey's Descent into the Underworld," *Southern Quarterly* 12(3), April 1974, 241-42.

"Hunting Civil War Relics at Nimblewill Creek"

DAVID C. BERRY. "Harmony with the Dead: James Dickey's Descent into the Underworld," *Southern Quarterly* 12(3), April 1974, 239-40.

JOHN WILLIAM CORRINGTON. "James Dickey's Poems: 1957-1967: A Personal Appraisal," *Georgia Review* 22(1), Spring 1968, 16-19.

"The Ice Skin"

MARTIN DODSWORTH. "Introduction: The Survival of Poetry," in *The Survival of Poetry*, pp. 16-17.

"In the Lupanar at Pompeii"

NORMAN FRIEDMAN. "The Wesleyan Poets — II," *Chicago Review* 19(1), 1966, 57-58.

"In the Mountain Tent"

WALTON BEACHAM. *The Meaning of Poetry*, pp. 237-40.

"In the Tree House at Night"

LAURENCE LIEBERMAN. *Unassigned Frequencies*, pp. 91-93.

"The Island"

DAVID C. BERRY. "Harmony with the Dead: James Dickey's Descent into the Underworld," *Southern Quarterly* 12(3), April 1974, 240.

"The Jewel"

LAURENCE LIEBERMAN. *Unassigned Frequencies*, p. 85.

"Kudzu"

JOAN BOBBITT. "Unnatural Order in the Poetry of James Dickey," *Concerning Poetry* 11(1), Spring 1978, 39-41.

"The Lifeguard"

LAURENCE LIEBERMAN. *Unassigned Frequencies* pp. 92-93.

LAURENCE PERRINE. *100 American Poems of the Twentieth Century*, pp. 277-80.

NORMAN SILVERSTEIN. "James Dickey's Muscular Eschatology," *Salmagundi* 22-23 (Spring-Summer 1973), 263. Reprinted in: *Contemporary Poetry in America*, p. 308.

"Living There"
see "Two Poems of Going Home: Living There"

"Looking for the Buckhead Boys"
see "Two Poems of Going Home: Looking for the Buckhead Boys"

"May Day Sermon to the Women of Gilmer County, by a Woman Preacher Leaving the Baptist Church"

CHRISTOPHER CLAUSEN. "Grecian Thoughts in the Home Fields: Reflections on Southern Poetry," *Georgia Review* 32(2), Summer 1978, 299-301.

JOYCE CAROL OATES. "Out of Stone into Flesh: The Imagination of James Dickey," *Modern Poetry Studies* 5(2), Autumn 1974, 119-21.

"Mercy"

RONALD BAUGHMAN. "James Dickey's *The Eye-Beaters*: 'An Agonizing New Life,'" *South Carolina Review* 10(2), April 1978, 84.

"Messages: Butterflies"

RONALD BAUGHMAN. "James Dickey's *The Eye-Beaters*: 'An Agonizing New Life,'" *South Carolina Review* 10(2), April 1978, 82-83.

"Messages: Giving a Son to the Sea"

RONALD BAUGHMAN. "James Dickey's *The Eye-Beaters*: 'An Agonizing New Life,'" *South Carolina Review* 10(2), April 1978, 83.

"On the Coosawattee"

BRUCE CARNES. "Deliverance in James Dickey's 'On the Coosawattee' and *Deliverance*," *Notes on Contemporary Literature* 7(2), March 1977, 2-4.

"Orpheus Before Hades"

DAVID C. BERRY. "Harmony with the Dead: James Dickey's Descent into the Underworld," *Southern Quarterly* 12(3), April 1974, 234-35.

"The Owl King"

JOYCE CAROL OATES. "Out of Stone into Flesh: The Imagination of James Dickey," *Modern Poetry Studies* 5(2), Autumn 1974, 105-6.

DICKEY, JAMES *(Cont.)*

"The Owl King" *(cont.)*

 RAYMOND SMITH. "The Poetic Faith of James Dickey," *Modern Poetry Studies* 2(6), 1972, 265-69.

"The Performance"

 LAURENCE LIEBERMAN. *Unassigned Frequencies,* pp. 84-85.

"Pine"

 RONALD BAUGHMAN. "James Dickey's *The Eye-Beaters*: 'An Agonizing New Life,'" *South Carolina Review* 10(2), April 1978, 86.

"Poem" *(Into the Stone)*

 DAVID C. BERRY. "Harmony with the Dead: James Dickey's Descent into the Underworld," *Southern Quarterly* 12(3), April 1974, 236.

"Power and Light"

 RICHARD CALHOUN. "James Dickey: The Expansive Imagination," in *Modern American Poetry,* ed. by Guy Owen, p. 251.

 LAURENCE LIEBERMAN. *Unassigned Frequencies,* pp. 75-76.

"Pursuit from Under"

 NORMAN FRIEDMAN. "The Wesleyan Poets — II," *Chicago Review* 19(1), 1966, 63-64.

 H. L. WEATHERBY. "The Way of Exchange in James Dickey's Poetry," *Sewanee Review* 74(3), Summer 1966, 676-77.

"Reincarnation 2"

 LAURENCE LIEBERMAN. *Unassigned Frequencies,* p. 98.

"The Shark's Parlor"

 H. L. WEATHERBY. "The Way of Exchange in James Dickey's Poetry," *Sewanee Review* 74(3), Summer 1966, 677.

"The Sheep Child"

 JOAN BOBBITT. "Unnatural Order in the Poetry of James Dickey," *Concerning Poetry* 11(1), Spring 1978, 41-42.

 RICHARD CALHOUN. "James Dickey: The Expansive Imagination," in *Modern American Poetry,* ed. by Guy Owen, pp. 249-50.

 LAURENCE LIEBERMAN. *Unassigned Frequencies,* pp. 79-80, 98-99.

"Slave Quarters"

 NORMAN FRIEDMAN. "The Wesleyan Poets — II," *Chicago Review* 19(1), 1966, 66.

 RICHARD HOWARD. "On James Dickey," *Partisan Review* 33(3), Summer 1966, 484-85.

"Sled Burial, Dream Country"

 WILLIAM HEYEN, ED. "A Conversation with James Dickey," *Southern Review,* n.s., 9(1), Winter 1973, 149-50.

"Sleeping Out at Easter"

 JOYCE CAROL OATES. "Out of Stone into Flesh: The Imagination of James Dickey," *Modern Poetry Studies* 5(2), Autumn 1974, 102-3.

"Snakebite"

 LAURENCE LIEBERMAN. *Unassigned Frequencies,* pp. 77-78.

"Springer Mountain"

 NORMAN FRIEDMAN. "The Wesleyan Poets — II," *Chicago Review* 19(1), 1966, 65.

 LAURENCE LIEBERMAN. *Unassigned Frequencies,* pp. 96-97.

 H. L. WEATHERBY. "The Way of Exchange in James Dickey's Poetry," *Sewanee Review* 74(3), Summer 1966, 673.

"The String"

 DAVID C. BERRY. "Harmony with the Dead: James Dickey's Descent into the Underworld," *Southern Quarterly* 12(3), April 1974, 236-37.

 LAURENCE LIEBERMAN. *Unassigned Frequencies,* pp. 89-91.

"Sun"

 NORMAN SILVERSTEIN. "James Dickey's Muscular Eschatology," *Salmagundi* 22-23 (Spring-Summer 1973), 264-66. Reprinted in: *Contemporary Poetry in America,* pp. 309-11.

"Trees and Cattle"

 RAYMOND SMITH. "The Poetic Faith of James Dickey," *Modern Poetry Studies* 2(6), 1972, 261-63.

"Turning Away"

 RONALD BAUGHMAN. "James Dickey's *The Eye-Beaters*: 'An Agonizing New Life,'" *South Carolina Review* 10(2), April 1978, 86-88.

 JOYCE CAROL OATES. "Out of Stone into Flesh: The Imagination of James Dickey," *Modern Poetry Studies* 5(2), Autumn 1974, 139-42.

"Two Poems of Going Home: Living There"

 RONALD BAUGHMAN. "James Dickey's *The Eye-Beaters*: 'An Agonizing New Life,'" *South Carolina Review* 10(2), April 1978, 83.

"Two Poems of Going Home: Looking for the Buckhead Boys"

 RONALD BAUGHMAN. "James Dickey's *The Eye-Beaters*: 'An Agonizing New Life,'" *South Carolina Review* 10(2), April 1974, 83-84.

"The Underground Stream"

 DAVID C. BERRY. "Harmony with the Dead: James Dickey's Descent into the Underworld," *Southern Quarterly* 12(3), April 1974, 237-38.

"The Vegetable King"

 GEORGE S. LENSING. "The Neo-Romanticism of James Dickey," *South Carolina Review* 10(2), April 1978, 22-23.

"Victory"

 RONALD BAUGHMAN. "James Dickey's *The Eye-Beaters*: 'An Agonizing New Life,'" *South Carolina Review* 10(2), April 1978, 82.

"A View of Fujiyama After the War"

 DAVID C. BERRY. "Harmony with the Dead: James Dickey's Descent into the Underworld," *Southern Quarterly* 12(3), April 1974, 240-41.

"The War Wound"

 NORMAN FRIEDMAN. "The Wesleyan Poets — II," *Chicago Review* 19(1), 1966, 64-65.

"Winter Trout"

 NORMAN FRIEDMAN. "The Wesleyan Poets — II," *Chicago Review* 19(1), 1966, 60-61.

DICKEY, WILLIAM

"Those Who Have Burned"

 JUDSON JEROME. "Introduction to the Poems of William Dickey," *Antioch Review* 23(1), Spring 1963, 52-53.

DICKINSON, EMILY

"The admirations and contemps of time"
ROLAND HAGENBÜCHLE. "Precision and Indeterminacy in the Poetry of Emily Dickinson," *ESQ* 20(1), First Quarter 1974, 45.

JAMES M. HUGHES. "Dickinson as 'Time's Sublimest Target,'" *Dickinson Studies* 34, Second Half 1978, 32-35.

ERNEST SANDEEN. "Delight Deterred by Retrospect: Emily Dickinson's Late-Summer Poems," *New England Quarterly* 40(4), December 1967, 492.

"After a hundred years"
FREDERICK L. MOREY. "Hundred Best Poems of Emily Dickinson," *Emily Dickinson Bulletin* 27, First Half 1975, 32.

"After great pain a formal feeling comes"
JEROME BEATY and WILLIAM H. MATCHETT. *Poetry from Statement to Meaning,* pp. 28-34.

CLEANTH BROOKS and ROBERT PENN WARREN. *Understanding Poetry,* pp. 468-71; revised ed., pp. 325-27.

STANLEY E. CLAYES and JOHN GERRIETTS. *Ways to Poetry,* p. 124.

ELIZABETH DREW. *Poetry,* pp. 124-25.

FRANCIS MANLEY. "An Explication of Dickinson's 'After Great Pain,'" *Modern Language Notes* 73(4), April 1958, 260-64.

WILLIAM BYSSHE STEIN. "Emily Dickinson's Parodic Masks," *University Review* 36(1), Autumn 1969, 54-55.

"An altered look about the hills"
JO ANN DE LAVAN WILLIAMS. "Spiders In The Attic: A Suggestion of Synthesis in the Poetry of Emily Dickinson," *Emily Dickinson Bulletin* 29, First Half 1976, 27.

"Ample make this bed"
FREDERICK L. MOREY. "Hundred Best Poems of Emily Dickinson," *Emily Dickinson Bulletin* 27, First Half 1975, 31.

"Angels in the early morning"
NANCY LAMPERT. "Dew Imagery in Emily Dickinson's Poetry," *Emily Dickinson Bulletin* 29, First Half 1976, 46.

"Apparently with no surprise"
HERBERT R. COURSEN, JR. "Nature's Center," *College English* 24(6), March 1963, 468-69.

LAURENCE PERRINE. *Sound and Sense,* pp. 126-27; second ed., pp. 138-39; third ed., pp. 165-66; fourth ed., pp. 155-56.

"'Arcturus' is his other name"
MARLENE SPRINGER. "Emily Dickinson's Humorous Road to Heaven," *Renascence* 23(3), Spring 1971, 132-34.

"Are friends delight or pain?"
CYNTHIA CHALIFF. "The Psychology of Economics in Emily Dickinson," *Literature and Psychology* 18(2-3), 1968, 95-96.

"Artists wrestled here"
GEORGE H. SOULE, JR. "ED and Jacob: 'Pugilist and Poet' Wrestling to the Dawn," *Emily Dickinson Bulletin* 31, First Half 1977, 52-53.

"As by the dead we love to sit"
EDGAR F. DANIELS. *Explicator* 35(2), Winter 1976, 10-11.

NAT HENRY. *Explicator* 31(5), January 1973, Item 35.

ROBERT L. LAIR. *Explicator* 25(7), March 1967, Item 58.

LAURENCE PERRINE. *Explicator* 33(6), February 1975, Item 49.

LAURENCE PERRINE. *Explicator* 36(3), Spring 1978, 32-33.

"As from the earth the light balloon"
MARIO L. D'AVANZO. "The Emersonian Context of Three Poems of ED," *Emily Dickinson Bulletin* 16(March 1971), 2-4.

"As if the sea should part"
SUZANNE JUHASZ. *Naked and Fiery Forms,* pp. 28-29.

"As imperceptibly as grief"
WALTER BLAIR. *The Literature of the United States,* II: 751.

SUZANNE JUHASZ. *Naked and Fiery Forms,* pp. 18-20.

FREDERICK L. MOREY. "Hundred Best Poems of Emily Dickinson," *Emily Dickinson Bulletin* 27, First Half 1975, 40-41.

"As watchers hang upon the east"
LAURENCE PERRINE. *Explicator* 35(2), Winter 1976, 4-5.

"At half past three a single bird"
ROBERT W. RUSSELL. *Explicator* 16(1), October 1957, Item 3.

"Aurora is the effort"
KENNETH B. NEWELL. *Explicator* 20(1), September 1961, Item 5.

"Awake ye muses nine"
VIVIAN R. POLLAK. "Emily Dickinson's Valentines," *American Quarterly* 26(1), March 1974, 66-72.

"Because I could not stop for death"
GÉMINO H. ABAD. *A Formal Approach to Lyric Poetry,* pp. 141-43.

WALTER BLAIR. *The Literature of the United States,* II: 750.

HAROLD BLOOM. *A Map of Misreading,* pp. 184-86.

RICHARD CHASE. *Emily Dickinson,* pp. 249-51. Abridged in: *The Case for Poetry,* pp. 105-6; second ed., pp. 91-92. Reprinted in: Cleanth Brooks and Robert Penn Warren. *Understanding Poetry,* third ed., pp. 327-28.

DAVID DAICHES and WILLIAM CHARVAT. *Poems in English,* p. 727.

DENIS DONOGHUE. "Emily Dickinson," in *Six American Poets from Emily Dickinson to the Present,* pp. 38-40.

PAUL J. FERLAZZO. "The Deadly Beau in Two Poems by Emily Dickinson," *Emily Dickinson Bulletin* 19 (December 1971), 133-36.

EUNICE GLENN. "Emily Dickinson's Poetry: A Revaluation," *Sewanee Review* 51(4), Autumn 1943, 585-88.

THEODORE C. HOEPFNER. "'Because I Could Not Stop for Death,'" *American Literature* 29(1), March 1957, 96. Abridged in: *The Case for Poetry,* second ed., p. 92.

WILLIAM R. MANIERRE. "E.D.: Visions and Revisions," *Texas Studies in Literature and Language* 5(1), Spring 1963, 6-11.

LOUIS L. MARTZ. *The Poem of the Mind,* pp. 94-95.

VIRGINIA POLANSKI. "His Poem or Mine?" *English Journal* 67(2), February 1978, 39-41.

KENNETH L. PRIVRATSKY. "Irony in Emily Dickinson's 'Because I Could Not Stop for Death,'" *Concerning Poetry* 11(2), Fall 1978, 25-30.

DICKINSON, EMILY *(Cont.)*

"Because I could not stop for death" *(cont.)*

JAMES REEVES. "Emily Dickinson," in *Commitment to Poetry*, p. 205.

D. S. SAVAGE. "Dickinson: Death: A Sequence of Poems," in *Master Poems of the English Language*, pp. 753-55.

ALLEN TATE. *Reactionary Essays on Poetry and Ideas*, pp. 14-16. Reprinted in: Cleanth Brooks and Robert Penn Warren. *Understanding Poetry*, third ed., p. 327. Also: Allen Tate. *On the Limits of Poetry*, pp. 205-7. Also: Charles Feidelson, Jr. and Paul Brodtkorb, Jr. *Interpretations of American Literature*, pp. 204-5. Also: Allen Tate. *Essays of Four Decades*, pp. 289-91. Also: *Readings for Liberal Education*, II: 173-74; revised ed., II: 165-66; third ed., II: 158-59. Abridged in: *The Case for Poetry*, p. 105; second ed., pp. 90-91.

LEONARD UNGER and WILLIAM VAN O'CONNOR. *Poems for Study*, pp. 547-48.

JOHN WHEATCROFT. "Emily Dickinson's Poetry and Jonathan Edwards on the Will," *Bucknell Review* 10(2), December 1961, 108-14.

YVOR WINTERS. *Maule's Curse*, pp. 154-56. Reprinted in: Yvor Winters. *In Defense of Reason*, pp. 288-90. Abridged in: *The Case for Poetry*, p. 105; second ed., p. 91.

"Because 'twas riches I could own"

CYNTHIA CHALIFF. "The Psychology of Economics in Emily Dickinson," *Literature and Psychology* 18(2-3), 1968, 95.

"Before I got my eye put out"

EVAN CARTON. "Dickinson and the Divine: The Terror of Integration, the Terror of Detachment," *ESQ* 24(4), Fourth Quarter 1978, 243-45.

JULE S. KAUFMAN. "Emily Dickinson and the Involvement of Retreat," *Tulane Studies in English* 21 (1974), 80-81.

THORNTON H. PARSONS. "The Indefatigable Casuist," *University of Kansas City Review* 30(1), Autumn 1963, 23.

"Behind me dips eternity"

SHARON CAMERON. " 'A Loaded Gun': Dickinson and the Dialectic of Rage," *PMLA* 93(3), May 1978, 430.

EVAN CARTON. "Dickinson and the Divine: The Terror of Integration, the Terror of Detachment," *ESQ* 24(4), Fourth Quarter 1978, 245-46.

FREDERICK L. MOREY. "Hundred Best Poems of Emily Dickinson," *Emily Dickinson Bulletin* 27, First Half 1975, 39.

"Belshazzar had a letter"

JEROME BEATY and WILLIAM H. MATCHETT. *Poetry From Statement to Meaning*, pp. 130-31.

"Bereaved of all, I went abroad"

JANET E. DeROSA. "J. 784: Bereaved of All, I Went Abroad," *Emily Dickinson Bulletin* 31, First Half 1977, 70-76.

"Besides the autumn poets sing"

VIVIAN R. POLLAK. "Emily Dickinson's Literary Allusions," *Essays in Literature* 1(1), Spring 1974, 57.

"The Bible is an antique volume"

ALBERT GELPI. *The Tenth Muse*, pp. 235-36.

CHAD and EVA T. WALSH. *Twice Ten*, pp. 111-13.

"A bird came down the walk"

J. BROOKS BOUSON. "ED and the Riddle of Containment," *Emily Dickinson Bulletin* 31, First Half 1977, 37.

FREDERIC I. CARPENTER. "Emily Dickinson and the Rhymes of Dream," *University of Kansas City Review* 20(2), Winter 1953, 119-20.

FREDERICK L. MOREY. "The Fifty Best Poems of Emily Dickinson (a three chapter study)," *Emily Dickinson Bulletin* 25, First Half 1974, 33.

ELEANOR WILNER. "The Poetics of Emily Dickinson," *ELH* 38(1), March 1971, 146-54.

"The brain is wider than the sky"

EVAN CARTON. "Dickinson and the Divine: The Terror of Integration, the Terror of Detachment," *ESQ* 24(4), Fourth Quarter 1978, 248.

LOUIS L. MARTZ. *The Poem of the Mind*, pp. 103-4.

FREDERICK L. MOREY. "Hundred Best Poems of Emily Dickinson," *Emily Dickinson Bulletin* 27, First Half 1975, 16.

"The bustle in a house"

DENIS DONOGHUE. "Emily Dickinson," in *Six American Poets from Emily Dickinson to the Present*, p. 40.

RAYMOND J. JORDAN. *Explicator* 21(6), February 1963, Item 49.

"The child's faith is new"

CYNTHIA CHALIFF. "ED as the Deprived Child," *Emily Dickinson Bulletin* 13 (June 1970), 37-38.

"A clock stopped"

EARL ROY MINER. *Explicator* 13(3), December 1954, Item 18.

FREDERICK L. MOREY. "The Fifty Best Poems of Emily Dickinson (a three chapter study)," *Emily Dickinson Bulletin* 25, First Half 1974, 16.

FREDERICK L. MOREY. "Hundred Best Poems of Emily Dickinson," *Emily Dickinson Bulletin* 27, First Half 1975, 32.

WILLIAM ROSSKY. *Explicator* 22(1), September 1963, Item 3.

"Come slowly, Eden"

SUZANNE JUHASZ. *Naked and Fiery Forms*, p. 25.

"The crickets sang"

SIMON TUGWELL. *Explicator* 23(6), February 1965, Item 46.

"Crumbling is not an instant's act"

CHARLES R. ANDERSON. "The Conscious Self in Emily Dickinson's Poetry," *American Literature* 31(3), November 1959, 297-98.

"Death is a dialogue between"

VIRGINIA H. ADAIR. *Explicator* 27(7), March 1969, Item 52.

LEE J. RICHMOND. "Dickinson's 'Death is a Dialogue,' " *Emily Dickinson Bulletin* 23, First Half 1973, 171.

"Death is a supple suitor"

PAUL J. FERLAZZO. "The Deadly Beau in Two Poems by Emily Dickinson," *Emily Dickinson Bulletin* 19 (December 1971), 136-38.

"A deed knocks first at thought"

JOHN WHEATCROFT. "Emily Dickinson's Poetry and Jonathan Edwards on the Will," *Bucknell Review* 10(2), December 1961, 103-4.

"The devil had he fidelity"

JOHN WHEATCROFT. " 'Holy Ghosts in Cages' — A Serious View of Humor in Emily Dickinson's Poetry," *American Transcendental Quarterly* 22(3), Spring 1974, 102.

"Did our best moment last"

DENIS DONOGHUE. *Connoisseurs of Chaos*, pp. 117-18.

"The difference between despair"

DOUGLAS A. NOVERR. "Emily Dickinson and the Art of Despair," *Emily Dickinson Bulletin* 23, First Half 1973, 162-63.

"A door just opened on a street"

THORNTON H. PARSONS. "The Indefatigable Casuist," *University of Kansas City Review* 30(1), Autumn 1963, 20.

"The drop that wrestles in the sea"

GEORGE H. SOULE, JR. "ED and Jacob: 'Pugilist and Poet' Wrestling to the Dawn," *Emily Dickinson Bulletin* 31, First Half 1977, 55-56.

"Dust is the only secret"

MARTIN BICKMAN. "Kora in Heaven: Love and Death in the Poetry of Emily Dickinson," *Emily Dickinson Bulletin* 32, Second Half 1977, 83.

"A dying tiger moaned for drink"

ELEANOR WILNER. "The Poetics of Emily Dickinson," *ELH* 38(1), March 1971, 129.

"Each life converges to some centre"

SALLY BURKE. "A Religion of Poetry: The Prayer Poems of Emily Dickinson," *Emily Dickinson Bulletin* 33, First Half 1978, 17-18.

ALBERT GELPI. *The Tenth Muse*, pp. 273-74.

AMY HORIUCHI. "Emily Dickinson's Existentialism," *Emily Dickinson Bulletin* 19 (December 1971), 112-13.

"Eden is that old-fashioned house"

ROY HARVEY PEARCE. *The Continuity of American Poetry*, pp. 186-87.

"Elysium is as far as to"

ROLAND HAGENBÜCHLE. "Precision and Indeterminacy in the Poetry of Emily Dickinson," *ESQ* 20(1), First Quarter 1974, 48-49.

JOHN F. LYNEN. "Three Uses of the Present: The Historian's, the Critic's, and Emily Dickinson's," *College English* 28(2), November 1966, 135.

STEPHEN WHICHER. *Explicator* 19(7), April 1961, Item 45.

"Escaping backward to perceive"

EVAN CARTON. "Dickinson and the Divine: The Terror of Integration, the Terror of Detachment," *ESQ* 24(4), Fourth Quarter 1978, 246-47.

"Essential oils are wrung"

FREDERICK L. MOREY. "Hundred Best Poems of Emily Dickinson," *Emily Dickinson Bulletin* 27, First Half 1975, 26.

"Except the smaller size"

CHARLES R. ANDERSON. "The Conscious Self in Emily Dickinson's Poetry," *American Literature* 31(3), November 1959, 295-96.

" 'Faith' is a fine invention"

MARIO L. D'AVANZO. "The Emersonian Context Of Three Poems of ED," *Emily Dickinson Bulletin* 16 (March 1971), 4-6.

PAUL WITHERINGTON. *Explicator* 26(8), April 1968, Item 62.

"The farthest thunder that I heard"

OLIVE H. RABE. "Emily Dickinson as mystic," *Colorado Quarterly* 14(3), Winter 1966, 280-84.

"The feet of people walking home"

TED-LARRY PEBWORTH and JAY CLAUDE SUMMERS. *Explicator* 27(9), May 1969, Item 76.

"A field of stubble lying sere"

ANDREA GOUDIE. "Another Path to Reality: Emily Dickinson's Birds," *Concerning Poetry* 7(1), Spring 1974, 32.

"The first day's night had come"

DENIS DONOGHUE. *Connoisseurs of Chaos*, pp. 110-11.

SIMON A. GROLNICK. "Article Review: Emily and the Psychobiographer," *Literature and Psychology* 23(2), 1973, 79.

CONSTANCE ROOKE. " 'The first Day's Night had come — ' an explication of J. 410," *Emily Dickinson Bulletin* 24, Second Half 1973, 221-23.

"For each extatic instant"

JULE S. KAUFMAN. "Emily Dickinson and the Involvement of Retreat," *Tulane Studies in English* 21 (1974), 82-83.

"For every bird a nest"

BARTON LEVI ST. ARMAND. *Explicator* 35(3), Spring 1977, 34-35.

GEORGE MONTEIRO. *Explicator* 37(1), Fall 1978, 28-29.

"Forever is composed of nows"

JOHN F. LYNEN. "Three Uses of the Present: The Historian's, the Critic's, and Emily Dickinson's," *College English* 28(2), November 1966, 130-31.

"Four trees upon a solitary acre"

CAROLE ANNE TAYLOR. "Kierkegaard and the Ironic Voices of Emily Dickinson," *Journal of English and Germanic Philology* 77(4), October 1978, 571.

"From a cocoon forth a butterfly"

SISTER CHARLOTTE DOWNEY. "Antithesis: How ED uses Style to Express Inner Conflict," *Emily Dickinson Bulletin* 33, First Half 1978, 10-11.

AUDRY S. EYLER. "An Explication of Poem 354 'Some keep the Sabbath going to Church,' " *Emily Dickinson Bulletin* 29, First Half 1976, 40-43.

"Funny to be a century"

PAUL W. ANDERSON. "The Metaphysical Mirth of Emily Dickinson," *Georgia Review* 20(1), Spring 1966, 77.

"Further in summer than the birds"

FREDERIC I. CARPENTER. "Emily Dickinson and the Rhymes of Dream," *University of Kansas City Review* 20(2), Winter 1953, 118.

FREDERIC I. CARPENTER. *Explicator* 8(5), March 1950, Item 33.

ROBERT H. ELIAS and HELEN L. ELIAS. *Explicator* 11(1), October 1952, Item 5.

SIDNEY E. LIND. "Emily Dickinson's 'Further in Summer than the Birds' and Nathaniel Hawthorne's 'The Old Manse,' " *American Literature* 39(2), May 1967, 163-69.

DAVID PORTER. "The Crucial Experience in Emily Dickinson's Poetry," *ESQ* 20(4), Fourth Quarter 1974, 288-89.

RENÉ RAPIN. *Explicator* 12(4), February 1954, Item 24.

ERNEST SANDEEN. "Delight Deferred by Retrospect: Emily Dickinson's Late-Summer Poems," *New England Quarterly* 40(4), December 1967, 496-97.

DICKINSON, EMILY *(Cont.)*

"Further in summer than the birds" *(cont.)*

> MARSHALL VAN DEUSEN. *Explicator* 13(5), March 1955, Item 33.

> YVOR WINTERS. *Maule's Curse*, pp. 159-60. Reprinted in: *The Literature of the United States*, II: 752. Also: Yvor Winters. *In Defense of Reason*, pp. 292-93.

"The gentian weaves her fringes"

> ERNEST SANDEEN. "Delight Deferred by Retrospect: Emily Dickinson's Late-Summer Poems," *New England Quarterly* 40(4), December 1967, 486-87.

"Go not too near a house of rose"

> WARREN BECK. "Poetry's Chronic Disease," *English Journal* 33(7), September 1944, 362-63.

> JAMES REEVES. "Emily Dickinson," in *Commitment to Poetry*, p. 196.

> MACKLIN THOMAS. "Analysis of the Experience in Lyric Poetry," *College English* 9(6), March 1948, 320-21.

> DAVID W. THOMPSON. "Interpretative Reading as Symbolic Action," *Quarterly Journal of Speech* 42(4), December 1956, 395-96.

"Go thy great way"

> ROLAND HAGENBÜCHLE. "Precision and Indeterminacy in the Poetry of Emily Dickinson," *ESQ* 20(1), First Quarter 1974, 43.

> ELEANOR WILNER. "The Poetics of Emily Dickinson," *ELH* 38(1), March 1971, 138-39.

"God is a distant, stately lover"

> CAROLE ANNE TAYLOR. "Kierkegaard and the Ironic Voices of Emily Dickinson," *Journal of English and Germanic Philology* 77(4), October 1978, 578-79.

"God permits industrious angels"

> MARLENE SPRINGER. "Emily Dickinson's Humorous Road to Heaven," *Renascence* 23(3), Spring 1971, 132.

"The grass so little has to do"

> PAUL W. ANDERSON. "The Metaphysical Mirth of Emily Dickinson," *Georgia Review* 20(1), Spring 1966, 75-76.

"A great hope fell"

> DOUGLAS A. NOVERR. "Emily Dickinson and the Art of Despair," *Emily Dickinson Bulletin* 23, First Half 1973, 163-64.

"The harm of years is on him"

> CHARLES R. ANDERSON. "The Conscious Self in Emily Dickinson's Poetry," *American Literature* 31(3), November 1959, 296-97.

"He fumbles at your soul"

> MARTIN BICKMAN. "Kora in Heaven: Love and Death in the Poetry of Emily Dickinson," *Emily Dickinson Bulletin* 32, Second Half 1977, 81.

> RICHARD CHASE. *Emily Dickinson*, pp. 204-5.

> CLARK GRIFFITH. "Emily Dickinson's Love Poetry," *University of Kansas City Review* 27(2), Winter 1960, 99-100.

> FREDERICK L. MOREY. "The Fifty Best Poems of Emily Dickinson (a three chapter study)," *Emily Dickinson Bulletin* 25, First Half 1974, 18.

"He put the belt around my life"

> EUNICE GLENN. "Emily Dickinson's Poetry: A Revaluation," *Sewanee Review* 51(4), Autumn 1943, 580-82.

"He touched me, so I live to know"

> CHESTER P. SADOWY. *Explicator* 37(1), Fall 1978, 4-5.

"The heart asks pleasure first"

> FREDERIC I. CARPENTER. "Emily Dickinson and the Rhymes of Dream," *University of Kansas City Review* 20(2), Winter 1953, 115.

" 'Heavenly Father,' take to thee"

> SOPHIA M. DAVIS. " 'Heavenly Father' — take to thee (An explication of poem J1461)," *Emily Dickinson Bulletin* 33, First Half 1978, 40-44.

> ALBERT GELPI. *The Tenth Muse*, pp. 236-37.

> DAVID A. ROBERTS. "Emily Dickinson's 'woe of ecstasy,' " *Colorado Quarterly* 23(4), Spring 1975, 514-15.

> CAROLE ANNE TAYLOR. "Kierkegaard and the Ironic Voices of Emily Dickinson," *Journal of English and Germanic Philology* 77(4), October 1978, 574.

> JOHN WHEATCROFT. " 'Holy Ghosts in Cages' — A Serious View of Humor in Emily Dickinson's Poetry," *American Transcendental Quarterly* 22(3), Spring 1974, 101-2.

"His mind like fabrics of the East"

> VIVIAN R. POLLAK. " 'That Fine Prosperity': Economic Metaphors in Emily Dickinson's Poetry," *Modern Language Quarterly* 34(2), June 1973, 173.

"Hope is a strange invention"

> CHARLES R. ANDERSON. "The Conscious Self in Emily Dickinson's Poetry," *American Literature* 31(3), November 1959, 301-2.

" 'Hope' is the thing with feathers"

> ANDREA GOUDIE. "Another Path to Reality: Emily Dickinson's Birds," *Concerning Poetry* 7(1), Spring 1974, 35-36.

"A house upon the height"

> LAURENCE PERRINE. *Explicator* 36(3), Spring 1978, 14-15.

> ELEANOR WILNER. "The Poetics of Emily Dickinson," *ELH* 38(1), March 1971, 140-41.

"How dare the robins sing"

> GEORGE H. SOULE, JR. "ED and Jacob: 'Pugilist and Poet' Wrestling to the Dawn," *Emily Dickinson Bulletin* 31, First Half 1977, 53-54.

"How happy I was if I could forget"

> SUZANNE JUHASZ. " 'I Dwell in Possibility' ED in the Subjunctive Mood," *Emily Dickinson Bulletin* 32, Second Half 1977, 107.

"How happy is the little stone"

> JOHN F. LYNEN. "Three Uses of the Present: The Historian's, the Critics, and Emily Dickinson's," *College English* 28(2), November 1966, 135-36.

"I asked no other thing"

> J. A. LAVIN. "Replies: Emily Dickinson and Brazil," *Notes & Queries*, n.s., 7(7), July 1960, 270-71.

> VIVIAN R. POLLAK. " 'That Fine Prosperity': Economic Metaphors in Emily Dickinson's Poetry," *Modern Language Quarterly* 34(2), June 1973, 169-70.

"I can wade grief"

> JOHN CODY. *Explicator* 37(1), Fall 1978, 15-16.

> WILLIAM HOWARD. *Explicator* 14(3), December 1955, Item 17.

> THORNTON H. PARSONS. "The Indefatigable Casuist," *University of Kansas City Review* 30(1), Autumn 1963, 22.

"I cannot dance upon my toes"

DAVID T. PORTER. "Emily Dickinson: The Formative Years," *Massachusetts Review* 6(3), Spring-Summer 1965, 565-66.

"I cannot live with you"

SHARON CAMERON. " 'A Loaded Gun': Dickinson and the Dialectic of Rage," *PMLA* 93(3), May 1978, 431-33.

EUNICE GLENN. "Emily Dickinson's Poetry: A Revaluation," *Sewanee Review* 51(4), Autumn 1943, 582-85.

FREDERICK L. MOREY. "The Fifty Best Poems of Emily Dickinson (a three chapter study)," *Emily Dickinson Bulletin* 25, First Half 1974, 12.

FREDERICK L. MOREY. "Hundred Best Poems of Emily Dickinson," *Emily Dickinson Bulletin* 27, First Half 1975, 23.

J. ANNE NEFF. "The Door Ajar," *Emily Dickinson Bulletin* 21 (June 1972), 78-81.

"I cautious scanned my little life"

DAVID A. ROBERTS. "Emily Dickinson's 'woe of ecstasy,' " *Colorado Quarterly* 23(4), Spring 1975, 506.

"I died for beauty, but was scarce"

GÉMINO H. ABAD. *A Formal Approach to Lyric Poetry,* pp. 139-41.

FREDERIC I. CARPENTER. "Emily Dickinson and the Rhymes of Dream," *University of Kansas City Review* 20(2), Winter 1953, 116-17.

FREDERICK L. MOREY. "Hundred Best Poems of Emily Dickinson," *Emily Dickinson Bulletin* 27, First Half 1975, 21.

"I dreaded that first robin so"

JOHN S. MANN. "Emily Dickinson, Emerson, and the Poet as Namer," *New England Quarterly* 51(4), December 1978, 486-88.

FREDERICK L. MOREY. "The Fifty Best Poems of Emily Dickinson (a three chapter study)," *Emily Dickinson Bulletin* 25, First Half 1974, 33-34.

"I dwell in possibility"

SUZANNE JUHASZ. " 'I Dwell in Possibility': ED in the Subjunctive Mood," *Emily Dickinson Bulletin* 32, Second Half 1977, 105.

"I felt a cleaving in my mind"

R. BETSY TENENBAUM. "Varieties of 'Extremity' in ED's Poetry," *Emily Dickinson Bulletin* 32, Second Half 1977, 120.

"I felt a funeral in my brain"

J. BROOKS BOUSON. "ED and the Riddle of Containment," *Emily Dickinson Bulletin* 31, First Half 1977, 45-46.

JOSEPH M. GARRISON, JR. "Emily Dickinson: From Ballerina to Gymnast," *ELH* 42(1), Spring 1975, 115-16.

SUZANNE JUHASZ. *Naked and Fiery Forms,* pp. 27-28.

GEORGE MONTEIRO. "Traditional Ideas in Dickinson's 'I Felt a Funeral in My Brain,' " *Modern Language Notes* 75(8), December 1960, 656-63.

FREDERICK L. MOREY. "The Fifty Best Poems of Emily Dickinson (a three chapter study)," *Emily Dickinson Bulletin* 25, First Half 1974, 25, 27.

FREDERICK L. MOREY. "Hundred Best Poems of Emily Dickinson," *Emily Dickinson Bulletin* 27, First Half 1975, 28.

DAVID A. ROBERTS. "Emily Dickinson's 'woe of ecstasy,' " *Colorado Quarterly* 23(4), Spring 1975, 507-9.

WILLIAM BYSSHE STEIN. "Emily Dickinson's Parodic Masks," *University Review* 36(1), Autumn 1969, 52-54.

R. BETSEY TENENBAUM. "Varieties of 'Extremity' in E.D.'s Poetry," *Emily Dickinson Bulletin* 32, Second Half 1977, 120.

"I found the words to every thought"

FREDERICK L. MOREY. "Hundred Best Poems of Emily Dickinson," *Emily Dickinson Bulletin* 27, First Half 1975, 38.

"I gave myself to him"

FREDERICK L. MOREY. "Hundred Best Poems of Emily Dickinson," *Emily Dickinson Bulletin* 27, First Half 1975, 36.

VIVIAN R. POLLAK. " 'That Fine Prosperity': Economic Metaphors in Emily Dickinson's Poetry," *Modern Language Quarterly* 34(2), June 1973, 173.

"I had a guinea golden"

VIVIAN R. POLLAK. "Emily Dickinson's Literary Allusions," *Essays in Literature* 1(1), Spring 1974, 55-57.

"I had been hungry all the years"

THORNTON H. PARSONS. "The Indefatigable Casuist," *University of Kansas City Review* 30(1), Autumn 1963, 20-21.

"I had not minded walls"

E. MILLER BUDICK. " 'I Had Not Minded — Walls — ': The Method and Meaning of Emily Dickinson's Symbolism," *Concerning Poetry* 9(2), Fall 1976, 5-12.

ROBERT MERIDETH. *Explicator* 23(3), November 1964, Item 25.

REBECCA PATTERSON. "Emily Dickinson's 'Double' Tim: Masculine Identification," *American Imago* 28(4), Winter 1971, 340-42.

MARK VAN DOREN. *Introduction to Poetry,* pp. 12-16.

"I have a king who does not speak"

VIRGINIA OGDEN BIRDSALL. "Emily Dickinson's Intruder in the Soul," *American Literature* 37(1), March 1965, 54-55.

"I heard a fly buzz when I died"

RONALD BECK. *Explicator* 26(4), December 1967, Item 31.

JOHN CIARDI. *Explicator* 14(4), January 1956, Item 22. (P) Reprinted in: Chad and Eva T. Walsh. *Twice Ten,* p. 119.

DENIS DONOGHUE. "Emily Dickinson," in *Six American Poets from Emily Dickinson to the Present,* pp. 37-38.

GERHARD FRIEDRICH. *Explicator* 13(6), April 1955, Item 35. Reprinted in: Chad and Eva T. Walsh, *Twice Ten,* pp. 118-19.

CLARENCE L. GOHDES. "Emily Dickinson's Blue Fly," *New England Quarterly* 51(3), September 1978, 423-31.

CAROLINE HOGUE. *Explicator* 20(3), November 1961, Item 26.

EUGENE HOLLAHAN. *Explicator* 25(1), September 1966, Item 6.

BENJAMIN T. SPENCER. "Criticism: Centrifugal and Centripetal," *Criticism* 8(2), Spring 1966, 141-43.

MELVIN G. WILLIAMS. "I. A. Richards on Dickinson: A Conjecture," *Emily Dickinson Bulletin* 26, Second Half 1974, 61-63.

DICKINSON, EMILY *(Cont.)*

"I held a jewel in my fingers"

    CYNTHIA CHALIFF. "The Psychology of Economics in Emily Dickinson," *Literature and Psychology* 18(2-3), 1968, 97.

"I know some lonely houses off the road"

    VIRGINIA OGDEN BIRDSALL. "Emily Dickinson's Intruder in the Soul," *American Literature* 37(1), March 1965, 56-59.

    MYRON OCHSHORN. *Explicator* 11(2), November 1952, Item 12.

"I know that he exists"

    EVAN CARTON. "Dickinson and the Divine: The Terror of Integration, the Terror of Detachment," *ESQ* 24(4), Fourth Quarter 1978, 249-50.

    GARY D. ELLIOTT. "The Solitary Dissenter: A Study of Emily Dickinson's Concept of God," *Emily Dickinson Bulletin* 20 (March 1972), 39-40.

    DAVID A. ROBERTS. "Emily Dickinson's 'woe of ecstasy,' " *Colorado Quarterly* 23(4), Spring 1975, 513-14.

"I like to see it lap the miles"

    GÉMINO H. ABAD. *A Formal Approach to Lyric Poetry,* pp. 277, 342-44.

    MARIO L. D'AVANZO. "J. 585: I like to see it lap the miles," *Emily Dickinson Bulletin* 31, First Half 1977, 59-61.

    FREDERICK J. HOFFMAN. "The Technological Fallacy in Contemporary Poetry: Hart Crane and MacKnight Black," *American Literature* 21(1), March 1949, 97. Reprinted in: Norman C. Stageberg and Wallace L. Anderson. *Poetry as experience,* p. 460.

    ROBERT E. LOWREY. " 'Boanerges': An Encomium for Edward Dickinson," *Arizona Quarterly* 26(1), Spring 1970, 54-58.

    JAMES MCNALLY. "Perspective in Movement — A Poem by Emily Dickinson," *CEA Critic* 26(2), November 1963, 9-10.

    FREDERICK L. MOREY. "The Fifty Best Poems of Emily Dickinson (a three chapter study)," *Emily Dickinson Bulletin* 25, First Half 1974, 35.

    "I. O. N.," *Explicator* 2(7), May 1944, Q31.

"I make this crescent fill or lack"

    EVAN CARTON. "Dickinson and the Divine: The Terror of Integration, the Terror of Detachment'," " *ESQ* 24(4), Fourth Quarter 1978, 248.

"I meant to have but modest needs"

    SALLY BURKE. "A Religion of Poetry: The Prayer Poems of Emily Dickinson," *Emily Dickinson Bulletin* 33, First Half 1978, 20-21.

    ROBERT GILLESPIE. "A Circumference of Emily Dickinson," *New England Quarterly* 46(2), June 1973, 260-61.

    VIVIAN R. POLLAK. " 'That Fine Prosperity': Economic Metaphors in Emily Dickinson's Poetry," *Modern Language Quarterly* 34(2), June 1973, 170-71.

"I never felt at home below"

    MARLENE SPRINGER. "Emily's Dickinson's Humorous Road to Heaven," *Renascence* 23(3), Spring 1971, 134-35.

"I never hear that one is dead"

    MYRON OCHSHORN. "In Search of Emily Dickinson," *New Mexico Quarterly Review* 23(1), Spring 1953, 101-2, 104. (P)

"I never hear the word 'escape' "

    THORNTON H. PARSONS. "The Indefatigable Casuist," *University of Kansas City Review* 30(1), Autumn 1963, 19.

"I never lost as much but twice"

    GARY D. ELLIOTT. "The Solitary Dissenter: A Study of Emily Dickinson's Concept of God," *Emily Dickinson Bulletin* 20 (March 1972), 42.

    ALLEN D. LACKEY. *Explicator* 34(3), November 1975, Item 18.

    GEORGE MONTEIRO. *Explicator* 30(1), September 1971, Item 7.

    VIVAIN R. POLLAK. " 'That Fine Prosperity': Economic Metaphors in Emily Dickinson's Poetry," *Modern Language Quarterly* 34(2), June 1973, 168-69.

    RENÉ RAPIN. *Explicator* 31(7), March 1973, Item 52.

"I never saw a moor"

    ROBERT F. FLEISSNER. "Dickinson's 'Moor,' " *Dickinson Studies* 34, Second Half 1978, 8.

    ROBERT MERIDETH. "Emily Dickinson and the Acquisitive Society," *New England Quarterly* 37(4), December 1964, 448-51.

"I read my sentence steadily"

    FREDERICK L. MOREY. "Hundred Best Poems of Emily Dickinson," *Emily Dickinson Bulletin* 27, First Half 1975, 39.

"I reason earth is short"

    DENIS DONOGHUE. *Connoisseurs of Chaos,* pp. 109-10.

    THORNTON H. PARSONS. "The Indefatigable Casuist," *University of Kansas City Review* 30(1), Autumn 1963, 25.

    CAROLE ANNE TAYLOR. "Kierkegaard and the Ironic Voices of Emily Dickinson," *Journal of English and Germanic Philology* 77(4), October 1978, 575-76.

"I rose because he sank"

    ALBERT GELPI. *The Tenth Muse,* pp. 253-54.

"I saw no way — the heavens were stitched"

    F. K. BARTSCH. "J. 378: I saw no way — The Heavens were stitched," *Emily Dickinson Bulletin* 31, First Half 1977, 62-64.

    ALBERT GELPI. *The Tenth Muse,* p. 272.

"I should have been too glad, I see"

    SHARON CAMERON. " 'A Loaded Gun': Dickinson and the Dialectic of Rage," *PMLA* 93(3), May 1978, 424-25.

    SCOTT DONALDSON. "Minding Emily Dickinson's Business," *New England Quarterly* 41(4), December 1968, 578-79.

    FREDERICK L. MOREY. "Hundred Best Poems of Emily Dickinson," *Emily Dickinson Bulletin* 27(First half, 1975), 25.

    MYRON OCHSHORN. "In Search of Emily Dickinson," *New Mexico Quarterly Review* 23(1), Spring 1953, 97-98.

"I started early, took my dog"

    VIRGINIA OGDEN BIRDSALL. "Emily Dickinson's Intruder in the Soul," *American Literature* 37(1), March 1965, 61-64.

    ERIC W. CARLSON. *Explicator* 20(9), May 1962, Item 72.

    WALTER H. EITNER. "ED: Another Daphne?" *Emily Dickinson Bulletin* 33, First Half 1978, 35-39.

    KATE FLORES. *Explicator* 9(7), May 1951, Item 47.

    GEORGE S. LENSING. *Explicator* 31(4), December 1972, Item 30.

FREDERICK L. MOREY. "The Fifty Best Poems of Emily Dickinson (a three chapter study)," *Emily Dickinson Bulletin* 25, First Half 1974, 25.

LAURENCE PERRINE. *Explicator* 10(4), February 1952, Item 28.

JAMES REEVES. "Emily Dickinson," in *Commitment to Poetry*, pp. 204-5.

"I stepped from plank to plank"

DAVID A. ROBERTS. "Emily Dickinson's 'woe of ecstasy,'" *Colorado Quarterly* 23(4), Spring 1975, 509-10.

"I taste a liquor never brewed"

JOHN CODY. *Explicator* 36(3), Spring 1978, 7-8.

LLOYD M. DAVIS. *Explicator* 23(7), March 1965, Item 53.

CECIL B. EBY. "'I Taste a Liquor Never Brewed': A Variant Reading," *American Literature* 36(4), January 1965, 516-18.

NANCY LAMPERT. "Dew Imagery in Emily Dickinson's Poetry," *Emily Dickinson Bulletin* 29, First Half 1976, 48-49.

WILLIAM BYSSHE STEIN. "Emily Dickinson's Parodic Masks," *University Review* 36(1), Autumn 1969, 49-52.

"I think the hemlock likes to stand"

THORNTON H. PARSONS. "The Indefatigable Casuist," *University of Kansas City Review* 30(1), Autumn 1963, 21-22.

"I tie my hat, I crease my shawl"

SHARON CAMERON. "'A Loaded Gun': Dickinson and the Dialectic of Rage," *PMLA* 93(3), May 1978, 431.

DAVID A. ROBERTS. "Emily Dickinson's 'woe of ecstasy,'" *Colorado Quarterly* 23(4), Spring 1975, 510-12.

"I would not paint a picture"

ALBERT GELPI. *The Tenth Muse*, pp. 289-90.

SUZANNE JUHASZ. *Naked and Fiery Forms*, p. 13. (P)

"I years had been from home"

STEVEN AXELROD. "Terror in the Everyday: Emily Dickinson's 'I Years Had Been From Home' (609)," *Concerning Poetry* 6(1), Spring 1973, 53-56.

J. BROOKS BOUSON. "ED and the Riddle of Containment," *Emily Dickinson Bulletin* 31, First Half 1977, 47.

JAMES E. MILLER, JR. "Emily Dickinson's The Thunder's Tongue," *Minnesota Review* 2(3), Spring 1962, 303. Reprinted in: James E. Miller, Jr. *Quests Surd and Absurd*, pp. 154-58.

FREDERICK L. MOREY. "Hundred Best Poems of Emily Dickinson," *Emily Dickinson Bulletin* 27, First Half 1975, 29.

JOHN TIMMERMAN. "God and Image of God in J. 609: A Brief Analysis," *Emily Dickinson Bulletin* 28, Second Half 1975, 124-26.

"If anybody's friend be dead"

FREDERICK L. MOREY. "Hundred Best Poems of Emily Dickinson," *Emily Dickinson Bulletin* 27, First Half 1975, 33.

"If I could bribe them by a rose"

CYNTHIA CHALIFF. "The Psychology of Economics in Emily Dickinson," *Literature and Psychology* 18(2-3), 1968, 93-94.

"If I should die"

VIVIAN R. POLLAK. "'That Fine Prosperity': Economic Metaphors in Emily Dickinson's Poetry," *Modern Language Quarterly* 34(2), June 1973, 164-66.

"If pain for peace prepares"

SUZANNE JUHASZ. "'I Dwell in Possibility' ED in the Subjunctive Mood," *Emily Dickinson Bulletin* 32, Second Half 1977, 107-8.

"If recollecting were forgetting"

SUZANNE JUHASZ. "'I Dwell in Possibility' ED in the Subjunctive Mood," *Emily Dickinson Bulletin* 32, Second Half 1977, 107.

"If you were coming in the fall"

FREDERICK KEEFER and DEBORAH VLAHOS. *Explicator* 29 (3), November 1970, Item 23.

LEE J. RICHMOND. "Emily Dickinson's 'If you were coming in the Fall': An Explication," *English Journal* 59(6), September 1970, 771-73.

"I'll tell you how the sun rose"

WILBUR SCOTT. *Explicator* 7(2), November 1948, Item 14.

"I'm ceded, I've stopped being theirs"

GLAUCO CAMBON. "Violence and Abstraction in Emily Dickinson," *Sewanee Review* 68(3), Summer 1960, 451-52. (P)

ALBERT GELPI. *The Tenth Muse*, p. 255.

FREDERICK L. MOREY. "Hundred Best Poems of Emily Dickinson," *Emily Dickinson Bulletin* 27, First Half 1975, 36.

"I'm 'wife' — I've finished that"

ALBERT GELPI. *The Tenth Muse*, p. 249. (P)

"Image of light, adieu"

ROLAND HAGENBÜCHLE. "Precision and Indeterminacy in the Poetry of Emily Dickinson," *ESQ* 20(1), First Quarter 1974, 38.

"Immured in heaven"

THOMAS H. JACKSON. *Explicator* 11(5), March 1953, Item 36.

"In snow thou comest"

ARCHIBALD MACLEISH. *Poetry and Experience*, pp. 109-10.

"In winter in my room"

JOHN S. MANN. "Dream in Emily Dickinson's Poetry," *Dickinson Studies* 34, Second Half 1978, 24-25.

"Is bliss then such abyss"

ROBERT MERIDETH. "Emily Dickinson and the Acquisitive Society," *New England Quarterly* 37(4), December 1964, 441-42.

"It always felt to me a wrong"

GARY D. ELLIOTT. "The Solitary Dissenter: A Study of Emily Dickinson's Concept of God," *Emily Dickinson Bulletin* 20 (March 1972), 43-44.

ALBERT GELPI. *The Tenth Muse*, p. 234.

REBECCA PATTERSON. "Emily Dickinson's 'Double' Tim: Masculine Identification," *American Imago* 28(4), Winter 1971, 356-57.

"It don't sound so terrible, quite, as it did"

THOMAS W. FORD. "Emily Dickinson and the Civil War," *University Review* 31(3), Spring 1965, 201-2.

DICKINSON, EMILY (Cont.)

"It dropped so low in my regard"

ARCHIBALD A. HILL. "Figurative Structure and Meaning: Two Poems by Emily Dickinson," *Texas Studies in Literature and Language* 16(1), Spring 1974, 206-8. Reprinted in: Archibald A. Hill. *Constituent and Pattern in Poetry*, pp. 133-35.

TED-LARRY PEBWORTH. "The Lusterware on Dickinson's Silver Shelf," *American Notes & Queries*, n.s., 12(2), October 1973, 18.

"It feels a shame to be alive"

THOMAS W. FORD. "Emily Dickinson and the Civil War," *University Review* 31(3), Spring 1965, 202.

"It is an honorable thought"

CHAD and EVA T. WALSH. *Twice Ten*, pp. 110-11.

"It might be lonelier"

SUZANNE JUHASZ. *Naked and Fiery Forms*, pp. 21-23.

"It was not death, for I stood up"

JOHN K. CRABBE. "A Thing Without Feathers (J. 510)," *Dickinson Studies* 34, Second Half 1978, 3-6.

DOUGLAS A. NOVERR. "Emily Dickinson and the Art of Despair," *Emily Dickinson Bulletin* 23, First Half 1973, 165-66.

"It would have starved a gnat"

CYNTHIA CHALIFF. "ED as a Deprived Child," *Emily Dickinson Bulletin* 13 (June 1970), 34-35.

"It would never be common more, I said"

PATRICK O'DONNELL. "Zones of the Soul: Emily Dickinson's Geographical Imagery," *CLA Journal* 21(1), September 1977, 64. (P)

"It's easy to invent a life"

VIVIAN R. POLLAK. " 'That Fine Prosperity': Economic Metaphors in Emily Dickinson's Poetry," *Modern Language Quarterly* 34(2), June 1973, 167-68.

DAVID A. ROBERTS. "Emily Dickinson's 'woe of ecstasy,' " *Colorado Quarterly* 23(4), Spring 1975, 514.

"It's like the light"

JAMES ASHBROOK PERKINS. "What Is It That Is Like the Light: A Consideration of J. 297," *Emily Dickinson Bulletin* 28, Second Half 1975, 129-31.

"I've dropped my brain — my soul is numb"

CHARLES R. ANDERSON. "The Conscious Self in Emily Dickinson's Poetry," *American Literature* 31(3), November 1959, 299-301.

"I've seen a dying eye"

MARIO D'AVANZO. "Emily Dickinson's 'Dying Eye,' " *Renascence* 19(2), Winter 1967, 110-11.

"Just lost, when I was saved"

KATHERINE W. SNIPES. "Emily Dickinson's Odd Secrets of the Line," *Emily Dickinson Bulletin* 11 (December 1969), 119.

JEFFREY STEINBRINK. "Emily Dickinson and Sylvia Plath: The Values of Mortality," *Women & Literature* 4(1), Spring 1976, 47-48.

"Lad of Athens, faithful be"

HYATT H. WAGGONER. *American Poets*, p. 203.

"The lamp burns sure within"

STUART LEWIS. *Explicator* 28(1), September 1969, Item 4.

"The last night that she lived"

GÉMINO H. ABAD. *A Formal Approach to Lyric Poetry*, pp. 161-63.

GÉMINO H. ABAD. *In Another Light*, pp. 158-61.

HARRY MODEAN CAMPBELL. *Explicator* 8(7), May 1950, Item 54.

DENIS DONOGHUE. *Connoisseurs of Chaos*, pp. 120-21.

DENIS DONOGHUE. "Emily Dickinson," in *Six American Poets from Emily Dickinson to the Present*, pp. 36-37.

JAMES REEVES. "Emily Dickinson," in *Commitment to Poetry*, p. 204.

"The last of summer is delight"

ERNEST SANDEEN. "Delight Deferred by Retrospect: Emily Dickinson's Late-Summer Poems," *New England Quarterly* 40(4), December 1967, 490-91.

"Lay this laurel on the one"

ARCHIBALD MACLEISH. *Poetry and Experience*, p. 99.

"Let me not mar that perfect dream"

FREDERICK L. MOREY. "Hundred Best Poems of Emily Dickinson," *Emily Dickinson Bulletin* 27, First Half 1975, 30.

"A light exists in spring"

CLARK GRIFFITH. "Frost and the American View of Nature," *American Quarterly* 20(1), Spring 1968, 27-28.

"Like rain it sounded till it curved"

HYATT H. WAGGONER. *American Poets*, pp. 216-19.

"A little east of Jordan"

REBECCA PATTERSON. "Emily Dickinson's 'Double' Tim: Masculine Identification," *American Imago* 28(4), Winter 1971, 355.

GEORGE H. SOULE, JR. "ED and Jacob: 'Pugilist and Poet' Wrestling to the Dawn," *Emily Dickinson Bulletin* 31, First Half 1977, 50-52.

"The Malay took the pearl"

ELEANOR WILNER. "The Poetics of Emily Dickinson," *ELH* 38(1), March 1971, 143-44.

"Many a phrase has the English language"

JAMES E. MILLER, JR. *Quests Surd and Absurd*, p. 148.

"Me prove it now, whoever doubt"

MARCUS K. BILLSON III. "Drama of Doubt, Dialectics of Pain (ED's 'Me prove it now'; a scene in her poetry)," *Emily Dickinson Bulletin* 30, Second Half 1976, 83-94.

EVAN CARTON. "Dickinson and the Divine: The Terror of Integration, the Terror of Detachment," *ESQ* 24(4), Fourth Quarter 1978, 247-48.

"The merchant of the picturesque"

ROBERT MERIDETH. "Emily Dickinson and the Acquisitive Society," *New England Quarterly* 37(4), December 1964, 439-40.

"Midsummer was it when they died"

MARTIN BICKMAN. "Kora in Heaven: Love and Death in the Poetry of Emily Dickinson," *Emily Dickinson Bulletin* 32, Second Half 1977, 98-99.

"A mien to move a queen"

F. DEWOLFE MILLER. "Emily Dickinson: Self-Portrait in the Third Person," *New England Quarterly* 46(1), March 1973, 119-24.

"Mine by the right of the white election"

FREDERICK L. MOREY. "Hundred Best Poems of Emily Dickinson," *Emily Dickinson Bulletin* 27, First Half 1975, 37.

"A mine there is no man would own"

VIVIAN R. POLLAK. "'That Fine Prosperity': Economic Metaphors in Emily Dickinson's Poetry," *Modern Language Quarterly* 34(2), June 1973, 177-78.

"More life went out when he went"

R. P. BLACKMUR. "Emily Dickinson: Notes on Prejudice and Fact," *Southern Review* 3(2), Autumn 1937, 337-41.

R. P. BLACKMUR. *Expense of Greatness*, pp. 126-30. Reprinted in: R. P. Blackmur. *Language as Gesture*, pp. 40-43.

"The morns are meeker than they were"

PAUL W. ANDERSON. "The Metaphysical Mirth of Emily Dickinson," *Georgia Review* 20(1), Spring 1966, 74-75.

"Much madness is divinest sense"

GÉMINO H. ABAD. *A Formal Approach to Lyric Poetry*, pp. 132-33.

D. BRUCE LOCKERBIE. "Solomon was Wrong," *English Journal* 52(8), November 1963, 598.

FREDERICK L. MOREY. "Hundred Best Poems of Emily Dickinson," *Emily Dickinson Bulletin* 27, First Half 1975, 20-21.

CYNTHIA GRIFFIN WOLFF. *Explicator* 36(4), Summer 1978, 3-4.

"My cocoon tightens, colors tease"

HYATT H. WAGGONER. *American Poets*, pp. 201-2.

"My first well day since many ill"

ERNEST SANDEEN. "Delight Deferred by Retrospect: Emily Dickinson's Late-Summer Poems," *New England Quarterly* 40(4), December 1967, 491-92.

"My life closed twice before its close"

M. D. FABER. "Psychoanalytic Remarks on a Poem by Emily Dickinson," *Psychoanalytic Review* 56(2), 1969, 247-64.

FREDERICK L. MOREY. "The Fifty Best Poems of Emily Dickinson (a three chapter study)," *Emily Dickinson Bulletin* 25, First Half 1974, 15-16.

FREDERICK L. MOREY. "Hundred Best Poems of Emily Dickinson," *Emily Dickinson Bulletin* 27, First Half 1975, 32-33.

"My life had stood a loaded gun"

CHARLES R. ANDERSON. "A Brilliant Failure: Emily Dickinson's 'My Life Had Stood — A Loaded Gun,'" in *The Dimensions of Poetry*, pp. 618-21.

SHARON CAMERON. "'A Loaded Gun': Dickinson and the Dialectic of Rage," *PMLA* 93(3), May 1978, 425-29.

JOHN CODY. "Emily Dickinson's Vesuvian Face," *American Imago* 24(3), Fall 1967, 161-80.

C. J. FISHER. "Emily Dickinson as a Latter-Day Metaphysical Poet," *American Transcendental Quarterly* 1(2), First Quarter 1969, 78.

FREDERICK L. MOREY. "Hundred Best Poems of Emily Dickinson," *Emily Dickinson Bulletin* 27, First Half 1975, 21.

THE POETRY WORKSHOP, COLUMBUS, GEORGIA. *Explicator* 15(8), May 1957, Item 51.

"My period had come for prayer"

J. BROOKS BOUSON. "ED and the Riddle of Containment," *Emily Dickinson Bulletin* 31, First Half 1977, 38-39.

SALLY BURKE. "A Religion of Poetry: The Prayer Poems of Emily Dickinson," *Emily Dickinson Bulletin* 33, First Half 1978, 20.

"My wheel is in the dark"

MABEL HOWARD, WILLIAM HOWARD, and EMILY HARVEY. *Explicator* 17(2), November 1958, Item 12.

"A narrow fellow in the grass"

PAUL W. ANDERSON. "The Metaphysical Mirth of Emily Dickinson," *Georgia Review* 20(1), Spring 1966, 79-80.

WALTER BLAIR and W. K. CHANDLER. *Approaches to Poetry*, second ed., pp. 258-60.

CHAD and EVA T. WALSH. *Twice Ten*, pp. 113-15.

"The nearest dream recedes unrealized"

DAVID T. PORTER. "Emily Dickinson: The Formative Years," *Massachusetts Review* 6(3), Spring-Summer 1965, 566-67.

"No brigadier throughout the year"

SISTER VICTORIA MARIE FORDE. *Explicator* 27(6), February 1969, Item 41.

"No man can compass a despair"

DOUGLAS A. NOVERR. "Emily Dickinson and the Act of Despair," *Emily Dickinson Bulletin* 23, First Half 1973, 164-65.

"No rack can torture me"

EUNICE GLENN. "Emily Dickinson's Poetry: A Revaluation," *Sewanee Review* 51(4), Autumn 1943, 577-78.

ANDREA GOUDIE. "Another Path to Reality: Emily Dickinson's Birds," *Concerning Poetry* 7(1), Spring 1974, 36.

FREDERICK L. MOREY. "Hundred Best Poems of Emily Dickinson," *Emily Dickinson Bulletin* 27, First Half 1975, 17.

"Not with a club the heart is broken"

MORDECAI MARCUS. *Explicator* 20(7), March 1962, Item 54.

"Of all the souls that stand create"

GÉMINO H. ABAD. *A Formal Approach to Lyric Poetry*, pp. 137-39.

RICHARD WILBUR. *Responses*, p. 13.

"Of bronze and blaze"

DAVID HIATT. *Explicator* 21(1), September 1962, Item 6.

JO C. SEARLES. "The Art of Dickinson's 'Household Thought,'" *Concerning Poetry* 6(1), Spring 1973, 46-51.

"Of course I prayed"

PAUL W. ANDERSON. "The Metaphysical Mirth of Emily Dickinson," *Georgia Review* 20(1), Spring 1966, 78.

GARY D. ELLIOTT. "The Solitary Dissenter: A Study of Emily Dickinson's Concept of God," *Emily Dickinson Bulletin* 20 (March 1972), 40.

ANDREA GOUDIE. "Another Path to Reality: Emily Dickinson's Birds," *Concerning Poetry* 7(1), Spring 1974, 33.

"Of death I try to think like this"

MARTIN BICKMAN. "Kora in Heaven: Love and Death in the Poetry of Emily Dickinson," *Emily Dickinson Bulletin* 32, Second Half 1977, 91-93.

NANCY MCCLARAN. *Explicator* 35(2), Winter 1976, 18-19.

REBECCA PATTERSON. "Emily Dickinson's 'Double' Tim: Masculine Identification," *American Imago* 28(4), Winter 1971, 349-50.

DICKINSON, EMILY *(Cont.)*

"Of death I try to think like this" *(cont.)*

WOLFGANG E. H. RUDAT. "Dickinson and Immortality: Virgilian and Miltonic Allusions in *Of Death I Try to Think Like This*," *American Notes & Queries*, n.s., 16(6), February 1978, 85-87.

ELEANOR WILNER. "The Poetics of Emily Dickinson," *ELH* 38(1), March 1971, 140.

"Of God we ask one favor"

FREDERICK L. MOREY. "Hundred Best Poems of Emily Dickinson," *Emily Dickinson Bulletin* 27, First Half 1975, 34-35.

"On this wondrous sea"

DENNIS GRUNES. "Child and Stranger," *Emily Dickinson Bulletin* 32, Second Half 1977, 135-40.

GEORGE MONTEIRO. *Explicator* 33(9), May 1975, Item 74.

"One blessing had I than the rest"

VIVIAN R. POLLAK. " 'That Fine Prosperity': Economic Metaphors in Emily Dickinson's Poetry," *Modern Language Quarterly* 34(2), June 1973, 178-79.

CAROLE ANNE TAYLOR. "Kierkegaard and the Ironic Voices of Emily Dickinson," *Journal of English and Germanic Philology* 77(4), October 1978, 572-73.

"One day is there of the series"

VIRGINIA H. ADAIR. "Dickinson's 'One Day Is There of the Series,' " *American Notes & Queries*, n.s., 5(3), November 1966, 35.

PAUL O. WILLIAMS. *Explicator* 23(4), December 1964, Item 28.

"One dignity delays for all"

ERHARDT H. ESSIG. *Explicator* 23(2), October 1964, Item 16.

FREDERICK L. MOREY. "Hundred Best Poems of Emily Dickinson," *Emily Dickinson Bulletin* 27, First Half 1975, 30.

"One need not be a chamber to be haunted"

CHARLES R. ANDERSON. "The Conscious Self in Emily Dickinson's Poetry," *American Literature* 31(3), November 1959, 304-5.

J. BROOKS BOUSON. "ED and the Riddle of Containment," *Emily Dickinson Bulletin* 31, First Half 1977, 46-47.

"The only news I know"

RALPH MARCELLINO. "Emily Dickinson," *College English* 7(2), November 1945, 102-3. (P)

"Our journey had advanced"

HAROLD BLOOM. "Poetic Crossing, II: American Stances," *Georgia Review* 30(4), Winter 1976, 788-90.

ROBERT GILLESPIE. "A Circumference of Emily Dickinson," *New England Quarterly* 46(2), June 1973, 267-71.

GEOFFREY H. HARTMAN. *Beyond Formalism*, pp. 349-51.

FREDERICK L. MOREY. "Hundred Best Poems of Emily Dickinson," *Emily Dickinson Bulletin* 27, First Half 1975, 29.

"Our lives are Swiss"

THORNTON H. PARSONS. "The Indefatigable Casuist," *University of Kansas City Review* 30(1), Autumn 1963, 19-20.

"Papa above"

PAUL W. ANDERSON. "The Metaphysical Mirth of Emily Dickinson," *Georgia Review* 20(1), Spring 1966, 73-74.

GARY D. ELLIOTT. "The Solitary Dissenter: A Study of Emily Dickinson's Concept of God," *Emily Dickinson Bulletin* 20 (March 1972), 41.

ALBERT GELPI. *The Tenth Muse*, p. 232.

DAVID A. ROBERTS. "Emily Dickinson's 'woe of ecstasy,' " *Colorado Quarterly* 23(4), Spring 1975, 512-13.

MARLENE SPRINGER. "Emily Dickinson's Humorous Road to Heaven," *Renascence* 23(3), Spring 1971, 131-32.

"Paradise is of the option"

JOHN WHEATCROFT. "Emily Dickinson's Poetry and Jonathan Edwards on the Will," *Bucknell Review* 10(2), December 1961, 118-20.

"The pattern of the sun"

ALBERT GELPI. *The Tenth Muse*, pp. 282-83.

"Perhaps I asked too large"

SUZANNE JUHASZ. *Naked and Fiery Forms*, pp. 30-31.

"A pit but heaven over it"

DAVID ROBINSON. "Text and Meaning in ED's 'A Pit — but Heaven over it — ' (J1712)," *Emily Dickinson Bulletin* 33, First Half 1978, 45-52.

"The poets light but lamps"

STUART LEWIS. *Explicator* 28(1), September 1969, Item 4.

BARTON LEVI ST. ARMAND. "Emily Dickinson and the Occult: The Rosicrucian Connection," *Prairie Schooner* 51(4), Winter 1977/78, 351-56.

"Portraits are to daily faces"

SIMON TUGWELL. "Notes on Two Poems by Emily Dickinson," *Notes & Queries*, n.s., 13(9), September 1966, 342.

"Praise it, 'tis dead"

JAMES S. MULLICAN. *Explicator* 27(8), April 1969, Item 62.

"Prayer is the little implement"

MARIO L. D'AVANZO. "The Emersonian Context of Three Poems of ED," *Emily Dickinson Bulletin* 16 (March 1971), 6-7.

"Presentiment is that long shadow on the lawn"

GÉMINO H. ABAD. *A Formal Approach to Lyric Poetry*, pp. 39-40.

DAVID H. HIRSCH. "Emily Dickinson's 'Presentiment,' " *American Notes & Queries*, n.s., 1(3), November 1962, 36-37.

FREDERICK L. MOREY. "The Fifty Best Poems of Emily Dickinson (a three chapter study)," *Emily Dickinson Bulletin* 25, First Half 1974, 36.

LAURENCE PERRINE and DAVID H. HIRSCH. "Emily Dickinson's 'Presentment' Again," *American Notes & Queries*, n.s., 3(8), April 1965, 119-20.

"The props assist the house"

J. BROOKS BOUSON. "ED and the Riddle of Containment," *Emily Dickinson Bulletin* 31, First Half 1977, 41-42.

"Publication is the auction"

MARIO L. D'AVANZO. " 'Unto the White Creator': The Snow of Dickinson and Emerson," *New England Quarterly* 45(2), June 1972, 278-80.

FREDERICK L. MOREY. "Hundred Best Poems of Emily Dickinson," *Emily Dickinson Bulletin* 27, First Half 1975, 17-18.

VIVIAN R. POLLAK. " 'That Fine Prosperity': Economic Metaphors in Emily Dickinson's Poetry," *Modern Language Quarterly* 34(2), June 1973, 176-77.

" 'Remember me' implored the thief"
VIVIAN R. POLLAK. "Emily Dickinson's Literary Allusions," *Essays in Literature* 1(1), Spring 1974, 59.

"Renunciation is a piercing virtue"
R. P. BLACKMUR. "Emily Dickinson: Notes on Prejudice and Fact," *Southern Review* 3(2), Autumn 1937, 333-36.
R. P. BLACKMUR. *Expense of Greatness*, pp. 119-23.
JOHN WHEATCROFT. "Emily Dickinson's Poetry and Jonathan Edwards on the Will," *Bucknell Review* 10(2), December 1961, 114-18.

"The reticent volcano keeps"
MARIO L. D'AVANZO. "Dickinson's 'The Reticent Volcano' and Emerson," *American Transcendental Quarterly* 14(1), Spring 1972, 11-12.
FREDERICK L. MOREY. "Hundred Best Poems of Emily Dickinson," *Emily Dickinson Bulletin* 27, First Half 1975, 38.

"Reverse cannot befall"
CHARLES R. ANDERSON. *Explicator* 18(8), May 1960, Item 46. Reprinted in: *Readings for Liberal Education*, fifth ed., II: 133-34.

"The robin is the one"
LAURENCE PERRINE. *Explicator* 33(4), December 1974, Item 33.

"A route of evanescence"
FRANK DAVIDSON. "A Note on Emily Dickinson's Use of Shakespeare," *New England Quarterly* 18(3), September 1945, 407-8.
KENNETH E. FISH, JR. in *The Case for Poetry*, 2d ed., pp. 93-94.
ROLAND HAGENBÜCHLE. "Precision and Indeterminacy in the Poetry of Emily Dickinson," *ESQ* 20(1), First Quarter 1974, 33-40.
JOHN F. LYNEN. "Three Uses of the Present: The Historian's, the Critic's, and Emily Dickinson's," *College English* 28(2), November 1966, 131-32.
ERNEST SANDEEN. "Delight Deferred by Retrospect: Emily Dickinson's Late-Summer Poems," *New England Quarterly* 40(4), December 1967, 498-99.
WAYNE SHUMAKER. "A Modest Proposal for Critics," *Contemporary Literature* 9(3), Summer 1968, 342-43.
GROVER SMITH. *Explicator* 7(7), May 1949, Item 54. Abridged in: *The Case for Poetry*, p. 109; second ed., p. 93.
LINDA J. TAYLOR. "Shakespeare and Circumference: Dickinson's Hummingbird and *The Tempest*," *ESQ* 23(4), Fourth Quarter 1977, 252-61.
HYATT H. WAGGONER. *American Poets*, pp. 197-98.
GEORGE F. WHICHER. *This Was a Poet*, p. 262. Abridged in: *The Case for Poetry*, p. 109; second ed., p. 93.

"Safe despair it is that raves"
DOUGLAS A. NOVERR. "Emily Dickinson and the Art of Despair," *Emily Dickinson Bulletin* 23, First Half 1973, 162.

"Safe in their alabaster chambers"
MOTHER ANGELA CARSON. *Explicator* 17(9), June 1959, Item 62.
WILLIAM HOWARD. *Explicator* 17(9), June 1959, Item 62. (P)

JAMES REEVES and MARTIN SEYMOUR-SMITH. *Inside Poetry*, pp. 66-67.
ROBERT H. WEST. "Literature and Knowledge," *Georgia Review* 25(2), Summer 1971, 141-43.

"Savior! I've no one else to tell"
CAROLE ANNE TAYLOR. "Kierkegaard and the Ironic Voices of Emily Dickinson," *Journal of English and Germanic Philology* 77(4), October 1978, 571-72.

"She bore it till the simple veins"
ARCHIBALD MACLEISH. *Poetry and Experience*, pp. 100-1.

"She rose to his requirement, dropt"
SUZANNE JUHASZ. *Naked and Fiery Forms*, p. 12.
FREDERICK L. MOREY. "Hundred Best Poems of Emily Dickinson," *Emily Dickinson Bulletin* 27, First Half 1975, 36-37.

"She sweeps with many-colored brooms"
LINDA MIZEJEWSKI. "Reply to Laurence Perrine," *College English* 36(2), October 1974, 213.
LINDA MIZEJEWSKI. "Sappho to Sexton: Womanhood Uncontained," *College English* 35(3), December 1973, 343-44.
LAURENCE PERRINE. "Dickinson Distorted," *College English* 36(2), October 1974, 212-13.

"She went as quiet as the dew"
NANCY LAMPERT. "Dew Imagery in Emily Dickinson's Poetry," *Emily Dickinson Bulletin* 29, First Half 1976, 51.

" 'Sic transit gloria mundi' "
VIVIAN R. POLLAK. "Emily Dickinson's Valentines," *American Quarterly* 26(1), March 1974, 72-78.

"A single clover plank"
PAUL W. ANDERSON. "The Metaphysical Mirth of Emily Dickinson," *Georgia Review* 20(1), Spring 1966, 82-83.
SCOTT DONALDSON. "Minding Emily Dickinson's Business," *New England Quarterly* 41(4), December 1968, 579-80.

"The snow that never drifts"
RALPH MARCELLINO. *Explicator* 13(6), April 1955, Item 36.

"So large my will"
JOHN WHEATCROFT. "Emily Dickinson's Poetry and Jonathan Edwards on the Will," *Bucknell Review* 10(2), December 1961, 105-6.

"A solemn thing it was I said"
MARTIN BICKMAN. "Kora in Heaven: Love and Death in the Poetry of Emily Dickinson," *Emily Dickinson Bulletin* 32, Second Half 1977, 96-97.
ALBERT GELPI. *The Tenth Muse*, pp. 266-67.

"Some keep the Sabbath going to church"
SALLY BURKE. "A Religion of Poetry: The Prayer Poems of Emily Dickinson," *Emily Dickinson Bulletin* 33, First Half 1978, 19.

"The soul has bandaged moments"
SISTER THERESE DELORES MCFADDEN. "Emily Dickinson: A Poet for the *Now* Generation," *English Journal* 60(4), April 1971, 463.

"The soul selects her own society"
GÉMINO H. ABAD. *A Formal Approach to Lyric Poetry*, pp. 135-37.
ELIZABETH BOWMAN. *Explicator* 29(2), October 1970, Item 13.

DICKINSON, EMILY *(Cont.)*

"The soul selects her own society" *(cont.)*

CARLOS DAGHLIAN. "Emily Dickinson in the Brazilian Classroom," *Emily Dickinson Bulletin* 24, Second Half 1973, 227-29.

C. J. FISHER. "Emily Dickinson as a Latter-Day Metaphysical Poet," *American Transcendental Quarterly* 1(2), First Quarter 1969, 77-78.

ALBERT GELPI. *The Tenth Muse,* p. 243.

ARCHIBALD A. HILL. "Figurative Structure and Meaning: Two Poems by Emily Dickinson," *Texas Studies in Literature and Language* 16(1), Spring 1974, 195-206. Reprinted in: Archibald A. Hill. *Constituent and Pattern in Poetry,* pp. 123-33.

WILL C. JUMPER. *Explicator* 29(1), September 1970, Item 5.

JULE S. KAUFMAN. "Emily Dickinson and the Involvement of Retreat," *Tulane Studies in English* 21 (1974), 77-78.

LARRY RUBIN. *Explicator* 30(8), April 1972, Item 67.

SIMON TUGWELL. *Explicator* 27(5), January 1968, Item 37.

MARK VAN DOREN. *Introduction to Poetry,* pp. 39-42.

PAUL WITHERINGTON. "The Neighborhood Humor of Dickinson's 'The Soul Selects Her Own Society,' " *Concerning Poetry* 2(2), Fall 1969, 5-9.

"The soul should always stand ajar"

VIRGINIA OGDEN BIRDSALL. "Emily Dickinson's Intruder in the Soul," *American Literature* 37(1), March 1965, 59-60.

"The soul unto itself"

FREDERICK L. MOREY. "Hundred Best Poems of Emily Dickinson," *Emily Dickinson Bulletin* 27, First Half 1975, 17.

" 'Sown in dishonor' "

VIVIAN R. POLLAK. "Emily Dickinson's Literary Allusions," *Essays in Literature* 1(1), Spring 1974, 57-58.

"The spider as an artist"

JOANNE DE LAVAN WILLIAMS. "Spiders In The Attic: A Suggestion of Synthesis in the Poetry of Emily Dickinson," *Emily Dickinson Bulletin* 29, First Half 1976, 27.

"The spider holds a silver ball"

JOANNE DE LAVAN WILLIAMS. "Spiders In The Attic: A Suggestion of Synthesis in the Poetry of Emily Dickinson," *Emily Dickinson Bulletin* 29, First Half 1976, 21-24.

"A spider sewed at night"

ALBERT GELPI. *The Tenth Muse,* pp. 297-98.

JOANNE DE LAVAN WILLIAMS. "Spiders In The Attic: A Suggestion of Synthesis in the Poetry of Emily Dickinson," *Emily Dickinson Bulletin* 29, First Half 1976, 24-26.

"The spirit lasts, but in what mode"

VIVIAN R. POLLAK. "After Calvary: The Last Years of ED's 'Dearest Earthly Friend,' " *Dickinson Studies* 34, Second Half 1978, 16.

"Success is counted sweetest"

GÉMINO H. ABAD. *A Formal Approach to Lyric Poetry,* pp. 134-35.

ROBERT MERIDETH. "Emily Dickinson and the Acquisitive Society," *New England Quarterly* 37(4), December 1964, 446-47.

FREDERICK L. MOREY. "Hundred Best Poems of Emily Dickinson," *Emily Dickinson Bulletin* 27, First Half 1975, 25.

THORNTON H. PARSONS. "The Indefatigable Casuist," *University of Kansas City Review* 30(1), Autumn 1963, 23.

RICHARD WILBUR. *Responses,* pp. 9-10.

"Summer has two beginnings"

LAWRENCE A. WALZ. *Explicator* 33(2), October 1974, Item 16.

"The sun just touched the morning"

ALBERT GELPI. *The Tenth Muse,* pp. 240-41.

"Superfluous were the sun"

BRITA LINDBERG. "Further Notes on a Poem by Emily Dickinson," *Notes & Queries,* n.s., 15(5), May 1968, 179-80.

SIMON TUGWELL. "Notes on Two Poems by Emily Dickinson," *Notes & Queries,* n.s., 13(9), September 1966, 342-43.

"That after horror, that 'twas us"

KATHERINE W. SNIPES. "Emily Dickinson's Odd Secrets of the Line," *Emily Dickinson Bulletin* 11 (December 1969), 117-19.

"There are two ripenings — one of sight"

LAURENCE PERRINE. *Explicator* 31(8), April 1973, Item 65.

"There came a day at summer's full"

MOTHER MARY ANTHONY. "Emily Dickinson's Scriptural Echoes," *Massachusetts Review* 2(3), Spring 1961, 557-61.

ALBERT GELPI. *The Tenth Muse,* pp. 244-45.

CLARK GRIFFITH. "Emily Dickinson's Love Poetry," *University of Kansas City Review* 27(2), Winter 1960, 95-96.

CAROLINE HOGUE. *Explicator* 11(3), December 1952, Item 17.

WILLIAM HOWARD. *Explicator* 12(6), April 1954, Item 41.

FREDERICK L. MOREY. "The Fifty Best Poems of Emily Dickinson (a three chapter study)," *Emily Dickinson Bulletin* 25, First Half 1974, 12.

DAVID T. PORTER. "Emily Dickinson: The Formative Years," *Massachusetts Review* 6(3), Spring-Summer 1965, 567-68.

"There came a wind like a bugle"

MARIO L. D'AVANZO. " 'Came a Wind Like a Bugle': Dickinson's Poetic Apocalypse," *Renascence* 17(1), Fall 1964, 29-31.

"There is a word"

JAMES M. HUGHES. "Dickinson as 'Time's Sublimest Target,' " *Dickinson Studies* 34, Second Half 1978, 29-31.

"There is no frigate like a book"

LAURENCE PERRINE. *Sound and Sense,* p. 32; second ed., p. 33; third ed., p. 39; fourth ed., p. 36.

"There's a certain slant of light"

DENIS DONOGHUE. "Emily Dickinson," in *Six American Poets from Emily Dickinson to the Present,* pp. 33-34.

DONALD EULERT. "Emily Dickinson's Certain Slant of Light," *American Transcendental Quarterly* 14(4), Spring 1972, 164-66.

GEORGE MONTEIRO. *Explicator* 31(2), October 1972, Item 13.

FREDERICK L. MOREY. "The Fifty Best Poems of Emily Dickinson (a three chapter study)," *Emily Dickinson Bulletin* 25, First Half 1974, 27-28.

FREDERICK L. MOREY. "Hundred Best Poems of Emily Dickinson," *Emily Dickinson Bulletin* 27, First Half 1975, 41-42.

LAURENCE PERRINE. *Explicator* 11(7), May 1953, Item 50.

"There's been a death in the opposite house"

JAMES REEVES and MARTIN SEYMOUR-SMITH. *Inside Poetry*, pp. 10-12.

"These are the days when birds come back"

GEORGE ARMS. *Explicator* 2(4), February 1944, Item 29.

ROBERT L. BERNER. *Explicator* 30(9), May 1972, Item 78.

MARTIN BICKMAN. "Kora in Heaven: Love and Death in the Poetry of Emily Dickinson," *Emily Dickinson Bulletin* 32, Second Half 1977, 100.

FREDERICK L. MOREY. "Hundred Best Poems of Emily Dickinson," *Emily Dickinson Bulletin* 27, First Half 1975, 40-41.

MARSHALL VAN DEUSEN. *Explicator* 12(6), April 1954, Item 40.

"These are the signs to nature's inns"

LEE J. RICHMOND. "Emersonian Echoes in Dickinson's 'These Are the Signs,'" *American Transcendental Quarterly* 29(1), Winter 1976, 2-3.

"They dropped like flakes"

THOMAS W. FORD. "Emily Dickinson and the Civil War," *University Review* 31(3), Spring 1965, 201.

"'They have not chosen me,' he said"

J. K. PACKARD. "The Christ Figure in Dickinson's Poetry," *Renascence* 22(1), Autumn 1969, 27.

"They leave us with the infinite"

CAROLE ANNE TAYLOR. "Kierkegaard and the Ironic Voices of Emily Dickinson," *Journal of English and Germanic Philology* 77(4), October 1978, 579-80.

"They say that 'Time assuages'"

FREDERICK L. MOREY. "Hundred Best Poems of Emily Dickinson," *Emily Dickinson Bulletin* 27, First Half 1975, 26-27.

"They shut me up in prose"

SUZANNE JUHASZ. *Naked and Fiery Forms*, pp. 12-13.

"This consciousness that is aware"

CHARLES R. ANDERSON. "The Conscious Self in Emily Dickinson's Poetry," *American Literature* 31(3), November 1959, 306-7.

HAROLD BLOOM. *Figures of Capable Imagination*, pp. 94-95.

ARCHIBALD MACLEISH. *Poetry and Experience*, pp. 107-9.

"This was a Poet — It is that"

GEORGE E. FORTENBERRY. *Explicator* 35(3), Spring 1977, 26-27.

ELEANOR WILNER. "The Poetics of Emily Dickinson," *ELH* 38(1), March 1971, 134-35.

"This world is not conclusion"

GARY D. ELLIOTT. "The Solitary Dissenter: A Study of Emily Dickinson's Concept of God," *Emily Dickinson Bulletin* 20 (March 1972), 38-39.

FREDERICK L. MOREY. "Hundred Best Poems of Emily Dickinson," *Emily Dickinson Bulletin* 27, First Half 1975, 33.

"Those dying then"

CAROLE ANNE TAYLOR. "Kierkegaard and the Ironic Voices of Emily Dickinson," *Journal of English and Germanic Philology* 77(4), October 1978, 573-74.

"Those not live yet"

DOROTHY WAUGH. *Explicator* 15(4), January 1957, Item 22.

"The thought beneath so slight a film"

LAURENCE PERRINE. "Sea and Surging Bosom," *CEA Critic* 30(2), November 1967, 9. (P)

JAMES E. WHITE. "Emily Dickinson: Metaphysician and Miniaturist," *CEA Critic* 29(6), March 1967, 17-18.

JAMES E. WHITE. "Sea and Surging Bosom," *CEA Critic* 30(2), November 1967, 9. (P)

"Through the strait pass of suffering"

SHARON CAMERON. "'A Loaded Gun': Dickinson and the Dialectic of Rage," *PMLA* 93(3), May 1978, 433-34.

"Tie the strings to my life, my Lord"

LESLIE H. PALMER. "ED's 'Father's Ground' — The Travel Motif of a Recluse Poet," *Emily Dickinson Bulletin* 30, Second Half 1976, 99-100.

"Time feels so vast that were it not"

ALBERT GELPI. *The Tenth Muse*, pp. 269-71.

"The tint I cannot take is best"

SISTER ELLEN FITZGERALD. *Explicator* 28(3), November 1969, Item 29.

"'Tis not the dying hurts us so"

ANDREA GOUDIE. "Another Path to Reality: Emily Dickinson's Birds," *Concerning Poetry* 7(1), Spring 1974, 33.

"'Tis so appalling, it exhilarates"

CAROLE ANNE TAYLOR. "Kierkegaard and the Ironic Voices of Emily Dickinson," *Journal of English and Germanic Philology* 77(4), October 1978, 577-78.

"'Tis true they shut me in the cold"

CYNTHIA CHALIFF. "ED as the Deprived Child," *Emily Dickinson Bulletin* 13 (June 1970), 36-37.

"Title divine is mine"

SHARON CAMERON. "'A Loaded Gun': Dickinson and the Dialectic of Rage," *PMLA* 93(3), May 1978, 434-35.

ALBERT GELPI. *The Tenth Muse*, pp. 246-47.

FREDERICK L. MOREY. "Hundred Best Poems of Emily Dickinson," *Emily Dickinson Bulletin* 27, First Half 1975, 37.

J. K. PACKARD. "The Christ Figure in Dickinson's Poetry," *Renascence* 22(1), Autumn 1969, 30-32.

LAURENCE PERRINE. "Dickinson Distorted," *College English* 36(2), October 1974, 212-13.

"To hear an oriole sing"

FREDERICK L. MOREY. "Hundred Best Poems of Emily Dickinson," *Emily Dickinson Bulletin* 27, First Half 1975, 21.

"To learn the transport by the pain"

THORNTON H. PARSONS. "The Indefatigable Casuist," *University of Kansas City Review* 30(1), Autumn 1963, 24-25.

"To make one's toilette after death"

ARCHIBALD MACLEISH. *Poetry and Experience*, pp. 96-97.

DICKINSON, EMILY *(Cont.)*

"To my quick ear the leaves conferred"
> CLARK GRIFFITH. "Frost and the American View of Nature," *American Quarterly* 20(1), Spring 1968, 33-34.

"To my small hearth his fire came"
> MARTIN BICKMAN. "Kora in Heaven: Love and Death in the Poetry of Emily Dickinson," *Emily Dickinson Bulletin* 32, Second Half 1977, 86-88.

"To own the art within the soul"
> SUZANNE JUHASZ. *Naked and Fiery Forms*, pp. 15-16.

"To pile like thunder to its close"
> JAMES E. MILLER, JR. *Quests Surd and Absurd*, pp. 146-47.

"To undertake is to achieve"
> RICHARD B. SEWALL. *Explicator* 6(8), June 1948, Item 51.

"A toad can die of light"
> REBECCA PATTERSON. "Emily Dickinson's Jewel Imagery," *American Literature* 42(4), January 1971, 506.

"'Twas like a maelstrom with a notch"
> MARTHA FODASKI. *Explicator* 19(4), January 1961, Item 24.
> JOHN S. MANN. "Dream in Emily Dickinson's Poetry," *Dickinson Studies* 34, Second Half 1978, 23-24.
> MYRON OCHSHORN. "In Search of Emily Dickinson," *New Mexico Quarterly Review* 23(1), Spring 1953, 103-6.
> KATHERINE W. SNIPES. "Emily Dickinson's Odd Secrets of the Line," *Emily Dickinson Bulletin* 11 (December 1969), 119-20.

"Twice had summer her fair verdure"
> ANDREA GOUDIE. "Another Path to Reality: Emily Dickinson's Birds," *Concerning Poetry* 7(1), Spring 1974, 32-33.

"Two butterflies went out at noon"
> LAURENCE PERRINE. "The Importance of Tone in the Interpretation of Literature," *College English* 24(5), February 1963, 389-90.

"Two swimmers wrestled on the spar"
> JOANNE FEIT DIEHL. "Emerson, Dickinson, and the Abyss," *ELH* 44(4), Winter 1977, 695-96.
> GEORGE H. SOULE, JR. "ED and Jacob: 'Pugilist and Poet' Wrestling to the Dawn," *Emily Dickinson Bulletin* 31, First Half 1977, 34-35.

"Undue significance a starving man attaches"
> RICHARD WILBUR. *Responses*, p. 8.

"'Unto me?' I do not know you"
> VIVIAN R. POLLAK. "Emily Dickinson's Literary Allusions," *Essays in Literature* 1(1), Spring 1974, 60.

"Water makes many beds"
> JAMES S. MULLICAN. *Explicator* 27(3), November 1968, Item 23.
> JOHN WHEATCROFT. "Emily Dickinson's Poetry and Jonathan Edwards on the Will," *Bucknell Review* 10(2), December 1961, 107-8.

"The way I read a letter's this"
> MARIO L. D'AVANZO. "Emersonian Revelation in 'The Way I Read a Letter's — This — ,'" *American Transcendental Quarterly* 17(1), Winter 1973, 14-15.

"We don't cry, Tim and I"
> ALBERT GELPI. *The Tenth Muse*, pp. 248-49.

"We dream — it is good we are dreaming"
> JOHN S. MANN. "Dream in Emily Dickinson's Poetry," *Dickinson Studies* 34, Second Half 1978, 23.

"We play at paste"
> ROLAND HAGENBÜCHLE. "Precision and Indeterminacy in the Poetry of Emily Dickinson," *ESQ* 20(1), First Quarter 1974, 44-45.
> FREDERICK L. MOREY. "Hundred Best Poems of Emily Dickinson," *Emily Dickinson Bulletin* 27, First Half 1975, 35.

"We should not mind so small a flower"
> KENNETH B. NEWELL. *Explicator* 19(9), June 1961, Item 65.

"We thirst at first — 'tis nature's act"
> SIMON A. GROLNICK. "Article Review: Emily and the Psychobiographer," *Literature and Psychology* 23(2), 1973, 75-76.
> FREDERICK L. MOREY. "Hundred Best Poems of Emily Dickinson," *Emily Dickinson Bulletin* 27, First Half 1975, 39.

"What I see not, I better see"
> JANE F. CROSTHWAITE. *Explicator* 36(3), Spring 1978, 10-12.

"What mystery pervades a well"
> INDER NATH KHER. "'An Abyss's Face': The Structure of Emily Dickinson's Poem," *Emily Dickinson Bulletin* 9 (June 1969), 52-55.
> REBECCA PATTERSON. "Emily Dickinson's 'Double' Tim: Masculine Identification," *American Imago* 28(4), Winter 1971, 348-49.

"What soft, cherubic creatures"
> NANCY LENZ HARVEY. *Explicator* 28(2), October 1969, Item 17.
> FREDERICK L. MOREY. "The Fifty Best Poems of Emily Dickinson (a three chapter study)," *Emily Dickinson Bulletin* 25, First Half 1974, 35-36.

"When I hoped I feared"
> WILSON O. CLOUGH. *Explicator* 10(2), November 1951, Item 10.
> CAROLINE HOGUE. *Explicator* 10(7), May 1952, Item 49.

"Where ships of purple gently toss"
> LAURENCE PERRINE. "The Nature of Proof in the Interpretation of Poetry," *English Journal* 51(6), September 1962, 394-96.

"Who abdicates ambush"
> ELEANOR WILNER. "The Poetics of Emily Dickinson," *ELH* 38(1), March 1971, 139.

"A wife at daybreak I shall be"
> MARTIN BICKMAN. "Kora in Heaven: Love and Death in the Poetry of Emily Dickinson," *Emily Dickinson Bulletin* 32, Second Half 1977, 94-95.
> ELIZABETH BUZZELLI. "An Explication: A Wife-at Daybreak I shall be- (461)," *Emily Dickinson Bulletin* 29, First Half 1976, 36-39.

"Wild nights — wild nights"
> MARTIN BICKMAN. "Kora in Heaven: Love and Death in the Poetry of Emily Dickinson," *Emily Dickinson Bulletin* 32, Second Half 1977, 80-81.
> JAMES T. CONNELLY. *Explicator* 25(5), January 1967, Item 44.
> PAUL FARIS. "Eroticism in Emily Dickinson's 'Wild Nights!'" *New England Quarterly* 40(2), June 1967, 269-74.

ALBERT GELPI. *The Tenth Muse*, p. 242.

SUZANNE JUHASZ. "'I Dwell in Possibility' ED in the Subjunctive Mood," *Emily Dickinson Bulletin* 32, Second Half 1977, 108-9.

SUZANNE JUHASZ. *Naked and Fiery Forms*, p. 24.

CHRISTOF WEGELIN. *Explicator* 26(3), November 1967, Item 25.

"The wind begun to rock the grass"

AIDA A. FARRAG. "J. 824: The Wind begun to rock the Grass," *Emily Dickinson Bulletin* 31, First Half 1977, 65-69.

"The wind drew off"

CONNIE M. DOYLE. "Emily Dickinson's 'The Wind Drew Off,'" *English Language Notes* 12(3), March 1975, 182-84. (P)

"The wind tapped like a tired man"

VIRGINIA OGDEN BIRDSALL. "Emily Dickinson's Intruder in the Soul," *American Literature* 37(1), March 1965, 60-61.

"With pinions of disdain"

ANDREA GOUDIE. "Another Path to Reality: Emily Dickinson's Birds," *Concerning Poetry* 7(1), Spring 1974, 36-37.

"Within my garden rides a bird"

ROLAND HAGENBÜCHLE. "Precision and Indeterminacy in the Poetry of Emily Dickinson," *ESQ* 20(1), First Quarter 1974, 35-36.

"Wonder is not precisely knowing"

KIMON FRIAR and JOHN MALCOLM BRINNIN. *Modern Poetry*, pp. 456-57.

"You constituted time"

CYNTHIA CHALIFF. "The Psychology of Economics in Emily Dickinson," *Literature and Psychology* 18(2-3), 1968, 98.

"You left me, sire, two legacies"

SUZANNE JUHASZ. *Naked and Fiery Forms*, p. 23.

"Your riches taught me poverty"

PATRICK O'DONNELL. "Zones of the Soul: Emily Dickinson's Geographical Imagery," *CLA Journal* 21(1), September 1977, 63. (P)

VIVIAN R. POLLAK. "'That Fine Prosperity': Economic Metaphors in Emily Dickinson's Poetry," *Modern Language Quarterly* 34(2), June 1973, 174-75.

"You're right — 'the way is narrow'"

ROBERT MERIDETH. "Emily Dickinson and the Acquisitive Society," *New England Quarterly* 37(4), December 1964, 447-48.

VIVIAN R. POLLAK. "'That Fine Prosperity': Economic Metaphors in Emily Dickinson's Poetry," *Modern Language Quarterly* 34(2), June 1973, 167.

DOBELL, SYDNEY

"Balder"

JOSEPH J. COLLINS. "Tennyson and the Spasmodics," *Victorian Newsletter* 43 (Spring 1973), 25-26.

DOROTHY F. DONELLY. "Philistine Taste in Victorian Poetry," *Victorian Poetry* 16(1-2), Spring-Summer 1978, 100-11.

DODGSON, CHARLES

"The Hunting of the Snark"

RICHARD HOWARD. "Carroll: The Hunting of the Snark," in *Master Poems of the English Language*, pp. 773-76.

"Jabberwocky"

JOHN CIARDI. *How Does a Poem Mean?* pp. 705-8; second ed., pp. 45-47.

RAYMOND J. RUNDUS. "'O Frabjous Day!': Introducing Poetry," *English Journal* 56(7), October 1967, 958-59.

AGNES STEIN. *The Uses of Poetry*, pp. 74-76.

"The Walrus and the Carpenter"

ERNEST EARNEST. "The Walrus and the Carpenter," *CEA Critic* 26(3), December 1963, 1, 6-7.

DONNE, JOHN

"Aire and Angels"

JOAN BENNETT. "The Love Poetry of John Donne: A Reply to Mr. C. S. Lewis," in *Seventeenth Century English Poetry*, first ed., pp. 124-28.

JOHN M. COUPER. "*Aire and Angels*," *American Notes & Queries*, n.s., 15(8), April 1977, 104-6.

HUGH SYKES DAVIES. "Text or Context?" *Review of English Literature* 6(1), January 1965, 93-107.

WILLIAM EMPSON. "Donne the Space Man," *Kenyon Review* 19(3), Summer 1957, 381-89.

HELEN GARDNER. *The Business of Criticism*, pp. 62-75.

FRANK L. HUNTLEY. *Explicator* 6(8), June 1948, Item 53.

J. B. LEISHMAN. *The Metaphysical Poets*, pp. 43-44.

LOUIS L. MARTZ. *The Wit of Love*, pp. 37-38.

EARL MINER. *The Metaphysical Poets from Donne to Cowley*, pp. 137-38.

EARL MINER. "Wit: Definition and Dialectic," in *Seventeenth Century English Poetry*, revised ed., p. 59.

KERBY NEILL. *Explicator* 6(2), November 1947, Item 8.

RAMAN SELDEN. "John Donne's 'Incarnational Conviction,'" *Critical Quarterly* 17(1), Spring 1975, 65-66.

MARTIN TURNELL. "John Donne and the Quest for Unity," *Nineteenth Century and After* 147(878), April 1950, 266-67.

LEONARD UNGER. *Donne's Poetry and Modern Criticism*, pp. 42-44. Reprinted in: Leonard Unger. *The Man in the Name*, pp. 64-67.

LEONARD UNGER and WILLIAM VAN O'CONNOR. *Poems for Study*, pp. 119-21.

GEORGE WILLIAMSON. *Six Metaphysical Poets*, pp. 63-64.

GEORGE WILLIAMSON. "Textual Difficulties in the Interpretation of Donne's Poetry," *Modern Philology* 38(1), August 1940, 42-45.

"The Anagram" (Elegy II)

DONALD L. GUSS. "Donne's 'The Anagram': Sources and Analogues," *Huntington Library Quarterly* 28(1), November 1964, 79-82.

"Anatomie of the World"

see "The First Anniversary"

"The Anniversarie" ("All Kings, and all their favorites")

ANNE FERRY. *All in War with Time*, pp. 101-6.

J. B. LEISHMAN. *The Metaphysical Poets*, pp. 36-37.

MICHAEL MCCANLES. *Dialectical Criticism and Renaissance Literature*, pp. 66-67.

LOUIS L. MARTZ. *The Wit of Love*, pp. 45-47.

DOUGLAS L. PETERSON. *The English Lyric from Wyatt to Donne*, pp. 329-30.

RAMAN SELDEN. "John Donne's 'Incarnational Conviction,'" *Critical Quarterly* 17(1), Spring 1975, 70-71.

CHAD and EVA T. WALSH. *Twice Ten*, pp. 8-11.

DONNE, JOHN *(Cont.)*

"The Anniversarie" ("All Kings, and all their favorites") *(cont.)*

> FRANK J. WARNKE. *Explicator* 16(2), November 1957, Item 12.

> GEORGE WILLIAMSON. *Six Metaphysical Poets*, p. 64.

"The Annunciation and Passion"

> HUGH KIRKPATRICK. *Explicator* 30(5), January 1972, Item 39.

"The Apparition"

> PATRICIA BEER. *An Introduction to the Metaphysical Poets*, pp. 7-11.

> SAMUEL S. BICKFORD, JR. "A Note on Donne's 'The Apparition,'" *Concerning Poetry* 4(1), Spring 1971, 13-14.

> ROBERT G. COLLMER. "Another Look at 'The Apparition,'" *Concerning Poetry* 7(2), Fall 1974, 34-40.

> WILLIAM EMPSON. *Seven Types of Ambiguity*, pp. 184-86; second ed., pp. 146-47; third ed., pp. 146-47.

> WILLIAM EVERSON. *Explicator* 4(8), June 1946, Item 56.

> STANLEY FRIEDMAN. *Explicator* 30(2), October 1971, Item 15.

> C. WILLIAM MILLER and DAN S. NORTON. *Explicator* 4(4), February 1946, Item 24.

> LAURENCE PERRINE. "On Donne's 'The Apparition,'" *Concerning Poetry* 9(1), Spring 1976, 21-24.

"At the round earth's imagin'd corners blow" ("Holy Sonnets," VII)

> see also "Holy Sonnets"

> STANLEY ARCHER. "Meditation and the Structure of Donne's 'Holy Sonnets,'" *ELH* 28(2), June 1961, 140-41.

> REUBEN ARTHUR BROWER. *The Fields of Light*, pp. 67-70. Reprinted in: *Readings for Liberal Education*, third ed., II: 29-32; fourth ed., II: 27-30; fifth ed., II: 26-29.

> LOUIS L. MARTZ. *The Poetry of Meditation*, pp. 50-52.

> I. A. RICHARDS. *Practical Criticism*, pp. 43-50.

> GEORGE WILLIAMSON. *Six Metaphysical Poets*, pp. 84-85.

"The Autumnall" (Elegy IX)

> ALAN ARMSTRONG. "The Apprenticeship of John Donne: Ovid and *The Elegies*," *ELH* 44(3), Fall 1977, 435-39.

> KITTY DATTA. "Love and asceticism in Donne's poetry: the divine analogy," *Critical Quarterly* 19(2), Summer 1977, 21.

> D. W. HARDING. "Donne's Anticipation of Experience," in *Experience Into Words*, pp. 23-24.

> LOUIS L. MARTZ. *The Wit of Love*, pp. 54-56.

> EARL MINER. *The Metaphysical Mode from Donne to Cowley*, pp. 136-37.

> CAROL MARKS SICHERMAN. "Donne's Discoveries," *Studies in English Literature 1500-1900* 11(1), Winter 1974, 74-78.

"The Baite"

> HEATHER DUBROW OUSBY. "John Donne's Versions of Pastoral," *Durham University Journal*, n.s., 38(1), December 1976, 33-37.

"Batter my heart, three person'd God" ("Holy Sonnets," XIV)

> see also "Holy Sonnets"

> PATRICIA BEER. *An Introduction to the Metaphysical Poets*, pp. 45-49.

> ARTHUR L. CLEMENTS. "Donne's Holy Sonnet XIV," *Modern Language Notes* 76(6), June 1961, 484-89.

> DAVID K. CORNELIUS. *Explicator* 24(3), November 1965, Item 25.

> ELIZABETH DREW. *Poetry*, pp. 58-60.

> GEORGE HERMAN. *Explicator* 12(3), December 1953, Item 18.

> FRANK KERMODE. *Shakespeare, Spenser, Donne*, pp. 146-47.

> WILLIAM KERRIGAN. "The Fearful Accommodations of John Donne," *English Literary Renaissance* 4(3), Autumn 1974, 351-56.

> GEORGE KNOX. *Explicator* 15(1), October 1956, Item 2.

> J. C. LEVENSON. *Explicator* 11(5), March 1953, Item 31.

> WILLIAM R. MUELLER. "Donne's Adulterous Female Town," *Modern Language Notes* 76(4), April 1961, 312-14.

> JOHN E. PARISH. "No. 14 of Donne's *Holy Sonnets*," *College English* 24(4), January 1963, 299-302.

> ELIAS SCHWARTZ. *Explicator* 26(3), November 1967, Item 27.

> THOMAS J. STEELE. *Explicator* 29(9), May 1971, Item 74.

> AGNES STEIN. *The Uses of Poetry*, pp. 345-47.

> CHAD WALSH. *Doors into Poetry*, pp. 23-25.

> MARY TENNEY WANNINGER. *Explicator* 28(4), December 1969, Item 37.

> GEORGE WILLIAMSON. *Six Metaphysical Poets*, pp. 86-87.

"The Blossome"

> CLEANTH BROOKS and ROBERT PENN WARREN. *Understanding Poetry*, pp. 370-74; revised ed., pp. 247-50.

> BARBARA HARDY. *The Advantage of Lyric*, pp. 25-26.

> J. B. LEISHMAN. *The Metaphysical Poets*, pp. 23-24.

> EARL MINER. "Wit: Definition and Dialectic," in *Seventeenth Century English Poetry*, revised ed., p. 53.

> DOUGLAS L. PETERSON. *The English Lyric from Wyatt to Donne*, pp. 301-3.

> SILVIA RUFFO-FIORE. "The Unwanted Heart In Petrarch and Donne," *Comparative Literature* 24(4), Fall 1972, 321-24.

> E. M. W. TILLYARD. *The Metaphysicals and Milton*, pp. 14-20.

> GEORGE WILLIAMSON. *Six Metaphysical Poets*, p. 76.

"The Bracelet" (Elegy XI)

> ALAN ARMSTRONG. "The Apprenticeship of John Donne: Ovid and *The Elegies*," *ELH* 44(3), Fall 1977, 428-30.

> ROBERT A. BRYAN. "John Donne's Use of the Anathema," *Journal of English and Germanic Philology* 61(2), April 1962, 310-11.

"The broken heart"

> SILVIA RAFFO-FIORE. "The Unwanted Heart in Petrarch and Donne," *Comparative Literature* 24(4), Fall 1972, 324-27.

> ROSEMOND TUVE. *Elizabethan and Metaphysical Imagery*, pp. 168-69.

"The Calme"

> MARGARET MAURER. "John Donne's Verse Letters," *Modern Language Quarterly* 37(3), September 1976, 246-47.

LINDA MIZEJEWSKI. "Darkness and Disproportion: A Study of Donne's 'Storme' and 'Calme,' " *Journal of English and Germanic Philology* 76(2), April 1977, 226-30.

GARY STORHOFF. "Metaphors of Despair in Donne's 'The Storme' and 'The Calme,' " *Concerning Poetry* 9(2), Fall 1976, 41-45.

"The Canonization"

JOHN BERNARD. "Orthodoxia Epidemica: Donne's Poetics and 'A Valediction: of my Name in the Window,' " *South Atlantic Quarterly* 71(3), Summer 1972, 382-83.

CLEANTH BROOKS. *The Well Wrought Urn*, pp. 11-18; revised ed., pp. 7-13. Reprinted in: *Criticism*, pp. 361-65. Also: *Critiques and Essays in Criticism*, pp. 71-76. Also: *The Language of Poetry*, pp. 46-59. Also: *American Literary Criticism*, pp. 523-28. Also: Chad and Eva T. Walsh. *Twice Ten*, pp. 22-26. Also: *The Study of Literature*, pp. 179-86. Abridged in: *The Case for Poetry*, p. 113; second ed., pp. 98-99.

CLEANTH BROOKS and ROBERT PENN WARREN. *Understanding Poetry*, fourth ed., pp. 134-37.

A. B. CHAMBERS. "The Fly in Donne's 'Canonization,' " *Journal of English and Germanic Philology* 65(2), April 1966, 252-59.

JOHN A. CLAIR. "Donne's 'The Canonization,' " *PMLA* 80(3), June 1965, 300-2.

CARVEL COLLINS. *Explicator* 12(1), October 1953, Item 3.

DAVID DAICHES and WILLIAM CHARVAT. *Poems in English*, pp. 657-58.

BETTIE ANNE DOEBLER. "Donne's Incarnate Venus," *South Atlantic Quarterly* 71(4), Autumn 1972, 511-12.

ANNE FERRY. *All in War with Time*, pp. 113-25.

EDWIN HONIG. "Donne: The Canonization," in *Master Poems of the English Language*, pp. 106-8.

MURRAY KRIEGER. *The New Apologists for Poetry*, pp. 13-18.

ALBERT C. LABRIOLA. "Donne's 'The Canonization': Its Theological Context and Its Religious Imagery," *Huntington Library Quarterly* 36(4), August 1973, 327-39.

PIERRE LEGOUIS. *Donne the Craftsman*, pp. 55-61. Abridged in: *The Case for Poetry*, pp. 111, 113; second ed., pp. 97-98.

MICHAEL MCCANLES. *Dialectical Criticism and Renaissance Literature*, pp. 63-66.

ROBERT NYE. "The body of his book: the poetry of John Donne," *Critical Quarterly* 14(4), Winter 1972, 350-51.

JOHN OLIVER PERRY. *The Experience of Poems*, pp. 184-87.

DOUGLAS L. PETERSON. *The English Lyric from Wyatt to Donne*, pp. 295-96, 318-19.

WILLIAM J. ROONEY. " 'The Canonization' — the Language of Paradox Reconsidered," *Journal of English Literary History* 23(1), March 1956, 36-47.

LEONARD UNGER. *Donne's Poetry and Modern Criticism*, pp. 26-30. Reprinted in: Leonard Unger. *The Man in the Name*, pp. 49-53.

GEORGE WILLIAMSON. *Six Metaphysical Poets*, pp. 60-61.

G. R. WILSON, JR. "The Interplay of Perception and Reflection: Mirror Imagery in Donne's Poetry," *Studies in English Literature 1500-1900* 9(1), Winter 1969, 113-15.

"Change" (Elegy III)

WILLIAM ROCKETT. "John Donne: The Ethical Argument of *Elegy III*," *Studies in English Literature 1500-1900* 15(1), Winter 1975, 57-69.

CAROL MARKS SICHERMAN. "The Mocking Voices of Donne and Marvell," *Bucknell Review* 17(2), May 1969, 37.

"Communitie"

MICHAEL MCCANLES. "Paradox in Donne," *Studies in the Renaissance* 13 (1966), 282-83.

DOUGLAS L. PETERSON. *The English Lyric from Wyatt to Donne*, pp. 298-300.

LEONARD UNGER. *Donne's Poetry and Modern Criticism*, pp. 41-42. Reprinted in: Leonard Unger. *The Man in the Name*, pp. 63-64.

"The Comparison" (Elegy VIII)

EARL MINER. *The Metaphysical Mode from Donne to Cowley*, pp. 128-29. (P)

EARL MINER. "Wit: Definition and Dialectic," in *Seventeenth Century English Poetry*, revised ed., pp. 52-53.

"The Computation"

LEE BALL, JR. *Explicator* 8(6), April 1950, Item 44.

"Confined Love"

MICHAEL MCCANLES. "Paradox in Donne," *Studies in the Renaissance* 13 (1966), 278-80. (P)

CAROL MARKS SICHERMAN. "The Mocking Voices of Donne and Marvell," *Bucknell Review* 17(2), May 1969, 34-36.

LEONARD UNGER. *The Man in the Name*, p. 61.

"La Corona"
see also "Temple"

HELEN GARDNER. "The Religious Poetry of John Donne," in *The Metaphysical Poets*, pp. 210-12.

ANTHONY LOW. *Love's Architecture*, pp. 42-51.

H. R. SWARDSON. *Poetry and the Fountain of Light*, pp. 66-67.

"The Crosse"

WILLIAM EMPSON. "Donne the Space Man," *Kenyon Review* 19(3), Summer 1957, 379-80.

SAMUEL HAZO. "Donne's Divine Letter," in *Essays and Studies in Language and Literature*, pp. 38-43.

GEORGE WILLIAMSON. "Textual Difficulties in the Interpretation of Donne's Poetry," *Modern Philology* 38(1), August 1940, 64-66. (P) Reprinted in: George Williamson. *Seventeenth Century Contexts*, pp. 109-12.

"The Curse"

ROBERT A. BRYAN. "John Donne's Use of the Anathema," *Journal of English and Germanic Philology* 61(2), April 1962, 310.

FRANK KERMODE. *Shakespeare, Spenser, Donne*, pp. 129-30.

"The Dampe"

ROGER A. COGNARD. *Explicator* 36(2), Winter 1978, 19-20.

GERALD GALLANT and A. L. CLEMENTS. "Harmonized Voices in Donne's 'Songs and Sonets': 'The Dampe,' " *Studies in English Literature 1500-1900* 15(1), Winter 1975, 71-82.

DONALD L. GUSS. "Donne's Conceit and Petrarchan Wit," *PMLA* 78(4), September 1963, 312-14.

DONNE, JOHN *(Cont.)*

"Death"

    BARBARA K. LEWALSKI. "Donne's Poetry of Compliment: The Speaker's Stance and the Topoi of Praise," in *Seventeenth-Century Imagery*, pp. 53-54.

"Death be not proud though some have called thee" ("Holy Sonnets," X)

    see also "Holy Sonnets"

    T. R. BARNES. *English Verse*, pp. 72-73.

    EDWARD A. BLOOM. "Charles H. Philbrick, and Elmer M. Blistein," *The Order of Poetry*, pp. viii-x.

    EARL DANIELS. *The Art of Reading Poetry*, pp. 275-78.

    JUDSON JEROME. "On Decoding Humor," *Antioch Review* 20(4), Winter 1960-61, 488-90.

    C. N. MANLOVE. *Literature and Reality*, pp. 11-12.

    EMERSON R. MARKS. "The Poetic Equivalent: *Mimesis* and the Literary Idea," *Western Humanities Review* 18(2), Spring 1964, 171-72.

    RALPH HAVEN WOLFE and EDGAR F. DANIELS. "Rime and Idea in Donne's Holy Sonnet X," *American Notes & Queries*, n.s., 5(8), April 1967, 116-17.

"The Dissolution"

    ROBERTS W. FRENCH. "Donne's 'Dissolution': What Does a Poem Mean, and Is It Any Good?" *CEA Critic* 38(2), January 1976, 11-15, 46.

    JAY ARNOLD LEVINE. "'The Dissolution': Donne's Twofold Elegy," *ELH* 28(4), December 1961, 301-15.

"The Dreame"

    FREDSON T. BOWERS. "An Interpretation of Donne's Tenth Elegy," *Modern Language Notes* 54(4), April 1939, 280-82.

    J. B. LEISHMAN. *The Metaphysical Poets*, p. 37.

    LAURENCE LERNER. *An Introduction to English Poetry*, pp. 42-50.

    ELIAS SCHWARTZ. *Explicator* 19(9), June 1961, Item 67.

    GEORGE WILLIAMSON. *Six Metaphysical Poets*, pp. 68-69.

"Elegie: The Anagram"

    see "The Anagram"

"Elegie: The Bracelet"

    see "The Bracelet"

"Elegie: Change"

    see "Change"

"Elegie: The Comparison"

    see "The Comparison"

"Elegie: Death"

    see "Death"

"Elegie: Going to Bed"

    see "Going to Bed"

"Elegie: His parting from her"

    see "His parting from her"

"Elegie: His Picture"

    see "His Picture"

"Elegie: Jealosie"

    see "Jealosie"

"Elegie: Loves Progress"

    see "Loves Progress"

"Elegie: Loves Warre"

    see "Loves Warre"

"Elegie: On his Mistris"

    see "On his Mistris"

"Elegie on Mris. Boulstred"

    BARBARA K. LEWALSKI. "Donne's Poetry of Compliment: The Speaker's Stance and the Topoi of Praise," in *Seventeenth-Century Imagery*, p. 53.

    C. N. MANLOVE. *Literature and Reality*, p. 12.

    ROSEMOND TUVE. *Elizabethan and Metaphysical Imagery*, pp. 201-2. Reprinted in: *The Metaphysical Poets*, pp. 98-99.

"Elegie on the L. C."

    JOSEPHINE MILES. *The Primary Language of Poetry in the 1640's*, pp. 90-92.

"Elegie on the Lady Marckham"

    BARBARA K. LEWALSKI. "Donne's Poetry of Compliment: The Speaker's Stance and the Topoi of Praise," in *Seventeenth-Century Imagery*, p. 52.

"Elegie On the untimely Death of the incomparable Prince, Henry"

    BARBARA K. LEWALSKI. "Donne's Poetry of Compliment: The Speaker's Stance and the Topoi of Praise," in *Seventeenth-Century Imagery*, pp. 63-65.

    TERRY G. SHERWOOD. "Reason, Faith, and Just Augustinian Lamentation in Donne's Elegy on Prince Henry," *Studies in English Literature 1500-1900* 13(1), Winter 1973, 53-67.

    LEONARD D. TOURNEY. "Convention and Wit in Donne's *Elegie* on Prince Henry," *Studies in Philology* 71(4), October 1974, 473-83.

    RUTH C. WALLERSTEIN. "Rhetoric in the English Renaissance: Two Elegies," *English Institute Essays*, 1948, pp. 166-70.

"Elegie: The Perfume"

    see "The Perfume"

"Elegie to the Lady Bedford"

    BARBARA K. LEWALSKI. "Donne's Poetry of Compliment: The Speaker's Stance and the Topoi of Praise," in *Seventeenth-Century Imagery*, pp. 58-59.

"Elegie: Variety"

    see "Variety"

"Epitaph on Himselfe"

    LOUIS L. MARTZ. *The Wit of Love*, pp. 56-58.

"Epithalamion made at Lincolnes Inne"

    HEATHER DUBROW OUSBY. "Donne's 'Epithalamion made at Lincolnes Inne': An Alternative Interpretation," *Studies in English Literature 1500-1900* 16(1), Winter 1976, 131-43.

"The Expiration"

    A. J. SMITH. "Donne's Invention," in *The Metaphysical Poets*, pp. 194-95.

    PATRICIA THOMSON. *Elizabethan Lyrical Poets*, p. 196.

"The Expostulation" (Elegy XV)

    ROBERT A. BRYAN. "John Donne's Use of the Anathema," *Journal of English and Germanic Philology* 61(2), April 1962, 311-12.

"The Extasie"

    ROBERT J. BAUER. "The Great Prince in Donne's 'The Extasie,'" *Tennessee Studies in Literature* 14 (1969), 93-102.

    JOAN BENNETT. "The Love Poetry of John Donne: A Reply to Mr. C. S. Lewis," in *Seventeenth Century English Poetry*, first ed., 120-22.

    MARIUS BEWLEY. *Masks & Mirrors*, pp. 10-14.

REUBEN ARTHUR BROWER. *The Fields of Light,* pp. 77-83.

FRANK A. DOGGETT. "Donne's Platonism," *Sewanee Review* 42(3), July-September 1934, 284-90.

WILLIAM EMPSON. *English Pastoral Poetry,* pp. 132-35. Reprinted in: *Criticism,* pp. 347-49.

RENÉ GRAZIANI. "John Donne's 'The Extasie' and Ecstasy," *Review of English Studies,* n.s., 19(74), May 1968, 121-36.

MERRITT Y. HUGHES. "Some of Donne's 'Ecstasies,' " *PMLA* 75(5), December 1960, 509-18.

MICHAEL MCCANLES. *Dialectical Criticism and Renaissance Literature,* pp. 67-69.

MICHAEL MCCANLES. "Distinguish in Order to Unite: Donne's 'The Extasie,' " *Studies in English Literature 1500-1900* 6(1), Winter 1966, 59-75.

ELIZABETH MCLAUGHLIN. " 'The Extasie' — Deceptive or Authentic?" *Bucknell Review* 18(3), Winter 1970, 55-78.

ARTHUR P. MAROTTI. "Donne and 'The Extasie,' " in *The Rhetoric of Renaissance Poetry,* pp. 140-73.

JOHN MARSHALL. "The Extasie," *Hound and Horn* 3(1), October-December 1929, 123-24.

LOUIS L. MARTZ. *The Wit of Love,* pp. 48-50.

EARL MINER. *The Metaphysical Mode from Donne to Cowley,* pp. 76-83.

CHARLES MITCHELL. "Donne's 'The Extasie': Love's Sublime Knot," *Studies in English Literature 1500-1900* 8(1), Winter 1968, 91-101.

ROBERT NYE. "The body is his book: the poetry of John Donne," *Critical Quarterly* 14(4), Winter 1972, 352-54.

I. A. RICHARDS. "Donne: The Extasie," in *Master Poems of the English Language,* pp. 116-22.

I. A. RICHARDS. *Poetries: Their Media and Ends,* pp. 85-94.

LEO SPITZER. *Essays on English and American Literature,* pp. 142-53.

LEO SPITZER. *A Method of Interpreting Literature,* pp. 5-21. Reprinted in: *The Metaphysical Poets,* pp. 116-28.

THOMAS R. THORNBURG. "Donne's *The Extasie*: A Definition of Love," *Ball State University Forum* 11(4), Autumn 1970, 66-69.

E. M. W. TILLYARD. *The Metaphysicals and Milton,* pp. 79-84.

MARTIN TURNELL. "John Donne and the Quest for Unity," *Nineteenth Century and After* 147(878), April 1950, 267-68.

PHILIP WHEELWRIGHT. *The Burning Fountain,* pp. 72-73.

GEORGE WILLIAMSON. *Seventeenth Century Contexts,* pp. 63-77. Reprinted in: *Seventeenth Century English Poetry,* pp. 132-43; revised ed., pp. 106-17.

GEORGE WILLIAMSON. *Six Metaphysical Poets,* pp. 73-74.

GEORGE WILLIAMSON. "Textual Difficulties in the Interpretation of Donne's Poetry," *Modern Philology* 38(1), August 1940, 55-59. Reprinted in: *Seventeenth Century Contexts,* pp. 99-103.

G. R. WILSON, JR. "The Interplay of Perception and Reflection: Mirror Imagery in Donne's Poetry," *Studies in English Literature 1500-1900* 9(1), Winter 1969, 111-13.

"Farewell to love"

HELEN GARDNER. "A Crux in Donne," *Times Literary Supplement,* 10 June 1949, p. 381.

LESLIE HOTSON. "A Crux in Donne," *Times Literary Supplement,* 16 April 1949, p. 249. (P)

J. C. MAXWELL. "A Crux in Donne," *Times Literary Supplement,* 6 May 1949, p. 297. (P)

DOUGLAS L. PETERSON. *The English Lyric from Wyatt to Donne,* pp. 311-13.

D. F. RAUBER. "Donne's 'Farewell to Love': A Crux Revisited," *Concerning Poetry* 3(2), Fall 1970, 51-63.

GEORGE WILLIAMSON. "Donne's 'Farewell to Love,' " *Modern Philology* 36(3), February 1939, 301-3. (P)

GEORGE WILLIAMSON. *Six Metaphysical Poets,* pp. 79-80.

GEORGE WILLIAMSON. "Textual Difficulties in the Interpretation of Donne's Poetry," *Modern Philology* 38(1), August 1940, 39-41. (P) Reprinted in: George Williamson. *Seventeenth Century Contexts,* pp. 81-83.

"Father, part of his double interest" ("Holy Sonnets," XVI)

GEORGE WILLIAMSON. *Seventeenth Century Contexts,* pp. 107-9.

GEORGE WILLIAMSON. *Six Metaphysical Poets,* p. 87.

GEORGE WILLIAMSON. "Textual Difficulties in the Interpretation of Donne's Poetry," *Modern Philology* 38(1), August 1940, 62-64.

"A Feaver"

JAMES REEVES and MARTIN SEYMOUR-SMITH. *Inside Poetry,* pp. 43-45.

LEONARD UNGER. *Donne's Poetry and Modern Criticism* pp. 54-55. Reprinted in: Leonard Unger. *The Man in the Name,* pp. 74-75.

GEORGE WILLIAMSON. *Six Metaphysical Poets,* pp. 62-63.

"The First Anniversary"

RAYMOND A. ANSELMENT. " 'Ascensio Mendax, Decensio Crudelis': The Image of Babel in the *Anniversaries,*" *ELH* 38(2), June 1971, 188-98.

ANTHONY F. BELLETTE. "Art and Imitation in Donne's *Anniversaries,*" *Studies in English Literature 1500-1900* 15(1), Winter 1975, 83-96.

ROBERT M. BENDER. "Donne: The First Anniversary," in *Master Poems of the English Language,* pp. 100-3.

MARIUS BEWLEY. *Masks & Mirrors,* pp. 32-47.

MARIUS BEWLEY. "Religious Cynicism in Donne's Poetry," *Kenyon Review* 14(1), Autumn 1952, 621-35.

R. L. COLIE. "The Rhetoric of Transcendence," *Philological Quarterly* 43(2), April 1964, 159-64.

PATRICK CRUTTWELL. *The Shakespearean Moment,* pp. 74-83.

KITTY DATTA. "Love and asceticism in Donne's poetry: the divine analogy," *Critical Quarterly* 19(2), Summer 1977, 13-19.

LEONARD DEAN. *English Masterpieces,* edited by William Frost, Maynard Mack, and Leonard Dean, vol. 3: *Renaissance Poetry,* p. 13.

JOHN G. DEMARAY. "Donne's Three Steps to Death," *Personalist* 46(3), Summer 1965, 372-75.

RUTH A. FOX. "Donne's *Anniversaries* and the Art of Living," *ELH* 38(4), December 1971, 528-41.

D. W. HARDING. *Experience Into Words,* pp. 17-20.

RICHARD E. HUGHES. "The Woman in Donne's *Anniversaries,*" *ELH* 34(3), September 1967, 307-26.

J. B. LEISHMAN. *The Metaphysical Poets,* pp. 54-76.

HAROLD LOVE. "The Argument of Donne's *First Anniversary,*" *Modern Philology* 64(2), November 1966, 125-31.

DONNE, JOHN *(Cont.)*

"The First Anniversary" *(cont.)*

PATRICK MAHONEY. "The *Anniversaries*: Donne's Rhetorical Approach to Evil," *Journal of English and Germanic Philology* 68(3), July 1969, 407-13.

PATRICK MAHONEY. "The Structure of Donne's *Anniversaries* as Companion Poems," *Genre* 5(3), September 1972, 235-56.

LOUIS L. MARTZ. "John Donne in Meditation: The *Anniversaries*," *English Literary History* 14(4), December 1947, 248-62. Reprinted in: Louis L. Martz. *The Poetry of Meditation*, pp. 221-31; revised ed., pp. 221-35. Also: *Seventeenth Century English Poetry*, pp. 152-63.

EARL MINER. *The Metaphysical Mode from Donne to Cowley*, pp. 63-69, 182-86.

MARJORIE HOPE NICOLSON. *The Breaking of the Circle*, pp. 65-104; revised ed., pp. 81-122.

DENNIS QUINN. "Donne's *Anniversaries* as Celebration," *Studies in English Literature 1500-1900* 9(1), Winter 1969, 97-105.

I. A. RICHARDS. "The Interaction of Words," in *The Language of Poetry*, pp. 75-87. Reprinted in: *Modern Literary Criticism*, pp. 85-93.

DANIEL R. SCHWARTZ. "The Unity of Eliot's 'Gerontion': The Failure of Meditation," *Bucknell Review* 19(1), Spring 1971, 60-64.

CAROL M. SICHERMAN. "Donne's Timeless *Anniversaries*," *University of Toronto Quarterly* 39(2), January 1970, 128-33.

GEORGE WILLIAMSON. "The Design of Donne's *Anniversaries*," *Modern Philology* 60(3), February 1963, 183-91. Reprinted in: George Williamson. *Milton & Others*, pp. 150-64.

GEORGE WILLIAMSON. *Seventeenth Century Contexts*, pp. 33-34.

GEORGE WILLIAMSON. *Six Metaphysical Poets*, pp. 35-37.

"The Flea"

JEROME BEATY and WILLIAM H. MATCHETT. *Poetry From Statement to Meaning*, pp. 81-84.

S. L. BETHEL. "The Nature of Metaphysical Wit (1953)," in *The Metaphysical Poets*, pp. 155-56.

H. DAVID BRUMBLE III. "John Donne's 'The Flea': Some Implications of the Encyclopedic and Poetic Flea Traditions," *Critical Quarterly* 15(2), Summer 1973, 147-54.

TOSHIHIKO KAWASAKI. "Donne's Microcosm," in *Seventeenth-Century Imagery*, pp. 33-34.

MICHAEL MCCANLES. "Paradox in Donne," *Studies in the Renaissance* 13 (1966), 280-82.

C. N. MANLOVE. *Literature and Reality*, p. 3.

EARL MINER. *The Metaphysical Mode from Donne to Cowley*, pp. 132-35.

EARL MINER. "Wit: Definition and Dialectic," in *Seventeenth Century English Poetry*, revised ed., pp. 56-57.

PATRICIA MEYER SPACKS. "In Search of Sincerity," *College English* 29(8), May 1968, 591-602.

ROSEMOND TUVE. *Elizabethan and Metaphysical Imagery*, pp. 172-73.

LEONARD UNGER. *Donne's Poetry and Modern Criticism*, pp. 60-61. Reprinted in: Leonard Unger. *The Man in the Name*, pp. 79-80.

"The Funerall"

ROBERT M. ADAMS. *Strains of Discord*, pp. 109.

PATRICIA BEER. *An Introduction to the Metaphysical Poets*, pp. 41-44.

J. E. V. CROFTS. "John Donne," *Essays and Studies* 22 (1936), 141-42.

CLYDE S. KILBY. *Poetry and Life*, pp. 159-60.

LOUIS L. MARTZ. *The Wit of Love*, pp. 42-43.

DONALD STAUFFER. *The Nature of Poetry*, pp. 86-87.

ALLEN TATE. "Poetry and the Absolute," *Sewanee Review* 35(1), January 1927, 41-43.

GEORGE WILLIAMSON. *Six Metaphysical Poets*, pp. 75-76.

"A Funerall Elegie"

RUTH A. FOX. "Donne's *Anniversaries* and the Art of Living," *ELH* 38(4), December 1971, 530-32.

W. M. LEBANS. "Donne's *Anniversaries* and the Tradition of Funeral Elegy," *ELH* 39(4), December 1972, 547-59.

PAUL A. PARRISH. "Donne's 'A Funerall Elegie,'" *Papers on Language and Literature* 11(1), Winter 1975, 83-87.

"Go and Catch a Falling Star"

see "Song: Goe and Catch a Falling Star"

"Going to Bed" (Elegy XIX)

JOAN BENNETT. "The Love Poetry of John Donne: A Reply to Mr. C. S. Lewis," in *Seventeenth Century English Poetry*, first ed., pp. 112-13.

VINCENT BUCKLEY. *Poetry and the Sacred*, p. 107.

KITTY DATTA. "Love and asceticism in Donne's poetry: the divine analogy," *Critical Quarterly* 19(2), Summer 1977, 7-8.

WILLIAM EMPSON. "Donne the Space Man," *Kenyon Review* 19(2), Summer 1957, 362-67.

E. R. GREGORY, JR. "The Balance of Parts: Imagistic Unity in Donne's 'Elegie XIX,'" *University Review* 35(1), Autumn 1968, 51-54.

W. W. MAIN. *Explicator* 10(2), November 1951, Item 14.

"Goodfriday, 1613. Riding Westward"

T. R. BARNES. *English Verse*, pp. 70-72.

A. B. CHAMBERS. "Goodfriday, 1613. Riding Westward: The Poem and the Tradition," *ELH* 28(1), March 1961, 31-53.

W. NELSON FRANCIS. *Explicator* 13(4), February 1955, Item 21.

DONALD M. FRIEDMAN. "Memory and the Art of Salvation in Donne's Good Friday Poem," *English Literary Renaissance* 3(3), Autumn 1973, 418-42.

JONATHAN GOLDBERG. "Donne's Journey East: Aspects of a Seventeenth-Century Trope," *Studies in Philology* 68(4), October 1971, 470-83.

WILLIAM H. HALEWOOD. *The Poetry of Grace*, pp. 26-32.

GEORGE HERMAN. *Explicator* 14(9), June 1956, Item 60.

FRANK KERMODE and A. J. SMITH. "The Metaphysical Poets," in *English Poetry*, edited by Alan Sinfield, pp. 60-61.

ANTHONY LOW. *Love's Architecture*, pp. 71-74.

C. N. MANLOVE. *Literature and Reality*, pp. 8-10.

LOUIS L. MARTZ. *The Poetry of Meditation*, pp. 54-56.

ROBERT NYE. "The body is his book: the poetry of John Donne," *Critical Quarterly* 14(4), Winter 1972, 358.

GEORGE A. E. PARFITT. "Donne, Herbert and the Matter of Schools," *Essays in Criticism* 22(4), October 1972, 387.

M. L. ROSENTHAL and A. J. M. SMITH. *Exploring Poetry*, pp. 479-83; second ed., pp. 283-85.

CAROL MARKS SICHERMAN. "Donne's Discoveries," *Studies in English Literature 1500-1900* 11(1), Winter 1971, 69-74.

A. J. SMITH. "The Poetry of John Donne," in *English Poetry and Prose*, ed. by Christopher Ricks, pp. 167-69.

GEORGE WILLIAMSON. *Six Metaphysical Poets*, pp. 88-90.

"The good-morrow"

PATRICIA BEER. *An Introduction to the Metaphysical Poets*, pp. 49-52.

JOHN BERNARD. "Orthodoxia Epidemica: Donne's Poetics and 'A Valediction: of my Name in the Window,'" *South Atlantic Quarterly* 71(3), Summer 1972, 381-82.

CLEANTH BROOKS, JOHN THIBAUT PURSER, and ROBERT PENN WARREN. *An Approach to Literature*, third ed., pp. 374-76; fourth ed., pp. 366-68; fifth ed., pp. 414-16.

HARRY BROWN and JOHN MILSTEAD. *What the Poem Means*, p. 64.

DAVID DAICHES and WILLIAM CHARVAT. *Poems in English*, pp. 656-57.

ANNE FERRY. *All in War with Time*, pp. 71-78.

DENNIS GRUNES. "John Donne's 'The Good Morrow,'" *American Imago* 33(3), Fall 1976, 261-65.

MYRL G. JONES. *Explicator* 33(5), January 1975, Item 37.

WILLIAM E. MORRIS. "Donne's Use of Enallage in 'The Good Morrow,'" *American Notes & Queries*, n.s., 11(2), October 1972, 19-20.

DOUGLAS L. PETERSON. *The English Lyric from Wyatt to Donne*, pp. 314-16.

JAMES SMITH. "On Metaphysical Poetry," *Scrutiny* 2(3), December 1933, 229-30.

LEONARD UNGER. *Donne's Poetry and Modern Criticism*, pp. 22-25. Reprinted in: Leonard Unger. *The Man in the Name*, pp. 46-49.

GEORGE WILLIAMSON. *Six Metaphysical Poets*, pp. 58-59.

G. R. WILSON, JR. "The Interplay of Perception and Reflection: Mirror Imagery in Donne's Poetry," *Studies in English Literature 1500-1900* 9(1), Winter 1969, 109-11.

"His parting from her"

LOWRY NELSON, JR. *Baroque Lyric Poetry*, pp. 130-32.

"His Picture" (Elegy V)

T. R. BARNES. *English Verse*, pp. 60-61.

HELEN L. GARDNER. "John Donne: A Note on Elegie V, 'His Picture,'" *Modern Language Review* 39(4), October 1944, 333-37. (P)

LOUIS L. MARTZ. *The Poem of the Mind*, pp. 10-11.

"Holy Sonnets"

see also first lines of sonnets, e.g., "Batter my heart, three person'd God" and "Death be not proud, though some have called thee"

ANTHONY LOW. *Love's Architecture*, pp. 57-71.

DOUGLAS L. PETERSON. "John Donne's *Holy Sonnets* and the Angelican Doctrine of Contrition," *Studies in Philology* 56(3), July 1959, 504-18.

DON M. RICKS. "The Westmoreland Manuscript and the Order of Donne's 'Holy Sonnets,'" *Studies in Philology* 63(2), April 1966, 187-95.

JOHN N. WALL, JR. "Donne's Wit of Redemption: The Drama of Prayer in the *Holy Sonnets*," *Studies in Philology* 73(2), April 1976, 189-203.

"A Hymne to Christ, at the Authors last going into Germany"

KITTY DATTA. "Love and asceticism in Donne's poetry: the divine analogy," *Critical Quarterly* 19(2), Summer 1977, 22.

ANTHONY LOW. *Love's Architecture*, pp. 78-80.

PHILIP C. MCGUIRE. "Private Prayer and English Poetry in the Early Seventeenth Century," *Studies in English Literature 1500-1900* 14(1), Winter 1974, 71-72.

HARRY MORRIS. "John Donne's Terrifying Pun," *Papers on Language and Literature* 9(2), Spring 1973, 135-36.

GEORGE WILLIAMSON. *Six Metaphysical Poets*, pp. 90-91.

A. S. P. WOODHOUSE. *The Poet and His Faith*, pp. 64-65.

"Hymne to God my God, in my sicknesse"

DONALD K. ANDERSON, JR. "Donne's 'Hymne to God my God, in my sicknesse' and the T-in-O Maps," *South Atlantic Quarterly* 71(4), Autumn 1972, 465-72.

VINCENT BUCKLEY. *Poetry and the Sacred*, pp. 108-13.

HARRY M. CAMPBELL. "Donne's 'Hymn to God, My God, in My Sickness,'" *College English* 5(4), January 1944, 192-96. Reprinted in: *Readings for Liberal Education*, II: 500-4; revised ed., II: 32-36.

CONRAD HILBERRY. "The First Stanza of Donne's 'Hymne to God My God, In My Sickness,'" *Notes and Queries*, n.s., 4(8), August 1957, 336-37.

TERENCE L. LISBETH. *Explicator* 29(8), April 1971, Item 66.

ANTHONY LOW. *Love's Architecture*, pp. 76-80.

MICHAEL MCCANLES. *Dialectical Criticism and Renaissance Literature*, pp. 71-72.

LOUIS L. MARTZ. "Donne: Hymne to God My God, in My Sicknesse,'" in *Master Poems of the English Language*, pp. 137-40.

LOUIS L. MARTZ. *The Poem of the Mind*, pp. 40-43.

HARRY MORRIS. "*In Articulo Mortis*," *Tulane Studies in English* 11 (1961), 33-37.

ROBERT NYE. "The body is his book: the Poetry of John Donne," *Critical Quarterly* 14(4), Winter 1972, 358.

GEORGE WILLIAMSON. *Six Metaphysical Poets*, pp. 92-93.

"A Hymne to God the Father"

VINCENT BUCKLEY. *Poetry and the Sacred*, pp. 108-9.

D. W. HARDING. *Experience Into Words*, pp. 29-30.

DAVID J. LEIGH. "Donne's 'A Hymne to God the Father': New Dimensions," *Studies in Philology* 75(1), Winter 1978, 84-92.

ANTHONY LOW. *Love's Architecture*, pp. 77-80.

PHILIP C. MCGUIRE. "Private Prayer and English Poetry in the Early Seventeenth Century," *Studies in English Literature 1500-1900* 14(1), Winter 1974, 70-71.

HARRY MORRIS. "John Donne's Terrifying Pun," *Papers on Language and Literature* 9(2), Spring 1973, 128-37.

ROBERT NYE. "The body is his book: the poetry of John Donne," *Critical Quarterly* 14(4), Winter 1972, 358-59.

A. J. SMITH. "The Poetry of John Donne," in *English Poetry and Prose*, ed. by Christopher Ricks, p. 169.

CHAD and EVA T. WALSH. *Twice Ten*, pp. 16-18.

GEORGE WILLIAMSON. *Six Metaphysical Poets*, pp. 91-92.

DONNE, JOHN *(Cont.)*

"I am a little world made cunningly" ("Holy Sonnets," V)
see also "Holy Sonnets"

HARRY BROWN and JOHN MILSTEAD. *What the Poem Means*, p. 61.

WILLIAM EMPSON. "Donne the Space Man," *Kenyon Review* 19(3), Summer 1957, 374-76. (P)

WILLIAM EMPSON. *English Pastoral Poetry*, pp. 74-76.

CHAD and EVA T. WALSH. *Twice Ten*, pp. 12-14.

GEORGE WILLIAMSON. *Six Metaphysical Poets*, p. 84.

"If faithfull soules be alike glorifi'd" ("Holy Sonnets," VIII)
see also "Holy Sonnets"

GEORGE WILLIAMSON. *Six Metaphysical Poets*, p. 85.

"If poysonous mineralls, and if that tree" ("Holy Sonnets," IX)

see also "Holy Sonnets"

CLEANTH BROOKS and ROBERT PENN WARREN. *Understanding Poetry*, pp. 520-24; revised ed., pp. 380-86; third ed., pp. 355-61.

SUSAN LINVILLE. *Explicator* 36(4), Summer 1978, 21-22.

LOUIS L. MARTZ. "The Action of the Self: Devotional Poetry in the Seventeenth Century," in *Metaphysical Poetry*, edited by Malcolm Bradbury and David Palmer, pp. 105-6.

LOUIS L. MARTZ. *The Poetry of Meditation*, p. 52.

GEORGE WILLIAMSON. *Six Metaphysical Poets*, pp. 85-86.

"Ignatius His Conclave"
see "Satyre V"

"The Indifferent"

HARRY BROWN and JOHN MILSTEAD. *What the Poem Means*, p. 64.

NORMAN N. HOLLAND. "Clinical, Yes. Healthy, No," *Literature and Psychology* 14(3-4), Summer-Fall 1964, 124-25.

EARL MINER. *The Metaphysical Mode from Donne to Cowley*, pp. 15-18.

CAROL MARKS SICHERMAN. "The Mocking Voices of Donne and Marvell," *Bucknell Review* 17(2), May 1969, 36.

LEONARD UNGER. *The Man in the Name*, p. 61.

"Jealosie" (Elegy I)

ALAN ARMSTRONG. "The Apprenticeship of John Donne: Ovid and *The Elegies*," *ELH* 44(3), Fall 1977, 426-27.

A. LABRANCHE. " 'Blanda Elegeia': The Background to Donne's 'Elegies,' " *Modern Language Review* 61(3), July 1966, 361-62.

LOUIS L. MARTZ. "John Donne: the Meditative Voice," *Massachusetts Review* 1(2), Winter 1960, 331-32.

"A Jeat Ring sent"

MYRTLE PIHLMAN POPE. *Explicator* 34(6), February 1976, Item 44.

ROSEMOND TUVE. *Elizabethan and Metaphysical Imagery*, pp. 290-91.

THOMAS J. WERTENBAKER, JR. *Explicator* 35(4), Summer 1977, 27-28.

"Lecture upon the Shadow"

M. A. GOLDBERG. *Explicator* 14(8), May 1956, Item 50.

NAT HENRY. *Explicator* 20(7), March 1962, Item 60.

FREDERICK KILEY. "A Larger Reading of Donne's 'A Lecture Upon the Shadow,' " *CEA Critic* 30(7), April 1968, 16-17.

MICHAEL MCCANLES. *Dialectical Criticism and Renaissance Literature*, pp. 61-63.

LOUIS L. MARTZ. *The Wit of Love*, pp. 52-54.

LYNNE MOLELLA. "Donne's 'A Lecture Upon the Shadow,' " *Thoth* 3(2), Spring 1962, 69-77.

PETER R. MOODY. *Explicator* 20(7), March 1962, Item 60.

OLIVIA MURRAY NICHOLS. *Explicator* 32(7), March 1974, Item 52.

DOUGLAS L. PETERSON. *The English Lyric from Wyatt to Donne*, pp. 317-18.

JOHN D. RUSSELL. *Explicator* 17(2), November 1958, Item 9.

JOHN T. SHAWCROSS. "Donne's 'A Lecture Upon the Shadow,' " *English Language Notes* 1(3), March 1964, 187-88.

LEONARD UNGER. *Donne's Poetry and Modern Criticism*, pp. 56-57. Reprinted in: Leonard Unger. *The Man in the Name*, pp. 76-77.

MARK VAN DOREN. *Introduction to Poetry*, pp. 26-31.

"The Legacie"

BARBARA HARDY. *The Advantage of Lyric*, pp. 26-28.

"A Letter to the Lady Carey, and Mrs. Essex Riche, From Amyens"

BARBARA K. LEWALSKI. "Donne's Poetry of Compliment: The Speaker's Stance and the Topoi of Praise," in *Seventeenth-Century Imagery*, pp. 59-60.

LAURENCE STAPLETON. "The Theme of Virtue in Donne's Verse Epistles," *Studies in Philology* 55(2), April 1958, 197.

"A Litanie"

HELEN GARDNER. "The Religious Poetry of John Donne," in *The Metaphysical Poets*, pp. 212-17.

ANTHONY LOW. *Love's Architecture*, pp. 51-57.

"Lovers Infiniteness"
see "Loves infinitenesse"

"Loves Alchymie"

W. A. MURRAY. "Donne and Paracelsus: An Essay in Interpretation," *Review of English Studies* 25(98), April 1949, 115-18.

GEORGE WILLIAMSON. *Seventeenth Century Contexts*, pp. 98-99. (P)

GEORGE WILLIAMSON. *Six Metaphysical Poets*, p. 70.

"Loves Deitie"

ARTHUR K. MOORE. "Donne's 'Love's Deitie' and *De Planctu Naturae*," *Philological Quarterly* 42 (4 Suppl.), October 1963, 102-5.

JOHN L. SWEENEY. "Basic in Reading," *Kenyon Review* 5(1), Winter 1943, 55-59. (P) Reprinted in: *The Dimensions of Poetry*, pp. 225-28.

"Loves diet"

JOHN V. HAGOPIAN. *Explicator* 17(1), October 1958, Item 5. (P)

BARBARA HARDY. *The Advantage of Lyric*, pp. 24-25.

LAURENCE PERRINE. *Explicator* 35(3), Spring 1977, 20-21.

DOUGLAS L. PETERSON. *The English Lyric from Wyatt to Donne*, pp. 306-7.

LEONARD UNGER. *Donne's Poetry and Modern Criticism*, pp. 55-56. Reprinted in: Leonard Unger. *The Man in the Name*, pp. 75-76.

"Loves exchange"

GEORGE WILLIAMSON. *Six Metaphysical Poets*, pp. 67-68.

"Loves growth"

SISTER MARY ALPHONSE. *Explicator* 25(5), January 1967, Item 43.

JOHN BERNARD. "Orthodoxia Epidemica: Donne's Poetics and 'A Valediction: of my Name in the Window,'" *South Atlantic Quarterly* 71(3), Summer 1972, 380-81.

ALAN BLANKENSHIP. *Explicator* 31(9), May 1973, Item 73.

BARBARA HARDY. *The Advantage of Lyric*, pp. 20-23.

JUDY Z. KRONENFELD. "The Asymmetrical Arrangement of Donne's 'Love's Growth' as an Emblem of its Meaning," *Concerning Poetry* 9(2), Fall 1976, 53-58.

J. B. LEISHMAN. *The Metaphysical Poets*, pp. 44-45.

LOUIS L. MARTZ. *The Wit of Love*, pp. 39-41.

LOWRY NELSON, JR. *Baroque Lyric Poetry*, pp. 122-24, 129-30.

DOUGLAS L. PETERSON. *The English Lyric from Wyatt to Donne*, pp. 303-5.

BARBARA TRAISTER. *Explicator* 34(8), April 1976, Item 60.

ROSEMOND TUVE. *Elizabethan and Metaphysical Imagery*, pp. 174-75.

GEORGE WILLIAMSON. *Six Metaphysical Poets*, p. 67.

"Loves infinitenesse"

WILLIAM FREEDMAN. *Explicator* 31(1), September 1972, Item 6.

MICHAEL MCCANLES. *Dialectical Criticism and Renaissance Literature*, pp. 59-61.

DONALD STAUFFER. *The Nature of Poetry*, pp. 240-41.

E. M. W. TILLYARD. *The Metaphysicals and Milton*, pp. 30-35.

GEORGE WILLIAMSON. *Six Metaphysical Poets*, pp. 61-62.

"Loves Progress" (Elegy XVIII)

DOUGLAS L. PETERSON. *The English Lyric from Wyatt to Donne*, pp. 300-1.

"Loves Usury"

ROBERT F. GLECKNER and GERALD SMITH. *Explicator* 8(6), April 1950, Item 43.

D. W. HARDING. *Experience Into Words*, pp. 25-26.

LARRY D. TJARKS. "Donne's 'Loves Usury' and a Self-Deceived Persona," *Southern Quarterly* 14(3), April 1976, 207-13.

LEONARD UNGER. *Donne's Poetry and Modern Criticism*, pp. 57-58. Reprinted in: Leonard Unger. *The Man in the Name*, p. 77.

GEORGE WILLIAMSON. *Six Metaphysical Poets*, p. 60.

"Loves Warre" (Elegy XX)

ALAN ARMSTRONG. "The Apprenticeship of John Donne: Ovid and *The Elegies*," *ELH* 44(3), Fall 1977, 421-25.

"The Message"

JOHN T. SHAWCROSS. "The Poet as Orator: One Phase of His Judicial Pose," in *The Rhetoric of Renaissance Poetry*, pp. 24-25.

"Metempsychosis"

MARIUS BEWLEY. *Masks & Mirrors*, pp. 28-31.

MARIUS BEWLEY. "Religious Cynicism in Donne's Poetry," *Kenyon Review* 14(4), Autumn 1952, 623-24.

JANEL M. MUELLER. "Donne's Epic Venture in the *Metempsychosis*," *Modern Philology* 70(2), November 1972, 109-37.

M. VAN WYK SMITH. "John Donne's *Metempsychosis*," *Review of English Studies*, n.s., 24(93), February 1973, 17-25; 24 (94), May 1973, 141-52.

SUSAN SNYDER. "Donne and Du Bartas: *The Progresse of the Soule* as Parody," *Studies in Philology* 70(4), October 1973, 392-407.

GEORGE WILLIAMSON. "Donne's Satirical *Progresse of the Soule*," *ELH* 36(1), March 1969, 250-64.

GEORGE WILLIAMSON. *Milton & Others*, pp. 154-58.

"Negative love"

HELEN GARDNER. *The Business of Criticism*, pp. 63-64.

WALTER GIERASCH. *Explicator* 9(2), November 1950, Item 13.

J. B. LEISHMAN. *The Metaphysical Poets*, p. 20.

H. M. RICHMOND. "The Intangible Mistress," *Modern Philology* 56(4), May 1959, 217-20.

GEORGE WILLIAMSON. *Six Metaphysical Poets*, pp. 78-79.

"A nocturnall upon S. Lucies day. Being the shortest day"

A. ALVAREZ. *The School of Donne*, American ed., pp. 17-20.

C. B. COX and A. E. DYSON. *The Practical Criticism of Poetry*, pp. 57-65.

DAVID DAICHES and WILLIAM CHARVAT. *Poems in English*, pp. 658-59.

WILLIAM EMPSON. "Donne the Space Man," *Kenyon Review* 19(3), Summer 1957, 390-91.

MICHAEL V. FOX. *Explicator* 36(2), Winter 1978, 24-25.

FRANK KERMODE. *Shakespeare, Spenser, Donne*, pp. 130-32.

J. B. LEISHMAN. *The Metaphysical Poets*, pp. 55-58.

LOUIS L. MARTZ. "John Donne: the Meditative Voice," *Massachusetts Review* 1(2), Winter 1960, 340-42. Reprinted in: *The Poem of the Mind*, pp. 17-20.

CLARENCE H. MILLER. "Donne's 'A Nocturnall upon S. Lucies Day' and the Nocturns of Matins," *Studies in English Literature 1500-1900* 6(1), Winter 1966, 77-86.

EARL MINER. *The Metaphysical Mode from Donne to Cowley*, pp. 57-58.

W. A. MURRAY. "Donne and Paracelsus: An Essay in Interpretation," *Review of English Studies* 25(98), April 1949, 118-23.

HENRY WINFIELD PETER. "Donne's 'Nocturnall' and the *Nigredo*," *Thoth* 9(2), Spring 1968, 48-57.

DOUGLAS L. PETERSON. *The English Lyric from Wyatt to Donne*, pp. 326-29.

JOHN T. SHAWCROSS. *Explicator* 23(7), March 1965, Item 56.

CAROL MARKS SICHERMAN. "Donne's Discoveries," *Studies in English Literature 1500-1900* 11(1), Winter 1971, 81-83.

RICHARD SLEIGHT. "John Donne: A Nocturnall Upon S. Lucies Day, Being the Shortest Day," in *Interpretations*, pp. 32-58.

E. M. W. TILLYARD. *The Metaphysicals and Milton*, pp. 20-22.

MARTIN TURNELL. "John Donne and the Quest for Unity," *Nineteenth Century and After* 147(878), April 1950, 265-66.

LEONARD UNGER. *Donne's Poetry and Modern Criticism*, pp. 46-50. Reprinted in: Leonard Unger. *The Man in the Name*, pp. 67-71.

DONNE, JOHN *(Cont.)*

"A nocturnall upon S. Lucies day. Being the shortest day" *(cont.)*

> DENNIS M. WELCH. "The Meaning of Nothingness in Donne's 'Nocturnall upon S. Lucies Day,' " *Bucknell Review* 22(1), April 1976, 48-56.
>
> GEORGE WILLIAMSON. *Six Metaphysical Poets*, pp. 70-72.

"O might those signes and teares returne again" ("Holy Sonnets," III)

> see also "Holy Sonnets"
>
> GEORGE WILLIAMSON. *Seventeenth Century Contexts*, pp. 105-6. (P)
>
> GEORGE WILLIAMSON. *Six Metaphysical Poets*, pp. 83-84.

"Obsequies to the Lord Harrington"

> PHILIP C. KOLIN. "Donne's 'Obsequies to the Lord Harrington': Theme, Structure, and Image," *Southern Quarterly* 13(1), October 1974, 65-82.
>
> BARBARA K. LEWALSKI. "Donne's Poetry of Compliment: The Speaker's Stance and the Topoi of Praise," in *Seventeenth-Century Imagery*, pp. 65-67.

"Oh, to vex me, contraryes meete in one" ("Holy Sonnets," XIX)

> see also "Holy Sonnets"
>
> MICHAEL MCCANLES. *Dialectical Criticism and Renaissance Literature*, pp. 70-71.
>
> LOUIS L. MARTZ. *The Wit of Love*, pp. 29-30.
>
> DOUGLAS L. PETERSON. *The English Lyric from Wyatt to Donne*, pp. 346-47.
>
> GEORGE WILLIAMSON. *Six Metaphysical Poets*, p. 88.

"On his Mistris" (Elegy XVI)

> JOAN BENNETT. "The Love Poetry of John Donne: A Reply to Mr. C. S. Lewis," in *Seventeenth Century English Poetry*, first ed., pp. 122-24.
>
> VINCENT BUCKLEY. *Poetry and the Sacred*, pp. 104-6. (P)

"The Paradox"

> MICHAEL MCCANLES. "Paradox in Donne," *Studies in the Renaissance* 13 (1966), 283-86.

"The Perfume" (Elegy IV)

> A. LABRANCHE. " 'Blanda Elegeia': The Background to Donne's 'Elegies,' " *Modern Language Review* 61(3), July 1966, 362-63.
>
> EARL MINER. *The Metaphysical Mode from Donne to Cowley*, pp. 215-31.
>
> ARTHUR MINTON. *Explicator* 4(7), May 1946, Item 50.
>
> CAROL MARKS SICHERMAN. "The Mocking Voices of Donne and Marvell," *Bucknell Review* 17(2), May 1969, 37-38.
>
> HENRY TEN EYCK PERRY. *Explicator* 5(2), November 1946, Item 10.

"The Primrose"

> EDWARD D. CLEVELAND. *Explicator* 8(1), October 1949, Item 4.
>
> R. A. DURR. "Donne's 'The Primrose,' " *Journal of English and Germanic Philology* 59(2), April 1960, 218-22.
>
> DOUGLAS L. PETERSON. *The English Lyric from Wyatt to Donne*, pp. 301-3.
>
> RAMAN SELDEN. "John Donne's 'Incarnational Conviction,' " *Critical Quarterly* 17(1), Spring 1975, 68-70.
>
> GEORGE WILLIAMSON. *Six Metaphysical Poets*, pp. 76-77.

"The Progresse of the Soule"

> see "Metempsychosis" or "The Second Anniversary"

"The Prohibition"

> JOHN T. SHAWCROSS. "The Poet as Orator: One Phase of His Judicial Pose," in *The Rhetoric of Renaissance Poetry*, p. 25.
>
> LEONARD UNGER. *Donne's Poetry and Modern Criticism*, pp. 40-41. Reprinted in: Leonard Unger. *The Man in the Name*, pp. 61-63.
>
> ELIZABETH LEWIS WIGGINS. "Logic in the Poetry of John Donne," *Studies in Philology* 42(1), January 1945, 58-59.

"Pyramus and Thisbe"

> EDGAR F. DANIELS. *Explicator* 36(2), Winter 1978, 31.

"The Relique"

> ANNE FERRY. *All in War with Time*, pp. 106-12.
>
> DAVID V. HARRINGTON. *Explicator* 25(3), November 1966, Item 22.
>
> NORMAN N. HOLLAND. "Clinical, Yes. Healthy, No," *Literature and Psychology* 14(3-4), Summer-Fall, 1964, 123-24.
>
> LAURENCE LERNER. *An Introduction to English Poetry*, pp. 46-49.
>
> LOUIS L. MARTZ. *The Wit of Love*, pp. 43-45.
>
> MARVIN MORILLO. "Donne's 'The Relique' as Satire," *Tulane Studies in English* 21 (1974), 47-55.
>
> ROBERT ROGERS. "Literary Value and the Clinical Fallacy," *Literature and Psychology* 14(3-4), Summer-Fall 1964, 119-21.
>
> A. J. SMITH. "Donne's Invention," in *The Metaphysical Poets*, p. 199. (P)
>
> CHAD and EVA T. WALSH. *Twice Ten*, pp. 15-16.
>
> GEORGE WILLIAMSON. *Six Metaphysical Poets*, pp. 77-78.

"Resurrection, imperfect"

> RUTH E. FALK. *Explicator* 17(3), December 1958, Item 24.

"Sapho to Philaenis"

> G. R. WILSON, JR. "The Interplay of Perception and Reflection: Mirror Imagery in Donne's Poetry," *Studies in English Literature 1500-1900* 9(1), Winter 1969, 118-19.

"Satyre I"

> N. J. C. ANDREASON. "Theme and Structure in Donne's *Satyres*," *Studies in English Literature 1500-1900* 3(1), Winter 1963, 59-67.
>
> EMORY ELLIOTT. "The Narrative and Allusive Unity of Donne's *Satyres*," *Journal of English and Germanic Philology* 75(1-2), January-April 1976, 110-12.
>
> SISTER M. GERALDINE. "Donne's *Notitia*: The Evidence of the Satires," *University of Toronto Quarterly* 36(1), October 1966, 26-27.
>
> M. THOMAS HESTER. " 'Zeal' as Satire: The Decorum of Donne's *Satyres*," *Genre* 10(2), Summer 1977, 188.
>
> EJNER J. JENSEN. "The Wit of Renaissance Satire," *Philological Quarterly* 51(2), April 1972, 403-5.
>
> S. F. JOHNSON. *Explicator* 11(8), June 1953, Item 53.
>
> JOHN R. LAURITSEN. "Donne's *Satyres*: The Drama of Self-Discovery," *Studies in English Literature 1500-1900* 16(1), Winter 1976, 121-23.
>
> CAROL MARKS SICHERMAN. "The Mocking Voices of Donne and Marvell," *Bucknell Review* 17(2), May 1969, 38-40.

"Satyre II"

N. J. C. ANDREASON. "Theme and Structure in Donne's *Satyres,*" *Studies in English Literature 1500-1900* 3(1), Winter 1963, 59-64, 67-69.

EMORY ELLIOTT. "The Narrative and Allusive Unity of Donne's *Satyres,*" *Journal of English and Germanic Philology* 75(1,2), January-April 1976, 112.

SISTER M. GERALDINE. "Donne's *Notitia*: The Evidence of the Satires," *University of Toronto Quarterly* 36(1), October 1966, 27.

M. THOMAS HESTER. " 'Zeal' as Satire: The Decorum of Donne's *Satyres,*" *Genre* 10(2), Summer 1977, 188-89.

JOHN R. LAURITSEN. "Donne's *Satyres*: The Drama of Self-Discovery," *Studies in English Literature 1500-1900* 16(1), Winter 1976, 123-25.

"Satyre III"

ROBERT M. ADAMS. *Strains of Discord,* pp. 11-13.

N. J. C. ANDREASEN. "Theme and Structure in Donne's *Satyres,*" *Studies in English Literature 1500-1900* 3(1), Winter 1963, 59-64, 69-71.

A. F. BELLETTE. "The Originality of Donne's *Satires,*" *University of Toronto Quarterly* 44(2), Winter 1975, 135-39.

KITTY DATTA. "Love and asceticism in Donne's poetry: the divine analogy," *Critical Quarterly* 19(2), Summer 1977, 9.

EMORY ELLIOTT. "The Narrative and Allusive Unity of Donne's *Satyres,*" *Journal of English and Germanic Philology* 75(1-2), January-April 1976, 112-13.

SISTER M. GERALDINE. "Donne's *Notitia*: The Evidence of the Satires," *University of Toronto Quarterly* 36(1), October 1966, 27-29.

SISTER M. GERALDINE. "John Donne and the Mindes Indeavours," *Studies in English Literature 1500-1900* 5(1), Winter 1965, 116-19.

M. THOMAS HESTER. " 'All Our Soules Devotion': Satire as Religion in Donne's *Satyre III,*" *Studies in English Literature 1500-1900* 18(1), Winter 1978, 35-55.

M. THOMAS HESTER. " 'Zeal' as Satire: The Decorum of Donne's *Satyres,*" *Genre* 10(2), Summer 1977, 189-90.

JOHN R. LAURITSEN. "Donne's *Satyres*: The Drama of Self-Discovery," *Studies in English Literature 1500-1900* 16(1), Winter 1976, 125-27.

LOUIS L. MARTZ. *The Poem of the Mind,* pp. 13-15.

THOMAS V. MOORE. "Donne's Use of Uncertainty as a Vital Force in *Satyre III,*" *Modern Philology* 67(1), August 1969, 41-49.

ROBERT NYE. "The body is his book: the poetry of John Donne," *Critical Quarterly* 14(4), Winter 1972, 346-47.

JOHN R. ROBERTS. "Donne's *Satyre III* Reconsidered," *CLA Journal* 12(2), December 1968, 105-15.

CAMILLE SLIGHTS. " 'To Stand Inquiring Right': The Casuistry of Donne's 'Satyre III,' " *Studies in English Literature 1500-1900* 12(1), Winter 1972, 85-101.

HALLETT SMITH. *Elizabethan Poetry,* pp. 224-25.

"Satyre IV"

N. J. C. ANDREASON. "Theme and Structure in Donne's *Satyres,*" *Studies in English Literature 1500-1900* 3(1), Winter 1963, 59-64, 71-73.

A. F. BELLETTE. "The Originality of Donne's *Satires,*" *University of Toronto Quarterly* 44(2), Winter 1975, 134-35.

EMORY ELLIOTT. "The Narrative and Allusive Unity of Donne's *Satyres,*" *Journal of English and Germanic Philology* 75(1-2), January-April 1976, 113-15.

SISTER M. GERALDINE. "Donne's *Notitia*: The Evidence of the Satires," *University of Toronto Quarterly* 36(1), October 1966, 29-31.

M. THOMAS HESTER. " 'Zeal' as Satire: The Decorum of Donne's *Satyres,*" *Genre* 10(2), Summer 1977, 191-92.

JOHN R. LAURITSEN. "Donne's *Satyres*: The Drama of Self-Discovery," *Studies in English Literature 1500-1900* 16(1), Winter 1976, 127-29.

WILLIAM YOUNGREN. "Generality in Augustan Satire," in *In Defense of Reading,* pp. 207-17.

"Satyre V"

N. J. C. ANDREASEN. "Theme and Structure in Donne's *Satyres,*" *Studies in English Literature 1500-1900* 3(1), Winter 1963, 59-64, 73-74.

EMORY ELLIOTT. "The Narrative and Allusive Unity of Donne's *Satyres,*" *Journal of English and Germanic Philology* 75(1,2), January-April 1976, 115.

SISTER M. GERALDINE. "Donne's *Notitia*: The Evidence of the Satires," *University of Toronto Quarterly* 36(1), October 1966, 31-34.

M. THOMAS HESTER. "The Satirist as Exegete: John Donne's *Satyre V,*" *Texas Studies in Literature and Language* 20(3), Fall 1978, 347-66.

M. THOMAS HESTER. " 'Zeal' as Satire: The Decorum of Donne's *Satyres,*" *Genre* 10(2), Summer 1977, 192-93.

JOHN R. LAURITSEN. "Donne's *Satyres*: The Drama of Self-Discovery," *Studies in English Literature 1500-1900* 16(1), Winter 1976, 129-30.

"The Second Anniversary"

RAYMOND A. ANSELMENT. " 'Ascensio Mendax, Decensio Crudelis': The Image of Babel in the *Anniversaries,*" *ELH* 38(2), June 1971, 198-205.

ANTHONY F. BELLETTE. "Art and Imitation in Donne's *Anniversaries,*" *Studies in English Literature 1500-1900* 15(1), Winter 1975, 83-96.

MARIUS BEWLEY. *Masks & Mirrors,* pp. 32-47.

MARIUS BEWLEY. "Religious Cynicism in Donne's Poetry," *Kenyon Review* 14(4), Autumn 1952, 621-35.

R. L. COLIE. "The Rhetoric of Transcendence," *Philological Quarterly* 43(2), April 1964, 165-70.

PATRICK CRUTTWELL. *The Shakespearean Moment,* pp. 74-94.

KITTY DATTA. "Love and asceticism in Donne's poetry: the divine analogy," *Critical Quarterly* 19(2), Summer 1977, 13-19.

JOHN G. DEMARAY. "Donne's Three Steps to Death," *Personalist* 46(3), Summer 1965, 375-78.

RUTH A. FOX. "Donne's *Anniversaries* and the Art of Living," *ELH* 38(4), December 1971, 528-41.

RICHARD E. HUGHES. "The Woman in Donne's *Anniversaries,*" *ELH* 34(3), September 1967, 307-26.

W. M. LEBANS. "Donne's *Anniversaries* and the Tradition of Funeral Elegy," *ELH* 39(4), December 1972, 545-59.

J. B. LEISHMAN. *The Metaphysical Poets,* pp. 54-76.

JOHN L. MAHONEY. "Donne and Greville: Two Christian Attitudes Toward the Renaissance Idea of Mutability and Decay," *CLA Journal* 5(3), March 1962, 205-9.

PATRICK MAHONEY. "The *Anniversaries*: Donne's Rhetorical Approach to Evil," *Journal of English and Germanic Philology* 68(3), July 1969, 407-13.

DONNE, JOHN *(Cont.)*

"The Second Anniversary" *(cont.)*

PATRICK MAHONEY. "The Structure of Donne's *Anniversaries* as Companion Poems," *Genre* 5(3), September 1972, 235-56.

LOUIS L. MARTZ. "John Donne in Meditation: The *Anniversaries*," *English Literary History* 14(4), December 1947, 262-73. Reprinted in: *Seventeenth Century English Poetry*, pp. 163-73; revised ed., pp. 137-47.

LOUIS L. MARTZ. *The Poetry of Meditation*, pp. 236-48.

EARL MINER. *The Metaphysical Mode from Donne to Cowley*, pp. 69-75, 182-86.

MARJORIE HOPE NICHOLSON. *The Breaking of the Circle*, pp. 65-104; revised ed., pp. 81-122.

DENNIS QUINN. "Donne's *Anniversaries* as Celebration," *Studies in English Literature 1500-1900* 9(1), Winter 1969, 97-105.

DANIEL R. SCHWARTZ. "The Unity of Eliot's 'Gerontion': The Failure of Meditation," *Bucknell Review* 19(1), Spring 1971, 60-64.

RAMAN SELDEN. "John Donne's 'Incarnational Conviction,'" *Critical Quarterly* 17(1), Spring 1975, 71-72.

CAROL M. SICHERMAN. "Donne's Timeless *Anniversaries*," *University of Toronto Quarterly* 39(2), January 1970, 133-41.

P. G. STANWOOD. "'Essentiall Joye' in Donne's *Anniversaries*," *Texas Studies in Literature and Language* 13(2), Summer 1971, 227-38.

MICHAEL TEPPER. "John Donne's Fragment Epic: 'The Progresse of the Soule,'" *English Language Notes* 13(4), June 1976, 262-66.

GEORGE WILLIAMSON. "The Design of Donne's *Anniversaries*," *Modern Philology* 60(3), February 1963, 183-91.

"Show me deare Christ, thy spouse so bright and clear" ("Holy Sonnets," XVIII)

see also "Holy Sonnets"

REUBEN ARTHUR BROWER. *The Fields of Light*, pp. 24-25.

REUBEN ARTHUR BROWER. "The Speaking Voice," in *The Study of Literature*, pp. 165-69.

WILLIAM KERRIGAN. "The Fearful Accommodations of John Donne," *English Literary Renaissance* 4(3), Autumn 1974, 356-60.

DOUGLAS L. PETERSON. *The English Lyric from Wyatt to Donne*, pp. 344-45.

JOHN CROWE RANSOM. "A Postscript on Shakespeare's Sonnets," *Kenyon Review* 30(4), 1968, 526-27.

STANLEY STEWART. *The Enclosed Garden*, pp. 19-21.

PATRICIA THOMSON. *Elizabethan Lyrical Poets*, pp. 198-99.

CHAD and EVA T. WALSH. *Twice Ten*, p. 27.

"Since she whom I lov'd, hath paid her last debt" ("Holy Sonnets," VII)

see also "Holy Sonnets"

HELEN GARDNER. "Another Note on Donne: 'Since She Whom I Lov'd,'" *Modern Language Review* 52(4), October 1957, 564-65.

LOUIS L. MARTZ. "The Action of the Self: Devotional Poetry in the Seventeenth Century," in *Metaphysical Poetry*, edited by Malcolm Bradbury and David Palmer, pp. 106-8.

HARRY MORRIS. "John Donne's Terrifying Pun," *Papers on Language and Literature* 9(2), Spring 1973, 133-34.

DOUGLAS L. PETERSON. *The English Lyric from Wyatt to Donne*, pp. 345-46.

E. M. W. TILLYARD. *The Metaphysicals and Milton*, pp. 3-7, 77-78.

GEORGE WILLIAMSON. *Six Metaphysical Poets*, pp. 87-88.

"Song: Goe and Catch a Falling Star"

ROBERT HAWKINS. *Preface to Poetry*, pp. 103-5.

LOUIS J. LOCKE. *Explicator* 1(4), February 1943, Item 29. Reprinted in: Norman C. Stageberg and Wallace L. Anderson. *Poetry as Experience*, pp. 472-73.

JOHN PETER. "Crashaw and 'The Weeper,'" *Scrutiny* 19(4), October 1953, 261-62.

DOUGLAS L. PETERSON. *The English Lyric from Wyatt to Donne*, p. 297.

M. L. ROSENTHAL, W. C. HUMMEL, and V. E. LEICHTY. *Effective Reading*, pp. 406-10.

"Song: Sweetest love, I do not goe"

HARRY BROWN and JOHN MILSTEAD. *What the Poem Means*, p. 63.

"Sonnet. The Token"

FRANCIS MANLEY. "Chaucer's Rosary and Donne's Bracelet: Ambiguous Coral," *Modern Language Notes* 74(5), May 1959, 385-88.

"Spit in my face, yee Jewes, and pierce my side" ("Holy Sonnets," XI)

PATRICK GRANT. "Augustinian Spirituality and the *Holy Sonnets* of John Donne," *ELH* 38(4), December 1971, 542-44.

LOUIS L. MARTZ. *The Poetry of Meditation*, pp. 49-50.

"The Storme"

CLAYTON D. LEIN. "Donne's 'The Storme': The Poem and the Tradition," *English Literary Renaissance* 4(1), Winter 1974, 137-63.

MARGARET MAURER. "John Donne's Verse Letters," *Modern Language Quarterly* 37(3), September 1976, 246-47.

LINDA MIZEJEWSKI. "Darkness and Disproportion: A Study of Donne's 'Storme' and 'Calme,'" *Journal of English and Germanic Philology* 76(2), April 1977, 217-26.

GARY STORHOFF. "Metaphors of Despair in Donne's 'The Storme' and 'The Calme,'" *Concerning Poetry* 9(2), Fall 1976, 41-45.

"The Sunne Rising"

STANLEY ARCHER. "Meditation and the Structure of Donne's 'Holy Sonnets,'" *ELH* 28(2), June 1961, 142.

GLENN J. CHRISTENSEN. *Explicator* 7(1), October 1948, Item 3.

STANLEY E. CLAYES and JOHN GERRIETTS. *Ways to Poetry*, pp. 182-84.

DAVID DAICHES and WILLIAM CHARVAT. *Poems in English*, p. 657.

LEONARD DEAN. *English Masterpieces*, edited by William Frost, Maynard Mack, and Leonard Dean, vol. 3: *Renaissance Poetry*, p. 11.

ELIZABETH DREW. *Poetry*, pp. 199-200.

A. E. DYSON and JULIAN LOVELOCK. *Masterful Images*, pp. 21-28.

ANNE FERRY. *All in War with Time*, pp. 78-85.

LLOYD FRANKENBERG. *Invitation to Poetry*, p. 212.

WALTER GIERASCH. *Explicator* 6(7), May 1948, Item 47.

TOSHIHIKO KAWASAKI. "Donne's Microcosm," in *Seventeenth-Century Imagery,* p. 29.

LOWRY NELSON, JR. *Baroque Lyric Poetry,* pp. 124-30.

DOUGLAS L. PETERSON. *The English Lyric from Wyatt to Donne,* pp. 291-94.

ELIZABETH POMEROY. *Explicator* 27(1), September 1968, Item 4.

M. L. ROSENTHAL and A. J. M. SMITH. *Exploring Poetry,* pp. 477-79; second ed., pp. 280-83.

MARTIN TURNELL. "John Donne and the Quest for Unity," *Nineteenth Century and After* 147(878), April 1950, 263-64.

LEONARD UNGER. *Donne's Poetry and Modern Criticism,* pp. 38-39. Reprinted in: Leonard Unger. *The Man in the Name,* pp. 60-61.

GEORGE WILLIAMSON. *Six Metaphysical Poets,* p. 60.

"Temple"
see also "La Corona"

A. B. CHAMBERS. "The Meaning of 'The Temple' in Donne's *La Corona,*" *Journal of English and Germanic Philology* 59(2), April 1960, 212-17.

"This is my playes last scene, here heavens appoint" ("Holy Sonnets," VI)
see also "Holy Sonnets"

J. MAX PATRICK. *Explicator* 31(2), October 1972, Item 12.

ARTHUR W. PITTS, JR. *Explicator* 29(5), January 1971, Item 39.

"Thou hast made me, And shall thy work decay?" ("Holy Sonnets," I)
see also "Holy Sonnets"

PHILIP C. MCGUIRE. "Private Prayer and English Poetry in the Early Seventeenth Century," *Studies in English Literature 1500-1900* 14(1), Winter 1974, 67-68.

ELIAS SCHWARTZ. "*Mimesis* and the Theory of Signs," *College English* 29(5), February 1968, 351-52.

GEORGE WILLIAMSON. *Six Metaphysical Poets,* p. 83.

YVOR WINTERS. "The Poetry of Gerard Manley Hopkins (I)," *Hudson Review* 1(4), Winter 1949, 457-60. Reprinted in: Yvor Winters. *The Function of Criticism,* pp. 104-7.

"To E. of D. with six holy Sonnets"

THOMAS O. SLOAN. "The Crossing of Rhetoric and Poetry in the English Renaissance," in *The Rhetoric of Renaissance Poetry,* pp. 223-25.

"To Mr. R. W." ("If, as mine is, thy life a slumber be")

ALLEN BARRY CAMERON. "Donne's Deliberative Verse Epistles," *English Literary Renaissance* 6(3), Autumn 1976, 390-93.

KITTY DATTA. "Love and asceticism in Donne's poetry: the divine analogy," *Critical Quarterly* 19(2), Summer 1977, 12.

MARGARET MAURER. "John Donne's Verse Letters," *Modern Language Quarterly* 37(3), September 1976, 245-46.

"To Mr. Rowland Woodward" ("Like one who in her third widdowhood doth professe")

ALLEN BARRY CAMERON. "Donne's Deliberative Verse Epistles," *English Literary Renaissance* 6(3), Autumn 1976, 393-97.

GARY P. STORHOFF. "Social Mode and Poetic Strategies: Donne's Verse Letters to His Friends," *Essays in Literature* 4(1), Spring 1977, 12.

"To Mr. T. W." ("Haste thee harsh verse as fast as thy lame measure")

MICHAEL SMALLING. "The Personae in Donne's Epideictic Verse: A Second Opinion," *Southern Quarterly* 14(3), April 1976, 204-5.

"To Mr. Tilman, after he had taken orders"

ALLEN BARRY CAMERON. "Donne's Deliberative Verse Epistles," *English Literary Renaissance* 6(3), Autumn 1976, 398-402.

"To Sr. Edward Herbert. At Julyers"

ALLEN BARRY CAMERON. "Donne's Deliberative Verse Epistles," *English Literary Renaissance* 6(3), Autumn 1976, 386-89.

BARBARA K. LEWALSKI. "Donne's Poetry of Compliment: The Speaker's Stance and the Topoi of Praise," in *Seventeenth-Century Imagery,* pp. 50-51.

"To Sir H. W. at his going Ambassador to Venice"

GARY P. STORHOFF. "Social Mode and Poetic Strategies: Donne's Verse Letters to His Friends," *Essays in Literaure* 4(1), Spring 1977, 13-14.

"To Sir Henry Goodyere" ("Who makes the Past, a patterne for next yeare")

ALLEN BARRY CAMERON. "Donne's Deliberative Verse Epistles," *English Literary Renaissance* 6(3), Autumn 1976, 382-86.

JAY ARNOLD LEVINE. "The Status of the Verse Epistle Before Pope," *Studies in Philology* 59(4), October 1962, 674-75.

GARY P. STORHOFF. "Social Mode and Poetic Strategies: Donne's Verse Letters to His Friends," *Essays in Literature* 4(1), Spring 1977, 15-17.

"To Sr. Henry Wotton" ("Here's no more news, than vertue, I may as well")

ALLEN BARRY CAMERON. "Donne's Deliberative Verse Epistles," *English Literary Renaissance* 6(3), Autumn 1976, 381-82.

"To Sr. Henry Wotton" ("Sir, more than kisses, letters mingle soules")

ALLEN BARRY CAMERON. "Donne's Deliberative Verse Epistles," *English Literary Renaissance* 6(3), Autumn 1976, 375-81.

GARY P. STORHOFF. "Social Mode and Poetic Strategies: Donne's Verse Letters to His Friends," *Essays in Literature* 4(1), Spring 1977, 14-15.

"To the Countesse of Bedford" ("Honour is so sublime perfection")

BARBARA K. LEWALSKI. "Donne's Poetry of Compliment: The Speaker's Stance and the Topoi of Praise," in *Seventeenth-Century Imagery,* pp. 56-57.

"To the Countesse of Bedford" ("Reason is our Soules left hand, Faith her right")

BARBARA K. LEWALSKI. "Donne's Poetry of Compliment: The Speaker's Stance and The Topoi of Praise," in *Seventeenth-Century Imagery,* pp. 60-61.

MARGARET MAURER. "John Donne's Verse Letters," *Modern Language Quarterly* 37(3), September 1976, 253-55.

"To the Countesse of Bedford" ("T'have written then, when you writ, seem'd to mee")

DAN S. COLLINS. *Explicator* 31(3), November 1972, Item 19.

BARBARA K. LEWALSKI. "Donne's Poetry of Compliment: The Speaker's Stance and the Topoi of Praise," in *Seventeenth-Century Imagery,* p. 56.

DONNE, JOHN (*Cont.*)

"To the Countesse of Bedford" ("You have refin'd mee, and to worthyest things")

>   BARBARA K. LEWALSKI. "Donne's Poetry of Compliment: The Speaker's Stance and the Topoi of Praise," in *Seventeenth-Century Imagery*, pp. 57-58.

"To the Countesse of Bedford. On New-yeares day"

>   BARBARA K. LEWALSKI. "Donne's Poetry of Compliment: The Speaker's Stance and the Topoi of Praise," in *Seventeenth-Century Imagery*, p. 57.

"To the Countesse of Huntingdon" ("Man to Gods image, Eve, to mans was made")

>   ROBERT HARRISON. *Explicator* 25(4), December 1966, Item 33.

>   BARBARA K. LEWALSKI. "Donne's Poetry of Compliment: The Speaker's Stance and the Topoi of Praise,," in *Seventeenth-Century Imagery*, p. 55.

"To the Countesse of Huntingdon" ("That unripe side of earth, that heavy clime")

>   BARBARA K. LEWALSKI. "Donne's Poetry of Compliment: The Speaker's Stance and the Topoi of Praise," in *Seventeenth-Century Imagery*, p. 51.

"To the Countesse of Salisbury. August 1614"

>   BARBARA K. LEWALSKI. "Donne's Poetry of Compliment: The Speaker's Stance and the Topoi of Praise," in *Seventeenth-Century Imagery*, pp. 62-63.

"Twicknam garden"

>   LOUIS L. MARTZ. "John Donne: the Meditative Voice," *Massachusetts Review* 1(2), Winter 1960, 338-39. Reprinted in: Louis L. Martz. *The Poem of the Mind*, pp. 16-17.

>   EARL MINER. *The Metaphysical Mode from Donne to Cowley*, pp. 55-57.

>   LOWRY NELSON, JR. *Baroque Lyric Poetry*, pp. 132-36.

>   LEONARD UNGER. *Donne's Poetry and Modern Criticism*, pp. 30-37. Reprinted in: Leonard Unger. *The Man in the Name*, pp. 53-59.

>   GEORGE WILLIAMSON. *Six Metaphysical Poets*, pp. 64-65.

"The undertaking"

>   NOAM FLINKER. *Explicator* 36(3), Spring 1978, 17-18.

>   THOMAS O. SLOAN. "The Rhetoric in the Poetry of John Donne," *Studies in English Literature 1500-1900* 3(1), Winter 1963, 39-41.

>   GEORGE WILLIAMSON. *Six Metaphysical Poets*, p. 59.

"Upon the Annunciation and Passion Falling Upon One Day. 1608"

see "The Annunciation and Passion"

"Upon the translation of the Psalmes by Sir Philip Sydney, and the Countesse of Pembroke his Sister"

>   ANTHONY LOW. *Love's Architecture*, pp. 74-76.

"A Valediction forbidding mourning"

>   GÉMINO H. ABAD. *A Formal Approach to Lyric Poetry*, pp. 327-32.

>   ROBERT M. ADAMS. *Strains of Discord*, pp. 109-11.

>   T. R. BARNES. *English Verse* pp. 61-64.

>   JOHN CIARDI. *Dialogue with an Audience*, pp. 245-51.

>   JOHN CIARDI. *How Does a Poem Mean?* pp. 873-75; second ed., pp. 248-50.

>   EARL DANIELS. *The Art of Reading Poetry*, pp. 213-16.

>   KITTY DATTA. "Love and asceticism in Donne's poetry: the divine analogy," *Critical Quarterly* 19(2), Summer 1977, 20-21.

JAY DEAN DIVINE. "Compass and Circle in Donne's 'A Valediction: Forbidding Mourning,'" *Papers on Language and Literature* 9(1), Winter 1973, 78-80.

ANNE FERRY. *All in War with Time*, pp. 90-101.

ALISTAIR FOWLER. *Conceitful Thought*, pp. 103-4.

NIGEL FOXELL. *Ten Poems Analyzed*, pp. 1-12.

JOHN FRECCERO. "Donne's 'Valediction: Forbidding Mourning,'" *ELH* 30(4), December 1963, 335-76.

T. R. HENN. *The Apple and the Spectroscope*, pp. 20-24.

BROTHER JOSEPH. *Explicator* 16(7), April 1958, Item 43.

FRANK KERMODE and A. J. SMITH. "The Metaphysical Poets," in *English Poetry*, edited by Alan Sinfield, pp. 63-66.

JAMES R. KREUZER. *Elements of Poetry*, pp. 84-86.

C. N. MANLOVE. *Literature and Reality*, pp. 4-8.

LOUIS L. MARTZ. *The Wit of Love*, pp. 47-48.

FRED B. MILLETT. *Reading Poetry*, pp. 61-63; second ed., pp. 74-77.

I. A. RICHARDS. "Donne: A Valediction: Forbidding Mourning," in *Master Poems of the English Language*, pp. 111-13.

CAROL MARKS SICHERMAN. "Donne's Discoveries," *Studies in English Literature 1500-1900* 11(1), Winter 1971, 78-81.

PATRICIA MEYER SPACKS. "In Search of Sincerity," *College English* 29(8), May 1968, 594-95.

ALLEN TATE. "The Point of Dying: Donne's 'Virtuous Men,'" *Sewanee Review* 61(1), Winter 1953, 76-81. Reprinted in: Allen Tate. *Essays of Four Decades*, pp. 247-52.

LEONARD UNGER. *Donne's Poetry and Modern Criticism*, pp. 53-54. Reprinted in: Leonard Unger. *The Man in the Name*, pp. 61-62.

CHAD WALSH. *Doors into Poetry*, pp. 111-15.

PHILIP WHEELWRIGHT. *The Burning Fountain*, pp. 103-4.

GEORGE WILLIAMSON. *Six Metaphysical Poets*, pp. 72-73.

"A Valediction of my name in the window"

>   JOHN BERNARD. "Orthodoxia Epedemica: Donne's Poetics and 'A Valediction: of my Name in the Window,'" *South Atlantic Quarterly* 71(3), Summer 1972, 384-88.

>   CLEANTH BROOKS. *Modern Poetry and the Tradition*, pp. 24-25.

>   BARBARA HARDY. *The Advantage of Lyric*, pp. 28-32.

>   DOUGLAS L. PETERSON. *The English Lyric from Wyatt to Donne*, pp. 321-26.

>   LEONARD UNGER. *Donne's Poetry and Modern Criticism*, pp. 61-62. Reprinted in: Leonard Unger. *The Man in the Name*, pp. 80-81.

>   G. R. WILSON, JR. "The Interplay of Perception and Reflection: Mirror Imagery in Donne's Poetry," *Studies in English Literature 1500-1900* 9(1), Winter 1969, 117-18.

"Valediction of the booke"

>   RHODES DUNLAP. "Donne As Navigator," *Times Literary Supplement*, 28 December 1946, p. 643. (P)

>   LEONARD UNGER. *Donne's Poetry and Modern Criticism*, pp. 58-59. Reprinted in: Leonard Unger. *The Man in the Name*, pp. 77-78.

>   GEORGE WILLIAMSON. *Six Metaphysical Poets*, pp. 65-66.

"A Valediction of weeping"

STANLEY ARCHER. "Meditation and the Structure of Donne's 'Holy Sonnets,'" *ELH* 28(2), June 1961, 141-42.

T. R. BARNES. *English Verse*, pp. 64-65.

EARL DANIELS. *The Art of Reading Poetry*, pp. 216-17.

WILLIAM EMPSON. *Seven Types of Ambiguity*, pp. 175-83; second and third eds., pp. 139-45. Reprinted in: *The Modern Critical Spectrum*, pp. 97-101.

ANNE FERRY. *All in War with Time*, pp. 85-90.

JOHN HOLLOWAY. "The Simplicities of Poetry," *Essays by Divers Hands*, 3rd series, 31 (1962), 92-93.

CHAD and EVA T. WALSH. *Twice Ten*, pp. 18-20.

GEORGE WILLIAMSON. *Six Metaphysical Poets*, pp. 69-70.

G. R. WILSON, JR. "The Interplay of Perception and Reflection: Mirror Imagery in Donne's Poetry," *Studies in English Literature 1500-1900* 9(1), Winter 1969, 119-20.

"Variety" (Elegy XVII)

DOUGLAS L. PETERSON. *The English Lyric from Wyatt to Donne*, pp. 307-11.

"What if this present were the world's last night?" ("Holy Sonnets," XIII)

see also "Holy Sonnets"

WILLIAM EMPSON. *Seven Types of Ambiguity*, pp. 183-84; second ed., pp. 145-46; third ed., pp. 145-46. Reprinted in: *The Modern Critical Spectrum*, pp. 101-2.

LOUIS L. MARTZ. "John Donne: the Meditative Voice," *Massachusetts Review* 1(2), Winter 1960, 329-30. Reprinted in: Louis L. Martz. *The Poem of the Mind*, pp. 6-7.

JOHN E. PARISH. *Explicator* 22(3), November 1963, Item 19.

DOUGLAS L. PETERSON. *The English Lyric from Wyatt to Donne*, pp. 341-42.

GEORGE WILLIAMSON. *Six Metaphysical Poets*, p. 86.

"Why are we by all creatures waited on?" ("Holy Sonnets," XII)

see also "Holy Sonnets"

M. E. GRENANDER. *Explicator* 13(7), May 1955, Item 42.

LOUIS L. MARTZ. *The Poetry of Meditation*, first ed., pp. 53-54.

ARTHUR L. SIMPSON, JR. *Explicator* 27(9), May 1969, Item 75.

"The Will"

ROSEMOND TUVE. *Elizabethan and Metaphysical Imagery*, pp. 170-71.

LEONARD UNGER. *Donne's Poetry and Modern Criticism*, pp. 59-60. Reprinted in: Leonard Unger. *The Man in the Name*, pp. 78-79.

GEORGE WILLIAMSON. *Six Metaphysical Poets*, pp. 74-75.

"Witchcraft by a picture"

G. R. WILSON, JR. "The Interplay of Perception and Reflection: Mirror Imagery in Donne's Poetry," *Studies in English Literature 1500-1900* 9(1), Winter 1969, 115-16.

"Womans constancy"

JAMES R. KREUZER. *Elements of Poetry*, pp. 145-46.

DOUGLAS L. PETERSON. *The English Lyric from Wyatt to Donne*, pp. 297-98.

DOOLITTLE, HILDA ("H.D.")

"Demeter"

LILLIAN FEDER. *Ancient Myth in Modern Poetry*, pp. 17-18.

"The Flowering of the Rod"

L. S. DEMBO. *Conceptions of Reality in Modern American Poetry*, pp. 32-33.

"The God"

BERNARD F. ENGEL. "H. D.: Poems That Matter and Dilutations," *Contemporary Literature* 10(4), Autumn 1969, 515.

"Heat"

HARRY BROWN and JOHN MILSTEAD. *What the Poem Means*, p. 65.

"Heliodora"

JOSEPH N. RIDDEL. "H. D. and the Poetics of 'Spiritual Realism,'" *Contemporary Literature* 10(4), Autumn 1969, 455-56.

"Hermetic Definition"

VINCENT QUINN. "H. D.'s 'Hermetic Definition': The Poet as Archetypal Mother," *Contemporary Literature* 18(1), Winter 1977, 51-61.

"The Islands"

E. B. GREENWOOD. "H. D. and The Problem of Escapism," *Essays in Criticism* 21(4), October 1971, 370-72.

"Lethe"

HARRY BROWN and JOHN MILSTEAD. *What the Poem Means*, p. 65.

"Loss"

JOSEPH N. RIDDEL. "H. D. and the Poetics of 'Spiritual Realism,'" *Contemporary Literature* 10(4), Autumn 1969, 453-54.

"Oread"

EARL DANIELS. *The Art of Reading Poetry*, pp. 198-99.

WILLIS D. JACOBS. *Explicator* 10(7), May 1952, Item 45.

MACKLIN THOMAS. "Analysis of the Experience in Lyric Poetry," *College English* 9(6), March 1948, 320.

"Pear Tree"

CLEANTH BROOKS, JOHN THIBAUT PURSER, and ROBERT PENN WARREN. *An Approach to Literature*, fifth edition, pp. 356-57.

"The Pool"

EARL DANIELS. *The Art of Reading Poetry*, pp. 196-97. Reprinted in: Norman C. Stageberg and Wallace L. Anderson. *Poetry as Experience*, p. 29.

"Sea Gods"

L. S. DEMBO. *Conceptions of Reality in Modern American Poetry*, p. 26.

"Tribute to the Angels"

L. S. DEMBO. *Conceptions of Reality in Modern American Poetry*, pp. 30-32.

DORN, EDWARD

"Idaho Out"

WILLIAM J. LOCKWOOD. "Ed Dorn's Mystique of the Real: His Poems for North America," *Contemporary Literature* 19(1), Winter 1978, 67-75.

"Mourning Letter, March 29, 1963"

DONALD DAVIE. *The Poet in the Imaginary Museum*, p. 148.

DORN, EDWARD (*Cont.*)

"Oxford"

> DONALD DAVIE. "The Black Mountain Poets: Charles Olson and Edward Dorn," in *The Survival of Poetry*, pp. 228-33.

DOUGLAS, KEITH

"Adams"

> DAVID ORMEROD. "Keith Douglas and The Name of the Poem I Can't Write," *Ariel* 9(2), April 1978, 16-17.

"Cairo Jag"

> GEORGE FRASER. *Essays on Twentieth-Century Poets*, pp. 227-28.
>
> VERNON SCANNELL. *Not Without Glory*, pp. 42-43.

"How to Kill"

> DAVID ORMEROD. "Keith Douglas and The Name of the Poem I Can't Write," *Ariel* 9(2), April 1978, 20-21.
>
> VERNON SCANNELL. *Not Without Glory*, pp. 46-47.

"The Knife"

> DAVID ORMEROD. "Keith Douglas and The Name of the Poem I Can't Write," *Ariel* 9(2), April 1978, 18.

"Leukothea"

> GEORGE FRASER. *Essays on Twentieth-Century Poets*, pp. 224-25.

"Simplify Me When I'm Dead"

> DAVID ORMEROD. "Keith Douglas and The Name of the Poem I Can't Write," *Ariel* 9(1), April 1978, 13-14.

"Time Eating"

> DAVID ORMEROD. "Keith Douglas and The Name of the Poem I Can't Write," *Ariel* 9(2), April 1978, 15.

"Vergissmeinicht"

> VERNON SCANNELL. *Not Without Glory*, pp. 44-46.

DOWSON, ERNEST

"Benedicto Domini"

> RICHARD BENVENUTO. "The Function of Language in the Poetry of Ernest Dowson," *English Literature in Transition* 21(3), 1978, 162.

"Carthusians"

> RAZA ALI. "The 'Decadent' View of Life and Dowson's Poetry," *Thoth* 13(1), Winter 1972-73, 30-31.

"In Tempore Senectutis"

> THEO STEINMAN. "The Two-Dimensional Structure of Dowson's 'In Tempore Senectutis,'" *Concerning Poetry* 7(2), Fall 1974, 49-53.

"Non Sum Qualis Eram Bonae Sub Regno Cynarae"

> MARK LONGAKER. *Explicator* 9(7), May 1951, Item 48.
>
> JAMES G. NELSON. "The Nature of Aesthetic Experience in the Poetry of the Nineties: Ernest Dowson, Lionel Johnson and John Gray," *English Literature in Transition* 17(4), 1974, 227-29.

"Nuns of the Perpetual Adoration"

> RICHARD BENVENUTO. "The Function of Language in the Poetry of Ernest Dowson," *English Literature in Transition* 21(3), 1978, 160-61.

"The Pierrot of the Minute"

> JOHN R. REED. "Bedlamite and Pierrot: Ernest Dowson's Esthetic of Futility," *ELH* 35(1), March 1968, 109-12.

"To One in Bedlam"

> RICHARD BENVENUTO. "The Function of Language in the Poetry of Ernest Dowson," *English Literature in Transition* 21(3), 1978, 162-63.
>
> JOHN R. REED. "Bedlamite and Pierrot: Ernest Dowson's Esthetic of Futility," *ELH* 35(1), March 1968, 112-13.

"Villanelle of His Lady's Treasures"

> JAN B. GORDON. "Poetic Pilgrimage of Dowson," *Renascence* 20(1), Autumn 1967, 5-6.

"Yvonne of Brittany"

> RICHARD BENVENUTO. "The Function of Language in the Poetry of Ernest Dowson," *English Literature in Transition* 21(3), 1978, 161-62.

DRAYTON, MICHAEL

"Agincourt"

> EARL DANIELS. *The Art of Reading Poetry*, pp. 163-68.

"Another to the River Ankor"

> ROSEMOND TUVE. *Elizabethan and Metaphysical Imagery*, pp. 62-63.

"Cleer Ankor, on whose silver-sanded shore"

> see "Another to the River Ankor"

"How many paltry, foolish, painted things" (*Idea*, 6)

> WALTER R. DAVIS. " 'Fantastickly I Sing': Drayton's *Idea* of 1619," *Studies in Philology* 66(2), April 1969, 213-14.

"I heare some say, this man is not in love" (*Idea*, 24)

> WALTER R. DAVIS. " 'Fantastickly I Sing': Drayton's *Idea* of 1619," *Studies in Philology* 66(2), April 1969, 207.

"Like an adventurous seafarer am I"

> ROSEMOND TUVE. *Elizabethan and Metaphysical Imagery*, pp. 61-62.

"Love's Farewell"

> PAUL O. CLARK. "Other Visits to Love's Deathbed," *CEA Critic* 37(1), November 1974, 30-31.
>
> DAVID LEON HIGDON. "Love's Deathbed Revisited," *CEA Critic* 36(1), November 1973, 35.
>
> LAURENCE PERRINE. "A Drayton Sonnet," *CEA Critic* 25(9), June 1963, 8.
>
> JOHN S. PHILLIPSON. "A Drayton Sonnet," *CEA Critic* 25(7), April 1963, 3.
>
> OWEN J. REAMER. "Come Back to Love's Deathbed," *CEA Critic* 37(1), November 1974, 28-29.
>
> GARY STRINGER. "Love's Deathbed One More Time: A Reply to Mr. Leon Higdon," *CEA Critic* 37(1), November 1974, 27-28.

"Since ther's no helpe, come let us kisse and part" (*Idea*, 61)

> WALTER R. DAVIS. " 'Fantastickly I Sing': Drayton's *Idea* of 1619," *Studies in Philology* 66(2), April 1969, 214-15.
>
> LEONARD DEAN. *English Masterpieces*, edited by William Frost, Maynard Mack, and Leonard Dean, vol. 3: *Renaissance Poetry*, p. 4.

"To My Most Dearely-loved Friend Henery Reynolds Esquire: of Poets and Poesie"

> D. J. PALMER. "The Verse Epistle," in *Metaphysical Poetry*, edited by Malcolm Bradbury and David Palmer, pp. 97-98.

"To the Cambro-Britons and their harp, his ballad of Agincourt"

> see "Agincourt"

"To the Reader of these Sonnets" (*Idea*)

> WALTER R. DAVIS. " 'Fantastickly I Sing': Drayton's *Idea* of 1619," *Studies in Philology* 66(2), April 1969, 205-6.

DREW, JOHN

"Poem for Chandravan Mehta"

> JEFFREY WAINWRIGHT. "Jeffrey Wainwright on John Drew," *Iowa Review* 6(3-4), Summer-Fall 1975, 195-96.

"Two Aspects of Paternity"

> JEFFREY WAINWRIGHT. "Jeffrey Wainwright on John Drew," *Iowa Review* 6(3-4), Summer-Fall 1975, 195-96.

DRINKWATER, JOHN

"The Carver in Stone"

> " 'Some Poets of Today,' S. P. B. Mais, 'The Nineteenth Century,' " in *Georgian Poetry,* pp. 168-69.

DRYDEN, JOHN

"Absalom and Achitophel"

> JOEL BLAIR. "Dryden's Ceremonial Hero," *Studies in English Literature 1500-1900* 9(3), Summer 1969, 389-90.
>
> REUBEN ARTHUR BROWER. *The Fields of Light,* pp. 51-56.
>
> SANFORD BUDICK. *Poetry of Civilization,* pp. 86-105.
>
> A. E. DYSON and JULIAN LOVELOCK. *Masterful Images,* pp. 71-96.
>
> DAVID FARLEY-HILLS. *The Benevolence of Laughter,* pp. 114-31.
>
> P. J. C. FIELD. "Authoritative Echo in Dryden," *Durham University Journal,* n.s., 31(3), June 1970, 143-48.
>
> LEON M. GUILHAMET. "Dryden's Debasement of Scripture in *Absalom and Achitophel,*" *Studies in English Literature 1500-1900* 9(3), Summer 1969, 395-413.
>
> IAN JACK. *Augustan Satire,* pp. 53-76.
>
> GEORGE R. LEVINE. "Dryden's 'Inarticulate Poesy': Music and the Davidic King in *Absalom and Achitophel,*" *Eighteenth Century Studies* 1(4), Summer 1968, 291-312.
>
> BARBARA KIEFER LEWALSKI. "The Scope and Function of Biblical Allusion in *Absalom and Achitophel,*" *English Language Notes* 3(1), September 1965, 29-35.
>
> MAYNARD MACK. *English Masterpieces,* edited by William Frost, Maynard Mack, and Leonard Dean, vol. 5: *The Augustans,* pp. 6-10.
>
> THOMAS E. MARESCA. "The Context of Dryden's *Absalom and Achitophel,*" *ELH* 41(3), Fall 1974, 340-58.
>
> REBECCA PRICE PARKIN. "Some Rhetorical Aspects of Dryden's Biblical Allusions," *Eighteenth Century Studies* 2(4), Summer 1969, 347-60.
>
> R. G. PETERSON. "Larger Manners and Events: Sallust and Virgil in *Absalom and Achitophel,*" *PMLA* 82(2), May 1967, 236-44.
>
> CHRISTOPHER RICKS. "Dryden's Absalom," *Essays in Criticism* 11(3), July 1961, 273-89.
>
> RICHARD WENDORF. "Dryden, Charles II, and the Interpretation of Historical Character," *Philological Quarterly* 56(1), Winter 1977, 96-98.

"Alexander's Feast"

> ISAAC ASIMOV. *Familiar Poems, Annotated,* pp. 19-34.
>
> NIGEL FOXEL. *Ten Poems Analyzed,* pp. 23-40.
>
> BESSIE PROFFITT. "Political Satire in Dryden's *Alexander's Feast,*" *Texas Studies in Literature and Language* 11(4), Winter 1970, 1307-16.
>
> RUTH SMITH. "The Argument and Contexts of Dryden's *Alexander's Feast,*" *Studies in English Literature 1500-1900* 18(3), Summer 1978, 465-90.

"Astraea Redux"

> A. E. WALLACE MAURER. "The Structure of Dryden's *Astraea Redux,*" *Papers on Language and Literature* 2(1), Winter 1966, 13-20.
>
> DAVID M. VIETH. "Divided Consciousness: The Trauma and Triumph of Restoration Culture," *Tennessee Studies in Literature* 22 (1977), 49-50.
>
> GEORGE R. WASSERMAN. "The Domestic Metaphor in *Astrae Redux,*" *English Language Notes* 3(2), December 1965, 106-11.
>
> RICHARD WENDORF. "Dryden, Charles II, and the Interpretation of Historical Character," *Philological Quarterly* 56(1), Winter 1977, 93-95.
>
> STEVEN N. ZWICKER. "The King and Christ: Figural Imagery in Dryden's Restoration Panegyrics," *Philological Quarterly* 50(4), October 1971, 584-91.

"Baucis and Philemon"

> D. W. HOPKINS. "Dryden's 'Baucis and Philemon,' " *Comparative Literature* 28(2), Spring 1976, 135-43. (P)

"Ceyx and Aleyone"

> JUDITH SLOMAN. "An Interpretation of Dryden's Fables," *Eighteenth Century Studies* 4(2), Winter 1971, 200-1.

"The Character of a Good Parson"

> JUDITH SLOMAN. "An Interpretation of Dryden's Fables," *Eighteenth Century Studies* 4(2), Winter 1971, 208-9.

"The Cock and the Fox"

> CHARLES H. HINNANT. "Dryden's Gallic Rooster," *Studies in Philology* 65(4), July 1968, 647-56.
>
> C. N. MANLOVE. *Literature and Reality,* pp. 64-75.
>
> EARL MINER. *The Restoration Mode from Milton to Dryden,* pp. 547-49.

"Cymon and Iphigenia"

> JUDITH SLOMAN. "An Interpretation of Dryden's Fables," *Eighteenth Century Studies* 4(2), Winter 1971, 210-11.

"Eleonora"

> DONALD R. BENSON. "Platonism and Neoclassic Metaphor: Dryden's *Eleonora* and Donne's *Anniversaries,*" *Studies in Philology* 68(3), July 1971, 340-56.

"Epilogue Spoken to the King at the opening of the Play-House at Oxford on Saturday last. Being March the Nineteenth 1681"

> SANFORD BUDICK. *Poetry of Civilization,* pp. 83-86.

"The Flower and the Leaf"

> JUDITH SLOMAN. "An Interpretation of Dryden's Fables," *Eighteenth Century Studies* 4(2), Winter 1971, 200-2.

"Heroique Stanzas"

> DAVID M. VIETH. "Divided Consciousness: The Trauma and Triumph of Restoration Culture," *Tennessee Studies in Literature* 22 (1977), 49.

DRYDEN, JOHN *(Cont.)*

"Heroique Stanzas" *(cont.)*

MICHAEL WEST. "Shifting Concepts of Heroism in Dryden's Panegyrics," *Papers on Language and Literature* 10(4), Fall 1974, 379-83.

"Mac Flecknoe"

MICHAEL W. ALSSID. "Shadwell's *MacFlecknoe*," *Studies in English Literature 1500-1900* 7(3), Summer 1967, 387-402.

DAVID DAICHES and WILLIAM CHARVAT. *Poems in English*, pp. 673-75.

JEROME DONNELLY. "Movement and Meaning in Dryden's *MacFlecknoe*," *Texas Studies in Literature and Language* 12(4), Winter 1971, 569-82.

MOTHER MARY ELEANOR. "*Anne Killigrew* and *MacFlecknoe*," *Philolgical Quarterly* 43(1), January 1964, 47-54.

PAUL GOODMAN. *The Structure of Literature*, pp. 117-26.

DAVID FARLEY-HILLS. *The Benevolence of Laughter*, pp. 110-14.

P. J. C. FIELD. "Authoritative Echo in Dryden," *Durham University Journal*, n.s., 31(3), June 1970, 149-51.

IAN JACK. "Mock Heroic: *MacFlecknoe*," in *Seventeenth Century English Poetry*, pp. 425-34; revised ed., pp. 464-73.

GEORGE MCFADDEN. "Elkanah Settle and the Genesis of *Mac Flecknoe*," *Philological Quarterly* 43(1), January 1964, 55-72.

MAYNARD MACK. *English Masterpieces*, edited by William Frost, Maynard Mack, and Leonard Dean, vol. 5: *The Augustans*, pp. 5-6.

EARL MINER. *The Restoration Mode from Milton to Dryden*, pp. 319-20, 344-47, 440-48, 453-54.

TOM H. TOWERS. "The Lineage of Shadwell: An Approach to *MacFlecknoe*," *Studies in English Literature 1500-1900* 3(3), Summer 1963, 323-34.

DAVID M. VIETH. "Divided Consciousness: The Trauma and Triumph of Restoration Culture," *Tennessee Studies in Literature* 22 (1977), 55-56.

MICHAEL WILDING. "Allusion and Innuendo in *MacFlecknoe*," *Essays in Criticism* 19(4), October 1969, 355-70.

"The Medal"

SANFORD BUDICK. *Poetry of Civilization*, pp. 105-10.

THOMAS R. EDWARDS. *Imagination and Power*, pp. 86-102.

A. E. WALLACE MAURER. "The Design of Dryden's *The Medall*," *Papers on Language and Literature* 2(4), Fall 1966, 293-304.

EARL MINER. *The Restoration Mode from Milton to Dryden*, pp. 320-22, 442-48, 451-53.

ALAN H. ROPER. "Dryden's *Medal* and the Divine Analogy," *ELH* 29(4), December 1962, 396-417.

"Ode: To the Pious Memory of the Accomplished Young Lady, Mrs. Anne Killigrew"

ROBERT DALY. "Dryden's Ode to Anne Killigrew and the Communal Work of Poets," *Texas Studies in Literature and Language* 18(2), Summer 1976, 184-97.

MOTHER MARY ELEANOR. "*Anne Killigrew* and *Mac Flecknoe*," *Philological Quarterly* 43(1), January 1964, 47-54.

JUDSON JEROME. "On Decoding Humor," *Antioch Review* 20(4), Winter 1960-61, 486-87.

JEFFRY B. SPENCER. *Heroic Nature*, pp. 178-82.

E. M. W. TILLYARD. *Five Poems, 1470-1870*, pp. 49-65. Reprinted in: *Essays in Modern Literary Criticism*, pp. 353-65.

DAVID M. VIETH. "Irony in Dryden's Ode to Anne Killigrew," *Studies in Philology* 62(1), January 1965, 91-100.

RUTH WALLERSTEIN. "On the Death of Mrs. Killigrew: The Perfecting of a Genre," in *Seventeenth Century English Poetry*, pp. 415-24; revised ed., pp. 454-63.

"On the Marriage of the Fair and Vertuous Lady, Mrs. Anastasia Stafford, with That Truly Worthy Gent. George Holman, Esq."

EARL MINER. "Dryden's Ode on Mrs. Anastasia Stafford," *Huntington Library Quarterly* 30(2), February 1967, 103-11.

"On the Monument of a fair Maiden Lady, who died at Bath, and is there interred"

JUDITH SLOMAN. "An Interpretation of Dryden's Fables," *Eighteenth Century Studies* 4(2), Winter 1971, 210.

"Religio Laici"

G. DOUGLAS ATKINS. "Dryden's *Religio Laici*: A Reappraisal," *Studies in Philology* 75(3), July 1978, 347-70.

DONALD R. BENSON. "Theology and Politics in Dryden's Conversion," *Studies in English Literature 1500-1900* 4(3), Summer 1964, 395-401.

DONALD R. BENSON. "Who 'Bred' *Religio Laici*?" *Journal of English and Germanic Philology* 65(2), April 1966, 238-51.

JIM W. CORDER. "Rhetoric and Meaning in *Religio Laici*," *PMLA* 82(2), May 1967, 245-49.

WILLIAM EMPSON. "A Deist Tract by Dryden," *Essays in Criticism* 25(1), January 1975, 74-100.

WILLIAM EMPSON. "Dryden's Apparent Scepticism," *Essays in Criticism* 20(2), April 1970, 172-81.

THOMAS H. FUJIMURA. "Dryden's *Religio Laici*: An Anglican Poem," *PMLA* 76(3), June 1961, 205-17.

JEROME MCGANN. "The Argument of Dryden's *Religio Laici*," *Thoth* 3(2), Spring 1962, 78-89.

REBECCA PRICE PARKIN. "Some Rhetorical Aspects of Dryden's Biblical Allusions," *Eighteenth Century Studies* 2(4), Summer 1969, 360-66.

FRANCES MAYHEW RIPPY. "Imagery, John Dryden, and 'The Poetry of Statement,'" *Ball State Teachers College Forum* 1(2), Winter 1960-61, 13-20.

"Secular Masque"

ALAN H. ROPER. "Dryden's 'Secular Masque,'" *Modern Language Quarterly* 23(1), March 1962, 29-40.

"Sigismonda and Guiscardo"

EARL MINER. *The Restoration Mode from Milton to Dryden*, pp. 511-13.

JUDITH SLOMAN. "Dryden's Originality in *Sigismonda and Guiscardo*," *Studies in English Literature 1500-1900* 12(3), Summer 1972, 445-57.

"A Song for St. Cecilia's Day, 1687"

DAVID DAICHES. "Dryden: A Song for St. Cecilia's Day," in *Master Poems of the English Language*, pp. 232-37.

ALASTAIR FOWLER and DOUGLAS BROOKS. "The Structure of Dryden's 'Song for St. Cecilia's Day, 1687,'" *Essays in Criticism* 17(4), October 1967, 434-47. Reprinted in: *Silent Poetry*, pp. 185-200.

H. JAMES JENSON. "Comparing the Arts in the Age of Baroque," *Eighteenth Century Studies* 6(3), Spring 1973, 334-47.

DOUGLAS MURRAY. "The Musical Structure of Dryden's 'Song for St. Cecilia's Day,'" *Eighteenth Century Studies* 10(3), Spring 1977, 326-34.

EARL R. WASSERMAN. "Pope's *Ode for Musick*," *ELH* 28(2), June 1961, 165-69.

"Threnodia Augustalis"

RICHARD WENDORF. "Dryden, Charles II, and the Interpretation of Historical Character," *Philological Quarterly* 56(1), Winter 1977, 98-99.

"To Her Grace the Duchess of Ormond with the Following Poem of Palamon and Arcite"

EARL MINER. *The Restoration Mode from Milton to Dryden*, pp. 450-51.

JUDITH SLOMAN. "An Interpretation of Dryden's Fables," *Eighteenth Century Studies* 4(2), Winter 1971, 204.

"To His Sacred Majesty"

JOEL BLAIR. "Dryden's Ceremonial Hero," *Studies in English Literature 1500-1900* 9(3), Summer 1969, 382-83.

RICHARD WENDORF. "Dryden, Charles II, and the Interpretation of Historical Character," *Philological Quarterly* 56(1), Winter 1977, 95.

STEVEN N. ZWICKER. "The King and Christ: Figural Imagery in Dryden's Restoration Panegyrics," *Philological Quarterly* 50(4), October 1971, 591-98.

"To My Dear Friend Mr. Congreve, on his Comedy called *The Double-Dealer*"

JAY ARNOLD LEVINE. "The Status of the Verse Epistle Before Pope," *Studies in Philology* 59(4), October 1962, 682-83.

EARL MINER. *The Restoration Mode from Milton to Dryden*, pp. 30-31.

"To my Honour'd Friend, Dr. Charleton"

JOEL BLAIR. "Dryden's Ceremonial Hero," *Studies in English Literature 1500-1900* 9(3), Summer 1969, 383.

EARL R. WASSERMAN. *The Subtler Language*, pp. 15-33.

"To my Honored Friend, Sir Robert Howard, On his Excellent Poems"

JAMES WILLIAM JOHNSON. "Dryden's Epistle to Robert Howard," *Ball State Teachers College Forum* 2(1), Spring 1961, 20-24.

DAVID M. VIETH. "Irony in Dryden's Verses to Sir Robert Howard," *Essays in Criticism* 22(3), July 1972, 239-43.

"To My Honour'd Kinsman, John Driden, of Chesterton, in the County of Huntingdon, Esquire"

J. DOUGLAS CANFIELD. "The Image of the Circle in Dryden's 'To My Honour'd Kinsman,'" *Papers on Language and Literature* 11(2), Spring 1975, 168-76.

JAY ARNOLD LEVINE. "John Dryden's Epistle to John Driden," *Journal of English and Germanic Philology* 63(3), July 1964, 450-74.

EARL MINER. *The Restoration Mode from Milton to Dryden*, pp. 152-57. (P)

JUDITH SLOMAN. "An Interpretation of Dryden's Fables," *Eighteenth Century Studies* 4(2), Winter 1971, 205-7.

"To Sir Godfrey Kneller"

ACHSAH GUIBBORY. "Dryden's Views of History," *Philological Quarterly* 52(2), April 1973, 203-4.

JAY ARNOLD LEVINE. "The Status of the Verse Epistle Before Pope," *Studies in Philology* 59(4), October 1962, 682-84.

EARL MINER. "Dryden's *Eikon Basilike: To Sir Godfrey Kneller*," in *Seventeenth-Century Imagery*, pp. 151-67.

EARL MINER. *The Restoration Mode from Milton to Dryden*, pp. 532-35.

"To the Memory of Mr. Oldham"

WILLIAM B. BACHE. "Dryden and Oldham: Hail and Farewell," *CLA Journal* 12(3), March 1969, 237-43.

WALLACE CABLE BROWN. "The 'Heresy' of the Didactic," *University of Kansas City Review* 11(3), Spring 1945, 182-84. Reprinted in: *The Dimensions of Poetry*, pp. 289-90.

JOHN R. CLARK. "'To the Memory of Mr. Oldham': Dryden's Disquieting Lines," *Concerning Poetry* 3(1), Spring 1970, 43-49.

EARL DANIELS. *The Art of Reading Poetry*, pp. 377-79.

DUSTIN GRIFFIN. "Dryden's 'Oldham' and the Perils of Writing," *Modern Language Quarterly* 37(2), June 1976, 133-50.

R. G. PETERSON. "The Unavailing Gift: Dryden's Roman Farewell to Mr. Oldham," *Modern Philology* 66(3), February 1969, 232-36.

MARK VAN DOREN. *Introduction to Poetry*, pp. 93-98.

"To the Pious Memory of the Accomplished Young Lady, Mrs. Anne Killigrew"

see "Ode: To the Pious Memory of the Accomplished Young Lady, Mrs. Anne Killigrew"

"To William Congreve"

EARL MINER. *The Restoration Mode from Milton to Dryden*, pp. 535-39.

"Upon the Death of the Lord Hastings"

JOSEPHINE MILES. *The Primary Language of Poetry in the 1640's*, pp. 92-94.

ROSEMOND TUVE. *Elizabethan and Metaphysical Imagery*, pp. 318-19. (P)

"Whil'st Alexis lay prest" (*Marriage a la Mode*)

DAVID FARLEY-HILLS. *The Benevolence of Laughter*, p. 110.

"Zambra Dance" (*The Conquest of Granada*)

BETTY GAY COSHOW. *Explicator* 16(3), December 1957, Item 16.

BRUCE KING. *Explicator* 18(3), December 1959, Item 18.

DU BOIS, W. E. B.

"Children of the Moon"

WILSON J. MOSES. "The Poetics of Ethiopianism: W. E. B. Du Bois and Literary Black Nationalism," *American Literature* 47(3), November 1975, 418-20.

"The Riddle of the Sphinx"

WILSON J. MOSES. "The Poetics of Ethiopianism: W. E. B. Du Bois and Literary Black Nationalism," *American Literature* 47(3), November 1975, 415.

DUCK, STEPHEN

"Avaro and Amanda"

ALAN WARNER. "Stephen Duck, the Thresher Poet," *Review of English Literature* 8(2), April 1967, 44-45.

DUFAULT, PETER KANE

"General Salute"

> JOHN CLARK PRATT. *The Meaning of Modern Poetry*, pp. 88-89, 94, 90-91, 98-99, 110.

DUGAN, ALAN

"Adultery"

> ROBERT BOYERS. "Alan Dugan: The Poetry of Survival," in *Contemporary Poetry in America*, pp. 341-43.
>
> ROBERT BOYERS. *Excursions*, pp. 195-97.

"Not to Choose"

> ROBERT BOYERS. "Alan Dugan: The Poetry of Survival," in *Contemporary Poetry in America*, p. 343.

"Tribute to Kafka for Someone Taken"

> ROBERT BOYERS. "Alan Dugan: The Poetry of Survival," in *Contemporary Poetry in America*, p. 345.
>
> ROBERT BOYERS. *Excursions*, pp. 198-99.

DUKE, RICHARD

"A Panegyric upon Oates"

> P. J. C. FIELD. "Authoritative Echo in Dryden," *Durham University Journal*, n.s., 31(3), June 1970, 138-39.

DUNBAR, PAUL LAWRENCE

"The Haunted Oak"

> CLEANTH BROOKS and ROBERT PENN WARREN. *Understanding Poetry*, fourth ed., pp. 64-66.

"We Wear the Mask"

> TODD M. LIEBER. "Ralph Ellison and the Metaphor of Invisibility in Black Literary Tradition," *American Quarterly* 24(1), March 1972, 92-94.

DUNBAR, WILLIAM

"Ane Blak Moir"

> JACK BARNWELL. "A Footnote to *White Over Black*," *Southern Quarterly* 15(2), January 1977, 195-97.

"Ane Ballat of the Fenʒeit Freir of Tungland How he fell in the Myre fleand to Turkiland"

> BRYAN S. HAY. "William Dunbar's Flying Abbot: Apocalypse Made to Order," *Studies in Scottish Literature* 11(4), April 1974, 221-25.

"The Antichrist"

> BRYAN S. HAY. "William Dunbar's Flying Abbot: Apocalypse Made to Order," *Studies in Scottish Literature* 11(4), April 1974, 218-21.

"The Fenyeit Freir of Tungland"

> see "Ane Ballet of the Fenʒeit Freir of Tungland How he fell in the Myre fleand to Turkiland"

"The Flyting of Dunbar and Kennedie"

> JOHN LEYERLE. "The Two Voices of William Dunbar," *University of Toronto Quarterly* 31(3), April 1962, 334-37.

"The Golden Targe"

> LOIS A. EBIN. "The Theme of Poetry in Dunbar's 'Golden Targe,'" *Chaucer Review* 7(2), Fall 1972, 147-59.
>
> R. J. LYALL. "Moral Allegory in Dunbar's 'Goldyn Targe,'" *Studies in Scottish Literature* 11(1&2), July-October 1973, 47-65.
>
> WALTER SCHEPS. "*The Golden Targe*: Dunbar's Comic Psychomachia," *Papers on Language and Literature* 11(4), Fall 1975, 339-56.

FRANK SHUFFELTON. "An Imperial Flower: Dunbar's *The Golden Targe* and the Court Life of James IV of Scotland," *Studies in Philology* 72(2), April 1975, 193-207.

> A. C. SPEARING. *Medieval Dream-Poetry*, pp. 196-97.
>
> E. ALLEN TILLEY. "The Meaning of Dunbar's 'The Golden Targe,'" *Studies in Scottish Literature* 10(4), April 1973, 220-31.

"In Secreit Place"

> PRISCILLA BAWCUTT. "Aspects of Dunbars Imagery," in *Chaucer and Middle English Studies in Honor of Rossell Hope Robbins*, pp. 195-96.

"Lament for the Makaris"

> R. D. DREXLER. "Dunbar's 'Lament for the Makaris' and the Dance of Death Tradition," *Studies in Scottish Literature* 13(1978), 144-58.
>
> DOUGLAS L. PETERSON. *The English Lyric from Wyatt to Donne*, pp. 21-23.

"The Magryme"

> ARTHUR K. MOORE. *The Secular Lyric in Middle English*, pp. 205-7.

"Meditatioun in Wynter"

> A. M. KINGHORN. "Dunbar and Villon — A Comparison and a Contrast," *Modern Language Rivew* 62(2), April 1967, 204.
>
> ARTHUR K. MOORE. *The Secular Lyric in Middle English*, pp. 207-8.
>
> JOHN SPEIRS. "William Dunbar," *Scrutiny* 7(1), June 1938, 67-68.

"My heid did ʒak ʒester nicht"

> see "The Magryme"

"Petition of the Gray Horse"

> ARTHUR K. MOORE. *The Secular Lyric in Middle English*, pp. 209-13.

"Qulone Mony Benefices Vakit"

> PRISCILLA BAWCUTT. "Aspects of Dunbar's Imagery," in *Chaucer and Middle English Studies in Honor of Rossell Hope Robbins*, p. 193.

"The Thrissil and the Rois"

> A. C. SPEARING. *Medieval Dream-Poetry*, pp. 192-96.

"To a Lady"

> WALTER GIERASCH. *Explicator* 6(3), December 1947, Item 21.
>
> ARTHUR K. MOORE. *The Secular Lyric in Middle English*, pp. 201-3.

"The Tretis of the Tua Mariit Wemen and the Wedo"

> PRISCILLA BAWCUTT. "Aspects of Dunbar's Imagery," in *Chaucer and Middle English Studies in Honor of Rossell Hope Robbins*, pp. 196-99.
>
> LOIS A. EBIN. "The Theme of Poetry in Dunbar's 'Golden Targe,'" *Chaucer Review* 7(2), Fall 1972, 157-58.
>
> JOHN LEYERLE. "The Two Voices of William Dunbar," *University of Toronto Quarterly* 31(3), April 1962, 331-34.
>
> JOHN SPEIRS. "William Dunbar," *Scrutiny* 7(1), June 1938, 59-61.

DUNCAN, ROBERT

"Bending the Bow"

> A. K. WEATHERHEAD. "Robert Duncan and the Lyric," *Contemporary Literature* 16(2), Spring 1975, 166-67.

"Doves"

 L. S. Dembo. *Conceptions of Reality in Modern American Poetry*, pp. 215-16.

"Fire"

 Robert C. Weber. "Robert Duncan and the Poem of Resonance," *Concerning Poetry* 11(1), Spring 1978, 67-73.

"Lammas Dream Poem"

 Samuel Charters. *Some Poems/Poets*, pp. 47-55.

"Strains of Sight"

 M. L. Rosenthal. "Dynamics of Form and Motive in Some Representative Twentieth-Century Lyric Poems," *ELH* 37(1), 141-44.

DURRELL, LAWRENCE

"Alexandria"

 Joan Goulianos. "Lawrence Durrell and Alexandria," *Virginia Quarterly Review* 45(4), Autumn 1969, 669-70.

"At Epidaurus"

 Kimon Friar and John Malcolm Brinnin. *Modern Poetry*, pp. 457-58.

"Conon in Alexandria"

 Joan Goulianos. "Lawrence Durrell and Alexandria," *Virginia Quarterly Review* 45(4), Autumn 1969, 670-71.

"Delos"

 George Fraser. *Essays on Twentieth-Century Poets*, pp. 177-79.

"Je Est Un Autre"

 George Fraser. *Essays on Twentieth-Century Poets*, pp. 179-80.

"Levant"

 Joan Goulianos. "Lawrence Durrell and Alexandria," *Virginia Quarterly Review* 45(4), Autumn 1969, 666.

"On Seeming to Presume"

 George Fraser. *Essays on Twentieth-Century Poets*, p. 180.

"Song for Zarathustra"

 Norman Silverstein and Arthur L. Lewis. *Explicator* 21(2), October 1962, Item 10.

"Style"

 George Fraser. *Essays on Twentieth-Century Poets*, pp. 176-77.

"To Argos"

 Kimon Friar and John Malcolm Brinnin. *Modern Poetry*, pp. 457-58.

DWIGHT, TIMOTHY

"An Extract from 'The Retrospect' "

 Robert Edson Lee. "Timothy Dwight and the Boston *Palladium*," *New England Quarterly* 35(2), June 1962, 230.

"Greenfield Hill"

 John Griffith. "*The Columbiad* and *Greenfield Hill*: History, Poetry, and Ideology in the Late Eighteenth Century," *Early American Literature* 10(3), Winter 1975/76, 243-49.

DYER, EDWARD

"A Modest Love"

 Dorothy Pettit. "To Deepen Delight Through Study," *English Journal* 53(1), January 1964, 57-58.

DYLAN, BOB

"Love Minus Zero/No Limit"

 Leland A. Poague. "Dylan as *Auteur*: Theoretical Notes, and an Analysis of 'Love Minus Zero/No Limit,' " *Journal of Popular Culture* 8(1), Summer 1974, 53-58.

DYMENT, CLIFFORD

"Saint Augustine at Thirty-Two"

 Robin Skelton. *The Poetic Pattern*, pp. 80-84.

E

EBERHART, RICHARD

"Aesthetics after War"

HARRY J. CARGAS. *Daniel Berrigan and Contemporary Protest Poetry*, pp. 27-28.

"Am I My Neighbor's Keeper?"

LOUISE BOGAN, PHILIP BOOTH, WILLIAM STAFFORD and RICHARD EBERHART. "On Richard Eberhart's 'Am I My Neighbor's Keeper?'" in *The Contemporary Poet as Artist and Critic*, pp. 142-66.

"Autumnal"

RALPH J. MILLS, JR. "Richard Eberhart," in *Seven American Poets from MacLeish to Nemerov*, pp. 88-89.

"The Brotherhood of Men"

RALPH J. MILLS, JR. *Contemporary American Poetry*, p. 28.

"The Critic"

RICHARD EBERHART. "Will and Psyche in Poetry," in *The Moment of Poetry*, pp. 51-54.

"Dam Neck, Virginia"

HARRY BROWN and JOHN MILSTEAD. *What the Poem Means*, p. 68.

RICHARD J. FEIN. "The Cultivation of Paradox: The War Poetry of Richard Eberhart," *Ball State University Forum* 10(2), Spring 1969, 56-60.

"Drinking Song"

VERNON SCANNELL. *Not Without Glory*, pp. 225-26.

"Experience Evoked"

SEAMUS COONEY. *Explicator* 32(5), January 1974, Item 39.

RICHARD EBERHART. *Explicator* 32(9), May 1974, Item 76.

"A Fable of the War"

VERNON SCANNELL. *Not Without Glory*, pp. 226-27.

"For a Lamb"

RALPH J. MILLS, JR. "Richard Eberhart," in *Seven American Poets from MacLeish to Nemerov*, p. 71.

"Fragment of New York, 1929"

RALPH J. MILLS, JR. "Richard Eberhart," in *Seven American Poets from MacLeish to Nemerov*, pp. 82-83.

"The Fury of Aerial Bombardment"

JO ALLEN BRADHAM. *Explicator* 22(9), May 1964, Item 71.

JOHN CIARDI. *How Does a Poem Mean?* p. 999; second ed., p. 364. Reprinted in: Harry J. Cargas. *Daniel Berrigan and Contemporary Protest Poetry*, p. 20.

RICHARD J. FEIN. "The Cultivation of Paradox: The War Poetry of Richard Eberhart," *Ball State University Forum* 10(2), Spring 1969, 62-64.

DAN JAFFE. "Poets in the Inferno: Civilians, C.O.'s and Combatants," in *The Forties*, pp. 38-39.

FRED B. MILLETT, ARTHUR W. HOFFMAN, and DAVID R. CLARK. *Reading Poetry*, second ed., pp. 85-87.

RALPH J. MILLS, JR. "Richard Eberhart," in *Seven American Poets from MacLeish to Nemerov*, pp. 80-81.

"The Goal of Intellectual Man"

RALPH J. MILLS, JR. "Richard Eberhart," in *Seven American Poets from MacLeish to Nemerov*, pp. 69-70.

"Grave Piece"

RICHARD EBERHART. *Explicator* 6(4), February 1948, Item 23. Reprinted in: *Reading Modern Poetry*, pp. 273-74; revised ed., pp. 264-65.

RALPH J. MILLS, JR. "Richard Eberhart," in *Seven American Poets from MacLeish to Nemerov*, p. 76.

"The Groundhog"

GÉMINO H. ABAD. *A Formal Approach to Lyric Poetry*, pp. 54-59.

GÉMINO H. ABAD. *In Another Light*, pp. 219-48.

AEROL ARNOLD. *Explicator* 15(1), October 1956, Item 3.

HARRY J. CARGAS. *Daniel Berrigan and Contemporary Protest Poetry*, pp. 23-25.

ALICE C. COLEMAN. "Amid the Golden Fields," *English Journal* 52(4), April 1963, 300-2.

BABETTE DEUTSCH. *Poetry in Our Time*, pp. 216-17; second ed., pp. 236-37.

BREWSTER GHISELIN. "Eberhart: The Groundhog," in *Master Poems of the English Language*, pp. 1010-12.

LOIS GORDON. "Richard Eberhart: Romantic Poet and Love Child," in *The Fifties*, pp. 191-92.

SYDNEY MENDEL. *Explicator* 17(9), June 1959, Item 64.

RALPH J. MILLS, JR. "Richard Eberhart," in *Seven American Poets from MacLeish to Nemerov*, pp. 71-75.

JAMES M. REID. *100 American Poems of the Twentieth Century*, pp. 192-94.

M. L. ROSENTHAL. *The Modern Poets*, pp. 246-47.

M. L. ROSENTHAL. "Three Poets in Focus," *New Republic* 125(24), 10 December 1951, 27.

PETER L. THORSLEV, JR. "The Poetry of Richard Eberhart," in *Poets in Progress,* pp. 85-86.

"The Horse Chestnut Tree"

JAMES M. REID. *100 American Poems of the Twentieth Century,* pp. 194-96.

"I Walked Out to the Graveyard to See the Dead"

KIMON FRIAR and JOHN MALCOLM BRINNIN. *Modern Poetry,* pp. 458-59. (Quoting Richard Eberhart)

DANIEL HOFFMAN. "Hunting a Master Image: The Poetry of Richard Eberhart," *Hollins Critic* 1(4), October 1964, 3-4.

"If I could only live at the Pitch that is near Madness"

BABETTE DEUTSCH. *Poetry in Our Time,* p. 217; second ed., p. 237.

RALPH J. MILLS, JR. "Richard Eberhart," in *Seven American Poets from MacLeish to Nemerov,* pp. 64-66.

"Imagining How it would be to be Dead"

RALPH J. MILLS, JR. "Richard Eberhart," in *Seven American Poets from MacLeish to Nemerov,* pp. 76-77.

"Life as Visionary Spirit"

RALPH J. MILLS, JR. "Richard Eberhart," in *Seven American Poets from MacLeish to Nemerov,* pp. 87-88.

"Light from Above"

RALPH J. MILLS, JR. "Richard Eberhart," in *Seven American Poets from MacLeish to Nemerov,* pp. 89-90.

"Maze"

RALPH J. MILLS, JR. "Richard Eberhart," in *Seven American Poets from MacLeish to Nemerov,* pp. 63-64.

"A Meditation"

RALPH J. MILLS, JR. "Richard Eberhart," in *Seven American Poets from MacLeish to Nemerov,* pp. 77-79.

J. L. SWEENEY. "Two letters from J. L. Sweeney to Richard Eberhart anent the *Meditation,*" *Furioso* 1(3), Spring 1940, 42-43.

"New Hampshire, February"

RALPH J. MILLS, JR. *Contemporary American Poetry,* pp. 13-15.

"On a Squirrel Crossing the Road in Autumn, in New England"

JAMES M. REID. *100 American Poems of the Twentieth Century,* pp. 196-98.

"On Shooting Particles beyond the World"

HARRY J. CARGAS. *Daniel Berrigan and Contemporary Protest Poetry,* pp. 20-21.

"Orchard"

RALPH J. MILLS, JR. *Contemporary American Poetry,* pp. 19-20.

"The Preacher Sought to Find Out Acceptable Words"

RICHARD J. FEIN. "The Cultivation of Paradox: The War Poetry of Richard Eberhart," *Ball State University Forum* 10(2), Spring 1969, 60-62.

"Request for Offering"

RALPH J. MILLS, JR. "Richard Eberhart," in *Seven American Poets from MacLeish to Nemerov,* p. 64.

"Seals, Terns, Time"

RICHARD EBERHART. *Explicator* 30(4), December 1971, Item 29.

ALVIN SULLIVAN. *Explicator* 30(1), September 1971, Item 8.

ALVIN SULLIVAN. *Explicator* 30(4), December 1971, Item 29.

"Sestina"

PAUL CUMMINS. "The Sestina in the 20th Century," *Concerning Poetry* 11(1), Spring 1978, 20.

"The Skier and the Mountain"

RALPH J. MILLS, JR. "Richard Eberhart," in *Seven American Poets from MacLeish to Nemerov,* pp. 67-79.

"The Soul Longs to Return whence it Came"

DANIEL HOFFMAN. "Hunting a Master Image: The Poetry of Richard Eberhart," *Hollins Critic* 1(4), October 1964, 4.

"This fevers me, this sun on green"

RALPH J. MILLS, JR. *Contemporary American Poetry,* p. 17.

"Throwing the Apple"

RICHARD F. BAUERLE. *Explicator* 27(3), November 1968, Item 21.

"Ur Burial"

RICHARD F. BAUERLE. *Explicator* 16(7), April 1958, Item 38.

"The Young Hunter"

RICHARD EBERHART. *Explicator* 6(4), February 1948, Item 24.

EBERMAN, WILLIS

"After Illness"

GEORGE ABBE. *You and Contemporary Poetry,* pp. 12-13; 1965 ed., pp. 13-14.

EDSON, RUSSELL

"One Wonders"

ALBERTA T. TURNER. "Implied Metaphor: A Problem in Evaluating Contemporary Poetry," *Iowa Review* 5(1), Winter 1974, 116-17.

EIGNER, LARRY

"It Sounded"

SAMUEL CHARTERS. *Some Poems/Poets,* pp. 115-16.

"the knowledge of death and now"

SAMUEL CHARTERS. *Some Poems/Poets,* pp. 114-15.

EISELEY, LOREN

"Arrowhead"

E. FRED CARLISLE. "The Poetic Achievement of Loren Eiseley," *Prairie Schooner* 51(2), Summer 1977, 126-27.

"The Old Ones"

E. FRED CARLISLE. "The Poetic Achievement of Loren Eiseley," *Prairie Schooner* 51(2), Summer 1977, 123.

"Timberline"

E. FRED CARLISLE. "The Poetic Achievement of Loren Eiseley," *Prairie Schooner* 51(2), Summer 1977, 122. (P)

EISELEY, LOREN *(Cont.)*

"White Night"

> E. Fred Carlisle. "The Poetic Achievement of Loren Eiseley," *Prairie Schooner* 51(2), Summer 1977, 124-26.

ELIOT, GEORGE

"I Grant You Ample Leave"

> Bernard J. Paris. "George Eliot's Unpublished Poetry," *Studies in Philology* 56(3), July 1959, 551-54.

"In a London Drawing Room"

> Bernard J. Paris. "George Eliot's Unpublished Poetry," *Studies in Philology* 56(3), July 1959, 549-51.

ELIOT, T. S.

"The Ad-dressing of Cats"

> Felix Clowder. "The Bestiary of T. S. Eliot," *Prairie Schooner* 34(1), Spring 1960, 35-36.

"Animula"

> Melvin W. Askew. "Form and Process in Lyric Poetry," *Sewanee Review* 72(2), Spring 1964, 294-95.
>
> Harry Brown and John Milstead. *What the Poem Means*, p. 71.
>
> Karen T. Romer. "T. S. Eliot and the Language of Liturgy," *Renascence* 24(3), Spring 1972, 129-30.
>
> Grover Smith. "Visions and Revisions: the 'Ariel Poems,' " in *Modern Poetry*, pp. 307-10.
>
> T. A. Stroud. *Explicator* 28(2), October 1969, Item 14.

"Ash Wednesday"

> Charles Altieri. "Steps of the Mind in T. S. Eliot's Poetry," *Bucknell Review* 22(2), Fall 1976, 199-205.
>
> James Benziger. *Images of Eternity*, pp. 244-45.
>
> R. P. Blackmur. *The Double Agent*, pp. 190-96. Reprinted in: R. P. Blackmur. *Language as Gesture*, pp. 168-71.
>
> Gwenn R. Boardman. "*Ash Wednesday*: Eliot's Lenten Mass Sequence," *Renascence* 15(1), Fall 1962, 28-36.
>
> Harry Brown and John Milstead. *What the Poem Means*, pp. 71-72.
>
> Vincent Buckley. *Poetry and the Sacred*, pp. 213-19.
>
> Sister M. Cleophas. "*Ash Wednesday*: The *Purgatorio* in a Modern Mode," *Comparative Literature* 11(4), Fall 1959, 329-39.
>
> Clifford Davidson. "Types of Despair In 'Ash Wednesday,' " *Renascence* 18(4), Summer 1966, 216-18.
>
> Paul J. Dolan. "*Ash Wednesday*: A Catechumenical Poem," *Renascence* 19(4), Summer 1967, 198-207.
>
> F. Peter Dzwonkoski, Jr. " 'The Hollow Men' and *Ash-Wednesday*: Two Dark Nights," *Arizona Quarterly* 30(1), Spring 1974, 23-42.
>
> Genevieve W. Foster. "The Archetypal Imagery of T. S. Eliot," *PMLA* 60(2), June 1945, 580-82.
>
> Warren French. "The Age of Eliot: The Twenties as Waste Land," in *The Twenties*, edited by Warren French, pp. 17-18.
>
> Kimon Friar and John Malcolm Brinnin. *Modern Poetry*, pp. 465-72.
>
> Nancy D. Hargrove. "Landscape as Symbol in T. S. Eliot's *Ash-Wednesday*," *Arizona Quarterly* 30(1), Spring 1974, 53-62.
>
> Hugh Kenner. "Eliot's Moral Dialectic," *Hudson Review* 2(3), Autumn 1949, 439-46.

F. R. Leavis. *New Bearings in English Poetry*, pp. 117-29.

J. Hillis Miller. *Poets of Reality*, pp. 182-84.

Theodore Morrison. "*Ash Wednesday*: A Religious History," *New England Quarterly* 11(2), June 1938, 266-86.

Roy Harvey Pearce. *The Continuity of American Poetry*, pp. 309-12.

Karen T. Romer. "T. S. Eliot and the Language of Liturgy," *Renascence* 24(3), Spring 1972, 132-35.

M. L. Rosenthal. *Sailing into the Unknown*, pp. 189-91.

Elisabeth Schneider. "Prufrock and After: The Theme of Change," *PMLA* 87(5), October 1972, 1109-13.

Margaret Patrice Slattery. "Structural Unity in Eliot's 'Ash Wednesday,' " *Renascence* 20(3), Spring 1968, 147-52.

Gordon Symes. "T. S. Eliot and Old Age," *Fortnightly* 169(3), March 1951, 191-92.

Allen Tate. *Reactionary Essays on Poetry and Ideas*, pp. 210-20. Reprinted in: Allen Tate. *On the Limits of Poetry*, pp. 344-49. Also: Allen Tate. *Essays of Four Decades*, pp. 462-70.

Raymond Tschumi. *Thought in Twentieth-Century English Poetry*, pp. 144-46.

Leonard Unger. *The Man in the Name*, pp. 141-67.

Leonard Unger. "Notes on *Ash Wednesday*," *Southern Review* 4(4), Spring 1939, 745-70.

Leonard Unger. "T. S. Eliot's Rose Garden: A Persistent Theme," *Southern Review* 7(4), Spring 1942, 675-76.

A. S. P. Woodhouse. *The Poet and His Faith*, pp. 266-70.

Carl Wooton. "The Mass: 'Ash-Wednesday's' Objective Correlative," *Arizona Quarterly* 17(1), Spring 1961, 31-42.

"Aunt Helen"

> Gémino H. Abad. *In Another Light*, pp. 156-58. Reprinted in: Gémino H. Abad. *A Formal Approach to Lyric Poetry*, pp. 159-60.

"The *Boston Evening Transcript*"

> T. R. Barnes. *English Verse*, pp. 280-82.
>
> Wallace Cable Brown. " 'A Poem Should Not Mean But Be,' " *University of Kansas City Review* 15(1), Autumn 1948, 61-62.
>
> Chad Walsh. *Doors into Poetry*, p. 27.

"Burbank with a Baedeker; Bleistein with a Cigar"

> Robert Alter. "Eliot, Lawrence & the Jews," *Commentary* 50(4), October 1970, 83-86.
>
> John R. Harrison. *The Reactionaries*, pp. 150-52.
>
> L. G. Locke. *Explicator* 3(7), May 1945, Item 53.
>
> Laura Riding and Robert Graves. *A Survey of Modernist Poetry*, pp. 235-42.
>
> Jane Worthington. "The Epigraphs to the Poetry of T. S. Eliot," *American Literature* 21(1), March 1949, 6-7.

"Burnt Norton"

see also "Four Quartets"

> David Daiches and William Charvat. *Poems in English*, pp. 741-42.
>
> Elizabeth Drew. *T. S. Eliot: The Design of His Poetry*, pp. 151-62. Reprinted in: *Readings for Liberal Education*, revised ed., II: 225-32; third ed., II: 216-22; fourth ed., II: 218-24; fifth ed., II: 200-7.

ELIZABETH DREW and JOHN L. SWEENEY. *Directions in Modern Poetry*, pp. 138-40.

BARBARA EVERETT. "A Visit to Burnt Norton," *Critical Quarterly* 16(3), Autumn 1974, 199-224.

KIMON FRIAR and JOHN MALCOLM BRINNIN. *Modern Poetry*, pp. 461-65.

D. W. HARDING. *Experience Into Words*, pp. 107-9.

F. R. LEAVIS. *Education and the University*, pp. 94-98.

F. R. LEAVIS. "Eliot's Later Poetry," *Scrutiny* 11(1), Summer 1942, 65-67.

H. Z. MACCOBY. "A Commentary on 'Burnt Norton,'" *Notes & Queries*, n.s., 15(2), February 1968, 50-57; 17(2), February 1970, 53-59; 17(12), December 1970, 458-64.

M. L. ROSENTHAL. *Sailing into the Unknown*, pp. 169-203.

RAYMOND TSCHUMI. *Thought in Twentieth-Century English Poetry*, pp. 149-54.

LEONARD UNGER. *The Man in the Name*, pp. 177-81.

LEONARD UNGER. "T. S. Eliot's Rose Garden: A Persistent Theme," *Southern Review* 7(4), Spring 1942, 677-81.

PHILIP WHEELWRIGHT. *The Burning Fountain*, pp. 333-36.

PHILIP WHEELWRIGHT. "The Burnt Norton Trilogy," *Chimera* 1(2), Autumn 1942, 7-12.

JANE WORTHINGTON. "The Epigraphs to the Poetry of T. S. Eliot," *American Literature* 21(1), March 1949, 16-17.

"Burnt Norton II"

LINDA BRADLEY SALAMON. "The Orchestration of 'Burnt Norton, II,'" *University of Toronto Quarterly* 45(1), Fall 1975, 50-66.

"A Cooking Egg"

DONALD DAVIE. "Pound and Eliot: A Distinction," in *The Poet in the Imaginary Museum*, pp. 201-4.

ELIZABETH DREW. *Discovering Poetry*, pp. 113-14.

JAMES F. LOUCKS. "T. S. Eliot's 'A Cooking Egg': An Echo from Thomas Hood," *Notes & Queries*, n.s., 23(7), July 1976, 299-300.

I. A. RICHARDS. *Principles of Literary Criticism*, pp. 293-94.

GROVER SMITH, JR. "Getting Used to T. S. Eliot," *English Journal* 49(1), January 1960, 8-9.

E. M. W. TILLYARD, ET. AL. "'A Cooking Egg,'" *Essays in Criticism* 3(3), July 1953, 345-57.

JANE WORTHINGTON. "The Epigraphs to the Poetry of T. S. Eliot," *American Literature* 21(1), March 1949, 9-10.

"Coriolan"

see also "Difficulties of a Statesman" and "Triumphal March"

THOMAS R. EDWARDS. *Imagination and Power*, pp. 197-203.

LILLIAN FEDER. *Ancient Myth in Modern Poetry*, pp. 312-15.

GILBERT HIGHET. *The Powers of Poetry*, pp. 293-300.

DONALD F. THEALL. "Traditional Satire in Eliot's 'Coriolan,'" *Accent* 11(4), Autumn 1951, 194-206.

"Dans le Restaurant"

WILLIAM ARROWSMITH. "Daedal Harmonies: A Dialogue on Eliot and the Classics," *Southern Review*, n.s., 13(1), Winter 1977, 1-47.

LLOYD FRANKENBERG. *Pleasure Dome*, pp. 72-76.

LEONARD UNGER. *The Man in the Name*, pp. 169-71.

GEORGE WHITESIDE. "T. S. Eliot's *Dans le Restaurant*," *American Imago* 33(2), Summer 1976, 155-73.

"The Death of Saint Narcissus"

LILLIAN FEDER. "Narcissus as Saint and Dancer," *T. S. Eliot Review* 3(1-2), 1976, 13-19.

"Dificulties of a Statesman"

see also "Coriolan"

F. R. LEAVIS. *Education and the University*, p. 94.

"The Dry Salvages"

see also "Four Quartets"

JOHN D. BOYD. "*The Dry Salvages*: Topography as Symbol," *Renascence* 20(3), Spring 1968, 119-33, 161.

LOIS A. CUDDY. "Eliot and *Huck Finn*: River and Sea in 'The Dry Salvages,'" *T. S. Eliot Review* 3(1-2), 1976, 3-12.

F. R. LEAVIS. *Education and the University*, pp. 99-103.

F. R. LEAVIS. "Eliot's Later Poetry," *Scrutiny* 11(1), Summer 1942, 68-71.

AUDREY T. RODGERS. "The Mythic Perspective of Eliot's 'The Dry Salvages,'" *Arizona Quarterly* 30(1), Spring 1974, 74-94.

LEONARD UNGER. *The Man in the Name*, pp. 186-88.

LEONARD UNGER. "T. S. Eliot's Rose Garden: A Persistent Theme," *Southern Review* 7(4), Spring 1942, 687-88.

HYATT HOWE WAGGONER. *The Heel of Elohim*, pp. 90-99.

PHILIP WHEELWRIGHT. "The Burnt Norton Trilogy," *Chimera* 1(2), Autumn 1942, 13-18.

"East Coker"

see also "Four Quartets"

CURTIS BRADSFORD. "Footnotes to East Coker: A Reading," *Sewanee Review* 52(2), Spring 1944, 169-75.

D. BOSLEY BROTMAN. "T. S. Eliot: 'The Music of Ideas,'" *The University of Toronto Quarterly* 18(1), October 1948, 20-29.

H. W. HÄUSERMANN. "'East Coker' and 'The Family Reunion,'" *Life and Letters* 47(1), October 1945, 32-38.

JACK KLIGERMAN. "An Interpretation of T. S. Eliot's 'East Coker,'" *Arizona Quarterly* 18(2), Summer 1962, 101-12.

JAMES JOHNSON SWEENEY. "East Coker: A Reading," *Southern Review* 6(4), Spring 1941, 771-91.

LEONARD UNGER. *The Man in the Name*, pp. 185-86.

LEONARD UNGER. "T. S. Eliot's Rose Garden: A Persistent Theme," *Southern Review* 7(4), Spring 1942, 686-87.

"La Figlia che Piange"

RON D. K. BANERJEE. "Dante Through the Looking Glass: Rossetti, Pound and Eliot," *Comparative Literature* 24(2), Spring 1972, 144-49.

L. S. DEMBO. *Conceptions of Reality in Modern American Poetry*, pp. 191-92.

VERNON HALL, JR. *Explicator* 5(2), November 1946, Item 16.

MARTIN SCOFIELD. "'A gesture and a pose': T. S. Eliot's images of love," *Critical Quarterly* 18(3), Autumn 1976, 11-14.

JOHN B. VICKERY. "Eliot's Poetry: The Quest and the Way (Part 1)," *Renascence* 10(1), Autumn 1957, 5.

HYATT H. WAGGONER. *American Poets*, p. 420.

ELIOT, T. S. (*Cont.*)

"Four Quartets"

see also "Burnt Norton," "The Dry Salvages," "East Coker," and "Little Gidding"

R. P. BLACKMUR. *Form and Value in Modern Poetry,* pp. 153-82.

R. P. BLACKMUR. *Language as Gesture,* pp. 192-220.

R. P. BLACKMUR. "Unappeasable and Peregrine: Behavior and the Four Quartets," *Thought* 26(100), Spring 1951, 50-76.

WILLIAM BLISSETT. "The Argument of T. S. Eliot's *Four Quartets,*" *University of Toronto Quarterly* 15(2), January 1946, 115-26.

JOHN M. BRADBURY. "*Four Quartets*: The Structural Symbolism," *Sewanee Review* 59(2), Spring 1951, 254-70.

CURTIS B. BRADSFORD. "Journeys to Byzantium," *Virginia Quarterly Review* 25(2), Spring 1949, 216-24.

R. L. BRETT. *Reason and Imagination,* pp. 120-35.

HARRY BROWN and JOHN MILSTEAD. *What the Poem Means,* pp. 72-76.

VINCENT BUCKLEY. *Poetry and the Sacred,* pp. 219-37.

P. H. BUTTER. "*Four Quartets*: some yes-buts to Dr Leavis," *Critical Quarterly* 18(1), Spring 1976, 31-40.

RIVERS CAREW. "George Rouault and T. S. Eliot: A Note," *Hibbert Journal* 60(3), April 1962, 234-35.

MERREL D. CLUBB, JR. "The Heraclitean Element in Eliot's *Four Quartets,*" *Philological Quarterly* 40(1), January 1961, 19-33.

DONALD DAVIE. "Pound and Eliot: A Distinction," in *The Poet in the Imaginary Museum,* pp. 192-99.

DONALD DAVIS. "T. S. Eliot: The End of an Era," *Twentieth Century* 159(950), April 1956, 350-62.

VIVIAN DE SOLA PINTO. *Crisis in English Poetry,* pp. 180-84; fifth ed., pp. 161-65.

L. S. DEMBO. *Conceptions of Reality in Modern American Poetry,* pp. 200-7.

BABETTE DEUTSCH. *Poetry in Our Time,* pp. 164-66, 170-72, 177-80; second ed., pp. 178-80, 184-86, 191-94.

DENIS DONOGHUE. *The Ordinary Universe,* pp. 242-66.

ARNOLD P. DREW. "Hints and Guesses in *Four Quartets,*" *University of Kansas City Review* 20(3), Spring 1954, 171-75.

BERNARD DUFFEY. *Poetry in America,* pp. 308-11.

LILLIAN FEDER. *Ancient Myth in Modern Poetry,* pp. 236-42, 315-16.

R. W. FLINT. "The *Four Quartets* Reconsidered," *Sewanee Review* 56(1), Winter 1948, 69-81.

KIMON FRIAR and JOHN MALCOLM BRINNIN. *Modern Poetry,* pp. 426-27, 459-61.

LLOYD FRANKENBERG. *Pleasure Dome,* pp. 98-117.

GEORGE FRASER. *Essays on Twentieth-Century Poets,* pp. 117-22.

HELEN L. GARDNER. "'Four Quartets': A Commentary," in *Critiques and Essays in Criticism,* pp. 181-97.

HELEN L. GARDNER. "The Landscapes of Eliot's Poetry," *Critical Quarterly* 10(4), Winter 1968, 320-30.

SISTER MARY GERARD. "Eliot of the Circle and John of the Cross," *Thought* 34(132), Spring 1959, 107-27.

CHRISTOPHER GILLIE. *Movements in English Literature,* pp. 160-63.

HARVEY GROSS. "T. S. Eliot," in *The Contrived Corridor,* pp. 58-73.

DAVID D. HIRSCH. "T. S. Eliot and the Vexation of Time," *Southern Review,* n.s., 3(3), Summer 1967, 620-24.

GRAHAM HOUGH. "Vision and Doctrine in *Four Quartets,*" *Critical Quarterly* 15(2), Summer 1973, 107-27.

G. WILSON KNIGHT. *Neglected Powers,* pp. 374-82.

G. WILSON KNIGHT. *Neglected Powers,* pp. 394-96.

GEORGE A. KNOX. "Quest for the Word in Eliot's *Four Quartets,*" *Journal of English Literary History* 18(4), December 1951, 310-21.

WILLIAM F. LYNCH. "The Theological Imagination," in *The New Orpheus,* pp. 122-30.

F. O. MATTHIESSEN. "Eliot's Quartets," *Kenyon Review* 5(2), Spring 1943, 161-78.

F. O. MATTHIESSEN. "T. S. Eliot: The Four Quartets," in *Literary Opinion in America,* third ed., pp. 282-95.

J. HILLIS MILLER. *Poets of Reality,* pp. 187-89.

JAMES E. MILLER, JR. *Quests Surd and Absurd,* pp. 119-24.

JAMES E. MILLER, JR. "Whitman and Eliot: The Poetry of Mysticism," *Southwest Review* 43(2), Spring 1958, 113.

THOMAS J. MORRISSEY. "'Intimate and Unidentifiable': The Voices of Fragmented Reality in the Poetry of T. S. Eliot," *Centennial Review* 22(1), Winter 1978, 18-27.

ROY HARVEY PEARCE. *The Continuity of American Poetry,* pp. 312-17.

M. GILBERT PORTER. "Narrative Stance in *Four Quartets*: Choreography and Commentary," *University Review* 36(1), Autumn 1969, 57-66.

SISTER M. BERNETTA QUINN. *The Metamorphic Tradition,* pp. 143-47.

THOMAS R. REES. "The Orchestration of Meaning in T. S. Eliot's *Four Quartets,*" *Journal of Aesthetics and Art Criticism* 28(1), Fall 1969, 63-69.

M. L. ROSENTHAL. *The Modern Poets,* pp. 88-89, 94-103.

MALCOLM ROSS. "The Writer as Christian,," in *The New Orpheus* pp. 91-92.

JAMES P. SEXTON. "*Four Quartets* and the Christian Calendar," *American Literature* 43(2), May 1971, 279-81.

T. B. SHEPHERD. "The *Four Quartets* Re-examined," *London Quarterly and Holborn Review* 175 (July 1950), 228-39.

WILLIAM V. SPANOS. "Hermeneutics and Memory: Destroying T. S. Eliot's *Four Quartets,*" *Genre* 11(4), Winter 1978, 523-73.

NARSINGH SRIVASTAVA. "The Ideas of The *Bhagavad Gita* in *Four Quartets,*" *Comparative Literature* 29(2), Spring 1977, 97-108.

LEONARD UNGER. "T. S. Eliot," in *Seven Modern American Poets,* pp. 213-16.

ROBERT D. WAGNER. "The Meaning of Eliot's Rose-Garden," *PMLA* 69(1), March 1954, 22-23.

HAROLD H. WATTS. *Hound and Quarry,* pp. 226-38.

A. KINGSLEY WEATHERHEAD. "*Four Quartets*: Setting Love in Order," *Wisconsin Studies in Contemporary Literature* 3(2), Spring-Summer 1962, 32-49.

MORRIS WEITZ. "T. S. Eliot: Time as a Mode of Salvation," *Sewanee Review* 60(1), Winter 1952, 48-64.

A. S. P. WOODHOUSE. *The Poet and His Faith,* pp. 270-83.

"Fragment of an Agon"

M. L. ROSENTHAL. *The Modern Poets,* pp. 75-76.

"Gerontion"

R. P. BLACKMUR. "T. S. Eliot," *Hound and Horn* 1(3), March 1928, 201-3.

ALEC BROWN. "The Lyric Impulse in the Poetry of T. S. Eliot," in *Scrutinies*, II: 7-12.

HARRY BROWN and JOHN MILSTEAD. *What the Poem Means*, pp. 76-77.

DAVID DAICHES. "Some Aspects of T. S. Eliot," *College English* 9(3), December 1947, 117-20.

DAVID DAICHES and WILLIAM CHARVAT. *Poems in English*, pp. 738-40.

L. S. DEMBO. *Conceptions of Reality in Modern American Poetry*, pp. 192-93.

WALLACE DOUGLAS, ROY LAMSON and HALLETT SMITH. *The Critical Reader*, pp. 125-30.

ELIZABETH DREW and JOHN L. SWEENEY. *Directions in Modern Poetry*, pp. 42-44.

F. DYE. *Explicator* 18(7), April 1960, Item 39.

WILLIAM R. ESHELMAN. *Explicator* 4(6), April 1946, Item 44.

LILLIAN FEDER. *Ancient Myth in Modern Poetry*, pp. 308-10.

LLOYD FRANKENBERG. *Pleasure Dome*, pp. 52-55.

KIMON FRIAR and JOHN MALCOLM BRINNIN. *Modern Poetry*, pp. 497-98.

CLARK GRIFFITH. *Explicator* 21(6), February 1963, Item 46.

HARVEY GROSS. "*Gerontion* and the Meaning of History," *PMLA* 73(3), June 1958, 299-304. Reprinted in: *The Dimensions of Poetry*, pp. 688-96.

HARVEY GROSS. "T. S. Eliot," in *The Contrived Corridor*, pp. 32-44.

JOHN HALVERSON. "Prufrock, Freud, and Others," *Sewanee Review* 76(4), Autumn 1968, 580-87.

F. R. LEAVIS. *New Bearings on English Poetry*, pp. 79-87.

ARTHUR MIZENER. "To Meet Mr. Eliot," *Sewanee Review* 65(1), Winter 1957, 42-44.

ROY HARVEY PEARCE. *The Continuity of American Poetry*, pp. 299-300.

JOHN CROWE RANSOM. "Gerontion," *Sewanee Review* 74(2), Spring 1966, 389-414.

M. L. ROSENTHAL. *The Modern Poets*, pp. 84-88.

M. L. ROSENTHAL and A. J. M. SMITH. *Exploring Poetry*, pp. 638-44; second ed., 460-64.

E. SAN JUAN, JR. "Form and Meaning in 'Gerontion,' " *Renascence* 22(3), Spring 1970, 115-26.

DANIEL R. SCHWARTZ. "The Unity of Eliot's 'Gerontion': The Failure of Meditation," *Bucknell Review* 19(1), Spring 1971, 55-76.

ZOREH TAWAKULI SULLIVAN. "Memory and Meditative Structure in T. S. Eliot's Early Poetry," *Renascence* 29(2), Winter 1977, 102-5.

LEONARD UNGER. *The Man in the Name*, pp. 172-73.

LEONARD UNGER. "T. S. Eliot's Rose Garden: A Persistent Theme," *Southern Review* 7(4), Spring 1942, 672-73.

CHAD WALSH. *Doors into Poetry*, pp. 100-4.

PHILIP WHEELWRIGHT. *The Burning Fountain*, pp. 336-38.

MERVYN W. WILLIAMSON. "T. S. Eliot's 'Gerontion': A Study in Thematic Repetition and Development," *Texas University Studies in English* 36 (1957), 111-26.

JANE WORTHINGTON. "The Epigraphs to the Poetry of T. S. Eliot," *American Literature* 21(1), March 1949, 5-6.

"Growltiger's Last Stand"

OWEN KERR. "Old Possum's Book of Practical Cats by T. S. Eliot," *English Journal* 65(1), January 1976, 66.

"The Hippopotamus"

GÉMINO H. ABAD. *A Formal Approach to Lyric Poetry*, pp. 306-7.

HERBERT MARSHALL MCLUHAN. *Explicator* 2(7), May 1944, Item 50.

ROBERT SPRICH. "Theme and Structure in Eliot's 'The Hippopotamus,' " *CEA Critic* 31(7), April 1969, 8.

FRANCIS LEE UTLEY. *Explicator* 3(2), November 1944, Item 10.

JANE WORTHINGTON. "The Epigraphs to the Poetry of T. S. Eliot," *American Literature* 21(1), March 1949, 10-11.

"The Hollow Men"

ALEC BROWN. "The Lyric Impulse in the Poetry of T. S. Eliot," in *Scrutinies*, II: 48-51.

HARRY BROWN and JOHN MILSTEAD. *What the Poem Means*, p. 79.

ELIZABETH DREW and JOHN L. SWEENEY. *Directions in Modern Poetry*, pp. 134-36.

F. PETER DZWONKOSKI, JR. " 'The Hollow Men' and *Ash-Wednesday*: Two Dark Nights," *Arizona Quarterly* 30(1), Spring 1974, 16-23.

LILLIAN FEDER. *Ancient Myth in Modern Poetry*, pp. 231-36.

GENEVIEVE W. FOSTER. "The Archetypal Imagery of T. S. Eliot," *PMLA* 60(2), June 1945, 576-78.

WARREN FRENCH. "The Age of Eliot: The Twenties as Waste Land," in *The Twenties*, edited by Warren French, pp. 15-17.

EVERETT GILLIS. "The Spiritual Status of T. S. Eliot's Hollow Men," *Texas Studies in Literature and Language* 2(4), Winter 1961, 464-75.

J. G. KEOGH. "Eliot's *Hollow Men* as Graveyard Poetry," *Renascence* 21(3), Spring 1969, 115-18.

ROBERT S. KINSMAN. *Explicator* 8(6), April 1950, Item 48.

SYDNEY J. KRAUSE. "Hollow Men and False Horses," *Texas Studies in Literature and Language* 2(3), Autumn 1960, 368-77.

J. HILLIS MILLER. *Poets of Reality*, pp. 180-82.

KAREN T. ROMER. "T. S. Eliot and the Language of Liturgy," *Renascence* 24(3), Spring 1972, 130-32.

M. L. ROSENTHAL. *Sailing into the Unknown*, pp. 183-88.

GROVER SMITH, JR. "Getting Used to T. S. Eliot," *English Journal* 49(1), January 1960, 9, 15.

JOHN B. VICKERY. "Eliot's Poetry: The Quest and the Way (Part I)," *Renascence* 10(1), Autumn 1957, 8-9.

"Hysteria"

HENRY CHRISTIAN. "Thematic Development in T. S. Eliot's 'Hysteria,' " *Twentieth Century Literature* 6(2), July 1960, 76-80.

L. S. DEMBO. *Conceptions of Reality in Modern American Poetry*, pp. 189-90.

M. L. ROSENTHAL. *Sailing into the Unknown*, pp. 158-60.

"Jellicle Cats"

FELIX CLOWDER. "The Bestiary of T. S. Eliot," *Prairie Schooner* 34(1), Spring 1960, 31-33.

"Journey of the Magi"

WALTON BEACHAM. *The Meaning of Poetry*, pp. 284-92.

ELIOT, T. S. *(Cont.)*

"Journey of the Magi" *(cont.)*

R. D. BROWN. "Revelation in T. S. Eliot's 'Journey of the Magi,'" *Renascence* 24(3), Spring 1972, 136-40.

DAVID DAICHES and WILLIAM CHARVAT. *Poems in English*, p. 740.

ELIZABETH DREW. *Poetry*, pp. 237-40.

GENEVIEVE W. FOSTER. "The Archetypal Imagery of T. S. Eliot," *PMLA* 60(2), June 1945, 578-80.

ROBERT HAWKINS. *Preface to Poetry*, pp. 113-16.

JOHN T. HIERS. "Birth or Death: Eliot's 'Journey of the Magi' and 'A Song for Simeon,'" *South Carolina Review* 8(2), April 1976, 41-46.

ROBERT B. KAPLAN and RICHARD J. WALL. *Explicator* 19(2), November 1960, Item 8.

LAURENCE PERRINE. *100 American Poems of the Twentieth Century*, pp. 132-34.

M. L. ROSENTHAL. *Sailing into the Unknown*, pp. 191-93.

ELISABETH SCHNEIDER. "Prufrock and After: The Theme of Change," *PMLA* 87(5), October 1972, 1113-14.

GROVER SMITH. "Visions and Revisions: the 'Ariel Poems,'" in *Modern Poetry*, pp. 302-4, 306-7.

LOUIS UNTERMEYER. *50 Modern American & British Poets*, pp. 250-51.

JOHN HOWARD WILLS. *Explicator* 2(5), March 1954, Item 32.

A. S. P. WOODHOUSE. *The Poet and His Faith*, pp. 265-66.

"Lines for an Old Man"

M. L. ROSENTHAL. *Sailing into the Unknown*, pp. 6-8.

"Little Gidding"

see also "Four Quartets"

CHRISTOPHER CLAUSEN. "Tintern Abbey to Little Gidding: The Past Recaptured," *Sewanee Review* 84(3), Summer 1976, 419-20.

D. W. HARDING. *Experience Into Words*, pp. 121-25.

M. L. ROSENTHAL. *Sailing into the Unknown*, pp. 45-66.

M. L. ROSENTHAL and A. J. M. SMITH. *Exploring Poetry*, pp. 696-704.

JOHN SHAND. "Around 'Little Gidding,'" *Nineteenth Century and After* 136(811), September 1944, 120-32.

JAMES JOHNSON SWEENEY. "Little Gidding: Introductory to a Reading," *Poetry* 62(4), July 1943, 214-23.

"The Love Song of J. Alfred Prufrock"

ROBERT M. ADAMS. *Strains of Discord*, pp. 112-13.

CHARLES ALTIERI. "Steps of the Mind in T. S. Eliot's Poetry," *Bucknell Review* 22(2), Fall 1976, 185-89.

RUSSELL AMES. "Decadence in the Art of T. S. Eliot," *Science and Society* 16(3), Summer 1952, 193-221.

T. R. BARNES. *English Verse*, pp. 282-90.

ROY P. BASLER. "Psychological Pattern in 'The Love Song of J. Alfred Prufrock,'" *Twentieth Century English*, 1946, pp. 384-400.

ROY P. BASLER. *Sex, Symbolism, and Psychology in Literature*, pp. 203-21.

JOHN BERRYMAN. *The Freedom of the Poet*, pp. 270-78.

MARGARET MORTON BLUM. "The *Fool* in 'The Love Song of J. Alfred Prufrock,'" *Modern Language Notes* 72(6), June 1957, 424-26.

CLEANTH BROOKS and ROBERT PENN WARREN. *Understanding Poetry*, pp. 589-96; revised ed., pp. 433-44; third ed., pp. 370-99. Reprinted in: *The Creative Reader;* pp. 878-85; second ed., pp. 935-42.

HARRY BROWN and JOHN MILSTEAD. *What the Poem Means*, pp. 79-80.

JOHN CLENDENNING. "Time, Doubt and Vision: Notes on Emerson and T. S. Eliot," *American Scholar* 36(1), Winter 1966/67, 130-31.

R. G. COLLINGWOOD. *The Principles of Art*, p. 310.

MICHAEL J. COLLINS. "Formal Allusion in Modern Poetry," *Concerning Poetry* 9(1), Spring 1976, 5-6.

IAN S. DUNN. *Explicator* 22(1), September 1963, Item 1.

J. PETER DYSON. "Word Heard: Prufrock Asks His Question," *Yeats Eliot Review* 5(2), 1978, 33-35. (P)

PAUL ENGLE. "Eliot's The Love Song of J. Alfred Prufrock," in *Reading Modern Poetry*, pp. 167-74; revised ed., pp. 148-55.

BARBARA EVERETT. "In Search of Prufrock," *Critical Quarterly* 16(2), Summer 1974, 101-21.

LILLIAN FEDER. *Ancient Myth in Modern Poetry*, pp. 123-25, 219-22.

CLIFFORD J. FISH. *Explicator* 8(3), June 1950, Item 62.

GEORGE FORTENBERRY. "Prufrock and the Fool Song," *Ball State University Forum* 8(1), Winter 1967, 51-54.

LLOYD FRANKENBERG. *Pleasure Dome*, pp. 40-42, 45-49.

JOHN E. GURKA. "The Voices of Ulysses and Prufrock," *English Journal* 55(2), February 1966, 205-7.

JOHN HALVERSON. "Prufrock, Freud, and Others," *Sewanee Review* 76(4), Autumn 1968, 571-80.

DAVID D. HIRSCH. "T. S. Eliot and the Vexation of Time," *Southern Review*, n.s., 3(3), Summer 1967, 608-20.

JAMES F. KNAPP. "Eliot's 'Prufrock' and the Form of Modern Poetry," *Arizona Quarterly* 30(1), Spring 1974, 5-14.

ROBERT LANGBAUM. *The Poetry of Experience*, pp. 189-92, 198-202.

ARTHUR C. McGILL. *The Celebration of Flesh*, pp. 45-46.

MINOR WALLACE MAJOR. "A St. Louisan's View of Prufrock," *CEA Critic* 23(6), September 1961, 5.

JOSEPH MARGOLIS. *Interpretations*, John Wain, ed., pp. 183-93.

J. HILLIS MILLER. *Poets of Reality*, pp. 137-41.

ROY HARVEY PEARCE. *The Continuity of American Poetry*, pp. 297-98.

LAURENCE PERRINE. *100 American Poems of the Twentieth Century*, pp. 105-12.

JOHN OLIVER PERRY. *The Experience of Poems*, pp. 63-68.

JOHN OLIVER PERRY. "The Relationships of Disparate Voices in Poems," *Essays in Criticism* 15(1), January 1965, 56-57.

R. G. PETERSON. "Concentric Structure and 'The Love Song of J. Alfred Prufrock,'" *T. S. Eliot Review* 3(1-2), 1976, 25-28.

JOHN C. POPE. "Prufrock and Raskolnikov," *American Literature* 17(3), November 1945, 213-30; 18(4), January 1947, 319-21.

M. L. ROSENTHAL and A. J. M. SMITH. *Exploring Poetry*, pp. 376-77; second ed., pp. 152-53.

THOMAS C. RUMBLE. "Some Grail Motifs in Eliot's Prufrock," in *Studies in American Literature*, pp. 95-103.

ELISABETH SCHNEIDER. "Prufrock and After: The Theme of Change," *PMLA* 87(5), October 1972, 1103-6.

MARTIN SCOFIELD. " 'A gesture and a pose': T. S. Eliot's images of love," *Critical Quarterly* 18(3), Autumn 1976, 9-10.

KARL SHAPIRO. "T. S. Eliot: The Death of Literary Judgment," in *In Defense of Ignorance*, pp. 45-47.

GROVER SMITH, JR. "Getting Used to T. S. Eliot," *English Journal* 49(1), January 1960, 6-7.

ZOREH TAWAKULI SULLIVAN. "Memory and Meditative Structure in T. S. Eliot's Early Poetry," *Renascence* 29(2), Winter 1977, 99-100.

GORDON SYMES. "T. S. Eliot and Old Age," *Fortnightly* 169(3), March 1951, 188-89.

WRIGHT THOMAS and STUART GERRY BROWN. *Reading Poems: An Introduction to Critical Study*, pp. 698-700.

RAYMOND TSCHUMI. *Thought in Twentieth-Century English Poetry*, pp. 127-32.

W. ARTHUR TURNER. "The Not So Coy Mistress of J. Alfred Prufrock," *South Atlantic Quarterly* 54(4), October 1955, 516-22.

LEONARD UNGER. "T. S. Eliot," in *Seven Modern American Poets*, pp. 206-7.

CHARLES CHILD WALCUTT. "Eliot's 'The Love Song of J. Alfred Prufrock,' " *College English* 19(2), November 1957, 71-72.

LEON WALDOFF. "Prufrock's Defenses and Our Response," *American Imago* 26(2), Summer 1969, 182-93.

MORRIS WEITZ. *Philosophy of the Arts*, pp. 94-107.

ARTHUR WORMHOUDT. "A Psychoanalytic Interpretation of 'The Love Song of J. Alfred Prufrock,' " *Perspective* 2 (Winter 1949), 109-17.

"Macavity: The Mystery Cat"

PRISCILLA PRESTON. "A Note on T. S. Eliot and Sherlock Holmes," *Modern Language Review* 54(3), July 1959, 398-99.

"Marina"

W. J. BARNES. "T. S. Eliot's 'Marina': Image and Symbol," *University of Kansas City Review* 29(4), Summer 1963, 297-305.

JAMES BENZIGER. *Images of Eternity*, pp. 245-46.

HARRY BROWN and JOHN MILSTEAD. *What the Poem Means*, p. 77.

ELSPETH CAMERON. "T. S. Eliot's 'Marina': An Exploration," *Queen's Quarterly* 77(2), Summer 1970, 180-89.

C. B. COX and A. E. DYSON. *Modern Poetry*, pp. 72-79.

DAVID DAICHES and WILLIAM CHARVAT. *Poems in English*, p. 741.

BABETTE DEUTSCH. *Poetry in Our Time*, pp. 175-76; second ed., pp. 188-90.

PAUL J. DOLAN. "Eliot's *Marina*: A Reading," *Renascence* 21(4), Summer 1969, 203-6, 222.

GENEVIEVE W. FOSTER. "The Archetypal Imagery of T. S. Eliot," *PMLA* 60(2), June 1945, 582-83.

CHRISTOPHER GILLIE. *Movements in English Literature*, pp. 159-60.

G. WILSON KNIGHT. *Neglected Powers*, p. 372.

F. R. LEAVIS. *Education and the University*, 90-92.

F. R. LEAVIS. "Eliot's Later Poetry," *Scrutiny* 11(1), Summer 1942, 61-63.

F. R. LEAVIS. *New Bearings on English Poetry*, pp. 129-31.

Y. B. OLSSON. "T. S. Eliot's *Marina*: A Study in Poetic Cohesion," *Durham University Journal*, n.s., 33(2), March 1972, 115-19.

KAREN T. ROMER. "T. S. Eliot and the Language of Liturgy," *Renascence* 24(3), Spring 1972, 127-30.

M. L. ROSENTHAL. *Sailing into the Unknown*, pp. 194-95.

ELISABETH SCHNEIDER. "Prufrock and After: The Theme of Change," *PMLA* 87(5), October 1972, 1114-16.

MARTIN SCOFIELD. " 'A gesture and a pose': T. S. Eliot's images of love," *Critical Quarterly* 18(3), Autumn 1976, 22-25.

GROVER SMITH. "Visions and Revisions: the 'Ariel Poems,' " in *Modern Poetry*, pp. 310-15.

"Mr. Apollinax"

ALEC BROWN. "The Lyric Impulse in the Poetry of T. S. Eliot," in *Scrutinies*, II: 29-31.

LILLIAN FEDER. *Ancient Myth in Modern Poetry*, pp. 125-26.

GROVER SMITH, JR. "Getting Used to T. S. Eliot," *English Journal* 49(1), January 1960, 8.

"Mr. Eliot's Sunday Morning Service"

GÉMINO H. ABAD. *A Formal Approach to Lyric Poetry*, pp. 332-36.

CHARLES ALTIERI. "Steps of the Mind in T. S. Eliot's Poetry," *Bucknell Review* 22(2), Fall 1976, 193-94.

ANSELM ATKINS. "Mr. Eliot's Sunday Morning Parody," *Renascence* 21(1), Autumn 1968, 41-43, 54.

DAVID HOLBROOK. *Llareggub Revisited*, pp. 80-82.

DAVID HOLBROOK. "Mr. Eliot's Chinese Wall," *Essays in Criticism* 5(4), October 1955, 418-26.

GEORGE MONTEIRO. "Christians and Jews in 'Mr. Eliot's Sunday Morning Service,' " *T. S. Eliot Review* 3(1-2), 1976, 20-22.

ERNEST SCHANZER. " 'Mr. Eliot's Sunday Morning Service,' " *Essays in Criticism* 5(2), April 1955, 153-58.

ARVID SHULENBERGER. *Explicator* 10(4), February 1952, Item 29.

HYATT H. WAGGONER. *American Poets*, p. 421.

JANE WORTHINGTON. "The Epigraphs to the Poetry of T. S. Eliot," *American Literature* 21(1), March 1949, 11-12.

"The Naming of Cats"

FELIX CLOWDER. "The Bestiary of T. S. Eliot," *Prairie Schooner* 34(1), Spring 1960, 34-35.

"Ode" (*Ara Vos Prec*)

E. P. BOLLIER. "A Broken Coriolanus: A Note on T. S. Eliot's *Coriolan*," *Southern Review*, n.s., 3(3), Summer 1967, 628-29.

E. P. BOLLIER. "T. S. Eliot's 'Lost' Ode of Dejection," *Bucknell Review* 16(1), March 1968, 1-17.

M. L. ROSENTHAL. *Sailing into the Unknown*, pp. 160-62.

"Old Deuteronomy"

FELIX CLOWDER. "The Bestiary of T. S. Eliot," *Prairie Schooner* 34(1), Spring 1960, 33-34.

"Portrait of a Lady"

SARA deSAUSSURE DAVIS. "Two Portraits of a Lady: Henry James and T. S. Eliot," *Arizona Quarterly* 32(4), Winter 1976, 367-80.

L. S. DEMBO. *Conceptions of Reality in Modern American Poetry*, pp. 187-89.

ELIOT, T. S. *(Cont.)*

"Portrait of a Lady" *(cont.)*

RICHARD J. GIANNONE. "Eliot's 'Portrait of a Lady' and Pound's 'Portrait d'une Femme,'" *Twentieth Century Literature* 5(3), October 1959, 131-34.

MARTIN SCOFIELD. "'A gesture and a pose': T. S. Eliot's images of love," *Critical Quarterly* 18(3), Autumn 1976, 10-11.

KARL SHAPIRO. *In Defense of Ignorance*, pp. 47-48.

PATRICIA MEYER SPACKS. "In Search of Sincerity," *College English* 29(8), May 1968, 599-601.

W. ARTHUR TURNER. "The Not So Coy Mistress of J. Alfred Prufrock," *South Atlantic Quarterly* 54(4), October 1955, 517-18.

HYATT H. WAGGONER. *American Poets*, pp. 418-20.

"Preludes"

JACK BEHAR. "Eliot and the Language of Gesture: The Early Poems," *Twentieth Century Literature* 23(4), December 1977, 492-96.

CLEANTH BROOKS, JOHN THIBAUT PURSER, and ROBERT PENN WARREN. *An Approach to Literature*, fifth ed., pp. 452-53.

CLEANTH BROOKS and ROBERT PENN WARREN. *Understanding Poetry*, fourth ed., pp. 91-93.

HARRY BROWN and JOHN MILSTEAD. *What the Poem Means*, p. 78.

LAURENCE LERNER. "Reading Modern Poetry," in *English Poetry*, edited by Alan Sinfield, pp. 151-54.

A. A. MENDILOW. "T. S. Eliot's 'Long Unlovely Street,'" *Modern Language Review* 63(2), April 1968, 320-22.

J. HILLIS MILLER. *Poets of Reality*, pp. 144-45, 172-73.

THOMAS J. MORRISSEY. "'Intimate and Unidentifiable': The Voices of Fragmented Reality in the Poetry of T. S. Eliot," *Centennial Review* 22(1), Winter 1978, 8-18.

LAURENCE PERRINE. *100 American Poems of the Twentieth Century*, pp. 103-5.

"Rhapsody on a Windy Night"

L. S. DEMBO. *Conceptions of Reality in Modern American Poetry*, pp. 186-87.

JOHN F. LYNEN. "Forms of Time in Modern Poetry," *Queen's Quarterly* 82(3), Autumn 1975, 355-57.

A. A. MENDILOW. "T. S. Eliot's 'Long Unlovely Street,'" *Modern Language Review* 63(2), April 1968, 322-26.

J. HILLIS MILLER. *Poets of Reality*, p. 146.

M. L. ROSENTHAL. *The Modern Poets*, pp. 6-7.

KARL SHAPIRO. *In Defense of Ignorance*, p. 49.

ZOREH TAWAKULI SULLIVAN. "Memory and Meditative Structure in T. S. Eliot's Early Poetry," *Renascence* 29(2), Winter 1977, 101-2.

"The Rock"

WARREN FRENCH. "The Age of Eliot: The Twenties as Waste Land," in *The Twenties*, edited by Warren French, pp. 19-21.

D. W. HARDING. *Experience Into Words*, pp. 112-16.

"A Song for Simeon"

GENEVIEVE W. FOSTER. "The Archetypal Imagery of T. S. Eliot," *PMLA* 60(2), June 1945, 578-80.

MALCOLM S. GLASS. "T. S. Eliot: Christian Poetry Through Liturgical Allusion," in *The Twenties*, edited by Richard E. Langford and William E. Taylor, pp. 42-45.

JOHN T. HIERS. "Birth or Death: Eliot's 'Journey of the Magi' and 'A Song for Simeon,'" *South Carolina Review* 8(2), April 1976, 41-46.

HUGH KENNER. "Eliot's Moral Dialectic," *Hudson Review* 2(3), Autumn 1949, 424-28.

GROVER SMITH. "Visions and Revisions: the 'Ariel Poems,'" in *Modern Poetry*, pp. 304-7.

"Sweeney Agonistes"

MORRIS FREEDMAN. "Jazz Rhythms and T. S. Eliot," *South Atlantic Quarterly* 51(3), July 1952, 428-32.

MORRIS FREEDMAN. "The Meaning of T. S. Eliot's Jew," *South Atlantic Quarterly* 55(2), April 1956, 200-1.

SEARS JAYNE. "Mr. Eliot's Agon," *Philological Quarterly* 34(4), October 1955, 395-414.

WILLIAM V. SPANOS. "'Wanna Go Home, Baby?': *Sweeney Agonistes* as Drama of the Absurd," *PMLA* 85(1), January 1970, 8-20.

LEONARD UNGER. "T. S. Eliot," in *Seven Modern American Poets*, p. 212.

"Sweeney Among the Nightingales"

HARRY BROWN and JOHN MILSTEAD. *What the Poem Means*, pp. 78-79.

JAMES DAVIDSON. "The End of Sweeney," *College English* 27(5), February 1966, 400-3.

BABETTE DEUTSCH. *Poetry in Our Time*, pp. 168-70; second ed., pp. 181-83.

ELIZABETH DREW. *T. S. Eliot: The Design of His Poetry*, pp. 42-46. Abridged in: *The Case for Poetry*, pp. 133-35; second ed., p. 114.

DOROTHY EDMONDS. "T. S. Eliot: Toward the 'Still Point,'" *Ball State Teachers College Forum* 5(2), Spring 1964, 50-51.

LILLIAN FEDER. *Ancient Myth in Modern Poetry*, pp. 126-28.

LLOYD FRANKENBERG. *Invitation to Poetry*, pp. 241-42.

EVERETT A. GILLIS. "Religion in a Sweeney World," *Arizona Quarterly* 20(1), Spring 1964, 55-63.

ELIZABETH RUDISILL HOMANN. *Explicator* 17(5), February 1959, Item 34.

STANLEY EDGAR HYMAN. "Poetry and Criticism: T. S. Eliot," *American Scholar* 30(1), Winter 1960-1, 43-49.

P. G. MUDFORD. "Sweeney among the Nightingales," *Essays in Criticism* 19(3), July 1969, 285-91.

JOHN OWER. "Pattern and Value in 'Sweeney among the Nightingales,'" *Renascence* 23(3), Spring 1971, 151-58.

DONALD A. STAUFFER. *The Nature of Poetry*, pp. 78-80. Abridged in: *The Case for Poetry*, p. 135; second ed., pp. 114-15.

GEORGE WHITESIDE. "A Freudian Dream Analysis of 'Sweeney Among the Nightingales,'" *Yeats Eliot Review* 5(1), 1978, 14-17.

GEORGE WILLIAMSON. *A Reader's Guide to T. S. Eliot*, pp. 97-99. Abridged in: *The Case for Poetry*, p. 133; second ed., p. 113.

"Sweeney Erect"

ARTHUR MIZENER. "To Meet Mr. Eliot," *Sewanee Review* 65(1), Winter 1957, 41-42.

CHARLES CHILD WALCUTT. *Explicator* 35(2), Winter 1976, 31-32.

JANE WORTHINGTON. "The Epigraphs to the Poetry of T. S. Eliot," *American Literature* 21(1), March 1949, 7-9.

"To the Indians Who Died in Africa"

K. S. NARAYANA RAO. "T. S. Eliot and the *Bhagavad-Gita*," *American Quarterly* 15(4), Winter 1963, 572-78.

"Triumphal March"

see also "Coriolan"

EARL DANIELS. *The Art of Reading Poetry*, pp. 406-8.

GENEVIEVE W. FOSTER. "The Archetypal Imagery of T. S. Eliot," *PMLA* 60(2), June 1945, 583-84.

F. R. LEAVIS. *Education and the University*, pp. 92-93.

F. R. LEAVIS. "Eliot's Later Poetry," *Scrutiny* 11(1), Summer 1942, 63-64.

"The Waste Land"

ROBERT J. ANDREACH. "*Paradise Lost* and the Christian Configuration of *The Waste Land*," *Papers on Language and Literature* 5(3), Summer 1969, 296-309.

RAYMOND BENOIT. *Single Nature's Double Name*, pp. 108-18.

A. F. BERINGAUSE. "Journey Through *The Waste Land*," *South Atlantic Quarterly* 56(1), January 1957, 79-90.

R. P. BLACKMUR. "T. S. Eliot," *Hound and Horn* 1(3), March 1928, 190-96.

MAUD BODKIN. *Archetypal Patterns in Poetry*, pp. 310-14.

C. M. BOWRA. *The Creative Experiment*, pp. 159-88.

EDWARD BRANDABUR. "Eliot and the Myth of Mute Speech," *Renascence* 22(3), Spring 1970, 141-50.

CLEANTH BROOKS. "Eliot: The Waste Land," in *Master Poems of the English Language*, pp. 958-81.

CLEANTH BROOKS. *Modern Poetry and the Tradition*, pp. 136-72.

CLEANTH BROOKS, JR. *Understanding Poetry*, fourth ed., pp. 306-10.

CLEANTH BROOKS, JR. "The Waste Land: An Analysis," *Southern Review* 3(1), Summer 1937, 106-36.

ALEC BROWN. "The Lyric Impulse in the Poetry of T. S. Eliot," in *Scrutinies*, II: 34-48.

HARRY BROWN and JOHN MILSTEAD. *What the Poem Means*, pp. 80-82.

VINCENT BUCKLEY. *Poetry and the Sacred*, pp. 209-13.

DOUGLAS BUSH. *Pagan Myth and Christian Tradition in English Poetry*, pp. 86-89.

OSCAR CARGILL. "Death in a Handful of Dust," *Criticism* 11(3), Summer 1969, 275-96.

DAVID CRAIG. "The Defeatism of *The Waste Land*," *Critical Quarterly* 2(3), Autumn 1960, 241-52.

VIVIAN DE SOLA PINTO. *Crisis in English Poetry*, pp. 170-75; fifth ed., pp. 151-56.

L. S. DEMBO. *Conceptions of Reality in Modern American Poetry*, pp. 194-200.

BABETTE DEUTSCH. *Poetry in Our Time*, pp. 160-64; second ed., pp. 173-78.

BABETTE DEUTSCH. *This Modern Poetry*, pp. 118-27.

ELIZABETH DREW and JOHN L. SWEENEY. *Directions in Modern Poetry*, pp. 40-42, 44-48.

DOROTHY EDMONDS. "T. S. Eliot: Toward the 'Still Point,'" *Ball State Teachers College Forum* 5(2), Spring 1974, 51-53.

BARBARA EVERETT. "Eliot In and Out of *The Waste Land*," *Critical Quarterly* 17(1), Spring 1975, 7-30.

WILLIAM J. FARRELL. "*The Waste Land* as Rhetoric," *Renascence* 22(3), Spring 1970, 127-40.

LILLIAN FEDER. *Ancient Myth in Modern Poetry*, pp. 128-36, 222-31, 311-12, 346-47.

GENEVIEVE W. FOSTER. "The Archetypal Imagery of T. S. Eliot," *PMLA* 60(2), June 1945, 568-76.

STEVEN FOSTER. "Relativity and *The Waste Land*: A Postulate," *Texas Studies in Literature and Language* 7(1), Spring 1965, 77-95.

LLOYD FRANKENBERG. *Pleasure Dome*, pp. 64-77.

G. S. FRASER. "The Waste Land Revisited," in *Vision and Rhetoric*, pp. 98-112. Reprinted in: George Fraser. *Essays on Twentieth Century Poets*, pp. 89-98.

WARREN FRENCH. "The Age of Eliot: The Twenties as Waste Land," in *The Twenties*, edited by Warren French, pp. 7-14, 22-26.

KIMON FRIAR and JOHN MALCOLM BRINNIN. *Modern Poetry*, pp. 425-26, 472-97.

EDWIN FUSSELL. *Lucifer in Harness*, pp. 80-83, 145-50.

HARVEY GROSS. "T. S. Eliot," in *The Contrived Corridor*, pp. 44-45.

IAN HAMILTON. "The Waste Land," in *A Poetry Chronicle*, pp. 19-29.

CAROL CLANCY HARTER. "Strange Bedfellows: *The Waste Land* and *An American Tragedy*," in *The Twenties*, edited by Warren French, pp. 51-64.

RICHARD D. HATHAWAY. "*The Waste Land's* Benediction," *American Notes & Queries*, n.s., 2(4), December 1963, 53-54.

GILBERT HIGHET. *The Powers of Poetry*, pp. 323-29.

FREDERICK J. HOFFMAN. *The Twenties*, pp. 291-303; revised ed., pp. 330-43.

DAVID HOLBROOK. *Lost Bearings in English Poetry*, pp. 93-98.

FLORENCE JONES. "T. S. Eliot Among the Prophets," *American Literature* 38(3), November 1966, 285-302.

F. R. LEAVIS. *New Bearings in English Poetry*, pp. 90-114.

JOHN LUCAS and WILLIAM MYERS. "*The Waste Land* Today," *Essays in Criticism* 19(2), April 1969, 193-209.

ARTHUR C. MCGILL. *The Celebration of Flesh*, pp. 52-85.

JULIET MCLAUCHLAN. "Allusion in *The Waste Land*," *Essays in Criticism* 19(4), October 1969, 454-60.

FLORENCE MARSH. "The Ocean-Desert: *The Ancient Mariner* and *The Waste Land*," *Essays in Criticism* 9(2), April 1959, 126-33.

MILTON MILLER. "What the Thunder Meant," *ELH* 36(2), June 1969, 440-54.

MARION MONTGOMERY. "The Awful Daring: The Self Surrendered in *The Waste Land*," *Arizona Quarterly* 30(1), Spring 1974, 43-52.

CHARLES MOORMAN. "Myth and Organic Unity in *The Waste Land*," *South Atlantic Quarterly* 57(2), Spring 1958, 194-203.

GABRIEL MOTOLA. " 'The Waste Land': Symbolism and Structure," *Literature and Psychology* 18(4), 1968, 205-12.

WILLIAM T. MOYNIHAN. "The Goal of the Waste Land Quest," *Renascence* 13(4), Summer 1961, 171-79.

GERTRUDE PATTERSON. " 'The Waste Land' in the Making," *Critical Quarterly* 14(3), Autumn 1972, 269-83.

ROY HARVEY PEARCE. *The Continuity of American Poetry*, pp. 306-9.

LAURENCE PERRINE. *100 American Poems of the Twentieth Century*, pp. 112-32.

ELIOT, T. S. *(Cont.)*

"The Waste Land" *(cont.)*

JOHN PETER. "A New Interpretation of *The Waste Land*," *Essays in Criticism* 19(2), April 1969, 140-65.

WILLIAM H. PRITCHARD. "Reading *The Waste Land* Today," *Essays in Criticism* 19(2), April 1969, 176-92.

HARRY PUCKETT. "T. S. Eliot on Knowing: The Word Unheard," *New England Quarterly* 44(2), June 1971, 179-96.

SISTER M. BERNETTA QUINN. *The Metamorphic Tradition,* pp. 130-42.

M. L. ROSENTHAL. *The Modern Poets,* pp. 88-94.

M. L. ROSENTHAL. *Sailing into the Unknown,* pp. 162-78.

ELISABETH SCHNEIDER. "Prufrock and After: The Theme of Change," *PMLA* 87(5), October 1972, 1106-7.

DELMORE SCHWARTZ. "T. S. Eliot as the International Hero," *Partisan Review* 12(2), Spring 1945, 199-206.

NATHAN A. SCOTT. *Rehearsals of Discomposure,* pp. 203-25.

WALTER SUTTON. "*Mauberley, The Waste Land,* and the Problem of Unified Form," *Contemporary Literature* 9(1), Winter 1968, 15-35.

RONALD TAMPLIN. "*The Tempest* and *The Waste Land*," *American Literature* 39(3), November 1967, 352-72.

WRIGHT THOMAS and STUART GERRY BROWN. *Reading Poems: An Introduction to Critical Study,* pp. 716-31, 749-51.

RAYMOND TSCHUMI. *Thought in Twentieth-Century English Poetry,* pp. 132-44.

JOHN B. VICKERY. "Eliot's Poetry: The Quest and the Way (Part I)," *Renascence* 10(1), Autumn 1957, 5-8.

PHILIP WHEELWRIGHT. *The Burning Fountain,* pp. 338-51.

GEORGE WILLIAMSON. "The Structure of *The Waste Land*," *Modern Philology* 47(3), February 1950, 191-206.

EDMUND WILSON. *Axel's Castle,* pp. 104-11. Reprinted in: *Literary Opinion in America,* pp. 186-93; revised ed., pp. 213-18, third ed., pp. 213-18.

"Whispers of Immortality"

JAMES R. CALDWELL. "States of Mind: States of Consciousness," *Essays in Criticism* 4(2), April 1954, 171-74.

SISTER M. CLEOPHAS. *Explicator* 8(3), December 1949, Item 22.

WILLIAM EMPSON. *Seven Types of Ambiguity,* second and third eds., pp. 78-79.

VICTOR STRANDBERG. *Explicator* 17(8), May 1959, Item 53.

CHARLES C. WALCUTT. *Explicator* 7(2), November 1948, Item 11.

EMERSON, RALPH WALDO

"Alphonso of Castile"

WILLIAM SLOANE KENNEDY. *Clews to Emerson's Mystic Verse.* Reprinted in *American Transcendental Quarterly* 29(3), Winter 1976, 13.

"The Apology"

CHARLES MALLOY. *A Study of Emerson's Major Poems.* Reprinted in *American Transcendental Quarterly* 23(1-3), Summer 1974, 55-59.

"April"

CARL F. STRAUCH. "Hatred's Swift Repulsions: Emerson, Margaret Fuller, and Others," *Studies in Romanticism* 7(2), Winter 1968, 75-76.

"Astraea"

CARL F. STRAUCH. "Hatred's Swift Repulsions: Emerson, Margaret Fuller, and Others," *Studies in Romanticism* 7(2), Winter 1968, 99-101.

"Bacchus"

HAROLD BLOOM. "Bacchus and Merlin: The Dialectic of Romantic Poetry in America," *Southern Review,* n.s., 7(1), Winter 1970, 151-52.

MICHAEL H. COWAN. "The Loving Proteus: Metamorphosis in Emerson's Poetry," *American Transcendental Quarterly* 25(1), Winter 1975, 16-17.

CHARLES MALLOY. *A Study of Emerson's Major Poems.* Reprinted in *American Transcendental Quarterly* 23(1-3), Summer 1974, 39-43.

BERNARD J. PARIS. "Emerson's 'Bacchus,'" *Modern Language Quarterly* 23(2), June 1962, 150-59.

ROY HARVEY PEARCE. *The Continuity of American Poetry,* p. 158.

"Beauty"

STANLEY BRODWIN. "Emerson's Version of Plotinus: The Flight to Beauty," *Journal of the History of Ideas* 35(3), July-September 1974, 477.

"The Bohemian Hymn"

RICHARD E. AMACHER. *Explicator* 5(8), June 1947, Item 55.

ERIC W. CARLSON. "Emerson's 'The Bohemian Hymn,'" *Emerson Society Quarterly* 6(1), First Quarter 1957, 6-7.

"Brahma"

GÉMINO H. ABAD. *A Formal Approach to Lyric Poetry,* pp. 131-32.

K. R. CHANDRASEKHARAN. "Emerson's *Brahma*: An Indian Interpretation," *New England Quarterly* 33(4), December 1960, 506-12.

RICHARD LEE FRANCIS. "Archangel in the Pleached Garden: Emerson's Poetry," *ELH* 33(4), December 1966, 469-71.

CHARLES MALLOY. "An Interpretation of Emerson's 'Brahma,'" *American Transcendental Quarterly* 23(3), Summer 1974, 119-21.

CHARLES MALLOY. *A Study of Emerson's Major Poems.* Reprinted in *American Transcendental Quarterly* 23(1-3), Summer 1974, 60-66.

WILLIAM BYSSHE STEIN, JOHN D. RUSSELL, MARILYN BALDWIN, and GAYLORD C. LEROY. *Explicator* 20(4), November 1961, Item 29. (P)

MARK VAN DOREN. *Introduction to Poetry,* pp. 90-93.

ROBERT L. WHITE. *Explicator* 21(8), April 1963, Item 63.

"Celestial Love"

see also "Initial, Daemonic, and Celestial Love"

CHARLES MALLOY. *A Study of Emerson's Major Poems.* Reprinted in *American Transcendental Quarterly* 23(1-3), Summer 1974, 72-79.

"Circles"

CARL F. STRAUCH. "Emerson and the Doctrine of Sympathy," *Studies in Romanticisim* 6(3), Spring 1967, 155-56.

"Concord Hymn"

GEORGE ARMS. *Explicator* 1(3), December 1942, Item 23.

Isaac Asimov. *Familiar Poems, Annotated,* pp. 149-51.

"Days"

George Arms. *Explicator* 4(2), November 1945, Item 8. Abridged in: *The Case for Poetry,* p. 140; second ed., pp. 118-19.

John Clendenning. "Emerson's 'Days': A Psychoanalytic Study," *American Transcendental Quarterly* 25(1), Winter 1975, 6-11.

John Clendenning. "Time, Doubt and Vision: Notes on Emerson and T. S. Eliot," *American Scholar* 36(1), Winter 1966/67, 129-30.

David Daiches and William Charvat. *Poems in English,* p. 719.

Mario L. D'Avanzo. "Emerson's 'Days' and Proverbs," *American Transcendental Quarterly* 1(2), First Quarter 1969, 83-85.

Edward G. Fletcher. *Explicator* 5(6), April 1947, Item 41.

Richard Lee Francis. "Archangel in the Pleached Garden: Emerson's Poetry," *ELH* 33(4), December 1966, 468-69.

Seymour L. Gross. "Emerson and Poetry," *South Atlantic Quarterly* 54(1), January 1955, 93-94.

Joseph Jones. *Explicator* 4(6), April 1946, Item 47. Abridged in: *The Case for Poetry,* p. 140; second ed., p. 118.

Richard Ray Kirk and Roger Philip McCutcheon. *An Introduction to the Study of Poetry,* pp. 35-36. Abridged in: *The Case for Poetry,* p. 139; second ed., p. 118.

Charles Malloy. *A Study of Emerson's Major Poems.* Reprinted in *American Transcendental Quarterly* 23(1-3), Summer 1974, 25-28, 66-69.

F. O. Matthiessen. *American Renaissance,* pp. 59-60.

Richard Tuerk. "Emerson's Darker Vision: 'Hamatreya' and 'Days,'" *American Transcendental Quarterly* 25(1&2), Winter 1975, 28-33.

"Destiny"

Carl F. Strauch. "Hatred's Swift Repulsions: Emerson, Margaret Fuller, and Others," *Studies in Romanticism* 7(2), Winter 1968, 92-93.

"Each and All"

George Arms. "The Dramatic Movement in Emerson's 'Each and All,'" *English Language Notes* 1(3), March 1964, 207-11.

Walter Blair and Clarence Faust. "Emerson's Literary Method," *Modern Philology* 42(2), November 1944, 89-91.

Seymour L. Gross. "Emerson and Poetry," *South Atlantic Quarterly* 54(1), January 1955, 89-91.

Carl F. Strauch. "Emerson and the Doctrine of Sympathy," *Studies in Romanticism* 6(3), Spring 1967, 157.

"Étienne de la Boéce"

Charles Malloy. *A Study of Emerson's Major Poems.* Reprinted in *American Transcendental Quarterly* 23(1-3), Summer 1974, 66-69.

Carl F. Strauch. "Hatred's Swift Repulsions: Emerson, Margaret Fuller, and Others," *Studies in Romanticism* 7(2), Winter 1968, 89-90.

"Ever the Rock of Ages melts"

Karl Keller. "From Christianity to Transcendentalism: A Note on Emerson's Use of the Conceit," *American Literature* 39(1), March 1967, 94-98.

"Experience"

William Sloane Kennedy. *Clews to Emerson's Mystic Verse.* Reprinted in *American Transcendental Quarterly* 29(3), Winter 1976, 10-11.

"Fable"

Gémino H. Abad. *A Formal Approach to Lyric Poetry,* pp. 130-31.

"Forbearance"

John Newell Sanborn. "Thoreau in Emerson's 'Forbearance,'" *Thoreau Journal Quarterly* 9(4), October 1977, 22-23.

Carl F. Strauch. "Emerson and the Doctrine of Sympathy," *Studies in Romanticism* 6(3), Spring 1967, 158-61.

"Forerunners"

Stanley Brodwin. "Emerson's Version of Plotinus: The Flight to Beauty," *Journal of the History of Ideas* 35(3), July-September 1974, 477.

"Friendship"

Franklin Benjamin Sanborn. *Lectures on Literature and Philosophy.* Reprinted in *American Transcendental Quarterly* 34(2), Spring 1977, 70.

"Give All to Love"

Harry Brown and John Milstead. *What the Poem Means,* pp. 83-84.

Michael H. Cowan. *Explicator* 18(8), May 1960, Item 49.

Michael H. Cowan. "The Loving Proteus: Metamorphosis in Emerson's Poetry," *American Transcendental Quarterly* 25(1), Winter 1975, 21.

David Daiches and William Charvat. *Poems in English,* p. 719.

Carl F. Strauch. "Hatred's Swift Repulsions: Emerson, Margaret Fuller, and Others," *Studies in Romanticism* 7(2), Winter 1968, 87-88.

"God is All"

William Sloane Kennedy. *Clews to Emerson's Mystic Verse.* Reprinted in *American Transcendental Quarterly* 29(3), Winter 1976, 12.

"Guy"

William Sloane Kennedy. *Clews to Emerson's Mystic Verse.* Reprinted in *American Transcendental Quarterly* 29(3), Winter 1976, 15.

Carl F. Strauch. "Emerson and the Doctrine of Sympathy," *Studies in Romanticism* 6(3), Spring 1967, 168-70.

"Hamatreya"

Albert Gelpi. *The Tenth Muse,* pp. 98-102.

Hohan Lal Sharma. *Explicator* 26(8), April 1968, Item 63.

Carl F. Strauch. "Emerson and the Doctrine of Sympathy," *Studies in Romanticism* 6(3), Spring 1967, 172-74.

Richard Tuerk. "Emerson's Darker Vision: 'Hamatreya' and 'Days,'" *American Transcendental Quarterly* 25(1&2), Winter 1975, 28-30.

"Hermione"

William Sloane Kennedy. *Clews to Emerson's Mystic Verse.* Reprinted in *American Transcendental Quarterly* 29(3), Winter 1976, 14.

Charles Malloy. *A Study of Emerson's Major Poems.* Reprinted in *American Transcendental Quarterly* 23(1-3), Summer 1974, 44-52.

EMERSON, RALPH WALDO *(Cont.)*

"Initial, Daemonic, and Celestial Love"

see also "Celestial Love," "Initial Love"

BERNARD DUFFEY. *Poetry in America,* pp. 46-47.

WILLIAM SLOANE KENNEDY. *Clews to Emerson's Mystic Verse.* Reprinted in *American Transcendental Quarterly* 29(3), Winter 1976, 3-6.

FRANKLIN BENJAMIN SANBORN. *Lectures on Literature and Philosophy.* Reprinted in *American Transcendental Quarterly* 34(1-2), Spring 1977, 71-73.

CARL F. STRAUCH. "Hatred's Swift Repulsions: Emerson, Margaret Fuller, and Others," *Studies in Romanticism* 7(2), Winter 1968, 81-87.

"Initial Love"

see also "Initial, Daemonic, and Celestial Love"

"The Initial Love"

CARL F. STRAUCH. "Emerson's Adaptation of Myth in 'The Initial Love,'" *American Transcendental Quarterly* 25(2), Winter 1975, 51-65.

"Letters"

GILBERT HIGHET. *The Powers of Poetry,* p. 102.

"Limits"

ALBERT GELPI. *The Tenth Muse,* pp. 102-4.

"May-Day"

MICHAEL H. COWAN. "The Loving Proteus: Metamorphosis in Emerson's Poetry," *American Transcendental Quarterly* 25(1), Winter 1975, 21-22.

"Merlin"

HAROLD BLOOM. "Bacchus and Merlin: The Dialectic of Romantic Poetry in America," *Southern Review,* n.s., 7(1), Winter 1970, 152-56.

HAROLD BLOOM. "Poetic Crossing, II: American Stances," *Georgia Review* 30(4), Winter 1976, 780-81.

WILLIAM SLOAN KENNEDY. *Clews to Emerson's Mystic Verse.* Reprinted in *American Transcendental Quarterly* 29(3), Winter 1976, 8-9.

CHARLES MALLOY. *A Study of Emerson's Major Poems.* Reprinted in *American Transcendental Quarterly* 23(1-3), Summer 1974, 96-103.

"Mithridates"

WILLIAM SLOANE KENNEDY. *Clews to Emerson's Mystic Verse.* Reprinted in *American Transcendental Quarterly* 29(3), Winter 1976, 13-14.

CHARLES MALLOY. *A Study of Emerson's Major Poems.* Reprinted in *American Transcendental Quarterly* 23(1-3), Summer 1974, 53-55.

CHARLES MALLOY. "What Bearing Upon Emerson's Poems Have Their Titles?" *American Transcendental Quarterly* 23(3), Summer 1974, 111-13.

JAMES E. MULQUEEN. "Emersonian Transcendentalism: Over-Soul or Over-Self?" *Tennessee Studies in Literature* 21(1976), 24.

"Monadnoc"

HAROLD BLOOM. "Bacchus and Merlin: The Dialectic of Romantic Poetry in America," *Southern Review,* n.s., 7(1), Winter 1970, 143-46.

CHARLES MALLOY. *A Study of Emerson's Major Poems.* Reprinted in *American Transcendental Quarterly* 23(1-3), Summer 1974, 80-96.

CARL F. STRAUCH. "Hatred's Swift Repulsions: Emerson, Margaret Fuller, and Others," *Studies in Romanticism* 7(2), Winter 1968, 76-78.

"The Nun's Aspiration"

WILLIAM SLOANE KENNEDY. *Clews to Emerson's Mystic Verse.* Reprinted in *American Transcendental Quarterly* 29(3), Winter 1976, 9.

"Ode, Inscribed to W. H. Channing"

GEORGE ARMS. "Emerson's 'Ode Inscribed to W. H. Channing,'" *College English* 22(6), March 1961, 407-9.

HARRY BROWN and JOHN MILSTEAD. *What the Poem Means,* p. 84.

"Ode to Beauty"

STANLEY BRODWIN. "Emerson's Version of Plotinus: The Flight to Beauty," *Journal of the History of Ideas* 35(3), July-September 1974, 475-77.

MICHAEL H. COWAN. "The Loving Proteus: Metamorphosis in Emerson's Poetry," *American Transcendental Quarterly* 25(1), Winter 1975, 20-21.

"Painting and Sculpture"

CARL F. STRAUCH. "Hatred's Swift Repulsions: Emerson, Margaret Fuller, and Others," *Studies in Romanticism* 7(2), Winter 1968, 80.

"The Park"

CARL F. STRAUCH. "Hatred's Swift Repulsions: Emerson, Margaret Fuller, and Others," *Studies in Romanticism* 7(2), Winter 1968, 91-92.

"The Poet"

CHARLES W. MIGNON. "Starsown Poet, Abstemious Muse," *American Transcendental Quarterly* 25(2), Winter 1975, 33-41.

"Power"

WILLIAM K. BOTTORFF. *Explicator* 31(6), February 1973, Item 45.

"The Problem"

CARL DENNIS. "Emerson's Poetics of Inspiration," *American Transcendental Quarterly* 25(1), Winter 1975, 25-26.

CHARLES MALLOY. *A Study of Emerson's Major Poems.* Reprinted in *American Transcendental Quarterly* 23(1-3), Summer 1974, 29-36.

CHARLES MALLOY. "What Bearing Upon Emerson's Poems Have Their Titles?" *American Transcendental Quarterly* 23(3), Summer 1974, 113-14.

"The Rhodora"

STEVEN G. AXELROD. "Teaching Emerson's 'The Rhodora,'" *CEA Critic* 36(4), May 1974, 34-35.

BERNARD DUFFEY. *Poetry in America,* pp. 14-15.

SEYMOUR L. GROSS. "Emerson and Poetry," *South Atlantic Quarterly* 54(1), January 1955, 91-93.

R. A. YODER. "Toward the 'Titmouse Dimension': The Development of Emerson's Poetic Style," *PMLA* 87(2), March 1972, 257.

"The River"

HAROLD BLOOM. "The Central Man: Emerson, Whitman, Wallace Stevens," *Massachusetts Review* 7(1), Winter 1966, 26-30.

"Rubies"

CHARLES MALLOY. *A Study of Emerson's Major Poems.* Reprinted in *American Transcendental Quarterly* 23(1-3), Summer 1974, 59-60.

"Saadi"

CHARLES MALLOY. *A Study of Emerson's Major Poems.* Reprinted in *American Transcendental Quarterly* 23(1-3), Summer 1974, 103-10.

"Seashore"

MICHAEL H. COWAN. "The Loving Proteus: Metamorphosis in Emerson's Poetry," *American Transcendental Quarterly* 25(1), Winter 1975, 19.

ROY HARVEY PEARCE. *The Continuity of American Poetry*, pp. 154-55.

"The Snow-Storm"

DAVID DAICHES and WILLIAM CHARVAT. *Poems in English*, pp. 719-20.

ALBERT GELPI. *The Tenth Muse*, pp. 96-98.

F. O. MATTHIESSEN. *American Renaissance*, pp. 138-39. Reprinted in: Norman C. Stageberg and Wallace L. Anderson. *Poetry as Experience*, pp. 485-86.

DAVID PORTER. " 'Threnody' and Emerson's Poetics of Failure," *ESQ* 22(1), First Quarter 1976, 6.

SISTER PAULA REITEN. *Explicator* 22(5), January 1964, Item 39.

HYATT H. WAGGONER. *American Poets*, p. 77.

"The Sphinx"

LAWRENCE BUELL. *Literary Transcendentalism*, pp. 182-83.

WILLIAM SLOANE KENNEDY. *Clews to Emerson's Mystic Verse*. Reprinted in *American Transcendental Quarterly* 29(3), Winter 1976, 7-8.

CHARLES MALLOY. *A Study of Emerson's Major Poems*. Reprinted in *American Transcendental Quarterly* 23(1-3), Summer 1974, 5-25.

JAMES B. REECE. "Emerson's 'The Sphinx' and the Perception of Identity," *ESQ* 24(1), First Quarter, 1978, 12-19.

DAVID ROBINSON. "The Romantic Quest in Poe and Emerson: 'Ulalume' and 'The Sphinx,' " *American Transcendental Quarterly* 26 (Suppl.), Spring 1975, 26-30.

E. J. ROSE. "Melville, Emerson, and the Sphinx," *New England Quarterly* 36(2), June 1963, 249-58.

CARL F. STRAUCH. "Emerson and the Doctrine of Sympathy," *Studies in Romanticism* 6(3), Spring 1967, 154-56.

CHARLES CHILD WALCUTT. *Explicator* 31(3), November 1972, Item 20.

DAVID H. WATTERS. "Emerson, Dickinson, and the Atomic Self," *Emily Dickinson Bulletin* 32 (Second half, 1977), 124-25.

THOMAS R. WHITAKER. "The Riddle of Emerson's 'Sphinx,' " *American Literature* 27(2), May 1955, 179-95.

"Terminus"

AUGUST H. MASON. *Explicator* 4(5), March 1946, Item 37.

"Threnody"

WALTER BLAIR and CLARENCE FAUST. "Emerson's Literary Method," *Modern Philology* 42(2), November 1944, 91-95.

MICHAEL H. COWAN. "The Loving Proteus: Metamorphosis in Emerson's Poetry," *American Transcendental Quarterly* 25(1), Winter 1975, 14-15.

BERNARD DUFFEY. *Poetry in America*, pp. 25-27.

RICHARD LEE FRANCIS. "Archangel in the Pleached Garden: Emerson's Poetry," *ELH* 33(4), December 1966, 464-66.

DAVID PORTER. " 'Threnody' and Emerson's Poetics of Failure," *ESQ* 22(1), First Quarter 1976, 1-13.

MARY EDRICH REDDING. "Emerson's 'Instant Eternity': A Existential Approach," *American Transcendental Quarterly* 9(2), Winter 1971, 49.

"The Titmouse"

DAVID PORTER. " 'Threnody' and Emerson's Poetics of Failure," *ESQ* 22(1), First Quarter 1976, 6-7.

HYATT H. WAGGONER. *American Poets*, pp. 296-300.

"To Rhea"

WILLIAM SLOANE KENNEDY. *Clews to Emerson's Mystic Verse*. Reprinted in *American Transcendental Quarterly* 29(3), Winter 1976, 17-18.

DAVID PORTER. " 'Threnody' and Emerson's Poetics of Failure," *ESQ* 22(1), First Quarter 1976, 5-6.

"Two Rivers"

RICHARD LEE FRANCIS. "Archangel in the Pleached Garden: Emerson's Poetry," *ELH* 33(4), December 1966, 471-72.

"Uriel"

RICHARD LEE FRANCIS. "Archangel in the Pleached Garden: Emerson's Poetry," *ELH* 33(4), December 1966, 466-68.

ALBERT GELPI. *The Tenth Muse*, pp. 71-72.

E. T. HELMICK. "Emerson's 'Uriel' as Poetic Theory," *American Transcendental Quarterly* 1(1), First Quarter 1969, 35-38.

WILLIAM SLOANE KENNEDY. *Clews to Emerson's Mystic Verse*. Reprinted in *American Transcendental Quarterly* 29(3), Winter 1976, 18.

CHARLES MALLOY. *A Study of Emerson's Major Poems*. Reprinted in *American Transcendental Quarterly* 23(1-3), Summer 1974, 36-39.

HUGH H. WITEMAYER. " 'Line' and 'Round' in Emerson's 'Uriel,' " *PMLA* 82(1), March 1967, 98-103.

"The Visit"

CHARLES MALLOY. "What Bearing Upon Emerson's Poems Have Their Titles?" *American Transcendental Quarterly* 23(3), Summer 1974, 114.

CARL F. STRAUCH. "Hatred's Swift Repulsions: Emerson, Margaret Fuller, and Others," *Studies in Romanticism* 7(2), Winter 1968, 93-94.

"Wealth"

MICHAEL H. COWAN. "The Loving Proteus: Metamorphosis in Emerson's Poetry," *American Transcendental Quarterly* 25(1), Winter 1975, 17-18.

WILLIAM SLOANE KENNEDY. *Clews to Emerson's Mystic Verse*. Reprinted in *American Transcendental Quarterly* 29(3), Winter 1976, 11-12.

"Woodnotes I"

CARL F. STRAUCH. "Emerson and the Doctrine of Sympathy," *Studies in Romanticism* 6(3), Spring 1967, 161-67.

"Woodnotes II"

JOHN Q. ANDERSON. "Emerson's 'Eternal Pan' — The Re-Creation of a Myth," *American Transcendental Quarterly* 25(1), Winter 1975, 4-5.

"Xenophanes"

WILLIAM SLOANE KENNEDY. *Clews to Emerson's Mystic Verse*. Reprinted in *American Transcendental Quarterly* 29(3), Winter 1976, 15-16.

EMPSON, WILLIAM

"The Ants"

GEOFFREY THURLEY. *The Ironic Harvest*, pp. 41-42.

JOHN WAIN. *Professing Poetry*, pp. 284-90.

"Arachne"

JOHN WAIN. *Professing Poetry*, pp. 296-98.

EMPSON, WILLIAM *(Cont.)*

"Aubade"

"William Empson in Conversation with Christopher Ricks," in *The Modern Poet*, edited by Ian Hamilton, pp. 181-82.

JOHN WAIN. *Professing Poetry*, pp. 315-16.

"Autumn on Nan-yueh"

WILLIAM EMPSON. *The Gathering Storm*, pp. 70-71.

"Bacchus"

WILLIAM EMPSON. *The Gathering Storm*, pp. 56-62.

"The Beautiful Train"

HARTMUT BREITKREUZ. *Explicator* 31(2), October 1972, Item 9.

WILLIAM EMPSON. *The Gathering Storm*, p. 66.

"Camping Out"

GEOFFREY THURLEY. *The Ironic Harvest*, pp. 47-48.

"China"

WILLIAM EMPSON. *The Gathering Storm*, pp. 67-70.

"Four Legs, Two Legs, Three Legs"

WILLIAM EMPSON. *The Gathering Storm*, pp. 63-64. Reprinted in: Kimon Friar and John Malcolm Brinnin. *Modern Poetry*, p. 499.

"High Dive"

GEOFFREY THURLEY. *The Ironic Harvest*, pp. 43-44.

"Invitation and Juno"

DAVID ORMEROD. *Explicator* 25(2), October 1966, Item 13.

"Just a smack at Auden"

GEOFFREY THURLEY. *The Ironic Harvest*, p. 56.

"Let It Go"

COLIN FALCK. "William Empson," in *The Modern Poet*, edited by Ian Hamilton, pp. 61-62.

" 'Not Wrongly Moved . . .,' " *Times Literary Supplement*, 7 October 1955, p. 588. Reprinted in: G. S. Fraser. *Vision and Rhetoric*, pp. 193-95. Also: George Fraser. *Essays on Twentieth-Century Poets*, pp. 162-63.

"William Empson in Conversation with Christopher Ricks," in *The Modern Poet*, edited by Ian Hamilton, p. 183.

"Missing Dates"

ELIZABETH DREW. *Poetry*, pp. 138-41.

KIMON FRIAR and JOHN MALCOLM BRINNIN. *Modern Poetry*, pp. 498-99. (Quoting William Empson)

ROBERT DONALD SPECTOR. "Form and Content in Empson's 'Missing Dates,' " *Modern Language Notes* 74(4), April 1959, 310-11.

GEOFFREY THURLEY. *The Ironic Harvest*, pp. 52-53.

"Note on Local Flora"

ELIZABETH DREW and JOHN L. SWEENEY. *Directions in Modern Poetry*, pp. 81-83. (Quoting William Empson)

JOHN WAIN. *Professing Poetry*, pp. 298-99.

"Plenum and Vacuum"

IAN HAMILTON. "William Empson," in *A Poetry Chronicle*, pp. 38-40.

"Reflection from Anita Loos"

WILLIAM EMPSON. *The Gathering Storm*, pp. 66-67.

"Reflection from Rochester"

WILLIAM EMPSON. *The Gathering Storm*, pp. 64-65.

"Rolling the Lawn"

GEOFFREY THURLEY. *The Ironic Harvest*, p. 42.

"Sleeping out in the College Cloister"

GEOFFREY THURLEY. *The Ironic Harvest*, pp. 44-47.

"Success"

JOHN WAIN. *Professing Poetry*, pp. 312-14.

"The Teasers"

G. S. FRASER. *Interpretations*, John Wain, ed., pp. 225-34.

"William Empson in Conversation with Christopher Ricks," in *The Modern Poet*, edited by Ian Hamilton, pp. 179-80.

"This Last Pain"

RICHARD EBERHART. "Empson's Poetry," *Accent* 4(4), Summer 1944, 203-6.

"To an Old Lady"

GEOFFREY THURLEY. *The Ironic Harvest*, pp. 39-40.

"Value Is in Activity"

JOHN WAIN. *Professing Poetry*, pp. 294-96.

"Your Teeth Are Ivory Towers"

WILLIAM EMPSON. *The Gathering Storm*, pp. 62-63.

ETHEREGE, GEORGE

"To a Lady Asking Him How Long He Would Love Her"

RACHEL TRICKETT. "Samuel Butler and the Minor Restoration Poets," in *English Poetry and Prose*, ed. by Christopher Ricks, p. 331.

EVANS, DONALD

"En Monocle"

KENNETH FIELDS. "Past Masters: Walter Conrad Arensberg and Donald Evans," *Southern Review*, n.s., 6(2), Spring 1970, 336-37.

EVANS, MARI

"Vive Noir!"

ROBERT P. SEDLACK. "Mari Evans: Consciousness and Craft," *CLA Journal* 15(4), June 1972, 465-75.

EVERSON, WILLIAM

"Canticle to the Water Birds"

PAUL A. LACEY. *The Inner War*, p. 94.

"Chronicle of Division"

RALPH J. MILLS, JR. *Contemporary American Poetry*, p. 90.

"The Flight in the Desert"

RALPH J. MILLS, JR. *Contemporary American Poetry*, pp. 95-97.

"A Frost Lay White on California"

PAUL A. LACEY. *The Inner War*, pp. 102-3.

"Gethsemani"

PAUL A. LACEY. *The Inner War*, pp. 92-93.

"God Germed in Raw Granite"

PAUL A. LACEY. *The Inner War*, p. 104.

"In All These Acts"

PAUL A. LACEY. *The Inner War*, pp. 103-4.

"Invocation"

PAUL A. LACEY. *The Inner War*, p. 85.

"Jacob and the Angel"

PAUL A. LACEY. *The Inner War*, pp. 99-101.

"The Roots"
> Ralph J. Mills, Jr. *Contemporary American Poetry,* pp. 88-89.

"A Savagery of Love"
> Paul A. Lacey. *The Inner War,* p. 95.

"The Sides of a Mind"
> Paul A. Lacey. *The Inner War,* pp. 84-85.

"The Uncouth"
> Paul A. Lacey. *The Inner War,* pp. 88-90.

EWING, SAMUEL

"American Miracle"
> Irving N. Rothman. "Structure and Theme in Samuel Ewing's Satire, the 'American Miracle,'" *American Literature* 40(3), November 1968, 294-308.

F

FANSHAWE, RICHARD

"An Ode, upon his Majesties Proclamation in the Year 1630"
GEOFFREY WALTON. "The Tone of Ben Jonson's Poetry," in *Seventeenth Century English Poetry*, pp. 206-7; revised ed., pp. 165-66.

FAULKNER, WILLIAM

"The Lilacs"
MARGARET YONCE. " 'Shot Down Last Spring': The Wounded Aviators of Faulkner's Wasteland," *Mississippi Quarterly* 31(3), Summer 1978, 359-68.

"My health? My health's a fevered loud distress"
CLEANTH BROOKS. "The Image of Helen Baird in Faulkner's Early Poetry and Fiction," *Sewanee Review* 85(2), Spring 1977, 221-22.

"Proposal"
CLEANTH BROOKS. "The Image of Helen Baird in Faulkner's Early Poetry and Fiction," *Sewanee Review* 85(2), Spring 1977, 221.

"Spring"
MARY JANE DICKERSON. "Faulkner's Golden Steed," *Mississippi Quarterly* 31(3), Summer 1978, 370-71.

FAWCETT, JOSEPH

"Advertisement by the Editor"
EDMUND G. MILLER. "Hazlitt and Fawcett," *Wordsworth Circle* 8(4), Autumn 1977, 379-80.

FEARING, KENNETH

"Ad"
CHAD WALSH. *Doors into Poetry,* p. 26.

"Green Light"
MACHA ROSENTHAL. "The Meaning of Kenneth Fearing's Poetry," *Poetry* 64(4), July 1944, 211-12.
M. L. ROSENTHAL. *The Modern Poets,* pp. 237-38.

"Hold the Wire"
JOSEPH WARREN BEACH. *Obsessive Images,* pp. 245-46.

"Homage"
HARRY BROWN and JOHN MILSTEAD. *What the Poem Means,* pp. 84-85.

"Obituary"
MACHA ROSENTHAL. "The Meaning of Kenneth Fearing's Poetry," *Poetry* 64(4), July 1944, 214.

"Portrait"
JAMES M. REID. *100 American Poems of the Twentieth Century,* pp. 184-86.

"Radio Blues"
MACHA ROSENTHAL. "The Meaning of Kenneth Fearing's Poetry," *Poetry* 64(4), July 1944, 220.

"What if Mr. Jesse James Should Someday Die?"
MACHA ROSENTHAL. "The Meaning of Kenneth Fearing's Poetry," *Poetry* 64(4), July 1944, 214-15.

"Yes, the Serial Will be Continued"
WALTER GIERASCH. "Reading Modern Poetry," *College English* 2(1), October 1940, 34-35.

FEINMAN, ALVIN

"Circumferences"
HAROLD BLOOM. "Bacchus and Merlin: The Dialectic of Romantic Poetry in America," *Southern Review,* n.s., 7(1), Winter 1970, 174-75.

"November Sunday Morning"
HAROLD BLOOM. "Bacchus and Merlin: The Dialectic of Romantic Poetry in America," *Southern Review,* n.s., 7(1), Winter 1970, 166-67.

"Pilgrim Heights"
HAROLD BLOOM. "Bacchus and Merlin: The Dialectic of Romantic Poetry in America," *Southern Review,* n.s., 7(1), Winter 1970, 170-71.

FELDMAN, IRVING

"My Olson Elegy"
ROBERT BOYERS. "Promise and Faithfulness: The Poems of Irving Feldman," *Modern Poetry Studies* 4(3), Winter 1973, 273.

"Our Leaders"
ROBERT BOYERS. "Promise and Faithfulness: The Poems of Irving Feldman," *Modern Poetry Studies* 4(3), Winter 1973, 275-78.

"X"
ROBERT BOYERS. "Promise and Faithfulness: The Poems of Irving Feldman," *Modern Poetry Studies* 4(3), Winter 1973, 279-80.

FERGUSSON, ROBERT

"Auld Reikie"
DAVID DAICHES. "Eighteenth-Century Vernacular Poetry," in *Scottish Poetry: A Critical Survey,* pp. 183-84.

ALLAN H. MACLAINE. "Robert Fergusson's *Auld Reikie* and the Poetry of City Life," *Studies in Scottish Literature* 1(2), October 1963, 99-110.

"The Daft Days"

DAVID DAICHES. "Eighteenth-Century Vernacular Poetry," in *Scottish Poetry: A Critical Survey*, pp. 172-73.

"The Farmer's Ingle"

DAVID DAICHES. "Eighteenth-Century Vernacular Poetry," in *Scottish Poetry: A Critical Survey*, pp. 180-81.

"Hallow-fair"

ALLAN H. MACLAINE. "The *Christis Kirk* Tradition: Its Evolution in Scots Poetry To Burns," *Studies in Scottish Literature* 2(3), January 1965, 172-77.

"The King's Birthday in Edinburgh"

DAVID DAICHES. "Eighteenth-Century Vernacular Poetry," in *Scottish Poetry: A Critical Survey*, pp. 175-76.

"Leith Races"

ALLAN H. MACLAINE. "The *Christis Kirk* Tradition: Its Evolution in Scots Poetry To Burns," *Studies in Scottish Literature* 2(3), January 1965, 177-80.

FERLINGHETTI, LAWRENCE

"Constantly risking absurdity" (*Coney Island of the Mind*, 15)

JAMES A. BUTLER. "Ferlinghetti: Dirty Old Man?" *Renascence* 18(3), Spring 1966, 119-21.

R. P. DICKEY. "The New Genteel Tradition in American Poetry," *Sewanee Review* 82(4), Fall 1974, 735-36.

BROTHER EDWARD KENT. "Daredevil Poetics: Ferlinghetti's Definition of a Poet," *English Journal* 59(9), December 1970, 1243-44.

"Hidden Door"

L. A. IANNI. "Lawrence Ferlinghetti's Fourth Person Singular and the Theory of Relativity," *Wisconsin Studies in Contemporary Literature* 8(3), Summer 1967, 397-98.

"In Goya's greatest scenes we seem to see the people of the world"

JAMES G. KENNEDY. "The Two European Cultures and the Necessary New Sense of Literature," *College English* 31(6), March 1970, 584-85.

"One Thousand Fearful Words For Fidel Castro"

SAMUEL CHARTERS. *Some Poems/Poets*, pp. 77-83.

"Sarolla's women in their picture hats"

JOHN CLARK PRATT. *The Meaning of Modern Poetry*, pp. 329, 316, 324, 326, 328-29, 337, 330-31, 350-51, 340-41.

FERRIL, THOMAS HORNSBY

"Nothing Is Long Ago"

JAY GURIAN. "The possibility of a Western poetics," *Colorado Quarterly* 15(1), Summer 1966, 80-81.

FERRY, DAVID

"My Parents en Route"

NORMAN FRIEDMAN. "The Wesleyan Poets — I," *Chicago Review* 18(3-4), 1966, 70.

"On the Way to the Island"

NORMAN FRIEDMAN. "The Wesleyan Poets — I," *Chicago Review* 18(3-4), 1966, 69-70.

"The Soldier"

ROBERT PINSKY. *The Situation of Poetry*, pp. 172-74.

FIELD, EDWARD

"The Life of Joan Crawford"

CHARLES STETLER and GERALD LOCKLIN. "Edward Field, Stand-Up Poet," *Minnesota Review* 9(1), 1969, 66-67.

"Tailspin"

CHARLES STETLER and GERALD LOCKLIN. "Edward Field, Stand-Up Poet," *Minnesota Review* 9(1), 1969, 69.

"What happened to May Caspar?"

CHARLES STETLER and GERALD LOCKLIN. "Edward Field, Stand-Up Poet," *Minnesota Review* 9(1), 1969, 67.

"White Jungle Queen"

CHARLES STETLER and GERALD LOCKLIN. "Edward Field, Stand-Up Poet," *Minnesota Review* 9(1), 1969, 67-68.

FIELDING, HENRY

"The Masquerade"

L. P. GOGGIN. "Fielding's 'The Masquerade,' " *Philological Quarterly* 36(4), October 1957, 475-87.

J. OATES SMITH. "Masquerade and Marriage: Fielding's Comedies of Identity," *Ball State University Forum* 6(3), Autumn 1965, 10-11.

FIELDS, JAMES T.

"The Captain's Daughter"

EARL DANIELS. *The Art of Reading Poetry*, pp. 85-88.

"The Owl Critic"

LOUIS D. RUBIN, JR. " 'The Barber Kept on Shaving': The Two Perspectives of American Humor," *Sewanee Review* 81(4), Autumn 1973, 693-94.

FINKEL, DONALD

"Hunting Song"

RICHARD HOWARD. "Donald Finkel: 'There Is No Perfection Possible. But There is Tomorrow,' " *Perspective* 16(1), Winter-Spring 1969, 6-7.

"Simeon"

RICHARD HOWARD. "Donald Finkel: 'There Is No Perfection Possible. But There is Tomorrow,' " *Perspective* 16(1), Winter-Spring 1969, 8-9.

FINLAY, IAN HAMILTON

"Redboat/bedboat"

ALICIA OSTRIKER. "Poem Objects," *Partisan Review* 40(1), Winter 1973, 103-4.

FISKE, JOHN

"In Fanne: Rig"

JAMES BRAY. "John Fiske: Puritan Precursor of Edward Taylor," *Early American Literature* 9(1), Spring 1974, 31-32. (P)

"Upon the much-to-be lamented desease of the Reverend Mr. John Cotton late Teacher to the Church at Boston, N.E. who departed this Life 23 of 10.52"

ASTRIC SCHMITT-V. MÜHLENFELS. "John Fiske's Funeral Elegy on John Cotton," *Early American Literature* 12(1), Spring 1977, 49-62.

FITZGERALD, EDWARD

"The Rubáiyát of Omar Khayyám"

C. M. Bowra. "Edward Fitzgerald," in *In General and Particular*, pp. 173-91. Reprinted in: *Master Poems of the English Language*, pp. 625-40.

William Cadbury. "Fitzgerald's *Rubáiyát* as a Poem," *ELH* 34(4), December 1967, 541-63.

David Sonstroem. "Abandon the Day: Fitzgerald's *Rubáiyát of Omar Khayyám*," *Victorian Newsletter* 36 (Fall 1969), 10-13.

FLETCHER, PHINEAS

"Elisa"

Joan Grundy. *The Spenserian Poets*, pp. 191-92.

FLINT, F. S.

"Chrysanthemums"

L. S. Dembo. *Conceptions of Reality in Modern American Poetry*, p. 22.

"Otherworld"

Norman T. Gates. "Richard Aldington and F. S. Flint: Poets' Dialogue," *Papers on Language and Literature* 8(1), Winter 1972, 66-68. (P)

"Soldiers"

Norman T. Gates. "Richard Aldington and F. S. Flint: Poets' Dialogue," *Papers on Language and Literature* 8(1), Winter 1972, 65-66.

FORDE, THOMAS

"Lusus Fortunae"

George Williamson. "Mutability, Decay and Jacobean Melancholy," in *Seventeenth Century Contexts*, pp. 36-38.

FRANCIS, ROBERT

"Pitcher"

Stephen Dunning and Robert Francis. "Poetry as (Disciplined) Play," *English Journal* 52(8), November 1963, 607-9.

"Two Wrestlers"

Norman Friedman. "The Wesleyan Poets — IV," *Chicago Review* 19(3), June 1967, 69-70.

FRANKENBERG, LLOYD

"I Lazarus"

Nelson Algren. "Lloyd Frankenberg's Poems," *Poetry* 66(1), April 1940, 47-48.

FRASER, G. S.

"Instead of an Elegy"

G. Wilson Knight. *Neglected Powers*, p. 78.

FREEMAN, JOHN

"The Pigeons"

" 'Georgian Poetry', Unsigned Review, 'The Times Literary Supplement,' " in *Georgian Poetry*, p. 210.

FRENEAU, PHILIP

"The American Village"

William L. Andrews. "Goldsmith and Freneau in 'The American Village,' " *Early American Literature* 5(2), Fall 1970, 14-23.

"The Beauties of Santa Cruz"

Edwin H. Cady. "Philip Freneau as Archetypal American Poet," in *Literature and Ideas in America*, pp. 15-18.

Jane Donahue Eberwain. "Freneau's 'The Beauties of Santa Cruz,' " *Early American Literature* 12(3), Winter 1977/78, 271-76.

"The House of Night"

Edwin H. Cady. "Philip Freneau as Archetypal American Poet," in *Literature and Ideas in America*, pp. 12-14.

Lewis Leary. "The Dream Visions of Philip Freneau," *Early American Literature* 11(2), Fall 1976, 160-66.

Lewis Leary. "Literature in New York, 1775," *Early American Literature* 11(1), Spring 1976, 16.

"The Indian Burying Ground"

George Arms. *Explicator* 2(7), May 1944, Item 55.

Martin E. Itzkowitz. "Freneau's 'Indian Burying Ground' and Keats' 'Grecian Urn,' " *Early American Literature* 6(3), Winter 1971-72, 258-62.

George R. Wasserman. *Explicator* 20(5), January 1962, Item 43.

"On the Uniformity and Perfection of Nature"

Roy Harvey Pearce. *The Continuity of American Poetry*, pp. 201-2.

"The Pictures of Columbus"

Carol A. Kyle. "That Poet Freneau: A Study of the Imagistic Success of *The Pictures of Columbus*," *Early American Literature* 9(1), Spring 1974, 62-70.

"A Political Litany"

William L. Andrews. "Freneau's 'A Political Litany': A Note on Interpretation," *Early American Literature* 12(2), Fall 1977, 193-96.

"The Wild Honey Suckle"

Robert D. Arner. "Neoclassicism and Romanticism: A Reading of Freneau's 'The Wild Honey Suckle,' " *Early American Literature* 9(1), Spring 1974, 53-61.

FRIEBERT, STUART

"The Apron"

Alberta T. Turner. "The Smaller Camels and the Needle's Eye: Poet and Magazine Editor in 1976," *College English* 38(6), February 1977, 595-97.

FROST, FRANCES

"Cradle Song"

John Ciardi. "Sensitivity Without Discipline," *Nation* 179(23), 4 December 1954, 490-92.

FROST, ROBERT

"Accidentally on Purpose"

Claude M. Simpson. "Robert Frost and Man's 'Royal Role,' " in *Aspects of American Poetry* pp. 135-36.

Robert B. Thompson. *Explicator* 36(2), Winter 1978, 17.

"Acquainted with the Night"

Charles R. Anderson. "Robert Frost: 1874-1963," *Saturday Review* 46(8), 23 February 1963, 18.

Malcolm Brown. "The Sweet Crystalline Cry," *Western Review* 16(4), Summer 1952, 266.

Denis Donoghue. *Connoisseurs of Chaos*, pp. 174-75.

Joseph H. Friend. "Teaching the 'Grammar of Poetry,' " *College English* 27(5), February 1966, 363-64.

Nat Henry. *Explicator* 35(3), Spring 1977, 28-29.

Laurence Perrine. *Explicator* 37(1), Fall 1978, 13-14.

"After Apple-Picking"

James Bruce Anderson. "Frost and Sandburg: A Theological Criticism," *Renascence* 19(4), Summer 1967, 175-76.

Walton Beacham. *The Meaning of Poetry*, pp. 115-17.

Cleanth Brooks. *Modern Poetry and the Tradition*, pp. 114-16.

Cleanth Brooks and Robert Penn Warren. *Understanding Poetry*, revised ed., pp. 389-97; third ed., pp. 363-69.

Reginald L. Cook. "Frost as a Parablist," *Accent* 10(1), Autumn 1949, 36.

Peter W. Dowell. "Counter-Images and Their Function in the Poetry of Robert Frost," *Tennessee Studies in Literature* 14 (1969), 18-20.

Joe M. Ferguson, Jr. *Explicator* 22(7), March 1964, Item 53.

Robert Langbaum. "The New Nature Poetry,," in *The Modern Spirit*, pp. 106-7.

Josephine Miles. "Reading Poems," *English Journal* 52(3), March 1963, 157-58.

George Monteiro. *Explicator* 30(7), March 1972, Item 62.

Kenneth T. Reed. "Longfellow's 'Sleep' and Frost's 'After Apple-Picking,'" *American Notes & Queries*, n.s., 10(9), May 1972, 134-35.

Doug Schroeder. "Robert Frost's Use of Symbol in 'After Apple-Picking'," in Walton Beacham, *The Meaning of Poetry*, pp. 70-71.

William Bysshe Stein. "'After Apple-Picking': Echoic Parody," *University Review* 34(4), Summer 1969, 301-5.

Floyd C. Watkins. "Going and Coming Back: Robert Frost's Religious Poetry," *South Atlantic Quarterly* 73(4), Autumn 1974, 448-49.

"Afterflakes"

Darrel Abel. "Emerson's 'Apparition of God' and Frost's 'Apparition of the Mind,'" *University of Toronto Quarterly* 48(1), Fall 1978, 46.

"All Revelation"

Darrel Abel. "Emerson's 'Apparition of God' and Frost's 'Apparition of the Mind,'" *University of Toronto Quarterly* 48(1), Fall 1978, 43-45.

Theodore Morrison. "Frost: Country Poet and Cosmopolitan Poet," *Yale Review* 59(2), December 1969, 193-96.

Lawrance Thompson. "Robert Frost," in *Seven Modern American Poets*, pp. 26-29.

Harold E. Toliver. *Pastoral Forms and Attitudes*, p. 337.

"America Is Hard to See"

John Ciardi. "Robert Frost: American Bard," *Saturday Review* 45(12), 12 March 1962, 53.

"And All We Call American"

Claude M. Simpson. "Robert Frost and Man's 'Royal Role,'" in *Aspects of American Poetry* pp. 126-28.

"The Armful"

Carl Lindner. "Robert Frost: 'In the American Grain,'" *Colorado Quarterly* 22(4), Spring 1974, 477-78.

"At Woodward's Garden"

Bob Dowell. "Revealing Incident as Technique in the Poetry of Robert Frost," *CEA Critic* 31(3), December 1968, 12.

"Atmosphere"

Darrel Abel. "Emerson's 'Apparition of God' and Frost's 'Apparition of the Mind,'" *University of Toronto Quarterly* 48(1), Fall 1978, 47.

"Auspex"

Jan B. Gordon. "Robert Frost's Circle of Enchantment," in *Modern American Poetry* edited by Jerome Mazzaro, pp. 87-88.

"Away"

Richard Eberhart. "Robert Frost in the Clearing," *Southern Review*, n.s., 11(2), Spring 1975, 264-66.

"The Axe-Helve"

Charles R. Anderson. "Robert Frost, 1874-1963," *Saturday Review* 46(8), 23 February 1963, 20.

Arthur C. McGill. *The Celebration of Flesh*, pp. 109-10.

George Monteiro. "Redemption Through Nature: A Recurring Theme in Thoreau, Frost and Richard Wilbur," *American Quarterly* 20(4), Winter 1968, 796-804.

James R. Vitelli. "Robert Frost: The Contrarieties of Talent and Tradition," *New England Quarterly* 47(3), September 1974, 363-65.

"The Bear"

Hyatt H. Waggoner. *American Poets*, pp. 309-11.

Harold H. Watts. "Robert Frost and the Interrupted Dialogue," *American Literature* 27(1), March 1955, 76-77.

Yvor Winters. *The Function of Criticism*, pp. 166-67.

"Beech"

Harold E. Toliver. *Pastoral Forms and Attitudes*, pp. 338-40.

"Bereft"

Clark Griffith. "Frost and the American View of Nature," *American Quarterly* 20(1), Spring 1968, 32-33.

"Birches"

Harry Berger, Jr. "Poetry as Revision: Interpreting Robert Frost," *Criticism* 10(1), Winter 1968, 18-22.

Harry Brown and John Milstead. *What the Poem Means*, pp. 89-90.

Jeffrey Hart. "Frost and Eliot," *Sewanee Review* 84(3), Summer 1976, 435-37.

Lewis H. Miller, Jr. "The Poet as Swinger: Fact and Fancy in Robert Frost," *Criticism* 16(1), Winter 1974, 59-64.

George Monteiro. "Birches in Winter: Notes on Thoreau and Frost," *CLA Journal* 12(2), December 1968, 129-33.

James M. Reid. *100 American Poems of the Twentieth Century*, pp. 33-36.

Ruthe T. Sheffey. "From Delight to Wisdom: Thematic Progression in the Poetry of Robert Frost," *CLA Journal* 8(1), September 1964, 53-54.

Richard Wilbur. "Poetry and Happiness," in his *Responses*, pp. 110-14.

"The Birthplace"

Peter W. Dowell. "Counter-Images and Their Function in the Poetry of Robert Frost," *Tennessee Studies in Literature* 14 (1969), 17-18.

"The Black Cottage"

Malcolm Cowley. *A Many-Windowed House*, pp. 206-7.

FROST, ROBERT *(Cont.)*

"The Black Cottage" *(cont.)*

    C. C. CUNNINGHAM. *Literature as a Fine Art,* pp. 152-53.

    PETER W. DOWELL. "Counter-Images and Their Function in the Poetry of Robert Frost," *Tennessee Studies in Literature* 14 (1969), 27-28.

    WILLIAM H. PRITCHARD. "*North of Boston*: Frost's Poetry of Dialogue," in *In Defense of Reading,* pp. 49-51.

"Bond and Free"

    MORDECAI MARCUS. "Robert Frost's 'Bond and Free': Structure and Meaning," *Concerning Poetry* 8(1), Spring 1975, 61-64.

"A Boundless Moment"

    DARREL ABEL. "Emerson's 'Apparition of God' and Frost's 'Apparition of the Mind,'" *University of Toronto Quarterly* 48(1), Fall 1978, 50.

    NINA BAYM. "An Approach to Robert Frost's Nature Poetry," *American Quarterly* 17(4), Winter 1965, 716-17.

    HAROLD E. TOLIVER. *Pastoral Forms and Attitudes,* pp. 353-54.

"A Brook in the City"

    HAROLD E. TOLIVER. *Pastoral Forms and Attitudes,* p. 342.

    ARNOLD WHITRIDGE. "Robert Frost and Carl Sandburg: The Two Elder Statesmen of American Poetry," *New York Public Library Bulletin* 66(3), March 1962, 167.

"Brown's Descent"

    WALTER GIERASCH. *Explicator* 11(8), June 1953, Item 60.

"Build Soil"

    NINA BAYM. "An Approach to Robert Frost's Nature Poetry," *American Quarterly* 17(4), Winter 1965, 715.

"A Cabin in the Clearing"

    JOHN CIARDI. "Robert Frost: American Bard," *Saturday Review* 45(12), 12 March 1962, 53. Reprinted in: John Ciardi. *Dialogue with an Audience,* pp. 193-94.

    CLAUDE M. SIMPSON. "Robert Frost and Man's 'Royal Role,'" in *Aspects of American Poetry,* pp. 122-23.

"Canis Major"

    HYATT H. WAGGONER. *American Poets,* pp. 304-5.

"Carpe Diem"

    KEITH D. G. JOHNSON. "'Gather ye rosebuds . . .?'" *English Journal* 54(2), February 1965, 136-37.

"The Census-Taker"

    JEFFREY HART. "Frost and Eliot," *Sewanee Review* 84(3), Summer 1976, 428-29.

    GLEN A. LOVE. "Frost's 'The Census-Taker' and de la Mare's 'The Listeners,'" *Papers on Language and Literature* 4(2), Spring 1968, 198-200.

"The Cocoon"

    RICHARD POIRIER. "Soundings for Home: Frost's Poetry of Extravagance and Return," *Georgia Review* 31(2), Summer 1977, 299-300.

"Come In"

    CLEANTH BROOKS, JOHN THIBAUT PURSER, and ROBERT PENN WARREN. *An Approach to Literature,* fourth ed., pp. 425-26; fifth ed., p. 490.

    BABETTE DEUTSCH. *Poetry in Our Time,* pp. 75-76; second ed., pp. 82-83.

THOMAS W. FORD. "Invitation from a Thrush: Frost Versus Whitman," *Walt Whitman Review* 22(4), December 1976, 166-67.

JAMES G. HEPBURN. "Robert Frost and His Critics," *New England Quarterly* 35(3), September 1962, 369-71.

ROBERT KERN. "Toward a New Nature Poetry," *Centennial Review* 19(3), Summer 1975, 208-10.

ROBERT ORNSTEIN. *Explicator* 15(9), June 1957, Item 61.

"A Concept Self-Conceived"

    JOSEPH KAU. *Explicator* 35(3), Spring 1977, 19.

"A Considerable Speech"

    BABETTE DEUTSCH. *Poetry in Our Time,* pp. 72-73; second ed., pp. 77-78.

"The Cow in Apple Time"

    ARTHUR C. MCGILL. *The Celebration of Flesh,* pp. 103-4.

"The Death of the Hired Man"

    GÉMINO H. ABAD. *A Formal Approach to Lyric Poetry,* pp. 379-80.

    JAMES K. BOWEN. "Propositional and Emotional Knowledge in Robert Frost's 'The Death of the Hired Man,' 'The Fear,' and 'Home Burial,'" *CLA Journal* 12(2), December 1968, 155-57.

    C. M. BOWRA. "Reassessments I: Robert Frost," *Adelphi* 27 (November 1950), 54-55.

    C. C. CUNNINGHAM. *Literature as a Fine Art: Analysis and Interpretation,* pp. 106-10.

    BESS COOPER HOPKINS. "A Study of 'The Death of the Hired Man,'" *English Journal* 43(4), April 1954, 175-76.

    JULIAN MASON. "Frost's Conscious Accommodation of Contraries," *CEA Critic* 38(3), March 1976, 28.

    LAURENCE PERRINE. *100 American Poems of the Twentieth Century,* pp. 26-33.

    WILLIAM H. PRITCHARD. "*North of Boston*: Frost's Poetry of Dialogue," in *In Defense of Reading,* pp. 51-55.

    ANDREI SINYAVSKY. "On Robert Frost's Poems," tr. by Laszlo Tikos and Frederick C. Ellert, *Massachusetts Review* 7(3), Summer 1966, 436-37.

    CHARLES C. WALCUTT. *Explicator* 3(1), October 1944, Item 7.

"The Demiurge's Laugh"

    EBEN BASS. "Frost's Poetry of Fear," *American Literature* 43(4), January 1972, 603-4.

    WALTER BLAIR. *The Literature of the United States,* II: 933.

    ROBERT F. FLEISSNER. "Frost's Response to Keats' Risibility," *Ball State University Forum* 11(1), Winter 1970, 40-43.

"Departmental or, The End of My Ant Jerry"

    MARIO L. D'AVANZO. "Frost's 'Departmental' and Emerson: A Further Range of Satire," *Concerning Poetry* 10(2), Fall 1977, 67-69.

"Desert Places"

    HARRY BERGER, JR. "Poetry as Revision: Interpreting Robert Frost," *Criticism* 10(1), Winter 1968, 12-15.

    CLEANTH BROOKS and ROBERT PENN WARREN. *Understanding Poetry,* pp. 193-94; second ed., pp. 87-88; third ed., pp. 105-6; fourth ed., pp. 203-5.

    WALLACE CABLE BROWN. "'A Poem Should Not Mean But Be,'" *University of Kansas City Review* 15(1), Autumn 1948, 62-63.

CHARLES B. HANDS. "The Hidden Terror of Robert Frost," *English Journal* 58(8), November 1969, 1166-68.

CARL M. LINDNER. "Robert Frost: Dark Romantic," *Arizona Quarterly* 29(3), Autumn 1973, 243-44.

RONALD L. LYCETTE. "The Vortex Points of Robert Frost," *Ball State University Forum* 14(3), Summer 1973, 56.

LEWIS H. MILLER, JR. "Two Poems of Winter," *College English* 28(4), January 1967, 314-16.

"Design"

ARNOLD G. BARTINI. "Robert Frost and Moral Neutrality," *CEA Critic* 38(2), January 1976, 22.

BABETTE DEUTSCH. *Poetry in Our Time,* second ed., p. 79.

BOB DOWELL. "Revealing Incident as Technique in the Poetry of Robert Frost," *CEA Critic* 31(3), December 1968, 12-13.

ELIZABETH DREW. *Poetry,* pp. 186-88. Abridged in: *The Case for Poetry,* second ed., pp. 127-28.

DAVID HIATT. *Explicator* 28(5), January 1970, Item 41.

LEE A. JACOBUS and WILLIAM T. MOYNIHAN. *Poems in Context,* pp. 5-13.

RANDALL JARRELL. "To the Laodiceans," *Kenyon Review* 14(1), Autumn 1952, 542-45.

CARL M. LINDNER. "Robert Frost: Dark Romantic," *Arizona Quarterly* 29(3), Autumn 1973, 240-43.

RONALD L. LYCETTE. "The Vortex Points of Robert Frost," *Ball State University Forum* 14(3), Summer 1973, 57.

JOHN F. LYNEN. "The Poet's Meaning and the Poem's World," in *Modern Poetry,* pp. 497-98.

RICHARD OHMANN. "The Size and Structure of Academic Field: Some Perplexities," *College English* 28(5), February 1967, 364-65.

LAURENCE PERRINE. *100 American Poems of the Twentieth Century,* pp. 45-47.

JOHN OLIVER PERRY. *The Experience of Poems,* pp. 270-71.

JANIS P. STOUT. "Convention and Variation in Frost's Sonnets," *Concerning Poetry* 11(1), Spring 1978, 29-30.

CHAD and EVA T. WALSH. *Twice Ten,* pp. 161-63.

FLOYD C. WATKINS. "Going and Coming Back: Robert Frost's Religious Poetry," *South Atlantic Quarterly* 73(4), Autumn 1974, 458.

"Devotion"

WALTER GIERASCH. *Explicator* 10(7), May 1952, Item 50.

"Directive"

MARGARET M. BLUM. "Robert Frost's 'Directive': A Theological Reading," *Modern Language Notes* 76(6), June 1961, 524-25.

PHILIP BOOTH. "Frost: Directive," in *Master Poems of the English Language,* pp. 884-88.

MARIE BORROFF. "Robert Frost's New Testament: Language and the Poem," *Modern Philology* 69(1), August 1971, 50-54.

PEARLANNA BRIGGS. *Explicator* 21(9), May 1963, Item 71.

DAVID RIDGLEY CLARK. *Lyric Resonance,* pp. 106-17, 132-33.

JAMES M. COX. "Robert Frost and the Edge of the Clearing," *Virginia Quarterly Review* 35(11), Winter 1959, 85-87.

BABETTE DEUTSCH. *Poetry in Our Time,* p. 75; second ed., pp. 81-82.

LYLE DOMINA. "Thoreau and Frost: The Search for Reality," *Ball State University Forum* 19(4), Autumn 1978, 71-72.

JAMES P. DOUGHERTY. "Robert Frost's 'Directive' to the Wilderness," *American Quarterly* 18(2), Summer 1966, 208-19.

JOHN ROBERT DOYLE, JR. "A Reading of Robert Frost's 'Directive,' " *Georgia Review* 22(4), Winter 1968, 501-8.

ELIZABETH DREW. *Poetry,* pp. 229-33.

S. P. C. DUVALL. "Robert Frost's 'Directive' out of *Walden,*" *American Literature* 31(4), January 1960, 482-88.

JAN B. GORDON. "Robert Frost's Circle of Enchantment," in *Modern American Poetry,* edited by Jerome Mazzaro, pp. 79-81.

JEFFREY HART. "Frost and Eliot," *Sewanee Review* 84(3), Summer 1976, 443-46.

MILDRED E. HARTSOCK. *Explicator* 16(7), April 1958, Item 42.

J. DENNIS HUSTON. " 'The Wonder of Unexpected Supply': Robert Frost and a Poetry Beyond Confusion," *Centennial Review* 13(3), Summer 1969, 325-29.

TODD M. LIEBER. "Robert Frost and Wallace Stevens: 'What to Make of a Diminished Thing,' " *American Literature* 47(1), March 1975, 81-82.

ROY HARVEY PEARCE. *The Continuity of American Poetry,* pp. 274-75.

ROBERT PETERS. "The Truth of Frost's 'Directive,' " *Modern Language Notes* 75(1), January 1960, 29-32.

WILLIAM H. PRITCHARD. "Diminished Nature," *Massachusetts Review* 1(3), Spring 1960, 488-92.

ARTHUR M. SAMPLEY. "The Myth and the Quest; The Stature of Robert Frost," *South Atlantic Quarterly* 70(3), Summer 1971, 295.

ROBERT G. TWOMBLY. "The Poetics of Demur: Lowell and Frost," *College English* 37(4), December 1976, 388-89.

GEORGE WATERS. " 'Directive': Frost's Magical Mystery Tour," *Concerning Poetry* 9(1), Spring 1976, 33-38.

"Does No One But Me At All Ever Feel This Way in the Least"

CLAUDE M. SIMPSON. "Robert Frost and Man's 'Royal Role,' " in *Aspects of American Poetry,* pp. 124-26.

"Doom to Bloom"

CLAUDE M. SIMPSON. "Robert Frost and Man's 'Royal Role,' " in *Aspects of American Poetry,* pp. 128-29.

"The Draft Horse"

EBEN BASS. "Frost's Poetry of Fear," *American Literature* 43(4), January 1972, 613-15.

MARGARET M. BLUM. *Explicator* 24(9), May 1966, Item 79.

PAUL BURRELL. *Explicator* 25(7), March 1967, Item 60.

The Case for Poetry, second ed., pp. 131-35.

FREDERICK L. GWYNN. "Analysis and Synthesis of Frost's 'The Draft Horse,' " *College English* 26(3), December 1964, 223-25.

JAMES HOETKER. "Frost's 'The Draft Horse,' " *College English* 26(6), March 1965, 485.

LAURENCE PERRINE. *Explicator* 24(9), May 1966, Item 79.

FROST, ROBERT *(Cont.)*

"The Draft Horse" *(cont.)*

MARTHA C. STONE. "Can Teachers Learn From Their Students?" *CEA Critic* 25(4), February 1963, 7-8.

"A Dream of Julius Caesar"

JAN B. GORDON. "Robert Frost's Circle of Enchantment," in *Modern American Poetry,* edited by Jerome Mazzaro, pp. 60-61.

"A Dream Pang"

DONALD T. HAYNES. "The Narrative Unity of *A Boy's Will,*" *PMLA* 87(3), May 1972, 459-60.

"A Drumlin Woodchuck"

LAWRANCE THOMPSON. "Robert Frost," in *Seven Modern American Poets,* pp. 25-26.

"Dust of Snow"

NORBERT ARTZT. "The Poetry Lesson," *College English* 32(7), April 1971, 740-42.

HARRY BERGER, JR. "Poetry as Revision: Interpreting Robert Frost," *Criticism* 10(1), Winter 1968, 2-4.

EDGAR H. KNAPP. *Explicator* 28(1), September 1969, Item 9.

LAURENCE PERRINE. "Dust of Snow Gets In Our Eyes (Comment on Norbert Artzt, 'The Poetry Lesson' CE April 1971)," *College English* 33(5), February 1972, 589-90.

LAURENCE PERRINE. *Explicator* 29(7), March 1971, Item 61.

HYATT H. WAGGONER. *American Poets,* pp. 301-2.

"The Egg and the Machine"

HARSHARAN SINGH AHLUWALIA. "The 'Conservatism' of Robert Frost," *Bulletin of the New York Public Library* 70(8), October 1966, 487.

PETER W. DOWELL. "Counter-Images and Their Function in the Poetry of Robert Frost," *Tennessee Studies in Literature* 14 (1969), 23-25.

YVOR WINTERS. "Robert Frost: Or, The Spiritual Drifter as Poet," *Sewanee Review* 56(4), Autumn 1948, 577-79.

"An Empty Threat"

LAURENCE PERRINE. *Explicator* 30(8), April 1972, Item 63.

LAWRANCE THOMPSON. "Robert Frost," in *Seven Modern American Poets,* p. 25.

"An Encounter"

EBEN BASS. "Frost's Poetry of Fear," *American Literature* 43(4), January 1972, 605.

"Escapist-Never"

DARREL ABEL. "Robert Frost's 'True Make-Believe,'" *Texas Studies in Literature and Language* 20(4), Winter 1978, 574-75.

"Etherealizing"

TODD M. LIEBER. "Robert Frost and Wallace Stevens: 'What to Make of a Diminished Thing,'" *American Literature* 47(1), March 1975, 75-76.

"The Exposed Nest"

SISTER CATHERINE THERESA. "New Testament Interpretations of Robert Frost's Poems," *Ball State University Forum* 11(1), Winter 1970, 51-52.

"The Fear"

EBEN BASS. "Frost's Poetry of Fear," *American Literature* 43(4), January 1972, 611-12.

JAMES K. BOWEN. "Propositional and Emotional Knowledge in Robert Frost's 'The Death of the Hired Man,' 'The Fear,' and 'Home Burial,'" *CLA Journal* 12(2), December 1968, 157-58.

"The Figure in the Doorway"

PETER W. DOWELL. "Counter-Images and Their Function in the Poetry of Robert Frost," *Tennessee Studies in Literature* 14 (1969), 22-23.

RICHARD POIRIER. "Soundings for Home: Frost's Poetry of Extravagance and Return," *Georgia Review* 31(2), Summer 1977, 303-4.

"Fire and Ice"

WALTER BEACHAM. *The Meaning of Poetry,* p. 231.

"For Once, Then, Something"

DARREL ABEL. "Emerson's 'Apparition of God' and Frost's 'Apparition of the Mind,'" *University of Toronto Quarterly* 48(1), Fall 1978, 45-46.

HELEN BACON. "Dialogue of Poets: *Mens Animi* and the Renewal of Words," *Massachusetts Review* 19(2), Summer 1978, 327-33.

CHARLES B. HANDS. "The Hidden Terror of Robert Frost," *English Journal* 58(8), November 1969, 1163-64.

JEFFREY HART. "Frost and Eliot," *Sewanee Review* 84(3), Summer 1976, 442-43.

DAN G. HOFFMAN. *Explicator* 9(2), November 1950, Item 17.

JOHN F. LYNEN. "The Poet's Meaning and the Poem's World," in *Modern Poetry,* p. 497.

LAWRANCE THOMPSON. "Robert Frost," in *Seven Modern American Poets,* pp. 20-21.

HYATT H. WAGGONER. *American Poets,* p. 301.

"Forgive, O Lord, my little jokes on Thee"

HOWELL D. CHICKERING, JR. "Robert Frost, Romantic Humorist," *Literature and Psychology* 16(3-4), 1966, 148.

RICHARD EBERHART. "Robert Frost in the Clearing," *Southern Review,* n.s., 11(2), Spring 1975, 263-64.

WILLIAM G. O'DONNELL. "Robert Frost at Eighty-Eight," *Massachusetts Review* 4(1), Autumn 1962, 217.

"The Freedom of the Moon"

DOROTHY JUDD HILL. "Painterly Qualities in Frost's Lyric Poetry," *Ball State University Forum* 11(1), Winter 1970, 9-10.

"Gathering Leaves"

LAURENCE PERRINE. "Frost's 'Gathering Leaves,'" *CEA Critic* 34(1), November 1971, 29.

"Ghost House"

EBEN BASS. "Frost's Poetry of Fear," *American Literature* 43(4), January 1972, 608.

DENNIS VAIL. *Explicator* 30(2), October 1971, Item 11.

"The Gift Outright"

HAMIDA BOSMAJIAN. "Robert Frost's 'The Gift Outright': Wish and Reality in History and Poetry," *American Quarterly* 22(1), Spring 1970, 95-105.

JAMES R. KREUZER. *Elements of Poetry,* pp. 153-55.

"Good-bye and Keep Cold"

RICHARD FOSTER. "Leaves Compared with Flowers: A Reading in Robert Frost's Poems," *New England Quarterly* 46(3), September 1973, 416-17.

"The Grindstone"

REGINALD L. COOK. "Frost as Parablist," *Accent* 10(1), Autumn 1949, 37-38.

"The Gum-Gatherer"

RICHARD WILBUR. "On Robert Frost's 'The Gum-Gatherer,' " in his *Responses*, pp. 185-89.

"Happiness Makes up in Height"

W. G. O'DONNELL. "Robert Frost and New England: A Revaluation," *Yale Review* 37(4), Summer 1948, 707-8.

"Hard Not to Be King"

SISTER MARY JEREMY. "Contrarieties in Robert Frost," *Catholic World* 192(1,149), December 1960, 167-70.

"The Hill Wife"

EBEN BASS. "Frost's Poetry of Fear," *American Literature* 43(4), January 1972, 609-11.

WILLIAM H. PRITCHARD. "*North of Boston*: Frost's Poetry of Dialogue," in *In Defense of Reading*, p. 41.

"A Hillside Thaw"

CARL LINDNER. "Robert Frost: 'In the American Grain,' " *Colorado Quarterly* 22(4), Spring 1974, 475-76.

DAVID ALAN SANDERS. "Words in the Rush of Everything to Waste: A Poetic Theme in Frost," *South Carolina Review* 7(1), November 1977, 40-47.

"Home Burial"

GÉMINO H. ABAD. *A Formal Approach to Lyric Poetry*, pp. 81-93.

EBEN BASS. "Frost's Poetry of Fear," *American Literature* 43(4), January 1972, 608-9.

JAMES K. BOWEN. "Propositional and Emotional Knowledge in Robert Frost's 'The Death of the Hired Man,' 'The Fear,' and 'Home Burial,' " *CLA Journal* 12(2), December 1968, 158-59.

RANDALL JARRELL. "Robert Frost's 'Home Burial,' " in *The Moment of Poetry*, pp. 99-132.

WILLIAM H. PRITCHARD. "*North of Boston*: Frost's Poetry of Dialogue," in *In Defense of Reading*, pp. 42-46.

LAURENCE J. SASSO, JR. "Robert Frost: Love's Question," *New England Quarterly* 42(1), March 1969, 101-2.

ROBERT H. SWENNES. "Man and Wife: The Dialogue of Contraries in Robert Frost's Poetry," *American Literature* 42(3), November 1970, 365-68.

"Hyla Brook"

HELEN H. BACON. "In- and Outdoor Schooling: Robert Frost and the Classics," *American Scholar* 43(4), Autumn 1974, 646-47.

WILLIAM H. PRITCHARD. "Diminished Nature," *Massachusetts Review* 1(3), Spring 1960, 482-85.

DAVID ALAN SANDERS. "Words in the Rush of Everything to Waste: A Poetic Theme in Frost," *South Carolina Review* 7(1), November 1974, 36-37.

HAROLD E. TOLIVER. *Pastoral Forms and Attitudes*, pp. 355-57.

ISADORE TRASCHEN. "Robert Frost: Some Divisions in a Whole Man," *Yale Review* 55(1), October 1965, 58-59.

"I Could Give All to Time"

THEODORE MORRISON. "Frost: Country Poet and Cosmopolitan Poet," *Yale Review* 59(2), December 1969, 190-93.

"I Will Sing You One-O"

ANNA K. JUHNKE. "Religion in Robert Frost's Poetry: The Play for Self-Possession," *American Literature* 36(2), May 1964, 154-55.

JOHN F. LYNEN. "Forms of Time in Modern Poetry," *Queen's Quarterly* 82(3), Autumn 1975, 353-57.

LAURENCE PERRINE. *Explicator* 34(6), February 1976, Item 48.

FLOYD C. WATKINS. "Going and Coming Back: Robert Frost's Religious Poetry," *South Atlantic Quarterly* 73(4), Autumn 1974, 454-55.

"In a Vale"

DONALD T. HAYNES. "The Narrative Unity of *A Boy's Will*," *PMLA* 87(3), May 1972, 459-60.

"In Hardwood Groves"

DAVID ALAN SANDERS. "Words in the Rush of Everything to Waste: A Poetic Theme in Frost," *South Carolina Review* 7(1), November 1974, 37-38.

"In the Home Stretch"

RICHARD FOSTER. "Leaves Compared with Flowers: A Reading in Robert Frost's Poems," *New England Quarterly* 46(3), September 1973, 411-12.

ROY HARVEY PEARCE. *The Continuity of American Poetry*, p. 282.

ROY HARVEY PEARCE. "Frost's Momentary Stay," in *Modern American Poetry*, edited by Guy Owen, pp. 33-34.

"In White"

GEORGE MONTEIRO. "Emily Dickinson and Robert Frost," *Prairie Schooner* 51(4), Winter 1977/78, 377-79.

"Into My Own"

HOWELL D. CHICKERING, JR. "Robert Frost, Romantic Humorist," *Literature and Psychology* 16(3-4), 1966, 146.

DONALD T. HAYNES. "The Narrative Unity of *A Boy's Will*," *PMLA* 87(3), May 1972, 454-55.

"The Investment"

BOB DOWELL. "Revealing Incident as Technique in the Poetry of Robert Frost," *CEA Critic* 31(3), December 1968, 12.

M. L. ROSENTHAL. *Poetry and the Common Life*, pp. 6-10.

"Iota Subscript"

WARD ALLEN. "Robert Frost's 'Iota Subscript,' " *English Language Notes* 6(4), June 1969, 285-87.

"Iris by Night"

HARRY BERGER, JR. "Poetry as Revision: Interpreting Robert Frost," *Criticism* 10(1), Winter 1968, 4-7.

"The Kitchen Chimney"

MARIO L. D'AVANZO. "How to Build a Chimney: Frost Gleans Thoreau," *Thoreau Journal Quarterly* 9(4), October 1977, 24-26.

"Kitty Hawk"

HELEN BACON. "Dialogue of Poets: *Mens Animi* and the Renewal of Words," *Massachusetts Review* 19(2), Summer 1978, 319-26.

JOHN CIARDI. *Dialogue with an Audience*, p. 170.

JOHN CIARDI. "Robert Frost: American Bard," *Saturday Review* 45(12), 12 March 1962, 52-53. Reprinted in: John Ciardi. *Dialogue with an Audience*, pp. 189-91.

FROST, ROBERT *(Cont.)*

"Kitty Hawk" *(cont.)*

LAURENCE GOLDSTEIN. "'Kitty Hawk' and the Question of American Destiny," *Iowa Review* 9(1), Winter 1978, 41-49.

JOHN T. HIERS. "Robert Frost's Quarrel with Science and Technology," *Georgia Review* 25(2), Summer 1971, 201-5.

CLAUDE M. SIMPSON. "Robert Frost and Man's 'Royal Role,'" in *Aspects of American Poetry,* pp. 137-47.

"The Last Mowing"

WALTER GIERASCH. *Explicator* 10(4), February 1952, Item 25.

HAROLD E. TOLIVER. *Pastoral Forms and Attitudes,* pp. 359-60.

YVOR WINTERS. "Robert Frost: Or, The Spiritual Drifter as Poet," *Sewanee Review* 56(4), Autumn 1948, 589-90.

"A Leaf Treader"

CLEANTH BROOKS, JOHN THIBAUT PURSER, and ROBERT PENN WARREN. *An Approach to Literature,* fourth ed., pp. 423-24; fifth ed., pp. 488-90.

"Leaves Compared with Flowers"

RICHARD FOSTER. "Leaves Compared with Flowers: A Reading in Robert Frost's Poems," *New England Quarterly* 46(3), September 1973, 422-23.

"The Lesson for Today"

MALCOLM COWLEY. *A Many-Windowed House,* pp. 209-10.

BABETTE DEUTSCH. *Poetry in Our Time,* p. 77; second ed., p. 83.

RUSSELL KIRK. "The Poet As Conservative," *Critic* 18(4), February-March 1960, 19-20, 84.

TODD M. LIEBER. "Robert Frost and Wallace Stevens: 'What to Make of a Diminished Thing,'" *American Literature* 47(1), March 1975, 69-70.

YVOR WINTERS. "Robert Frost: Or, The Spiritual Drifter as Poet," *Sewanee Review* 56(4), Autumn 1948, 585-86. Reprinted in: Yvor Winters. *The Function of Criticism,* pp. 177-78. Also: *Literary Opinion in America,* revised and third eds., pp. 431-32.

"The Line-Gang"

JOHN T. HIERS. "Robert Frost's Quarrel with Science and Technology," *Georgia Review* 25(2), Summer 1971, 192-93.

"A Line-Storm Song"

LAURENCE PERRINE. *100 American Poems of the Twentieth Century,* pp. 43-45.

"The Literate Farmer and the Planet Venus"

LAURENCE PERRINE. "The Tone of Frost's 'The Literate Farmer and the Planet Venus,'" *Notes on Contemporary Literature* 5(2), March 1975, 10-13.

FRED C. SCHUTZ. "Frost's 'The Literate Farmer and the Planet Venus': Why 1926?" *Notes on Contemporary Literature* 4(5), November 1974, 8-10.

"A Lone Striker"

HARSHARAN SINGH AHLUWALIA. "The 'Conservatism' of Robert Frost," *Bulletin of the New York Public Library* 70(8), October 1966, 487-88.

FREDERICK L. GWYNN. "Poetry Crisis at Corning," *CEA Critic* 15(9), December 1953, 1, 3.

SISTER CATHERINE THERESA. "New Testament Interpretations of Robert Frost's Poems," *Ball State University Forum* 11(1), Winter 1970, 53-54.

HAROLD H. WATTS. "Robert Frost and the Interrupted Dialogue," *American Literature* 27(1), March 1955, 77-78.

"The Lost Follower"

HELEN H. BACON. "In- and Outdoor Schooling: Robert Frost and the Classics," *American Scholar* 43(4), Autumn 1974, 648-49.

WILLIAM H. PRITCHARD. "Wildness of Logic in Modern Lyric," in *Forms of Lyric,* pp. 132-34.

"Love and a Question"

MICHAEL J. COLLINS. "A Note on Frost's 'Love and a Question,'" *Concerning Poetry* 8(1), Spring 1975, 57-58.

LAURENCE PERRINE. "The Dilemma in Frost's 'Love and a Question,'" *Concerning Poetry* 5(2), Fall 1972, 5-8.

"The Lovely Shall Be Choosers"

ELIZABETH NITCHIE. *Explicator* 13(6), April 1955, Item 39.

EDWARD SCHWARTZ. *Explicator* 13(1), October 1954, Item 3.

W. L. WERNER. *Explicator* 13(6), April 1955, Item 39.

"Maple"

DARREL ABEL. "Robert Frost's 'True Make-Believe,'" *Texas Studies in Literature and Language* 20(4), Winter 1978, 556-62.

FLOYD C. WATKINS. "Going and Coming Back: Robert Frost's Religious Poetry," *South Atlantic Quarterly* 73(4), Autumn 1974, 451.

"A Masque of Mercy"

HEYWARD BROCK. "Robert Frost's Masques Reconsidered," *Renascence* 30(3), Spring 1978, 137-51.

SISTER MARY JEREMY FINNEGAN. "Frost's *Masque of Mercy,*" *Catholic World* 186 (February 1958), 359-61.

W. R. IRWIN. "The Unity of Frost's Masques," *American Literature* 32(3), November 1960, 302-12.

JUDSON JEROME. "Three Faces of Jonah: A Parable for Prosperous Times," *Virginia Quarterly Review* 42(3), Summer 1966, 460-75.

ANNA K. JUHNKE. "Religion in Robert Frost's Poetry: The Play for Self-Possession," *American Literature* 36(2), May 1964, 161-63.

LAWRANCE THOMPSON. "Robert Frost," in *Seven Modern American Poets,* pp. 37-40.

"A Masque of Reason"

DARREL ABEL. "Emerson's 'Apparition of God' and Frost's 'Apparition of the Mind,'" *University of Toronto Quarterly* 48(1), Fall 1978, 42-43.

HEYWARD BROCK. "Robert Frost's Masques Reconsidered," *Renascence* 30(3), Spring 1978, 137-51.

W. R. IRWIN. "The Unity of Frost's Masques," *American Literature* 32(3), November 1960, 302-12.

JUDSON JEROME. "Three Faces of Jonah: A Parable for Prosperous Times," *Virginia Quarterly Review* 42(3), Summer 1966, 460-62.

ANNA K. JUHNKE. "Religion in Robert Frost's Poetry: The Play for Self-Possession," *American Literature* 36(2), May 1964, 160-61.

LAWRANCE THOMPSON. "Robert Frost," in *Seven Modern American Poets,* pp. 34-37.

RUTH TODASCO. "Dramatic Characterization in Frost: *A Masque of Reason,*" *University of Kansas City Review* 29(3), Spring 1963, 227-30.

HAROLD E. TOLIVER. *Pastoral Forms and Attitudes,* pp. 379-80.

"Meeting and Passing"

LAURENCE J. SASSO, JR. "Robert Frost: Love's Question," *New England Quarterly* 42(1), March 1969, 106-7.

JANIS P. STOUT. "Convention and Variation in Frost's Sonnets," *Concerning Poetry* 11(1), Spring 1978, 30.

"Mending Wall"

JOSEPH WARREN BEACH. "Robert Frost," *Yale Review* 43(2), Winter 1954, 210-11.

MARIE BORROFF. "Robert Frost's New Testament: Language and the Poem," *Modern Philology* 69(1), August 1971, 37-39.

JAMES K. BOWEN. "The *Persona* in Frost's 'Mending Wall': Mended or Amended?" *CEA Critic* 31(2), November 1968, 14.

JOHN C. BRODERICK. *Explicator* 14(4), January 1956, Item 24.

BABETTE DEUTSCH. *This Modern Poetry*, p. 42.

S. L. DRAGLAND. *Explicator* 25(5), January 1967, Item 39.

CARSON GIBB. *Explicator* 20(6), February 1962, Item 48.

JAN B. GORDON. "Robert Frost's Circle of Enchantment," in *Modern American Poetry*, edited by Jerome Mazzaro, pp. 68-69.

ROBERT HUNTING. "Who Needs Mending?" *Western Humanities Review* 17(1), Winter 1963, 88-89.

EDWARD JAYNE. "Up Against the 'Mending Wall': The Psychoanalysis of a Poem by Frost," *College English* 34(7), April 1973, 934-51.

FRANK LENTRICCHIA. "Experience as Meaning: Robert Frost's 'Mending Wall,'" *CEA Critic* 34(4), May 1972, 8-12.

CARL LINDNER. "Robert Frost: 'In the American Grain,'" *Colorado Quarterly* 22(4), Spring 1974, 474-75.

RONALD L. LYCETTE. "The Vortex Points of Robert Frost," *Ball State University Forum* 14(3), Summer 1973, 56.

JULIAN MASON. "Frost's Conscious Accommodation of Contraries," *CEA Critic* 38(3), March 1976, 29.

GEORGE MONTEIRO. "Robert Frost's Linked Analogies," *New England Quarterly* 46(3), September 1973, 466.

GEORGE MONTEIRO. "Unlinked Myth in Frost's 'Mending Wall,'" *Concerning Poetry* 7(2), Fall 1974, 10-12.

MARION MONTGOMERY. "Robert Frost and His Use of Barriers: Man *vs* Nature Toward God," *South Atlantic Quarterly* 57(3), Summer 1958, 349-50.

WILLIAM H. PRITCHARD. "The Grip of Frost," *Hudson Review* 29(2), Summer 1976, 190-92.

JAMES REEVES and MARTIN SEYMOUR-SMITH. *Inside Poetry*, pp. 23-25.

M. L. ROSENTHAL and A. J. M. SMITH. *Exploring Poetry*, pp. 5-6; second ed., pp. 4-6.

THOMAS J. SHALVEY. "Valéry and Frost: Two Views of Subjective Reality," *Renascence* 11(4), Summer 1959, 187.

LOUIS UNTERMEYER. *50 Modern American & British Poets*, pp. 227-28.

DENNIS VAIL. "Tree Imagery in Frost's 'Mending Wall,'" *Notes on Contemporary Literature* 3(4), September 1973, 9-11.

WILLIAM S. WARD. "Lifted Pots and Unmended Walls," *College English* 27(5), February 1966, 428-29.

CHARLES N. WATSON, JR. "Frost's Wall: The View from the Other Side," *New England Quarterly* 44(4), December 1971, 653-56.

"Misgiving"

ARTHUR C. MCGILL. *The Celebration of Flesh*, pp. 105-7.

"Moon Compasses"

ROGER L. SLAKEY. *Explicator* 37(1), Fall 1978, 22-23.

CHAD and EVA T. WALSH. *Twice Ten*, pp. 166-68.

"The Most of It"

HELEN BACON. "Dialogue of Poets: *Mens Animi* and the Renewal of Words," *Massachusetts Review* 19(2), Summer 1978, 327-33.

ROY HARVEY PEARCE. *The Continuity of American Poetry*, p. 280.

ROY HARVEY PEARCE. "Frost's Momentary Stay," in *Modern American Poetry*, ed. by Guy Owen, pp. 31-32.

ROBERT PINSKY. *The Situation of Poetry*, pp. 65-69.

RICHARD POIRIER. "Soundings for Home: Frost's Poetry of Extravagance and Return," *Georgia Review* 31(2), Summer 1977, 304-15.

WILLIAM H. PRITCHARD. "The Grip of Frost," *Hudson Review* 29(2), Summer 1976, 200-3.

HAROLD E. TOLIVER. *Pastoral Forms and Attitudes*, pp. 350-52.

YVOR WINTERS. "Robert Frost: Or, The Spiritual Drifter as Poet," *Sewanee Review* 56(4), Autumn 1958, 591-92. Reprinted in: *Literary Opinion in America*, revised ed., pp. 435-36; third ed., pp. 435-36. Also: Yvor Winters. *The Function of Criticism*, pp. 182-83.

"The Mountain"

HELEN H. BACON. "In- and Outdoor Schooling: Robert Frost and the Classics," *American Scholar* 43(4), Autumn 1974, 644-46.

LAURENCE PERRINE. "Frost's 'The Mountain': Concerning Poetry," *Concerning Poetry* 4(1), Spring 1971, 5-11.

FLOYD C. WATKINS. "Going and Coming Back: Robert Frost's Religious Poetry," *South Atlantic Quarterly* 73(4), Autumn 1974, 450-51.

"Mowing"

DARREL ABEL. "Emerson's 'Apparition of God' and Frost's 'Apparition of the Mind,'" *University of Toronto Quarterly* 48(1), Fall 1978, 48.

HELEN H. BACON. "In- and Outdoor Schooling: Robert Frost and the Classics," *American Scholar* 43(4), Autumn 1974, 647-48.

CLEANTH BROOKS and ROBERT PENN WARREN. *Understanding Poetry*, third ed., pp. 369-71.

DONALD T. HAYNES. "The Narrative Unity of *A Boy's Will*," *PMLA* 87(3), May 1972, 460.

LEWIS H. MILLER, JR. "The Poet as Swinger: Fact and Fancy in Robert Frost," *Criticism* 16(1), Winter 1974, 64-67.

WILLIAM H. PRITCHARD. "The Grip of Frost," *Hudson Review* 29(2), Summer 1976, 188-90.

LAWRANCE THOMPSON. "Robert Frost," in *Seven Modern American Poets*, pp. 42-43.

HAROLD E. TOLIVER. *Pastoral Forms and Attitudes*, pp. 344-45.

DENNIS VAIL. "Frost's 'Mowing': Work and Poetry," *Notes on Contemporary Literature* 4(1), January 1974, 4-7.

FROST, ROBERT *(Cont.)*

"My Butterfly"

> GEORGE MONTEIRO. "Emily Dickinson and Robert Frost," *Prairie Schooner* 51(4), Winter 1977/78, 373-76.

"The Need of Being Versed in Country Things"

> CLEANTH BROOKS, JOHN THIBAUT PURSER, and ROBERT PENN WARREN. *An Approach to Literature,* third ed., pp. 346-47; fourth ed., pp. 343-45; fifth ed., pp. 491-93.

> WILLIAM H. PRITCHARD. "Diminished Nature," *Massachusetts Review* 1(3), Spring 1960, 485-88.

"Neither Out Far Nor In Deep"

> REGINALD L. COOK. "Frost the Diversionist," *New England Quarterly* 40(3), September 1967, 334-38.

> HAROLD H. CORBIN, JR. *Explicator* 1(7), May 1943, Item 58.

> CLARK GRIFFITH. "Frost and the American View of Nature," *American Quarterly* 20(1), Spring 1968, 30-32.

> CECILIA HENNEL HENDRICKS. *Explicator* 1(7), May 1943, Item 58.

> RANDALL JARRELL. "To the Laodiceans," *Kenyon Review* 14(4), Autumn 1952, 538-40.

> D. J. LEPORE. "Robert Frost — The Middle-Ground: An Analysis of 'Neither Out Far Nor In Deep,'" *English Journal* 53(3), March 1964, 215-16.

> JOHN F. LYNEN. "The Poet's Meaning and the Poem's World," in *Modern Poetry,* pp. 493-96.

> LAURENCE PERRINE. *Explicator* 7(6), April 1949, Item 46.

> R. W. STALLMAN. "The Position of Poetry Today," *English Journal* 46(5), May 1957, 247-48.

> HYATT H. WAGGONER. *American Poets,* pp. 315-16.

> FLOYD C. WATKINS. "Going and Coming Back: Robert Frost's Religious Poetry," *South Atlantic Quarterly* 73(4), Autumn 1974, 458-59.

"Never Again Would Birds' Song Be the Same"

> RICHARD POIRIER. "Soundings for Home: Frost's Poetry of Extravagance and Return," *Georgia Review* 31(2), Summer 1977, 313-14.

> WILLIAM H. PRITCHARD. "Wildness of Logic in Modern Lyric," in *Forms of Lyric,* pp. 131-32.

"New Hampshire"

> NINA BAYM. "An Approach to Robert Frost's Nature Poetry," *American Quarterly* 17(4), Winter 1965, 714-15.

> JEFFREY HART. "Frost and Eliot," *Sewanee Review* 84(3), Summer 1976, 429-32.

> JAMES R. VITELLI. "Robert Frost: The Contrarieties of Talent and Tradition," *New England Quarterly* 47(3), September 1974, 361-62. (P)

"Not All There"

> ROBERT F. FLEISSNER. *Explicator* 31(5), January 1973, Item 33.

"Nothing Gold Can Stay"

> CHARLES R. ANDERSON. *Explicator* 22(8), April 1964, Item 63.

> WARREN BECK. "Poetry's Chronic Disease," *English Journal* 33(7), September 1944, 363.

> SISTER M. BERNETTA QUINN. "Symbolic Landscape in Frost's 'Nothing Gold Can Stay,'" *English Journal* 55(5), May 1966, 621-24.

> DAVID ALAN SANDERS. "Words in the Rush of Everything to Waste: A Poetic Theme in Frost," *South Carolina Review* 7(1), November 1974, 36.

> JAMES G. SOUTHWORTH. *Some Modern American Poets,* pp. 84-85.

> WALTER SUTTON. "The Contextualist Dilemma — or Fallacy?" *Journal of Aesthetics and Art Criticism* 17(2), December 1958, 225-26.

"The Objection to Being Stepped On"

> CLAUDE M. SIMPSON. "Robert Frost and Man's 'Royal Role,'" in *Aspects of American Poetry,* p. 129.

"An Old Man's Winter Night"

> EBEN BASS. "Frost's Poetry of Fear," *American Literature* 43(4), January 1972, 606-7.

> HARRY BROWN and JOHN MILSTEAD. *What the Poem Means,* p. 89.

> CHARLES G. DAVIS. *Explicator* 27(3), November 1968, Item 19.

> ROBERT LANGBAUM. "The New Nature Poetry," in *The Modern Spirit,* pp. 106-7.

"On a Tree Fallen Across the Road"

> EBEN BASS. "Frost's Poetry of Fear," *American Literature* 43(4), January 1972, 613.

> PETER W. DOWELL. "Counter-Images and Their Function in the Poetry of Robert Frost," *Tennessee Studies in Literature* 14 (1969), 25-27.

> HAROLD E. TOLIVER. *Pastoral Forms and Attitudes,* pp. 335-36.

"On Looking Up By Chance at the Constellations"

> SISTER CATHERINE THERESA. "New Testament Interpretations of Robert Frost's Poems," *Ball State University Forum* 11(1), Winter 1970, 54.

> CARL M. LINDNER. "Robert Frost: Dark Romantic," *Arizona Quarterly* 29(3), Autumn 1973, 238-40.

"On the Heart's Beginning to Cloud the Mind"

> HARRY BERGER, JR. "Poetry as Revision: Interpreting Robert Frost," *Criticism* 10(1), Winter 1968, 16-18.

> RICHARD POIRIER. "Soundings for Home: Frost's Poetry of Extravagance and Return," *Georgia Review* 31(2), Summer 1977, 301-3.

"Once by the Pacific"

> GÉMINO H. ABAD. *A Formal Approach to Lyric Poetry,* p. 267.

> HARRY BROWN and JOHN MILSTEAD. *What the Poem Means,* pp. 91-92.

> CLARK GRIFFITH. "Frost and the American View of Nature," *American Quarterly* 20(1), Spring 1968, 34-35.

> D. S. J. PARSONS. "Night of Dark Intent," *Papers on Language and Literature* 6(2), Spring 1970, 205-10.

> MARK VAN DOREN. *Introduction to Poetry,* pp. 77-80.

"One More Brevity"

> CLAUDE M. SIMPSON. "Robert Frost and Man's 'Royal Role,'" in *Aspects of American Poetry,* pp. 130-32.

"The Onset"

> WILLIAM W. BETTS, JR. "The Poem in the Classroom," *Studies in the Humanities* 1(1), March 1969, 6.

> CHAD and EVA T. WALSH. *Twice Ten,* pp. 163-66.

"'Out, Out — '"

> GÉMINO H. ABAD. *A Formal Approach to Lyric Poetry,* pp. 233-34.

> MARIE BORROFF. "Robert Frost's New Testament: Language and the Poem," *Modern Philology* 69(1), August 1971, 47-48.

WILLIAM S. DOXEY. *Explicator* 29(8), April 1971, Item 70.

ROBERT HAWKINS. *Preface to Poetry*, pp. 43-45.

ARCHIBALD HENDERSON. "Robert Frost's " 'Out, Out — ' "," *American Imago* 34(1), Spring 1977, 12-27.

LEE A. JACOBUS and WILLIAM T. MOYNIHAN. *Poems in Context*, pp. 20-23.

LAURENCE PERRINE. *Sound and Sense*, pp. 108-9; second ed., pp. 115-16; third ed., pp. 136-37; fourth ed., pp. 127-28.

WILLIAM H. PRITCHARD. "The Grip of Frost," *Hudson Review* 29(2), Summer 1976, 195-97.

WELDON THORNTON. *Explicator* 25(9), May 1967, Item 71.

"The Oven Bird"

CLEANTH BROOKS, JOHN THIBAUT PURSER, and ROBERT PENN WARREN. *An Approach to Literature*, fourth ed., pp. 426-27; fifth ed., pp. 490-91.

C. R. B. COMBELLACK. *Explicator* 22(3), November 1963, Item 17.

FRED DURDEN. "Thoreau and Frost: Birds of a Feather," *Thoreau Journal Quarterly* 9(4), October 1977, 30-32.

JERRY A. HERNDON. *Explicator* 28(8), April 1970, Item 64.

GEORGE MONTEIRO. "Robert Frost's Solitary Singer," *New England Quarterly* 44(1), March 1971, 134-40.

WILLIAM R. OSBORNE. *Explicator* 26(6), February 1968, Item 47.

JOHN CLARK PRATT. *The Meaning of Modern Poetry*, pp. 131, 137, 133, 138, 154, 139, 146-47, 158.

WILLIAM H. PRITCHARD. "Diminished Nature," *Massachusetts Review* 1(3), Spring 1960, 477-82.

DAVID ALAN SANDERS. "Words in the Rush of Everything to Waste: A Poetic Theme in Frost," *South Carolina Review* 7(1), November 1974, 38-40.

MARK VAN DOREN. *Introduction to Poetry*, pp. 73-77.

HYATT H. WAGGONER. *American Poets*, pp. 297-300.

"Pan with Us"

DONALD T. HAYNES. "The Narrative Unity of *A Boy's Will*," *PMLA* 87(3), May 1972, 461.

"The Pasture"

HELEN H. BACON. "In- and Outdoor Schooling: Robert Frost and the Classics," *American Scholar* 43(4), Autumn 1974, 647.

LYLE DOMINA. "Thoreau and Frost: The Search for Reality," *Ball State University Forum* 19(4), Autumn 1978, 68-70.

WILLIAM FREEDMAN. *Explicator* 29(9), May 1971, Item 80.

ROD W. HORTON. "The Pasture," *CEA Critic* 11(5), February 1949, 4.

WILLIAM S. LONG. "Frost," *CEA Critic* 10(2), November 1948, 4.

M. L. ROSENTHAL. *Poetry and the Common Life*, p. 11.

SISTER CATHERINE THERESA. "New Testament Interpretations of Robert Frost's Poems," *Ball State University Forum* 11(1), Winter 1970, 50.

LAWRANCE THOMPSON. " 'All . . . Love Poems,' " *CEA Critic* 11(5), February 1949, 4-5.

CHAD WALSH. *Doors into Poetry*, pp. 92-93.

"Paul's Wife"

FLOYD C. WATKINS. "Going and Coming Back: Robert Frost's Religious Poetry," *South Atlantic Quarterly* 73(4), Autumn 1974, 451-53.

"The Pauper Witch of Grafton"

MORDECAI MARCUS. "The Whole Pattern of Frost's 'Two Witches': Contrasting Psycho-Sexual Modes," *Literature and Psychology* 26(2), 1976, 74-78.

"The Peaceful Shepherd"

DENNIS VAIL. "Point of View in Frost's 'The Peaceful Shepherd,' " *Notes on Contemporary Literature* 4(5), November 1974, 2-4.

"Provide, Provide"

RANDALL JARRELL. "To the Laodiceans," *Kenyon Review* 14(4), Autumn 1952, 540-42.

LAURENCE PERRINE. "Frost's 'Provide, Provide,' " *Notes on Contemporary Literature* 8(2), March 1978, 9.

JOHN OLIVER PERRY. *The Experience of Poems*, pp. 61-62.

ROBERT G. TWOMBLY. "The Poetics of Demur: Lowell and Frost," *College English* 38(4), December 1976, 391-92.

"Putting in the Seed"

DANIEL R. BARNES. *Explicator* 31(8), April 1973, Item 59.

"Quandry"

THOMAS K. HEARN, JR. "Making Sweetbreads Do: Robert Frost and Moral Empiricism," *New England Quarterly* 49(1), March 1976, 73-74.

"The Quest of the Purple-Fringed"

MICHAEL WEST. "Versifying Thoreau: Frost's 'The Quest of the Purple-Fringed' and 'Fire and Ice,' " *English Language Notes* 16(1), September 1978, 42-44.

"Questioning Faces"

DOROTHY JUDD HALL. "Painterly Qualities in Frost's Lyric Poetry," *Ball State University Forum* 11(1), Winter 1970, 10.

"Range-Finding"

ARNOLD G. BARTINI. "Robert Frost and Moral Neutrality," *CEA Critic* 38(2), January 1976, 23.

CLEANTH BROOKS. "I. A. Richards and the Concept of Tension," in *I. A. Richards: Essays in His Honor*, pp. 154-56.

PETER W. DOWELL. "Counter-Images and Their Function in the Poetry of Robert Frost," *Tennessee Studies in Literature* 14 (1969), 20-22.

DARRELL MANSELL, JR. *Explicator* 24(7), March 1966, Item 63.

JANIS P. STOUT. "Convention and Variation in Frost's Sonnets," *Concerning Poetry* 11(1), Spring 1978, 29.

"Reluctance"

JAMES BRUCE ANDERSON. "Frost and Sandburg: A Theological Criticism," *Renascence* 19(4), Summer 1967, 172-73.

HARRY BROWN and JOHN MILSTEAD. *What the Poem Means*, p. 92.

JAN B. GORDON. "Robert Frost's Circle of Enchantment," in *Modern American Poetry*, edited by Jerome Mazzaro, p. 68.

"Revelation"

SISTER CATHERINE THERESA. "New Testament Interpretations of Robert Frost's Poems," *Ball State University Forum* 11(1), Winter 1970, 51.

"The Road Not Taken"

GÉMINO H. ABAD. *A Formal Approach to Lyric Poetry*, pp. 234-35.

FROST, ROBERT *(Cont.)*

"The Road Not Taken" *(cont.)*

DARREL ABEL. "Robert Frost's 'True Make-Believe,' " *Texas Studies in Literature and Language* 20(4), Winter 1978, 555-56.

WILLIAM B. BACHE. "Rationalization in Two Frost Poems," *Ball State University Forum* 11(1), Winter 1970, 33-34.

WILLIAM W. BETTS, JR. "The Poem in the Classroom," *Studies in the Humanities* 1(1), March 1969, 5.

LARRY L. FINGER. "Frost's 'The Road Not Taken': A 1925 Letter Come to Light," *American Literature* 50(3), November 1978, 478-79.

BEN W. GRIFFITH, JR. *Explicator* 12(8), June 1954, Item 55.

R. G. MALBONE. *Explicator* 24(3), November 1965, Item 27.

LAURENCE PERRINE. *Explicator* 19(5), February 1961, Item 28.

ELEANOR M. SICKELS. *Explicator* 19(5), February 1961, Item 28.

"The Rose Family"

LAURENCE PERRINE. *Explicator* 26(5), January 1968, Item 43.

"Rose Pogonias"

JAN B. GORDON. "Robert Frost's Circle of Enchantment," in *Modern American Poetry,* edited by Jerome Mazzaro, pp. 64-65.

"The Runaway"

CHARLES B. HANDS. "The Hidden Terror of Robert Frost," *English Journal* 58(8), November 1969, 1165-66.

MARK VAN DOREN. "The Permanence of Robert Frost," *American Scholar* 5(2), Spring 1936, 196.

"Sand Dunes"

LAURENCE PERRINE. *Explicator* 14(6), March 1956, Item 38.

R. W. STALLMAN. "The Position of Poetry Today," *English Journal* 46(5), May 1957, 246-47.

HYATT H. WAGGONER. *American Poets,* pp. 303-4.

"The Self-Seeker"

DARREL ABEL. "Robert Frost's 'True Make-Believe,' " *Texas Studies in Literature and Language* 20(4), Winter 1978, 562-63.

LAURENCE PERRINE. "The Sense of Frost's 'The Self-Seeker,' " *Concerning Poetry* 7(2), Fall 1974, 5-8.

HAROLD E. TOLIVER. *Pastoral Forms and Attitudes,* pp. 341-42.

"A Servant to Servants"

DENIS DONOGHUE. "A Mode of Communication: Frost and the 'Middle' Style," *Yale Review* 52(2), December 1962, 215-16.

STUART B. JAMES. "The Home's Tyranny: Robert Frost's 'A Servant to Servants' and Andrew Wyeth's 'Christina's World,' " *South Dakota Review* 1(2), May 1964, 8-13.

DONALD JONES. "Kindred Entanglements in Frost's 'A Servant to Servants,' " *Papers on Language and Literature* 2(2), Spring 1966, 150-61.

"The Silken Tent"

WALTON BEACHAM. *The Meaning of Poetry,* pp. 51-54.

WALTER GIERASCH. *Explicator* 30(1), September 1971, Item 10.

RONALD L. LYCETTE. "The Vortex Points of Robert Frost," *Ball State University Forum* 14(3), Summer 1973, 58.

"Sitting by a Bush in Broad Daylight"

HARRY MODEAN CAMPBELL. *Explicator* 5(3), December 1946, Item 18.

ANNA K. JUHNKE. "Religion in Robert Frost's Poetry: The Play for Self-Possession," *American Literature* 36(2), May 1964, 156-57.

"Snow"

EBEN BASS. "Frost's Poetry of Fear," *American Literature* 43(4), January 1972, 604-5.

"A Soldier"

JANIS P. STOUT. "Convention and Variation in Frost's Sonnets," *Concerning Poetry* 11(1), Spring 1978, 28-29.

"Something for Hope"

HELEN H. BACON. "In- and Outdoor Schooling: Robert Frost and the Classics," *American Scholar* 43(4), Autumn 1974, 643.

"The Span of Life"

JOHN CIARDI. *How Does a Poem Mean?* pp. 994-95; second ed., p. 360.

"Spring Pools"

C. R. B. COMBELLACK. *Explicator* 30(3), November 1971, Item 27.

MICHAEL HANCHER. "Understanding Poetic Speech Arts," *College English* 36(6), February 1975, 637-38.

HAROLD E. TOLIVER. *Pastoral Forms and Attitudes,* pp. 354-55.

DAVID TOOR. *Explicator* 28(3), November 1969, Item 28.

ROBERT G. TWOMBLY. "The Poetics of Demur; Lowell and Frost," *College English* 37(4), December 1976, 389-91.

"The Star-Splitter"

SISTER CATHERINE THERESA. "New Testament Interpretations of Robert Frost's Poems," *Ball State University Forum* 11(1), Winter 1970, 52-53.

"Stopping by Woods on a Snowy Evening"

GÉMINO H. ABAD. *A Formal Approach to Lyric Poetry,* pp. 51-54.

GÉMINO H. ABAD. *In Another Light,* pp. 96-97, 100-14.

JAMES ARMSTRONG. "The 'Death Wish' in 'Stopping by Woods,' " *College English* 25(6), March 1964, 440, 445.

JEROME BEATY and WILLIAM H. MATCHETT. *Poetry From Statement to Meaning,* pp. 6-8.

WALTER BLAIR and JOHN C. GERBER. *Better Reading 2: Literature,* pp. 156-57.

CLEANTH BROOKS. "Poetry Since *The Waste Land,*" *Southern Review,* n.s., 1(3), Summer 1965, 495-96.

JOHN CIARDI. *How Does a Poem Mean?* pp. 671-76; second ed., pp. 6-10.

JOHN CIARDI. "Robert Frost: The Way to a Poem," *Saturday Review* 41(12 April 1958), 13-15. Reprinted in: John Ciardi. *Dialogue with an Audience,* pp. 147-57. Also: Chad and Eva T. Walsh. *Twice Ten,* pp. 176-79.

CHARLES W. COOPER and JOHN HOLMES. *Preface to Poetry,* pp. 605-7.

JAMES M. COX. "Robert Frost and the Edge of the Clearing," *Virginia Quarterly Review* 35(1), Winter 1959, 82-84.

EARL DANIELS. *The Art of Reading Poetry,* pp. 16-18. Reprinted in: *The Creative Reader,* pp. 875-78; second ed., pp. 932-35.

LLOYD N. DENDINGER. "The Irrational Appeal of Frost's Dark Deep Woods," *Southern Review,* n.s., 2(4), Autumn 1966, 822-29.

BOB DOWELL. "Revealing Incident as Technique in the Poetry of Robert Frost," *CEA Critic* 31(3), December 1968, 12.

NORMAN FRIEDMAN. "Three Views of Poetic Form," *College English* 26(7), April 1965, 496-97.

CHARLES B. HANDS. "The Hidden Terror of Robert Frost," *English Journal* 58(8), November 1969, 1164-65.

NAT HENRY. *Explicator* 37(1), Fall 1978, 37-38.

JAMES G. HEPBURN. "Robert Frost and His Critics," *New England Quarterly* 35(3), September 1962, 367-69.

D. J. LEPORE. "Setting and/or Statement," *English Journal* 55(5), May 1966, 624-26.

ARTHUR C. MCGILL. *The Celebration of Flesh,* pp. 100-3.

CHARLES A. MCLAUGHLIN. "Two Views of Poetic Unity," *University of Kansas City Review* 22(4), Summer 1956, 312-15.

THEODORE MORRISON. "Frost: Country Poet and Cosmopolitan Poet," *Yale Review* 59(2), December 1969, 181-89.

JOHN T. OLGILVIE. "From Woods to Stars: A Pattern of Imagery in Robert Frost's Poetry," in *The Dimensions of Poetry,* pp. 668-72.

LAURENCE PERRINE. *Sound and Sense,* p. 117; second ed., p. 126; third ed., p. 151; fourth ed., p. 142.

JAMES M. REID. "An Adventure in Programing Literature," *English Journal* 52(9), December 1963, 661-67.

JAMES M. REID. *100 American Poems of the Twentieth Century,* pp. 24-26.

WILLIAM H. SHURR. "Once More to the 'Woods': A New Point of Entry into Frost's Most Famous Poem," *New England Quarterly* 47(4), December 1974, 584-94.

LEONARD UNGER and WILLIAM VAN O'CONNOR. *Poems for Study,* pp. 597-600.

CHARLES CHILD WALCUTT. "Interpreting the Symbol," *College English* 14(8), May 1953, 450.

JAMES WRIGHT. "Frost: Stopping by Woods on a Snowy Evening," in *Master Poems of the English Language,* pp. 877-81.

"Storm Fear"

JAN B. GORDON. "Robert Frost's Circle of Enchantment," in *Modern American Poetry,* edited by Jerome Mazzaro, pp. 63-64.

CARL M. LINDNER. "Robert Frost: Dark Romantic," *Arizona Quarterly* 29(3), Autumn 1973, 236-37.

ARTHUR C. MCGILL. *The Celebration of Flesh,* pp. 98-99.

"The Strong Are Saying Nothing?"

ANN K. JUHNKE. "Religion in Robert Frost's Poetry: The Play for Self-Possession," *American Literature* 36(2), May 1964, 156.

"The Subverted Flower"

HOWARD MUNFORD. *Explicator* 17(4), January 1959, Item 31.

ROY SCHEELE. "Sensible Confusion in Frost's 'The Subverted Flower,'" *South Carolina Review* 10(1), November 1977, 89-98.

DONALD B. STAUFFER. *Explicator* 15(6), March 1957, Item 38.

"The Thatch"

EBEN BASS. "Frost's Poetry of Fear," *American Literature* 43(4), January 1972, 607-8.

DAVID RIDGLEY CLARK. *Lyric Resonance,* pp. 117-32.

LAURENCE J. SASSO, JR. "Robert Frost: Love's Question," *New England Quarterly* 42(1), March 1969, 102-3.

"There are Roughly Zones"

CARL LINDNER. "Robert Frost: 'In the American Grain,'" *Colorado Quarterly* 22(4), Spring 1974, 471-74.

"They say the truth will make you free"

LAWRANCE THOMPSON. "Robert Frost," in *Seven Modern American Poets,* p. 22.

"The Times Table"

EBEN BASS. "Frost's Poetry of Fear," *American Literature* 43(4), January 1972, 613.

"To a Young Wretch"

JULIAN MASON. "Frost's Conscious Accommodation of Contraries," *CEA Critic* 38(3), March 1976, 30.

"To Earthward"

CLEANTH BROOKS, JOHN THIBAUT PURSER, and ROBERT PENN WARREN. *An Approach to Literature,* fourth ed., pp. 424-25.

DONALD HALL. "Vanity, Fame, Love, and Robert Frost," *Commentary* 64(6), December 1977, 52.

WILBUR S. SCOTT. *Explicator* 16(4), January 1958, Item 23.

"To the Thawing Wind"

HOWELL D. CHICKERING, JR. "Robert Frost, Romantic Humorist," *Literature and Psychology* 16(3-4), 1966, 147-48.

BRUCE STILLIANS. *Explicator* 31(4), December 1972, Item 31.

"Too Anxious for Rivers"

GEORGE KNOX. "A Backward Motion Toward the Source," *Personalist* 47(3), Summer 1966, 380-81.

LAWRANCE THOMPSON. "Robert Frost," in *Seven Modern American Poets,* 29-30.

"Tree at my Window"

EBEN BASS. "Frost's Poetry of Fear," *American Literature* 43(4), January 1972, 607.

HARRY BROWN and JOHN MILSTEAD. *What the Poem Means,* pp. 93-94.

R. W. STALLMAN. "The Position of Poetry Today," *English Journal* 46(5), May 1957, 248-49.

"Trespass"

MARJORIE COOK. "The Complexity of Boundaries: 'Trespass' by Robert Frost," *Notes on Contemporary Literature* 5(1), January 1975, 2-5.

"The Tuft of Flowers"

JAMES BRUCE ANDERSON. "Frost and Sandburg: A Theological Criticism," *Renascence* 19(4), Summer 1967, 176-77.

MICHAEL J. COLLINS. "Formal Allusion in Modern Poetry," *Concerning Poetry* 9(1), Spring 1976, 6-7.

BABETTE DEUTSCH. *Poetry in Our Time,* p. 70; second ed., pp. 74-75.

DONALD T. HAYNES. "The Narrative Unity of *A Boy's Will,*" *PMLA* 87(3), May 1972, 460-61.

FROST, ROBERT *(Cont.)*

"The Tuft of Flowers" *(cont.)*

GEORGE MONTIERO. "Robert Frost's Linked Analogies," *New England Quarterly* 46(3), September 1973, 463-66.

HAROLD E. TOLIVER. *Pastoral Forms and Attitudes*, pp. 342-43.

"Two Look at Two"

JAN B. GORDON. "Robert Frost's Circle of Enchantment," in *Modern American Poetry*, edited by Jerome Mazzaro, pp. 71-72.

LAURENCE J. SASSO, JR. "Robert Frost: Love's Question," *New England Quarterly* 42(1), March 1969, 105-6.

"Two Tramps in Mud Time"

GÉMINO H. ABAD. *A Formal Approach to Lyric Poetry*, pp. 185-86, 232-33.

WILLIAM B. BACHE. "Rationalization in Two Frost Poems," *Ball State University Forum* 11(1), Winter 1970, 34-35.

WALTER BLAIR. *The Literature of the United States*, II: 940.

ALBERT BRAVERMAN and BERNARD EINBOND. *Explicator* 29(3), November 1970, Item 25.

CLEANTH BROOKS. *Modern Poetry and the Tradition*, pp. 112-13.

HARRY BROWN and JOHN MILSTEAD. *What the Poem Means*, p. 94.

MALCOLM COWLEY. *A Many-Windowed House*, pp. 208-9.

DENIS DONOGHUE. *Connoisseurs of Chaos*, pp. 182-83.

RICHARD FOSTER. "Leaves Compared with Flowers: A Reading in Robert Frost's Poems," *New England Quarterly* 46(3), September 1973, 418-20.

CHARLES KAPLAN. *Explicator* 12(8), June 1954, Item 51.

GEORGE MONTEIRO. "Robert Frost and the Politics of Self," *New York Public Library Bulletin* 73(5), May 1969, 309-14.

LAWRANCE THOMPSON. "Robert Frost," in *Seven Modern American Poets*, p. 33.

ROBERT PENN WARREN. "Frost: Two Tramps in Mud Time," in *Master Poems of the English Language*, pp. 871-75.

GEORGE F. WHICHER. "Frost at Seventy," *American Scholar* 14(4), Autumn 1945, 412-14.

"Unharvested"

HAROLD E. TOLIVER. *Pastoral Forms and Attitudes*, pp. 346-47.

"The Vanishing Red"

C. M. BOWRA. "Reassessments I: Robert Frost," *Adelphi* 27 (November 1950), 55.

"The Vantage Point"

REGINALD L. COOK. "Robert Frost: An Equilibrist's Field of Vision," *Massachusetts Review* 15(3), Summer 1974, 393.

JAN B. GORDON. "Robert Frost's Circle of Enchantment," in *Modern American Poetry*, edited by Jerome Mazzaro, pp. 69-70.

"Version"

JOSEPH KAU. "Two Notes on Robert Frost Poems: Frost's 'Version' of Zeno's Arrow," *Notes on Modern American Literature* 1(4), Fall 1977, Item 33.

"The Vindictives"

J. M. LINEBARGER. "Sources of Frost's 'The Vindictives,'" *American Notes & Queries*, n.s., 12(9-10), May-June 1974, 150-54.

"Waiting: Afield at Dusk"

DARREL ABEL. "Emerson's 'Apparition of God' and Frost's 'Apparition of the Mind,'" *University of Toronto Quarterly* 48(1), Fall 1978, 48.

JAN B. GORDON. "Robert Frost's Circle of Enchantment," in *Modern American Poetry*, edited by Jerome Mazzaro, pp. 67-68.

DONALD T. HAYNES. "The Narrative Unity of *A Boy's Will*," *PMLA* 87(3), May 1972, 459.

"We Vainly Wrestle"

JOSEPH KAU. "Two Notes on Robert Frost Poems: Blind Optimism in Frost's 'We Vainly Wrestle,'" *Notes on Modern American Literature* 1(4), Fall 1977, Item 33.

"West-Running Brook"

JAN B. GORDON. "Robert Frost's Circle of Enchantment," in *Modern American Poetry*, edited by Jerome Mazzaro, pp. 74-76.

GEORGE KNOX. "A Backward Motion Toward the Source," *Personalist* 47(3), Summer 1966, 378-80.

TODD M. LIEBER. "Robert Frost and Wallace Stevens: 'What to Make of a Diminished Thing,'" *American Literature* 47(1), March 1975, 76.

RICHARD D. LORD. "Frost and Cyclicism," *Renascence* 10(1), Autumn 1957, 19-25, 31.

RONALD L. LYCETTE. "The Vortex Points of Robert Frost," *Ball State University Forum* 14(3), Summer 1973, 57-58.

PATRICK MORROW. "The Greek Nexus in Robert Frost's 'West-Running Brook,'" *Personalist* 49(1), Winter 1968, 24-33.

LAURENCE J. SASSO, JR. "Robert Frost: Love's Question," *New England Quarterly* 42(1), March 1969, 98-99.

ROBERT H. SWENNES. "Man and Wife: The Dialogue of Contraries in Robert Frost's Poetry," *American Literature* 42(3), November 1970, 369-71.

LAWRANCE THOMPSON. "Robert Frost," in *Seven Modern American Poets*, pp. 30-32.

HAROLD E. TOLIVER. *Pastoral Forms and Attitudes*, pp. 357-59.

CHAD and EVA T. WALSH. *Twice Ten*, pp. 170-75.

HAROLD H. WATTS. "Robert Frost and the Interrupted Dialogue," *American Literature* 27(1), March 1955, 70-74, *passim*.

H. T. WEBSTER. *Explicator* 8(4), February 1950, Item 32.

"The White-Tailed Hornet"

HARRY BERGER, JR. "Poetry as Revision: Interpreting Robert Frost," *Criticism* 10(1), Winter 1968, 9-11.

SISTER CATHERINE THERESA. "New Testament Interpretations of Robert Frost's Poems," *Ball State University Forum* 11(1), Winter 1970, 53.

"Wild Grapes"

HELEN BACON. "For Girls: From 'Birches' to 'Wild Grapes,'" *Yale Review* 67(1), Autumn 1977, 13-29.

LAURENCE PERRINE. "Letting Go With the Heart: Frost's 'Wild Grapes,'" *Notes on Modern American Literature* 2(3), Summer 1978, Item 20.

"A-Wishing Well"

A. R. FERGUSON. "Frost, Sill, and 'A-Wishing Well,' " *American Literature* 33(3), November 1961, 370-73.

CLAUDE M. SIMPSON. "Robert Frost and Man's 'Royal Role,' " in *Aspects of American Poetry,* pp. 133-35.

"The Witch of Coös"

EBEN BASS. "Frost's Poetry of Fear," *American Literature* 43(4), January 1972, 612-13.

MORDECAI MARCUS. "The Whole Pattern of Frost's 'Two Witches': Contrasting Psycho-Sexual Modes," *Literature and Psychology* 26(2), 1976, 69-74.

LAURENCE PERRINE. *100 American Poems of the Twentieth Century,* pp. 36-43.

FRED C. SCHUTZ. *Explicator* 33(3), November 1974, Item 19.

CAMILLE SLIGHTS and WILLIAM SLIGHTS. *Explicator* 27(6), February 1969, Item 40.

LAWRANCE THOMPSON. "Robert Frost," in *Seven Modern American Poets,* p. 17.

THOMAS R. THORNBURG. "Mother's Private Ghost: A Note on Frost's 'The Witch of Coös,' " *Ball State University Forum* 11(1), Winter 1970, 16-20.

"The Wood-Pile"

FERMAN BISHOP. *Explicator* 18(9), June 1960, Item 58.

CLEANTH BROOKS. *Modern Poetry and the Tradition,* pp. 113-14.

CLEANTH BROOKS, JOHN THIBAUT PURSER, and ROBERT PENN WARREN. *An Approach to Literature,* pp. 453-54; second ed., pp. 453-54; third ed., pp. 305-7; fourth ed., pp. 421-23; fifth ed., pp. 487-88.

BABETTE DEUTSCH. *Poetry in Our Time,* p. 70; second ed., p. 75.

ALEXANDER C. KERN. *Explicator* 28(6), February 1970, Item 49.

LAURENCE LERNER. "An Essay on Pastoral," *Essays in Criticism* 20(3), July 1970, 275-77. Reprinted in: Laurence Lerner. *The Uses of Pastoral,* pp. 11-13.

LAURENCE LERNER. *The Uses of Nostalgia,* pp. 11-13.

LEWIS H. MILLER, JR. "The Poet as Swinger: Fact and Fancy in Robert Frost," *Criticism* 16(1), Winter 1974, 67-72.

ROBERT NARVESON. "On Frost's 'The Wood-Pile,' " *English Journal* 57(1), January 1968, 39-40.

RICHARD POIRIER. "Soundings for Home: Frost's Poetry of Extravagance and Return," *Georgia Review* 31(2), Summer 1977, 289-93.

HAROLD E. TOLIVER. *Pastoral Forms and Attitudes,* pp. 348-49.

HYATT H. WAGGONER. *American Poets,* pp. 308-9.

FLOYD C. WATKINS. "Going and Coming Back: Robert Frost's Religious Poetry," *South Atlantic Quarterly* 73(4), Autumn 1974, 449-50.

"A Young Birch"

MARIO L. D'AVANZO. "Frost's 'A Young Birch': A Thing of Beauty," *Concerning Poetry* 3(2), Fall 1970, 69-70.

FROUDE, JAMES ANTHONY

"Confessio fidei"

FREDERICK L. MULHAUSER. "An Unpublished Poem of James Anthony Froude," *English Language Notes* 12(1), September 1974, 26-30.

FULLER, ROY

"Amateur Film-Making"

GRAHAM MARTIN. "Roy Fuller," in *The Modern Poet,* edited by Ian Hamilton, pp. 29-30.

"Eclipse"

GEOFFREY THURLEY. *The Ironic Harvest,* p. 140.

"The Historian"

IAN HAMILTON. *A Poetry Chronicle,* pp. 90-91.

"The Image"

JOHN PRESS. "English Verse Since 1945," *Essays by Divers Hands,* 3rd series, 31 (1962), 160-61.

"The Perturbation of Uranus"

GRAHAM MARTIN. "Roy Fuller," in *The Modern Poet,* edited by Ian Hamilton, pp. 26-27.

"Spring 1942"

VERNON SCANNELL. *Not Without Glory,* pp. 98-99.

"The Statue"

GRAHAM MARTIN. "Roy Fuller," in *The Modern Poet,* edited by Ian Hamilton, pp. 27-28.

"What is Terrible"

VERNON SCANNELL. *Not Without Glory,* pp. 105-6.

"Winter in Camp"

VERNON SCANNELL. *Not Without Glory,* pp. 108-12.

FUNAROFF, SOL

"Factory Night"

ESTELLE GERSHGOREN NOVAK. "The Dynamo School of Poets," *Contemporary Literature* 11(4), Autumn 1970, 529.

"What the Thunder Said: A Fire Sermon"

ESTELLE GERSHGOREN NOVAK. "The Dynamo School of Poets," *Contemporary Literature* 11(4), Autumn 1970, 530-31.

G

GALLER, DAVID

"The Dybbuk"

LAURENCE LIEBERMAN. *Unassigned Frequencies,* pp. 198-99.

GARDNER, ISABELLA

"At the Zoo"

RALPH J. MILLS, JR. *Contemporary American Poetry,* pp. 124-26.

"Of Flesh and Bone"

RALPH J. MILLS, JR. *Contemporary American Poetry,* pp. 127-29.

"On Looking in the Looking Glass"

RALPH J. MILLS, JR. *Contemporary American Poetry,* pp. 131-33.

"The Panic Vine"

RALPH J. MILLS, JR. *Contemporary American Poetry,* pp. 129-30.

"Part of the Darkness"

PAUL CARROLL. *The Poem In Its Skin,* p. 213.

"Summer Remembered"

LAURENCE PERRINE. *100 American Poems of the Twentieth Century,* pp. 235-37.

"To Thoreau on Rereading Walden"

RALPH J. MILLS, JR. *Contemporary American Poetry,* p. 126.

"The Widow's Yard"

PAUL CARROLL. *The Poem In Its Skin,* pp. 53-62.

"Zei Gesund"

RALPH J. MILLS, JR. *Contemporary American Poetry,* p. 130.

GARDONS, S. S.

"The Survivors"

WILLIAM HEYEN. "A Note on S. S. Gardons," *Western Humanities Review* 25(3), Summer 1971, 254-55.

GARFITT, ROGER

"Rosehill"

EDWARD BRUNNER. "Uncomely Relations," *Iowa Review* 6(3-4), Summer-Fall 1975, 235-37.

GARRIGUE, JEAN

"Dialog for Belvedere"

JOSEPH WARREN BEACH. "The Cancelling Out — A Note on Recent Poetry," *Accent* 7(4), Summer 1947, 246-48. (P)

"The Flux of Autumn"

LAURENCE LIEBERMAN. *Unassigned Frequencies,* p. 108.

"For Such a Bird He Had No Convenient Cage"

LAURENCE LIEBERMAN. *Unassigned Frequencies,* p. 113.

"For the Fountains and Fountaineers of Villa d'Este"

GRACE SCHULMAN. "To Create the Self," *Twentieth Century Literature* 23(3), October 1977, 309-10.

"Pays Perdu"

GRACE SCHULMAN. "To Create the Self," *Twentieth Century Literature* 23(3), October 1977, 310-11.

"Studies for an Actress"

LAURENCE LIEBERMAN. *Unassigned Frequencies,* pp. 108-10.

"Why the Heart Has Dreams Is Why the Mind Goes Mad"

LAURENCE LIEBERMAN. *Unassigned Frequencies,* pp. 110-11.

GASCOIGNE, GEORGE

"Dan Bartholomew's Dolorous Discourses"

ROBERT PINSKY. *The Situation of Poetry,* pp. 170-72.

"Gascoigne's Good Morrow"

MALCOLM MACKENZIE ROSS. "History and Poetry: Decline of the Historical Concrete," *Thought* 26(102), Autumn 1951, 437-38.

"Gascoignes woodmanship"

DOUGLAS L. PETERSON. *The English Lyric from Wyatt to Donne,* pp. 154-60.

YVOR WINTERS. "The 16th Century Lyric in England: A Critical and Historical Reinterpretation," in *Elizabethan Poetry,* edited by Paul J. Alpers, pp. 100-2.

"The common speech is, spend and God will send" (Gascoigne's Memories, III)

DOUGLAS L. PETERSON. *The English Lyric from Wyatt to Donne,* pp. 153-54.

YVOR WINTERS. "The 26th Century Lyric in England: A Critical and Historical Reinterpretation," in *Elizabethan Poetry,* edited by Paul J. Alpers, pp. 98-99.

"The constancie of a lover hath thus sometimes bene briefly declared"
> DOUGLAS L. PETERSON. *The English Lyric from Wyatt to Donne*, pp. 152-53.
> JOHN T. SHAWCROSS. "The Poet as Orator: One Phase of His Judicial Pose," in *The Rhetoric of Renaissance Poetry*, pp. 13-14.

"The Lullabie of a Lover"
> LEONARD NATHAN. "Gascoigne's 'Lullabie' and Structures in the Tudor Lyric," in *The Rhetoric of Renaissance Poetry*, pp. 58-72.
> DOUGLAS L. PETERSON. *The English Lyric from Wyatt to Donne*, pp. 160-62.

GASCOYNE, DAVID

"Andante Amoroso"
> SISTER BERNETTA QUINN. "Symbolic Landscape in David Gascoyne," *Contemporary Literature* 12(4), Autumn 1971, 484-85.

"An Autumn Park"
> SISTER BERNETTA QUINN. "Symbolic Landscape in David Gascoyne," *Contemporary Literature* 12(4), Autumn 1971, 487.

"Chambre d'Hotel"
> GEOFFREY THURLEY. *The Ironic Harvest*, pp. 107-8.

"The Diabolical Principle"
> ROB JACKAMAN. "View From The White Cliffs: A Close Look at One Manifestation of English Surrealism," *Twentieth Century Literature* 21(1), February 1975, 75-79.

"Eclipse of the Moon"
> SISTER BERNETTA QUINN. "Symbolic Landscape in David Gascoyne," *Contemporary Literature* 12(4), Autumn 1971, 469.

"Epilogue"
> SISTER BERNETTA QUINN. "Symbolic Landscape in David Gascoyne," *Contemporary Literature* 12(4), Autumn 1971, 479-80.

"Evening Again"
> SISTER BERNETTA QUINN. "Symbolic Landscape in David Gascoyne," *Contemporary Literature* 12(4), Autumn 1971, 492.

"Figure in a Landscape"
> SISTER BERNETTA QUINN. "Symbolic Landscape in David Gascoyne," *Contemporary Literature* 12(4), Autumn 1971, 477-78.

"The Gravel-Pit Field"
> SISTER BERNETTA QUINN. "Symbolic Landscape in David Gascoyne," *Contemporary Literature* 12(4), Autumn 1971, 489-90.

"Inferno"
> SISTER BERNETTA QUINN. "Symbolic Landscape in David Gascoyne," *Contemporary Literature* 12(4), Autumn 1971, 484.

"Jardin du Palais Royal"
> GEOFFREY THURLEY. *The Ironic Harvest*, pp. 108-9.

"Landscape"
> SISTER BERNETTA QUINN. "Symbolic Landscape in David Gascoyne," *Contemporary Literature* 12(4), Autumn 1971, 493-94.

"Mozart Sursum Corda"
> SISTER BERNETTA QUINN. "Symbolic Landscape in David Gascoyne," *Contemporary Literature* 12(4), Autumn 1971, 483.

"Noctambules"
> GEOFFREY THURLEY. *The Ironic Harvest*, p. 106.

"Orpheus in the Underworld"
> SISTER BERNETTA QUINN. "Symbolic Landscape in David Gascoyne," *Contemporary Literature* 12(4), Autumn 1971, 479.

"Renaissance"
> SISTER BERNETTA QUINN. "Symbolic Landscape in David Gascoyne," *Contemporary Literature* 12(4), 470-71.

"Reported Missing"
> GEOFFREY THURLEY. *The Ironic Harvest*, p. 112.

"Salvador Dali"
> SISTER BERNETTA QUINN. "Symbolic Landscape in David Gascoyne," *Contemporary Literature* 12(4), Autumn 1971, 491-92.

"Slate"
> SISTER BERNETTA QUINN. "Symbolic Landscape in David Gascoyne," *Contemporary Literature* 12(4), Autumn 1971, 491.

"Tenebrae"
> SISTER BERNETTA QUINN. "Symbolic Landscape in David Gascoyne," *Contemporary Literature* 12(4), Autumn 1971, 479.

"A Vagrant"
> GEOFFREY THURLEY. *The Ironic Harvest*, pp. 112-15.

"The Very Image"
> GEOFFREY THURLEY. *The Ironic Harvest*, p. 102.

"Vista"
> SISTER BERNETTA QUINN. "Symbolic Landscape in David Gascoyne," *Contemporary Literature* 12(4), Autumn 1971, 468.

"Walking at Whitaun"
> SISTER BERNETTA QUINN. "Symbolic Landscape in David Gascoyne," *Contemporary Literature* 12(4), Autumn 1971, 488.

"The Wall"
> GEOFFREY THURLEY. *The Ironic Harvest*, p. 105.

"A Wartime Dawn"
> GEOFFREY THURLEY. *The Ironic Harvest*, pp. 110-11.

"Winter Garden"
> C. DAY LEWIS. *The Poetic Image*, pp. 131-33.

"The worlds are breaking in my head"
> SISTER BERNETTA QUINN. "Symbolic Landscape in David Gascoyne," *Contemporary Literature* 12(4), Autumn 1971, 476.

GAY, JOHN

"Epistle to Pulteney"
> PATRICIA MEYER SPACKS. "John Gay: A Satirist's Progress," *Essays in Criticism* 14(2), April 1964, 158-61.

"Epistle to the Right Honourable Paul Methuen, Esq."
> PATRICIA MEYER SPACKS. "John Gay: A Satirist's Progress," *Essays in Criticism* 14(2), April 1964, 161-62.

GAY, JOHN *(Cont.)*

"Panegyrical Epistle to Mr. Thomas Snow"

> PATRICIA MEYER SPACKS. "John Gay: A Satirist's Progress," *Essays in Criticism* 14(2), April 1964, 162-63.

"The Poet and the Rose"

> LYNA LEE MONTGOMERY. "The Phoenix: Its Use as a Literary Device in English from the Seventeenth Century to the Twentieth Century," *D. H. Lawrence Review* 5(3), Fall 1972, 290-91.

"Rural Sports"

> MARTIN C. BATTESTIN. "Menalcas' Song: The Meaning of Art and Artifice in Gay's Poetry," *Journal of English and Germanic Philology* 65(4), October 1966, 665-66.

"Saturday" (*The Shepherd's Week*)

> JOHN ROBERT MOORE. "Gay's Burlesque of Sir Richard Blackmore's Poetry," *Journal of English and Germanic Philology* 50(1), January 1951, 83-89.

"The Shepherd's Week"

> HAROLD E. TOLIVER. *Pastoral Forms and Attitudes*, pp. 193-94.

"The Wild Boar and the Ram"

> PATRICIA MEYER SPACKS. "John Gay: A Satirist's Progress," *Essays in Criticism* 14(2), April 1964, 167-69.

GERSHON, KAREN

"Swiss Morning"

> BERNARD KNIEGER. *Explicator* 30(5), January 1972, Item 42.

GERSHWIN, IRA

"I Can't Get Started"

> DAVID RUSSELL. "Imagery and Illusion in 'I Can't Get Started,'" *CEA Critic* 26(5), February 1964, 8.
> GEORGE A. TEST. "'I Can't Get Started' Reconsidered," *CEA Critic* 26(2), November 1963, 11.

GHISELIN, BREWSTER

"Bath of Aphrodite"

> BREWSTER GHISELIN. "The Birth of a Poem," *Poetry* 69(1), October 1946, 30-43. Reprinted in: *Readings for Liberal Education*, third ed., II: 239-46.

"Gull in the Great Basin"

> RAY B. WEST. *Writing in the Rocky Mountains*, pp. 58-59.

GIBSON, MORGAN

"The Desire To Run Their Lives"

> ANNE HALLEY. "Recent American Poetry: Outside Relevancies," *Massachusetts Review* 9(4), Autumn 1968, 701-2.

GIBSON, WALKER

"Billiards"

> GEORGE ABBE. *You and Contemporary Poetry*, pp. 40-41; second ed., pp. 55-56.

"Thaw"

> GEORGE ABBE. *You and Contemporary Poetry*, p. 39; second ed., pp. 53-55.

GIBSON, WILLIAM

"The Ice-Cart"

> RODERICK A. JACOBS. "A Poem for the Junior High," *English Journal* 55(1), January 1966, 99-100.

"Winter Piece"

> EUGENE R. KINTGEN. "Perceiving Poetic Syntax," *College English* 40(1), September 1978, 17-27.

GINSBERG, ALLEN

"America"

> KINGSLEY WIDMER. "The Beat in the Rise of the Populist Culture," in *The Fifties*, p. 169.

"American Change"

> SAMUEL CHARTERS. *Some Poems/Poets*, pp. 71-76.

"Cafe in Warsaw"

> CHAD and EVA T. WALSH. *Twice Ten*, pp. 288-89.

"Death to Van Gogh's Ear!"

> KINGSLEY WIDMER. "The Beat in the Rise of the Populist Culture," in *The Fifties*, pp. 168-69.

"Howl"

> ROBERT HENSON. "'Howl' In The Classroom," *CEA Critic* 23(2), February 1961, 1, 8-9.
> LOUIS SIMPSON. *A Revolution in Taste*, pp. 72-74.
> WALTER SUTTON. *American Free Verse*, pp. 182-84.

"Message"

> PAUL CARROLL. *The Poem In Its Skin*, pp. 246-49.

"A Supermarket in California"

> JAMES E. MILLER. "Walt Whitman and the Secret of History," in *Start with the Sun*, pp. 16-17.
> ROBERT PINSKY. *The Situation of Poetry*, pp. 169-70.

"The Trembling of the Veil"

> CHAD and EVA T. WALSH. *Twice Ten*, pp. 275-77.

"Who Be Kind To"

> MORRIS DICKSTEIN. "Allen Ginsberg and the 60's," *Commentary* 49(1), January 1970, 70.

"Wichita Vortex Sutra"

> HARRY J. CARGAS. *Daniel Berrigan and Contemporary Protest Poetry*, pp. 67-76.
> PAUL CARROLL. *The Poem In Its Skin*, pp. 81-109.

GIOVANNI, NIKKI

"all i gotta do"

> SUZANNE JUHASZ. *Naked and Fiery Forms*, pp. 161-64.

"Beautiful Black Men (with compliments and apologies to all not mentioned by name)"

> SUZANNE JUHASZ. *Naked and Fiery Forms*, pp. 158-59.

"Legacies"

> SUZANNE JUHASZ. *Naked and Fiery Forms*, pp. 169-70.

"My House"

> SUZANNE JUHASZ. *Naked and Fiery Forms*, pp. 171-74.

"Poem (No Name No. 3)"

> WILLIAM J. REEVES. "The Significance of Audience in Black Poetry," *Negro American Literature Forum* 9(1), Spring 1975, 31.

"Revolutionary Dreams"

> SUZANNE JUHASZ. *Naked and Fiery Forms*, pp. 167-68.

GLÜCK, LOUISE

"For My Mother"

> LOUISE GLÜCK. "Louise Glück's Response," *Iowa Review* 4(4), Fall 1973, 74.

> STANLEY PLUMLY. "Gemini," *Iowa Review* 4(4), Fall 1973, 74. (P)

"Gemini"

> STANLEY PLUMLY. "Gemini," *Iowa Review* 4(4), Fall 1973, 73.

"The Pond"

> STANLEY PLUMLY. "Gemini," *Iowa Review* 4(4), Fall 1973, 72-73.

GODSEY, EDWIN

"Day in School"

> THOMAS H. LANDESS. "Edwin Godsey's *Cabin Fever* and the Aesthetics of Virtue," *Georgia Review* 23(3), Fall 1969, 349-51.

"Epilogue: The Wilderness"

> THOMAS H. LANDESS. "Edwin Godsey's *Cabin Fever* and the Aesthetics of Virtue," *Georgia Review* 23(3), Fall 1969, 345-46.

"Euphrosyne"

> THOMAS H. LANDESS. "The Present Course of Southern Fiction: *Everynegro* and Other Alternatives," *Arlington Quarterly* 1(2), Winter 1967-1968, 79.

"For Grandfather Corns (1852-1936)"

> THOMAS H. LANDESS. "The Present Course of Southern Fiction: *Everynegro* and Other Alternatives," *Arlington Quarterly* 1(2), Winter 1967-1968, 79-80.

"Hoppy"

> THOMAS H. LANDESS. "The Present Course of Southern Fiction: *Everynegro* and Other Alternatives," *Arlington Quarterly* 1(2), Winter 1967-68, 80-81.

"Stillness: an Eclogue"

> THOMAS H. LANDESS. "The Present Course of Southern Fiction: *Everynegro* and Other Alternatives," *Arlington Quarterly* 1(2), Winter 1967-1968, 82-83.

"Words on Sunday"

> THOMAS H. LANDESS. "The Present Course of Southern Fiction: *Everynegro* and Other Alternatives," *Arlington Quarterly* 1(2), Winter 1967-1968, 77-78.

GOGARTY, OLIVER

"The Crab Tree"

> DAVID RIDGLEY CLARK. *Lyric Resonance,* pp. 69-74.

"Golden Stockings"

> DAVID RIDGLEY CLARK. *Lyric Resonance,* pp. 68-69.

"Non Dolet"

> DAVID RIDGLEY CLARK. *Lyric Resonance,* pp. 66-67.

"The Old Goose"

> D. J. HUXLEY. "Yeats and Dr Gogarty," *Ariel* 3(3), July 1972, 37-38.

"Per Iter Tenebroscium"

> DAVID RIDGLEY CLARK. *Lyric Resonance,* p. 68.

"To a Cock"

> D. J. HUXLEY. "Yeats and Dr Gogarty," *Ariel* 3(3), July 1972, 35-36.

GOLDSMITH, OLIVER

"Ballad" (*The Vicar of Wakefield*)

> ROBERT HUNTING. "The Poems in 'The Vicar of Wakefield,'" *Criticism* 15(3), Summer 1973, 235-38.

"The Deserted Village"

> HOWARD J. BELL, JR. "*The Deserted Village* and Goldsmith's Social Doctrines," *PMLA* 59(3), September 1944, 747-72.

> THOMAS R. EDWARDS. *Imagination and Power,* pp. 129-37.

> RICHARD EVERSOLE. "The Oratorical Design of *The Deserted Village*," *English Language Notes* 4(2), December 1966, 99-104.

> MORRIS GOLDEN. "The Broken Dreams of *The Deserted Village*," *Literature and Psychology* 9(3 & 4), Summer & Fall 1959, 41-44.

> LAURENCE GOLDSTEIN. "The Auburn Syndrome: Change and Loss in 'The Deserted Village' and Wordsworth's Grasmere," *ELH* 40(3), Fall 1973, 354-59.

> RICHARD J. JAARSMA. "Ethics in the Wasteland: Image and Structure in Goldsmith's *The Deserted Village*," *Texas Studies in Literature and Language* 13(3), Fall 1971, 447-59.

> ROBERT MAHONY. "Lyrical Antithesis: The Moral Style of The Deserted Village," *Ariel* 8(2), April 1977, 33-47.

> C. N. MANLOVE. *Literature and Reality,* pp. 177-80.

> DESMOND PACEY. "The Goldsmiths and Their Villages," *University of Toronto Quarterly* 21(1), October 1951, 27-38.

> RICARDO QUINTANA. "*The Deserted Village*: Its Logical and Rhetorical Elements," *College English* 26(3), December 1964, 204-14.

> LEO F. STORM. "Literary Convention in Goldsmith's Deserted Village," *Huntington Library Quarterly* 33(3), May 1970, 243-56.

> CHARLES TOMLINSON. "Goldsmith: The Deserted Village," in *Master Poems of the English Language,* pp. 353-58.

> RAYMOND WILLIAMS. " 'Nature's Threads,' " *Eighteenth Century Studies* 2(1), Fall 1968, 45-57.

"An Elegy on the Death of a Mad Dog"

> ROBERT HUNTING. "The Poems in 'The Vicar of Wakefield,'" *Criticism* 15(3), Summer 1973, 238-39.

"The Traveller"

> RICHARD J. JAARSMA. "Satire, Theme, and Structure in *The Traveller*," *Tennessee Studies in Literature* 16 (1971), 47-65.

> ALAN D. McKILLOP. "Local Attachment and Cosmopolitanism — The Eighteenth-Century Pattern," in *From Sensibility to Romanticism,* pp. 200-4.

> LEO STORM. "Conventional Ethics in Goldsmith's *The Traveller*," *Studies in English Literature 1500-1900* 17(3), Summer 1977, 463-76.

GONZALEZ, RODOLFO

"I Am Joáquin"

> JOEL HANCOCK. "The Emergence of Chicano Poetry: A Survey of Sources, Themes, and Techniques," *Arizona Quarterly* 29(1), Spring 1973, 64-65.

GOODMAN, PAUL

"Long Lines"

> M. L. ROSENTHAL. *Poetry and the Common Life,* pp. 121-22.

GOODWIN, LEROY

"Fired-eyed Southpaw"

ANNE HALLEY. "Recent American Poetry: Outside Relevancies," *Massachusetts Review* 9(4), Autumn 1968, 706-8.

GOODYERE, HENRY

"On the untimely Death of the incomparable Prince Henry"

TERRY G. SHERWOOD. "Reason, Faith, and Just Augustinian Lamentation in Donne's Elegy on Prince Henry," *Studies in English Literature 1500-1900* 13(1), Winter 1973, 57-60.

GOOGE, BARNABY

"Cupido Conquered"

WILLIAM E. SHEIDLEY. "A Timely Anachronism: Tradition and Theme in Barnaby Googe's 'Cupido Conquered,' " *Studies in Philology* 69(2), April 1972, 150-66.

"An Epytaphe of Lord Sheffeldes death"

DOUGLAS L. PETERSON. *The English Lyric from Wyatt to Donne*, pp. 139-41.

"An Epytaphe of M. Shelley"

DOUGLAS L. PETERSON. *The English Lyric from Wyatt to Donne*, pp. 139-41.

"An Epytaphe of the Death of Nicolas Grimaold"

DOUGLAS L. PETERSON. *The English Lyric from Wyatt to Donne*, pp. 142-43.

"Of Maistres D. S."

DOUGLAS L. PETERSON. *The English Lyric from Wyatt to Donne*, pp. 141-42.

"Of Money"

DOUGLAS L. PETERSON. *The English Lyric from Wyatt to Donne*, pp. 136-37.

GRAHAM, HENRY

"Cat Poem"

AGNES STEIN. *The Uses of Poetry*, p. 224.

GRAHAM, W. S.

"At last it's all so still" (*Nightfishing*)

JAMES DICKEY. "W. S. Graham," in *Babel to Byzantium*, pp. 44-45.

"Letter V"

CALVIN BEDIENT. *Eight Contemporary Poets*, p. 175.

"The Nightfishing"

CALVIN BEDIENT. *Eight Contemporary Poets*, pp. 168-70.

"Since All My Steps Taken"

CALVIN BEDIENT. *Eight Contemporary Poets*, p. 164.

"The White Threshold"

LEONIE ADAMS. "First Poems of Celebration," *Poetry* 82(5), August 1953, 275-76.

GRAVES, ROBERT

"Alice"

DANIEL HOFFMAN. *Barbarous Knowledge*, pp. 170-71.

"Apple Island"

DAVID ORMEROD. *Explicator* 32(7), March 1974, Item 53.

"A Ballad of Nursery Rhyme"

MYRON SIMON. "The Georgian Infancy of Robert Graves," *Focus on Robert Graves* 4 (June 1974), 61-62.

"The Bards"

DANIEL HOFFMAN. *Barbarous Knowledge*, pp. 166-68.

"The Beast"

MICHAEL KIRKHAM. "The 'Poetic Liberation' of Robert Graves," *Minnesota Review* 6(3), 1966, 250-51.

"The Castle"

DANIEL HOFFMAN. *Barbarous Knowledge*, p. 173.

"Certain Mercies"

M. C. KIRKHAM. "Incertitude and the White Goddess," *Essays in Criticism* 16(1), January 1966, 64-65.

"The Cool Web"

DANIEL HOFFMAN. *Barbarous Knowledge*, pp. 178-79.

"Counting the Beats"

SYDNEY BOLT. "Robert Graves," in *Criticism in Action*, pp. 108-12.

"The Cuirassiers of the Frontier"

DANIEL HOFFMAN. *Barbarous Knowledge*, pp. 184-85.

"Dethronement"

M. C. KIRKHAM. "Incertitude and the White Goddess," *Essays in Criticism* 16(1), January 1966, 70-71.

"End of Play"

SYDNEY BOLT. "Robert Graves," in *Criticism in Action*, pp. 112-16.

M. C. KIRKHAM. "Incertitude and the White Goddess," *Essays in Criticism* 16(1), January 1966, 65-67.

MICHAEL KIRKHAM. "Robert Grave's Debt to Laura Riding," *Focus on Robert Graves* 3 (December 1973), 40-41.

"An English Wood"

M. C. KIRKHAM. "Incertitude and the White Goddess," *Essays in Criticism* 16(1), January 1966, 59-61.

"Escape"

LILLIAN FEDER. *Ancient Myth in Modern Poetry*, p. 17.

"The Glutton"

see "The Beast"

"The Haunted House"

M. C. KIRKHAM. "Incertitude and the White Goddess," *Essays in Criticism* 16(1), January 1966, 58-59.

"In Dedication"

LILLIAN FEDER. *Ancient Myth in Modern Poetry*, pp. 366-67.

"In Her Praise"

LILLIAN FEDER. *Ancient Myth in Modern Poetry*, pp. 363-64.

"Language of the Seasons"

MICHAEL KIRKHAM. "The 'Poetic Liberation' of Robert Graves," *Minnesota Review* 6(3), 1966, 254.

"The Leveller"

S. H. BURTON. *The Criticism of Poetry*, pp. 11-13.

"Love in Barrenness"

DANIEL HOFFMAN. *Barbarous Knowledge*, pp. 186-87.

"A Love Story"

GEORGE FRASER. *Essays on Twentieth-Century Poets*, pp. 133-34.

MICHAEL KIRKHAM. "The 'Poetic Liberation' of Robert Graves," *Minnesota Review* 6(3), 1966, 251-52.

"Mid-Winter Waking"

M. C. Kirkham. "Incertitude and the White Goddess," *Essays in Criticism* 16(1), January 1966, 67-68.

"The Naked and the Nude"

Eugene Hollahan. "Sir Kenneth Clark's *The Nude*: Catalyst for Robert Graves's 'The Naked and the Nude'?" *PMLA* 87(3), May 1972, 443-51.

"The Next Time"

Michael Kirkham. "Robert Graves's Debt to Laura Riding," *Focus on Robert Graves* 3 (December 1973), 42-43.

"The Oath"

Michael Kirkham. "The 'Poetic Liberation' of Robert Graves," *Minnesota Review* 6(3), 1966, 248-49.

"On Dwelling"

John Clark Pratt. *The Meaning of Modern Poetry*, pp. 249, 260, 271, 265, 276.

"Outlaws"

Lillian Feder. *Ancient Myth in Modern Poetry*, pp. 357-58.

"Pure Death"

Daniel Hoffman. *Barbarous Knowledge*, pp. 187-88.

"Recalling War"

M. L. Rosenthal. *Poetry and the Common Life*, p. 89.

"Rocky Acres"

Daniel Hoffman. *Barbarous Knowledge*, pp. 164-66.

Myron Simon. "The Georgian Infancy of Robert Graves," *Focus on Robert Graves* 4 (June 1974), 57-58.

"Saint"

Patricia Lacerva. *Explicator* 29(4), December 1970, Item 31.

"The Second-Fated"

Daniel Hoffman. *Barbarous Knowledge*, pp. 10-12.

"The Shot"

Michael Kirkham. "The 'Poetic Liberation' of Robert Graves," *Minnesota Review* 6(3), 1966, 249-50.

"Sick Love"

Ronald Hayman. "Robert Graves," *Essays in Criticism* 5(1), January 1955, 38.

Daniel Hoffman. *Barbarous Knowledge*, pp. 188-89.

"The Survivor"

Ronald Hayman. "Robert Graves," *Essays in Criticism* 5(1), January 1955, 39-40.

"The Terraced Valley"

Ronald Hayman. "Robert Graves," *Essays in Criticism* 5(1), January 1955, 34-35.

"Theseus and Ariadne"

Ronald Hayman. "Robert Graves," *Essays in Criticism* 5(1), January 1955, 36-37.

"To Juan at the Winter Solstice"

Lillian Feder. *Ancient Myth in Modern Poetry*, pp. 365-66.

Kimon Friar and John Malcolm Brinnin. *Modern Poetry*, pp. 500-1. (Quoting Robert Graves)

Daniel Hoffman. *Barbarous Knowledge*, pp. 214-17.

Bruce A. Rosenberg. *Explicator* 21(1), September 1962, Item 3.

"To Sleep"

Michael Kirkham. "The 'Poetic Liberation' of Robert Graves," *Minnesota Review* 6(3), 1966, 253-54.

"Ulysses"

Lillian Feder. *Ancient Myth in Modern Poetry*, pp. 413-14.

G. S. Fraser. *Vision and Rhetoric*, pp. 135-37. Reprinted in: George Fraser. *Essays on Twentieth-Century Poets*, pp. 125-26.

Yvonne Rodax. "In Defense of Circe," *Virginia Quarterly Review* 47(4), Autumn 1971, 593.

Roger Rosenblatt. "The People versus Literature," *American Scholar* 43(4), Autumn 1974, 599-602.

"Vanity"

C. B. Cox and A. E. Dyson. *Modern Poetry*, pp. 116-21.

M. C. Kirkham. "Incertitude and the White Goddess," *Essays in Criticism* 16(1), January 1966, 61-63.

"Warning to Children"

Daniel Hoffman. *Barbarous Knowledge*, p. 169.

"The White Goddess"

Daniel Hoffman. *Barbarous Knowledge*, pp. 198-200.

"The Worms of History"

Michael Kirkham. "The 'Poetic Liberation' of Robert Graves," *Minnesota Review* 6(3), 1966, 247-48.

GRAY, JOHN

"The Barber"

James G. Nelson. "The Nature of Aesthetic Experience in the Poetry of the Nineties: Ernest Dowson, Lionel Johnson, and John Gray," *English Literature in Transition* 17(4), 1974, 226.

"Miska"

James G. Nelson. "The Nature of Aesthetic Experience in the Poetry of the Nineties: Ernest Dowson, Lionel Johnson, and John Gray," *English Literature in Transition* 17(4), 1974, 225-26.

"On a Picture"

James G. Nelson. "The Nature of Aesthetic Experience in the Poetry of the Nineties: Ernest Dowson, Lionel Johnson, and John Gray," *English Literature in Transition* 17(4), 1974, 227.

GRAY, THOMAS

"The Bard"

Dustin Griffin. "Gray's Audiences," *Essays in Criticism* 28(3), July 1978, 213-14.

Charles H. Hinnant. "Changing Perspectives on the Past: The Reception of Thomas Gray's *The Bard*," *Clio* 3(3), June 1974, 315-29.

Karl Kroeber. *Romantic Narrative Art*, pp. 30-32.

Patricia Meyer Spacks. "'Artful Strife': Conflict in Gray's Poetry," *PMLA* 81(1), March 1966, 66-68.

Patricia Meyer Spacks. "Thomas Gray: Action and Image," in *The Poetry of Vision*, pp. 110-12.

"Elegy Written in a Country Churchyard"

F. W. Bateson. *English Poetry*, pp. 181-93.

Frank Brady. "Structure and Meaning in Gray's *Elegy*," in *From Sensibility to Romanticism*, pp. 177-89.

Bertrand H. Bronson. "On a Special Decorum in Gray's *Elegy*," in *From Sensibility to Romanticism*, pp. 171-76.

Cleanth Brooks. "Gray: Elegy Written in a Country Churchyard," in *Master Poems of the English Language*, pp. 309-22.

GRAY, THOMAS (*Cont.*)

"Elegy Written in a Country Churchyard" (*cont.*)

CLEANTH BROOKS. *The Well Wrought Urn*, pp. 105-23; revised ed., pp. 85-100. Abridged in: *The Case for Poetry*, pp. 157, 159; second ed., pp. 139-40.

HARRY BROWN and JOHN MILSTEAD. *What the Poem Means*, pp. 95-96.

THOMAS R. CARPER. "Gray's Personal Elegy," *Studies in English Literature 1500-1900* 17(3), Summer 1977, 451-62.

DAVID DAICHES and WILLIAM CHARVAT. *Poems in English*, p. 684.

A. E. DYSON. "The Ambivalence of Gray's Elegy," *Essays in Criticism* 7(3), July 1957, 257-61.

THOMAS R. EDWARDS. *Imagination and Power*, pp. 118-37.

FRANK H. ELLIS. "Gray's *Elegy*: The Biographical Problem in Literary Criticism," *PMLA* 66(6), December 1951, 971-1008. Abridged in: *The Case for Poetry*, pp. 161, 163; second ed., pp. 140-41.

LYLE GLAZIER. "Gray's Elegy: 'The Skull Beneath the Skin,'" *University of Kansas City Review* 19(3), Spring 1953, 174-80.

DUSTIN GRIFFIN. "Gray's Audiences," *Essays in Criticism* 28(3), July 1978, 211-13.

CURT HARTOG. "Psychic Resolution in Gray's *Elegy*," *Literature and Psychology* 25(1), 1975, 5-16.

GILBERT HIGHET. *The Powers of Poetry*, pp. 278-85.

IAN JACK. "Gray's *Elegy* Reconsidered," in *From Sensibility to Romanticism*, pp. 139-69.

MYRDDIN JONES. "Gray, Jaques, and the Man of Feeling," *Review of English Studies*, n.s., 25(97), February 1974, 39-48.

JAMES M. KUIST. "The Conclusion of Gray's Elegy," *South Atlantic Quarterly* 70(2), Spring 1971, 203-14.

C. N. MANLOVE. *Literature and Reality*, pp. 149-62.

PATRICIA MEYER SPACKS. "Thomas Gray: Action and Image," in *The Poetry of Vision*, pp. 115-16.

HERBERT W. STARR. "'A Youth to Fortune and to Fame Unknown': A Re-Estimation," *Journal of English and Germanic Philology* 48(1), January 1949, 97-107.

RICHARD P. SUGG. "The Importance of Voice: Gray's *Elegy*," *Tennessee Studies in Literature* 19 (1974), 115-20.

P. F. VERNON. "The Structure of Gray's Early Poems," *Essays in Criticism* 15(4), October 1965, 390-93.

LEONE VIVANTE. *English Poetry*, pp. 80-82.

HOWARD D. WEINBROT. "Gray's *Elegy*: A Poem of Moral Choice and Resolution," *Studies in English Literature 1500-1900* 18(3), Summer 1978, 537-51.

W. K. WIMSATT. "Imitation as Freedom: 1717-1798," in *Forms of Lyric*, pp. 52-59.

GEORGE T. WRIGHT. "Stillness and the Argument of Gray's *Elegy*," *Modern Philology* 74(4), May 1977, 381-89.

"Ode on a Distant Prospect of Eton College"

M. H. ABRAMS. "Structure and Style In the Greater Romantic Lyric," in *From Sensibility to Romanticism*, pp. 538-39. Reprinted in: *Romanticism and Consciousness*, pp. 211-12.

MARSHALL BROWN. "The Urbane Sublime," *ELH* 45(2), Summer 1978, 238-42.

DAVID DAICHES and WILLIAM CHARVAT. *Poems in English*, p. 683.

FRANK H. ELLIS. "Gray's Eton College Ode: The Problem of Tone," *Papers on Language and Literature* 5(2), Spring 1969, 130-38.

NIGEL FOXELL. *Ten Poems Analyzed*, pp. 103-21.

DUSTIN GRIFFIN. "Gray's Audiences," *Essays in Criticism* 28(3), July 1978, 210-11.

GEOFFREY H. HARTMAN. *Beyond Formalism*, pp. 315-16, 320-21.

ALBERT M. LYLES. "Historical Perspective in Gray's Eton College Ode," *Tennessee Studies in Literature* 9 (1964), 57-61.

MARTIN PRICE. "The Inquisition of Truth: Memory and Freedom in Gibbon's Memoirs," *Philological Quarterly* 54(1), Winter 1975, 392-94.

PATRICIA MEYER SPACKS. "Statement and Artifice in Thomas Gray," *Studies in English Literature 1500-1900* 5(3), Summer 1965, 527-32.

PATRICIA MEYER SPACKS. "Thomas Gray: Action and Image," in *The Poetry of Vision*, pp. 98-103.

KARL F. THOMPSON. *Explicator* 9(4), February 1951, Item 28.

P. F. VERNON. "The Structure of Gray's Early Poems," *Essays in Criticism* 15(4), October 1965, 387-90.

FREDERICK C. WILKINS. *Explicator* 25(8), April 1967, Item 66.

"Ode on the Death of a Favorite Cat"

WILLIAM EMPSON. *Seven Types of Ambiguity*, pp. 97-99, 154-55; second and third eds., pp. 77, 121-23.

ELEANOR N. HUTCHENS. "Gray's Cat and Pope's Belinda," *Tennessee Studies in Literature*, 6 (1961), 103-8.

"Ode on the Spring"

PATRICIA MEYER SPACKS. "Statement and Artifice in Thomas Gray," *Studies in English Literature 1500-1900* 5(3), Summer 1965, 520-24.

PATRICIA MEYER SPACKS. "Thomas Gray: Action and Image," in *The Poetry of Vision*, pp. 91-95.

P. F. VERNON. "The Structure of Gray's Early Poems," *Essays in Criticism* 15(4), October 1965, 382-87.

"The Progress of Poesy"

ARTHUR DICKSON. *Explicator* 9(7), May 1951, Item 49.

PATRICIA MEYER SPACKS. "Thomas Gray: Action and Image," in *The Poetry of Vision*, pp. 103-10.

"Sonnet on the Death of Richard West"

WILLIAM B. BACHE. "Gray's 'Sonnet: On The Death of Richard West,'" *CEA Critic* 31(2), November 1968, 12.

JOSEPH FOLADARE. "Gray's 'Frail Memorial' To West," *PMLA* 75(1), March 1960, 61-65.

DUSTIN GRIFFIN. "Gray's Audiences," *Essays in Criticism* 28(3), July 1978, 208-10.

DONALD C. MELL, JR. "Form as Meaning in Augustan Elegy: A Reading of Thomas Gray's 'Sonnet on the Death of Richard West,'" *Papers on Language and Literature* 4(2), Spring 1968, 131-43.

JUDITH K. MOORE. "Thomas Gray's 'Sonnet on the Death of Richard West': The Circumstances and the Diction," *Tennessee Studies in Literature* 19 (1974), 107-13.

PATRICIA MEYER SPACKS. "Statement and Artifice in Thomas Gray," *Studies in English Literature 1500-1900* 5(3), Summer 1965, 524-27.

PATRICIA MEYER SPACKS. "Thomas Gray: Action and Image," in *The Poetry of Vision*, pp. 95-98.

GREENE, ROBERT

"Maesia's Song"

CLEANTH BROOKS and ROBERT PENN WARREN. *Understanding Poetry*, fourth ed., pp. 131-33.

"Sweet Are the Thoughts That Savor of Content"

GEORGE ARMS and L. G. LOCKE. *Explicator* 3(4), February 1945, Item 27.

GREGOR, ARTHUR

"Assisi and Environs"

GRACE SCHULMAN. "To Create the Self," *Twentieth Century Literature* 23(3), October 1977, 301-2.

"Horizon's West"

GRACE SCHULMAN. "To Create the Self," *Twentieth Century Literature* 23(3), October 1977, 302-3.

"Like Laocoön"

GRACE SCHULMAN. "To Create the Self," *Twentieth Century Literature* 23(3), October 1977, 303-4.

"One Wintry Day Sunny and Clear"

GRACE SCHULMAN. "To Create the Self," *Twentieth Century Literature* 23(3), October 1977, 301.

GREGORY, HORACE

"Advice"

WILLIAM M. DAVIS. "Figures of Nightmare," *Modern Poetry Studies* 4(1), Spring 1973, 57.

"Birthday in April"

ROBERT K. MORRIS. "The Resurrected Vision: Horace Gregory's Thirties Poems," *Modern Poetry Studies* 4(1), Spring 1973, 87-88.

"Bridgewater Jones: Impromptu in a Speakeasy"

ROBERT K. MORRIS. "The Resurrected Vision: Horace Gregory's Thirties Poems," *Modern Poetry Studies* 4(1), Spring 1973, 82-83.

"Dempsey, Dempsey"

ROBERT K. MORRIS. "The Resurrected Vision: Horace Gregory's Thirties Poems," *Modern Poetry Studies* 4(1), Spring 1973, 79-80.

"Elizabeth at the Piano"

M. L. ROSENTHAL. "The 'Pure' Poetry of Horace Gregory," *Modern Poetry Studies* 4(1), Spring 1973, 54.

"For you, my son"

JOSEPH WARREN BEACH. *Obsessive Images*, pp. 69-71.

"Fortune for Mirabel"

ROBERT PHILLIPS. "The Quick-Change Artist: Notes on Horace Gregory's Poetic Imagery," *Modern Poetry Studies* 4(1), Spring 1973, 71-72.

"Four Monologues from *The Passion of M'Phail*"

VICTOR A. KRAMER. "Contemplative Need In Horace Gregory's Poetry," *Modern Poetry Studies* 4(1), Spring 1973, 34-37.

M. L. ROSENTHAL. "The 'Pure' Poetry of Horace Gregory," *Modern Poetry Studies* 4(1), Spring 1973, 51-54.

"Interior: The Suburbs"

M. L. ROSENTHAL. "The 'Pure' Poetry of Horace Gregory," *Modern Poetry Studies* 4(1), Spring 1973, 46-47.

"Longface Mahoney Discusses Heaven"

M. L. ROSENTHAL. "The 'Pure' Poetry of Horace Gregory," *Modern Poetry Studies* 4(1), Spring 1973, 47-49.

"McAlpine Garfinkel, Poet"

ROBERT K. MORRIS. "The Resurrected Vision: Horace Gregory's Thirties Poems," *Modern Poetry Studies* 4(1), Spring 1973, 80-81.

"Mutum Est Pictura Poema"

VICTOR A. KRAMER. "Contemplative Need In Horace Gregory's Poetry," *Modern Poetry Studies* 4(1), Spring 1973, 41.

"O Metaphysical Read"

ROBERT K. MORRIS. "The Resurrected Vision: Horace Gregory's Thirties Poems," *Modern Poetry Studies* 4(1), Spring 1973, 81-82.

"O Mors Aeterna"

ROBERT K. MORRIS. "The Resurrected Vision: Horace Gregory's Thirties Poems," *Modern Poetry Studies* 4(1), Spring 1973, 84-85.

"Opera, Opera!"

JOSEPH WARREN BEACH. *Obsessive Images*, pp. 288-89.

M. L. ROSENTHAL. "The 'Pure' Poetry of Horace Gregory," *Modern Poetry Studies* 4(1), Spring 1973, 54-55.

"Prisoner's Song"

WILLIAM V. DAVIS. "Figures of Nightmare," *Modern Poetry Studies* 4(1), Spring 1973, 58.

"Stanzas for My Daughter"

ROBERT K. MORRIS. "The Resurrected Vision: Horace Gregory's Thirties Poems," *Modern Poetry Studies* 4(1), Spring 1973, 86-87.

"Suburban Hostel: Hudson River View"

VICTOR A. KRAMER. "Contemplative Need In Horace Gregory's Poetry," *Modern Poetry Studies* 4(1), Spring 1973, 43.

"Under the Stone I Saw Them Flow" (Chorus for Survival VI)

WALTER GIERASCH. *Explicator* 3(8), June 1945, Item 63.

WALTER GIERASCH. "Reading Modern Poetry," *College English* 2(1), October 1940, 33-34.

"Voices of Heroes"

JOSEPH WARREN BEACH. *Obsessive Images*, p. 232.

"A Wreath for Margery"

ROBERT K. MORRIS. "The Resurrected Vision: Horace Gregory's Thirties Poems," *Modern Poetry Studies* 4(1), Spring 1973, 88-89.

"The Young Wife"

WILLIAM V. DAVIS. "Figures of Nightmare," *Modern Poetry Studies* 4(1), Spring 1973, 58-59.

GRENFELL, JULIAN

"Into Battle"

BERNARD BERGONZI. *Heroes' Twilight*, pp. 49-51.

JON SILKIN. *Out of Battle*, pp. 72-73.

GREVILLE, FULKE

"Alas poore soule, thinke you to master *Love*" (*Caelica*, XLI)

RONALD A. REBHOLZ. "Love's Newfangleness: A Comparison of Greville and Wyatt," *Studies in the Literary Imagination* 11(1), Spring 1978, 28-30.

GREVILLE, FULKE *(Cont.)*

"Away with these selfe-loving lads" *(Caelica, LII)*
> MURRAY KRIEGER. *The Classic Vision,* pp. 74-75.

"Caelica, I overnight was finely used" *(Caelica, XXXVIII)*
> PETER HEIDTMANN. "The Lyrics of Fulke Greville," *Ohio University Review* 10 (1968), 34-36.

"Downe in the depth of mine iniquity" *(Caelica, XCIX)*
> PETER HEIDTMANN. "The Lyrics of Fulke Greville," *Ohio University Review* 10 (1968), 38-40.
> DOUGLAS L. PETERSON. *The English Lyric from Wyatt to Donne,* pp. 282-83.

"The earth with thunder torne, with fire blasted" *(Caelica, LXXXVI)*
> PETER HEIDTMANN. "The Lyrics of Fulke Greville," *Ohio University Review* 10 (1968), 37-38.

"Eternall Truth, almighty, infinite" *(Caelica, XCVII)*
> DOUGLAS L. PETERSON. *The English Lyric from Wyatt to Donne,* pp. 277-81.

"Eyes, why did you bring unto me those graces" *(Caelica, VI)*
> DOUGLAS L. PETERSON. *The English Lyric from Wyatt to Donne,* pp. 257-58.

"Faire Dog, which so my heart dost teare asunder" *(Caelica, II)*
> DOUGLAS L. PETERSON. *The English Lyric from Wyatt to Donne,* pp. 254-55.

"Fye, foolish Earth, thinke you the heaven wants glory" *(Caelica, XVI)*
> MURRAY KRIEGER. *The Classic Vision,* pp. 75-77.
> DOUGLAS L. PETERSON. *The English Lyric from Wyatt to Donne,* pp. 260-61.
> JOHN T. SHAWCROSS. "The Poet as Orator: One Phase in His Judicial Pose," in *The Rhetoric of Renaissance Poetry,* pp. 19-21.

"I with whose colours Myra drest her head" *(Caelica, XXII)*
> DAVID DAICHES and WILLIAM CHARVAT. *Poems in English,* p. 648.

"In night when colours all to blacke are cast" *(Caelica, C)*
> NEIL POWELL. "The Abstract Joy: Thom Gunn's Early Poetry," *Critical Quarterly* 13(3), Autumn 1971, 219-20.

"In the time when herbs and flowers" *(Caelica, LXXV)*
> GEORGE WILLIAMSON. *Seventeenth Century Contexts,* pp. 66-67.

"Love is the Peace, whereto all thoughts doe strive" *(Caelica, LXXXV)*
> DOUGLAS L. PETERSON. *The English Lyric from Wyatt to Donne,* pp. 271-72.

"Love, of mans wandring thoughts the restlesse being" *(Caelica, X)*
> DOUGLAS L. PETERSON. *The English Lyric from Wyatt to Donne,* p. 259.

"Love, the delight of all well-thinking minds" *(Caelica, I)*
> DAVID DAICHES and WILLIAM CHARVAT. *Poems in English,* p. 648.
> DOUGLAS L. PETERSON. *The English Lyric from Wyatt to Donne,* pp. 254-55.

"Man, dreame no more of curious mysteries" *(Caelica, LXXXVIII)*
> DOUGLAS L. PETERSON. *The English Lyric from Wyatt to Donne,* pp. 272-73.

"The Manicheans did no Idols make" *(Caelica, LXXXIX)*
> DOUGLAS L. PETERSON. *The English Lyric from Wyatt to Donne,* pp. 273-74.

"A Treatie of Humane Learning"
> R. L. COLIE. "The Rhetoric of Transcendence," *Philological Quarterly* 43(2), April 1964, 156-58.
> JOHN L. MAHONEY. "Donne and Greville: Two Christian Attitudes Toward the Renaissance Idea of Mutability and Decay," *CLA Journal* 5(3), March 1962, 209-12.

"The Turkish gouernment allowes no Law" *(Caelica, XC)*
> DOUGLAS L. PETERSON. *The English Lyric from Wyatt to Donne,* p. 274.

"When as Mans life, the light of humane lust" *(Caelica, LXXXVII)*
> ODETTE DE MOURGES. *Metaphysical Baroque & Precieux Poetry,* pp. 24-25.

"Who trusts for trust, or hopes of love for love" *(Caelica, V)*
> DOUGLAS L. PETERSON. *The English Lyric from Wyatt to Donne,* p. 257.

"The World, that all containes, is ever moving" *(Caelica, VII)*
> MURRAY KRIEGER. *The Classic Vision,* pp. 71-72.
> GARY L. LITT. " 'Images of Life': A Study of Narrative and Structure in Fulke Greville's *Caelica,*" *Studies in Philology* 69(2), April 1972, 218-19.

"Wrapt up, O Lord, in mans degeneration" *(Caelica, XCVIII)*
> DOUGLAS L. PETERSON. *The English Lyric from Wyatt to Donne,* pp. 281-82.

"You little starres that live in skyes" *(Caelica, IV)*
> PETER HEIDTMANN. "The Lyrics of Fulke Greville," *Ohio University Review* 10 (1968), 33-34.
> MURRAY KRIEGER. *The Classic Vision,* pp. 72-73.
> DOUGLAS L. PETERSON. *The English Lyric from Wyatt to Donne,* pp. 256-57.

GUNN, THOM

"Back to Life"
> LAWRENCE R. RIES. *Wolf Masks,* pp. 90-91.
> PATRICK SWINDEN. "Thom Gunn's Castle," *Critical Quarterly* 19(3), Autumn 1977, 55-56.

"The Bath House"
> CATHERINE R. STIMPSON. "Thom Gunn: The Redefinition of Place," *Contemporary Literature* 18(3), Summer 1977, 402-3.

"The Beach Head"
> NEIL POWELL. "The Abstract Joy: Thom Gunn's Early Poetry," *Critical Quarterly* 13(3), Autumn 1971, 222-23.

"The Beaters"
> LAWRENCE R. RIES. *Wolf Masks,* pp. 76-77.

"The Byrnies"
> JOHN MILLER. "The Stipulative Imagination of Thom Gunn," *Iowa Review* 4(1), Winter 1973, 67-68.

"Captain in Time of Peace"
> LAWRENCE R. RIES. *Wolf Masks,* pp. 65-67.

"Carnal Knowledge"
> GEORGE FRASER. *Essays on Twentieth-Century Poets,* p. 237.

NEIL POWELL. "The Abstract Joy: Thom Gunn's Early Poetry," *Critical Quarterly* 13(3), Autumn 1971, 223-25.

LAWRENCE R. RIES. *Wolf Masks,* p. 68.

"Claus von Stauffenberg"

LAWRENCE R. RIES. *Wolf Masks,* pp. 83-84.

"Considering the Snail"

C. B. COX and A. E. DYSON. *Modern Poetry,* pp. 147-52.

"The Corridor"

LAWRENCE R. RIES. *Wolf Masks,* pp. 79-80.

"The Court Revolt"

LAWRENCE R. RIES. *Wolf Masks,* pp. 68-69.

"Elegy on the Dust"

MERLE E. BROWN. "A Critical Performance of Thom Gunn's 'Misanthropos,' " *Iowa Review* 4(1), Winter 1973, 80-83.

"Flying above California"

MARTIN DODSWORTH. "Thom Gunn: Poetry as Action and Submission," in *The Survival of Poetry,* pp. 203-4.

"The Garden of the Gods"

CATHERINE R. STIMPSON. "Thom Gunn: The Redefinition of Place," *Contemporary Literature* 18(3), Summer 1977, 402.

"Helen's Rape"

GEORGE FRASER. *Essays on Twentieth-Century Poets,* pp. 236-37.

LAWRENCE R. RIES. *Wolf Masks,* p. 67, 69.

"In Santa Maria del Populo"

LAWRENCE R. RIES. *Wolf Masks,* p. 81.

PATRICK SWINDEN. "Old Lines, New Lines: The Movement Ten Years After," *Critical Quarterly* 9(4), Winter 1967, 352.

"In the Tank"

MARTIN DODSWORTH. "Thom Gunn: Poetry as Action and Submission," in *The Survival of Poetry,* pp. 204-5.

"Incident on a Journey"

LAWRENCE R. RIES. *Wolf Masks,* pp. 70-71.

"Innocence"

LAWRENCE R. RIES. *Wolf Masks,* pp. 82-83.

"Inside the moon I see a hell of love"

GEORGE FRASER. *Essays on Twentieth-Century Poets,* pp. 237-39.

"Lazarus Not Raised"

MARTIN DODSWORTH. "Thom Gunn: Poetry as Action and Submission," in *The Survival of Poetry,* pp. 208-9.

"Lebensraum"

JAMES G. KENNEDY. "The Two European Cultures and the Necessary New Sense of Literature," *College English* 31(6), March 1970, 582-83.

"Legal Reform"

LAWRENCE R. RIES. *Wolf Masks,* pp. 78-79.

"Lerici"

JOHN FULLER. "Thom Gunn," in *The Modern Poet,* edited by Ian Hamilton, pp. 18-19.

LAWRENCE R. RIES. *Wolf Masks,* p. 70.

"Lights Among Redwood"

MARTIN DODSWORTH. "Thom Gunn: Poetry as Action and Submission," in *The Survival of Poetry,* pp. 211-14.

CATHERINE R. STIMPSON. "Thom Gunn: The Redefinition of Place," *Contemporary Literature* 18(3), Summer 1977, 401-2.

PATRICK SWINDEN. "Thom Gunn's Castle," *Critical Quarterly* 19(3), Autumn 1977, 51-52.

"Lines for a Book"

MARTIN DODSWORTH. "Thom Gunn: Poetry as Action and Submission," in *The Survival of Poetry,* pp. 197-99.

LAWRENCE R. RIES. *Wolf Masks,* pp. 75-76.

"Lofty in the Palais de Danse"

LAWRENCE R. RIES. *Wolf Masks,* pp. 67-68.

"Market At Turk"

JOHN MILLER. "The Stipulative Imagination of Thom Gunn," *Iowa Review* 4(1), Winter 1973, 59-60.

"Merlin in the Cave: He Speculates Without a Book"

JOHN MILLER. "The Stipulative Imagination of Thom Gunn," *Iowa Review* 4(1), Winter 1973, 61-62.

"A Mirror for Poets"

JOHN MILLER. "The Stipulative Imagination of Thom Gunn," *Iowa Review* 4(1), Winter 1973, 57-58.

LAWRENCE R. RIES. *Wolf Masks,* pp. 63-65.

" 'On the Move' "

C. B. COX and A. E. DYSON. *The Practical Criticism of Poetry,* pp. 87-94, 99.

G. S. FRASER. "The Poetry of Thom Gunn," *Critical Quarterly* 3(4), Winter 1961, 364-67. Reprinted in: George Fraser. *Essays on Twentieth-Century Books,* pp. 240-42.

JOHN MILLER. "The Stipulative Imagination of Thom Gunn," *Iowa Review* 4(1), Winter 1973, 60.

LAWRENCE R. RIES. *Wolf Masks,* pp. 73-75.

"A Plan of Self-Subjection"

LAWRENCE R. RIES. *Wolf Masks,* pp. 71-72.

"La Prisonnière"

LAWRENCE R. RIES. *Wolf Masks,* pp. 66-67.

"Sunlight"

MERLE BROWN. "Larkin and His Audience," *Iowa Review* 8(4), Fall 1977, 120.

"Tamer and Hawk"

NEIL POWELL. "The Abstract Joy: Thom Gunn's Early Poetry," *Critical Quarterly* 13(3), Autumn 1971, 223.

"To His Cynical Mistress"

LAWRENCE R. RIES. *Wolf Masks,* p. 65.

"To Yvor Winters, 1955"

LAWRENCE R. RIES. *Wolf Masks,* pp. 72-73.

CATHERINE R. STIMPSON. "Thom Gunn: The Redefinition of Place," *Contemporary Literature* 18(3), Summer 1977, 401.

"Touch"

MARTIN DODSWORTH. "Thom Gunn: Poetry as Action and Submission," in *The Survival of Poetry,* pp. 199-203.

PATRICK SWINDEN. "Thom Gunn's Castle," *Critical Quarterly* 19(3), Autumn 1977, 53-55.

GUNN, THOM *(Cont.)*

"The Unsettled Motorcyclist's Vision of His Death"
> JOHN MILLER. "The Stipulative Imagination of Thom Gunn," *Iowa Review* 4(1), Winter 1973, 60-61.

"Vox Humana"
> JOHN MILLER. "The Stipulative Imagination of Thom Gunn," *Iowa Review* 4(1), Winter 1973, 63.

"The Wound"
> JOHN FULLER. "Thom Gunn," in *The Modern Poet,* edited by Ian Hamilton, pp. 19-22.
> JOHN FULLER. "The Stipulative Imagination of Thom Gunn," *Iowa Review* 4(1), Winter 1973, 58.
> NEIL POWELL. "The Abstract Joy: Thom Gunn's Early Poetry," *Critical Quarterly* 13(3), Autumn 1971, 221-22.

GURNEY, IVOR

"Lock Keeper"
> E. D. MACKERNESS. "The Poetry of Ivor Gurney," *Review of English Literature* 3(2), April 1962, 75-77.

"The Silent One"
> JON SILKIN. *Out of Battle,* pp. 124-25.

"To His Love"
> JON SILKIN. *Out of Battle,* pp. 122-24.

GUTHRIE, RAMON

"Anaut Daniel"
> SALLY M. GALL. "Ramon Guthrie's Forgotten Book," *Modern Poetry Studies* 9(1), Spring 1978, 70-71.

"The Christoi"
> SALLY M. GALL. "Ramon Guthrie's Forgotten Book," *Modern Poetry Studies* 9(1), Spring 1978, 66.

"Desnos"
> SALLY M. GALL. "Ramon Guthrie's Forgotten Book," *Modern Poetry Studies* 9(1), Spring 1978, 67-68.

"High Abyss"
> SALLY M. GALL. "Ramon Guthrie's Forgotten Book," *Modern Poetry Studies* 9(1), Spring 1978, 75-76.

"Inventory"
> SALLY M. GALL. "Ramon Guthrie's Forgotten Book," *Modern Poetry Studies* 9(1), Spring 1978, 62-63.

"Judgement Day"
> SALLY M. GALL. "Ramon Guthrie's Forgotten Book," *Modern Poetry Studies* 9(1), Spring 1978, 73-74.

"Loin de Moi"
> SALLY M. GALL. "Ramon Guthrie's Forgotten Book," *Modern Poetry Studies* 9(1), Spring 1978, 63-64.

"The Making of the Bear"
> SALLY M. GALL. "Ramon Guthrie's Forgotten Book," *Modern Poetry Studies* 9(1), Spring 1978, 74-75.

"Maximum Security Ward #1"
> M. L. ROSENTHAL. "Some Thoughts on American Poetry Today," *Salmagundi* 22-23 (Spring-Summer 1973), 67. Reprinted in: *Contemporary Poetry in America,* p. 26.

"People Walking"
> SALLY M. GALL. "Ramon Guthrie's Forgotten Book," *Modern Poetry Studies* 9(1), Spring 1978, 71-72.

"Polar Bear"
> M. L. ROSENTHAL and A. J. M. SMITH. *Exploring Poetry,* second ed., pp. 118-21.

"Today Is Friday"
> SALLY M. GALL. "Ramon Guthrie's Forgotten Book," *Modern Poetry Studies* 9(1), Spring 1978, 60-61.

" 'Visse, Scrisse, Amo' "
> SALLY M. GALL. "Ramon Guthrie's Forgotten Book," *Modern Poetry Studies* 9(1), Spring 1978, 72-73.

H

HABINGTON, WILLIAM

"To Roses in the bosome of Castara"

A. J. SMITH. "The Failure of Love: Love Lyrics after Donne," in *Metaphysical Poetry,* edited by Malcolm Bradbury and David Palmer, pp. 44-45.

HALL, DONALD

"The Alligator Bride"

RALPH J. MILLS, JR. "Donald Hall's Poetry," *Iowa Review* 2(1), Winter 1971, 113-16. Reprinted in: Ralph J. Mills, Jr. *Cry of the Human,* pp. 236-40.

"Apples"

RALPH J. MILLS, JR. "Donald Hall's Poetry," *Iowa Review* 2(1), Winter 1971, 120-21. Reprinted in: Ralph J. Mills, Jr. *Cry of the Human,* pp. 246-48.

"At Thirty-Five"

RALPH J. MILLS, JR. "Donald Hall's Poetry," *Iowa Review* 2(1), Winter 1971, 106-8. Reprinted in: Ralph J. Mills, Jr. *Cry of the Human,* pp. 226-29.

"The Body Politic"

LAURENCE PERRINE. *100 American Poems of the Twentieth Century,* pp. 272-74.

"The Child"

RALPH J. MILLS, JR. "Donald Hall's Poetry," *Iowa Review* 2(1), Winter 1971, 100-1. Reprinted in: Ralph J. Mills, Jr. *Cry of the Human,* pp. 217-18.

"Christmas Eve in Whitneyville"

RALPH J. MILLS, JR. "Donald Hall's Poetry," *Iowa Review* 2(1), Winter 1971, 87-88. Reprinted in: Ralph J. Mills, Jr. *Cry of the Human,* pp. 199-200.

"Cold Water"

RALPH J. MILLS, JR. "Donald Hall's Poetry," *Iowa Review* 2(1), Winter 1971, 108-11. Reprinted in: Ralph J. Mills, Jr. *Cry of the Human,* pp. 229-32.

"Digging"

RALPH J. MILLS, JR. "Donald Hall's Poetry," *Iowa Review* 2(1), Winter 1971, 104-5. Reprinted in: Ralph J. Mills, Jr. *Cry of the Human,* pp. 223-25.

"Elegy for Wesley Wells"

RALPH J. MILLS, JR. "Donald Hall's Poetry," *Iowa Review* 2(1), Winter 1971, 83-85. Reprinted in: Ralph J. Mills, Jr. *Cry of the Human,* pp. 194-96.

"Exile"

RALPH J. MILLS, JR. "Donald Hall's Poetry," *Iowa Review* 2(1), Winter 1971, 85-86. Reprinted in: Ralph J. Mills, Jr. *Cry of the Human,* pp. 196-97.

"The Grass"

RALPH J. MILLS, JR. "Donald Hall's Poetry," *Iowa Review* 2(1), Winter 1971, 98-99. Reprinted in: Ralph J. Mills, Jr. *Cry of the Human,* pp. 215-16.

"The Man in the Dead Machine"

RALPH J. MILLS, JR. "Donald Hall's Poetry," *Iowa Review* 2(1), Winter 1971, 112-13. Reprinted in: Ralph J. Mills, Jr. *Cry of the Human,* pp. 234-36.

"The Poem" (*A Roof of Tiger Lilies*)

RALPH J. MILLS, JR. "Donald Hall's Poetry," *Iowa Review* 2(1), Winter 1971, 95-96. Reprinted in: Ralph J. Mills, Jr. *Cry of the Human,* pp. 210-12.

"Sleeping"

RALPH J. MILLS, JR. "Donald Hall's Poetry," *Iowa Review* 2(1), Winter 1971, 101-2. Reprinted in: Ralph J. Mills, Jr. *Cry of the Human,* pp. 219-20.

"The Snow"

RALPH J. MILLS, JR. "Donald Hall's Poetry," *Iowa Review* 2(1), Winter 1971, 96-98. Reprinted in: Ralph J. Mills, Jr. *Cry of the Human,* pp. 212-15.

"The Stump"

RALPH J. MILLS, JR. "Donald Hall's Poetry," *Iowa Review* 2(1), Winter 1971, 102-4. Reprinted in: Ralph J. Mills, Jr. *Cry of the Human,* pp. 221-23.

"Swan"

RALPH J. MILLS, JR. "Donald Hall's Poetry," *Iowa Review* 2(1), Winter 1971, 117-20. Reprinted in: Ralph J. Mills, Jr. *Cry of the Human,* pp. 241-45.

"The Three Movements"

RALPH J. MILLS, JR. "Donald Hall's Poetry," *Iowa Review* 2(1), Winter 1971, 91-92. Reprinted in: Ralph J. Mills, Jr. *Cry of the Human,* pp. 204-6.

"Wedding Party"

RALPH J. MILLS, JR. "Donald Hall's Poetry," *Iowa Review* 2(1), Winter 1971, 86-87. Reprinted in: Ralph J. Mills, Jr. *Cry of the Human,* pp. 197-99.

"Wells"

RALPH J. MILLS, JR. "Donald Hall's Poetry," *Iowa Review* 2(1), Winter 1971, 105-6. Reprinted in: Ralph J. Mills, Jr. *Cry of the Human,* pp. 225-26.

HALL, JOHN

"The Call"

> A. J. SMITH. "The Failure of Love: Love Lyrics after Donne," in *Metaphysical Poetry*, edited by Malcolm Bradbury and David Palmer, pp. 48-49.

"Of Beauty"

> STANLEY STEWART. *The Enclosed Garden*, pp. 140-41. (P)

HALL, JOSEPH

"Harbinger to the Progress"

> LEONARD D. TOURNEY. "Joseph Hall and the *Anniversaries*," *Papers on Language and Literature* 13(1), Winter 1977, 28-29.

"To the Praise of the Dead"

> LEONARD D. TOURNEY. "Joseph Hall and the *Anniversaries*," *Papers on Language and Literature* 13(1), Winter 1977, 27-28.

HALLEY, ANNE

"Dear God, the Day Is Grey"

> LAURENCE PERRINE. *100 American Poems of the Twentieth Century*, pp. 287-89.

HALLEY, EDMOND

"On this Mathematico-Physical Work, a Singular Glory of Our Age and Nature, By a Most Illustrious Man, Mr. Isaac Newton"

> W. R. ALBURY. "Halley's Ode on the *Principia* of Newton and the Epicurean Revival in England," *Journal of the History of Ideas* 39(1), January-March 1978, 24-43.

HARDS, TERENCE

"Hansey"

> JAMES REEVES and MARTIN SEYMOUR-SMITH. *Inside Poetry*, pp. 17-19.

HARDY, THOMAS

"After a Journey"

> C. B. COX and A. E. DYSON. *Modern Poetry*, pp. 33-40.

> DAVID HOLBROOK. *Lost Bearings in English Poetry*, pp. 204-16.

> F. R. LEAVIS. "Reality and Sincerity: Notes in the Analysis of Poetry," *Scrutiny* 19(2), Winter 1952-3, 92-98.

> MAIRE A. QUINN. "The Personal Past in the Poetry of Thomas Hardy and Edward Thomas," *Critical Quarterly* 16(1), Spring 1974, 12-13.

"Afterwards"

> CHARLES MITCHELL. "Hardy's 'Afterwards,' " *Victorian Poetry* 1(1), January 1963, 68-70.

> JAMES REEVES. "Paradoxes of Poetic Understanding," in *Commitment to Poetry*, pp. 31-32.

> DAVID S. THATCHER. "Another Look at Hardy's 'Afterwards,' " *Victorian Newsletter* 38 (Fall 1970), 14-18.

"Ah, Are You Digging on My Grave?"

> ANTHONY LOW. "The Friendly Dog: Eliot and Hardy," *American Notes & Queries*, n.s., 12(7), March 1974, 107.

"An Ancient to Ancients"

> BABETTE DEUTSCH. *Poetry in Our Time*, pp. 7-8.

"And There Was a Great Calm"

> JOHN CROWE RANSOM. "Thomas Hardy's Poems, and the Religious Difficulties of a Naturalist," *Kenyon Review* 22(2), Spring 1960, 178-80.

"At a Seaside Town in 1869"

> THEODORE HOLMES. "Thomas Hardy's City of the Mind," *Sewanee Review* 75(2), Spring 1967, 290-92.

"At Castle Bottrell"

> T. R. BARNES. *English Verse*, pp. 263-65.

"At the Railway Station, Upway"

> GEOFFREY HARVEY. "Thomas Hardy's Poetry of Transcendence," *Ariel* 9(4), October 1978, 11-12.

"The Ballad of Love's Skeleton"

> LAURENCE LERNER. *An Introduction to English Poetry*, pp. 177-79.

"Beeny Cliff"

> DONALD DAVIE. "Hardy's Virgilian Purples," in *The Poet in the Imaginary Museum*, pp. 221-28.

> ALAN WARREN FRIEDMAN. " 'Beeny Cliff' and 'Under the Waterfall': An Approach to Hardy's Love Poetry," *Victorian Poetry* 5(3), Autumn 1967, 224-28.

"Channel Firing"

> CLEANTH BROOKS, JOHN THIBAUT PURSER, and ROBERT PENN WARREN. *An Approach to Literature*, fifth ed., pp. 380-81.

> CLEANTH BROOKS and ROBERT PENN WARREN. *Understanding Poetry*, pp. 309-11; revised ed., pp. 164-66; third ed., pp. 191-93; fourth ed., pp. 45-47, 95-96.

> BABETTE DEUTSCH. *Poetry in Our Time*, first ed., pp. 9-10.

> ROSS MURFIN. " 'Channel Firing': An Introduction to Hardy's Special Cosmos," *Thoth* 13(3), Fall 1973, 27-36.

> JOHN CROWE RANSOM. "Thomas Hardy's Poems, and the Religious Difficulties of a Naturalist," *Kenyon Review* 22(2), Spring 1960, 170-73.

> M. L. ROSENTHAL and A. J. M. SMITH. *Exploring Poetry*, second ed., p. 8.

> RODGER L. TARR. *Explicator* 36(4), Summer 1978, 17-18.

"The Children and Sir Nameless"

> VERN B. LENTZ and DOUGLAS D. SHORT. "Hardy, Shelley, and the Statues," *Victorian Poetry* 12(4), Winter 1974, 370-72.

"Come Not: Yet Come!"

> MRS. PHILPOTT. "Thomas Hardy — Light and Shade," *Thomas Hardy Yearbook* 5 (1975), 69.

"A Commonplace Day"

> F. R. LEAVIS. "Hardy the Poet," *Southern Review* 6(1), Summer 1940, 95-97.

"Compassion"

> HAROLD OREL. "Hardy and the Animal World," *Thomas Hardy Society Review* 1(1), 1975, 10-11.

"The Convergence of the Twain"

> CLEANTH BROOKS. *Modern Poetry and the Tradition*, p. 243.

> CLEANTH BROOKS, JOHN THIBAUT PURSER, and ROBERT PENN WARREN. *An Approach to Literature*, pp. 490-91; second ed., pp. 490-91; third ed., pp. 380-82; fourth ed., pp. 375-77; fifth ed., pp. 425-27.

> JOHN R. COMBS. "*Cleaving* in Hardy's 'The Convergence of the Twain,' " *CEA Critic* 37(1), November 1974, 22-23.

D. E. MAYERS. "Dialectical Structures in Hardy's Poems," *Victorian Newsletter* 27 (Spring 1965), 17.

PAUL N. SIEGEL. *Explicator* 11(2), November 1952, Item 13.

"The Country Wedding: A Fiddler's Story"

CLEANTH BROOKS and ROBERT PENN WARREN. *Understanding Poetry,* fourth ed., pp. 280-81.

"The Curate's Kindness"

BABETTE DEUTSCH. *Poetry in Our Time,* pp. 4-5; second ed., p. 5.

"The Darkling Thrush"

JEROME BEATY and WILLIAM H. MATCHETT. *Poetry From Statement to Meaning,* pp. 94-98.

JOHN BERRYMAN. "Hardy and His Thrush," in *The Freedom of the Poet,* pp. 242-44.

JOHN BERRYMAN. "Hardy: The Darkling Thrush,," in *Master Poems of the English Language,* pp. 788-90.

R. A. BURNS. "Imagery in Hardy's 'The Darkling Thrush,'" *Concerning Poetry* 10(1), Spring 1977, 87-89.

S. H. BURTON. *The Criticism of Poetry,* pp. 132-35.

FRANK DOGGETT. "Romanticism's Singing Bird," *Studies in English Literature 1500-1900* 14(4), Autumn 1974, 560-61.

GEOFFREY HARVEY. "Thomas Hardy's Poetry of Transcendence," *Ariel* 9(4), October 1978, 8-10.

DAVID PERKINS. "Hardy and the Poetry of Isolation," *ELH* 26(2), June 1959, 262-67.

"A Dream or No"

ALBERT J. GUERARD. "The Illusion of Simplicity: The Shorter Poems of Thomas Hardy," *Sewanee Review* 72(3), Summer 1964, 386-88.

"A Drizzling Easter Morning"

DELMORE SCHWARTZ. "Poetry and Belief in Thomas Hardy," *Southern Review* 6(1), Summer 1940, 73-74. Reprinted in: *The Critic's Notebook,* pp. 201-3. Also: *Critiques and Essays in Criticism,* p. 342. Also: *Modern Literary Criticism,* pp. 347-48. Also: Delmore Schwartz. *Selected Essays of Delmore Schwartz,* pp. 67-68.

"Drummer Hodge"

CHRISTOPHER GILLIE. *Movements in English Literature,* pp. 66-67.

MARK VAN DOREN. *Introduction to Poetry,* pp. 98-102.

"During Wind and Rain"

JONATHAN DOLLIMORE. "The Poetry of Hardy and Edward Thomas," *Critical Quarterly* 17(3), Autumn 1975, 204.

GEOFFREY HARVEY. "Thomas Hardy's Poetry of Transcendence," *Ariel* 9(4), October 1978, 16-18.

JAMES R. KREUZER. *Elements of Poetry,* pp. 162-64.

MARGARET MAHAR. "Hardy's Poetry of Renunciation," *ELH* 45(2), Summer 1978, 311-13.

MORDECAI and ERIN MARCUS. *Explicator* 19(3), December 1960, Item 14.

HAROLD E. TOLIVER. *Pastoral Forms and Attitudes,* pp. 298-300.

"The Fallow Deer at the Lonely House"

CLYDE S. KILBY. *Poetry and Life,* pp. 5-6.

"The Farm-Woman's Winter"

T. R. BARNES. *English Verse,* pp. 269-71.

"Former Beauties"

PETER F. NEUMEYER. "The Transfiguring Vision," *Victorian Poetry* 3(4), Autumn 1965, 263-66.

"Friends Beyond"

JOHN CROWE RANSOM. "Hardy — Old Poet," *New Republic* 126(19), 12 May 1952, 30-31.

"The Garden Seat"

JOHN CROWE RANSOM. "Honey and Gall," *Southern Review* 6(1), Summer 1940, 7-9.

"George Meredith"

I. A. RICHARDS. *Practical Criticism,* pp. 147-53, *passim.*

"God-Forgotten"

LAURENCE PERRINE. "Thomas Hardy's 'God-Forgotten,'" *Victorian Poetry* 6(2), Summer 1968, 187-88.

"God's Funeral"

ROSE MURFIN. "'Channel Firing': An Introduction to Hardy's Special Cosmos," *Thoth* 13(3), Fall 1973, 32-34, *passim.*

"The Going"

DWAYNE HOWELL. "Dogma and Belief in the Poetry of Thomas Hardy," *English Literature in Transition* 19(1), 1976, 10-11.

MARGARET MAHAR. "Hardy's Poetry of Renunciation," *ELH* 45(2), Summer 1978, 307-8.

"Going and Staying"

PHILIP K. JASON. "A Possible Allusion in Thomas Hardy's 'Going and Staying,'" *Victorian Poetry* 14(3), Autumn 1976, 261-63.

"Hap"

JAMES R. KINCAID. "'Why Unblooms the Best Hope?': Victorian Narrative Forms and the Explanation of Calamity," *Victorian Newsletter* 53 (Spring 1978), 1-2.

"He Abjures Love"

V. H. COLLINS. "The Love Poetry of Thomas Hardy," *Essays and Studies* 28 (1942), 71-72.

"He Resolves To Say No More"

HAROLD BLOOM. *A Map of Misreading,* p. 23.

"Her Father"

LAWRENCE RICHARD HOLMES. *Explicator* 14(8), May 1956, Item 53. (P)

"How She Went to Ireland"

MARGARET MAHAR. "Hardy's Poetry of Renunciation," *ELH* 45(2), Summer 1978, 305-6.

"I Found Her out There"

ALBERT J. GUERARD. "The Illusion of Simplicity: The Shorter Poems of Thomas Hardy," *Sewanee Review* 72(3), Summer 1964, 383-86.

ANTONY H. HARRISON. "Hardy's Poetry: The Uses of Nature," *Ball State University Forum* 19(1), Winter 1978, 69.

"If You Had Known"

ALBERT J. GUERARD. "The Illusion of Simplicity: The Shorter Poems of Thomas Hardy," *Sewanee Review* 72(3), Summer 1964, 368-70.

"In Tenebris, I"

WALTER GIERASCH. *Explicator* 4(6), April 1946, Item 45.

HARDY, THOMAS (*Cont.*)

"In the Days of Crinoline"

R. P. BLACKMUR. "The Shorter Poems of Thomas Hardy," *Southern Review* 6(1), Summer 1940, 39. Reprinted in: R. P. Blackmur. *Expense of Greatness*, pp. 62-63. Also: R. P. Blackmur. *Language as Gesture*, pp. 70-71. Also: R. P. Blackmur. *Form and Value in Modern Poetry*, p. 22. Also: *Modern Poetry*, pp. 167-68.

"In Time of 'The Breaking of Nations' "

DeLANCEY FERGUSON. *Explicator* 4(4), February 1946, Item 25.

JOHN OLIVER PERRY. *The Experience of Poems*, pp. 44-45.

"The Lacking Sense"

GILBERT NEIMAN. "Was Hardy Anthropomorphic?" *Twentieth Century Literature* 2(2), July 1956, 86-91.

"The Lady in the Furs"

HAROLD OREL. "Hardy and the Animal World," *Thomas Hardy Society Review* 1(1), 1975, 11.

"Last Words to a Dumb Friend"

R. P. BLACKMUR. "The Shorter Poems of Thomas Hardy," *Southern Review* 6(1), Summer 1940, 44-47. Reprinted in: R. P. Blackmur. *Expense of Greatness*, pp. 68-72. Also: R. P. Blackmur. *Form and Value in Modern Poetry*, pp. 27-29. Also: R. P. Blackmur. *Language as Gesture*, pp. 76-78. Also: *Modern Poetry*, pp. 172-74.

JAMES REEVES and MARTIN SEYMOUR-SMITH. *Inside Poetry*, pp. 62-65.

"Love Watches a Window"

MARGARET MAHAR. "Hardy's Poetry of Renunciation," *ELH* 45(2), Summer 1978, 317-18.

"Lying Awake"

DENNIS TAYLOR. "The Patterns in Hardy's Poetry," *ELH* 42(2), Summer 1975, 272-73.

"A Man"

T. R. BARNES. *English Verse*, pp. 259-61.

"The Man He Killed"

DAVID PERKINS. "Hardy and the Poetry of Isolation," *ELH* 26(2), June 1959, 254-56.

LAURENCE PERRINE. *Sound and Sense*, pp. 21-22; revised ed., pp. 21-22; third ed., pp. 23-26; fourth ed., pp. 21-24.

"The Masked Face"

DELMORE SCHWARTZ. "Poetry and Belief in Thomas Hardy," *Southern Review* 6(1), Summer 1940, 71-72. Reprinted in: *Critiques and Essays in Criticism*, pp. 340-41. Also: *Modern Literary Criticism*, pp. 345-46. Also: Delmore Schwartz. *Selected Essays of Delmore Schwartz*, pp. 65-66.

DENNIS TAYLOR. "Victorian Philology and Victorian Poetry," *Victorian Newsletter* 53 (Spring 1978), 14.

"Men Who March Away"

JON SILKIN. *Out of Battle*, pp. 51-52.

"The Minute before Meeting"

V. H. COLLINS. "The Love Poetry of Thomas Hardy," *Essays and Studies* 28 (1942), 73-74.

"Moments of Vision"

GEOFFREY HARVEY. "Thomas Hardy's Poetry of Transcendence," *Ariel* 9(4), October 1978, 7-8.

"The Moth-Signal"

R. P. BLACKMUR. "The Shorter Poems of Thomas Hardy," *Southern Review* 6(1), Summer 1940, 36-38. Reprinted in: R. P. Blackmur. *Form and Value in Modern Poetry*, pp. 19-21. Also: R. P. Blackmur. *The Expense of Greatness*, pp. 59-61. Also: R. P. Blackmur. *Language as Gesture*, pp. 68-69. Also: *Modern Poetry*, pp. 165-66.

"Nature's Questioning"

J. O. BAILEY. "Evolutionary Meliorism in the Poetry of Thomas Hardy," *Studies in Philology* 60(3), July 1963, 572-73.

ALLEN TATE. "Hardy's Philosophic Metaphors," *Southern Review* 6(1), Summer 1940, 104-7. Reprinted in: *Criticism*, pp. 185-86. Also: Allen Tate. *Reason in Madness*, pp. 125-29. Also: Allen Tate. *On the Limits of Poetry*, pp. 191-94. Also: Allen Tate. *Essays of Four Decades*, pp. 335-39.

"Neutral Tones"

CLEANTH BROOKS, JOHN THIBAUT PURSER, and ROBERT PENN WARREN. *An Approach to Literature*, pp. 460-61; second ed., pp. 460-61; third ed., pp. 329-31; fourth ed., pp. 327-28; fifth ed., pp. 397-98.

PAUL C. DOHERTY and E. DENNIS TAYLOR. "Syntax in Hardy's 'Neutral Tones,' " *Victorian Poetry* 12(3), Autumn 1974, 289.

ALBERT J. GUERARD. "The Illusion of Simplicity: The Shorter Poems of Thomas Hardy," *Sewanee Review* 72(3), Summer 1964, 368-69.

JAMES HAZEN. "The God-Curst Sun: Love in 'Neutral Tones,' " *Victorian Poetry* 9(3), Autumn 1971, 331-36.

LEONARD UNGER and WILLIAM VAN O'CONNOR. *Poems for Study*, p. 568.

"The Newcomer's Wife"

LEONARD UNGER and WILLIAM VAN O'CONNOR. *Poems for Study*, p. 568.

"A Night in November"

MAIRE A. QUINN. "The Personal Past in the Poetry of Thomas Hardy and Edward Thomas," *Critical Quarterly* 16(1), Spring 1974, 10-11.

"A Nightmare, and the Next Thing"

MARGARET MAHAR. "Hardy's Poetry of Renunciation," *ELH* 45(2), Summer 1978, 319-20.

"Nobody Comes"

LEONARD UNGER and WILLIAM VAN O'CONNOR. *Poems for Study*, pp. 574-75.

"Old Furniture"

GEOFFREY HARVEY. "Thomas Hardy's Poetry of Transcendence," *Ariel* 9(4), October 1978, 12-14.

"On a Heath"

WALTER F. WRIGHT. "A Hardy Perennial," *Prairie Schooner* 48(3), Fall 1974, 255-57. (P)

"On an Invitation to the United States"

CLEANTH BROOKS, JOHN THIBAUT PURSER, and ROBERT PENN WARREN. *An Approach to Literature*, pp. 464-67; second ed., pp. 464-67; third ed., pp. 336-40; fourth ed., pp. 334-38.

"On Sturminster Foot-bridge"

T. R. BARNES. "Thomas Hardy," in *Criticism in Action*, pp. 55-57.

"On the Departure Platform"

V. H. COLLINS. "The Love Poetry of Thomas Hardy," *Essays and Studies* 28 (1942), 73.

WALTER GIERASCH. *Explicator* 4(2), November 1945, Item 10.

"On the Palatine"

J. O. BAILEY. "Hardy's 'Poems of Pilgrimage,' " *English Literature in Transition* 9(4), 1967, 191-92.

"Overlooking the River Stour"

T. R. BARNES. "Thomas Hardy," in *Criticism in Action*, pp. 52-55.

"The Oxen"

JOHN CLARK PRATT. *The Meaning of Modern Poetry*, pp. 235, 239-40, 250, 248.

DELMORE SCHWARTZ. "Poetry and Belief in Thomas Hardy," *Southern Review* 6(1), Summer 1940, 70-71. Reprinted in: *Critiques and Essays in Criticism*, pp. 339-40. Also: *Modern Literary Criticism*, pp. 344-45. Also: Delmore Schwartz. *Selected Essays of Delmore Schwartz*, pp. 64-65.

"Panthera"

FRANK R. GIORDANO. "Chance and Choice in Thomas Hardy's 'Panthera,' " *English Literature in Transition* 14(4), 1971, 249-56.

WILLIAM W. MORGAN. " 'Panthera' and the Criticism of Hardy's Poetry," *Thomas Hardy Yearbook* 3 (1972-3), 44-51.

"The Phantom Horsewoman"

GEOFFREY HARVEY. "Thomas Hardy's Poetry of Transcendence," *Ariel* 9(4), October 1978, 15.

"Proud Songsters"

ANTONY H. HARRISON. "Hardy's Poetry: The Uses of Nature," *Ball State University Forum* 19(1), Winter 1978, 66.

"The Reminder"

MICHAEL J. COLLINS. "Formal Allusion in Modern Poetry," *Concerning Poetry* 9(1), Spring 1976, 7-8.

"The Roman Gravemounds"

R. P. BLACKMUR. "The Shorter Poems of Thomas Hardy," *Southern Review* 6(1), Summer 1940, 44-46. Reprinted in: R. P. Blackmur. *Expense of Greatness*, p. 69. Also: R. P. Blackmur. *Form and Value in Modern Poetry*, pp. 27-28. Also: *Modern Poetry*, p. 172.

"The Roman Road"

MARK VAN DOREN. *Introduction to Poetry*, pp. 107-10.

"The Ruined Maid"

LAURENCE LERNER. *An Introduction to English Poetry*, pp. 179-85.

"The Sacrilege"

RICHARD L. PURDY. *Explicator* 3(4), February 1945, Item 28. (P)

MAIRE A. QUINN. "Hardy as Balladist — 'The Sacrilege,' " *Thomas Hardy Yearbook* 6(1976), 28-29.

"Seen by the Waits"

R. P. BLACKMUR. "The Shorter Poems of Thomas Hardy," *Southern Review* 6(1), Summer 1940, 38-39. Reprinted in: R. P. Blackmur. *Expense of Greatness*, pp. 61-62. Also: R. P. Blackmur. *Form and Value in Modern Poetry*, pp. 21-22. Also: R. P. Blackmur. *Language as Gesture*, pp. 69-70. Also: *Modern Poetry*, pp. 166-67.

"The Self-Unseeing"

CHRISTOPHER GILLIE. *Movements in English Literature*, p. 69.

GEOFFREY HARVEY. "Thomas Hardy's Poetry of Transcendence," *Ariel* 9(4), October 1978, 10-11.

"The Shadow on the Stone"

C. B. COX and A. E. DYSON. *The Practical Criticism of Poetry*, pp. 71-86.

JONATHAN DOLLIMORE. "The Poetry of Hardy and Edward Thomas," *Critical Quarterly* 17(3), Autumn 1975, 203-4.

ERNEST L. FONTANA. *Explicator* 37(1), Fall 1978, 17-18.

MAIRE A. QUINN. "The Personal Past in the Poetry of Thomas Hardy and Edward Thomas," *Critical Quarterly* 16(1), Spring 1974, 11.

"The Sheep Boy"

T. R. BARNES. "Thomas Hardy," in *Criticism in Action*, pp. 57-58.

ANTONY H. HARRISON. "Hardy's Poetry: The Uses of Nature," *Ball State University Forum* 19(1), Winter 1978, 66-67.

"Shelley's Skylark"

HAROLD BLOOM. *A Map of Misreading*, p. 22.

IRIS TILLMAN-HILL. "Hardy's Skylark and Shelley's," *Victorian Poetry* 10(1), Spring 1972, 79-83.

"A Sign-Seeker"

MARGARET MAHAR. "Hardy's Poetry of Renunciation," *ELH* 45(2), Summer 1978, 318-19.

"Snow in the Suburbs"

ANTONY H. HARRISON. "Hardy's Poetry: The Uses of Nature," *Ball State University Forum* 19(1), Winter 1978, 68.

"The Souls of the Slain"

JON SILKIN. *Out of Battle*, pp. 48-49.

"The Subalterns"

JOHN CROWE RANSOM. "Thomas Hardy's Poems, and the Religious Difficulties of a Naturalist," *Kenyon Review* 22(2), Spring 1960, 173-78.

"The Telegram"

R. P. BLACKMUR. *The Expense of Greatness*, pp. 56-59. Reprinted in: R. P. Blackmur. *Form and Value in Modern Poetry*, pp. 17-19. Also: R. P. Blackmur. *Language as Gesture*, 66-67. Also: *Modern Poetry*, pp. 163-65.

"To an Unborn Pauper Child"

C. DAY LEWIS. *The Poetic Image*, pp. 150-53. Reprinted in: *Reading Modern Poetry*, pp. 48-50.

"To My Father's Violin"

DWAYNE HOWELL. "Dogma and Belief in the Poetry of Thomas Hardy," *English Literature in Transition* 19(1), 1976, 7-9.

"The Torn Letter"

D. E. MAYERS. "Dialectical Structures in Hardy's Poems," *Victorian Newsletter* 27 (Spring 1965), 17-18.

"Transformations"

ANTONY H. HARRISON. "Hardy's Poetry: The Uses of Nature," *Ball State University Forum* 19(1), Winter 1978, 69.

"Under the Waterfall"

ALAN WARREN FRIEDMAN. " 'Beeny Cliff' and 'Under the Waterfall': An Approach to Hardy's Love Poetry," *Victorian Poetry* 5(3), Autumn 1967, 224-28.

MARGARET MAHAR. "Hardy's Poetry of Renunciation," *ELH* 45(2), Summer 1978, 314-15.

HARDY, THOMAS *(Cont.)*

"Under the Waterfall" *(cont.)*

     MAIRE A. QUINN. "The Personal Past in the Poetry of Thomas Hardy and Edward Thomas," *Critical Quarterly* 16(1), Spring 1974, 20.

"Valenciennes"

     FRANK R. GIORDANO, JR. "A Source for Thomas Hardy's 'Valenciennes,'" *Victorian Poetry* 14(4), Winter 1976, 349-55.

"The Vatican: Sala Delle Muse"

     J. O. BAILEY. "Hardy's Poems of Pilgrimage," *English Literature in Transition* 9(4), 1967, 192-93.

"The Voice"

     MAIRE A. QUINN. "The Personal Past in the Poetry of Thomas Hardy and Edward Thomas," *Critical Quarterly* 16(1), Spring 1974, 11-12.

"We Are Getting to the End"

     HAROLD BLOOM. *A Map of Misreading*, p. 23.

"The Well-Beloved"

     V. H. COLLINS. "The Love Poetry of Thomas Hardy," *Essays and Studies* 28 (1942), 74-75.

"Wessex Heights"

     J. O. BAILEY and NORMAN PAGE. "'Wessex Heights' Visited and Revisited: Professors J. O. Bailey and Norman Page," *English Literature in Transition* 15(1), 1972, 57-62.

     FRANK R. GIORDANO, JR. "Hardy's Farewell to Fiction: The Structure of 'Wessex Heights,'" *Thomas Hardy Yearbook* 5 (1975), 58-66.

     J. HILLIS MILLER. "History as Repetition in Thomas Hardy's Poetry: The Example of 'Wessex Heights,'" in *Victorian Poetry*, pp. 223-53.

     J. HILLIS MILLER. "'Wessex Heights': The Persistence of the Past in Hardy's Poetry," *Critical Quarterly* 10(4), Winter 1968, 339-59.

     ROSS MURFIN. "'Channel Firing': An Introduction to Hardy's Special Cosmos," *Thoth* 13(3), Fall 1973, 27-36.

"Where the Picnic Was"

     DONALD DAVIE. "Hardy's Virgilian Purples," in *The Poet in the Imaginary Museum*, pp. 233-34.

     MARGARET MAHAR. "Hardy's Poetry of Renunciation," *ELH* 45(2), Summer 1978, 308-9.

"The Wind Blew Words"

     HAROLD OREL. "Hardy and the Animal World," *Thomas Hardy Society Review* 1(1), 1975, 9-10.

"The Wind's Prophecy"

     J. HILLIS MILLER. "History as Repetition in Thomas Hardy's Poetry: The Example of 'Wessex Heights,'" in *Victorian Poetry*, p. 231.

"The Woman I Met"

     FRANK R. GIORDANO, JR. "The Repentant Magdalen in Thomas Hardy's 'The Woman I Met,'" *English Literature in Transition* 15(2), 1972, 136-43.

"The Workbox"

     CLEANTH BROOKS and ROBERT PENN WARREN. *Understanding Poetry*, fourth ed., pp. 42-43.

"The Year's Awakening"

     DAVID PERKINS. "Hardy and the Poetry of Isolation," *ELH* 26(2), June 1959, 261-62.

"Your Last Drive"

     DWAYNE HOWELL. "Dogma and Belief in the Poetry of Thomas Hardy," *English Literature in Transition* 19(1), 1976, 11-13.

HARPER, MICHAEL

"Afterward: A Film"

     ROBERT B. STEPTO. "*I Thought I Know These People*: Richard Wright & the Afro-American Literary Tradition," *Massachusetts Review* 18(3), Autumn 1977, 539-41.

"Alice"

     ROBERT B. STEPTO. "Michael Harper's Extended Tree: John Coltrane and Sterling Brown," *Hollins Critic* 13(3), June 1976, 13-14. (P)

"American History"

     ROBERT B. STEPTO. "Michael S. Harper, Poet as Kinsman: The Family Sequences," *Massachusetts Review* 17(3), Autumn 1976, 478-79.

"Brother John"

     ROBERT B. STEPTO. "Michael Harper's Extended Tree: John Coltrane and Sterling Brown," *Hollins Critic* 13(3), June 1976, 3-4.

"Dear John, Dear Coltrane"

     ROBERT B. STEPTO. "Michael Harper's Extended Tree: John Coltrane and Sterling Brown," *Hollins Critic* 13(3), June 1976, 5-6.

"Deathwatch"

     ROBERT B. STEPTO. "Michael S. Harper, Poet as Kinsman: The Family Sequences," *Massachusetts Review* 17(3), Autumn 1976, 479-80.

"Debridement"

     LAURENCE LIEBERMAN. "Derek Walcott and Michael S. Harper: The Muse of History," in *Unassigned Frequencies*, pp. 294-96.

"Dirge for Trane"

     ROBERT B. STEPTO. "Michael Harper's Extended Tree: John Coltrane and Sterling Brown," *Hollins Critic* 13(3), June 1976, 9-10.

"Grandfather"

     ROBERT B. STEPTO. "Michael S. Harper, Poet as Kinsman: The Family Sequences," *Massachusetts Review* 17(3), Autumn 1976, 502.

"Here Where Coltrane Is"

     ROBERT B. STEPTO. "Michael Harper's Extended Tree: John Coltrane and Sterling Brown," *Hollins Critic* 13(3), June 1976, 6-7.

"Homage to the New World"

     ROBERT B. STEPTO. "Michael S. Harper, Poet as Kinsman: The Family Sequences," *Massachusetts Review* 17(3), Autumn 1976, 488-95.

"Kin"

     ROBERT B. STEPTO. "Michael S. Harper, Poet as Kinsman: The Family Sequences," *Massachusetts Review* 17(3), Autumn 1976, 495-99.

"Ode to Tenochtitlan"

     ROBERT B. STEPTO. "Michael Harper's Extended Tree: John Coltrane and Sterling Brown," *Hollins Critic* 13(3), June 1976, 10-11.

"Operation Harvest Moon"

     LAURENCE LIEBERMAN. "Derek Walcott and Michael S. Harper: The Muse of History," in *Unassigned Frequencies*, p. 295.

"Remember Mexico"
>ROBERT B. STEPTO. "Michael Harper's Extended Tree: John Coltrane and Sterling Brown," *Hollins Critic* 13(3), June 1976, 7-8.

"Ruth's Blues"
>ROBERT B. STEPTO. "Michael S. Harper, Poet as Kinsman: The Family Sequences," *Massachusetts Review* 17(3), Autumn 1976, 483-86.

"WARS: DEBTS"
>ROBERT B. STEPTO. "Michael Harper's Extended Tree: John Coltrane and Sterling Brown," *Hollins Critic* 13(3), June 1976, 14-15.

"Zocalo"
>ROBERT B. STEPTO. "Michael Harper's Extended Tree: John Coltrane and Sterling Brown," *Hollins Critic* 13(3), June 1976, 8-9.

HARRIS, WILSON

"Behring Straits"
>W. J. HOWARD. "Wilson Harris's 'Guiana Quartet': from personal myth to national identity," *Ariel* 1(1), January 1970, 54-55.

HARVEY, CHRISTOPHER

"The Synagogue"
>STANLEY STEWART. *The Enclosed Garden*, pp. 50-51.

HARVEY, GABRIEL

"Glosse"
>HALE MOORE. "Gabriel Harvey's References to Marlowe," *Studies in Philology* 23(3), July 1926, 343-57.

"Sonnet, *Gorgon*, or the Wonderful Year"
>HALE MOORE. "Gabriel Harvey's References to Marlowe," *Studies in Philology* 23(3), July 1926, 343-57.

"A/Stanza Declarative: to the Lovers of Admirable Works"
>HALE MOORE. "Gabriel Harvey's References to Marlowe," *Studies in Philology* 23(3), July 1926, 343-57.

"The Writer's Postscript; or, a Friendly Caveat to the *Second Shakerley* of Powles"
>HALE MOORE. "Gabriel Harvey's References to Marlowe," *Studies in Philology* 23(3), July 1926, 343-57.

HAUSMAN, GERALD

"Sleeping Out"
>SUZANNE JUHASZ. *Naked and Fiery Forms*, pp. 139-40.

HAY, JOHN

"Jim Bludso"
>EARL DANIELS. *The Art of Reading Poetry*, pp. 88-92.

HAYDEN, ROBERT

"The Ballad of Nat Turner"
>CHARLES T. DAVIS. "Robert Hayden's Use of History," in *Modern Black Poets*, pp. 103-4.
>CONSTANCE J. POST. "Image and Idea in the Poetry of Robert Hayden," *CLA Journal* 20(2), December 1976, 172-73.

"Beginning"
>WILBURN WILLIAMS, JR. "Covenant of Timelessness & Time: Symbolism & History in Robert Hayden's *Angle of Ascent*," *Massachusetts Review* 18(4), Winter 1977, 747-48.

"The Diver"
>MAURICE J. O'SULLIVAN, JR. "The Mask of Allusion in Robert Hayden's 'The Diver,'" *CLA Journal* 17(1), September 1973, 85-92.

"The Dream"
>CHARLES T. DAVIS. "Robert Hayden's Use of History," in *Modern Black Poets*, pp. 107-8.

"El-Hajj Malik El-Shatuzz"
>CHARLES T. DAVIS. "Robert Hayden's Use of History," in *Modern Black Poets*, pp. 96-111.

"Electrical Storm"
>CONSTANCE J. POST. "Image and Idea in the Poetry of Robert Hayden," *CLA Journal* 20(2), December 1976, 169-70.

"Figure"
>SANDRA GOVAN. "The Poetry of Black Experience As Counterpoint to the Poetry of the Black Aesthetic," *Negro American Literature Forum* 8(4), Winter 1974, 291.

"For a Young Artist"
>HOWARD FAULKNER. "'Transformed by Steeps of Flight': The Poetry of Robert Hayden," *CLA Journal* 21(2), December 1977, 284-85.

"Frederick Douglass"
>CHARLES T. DAVIS. "Robert Hayden's Use of History," in *Modern Black Poets*, p. 106.
>FRED M. FETROW. "Robert Hayden's 'Frederick Douglass': Form and Meaning in a Modern Sonnet," *CLA Journal* 17(1), September 1973, 79-84.

"Full Moon"
>WILBURN WILLIAMS, JR. "Covenant of Timelessness & Time: Symbolism & History in Robert Hayden's *Angle of Ascent*," *Massachusetts Review* 18(4), Winter 1977, 743-45.

"Homage to the Empress of the Blues"
>CONSTANCE J. POST. "Image and Idea in the Poetry of Robert Hayden," *CLA Journal* 20(2), December 1976, 175.

"'Lear is Gay'"
>CONSTANCE J. POST. "Image and Idea in the Poetry of Robert Hayden," *CLA Journal* 20(2), December 1976, 174-75.

"Market"
>RICHARD O. LEWIS. "A Literary-Psychoanalytic Interpretation of Robert Hayden's 'Market,'" *Negro American Literature Forum* 9(1), Spring 1975, 21-24.

"Middle Passage"
>CHARLES T. DAVIS. "Robert Hayden's Use of History," in *Modern Black Poets*, pp. 98-103.
>HOWARD FAULKNER. "'Transformed by Steeps of Flight': The Poetry of Robert Hayden," *CLA Journal* 21(2), December 1977, 290.

"The Night-Blooming Cereus"
>CONSTANCE J. POST. "Image and Idea in the Poetry of Robert Hayden," *CLA Journal* 20(2), December 1976, 172.
>WILBURN WILLIAMS, JR. "Covenant of Timelessness & Time: Symbolism & History in Robert Hayden's *Angle of Ascent*," *Massachusetts Review* 18(4), Winter 1977, 745-46.

"Night, Death, Mississippi"
>HOWARD FAULKNER. "'Transformed by Steeps of Flight': The Poetry of Robert Hayden," *CLA Journal* 21(2), December 1977, 289.

HAYDEN, ROBERT *(Cont.)*

"O Daedalus, Fly Away Home"

> CHARLES T. DAVIS. "Robert Hayden's Use of History," in *Modern Black Poets,* pp. 96-111.

"The Peacock Room"

> WILBURN WILLIAMS, JR. "Covenant of Timelessness & Time: Symbolism & History in Robert Hayden's *Angle of Ascent," Massachusetts Review* 18(4), Winter 1977, 746-47.

"The Performers"

> HOWARD FAULKNER. " 'Transformed by Steeps of Flight': The Poetry of Robert Hayden," *CLA Journal* 21(2), December 1977, 285.

"The Rabbi"

> WILBURN WILLIAMS, JR. "Covenant of Timelessness & Time: Symbolism & History in Robert Hayden's *Angle of Ascent," Massachusetts Review* 18(4), Winter 1977, 741-42. (P)

"Runagate, Runagate"

> CHARLES T. DAVIS. "Robert Hayden's Use of History," in *Modern Black Poets,* pp. 103-5.
>
> HOWARD FAULKNER. " 'Transformed by Steeps of Flight': The Poetry of Robert Hayden," *CLA Journal* 21(2), December 1977, 291.

"Stars"

> CONSTANCE J. POST. "Image and Idea in the Poetry of Robert Hayden," *CLA Journal* 20(2), December 1976, 165-68.

"Theme and Variation"

> CONSTANCE J. POST. "Image and Idea in the Poetry of Robert Hayden," *CLA Journal* 20(2), December 1976, 170.

HAYES, ALFRED

"Epistle to Gentiles"

> JOSEPH WARREN BEACH. *Obsessive Images,* pp. 36-37.

HAYNE, PAUL HAMILTON

"My Mother-Land"

> EDWARD IFKOVIC. "Two Poems for Paul Hamilton Hayne," *American Notes & Queries,* n.s., 6(5), January 1968, 71-72.

HEANEY, SEAMUS

"The Backward Look"

> JOHN WILSON FOSTER. "The Poetry of Seamus Heaney," *Critical Quarterly* 16(1), Spring 1974, 44.

"Death of a Naturalist"

> JULIAN GITZEN. "An Irish Imagist," *Studies in the Humanities* 4(2), February 1975, 10-11.

"Docker"

> JOHN WILSON FOSTER. "The Poetry of Seamus Heaney," *Critical Quarterly* 16(1), Spring 1974, 37-38.

"A Lough Neagh Sequence"

> JOHN WILSON FOSTER. "The Poetry of Seamus Heaney," *Critical Quarterly* 16(1), Spring 1974, 41.

"A New Song"

> JOHN WILSON FOSTER. "The Poetry of Seamus Heaney," *Critical Quarterly* 16(1), Spring 1974, 45-46.

"The Outlaw"

> BENEDICT KIELY. "A Raid Into Dark Corners: The Poems of Seamus Heaney," *Hollins Critic* 7(4), October 1970, 6.

"Personal Helicon"

> BENEDICT KIELY. "A Raid Into Dark Corners: The Poems of Seamus Heaney," *Hollins Critic* 7(4), October 1970, 8.

"Traditions"

> JOHN WILSON FOSTER. "The Poetry of Seamus Heaney," *Critical Quarterly* 16(1), Spring 1974, 44-45.

HEATH-STUBBS, JOHN

"For the New Cosmology"

> ROBIN SKELTON. *The Poetic Pattern,* pp. 68-69. (Quoting John Heath-Stubbs)

HECHT, ANTHONY

" 'It Out-Herods Herod. I Pray You, Avoid It' "

> LOUIS UNTERMEYER. *50 Modern American & British Poets,* p. 318.

" 'More Light! More Light!' "

> LOUIS UNTERMEYER. *50 Modern American & British Poets,* p. 318.

"Ostia Antica"

> NICHOLAS JOOST. *Explicator* 20(2), October 1961, Item 14.

"Samuel Sewall"

> LAURENCE PERRINE. *100 American Poems of the Twentieth Century,* pp. 262-64.

"The Vow"

> GLAUCO CAMBON. *Recent American Poetry,* pp. 22-23.

HEMANS, FELICIA DOROTHEA

"The Landing of the Pilgrim Fathers"

> ISAAC ASIMOV. *Familiar Poems, Annotated,* pp. 114-20.

HEMINGWAY, ERNEST

"They All Made Peace — What is Peace?"

> E. SAN JUAN, JR. "Integrity of Composition in the Poems of Ernest Hemingway," *University Review* 32(1), Autumn 1965, 57-58.

HENLEY, WILLIAM ERNEST

"Invictus"

> ISAAC ASIMOV. *Familiar Poems, Annotated,* pp. 229-33.
>
> HERBERT MARSHALL MCLUHAN. *Explicator* 3(3), December 1944, Item 22. Reprinted in: *The Creative Reader,* pp. 874-75; second ed., pp. 294-95.
>
> J. M. PURCELL. *Explicator* 4(2), November 1945, Item 13.

"Space and Dread and the Dark"

> GEORGE HERMAN. *Explicator* 22(2), October 1963, Item 14.

"The Ways of Death"

> RAY L. ARMSTRONG. *Explicator* 14(4), January 1956, Item 21.
>
> EARL DANIELS. *The Art of Reading Poetry,* pp. 268-69.

HENRI, ADRIAN

"Me (if you weren't you, who would you like to be?)"

GREVEL LINDOP. "Poetry, Rhetoric and the Mass Audience: The Case of the Liverpool Poets," in *British Poetry Since 1960*, p. 99.

HENRYSON, ROBERT

"The Abbay Walk"

I. W. A. JAMIESON. "The Minor Poems of Robert Henryson," *Studies in Scottish Literature* 9(2-3), Oct.-Jan. 1971-2, 132-34.

"Aganis Haisty Credence of Titlaris"

I. W. A. JAMIESON. "The Minor Poems of Robert Henryson," *Studies in Scottish Literature* 9(2-3), Oct.-Jan. 1971-2, 136-39.

"The Annunciation"

CHARLES A. HALLETT. "Theme and Structure in Henryson's 'The Annunciation,'" *Studies in Scottish Literature* 10(3), January 1973, 165-74.

"The Bludy Serk"

I. W. A. JAMIESON. "The Minor Poems of Robert Henryson," *Studies in Scottish Literature* 9(2-3), Oct.-Jan. 1971-2, 143-45.

A. M. KINGHORN. "The Minor Poems of Robert Henryson," *Studies in Scottish Literature* 3(1), July 1965, 32.

GEORGE S. PEEK. "Robert Henryson's View of Original Sin in 'The Bludy Serk,'" *Studies in Scottish Literature* 10(4), April 1973, 199-206.

"The Cock and the Jewel"

see "The Taill of the Cok and Jasp"

"Confessio Reynardi"

JOHN BLOCK FRIEDMAN. "Henryson, the Friars, and the *Confessio Reynardi*," *Journal of English and Germanic Philology* 66(4), October 1967, 550-61.

"The Garmont of Gud Ladeis"

I. W. A. JAMIESON. "The Minor Poems of Robert Henryson," *Studies in Scottish Literature* 9(2-3), Oct.-Jan. 1971-2, 135-36.

"Orpheus and Eurydice"

A. M. KINGHORN. "The Minor Poems of Robert Henryson," *Studies in Scottish Literature* 3(1), July 1965, 32-34.

R. J. MANNING. "A Note On Symbolic Identification in Henryson's 'Orpheus and Eurydice,'" *Studies in Scottish Literature* 8(4), April 1971, 265-71.

"The Praise of Aige"

I. W. A. JAMIESON. "The Minor Poems of Robert Henryson," *Studies in Scottish Literature* 9(2-3), Oct.-Jan. 1971-2, 126-27, 129-31.

"Ane Prayer for the Pest"

I. W. A. JAMIESON. "The Minor Poems of Robert Henryson," *Studies in Scottish Literature* 9(2-3), Oct.-Jan. 1971-2, 141-43.

A. M. KINGHORN. "The Minor Poems of Robert Henryson," *Studies in Scottish Literature* 3(1), July 1965, 36.

"The Preiching of the Swallow"

J. A. BURROW. "Henryson: *The Preaching of the Swallow*," *Essays in Criticism* 25(1), January 1975, 25-37.

GEORGE CLARK. "Henryson and Aesop: The Fable Transformed," *ELH* 43(1), Spring 1976, 10-17.

DENTON FOX. "Henryson's *Fables*," *ELH* 29(4), December 1962, 348-55.

"Prologue" (*The Morall Fabillis of Esope the Phrygian*)

DENTON FOX. "Henryson's *Fables*," *ELH* 29(4), December 1962, 339-41.

"The Ressoning betwix Aige and Yowth"

I. W. A. JAMIESON. "The Minor Poems of Robert Henryson," *Studies in Scottish Literature* 9(2-3), Oct.-Jan. 1971-2, 126-29.

"The Ressoning betwix Deth and Man"

A. M. KINGHORN. "The Minor Poems of Robert Henryson," *Studies in Scottish Literature* 3(1), July 1965, 34-35.

"Robene and Makyne"

A. M. KINGHORN. "The Minor Poems of Robert Henryson," *Studies in Scottish Literature* 3(1), July 1965, 30-31.

ARTHUR K. MOORE. *The Secular Lyric in Middle English*, pp. 188-94.

"Sum Practysis of Medecyne"

I. W. A. JAMIESON. "The Minor Poems of Robert Henryson," *Studies in Scottish Literature* 9(2-3), Oct.-Jan. 1971-2, 139-41.

A. M. KINGHORN. "The Minor Poems of Robert Henryson," *Studies in Scottish Literature* 3(1), July 1965, 37-39.

"The Taill how this foirsaid Tod maid his Confessioun to Freir Wolf Waitskaith"

see "Confessio Reynardi"

"The Taill of the Cok and Jasp"

GEORGE CLARK. "Henryson and Aesop: The Fable Transformed," *ELH* 43(1), Spring 1976, 6-10.

DENTON FOX. "Henryson's *Fables*," *ELH* 29(4), December 1962, 341-48.

"Taill of the Wolf and the Wedder"

I. W. A. JAMIESON. "Henryson's *Taill of the Wolf and the Wedder*," *Studies in Scottish Literature* 6(4), April 1969, 248-57.

"The Testament of Cresseid"

E. DUNCAN ASWELL. "The Role of Fortune in *The Testament of Cresseid*," *Philological Quarterly* 46(4), October 1967, 471-87.

DOUGLAS DUNCAN. "Henryson's *Testament of Cresseid*," *Essays in Criticism* 11(2), April 1961, 128-35.

RALPH HANNA III. "Cresseid's Dream and Henryson's *Testament*," in *Chaucer and Middle English Studies in Honor of Rossell Hope Robbins*, pp. 288-97.

SYDNEY HARTH. "Henryson Reinterpreted," *Essays in Criticism* 11(4), October 1961, 471-80.

ALDOUS HUXLEY. "Exhumations I. Huxley's 'Chaucer,'" *Essays in Criticism* 15(1), January 1965, 20-21.

C. W. JENTOFT. "Henryson as Authentic 'Chaucerian': Narrator, Character, and Courtley Love in *The Testament of Cresseid*," *Studies in Scottish Literature* 10(2), October 1972, 94-102.

JOHN MCNAMARA. "Divine Justice in Henryson's *Testament of Cresseid*," *Studies in Scottish Literature* 11(1&2), July-October 1973, 99-107.

DELORES L. NOLL. "*The Testament of Cresseid*; Are Christian Interpretations Valid?" *Studies in Scottish Literature* 9(1), July 1971, 16-25.

LEE W. PATTERSON. "Christian and Pagan in *The Testament of Cresseid*," *Philological Quarterly* 52(4), October 1973, 696-714.

HENRYSON, ROBERT *(Cont.)*

"The Testament of Cresseid" *(cont.)*

> LARRY M. SKLUTE. "Phoebus Descending: Rhetoric and Moral Vision in Henryson's *Testament of Cresseid*," *ELH* 44(2), Summer 1977, 189-204.
>
> A. C. SPEARING. "Conciseness and The Testament of Cresseid," in *Criticism and Medieval Poetry*, pp. 118-44; second ed., 157-92.
>
> E. M. W. TILLYARD. *Five Poems, 1470-1870*, pp. 5-29.

"The Thre Deid-Pollis"

> I. W. A. JAMIESON. "The Minor Poems of Robert Henryson," *Studies in Scottish Literature* 9(2-3), Oct.-Jan. 1971-2, 126-27, 131-32.

HERBERT, EDWARD

"An Appeal to his hopes not to fail him"

> CATHERINE A. HEBERT. "The Platonic Love Poetry of Lord Herbert of Cherbury," *Ball State University Forum* 11(4), Autumn 1970, 49.

"Elegy for Doctor Dunn"

> MICHAEL MURRIN. "Poetry as Literary Criticism," *Modern Philology* 65(3), February 1968, 205.

"Elegy for the Prince"

> TERRY G. SHERWOOD. "Reason, Faith, and Just Augustinian Lamentation in Donne's Elegy on Prince Henry," *Studies in English Literature 1500-1900* 13(1), Winter 1973, 55-56.

"Elegy over a Tomb"

> C. B. COX and A. E. DYSON. *The Practical Criticism of Poetry*, pp. 71-86.

"An Ode Upon a Question Moved, whether Love Should Continue For Ever"

> A. ALVAREZ. *The School of Donne*, English ed., 53-56; American ed., pp. 61-64.
>
> GEORGE WILLIAMSON. *Seventeenth Century Contexts*, pp. 69-72.

"Platonick Love (I)"

> CATHERINE A. HEBÉRT. "The Platonic Love Poetry of Lord Herbert of Cherbury," *Ball State University Forum* 11(4), Autumn 1970, 47-48.

"Platonick Love (II)"

> CATHERINE A. HEBÉRT. "The Platonic Love Poetry of Lord Herbert of Cherbury," *Ball State University Forum* 11(4), Autumn 1970, 48-49.

"Platonick Love (III)"

> CATHERINE A. HEBÉRT. "The Platonic Love Poetry of Lord Herbert of Cherbury," *Ball State University Forum* 11(4), Autumn 1970, 49.

"Sonnet of Black Beauty"

> STANLEY STEWART. *The Enclosed Garden*, pp. 66-67.

"Tears, flow no more, or if you needs must flow"

> JOHN T. SHAWCROSS. "The Poet as Orator: One Phase of His Judicial Pose," in *The Rhetoric of Renaissance Poetry*, pp. 26-27.

"The Thought"

> LLOYD FRANKENBERG. *Invitation to Poetry*, pp. 390-91.

"To her Hair"

> JOHN T. SHAWCROSS. "The Poet as Orator: One Phase of His Judicial Pose," in *The Rhetoric of Renaissance Poetry*, pp. 27-28.

HERBERT, GEORGE

"Aaron"

> H. ANDREW HARNACK. "George Herbert's 'Aaron': The Aesthetics of Shaped Typology," *English Language Notes* 14(1), September 1976, 25-32.
>
> WILLIAM J. SCHEICK. "Typology and Allegory: A Comparative Study of George Herbert and Edward Taylor," *Essays in Literature* 2(1), Spring 1975, 78-82.
>
> JOSEPH H. SUMMERS. "The Poem as Hieroglyph," in *Seventeenth Century English Poetry*, pp. 226-27; revised ed., pp. 236-37.
>
> GEORGE WILLIAMSON. *Six Metaphysical Poets*, p. 116.

"Aethiopissa Ambit Cestum Diuersis Coloris Virum"

> PHILLIP DUST. "The Sorrow of a Black Woman in a Seventeenth Century New-Latin Poem," *CLA Journal* 18(4), June 1975, 516-20.
>
> ROBERT F. FLEISSNER. "Herbert's Aethiopesa and the Dark Lady: A Mannerist Parallel," *CLA Journal* 19(4), June 1976, 458-67.
>
> ELLIOT H. TOKSON. "The Image of the Negro in Four Seventeenth-Century Love Poems," *Modern Language Quarterly* 30(4), December 1969, 510-15.

"Affliction (I)"

> WILLIAM EMPSON. *Seven Types of Ambiguity*, second and third eds., pp. 183-84.
>
> BARBARA LEAH HARMAN. "George Herbert's 'Affliction (I)': The Limits of Representation," *ELH* 44(2), Summer 1977, 267-85.
>
> SISTER M. JOSELYN. "Herbert and Hopkins: Two Lyrics," *Renascence* 10(4), Summer 1958, 192-95.
>
> L. C. KNIGHTS. *Explorations*, pp. 141-44.
>
> L. C. KNIGHTS. "George Herbert," *Scrutiny* 12(3), Summer 1944, 180-83.
>
> BILL SMITHSON. "Herbert's 'Affliction' Poems," *Studies in English Literature 1500-1900* 15(1), Winter 1975, 125-30.
>
> HERMINE J. VAN NUIS. "Herbert's 'Affliction' Poems: A Pilgrim's Progress," *Concerning Poetry* 8(2), Fall 1975, 8-11.
>
> HELEN VENDLER. "The Re-invented Poem: George Herbert's Alternatives," in *Forms of Lyric*, pp. 34-35.
>
> GEORGE WILLIAMSON. *Six Metaphysical Poets*, pp. 96-98.

"Affliction (II)"

> BILL SMITHSON. "Herbert's 'Affliction' Poems," *Studies in English Literature 1500-1900* 15(1), Winter 1975, 137-38.
>
> HERMINE J. VAN NUIS. "Herbert's 'Affliction' Poems: A Pilgrim's Progress," *Concerning Poetry* 8(2), Fall 1975, 11-12.

"Affliction (III)"

> BILL SMITHSON. "Herbert's 'Affliction' Poems," *Studies in English Literature 1500-1900* 15(1), Winter 1975, 138-39.
>
> HERMINE J. VAN NUIS. "Herbert's 'Affliction' Poems: A Pilgrim's Progress," *Concerning Poetry* 8(2), Fall 1975, 12-13.

"Affliction (IV)"

> BILL SMITHSON. "Herbert's 'Affliction' Poems," *Studies in English Literature 1500-1900* 15(1), Winter 1975, 134-37.
>
> HERMINE J. VAN NUIS. "Herbert's 'Affliction' Poems: A Pilgrim's Progress," *Concerning Poetry* 8(2), Fall 1975, 13-14.

"Affliction (V)"

WILLIAM J. SCHEICK. "Typology and Allegory: A Comparative Study of George Herbert and Edward Taylor," *Essays in Literature* 2(1), Spring 1975, 82-83.

BILL SMITHSON. "Herbert's 'Affliction' Poems," *Studies in English Literature 1500-1900* 15(1), Winter 1975, 130-34.

HERMINE J. VAN NUIS. "Herbert's 'Affliction' Poems: A Pilgrim's Progress," *Concerning Poetry* 8(2), Fall 1975, 15-16.

"The Agonie"

EDGAR F. DANIELS. *Explicator* 30(2), October 1971, Item 16.

ANTHONY LOW. *Love's Architecture*, pp. 96-97.

LOUIS L. MARTZ. *The Poetry of Meditation*, pp. 84-85.

RENÉ RAPIN. *Explicator* 30(2), October 1971, Item 16. (P)

"The Altar"

STANLEY E. FISH. "Letting Go: The Reader in Herbert's Poetry," *ELH* 37(4), December 1970, 485-94.

BARBARA K. LEWALSKI. "Typology and Poetry: A Consideration of Herbert, Vaughan, and Marvell," in *Illustrious Evidence*, pp. 45-47.

ANTHONY LOW. *Love's Architecture*, pp. 93-94.

MICHAEL MCCANLES. *Dialectical Criticism and Renaissance Literature*, pp. 79-80.

PHILIP C. MCGUIRE. "Private Prayer and English Poetry in the Early Seventeenth Century," *Studies in English Literature 1500-1900* 14(1), Winter 1974, 75-76.

WILLIAM J. SCHEICK. "Typology and Allegory: A Comparative Study of George Herbert and Edward Taylor," *Essays in Literature* 2(1), Spring 1975, 83-84.

THOMAS B. STROUP. " 'A Reasonable, Holy, and Living Sacrifice': Herbert's 'The Altar,' " *Essays in Literature* 2(2), Fall 1975, 149-63.

JOSEPH H. SUMMERS. "The Poem as Hieroglyph," in *Seventeenth Century English Poetry*, pp. 229-32; revised ed., pp. 239-42.

"Anagram"

SISTER SARA WILLIAM HANLEY. "George Herbert's 'Ana$_{Army}^{Mary}$Gram,' " *English Language Notes* 4(1), September 1966, 16-19.

LOUIS H. LEITER. "George Herbert's Anagram," *College English* 26(7), April 1965, 543-44.

ROBERT E. REITER. "George Herbert's 'Anagram': A Reply to Professor Leiter," *College English* 28(1), October 1966, 59-60.

"The Answer"

SAM WESTGATE. "George Herbert: 'Wit's an Unruly Engine,' " *Journal of the History of Ideas* 38(2), April-June 1977, 293-95.

"Artillerie"

A. L. CLEMENTS. "Theme, Tone, and Tradition in George Herbert's Poetry," *English Literary Renaissance* 3(2), Spring 1973, 265-71.

EARL MINER. *The Metaphysical Mode from Donne to Cowley*, pp. 93-95.

"Assurance"

JANE E. WOLFE. "George Herbert's 'Assurance,' " *CLA Journal* 5(3), March 1962, 213-22.

"The Bag"

SAAD EL-GABALAWY. "The Pilgrimage: George Herbert's Favorite Allegorical Technique," *CLA Journal* 13(4), June 1970, 417-18.

JEANNE CLAYTON HUNTER. *Explicator* 35(3), Spring 1977, 14-15.

LOUIS L. MARTZ. "The Action of the Self: Devotional Poetry in the Seventeenth Century," in *Metaphysical Poetry*, edited by Malcolm Bradbury and David Palmer, pp. 111-12.

LOUIS L. MARTZ. *The Poetry of Meditation*, rev. ed., pp. 302-3.

"The Banquet"

MALCOLM M. ROSS. "A Note on the Metaphysicals," *Hudson Review* 6(1), Spring 1953, 111.

"The Bunch of Grapes"

STANLEY E. FISH. "Catechizing the Reader: Herbert's Socratean Rhetoric," in *The Rhetoric of Renaissance Poetry*, pp. 179-85.

BARBARA K. LEWALSKI. "Typology and Poetry: A Consideration of Herbert, Vaughan, and Marvell," in *Illustrious Evidence*, pp. 44-45.

LAURENCE LERNER. *An Introduction to English Poetry*, pp. 52-61.

F. C. MCGRATH. *Explicator* 29(2), October 1970, Item 15.

JOSEPH H. SUMMERS. "The Poem as Hieroglyph," in *Seventeenth Century English Poetry*, pp. 218-20; revised ed., pp. 228-30.

"Businesse"

ROBERT G. COLLMER. *Explicator* 16(3), November 1957, Item 11.

"Christmas"

ANTHONY LOW. *Love's Architecture*, pp. 83-84.

JEAN WILKINSON. "Three Sets of Religious Poems," *Huntington Library Quarterly* 36(3), May 1973, 218-19. (P)

"The Church-floore"

SARA WILLIAM HANLEY. "Temples in *The Temple*: George Herbert's Study of the Church," *Studies in English Literature 1500-1900* 8(1), Winter 1968, 128-31.

JOSEPH H. SUMMERS. "The Poem as Hieroglyph," in *Seventeenth Century English Poetry*, pp. 216-18; revised ed., pp. 226-28.

"Church-lock and key"

SARA WILLIAM HANLEY. "Temples in *The Temple*: George Herbert's Study of the Church," *Studies in English Literature 1500-1900* 8(1), Winter 1968, 127-31.

FRANK L. HUNTLEY. "A Crux in George Herbert's *The Temple*," *English Language Notes* 8(1), September 1970, 13-17.

"The Church Militant"

RAYMOND A. ANSELMENT. " 'The Church Militant': George Herbert and the Metamorphoses of Christian History," *Huntington Library Quarterly* 41(4), August 1978, 299-316.

VALERIE CARNES. "The Unity of George Herbert's *The Temple*: A Reconsideration," *ELH* 35(4), December 1968, 520-24.

STANLEY STEWART. "Time and *The Temple*," *Studies in English Literature 1500-1900* 6(1), Winter 1966, 105-10.

"Church-monuments"

ELISSA S. GURALNICK. *Explicator* 35(4), Summer 1977, 12-14.

HERBERT, GEORGE *(Cont.)*

"Church-monuments" *(cont.)*

FRANK KERMODE and A. J. SMITH. "The Metaphysical Poets," in *English Poetry*, edited by Alan Sinfield, p. 60.

M. M. MAHOOD. "Something Understood: The Nature of Herbert's Wit," in *Metaphysical Poetry*, edited by Malcolm Bradbury and David Palmer, pp. 134-35.

LOUIS L. MARTZ. *The Poetry of Meditation*, pp. 141-43. Reprinted in: *The Modern Critical Spectrum*, pp. 248-50.

JOSEPH H. SUMMERS. "The Poem as Hieroglyph," in *Seventeenth Century English Poetry*, pp. 220-25; revised ed., pp. 230-35.

"Church-musick"

SARA WILLIAM HANLEY. "Temples in *The Temple*: George Herbert's Study of the Church," *Studies in English Literature 1500-1900* 8(1), Winter 1968, 127-31.

"The Church-Porch"

SHERIDAN D. BLAU. "The Poet as Casuist: Herbert's 'Church-Porch,' " *Genre* 4(2), June 1971, 142-52.

VALERIE CARNES. "The Unity of George Herbert's *The Temple*: A Reconsideration," *ELH* 35(4), December 1968, 510-14.

MICHAEL MCCANLES. *Dialectical Criticism and Renaissance Literature*, pp. 77-79.

LOUIS L. MARTZ. *The Poetry of Meditation*, pp. 290-92.

THOMAS B. STROUP. " 'A Reasonable, Holy, and Living Sacrifice': Herbert's 'The Altar,' " *Essays in Literature* 2(2), Fall 1975, 150-51.

JOSEPH H. SUMMERS. *The Heirs of Donne and Jonson*, pp. 89-97, 99-100.

"Church-windows"

see *"The Windows"*

"The Collar"

G. P. V. AKRIGG. "George Herbert's 'Caller,' " *Notes and Queries*, n.s., 1(1), January 1954, 17.

JACK M. BICKHAM. *Explicator* 10(3), December 1951, Item 17.

WILLIAM J. BROWN. "Herbert's 'The Collar' and Shakespeare's *1 Henry IV*," *American Notes & Queries*, n.s., 6(4), December 1967, 51-53.

DAVID DAICHES and WILLIAM CHARVAT. *Poems in English*, p. 660.

C. DAY LEWIS. *The Poetic Image*, pp. 80-81. Reprinted in: *Readings for Liberal Education*, revised ed., II: 39-40.

DUDLEY FITTS. "Herbert: The Collar," in *Master Poems of the English Language*, pp. 149-51.

WILLIAM H. HALEWOOD. *The Poetry of Grace*, pp. 89-99.

BARBARA LEAH HARMAN. "The Fiction of Coherence: George Herbert's 'The Collar,' " *PMLA* 93(5), October 1978, 865-77.

JEFFREY HART. "Herbert's 'The Collar' Re-read," in *Seventeenth Century English Poetry*, revised ed., pp. 248-56.

LAURENCE LERNER. *An Introduction to English Poetry*, pp. 53-55.

PAUL M. LEVITT and KENNETH G. JOHNSTON. "Herbert's 'The Collar': A Nautical Metaphor," *Studies in Philology* 66(2), April 1969, 217-24.

PAUL M. LEVITT and KENNETH G. JOHNSTON. "Herbert's 'The Collar' and the Story of Job," *Papers on Language and Literature* 4(3), Summer 1968, 329-30.

M. M. MAHOOD. "Something Understood: The Nature of Herbert's Wit," in *Metaphysical Poetry*, edited by Malcolm Bradbury and David Palmer, p. 133.

DAN S. NORTON. *Explicator* 2(6), April 1944, Item 41.

DAN S. NORTON. *Explicator* 3(6), April 1945, Item 46.

H. R. SWARDSON. *Poetry and the Fountain of Light*, pp. 67-68.

GEORGE WILLIAMSON. *Six Metaphysical Poets*, pp. 114-15.

"Conscience"

LOUIS L. MARTZ. "The Action of the Self: Devotional Poetry in the Seventeenth Century," in *Metaphysical Poetry*, edited by Malcolm Bradbury and David Palmer, pp. 112-13.

"The Crosse"

ANTHONY LOW. *Love's Architecture*, pp. 107-8.

LOUIS L. MARTZ. *The Poetry of Meditation*, pp. 134-35.

"Death"

PATRICIA BEER. *An Introduction to the Metaphysical Poets*, pp. 67-70.

ARNOLD STEIN. "George Herbert: The Art of Plainness," in *The Poetic Tradition*, pp. 115-21.

ARNOLD STEIN. "George Herbert: The Art of Plainness," in *Seventeenth Century English Poetry*, revised ed., pp. 272-77.

GEORGE WILLIAMSON. *Six Metaphysical Poets*, p. 117.

"Deniall"

JOSEPH H. SUMMERS. "The Poem as Hieroglyph," in *Seventeenth Century English Poetry*, p. 226; revised ed., p. 236.

H. R. SWARDSON. *Poetry and the Fountain of Light*, pp. 78-79.

"Dialogue"

BERNARD KNIEGER. "The Purchase-Sale: Patterns of Business Imagery in the Poetry of George Herbert," *Studies in English Literature 1500-1900* 6(1), Winter 1966, 113-15.

MICHAEL MCCANLES. *Dialectical Criticism and Renaissance Literature*, pp. 83-85.

"Discipline"

JACOB H. ADLER. "Form and Meaning in Herbert's 'Discipline,' " *Notes and Queries*, n.s., 5(6), June 1958, 240-43.

HAMISH SWANSTON. "The Second 'Temple,' " *Durham University Journal*, n.s., 25(1), December 1963, 17-18.

"Divinitie"

GEORGE WILLIAMSON. *Six Metaphysical Poets*, pp. 113-14.

"Dooms Day"

CONRAD HILBERRY. *Explicator* 16(5), January 1958, Item 24.

"Dulnesse"

ROSEMARY FREEMAN. "Parody as a Literary Form: George Herbert and Wilfred Owen," *Essays in Criticism* 13(4), October 1963, 313-14.

HELEN VENDLER. "The Re-invented Poem: George Herbert's Alternatives," in *Forms of Lyric*, pp. 21-22.

JEAN WILKINSON. "Three Sets of Religious Poems," *Huntington Library Quarterly* 36(3), May 1973, 215-16.

"Easter"

ANTHONY LOW. *Love's Architecture*, pp. 85-87.

"Easter-Wings"

C. C. BROWN and W. P. INGOLDSBY. "George Herbert's 'Easter-Wings,'" *Huntington Library Quarterly* 35(2), February 1972, 131-42.

ROBERT HASTINGS. "'Easter Wings' as a Model of Herbert's Method," *Thoth* 4(1), Winter 1963, 15-23.

ANTHONY LOW. *Love's Architecture*, pp. 101-2.

JOSEPH H. SUMMERS. "The Poem as Hieroglyph," in *Seventeenth Century English Poetry*, pp. 232-33; revised ed., pp. 242-43.

"The Elixir"

CHARLES MOLESWORTH. "Herbert's 'The Elixir': Revision Towards Action," *Concerning Poetry* 5(2), Fall 1972, 12-20.

"Employment (I)"

WILLIAM H. HALEWOOD. *The Poetry of Grace*, pp. 107-9.

"Employment (II)"

BERNARD KNIEGER. "The Purchase-Sale: Patterns of Business Imagery in the Poetry of George Herbert," *Studies in English Literature 1500-1900* 6(1), Winter 1966, 120-22.

GEORGE WILLIAMSON. *Six Metaphysical Poets*, pp. 98-99.

"Even-Song"

SARA WILLIAM HANLEY. "Temples in *The Temple*: George Herbert's Study of the Church," *Studies in English Literature 1500-1900* 8(1), Winter 1968, 123-26.

SAM WESTGATE. "George Herbert: 'Wit's an Unruly Engine,'" *Journal of the History of Ideas* 38(2), April-June 1977, 291-93.

"Faith"

M. M. MAHOOD. "Something Understood: The Nature of Herbert's Wit," in *Metaphysical Poetry*, edited by Malcolm Bradbury and David Palmer, p. 125.

"The Flower"

M. H. ABRAMS. "Structure and Style In the Greater Romantic Lyric," in *From Sensibility to Romanticism*, pp. 554-55. Reprinted in: *Romanticism and Consciousness*, pp. 226-27.

A. L. CLEMENTS. "Theme, Tone, and Tradition in George Herbert's Poetry," *English Literary Renaissance* 3(2), Spring 1973, 280-83.

L. C. KNIGHTS. *Explorations*, pp. 146-47. Reprinted in: *Poems and Critics*, pp. 59-60.

L. C. KNIGHTS. "George Herbert," *Scrutiny* 12(3), Summer 1944, 185-86.

ANTHONY LOW. *Love's Architecture*, pp. 110-14.

EARL MINER. *The Metaphysical Mode from Donne to Cowley*, pp. 231-46.

STANLEY STEWART. "Time and *The Temple*," *Studies in English Literature 1500-1900* 6(1), Winter 1966, 100-3.

HAROLD E. TOLIVER. *Pastoral Forms and Attitudes*, pp. 124-25.

MARK VAN DOREN. *Introduction to Poetry*, pp. 69-73.

HELEN VENDLER. "The Re-invented Poem: George Herbert's Alternatives," in *Forms of Lyric*, 35-42.

GEORGE WILLIAMSON. *Six Metaphysical Poets*, pp. 115-16.

"The Forerunners"

PHILIP J. GALLAGHER. "George Herbert's 'The Forerunners,'" *English Language Notes* 15(1), September 1977, 14-18.

ARNOLD STEIN. "George Herbert: The Art of Plainness," in *The Poetic Tradition*, pp. 103-6.

ARNOLD STEIN. "George Herbert: The Art of Plainness," in *Seventeenth Century English Poetry*, revised ed., pp. 261-63.

H. R. SWARDSON. *Poetry and the Fountain of Light*, pp. 71-72.

HELEN VENDLER. "The Re-invented Poem: George Herbert's Alternatives," in *Forms of Lyric*, pp. 33-34.

"Frailtie"

SISTER SARA WILLIAM HANLEY. *Explicator* 25(2), October 1966, Item 18.

"Good Friday"

ANTHONY LOW. *Love's Architecture*, pp. 97-99.

"Grace"

HELEN VENDLER. "The Re-invented Poem: George Herbert's Alternatives," in *Forms of Lyric*, pp. 20-21.

"Grief"

ANTHONY LOW. *Love's Architecture*, pp. 106-7.

HELEN J. SCHWARTZ. *Explicator* 31(6), February 1973, Item 43.

"The H. Scriptures (I)"

VIRGINIA R. MOLLENKOTT. "George Herbert's Epithet-Sonnets," *Genre* 5(2), June 1972, 133-35.

SAM WESTGATE. "George Herbert: 'Wit's an Unruly Engine,'" *Journal of the History of Ideas* 38(2), April-June 1977, 289-90.

"Heaven"

HAROLD E. TOLIVER. *Pastoral Forms and Attitudes*, pp. 133-35.

"The Holdfast"

STANLEY E. FISH. "Letting Go: The Reader in Herbert's Poetry," *ELH* 37(4), December 1970, 480-82.

SISTER M. JOSELYN. "Herbert and Muir: Pilgrims of Their Age," *Renascence* 15(3), Spring 1963, 130-31.

"The Holy Communion"

MALCOLM M. ROSS. "A Note on the Metaphysicals," *Hudson Review* 6(1), Spring 1953, 110-11.

"Hope"

WILLIAM EMPSON. *Seven Types of Ambiguity*, pp. 150-53; second and third eds., pp. 118-20.

JOHN FREDERICK NIMS. *Western Wind*, p. 45.

"The Invitation"

HELEN VENDLER. "The Re-invented Poem: George Herbert's Alternatives," in *Forms of Lyric*, pp. 25-28.

"Jordan (I)"

T. R. BARNES. *English Verse*, pp. 74-76.

PATRICIA BEER. *An Introduction to the Metaphysical Poets*, pp. 63-67.

C. C. BROWN and W. P. INGOLDSBY. "George Herbert's 'Easter-Wings,'" *Huntington Library Quarterly* 35(2), February 1972, 139-40.

MACDONALD EMSLIE. *Explicator* 12(6), April 1954, Item 35.

ROSEMARY FREEMAN. "Parody as a Literary Form: George Herbert and Wilfred Owen," *Essays in Criticism* 13(4), October 1963, 310-11.

BARBARA LEAH HARMAN. "The Fiction of Coherence: George Herbert's 'The Collar,'" *PMLA* 93(5), October 1978, 865-66.

ANTHONY LOW. "Herbert's 'Jordan (I)' and the Court Masque," *Criticism* 14(2), Spring 1972, 109-18.

HERBERT, GEORGE *(Cont.)*

"Jordan (I)" *(cont.)*

> EARL MINER. *The Metaphysical Mode from Donne to Cowley,* pp. 135-36.
>
> EARL MINER. "Wit: Definition and Dialectic," in *Seventeenth Century English Poetry,* revised ed., pp. 57-58.
>
> MICHAEL MURRIN. "Poetry as Literary Criticism," *Modern Philology* 65(3), February 1968, 202-3.
>
> H. R. SWARDSON. *Poetry and the Fountain of Light,* pp. 69-70.

"Jordan (II)"

> ROSEMARY FREEMAN. "Parody as a Literary Form: George Herbert and Wilfred Owen," *Essays in Criticism* 13(4), October 1963, 310-12.
>
> BARBARA LEAH HARMAN. "The Fiction of Coherence: George Herbert's 'The Collar,' " *PMLA* 93(5), October 1978, 865-66.
>
> H. R. SWARDSON. *Poetry and the Fountain of Light,* pp. 70-71.

"Josephs Coat"

> JOSEPH H. SUMMERS. "The Poem as Hieroglyph," in *Seventeenth Century English Poetry,* p. 220; revised ed., p. 230.

"Judgement"

> DONALD E. STANFORD. "The Imagination of Death in the Poetry of Philip Pain, Edward Taylor, and George Herbert," *Studies in the Literary Imagination* 9(2), Fall 1976, 61-62.

"Justice (II)"

> WILLIAM H. HALEWOOD. *The Poetry of Grace,* pp. 104-6.

"Life"

> LOUIS L. MARTZ. *The Poetry of Meditation,* pp. 58-59.
>
> STANLEY STEWART. *The Enclosed Garden,* pp. 113-14.
>
> GEORGE WILLIAMSON. *Six Metaphysical Poets,* pp. 111-12.

"Love (I)"

> ARNOLD STEIN. "George Herbert: The Art of Plainness," in *Seventeenth Century English Poetry,* revised ed., p. 257.
>
> SAM WESTGATE. "George Herbert: 'Wit's an Unruly Engine,' " *Journal of the History of Ideas* 38(2), April-June 1977, 287-89.

"Love (II)"

> ARNOLD STEIN. "George Herbert: The Art of Plainness," in *Seventeenth Century English Poetry,* revised ed., p. 257.
>
> SAM WESTGATE. "George Herbert: 'Wit's an Unruly Engine,' " *Journal of the History of Ideas* 38(2), April-June 1977, 287-89.

"Love (III)"

> A. ALVAREZ. *The School of Donne,* English ed., pp. 79-81; American ed., pp. 87-89.
>
> CHANA BLOCH. "George Herbert and the Bible: A Reading of 'Love (III),' " *English Literary Renaissance* 8(3), Autumn 1978, 329-40.
>
> REUBEN ARTHUR BROWER. *The Fields of Light,* pp. 28-29.
>
> REUBEN ARTHUR BROWER. "The Speaking Voice," in *The Study of Literature,* pp. 169-71.
>
> GREG CROSSAN. *Explicator* 37(1), Fall 1978, 40-41.
>
> MICHAEL MCCANLES. *Dialectical Criticism and Renaissance Literature,* pp. 75-76.

> M. M. MAHOOD. "Something Understood: The Nature of Herbert's Wit," in *Metaphysical Poetry,* edited by Malcolm Bradbury and David Palmer, pp. 145-47.
>
> EARL MINER. *The Metaphysical Mode from Donne to Cowley,* pp. 95-97.
>
> ROBERT L. MONTGOMERY. "The Province of Allegory in George Herbert's Verse," *Texas Studies in Literature and Language* 1(4), Winter 1960, 460-71.
>
> NICHOLAS SHARP. *Explicator* 33(3), November 1974, Item 26.
>
> JAMES THORPE. *Explicator* 24(2), October 1965, Item 16.

"Love-joy"

> STANLEY E. FISH. "Catechizing the Reader: Herbert's Socratean Rhetoric," in *The Rhetoric of Renaissance Poetry,* pp. 177-78.

"Love unknown"

> IRA CLARK. " 'Lord, In Thee The *Beauty* Lies in the *Discovery*': 'Love Unknown' and Reading Herbert," *ELH* 39(4), December 1972, 560-84.
>
> ROBERT L. MONTGOMERY, JR. "The Province of Allegory in George Herbert's Verse," *Texas Studies in Literature and Language* 1(4), Winter 1960, 465-69.

"Man"

> VINCENT BUCKLEY. *Poetry and the Sacred,* pp. 45-47.
>
> LAWRENCE J. DESSNER. "A Reading of George Herbert's 'Man,' " *Concerning Poetry* 5(1), Spring 1972, 61-63.
>
> LOUIS L. MARTZ. *The Poetry of Meditation,* pp. 59-61.
>
> GEORGE WILLIAMSON. *Six Metaphysical Poets,* pp. 110-11.

"Mattens"

> SARA WILLIAM HANLEY. "Temples in *The Temple*: George Herbert's Study of the Church," *Studies in English Literature 1500-1900* 8(1), Winter 1968, 123-26.

"Mortification"

> HELEN GARDNER. "The Metaphysical Poets," in *Seventeenth Century English Poetry,* pp. 60-61; revised ed., pp. 43-44.
>
> M. M. MAHOOD. "Something Understood: The Nature of Herbert's Wit," in *Metaphysical Poetry,* edited by Malcolm Bradbury and David Palmer, pp. 133-34.
>
> GEORGE WILLIAMSON. *Six Metaphysical Poets,* p. 112.

"My God, where is that ancient heat toward thee"

> H. R. SWARDSON. *Poetry and the Fountain of Light,* pp. 64-65.

"Paradise"

> STANLEY STEWART. *The Enclosed Garden,* pp. 52-59.
>
> JOSEPH H. SUMMERS. "The Poem as Hieroglyph," in *Seventeenth Century English Poetry,* pp. 228-29; revised ed., pp. 238-39.
>
> R. DARBY WILLIAMS. "Two Baroque Game Poems on Grace: Herbert's 'Paradise' and Milton's 'On Time,' " *Criticism* 12(3), Summer 1970, 180-86.

"A Parodie"

> ROSAMOND TUVE. "Sacred 'Parody' of Love Poetry and Herbert," *Studies in the Renaissance* 8 (1961), 249-90.
>
> RAYMOND J. WILSON III. "George Herbert's 'A Parodie': Its Double Meanings," *American Imago* 34(2), Summer 1977, 154-57.

"Peace"

> SAAD EL-GABALAWY. "The Pilgrimage: George Herbert's Favorite Allegorical Technique," *CLA Journal* 13(4), June 1970, 413-14.
>
> SISTER M. JOSELYN. "Herbert and Muir: Pilgrims of Their Age," *Renascence* 15(3), Spring 1963, 127-28.
>
> MICHAEL WEST. "Ecclesiastical Controversy in George Herbert's 'Peace,'" *Review of English Studies*, n.s., 22(88), November 1971, 445-51.

"The Pearl"

> BERNARD KNIEGER. "Teaching George Herbert in Israel — and in America?" *CLA Journal* 10(2), December 1966, 146-47.
>
> M. M. MAHOOD. "Something Understood: The Nature of Herbert's Wit," in *Metaphysical Poetry*, edited by Malcolm Bradbury and David Palmer, pp. 129-31.
>
> ARNOLD STEIN. "George Herbert: The Art of Plainness," in *Seventeenth Century English Poetry*, revised ed., pp. 268-71.
>
> ARNOLD STEIN. "George Herbert: The Art of Plainness," in *The Poetic Tradition*, pp. 111-15.
>
> H. R. SWARDSON. *Poetry and the Fountain of Light*, pp. 74-76.
>
> GEORGE WILLIAMSON. *Six Metaphysical Poets*, pp. 109-10.

"The Pilgrimage"

> SAAD EL-GABALAWY. "The Pilgrimage: George Herbert's Favorite Allegorical Technique," *CLA Journal* 13(4), June 1970, 408-13.
>
> WILLIAM EMPSON. *Seven Types of Ambiguity*, pp. 163-65; second and third eds., pp. 129-31. (P) Reprinted in: *Poems and Critics*, pp. 60-62.
>
> SISTER M. JOSELYN. "Herbert and Muir: Pilgrims of Their Age," *Renascence* 15(3), Spring 1963, 131.
>
> L. C. KNIGHTS. *Explorations*, pp. 135-37. Reprinted in: *Poems and Critics*, pp. 57-58.
>
> LOUIS L. MARTZ. *The Poetry of Meditation*, pp. 304-6.

"Prayer (I)"

> E. B. GREENWOOD. "George Herbert's Sonnet 'Prayer': A Stylistic Study," *Essays in Criticism* 15(1), January 1965, 27-45.
>
> FRANK KERMODE and A. J. SMITH. "The Metaphysical Poets," in *English Poetry*, edited by Alan Sinfield, pp. 66-67.
>
> M. M. MAHOOD. "Something Understood: The Nature of Herbert's Wit," in *Metaphysical Poetry*, edited by Malcolm Bradbury and David Palmer, pp. 128-29.
>
> LOUIS L. MARTZ. *The Poetry of Meditation*, pp. 298-300.
>
> EARL MINER. "Wit: Definition and Dialectic," in *Seventeenth Century English Poetry*, revised ed., pp. 50-51.
>
> VIRGINIA R. MOLLENKOTT. "George Herbert's Epithet-Sonnets," *Genre* 5(2), June 1972, 135-36.
>
> HOWARD NEMEROV. "Speaking Silence," *Georgia Review* 29(4), Winter 1979, 870-77.
>
> HELEN VENDLER. "The Re-invented Poem: George Herbert's Alternatives," in *Forms of Lyric*, pp. 28-31.

"Prayer (II)"

> SAM WESTGATE. "George Herbert: 'Wit's an Unruly Engine,'" *Journal of the History of Ideas* 38(2), April-June 1977, 290-91.

"Providence"

> MICHAEL MCCANLES. *Dialectical Criticism and Renaissance Literature*, pp. 89-93.

> VIRGINIA R. MOLLENKOTT. "The Many and the One in George Herbert's 'Providence,'" *CLA Journal* 10(1), September 1966, 34-41.

"The Pulley"

> EARL DANIELS. *The Art of Reading Poetry*, pp. 208-10.
>
> JANE GRAYSON. "Bernardine Paranomasia in Herbert's 'The Pulley,'" *American Notes and Queries*, n.s., 15(4), December 1976, 52-53.
>
> D. S. MEAD. *Explicator* 4(3), December 1945, Item 17.
>
> M. L. ROSENTHAL and A. J. M. SMITH. *Exploring Poetry*, first ed., p. 545.
>
> GEORGE WILLIAMSON. *Six Metaphysical Poets*, p. 115.

"The Quidditie"

> JESS CLOUD. *Explicator* 34(4), December 1975, Item 32.
>
> HAROLD E. TOLIVER. *Pastoral Forms and Attitudes*, p. 131.

"The Quip"

> EDGAR F. DANIELS. "Herbert's *The Quip*, Line 23; 'Say, I am Thine,'" *English Language Notes* 2(1), September 1964, 10-12.
>
> M. M. MAHOOD. "Something Understood: The Nature of Herbert's Wit," in *Metaphysical Poetry*, edited by Malcolm Bradbury and David Palmer, p. 136.
>
> GEORGE WILLIAMSON. *Six Metaphysical Poets*, pp. 112-13.

"Redemption"

> PATRICIA BEER. *An Introduction to the Metaphysical Poets*, pp. 59-63.
>
> ILONA BELL. "'Setting Foot into Divinity': George Herbert and the English Reformation," *Modern Language Quarterly* 38(3), September 1977, 237-38.
>
> A. E. DYSON and JULIAN LOVELOCK. *Masterful Images*, pp. 29-35.
>
> SAAD EL-GABALAWY. "The Pilgrimage: George Herbert's Favorite Allegorical Technique," *CLA Journal* 13(4), June 1970, 414-15.
>
> BERNARD KNIEGER. *Explicator* 11(4), February 1953, Item 24.
>
> ANTHONY LOW. *Love's Architecture*, p. 99.
>
> LOUIS L. MARTZ. *The Poetry of Meditation*, rev. ed., pp. 307-9.
>
> VIRGINIA R. MOLLENKOTT. "George Herbert's 'Redemption,'" *English Language Notes* 10(4), June 1973, 262-67.
>
> GEORGE WILLIAMSON. *Six Metaphysical Poets*, pp. 106-7.

"Repentance"

> M. M. MAHOOD. "Something Understood: The Nature of Herbert's Wit," in *Metaphysical Poetry*, edited by Malcolm Bradbury and David Palmer, pp. 127-28.

"The Reprisall"

> ANTHONY LOW. *Love's Architecture*, p. 96.
>
> MICHAEL MCCANLES. *Dialectical Criticism and Renaissance Literature*, pp. 81-82.

"The Rose"

> DON CAMERON ALLEN. "George Herbert: 'The Rose,'" in *Image and Meaning*, pp. 67-79, revised ed., pp. 102-14.
>
> DONALD E. STANFORD. "The Imagination of Death in the Poetry of Philip Pain, Edward Taylor, and George Herbert," *Studies in the Literary Imagination* 9(2), Fall 1976, 59-60. (P)

HERBERT, GEORGE *(Cont.)*

"The Sacrifice"

ILONA BELL. " 'Setting Foot into Divinity': George Herbert and the English Reformation," *Modern Language Quarterly* 38(3), September 1977, 226-27.

WILLIAM EMPSON. "George Herbert and Miss Tuve," *Kenyon Review* 12(4), Autumn 1950, 735-38. (P)

WILLIAM EMPSON. *Seven Types of Ambiguity*, pp. 286-95; second and third eds., pp. 226-33.

ANTHONY LOW. *Love's Architecture*, pp. 94-95.

MICHAEL MCCANLES. *Dialectical Criticism and Renaissance Literature*, pp. 86-89.

LOUIS L. MARTZ. *The Poetry of Meditation*, pp. 91-96.

EARL MINER. *The Metaphysical Mode from Donne to Cowley*, pp. 190-91.

ROSAMOND TUVE. "On Herbert's 'Sacrifice,' " *Kenyon Review* 12(1), Winter 1950, 51-75.

"The Search"

ANTHONY LOW. *Love's Architecture*, pp. 103-6.

"Sepulchre"

ANTHONY LOW. *Love's Architecture*, pp. 99-100.

"Sinne (II)"

SARA WILLIAM HANLEY. "Temples in *The Temple*: George Herbert's Study of the Church," *Studies in English Literature 1500-1900* 8(1), Winter 1968, 123-26.

"The Sonne"

FREDERICK VON ENDE. "George Herbert's 'The Sonne': In Defense of the English Language," *Studies in English Literature* 12(1), Winter 1972, 173-82.

"Sunday"

ROBERT L. MONTGOMERY, JR. "The Province of Allegory in George Herbert's Verse," *Texas Studies in Literature and Language* 1(4), Winter 1960, 458-60.

STANLEY STEWART. *The Enclosed Garden*, pp. 147-48.

"Superluminaire"

ELIZABETH MCLAUGHLIN and GAIL THOMAS. "Communion in *The Temple*," *Studies in English Literature 1500-1900* 15(1), Winter 1975, 112-14.

"The Temper (I)"

FREDSON BOWERS. "Herbert's Sequential Imagery: 'The Temper,' " *Modern Philology* 59(3), February 1962, 202-13.

A. L. CLEMENTS. "Theme, Tone, and Tradition in George Herbert's Poetry," *English Literary Renaissance* 3(2), Spring 1973, 278-80.

ARNOLD STEIN. "George Herbert: The Art of Plainness," in *The Poetic Tradition*, pp. 108-11.

ARNOLD STEIN. "George Herbert: The Art of Plainness," in *Seventeenth Century English Poetry*, revised ed., pp. 265-68.

HAROLD E. TOLIVER. *Pastoral Forms and Attitudes*, pp. 135-37.

HELEN VENDLER. "The Re-invented Poem: George Herbert's Alternatives," in *Forms of Lyric*, pp. 31-33.

GEORGE WILLIAMSON. *Six Metaphysical Poets*, p. 107.

"The Thanksgiving"

ILONA BELL. " 'Setting Foot into Divinity': George Herbert and the English Reformation," *Modern Language Quarterly* 38(3), September 1977, 228-36.

ANTHONY LOW. *Love's Architecture*, p. 95.

MICHAEL MCCANLES. *Dialectical Criticism and Renaissance Literature*, pp. 80-81.

HAROLD E. TOLIVER. *Pastoral Forms and Attitudes*, pp. 121-23.

"Time"

STANLEY STEWART. *The Enclosed Garden*, p. 102.

"To all Angels and Saints"

LOUIS L. MARTZ. *The Poetry of Meditation*, pp. 97-98.

"Trinitie Sunday"

SARA WILLIAM HANLEY. "Temples in *The Temple*: George Herbert's Study of the Church," *Studies in English Literature 1500-1900* 8(1), Winter 1968, 131-33.

ANTHONY LOW. *Love's Architecture*, p. 87.

JOSEPH H. SUMMERS. *Explicator* 10(4), February 1952, Item 23.

"A True Hymne"

STANLEY E. FISH. "Letting Go: The Reader in Herbert's Poetry," *ELH* 37(4), December 1970, 482-85.

LLOYD FRANKENBERG. *Invitation to Poetry*, pp. 62-63.

ARNOLD STEIN. "George Herbert: The Art of Plainness," in *The Poetic Tradition*, pp. 100-3.

ARNOLD STEIN. "George Herbert: The Art of Plainness," in *Seventeenth Century English Poetry*, revised ed., pp. 258-61.

HAROLD E. TOLIVER. *Pastoral Forms and Attitudes*, p. 132.

HELEN VENDLER. "The Re-invented Poem: George Herbert's Alternatives," in *Forms of Lyric*, pp. 22-23.

"Vanitie (I)"

RONALD GASKELL. "Herbert's 'Vanitie,' " *Critical Quarterly* 3(4), Winter 1961, 313-15.

BERNARD KNIEGER. "Teaching George Herbert in Israel — and in America?" *CLA Journal* 10(2), December 1966, 146.

FRANK J. WARNKE. "Baroque and Metaphysical," in *The Metaphysical Poets*, pp. 105-6.

GEORGE WILLIAMSON. *Six Metaphysical Poets*, p. 108.

"Virtue"

EDWIN B. BENJAMIN. *Explicator* 9(2), November 1950, Item 12.

HERBERT MARSHALL MCLUHAN. *Explicator* 2(1), October 1943, Item 4. Reprinted in: *Readings for Liberal Education*, II: 534-35.

M. M. MAHOOD. "Something Understood: The Nature of Herbert's Wit," in *Metaphysical Poetry*, edited by Malcolm Bradbury and David Palmer, pp. 143-45.

LOUIS L. MARTZ. "The Action of the Self: Devotional Poetry in the Seventeenth Century," in *Metaphysical Poetry*, edited by Malcolm Bradbury and David Palmer, pp. 108-10.

EARL MINER. *The Metaphysical Mode from Donne to Cowley*, pp. 140-41.

EARL MINER. "Wit: Definition and Dialectic," in *Seventeenth Century English Poetry*, revised ed., pp. 61-62.

M. L. ROSENTHAL and A. J. M. SMITH. *Exploring Poetry*, first ed., pp. 416-17.

HAROLD E. TOLIVER. *Pastoral Forms and Attitudes*, pp. 126-28.

HELEN VENDLER. "George Herbert's 'Vertue,' " *Ariel* 1(2), April 1970, 54-70.

GEORGE WILLLIAMSON. *Six Metaphysical Poets*, pp. 108-9.

"The Windows"

T. R. BARNES. *English Verse*, pp. 73-74.

REUBEN ARTHUR BROWER. *The Fields of Light*, pp. 45-47.

R. A. FORSYTH. "Herbert, Clough, and their Church-Windows," *Victorian Poetry* 7(1), Spring 1969, 21-25.

SARA WILLIAM HANLEY. "Temples in *The Temple*: George Herbert's Study of the Church," *Studies in English Literature 1500-1900* 8(1), Winter 1968, 129-31.

GEORGE WILLIAMSON. *Six Metaphysical Poets*, pp. 107-8.

"The World"

EDWARD C. JACOBS. "Herbert's 'The World': A Study of Grace," *Concerning Poetry* 8(2), Fall 1975, 71-74.

"A Wreath"

MARGARET CARPENTER. "From Herbert to Marvell: Poetics in 'A Wreath' and 'The Coronet,' " *Journal of English and Germanic Philology* 69(1), January 1970, 50-62.

HERRICK, ROBERT

"Another Grace for a Child"

ROBIN SKELTON. *Poetry*, pp. 135-36.

"The Apparition of his Mistress calling him to Elysium"

JAY A. GERTZMAN. "Robert Herrick's Recreative Pastoral," *Genre* 7(2), June 1974, 188.

M. L. ROSENTHAL and A. J. M. SMITH. *Exploring Poetry*, pp. 251-52.

"The Argument of his Book"

JAY A. GERTZMAN. "Robert Herrick's Recreative Pastoral," *Genre* 7(2), June 1974, 185-87.

ROBERT B. HINMAN. "The Apotheosis of Faust: Poetry and New Philosophy in the Seventeenth Century," in *Metaphysical Poetry*, edited by Malcolm Bradbury and David Palmer, pp. 159-64.

EDWARD L. HIRSH. *Explicator* 2(2), November 1943, Item 11.

H. R. SWARDSON. *Poetry and the Fountain of Light*, pp. 46-47.

"The Bracelet to Julia"

CLYDE S. KILBY. *Poetry and Life*, p. 15.

"The Carkanet"

CHARLES A. HUTTAR. *Explicator* 24(4), December 1965, Item 35.

CHARLES SANDERS. *Explicator* 23(3), November 1964, Item 24.

"Cherrie-Ripe"

DAVID DAICHES. *A Study of Literature*, pp. 148-50.

"A Christmas Caroll, Sung to the King in the Presence at White-Hall"

LEAH SINANOGLOU MARCUS. "Herrick's *Noble Numbers* and the Politics of Playfulness," *English Literary Renaisssance* 7(1), Winter 1977, 119-20.

"The Comming of good luck"

F. W. BATESON. *English Poetry*, pp. 82-83.

"Corinna's going a Maying"

CLEANTH BROOKS. *The Well Wrought Urn*, pp. 67-75; revised ed., pp. 54-64. Reprinted in: *Essays in Modern Literary Criticism*, pp. 327-35.

ROBERT H. DEMING. "The Use of the Past: Herrick and Hawthorne," *Journal of Popular Culture* 2(2), Fall 1968, 284-87.

A. LEIGH DENEEF. "Herrick's 'Corina' and the Ceremonial Mode," *South Atlantic Quarterly* 70(4), Autumn 1971, 530-45.

JAY A. GERTZMAN. "Robert Herrick's Recreative Pastoral," *Genre* 7(2), June 1974, 189.

ROY HARVEY PEARCE. " 'Pure' Criticism and the History of Ideas," *Journal of Aesthetics and Art Criticism* 7(2), December 1948, 126-29.

ROGER B. ROLLIN. "The Decorum of Criticism and Two Poems by Herrick," *CEA Critic* 31(4), January 1969, 4-7.

H. R. SWARDSON. *Poetry and the Fountain of Light*, pp. 58-59.

"A Country Life: To his Brother, M. Tho. Herrick"

PAUL R. JENKINS. "Rethinking What Moderation Means to Robert Herrick," *ELH* 39(1), March 1972, 49-53.

ANTHONY LOW. *Love's Architecture*, pp. 210-11.

"Delight in Disorder"

F. W. BATESON. *English Poetry and the English Language*, pp. 42-43. Reprinted in: Cleanth Brooks and Robert Penn Warren. *Understanding Poetry*, p. 328; revised ed., p. 188; third ed., pp. 259-60. Also: Leonard Unger and William Van O'Connor. *Poems for Study*, p. 147. Also: *Readings for Liberal Education*, fourth ed., II: 35-36; fifth ed., II: 34-35.

ELIZABETH DREW. *Poetry*, pp. 78-79.

PAUL R. JENKINS. "Rethinking What Moderation Means to Robert Herrick," *ELH* 39(1), March 1972, 53-54.

C. N. MANLOVE. *Literature and Reality*, p. 27.

EDWARD W. ROSENHEIM, JR. *What Happens in Literature*, pp. 32-39.

JACK SHADOIAN. "Herrick's 'Delight in Disorder,' " *Studies in the Humanities* 2(2), Summer 1971, 23-25.

LEO SPITZER. "Herrick's 'Delight in Disorder,' " *Modern Language Notes* 76(3), March 1961, 209-14. Reprinted in: Leo Spitzer. *Essays on English and American Literature*, pp. 132-38.

"A Dirge upon the Death of the Right Valiant Lord, Bernard Stuart"

ROBERT H. DEMING. "Herrick's Funereal Poems," *Studies in English Literature 1500-1900* 9(1), Winter 1969, 162-65.

"Epilogue" (*Hesperides*)

JOHN L. KIMMEY. "Robert Herrick's Persona," *Studies in Philology* 67(2), April 1970, 223.

"The Fairie Temple; or, Oberons Chapell"

A. S. CHAMBERS. "Herrick and the Trans-shifting of Time," *Studies in Philology* 72(1), January 1975, 91-94.

ROBERT H. DEMING. "Robert Herrick's Classical Ceremony," *ELH* 34(3), September 1967, 332-39.

DANIEL H. WOODWARD. "Herrick's Oberon Poems," *Journal of English and Germanic Philology* 64(2), April 1965, 270-84.

"Farewell Frost, or Welcome the Spring"

EARL MINER. *The Cavalier Mode from Jonson to Cotton*, pp. 177-79.

"The Funerall Rites of the Rose"

ROBERT H. DEMING. "Herrick's Funereal Poems," *Studies in English Literature 1500-1900* 9(1), Winter 1969, 153-58.

WILLIAM EMPSON. *Seven Types of Ambiguity*, second and third eds., pp. 162-63. (P)

HERRICK, ROBERT *(Cont.)*

"The Funerall Rites of the Rose" *(cont.)*

THOMAS R. WHITAKER. "Herrick and the Fruits of the Garden," *Journal of English Literary History* 22(1), March 1955, 16-23.

"Good Friday: Rex Tragicus, or Christ going to His Crosse"

DON CAMERON ALLEN. "Robert Herrick: 'Rex Tragicus,'" in *Image and Meaning,* second ed., pp. 138-51.

A. B. CHAMBERS. "Herrick and the Trans-shifting of Time," *Studies in Philology* 72(1), January 1975, 87.

ANTHONY LOW. *Love's Architecture,* pp. 227-29.

"His age, dedicated to his peculiar friend, M. John Wickes, under the name of Postumus"

PAUL R. JENKINS. "Rethinking What Moderation Means to Robert Herrick," *ELH* 39(1), March 1972, 59-61.

"His Farwell unto Poetrie"

H. R. SWARDSON. *Poetry and the Fountain of Light,* pp. 44-45.

"His Grange, or private wealth"

JOHN L. KIMMEY. "Order and Form in Herrick's *Hesperides*," *Journal of English and Germanic Philology* 70(2), April 1971, 264-65.

"His Letanie to the Holy Spirit"

ANTHONY LOW. *Love's Architecture,* pp. 219-20.

"His Meditation upon Death"

ANTHONY LOW. *Love's Architecture,* pp. 226-27.

"His Poetrie his Pillar"

JOHN L. KIMMEY. "Order and Form in Herrick's *Hesperides*," *Journal of English and Germanic Philology* 70(2), April 1971, 262.

"His returne to London"

H. R. SWARDSON. *Poetry and the Fountain of Light,* pp. 55-56.

"His Winding-sheet"

THOMAS R. WHITAKER. "Herrick and the Fruits of the Garden," *Journal of English Literary History* 22(1), March 1955, 26-29.

"The Hock Cart"

RICHARD E. HUGHES. "Herrick's 'Hock Cart': Companion Piece to 'Corinna's Going A-Maying,'" *College English* 27(5), February 1966, 420-22.

EARL MINER. *The Cavalier Mode from Jonson to Cotton,* pp. 192-93.

ROGER B. ROLLIN. "The Decorum of Criticism and Two Poems by Herrick," *CEA Critic* 31(4), January 1969, 4-7.

"How Roses came red"

EDGAR SMITH ROSE. "The Anatomy of Imagination," *College English* 27(5), February 1966, 350.

"Julia's Petticoat"

ANTHONY LOW. *Love's Architecture,* p. 212.

ROSEMOND TUVE. *Elizabethan and Metaphysical Imagery,* p. 93.

"The Mad Maid's Song"

MARIO L. D'AVANZO. "Herrick's 'The Mad Maid's Song,'" *American Notes & Queries,* n.s., 4(4), December 1965, 55.

WILLIAM VAN O'CONNOR. "Tension and Structure of Poetry," *Sewanee Review* 51(4), Autumn 1943, 557-58.

LEONARD UNGER and WILLIAM VAN O'CONNOR. *Poems for Study,* p. 145.

"Mattens, or morning Prayer"

ROBERT H. DEMING. "Robert Herrick's Classical Ceremony," *ELH* 34(3), September 1967, 341-42.

"Meat without mirth"

H. R. SWARDSON. *Poetry and the Fountain of Light,* pp. 54-55.

"The New-yeeres Gift, or Circumcision Song, Sung to the King in the Presence at White-Hall"

ANTHONY LOW. *Love's Architecture,* p. 223.

"The Night-piece, to Julia"

WALLACE DOUGLAS, ROY LAMSON, and HALLETT SMITH. *The Critical Reader,* pp. 83-86.

"A Nuptiall Song, or Epithalamie, on Sir Clipseby Crew and his Lady"

JAY A. GERTZMAN. "Robert Herrick's Recreative Pastoral," *Genre* 7(2), June 1974, 189-90.

"Oberons Feast"

DANIEL H. WOODWARD. "Herrick's Oberon Poems," *Journal of English and Germanic Philology* 64(2), April 1965, 270-84.

"Oberons Palace"

DANIEL H. WOODWARD. "Herrick's Oberon Poems," *Journal of English and Germanic Philology* 64(2), April 1965, 270-84.

"A Paranaeticall, or Advisive Verse, to his friend, Master John Wicks"

EARL MINER. *The Cavalier Mode from Jonson to Cotton,* pp. 131-33.

"A Panegyrick to Sir Lewis Pemberton"

C. N. MANLOVE. *Literature and Reality,* pp. 27-29.

EARL MINER. *The Cavalier Mode from Jonson to Cotton,* pp. 276-78.

"The Perfume"

ROBERT H. DEMING. "Robert Herrick's Classical Ceremony," *ELH* 34(3), September 1967, 342-43.

"The Pillar of Fame"

JOHN L. KIMMEY. "Order and Form in Herrick's *Hesperides*," *Journal of English and Germanic Philology* 70(2), April 1971, 263-64.

"The Sacrifice, by way of Discourse betwixt himselfe and Julia"

ROBERT H. DEMING. "Robert Herrick's Classical Ceremony," *ELH* 34(3), September 1967, 330-32.

"A song upon Silvia"

ROSEMOND TUVE. *Elizabethan and Metaphysical Imagery,* p. 129.

"The Star-Song: A Caroll to the King: sung at White-Hall"

LEAH SINANOGLOU MARCUS. "Herrick's *Noble Numbers* and the Politics of Playfulness," *English Literary Renaissance* 7(1), Winter 1977, 119-20.

"A Ternary of Littles, Upon a Pipkin of Jelly Sent to a Lady"

ARCHIBALD A. HILL. *Constituent and Pattern in Poetry,* pp. 88-90.

"A Thanksgiving to God, for his House"

JOHN L. KIMMEY. "Order and Form in Herrick's *Hesperides*," *Journal of English and Germanic Philology* 70(2), April 1971, 265.

ANTHONY LOW. *Love's Architecture,* pp. 221-22.

EARL MINER. *The Cavalier Mode from Jonson to Cotton,* pp. 49-51.

"This Crosse-Tree"

JOHN L. KIMMEY. "Order and Form in Herrick's *Hesperides," Journal of English and Germanic Philology* 70(2), April 1971, 261-62.

"To Anthea lying in bed"

ROSEMOND TUVE. *Elizabethan and Metaphysical Imagery,* pp. 11-12.

"To Blossoms"

CLEANTH BROOKS and ROBERT PENN WARREN. *Understanding Poetry,* pp. 369-70, 374; revised ed., pp. 246-47.

"To Daffadills"

JEROME BEATY and WILLIAM H. MATCHETT. *Poetry From Statement to Meaning,* pp. 223-24.

SIGURD BURCKHARDT. "Poetry, Language, and the Condition of the Modern Man," *Centennial Review* 4(1), Winter 1960, 4-6.

A. B. CHAMBERS. "Herrick and the Trans-shifting of Time," *Studies in Philology* 72(1), January 1975, 100-5.

ARCHIBALD MACLEISH. *Poetry and Experience,* pp. 36-38.

MAREN-SOFIE RØSTVIG. "Andrew Marvell and the Caroline Poets," in *English Poetry and Prose,* ed. by Christopher Ricks, pp. 216-17.

WRIGHT THOMAS and STUART GERRY BROWN. *Reading Poems: An Introduction to Critical Study,* pp. 650-51, 695-97.

HAROLD E. TOLIVER. *Pastoral Forms and Attitudes,* pp. 129-30.

"To Electra"

HENNIG COHEN. *Explicator* 17(6), March 1959, Item 44.

"To Groves"

ROBERT H. DEMING. "Herrick's Funereal Poems," *Studies in English Literature 1500-1900* 9(1), Winter 1969, 165-67.

"To His Muse"

JAY A. GERTZMAN. "Robert Herrick's Recreative Pastoral," *Genre* 7(2), June 1974, 187. (P)

"To His Saviour. The New yeers gift"

LEAH SINANOGLOU MARCUS. "Herrick's *Noble Numbers* and the Politics of Playfulness," *English Literary Renaissance* 7(1), Winter 1977, 118-19.

"To his Saviours Sepulcher: his Devotion"

ANTHONY LOW. *Love's Architecture,* pp. 230-32.

"To his sweet Saviour"

ANTHONY LOW. *Love's Architecture,* pp. 225-26.

"To Julia, the Flaminica Dialis, or Queen-Priest"

ROBERT H. DEMING. "Robert Herrick's Classical Ceremony," *ELH* 34(3), September 1967, 339-41.

"To live merrily, and to trust to Good Verses"

LLOYD FRANKENBERG. *Invitation to Poetry,* pp. 48-50.

H. R. SWARDSON. *Poetry and the Fountain of Light,* pp. 49-50.

"To Meadows"

MARK VAN DOREN. *Introduction to Poetry,* pp. 65-69.

"To Perilla"

ROBERT H. DEMING. "Herrick's Funereal Poems," *Studies in English Literature 1500-1900* 9(1), Winter 1969, 158-60.

"To Phyllis, to love, and live with him"

JAY A. GERTZMAN. "Robert Herrick's Recreative Pastoral," *Genre* 7(2), June 1974, 188-89.

"To Silvia"

H. R. SWARDSON. *Poetry and the Fountain of Light,* pp. 50-51.

"To the reverend shade of his Religious Father"

ROBERT H. DEMING. "Herrick's Funereal Poems," *Studies in English Literature 1500-1900* 9(1), Winter 1969, 160-62.

"To the Virgins, to Make Much of Time"

GEORGE ARMS. *Explicator* 1(1), October 1942, Item 2.

WALTON BEACHAM. *The Meaning of Poetry,* pp. 235-37.

CLEANTH BROOKS, JOHN THIBAUT PURSER, and ROBERT PENN WARREN. *An Approach to Literature,* fifth ed., pp. 394-96.

ANTHONY OSTROFF. "Herrick: To the Virgins, to Make Much of Time," in *Master Poems of the English Language,* pp. 143-46.

RICHARD J. ROSS. "Herrick's Julia in Silks," *Essays in Criticism* 15(2), April 1965, 177-80.

H. R. SWARDSON. *Poetry and the Fountain of Light,* pp. 60-61.

E. M. W. TILLYARD. *The Metaphysicals and Milton,* pp. 53-57.

"To the Water Nymphs drinking at the Fountain"

H. R. SWARDSON. *Poetry and the Fountain of Light,* pp. 52-53.

"The Transfiguration"

A. B. CHAMBERS. "Herrick and the Trans-shifting of Time," *Studies in Philology* 72(1), January 1975, 94-100.

"Upon Julia's Clothes"

GÉMINO H. ABAD. *In Another Light,* pp. 164-65.

F. W. BATESON. *English Poetry,* p. 46.

LAWRENCE COFFIN. " 'Liquifaction' in Herrick's 'Upon Julia's Clothes,' " *Concerning Poetry* 6(2), Fall 1973, 56-59.

EARL DANIELS. *Explicator* 1(5), March 1943, Item 35. Reprinted in: *The Creative Reader,* pp. 852-53; second ed., pp. 906-7. Abridged in: *The Case for Poetry,* first ed., p. 175.

WILLIAM O. HARRIS. *Explicator* 21(4), December 1962, Item 29. Abridged in: *The Case for Poetry,* second ed., p. 153.

NAT HENRY. *Explicator* 5(6), April 1947, Item 46.

NAT HENRY. *Explicator* 14(3), December 1955, Item 15. Abridged in: *The Case for Poetry,* second ed., p. 152.

LOUIS H. LEITER. *Explicator* 25(5), January 1967, Item 41.

C. S. LEWIS. "An Open Letter to Dr. Tillyard," *Essays and Studies* 21 (1935), 160-61.

C. S. LEWIS. "The Personal Heresy in Criticism," *Essays and Studies* 19 (1933), 9-11.

GENE MONTAGUE. *Explicator* 36(3), Spring 1978, 21-22.

MICHAEL J. PRESTON. *Explicator* 30(9), May 1972, Item 82.

RICHARD J. ROSS. "Herrick's Julia in Silks," *Essays in Criticism* 15(2), April 1965, 171-77.

MAREN-SOFIE RØSTVIG. "Andrew Marvell and the Caroline Poets," in *English Poetry and Prose,* ed. by Christopher Ricks, p. 219.

ELISABETH SCHNEIDER. *Explicator* 13(5), March 1955, Item 30. Abridged in: *The Case for Poetry,* second ed., p. 152.

HERRICK, ROBERT *(Cont.)*

"Upon Julia's Clothes" *(cont.)*

J. D. SHUCHTER. *Explicator* 25(3), November 1966, Item 27.

DONALD STAUFFER. *The Nature of Poetry*, pp. 162-63.

E. M. W. TILLYARD. "The Personal Heresy in Criticism: A Rejoinder," *Essays and Studies* 20 (1934), 17-20. Abridged in: *The Case for Poetry*, p. 175; second ed., pp. 151-52. Reprinted in: *The Modern Critical Spectrum*, pp. 213-14.

LEWIS E. WEEKS, JR. "Julia Unveiled: A Note on Herrick's 'Upon Julia's Clothes,' " *CEA Critic* 25(9), June 1963, 8.

GAIL S. WEINBERG. *Explicator* 27(2), October 1968, Item 12.

"Upon Prig"

ROBERT W. HALLI, JR. *Explicator* 35(4), Summer 1977, 22.

"Upon Silvia"

see "A Song upon Silvia"

"The Vision"

ROSEMOND TUVE. *Elizabethan and Metaphysical Imagery*, pp. 87-88.

"When he would have his verses read"

H. R. SWARDSON. *Poetry and the Fountain of Light*, pp. 47-48.

"The White Island"

ANTHONY LOW. *Love's Architecture*, pp. 214-18.

HEY, PHILIP

"The First Planet After Her Death"

ALBERTA T. TURNER. "Implied Metaphor: A Problem in Evaluating Contemporary Poetry," *Iowa Review* 5(1), Winter 1974, 114-15.

"It is 6 A.M. in the Middle of Kansas And"

ALBERTA T. TURNER. "Implied Metaphor: A Problem in Evaluating Contemporary Poetry," *Iowa Review* 5(1), Winter 1974, 113-14.

HEYEN, WILLIAM

"Depth of Field"

"The Individual Voice: A Conversation with William Heyen," edited by Philip L. Gerber and Robert J. Gemmett, *Western Humanities Review* 23(3), Summer 1969, 225.

"Existential"

"The Individual Voice: A Conversation with William Heyen," edited by Philip L. Gerber and Robert J. Gemmett, *Western Humanities Review* 23(3), Summer 1969, 223-24.

"Windfall"

"The Individual Voice: A Conversation with William Heyen," edited by Philip L. Gerber and Robert J. Gemmett, *Western Humanities Review* 23(3), Summer 1969, 227-28.

HIGGINSON, THOMAS WENTWORTH

"The Baltimore Oriole"

JEROME BEATY and WILLIAM H. MATCHETT. *Poetry From Statement to Meaning*, pp. 250-53.

HILBERRY, CONRAD

"Hamster Cage"

MARGARET A. LARSON. "Instructive Destructive," *English Journal* 61(4), April 1972, 508-9.

HILL, GEOFFREY

"Annunciations"

HAROLD BLOOM. *Figures of Capable Imagination*, pp. 237-41.

"Funeral Music"

JON SILKIN. "The Poetry of Geoffrey Hill," *Iowa Review* 3(3), Summer 1972, 116-18. Reprinted in: *British Poetry Since 1960*, pp. 152-54.

A. K. WEATHERHEAD. "Geoffrey Hill," *Iowa Review* 8(4), Fall 1977, 106-9.

"Genesis"

WALLACE D. MARTIN. "Beyond Modernism: Christopher Middleton and Geoffrey Hill," *Contemporary Literature* 12(4), Autumn 1971, 431.

"History as Poetry"

WALLACE D. MARTIN. "Beyond Modernism: Christopher Middleton and Geoffrey Hill," *Contemporary Literature* 12(4), Autumn 1971, 433-34.

"Metamorphoses"

WALLACE D. MARTIN. "Beyond Modernism: Christopher Middleton and Geoffrey Hill," *Contemporary Literature* 12(4), Autumn 1971, 432.

"Picture of a Nativity"

LAWRENCE KRAMER. "The Wodwo Watches the Water Clock: Language in Postmodern British and American Poetry," *Contemporary Literature* 18(3), Summer 1977, 323-25.

"September Song"

JON SILKIN. "The Poetry of Geoffrey Hill," *Iowa Review* 3(3), Summer 1972, 119-21. Reprinted in: *British Poetry Since 1960*, pp. 145-47.

"The Songbook of Sebastian Arrurruz"

JON SILKIN. "The Poetry of Geoffrey Hill," *Iowa Review* 3(3), Summer 1972, 119-21. Reprinted in: *British Poetry Since 1960*, pp. 154-57.

"To the (supposed) Patron"

GEOFFREY THURLEY. *The Ironic Harvest*, pp. 154-55.

HILL, LESLIE PINCKNEY

"So Quietly"

MELVIN G. WILLIAMS. "Black Literature vs. Black Studies: Three Lynchings," *Black American Literature Forum* 11(3), Fall 1977, 104-5.

HINE, DARYL

"Tableau Vivant"

JEROME J. MCGANN. "The Beauty of the Medusa: A Study in Romantic Literary Iconology," *Studies in Romanticism* 11(1), Winter 1972, 23-25.

HITCHCOCK, GEORGE

"Scattering Flowers"

CARY NELSON. "Whitman in Vietnam: Poetry and History in Contemporary America," *Massachusetts Review* 16(1), Winter 1975, 58-60.

HOBSBAUM, PHILIP

"A Lesson in Love, Coming Out Fighting"

DAVID HOLBROOK. *Lost Bearings in English Poetry*, pp. 181-84.

HOCCLEVE, THOMAS

"Complaint"

JEROME MITCHELL. "The Autobiographical Element in Hoccleve," *Modern Language Quarterly* 28(3), September 1967, 280-82.

"Dialogue with a Friend"

JEROME MITCHELL. "The Autobiographical Element in Hoccleve," *Modern Language Quarterly* 28(3), September 1967, 282-83.

"La Male Regle"

JEROME MITCHELL. "The Autobiographical Element in Hoccleve," *Modern Language Quarterly* 28(3), September 1967, 276-77.

HODGSON, RALPH

"Appearance of the Muse"

"Ralph Hodgson: A Poet's Journey in Time," *Times Literary Supplement*, 13 February 1959, p. 78.

"February"

DARREL ABEL. "How to Teach Students to Read a Poem," *College English* 17(2), November 1955, 90-92.

"The Muse and the Mastiff"

"Ralph Hodgson: A Poet's Journey in Time," *Times Literary Supplement*, 13 February 1959, p. 78.

"Time"

"Ralph Hodgson: A Poet's Journey in Time," *Times Literary Supplement*, 13 February 1959, p. 78.

"To Deck a Woman"

"Ralph Hodgson: A Poet's Journey in Time," *Times Literary Supplement*, 13 February 1959, p. 77-78.

HODGSON, WILLIAM NOEL

"By All the Glories of the Day"

HERBERT PALMER. *Post-Victorian Poetry*, pp. 229-31.

HOFFMAN, DANIEL

"Awoke into a Dream of Singing"

JOHN ALEXANDER ALLEN. "Another Country: The Poetry of Daniel Hoffman," *Hollins Critic* 15(4), October 1978, 10.

"In the Pitch of Night"

JOHN ALEXANDER ALLEN. "Another Country: The Poetry of Daniel Hoffman," *Hollins Critic* 15(4), October 1978, 11.

"The Seals in Penobscot Bay"

JOHN ALEXANDER ALLEN. "Another Country: The Poetry of Daniel Hoffman," *Hollins Critic* 15(4), October 1978, 4.

"Ten Thousand Dreaming Seamen Proven Wrong"

JOHN ALEXANDER ALLEN. "Another Country: The Poetry of Daniel Hoffman," *Hollins Critic* 15(4), October 1978, 4.

"A Visitation"

JOHN ALEXANDER ALLEN. "Another Country: The Poetry of Daniel Hoffman," *Hollins Critic* 15(4), October 1978, 2-3.

HOGG, JAMES

"Kilmeny"

DOUGLAS S. MACK. "Hogg's Kilmeny: An Interpretation," *Studies in Scottish Literature* 4(1), July 1966, 42-45.

HOLLO, ANSELM

"The Struggle"

GEOFFREY THURLEY. *The Ironic Harvest*, pp. 201-2.

HOLMES, JOHN

"All's Well That Ends"

JOHN HOLMES. *Writing Poetry*, pp. 42-45.

"Chair in the Field"

JOHN HOLMES. *Writing Poetry*, pp. 39-42.

"Herself"

DORIS HOLMES. *Explicator* 28(9), May 1970, Item 77.

"The New View"

JOHN HOLMES. *Writing Poetry*, pp. 36-39.

"On a Magazine Picture of a Mass Burial"

LAURENCE LIEBERMAN. "John Holmes," in *Unassigned Frequencies*, p. 205.

HOLMES, OLIVER WENDELL

"The Chambered Nautilus"

GEORGE ARMS. *Explicator* 4(7), May 1946, Item 51.

GEORGE ARMS. *The Fields Were Green*, pp. 108-10.

HYATT H. WAGGONER. *American Poets*, pp. 53-55.

"The Deacon's Masterpiece"

GEORGE ARMS. *The Fields Were Green*, pp. 112-13.

ISAAC ASIMOV. *Familiar Poems, Annotated*, pp. 125-36.

HARRY BROWN and JOHN MILSTEAD. *What the Poem Means*, p. 105.

J. STANLEY MATTSON. "Oliver Wendell Holmes and 'The Deacon's Masterpiece': A Logical Story?" *New England Quarterly* 41(1), March 1968, 104-14.

HYATT H. WAGGONER. *American Poets*, pp. 55-57.

"The Living Temple"

GEORGE ARMS. *Explicator* 2(2), November 1943, Item 15.

GEORGE ARMS. *The Fields Were Green*, pp. 104-5.

"Old Ironsides"

ISAAC ASIMOV. *Familiar Poems, Annotated*, pp. 183-86.

"The Peau de Chagrin of State Street"

GEORGE ARMS. *The Fields Were Green*, p. 102.

"Two Sonnets: Harvard"

GEORGE ARMS. *The Fields Were Green*, pp. 113-14.

"The Two Streams"

GEORGE ARMS. *The Fields Were Green*, pp. 97-99.

GEORGE ARMS. " 'To Fix the Image All Unveiled and Warm,' " *New England Quarterly* 19(4), December 1946, 534-37.

"Urania: A Rhymed Lesson"

HYATT H. WAGGONER. *American Poets*, pp. 57-58.

HOOD, THOMAS

"Autumn"

AUDREY JENNINGS. "Hood's 'Autumn,' " *Times Literary Supplement*, 26 June 1953, p. 413.

HOOD, THOMAS (*Cont.*)

"The Death Bed"

>JEROME BEATY and WILLIAM H. MATCHETT. *Poetry From Statement to Meaning*, pp. 139-40. (P)

"The Dream of Eugene Aram"

>KARL KROEBER. *Romantic Narrative Art*, pp. 129-31.

"Hero and Leander"

>KARL KROEBER. *Romantic Narrative Art*, p. 127.

"The Last Man"

>KARL KROEBER. *Romantic Narrative Art*, p. 129.

"Miss Kilmansegg and Her Precious Leg"

>KARL KROEBER. *Romantic Narrative Art*, pp. 131-32.

HOPE, A. D.

"Agony Column"

>LAURENCE PERRINE. "A. D. Hope's 'Agony Column,' " *Notes on Contemporary Literature* 2(3), May 1972, 2-3.

"The Brides"

>LAURENCE PERRINE. "Four Forms of Metaphor," *College English* 33(2), November 1971, 136-37.

"Moschus Moschiferus, A Song for St. Cecilia's Day"

>WILLIAM JAY SMITH. "A. D. Hope and The Comic Vision: Four Recent Contributions," *Hollins Critic* 9(2), June 1972, 2-3.

>LOUIS UNTERMEYER. *50 Modern American & British Poets*, pp. 271-72.

"On An Engraving by Casserius"

>WILLIAM JAY SMITH. "A. D. Hope and The Comic Vision: Four Recent Contributions," *Hollins Critic* 9(2), June 1972, 3.

HOPKINS, GERARD MANLEY

"The Alchemist in the City"

>JAMES LEGGIO. "Hopkins and Alchemy," *Renascence* 29(3), Spring 1977, 117-18.

>FLORENCE K. RIDDLE. "Hopkins' Dramatic Monologues," *Hopkins Quarterly* 2(2), July 1975, 59-62.

"Andromeda"

>R. N. EGUDU. "Gerard Manley Hopkins' Poetry and the Christian Apostleship," *Hopkins Quarterly* 3(1), April 1976, 8-9.

>PAUL L. MARIANI. "Hopkins' 'Andromeda' and The New Aestheticism," *Victorian Poetry* 11(1), Spring 1973, 39-54.

"As kingfishers catch fire, dragonflies draw flame"

>KENT BEYETTE. "Grace and Time as Latent Structures in the Poetry of Gerard Manley Hopkins," *Texas Studies in Literature and Language* 16(4), Winter 1975, 705-14.

>WINSTON COLLINS. "Tennyson and Hopkins," *University of Toronto Quarterly* 38(1), October 1968, 88.

>GEOFFREY H. HARTMAN. *The Unmediated Vision*, pp. 58-59.

>BOYD LITZINGER. "The Pattern of Ascent in Hopkins," *Victorian Poetry* 2(1), Winter 1964, 43-45.

"Ashboroughs"

>JAMES FINN COTTER. "Hornlight Wound to the West': The Inscape of Passion in Hopkins' Poetry," *Victorian Poetry* 16(4), Winter 1978, 311-12.

"Binsey Poplars"

>BELL GALE CHEVIGNY. "Instress and Devotion in the Poetry of Gerard Manley Hopkins," *Victorian Studies* 9(2), December 1965, 148.

"The Blessed Virgin Compared to the Air We Breathe"

>TAD W. GUZIE. "Are Modern Poets Morbid?" *Catholic World* 185(1105), April 1957, 29-30.

>M. B. MCNAMEE. "The Ignatian Meditation Pattern in the Poetry of Gerard Manley Hopkins," *Hopkins Quarterly* 2(1), April 1975, 24-27.

"The Bugler's First Communion"

>R. N. EGUDU. "Gerard Manley Hopkins' Poetry and the Christian Apostleship," *Hopkins Quarterly* 3(1), April 1976, 12-14.

"The Caged Skylark"

>KIMON FRIAR and JOHN MALCOLM BRINNIN. *Modern Poetry*, pp. 503-4.

>MARGARET GIOVANNINI. *Explicator* 14(6), March 1956, Item 35.

>BARBARA HARDY. *The Advantage of Lyric*, pp. 60-62.

>FRANK JORDAN, JR. *Explicator* 28(9), May 1970, Item 80.

>GERALD MONSMAN. "Hopkins and the 'here/Buckle!' of Creation," *Hopkins Quarterly* 5(1), Spring 1978, 25-26.

"The Candle Indoors"

>BELL GALE CHEVIGNY. "Instress and Devotion in the Poetry of Gerard Manley Hopkins," *Victorian Studies* 9(2), December 1965, 149-50.

"Carrion Comfort"

>J. ANGELA CARSON. "The Metaphor of Struggle in 'Carrion Comfort,' " *Philological Quarterly* 49(4), October 1970, 547-57.

>BELL GALE CHEVIGNY. "Instress and Devotion in the Poetry of Gerard Manley Hopkins," *Victorian Studies* 9(2), December 1965, 152.

>MARIE CORNELIA. "Images and Allusion in Hopkins' 'Carrion Comfort,' " *Renascence* 27(1), Autumn 1974, 51-55.

>JAMES FINN COTTER. " 'Hornlight Wound to the West': The Inscape of Passion in Hopkins' Poetry," *Victorian Poetry* 16(4), Winter 1978, 307-8.

>BABETTE DEUTSCH. *Poetry in Our Time*, p. 302; second ed., pp. 337-38.

>DAVID ANTHONY DOWNES. "Beatific Landscapes in Hopkins," *Hopkins Quarterly* 1(4), January 1975, 195-96.

>R. N. EGUDU. "Gerard Manley Hopkins' Poetry and the Christian Apostleship," *Hopkins Quarterly* 3(1), April 1976, 11-12.

>KIMON FRIAR and JOHN MALCOLM BRINNIN. *Modern Poetry*, p. 502.

>SISTER M. JOSELYN. "Herbert and Hopkins: Two Lyrics," *Renascence* 10(4), Summer 1958, 192-95.

>PETER L. MCNAMARA. "Motivation and Meaning in the 'Terrible Sonnets,' " *Renascence* 16(2), Winter 1964, 80, 94.

>PHILIP PAGE. "Unity and Subordination in 'Carrion Comfort,' " *Victorian Poetry* 14(1), Spring 1976, 25-32.

>BERTRAND F. RICHARDS. "Meaning in Hopkins' 'Carrion Comfort,' " *Renascence* 27(1), Autumn 1974, 45-50.

>ALAN M. ROSE. "Hopkins' 'Carrion Comfort': The Artful Disorder of Prayer," *Victorian Poetry* 15(3), Autumn 1977, 207-17.

MALCOLM H. VILLARUBIA. "Two Wills Unwound in the 'Terrible' Sonnets," *Renascence* 27(2), Winter 1975, 73-75.

"'The Child is Father to the Man'"

A. THOMAS. "G. M. Hopkins: An Unpublished Triolet," *Modern Language Review* 61(2), April 1966, 186.

"Cockle's Antibilious Pills"

A. THOMAS. "G. M. Hopkins: An Unpublished Triolet," *Modern Language Review* 61(2), April 1966, 184-86.

NORMAN E. WHITE. "G. M. Hopkins's Triolet 'Cockle's Antibilious Pills,'" *Notes & Queries*, n.s., 15(5), May 1968, 183-84.

"Duns Scotus's Oxford"

YVOR WINTERS. "The Poetry of Gerard Manley Hopkins (II)," *Hudson Review* 2(1), Spring 1949, 64. Reprinted in: Yvor Winters. *The Function of Criticism*, pp. 126-27.

"Epithalamion"

LIONEL ADEY. "A Reading of Hopkins' 'Epithalamion,'" *Victorian Newsletter* 42 (Fall 1972), 16-20.

WENDELL STACY JOHNSON. *Sex and Marriage in Victorian Poetry*, pp. 72-74.

"The Escorial"

DONALD SUTHERLAND. "Hopkins Again," *Prairie Schooner* 35(3), Fall 1961, 200-2.

"Felix Randal"

HARRY BROWN and JOHN MILSTEAD. *What the Poem Means*, p. 106.

BELL GALE CHEVIGNY. "Instress and Devotion in the Poetry of Gerard Manley Hopkins," *Victorian Studies* 9(2), December 1965, 149.

JOSEPH EBLE. "Levels of Awareness: A Reading of Hopkins' 'Felix Randal,'" *Victorian Poetry* 13(2), Summer 1975, 129-35.

KIMON FRIAR and JOHN MALCOLM BRINNIN. *Modern Poetry*, p. 503.

PAUL L. MARIANI. "Hopkins' 'Felix Randall' As Sacramental Vision," *Renascence* 19(4), Summer 1967, 217-20.

"For a Picture of St. Dorothea"

FLORENCE K. RIDDLE. "Hopkins' Dramatic Monologues," *Hopkins Quarterly* 2(2), July 1975, 56-57.

"God's Grandeur"

RONALD BATES. "Hopkins' Embers Poems: A Liturgical Source," *Renascence* 17(1), Fall 1964, 35-36.

TODD K. BENDER. *Explicator* 21(7), March 1963, Item 55.

CLEANTH BROOKS, JOHN THIBAUT PURSER, and ROBERT PENN WARREN. *An Approach to Literature*, fifth ed., pp. 459-60.

BELL GALE CHEVIGNY. "Instress and Devotion in the Poetry of Gerard Manley Hopkins," *Victorian Studies* 9(2), December 1965, 145-46.

TERRY EAGLETON. "Nature and the Fall in Hopkins: A Reading of 'God's Grandeur,'" *Essays in Criticism* 23(1), January 1973, 68-75.

MARGARET GIOVANNINI. *Explicator* 24(4), December 1965, Item 36.

TAD W. GUZIE. "Are Modern Poets Morbid?" *Catholic World* 185(1105), April 1957, 30-31.

JAMES R. KINCAID. "'Why Unblooms the Best Hope?': Victorian Narrative Forms and the Explanation of Calamity," *Victorian Newsletter* 53 (Spring 1978), 3-4.

GERALD MONSMAN. "Hopkins and the 'here/Buckle!' of Creation," *Hopkins Quarterly* 5(1), Spring 1978, 27-30.

SISTER MARY NOEL. "Gathering to a Greatness: A Study of 'God's Grandeur,'" *English Journal* 53(4), April 1964, 285-87.

JOHN CLARK PRATT. *The Meaning of Modern Poetry*, 214, 218-19, 230-31, 228-29, 233, 220-21.

DONALD H. REIMAN. "Hopkins' 'Ooze of Oil' Rises Again," *Victorian Poetry* 4(1), Winter 1966, 39-42.

M. L. ROSENTHAL and A. J. M. SMITH. *Exploring Poetry*, pp. 94-97; second ed., pp. 115-17.

ROGER L. SLAKEY. "The Grandeur in Hopkins' 'God's Grandeur,'" *Victorian Poetry* 7(2), Summer 1969, 159-63.

GERTRUDE M. WHITE. "Hopkins's 'God's Grandeur': A Poetic Statement of Christian Doctrine," *Victorian Poetry* 4(4), Autumn 1966, 284-87.

BROOKS WRIGHT. *Explicator* 10(1), October 1951, Item 5.

"The Habit of Perfection"

FRANCIS J. GREINER. *Explicator* 21(3), November 1962, Item 19.

BOYD LITZINGER. *Explicator* 16(1), October 1957, Item 1.

"The Handsome Heart"

R. N. EGUDU. "Gerard Manley Hopkins' Poetry and the Christian Apostleship," *Hopkins Quarterly* 3(1), April 1976, 15-16.

"Harry Ploughman"

C. DAY LEWIS. *The Poetic Image*, pp. 125-28.

NORMAN C. STAGEBERG and WALLACE L. ANDERSON. *Poetry as Experience*, pp. 222-29.

WILLIAM B. THESING. "'Tom's Garland' and Hopkins' Inscapes of Humanity," *Victorian Poetry* 15(1), Spring 1977, 41-43.

"Heaven-Haven"

E. L. EPSTEIN. "Hopkins's 'Heaven-Haven': A Linguistic-Critical Description," *Essays in Criticism* 23(2), April 1973, 137-45.

BOYD LITZINGER. "The Genesis of Hopkins' 'Heaven-Haven,'" *Victorian Newsletter* 17 (Spring 1960), 31-33.

ALLAN RODWAY. "Hopkins's 'Heaven-Haven,'" *Essays in Criticism* 23(4), October 1973, 430-34.

"Henry Purcell"

T. R. BARNES. *English Verse*, pp. 255-57.

GERALD L. BRUNS. "The Idea of Energy in the Writings of Gerard Manley Hopkins," *Renascence* 29(1), Autumn 1976, 37-38.

BARBARA HARDY. *The Advantage of Lyric*, p. 58.

WILLIAM B. THESING. "'Tom's Garland' and Hopkins' Inscapes of Humanity," *Victorian Poetry* 15(1), Spring 1977, 39-41.

"Hurrahing in Harvest"

EDWARD A. BLOOM, CHARLES H. PHILBRICK, and ELMER M. BLISTEIN. *The Order of Poetry*, pp. 130-34.

BELL GALE CHEVIGNY. "Instress and Devotion in the Poetry of Gerard Manley Hopkins," *Victorian Studies* 9(2), December 1965, 147-48.

HOPKINS, GERARD MANLEY *(Cont.)*

"Hurrahing in Harvest" *(cont.)*

> KIMON FRIAR and JOHN MALCOLM BRINNIN. *Modern Poetry*, p. 504.
>
> BARBARA HARDY. *The Advantage of Lyric*, pp. 59-60.
>
> DONALD SUTHERLAND. "Hopkins Again," *Prairie Schooner* 35(3), Fall 1961, 229-41.

" — I am like a slip of comet"

> MARGARET C. PATTERSON. "Young Hopkins, Anglican Student: ' — I am like a slip of comet,'" *Hopkins Quarterly* 4(1), Spring 1977, 27-34.

"I wake and feel the fell of dark, not day"

> ALEXANDER W. ALLISON. *Explicator* 17(8), May 1959, Item 54.
>
> DAVID ANTHONY DOWNES. "Beatific Landscapes in Hopkins," *Hopkins Quarterly* 1(4), January 1975, 197.
>
> KIMON FRIAR and JOHN MALCOLM BRINNIN. *Modern Poetry*, pp. 502-3.
>
> STEPHEN C. PEPPER. *The Basis of Criticism in the Arts*, pp. 127-40.
>
> MALCOLM H. VILLARUBIA. "Two Wills Unwound in the 'Terrible' Sonnets," *Renascence* 27(2), Winter 1975, 75-76.

"In Honour of St. Alphonsus Rodriguez"

> W. H. GARDNER. "The Relgious Problem in G. M. Hopkins," *Scrutiny* 6(1), June 1937, 38.

"Inversnaid"

> T. R. BARNES. *English Verse*, pp. 251-53.
>
> CLEANTH BROOKS and ROBERT PENN WARREN. *Understanding Poetry*, fourth ed., pp. 83-84.

"The Lantern Out of Doors"

> JAMES FINN COTTER. " 'Hornlight Wound to the West': The Inscape of the Passion in Hopkins' Poetry," *Victorian Poetry* 16(4), Winter 1978, 304.

"The Leaden Echo and the Golden Echo"

> F. R. LEAVIS. *New Bearings on English Poetry*, pp. 172-75.
>
> R. K. R. THORNTON. "How Leaden Is Your Echo?" *Hopkins Quarterly* 5(1), Spring 1978, 33-41.
>
> CHAD WALSH. "Hopkins: The Leaden Echo and the Golden Echo," in *Master Poems of the English Language*, pp. 806-10.

"The Loss of the Eurydice"

> R. N. EGUDU. "Gerard Manley Hopkins' Poetry and the Christian Apostleship," *Hopkins Quarterly* 3(1), April 1976, 8. (P)
>
> RICHARD J. O'DEA. " 'The Loss of the Eurydice': A Possible Key to the Reading of Hopkins," *Victorian Poetry* 4(4), Autumn 1966, 291-93.
>
> ALFRED THOMAS. "Hopkinsharvest: The Meeting of the 'Wrecks,'" *Victorian Poetry* 12(1), Spring 1974, 71-73.

"Margaret Clitheroe"

> R. J. SCHOECK. "Peine Forte et Dure and Hopkins' 'Margaret Clitheroe,'" *Modern Language Notes* 74(3), March 1959, 220-24.

"My own heart let me more have pity on"

> HARRY BROWN and JOHN MILSTEAD. *What the Poem Means*, p. 107.
>
> ROBERT H. GOLDSMITH. "The Selfless Self: Hopkins' Late Sonnets," *Hopkins Quarterly* 3(2), July 1976, 75.
>
> BARBARA HARDY. *The Advantage of Lyric*, pp. 63-64.

> ELISABETH SCHNEIDER. *Explicator* 5(7), May 1947, Item 51.
>
> ELISABETH SCHNEIDER. *Explicator* 7(7), May 1949, Item 49. (P)
>
> MALCOLM H. VILLARUBIA. "Two Wills Unwound in the 'Terrible' Sonnets," *Renascence* 27(2), Winter 1975, 78-79.

"The Nix"

> HOWARD W. FULWEILER. "Gerard Manley Hopkins and the 'Stanching, Quenching Ocean of a Motionable Mind,'" *Victorian Newsletter* 30 (Fall 1966), 8.

" 'No news in the *Times* to-day' "

> A. THOMAS. "G. M. Hopkins: An Unpublished Triolet," *Modern Language Review* 61(2), April 1966, 184.

"No worst, there is none"

> JAMES FINN COTTER. " 'Hornlight Wound to the West': The Inscape of Passion in Hopkins' Poetry," *Victorian Poetry* 16(4), Winter 1978, 308.
>
> ROBERT A. DURR. *Explicator* 11(2), November 1952, Item 11.
>
> FRANCIS FIKE. "The Problem of Motivation in 'No Worst, There Is None,'" *Hopkins Quarterly* 2(4), January 1976, 175-78.
>
> KIMON FRIAR and JOHN MALCOLM BRINNIN. *Modern Poetry*, p. 502.
>
> ROBERT H. GOLDSMITH. "The Selfless Self: Hopkins' Late Sonnets," *Hopkins Quarterly* 3(2), July 1976, 73.
>
> SISTER MARCELLA M. HOLLOWAY. *Explicator* 14(8), May 1956, Item 51.
>
> SISTER MARY HUMILIATA. "Hopkins and the Prometheus Myth," *PMLA* 70(1), March 1955, 58-68.
>
> PETER L. MCNAMARA. "Motivation and Meaning In the 'Terrible Sonnets,'" *Renascence* 16(2), Winter 1964, 79-80.
>
> JAMES REEVES and MARTIN SEYMOUR-SMITH. *Inside Poetry*, pp. 80-83.
>
> YVOR WINTERS. "The Poetry of Gerard Manley Hopkins (I)," *Hudson Review* 1(4), Winter 1949, 460-66. Reprinted in: Yvor Winters. *The Function of Criticism*, pp. 107-13.

"On a Piece of Music"

> YVOR WINTERS. "The Poetry of Gerard Manley Hopkins (I)," *Hudson Review* 2(1), Spring 1949, 87-88. Reprinted in: Yvor Winters. *The Function of Criticism*, pp. 152-53.

"Patience, hard thing!"

> BELL GALE CHEVIGNY. "Instress and Devotion in the Poetry of Gerard Manley Hopkins," *Victorian Studies* 9(2), December 1965, 151-52.
>
> R. N. EGUDU. "Gerard Manley Hopkins' Poetry and the Christian Apostleship," *Hopkins Quarterly* 3(1), April 1976, 14-15.
>
> JOHN J. GLAVIN. " 'The Exercise of Saints': Hopkins, Milton, and Patience," *Texas Studies in Literature and Language* 20(2), Summer 1978, 139-52.
>
> ROBERT H. GOLDSMITH. "The Selfless Self: Hopkins' Late Sonnets," *Hopkins Quarterly* 3(2), July 1976, 74-75.
>
> BARBARA HARDY. *The Advantage of Lyric*, pp. 64-66.
>
> MALCOLM H. VILLARUBIA. "Two Wills Unwound in the 'Terrible' Sonnets," *Renascence* 27(2), Winter 1975, 76-78.

"Pied Beauty"

> JOHN BRITTON. " 'Pied Beauty' and the Glory of God," *Renascence* 11(2), Winter 1959, 72-75.

ELIZABETH D. DUNLAP. "Sound and Sense in 'Pied Beauty,'" *Hopkins Quarterly* 3(1), April 1976, 35-38.

LLOYD FRANKENBERG. *Invitation to Poetry*, pp. 294-96.

BARBARA HARDY. *The Advantage of Lyric*, pp. 56-57.

SISTER MARCELLA M. HOLLOWAY. "Hopkins' Theory of 'Antithetical Parallelism,'" *Hopkins Quarterly* 1(3), October 1974, 130-32.

SAMUEL KLIGER. "God's 'Plenitude' in the Poetry of Gerard Manley Hopkins," *Modern Language Notes* 59(6), June 1944, 408-10.

JOAQUIN KUHN. "The Completeness of 'Pied Beauty,'" *Studies in English Literature 1500-1900* 18(4), Autumn 1978, 677-92.

BOYD A. LITZINGER. "Hopkins' 'Pied Beauty' Once More," *Renascence* 13(3), Spring 1961, 136-38.

BOYD A. LITZINGER. "The Pattern of Ascent in Hopkins," *Victorian Poetry* 2(1), Winter 1964, 43-45.

AMY LOWENSTEIN. "Seeing 'Pied Beauty': A Key to Theme and Structure," *Victorian Poetry* 14(1), Spring 1976, 64-66.

ROBERT PREYER. "'The Fine Delight that Fathers Thought': Gerard Manley Hopkins and the Romantic Survival," in *Victorian Poetry*, pp. 180-81.

RICHARD WILBUR. *Responses*, pp. 94-95.

"Pilate"

FLORENCE K. RIDDLE. "Hopkins' Dramatic Monologues," *Hopkins Quarterly* 2(2), July 1975, 53-54.

"Rest"

HOWARD W. FULWEILER. "Gerard Manley Hopkins and the 'Stanching, Quenching Ocean of a Motionable Mind,'" *Victorian Newsletter* 30 (Fall 1966), 7-8.

BOYD LITZINGER. "The Genesis of Hopkins' 'Heaven-Haven,'" *Victorian Newsletter* 17 (Spring 1964), 31-33.

"Ribblesdale"

T. R. BARNES. *English Verse*, pp. 253-55.

"Rosa Mystica"

JEROME BUMP. "Hopkins' Imagery and Medievalist Poetics," *Victorian Poetry* 15(2), Summer 1977, 106-17.

"St. Alphonsus Rodriguez"

HERBERT MARSHALL MCLUHAN. "The Analogical Mirrors," *Kenyon Review* 6(3), Summer 1944, 329-30. (P)

WILLIAM A. MCQUEEN. "'The Windhover' and 'St. Alphonsus Rodriguez,'" *Victorian Newsletter* 23 (Spring 1963), 25-26.

"The Sea and the Skylark"

JEROME BUMP. "Hopkins, the Humanities, and the Environment," *Georgia Review* 28(2), Summer 1974, 237-38.

KATHLEEN RAINE. "Hopkins, Nature, and Human Nature," *Sewanee Review* 81(2), Spring 1973, 212-13.

"The Shepherd's Brow"

THOMAS K. BEYETTE. "Hopkins' Phenomenology of Art in 'The Shepherd's Brow,'" *Victorian Poetry* 11(3), Autumn 1973, 207-13.

SISTER M. MARY HUGH CAMPBELL. "The Silent Sonnet: Hopkins' 'Shepherd's Brow,'" *Renascence* 15(3), Spring 1963, 133-42.

ROBERT BOYKIN CLARK. "Hopkins's 'The Shepherd's Brow,'" *Victorian Newsletter* 28 (Fall 1965), 16-18.

PAUL L. MARIANI. "The Artistic and Tonal Integrity of Hopkins' 'The Shepherd's Brow,'" *Victorian Poetry* 6(1), Spring 1968, 63-68.

PAUL L. MARIANI. "The Sound of Oneself Breathing: The Burden of Theological Metaphor in Hopkins," *Hopkins Quarterly* 4(1), Spring 1977, 17-26.

"The Soldier"

R. N. EGUDU. "Gerard Manley Hopkins' Poetry and the Christian Apostleship," *Hopkins Quarterly* 3(1), April 1976, 10-11.

"A Soliloquy of One of the Spies left in the Wilderness"

FLORENCE K. RIDDLE. "Hopkins' Dramatic Monologues," *Hopkins Quarterly* 2(2), July 1975, 53.

"Spelt from Sibyl's Leaves"

JEROME BUMP. "Hopkins, the Humanities, and the Environment," *Georgia Review* 28(2), Summer 1974, 241-43.

JAMES FINN COTTER. "'Hornlight Wound to the West': The Inscape of Passion in Hopkins' Poetry," *Victorian Poetry* 16(4), Winter 1978, 305-6.

FRANCIS DOHERTY. "A Note on *Spelt from Sibyl's Leaves*," *Essays in Criticism* 14(4), October 1964, 428-32.

KIMON FRIAR and JOHN MALCOLM BRINNIN. *Modern Poetry*, p. 503.

ANDOR GOMME. "A Note on Two Hopkins Sonnets," *Essays in Criticism* 14(3), July 1964, 327-29.

F. R. LEAVIS. *New Bearings on English Poetry*, pp. 182-86. Reprinted in: *Poems and Critics*, pp. 212-14.

I. A. RICHARDS. "Gerard Hopkins," *Dial* 81(3), September 1926, 199-201.

WILLIAM JOSEPH ROONEY. "'Spelt from Sibyl's Leaves' — A Study in Contrasting Methods of Evaluation," *Journal of Aesthetics and Art Criticism* 13(4), June 1955, 507-19.

RAYMOND V. SCHODER. "Spelt from Sibyl's Leaves," *Thought* 19(75), December 1944, 634-48.

H. G. SHERWOOD. *Explicator* 15(1), October 1956, Item 5.

GARY L. STONUM. "The Hermeneutics of 'Spelt from Sibyl's Leaves,'" *Hopkins Quarterly* 3(3), October 1976, 117-29.

SISTER THERESE. *Explicator* 17(7), April 1959, Item 45.

NORMAN WHITE. *Explicator* 30(3), November 1971, Item 24.

NORMAN WHITE. "Hopkins' 'Spelt from Sibyl's Leaves,'" *Victorian Newsletter* 36 (Fall 1969), 27-28.

"Spring"

BELL GALE CHEVIGNY. "Instress and Devotion in the Poetry of Gerard Manley Hopkins," *Victorian Studies* 9(2), December 1965, 146.

SUSAN A. HALLGARTH. "A Study of Hopkins' Use of Nature," *Victorian Poetry* 5(1), Summer 1967, 87.

LOUIS RADER. "Romantic Structure and Theme in Hopkins' Poetry," *Hopkins Quarterly* 1(2), July 1974, 95-96.

"Spring and Fall: To a Young Child"

GÉMINO H. ABAD. *In Another Light*, pp. 248-50.

SIGURD BURCKHARDT. "Poetry, Language, and the Condition of the Modern Man," *Centennial Review* 4(1), Winter 1960, 6-7.

SISTER ESTELLE CASALANDRA. "The Three Margarets," *Sewanee Review* 81(2), Spring 1973, 225-28.

BABETTE DEUTSCH. *Poetry in Our Time*, p. 294; second ed., p. 329.

PAUL C. DOHERTY. "Hopkins' 'Spring and Fall: To A Young Child,'" *Victorian Poetry* 5(2), Summer 1967, 140-43.

HOPKINS, GERARD MANLEY *(Cont.)*

"Spring and Fall: To a Young Child" *(cont.)*

ELIZABETH DREW. *Poetry*, pp. 107-9.

WILLIAM EMPSON. *Seven Types of Ambiguity*, pp. 187-88; second and third eds., pp. 148-49. Reprinted in: *The Modern Critical Spectrum*, pp. 103-4.

C. ANTHONY GIFFARD. "The Springs of Goldengrove," *Victorian Poetry* 15(1), Spring 1977, 60-65.

JOHN A. MYERS. "Intimations of Mortality: An Analysis of Hopkins' 'Spring and Fall,'" *English Journal* 51(8), November 1962, 585-87.

I. A. RICHARDS. *Practical Criticism*, pp. 81-90.

JULIAN SMITH. *Explicator* 27(5), January 1969, Item 36.

PETER STAMBLER. "Selving: The Sense of Perfection in Hopkins," *Thoth* 12(2), Winter 1972, 30-33.

"The Starlight Night"

JAMES FINN COTTER. " 'Hornlight Wound to the West': The Inscape of the Passion in Hopkins' Poetry," *Victorian Poetry* 16(4), Winter 1978, 301-2.

GERALD MONSMAN. "Hopkins and the 'here/Buckle!' of Creation," *Hopkins Quarterly* 5(1), Spring 1978, 27.

EDWARD PROFFITT. "Tone and Contrast in Hopkins' 'The Starlight Night,'" *Hopkins Quarterly* 5(2), Summer 1978, 47-50.

FLORENCE K. RIDDLE. "Hopkins' Dramatic Monologues," *Hopkins Quarterly* 2(2), July 1975, 57-58.

YVOR WINTERS. "The Poetry of Gerard Manley Hopkins (II)," *Hudson Review* 2(1), Spring 1949, 63. Reprinted in: Yvor Winters. *The Function of Criticism*, pp. 125-26.

"That Nature Is a Heraclitian Fire and of the Comfort of the Resurrection"

BELL GALE CHEVIGNY. "Instress and Devotion in the Poetry of Gerard Manley Hopkins," *Victorian Studies* 9(2), December 1965, 152-53.

WINSTON COLLINS. "Tennyson and Hopkins," *University of Toronto Quarterly* 38(1), October 1968, 84-87.

JAMES FINN COTTER. " 'Hornlight Wound to the West': The Inscape of Passion in Hopkins' Poetry," *Victorian Poetry* 16(4), Winter 1978, 310-11.

KIMON FRIAR and JOHN MALCOLM BRINNIN. *Modern Poetry*, pp. 501-2.

JOSEPH E. GRENNEN. "Grammar As Thaumaturgy: Hopkins' 'Heraclitean Fire,'" *Renascence* 15(4), Summer 1963, 208-11.

SISTER MARCELLA M. HOLLOWAY. "Hopkins' Theory of 'Antithetical Parallelism,'" *Hopkins Quarterly* 1(3), October 1974, 135.

MICHAEL L. JOHNSON. "Hopkins, Heraclitus, Cosmic Instress and of the Comfort of the Resurrection," *Victorian Poetry* 10(3), Autumn 1972, 235-42.

BOYD LITZINGER. "The Pattern of Ascent in Hopkins," *Victorian Poetry* 2(1), Winter 1964, 43-47.

SISTER MARY DOMINIC STEVENS. *Explicator* 22(3), November 1963, Item 18.

"Thou art indeed just, Lord, if I contend"

T. R. BARNES. *English Verse*, pp. 258-59.

REUBEN ARTHUR BROWER. *The Fields of Light*, pp. 26-27. Reprinted in: *The Study of Literature*, pp. 165-69.

ELIZABETH DREW. *Poetry*, p. 141.

JAMES REEVES. "Paradoxes of Poetic Understanding," in *Commitment to Poetry*, pp. 24-25.

"To Oxford"

BERNARD RICHARDS. *Explicator* 33(3), November 1974, Item 24.

"To R. B."

LLOYD FRANKENBERG. *Invitation to Poetry*, pp. 65-68.

WILLIAM M. GIBSON. *Explicator* 6(2), November 1947, Item 12.

PAUL L. MARIANI. "The Sound of Oneself Breathing: The Burden of Theological Metaphor in Hopkins," *Hopkins Quarterly* 4(1), Spring 1977, 17-26.

EDWARD PROFITT. "The Metaphor of Gestation in Hopkins' 'To R. B.,'" *Victorian Poetry* 16(4), Winter 1978, 383-84.

"To seem the stranger lies my lot, my life"

DAVID ANTHONY DOWNES. "Beatific Landscapes in Hopkins," *Hopkins Quarterly* 1(4), January 1975, 197.

"Tom's Garland"

BABETTE DEUTSCH. *This Modern Poetry*, pp. 178-80.

RICHARD GUNTER. "Grammar, Semantics and the Poems of Gerard Manley Hopkins," *Hopkins Quarterly* 1(1), April 1974, 29-34.

HENRY SILVERSTEIN. "On 'Tom's Garland,'" *Accent* 7(2), Winter 1947, 67-81.

WILLIAM B. THESING. " 'Tom's Garland' and Hopkins' Inscapes of Humanity," *Victorian Poetry* 15(1), Spring 1977, 43-47.

"A Vision of the Mermaids"

HOWARD W. FULWEILER. "Gerard Manley Hopkins and the 'Stanching, Quenching Ocean of a Motionable Mind,'" *Victorian Newsletter* 30 (Fall 1966), 7.

SUSAN A. HALLGARTH. "A Study of Hopkins' Use of Nature," *Victorian Poetry* 5(2), Summer 1967, 81-82.

"A Voice from the World"

FLORENCE K. RIDDLE. "Hopkins' Dramatic Monologues," *Hopkins Quarterly* 2(2), July 1975, 54-56.

"The Windhover"

THOMAS J. ASSAD. "Hopkins' 'The Windhover,'" *Tulane Studies in English* 11 (1961), 87-95.

ROBERT W. AYERS. "Hopkins' *The Windhover*: A Further Simplification," *Modern Language Notes* 71(8), December 1956, 577-84.

RONALD BATES. "Hopkins' Embers Poems: A Liturgical Source," *Renascence* 17(1), Fall 1964, 32-35.

ROBERT BOYLE. "Time and Grace in Hopkins' Imagination," *Renascence* 29(1), Autumn 1976, 19-24.

LESLIE F. CHARD, II. "Once More Into *The Windhover*," *English Language Notes* 2(4), June 1965, 282-85.

BELL GALE CHEVIGNY. "Instress and Devotion in the Poetry of Gerard Manley Hopkins," *Victorian Studies* 9(2), December 1965, 146-47.

BABETTE DEUTSCH. *Poetry in Our Time*, pp. 295-300; second ed., pp. 330-36.

DENIS DONOGHUE. "The Bird as Symbol: Hopkins's Windhover," *Studies* 44(175), Autumn 1955, 291-99.

DENIS DONOGHUE. *The Ordinary Universe*, pp. 86-87.

DAVID ANTHONY DOWNES. "Beatific Landscapes in Hopkins," *Hopkins Quarterly* 1(4), January 1975, 190-92.

ELIZABETH DREW. *Poetry*, pp. 248-52.

LEON V. DRISKELL. "The Progressive Structure Of 'The Windhover,'" *Renascence* 19(1), Fall 1966, 30-36.

MOTHER MARY ELEANOR. "Hopkins' 'Windhover' and Southwell's Hawk," *Renascence* 15(1), Fall 1962, 21-22, 27.

WILLIAM EMPSON. *Seven Types of Ambiguity,* pp. 284-86; second and third eds., pp. 224-26. Reprinted in: *Poems and Critics,* pp. 211-12.

W. EMPSON. " 'The Windhover,' " *Times Literary Supplement,* 20 May 1955, p. 269.

KIMON FRIAR and JOHN MALCOLM BRINNIN. *Modern Poetry,* p. 504.

W. H. GARDNER. "The Religious Problem in G. M. Hopkins," *Scrutiny* 6(1), June 1937, 35-37. Reprinted in: *Critiques and Essays in Criticism,* pp. 349-53. Reprinted in: *Reading Modern Poetry,* pp. 337-41; revised ed., pp. 336-40.

W. H. GARDNER. "The 'Windhover,' " *Times Literary Supplement,* 24 June 1955, p. 349.

BROTHER FRANCIS GREINER. "Hopkins' 'The Windhover' Viewed as a Nature Poem," *Renascence* 15(2), Winter 1963, 68-75, 95.

FREDERICK L. GWYNN. "Hopkins' 'The Windhover': A New Simplification," *Modern Language Notes* 66(6), June 1951, 366-70.

GEOFFREY H. HARTMAN. *The Unmediated Vision,* pp. 49-67, 162.

ARCHIBALD A. HILL. "An Analysis of *The Windhover*: An Experiment in Structural Method," *PMLA* 70(5), December 1955, 968-78. Reprinted in: Archibald A. Hill. *Constituent and Pattern in Poetry,* pp. 28-38.

SISTER MARCELLA M. HOLLOWAY. "Hopkins Theory of 'Antithetical Parallelism," *Hopkins Quarterly* 1(3), October 1974, 133-34.

JOHN F. HUNTLEY. "Hopkins' 'The Windhover' As a Prayer of Request," *Renascence* 16(3), Spring 1964, 154-62.

CLYDE S. KILBY. *Poetry and Life,* pp. 208-9.

ROBERT LANGBAUM. *The Poetry of Experience,* pp. 66-69.

F. N. LEES. " 'The Windhover,' " *Scrutiny* 17(1), Spring 1950, 32-37.

PETER LISCA. "The Return of 'The Windhover,' " *College English* 19(3), December 1957, 124-26.

BOYD LITZINGER. "Once More, 'The Windhover,' " *Victorian Poetry* 5(3), Autumn 1967, 228-30.

HERBERT MARSHALL MCLUHAN. "The Analogical Mirrors," *Kenyon Review* 6(3), Summer 1944, 326-29.

WILLIAM A. MCQUEEN. " 'The Windhover' and 'St. Alphonsus Rodriguez,' " *Victorian Newsletter* 23(Spring 1963), 25-26.

BRUCE E. MILLER. "On 'The Windhover,' " *Victorian Poetry* 2(2), Spring 1964, 115-19.

GERALD MONSMAN. "Hopkins and the 'here/Buckle!' of Creation," *Hopkins Quarterly* 5(1), Spring 1978, 23-24.

GEORGE E. MONTAG. " 'The Windhover': Crucifixion and Redemption," *Victorian Poetry* 3(2), Spring 1965, 109-18.

GERARD L. NOLAN. "The 'Windhover,' " *Times Literary Supplement,* 24 June 1955, p. 349.

WALTER J. ONG. "Bird, Horse, and Chevalier in Hopkins' 'Windhover,' " *Hopkins Quarterly* 1(2), July 1974, 61-75.

MICHAEL PAYNE. "Syntactical Analysis and 'The Windhover,' " *Renascence* 19(2), Winter 1967, 88-92.

LOUIS RADER. "Romantic Structure and Theme in 'The Windhover,' " *Hopkins Quarterly* 2(2), July 1975, 79-92.

I. A. RICHARDS. "Gerard Hopkins," *The Dial* 81 (September 1926), 197-99.

J. G. RITZ. " 'The Windhover,' " *Times Literary Supplement,* 6 May 1955, p. 237.

ELISABETH SCHNEIDER. *Explicator* 18(4), January 1960, Item 22. Reprinted in: *The Dimensions of Poetry,* pp. 551-54. Also: *Readings for Liberal Education,* fourth ed., II: 162-64; fifth ed., II: 141-43.

F. X. SHEA. "Another Look at 'The Windhover,' " *Victorian Poetry* 2(4), Autumn 1964, 219-39.

NORMAN C. STAGEBERG and WALLACE L. ANDERSON. *Poetry as Experience,* pp. 493-96.

PETER STAMBLER. "Selving: The Sense of Perfection in Hopkins," *Thoth* 12(2), Winter 1972, 35-36.

DANIEL STEMPEL. "A Reading of 'The Windhover,' " *College English* 23(4), January 1962, 305-7.

ALISON G. SULLOWAY. "St. Ignatius Loyola and the Victorian Temper: Hopkins' Windhover as Symbol of 'Diabolic Gravity,' " *Hopkins Quarterly* 1(1), April 1974, 43-51.

ALFRED THOMAS. *Explicator* 33(4), December 1974, Item 31.

ALFRED THOMAS. "G. M. Hopkins: 'The Windhover'; Sources, 'Underthought', and Significance," *Modern Language Review* 70(3), July 1975, 497-507.

BRUCE WALLIS. " 'The Windhover' and the Patristic Exegetical Tradition," *University of Toronto Quarterly* 41(3), Spring 1972, 246-55.

DENNIS WARD. *Interpretations,* John Wain, ed., pp. 138-51.

YVOR WINTERS. *The Function of Criticism,* pp. 127-35.

CARL R. WOODRING. "Once More 'The Windhover,' " *Western Review* 15(1), Autumn 1950, 61-64.

EMILY K. YODER. "Evil and Idolatry in 'The Windhover,' " *Hopkins Quarterly* 2(1), April 1975, 33-46.

"The Wreck of the Deutschland"

MICHAEL R. BAKER. "The Logos in 'The Wreck of the Deutschland,' " *Hopkins Quarterly* 4(1), Spring 1977, 3-15.

ROBERT BOYLE. "Time and Grace in Hopkins' Imagination," *Renascence* 29(1), Autumn 1976, 7-19.

MICHAEL H. BRIGHT. "The Homiletic Structure of *The Wreck of the Deutschland,*" *Renascence* 25(2), Winter 1973, 95-102.

HARRY BROWN and JOHN MILSTEAD. *What the Poem Means,* pp. 109-10.

JEROME BUMP. " 'The Wreck of the Deutschland' and the Dynamic Sublime," *ELH* 41(1), Spring 1974, 106-29.

JAMES FINN COTTER. "Inscaping *The Wreck of the Deutschland,*" *Renascence* 21(3), Spring 1969, 124-33.

JAMES M. DEGEORGE. "The Dynamic Self in Gerard Manley Hopkins' *The Wreck of the Deutschland,*" *Studies in the Humanities* 3(1), October 1972, 4-11.

JAMES DICKEY. *Babel to Byzantium,* pp. 238-41.

JAMES DICKEY. "Hopkins: The Wreck of the Deutschland," in *Master Poems of the English Language,* pp. 801-3.

DAVID ANTHONY DOWNES. "Beatific Landscapes in Hopkins," *Hopkins Quarterly* 1(3), October 1974, 155-60.

DAVID ANTHONY DOWNES. "Grace and Beauty in 'The Wreck of the Deutschland': A Centenary Estimation," *Hopkins Quarterly* 3(4), January 1977, 139-55.

HOPKINS, GERARD MANLEY (Cont.)

"The Wreck of the Deutschland" (cont.)

R. N. EGUDU. "Gerard Manley Hopkins' Poetry and the Christian Apostleship," *Hopkins Quarterly* 3(1), April 1976, 5-6.

NIGEL FOXELL. *Ten Poems Analyzed*, pp. 203-54.

HOWARD W. FULWEILER. "Gerard Manley Hopkins and the 'Stanching, Quenching Ocean of a Motionable Mind,'" *Victorian Newsletter* 30 (Fall 1966), 9-13.

W. H. GARDNER. "Synopsis," in *The Dimensions of Poetry*, pp. 534-35.

W. H. GARDNER. "*The Wreck of the Deutschland*," *Essays and Studies* 21 (1935), 124-52.

SUSAN A. HALLGARTH. "A Study of Hopkins' Use of Nature," *Victorian Poetry* 5(1), Spring 1967, 84-85.

GEOFFREY H. HARTMAN. *Beyond Formalism*, pp. 236-37.

SISTER MARCELLA M. HOLLOWAY. "Hopkins' Theory of 'Antithetical Parallelism,'" *Hopkins Quarterly* 1(3), October 1974, 128-30.

SISTER MARCELLA M. HOLLOWAY. "An Immortalized Shipwreck: One Century Later," *Hopkins Quarterly* 2(4), January 1976, 153-60.

A. R. JONES. "G. M. Hopkins: Victorian," in *The Major Victorian Poets*, pp. 307-10.

THOMAS KRETZ. "Advents Three for Three: A Study of 'The Wreck of the Deutschland,'" *Victorian Poetry* 11(3), Autumn 1973, 252-54.

F. R. LEAVIS. *New Bearings on English Poetry*, pp. 175-80.

M. B. MCNAMEE. "Mastery and Mercy in *The Wreck of the Deutschland*," *College English* 23(4), January 1962, 267-76.

PETER MILWARD. "Biblical Imagery of Water in 'The Wreck of the Deutschland,'" *Hopkins Quarterly* 1(3), October 1974, 115-20.

PETER MILWARD. "Sacramental Symbolism in Hopkins and Eliot," *Renascence* 20(2), Winter 1968, 104-11.

JAMES W. PARINS. "Orion of Light: The Patmorean Flavor in Hopkins' 'Wreck,'" *Hopkins Quarterly* 3(1), April 1976, 23-33.

BROTHER ADELBERT SCHEVE. *Explicator* 17(9), June 1959, Item 60.

ELISABETH W. SCHNEIDER. "*The Wreck of the Deutschland*: A New Reading," *PMLA* 81(1), March 1966, 110-22.

F. X. SHEA. "The Art of Sinking in 'The Wreck of the Deutschland,'" *Hopkins Quarterly* 1(1), April 1974, 37-40.

PETER STAMBLER. "Selving: The Sense of Perfection in Hopkins," *Thoth* 12(2), Winter 1972, 34-35.

R. K. R. THORNTON. "The Diagram of a Mind," *Hopkins Quarterly* 3(2), July 1976, 47-58.

FRANCIS BEAUCHESNE THORNTON. "Essay on 'The Wreck of the Deutschland,'" *Catholic World* 160(955), October 1944, 41-46.

A. S. P. WOODHOUSE. *The Poet and His Faith*, pp. 245-49.

HORNE, FRANK

"He Won't Stay Put, A Carol for All Seasons"

RONALD PRIMEAU. "Frank Horne and the Second Echelon Poets of the Harlem Renaissance," in *The Harlem Renaissance Remembered*, p. 260.

"To All of You"

RONALD PRIMEAU. "Frank Horne and the Second Echelon Poets of the Harlem Renaissance," in *The Harlem Renaissance Remembered*, p. 251.

"To Chick"

RONALD PRIMEAU. "Frank Horne and the Second Echelon Poets of the Harlem Renaissance," in *The Harlem Renaissance Remembered*, pp. 252-53.

"To James"

RONALD PRIMEAU. "Frank Horne and the Second Echelon Poets of the Harlem Renaissance," in *The Harlem Renaissance Remembered*, pp. 249-51.

"To You"

RONALD PRIMEAU. "Frank Horne and the Second Echelon Poets of the Harlem Renaissance," in *The Harlem Renaissance Remembered*, pp. 253-54.

HORTON, GEORGE

"On Liberty and Slavery"

WILLIAM J. REEVES. "The Significance of Audience in Black Poetry," *Negro American Literature Forum* 9(1), Spring 1975, 30-32.

HOSKINS, JOHN

"Absence"

CLEANTH BROOKS. *Modern Poetry and the Tradition*, pp. 22-24.

CLEANTH BROOKS, JR. "Three Revolutions in Poetry: II. Wit and High Seriousness," *Southern Review* 1(2), Autumn 1935, 330. (P)

HOUSMAN, A. E.

"Be Still, My Soul"

GORDON PITTS. "Housman's 'Be Still, My Soul,'" *Victorian Poetry* 3(2), Spring 1965, 137-38. (P)

"Bredon Hill"

CLEANTH BROOKS. "Alfred Edward Housman," in *Anniversary Lectures 1959*, pp. 46-48.

"The Carpenter's Son"

S. G. ANDREWS. *Explicator* 19(1), October 1960, Item 3.

"The Chestnut Casts His Flambeaux"

HARRY BROWN and JOHN MILSTEAD. *What the Poem Means*, p. 114.

F. A. PHILBRICK. *Explicator* 4(3), December 1945, Item 20.

WARREN TAYLOR. *Explicator* 3(8), June 1945, Item 64.

"Crossing Alone the Nighted Ferry"

RANDALL JARRELL. "Texts from Housman," *Kenyon Review* 1(3), Summer 1939, 261-66. Reprinted in: *Modern Poetry*, pp. 141-45.

"Eight O'Clock"

CLEANTH BROOKS. "Alfred Edward Housman," in *Anniversary Lectures 1959*, pp. 42-43.

M. L. ROSENTHAL and A. J. M. SMITH. *Exploring Poetry*, pp. 69-71; second ed., pp. 84-86.

"1887"

CLEANTH BROOKS. "Alfred Edward Housman," in *Anniversary Lectures 1959*, pp. 48-51.

CLEANTH BROOKS, JOHN THIBAUT PURSER, and ROBERT PENN WARREN. *An Approach to Literature*, fifth ed., p. 439.

CLEANTH BROOKS and ROBERT PENN WARREN. *Understanding Poetry*, third ed., p. 350; fourth ed., pp. 117-19.

T. S. K. SCOTT-CRAIG, CHARLES C. WALCUTT, and CLEANTH BROOKS, JR. *Explicator* 2(5), March 1944, Item 34.

CHARLES CHILD WALCUTT. "Housman and the Empire: An Analysis of '1887,'" *College English* 5(5), February 1944, 255-58. Reprinted in: *Readings for Liberal Education*, II: 418-23; revised ed., II: 175-80. Also: *Reading Modern Poetry*, first ed., pp. 20-26.

"Epitaph on an Army of Mercenaries"

WALTON BEACHAM. *The Meaning of Poetry*, pp. 3-4.

CLEANTH BROOKS. "Alfred Edward Housman," in *Anniversary Lectures 1959*, pp. 40-41.

LEONARD UNGER and WILLIAM VAN O'CONNOR. *Poems for Study*, p. 39.

W. L. WERNER. *Explicator* 2(5), March 1944, Item 38.

RICHARD WILBUR. "Round About a Poem of Housman's," in *The Moment of Poetry*, pp. 78-90. Reprinted in: Richard Wilbur. *Responses*, pp. 21-32.

"Epithalamium"

GERARD REEDY. "Housman's Use of Classical Convention," *Victorian Poetry* 6(1), Spring 1968, 56-59.

"Farewell to Barn and Stack and Tree"

CLEANTH BROOKS and ROBERT PENN WARREN. *Understanding Poetry*, fourth ed., pp. 36-37.

"R. T. R." *Explicator* 1(6), April 1943, Q29.

WILBUR S. SCOTT. *Explicator* 5(2), November 1946, Item 11.

FRANK SULLIVAN. *Explicator* 2(5), March 1944, Item 36.

"The Farms of Home Lie Lost in Even"

ELLEN FRIEDMAN. "The Divided Self in the Poems of A. E. Housman," *English Literature in Transition* 20(1), 1977, 32-33.

"He Standing Hushed"

ROBERT BRAINARD PEARSALL. "Housman's 'He Standing Hushed,'" *Victorian Poetry* 7(1), Spring 1969, 62-64.

"Hell Gate"

CLEANTH BROOKS and ROBERT PENN WARREN. *Understanding Poetry*, third ed., pp. 55-59.

JOHN HAWLEY ROBERTS. *Explicator* 5(6), April 1947, Item 44.

"Her Strong Enchantments Failing"

CLYDE K. HYDER. *Explicator* 4(2), November 1945, Item 11.

"I to My Perils"

ELLEN FRIEDMAN. "The Divided Self in the Poems of A. E. Housman," *English Literature in Transition* 20(1), 1977, 29-30.

CHRISTOPHER RICKS. "The Nature of Housman's Poetry," *Essays in Criticism* 14(3), July 1964, 269-71.

"The Immortal Part"

LOUISE SCHUTZ BOAS. *Explicator* 2(5), March 1944, Item 37.

CLEANTH BROOKS. "Alfred Edward Housman," in *Anniversary Lectures 1959*, pp. 45-46.

CLEANTH BROOKS and ROBERT PENN WARREN. *Understanding Poetry*, revised ed., pp. 617-22; third ed., pp. 539-44; fourth ed., pp. 482-87.

HARRY MODEAN CAMPBELL. "Conflicting Metaphors: A Poem By A. E. Housman," *CEA Critic* 22(1), January 1960, 4.

ROBERT H. WEST. "Literature and Knowledge," *Georgia Review* 25(2), Summer 1971, 140-41.

"In the Morning"

ROBERT M. RYLEY. "Hermeneutics in the Classroom: E. D. Hirsch, Jr., and a Poem by Housman," *College English* 36(1), September 1974, 46-50.

"Into My Heart an Air That Kills"

DONALD STAUFFER. *The Nature of Poetry*, pp. 22-24, 156-59.

"Is My Team Ploughing?"

STANLEY E. CLAYES and JOHN GERRIETTS. *Ways to Poetry*, pp. 6-7.

LAURENCE PERRINE. *Sound and Sense*, p. 24; third ed., p. 27; fourth ed., p. 25.

"It Nods and Curtseys and Recovers"

RANDALL JARRELL. "Texts from Housman," *Kenyon Review* 1(3), Summer 1939, 266-70. Reprinted in: *Modern Poetry*, pp. 145-49.

"The Lent Lily"

BABETTE DEUTSCH. *Poetry in Our Time*, p. 17; second ed., pp. 17-18. (P)

MICHAEL MACKLEM. "The Elegiac Theme in Housman," *Queens Quarterly* 59(1), Spring 1952, 50-51.

"Loveliest of Trees"

GÉMINO H. ABAD. *A Formal Approach to Lyric Poetry*, pp. 47-48, 183, 197.

GEORGE ARMS. *Explicator* 1(7), May 1943, Item 57.

JEROME BEATY and WILLIAM H. MATCHETT. *Poetry From Statement to Meaning*, pp. 220-22.

WALTER BLAIR and W. K. CHANDLER. *Approaches to Poetry*, second ed., pp. 256-58.

B. J. LEGGETT. "The Poetry of Insight: Persona and Point of View in Housman," *Victorian Poetry* 14(4), Winter 1976, 329-31.

WINIFRED LYNSKEY. *Explicator* 4(8), June 1946, Item 59.

MICHAEL MACKLEM. "The Elegiac Theme in Housman," *Queens Quarterly* 59(1), Spring 1952, 41.

PATRICK STORY. "Housman's Cherry Trees: Toward the Practice of Marxist Explication," *Minnesota Review*, n.s., 5 (Fall 1975), 81-88.

WILLIAM L. WERNER. *Explicator* 1(7), June 1943, Item 69.

"The Merry Guide"

LOUISE SCHUTZ BOAS. *Explicator* 3(1), October 1944, Item 6.

"The Night Is Freezing Fast"

CLEANTH BROOKS. "Alfred Edward Housman," in *Anniversary Lectures 1959*, p. 44.

JAMES R. KREUZER. *Elements of Poetry*, pp. 220-21.

B. J. LEGGETT. "The Poetry of Insight: Persona and Point of View in Housman," *Victorian Poetry* 14(4), Winter 1976, 335-36.

"Now Dreary Dawns the Eastern Light"

ELLEN FRIEDMAN. "The Divided Self in the Poems of A. E. Housman," *English Literature in Transition* 20(1), 1977, 31-32.

"Now Hollow Fires Burn Out to Black"

TOM BURNS HABER. *Explicator* 11(5), March 1953, Item 35. (P)

"The Olive"

BABETTE DEUTSCH. *Poetry in Our Time*, pp. 17-18; second ed., pp. 18-19.

LAURENCE PERRINE. "Housman's 'The Olive,'" *Victorian Poetry* 11(4), Winter 1973, 340-41.

HOUSMAN, A. E. *(Cont.)*

"On the Idle Hill of Summer"

> CHRISTOPHER GILLIE. *Movements in English Literature*, pp. 65-66.

"On Wenlock Edge"

> SPIRO PETERSON. *Explicator* 15(7), April 1957, Item 46.

> ROBERT WOOSTER STALLMAN. *Explicator* 3(4), February 1945, Item 26.

"The Oracles"

> BREWSTER GHISELIN. *Explicator* 4(5), March 1946, Item 33.

> CLYDE K. HYDER. *Explicator* 4(1), October 1945, Item 5.

> EDWARD SPIVEY. *Explicator* 21(5), January 1963, Item 44.

"Others, I Am Not the First"

> B. J. LEGGETT. "The Point of Insight: Persona and Point of View in Housman," *Victorian Poetry* 14(4), Winter 1976, 332-33.

"The Recruit"

> B. J. LEGGETT. *Explicator* 25(3), November 1966, Item 25.

"Reveille"

> F. R. LEAVIS. "Imagery and Movement: Notes in the Analysis of Poetry," *Scrutiny* 13(2), September 1945, 132-34.

> DONALD STAUFFER. *The Nature of Poetry*, pp. 140-47.

"Revolution"

> F. A. PHILBRICK and RALPH P. BOAS. *Explicator* 2(5), March 1944, Item 35.

> JOHN W. STEVENSON. "The Martyr as Innocent: Housman's Lonely Lad," *South Atlantic Quarterly* 57(1), Winter 1958, 78-79.

"Stars I Have Seen Them Fall"

> EMERSON R. MARKS. "The Poetic Equivalent: *Mimesis* and the Literary Idea," *Western Humanities Review* 18(2), Spring 1964, 164-65.

"Tell Me Not Here"

> CLEANTH BROOKS. "Alfred Edward Housman," in *Anniversary Lectures 1959*, pp. 53-56.

> CHRISTOPHER RICKS. "The Nature of Housman's Poetry," *Essays in Criticism* 14(3), July 1964, 282-84.

"Terence, This Is Stupid Stuff"

> HARRY BROWN and JOHN MILSTEAD. *What the Poem Means*, pp. 113-14.

> B. J. LEGGETT. "The Miltonic Allusions in Housman's 'Terence, This Is Stupid Stuff,'" *English Language Notes* 5(3), March 1968, 202-7.

> RONALD E. MCFARLAND. "'The Tune the Old Cow Died Of': An Allusion in Housman," *Victorian Poetry* 11(1), Spring 1973, 60-61. (P)

> DOUGLAS JOHN MCREYNOLDS. *Explicator* 31(5), January 1973, Item 39. (P)

> JOHN W. STEVENSON. "The Pastoral Setting in the Poetry of A. E. Housman," *South Atlantic Quarterly* 55(4), October 1956, 494-96.

"To an Athlete Dying Young"

> WILLIAM BACHE. *Explicator* 10(1), October 1951, Item 6.

> JEROME BEATY and WILLIAM H. MATCHETT. *Poetry From Statement to Meaning*, pp. 172-74, 238-39.

> CLEANTH BROOKS and ROBERT PENN WARREN. *Understanding Poetry*, pp. 385-87; revised ed., pp. 267-69.

> C. R. B. COMBELLACK. *Explicator* 10(5), March 1952, Item 31. (P)

> ROBERT HAWKINS. *Preface to Poetry*, pp. 110-12.

> NAT HENRY. *Explicator* 12(7), May 1954, Item 48.

> JAMES L. KUGEL. *The Techniques of Strangeness in Symbolist Poetry*, pp. 39-40.

> B. J. LEGGETT. "The Poetry of Insight: Persona and Point of View in Housman," *Victorian Poetry* 14(4), Winter 1976, 336-37.

> WALTER L. MYERS. *Explicator* 11(4), February 1953, Item 23.

> LEONARD UNGER and WILLIAM VAN O'CONNOR. *Poems for Study*, pp. 8-9.

> CHARLES CHILD WALCUTT. "Interpreting the Symbol," *College English* 14(8), May 1953, 449-51.

"The True Lover"

> DARREL ABEL. *Explicator* 8(3), December 1949, Item 23.

> CLEANTH BROOKS, JOHN THIBAUT PURSER, and ROBERT PENN WARREN. *An Approach to Literature*, pp. 442-43; second ed., pp. 442-43; third ed., pp. 296-97; fourth ed., pp. 297-98; fifth ed., pp. 344-45.

> MAUDE M. HAWKINS. *Explicator* 8(8), June 1950, Item 61.

"The Vane on Hughley Steeple"

> T. R. BARNES. *English Verse*, pp. 269-70.

"Wake Not for the World Heard Thunder"

> ALLAN GRAY. "A Shakespearean Allusion in Housman, *Last Poems* XXIX," *English Language Notes* 8(1), September 1970, 36-39.

"We'll to the Woods No More"

> ELISABETH SCHNEIDER. *Aesthetic Motive*, pp. 97-103. Partial reprint in: *The Critic's Notebook*, p. 225.

"When I Came Last to Ludlow"

> ELLEN FRIEDMAN. "The Divided Self in the Poems of A. E. Housman," *English Literature in Transition* 20(1), 1977, 27-28.

"When I Was One-and-Twenty"

> EDWARD W. ROSENHEIM, JR. *What Happens in Literature*, pp. 5-13.

"When Israel Out of Egypt Came"

> L. G. LOCKE. *Explicator* 2(5), March 1944, Item 39.

"When Smoke Stood Up from Ludlow"

> DONALD STAUFFER. *The Nature of Poetry*, pp. 217-18.

"White in the Moon the Long Road Lies"

> JAMES R. KREUZER. *Elements of Poetry*, pp. 132-34.

"With Rue My Heart Is Laden"

> GÉMINO H. ABAD. *In Another Light*, p. 252.

> ELLEN FRIEDMAN. "The Divided Self in the Poems of A. E. Housman," *English Literature in Transition* 20(1), 1977, 30-31.

> WINIFRED LYNSKEY. "A Critic in Action: Mr. Ransom," *College English* 5(5), February 1944, 241-42.

> TRACEY PETERSON. "A. E. Housman's 'With Rue My Heart Is Laden': A Suggestion for Interpretation," *Papers on Language and Literature* 7(1), Winter 1971, 94-95.

> JOHN CROWE RANSOM. "Honey and Gall," *Southern Review* 6(1), Summer 1940, 6-8.

> WRIGHT THOMAS and STUART GERRY BROWN. *Reading Poems: An Introduction to Critical Study*, pp. 754-56.

"With Seed the Sowers Scatter"

WILLIAM EMPSON. "Emotions in Words Again," *Kenyon Review* 10(4), Autumn 1948, 587-89. Reprinted in: *The Kenyon Critics,* pp. 133-35.

HOWARD, HENRY

see SURREY, HENRY HOWARD, EARL OF

HOWARD, RICHARD

"The Chalk Cliffs of Rugen"

THOMAS WOLL. "Stasis Within Flux: Richard Howard's Findings," *Modern Poetry Studies* 4(3), Winter 1973, 268-69.

"From Beyoglu"

THOMAS WOLL. "Stasis Within Flux: Richard Howard's Findings," *Modern Poetry Studies* 4(3), Winter 1973, 267-68.

"From Tarragona"

THOMAS WOLL. "Stasis Within Flux: Richard Howard's Findings," *Modern Poetry Studies* 4(3), Winter 1973, 262-63.

"Giovanni da Fiesole on the Sublime, or Fra Angelico's Last Judgement"

THOMAS WOLL. "Stasis Within Flux: Richard Howard's Findings," *Modern Poetry Studies* 4(3), Winter 1973, 264.

"November, 1889"

THOMAS WOLL. "Stasis Within Flux: Richard Howard's Findings," *Modern Poetry Studies* 4(3), Winter 1973, 264-67.

"Queer's Song"

RICHARD WATSON. "Inside-Out Ceremonies: A Trope from *Quantities* and *The Damages* by Richard Howard," *Minnesota Review* 8(3), 1968, 226.

"The Return from Montauk"

NORMAN FRIEDMAN. "The Wesleyan Poets — I," *Chicago Review* 18(3-4), 1966, 62-63.

"Secular Games"

RICHARD WATSON. "Inside-Out Ceremonies: A Trope from *Quantities* and *The Damages* by Richard Howard," *Minnesota Review* 8(3), 1968, 226.

"Waiting for Ada"

THOMAS WOLL. "Stasis Within Flux: Richard Howard's Findings," *Modern Poetry Studies* 4(3), Winter 1973, 263-64.

HOWARD, ROGER

"Reply to Ma Chih-Yuan"

ROGER HOWARD. "Contradiction and the Poetic Image," *Minnesota Review,* n.s., 5 (Fall 1975), 89-90.

"Two Attitudes Towards Sparks"

ROGER HOWARD. "Contradiction and the Poetic Image," *Minnesota Review,* n.s., 5 (Fall 1975), 95-97.

HOWE, JULIA WARD

"The Battle Hymn of the Republic"

ISAAC ASIMOV. *Familiar Poems, Annotated,* pp. 209-15.

HOWELL, JAMES

"To the Knowing Reader touching Familiar Letters"

EARL MINER. *The Cavalier Mode from Jonson to Cotton,* pp. 262-63.

HOWELL, THOMAS

"Winter's Morning Muse"

ALAN T. BRAFORD. "Mirrors of Mutability: Winter Landscapes in Tudor Poetry," *English Literary Renaissance* 4(1), Winter 1974, 21-22.

HUGHES, LANGSTON

"As I Grew Older"

RAYMOND SMITH. "Langston Hughes: Evolution of the Poetic Persona," *Studies in the Literary Imagination* 7(2), Fall 1974, 54-55.

"A Black Pierrot"

JERRALD RANTA. "Geometry, Vision, and Poetic Form," *College English* 39(6), February 1978, 712-13.

"Border Line"

EARLENE D. GARBER. "Form as a Complement to Content in Three of Langston Hughes' Poems," *Negro American Literature Forum* 5(4), Winter 1971, 137-38.

"Bound No'th Blues"

EDWARD A. WALDRON. "The Blue Poetry of Langston Hughes," *Negro American Literature Forum* 5(4), Winter 1971, 147.

"Brass Spittoons"

BABETTE DEUTSCH. *Poetry in Our Time,* first ed., p. 358.

"Christ in Alabama"

ROBERT F. RICHARDS. "Literature and Politics," *Colorado Quarterly* 19(1), Summer 1970, 104.

"Cora"

R. BAXTER MILLER. "'No Crystal Stair': Unity, Archetype and Symbol in Langston Hughes's Poems on Women," *Negro American Literature Forum* 9(4), Winter 1975, 112-13.

"Cross"

HORTENSE E. THORNTON. "Sexism as Quagmire: Nella Larsen's *Quicksand,*" *CLA Journal* 16(3), March 1973, 288.

"Crowing-Hen Blues"

EDWARD A. WALDRON. "The Blue Poetry of Langston Hughes," *Negro American Literature Forum* 5(4), Winter 1971, 147.

"Dream"

EARLENE D. GARBER. "Form as a Complement to Content in Three of Langston Hughes' Poems," *Negro American Literature Forum* 5(4), Winter 1971, 138-39.

"Evenin' Air Blues"

ALLEN D. PROWLE. "Langston Hughes," in *The Black American Writer,* II: 83.

EDWARD A. WALDRON. "The Blue Poetry of Langston Hughes," *Negro American Literature Forum* 5(4), Winter 1971, 146.

"Hard Luck"

EDWARD A. WALDRON. "The Blue Poetry of Langston Hughes," *Negro American Literature Forum* 5(4), Winter 1971, 145-46.

HUGHES, LANGSTON (*Cont.*)

"Jitney"

> JAMES A. EMANUEL. "The Literary Experiments of Langston Hughes," *CLA Journal* 11(4), June 1968, 340-41.

"Lament over Love"

> DELLITA L. MARTIN. "Langston Hughes's Use of the Blues," *CLA Journal* 22(2), December 1978, 154-56.

"Listen Here Blues"

> EDWARD E. WALDRON. "The Blue Poetry of Langston Hughes," *Negro American Literature Forum* 5(4), Winter 1971, 144-45.

"Midwinter Blues"

> CLEANTH BROOKS, JOHN THIBAUT PURSER, and ROBERT PENN WARREN. *An Approach to Literature,* fifth ed., p. 399.

"Mississippi Levee"

> EDWARD A. WALDRON. "The Blue Poetry of Langston Hughes," *Negro American Literature Forum* 5(4), Winter 1971, 148.

"Morning After"

> EDWARD A. WALDRON. "The Blue Poetry of Langston Hughes," *Negro American Literature Forum* 5(4), Winter 1971, 147.

"Mother to Son"

> R. BAXTER MILLER. " 'No Crystal Stair': Unity, Archetype and Symbol in Langston Hughes's Poems on Women," *Negro American Literature Forum* 9(4), Winter 1975, 109-11.

"Negro Mother"

> R. BAXTER MILLER. " 'No Crystal Stair': Unity, Archetype and Symbol in Langston Hughes's Poems on Women," *Negro American Literature Forum* 9(4), Winter 1975, 111-12.

"Seven Moments of Love Sequence"

> EDWARD A. WALDRON. "The Blue Poetry of Langston Hughes," *Negro American Literature Forum* 5(4), Winter 1971, 143.

"Six-Bit Blues"

> EDWARD A. WALDRON. "The Blue Poetry of Langston Hughes," *Negro American Literature Forum* 5(4), Winter 1971, 146-47.

"Southern Mammy"

> R. BAXTER MILLER. " 'No Crystal Stair': Unity, Archetype and Symbol in Langston Hughes's Poems on Women," *Negro American Literature Forum* 9(4), Winter 1975, 113.

"Strange Hurt"

> R. BAXTER MILLER. " 'No Crystal Stair': Unity, Archetype and Symbol in Langston Hughes's Poems on Women," *Negro American Literature Forum* 9(4), Winter 1975, 112.

"Suicide"

> DELLITA L. MARTIN. "Langston Hughes's Use of the Blues," *CLA Journal* 22(2), December 1978, 153-54.

"Supper Time"

> ALLEN D. PROWLE. "Langston Hughes," in *The Black American Writer,* II: 83.

"Theme for English B"

> GARY F. SCHARNHORST. *Explicator* 32(4), December 1973, Item 27.

"The Weary Blues"

> EDWARD E. WALDRON. "The Blue Poetry of Langston Hughes," *Negro American Literature Forum* 5(4), Winter 1971, 148.

"Young Gal's Blues"

> DELLITA L. MARTIN. "Langston Hughes's Use of the Blues," *CLA Journal* 22(2), December 1978, 156-58.

> SHERLEY A. WILLIAMS. "The Blues Roots of Contemporary Afro-American Poetry," *Massachusetts Review* 18(3), Autumn 1977, 545-47.

HUGHES, TED

"Acrobats"

> DAVID RIFE. "Rectifying Illusion in the Poetry of Ted Hughes," *Minnesota Review* 10(4), 1970, 98-99.

"The Ancient Heroes and the Bomber Pilot"

> G. J. RAWSON. "Ted Hughes: A Reappraisal," *Essays in Criticism* 15(1), January 1965, 87-88.

> LAWRENCE R. RIES. *Wolf Masks,* pp. 122-23.

"Battle of Osfrontalis"

> J. BROOKS BOUSON. "A Reading of Ted Hughes's *Crow,*" *Concerning Poetry* 7(2), Fall 1974, 28.

> CHARLES V. FERNANDEZ. "Crow: A Mythology of the Demonic," *Modern Poetry Studies* 6(2), Autumn 1975, 154.

"Bayonet Charge"

> LAWRENCE R. RIES. *Wolf Masks,* pp. 104-5.

"Cadenza"

> ANTHONY LIBBY. "God's Lioness and the Priest of Sycorax: Plath and Hughes," *Contemporary Literature* 15(3), Summer 1974, 390-91.

"The Casualty"

> C. B. COX and A. E. DYSON. *Modern Poetry,* pp. 142-46.

> A. E. DYSON. "Ted Hughes," *Critical Quarterly* 1(3), Autumn 1959, 224-25.

"Childbirth"

> BRIAN JOHN. "Ted Hughes: Poet at the Master-Fulcrum of Violence," *Arizona Quarterly* 23(1), Spring 1967, 9-10.

"A Childish Prank"

> CLAIRE HAHN. "Crow and the Biblical creation narratives," *Critical Quarterly* 19(1), Spring 1977, 47.

> DAVID LODGE. " 'Crow' and the Cartoons," *Critical Quarterly* 13(1), Spring 1971, 37-38.

> JAROLD RAMSEY. "Crow: or the Trickster Transformed," *Massachusetts Review* 19(1), Spring 1978, 119-21.

"Cleopatra to the Asp"

> C. J. RAWSON. "Ted Hughes: A Reappraisal," *Essays in Criticism* 15(1), January 1965, 86.

"The Contender"

> CHARLES V. FERNANDEZ. "Crow: A Mythology of the Demonic," *Modern Poetry Studies* 6(2), Autumn 1975, 155.

"The Conversion of Reverend Skinner"

> LAWRENCE R. RIES. *Wolf Masks,* pp. 128-29.

"Criminal Ballad"

> DAVID HOLBROOK. *Lost Bearings in English Poetry,* p. 151.

"Crow and Mama"
  CLAIRE HAHN. "*Crow* and the Biblical creation narratives," *Critical Quarterly* 19(1), Spring 1977, 46-47.

"Crow and the sea"
  CLAIRE HAHN. "*Crow* and the Biblical creation narratives," *Critical Quarterly* 19(1), Spring 1977, 49-50.

"Crow blacker than ever"
  CLAIRE HAHN. "*Crow* and the Biblical creation narratives," *Critical Quarterly* 19(1), Spring 1977, 48-49.

"Crow communes"
  CLAIRE HAHN. "*Crow* and the Biblical creation narratives," *Critical Quarterly* 19(1), Spring 1977, 48.

"Crow Hears Fate Knock on the Door"
  JAROLD RAMSEY. "Crow: or the Trickster Transformed," *Massachusetts Review* 19(1), Spring 1978, 121-22.

"Crow Tyrannosaurus"
  JAROLD RAMSEY. "Crow: or the Trickster Transformed," *Massachusetts Review* 19(1), Spring 1978, 122.

"Crow's Account of St. George"
  CHARLES V. FERNANDEZ. "Crow: A Mythology of the Demonic," *Modern Poetry Studies* 6(2), Autumn 1975, 153-54.
  DAVID HOLBROOK. *Lost Bearings in English Poetry*, pp. 148-51.
  LAWRENCE R. RIES. *Wolf Masks*, pp. 109-10.

"Crow's First Lesson"
  CLAIRE HAHN. "*Crow* and the Biblical creation narratives," *Critical Quarterly* 19(1), Spring 1977, 47.

"Crow's Theology"
  AGNES STEIN. *The Uses of Poetry*, pp. 79-80.

"The Dove Breeder"
  DERWENT MAY. "Ted Hughes," in *The Survival of Poetry*, pp. 136-37.

"Egg-Head"
  C. J. RAWSON. "Ted Hughes: A Reappraisal," *Essays in Criticism* 15(1), January 1965, 83-86.
  LAWRENCE R. RIES. *Wolf Masks*, pp. 121-22.

"Full Moon and Little Frieda"
  DAVID HOLBROOK. *Lost Bearings in English Poetry*, pp. 127-28.

"Ghost Crabs"
  LAWRENCE R. RIES. *Wolf Masks*, pp. 107-9.

"Gog"
  DAVID HOLBROOK. *Lost Bearings in English Poetry*, pp. 110-26.
  GEOFFREY THURLEY. *The Ironic Harvest*, pp. 182-83.

"Grief for Dead Soldiers"
  A. E. DYSON. "Ted Hughes," *Critical Quarterly* 1(3), Autumn 1959, 223-24.

"The Hawk in the Rain"
  BRIAN JOHN. "Ted Hughes: Poet at the Master-Fulcrum of Violence," *Arizona Quarterly* 23(1), Spring 1967, 6-8.
  DERWENT MAY. "Ted Hughes," in *The Survival of Poetry*, pp. 141-44.
  C. J. RAWSON. "Ted Hughes: A Reappraisal," *Essays in Criticism* 15(1), January 1965, 79-81.
  C. J. RAWSON. "Ted Hughes and Violence," *Essays in Criticism* 16(1), January 1966, 124-25.

LAWRENCE R. RIES. *Explicator* 33(4), December 1974, Item 34.
  LAWRENCE R. RIES. *Wolf Masks*, pp. 110-12.
  DAVID RIFE. "Rectifying Illusion in the Poetry of Ted Hughes," *Minnesota Review* 10(4), 1970, 98.
  DONALD J. WATT. "Echoes of Hopkins in Ted Hughes's 'The Hawk in the Rain,' " *Notes on Contemporary Literature* 2(3), May 1972, 10-12.

"Hawk Roosting"
  ALLAN GRANT. "Ted Hughes," in *Criticism in Action*, pp. 101-2.
  C. J. RAWSON. "Ted Hughes and Violence," *Essays in Criticism* 16(1), January 1966, 126-28.
  DAVID RIFE. "Rectifying Illusion in the Poetry of Ted Hughes," *Minnesota Review* 10(4), 1970, 96-97.

"How Water Began to Play"
  JAROLD RAMSEY. "Crow: or the Trickster Transformed," *Massachusetts Review* 19(1), Spring 1978, 126.

"Invitation to the Dance"
  LAWRENCE R. RIES. *Wolf Masks*, pp. 125-27.

"The Jaguar"
  DAVID RIFE. "Rectifying Illusion in the Poetry of Ted Hughes," *Minnesota Review* 10(3-4), 1970, 97.

"A Kill"
  J. BROOKS BOUSON. "A Reading of Ted Hughes's *Crow*," *Concerning Poetry* 7(2), Fall 1974, 24.

"Law in the Country of the Cats"
  LAWRENCE R. RIES. *Wolf Masks*, p. 117.

"Littleblood"
  JAROLD RAMSEY. "Crow: or the Trickster Transformed," *Massachusetts Review* 19(1), Spring 1978, 126-27.

"The Lovepet"
  J. BROOKS BOUSON. "A Reading of Ted Hughes's *Crow*," *Concerning Poetry* 7(2), Fall 1974, 29.

"Lovesong"
  DAVID HOLBROOK. *Lost Bearings in English Poetry*, p. 142.

"Lupercalia"
  BRIAN JOHN. "Ted Hughes: Poet at the Master-Fulcrum of Violence," *Arizona Quarterly* 23(1), Spring 1967, 13.

"Macaw and Little Miss"
  LAWRENCE R. RIES. *Wolf Masks*, pp. 103-4.

"The Man Seeking Experience Enquires His Way of a Drop of Water"
  DERWENT MAY. "Ted Hughes," in *The Survival of Poetry*, pp. 138-39.
  C. J. RAWSON. "Ted Hughes: A Reappraisal," *Essays in Criticism* 15(1), January 1965, 89-91.

"The Martyrdom of Bishop Ferrar"
  LAWRENCE R. RIES. *Wolf Masks*, pp. 115-16.

"Mayday on Holderness"
  LAWRENCE R. RIES. *Wolf Masks*, pp. 114-15.

"A Modest Proposal"
  J. D. HAINSWORTH. "Ted Hughes and Violence," *Essays in Criticism* 15(3), July 1965, 358-59.
  C. J. RAWSON. "Ted Hughes and Violence," *Essays in Criticism* 16(1), January 1966, 128-29.

HUGHES, TED *(Cont.)*

"Nicholas Ferrer"

> Lawrence R. Ries. *Wolf Masks,* p. 106.

"November"

> Derwent May. "Ted Hughes," in *The Survival of Poetry,* pp. 147-48.
> Lawrence R. Ries. *Wolf Masks,* p. 114.

"October Dawn"

> Derwent May. "Ted Hughes," in *The Survival of Poetry,* pp. 134-36.

"Oedipus Crow"

> J. Brooks Bouson. "A Reading of Ted Hughes's *Crow,*" *Concerning Poetry* 7(2), Fall 1974, 28.

"Of Cats"

> Lawrence R. Ries. *Wolf Masks,* p. 118.

"An Otter"

> Allan Grant. "Ted Hughes," in *Criticism in Action,* pp. 103-4.

"Pike"

> Stuart Hirschberg. "An Encounter with the Irrational in Ted Hughes's 'Pike,'" *Concerning Poetry* 9(1), Spring 1976, 63-64.
> Robert Langbaum. "The New Nature Poetry," in *The Modern Spirit,* pp. 115-16.

"Public Bar TV"

> Derwent May. "Ted Hughes," in *The Survival of Poetry,* pp. 158-59.

"Relic"

> Lawrence R. Ries. *Wolf Masks,* p. 97.

"The Retired Colonel"

> Lawrence R. Ries. *Wolf Masks,* pp. 124-25.

"Six Young Men"

> C. B. Cox and A. E. Dyson. *The Practical Criticism of Poetry,* pp. 94-99.
> A. E. Dyson. "Ted Hughes," *Critical Quarterly* 1(3), Autumn 1959, 223.
> Lawrence R. Ries. *Wolf Masks,* p. 105.

"Skylarks"

> Derwent May. "Ted Hughes," in *The Survival of Poetry,* pp. 152-57.

"Song for a Phallus"

> David Holbrook. *Lost Bearings in English Poetry,* pp. 155-57.

"Song of a Rat"

> Stuart Hirschberg. "Hughes's New 'Rough Beast': The Malevolent New Order in 'Song of a Rat,'" *Concerning Poetry* 11(1), Spring 1978, 59-63.

"Sunstroke"

> Brian John. "Ted Hughes: Poet at the Master-Fulcrum of Violence," *Arizona Quarterly* 23(1), Spring 1967, 11-12.

"That Moment"

> M. L. Rosenthal. *Poetry and the Common Life,* pp. 110-11.

"Thistles"

> Lawrence R. Ries. *Wolf Masks,* pp. 106-7.

"Thrushes"

> Derwent May. "Ted Hughes," in *The Survival of Poetry,* pp. 146-47.

"Truth Kills Everybody"

> Jarold Ramsey. "Crow: or the Trickster Transformed," *Massachusetts Review* 19(1), Spring 1978, 125.

"Two Eskimo Songs"

> Jarold Ramsey. "Crow: or the Trickster Transformed," *Massachusetts Review* 19(1), Spring 1978, 126.

"Two legends"

> J. Brooks Bouson. "A Reading of Ted Hughes's Crow," *Concerning Poetry* 7(2), Fall 1974, 24.
> Claire Hahn. "*Crow* and the Biblical creation narratives," *Critical Quarterly* 19(1), Spring 1977, 45-46.

"Two Wise Generals"

> Lawrence R. Ries. *Wolf Masks,* pp. 116-17.

"Wilfred Owen's Photographs"

> Lawrence R. Ries. *Wolf Masks,* p. 123.

"Wings"

> Calvin Bedient. "On Ted Hughes," *Critical Quarterly* 14(2), Summer 1972, 105-6.

"Wodwo"

> Lawrence Kramer. "The Wodwo Watches the Water Clock: Language in Postmodern British and American Poetry," *Contemporary Literature* 18(3), Summer 1977, 336-37.
> Lawrence R. Ries. *Wolf Masks,* pp. 112-14.

"A Woman Unconscious"

> Lawrence R. Ries. *Wolf Masks,* pp. 123-24.

HUGO, RICHARD

"The Art of Poetry"

> Arthur Oberg. "Beyond Lichen and Rose: In Search of a Contemporary American Poetics," *Ohio Review* 17(1), Fall 1975, 58-59.

"The Squatter on Company Land"

> Richard Hugo. "How Poets Make a Living," *Iowa Review* 3(4), Fall 1972, 69-76.

HUMPHREYS, DAVID

"Ode to Laura"

> William K. Bottorff. "Humphreys' 'Ode to Laura': A Lost Satire," *Early American Literature Newsletter* 2(2), Fall 1967, 36-38.

HUMPHRIES, ROLFE

"Little Fugue"

> Harold E. Cook. *Explicator* 14(3), December 1955, Item 14.

"Polo Grounds"

> Laurence Perrine. *100 American Poems of the Twentieth Century,* pp. 168-71.

HUNT, LEIGH

"Abou Ben Adhem"

> Ernest E. Leisy. *Explicator* 5(2), November 1946, Item 9.
> T. O. Mabbott. *Explicator* 5(5), March 1947, Item 39.

"The Story of Rimini"

> Karl Kroeber. *Romantic Narrative Art,* pp. 122-26.

HUXLEY, ALDOUS

"Arabia Infelix"

> Donald Watt. "The Meditative Poetry of Aldous Huxley," *Modern Poetry Studies* 6(2), Autumn 1975, 121-22.

"The Birth of God"

> Donald Watt. "The Meditative Poetry of Aldous Huxley," *Modern Poetry Studies* 6(2), Autumn 1975, 118-19.

"The Cicadas"

> Donald Watt. "The Meditative Poetry of Aldous Huxley," *Modern Poetry Studies* 6(2), Autumn 1975, 125-26.

"Leda"

> Arthur Minton. *Explicator* 7(4), February 1949, Item 31.

"Mediterranean"

> Donald Watt. "The Meditative Poetry of Aldous Huxley," *Modern Poetry Studies* 6(2), Autumn 1975, 120.

"Orion"

> Donald Watt. "The Meditative Poetry of Aldous Huxley," *Modern Poetry Studies* 6(2), Autumn 1975, 123-25.

"The Reef"

> Donald Watt. "The Meditative Poetry of Aldous Huxley," *Modern Poetry Studies* 6(2), Autumn 1975, 117-18.

"Tide"

> Donald Watt. "The Meditative Poetry of Aldous Huxley," *Modern Poetry Studies* 6(2), Autumn 1975, 120-21.

"The Yellow Mustard"

> Donald Watt. "The Meditative Poetry of Aldous Huxley," *Modern Poetry Studies* 6(2), Autumn 1975, 126-28.

I

IGNATOW, DAVID

"Against the Evidence"
> RALPH J. MILLS, JR. "Earth Hard: The Poetry of David Ignatow," *Boundary 2* 2(3), Spring 1974, 414-15. Reprinted in: Ralph J. Mills, Jr. *Cry of the Human,* pp. 116-17.

"And Step"
> RALPH J. MILLS, JR. "Earth Hard: The Poetry of David Ignatow," *Boundary 2* 2(3), Spring 1974, 390. Reprinted in: Ralph J. Mills, Jr. *Cry of the Human,* p. 88.

"Blessing Myself"
> RALPH J. MILLS, JR. "Earth Hard: The Poetry of David Ignatow," *Boundary 2* 2(3), Spring 1974, 391. Reprinted in: Ralph J. Mills, Jr. *Cry of the Human,* p. 89.

"The Business Life"
> RALPH J. MILLS, JR. "Earth Hard: The Poetry of David Ignatow," *Boundary 2* 2(3), Spring 1974, 386-87. Reprinted in: Ralph J. Mills, Jr. *Cry of the Human,* pp. 84-85.

"Communion"
> RALPH J. MILLS, JR. "Earth Hard: The Poetry of David Ignatow," *Boundary 2* 2(3), Spring 1974, 384. Reprinted in: Ralph J. Mills, Jr. *Cry of the Human,* p. 80.

"The Dream"
> RALPH J. MILLS, JR. "Earth Hard: The Poetry of David Ignatow," *Boundary 2* 2(3), Spring 1974, 388-89. Reprinted in: Ralph J. Mills, Jr. *Cry of the Human,* pp. 86-87.

"Errand Boy I"
> RALPH J. MILLS, JR. "Earth Hard: The Poetry of David Ignatow," *Boundary 2* 2(3), Spring 1974, 385. Reprinted in: Ralph J. Mills, Jr. *Cry of the Human,* p. 82.

"First Coffin Poem"
> RALPH J. MILLS, JR. "Earth Hard: The Poetry of David Ignatow," *Boundary 2* 2(3), Spring 1974, 423-24. Reprinted in: Ralph J. Mills, Jr. *Cry of the Human,* pp. 127-29.

"A First on TV"
> RALPH J. MILLS, JR. "Earth Hard: The Poetry of David Ignatow," *Boundary 2* 2(3), Spring 1974, 405. Reprinted in: Ralph J. Mills, Jr. *Cry of the Human,* pp. 104-5.

"For One Moment"
> VICTOR CONTOSKI. "Time and Money: The Poetry of David Ignatow," *University Review* 34(3), Spring 1968, 211.

"From a Dream"
> RALPH J. MILLS, JR. "Earth Hard: The Poetry of David Ignatow," *Boundary 2* 2(3), Spring 1974, 410-11. Reprinted in: Ralph J. Mills, Jr. *Cry of the Human,* pp. 111-12.

"I Felt"
> RALPH J. MILLS, JR. "Earth Hard: The Poetry of David Ignatow," *Boundary 2* 2(3), Spring 1974, 378-79. Reprinted in: Ralph J. Mills, Jr. *Cry of the Human,* pp. 73-74.

"The Life Dance"
> RALPH J. MILLS, JR. "Earth Hard: The Poetry of David Ignatow," *Boundary 2* 2(3), Spring 1974, 419-20. Reprinted in: Ralph J. Mills, Jr. *Cry of the Human,* pp. 122-23.

"A Meditation on Violence"
> RALPH J. MILLS, JR. "Earth Hard: The Poetry of David Ignatow," *Boundary 2* 2(3), Spring 1974, 412-13. Reprinted in: Ralph J. Mills, Jr. *Cry of the Human,* pp. 113-15.

"The Moon"
> RALPH J. MILLS, JR. "Earth Hard: The Poetry of David Ignatow," *Boundary 2* 2(3), Spring 1974, 394. Reprinted in: Ralph J. Mills, Jr. *Cry of the Human,* pp. 92-94.

"Morning"
> RALPH J. MILLS, JR. "Earth Hard: The Poetry of David Ignatow," *Boundary 2* 2(3), Spring 1974, 425-27. Reprinted in: Ralph J. Mills, Jr. *Cry of the Human,* pp. 130-32.

"Noturne"
> RALPH J. MILLS, JR. "Earth Hard: The Poetry of David Ignatow," *Boundary 2* 2(3), Spring 1974, 382-83. Reprinted in: Ralph J. Mills, Jr. *Cry of the Human,* p. 79.

"Nourish the Crops"
> RALPH J. MILLS, JR. "Earth Hard: The Poetry of David Ignatow," *Boundary 2* 2(3), Spring 1974, 392-94. Reprinted in: Ralph J. Mills, Jr. *Cry of the Human,* pp. 91-92.

"The Open Boat"
> RALPH J. MILLS, JR. "Earth Hard: The Poetry of David Ignatow," *Boundary 2* 2(3), Spring 1974, 409-10. Reprinted in: Ralph J. Mills, Jr. *Cry of the Human,* pp. 110-11.

"Rescue the Dead"

RALPH J. MILLS, JR. "Earth Hard: The Poetry of David Ignatow," *Boundary 2* 2(3), Spring 1974, 395-99. Reprinted in: Ralph J. Mills, Jr. *Cry of the Human*, pp. 94-96.

"The Rightful One"

RALPH J. MILLS, JR. "Earth Hard: The Poetry of David Ignatow," *Boundary 2* 2(3), Spring 1974, 378-79. Reprinted in: Ralph J. Mills, Jr. *Cry of the Human*, pp. 73-75.

"Ritual One"

RALPH J. MILLS, JR. "Earth Hard: The Poetry of David Ignatow," *Boundary 2* 2(3), Spring 1974, 402-4. Reprinted in: Ralph J. Mills, Jr. *Cry of the Human*, pp. 101-3.

"Ritual Two"

RALPH J. MILLS, JR. "Earth Hard: The Poetry of David Ignatow," *Boundary 2* 2(3), Spring 1974, 404-7. Reprinted in: Ralph J. Mills, Jr. *Cry of the Human*, pp. 103-7.

"Ritual Three"

RALPH J. MILLS, JR. "Earth Hard: The Poetry of David Ignatow," *Boundary 2* 2(3), Spring 1974, 407-9. Reprinted in: Ralph J. Mills, Jr. *Cry of the Human*, pp. 107-10.

"The Room"

RALPH J. MILLS, JR. "Earth Hard: The Poetry of David Ignatow," *Boundary 2* 2(3), Spring 1974, 401-2. Reprinted in: Ralph J. Mills, Jr. *Cry of the Human*, pp. 99-101.

"Sales Talk"

RALPH J. MILLS, JR. "Earth Hard: The Poetry of David Ignatow," *Boundary 2* 2(3), Spring 1974, 386. Reprinted in: Ralph J. Mills, Jr. *Cry of the Human*, pp. 82-83.

"Say Pardon"

RALPH J. MILLS, JR. "Earth Hard: The Poetry of David Ignatow," *Boundary 2* 2(3), Spring 1974, 389-90. Reprinted in: Ralph J. Mills, Jr. *Cry of the Human*, pp. 87-88.

"Secret Histories"

JAMES DICKEY. *Babel to Byzantium*, pp. 25-27.

"Secretly"

RALPH J. MILLS, JR. "Earth Hard: The Poetry of David Ignatow," *Boundary 2* 2(3), Spring 1974, 418-19. Reprinted in: Ralph J. Mills, Jr. *Cry of the Human*, p. 122.

"Sediment"

RALPH J. MILLS, JR. "Earth Hard: The Poetry of David Ignatow," *Boundary 2* 2(3), Spring 1974, 400. Reprinted in: Ralph J. Mills, Jr. *Cry of the Human*, pp. 98-99.

"Six Movements on a Theme"

RALPH J. MILLS, JR. "Earth Hard: The Poetry of David Ignatow," *Boundary 2* 2(3), Spring 1974, 415-18. Reprinted in: Ralph J. Mills, Jr. *Cry of the Human*, pp. 117-22.

"The Song"

RALPH J. MILLS, JR. "Earth Hard: The Poetry of David Ignatow," *Boundary 2* 2(3), Spring 1974, 377. Reprinted in: Ralph J. Mills, Jr. *Cry of the Human*, pp. 71-72.

"A Suite for Marriage"

RALPH J. MILLS, JR. "Earth Hard: The Poetry of David Ignatow," *Boundary 2* 2(3), Spring 1974, 399-400. Reprinted in: Ralph J. Mills, Jr. *Cry of the Human*, pp. 96-98.

"They put a telephone in his coffin"

RALPH J. MILLS, JR. "Earth Hard: The Poetry of David Ignatow," *Boundary 2* 2(3), Spring 1974, 422-23. Reprinted in: Ralph J. Mills, Jr. *Cry of the Human*, pp. 126-27.

"Three in Transition"

RALPH J. MILLS, JR. "Earth Hard: The Poetry of David Ignatow," *Boundary 2* 2(3), Spring 1974, 420-21. Reprinted in: Ralph J. Mills, Jr. *Cry of the Human*, pp. 124-25.

IRWIN, JOHN

"Circles"

WYATT PRUNTY. "A Chromatic Poetry," *Southern Review*, n.s., 13(1), Winter 1977, 209-10.

J

JANDL, ERNST

"film"

ALICIA OSTRIKER. "Poem Objects," *Partisan Review* 40(1), Winter 1973, 104-5.

JARRELL, RANDALL

"Absent With Official Leave"

SISTER M. BERNETTA QUINN. *The Metamorphic Tradition*, pp. 196-97.

"Aging"

WILLIAM H. PRITCHARD. "Wildness of Logic in Modern Lyric," in *Forms of Lyric*, pp. 141-42.

"The Bad Music"

M. L. ROSENTHAL. "Randall Jarrell," in *Seven American Poets from MacLeish to Nemerov*, 136-37.

"La Belle au Bois Dormant"

SISTER M. BERNETTA QUINN. *The Metamorphic Tradition*, p. 202.

"The Bird of Night"

FRANCES C. FERGUSON. "Randall Jarrell and the Flotations of Voice," *Georgia Review* 28(3), Fall 1974, 438-39.

"The Black Swan"

SISTER M. BERNETTA QUINN. *The Metamorphic Tradition*, pp. 186-88.

M. L. ROSENTHAL. "Randall Jarrell," in *Seven American Poets from MacLeish to Nemerov*, pp. 157-58.

"The Blind Sheep"

SISTER M. BERNETTA QUINN. *The Metamorphic Tradition*, pp. 197-98.

"Burning the Letters"

CLEANTH BROOKS, JOHN THIBAUT PURSER, and ROBERT PENN WARREN. *An Approach to Literature*, fifth ed., pp. 354-55.

SISTER M. BERNETTA QUINN. *The Metamorphic Tradition*, pp. 198-99.

"A Camp in a Prussian Forest"

W. S. GRAHAM. "Jarrell's 'Losses': A Controversy: 'It All Comes Back to Me Now,'" *Poetry* 72(6), September 1948, 306.

LAURENCE PERRINE. *100 American Poems of the Twentieth Century*, pp. 227-30.

STEPHEN SPENDER. "Randall Jarrell's Landscape," *Nation* 166(18), 1 May 1948, 476.

"The Child of Courts"

M. L. ROSENTHAL. "Randall Jarrell," in *Seven American Poets from MacLeish to Nemerov*, pp. 153-55.

"Cinderella"

JOHN CROWE RANSOM. "The Rugged Way of Genius — A Tribute to Randall Jarrell," *Southern Review*, n.s., 3(2), Spring 1967, 276-78.

M. L. ROSENTHAL. "Randall Jarrell," in *Seven American Poets from MacLeish to Nemerov*, p. 165.

"The Dead Wingman"

M. L. ROSENTHAL. "Randall Jarrell," in *Seven American Poets from MacLeish to Nemerov*, p. 144-45.

"The Death of the Ball Turret Gunner"

PATRICK F. BASSETT. *Explicator* 36(3), Spring 1978, 20-21.

HARRY BROWN and JOHN MILSTEAD. *What the Poem Means*, pp. 116-17.

DAVID K. CORNELIUS. *Explicator* 35(3), Spring 1977, 3.

LEVEN M. DAWSON. *Explicator* 31(4), December 1972, Item 29.

PATRICK J. HORNER. *Explicator* 36(4), Summer 1978, 9-10.

ISABEL C. HUNGERLAND. "The Interpretation of Poetry," *Journal of Aesthetics and Art Criticism* 8(3), March 1955, 353-54.

JAMES R. KREUZER. *Elements of Poetry*, pp. 146-48.

JOHN CLARK PRATT. *The Meaning of Modern Poetry*, pp. 195, 202, 205, 212.

DAVID RAY. "The Lightning of Randall Jarrell," *Prairie Schooner* 35(1), Spring 1961, 45-52.

M. L. ROSENTHAL. *The Modern Poets*, p. 245.

M. L. ROSENTHAL. "Randall Jarrell," in *Seven American Poets from MacLeish to Nemerov*, pp. 137-38.

M. L. ROSENTHAL and A. J. M. SMITH. *Exploring Poetry*, pp. 547-49; second ed., pp. 354-55.

ROBERT WEISBERG. "Randall Jarrell: The Integrity of his Poetry," *Centennial Review* 17(3), Summer 1973, 239.

"The Dream of Waking"

SISTER M. BERNETTA QUINN. *The Metamorphic Tradition*, p. 196.

"Eighth Air Force"

CLEANTH BROOKS. "Irony as a Principle of Structure," in *Literary Opinion in America*, revised and third eds., pp. 738-40.

CLEANTH BROOKS, JOHN THIBAUT PURSER, and ROBERT PENN WARREN. *An Approach to Literature*, third ed., pp. 397-99; fourth ed., pp. 396-98; fifth ed., pp. 440-41.

FRANCES C. FERGUSON. "Randall Jarrell and the Flotations of Voice," *Georgia Review* 28(3), Fall 1974, 436-38.

M. L. ROSENTHAL. "Randall Jarrell," in *Seven American Poets from MacLeish to Nemerov*, pp. 142-44.

VERNON SCANNELL. *Not Without Glory*, pp. 194-95.

"The Elementary Scene"

M. L. ROSENTHAL. *Poetry and the Common Life*, pp. 23-25.

M. L. ROSENTHAL. "Randall Jarrell," in *Seven American Poets from MacLeish to Nemerov*, pp. 167-68.

"The Emancipators"

MORDECAI and ERIN MARCUS. *Explicator* 16(5), February 1958, Item 26.

"For an Emigrant"

M. L. ROSENTHAL. "Randall Jarrell," in *Seven American Poets from MacLeish to Nemerov*, pp. 139-40.

"A Front"

H. RUSSELL HILL. "Poetry and Experience," *English Journal* 55(2), February 1966, 162-68.

"A Game at Salzburg"

M. L. ROSENTHAL. "Randall Jarrell," in *Seven American Poets from MacLeish to Nemerov*, pp. 161-62.

"The Girl Dreams That She Is Giselle"

SISTER M. BERNETTA QUINN. *The Metamorphic Tradition*, pp. 188-91.

"A Girl in a Library"

JEROME MAZZARO. "Between Two Worlds: The Post-Modernism of Randall Jarrell," in *Contemporary Poetry in America*, p. 90.

"The Grown Up"

ROBERT WEISBERG. "Randall Jarrell: The Integrity of his Poetry," *Centennial Review* 17(3), Summer 1973, 241.

"Hohensalzburg: Fantastic Variations on a Theme of Romantic Character"

SISTER M. BERNETTA QUINN. *The Metamorphic Tradition*, pp. 174-81.

"Hope"

LAURENCE PERRINE. *100 American Poems of the Twentieth Century*, pp. 230-33.

"The House in the Wood"

AGNES STEIN. *The Uses of Poetry*, pp. 267-70.

ROBERT WEISBERG. "Randall Jarrell: The Integrity of his Poetry," *Centennial Review* 17(3), Summer 1973, 250-52.

"A Hunt in the Black Forest"

M. L. ROSENTHAL. "Randall Jarrell," in *Seven American Poets from MacLeish to Nemerov*, pp. 153-55.

ROBERT WEISBERG. "Randall Jarrell: The Integrity of his Poetry," *Centennial Review* 17(3), Summer 1973, 248-50.

"In the Ward: The Sacred Wood"

M. L. ROSENTHAL. "Randall Jarrell," in *Seven American Poets from MacLeish to Nemerov*, pp. 149-50.

"Jerome"

FRANCES C. FERGUSON. "Randall Jarrell and the Flotations of Voice," *Georgia Review* 28(3), Fall 1974, 432-35.

"King's Hunt"

SISTER M. BERNETTA QUINN. *The Metamorphic Tradition*, pp. 192-93.

"The Knight, Death, and the Devil"

WALTER B. RIDEOUT. " 'To Change, to Change!': The Poetry of Randall Jarrell," in *Poets in Progress*, pp. 172-73.

"Lady Bates"

M. L. ROSENTHAL. "Randall Jarrell," in *Seven American Poets from MacLeish to Nemerov*, pp. 155-56.

"Losses"

M. L. ROSENTHAL. "Randall Jarrell," in *Seven American Poets from MacLeish to Nemerov*, pp. 147-48.

"The Lost World"

ROBERT WEISBERG. "Randall Jarrell: The Integrity of his Poetry," *Centennial Review* 17(3), Summer 1973, 244-47.

"Love, In Its Separate Being"

JOSEPH WARREN BEACH. "The Cancelling Out — A Note on Recent Poetry," *Accent* 7(4), Summer 1947, 248-49.

"A Lullaby"

WALTER B. RIDEOUT. " 'To Change, to Change!': The Poetry of Randall Jarrell," in *Poets in Progress*, pp. 163-64.

"The Märchen"

M. L. ROSENTHAL. "Randall Jarrell," in *Seven American Poets from MacLeish to Nemerov*, pp. 151-53.

"Mail Call"

VERNON SCANNELL. *Not Without Glory*, pp. 193-94.

"The Metamorphosis"

SISTER M. BERNETTA QUINN. *The Metamorphic Tradition*, pp. 200-1.

"Next Day"

DENIS DONOGHUE. *The Ordinary Universe*, pp. 33-34.

"The Night Before the Night Before Christmas"

SISTER M. BERNETTA QUINN. *The Metamorphic Tradition*, pp. 182-85.

"90 North"

HARRY BROWN and JOHN MILSTEAD. *What the Poem Means*, p. 116.

"On the Railway Platform"

JOSEPH WARREN BEACH. *Obsessive Images*, pp. 178-80.

"The One Who Was Different"

ROBERT WEISBERG. "Randall Jarrell: The Integrity of his Poetry," *Centennial Review* 17(3), Summer 1973, 244-45.

"Orestes at Tauris"

M. L. ROSENTHAL. "Randall Jarrell," in *Seven American Poets from MacLeish to Nemerov*, p. 149.

"The Orient Express"

HARRY BROWN and JOHN MILSTEAD. *What the Poem Means*, p. 117.

"A Quilt-Pattern"

SISTER M. BERNETTA QUINN. *The Metamorphic Tradition*, pp. 192-95.

"A Rhapsody on Irish Themes"

SISTER M. BERNETTA QUINN. *The Metamorphic Tradition*, p. 191.

JARRELL, RANDALL (Cont.)

"2nd Air Force"

> M. L. ROSENTHAL. "Randall Jarrell," in *Seven American Poets from MacLeish to Nemerov*, p. 146.

"Seele im Raum"

> RUSSELL FOWLER. "Randall Jarrell's 'Eland': A Key to Motive and Technique in His Poetry," *Iowa Review* 5(2), Spring 1974, 118-26.
>
> BERTRAND F. RICHARDS. *Explicator* 33(3), November 1974, Item 22.
>
> M. L. ROSENTHAL. "Randall Jarrell," in *Seven American Poets from MacLeish to Nemerov*, pp. 158-60.

"The Skaters"

> M. L. ROSENTHAL. "Randall Jarrell," in *Seven American Poets from MacLeish to Nemerov*, pp. 135-37.

"The Sleeping Beauty: Variation of the Prince"

> SISTER M. BERNETTA QUINN. *The Metamorphic Tradition*, pp. 175-77.

"A Soul"

> SISTER M. BERNETTA QUINN. *The Metamorphic Tradition*, pp. 172-73.

"Thinking of the Lost World"

> JOHN CROWE RANSOM. "The Rugged Way of Genius — A Tribute to Randall Jarrell," *Southern Review*, n.s., 3(2), Spring 1967, 280-81.
>
> ROBERT WEISBERG. "Randall Jarrell: The Integrity of his Poetry," *Centennial Review* 17(3), Summer 1973, 252-55.

"To a Conscript of 1940"

> M. L. ROSENTHAL. "Randall Jarrell," in *Seven American Poets from MacLeish to Nemerov*, pp. 142-43.

"The Truth"

> M. L. ROSENTHAL. "Randall Jarrell," in *Seven American Poets from MacLeish to Nemerov*, pp. 155-57.

"The Venetian Blind"

> SISTER M. BERNETTA QUINN. *The Metamorphic Tradition*, pp. 191-92.

"A Well-to-do Invalid"

> JEROME MAZZARO. "Between Two Worlds: The Post-Modernism of Randall Jarrell," in *Contemporary Poetry in America*, p. 93.
>
> ROBERT WEISBERG. "Randall Jarrell: The Integrity of his Poetry," *Centennial Review* 17(3), Summer 1973, 242-44.

"Where the Rainbow Ends"

> PAUL WILLCOTT. "Randall Jarrell's Eschatological Vision," *Renascence* 18(4), Summer 1966, 210-15.

"Windows"

> M. L. ROSENTHAL. "Randall Jarrell," in *Seven American Poets from MacLeish to Nemerov*, pp. 167-68.

"The Woman at the Washington Zoo"

> CLEANTH BROOKS and ROBERT PENN WARREN. *Understanding Poetry*, fourth ed., pp. 476-82. (Quoting Randall Jarrell)
>
> STANLEY KUNITZ. "The New Books: Some Poets of the Year And Their Language of Transformation," *Harpers Magazine* 223(1335), August 1961, 88-89.
>
> LOUIS UNTERMEYER. *50 Modern American & British Poets*, p. 290.

JEFFERS, ROBINSON

"Apology for Bad Dreams"

> HARRY BROWN and JOHN MILSTEAD. *What the Poem Means*, pp. 117-18.
>
> FREDERIC I. CARPENTER. "Robinson Jeffers and the Torches of Violence," in *The Twenties*, edited by Richard E. Langford and William E. Taylor, p. 14.

"At the Birth of an Age"

> BABETTE DEUTSCH. *Poetry in Our Time*, p. 19; second ed., p. 20.

"The Bloody Sire"

> BENJAMIN W. GRIFFITH. "Robinson Jeffers' 'The Bloody Sire' and Stephen Crane's 'War Is Kind,'" *Notes on Contemporary Literature* 3(1), November 1973, 14-15.

"Christmas Card"

> BABETTE DEUTSCH. *Poetry in Our Time*, pp. 21-22; second ed., pp. 22-23.

"Credo"

> HARRY BROWN and JOHN MILSTEAD. *What the Poem Means*, p. 118.

"The Cruel Falcon"

> ROBERT BOYERS. "A Sovereign Voice: The Poetry of Robinson Jeffers," in *Modern American Poetry*, edited by Jerome Mazzaro, pp. 198-99.

"Crumbs or the Loaf"

> FREDERIC I. CARPENTER. "Robinson Jeffers and the Torches of Violence," in *The Twenties*, edited by Richard E. Langford and William E. Taylor, pp. 15-16.

"Fire on the Hills"

> GEORGE ARMS. *Explicator* 1(7), May 1943, Item 59.

"Hurt Hawks"

> VIRGINIA E. JORGENSEN. "Hearing the Night-Herons: A Lesson on Jeffers' 'Hurt Hawks,'" *English Journal* 51(6), September 1962, 440-42.

"The Inhumanist"

> STEPHEN BLUSTONE. "Robinson Jeffers and the Prophets: On *The Book of Jeremiah* and 'The Inhumanist,'" *Notes on Contemporary Literature* 5(4), September 1975, 2-3.

"Margrave"

> DAVID BULWER LUTYENS. *The Creative Encounter*, pp. 48-49.
>
> HYATT HOWE WAGGONER. *The Heel of Elohim*, pp. 121-29.

"May-June 1940"

> HARRY BROWN and JOHN MILSTEAD. *What the Poem Means*, pp. 119-20.

"Meditation on Saviours"

> WILLIAM SAVAGE. "The 'Savior' in the Poetry of Robinson Jeffers," *American Literature* 15(2), May 1943, 163-64.

"Nova"

> LAURENCE PERRINE. *100 American Poems of the Twentieth Century*, pp. 90-92.

"Ocean"

> LAURENCE PERRINE. *100 American Poems of the Twentieth Century*, pp. 87-90.

"The Purse Seine"

> HARRY BROWN and JOHN MILSTEAD. *What the Poem Means*, p. 121.

LAURENCE PERRINE. *100 American Poems of the Twentieth Century*, pp. 92-94.

M. L. ROSENTHAL. *The Modern Poets*, pp. 157-58.

"Rearmament"

ROBERT BOYERS. "A Sovereign Voice: The Poetry of Robinson Jeffers," *Sewanee Review* 77(3), Summer 1969, 505-7. Reprinted in: *Modern American Poetry*, edited by Jerome Mazzaro, pp. 201-3.

"Return"

ROBERT BOYERS. "A Sovereign Voice: The Poetry of Robinson Jeffers," in *Modern American Poetry*, edited by Jerome Mazzaro, pp. 195-96.

"Roan Stallion"

JOHN R. ALEXANDER. "Conflict in the Narrative Poetry of Robinson Jeffers," *Sewanee Review* 80(1), Winter 1972, 91-92.

HARRY BROWN and JOHN MILSTEAD. *What the Poem Means*, p. 120.

HYATT H. WAGGONER. *American Poets*, pp. 474-75.

"Science"

DELMORE SCHWARTZ. "The Enigma of Robinson Jeffers: I, Sources of Violence," *Poetry* 55(1), October 1939, 34-36. (P)

"Self-criticism in February"

DAVID BULWER LUTYENS. *The Creative Encounter*, pp. 45-46.

"Shine, Perishing Republic"

ROBERT BOYERS. "A Sovereign Voice: The Poetry of Robinson Jeffers," *Sewanee Review* 77(3), Summer 1969, 496-98.

HARRY BROWN and JOHN MILSTEAD. *What the Poem Means*, p. 121.

CHAD WALSH. *Doors into Poetry*, pp. 4-5.

"To the Stone-Cutters"

HARRY BROWN and JOHN MILSTEAD. *What the Poem Means*, pp. 121-22.

"The Tower Beyond Tragedy"

BABETTE DEUTSCH. *Poetry in Our Time*, pp. 19-20; second ed., pp. 20-21.

"Treasure"

HYATT H. WAGGONER. *American Poets*, p. 473.

JEROME, JUDSON

"Aubade"

JUDSON JEROME. "Rivalry with Madmen," *Yale Review* 48(3), March 1959, 346-50.

"From Beowulf to Thomas Hardy"

JUDSON JEROME. "Rivalry with Madmen," *Yale Review* 48(3), March 1959, 350-53.

JOHNSON, EDWARD

"Good News from New-England"

ROGER B. STEIN. "Seascape and the American Imagination: The Puritan Seventeenth Century," *Early American Literature* 7(1), Spring 1972, 26-27.

JOHNSON, JAMES WELDON

"The Creation"

LOIS MILLER. "And God Said, 'That's Good,': An Analysis of James Weldon Johnson's 'The Creation,'" *English Journal* 52(8), November 1963, 644-46.

JOHNSON, JOSEPHINE

"The Island"

DAN JAFFE. "Poets in the Inferno: Civilians, C.O.'s and Combatants," in *The Forties*, pp. 43-44. (P)

JOHNSON, LIONEL

"By the Statue of King Charles at Charing Cross"

F. R. LEAVIS. "'Thought' and Emotional Quality: Notes in the Analysis of Poetry," *Scrutiny* 13(1), Spring 1945, 62-65.

JAMES G. NELSON. "The Nature of Aesthetic Experience in the Poetry of the Nineties: Ernest Dowson, Lionel Johnson, and John Gray," *English Literature in Transition* 17(4), 1974, 230-31.

"Comely and Calm He Rides"

H. P. COLLINS. "A Note on the Classical Principle in Poetry," *Criterion* 3(2), April 1925, 391-94.

"The Dark Angel"

IAIN FLETCHER. "Lionel Johnson: The Dark Angel," in *Interpretations*, pp. 155-78.

"In Falmouth Harbour"

DANIEL RUTENBERG. "Crisscrossing the Bar: Tennyson and Lionel Johnson on Death," *Victorian Poetry* 10(2), Summer 1972, 179-80.

"Magic"

JOHN R. REED. "Mixing Memory and Desire in Late Victorian Literature," *English Literature in Transition* 14(1), 1971, 7.

"Oxford"

F. W. BATESON. *English Poetry*, pp. 235-39.

"Plato in London"

JAMES G. NELSON. "The Nature of Aesthetic Experience in the Poetry of the Nineties: Ernest Dowson, Lionel Johnson, and John Gray," *English Literature in Transition* 17(4), 1974, 230.

JOHN R. REED. "Mixing Memory and Desire in Late Victorian Literature," *English Literature in Transition* 14(1), 1971, 8-9.

"Upon a Drawing"

JOHN R. REED. "Mixing Memory and Desire in Late Victorian Literature," *English Literature in Transition* 14(1), 1971, 9-10.

JOHNSON, SAMUEL

"Battle of the Pygmies and Cranes"

CHRISTOPHER RICKS. "Johnson's 'Battle of the Pygmies and Cranes,'" *Essays in Criticism* 16(3), July 1966, 281-89.

"London"

EDWARD A. BLOOM and LILLIAN D. BLOOM. "Johnson's *London* and the Tools of Scholarship," *Huntington Library Quarterly* 34(2), February 1971, 115-39.

D. V. BOYD. "Vanity and Vacuity: A Reading of Johnson's Verse Satires," *ELH* 39(3), September 1972, 390-96.

J. P. HARDY. *Reinterpretations*, pp. 103-23.

R. T. WILKINSON. "Johnson's *London*: The Ironic Framework," *Concerning Poetry* 4(1), Spring 1971, 27-33.

"On the Death of Mr. Robert Levet"

T. R. BARNES. *English Verse*, pp. 132-33.

MURRAY KRIEGER. *The Classic Vision*, pp. 143-45.

JOHNSON, SAMUEL *(Cont.)*

"On the Death of Mr. Robert Levet" *(cont.)*

> DONALD C. MELL. "Johnson's Moral Elegiacs: Theme and Structure in 'On the Death of Robert Levet,'" *Genre* 5(3), September 1972, 293-306.

> JAMES REEVES and MARTIN SEYMOUR-SMITH. *Inside Poetry*, pp. 30-33.

> SUSIE I. TUCKER and HENRY GIFFORD. *Explicator* 15(7), April 1957, Item 45.

"The Vanity of Human Wishes"

> GEORGE T. AMIS. "The Style of *The Vanity of Human Wishes*," *Modern Language Quarterly* 35(1), March 1974. 16-29.

> Edward A. Bloom. "*The Vanity of Human Wishes*: Reason's Images," *Essays in Criticism* 15(2), April 1965, 181-92.

> D. V. BOYD. "Vanity and Vacuity: A Reading of Johnson's Verse Satires," *ELH* 39(3), September 1972, 396-403.

> WALLACE C. BROWN. "Dramatic Tension in Neoclassic Satire," *College English* 6(5), February 1945, 266-67.

> SANFORD BUDICK. *Poetry of Civilization*, pp. 156-72.

> LEOPOLD DAMROSCH, JR. "On Misreading Eighteenth Century Literature: A Defense," *Eighteenth Century Studies* 8(2), Winter 1974/75, 202-6.

> DONALD DAVIE. "Johnson: The Vanity of Human Wishes," in *Master Poems of the English Language*, pp. 300-3.

> HENRY GIFFORD. "*The Vanity of Human Wishes*," *Review of English Studies*, n.s., 6(22), April 1955, 157-65.

> DONALD GREENE. "On Misreading Eighteenth-Century Literature: A Rejoinder," *Eighteenth Century Studies* 9(1), Fall 1975, 108-18.

> JOHN HARDY. "Hope and Fear in Johnson," *Essays in Criticism* 26(4), October 1976, 292-99.

> FREDERICK W. HILLES. "Johnson's Poetic Fire," in *From Sensibility to Romanticism*, pp. 67-77.

> MURRAY KRIEGER. *The Classic Vision*, pp. 125-42.

> WILLIAM KUPERSMITH. "'More like an Orator than a Philosopher': Rhetorical Structure in *The Vanity of Human Wishes*," *Studies in Philology* 72(4), October 1975, 454-72.

> LAWRENCE LIPKING. "Learning to Read Johnson: *The Vision of Theodore* and *The Vanity of Human Wishes*," *ELH* 43(4), Winter 1976, 527-35.

> PAUL D. MCGLYNN. "Rhetoric as Metaphor in *The Vanity of Human Wishes*," *Studies in English Literature 1500-1900* 15(3), Summer 1975, 473-82.

> C. N. MANLOVE. *Literature and Reality*, pp. 163-66.

> PATRICK O'FLAHERTY. "Johnson as Satirist: A New Look at *The Vanity of Human Wishes*," *ELH* 34(1), March 1967, 78-91.

> PATRICIA MEYER SPACKS. "From Satire to Description," *Yale Review* 58(2), December 1968, 232-48.

> SUSIE I. TUCKER and HENRY GIFFORD. "Johnson's Poetic Imagination," *Review of English Studies*, n.s., 8(31), August 1957, 241-48.

> LEONARD UNGER and WILLIAM VAN O'CONNOR. *Poems for Study*, pp. 308-12.

"The Vision of Theodore"

> LAWRENCE LIPKING. "Learning to Read Johnson: *The Vision of Theodore* and *The Vanity of Human Wishes*," *ELH* 43(4), Winter 1976, 517-27.

JONES, DAVID

"The Dream of Private Clitus"

> Tony Stoneburner. "Notes on prophecy and apocalypse in a time of anarchy and revolution: a trying out," in *Literature in Revolution*, pp. 277-79.

"The Fatigue"

> PETER ORR. "Hear the Voice of the Bard," *Review of English Literature* 8(1), January 1967, 80-83.

> Tony Stoneburner. "Notes on prophecy and apocalypse in a time of anarchy and revolution: a trying out," in *Literature in Revolution*, p. 274.

"King Pellam's Launde"

> MONROE K. SPEARS. "Shapes and Surfaces: David Jones, With a Glance at Charles Tomlinson," *Contemporary Literature* 12(4), Autumn 1971, 408-9.

"The Lady of the Pool"

> MONROE K. SPEARS. "Shapes and Surfaces: David Jones, With a Glance at Charles Tomlinson," *Contemporary Literature* 12(4), Autumn 1971, 241.

"Middle-Sea and Lear-Sea"

> MONROE K. SPEARS. "Shapes and Surfaces: David Jones, With a Glance at Charles Tomlinson," *Contemporary Literature* 12(4), Autumn 1971, 412-13.

"Rite and Fore-Time"

> MONROE K. SPEARS. "Shapes and Surfaces: David Jones, With a Glance at Charles Tomlinson," *Contemporary Literature* 12(4), Autumn 1971, 411-12.

"The Tribune's Visitation"

> MONROE K. SPEARS. "Shapes and Surfaces: David Jones, With a Glance at Charles Tomlinson," *Contemporary Literature* 12(4), Autumn 1971, 415-16.

> Tony Stoneburner. "Notes on prophecy and apocalypse in a time of anarchy and revolution: a trying out," in *Literature in Revolution*, p. 281.

"The Tutelar of the Place"

> Tony Stoneburner. "Notes on prophecy and apocalypse in a time of anarchy and revolution: a trying out," in *Literature in Revolution*, pp. 279-80.

"The Wall"

> Tony Stoneburner. "Notes on prophecy and apocalypse in a time of anarchy and revolution: a trying out," in *Literature in Revolution*, pp. 275-77.

JONES, EBENEZER

"Emily"

> RUSSELL M. GOLDFARB. *Sexual Repression and Victorian Literature*, pp. 107-9.

"Zingalee"

> RUSSELL M. GOLDFARB. *Sexual Repression and Victorian Literature*, pp. 109-10.

JONES, LEROI

see BARAKA, IMAMU AMIRI

JONES, WILLIAM

"On parent knees, a naked newborn child"

> JEROME BEATY and WILLIAM H. MATCHETT. *Poetry From Statement to Meaning*, pp. 141-42.

JONG, ERICA

"The Eggplant Epithalamion"

> LOUIS UNTERMEYER. *50 Modern American & British Poets*, p. 351.

JONSON, BEN

"A Celebration of Charis"

R. V. LECLERCQ. "The Reciprocal Harmony of Jonson's 'A Celebration of Charis,'" *Texas Studies in Literature and Language* 16(4), Winter 1975, 627-50.

ARTHUR F. MAROTTI. "All About Jonson's Poetry," *ELH* 39(2), June 1972, 231-35.

RICHARD S. PETERSON. "Virtue Reconciled to Pleasure: Jonson's 'A Celebration of Charis,'" *Studies in the Literary Imagination* 6(1), April 1973, 219-67.

SARA VAN DEN BERG. "The Play of Wit and Love: Demetrius' *On Style* and Jonson's 'A Celebration of Charis,'" *ELH* 41(1), Spring 1974, 26-36.

G. J. WEINBERGER. "Jonson's Mock-Encomiastic 'Celebration of Charis,'" *Genre* 4(4), December 1971, 305-28.

"Clerimont's Song"
see "Still to be neat, still to be dressed"

"Drink to me only with thine eyes"
see "Song To Celia"

"Echo's Song"

WILLIAM V. SPANOS. "The Real Toad in the Jonsonian Garden: Resonance in the Nondramatic Poetry," *Journal of English and Germanic Philology* 68(1), January 1969, 10-11. Reprinted in: *Seventeenth Century English Poetry*, revised ed., pp. 209-10.

"An Elegy" ("Let me be what I am: as Virgil cold")
ANNE FERRY. *All in War with Time*, pp. 153-54.

BARBARA HUTCHISON. "Ben Jonson's 'Let Me Be What I Am': An Apology in Disguise," *English Language Notes* 2(3), March 1965, 185-90.

"An Elegy" ("Since you must go, and I must bid farewell")
EARL MINER. *The Cavalier Mode from Jonson to Cotton*, pp. 244-45.

"An Elegy" ("Though beauty be the mark of praise")
ANN FERRY. *All in War with Time*, pp. 168-72.

JUDITH K. GARDINER. "Syntax and the Platonic Ladder: Jonson's 'Though Beautie be the Marke of Praise,'" *Concerning Poetry* 8(1), Spring 1975, 35-40.

EARL MINER. *The Cavalier Mode from Jonson to Cotton*, pp. 11-12.

YVOR WINTERS. "Poetic Styles, Old and New," in *Four Poets on Poetry*, pp. 62-65.

"An Elegy on the Lady Jane Paulet, Marchioness of Winton"
JOHN LEMLY. "Masks and Self-Portraits in Jonson's Late Poetry," *ELH* 44(2), Summer 1977, 256-58.

GEOFFREY WALTON. "The Tone of Ben Jonson's Poetry," in *Seventeenth Century English Poetry*, pp. 211-12; revised ed., pp. 170-71.

"Epigram to a Friend, and Son" (*Underwood*, LXIX)
HUGH MACLEAN. "Ben Jonson's Poems: Notes on the Ordered Society," in *Seventeenth Century English Poetry*, revised ed., p. 179.

"An Epigram to William, Earl of Newcastle"
IRA CLARK. "Ben Jonson's Imitation," *Criticism* 20(2), Spring 1978, 126-27.

"An Epistle Answering to One that Asked to be Sealed of the Tribe of Ben" (*Underwood*, XLVII)
HUGH MACLEAN. "Ben Jonson's Poems: Notes on the Ordered Society," in *Seventeenth Century English Poetry*, revised ed., pp. 180-81.

"An Epistle Mendicant"
GEORGE BURKE JOHNSTON. "'An Epistle Mendicant' by Ben Jonson," *Notes & Queries*, n.s., 1(11), November 1954, 471. (P)

"An Epistle to a Friend" ("Sir, I am thankful, first to heaven for you")
HUGH MACLEAN. "Ben Jonson's Poems: Notes on the Ordered Society," in *Seventeenth Century English Poetry*, revised ed., p. 179.

"Epistle to a Friend" ("They are not sir, worst owers, that do pay")
HUGH MACLEAN. "Ben Jonson's Poems: Notes on the Ordered Society," in *Seventeenth Century English Poetry*, revised ed., pp. 179-80.

"An Epistle to a Friend, to Persuade Him to the Wars"
EARL MINER. *The Cavalier Mode from Jonson to Cotton*, pp. 171-74.

RICHARD C. NEWTON. "'Goe, quit 'hem all': Ben Jonson and Formal Verse Satire," *Studies in English Literature 1500-1900* 16(1), Winter 1976, 105-16.

"Epistle To Elizabeth, Countess of Rutland"
JAMES D. GARRISON. "Time and Value in Jonson's 'Epistle to Elizabeth Countesse of Rutland,'" *Concerning Poetry* 8(2), Fall 1975, 53-58.

ACHSAH GUIBBORY. "The Poet as Myth Maker: Ben Jonson's Poetry of Praise," *Clio* 5(3), Spring 1976, 315-17. (P)

HUGH MACLEAN. "Ben Jonson's Poems: Notes on the Ordered Society," in *Seventeenth Century English Poetry*, revised ed., pp. 196-97.

"Epistle To Katherine, Lady Aubigny"
ANTHONY LABRANCHE. "Samuel Daniel: A Voice of Thoughtfulness," in *The Rhetoric of Renaissance Poetry*, pp. 129-30.

HUGH MACLEAN. "Ben Jonson's Poems: Notes on the Ordered Society," in *Seventeenth Century English Poetry*, revised ed., p. 195.

EARL MINER. *The Cavalier Mode from Jonson to Cotton*, pp. 170-71.

"An Epistle to Master John Seldon"
EARL MINER. *The Cavalier Mode from Jonson to Cotton*, pp. 272-73.

"Epistle to My Lady Covell"
ANNE FERRY. *All in War with Time*, pp. 155-57.

"An Epistle to Sir Edward Sackville, now Earl of Dorset"
HUGH MACLEAN. "Ben Jonson's Poems: Notes on the Ordered Society," in *Seventeenth Century English Poetry*, revised ed., p. 194.

"Epitaph on Elizabeth, L. H."
HOWARD S. BABB. "The 'Epitaph on Elizabeth, L. H.' and Ben Jonson's Style," *Journal of English and Germanic Philology* 62(4), October 1963, 738-44.

JOHN M. MAJOR. "A Reading of Jonson's 'Epitaph on Elizabeth, L. H.,'" *Studies in Philology* 73(1), January 1976, 62-86.

STEPHEN E. TABACHNICK. *Explicator* 29(9), May 1971, Item 77.

"Epitaph on Salomon Pavy, a Child of Queen Elizabeth's Chapel"
ANNE FERRY. *All in War with Time*, pp. 201-3.

LOUIS F. MAY. *Explicator* 20(2), October 1961, Item 16.

"An Execration upon Vulcan"
EARL MINER. *The Cavalier Mode from Jonson to Cotton*, pp. 68-69.

JONSON, BEN *(Cont.)*

"A Fit of Rime Against Rime"
> GEORGE HEMPHILL. *Explicator* 12(8), June 1954, Item 50.

"The Ghyrlond of the Blessed Virgin Marie"
> PAUL M. CUBETA. "Ben Jonson's Religious Lyrics," *Journal of English and Germanic Philology* 62(1), January 1963, 98-100.

"Her Man Described by Her Own Dictamen"
> ANNE FERRY. *All in War with Time,* pp. 161-62.

"Her Triumph"
> MARIE BORROFF. "The Triumph of Charis: Through *Swards,* Not *Swords,*" *English Language Notes* 8(4), June 1971, 257-59.
> ANNE FERRY. *All in War with Time,* pp. 130-33.
> WILLIAM V. SPANOS. "The Real Toad in the Jonsonian Garden: Resonance in the Nondramatic Poetry," in *Seventeenth Century English Poetry,* revised ed., pp. 211-13.

"His Excuse for Loving"
> ANNE FERRY. *All in War with Time,* pp. 157-61.

"A Hymn on the Nativity of My Saviour"
> PAUL M. CUBETA. "Ben Jonson's Religious Lyrics," *Journal of English and Germanic Philology* 62(1), January 1963, 107-10.
> WILLIAM V. SPANOS. "The Real Toad in the Jonsonian Garden: Resonance in the Nondramatic Poetry," in *Seventeenth Century English Poetry,* revised ed., p. 211.

"Hymn to Cynthia"
> PHYLLIS RACKIN. "Poetry Without Paradox: Jonson's 'Hymne' to Cynthia," *Criticism* 4(3), Summer 1962, 186-96.

"Inviting a Friend to Supper"
> LEONARD DEAN. *English Masterpieces,* edited by William Frost, Maynard Mack, and Leonard Dean, vol. 3: *Renaissance Poetry,* p. 14.
> JACK SHADOIAN. "'Inviting a Friend to Supper': Aspects of Jonson's Craft and Personality," *Concerning Poetry* 3(2), Fall 1970, 29-35.

"It is not growing like a tree"
> JAMES E. MILLER, JR. and BERNICE SLOTE. "Meaning and Experience," in *The Dimensions of Poetry,* pp. 29-31.

"It was beauty that I saw"
> see "A Vision of Beauty"

"My Answer: The Poet to the Painter" (*Underwood* LII)
> ANNE FERRY. *All in War with Time,* pp. 149-51.

"My Picture Left in Scotland" (*Underwood* IX)
> ANNE FERRY. *All in War with Time,* pp. 172-76.

"An Ode" ("Helen, did Homer never see")
> ANNE FERRY. *All in War with Time,* pp. 135-37.
> ACHSAH GUIBBORY. "The Poet as Myth Maker: Ben Jonson's Poetry of Praise," *Clio* 5(3), Spring 1976, 323-24.

"An Ode" ("High-spirited friend")
> WALTER R. DAVIS. *Explicator* 31(9), May 1973, Item 70.
> SARA VAN DEN BERG. *Explicator* 35(2), Winter 1976, 24-26.

"An Ode, or Song, by all the Muses"
> WILLIAM V. SPANOS. "The Real Toad in the Jonsonian Garden: Resonance in the Nondramatic Poetry," in *Seventeenth Century English Poetry,* revised ed., pp. 208-9.

"Ode: To Sir William Sidney, on His Birthday"
> HUGH MACLEAN. "Ben Jonson's Poems: Notes on the Ordered Society," in *Seventeenth Century English Poetry,* revised ed., p. 191.
> D. S. J. PARSONS. "The Odes of Drayton and Jonson," *Queen's Quarterly* 75(4), Winter 1968, 679-81.

"On Cheverel the Lawyer"
> R. V. YOUNG, JR. "Style and Structure in Jonson's Epigrams," *Criticism* 17(3), Summer 1975, 216.

"On Gut" (*Epigrams,* CXVIII)
> R. V. YOUNG, JR. "Style and Structure in Jonson's Epigrams," *Criticism* 17(3), Summer 1975, 216-17.

"On Lieutenant Shift" (*Epigrams,* XII)
> R. V. YOUNG, JR. "Style and Structure in Jonson's Epigrams," *Criticism* 17(3), Summer 1975, 217-19.

"On Lucy, Countess of Bedford" (*Epigrams,* LXXVI)
> ANNE FERRY. *All in War with Time,* pp. 142-49.
> HARRIS FRIEDBERG. "Ben Jonson's Poetry: Pastoral, Georgic, Epigram," *English Literary Renaissance* 4(1), Winter 1974, 114-16.
> R. V. YOUNG, JR. "Style and Structure in Jonson's Epigrams," *Criticism* 17(3), Summer 1975, 210-11.

"On My First Daughter" (*Epigrams,* XXII)
> ROBERTS W. FRENCH. "Reading Jonson: *Epigrammes* 22 and 45," *Concerning Poetry* 10(1), Spring 1977, 5-9.
> WILLIAM V. SPANOS. "The Real Toad in the Jonsonian Garden: Resonance in the Nondramatic Poetry," *Journal of English and Germanic Philology* 68(1), January 1969, 11-12. Reprinted in: *Seventeenth Century English Poetry,* revised ed., pp. 210-11.

"On My First Son" (*Epigrams,* XLV)
> ROBERTS W. FRENCH. "Reading Jonson: *Epigrammes* 22 and 45," *Concerning Poetry* 10(1), Spring 1977, 9-11.
> WILLIAM B. BACHE. "Verbal Complexity in 'On My First Son,'" *CEA Critic* 32(4), January 1970, 12.
> L. A. BEAURLINE. "The Selective Principle in Jonson's Shorter Poems," *Criticism* 8(1), Winter 1966, 65-70.
> ANNE FERRY. *All in War with Time,* pp. 176-81.
> ROBERT W. FRENCH. "Reading Jonson: *Epigrammes* 22 and 45," *Concerning Poetry* 10(1), Spring 1977, 9-11.
> W. DAVID KAY. "The Christian Wisdom of Ben Jonson's 'On My First Sonne,'" *Studies in English Literature 1500-1900* 11(1), Winter 1971, 125-36.
> J. Z. KRONENFELD. "The Father Found: Consolation Achieved Through Love in Ben Jonson's 'On My First Sonne,'" *Studies in Philology* 75(1), Winter 1978, 64-83.
> MARY I. OATES. "Jonson's 'Ode Pindarick' and the Doctrine of Imitation," *Papers on Language and Literature* 11(2), Spring 1975, 134.
> ROBERT PINSKY. *The Situation of Poetry,* pp. 137-38.
> SHARON SANDERS RANDO. "'On My First Sonne': The Aesthetic Radical of Cavalier Poetry," *Concerning Poetry* 9(1), Spring 1976, 27-30.
> R. V. YOUNG, JR. "Style and Structure in Jonson's Epigrams," *Criticism* 17(3), Summer 1975, 205-7.

"On Something that Walks Somewhere" (*Epigrams,* XI)
> EDGAR F. DANIELS. *Explicator* 33(7), March 1975, Item 58.

RONALD E. MCFARLAND. *Explicator* 31(4), December 1972, Item 26.

"On Spies" (*Epigrams*, LIX)

G. A. E. PARFITT. "The Poetry of Ben Jonson," *Essays in Criticism* 18(1), January 1968, 18-31.

"On the Famous Voyage"

PETER E. MEDINE. "Object and Intent in Jonson's 'Famous Voyage,'" *Studies in English Literature 1500-1900* 15(1), Winter 1975, 97-110.

"On The Same Beast" (*Epigrams*, XXVI)

R. V. YOUNG, JR. "Style and Structure in Jonson's Epigrams," *Criticism* 17(3), Summer 1975, 215-16.

"On the Union" (*Epigrams*, V)

R. V. YOUNG, JR. "Style and Structure in Jonson's Epigrams," *Criticism* 17(3), Summer 1975, 207-8.

"The Pattern of Piety"

PERCY SIMPSON. "A Westminster Schoolboy and Ben Jonson," *Times Literary Supplement,* 27 November 1953, p. 761.

"The Sinner's Sacrifice"

PAUL M. CUBETA. "Ben Jonson's Religious Lyrics," *Journal of English and Germanic Philology* 62(1), January 1963, 103-7.

"A Song" ("Oh do not wanton with those eyes")

PETER STEESE. *Explicator* 21(4), December 1962, Item 31.

"Song To Celia" ("Drink to me only with thine eyes")

L. A. BEAURLINE. "The Selective Principle in Jonson's Shorter Poems," *Criticism* 8(1), Winter 1966, 72-73.

WILLIAM EMPSON. *Seven Types of Ambiguity,* pp. 306-7; second and third eds., pp. 242-43. (P)

MURRAY KRIEGER. *The Classic Vision,* pp. 69-71.

EARL MINER. *The Cavalier Mode from Jonson to Cotton,* pp. 102-3.

GERALD SANDERS and RALPH P. BOAS. *Explicator* 1(4), February 1943, Item 28.

WILLIAM V. SPANOS. "The Real Toad in the Jonsonian Garden: Resonance in the Nondramatic Poetry," *Journal of English and Germanic Philology* 68(1), January 1969, 7-8. Reprinted in: *Seventeenth Century English Poetry,* revised ed., pp. 206-7.

MARSHALL VAN DEUSEN. "Criticism and Ben Jonson's 'To Celia,'" *Essays in Criticism* 7(1), January 1957, 95-103.

"A Speech according to *Horace*"

RICHARD C. NEWTON. "'Goe, quit 'hem all': Ben Jonson and Formal Verse Satire," *Studies in English Literature 1500-1900* 16(1), Winter 1976, 114-15.

"Still to be neat, still to be dressed"

C. N. MANLOVE. *Literature and Reality,* pp. 16-18.

"To Benjamin Rudyard" (*Epigrams*, CXXII)

R. V. YOUNG, JR. "Style and Structure in Jonson's Epigrams," *Criticism* 17(3), Summer 1975, 213-14.

"To Fine Lady Would-Be" (*Epigrams*, LXII)

R. V. YOUNG, JR. "Style and Structure in Jonson's Epigrams," *Criticism* 17(3), Summer 1975, 219-21.

"To Heaven"

JEROME BEATY and WILLIAM H. MATCHETT. *Poetry From Statement to Meaning,* pp. 116-17.

PAUL M. CUBETA. "Ben Jonson's Religious Lyrics," *Journal of English and Germanic Philology* 62(1), January 1963, 101-2.

JUDITH K. GARDINER. "'To Heaven,'" *Concerning Poetry* 6(2), Fall 1973, 26-36.

WILLIAM KERRIGAN. "Ben Jonson Full of Shame and Scorn," *Studies in the Literary Imagination* 6(1), April 1973, 204-14.

PHILIP C. MCGUIRE. "Private Prayer and English Poetry in the Early Seventeenth Century," *Studies in English Literature 1500-1900* 14(1), Winter 1974, 72-75.

YVOR WINTERS. "Poetic Styles, Old and New," in *Four Poets on Poetry,* pp. 65-69.

"To His Lady, Then Mistress Cary" (*Epigrams* CXXVI)

ANNE FERRY. *All in War with Time,* pp. 134-35, 137-38.

"To John Donne" ("Donne, the delight of Phoebus, and each Muse")

STANLEY M. WIERSMA. *Explicator* 25(1), September 1966, Item 4.

"To Lucy, Countess of Bedford, with Mr. Donne's Satires"

HUGH MACLEAN. "Ben Jonson's Poems: Notes on the Ordered Society," in *Seventeenth Century English Poetry,* revised ed., pp. 192-93.

"To Mary Lady Wroth" ("How well, fair crown of your fair sex, might be")

PETER FELLOWES. *Explicator* 31(5), January 1973, Item 36.

ANNE FERRY. *All in War with Time,* pp. 138-42.

HARRIS FRIEDBERG. "Ben Jonson's Poetry: Pastoral, Georgic, Epigram," *English Literary Renaissance* 4(1), Winter 1974, 124-25.

"To My Muse" (*Epigrams*, LXV)

EDWARD PARTRIDGE. "Jonson's *Epigrammes*: The Named and the Nameless," *Studies in the Literary Imagination* 6(1), April 1973, 162-64.

"To Penshurst"

PAUL M. CUBETA. "A Jonsonian Ideal: 'To Penshurst,'" *Philological Quarterly* 42(4 Suppl.), October 1963, 14-24.

ALASTAIR FOWLER. "The 'Better Marks' of Jonson's *To Penshurst*," *Review of English Studies,* n.s., 24(95), August 1973, 266-82. Reprinted in: Alistair Fowler. *Conceitful Thought,* pp. 114-34.

HARRIS FRIEDBERG. "Ben Jonson's Poetry: Pastoral, Georgic, Epigram," *English Literary Renaissance* 4(1), Winter 1974, 127-36.

C. N. MANLOVE. *Literature and Reality,* pp. 19-26.

CHARLES MOLESWORTH. "'To Penshurst' and Jonson's Historical Imagination," *Clio* 1(2), February 1972, 5-13.

ANTHONY MORTIMER. "The Feigned Commonwealth in the Poetry of Ben Jonson," *Studies in English Literature 1500-1900* 13(1), Winter 1973, 73-79.

G. A. E. PARFITT. "Ethical Thought and Ben Jonson's Poetry," *Studies in English Literature 1500-1900* 9(1), Winter 1969, 123-26.

J. C. A. RATHMELL. "Jonson, Lord Lisle, and Penshurst," *English Literary Renaissance* 1(3), Autumn 1971, 250-60.

GAYLE EDWARD WILSON. "Jonson's Use of the Bible and the Great Chain of Being in 'To Penshurst,'" *Studies in English Literature 1500-1900* 8(1), Winter 1968, 77-89.

"To Pertinax Cob" (*Epigrams*, LXIX)

R. V. YOUNG, JR. "Style and Structure in Jonson's Epigrams," *Criticism* 17(3), Summer 1975, 214-15.

JONSON, BEN *(Cont.)*

"To Robert Cecil" ("Not glad, like those that have new hopes or suits")

> R. V. YOUNG, JR. "Style and Structure in Jonson's Epigrams," *Criticism* 17(3), Summer 1975, 208-10.

"To Sir Luckless Woo-All" *(Epigrams, XLVI)*

> ROBERT EARLEY. "Sir Luckless Woo-all's 'Wast Wife' and the *OED* (Jonson's *Epigramme* XLVI)," *English Language Notes* 12(4), June 1975, 265-68.

"To Sir Henry Nevil" *(Epigrams, CIX)*

> EDWARD PARTRIDGE. "Jonson's *Epigrammes*: The Named and the Nameless," *Studies in the Literary Imagination* 6(1), April 1973, 184-85.

"To Sir Henry Savile" *(Epigrams, XCV)*

> EDWARD PARTRIDGE. "Jonson's *Epigrammes*: The Named and the Nameless," *Studies in the Literary Imagination* 6(1), April 1973, 176-78.

"To Sir Robert Wroth"

> HUGH MACLEAN. "Ben Jonson's Poems: Notes on the Ordered Society," in *Seventeenth Century English Poetry,* revised ed., pp. 193-94.
>
> ANTHONY MORTIMER. "The Feigned Commonwealth in the Poetry of Ben Jonson," *Studies in English Literature 1500-1900* 13(1), Winter 1973, 76-79.

"To Susan, Countess of Montgomery" *(Epigrams, CIV)*

> HARRIS FRIEDBERG. "Ben Jonson's Poetry: Pastoral, Georgic, Epigram," *English Literary Renaissance* 4(1), Winter 1974, 125-26.
>
> EDWARD PARTRIDGE. "Jonson's *Epigrammes*: The Named and the Nameless," *Studies in the Literary Imagination* 6(1), April 1973, 189.

"To the Ghost of Martial" *(Epigrams, XXXVI)*

> IRA CLARK. "Ben Jonson's Imitation," *Criticism* 20(2), Spring 1978, 122-23.

"To the Immortal Memory and Friendship of That Noble Pair, Sir Lucius Cary and Sir H. Morison"

> IAN DONALDSON. "Jonson's Ode to Sir Lucius Cary and Sir H. Morison," *Studies in the Literary Imagination* 6(1), April 1973, 139-52.
>
> GEORGE HELD. "Jonson's Pindaric on Friendship," *Concerning Poetry* 3(1), Spring 1970, 29-41.
>
> WILLIAM KERRIGAN. "Ben Jonson Full of Shame and Scorn," *Studies in the Literary Imagination* 6(1), April 1973, 214-17.
>
> JOHN LEMLY. "Masks and Self-Portraits in Jonson's Late Poetry," *ELH* 44(2), Summer 1977, 258-63.
>
> EARL MINER. *The Cavalier Mode from Jonson to Cotton,* pp. 71-74, 153-54.
>
> MARY I. OATES. *Explicator* 33(1), September 1974, Item 6.
>
> MARY I. OATES. "Jonson's 'Ode Pindarick' and the Doctrine of Imitation," *Papers on Language and Literature* 11(2), Spring 1975, 126-48.
>
> JOSEPH H. SUMMERS. *The Heirs of Donne and Jonson,* pp. 37-39.
>
> SUSANNE WOODS. "Ben Jonson's Cary-Morison Ode: Some Observations on Structure and Form," *Studies in English Literature 1500-1900* 18(1), Winter 1978, 57-74.

"To the Memory of My Beloved, The Author, Mr. William Shakespeare, And What He Hath Left Us"

> FRED M. FEBROW. "Disclaimers Reclaimed: A Consideration of Jonson's Praise of Shakespeare," *Essays in Literature* 2(1), Spring 1975, 24-31.

> ACHSAH GUIBBORY. "The Poet as Myth Maker: Ben Jonson's Poetry of Praise," *Clio* 5(3), Spring 1976, 324-27.
>
> EARL MINER. *The Cavalier Mode from Jonson to Cotton,* pp. 137-41.
>
> AVON JACK MURPHY. "The Critical Elegy of Earlier Seventeenth-Century England," *Genre* 5(1), March 1972, 82-83. (P)
>
> JAMES REEVES and MARTIN SEYMOUR-SMITH. *Inside Poetry,* pp. 49-52.
>
> SARA VAN DEN BERG. " 'The Paths I Meant unto Thy Praise': Jonson's Poem for Shakespeare," *Shakespeare Studies* 11(1978), 207-18.

"To William, Earl of Pembroke"

> EARL MINER. *The Cavalier Mode from Jonson to Cotton,* pp. 273-74.
>
> EDWARD PARTRIDGE. "Jonson's *Epigrammes*: The Named and the Nameless," *Studies in the Literary Imagination* 6(1), April 1973, 154-55.

"To William Roe" *(Epigrams, CXXVIII)*

> EDWARD PARTRIDGE. "Jonson's *Epigrammes*: The Named and the Nameless," *Studies in the Literary Imagination* 6(1), April 1973, 197-98.
>
> R. V. YOUNG, JR. "Style and Structure in Jonson's Epigrams," *Criticism* 17(3), Summer 1975, 211-12.

"A Vision of Beauty"

> EARL DANIELS. *The Art of Reading Poetry,* pp. 200-1.
>
> BARBARA EVERETT. "Ben Jonson's 'A Vision of Beauty,' " *Critical Quarterly* 1(3), Autumn 1959, 238-44.

"Why I Write Not of Love"

> ANNE FERRY. *All in War with Time,* pp. 163-68, 171-72.

JOSSELYN, JOHN

"And the bitter storm augments; the wild winds rage"

> ROGER B. STEIN. "Seascape and the American Imagination: The Puritan Seventeenth Century," *Early American Literature* 7(1), Spring 1972, 29-30.

JOYCE, JAMES

"Chamber Music"

> ZACK BOWEN. "Goldenhair: Joyce's Archetypal Female," *Literature and Psychology* 17(4), 1967, 219-28.

"Ecce Puer"

> MARVIN FISHER. "James Joyce's 'Ecce Puer': The Return of the Prodding Gaul," *University of Kansas City Review* 25(4), Summer 1959, 265-71.
>
> LAWRENCE RICHARD HOLMES. *Explicator* 13(2), November 1954, Item 12.
>
> RICHARD M. KAIN. *Explicator* 14(5), February 1956, Item 29.

"Lean out of the Window"

> AGNES STEIN. *The Uses of Poetry,* pp. 10-13.

"Our broken cries and mournful lays"

> BARBARA HARDY. *The Advantage of Lyric,* pp. 8-10.

JUSTICE, DONALD

"Anonymous Drawing"

> PAT LAMORTE. "The 'Ancient Rules' — A Vanishing Species?" *Georgia Review* 27(4), Winter 1973, 499-500.

K

KAVANAGH, PATRICK

"The Great Hunger"

WILLIAM A. FAHEY. "Patrick Kavanagh: A Comment," *Renascence* 21(2), Winter 1969, 83-86.

BRENDAN KENNELLY. "Patrick Kavanagh," *Ariel* 1(3), July 1970, 12-16.

ALAN WARNER. "A Poet of the Countryside," *Review of English Literature* 5(3), July 1964, 80-83.

"Intimate Parnasus"

BRENDAN KENNELLY. "Patrick Kavanagh," *Ariel* 1(3), July 1970, 23-24.

"Primrose"

DUDLEY FITTS. "Loving Evocation of Irish Life," *New York Times Book Review*, 24 August 1947, p. 10.

"A Soul for Sale"

BRENDAN KENNELLY. "Patrick Kavanagh," *Ariel* 1(3), July 1970, 18.

KEATS, JOHN

"After Dark Vapours"

PAUL R. BAUMGARTNER. "Keats: Theme and Image in a Sonnet," *Keats-Shelley Journal* 8(1), Winter 1959, 11-14.

"La Belle Dame Sans Merci"

GÉMINO H. ABAD. *A Formal Approach to Lyric Poetry*, pp. 109-15.

FREDERICK L. BEATY. *Light from Heaven*, pp. 185-86.

HAROLD BLOOM. *The Visionary Company*, pp. 375-78.

BERNARD BREYER. *Explicator* 6(3), December 1947, Item 18.

C. DAY-LEWIS. *The Lyric Impulse*, pp. 68-69.

ROBERT GRAVES. "Keats: La Belle Dame Sans Merci," in *Master Poems of the English Language*, pp. 595-99.

DON A. KEISTER. *Explicator* 5(4), February 1947, Item 29.

KARL KROEBER. *Romantic Narrative Art*, pp. 36-41.

L. G. LOCKE. *Explicator* 5(1), October 1946, Item 1.

T. O. MABBOTT. *Explicator* 5(7), May 1947, Item 50.

FRED B. MILLET. *Reading Poetry*, pp. 64-65; second ed., pp. 81-82.

JAMES TWITCHELL. "La Belle Dame as Vampire," *CEA Critic* 37(4), May 1975, 31-33.

LEON WALDOFF. "Porphyro's Imagination and Keats's Romanticism," *Journal of English and Germanic Philology* 76(2), April 1977, 191.

EARL WASSERMAN. "La Belle Dame Sans Merci," in *English Romantic Poets*, pp. 365-79.

A. HYATT WILLIAMS. "Keats' 'La Belle Dame Sans Merci': The Bad-Breast Mother," *American Imago* 23(1), Spring 1966, 63-81.

ARTHUR WORMHOUDT. *The Demon Lover*, pp. 75-76.

"Bright Star"

F. W. BATESON. *English Poetry*, pp. 10-11.

RAYMOND BENOIT. *Single Nature's Double Name*, pp. 44-45.

HAROLD BLOOM. *The Visionary Company*, pp. 425-27.

CLEANTH BROOKS, JOHN THIBAUT PURSER, and ROBERT PENN WARREN. *An Approach to Literature*, pp. 481-82; second ed., pp. 481-82; third ed., pp. 358-59.

NEWELL F. FORD. "Holy Living and Holy Dying in Keats's Poetry," *Keats-Shelley Journal* 20 (1971), 49.

MARTIN KALLICH. "John Keats's Dispassionate Star: A Contextual Analysis," *Ball State Teachers College Forum* 5(1), Winter 1964, 11-16.

G. WILSON KNIGHT. *The Starlit Dome*, pp. 304-5.

DAVID ORMEROD. "Nature's Eremite: Keats and the Liturgy of Passion," *Keats-Shelley Journal* 16 (Winter 1967), 73-77.

M. L. ROSENTHAL. *Poetry and the Common Life*, pp. 123-25.

"The Cap and Bells"

HOWARD O. BROGAN. "'*The Cap and Bells*, or *The Jealousies*'?" *New York Public Library Bulletin* 77(3), Spring 1974, 298-313.

MARTIN HALPERN. "Keats and the 'Spirit that Laughest,'" *Keats-Shelley Journal* 15 (Winter 1966), 81-86.

"Epistle to John Hamilton Reynolds"

RICHARD BENVENUTO. "'The Balance of Good and Evil' in Keats's Letters and 'Lamia,'" *Journal of English and Germanic Philology* 71(1), January 1972, 3-4.

MICHAEL G. COOKE. *The Romantic Will*, pp. 161-64.

ALBERT GÉRARD. "Romance and Reality: Continuity and Growth in Keats's View of Art," *Keats-Shelley Journal* 11 (Winter 1962), 19-23.

MARTIN HALPERN. "Keats and the 'Spirit that Laughest,'" *Keats-Shelley Journal* 15 (Winter 1966), 73-75.

KEATS, JOHN *(Cont.)*

"Epistle to John Hamilton Reynolds" *(cont.)*

MARY VISICK. " 'Tease us out of thought': Keats's *Epistle to Reynolds* and the Odes," *Keats-Shelley Journal* 15 (Winter 1966), 87-98.

"The Eve of St. Agnes"

GÉMINO H. ABAD. *A Formal Approach to Lyric Poetry*, pp. 115-16.

G. DOUGLAS ATKINS. "*The Eve of St. Agnes* Reconsidered," *Tennessee Studies in Literature* 18 (1973), 113-32.

FREDERICK L. BEATY. *Light from Heaven*, pp. 183-85.

ARTHUR H. BELL. " 'The Depth of Things': Keats and Human Space," *Keats-Shelley Journal* 23 (1974), 82-87.

HAROLD BLOOM. *The Visionary Company*, pp. 369-75.

JAMES D. BOULGER. "Keats' Symbolism," *ELH* 28(3), September 1961, 254-59.

HARRY BROWN and JOHN MILSTEAD. *What the Poem Means*, pp. 125-26.

C. F. BURGESS. " 'The Eve of St. Agnes': One Way to the Poem," *English Journal* 54(5), May 1965, 389-94.

ARTHUR CARR. "John Keats' Other 'Urn,' " *University of Kansas City Review* 20(4), Summer 1954, 237-42.

ALICE CHANDLER. " 'The Eve of St. Agnes' and 'Porphyria's Lover,' " *Victorian Poetry* 3(4), Autumn 1965, 273-74.

MARIAN HOLLINGSWORTH CUSAC. "Keats as Enchanter: An Organizing Principle of *The Eve of St. Agnes*," *Keats-Shelley Journal* 17 (Winter 1968), 113-19.

R. H. FOGLE. "A Reading of Keats's 'Eve of St. Agnes,' " *College English* 6(6), March 1945, 325-28.

GAIL MCMURRAY GIBSON. "Ave Madeline: Ironic Annunciation in Keats's 'The Eve of St. Agnes,' " *Keats-Shelley Journal* 26 (1977), 39-50.

WILLIAM J. GRACE. "Teaching Poetic Appreciation Through Quantitative Analysis," *College English* 1(3), December 1939, 224-26.

BARRY EDWARD GROSS. "*The Eve of St. Agnes* and *Lamia*: Paradise Won, Paradise Lost," *Bucknell Review* 13(2), May 1965, 47-57.

PETER GRUDIN. "Keats' 'The Eve of Saint Agnes,' " *CEA Critic* 37(3), March 1975, 10-11.

JAMES R. KREUZER. *Elements of Poetry*, pp. 14-16, 125-32.

KARL KROEBER. *The Artifice of Reality*, pp. 108-10.

ROSEMARIE MAIER. "The Bitch and the Bloodhound: Generic Similarity in 'Christabel' and 'The Eve of St. Agnes,' " *Journal of English and Germanic Philology* 70(1), January 1971, 62-75.

NORMAN NATHAN. "Flesh Made Soul," *The Personalist* 42(2), Spring 1961, 198-202.

MICHAEL RAGUSSIS. "Narrative Structure and the Problem of the Divided Reader in *The Eve of St. Agnes*," *ELH* 42(3), Fall 1975, 378-94.

MICHAEL RAGUSSIS. *The Subterfuge of Art*, pp. 70-84.

ALLAN RODWAY. *The Romantic Conflict*, pp. 234-35.

LUCIO P. RUOTOLO. "Keats and Kierkegaard: The Tragedy of Two Worlds," *Renascence* 16(4), Summer 1964, 178-83.

ROGER SHARROCK. "Keats and the Young Lovers," *Review of English Literature* 2(1), January 1961, 80-85.

STUART M. SPERRY, JR. "Romance as Wish-Fulfillment: Keats's *The Eve of St. Agnes*," *Studies in Romanticism* 10(1), Winter 1971, 27-43.

WILLIAM STAFFORD. "Keats: The Eve of St. Agnes," in *Master Poems of the English Language*, pp. 609-12.

WILLIAM C. STEPHENSON. "The Performing Narrator in Keats's Poetry," *Keats-Shelley Journal* 26 (1977), 55-60.

JACK STILLINGER. "The Hoodwinking of Madeline: Scepticism in 'The Eve of St. Agnes,' " *Studies in Philology* 58(3), July 1961, 533-55.

JAMES B. TWITCHELL. "Porphyro as 'Famish'd Pilgrim': The Hoodwinking of Madeline Continued," *Ball State University Forum* 19(2), Spring 1978, 56-65.

LEON WALDOFF. "Porphyro's Imagination and Keats's Romanticism," *Journal of English and Germanic Philology* 76(2), April 1977, 177-89.

REGINALD R. WHIDDEN. *Explicator* 1(7), June 1943, Item 66.

ARTHUR WORMHOUDT. *The Demon Lover*, pp. 71-77.

HERBERT G. WRIGHT. "Has Keats's 'Eve of St. Agnes' a Tragic Ending?" *Modern Language Review* 40(2), April 1945, 90-94.

"The Eve of St. Mark"

WALTER E. HOUGHTON. "The Meaning of Keats's *Eve of St. Mark*," *English Literary History* 13(1), March 1946, 64-78.

DAVID LUKE. "*The Eve of Saint Mark*: Keats's 'ghostly Queen of Spades' and the Textual Superstition," *Studies in Romanticism* 9(3), Summer 1970, 161-75.

JACK STILLINGER. "The Meaning of 'Poor Cheated Soul' in Keats's 'The Eve of St. Mark,' " *English Language Notes* 5(3), March 1968, 193-96.

"Fairy's Song"

J. BURKE SEVERS. *Explicator* 14(1), October 1955, Item 3.

JACK STILLINGER. "The Context of Keats's 'Fairy's Song,' " *Keats-Shelley Journal* 10 (Winter 1961), 6-8.

"The Fall of Hyperion"

ARTHUR H. BELL. " 'The Depth of Things': Keats and Human Space," *Keats-Shelley Journal* 23 (1974), 91-94.

JAMES BENZIGER. *Images of Eternity*, pp. 130-37.

HAROLD BLOOM. "Keats and the Embarrassments of Poetic Tradition," in *From Sensibility to Romanticism*, pp. 521-24.

HAROLD BLOOM. *Poetry and Repression*, pp. 112-42.

HAROLD BLOOM. *The Visionary Company*, pp. 411-21.

EDWARD E. BOSTETTER. *The Romantic Ventriloquists*, pp. 136-40, 164-71.

LESLIE BRISMAN. *Romantic Origins*, pp. 92-102.

IRENE H. CHAYES. "Dreamer, Poet, and Poem in *The Fall of Hyperion*," *Philological Quarterly* 46(4), October 1967, 499-515.

MICHAEL G. COOKE. *The Romantic Will*, pp. 174-82.

GEOFFREY H. HARTMAN. "Spectral Symbolism and the Authorial Self: An Approach to Keats's *Hyperion*," *Essays in Criticism* 24(1), January 1974, 1-19.

HELEN E. HAWORTH. "The Titans, Apollo, and the Fortunate Fall in Keats's Poetry," *Studies in English Literature 1500-1900* 10(4), Autumn 1970, 637-49.

KARL KROEBER. *The Artifice of Reality*, pp. 146-53.

ANNE K. MELLOR. "Keats's Face of Moneta: Source and Meaning," *Keats-Shelley Journal* 25 (1976), 65-80.

KENNETH MUIR. "The Meaning of Hyperion," *Essays in Criticism* 2(1), January 1952, 63-75.

MICHAEL RAGUSSIS. *The Subterfuge of Art*, pp. 35-69.

ELIZABETH SEWELL. *The Human Metaphor*, pp. 127-36.

PAUL D. SHEATS. "Stylistic Discipline in *The Fall of Hyperion*," *Keats-Shelley Journal* 17 (Winter 1968), 75-88.

STUART M. SPERRY, JR. "Keats, Milton, and *The Fall of Hyperion*," *PMLA* 77(1), March 1962, 77-84.

WILLIAM C. STEPHENSON. "The Performing Narrator in Keats's Poetry," *Keats-Shelley Journal* 26 (1977), 66-70.

ROBERT D. WAGNER. "Keats: 'Ode to Psyche' and the Second 'Hyperion,' " *Keats-Shelley Journal* 13 (Winter 1964), 35-41.

"Happy is England! I could be content"

RAYMOND BENOIT. *Single Nature's Double Name*, pp. 43-44.

"Hyperion"

JAMES BENZIGER. *Images of Eternity*, pp. 130-37.

HAROLD BLOOM. *The Visionary Company*, pp. 381-89.

JAMES RALSTON CALDWELL. "The Meaning of *Hyperion*," *PMLA* 51(4), December 1936, 1080-97.

GEOFFREY H. HARTMAN. "Spectral Symbolism and the Authorial Self: An Approach to Keats's *Hyperion*," *Essays in Criticism* 24(1), January 1974, 1-19.

HELEN E. HAWORTH. "The Titans, Apollo, and the Fortunate Fall in Keats's Poetry," *Studies in English Literature 1500-1900* 10(4), Autumn 1970, 637-49.

EDWARD B. HUNGERFORD. *Shores of Darkness*, pp. 137-62.

G. WILSON KNIGHT. *The Starlit Dome*, pp. 282-88.

KARL KROEBER. *The Artifice of Reality*, pp. 137-46.

SHIV K. KUMAR. "The Meaning of *Hyperion*: A Reassessment," in *British Romantic Poets*, pp. 305-18.

BRUCE E. MILLER. "On the Incompleteness of Keats' *Hyperion*," *CLA Journal* 8(3), March 1965, 234-39.

KENNETH MUIR. "The Meaning of *Hyperion*," *Essays in Criticism* 2(1), January 1952, 54-75.

MICHAEL RAGUSSIS. *The Subterfuge of Art*, pp. 35-69.

JOHN HAWLEY ROBERTS. "Poetry of Sensation or of Thought?" *PMLA* 45(4), December 1930, 1134-36.

MARTHA HALE SHACKFORD. "*Hyperion*," *Studies in Philology* 22(1), January 1925, 48-60.

PAUL SHERWIN. "Dying into Life: Keats's Struggle with Milton in *Hyperion*," *PMLA* 93(3), May 1978, 383-95.

STUART M. SPERRY. "Some Versions of Keats," *Modern Language Quarterly* 38(2), June 1977, 182-83.

WILLIAM C. STEPHENSON. "The Performing Narrator in Keats's Poetry," *Keats-Shelley Journal* 26 (1977), 62-66.

PIERRE VITOUX. "Keats's Epic Design in *Hyperion*," *Studies in Romanticism* 14(2), Spring 1975, 165-83.

"I Stood Tip-Toe"

MARJORIE NORRIS. "Phenomenology and Process: Perception in Keats's 'I Stood Tip-Toe,' " *Keats-Shelley Journal* 25 (1976), 43-54.

JACK STILLINGER. "The Order of Poems in Keats's First Volume," *Philological Quarterly* 48(1), January 1969, 95-96.

"Isabella"

G. WILSON KNIGHT. *The Starlit Dome*, pp. 280-82.

ROGER SHARROCK. "Keats and The Young Lovers," *Review of English Literature* 2(1), January 1961, 80-83.

LOUISE Z. SMITH. "The Material Sublime: Keats and *Isabella*," *Studies in Romanticism* 13(4), Fall 1974, 299-311.

JACK STILLINGER. "Keats and Romance," *Studies in English Literature 1500-1900* 8(4), Autumn 1968, 593-605.

"The Jealousies"
see "The Cap and Bells"

"Lamia"

ROBERT M. ADAMS. *Strains of Discord*, pp. 62-63.

PATRICIA M. BALL. *The Central Self*, pp. 148-49.

JOSEPH WARREN BEACH. *A Romantic View of Poetry*, pp. 123-31.

FREDERICK L. BEATY. *Light from Heaven*, pp. 187-91.

ARTHUR H. BELL. " 'The Depth of Things': Keats and Human Space," *Keats-Shelley Journal* 23 (1974), 87-90.

RICHARD BENVENUTO. " 'The Balance of Good and Evil' in Keats's Letters and 'Lamia,' " *Journal of English and Germanic Philology* 71(1), January 1972, 6-11.

HAROLD BLOOM. *The Visionary Company*, pp. 378-81.

EDWARD E. BOSTETTER. *The Romantic Ventriloquists*, pp. 161-64.

JAMES D. BOULGER. "Keats' Symbolism," *ELH* 28(3), September 1961, 248-54.

LESLIE BRISMAN. *Romantic Origins*, pp. 59-66.

DOUGLAS BUSH. "Keats and His Ideas," in *English Romantic Poets*, p. 336.

DEREK COLVILLE. *Victorian Poetry and the Romantic Religion*, pp. 47-48.

GEORGIA S. DUNBAR. "The Significance of the Humor in 'Lamia,' " *Keats-Shelley Journal* 8(1), Winter 1959, 17-26.

BARRY EDWARD GROSS. "The *Eve of St. Agnes* and *Lamia*: Paradise Won, Paradise Lost," *Bucknell Review* 13(2), May 1965, 47-57.

DONALD H. REIMAN. "Keats and the Humanistic Paradox: Mythological History in *Lamia*," *Studies in English Literature 1500-1900* 11(4), Autumn 1971, 659-69.

JOHN HAWLEY ROBERTS. "The Significance of *Lamia*," *PMLA* 50(2), June 1935, 550-61.

LUCIO P. RUOTOLO. "Keats and Kierkegaard: The Tragedy of Two Worlds," *Renascence* 16(4), Summer 1964, 183-86.

ROGER SHARROCK. "Keats and the Young Lovers," *Review of English Literature* 2(1), January 1961, 80-81, 85-86.

WILLIAM CURTIS STEPHENSON. "The Fall from Innocence in Keats's 'Lamia,' " *Papers on Language and Literature* 10(1), Winter 1974, 35-50.

WILLIAM C. STEPHENSON. "The Performing Narrator in Keats's Poetry," *Keats-Shelley Journal* 26 (1977), 60-62.

WARREN STEVENSON. "*Lamia*: A Stab at the Gordian Knot," *Studies in Romanticism* 11(3), Summer 1972, 241-52.

GARRETT STEWART. "Lamia and the Language of Metamorphosis," *Studies in Romanticism* 15(1), Winter 1976, 3-41.

HAROLD E. TOLIVER. *Pastoral Forms and Attitudes*, pp. 270-73.

KEATS, JOHN *(Cont.)*

"Lamia" *(cont.)*

ARTHUR WORMHOUDT. *The Demon Lover,* pp. 77-82.

JACQUELINE ZEFF. "Strategies of Time in Keats's Narratives," *Studies in English Literature 1500-1900* 17(4), Autumn 1977, 632-36.

"Nebuchadnezzar's Dream"

AILEEN WARD. "Keats's Sonnet, 'Nebuchadnezzar's Dream,'" *Philological Quarterly* 34(2), April 1955, 177-88.

"Ode on a Grecian Urn"

M. H. ABRAMS. "Belief and Disbelief," *University of Toronto Quarterly* 27(2), January 1958, 124-27.

ROBERT M. ADAMS. *Strains of Discord,* pp. 68-71.

ROBERT M. ADAMS. *"Trompe-L'Oeil* in Shakespeare and Keats," *Sewanee Review* 61(2), Spring 1953, 251-53.

ALLEN AUSTIN. "Keats's Grecian Urn and the Truth of Eternity," *College English* 25(6), March 1964, 434-36.

ROY P. BASLER. *Explicator* 4(1), October 1945, Item 6.

F. W. BATESON. *English Poetry,* pp. 217-20.

GILLIAN BEER. "Aesthetic Debate in Keats's Odes," *Modern Language Review* 64(4), October 1969, 742-48.

RAYMOND BENOIT. *Single Nature's Double Name,* pp. 48-54.

JAMES BENZIGER. *Images of Eternity,* pp. 119-25.

ROBERT BERKELMAN. "Keats and the Urn," *South Atlantic Quarterly* 57(3), Summer 1958, 354-58.

PRATAP BISWAS. "Keats's Cold Pastoral," *University of Toronto Quarterly* 47(2), Winter 1977/8, 95-111.

HAROLD BLOOM. "Keats and the Embarrassments Of Poetic Tradition," in *From Sensibility to Romanticism,* pp. 520-21.

HAROLD BLOOM. *The Visionary Company,* pp. 406-10.

EDWARD E. BOSTETTER. *The Romantic Ventriloquists,* pp. 156-58.

C. M. BOWRA. *The Romantic Imagination,* pp. 126-48.

CLEANTH BROOKS, JR. "History Without Footnotes: An Account of Keats' Urn," *Sewanee Review* 52(1), Winter 1944, 89-101.

CLEANTH BROOKS. *The Well Wrought Urn,* pp. 151-66; revised ed., pp. 124-35. Reprinted in: *British Romantic Poets,* pp. 293-304. Also: *English Romantic Poets,* pp. 354-64. Also: *Five Approaches of Literary Criticism,* pp. 231-44.

CLEANTH BROOKS, JOHN THIBAUT PURSER, and ROBERT PENN WARREN. *An Approach to Literature,* fourth ed., pp. 415-18; fifth ed., pp. 480-82.

KENNETH BURKE. "Symbolic Action in a Poem by Keats," *Accent* 4(1), Autumn 1943, 30-42. Reprinted in: Kenneth Burke. *A Grammar of Motives,* pp. 447-63. Also: *Essays in Modern Literary Criticism,* pp. 396-411. Also: *The Modern Critical Spectrum,* pp. 58-69. Also: *Master Poems of the English Language,* pp. 569-82.

DAVID K. CORNELIUS. *Explicator* 20(7), March 1962, Item 57.

DAVID DAICHES and WILLIAM CHARVAT. *Poems in English,* p. 707.

MARIO L. D'AVANZO. " 'Ode on a Grecian Urn' and *The Excursion," Keats-Shelley Journal* 23(1974), 95-105.

A. E. DYSON and JULIAN LOVELOCK. *Masterful Images,* pp. 205-17.

WILLIAM EMPSON. *The Structure of Complex Words,* pp. 368-74.

RICHARD H. FOGLE. "Empathic Imagery in Keats and Shelley," *PMLA* 61(1), March 1946, 184-87.

NEWELL F. FORD. "Holy Living and Holy Dying in Keats's Poetry," *Keats-Shelley Journal* 20 (1971), 55-57.

ALBERT GÉRARD. "Romance and Reality: Continuity and Growth in Keats's View of Art," *Keats-Shelley Journal* 11 (Winter 1962), 23-29.

K. M. HAMILTON. "Time and the *Grecian Urn,"* *Dalhousie Review* 34(3), Autumn 1954, 246-54.

VICTOR M. HAMM. *Explicator* 3(7), May 1945, Item 56.

RAYMOND D. HAVENS. "Concerning the 'Ode on a Grecian Urn,'" *Modern Philology* 24(2), November 1926, 209-14.

GILBERT HIGHET. *The Powers of Poetry,* pp. 236-43.

ARCHIBALD A. HILL. *Constituent and Pattern in Poetry,* pp. 104-14.

JAMES L. HILL. "The Function of the Poem in Keats's 'Ode to a Grecian Urn' and Wordsworth's 'Resolution and Independence,'" *Centennial Review* 22(4), Fall 1978, 424-37.

VIRGIL HUTTON. *Explicator* 19(6), March 1961, Item 40.

BLAIR G. KENNEY. *Explicator* 27(9), May 1969, Item 69.

G. WILSON KNIGHT. *The Starlit Dome,* pp. 294-96.

ALICE FOX KORNBLUTH. *Explicator* 16(9), June 1958, Item 56.

KARL KROEBER. *The Artifice of Reality,* pp. 83-84.

F. R. LEAVIS. *Revaluation,* pp. 252-59.

F. R. LEAVIS. "Revaluations (IX): Keats," *Scrutiny* 4(4), March 1936, 384-88.

HERBERT MARSHALL McLUHAN. "Aesthetic Pattern in Keats's Odes," *University of Toronto Quarterly* 12(2), January 1943, 177-78.

MALCOLM MAGAW. "Yeats and Keats: The Poetics of Romanticism," *Bucknell Review* 13(3), December 1965, 87-96.

BRUCE E. MILLER. "Form and Substance in 'Grecian Urn,'" *Keats-Shelley Journal* 20 (1971), 62-70.

MARCO MINCOFF. "Beauty is Truth — Once More," *Modern Language Review* 65(2), April 1970, 267-71.

CHARLES I. PATTERSON. "Passion and Performance in Keats's *Ode on a Grecian Urn," Journal of English Literary History* 21(3), September 1954, 208-20.

RICHARD C. PETTIGREW. *Explicator* 5(2), November 1946, Item 13.

B. L. REID. "Keats and the Heart's Hornbook," *Massachusetts Review* 2(3), Spring 1961, 489-90.

STEPHEN A. REID. "Keats's Depressive Poetry," *Psychoanalytic Review* 58(3), 1971, 406-10.

ALLAN RODWAY. *The Romantic Conflict,* pp. 240-41.

LUCIO P. RUOTOLO. "Keats and Kierkegaard: The Tragedy of Two Worlds," *Renascence* 16(4), Summer 1964, 186-90.

JEAN-CLAUDE SALLÉ. "The Pious Frauds of Art: A Reading of The 'Ode on a Grecian Urn,'" *Studies in Romanticism* 11(2), Spring 1972, 79-93.

JAMES SHOKOFF. "Soul-Making in 'Ode on a Grecian Urn,'" *Keats-Shelley Journal* 24 (1975), 102-7.

DAVID SIMPSON. "Keats's Lady, Metaphor, and the Rhetoric of Neurosis," *Studies in Romanticism* 15(2), Spring 1976, 265-68.

ROYALL SNOW. "Heresy Concerning Keats," *PMLA* 43(4), December 1928, 1142-49.

LEO SPITZER. *Essays on English and American Literature,* pp. 67-97.

ROBERT WOOSTER STALLMAN. "Keats the Apollinian: The Time-and-Space Logic of His Poems as Paintings," *University of Toronto Quarterly* 16(2), January 1947, 155-56. Partial reprint in: *The Critic's Notebook*, pp. 188-89.

ROY ARTHUR SWANSON. "Form and Content in Keats's 'Ode on a Grecian Urn,'" *College English* 23(4), January 1962, 302-5.

WYLIE SYPHER. "Portrait of the Artist as John Keats," *Virginia Quarterly Review* 25(3), Summer 1949, 422-23.

ALLEN TATE. "A Reading of Keats (II)," *American Scholar* 15(2), Spring 1946, 194-97. Reprinted in: Allen Tate. *On the Limits of Poetry*, pp. 177-80. Also: Allen Tate. *Essays of Four Decades*, pp. 273-77.

WRIGHT THOMAS and STUART GERRY BROWN. *Reading Poems: An Introduction to Critical Study*, p. 660.

HAROLD E. TOLIVER. *Pastoral Forms and Attitudes*, pp. 267-70.

LEONARD UNGER. "Keats and the Music of Autumn," *Western Review* 14(4), Summer 1950, 281-83.

LEONARD UNGER. *The Man in the Name*, pp. 25-27.

LEONARD UNGER and WILLIAM VAN O'CONNOR. *Poems for Study*, pp. 457-58.

HELEN VENDLER. "The Experiential Beginnings of Keats's Odes," *Studies in Romanticism* 12(3), Summer 1973, 598-602.

MARY VISICK. "'Tease us out of thought': Keats's *Epistle to Reynolds* and the Odes," *Keats-Shelley Journal* 15 (Winter 1966), 87-98.

LEONE VIVANTE. *English Poetry*, pp. 196-203.

LEON WALDOFF. "Porphyro's Imagination and Keats's Romanticism," *Journal of English and Germanic Philology* 76(2), April 1977, 193.

WAYNE WARNCKE. *Explicator* 24(5), January 1966, Item 40.

JACOB D. WIGOD. "Keats's Ideal in the *Ode on a Grecian Urn*," *PMLA* 72(1), March 1957, 113-21.

STEWART C. WILCOX. "The Unity of 'Ode on a Grecian Urn,'" *Personalist* 31(2), Spring 1950, 149-56.

A. HYATT WILLIAMS. "Keats' 'La Belle Dame Sans Merci': The Bad-Breast Mother," *American Imago* 23(1), Spring 1966, 78-79.

"Ode on Indolence"

BERNARD BLACKSTONE. "The Mind of Keats in His Art," in *British Romantic Poets*, pp. 271-72.

HAROLD BLOOM. *The Visionary Company*, pp. 410-11.

EDWARD E. BOSTETTER. *The Romantic Ventriloquists*, pp. 155-56.

HOWARD H. HINKEL. "Growth Without Toil: Generative Indolence in Keats," *Tennessee Studies in Literature* 20 (1975), 26-36.

G. WILSON KNIGHT. *The Starlit Dome*, p. 296.

KARL KROEBER. *The Artifice of Reality*, pp. 80-83.

WILLIAM F. ZAK. "The Confirmation of Keats's Belief in Negative Capability: The 'Ode on Indolence,'" *Keats-Shelley Journal* 25 (1976), 55-64.

"Ode on Melancholy"

JOSEPH WARREN BEACH. *A Romantic View of Poetry*, pp. 91-94.

HAROLD BLOOM. *The Visionary Company*, pp. 403-6.

LESLIE BRISMAN. *Romantic Origins*, pp. 85-92.

CLEANTH BROOKS, JOHN THIBAUT PURSER, and ROBERT PENN WARREN. *An Approach to Literature*, pp. 479-81; second ed., pp. 479-81; third ed., pp. 355-58; fourth ed., pp. 349-52; fifth ed., pp. 420-23.

RICHARD D. EBERLY. *Explicator* 6(6), April 1948, Item 38. Reprinted in: *The Creative Reader*, pp. 856-58.

WILLIAM EMPSON. *Seven Types of Ambiguity*, pp. 272-75; second and third eds., pp. 214-17.

NEWELL F. FORD. "Holy Living and Holy Dying in Keats's Poetry," *Keats-Shelley Journal* 20 (1971), 57-59.

MARTIN HALPERN. "Keats and the 'Spirit that Laughest,'" *Keats-Shelley Journal* 15 (Winter 1966), 75-78.

DONALD E. HAYDEN. *Literary Studies*, pp. 50-56.

G. WILSON KNIGHT. *The Starlit Dome*, pp. 296-98.

KARL KROEBER. *The Artifice of Reality*, pp. 75-78.

F. R. LEAVIS. *Revaluation*, pp. 260-62.

F. R. LEAVIS. "Revaluations (IX): Keats," *Scrutiny* 4(4), March 1936, 390-92.

G. L. LITTLE. *Explicator* 25(6), February 1967, Item 46.

HORACE G. POSEY, JR. "Keats's 'Ode on Melancholy': Analogue of the Imagination," *Concerning Poetry* 8(2), 61-69.

ALLAN RODWAY. *The Romantic Conflict*, pp. 241-42.

ROBERT ROGERS. "Keats's Strenuous Tongue: A Study of 'Ode on Melancholy,'" *Literature and Psychology* 17(1), 1967, 2-12.

BARBARA HERRNSTEIN SMITH. "'Sorrow's Mysteries': Keats's 'Ode on Melancholy,'" *Studies in English Literature 1500-1900* 6(4), Autumn 1966, 679-91.

HELEN VENDLER. "The Experiential Beginnings of Keats's Odes," *Studies in Romanticism* 12(3), Summer 1973, 595-98.

LEON WALDOFF. "Porphyro's Imagination and Keats's Romanticism," *Journal of English and Germanic Philology* 76(2), April 1977, 193-94.

AILEEN WARD. "The Psychoanalytic Theory of Poetic Form: A Comment," *Literature and Psychology* 17(1), 1967, 33-35.

"Ode to a Nightingale"

ROBERT M. ADAMS. *Strains of Discord*, pp. 65-68.

ROBERT M. ADAMS. "*Trompe-L'Oeil* in Shakespeare and Keats," *Sewanee Review* 61(2), Spring 1953, 248-51.

W. H. AUDEN and NORMAN HOLMES PEARSON. *Poets of the English Language, IV: Blake to Poe*, xix-xx.

JEROME BEATY and WILLIAM H. MATCHETT. *Poetry From Statement to Meaning*, pp. 90-98.

GILLIAN BEER. "Aesthetic Debate in Keats's Odes," *Modern Language Review* 64(4), October 1969, 742-48.

ARTHUR H. BELL. "'The Depth of Things': Keats and Human Space," *Keats-Shelley Journal* 23 (1974), 90-91.

HARRY BELSHAW. "Keats on the Mount of Transfiguration," *London Quarterly and Holborn Review* 175 (October 1950), 320-24.

JAMES BENZIGER. *Images of Eternity*, pp. 119-29.

WALTER BLAIR and W. K. CHANDLER. *Approaches to Poetry*, pp. 552-56; second ed., pp. 578-82.

HAROLD BLOOM. "Keats and the Embarrassments Of Poetic Tradition," in *From Sensibility to Romanticism*, pp. 519-20.

HAROLD BLOOM. *The Visionary Company*, pp. 397-403.

EDWARD E. BOSTETTER. *The Romantic Ventriloquists*, pp. 158-59.

JAMES D. BOULGER. "Keats' Symbolism," *ELH* 28(3), September 1961, 245-48.

C. M. BOWRA. *The Romantic Imagination*, pp. 136-37.

LESLIE BRISMAN. *Romantic Origins*, pp. 78-85.

KEATS, JOHN *(Cont.)*

"Ode to a Nightingale" *(cont.)*

CLEANTH BROOKS. *Modern Poetry and the Tradition*, p. 31.

CLEANTH BROOKS, JOHN THIBAUT PURSER, and ROBERT PENN WARREN. *An Approach to Literature*, fourth ed., pp. 411-13; fifth ed., pp. 475-77.

CLEANTH BROOKS and ROBERT PENN WARREN. *Understanding Poetry*, pp. 409-15; revised ed., pp. 338-45; third ed., pp. 426-30; fourth ed., pp. 355-58. Reprinted in: *Master Poems of the English Language*, pp. 586-92.

HARRY BROWN and JOHN MILSTEAD. *What the Poem Means*, p. 124.

IRENE H. CHAYES. "Rhetoric as Drama: An Approach to the Romantic Ode," *PMLA* 79(1), March 1964, 74-77.

DEREK COLVILLE. *Victorian Poetry and the Romantic Religion*, pp. 49-50.

MICHAEL G. COOKE. *The Romantic Will*, pp. 166-70.

EARL DANIELS. *The Art of Reading Poetry*, pp. 366-72.

FRANK DOGGETT. "Romanticism's Singing Bird," *Studies in English Literature 1500-1900* 14(4), Autumn 1974, 553-57.

ELIZABETH DREW. *Poetry*, pp. 178-80.

DAVID EGGENSCHWILER. "Nightingales and Byzantine Birds, Something Less Than Kind," *English Language Notes* 8(3), March 1971, 186-91.

RICHARD HARTER FOGLE. "Keats's *Ode to a Nightingale*," *PMLA* 68(1), March 1953, 211-22.

RICHARD H. FOGLE. "A Note on Keats's *Ode to a Nightingale*," *Modern Language Quarterly* 8(1), March 1947, 81-84. Reprinted in: *English Romantic Poets*, pp. 380-84.

NEWELL F. FORD. "Holy Living and Holy Dying in Keats's Poetry," *Keats-Shelley Journal* 20 (1971), 46-49.

NEWELL F. FORD. "Keats, Empathy, and 'The Poetical Character,'" *Studies in Philology* 45(3), July 1948, 489-90.

BARRY GRADMAN. "*Measure for Measure* and Keats's 'Nightingale' Ode," *English Language Notes* 12(3), March 1975, 177-82.

ALBERT GUERARD, JR. "Prometheus and the Aeolian Lyre," *Yale Review* 33(3), Spring 1944, 495-96.

ANTHONY HECHT. "Shades of Keats and Marvell," *Hudson Review* 15(1), Spring 1962, 57-66.

ANDREW J. KAPPEL. "The Immortality of the Natural: Keats' 'Ode to a Nightingale,'" *ELH* 45(2), Summer 1978, 270-84.

G. WILSON KNIGHT. *The Starlit Dome*, pp. 298-300. Reprinted in: *Poems and Critics*, pp. 171-72.

MURRAY KRIEGER. "*Ekphrasis* and the Still Movement of Poetry; or *Laokoön* Revisited," in *The Poet as Critic*, pp. 19-20.

KARL KROEBER. *The Artifice of Reality*, pp. 78-80.

KARL KROEBER. *Romantic Narrative Art*, pp. 58-62.

F. R. LEAVIS. *Revaluation*, pp. 244-52.

F. R. LEAVIS. "Revaluations (IX): Keats," *Scrutiny* 4(4), March 1936, 378-84.

HERBERT MARSHALL MCLUHAN. "Aesthetic Pattern in Keats's Odes," *University of Toronto Quarterly* 12(2), January 1943, 167-77.

MALCOLM MAGAW. "Yeats and Keats: The Poetics of Romanticism," *Bucknell Review* 13(3), December 1965, 87-96.

LOWRY NELSON, JR. "The Rhetoric of Ineffability: Toward a Definition of Mystical Poetry," *Comparative Literature* 8(4), Fall 1956, 332-35.

DONALD PEARCE. "Flames Begotten of Flame," *Sewanee Review* 74(3), Summer 1966, 649-68.

JOHN OLIVER PERRY. *The Experience of Poems*, pp. 273-74, 299.

ROBERT PINSKY. *The Situation of Poetry*, pp. 47-60.

S. M. PITCHER. *Explicator* 3(5), March 1945, Item 39.

WILLIAM O. RAYMOND. "'The Mind's Internal Heaven' in Poetry," *University of Toronto Quarterly* 20(3), April 1951, 229-30.

STEPHEN A. REID. "Keats's Depressive Poetry," *Psychoanalytic Review* 58(3), 1971, 406-7, *passim*.

ALLAN RODWAY. *The Romantic Conflict*, pp. 239-40.

M. L. ROSENTHAL and A. J. M. SMITH. *Exploring Poetry*, pp. 505-7; second ed., pp. 358-60.

R. L. SMALLWOOD. "The Occasion of Keats's 'Ode to a Nightingale,'" *Durham University Journal*, n.s., 36(1), December 1974, 49-56.

JAMES SMITH. "Notes on the Criticism of T. S. Eliot," *Essays in Criticism* 22(4), October 1972, 344-45.

WYLIE SYPHER. "Portrait of the Artist as John Keats," *Virginia Quarterly Review* 25(3), Summer 1949, 425.

ALLEN TATE. "A Reading of Keats (II)," *American Scholar* 15(2), Spring 1946, 189-94. Reprinted in: Allen Tate. *On the Limits of Poetry*, pp. 171-77. Also: Allen Tate. *Essays of Four Decades*, pp. 267-77.

WRIGHT THOMAS and STUART GERRY BROWN. *Reading Poems: An Introduction to Critical Study*, pp. 658-60.

LEONARD UNGER. "Keats and the Music of Autumn," *Western Review* 14(4), Summer 1950, 281-83.

LEONARD UNGER and WILLIAM VAN O'CONNOR. *Poems for Study*, p. 458.

DOROTHY VAN GHENT. "The Passion of the Groves," *Sewanee Review* 52(2), Spring 1944, 226-46.

HELEN VENDLER. "The Experiential Beginnings of Keats's Odes," *Studies in Romanticism* 12(3), Summer 1973, 592-95.

MARY VISICK. "'Tease us out of thought': Keats's *Epistle to Reynolds* and the Odes," *Keats-Shelley Journal* 15 (Winter 1966), 87-98.

LEON VIVANTE. *English Poetry*, pp. 193-95.

LEON WALDOFF. "Porphyro's Imagination and Keats's Romanticism," *Journal of English and Germanic Philology* 76(2), April 1977, 192-93.

"Ode to Psyche"

ROBERT M. ADAMS. *Strains of Discord*, pp. 63-65.

ROBERT M. ADAMS. "*Trompe-L'Oeil* in Shakespeare and Keats," *Sewanee Review* 61(2), Spring 1953, 247-48.

KENNETH ALLOTT. "Keats's 'Ode to Psyche,'" *Essays in Criticism* 6(3), July 1956, 278-301.

FREDERICK L. BEATY. *Light from Heaven*, pp. 186-87.

GILLIAN BEER. "Aesthetic Debate in Keats's Odes," *Modern Language Review* 64(4), October 1969, 743-44.

HAROLD BLOOM. *A Map of Misreading*, pp. 152-56.

HAROLD BLOOM. *The Visionary Company*, pp. 389-97.

LESLIE BRISMAN. *Romantic Origins*, pp. 56-59.

HARRY BROWN and JOHN MILSTEAD. *What the Poem Means*, pp. 124-25.

JAMES H. BUNN. "Keats' *Ode to Psyche* and the Transformation of Mental Landscape," *ELH* 37(4), December 1970, 581-94.

DOUGLAS BUSH. *Pagan Myth and Christian Tradition in English Poetry*, p. 49.

MICHAEL G. COOKE. *The Romantic Will*, pp. 164-66.

LLOYD N. JEFFREY. "A Freudian Reading of Keats's *Ode to Psyche*," *Psychoanalytic Review* 55(2), Summer 1968, 289-306.

G. WILSON KNIGHT. *The Starlit Dome*, pp. 301-4.

KARL KROEBER. *The Artifice of Reality*, pp. 69-73.

LAURENCE LERNER. *The Uses of Nostalgia*, pp. 215-17.

MAX F. SCHULZ. "Keats's Timeless Order of Things: A Modern Reading of 'Ode to Psyche,' " *Criticism* 2(1), Winter 1960, 55-65.

WYLIE SYPHER. "Portrait of the Artist as John Keats," *Virginia Quarterly Review* 25(3), Summer 1949, 425-26.

ROBERT D. WAGNER. "Keats: 'Ode to Psyche' and the Second 'Hyperion,' " *Keats-Shelley Journal* 13 (Winter 1964), 29-34.

LEON WALDOFF. "Porphyro's Imagination and Keats's Romanticism," *Journal of English and Germanic Philology* 76(2), April 1977, 192.

LEON WALDOFF. "The Theme of Mutability in the 'Ode to Psyche,' " *PMLA* 92(3), May 1977, 410-19.

GEORGE YOST, JR. "An Identification in Keats's *Ode to Psyche*," *Philological Quarterly* 36(4), October 1957, 496-500.

"On First Looking into Chapman's Homer"

ISAAC ASIMOV. *Familiar Poems, Annotated*, pp. 172-76.

JOSEPH WARREN BEACH. "Keats's Realms of Gold," *PMLA* 49(1), March 1934, 246-57.

JAMES BENZIGER. *Images of Eternity*, pp. 110-11.

EARL DANIELS. *The Art of Reading Poetry*, pp. 210-11.

B. IFOR EVANS. "Keats's Approach to the Chapman Sonnet," *Essays and Studies* 16 (1930), 26-52.

G. GIOVANNINI. "Keats' Elysium of Poets," *Modern Language Notes* 63(1), January 1948, 19-25.

LYNN H. HARRIS. *Explicator* 4(5), March 1946, Item 35.

T. O. MABBOTT. *Explicator* 5(3), December 1946, Item 22.

J. MIDDLETON MURRY. "The Birth of a Great Poem," *Hibbert Journal* 27(1), October 1928, 93-110. Reprinted as: "When Keats Discovered Homer," *Bookman* 68(4), December 1928, 391-401.

BERNICE SLOTE. "Of Chapman's Homer and Other Books," *College English* 23(4), January 1962, 256-60. Reprinted in: *The Dimensions of Poetry*, pp. 461-68.

ROBERT WOOSTER STALLMAN. "Keats and the Apollinian: The Time-and-Space Logic of His Poems as Paintings," *University of Toronto Quarterly* 16(2), January 1947, 153-54.

WYLIE SYPHER. "Portrait of the Artist as John Keats," *Virginia Quarterly Review* 25(3), Summer 1949, 423-24.

LEON WALDOFF. "Porphyro's Imagination and Keats's Romanticism," *Journal of English and Germanic Philology* 76(2), April 1977, 189-90.

C. V. WICKER. "Cortez — Not Balboa," *College English* 17(7), April 1956, 383-87.

MELVIN G. WILLIAMS. "To Be or to Have Been: The Use of Verbs in Three Sonnets by John Keats," *CEA Critic* 32(3), December 1969, 12.

GARRY WILLS. "Classicism in Keats's Chapman Sonnet," *Essays in Criticism* 17(4), October 1967, 456-60.

CARL WOODRING. "On Looking into Keats's Voyagers," *Keats-Shelley Journal* 14 (Winter 1965), 15-22.

"On Seeing a Lock of Milton's Hair"

MICHAEL G. COOKE. *The Romantic Will*, pp. 156-58.

"On Seeing the Elgin Marbles"

JAMES BENZIGER. *Images of Eternity*, pp. 111-14.

EDWARD A. BLOOM, CHARLES H. PHILBRICK, and ELMER M. BLISTEIN. *The Order of Poetry*, pp. 94-95.

E. B. MURRAY. "Ambivalent Mortality in the Elgin Marbles Sonnet," *Keats-Shelley Journal* 20 (1971), 22-36.

MELVIN G. WILLIAMS. "To Be or to Have Been: The Use of Verbs in Three Sonnets by John Keats," *CEA Critic* 32(3), December 1969, 12.

"On Sitting Down to Read King Lear Once Again"

T. R. BARNES. *English Verse*, pp. 218-19.

LYNA LEE MONTGOMERY. "The Phoenix: Its Use as a Literary Device in English From the Seventeenth Century to the Twentieth Century," *D. H. Lawrence Review* 5(3), Fall 1972, 299.

"On Visiting the Tomb of Burns"

GEORGE YOST, JR. "A Source and Interpretation of Keats's Minos," *Journal of English and Germanic Philology* 57(2), April 1958, 220-29.

"Sleep and Poetry"

HAROLD BLOOM. *The Visionary Company*, pp. 354-59.

DEREK COLVILLE. *Victorian Poetry and the Romantic Religion*, pp. 43-44.

MICHAEL G. COOKE. *The Romantic Will*, pp. 152-55.

HELEN E. HAWORTH. "Keats and the Metaphor of Vision," *Journal of English and Germanic Philology* 67(3), July 1968, 371-94, *passim*.

ARCHIBALD LAMPMAN. "The Character and Poetry of Keats," *University of Toronto Quarterly* 15(4), July 1946, 361-63.

JOHN HAWLEY ROBERTS. "Poetry of Sensation or of Thought?" *PMLA* 45(4), December 1930, 1129-30.

ALLAN RODWAY. *The Romantic Conflict*, p. 238.

JACK STILLINGER. "The Order of Poems in Keats's First Volume," *Philological Quarterly* 48(1), January 1969, 100-1.

LIONEL TRILLING. "The Fate of Pleasure: Wordsworth to Dostoevsky," *Partisan Review* 30(2), Summer 1963, 175-76.

"Sonnet to Benjamin Haydon"

JAMES BENZIGER. *Images of Eternity*, p. 111.

"To Autumn"

T. R. BARNES. *English Verse*, pp. 222-24.

JAMES BENZIGER. *Images of Eternity*, pp. 129-30.

HAROLD BLOOM. *The Visionary Company*, pp. 421-25.

CLEANTH BROOKS, JOHN THIBAUT PURSER, and ROBERT PENN WARREN. *An Approach to Literature*, fourth ed., pp. 419-20; fifth ed., pp. 405-7.

REUBEN ARTHUR BROWER. *The Fields of Light*, pp. 39-41.

IRVING H. BUCHEN. "Keats's 'To Autumn': The Season of Optimum Form," *CEA Critic* 31(2), November 1968, 11.

MICHAEL G. COOKE. *The Romantic Will*, pp. 170-74.

DAVID DAICHES and WILLIAM CHARVAT. *Poems in English*, p. 707.

ROBERT DANIEL and MONROE C. BEARDSLEY. "Reading Takes a Whole Man," *College English* 17(1), October 1955, 31-32.

KEATS, JOHN *(Cont.)*

"To Autumn" *(cont.)*

NEWELL F. FORD. "Holy Living and Holy Dying in Keats's Poetry," *Keats-Shelley Journal* 20 (1971), 59-61.

EUGENE GREEN and ROSEMARY M. GREEN. "Keats's Use of Names in *Endymion* and in the Odes," *Studies in Romanticism* 16(1), Winter 1977, 32-34.

G. WILSON KNIGHT. *The Starlit Dome,* pp. 300-1. Reprinted in: *Poems and Critics,* pp. 172-74.

KARL KROEBER. *The Artifice of Reality,* pp. 114-16.

F. R. LEAVIS. *Revaluation,* pp. 262-64.

F. R. LEAVIS. "Revaluations (IX): Keats," *Scrutiny* 4(4), March 1936, 392-93.

JAMES LOTT. "Keats's *To Autumn*: The Poetic Consciousness and the Awareness of Process," *Studies in Romanticism* 9(2), Spring 1970, 71-81.

HERBERT MARSHALL MCLUHAN. "Aesthetic Pattern in Keats's Odes," *University of Toronto Quarterly* 12(2), January 1943, 178-79.

VIRGIL NEMOIANU. "The Dialectics of Movement in Keats's 'To Autumn,' " *PMLA* 93(2), March 1978, 205-14.

DONALD PEARCE. "Thoughts on the Autumn Ode of Keats," *Ariel* 6(3), July 1975, 3-19.

THOMAS PISON. "A Phenomenological Approach to Keats's 'To Autumn,' " *Bucknell Review* 22(1), April 1976, 37-47.

B. L. REID. "Keats and the Heart's Hornbook," *Massachusetts Review* 2(3), Spring 1961, 491-95.

STEPHEN A. REID. "Keats's Depressive Poetry," *Psychoanalytic Review* 58(3), 1971, 406, 411-15.

ALLAN RODWAY. *The Romantic Conflict,* pp. 242-44.

EDWARD W. ROSENHEIM, JR. *What Happens in Literature,* pp. 42-56.

B. C. SOUTHAM. "The Ode 'To Autumn,' " *Keats-Shelley Journal* 9(2), Autumn 1960, 91-98.

PATRICK SWINDEN. "John Keats: 'To Autumn,' " *Critical Quarterly* 20(4), Winter 1978, 57-60.

LEONARD UNGER. "Keats and the Music of Autumn," *Western Review* 14(4), Summer 1950, 275-84. Reprinted in: Leonard Unger. *The Man in the Name,* pp. 18-29.

LEONARD UNGER and WILLIAM VAN O'CONNOR. *Poems for Study,* pp. 454-57. Reprinted in: *Readings for Liberal Education,* fourth ed., II: 109-10; fifth ed., II: 102-3.

HELEN VENDLER. "The Experiential Beginnings of Keats's Odes," *Studies in Romanticism* 12(3), Summer 1973, 603-6.

"To Charles Cowden Clarke"

JOHN CIARDI. *How Does a Poem Mean?* p. 783; second ed., pp. 122-23. (P)

"To George Felton Matthew"

MICHAEL G. COOKE. *The Romantic Will,* pp. 150-52.

"To Homer"

THOMAS COOK. "Keats's Sonnet 'To Homer,' " *Keats-Shelley Journal* 11 (Winter 1962), 8-12.

"To Sleep"

NEWELL F. FORD. "Holy Living and Holy Dying in Keats's Poetry," *Keats-Shelley Journal* 20 (1971), 54-55.

"To Solitude"

STUART M. SPERRY, JR. "Keats's First Published Poem," *Huntington Library Quarterly* 29(2), February 1966, 191-97.

"What can I do to drive away"

HAROLD E. BRIGGS. "Keats, Robertson, and *That Most Hateful Land,*" *PMLA* 59(1), March 1944, 184-95.

JOHN ROBERT MOORE. "Keats's Lines to Fanny," *Times Literary Supplement,* 23 December 1949, p. 841. (P)

J. MIDDLETON MURRY. " 'Lines to Fanny,' " *Times Literary Supplement,* 18 November 1949, p. 751. (P)

RONALD PRIMEAU. "Chaucer's *Troilus and Criseyde* and the Rhythm of Experience in Keats's 'What can I do to drive away,' " *Keats-Shelley Journal* 23 (1974), 110-16.

"What the Thrush Said"

CLEANTH BROOKS, JOHN THIBAUT PURSER, and ROBERT PENN WARREN. *An Approach to Literature,* fourth ed., pp. 413-15; fifth ed., pp. 477-78.

MICHAEL G. COOKE. *The Romantic Will,* pp. 158-61.

"When I Have Fears That I May Cease to Be"

THOMAS E. CONNOLLY. *Explicator* 13(3), December 1954, Item 14.

NEWELL F. FORD. "Holy Living and Holy Dying in Keats's Poetry," *Keats-Shelley Journal* 20 (1971), 37-61.

M. A. GOLDBERG. "The 'Fears' of John Keats," *Modern Language Quarterly* 18(2), June 1957, 125-31.

MORLEY J. MAYS. *Explicator* 1(6), April 1943, Item 47.

MELVIN G. WILLIAMS. "To Be or to Have Been: The Use of Verbs in Three Sonnets by John Keats," *CEA Critic* 32(3), December 1969, 12.

"Why did I laugh to-night?"

NEWELL F. FORD. "Holy Living and Holy Dying in Keats's Poetry," *Keats-Shelley Journal* 20 (1971), 50-51.

MARTIN HALPERN. "Keats and the 'Spirit that Laughest,' " *Keats-Shelley Journal* 15 (Winter 1966), 78-79.

KEBLE, JOHN

"Christmas Day"

JEAN WILKINSON. "Three Sets of Religious Poems," *Huntington Library Quarterly* 36(3), May 1973, 222-24.

"Septuagesima Sunday"

JEAN WILKINSON. "Three Sets of Religious Poems," *Huntington Library Quarterly* 36(3), May 1973, 215.

"Tuesday in Easter Week: To the Snow-Drop"

JEAN WILKINSON. "Three Sets of Religious Poems," *Huntington Library Quarterly* 36(3), May 1973, 217-18.

KEES, WELDON

"After the Trial"

JOSEPH WARREN BEACH. *Obsessive Images,* pp. 335-36.

"For My Daughter"

CHARLES BAXTER. "Whatever Happened to Weldon Kees?" *Minnesota Review* 11(3), Fall 1972, 123-24.

"Report of the Meeting"

JOSEPH WARREN BEACH. *Obsessive Images,* pp. 287-88.

KENNEDY, G. A. STUDDERT

"Woodbine Willie"

    I. A. RICHARDS. *Practical Criticism*, pp. 53-61, 262-66.

KENNEDY, WALTER

"The Flyting of Dunbar and Kennedie"

    see entry under DUNBAR, WILLIAM

KENNEDY, X. J.

"Nude Descending a Staircase"

    NANCY SULLIVAN. "Perspective and the Poetic Process," *Wisconsin Studies in Contemporary Literature* 6(1), Winter-Spring 1965, 121-23.

KEY, FRANCIS SCOTT

"The Star-Spangled Banner"

    ISAAC ASIMOV. *Familiar Poems, Annotated*, pp. 163-71.

KEYES, SIDNEY

"The Foreign Gate"

    VERNON SCANNELL. *Not Without Glory*, pp. 87-92.

"Greenwich Observatory"

    LOIS T. MILLER. "A Single Goggling Eye: An Analysis of Sidney Keyes' 'Greenwich Observatory,' " *English Journal* 51(1), January 1962, 62-63.

KILMER, JOYCE

"Trees"

    WALTON BEACHAM. *The Meaning of Poetry*, pp. 2-3.

    CLEANTH BROOKS and ROBERT PENN WARREN. *Understanding Poetry*, pp. 387-91; revised ed., pp. 274-78; third ed., pp. 288-89.

    JEFFREY FLEECE. "Further Notes on a 'Bad' Poem," *College English* 12(6), March 1951, 314-20.

    PAUL SAWYER. "What Keeps 'Trees' Growing?" *CEA Critic* 33(1), November 1970, 17-19.

KING, HENRY

"The Boy's Answere to the Blackmore"

    ELLIOT H. TOKSON. "The Image of the Negro in Four Seventeenth-Century Love Poems," *Modern Language Quarterly* 30(4), December 1969, 510-18.

"An Exequy to his Matchless never to be Forgotten Friend"

    ROBERT F. GLECKNER. *Explicator* 12(7), May 1954, Item 46.

    JOSEPH H. SUMMERS. *The Heirs of Donne and Jonson*, pp. 84-85.

    GEORGE WILLIAMSON. *Six Metaphysical Poets*, pp. 244-48.

"The Labyrinth"

    ROSEMOND TUVE. *Elizabethan and Metaphysical Imagery*, pp. 357-58.

"Upon the Death of my ever Desired Friend Dr. Donne Deane of Paules"

    AVON JACK MURPHY. "The Critical Elegy of Earlier Seventeenth-Century England," *Genre* 5(1), March 1972, 91-93.

KINGSLEY, HENRY

"Magdalen at Michael's Gate"

    WILLIAM H. SCHEUERLE. " 'Magdalen at Michael's Gate': A Neglected Lyric," *Victorian Poetry* 5(2), Summer 1967, 144-46.

KINNELL, GALWAY

"Another Night in the Ruins"

    RALPH J. MILLS, JR. "A Reading of Galway Kinnell Part 2," *Iowa Review* 1(2), Spring 1970, 110-11. Reprinted in: Ralph J. Mills, Jr. *Cry of the Human*, pp. 175-76.

"The Avenue Bearing the Initial of Christ into the New World"

    RALPH J. MILLS, JR. "A Reading of Galway Kinnell Part 2," *Iowa Review* 1(2), Spring 1970, 102-5. Reprinted in: Ralph J. Mills, Jr. *Cry of the Human*, pp. 163-67.

    JANE TAYLOR. "The Poetry of Galway Kinnell," *Perspective* 15(3), Winter-Spring 1968, 199-200.

"The Bear"

    WILLIAM V. DAVIS. " 'The Rank Flavor of Blood': Galway Kinnell's 'The Bear,' " *Notes on Contemporary Literature* 7(2), March 1977, 4-6.

    " 'Deeper Than Personality': A Conversation With Galway Kinnell," edited by Philip L. Gerber and Robert J. Gemmett, *Iowa Review* 1(2), Spring 1970, 126-28.

    JOHN HOBBS. "Galway Kinnell's 'The Bear': Dream and Technique," *Modern Poetry Studies* 5(3), Winter 1974, 237-50.

    J. T. LEDBETTER. *Explicator* 33(8), April 1975, Item 63.

    RALPH J. MILLS, JR. "A Reading of Galway Kinnell Part 2," *Iowa Review* 1(2), Spring 1970, 119-21. Reprinted in: Ralph J. Mills, Jr. *Cry of the Human*, pp. 187-90.

    CHARLES MOLESWORTH. "The Rank Flavor of Blood: Galway Kinnell and American Poetry in the 1960's," *Western Humanities Review* 27(3), Summer 1973, 234-36.

"The Dead Shall Be Raised Incorruptible"

    M. L. ROSENTHAL. "Some Thoughts on American Poetry Today," *Salmagundi* 22-23 (Spring-Summer 1973), 65-66. Reprinted in: *Contemporary Poetry in America*, pp. 24-25.

"The Descent"

    RALPH J. MILLS, JR. "A Reading of Galway Kinnell," *Iowa Review* 1(1), Winter 1970, 78-82. Reprinted in: Ralph J. Mills, Jr. *Cry of the Human*, pp. 151-57.

    JANE TAYLOR. "The Poetry of Galway Kinnell," *Perspective* 15(3), Winter-Spring 1968, 194-95.

"Easter"

    GLAUCO CAMBON. *Recent American Poetry*, pp. 33-36.

    RALPH J. MILLS, JR. "A Reading of Galway Kinnell," *Iowa Review* 1(1), Winter 1970, 72-73. Reprinted in: Ralph J. Mills, Jr. *Cry of the Human*, pp. 143-44.

    JANE TAYLOR. "The Poetry of Galway Kinnell," *Perspective* 15(3), Winter-Spring 1968, 195-96.

"First Communion"

    RALPH J. MILLS, JR. "A Reading of Galway Kinnell," *Iowa Review* 1(1), Winter 1970, 68-69. Reprinted in: Ralph J. Mills, Jr. *Cry of the Human*, pp. 137-39.

"First Song"

    GENE H. KORETZ. *Explicator* 15(7), April 1957, Item 43.

    MELVIN WALKER LA FOLLETTE. *Explicator* 14(7), April 1956, Item 48.

    RALPH J. MILLS, JR. "A Reading of Galway Kinnell," *Iowa Review* 1(1), Winter 1970, 67-68. Reprinted in: Ralph J. Mills, Jr. *Cry of the Human*, pp. 136-37.

KINNELL, GALWAY *(Cont.)*

"Flower Herding on Mount Monadnock"

Ralph J. Mills, Jr. "A Reading of Galway Kinnell Part 2," *Iowa Review* 1(2), Spring 1970, 110. Reprinted in: Ralph J. Mills, Jr. *Cry of the Human,* pp. 174-75.

CHARLES MOLESWORTH. "The Rank Flavor of Blood: Galway Kinnell and American Poetry in the 1960's," *Western Humanities Review* 27(3), Summer 1973, 229-30.

"For Robert Frost"

CHARLES MOLESWORTH. "The Rank Flavor of Blood: Galway Kinnell and American Poetry in the 1960's," *Western Humanities Review* 27(3), Summer 1973, 227-28.

"How Many Nights"

" 'Deeper Than Personality': A Conversation With Galway Kinnell," edited by Philip L. Gerber and Robert J. Gemmett, *Iowa Review* 1(2), Spring 1970, 125-26. (P)

"In the Hotel of Lost Light"

M. L. ROSENTHAL. "Some Thoughts on American Poetry Today," *Salmagundi* 22-23 (Spring-Summer 1973), 64-65. Reprinted in: *Contemporary Poetry in America,* pp. 23-24.

"The Last River"

RALPH J. MILLS, JR. "A Reading of Galway Kinnell Part 2," *Iowa Review* 1(2), Spring 1970, 112-15. Reprinted in: Ralph J. Mills, Jr. *Cry of the Human,* pp. 177-82.

"Middle of the Way"

RALPH J. MILLS, JR. "A Reading of Galway Kinnell Part 2," *Iowa Review* 1(2), Spring 1970, 106-7. Reprinted in: Ralph J. Mills, Jr. *Cry of the Human,* pp. 168-70.

"The Porcupine"

RALPH J. MILLS, JR. "A Reading of Galway Kinnell Part 2," *Iowa Review* 1(2), Spring 1970, 117-19. Reprinted in: Ralph J. Mills, Jr. *Cry of the Human,* pp. 184-87.

"The River That is East"

JANE TAYLOR. "The Poetry of Galway Kinnell," *Perspective* 15(3), Winter-Spring 1968, 196-98.

"Seven Streams of Nevis"

RALPH J. MILLS, JR. "A Reading of Galway Kinnell," *Iowa Review* 1(1), Winter 1970, 73-76. Reprinted in: Ralph J. Mills, Jr. *Cry of the Human,* pp. 145-49.

"Spindrift"

RALPH J. MILLS, JR. "A Reading of Galway Kinnell Part 2," *Iowa Review* 1(2), Spring 1970, 108-10. Reprinted in: Ralph J. Mills, Jr. *Cry of the Human,* pp. 171-74.

JANE TAYLOR. "The Poetry of Galway Kinnell," *Perspective* 15(3), Winter-Spring 1968, 198-99.

LINDA WAGNER. "Spindrift: The World in a Seashell," *Concerning Poetry* 8(1), Spring 1975, 5-9.

"The Supper After the Last"

RALPH J. MILLS, JR. "A Reading of Galway Kinnell," *Iowa Review* 1(1), Winter 1970, 82-86. Reprinted in: Ralph J. Mills, Jr. *Cry of the Human,* pp. 158-62.

"Testament of the Thief"

RALPH J. MILLS, JR. "A Reading of Galway Kinnell Part 2," *Iowa Review* 1(2), Spring 1970, 115-17. Reprinted in: Ralph J. Mills, Jr. *Cry of the Human,* pp. 182-84.

"To Christ Our Lord"

RALPH J. MILLS, JR. "A Reading of Galway Kinnell," *Iowa Review* 1(1), Winter 1970, 69-71. Reprinted in: Ralph J. Mills, Jr. *Cry of the Human,* pp. 139-41.

"Vapor Trail Reflected in the Frog Pond"

" 'Deeper Than Personality': A Conversation With Galway Kinnell," edited by Philip L. Gerber and Robert J. Gemmett, *Iowa Review* 1(2), Spring 1970, 129-30.

"Westport"

RALPH J. MILLS, JR. "A Reading of Galway Kinnell," *Iowa Review* 1(1), Winter 1970, 71-72. Reprinted in: Ralph J. Mills, Jr. *Cry of the Human,* pp. 141-42.

JANE TAYLOR. "The Poetry of Galway Kinnell," *Perspective* 15(3), Winter-Spring 1968, 191-92.

"Where the Track Vanishes"

RALPH J. MILLS, JR. "A Reading of Galway Kinnell," *Iowa Review* 1(1), Winter 1970, 76-78. Reprinted in: Ralph J. Mills, Jr. *Cry of the Human,* pp. 149-51.

"The Wolves"

JOHN HOBBS. "Galway Kinnell's 'The Bear', Dream and Technique," *Modern Poetry Studies* 5(3), Winter 1974, 241.

KINSELLA, THOMAS

"Baggot Street Deserta"

DONALD T. TORCHIANA. "Contemporary Irish Poetry," *Chicago Review* 17(2-3), 1964, 162-63.

"A Country Walk"

CALVIN BEDIENT. *Eight Contemporary Poets,* pp. 129-33.

JOHN REES MOORE. "Thomas Kinsella's Nightwalker: A Phoenix in the Dark," *Hollins Critic* 5(4), October 1968, 10-11.

DONALD T. TORCHIANA. "Contemporary Irish Poetry," *Chicago Review* 17(2-3), 1964, 163-64.

"Downstream"

CALVIN BEDIENT. *Eight Contemporary Poets,* pp. 129-33.

DAVID RIDGLEY CLARK. *Lyric Resonance,* pp. 91-102.

"First Light"

BRUCE KELLNER. "The Wormwood Poems of Thomas Kinsella," *Western Humanities Review* 26(3), Summer 1972, 225-27.

"Folk Wisdom"

JOHN REES MOORE. "Thomas Kinsella's Nightwalker: A Phoenix in the Dark," *Hollins Critic* 5(4), October 1968, 4.

"Forsaken"

BRUCE KELLNER. "The Wormwood Poems of Thomas Kinsella," *Western Humanities Review* 26(3), Summer 1972, 224-25.

"Magnanimity"

JOHN REES MOORE. "Thomas Kinsella's Nightwalker: A Phoenix in the Dark," *Hollins Critic* 5(4), October 1968, 12-13.

"Mask of Love"

BRUCE KELLNER. "The Wormwood Poems of Thomas Kinsella," *Western Humanities Review* 26(3), Summer 1972, 222-24.

"Nightwalker"

CALVIN BEDIENT. *Eight Contemporary Poets,* pp. 126-29.

"Office of the Dead"

JOHN REES MOORE. "Thomas Kinsella's Nightwalker: A Phoenix in the Dark," *Hollins Critic* 5(4), October 1968, 3-4.

"On the Gift in the Shape of a Heart"

BRUCE KELLNER. "The Wormwood Poems of Thomas Kinsella," *Western Humanities Review* 26(3), Summer 1972, 230.

"Phoenix Park"

CALVIN BEDIENT. *Eight Contemporary Poets*, pp. 133-36.

"Remembering Old Wars"

BRUCE KELLNER. "The Wormwood Poems of Thomas Kinsella," *Western Humanities Review* 26(3), Summer 1972, 228-29.

"Ritual of Departure"

CALVIN BEDIENT. *Eight Contemporary Poets*, pp. 124-26.

"The Secret Garden"

BRUCE KELLNER. "The Wormwood Poems of Thomas Kinsella," *Western Humanities Review* 26(3), Summer 1972, 227-28.

"Soft Toy"

JOHN REES MOORE. "Thomas Kinsella's Nightwalker: A Phoenix in the Dark," *Hollins Critic* 5(4), October 1968, 3.

"Wormwood"

BRUCE KELLNER. "The Wormwood Poems of Thomas Kinsella," *Western Humanities Review* 26(3), Summer 1972, 221-22.

KIPLING, RUDYARD

"Danny Deever"

GÉMINO H. ABAD. *A Formal Approach to Lyric Poetry*, pp. 227-29.

LOUIS S. FRIEDLAND. *Explicator* 2(1), October 1943, Item 9.

"The Islanders"

JON SILKIN. *Out of Battle*, pp. 61-62. (P)

"M'Andrew's Hymn"

BABETTE DEUTSCH. *Poetry in Our Time*, p. 29; second ed., p. 32.

"Recessional"

ISAAC ASIMOV. *Familiar Poems, Annotated*, pp. 248-56.

CLEANTH BROOKS and ROBERT PENN WARREN. *Understanding Poetry*, fourth ed., pp. 120-22.

GEORGE ORWELL. "Rudyard Kipling," in *Five Approaches of Literary Criticism*, pp. 162-63.

JON SILKIN. *Out of Battle*, pp. 63-65. (P)

"The Secret of the Machines"

BABETTE DEUTSCH. *Poetry in Our Time*, p. 31; second ed., p. 34.

"Sestina of the Tramp-Royal"

JEROME BEATY and WILLIAM H. MATCHETT. *Poetry From Statement to Meaning*, pp. 143-45.

"The Storm Cone"

BABETTE DEUTSCH. *Poetry in Our Time*, p. 38; second ed., p. 40.

"The Story of Ung"

BABETTE DEUTSCH. *Poetry in Our Time*, first ed., p. 35.

KIRSTEIN, LINCOLN

"Big Deal"

VERNON SCANNELL. *Not Without Glory*, pp. 184-86.

"Rank"

VERNON SCANNELL. *Not Without Glory*, pp. 179-80.

KNIGHT, ETHERIDGE

"For Freckle-Faced Gerald"

H. BRUCE FRANKLIN. "The Literature of the American Prison," *Massachusetts Review* 18(1), Spring 1977, 70-71.

"Hard Rock Returns to Prison from the Hospital for the Criminal Insane"

H. BRUCE FRANKLIN. "The Literature of the American Prison," *Massachusetts Review* 18(1), Spring 1977, 68-70.

"The Idea of Ancestry"

AGNES STEIN. *The Uses of Poetry*, pp. 306-7.

KNOEPFLE, JOHN

"Country sweat"

LLOYD GOLDMAN. "Masks of Self-deception," *Minnesota Review* 8(3), 1968, 259-60.

"Drifting"

LLOYD GOLDMAN. "Masks of Self-deception," *Minnesota Review* 8(3), 1968, 261-62.

"Driftwood fire"

LLOYD GOLDMAN. "Masks of Self-deception," *Minnesota Review* 8(3), 1968, 259.

"In the late night"

RAYMOND BENOIT. "The Reflective Art of John Knoepfle," *Minnesota Review* 8(3), 1968, 257.

KOCH, KENNETH

"Permanently"

PAT LAMORTE. "The 'Ancient Rules' — A Vanishing Species?" *Georgia Review* 27(4), Winter 1973, 498-99.

KREYMBORG, ALFRED

"Every Morning"

CHARLES CHILD WALCUTT. "Critic's Taste or Artist's Intention," *University of Kansas City Review* 12(4), Summer 1948, 282-83.

KUNITZ, STANLEY

"Among the Gods"

GEORGE P. ELLIOTT. "The Poetry of Stanley Kunitz," *Accent* 18(4), Autumn 1958, 270.

"The Approach to Thebes"

JEAN H. HAGSTRUM. "The Poetry of Stanley Kunitz: An Introductory Essay," in *Poets in Progress*, pp. 56-57.

"As Flowers Are"

"An Interview with Stanley Kunitz," conducted by Cynthia Davis, *Contemporary Literature* 15(1), Winter 1974, 10.

"By Lamplight"

ROBERT WEISBERG. "Stanley Kunitz: The Stubborn Middle Way," *Modern Poetry Studies* 6(1), Spring 1975, 57-58.

KUNITZ, STANLEY *(Cont.)*

"Careless Love"

GEORGE P. ELLIOTT. "The Poetry of Stanley Kunitz," *Accent* 18(4), Autumn 1958, 268-69.

"Father and Son"

JEAN H. HAGSTRUM. "The Poetry of Stanley Kunitz: An Introductory Essay," in *Poets in Progress*, pp. 43-44.

JOSEPHINE MILES, ROBERT BELOOF, ROBERT LOWELL and STANLEY KUNITZ. "On Stanley Kunitz's 'Father and Son,'" in *The Contemporary Poet as Artist and Critic*, pp. 56-80.

"For the Word is Flesh"

JEAN H. HAGSTRUM. "The Poetry of Stanley Kunitz: An Introductory Essay," in *Poets in Progress*, pp. 43-44.

"Geometry of Moods"

RALPH J. MILLS, JR. *Contemporary American Poetry*, pp. 37-39.

"Green Ways"

ROBERT RUSSELL. "The Poet in the Classroom," *College English* 28(8), May 1967, 581.

"Hermetic Poem"

RALPH J. MILLS, JR. *Contemporary American Poetry*, pp. 39-40.

"Illumination"

ROBERT WEISBERG. "Stanley Kunitz: The Stubborn Middle Way," *Modern Poetry Studies* 6(1), Spring 1975, 70-71.

"Journal for My Daughter"

MARJORIE G. PERLOFF. "The Testing of Stanley Kunitz," *Iowa Review* 3(1), Winter 1972, 94-99.

"King of the River"

ROBERT WEISBERG. "Stanley Kunitz: The Stubborn Middle Way," *Modern Poetry Studies* 6(1), Spring 1975, 71-73.

"Night Letter"

RALPH J. MILLS, JR. *Contemporary American Poetry*, pp. 44-47.

"Off Point Lotus"

ROBERT WEISBERG. "Stanley Kunitz: The Stubborn Middle Way," *Modern Poetry Studies* 6(1), Spring 1975, 58-60.

"Open the Gates"

ROBERT WEISBERG. "Stanley Kunitz: The Stubborn Middle Way," *Modern Poetry Studies* 6(1), Spring 1975, 62-63.

"The Portrait"

MARJORIE G. PERLOFF. "The Testing of Stanley Kunitz," *Iowa Review* 3(1), Winter 1972, 103.

"Prophecy on Lethe"

ROBERT WEISBERG. "Stanley Kunitz: The Stubborn Middle Way," *Modern Poetry Studies* 6(1), Spring 1975, 67-69.

"Revolving Meditation"

ROBERT WEISBERG. "Stanley Kunitz: The Stubborn Middle Way," *Modern Poetry Studies* 6(1), Spring 1975, 69-70.

"The Science of the Night"

RALPH J. MILLS, JR. *Contemporary American Poetry*, pp. 33-35.

ROBERT RUSSELL. "The Poet in the Classroom," *College English* 28(8), May 1967, 581-82.

"The Scourge"

ROBERT WEISBERG. "Stanley Kunitz: The Stubborn Middle Way," *Modern Poetry Studies* 6(1), Spring 1975, 64-66.

"The Signal from the House"

ROBERT WEISBERG. "Stanley Kunitz: The Stubborn Middle Way," *Modern Poetry Studies* 6(1), Spring 1975, 60-62.

"Single Vision"

JEAN H. HAGSTRUM. "The Poetry of Stanley Kunitz: An Introductory Essay," in *Poets in Progress*, pp. 47-49.

"The Surgeons"

HARRY BROWN and JOHN MILSTEAD. *What the Poem Means*, p. 128.

RALPH J. MILLS, JR. *Contemporary American Poetry*, pp. 41-43.

"The Testing Tree"

CYNTHIA DAVIS. "Stanley Kunitz's 'The Testing Tree,'" *Concerning Poetry*, 8(1), Spring 1975, 43-46.

"The Thief"

JEAN H. HAGSTRUM. "The Poetry of Stanley Kunitz: An Introductory Essay," in *Poets in Progress*, p. 40.

"The Waltzer in the House"

JEROME BEATY and WILLIAM H. MATCHETT. *Poetry From Statement to Meaning*, pp. 227-28.

"The Way Down"

ROBERT RUSSELL. "The Poet in the Classroom," *College English* 28(8), May 1967, 583-84.

L

LAING, R. D.

"The Bird of Paradise"

> C. J. Rawson. " ' 'Tis only infinite below': Speculations on Swift, Wallace Stevens, R. D. Laing and others," *Essays in Criticism* 22(2), April 1972, 517-27.

LAMB, CHARLES

"The Old Familiar Faces"

> Leo Spitzer. "History of Ideas Versus Reading of Poetry," *Southern Review* 6(3), Winter 1941, 586-88.

LANDOR, WALTER SAVAGE

"Dirce"

> Gémino H. Abad. *A Formal Approach to Lyric Poetry*, pp. 37-38.

"Mild Is the Parting Year, and Sweet"

> Mary Ellen Rickey. *Explicator* 13(1), October 1954, Item 2.

"Mother, I Cannot Mind My Wheel"

> Gémino H. Abad. *A Formal Approach to Lyric Poetry*, p. 44.

"On His Seventy-Fifth Birthday"

> Lee A. Jacobus and William T. Moynihan. *Poems in Context*, pp. 51-52.

"On Lucretia Borgia's Hair"

> Gémino H. Abad. *A Formal Approach to Lyric Poetry*, p. 38.

"Past Ruin'd Ilion"

> Fred B. Millett, Arthur W. Hoffman and David R. Clark. *Reading Poetry*, second ed., pp. 14-15.

"Proud Word You Never Spoke"

> Richard Ray Kirk and Roger Philip McCutcheon. *An Introduction to the Study of Poetry*, pp. 15-16.

"Rose Aylmer"

> Cleanth Brooks and Robert Penn Warren. *Understanding Poetry*, pp. 270-73; revised ed., pp. 145-47; third ed., pp. 141-46; fourth ed., pp. 517-18.
>
> Richard Ray Kirk and Roger Philip McCutcheon. *An Introduction to the Study of Poetry*, pp. 90-92.
>
> R. H. Super. *Explicator* 3(4), February 1945, Item 31.

> Robert Penn Warren. "Pure and Impure Poetry," *Kenyon Review* 5(2), Spring 1943, 235-37. Reprinted in: *Criticism*, pp. 369-70. Also: *Critiques and Essays in Criticism*, pp. 90-92. Also: *Essays in Modern Literary Criticism*, pp. 251-53. Also: *The Kenyon Critics*, pp. 24-26.

"To Age"

> Laurence Perrine. "The Importance of Tone in the Interpretation of Literature," *College English* 24(5), February 1963, 392-93.

"Yes; I Write Verses"

> Laurence Perrine. "The Importance of Tone in the Interpretation of Literature," *College English* 24(5), February 1963, 392-95.

LANIER, SIDNEY

"Clover"

> Allen Tate. "A Southern Romantic," *New Republic* 76(978), 30 August 1933, 67-68.

"Corn"

> Roy Harvey Pearce. *The Continuity of American Poetry*, pp. 237-39.

"Evening Song"

> Cleanth Brooks and Robert Penn Warren. *Understanding Poetry*, fourth ed., pp. 247-49.

"The Marshes of Glynn"

> Roy Harvey Pearce. *The Continuity of American Poetry*, pp. 243-44.
>
> Owen J. Reamer. "Lanier's 'The Marshes of Glynn' Revisited," *Mississippi Quarterly* 23(1), Winter 1969-70, 57-63.
>
> Robert H. Ross. " 'The Marshes of Glynn': A Study in Symbolic Obscurity," *American Literature* 32(4), January 1961, 403-16.
>
> Hyatt H. Waggoner. *American Poets*, pp. 236-39.
>
> Harry R. Warfel. "Mystic Vision In 'The Marshes of Glynn,' " *Mississippi Quarterly* 19(1), Winter 1965-66, 34-40.

"My Springs"

> Cleanth Brooks and Robert Penn Warren. *Understanding Poetry*, pp. 442-45; revised ed., pp. 299-302; third ed., pp. 301-3.

"Night and Day"

> Edd Winfield Parks. "Lanier's 'Night and Day,' " *American Literature* 30(1), May 1958, 117-18.

LANIER, SIDNEY *(Cont.)*

"Sunrise"

    BERNARD DUFFEY. *Poetry in America*, pp. 104-6.

"The Symphony"

    HARRY BROWN and JOHN MILSTEAD. *What the Poem Means*, p. 130.

    ELISABETH J. HOGENES. *Explicator* 16(1), October 1957, Item 4.

    ROY HARVEY PEARCE. *The Continuity of American Poetry*, p. 239.

LARKIN, PHILIP

"Absences"

    MERLE BROWN. "Larkin and His Audience," *Iowa Review* 8(4), Fall 1977, 117-19.

"Ambulances"

    C. B. COX. "Philip Larkin, Anti-Heroic Poet," *Studies in the Literary Imagination* 9(1), Spring 1976, 161-62.

"Arrival"

    ROGER BOWEN. "Poet in Transition: Philip Larkin's *XX Poems*," *Iowa Review* 8(1), Winter 1977, 93-94.

"An Arundel Tomb"

    GEORGE FRASER. *Essays on Twentieth-Century Poets*, pp. 248-49.

    A. KINGSLEY WEATHERHEAD. "Philip Larkin of England," *ELH* 38(4), December 1971, 629-30.

"At Grass"

    CALVIN BEDIENT. *Eight Contemporary Poets*, p. 90.

    ROGER BOWEN. "Poet in Transition: Philip Larkin's *XX Poems*," *Iowa Review* 8(1), Winter 1977, 101-2.

    MERLE BROWN. "Larkin and His Audience," *Iowa Review* 8(4), Fall 1977, 121-23.

    C. B. COX and A. E. DYSON. *Modern Poetry*, pp. 137-41.

    JOAN E. HARTMAN. "Teaching Poetry: An Exercise in Practical Criticism," *College English* 35(1), October 1973, 17-31.

    MARTIN SCOFIELD. "The Poetry of Philip Larkin," *Massachusetts Review* 17(2), Spring 1976, 378-80.

"Church Going"

    WALTON BEACHAM. *The Meaning of Poetry*, pp. 34-38.

    CHRISTOPHER CLAUSEN. "Tintern Abbey to Little Gidding: The Past Recaptured," *Sewanee Review* 84(3), Summer 1976, 422-24.

    SUZANNE DE LESSEPS. "Dramatic Situation and Point of View in Philip Larkin's 'Church Going,' " in *The Meaning of Poetry*, pp. 293-94.

    BABETTE DEUTSCH. *Poetry in Our Time*, second ed., p. 399.

    G. S. FRASER. "Contemporary Poetry and the Anti-Romantic Idea," in *Vision and Rhetoric*, pp. 261-64.

    ALUN R. JONES. "The Poetry of Philip Larkin: A Note on Transatlantic Culture," *Western Humanities Review* 16(2), Spring 1962, 150.

    JAMES NAREMORE. "Philip Larkin's 'Lost World,' " *Contemporary Literature* 15(3), Summer 1974, 338-39.

    JOHN PRESS. "The Poetry of Philip Larkin," *Southern Review*, n.s., 13(1), Winter 1977, 138-39.

    KEITH SAGAR. "Philip Larkin," in *Criticism in Action*, pp. 121-24.

    ANTHONY THWAITE. "The Poetry of Philip Larkin," in *The Survival of Poetry*, pp. 48-50.

"Days"

    GEORGE FRASER. *Essays on Twentieth-Century Poets*, pp. 247-48.

    JOHN WAIN. *Professing Poetry*, pp. 170-71.

"Deceptions"

    CALVIN BEDIENT. *Eight Contemporary Poets*, pp. 85-86.

    ROGER BOWEN. "Poet in Transition: Philip Larkin's *XX Poems*," *Iowa Review* 8(1), Winter 1977, 92-93.

    JOHN PRESS. "The Poetry of Philip Larkin," *Southern Review*, n.s., 13(1), Winter 1977, 136-37.

"The Dedicated"

    ROGER BOWEN. "Poet in Transition: Philip Larkin's *XX Poems*," *Iowa Review* 8(1), Winter 1977, 98-99.

"Dockery and Son"

    PATRICK SWINDEN. "Old Lines, New Lines: The Movement Ten Years After," *Critical Quarterly* 9(4), Winter 1967, 348-49.

    GEOFFREY THURLEY. *The Ironic Harvest*, p. 147.

    A. KINGSLEY WEATHERHEAD. "Philip Larkin of England," *ELH* 38(4), December 1971, 625-28.

"Dry-Point"

    MARGARET BLUM. *Explicator* 32(6), February 1974, Item 48.

    ROGER BOWEN. "Poet in Transition: Philip Larkin's *XX Poems*," *Iowa Review* 8(1), Winter 1977, 97-98.

    STUART HIRSCHBERG. "Larkin's 'Dry-Point': Life Without Illusion," *Notes on Contemporary Literature* 8(1), January 1978, 5-6.

"Essential Beauty"

    COLIN FALCK. "Philip Larkin," in *The Modern Poet*, edited by Ian Hamilton, pp. 102-3.

"For Sidney Bechet"

    JOHN WAIN. "Engagement or Withdrawal? Some Notes on the Work of Philip Larkin," *Critical Quarterly* 6(2), Summer 1964, 170-71.

    JOHN WAIN. *Professing Poetry*, pp. 174-75.

"Going"

    ROGER BOWEN. "Poet in Transition: Philip Larkin's *XX Poems*," *Iowa Review* 8(1), Winter 1977, 100.

"Here"

    MERLE BROWN. "Larkin and His Audience," *Iowa Review* 8(4), Fall 1977, 127-30.

    JOHN WAIN. "Engagement or Withdrawal? Some Notes on the Work of Philip Larkin," *Critical Quarterly* 6(2), Summer 1964, 173-75.

"High Windows"

    C. B. COX. "Philip Larkin, Anti-Heroic Poet," *Studies in the Literary Imagination* 9(1), Spring 1976, 163-64.

"Homage to a Government"

    JOHN PRESS. "The Poetry of Philip Larkin," *Essays by Divers Hands*, 3rd Series, 39 (1977), 87-88.

    JOHN WAIN. *Professing Poetry*, p. 169.

"How Distant"

    JOHN WAIN. *Professing Poetry*, pp. 160-62.

"I put my mouth"

    JOHN WAIN. *Professing Poetry*, pp. 178-79.

"Lines on a Young Lady's Photograph Album"

    CALVIN BEDIENT. *Eight Contemporary Poets*, p. 84.

    C. B. COX and A. E. DYSON. *The Practical Criticism of Poetry*, pp. 46-57.

"Love Songs in Age"

D. J. ENRIGHT. *Conspirators and Poets,* p. 142.

"Maiden Name"

PATRICK SWINDEN. "Old Lines, New Lines: The Movement Ten Years After," *Critical Quarterly* 9(4), Winter 1967, 347-48.

"Mr. Bleaney"

IAN HAMILTON. "Philip Larkin," in *A Poetry Chronicle,* pp. 135-36.

GEOFFREY THURLEY. *The Ironic Harvest,* pp. 147-48.

"Modesties"

Roger Bowen. "Poet in Transition: Philip Larkin's *XX Poems,*" *Iowa Review* 8(1), Winter 1977, 90-91.

"Naturally The Foundation Will Bear Your Expenses"

JOHN WAIN. "Engagement or Withdrawal? Some Notes on the Work of Philip Larkin," *Critical Quarterly* 6(2), Summer 1964, 171-72.

JOHN WAIN. *Professing Poetry,* p. 169.

J. R. WATSON. "The other Larkin," *Critical Quarterly* 17(4), Winter 1975, 349-51.

"Next, Please"

ROGER BOWEN. "Poet in Transition: Philip Larkin's *XX Poems,*" *Iowa Review* 8(1), Winter 1977, 91-92.

C. B. COX. "Philip Larkin," *Critical Quarterly* 1(1), Spring 1959, 16.

ALUN R. JONES. "The Poetry of Philip Larkin: A Note on Transatlantic Culture," *Western Humanities Review* 16(2), Spring 1962, 149.

"No Road"

ROGER BOWEN. "Poet in Transition: Philip Larkin's *XX Poems,*" *Iowa Review* 8(1), Winter 1977, 95-96.

C. B. COX. "Philip Larkin," *Critical Quarterly* 1(1), Spring 1959, 16-17.

ALUN R. JONES. "The Poetry of Philip Larkin: A Note on Transatlantic Culture," *Western Humanities Review* 16(2), Spring 1962, 149-50.

"Posterity"

JOHN WAIN. *Professing Poetry,* pp. 168-69.

"Sad Steps"

BERNARD BERGONZI. "Davie, Larkin, and the State of England," *Contemporary Literature* 18(3), Summer 1977, 357-59.

"Solar"

MERLE BROWN. "Larkin and His Audience," *Iowa Review* 8(4), Fall 1977, 119-21.

"Toads"

ALUN R. JONES. "The Poetry of Philip Larkin: A Note on Transatlantic Culture," *Western Humanities Review* 16(2), Spring 1962, 147-48.

"Toads Revisited"

D. J. ENRIGHT. *Conspirators and Poets,* p. 142.

"Two Portraits of Sex: Etching"
see "Dry-Point"

"Two Portraits of Sex: Oils"

ROGER BOWEN. "Poet in Transition: Philip Larkin's *XX Poems,*" *Iowa Review* 8(1), Winter 1977, 97-98.

"Waiting for breakfast, while she brushed her hair"

JAMES NAREMORE. "Philip Larkin's 'Lost World,'" *Contemporary Literature* 15(3), Summer 1974, 334-35.

"Wants"

MERLE BROWN. "Larkin and His Audience," *Iowa Review* 8(4), Fall 1977, 125-26.

"Wedding-Wind"

ROGER BOWEN. "Poets in Transition: Philip Larkin's *XX Poems,*" *Iowa Review* 8(1), Winter 1977, 88-90.

KEITH SAGAR. "Philip Larkin," in *Criticism in Action,* pp. 125-26.

ANTHONY THWAITE. "The Poetry of Philip Larkin," in *The Survival of Poetry,* pp. 44-45.

"The Whitsun Weddings"

CALVIN BEDIENT. *Eight Contemporary Poets,* pp. 91-93.

MERLE BROWN. "Larkin and His Audience," *Iowa Review* 8(4), Fall 1977, 130-33.

DAVID HOLBROOK. *Lost Bearings in English Poetry,* pp. 164-74.

ALUN R. JONES. "The Poetry of Philip Larkin: A Note on Transatlantic Culture," *Western Humanities Review* 16(2), Spring 1962, 151-52.

JAMES NAREMORE. "Philip Larkin's 'Lost World,'" *Contemporary Literature* 15(3), Summer 1974, 339-43.

JOHN PRESS. "The Poetry of Philip Larkin," *Essays by Divers Hands,* 3rd series, 39 (1977), 86.

JOHN PRESS. "The Poetry of Philip Larkin," *Southern Review,* n.s., 13(1), Winter 1977, 140-41.

JOHN REIBETANZ. "'The Whitsun Weddings': Larkin's Reinterpretation of Time and Form in Keats," *Contemporary Literature* 17(4), Autumn 1976, 529-40.

MARTIN SCOFIELD. "The Poetry of Philip Larkin," *Massachusetts Review* 17(2), Spring 1976, 384-86.

"Wild Oats"

ROGER BOWEN. "Poet in Transition: Philip Larkin's *XX Poems,*" *Iowa Review* 8(1), Winter 1977, 96.

LATTIMORE, RICHMOND

"Witness to Death"

FORD T. SWETNAM, JR. *Explicator* 25(7), March 1967, Item 59.

LAUGHLIN, JAMES

"Go West Young Men"

LAURENCE PERRINE. *Explicator* 28(7), March 1970, Item 61.

LAWRENCE, D. H.

"Baby Tortoise"

LUCY M. BRASHEAR. "Lawrence's Companion Poems: 'Snake' and *Tortoises,*" *D. H. Lawrence Review* 5(1), Spring 1972, 55.

KEITH SAGAR. "'Little Living Myths': A Note on Lawrence's *Tortoises,*" *D. H. Lawrence Review* 3(2), Summer 1970, 162-63.

"Ballad of a Wilful Woman"

JUDITH MITCHELL. *Explicator* 36(4), Summer 1978, 4-6.

"Bavarian Gentians"

DAVID CAVITCH. "Solipsism and Death in D. H. Lawrence's Late Works," *Massachusetts Review* 7(3), Summer 1966, 505-7.

ELIZABETH CIPOLLA. "The *Last Poems* of D. H. Lawrence," *D. H. Lawrence Review* 2(2), Summer 1969, 108-9.

C. B. COX and A. E. DYSON. *Modern Poetry,* pp. 66-71.

LAWRENCE, D. H. *(Cont.)*

"Bavarian Gentians" *(cont.)*

JAMES E. MILLER, JR. and BERNICE SLOTE. *The Dimensions of Poetry*, pp. 30-31.

KEITH SAGAR. "The Genesis of 'Bavarian Gentians,'" *D. H. Lawrence Review* 8(1), Spring 1975, 47-53.

JOHN B. VICKERY. "D. H. Lawrence's Poetry: Myth and Matter," *D. H. Lawrence Review* 7(1), Spring 1974, 16-18.

"Bibbles"

BERNICE SLOTE. "The *Leaves* of D. H. Lawrence," in *Start with the Sun*, pp. 85-86.

"The Bride"

ROSEMARIE ARBUR. " 'Lilacs' and 'Sorrow': Whitman's Effect on the Early Poems of D. H. Lawrence," *Walt Whitman Review* 24(1), March 1978, 20-21.

"Brother and Sister"

EVELYN SHAKIR. " 'Secret Sin': Lawrence's Early Verse," *D. H. Lawrence Review* 8(2), Summer 1975, 163.

"Butterfly"

ELIZABETH CIPOLLA. "The *Last Poems* of D. H. Lawrence," *D. H. Lawrence Review* 2(2), Summer 1969, 108.

"Clerks"

EVELYN SHAKIR. " 'Secret Sin': Lawrence's Early Verse," *D. H. Lawrence Review* 8(2), Summer 1975, 169-70.

"Corot"

R. P. BLACKMUR. *The Double Agent*, pp. 112-15. Reprinted in: R. P. Blackmur. *Language as Gesture*, pp. 294-95. Also: R. P. Blackmur. *Form and Value in Modern Poetry*, pp. 261-62.

"End of Another Home Holiday"

A. ALVAREZ. "D. H. Lawrence: The Single State of Man," in *Modern Poetry*, pp. 288-92.

D. S. SAVAGE. *The Personal Principle*, p. 135.

"The Enkindled Spring"

ROBIN SKELTON. *The Poetic Pattern*, pp. 104-5.

"Excursion Train"

see "Honeymoon"

"Fish"

R. P. BLACKMUR. *Form and Value in Modern Poetry*, pp. 266-67.

DAVID CAVITCH. "Merging — With Fish and Others," *D. H. Lawrence Review* 7(2), Summer 1974, 172-78.

DEL IVAN JANIK. "Toward 'Thingness': Cézanne's Painting and Lawrence's Poetry," *Twentieth Century Literature* 19(2), April 1973, 123-27.

ROBERT KERN. "Toward a New Nature Poetry," *Centennial Review* 19(3), Summer 1975, 205-6.

ROBERT LANGBAUM. "Lords of Life, Kings in Exile: Identity and Sexuality in D. H. Lawrence," *American Scholar* 45(1), Winter 1975/76, 812.

JOYCE CAROL OATES. "The Hostile Sun: The Poetry of D. H. Lawrence," *Massachusetts Review* 13(4), Autumn 1972, 655-56.

"Glory of Darkness"

see "Bavarian Gentians"

"The Greeks are Coming!"

MICHAEL KIRKHAM. "D. H. Lawrence's *Last Poems*," *D. H. Lawrence Review* 5(2), Summer 1972, 117-18.

"The He-Goat"

JOYCE CAROL OATES. "The Hostile Sun: The Poetry of D. H. Lawrence," *Massachusetts Review* 13(4), Autumn 1972, 648.

"History"

JOHN B. VICKERY. "D. H. Lawrence's Poetry: Myth and Matter," *D. H. Lawrence Review* 7(1), Spring 1974, 9.

"Honeymoon"

EVELYN SHAKIR. " 'Secret Sin': Lawrence's Early Verse," *D. H. Lawrence Review* 8(2), Summer 1975, 163-64.

"Humming-bird"

JOYCE CAROL OATES. "The Hostile Sun: The Poetry of D. H. Lawrence," *Massachusetts Review* 13(4), Autumn 1972, 647-48.

"Hymn to Priapus"

M. L. ROSENTHAL. *The Modern Poets*, p. 162.

"Invocation to the Moon"

ELIZABETH CIPOLLA. "The *Last Poems* of D. H. Lawrence," *D. H. Lawrence Review* 2(2), Summer 1969, 108.

MICHAEL KIRKHAM. "D. H. Lawrence's *Last Poems*," *D. H. Lawrence Review* 5(2), Summer 1972, 108-9.

"Kisses in the Train"

EVELYN SHAKIR. " 'Secret Sin': Lawrence's Early Verse," *D. H. Lawrence Review* 8(2), Summer 1975, 171.

"Last Lesson of the Afternoon"

ANTHONY BEAL. "D. H. Lawrence," in *Criticism in Action*, pp. 93-95.

"Lightning"

JOHN B. VICKERY. "D. H. Lawrence's Poetry: Myth and Matter," *D. H. Lawrence Review* 7(1), Spring 1974, 8-9.

"Lord's Prayer"

MICHAEL KIRKHAM. "D. H. Lawrence's *Last Poems*," *D. H. Lawrence Review* 5(2), Summer 1972, 118-20.

"Lotus and Frost"

ROBIN SKELTON. *The Poetic Pattern*, pp. 103-4.

"Love on the Farm"

GÉMINO H. ABAD. *A Formal Approach to Lyric Poetry*, pp. 235-40.

DONALD GUTIERREZ. "Lapsing Out: Ideas of Mortality and Immortality in Lawrence," *Twentieth Century Literature* 24(2), Summer 1978, 178-80.

EVELYN SHAKIR. " 'Secret Sin': Lawrence's Early Verse," *D. H. Lawrence Review* 8(2), Summer 1975, 158-59.

JOHN B. VICKERY. "D. H. Lawrence's Poetry: Myth and Matter," *D. H. Lawrence Review* 7(1), Spring 1974, 8.

"The Man of Tyre"

MICHAEL KIRKHAM. "D. H. Lawrence's *Last Poems*," *D. H. Lawrence Review* 5(2), Summer 1972, 110-16.

"New Heaven and Earth"

JOYCE CAROL OATES. "The Hostile Sun: The Poetry of D. H. Lawrence," *Massachusetts Review* 13(4), Autumn 1972, 641-42.

M. L. ROSENTHAL. *The Modern Poets*, pp. 165-67.

BERNICE SLOTE. "The *Leaves* of D. H. Lawrence," in *Start with the Sun*, pp. 96-97.

"Pan in America"

WALLACE G. KAY. "Dionysius, D. H. Lawrence, and Jean Giono: Further Considerations," *Southern Quarterly* 6(4), July 1968, 407-9.

"Piano"

DAVID BLEICH. "The Determination of Literary Value," *Literature and Psychology* 17(1), 1967, 19-30.

F. R. LEAVIS. "'Thought' and Emotional Quality: Notes in the Analysis of Poetry," *Scrutiny* 13(1), Spring 1945, 55-58.

I. A. RICHARDS. *Practical Criticism,* pp. 105-17, *passim.*

M. L. ROSENTHAL. *Poetry and the Common Life,* pp. 20-21, 28.

MACKLIN THOMAS. "Analysis of the Experience in Lyric Poetry," *College English* 9(6), March 1948, 318-19.

AILEEN WARD. "The Psychoanalytic Theory of Poetic Form: A Comment," *Literature and Psychology* 17(1), 1967, 35-37.

"River Roses"

M. L. ROSENTHAL. *The Modern Poets,* pp. 163-64.

"Shadows"

DONALD GUTIERREZ. "Lapsing Out: Ideas of Mortality and Immortality in Lawrence," *Twentieth Century Literature* 24(2), Summer 1978, 181-86.

"She Said as Well to Me"

JOYCE CAROL OATES. "The Hostile Sun: The Poetry of D. H. Lawrence," *Massachusetts Review* 13(4), Autumn 1972, 651-52.

"The Ship of Death"

DAVID CAVITCH. "Solipsism and Death in D. H. Lawrence's Late Works," *Massachusetts Review* 7(3), Summer 1966, 507-8.

ELIZABETH CIPOLLA. "The *Last Poems* of D. H. Lawrence," *D. H. Lawrence Review* 2(2), Summer 1969, 103-19.

DONALD GUTIERREZ. "Circles and Arcs: The Rhythm of Circularity and Centrifugality in D. H. Lawrence's *Last Poems*," *D. H. Lawrence Review* 4(3), Fall 1971, 298-300.

EDWIN HONIG. "Lawrence: The Ship of Death," in *Master Poems of the English Language,* pp. 908-10.

JOYCE CAROL OATES. "The Hostile Sun: The Poetry of D. H. Lawrence," *Massachusetts Review* 13(4), Autumn 1972, 653-54.

"Snake"

ANTHONY BEAL. "D. H. Lawrence," in *Criticism in Action,* pp. 86-95.

LUCY M. BRASHEAR. "Lawrence's Companion Poems: 'Snake' and *Tortoises*," *D. H. Lawrence Review* 5(1), Spring 1972, 54-62.

HARRY BROWN and JOHN MILSTEAD. *What the Poem Means,* p. 132.

BABETTE DEUTSCH. *Poetry in Our Time,* pp. 89-91; second ed., pp. 96-98.

ROBERT LANGBAUM. "Lords of Life, Kings in Exile: Identity and Sexuality in D. H. Lawrence," *American Scholar* 45(1), Winter 1975/76, 813.

LESLIE B. MITTLEMAN. "Lawrence's 'Snake' not 'Sweet Georgian Brown,'" *English Literature in Transition* 9(1), 1966, 45-46.

"Snap Dragon"

EVELYN SHAKIR. "'Secret Sin': Lawrence's Early Verse," *D. H. Lawrence Review* 8(2), Summer 1975, 159-60.

"Song of a Man Who Has Come Through"

ROBERT HOGAN. *Explicator* 17(7), April 1959, Item 51.

M. L. ROSENTHAL. *The Modern Poets,* pp. 164-65.

ERWIN R. STEINBERG. "'Song of a Man Who Has Come Through' — A Pivotal Poem," *D. H. Lawrence Review* 11(1), Spring 1978, 50-62.

"Sorrow"

ROSEMARIE ARBUR. "'Lilacs' and 'Sorrow': Whitman's Effect on the Early Poems of D. H. Lawrence," *Walt Whitman Review* 24(1), March 1978, 18-20.

"Swan"

JOHN B. VICKERY. "D. H. Lawrence's Poetry: Myth and Matter," *D. H. Lawrence Review* 7(1), Spring 1974, 11-12.

"Tortoise Family Connections"

KEITH SAGAR. "'Little Living Myths': A Note on Lawrence's *Tortoises*," *D. H. Lawrence Review* 3(2), Summer 1970, 164-65.

"Tortoise Shell"

LUCY M. BRASHEAR. "Lawrence's Companion Poems: 'Snake' and *Tortoises*," *D. H. Lawrence Review* 5(1), Spring 1972, 55-56.

KEITH SAGAR. "'Little Living Myths': A Note on Lawrence's *Tortoises*," *D. H. Lawrence Review* 3(2), Summer 1970, 164.

"Tortoise Shout"

LUCY M. BRASHEAR. "Lawrence's Companion Poems: 'Snake' and *Tortoises*," *D. H. Lawrence Review* 5(1), Spring 1972, 58.

ROBERT LANGBAUM. "Lords of Life, Kings in Exile: Identity and Sexuality in D. H. Lawrence," *American Scholar* 45(1), Winter 1975/76, 812.

KEITH SAGAR. "'Little Living Myths': A Note on Lawrence's *Tortoises*," *D. H. Lawrence Review* 3(2), Summer 1970, 165-66.

"Trees in the Garden"

JOHN B. VICKERY. "D. H. Lawrence's Poetry: Myth and Matter," *D. H. Lawrence Review* 7(1), Spring 1974, 6-7. (P)

"Troth with the Dead"

SARAH YOUNGBLOOD. "Substance and Shadow: The Self in Lawrence's Poetry," *D. H. Lawrence Review* 1(2), Summer 1968, 123-24.

"The Turning Back"

DAVID FARMER. "D. H. Lawrence's 'The Turning Back': The Text and Its Genesis in Correspondence," *D. H. Lawrence Review* 5(2), Summer 1972, 125-26.

"Underneath"

JOHN C. ALEXANDER. "D. H. Lawrence and Teilhard de Chardin: A Study in Agreements," *D. H. Lawrence Review* 2(2), Summer 1969, 145-46.

"Vengeance is Mine"

LAURENCE LERNER. *An Introduction to English Poetry,* pp. 37-38.

"Virgin Youth"

EVELYN SHAKIR. "'Secret Sin': Lawrence's Early Verse," *D. H. Lawrence Review* 8(2), Summer 1975, 169.

LAWRENCE, D. H. *(Cont.)*

"Whales Weep Not!"

    JOHN B. VICKERY. "D. H. Lawrence's Poetry: Myth and Matter," *D. H. Lawrence Review* 7(1), Spring 1974, 15-16.

"Whether or Not"

    BABETTE DEUTSCH. *Poetry in Our Time*, pp. 5-6.

"The Wild Common"

    DEL IVAN JANIK. "Toward 'Thingness': Cézanne's Painting and Lawrence's Poetry," *Twentieth Century Literature* 19(2), April 1973, 121.

    SARAH YOUNGBLOOD. "Substance and Shadow: The Self in Lawrence's Poetry," *D. H. Lawrence Review* 1(2), Summer 1968, 118-20.

"Yesternight"

    EVELYN SHAKIR. "'Secret Sin': Lawrence's Early Verse," *D. H. Lawrence Review* 8(2), Summer 1975, 169-70.

"A Young Wife"

    JOHN B. VICKERY. "D. H. Lawrence's Poetry: Myth and Matter," *D. H. Lawrence Review* 7(1), Spring 1974, 10-11.

LAZARUS, EMMA

"The New Colossus"

    ISAAC ASIMOV. *Familiar Poems, Annotated*, pp. 243-47.

LEAR, EDWARD

"The Courtship of the Yonghy-Bonghy-Bo"

    INA RAE HARK. "Edward Lear: Eccentricity and Victorian *Angst*," *Victorian Poetry* 16(1-2), Spring-Summer 1978, 119-20.

"The Dong with a Luminous Nose"

    A. E. DYSON. "Method in Madness: A Note on Edward Lear," *English* 10(60), Autumn 1955, 223.

"The Jumblies"

    A. E. DYSON. "Method in Madness: A Note on Edward Lear," *English* 10(60), Autumn 1955, 222-23.

    INA RAE HARK. "Edward Lear: Eccentricity and Victorian *Angst*," *Victorian Poetry* 16(1-2), Spring-Summer 1978, 116-17.

"The Owl and the Pussycat"

    EDMUND MILLER. "Two Approaches to Edward Lear's Nonsense Songs," *Victorian Newsletter* 44 (Fall 1973), 5-6.

"The Pobble Who Has No Toes"

    EDMUND MILLER. "Two Approaches to Edward Lear's Nonsense Songs," *Victorian Newsletter* 44 (Fall 1973), 6-7.

LEE, DON L.

"But he was cool or: he even stopped for green lights"

    ANN COLLEY. "Don L. Lee's 'But He Was Cool Or: He Even Stopped for Green Lights': An Example of the New Black Aesthetic," *Concerning Poetry* 4(2), Fall 1971, 20-27.

    GENEVA SMITHERMAN. "The Power of the Rap: The Black Idiom and The New Black Poetry," *Twentieth Century Literature* 19(4), October 1973, 270.

"Poem to Complement Other Poems"

    GENEVA SMITHERMAN. "The Power of the Rap: The Black Idiom and The New Black Poetry," *Twentieth Century Literature* 19(4), October 1973, 271-72.

LEE-HAMILTON, EUGENE

"Mandolin"

    PHILIP HOBSBAUM. "The Rise of the Dramatic Monologue," *Hudson Review* 28(2), Summer 1975, 240-41.

LELAND, JOHN

"Laudatio Pacis"

    JAMES HUTTON. "John Leland's *Laudatio Pacis*," *Studies in Philology* 58(4), October 1961, 616-26.

LENNON, JOHN & MCCARTNEY, PAUL

"A Day in the Life"

    RICHARD POIRIER. "Learning from the Beatles," *Partisan Review* 34(4), Fall 1967, 541-42.

LEVERTOV, DENISE

"Adams's Complaint"

    DIANNE F. SADOFF. "Mythopoeia, The Moon, and Contemporary Women's Poetry," *Massachusetts Review* 19(1), Spring 1978, 101.

"Another Spring"

    DIANNE F. SADOFF. "Mythopoeia, The Moon, and Contemporary Women's Poetry," *Massachusetts Review* 19(1), Spring 1978, 99.

"At the Edge"

    THOMAS A. DUDDY. "To Celebrate: A Reading of Denise Levertov," *Criticism* 10(2), Spring 1968, 142-43.

"The Coming Fall"

    THOMAS A. DUDDY. "To Celebrate: A Reading of Denise Levertov," *Criticism* 10(2), Spring 1968, 148-49.

"The Crack"

    THOMAS A. DUDDY. "To Celebrate: A Reading of Denise Levertov," *Criticism* 10(2), Spring 1968, 150-51.

"Exchange"

    SUZANNE JUHASZ. *Naked and Fiery Forms*, pp. 64-65.

"The Five Day Rain"

    PATRICK MORROW. "Denise Levertov's 'The Five Day Rain,'" *Notes on Contemporary Literature* 2(1), January 1972, 4-6.

"From a Notebook: October '68-May '69"

    PAUL A. LACEY. *The Inner War*, pp. 127-29.

"From the Roof"

    SUZANNE JUHASZ. *Naked and Fiery Forms*, pp. 68-71.

"The Garden Wall"

    THOMAS A. DUDDY. "To Celebrate: A Reading of Denise Levertov," *Criticism* 10(2), Spring 1968, 146-48.

    CAROL A. KYLE. "Every Step an Arrival: *Six Variations* and the Musical Structure of Denise Levertov's Poetry," *Centennial Review* 17(3), Summer 1973, 291-92.

"The Goddess"

    THOMAS A. DUDDY. "To Celebrate: A Reading of Denise Levertov," *Criticism* 10(2), Spring 1968, 139-40.

"Illustrious Ancestors"

    PAUL A. LACEY. *The Inner War*, pp. 111-13.

"In Mind"

DIANNE F. SADOFF. "Mythopoeia, The Moon, and Contemporary Women's Poetry," *Massachusetts Review* 19(1), Spring 1978, 99-100.

"The Instant"

RALPH J. MILLS, JR. *Contemporary American Poetry*, pp. 189-91.

RALPH J. MILLS, JR. "Denise Levertov: The Poetry of the Immediate," in *Poets in Progress*, second ed., pp. 218-20.

"An Interim"

PAUL A. LACEY. *The Inner War*, p. 127.

"A Lamentation"

JEAN M. HUNT. "The New Grief-Language of Denise Levertov: *The Sorrow Dance*," *University Review* 34(2), Winter 1968, 152.

PAUL A. LACEY. *The Inner War*, pp. 120-21.

"Life at War"

JEAN M. HUNT. "Denise Levertov's New Grief-Language II: *The Sorrow Dance*," *University Review* 34(3), Spring 1969, 175-77, *passim*.

PAUL A. LACEY. *The Inner War*, pp. 124-25.

"Losing Track"

M. L. ROSENTHAL. "Dynamics of Form and Motive in Some Representative Twentieth-Century Lyric Poems," *ELH* 37(1), March 1970, 139-41.

M. L. ROSENTHAL and A. J. M. SMITH. *Exploring Poetry*, second ed., pp. 411-12.

"The Malice of Innocence"

CAROL A. KYLE. "Every Step an Arrival: *Six Variations* and the Musical Structure of Denise Levertov's Poetry," *Centennial Review* 17(3), Summer 1973, 294-95.

"Matins"

THOMAS A. DUDDY. "To Celebrate: A Reading of Denise Levertov," *Criticism* 10(2), Spring 1968, 144-45.

SUZANNE JUHASZ. *Naked and Fiery Forms*, pp. 71-74.

"The Mutes"

JEAN M. HUNT. "The New Grief-Language of Denise Levertov: *The Sorrow Dance*," *University Review* 35(2), Winter 1968, 150-51.

"O Taste and See"

LINDA WELSHIMER WAGNER. "'Sound of Direction,'" *Massachusetts Review* 8(1), Winter 1967, 219-20.

"Olga Poems"

JEAN M. HUNT. "Denise Levertov's New Grief-Language II: *The Sorrow Dance*," *University Review* 34(3), Spring 1969, 171-77.

SUZANNE JUHASZ. *Naked and Fiery Forms*, pp. 75-78.

PAUL A. LACEY. *The Inner War*, pp. 120-23.

CARY NELSON. "Whitman in Vietnam: Poetry and History in Contemporary America," *Massachusetts Review* 16(1), Winter 1975, 64-65.

"The Peachtree"

JEAN M. HUNT. "Denise Levertov's New Grief-Language II: *The Sorrow Dance*," *University Review* 34(3), Spring 1969, 175.

"Pleasures"

RALPH J. MILLS, JR. *Contemporary American Poetry*, pp. 181-82.

RALPH J. MILLS, JR. "Denise Levertov: The Poetry of the Immediate," in *Poets in Progress*, second ed., pp. 210-11.

"The Pulse"

NANCY JO HOFFMAN. "Reading Women's Poetry: The Meaning and Our Lives," *College English* 34(1), October 1972, 48-49.

"Relearning the Alphabet"

PAUL A. LACEY. *The Inner War*, pp. 130-31.

DIANNE F. SADOFF. "Mythopoeia, The Moon, and Contemporary Women's Poetry," *Massachusetts Review* 19(1), Spring 1978, 102.

WALTER SUTTON. *American Free Verse*, p. 179.

"The Ring of Changes"

CAROL A. KYLE. "Every Step an Arrival: *Six Variations* and the Musical Structure of Denise Levertov's Poetry," *Centennial Review* 17(3), Summer 1973, 289-90.

"Six Variations"

CAROL A. KYLE. "Every Step an Arrival: *Six Variations* and the Musical Structure of Denise Levertov's Poetry," *Centennial Review* 17(3), Summer 1973, 281-89.

"Something to Wear"

RALPH J. MILLS, JR. *Contemporary American Poetry*, pp. 185-88.

RALPH J. MILLS, JR. "Denise Levertov: The Poetry of the Immediate," in *Poets in Progress*, second ed., pp. 215-17.

"Song for Ishtar"

DIANNE F. SADOFF. "Mythopoeia, The Moon, and Contemporary Women's Poetry," *Massachusetts Review* 19(1), Spring 1978, 100.

"Staying Alive"

SUZANNE JUHASZ. *Naked and Fiery Forms*, pp. 78-82.

CARY NELSON. "Whitman in Vietnam: Poetry and History in Contemporary America," *Massachusetts Review* 16(1), Winter 1975, 63-65.

"A Stir in the Air"

CAROL A. KYLE. "Every Step an Arrival: *Six Variations* and the Musical Structure of Denise Levertov's Poetry," *Centennial Review* 17(3), Summer 1973, 292-93.

"To the Snake"

ENGLISH 692. "Poem Opening: An Invitation to Transactive Criticism," *College English* 40(1), September 1978, 2-16.

"The Tulips"

WALTER SUTTON. "A Conversation with Denise Levertov," *Minnesota Review* 5(4), October-December 1965, 330-31.

"Under a Blue Star"

SUZANNE JUHASZ. *Naked and Fiery Forms*, pp. 66-68.

"What Were They Like?"

JEAN M. HUNT. "Denise Levertov's New Grief-Language II: *The Sorrow Dance*," *University Review* 34(3), Spring 1969, 176.

"With Eyes at the Back of Our Heads"

RALPH J. MILLS, JR. *Contemporary American Poetry*, pp. 194-96.

RALPH J. MILLS, JR. "Denise Levertov: The Poetry of the Immediate," in *Poets in Progress*, second ed., pp. 224-26.

LEVINE, PHILIP

"The Poem Circling Hamtramck, Michigan All Night in Search of You"

    CHARLES MOLESWORTH. "The Burned Essential Oil: The Poetry of Philip Levine," *Hollins Critic* 12(5), December 1975, 14.

"Silent in America"

    RALPH J. MILLS, JR. *Cry of the Human*, pp. 254-57.

"They Feed They Lion"

    CHARLES MOLESWORTH. "The Burned Essential Oil: The Poetry of Philip Levine," *Hollins Critic* 12(5), December 1975, 9-10.

LEWIS, ALUN

"All Day it has Rained"

    VERNON SCANNELL. *Not Without Glory*, pp. 58-59.

"The Journey"

    VERNON SCANNELL. *Not Without Glory*, pp. 66-67.

"The Jungle"

    VERNON SCANNELL. *Not Without Glory*, pp. 68-73.

"The Mahratta Ghats"

    VERNON SCANNELL. *Not Without Glory*, pp. 65-66.

"Threnody on a Starry Night"

    RALPH HOUSTON. "The Broken Arch: A Study of the Poetry of Alun Lewis," *Adelphi* 28(4), Fourth Quarter, 1951, 407-8.

"The Way Back"

    JOHN PIKOULIS. "Alun Lewis: The Way Back," *Critical Quarterly* 14(2), Summer 1972, 145-66.

LEWIS, JAMES FRANKLIN

"Dawn in the Study"

    MARY GRAHAM LUND. *Explicator* 18(2), November 1959, Item 12.

"In Memoriam"

    MARY GRAHAM LUND. *Explicator* 18(4), January 1960, Item 23.

LEWIS, M. G.

"Alonzo the Brave and Fair Imogine" (*The Monk*)

    FREDERICK L. BEATY. *Light from Heaven*, pp. 200-1.

LEWIS, RICHARD

"Congratulatory Verses, wrote at the Arrival of Our Honourable Proprietary"

    J. A. LEO LEMAY. "Richard Lewis and Augustan American Poetry," *PMLA* 83(1), March 1968, 95-98.

"Food for Criticks"

    J. A. LEO LEMAY. "Richard Lewis and Augustan American Poetry," *PMLA* 83(1), March 1968, 89-91.

"A Journey from Patapsco to Annapolis"

    J. A. LEO LEMAY. "Richard Lewis and Augustan American Poetry," *PMLA* 83(1), March 1968, 85-89.

"A Rhapsody"

    J. A. LEO LEMAY. "Richard Lewis and Augustan American Poetry," *PMLA* 83(1), March 1968, 91-92.

"Verses to Mr. Ross, on Mr. Calvert's Departure from Maryland, May 10th, 1732"

    J. A. LEO LEMAY. "Richard Lewis and Augustan American Poetry," *PMLA* 83(1), March 1968, 92-95.

LEWIS, WYNDHAM

"The Enemy of the Stars"

    R. T. CHAPMAN. "'Edited by Wyndham Lewis,'" *Durham University Journal*, n.s., 36(1), December 1974, 15.

"One Way Song"

    JOHN R. HARRISON. *The Reactionaries*, pp. 80-81, 93. (P)

LIMÓN, JOSÉ

"Frost in the Rio Grande Valley"

    ALBERT D. TREVIÑO. "Frost in the Rio Grande Valley," *English Journal* 66(3), March 1977, 69.

LINDBERGH, ANNE MORROW

"The Man and the Child"

    JOHN CIARDI. *Dialogue with an Audience*, pp. 74-75.

LINDSAY, DAVID

"The Dream"

    RICHARD M. CLEWETT, JR. "Rhetorical Strategy and Structure in Three of Sir David Lindsay's Poems," *Studies in English Literature 1500-1900* 16(1), Winter 1976, 4-6.

"The Testament and Complaynt of Our Souerane Lordis Papyngo"

    RICHARD M. CLEWETT, JR. "Rhetorical Strategy and Structure in Three of Sir David Lindsay's Poems," *Studies in English Literature 1500-1900* 16(1), Winter 1976, 11-13.

LINDSAY, VACHEL

"Abraham Lincoln Walks at Midnight"

    JAMES M. REID. *100 American Poems of the Twentieth Century*, pp. 64-65.

    MARJORIE A. TAYLOR. "Vachel Lindsay and the Ghost of Abraham Lincoln," *Centennial Review* 22(1), Winter 1978, 113-17.

"The Congo"

    A. L. BADER. "Lindsay Explains 'The Congo,'" *Philological Quarterly* 27(2), April 1948, 190-92.

    WALTER BLAIR. *The Literature of the United States*, II: 946.

    HARRY BROWN and JOHN MILSTEAD. *What the Poem Means*, p. 134.

    LAURENCE PERRINE. *100 American Poems of The Twentieth Century*, pp. 55-64.

    AUSTIN WARREN. "The Case of Vachel Lindsay," *Accent* 6(4), Summer 1946, 237-39.

"General William Booth Enters into Heaven"

    WALTER BLAIR. *The Literature of the United States*, II: 944.

    AUSTIN WARREN. "The Case of Vachel Lindsay," *Accent* 6(4), Summer 1946, 237.

"The Santa Fe Trail"

    RICHARD E. AMACHER. *Explicator* 5(5), March 1947, Item 33.

    Richard E. Amacher. "Off 'The Santa Fé Trail,'" *American Literature* 20(3), November 1948, 337. (P)

    A. L. Bader. "Vachel Lindsay on 'The Santa Fé Trail,'" *American Literature* 19(4), January 1948, 360-62.

LISTER, R. P.

"Target"

LAURENCE PERRINE. "The Importance of Tone in the Interpretation of Literature," *College English* 24(5), February 1963, 390-92.

LODGE, THOMAS

"Epistle I" (*A Fig for Momus*)

JAY ARNOLD LEVINE. "The Status of the Verse Epistle Before Pope," *Studies in Philology* 59(4), October 1962, 671-72.

"Scillaes Metamorphosis"

ELIZABETH STORY DONNO. "The Epyllion," in *English Poetry and Prose,* ed. by Christopher Ricks, pp. 85-87.

LOGAN, JOHN

"Big Sur: Partington Cove"

CHARLES ALTIERI. "Poetry as Resurrection: John Logan's Structures of Metaphysical Solace," *Modern Poetry Studies* 3(5), 1973, 211-13.

"Cycle for Mother Cabrini"

HAROLD ISBELL. "Growth and Change: John Logan's Poems," *Modern Poetry Studies* 2(5), 1971, 213-16.

"Lines Against a Loved American Poet"

CHARLES ALTIERI. "Poetry as Resurrection: John Logan's Structures of Metaphysical Solace," *Modern Poetry Studies,* 3(5), 1973, 202.

"Lines for Michael in the Picture"

CHARLES ALTIERI. "Poetry as Resurrection: John Logan's Structures of Metaphysical Solace," *Modern Poetry Studies* 3(5), 1973, 219-20.

"Lines on Locks"

CHARLES ALTIERI. "Poetry as Resurrection: John Logan's Structures of Metaphysical Solace," *Modern Poetry Studies* 3(5), 1973, 213-14.

"Pagan Saturday"

HAROLD ISBELL. "Growth and Change: John Logan's Poems," *Modern Poetry Studies* 2(5), 1971, 216-17.

"The Picnic"

CHARLES ALTIERI. "Poetry as Resurrection: John Logan's Structures of Metaphysical Solace," *Modern Poetry Studies* 3(5), 1973, 205-7.

"Protest After a Dream"

CHARLES ALTIERI. "Poetry as Resurrection: John Logan's Structures of Metaphysical Solace," *Modern Poetry Studies* 3(5), 1973, 202-3.

"Recollection on the Day of a First Book"

CHARLES ALTIERI. "Poetry as Resurrection: John Logan's Structures of Metaphysical Solace," *Modern Poetry Studies* 3(5), 1973, 201-2.

"The Rescue"

CHARLES ALTIERI. "Poetry as Resurrection: John Logan's Structures of Metaphysical Solace," *Modern Poetry Studies* 3(5), 1973, 195-98.

"The Search"

HAROLD ISBELL. "Growth and Change: John Logan's Poems," *Modern Poetry Studies* 2(5), 1971, 222-23.

"Shore Scene"

CHARLES ALTIERI. "Poetry as Resurrection: John Logan's Structures of Metaphysical Solace," *Modern Poetry Studies* 3(5), 1973, 207-9.

"A Trip to Four or Five Towns"

CHARLES ALTIERI. "Poetry as Resurrection: John Logan's Structures of Metaphysical Solace," *Modern Poetry Studies* 3(5), 1973, 203-5.

"The Zoo"

CHARLES ALTIERI. "Poetry as Resurrection: John Logan's Structures of Metaphysical Solace," *Modern Poetry Studies* 3(5), 1973, 209-10.

LOGAN, PAUL

"A Century Piece for Poor Heine (1800-1856)"

PAUL CARROLL. *The Poem In Its Skin,* pp. 116-36.

LOMAX, JOHN AVERY

"Bronc Peeler's Song"

LAWRENCE CLAYTON. "Folk Song Comments on the End of an Era," *Southwestern American Literature* 5 (1975), 23-25.

"The Camp Fire Has Gone Out"

LAWRENCE CLAYTON. "Folk Song Comments on the End of an Era," *Southwestern American Literature* 5 (1975), 22-25.

LONGFELLOW, HENRY WADSWORTH

"Aftermath"

GEORGE ARMS. *The Fields Were Green,* pp. 213-14.

"The Bells of San Blas"

HYATT H. WAGGONER. *American Poets,* pp. 43-44.

"The Building of the Ship"

NEWTON ARVIN. "Early Longfellow," *Massachusetts Review* 3(1), Autumn 1961, 150-52.

"The Chamber over the Gate"

HYATT H. WAGGONER. *American Poets,* pp. 50-51.

"Chaucer"

AGNES STEIN. *The Uses of Poetry,* pp. 300-1.

NANCY L. TENFELDE. *Explicator* 22(7), March 1964, Item 55.

"The Children's Hour"

RICHARD RULAND. "Longfellow and the Modern Reader," *English Journal* 55(6), September 1966, 665.

"The Cross of Snow"

ROBERT A. DURR. *Explicator* 13(5), March 1955, Item 32.

"The Day is Done"

NEWTON ARVIN. "Early Longfellow," *Massachusetts Review* 3(1), Autumn 1961, 147.

"Excelsior"

WILLIAM E. BRIDGES. "Warm Hearth, Cold World: Social Perspectives on the Household Poets," *American Quarterly* 21(4), Winter 1969, 774-75.

"The Falcon of Ser Federigo"

GEORGE ARMS. *The Fields Were Green,* pp. 218-19.

"The Fire of Driftwood"

GEORGE ARMS. *The Fields Were Green,* p. 212.

NEWTON ARVIN. "Early Longfellow," *Massachusetts Review* 3(1), Autumn 1961, 152-53.

"Galgano"

STEVEN ALLABACK. "Longfellow's 'Galgano,'" *American Literature* 46(2), May 1974, 210-19.

"Hymn to the Night"

GEORGE ARMS. *Explicator* 1(1), October 1942, Item 7.

LONGFELLOW, HENRY WADSWORTH *(Cont.)*

"In the Churchyard at Cambridge"

GEORGE ARMS. *The Fields Were Green*, pp. 208-9.

FRANK D. MCCONNELL. "Film as Antipedagogy: Laughing at *Laura*, Cackling at *Kane*," *Massachusetts Review* 19(3), Autumn 1978, 577-78.

I. A. RICHARDS. *Practical Criticism*, pp. 163-76.

"The Jewish Cemetery at Newport"

DAVID DAICHES and WILLIAM CHARVAT. *Poems in English*, pp. 718-19.

"Jugurtha"

R. E. AMACHER. *Explicator* 6(4), February 1948, Item 29.

GEORGE ARMS. *The Fields Were Green*, p. 215.

"Mezzo Cammin"

WILLIAM E. BRIDGES. "Warm Hearth, Cold World: Social Perspectives on the Household Poets," *American Quarterly* 21(4), Winter 1969, 771-76.

"My Lost Youth"

GEORGE ARMS. "The Revision of 'My Lost Youth,'" *Modern Language Notes* 61(6), June 1946, 389-92.

"The Occultation of Orion"

NEWTON ARVIN. "Early Longfellow," *Massachusetts Review* 3(1), Autumn 1961, 154-55.

MICHAEL ZIMMERMAN. "War and Peace: Longfellow's 'The Occultation of Orion,'" *American Literature* 38(4), January 1967, 540-46.

"Oft Have I Seen at Some Cathedral Door" *(Divina Commedia, I)*

GEORGE ARMS. *Explicator* 2(1), October 1943, Item 7.

GEORGE ARMS. *The Fields Were Green*, p. 211.

"O star of morning and liberty" *(Divina Commedia, VI)*

RICHARD RULAND. "Longfellow and the Modern Reader," *English Journal* 55(6), September 1966, 667-68.

"Paul Revere's Ride"

ISAAC ASIMOV. *Familiar Poems, Annotated*, pp. 137-48.

"A Psalm of Life"

HYATT H. WAGGONER. *American Poets*, pp. 44-46.

"The Ropewalk"

HOWARD NEMEROV. *Poetry and Fiction*, pp. 156-57.

HYATT H. WAGGONER. *American Poets*, p. 51.

"Serenade" *(The Spanish Student)*

G. THOMAS TANSELLE. *Explicator* 23(6), February 1965, Item 48.

"Sleep"

KENNETH T. REED. "Longfellow's 'Sleep' and Frost's 'After Apple-Picking,'" *American Notes & Queries*, n.s., 10(9), May 1972, 134-35.

"Snow-Flakes"

GEORGE ARMS. *The Fields Were Green*, pp. 207-8.

NORMAN HOLMES PEARSON. "Both Longfellows," *University of Kansas City Review* 16(4), Summer 1950, 252-53.

"Tegnér's Drapa"

GERALD R. GRIFFIN. "Longfellow's 'Tegnér's Drapa': A Reappraisal," *American Transcendental Quarterly* 40(Fall 1978), 379-87.

LOVELACE, RICHARD

"Advice to my best Brother. Coll: Francis Lovelace"

BRUCE KING. "Green Ice and a Breast of Proof," *College English* 26(7), April 1965, 513-14. Reprinted in: *Seventeenth Century English Poetry*, revised ed., pp. 328-29.

"The Ant"

EARL MINER. *The Cavalier Mode from Jonson to Cotton*, pp. 112-14.

"La Bella Bona Roba"

A. ALVAREZ. *The School of Donne*, English ed., pp. 64-65; American ed., pp. 72-73.

MARIUS BEWLEY. *Masks & Mirrors*, pp. 56-58, 68-76.

GEORGE STEINER. "On Difficulty," *Journal of Aesthetics and Art Criticism* 36(3), Spring 1978, 268-69.

"A Black Patch on Lucasta's Face"

C. F. WILLIAMSON. "Two Notes on the Poems of Richard Lovelace," *Modern Language Review* 52(2), April 1957, 229.

"Cupid far gone"

THOMAS CLAYTON. *Explicator* 33(4), December 1974, Item 32. (P)

"Elinda's Glove"

PAULINA PALMER. "Lovelace's Treatment Of Some Marinesque Motifs," *Comparative Literature* 29(4), Fall 1977, 302-5.

"The Falcon"

RAYMOND A. ANSELMENT. "'Griefe Triumphant' and 'Victorious Sorrow': A Reading of Richard Lovelace's 'The Falcon,'" *Journal of English and Germanic Philology* 70(3), July 1971, 404-17.

"The Grasse-hopper"

DON CAMERON ALLEN. "An Explication of Lovelace's 'The Grasse-Hopper,'" *Modern Language Quarterly* 18(1), March 1957, 35-43. Reprinted in: Don Cameron Allen. *Image and Meaning*, pp. 152-64. Also: *Seventeenth Century English Poetry*, revised ed., pp. 280-89.

CLEANTH BROOKS. "Literary Criticism: Poet, Poem, and the Reader," in *Varieties of Literary Experience*, pp. 103-12.

BRUCE KING. "*The Grasse-hopper* and Allegory," *Ariel* 1(2), April 1970, 71-82.

BRUCE KING. "Green Ice and a Breast of Proof," *College English* 26(7), April 1965, 514-15.

EARL MINER. *The Cavalier Mode from Jonson to Cotton*, pp. 286-95.

"Gratiana dauncing and singing"

PAULINA PALMER. "Lovelace's Treatment of Some Marinsque Motifs," *Comparative Literature* 29(4), Fall 1977, 309-12.

JOHN T. SHAWCROSS. "The Poet as Orator: One Phase of His Judicial Pose," in *The Rhetoric of Renaissance Poetry*, pp. 30-31.

"Orpheus to Beasts"

MAREN-SOFIE RØSTVIG. "Andrew Marvell and the Caroline Poets," in *English Poetry and Prose*, ed. by Christopher Ricks, p. 210.

"The Scrutinie"

NORMAN H. HOLLAND. "Clinical, Yes. Healthy, No," *Literature and Psychology* 14(3-4), Summer-Fall 1964, 122.

NORMAN H. HOLLAND. "Literary Value: A Psychoanalytic Approach," *Literature and Psychology* 14(2), Spring 1964, 43-55.

"The Snayl"

RANDOLPH L. WADSWORTH, JR. "On 'The Snayl' by Richard Lovelace," *Modern Language Review* 65(4), October 1970, 750-60.

"To Althea, from Prison"

WILLIAM EMPSON. *Seven Types of Ambiguity*, pp. 266-67; second and third eds., pp. 209-11.

BRUCE KING. "Green Ice and a Breast of Proof," in *Seventeenth Century English Poetry*, revised ed., pp. 324-25.

JAMES R. KREUZER. *Elements of Poetry*, pp. 151-52.

A. J. SMITH. "The Failure of Love: Love Lyrics after Donne," in *Metaphysical Poetry*, edited by Malcolm Bradbury and David Palmer, pp. 60-61.

"To Fletcher reviv'd"

AVON JACK MURPHY. "The Critical Elegy of Earlier Seventeenth-Century England," *Genre* 5(1), March 1972, 86-87.

"To Lucasta From Prison"

A. J. SMITH. "The Failure of Love: Love Lyrics after Donne," in *Metaphysical Poetry*, edited by Malcolm Bradbury and David Palmer, p. 61.

"To Lucasta, Going to the Warres"

ROBERT HAWKINS. *Preface to Poetry*, pp. 106-8.

NORMAN N. HOLLAND. "Clinical, Yes. Healthy, No.," *Literature and Psychology* 14(3-4), Summer-Fall 1964, 122.

NORMAN N. HOLLAND. "Literary Value: A Psychoanalytic Approach," *Literature and Psychology* 14(2), Spring 1964, 50-55.

BRUCE KING. "Green Ice and a Breast of Proof," in *Seventeenth Century English Poetry*, revised ed., p. 326.

NORMAN HOLMES PEARSON. *Explicator* 7(8), June 1949, Item 58. Reprinted in: *Readings for Liberal Education*, revised ed., II: 57-59; third ed., II: 48-49.

MARK VAN DOREN. *Introduction to Poetry*, pp. 21-26.

"To Lucasta, Ode Lyrick"

JOHN T. SHAWCROSS. "The Poet as Orator: One Phase of His Judicial Pose," in *The Rhetoric of Renaissance Poetry*, pp. 29-30.

"To My Dear Friend Mr. E. R."

C. F. WILLIAMSON. "Two Notes on the Poems of Richard Lovelace," *Modern Language Review* April 1957, 227-28. (P)

"To my Worthy Friend, Mr. Peter Lilly: on that excellent Picture of His Majesty, and the Duke of Yorke"

EARL MINER. *The Cavalier Mode from Jonson to Cotton*, pp. 61-62.

"The Vintage to the Dungeon"

BRUCE KING. "Green Ice and a Breast of Proof," in *Seventeenth Century English Poetry*, revised ed., pp. 324-25.

LOVELING, BENJAMIN

"First Satire of Persius, Imitated"

CYNTHIA S. DESSEN. "An Eighteenth-Century Imitation of Persius, Satire I," *Texas Studies in Literature and Language* 20(3), Fall 1978, 433-56.

LOWBURY, EDWARD

"Nothing"

JOHN PRESS. "Edward Lowbury," *Southern Review*, n.s., 6(2), Spring 1970, 308-9.

"Surgery of a Burn"

JOHN PRESS. "Edward Lowbury," *Southern Review*, n.s., 6(2), Spring 1970, 303-5.

LOWELL, AMY

"The Book of Hours of Sister Clotilde"

L. S. DEMBO. *Conceptions of Reality in Modern American Poetry*, pp. 43-44.

"The Cremona Violin"

L. S. DEMBO. *Conceptions of Reality in Modern American Poetry*, p. 45.

"Night Clouds"

CHARLES W. COOPER and JOHN HOLMES. *Preface to Poetry*, pp. 141-42.

"Patterns"

CLEANTH BROOKS and ROBERT PENN WARREN. *Understanding Poetry*, pp. 139-43; revised ed., pp. 58-61.

HARRY BROWN and JOHN MILSTEAD. *What the Poem Means*, pp. 136-37.

JANET OVERMYER. "Which Broken Pattern? — A Note on Amy Lowell's 'Patterns,'" *Notes on Contemporary Literature* 1(4), September 1971, 14-15.

LAURENCE PERRINE. *100 American Poems of the Twentieth Century*, pp. 47-52.

"The Pond"

LEE A. JACOBUS and WILLIAM T. MOYNIHAN. *Poems in Context*, pp. 315-16.

"The Shadow"

L. S. DEMBO. *Conceptions of Reality in Modern American Poetry*, pp. 44-45.

"Sunshine"

EARL DANIELS. *The Art of Reading Poetry*, pp. 196-97.

"Sword Blades and Poppy Seed"

L. S. DEMBO. *Conceptions of Reality in Modern American Poetry*, pp. 42-43.

"Wind and Silver"

LAURENCE PERRINE. "Sinners in the Hands of an Angry Critic: 'But Deliver Us From Evil,'" *CEA Critic* 30(3), December 1967, 3-4.

LOWELL, JAMES RUSSELL

"After the Burial"

CLEANTH BROOKS and ROBERT PENN WARREN. *Understanding Poetry*, third ed., pp. 240-42.

"Agassiz"

GEORGE ARMS. *The Fields Were Green*, pp. 124-26.

IAN F. A. BELL. "Divine Patterns: Louis Agassiz and American Men of Letters. Some Preliminary Explorations," *Journal of American Studies* 10(3), December 1976, 356-58.

"Auspex"

RICHARD E. AMACHER. *Explicator* 9(5), March 1951, Item 37.

GEORGE ARMS. *The Fields Were Green*, pp. 133-34.

"The Cathedral"

GEORGE ARMS. *The Fields Were Green*, pp. 135-38.

LOWELL, JAMES RUSSELL *(Cont.)*

"Fitz Adam's Story"

GEORGE ARMS. *The Fields Were Green,* pp. 130-31.

HYATT H. WAGGONER. *American Poets,* pp. 61-62.

"Indian Summer: A Reverie"

BERNARD DUFFEY. *Poetry in America,* pp. 78-81.

"Memoriae Positum"

STEVEN AXELROD. "Colonel Shaw in American Poetry: 'For the Union Dead' and its Precursors," *American Quarterly* 24(4), October 1972, 528-30.

PAUL KAVANAGH. "The Nation Past and Present: A Study of Robert Lowell's 'For the Union Dead,'" *Journal of American Studies* 5(1), April 1971, 93-101.

"Ode Recited at the Harvard Commemoration"

GEORGE ARMS. *The Fields Were Green,* pp. 138-40.

HYATT H. WAGGONER. *American Poets,* pp. 578-80.

"Rhoecus"

HYATT H. WAGGONER. *American Poets,* pp. 64-65.

" 'Sunthin' in the Pastoral Line"

JOHN C. BRODERICK. "Lowell's 'Sunthin' in the Pastoral Line,'" *American Literature* 31(2), May 1959, 163-72.

BERNARD DUFFEY. *Poetry in America,* pp. 81-82.

ROY HARVEY PEARCE. *The Continuity of American Poetry,* pp. 219-20.

"To the Dandelion"

GEORGE ARMS. *The Fields Were Green,* pp. 132-33.

"The Washers of the Shroud"

JOHN Q. ANDERSON. "Lowell's 'The Washers of the Shroud' and the Celtic Legend of the Washer of the Ford," *American Literature* 35(3), November 1963, 361-63.

LOWELL, ROBERT

"Adam and Eve"

RALPH J. MILLS, JR. *Contemporary American Poetry,* pp. 144-46.

"After the Surprising Conversions"

JOHN AKEY. *Explicator* 9(8), June 1951, Item 51.

G. GIOVANNINI. *Explicator* 9(8), June 1951, Item 53.

GEORGE S. LENSING. "Robert Lowell and Jonathan Edwards: Poetry in the Hands of an Angry God," *South Carolina Review* 6(2), April 1974, 8-12.

DAVID BULWER LUTYENS. *The Creative Encounter,* pp. 174-75.

THOMAS VOGLER. "Robert Lowell: Payment Gat He Nane," *Iowa Review* 2(3), Summer 1971, 76-77.

DALLAS E. WIEBE. "Mr. Lowell and Mr. Edwards," *Wisconsin Studies in Contemporary Literature* 3(2), Spring-Summer 1962, 26-29.

"As a Plane Tree by the Water"

DAVID BULWER LUTYENS. *The Creative Encounter,* pp. 138-41.

DESALES STANDERWICK. "Notes on Robert Lowell," *Renascence* 8(2), Winter 1955, 80.

"Aswan Dam"

ROBERT PINSKY. *The Situation of Poetry,* pp. 21-23.

"At the Indian Killer's Grave"

DAVID BULWER LUTYENS. *The Creative Encounter,* pp. 149-50.

DESALES STANDERWICK. "Notes on Robert Lowell," *Renascence* 8(2), Winter 1955, 78-79.

AUSTIN WARREN. "A Double Discipline," *Poetry* 70(5), August 1947, 265.

"Between the Porch and the Altar"

MARIUS BEWLEY. "Aspects of Modern American Poetry," *Scrutiny* 17(4), March 1951, 345-47.

MARIUS BEWLEY. "Some Aspects of Modern American Poetry,," in *Modern Poetry,* pp. 260-61.

DAVID BULWER LUTYENS. *The Creative Encounter,* pp. 176-85.

JAY MARTIN. "Robert Lowell," in *Seven American Poets from MacLeish to Nemerov,* pp. 220-21.

M. L. ROSENTHAL. *The Modern Poets,* pp. 228-29.

THOMAS VOGLER. "Robert Lowell: Payment Gat He Nane," *Iowa Review* 2(3), Summer 1971, 78-82.

"Beyond the Alps"

CHARLES ALTIERI. "Poetry in a Prose World: Robert Lowell's 'Life Studies,'" *Modern Poetry Studies* 1(4), 1970, 182-83.

RALPH J. MILLS, JR. *Contemporary American Poetry,* pp. 149-51.

"The Bomber"

DAN JAFFE. "Poets in the Inferno: Civilians, C.O.'s and Combatants," in *The Forties,* p. 48.

"Caligula"

JOAN BOBBITT. "Lowell and Plath: Objectivity and the Confessional Mode," *Arizona Quarterly* 33(4), Winter 1977, 312-13.

"Central Park"

DONALD EULERT. "Robert Lowell and W. C. Williams: Sterility in 'Central Park,'" *English Language Notes* 5(2), December 1967, 129-35.

"Children of Light"

NEVILLE BRAYBROOKE. "The Poetry of Robert Lowell," *Catholic World* 198(1186), January 1964, 231-33.

"Christmas Eve Under Hooker's Statue"

RICHARD FEIN. "Mary and Bellona: The War Poetry of Robert Lowell," *Southern Review,* n.s., 1(4), Autumn 1965, 823-26.

DAVID BULWER LUTYENS. *The Creative Encounter,* pp. 168-70.

JAY MARTIN. "Robert Lowell," in *Seven American Poets from MacLeish to Nemerov,* p. 217.

THOMAS VOGLER. "Robert Lowell: Payment Gat He Nane," *Iowa Review* 2(3), Summer 1971, 77-78.

"Colloquy in Black Rock"

CHARLES ALTIERI. "Poetry in a Prose World: Robert Lowell's 'Life Studies,'" *Modern Poetry Studies* 1(4), 1970, 185.

HARRY BROWN and JOHN MILSTEAD. *What the Poem Means,* pp. 137-38.

DAVID BULWER LUTYENS. *The Creative Encounter,* pp. 142-43.

KENNETH JOHNSON. "The View from Lord Weary's Castle," in *The Forties,* p. 231.

JAY MARTIN. "Robert Lowell," in *Seven American Poets from MacLeish to Nemerov,* pp. 218-19.

RALPH J. MILLS, JR. *Contemporary American Poetry,* pp. 139-41.

THOMAS VOGLER. "Robert Lowell: Payment Gat He Nane," *Iowa Review* 2(3), Summer 1971, 73.

"Colonel Shaw and the Massachusetts 44th"

GEORGE W. NITCHIE. "The Importance of Robert Lowell," *Southern Review*, n.s., 8(1), Winter 1972, 121-22.

WALTER SUTTON. *American Free Verse*, pp. 158-59.

"Commander Lowell"

GEORGE MCFADDEN. "'Life Studies' — Robert Lowell's Comic Breakthrough," *PMLA* 90(1), January 1975, 100.

ROBERT PHILLIPS. *The Confessional Poets*, pp. 29-30.

"Concord"

DAVID ANTIN. "Modernism and Postmodernism: Approaching the Present in American Poetry," *Boundary 2* 1(1), Fall 1972, 109-10.

JEROME MAZZARO. "Robert Lowell's Early Politics of Apocalypse," in *Modern American Poetry*, edited by Jerome Mazzaro, pp. 327-28.

GABRIEL PEARSON. "Lowell's Marble Meanings," in *The Survival of Poetry*, pp. 61-63.

"The Crucifix"

DAVID BULWER LUTYENS. *The Creative Encounter*, pp. 143-46.

"David and Bathsheba in the Public Garden"

DAVID BULWER LUTYENS. *The Creative Encounter*, pp. 155-60.

"Dea Roma"

GLAUCO CAMBON. "Dea Roma and Robert Lowell," *Accent* 20(1), Winter 1960, 51-61.

DAVID BULWER LUTYENS. *The Creative Encounter*, pp. 155-60.

"The Dead in Europe"

HARRY J. CARGAS. *Daniel Berrigan and Contemporary Protest Poetry*, p. 53.

RICHARD FEIN. "Mary and Bellona: The War Poetry of Robert Lowell," *Southern Review*, n.s., 1(4), Autumn 1965, 832-33.

DAVID BULWER LUTYENS. *The Creative Encounter*, pp. 150-52.

"The Death of the Sheriff"

THOMAS VOGLER. "Robert Lowell: Payment Gat He Nane," *Iowa Review* 2(3), Summer 1971, 84-90.

A. KINGSLEY WEATHERHEAD. "Imagination and Fancy: Robert Lowell and Marianne Moore," *Texas Studies in Literature and Language* 6(2), Summer 1964, 192-96.

"The Dolphin"

STEVEN GOULD AXELROD. "Lowell's *The Dolphin* as a 'Book of Life,'" *Contemporary Literature* 18(4), Autumn 1977, 473-74.

ROBERT G. TWOMBLY. "The Poetics of Demur: Lowell and Frost," *College English* 38(4), December 1976, 387-88.

"Down the Nile"

DAVID KALSTONE. *Five Temperaments*, p. 71.

"The Drunken Fisherman"

HARRY BROWN and JOHN MILSTEAD. *What the Poem Means*, pp. 139-40.

THOMAS VOGLER. "Robert Lowell: Payment Gat He Nane," *Iowa Review* 2(3), Summer 1971, 75-76.

"Duc de Guise"

DAVID KALSTONE. *Five Temperaments*, pp. 68-69.

"Dunbarton"

ALAN HOLDER. "The Flintlocks of the Fathers: Robert Lowell's Treatment of the American Past," *New England Quarterly* 44(1), March 1971, 57-58.

ROBERT PHILLIPS. *The Confessional Poets*, pp. 27-29.

"During Fever"

GEORGE MCFADDEN. "'Life Studies' — Robert Lowell's Comic Breakthrough," *PMLA* 90(1), January 1975, 102-3.

ROBERT PHILLIPS. *The Confessional Poets*, p. 33.

"The Exile's Return"

SISTER ERIC MARIE BRUMLEVE. "Permanence and Change in the Poetry of Robert Lowell," *Texas Studies in Literature and Language*, 10(1), Spring 1968, 144-45.

RICHARD FEIN. "Mary and Bellona: The War Poetry of Robert Lowell," *Southern Review*, n.s., 1(4), Autumn 1965, 833-34.

KENNETH JOHNSON. "The View from Lord Weary's Castle," in *The Forties*, pp. 230-31.

JAY MARTIN. "Robert Lowell," in *Seven American Poets from MacLeish to Nemerov*, pp. 217-18.

PETER P. REMALEY. "Epic Machinery in Robert Lowell's *Lord Weary's Castle*," *Ball State University Forum* 18(2), Spring 1977, 59-64.

PETER P. REMALEY. "The Quest for Grace in Robert Lowell's *Lord Weary's Castle*," *Renascence* 28(3), Spring 1976, 116-19.

"Eye and Tooth"

JOAN BOBBITT. "Lowell and Plath: Objectivity and the Confessional Mode," *Arizona Quarterly* 33(4), Winter 1977, 313.

IAN HAMILTON. "Robert Lowell," in *A Poetry Chronicle*, p. 105.

DAVID KALSTONE. *Five Temperaments*, pp. 59-60.

CHRISTOPHER MORRIS. "The Ambivalence of Robert Lowell's 'For the Union Dead,'" *Modern Poetry Studies* 1(4), 1970, 202-3.

"Ezra Pound"

LAWRENCE KRAMER. "The Wodwo Watches the Water Clock: Language in Postmodern British and American Poetry," *Contemporary Literature* 18(3), Summer 1977, 326-28.

"Fall 1961"

STEVEN GOULD AXELROD. "Private and Public Worlds in Lowell's *For the Union Dead*," *Bucknell Review* 22(2), Fall 1976, 170-76.

STEPHEN C. MOORE. "Politics and the Poetry of Robert Lowell," *Georgia Review* 27(2), Summer 1973, 224-25.

GABRIEL PEARSON. "Lowell's Marble Meanings," in *The Survival of Poetry*, pp. 75-76.

"Falling Asleep over the Aeneid"

JAY MARTIN. "Robert Lowell," in *Seven American Poets from MacLeish to Nemerov*, pp. 223-24.

JEROME MAZZARO. "Robert Lowell's Early Politics of Apocalypse," in *Modern American Poetry*, edited by Jerome Mazzaro, pp. 348-49.

"The Fat Man in the Mirror"

DAVID BULWER LUTYENS. *The Creative Encounter*, pp. 190-96.

"Father"

DAVID KALSTONE. *Five Temperaments*, pp. 47-48.

LOWELL, ROBERT *(Cont.)*

"Father's Bedroom"

GEORGE MCFADDEN. "'Life Studies' — Robert Lowell's Comic Breakthrough," *PMLA* 90(1), January 1975, 101.

RALPH J. MILLS, JR. *Contemporary American Poetry,* p. 152.

ROBERT PHILLIPS. *The Confessional Poets,* p. 31.

"The First Study in Lent"

SISTER ERIC MARIE BRUMLEVE. "Permanence and Change in the Poetry of Robert Lowell," *Texas Studies in Literature and Language* 10(1), Spring 1966, 145-46.

RALPH J. MILLS, JR. *Contemporary American Poetry,* pp. 136-38.

"Fishnet"

STEVEN GOULD AXELROD. "Lowell's *The Dolphin* as a 'Book of Life,'" *Contemporary Literature* 18(4), Autumn 1977, 461-64.

"For Sale"

GEORGE MCFADDEN. "'Life Studies' — Robert Lowell's Comic Breakthrough," *PMLA* 90(1), January 1975, 101.

ROBERT PHILLIPS. *The Confessional Poets,* p. 31.

"For the Union Dead"

STEVEN AXELROD. "Baudelaire and the Poetry of Robert Lowell," *Twentieth Century Literature* 17(4), October 1971, 269-71.

STEVEN AXELROD. "Colonel Shaw in American Poetry: 'For the Union Dead' and its Precursors," *American Quarterly* 24(4), October 1972, 535-37.

STEVEN AXELROD. "Private and Public Worlds in Lowell's *For the Union Dead,*" *Bucknell Review* 22(2), Fall 1976, 176-79.

WILLIAM BEDFORD. "The Morality of Form in the Poetry of Robert Lowell," *Ariel* 9(1), January 1978, 10-13.

SISTER ERIC MARIE BRUMLEVE. "Permanence and Change in the Poetry of Robert Lowell," *Texas Studies in Literature and Language* 10(1), Spring 1968, 150-51.

PAUL C. DOHERTY. "The Poet as Historian: 'For the Union Dead' by Robert Lowell," *Concerning Poetry* 1(2), Fall 1968, 37-41.

IAN HAMILTON. *A Poetry Chronicle,* pp. 106-7.

GEOFFREY H. HARTMAN. *Beyond Formalism,* pp. 269-70.

JOHN C. HIRSH. "The Imagery of Dedication in Robert Lowell's 'For the Union Dead,'" *Journal of American Studies* 6(2), August 1972, 201-5.

DAVID HOLBROOK. *Lost Bearings in English Poetry,* pp. 48-57.

A. R. JONES. "Necessity and Freedom: The Poetry of Robert Lowell, Sylvia Plath and Anne Sexton," *Critical Quarterly* 7(1), Spring 1965, 18-21.

DAVID KALSTONE. *Five Temperaments,* pp. 132-33.

PAUL KAVANAGH. "The Nation Past and Present: A Study of Robert Lowell's 'For the Union Dead,'" *Journal of American Studies* 5(1), April 1971, 93-101.

JAY MARTIN. "Robert Lowell," in *Seven American Poets from MacLeish to Nemerov,* pp. 238-39.

GABRIEL PEARSON. "Lowell's Marble Meanings," in *The Survival of Poetry,* pp. 82-87.

GABRIEL PEARSON. "Robert Lowell: The Middle Years," in *Contemporary Poetry in America,* pp. 47-51.

ROBERT PINSKY. *The Situation of Poetry,* pp. 16-18.

JAMES M. REID. *100 American Poems of the Twentieth Century,* pp. 244-47.

PAUL SCHWABER. "Robert Lowell in Mid-Career," *Western Humanities Review* 25(4), Autumn 1971, 350-51.

"Fourth of July in Maine"

WILLIAM BEDFORD. "The Morality of Form in the Poetry of Robert Lowell," *Ariel* 9(1), January 1978, 14-15.

JAY MARTIN. "Robert Lowell," in *Seven American Poets from MacLeish to Nemerov,* p. 241.

"France (from the gibbet)"

THOMAS VOGLER. "Robert Lowell: Payment Gat He Nane," *Iowa Review* 2(3), Summer 1971, 73-74.

"The Ghost"

DAVID BULWER LUTYENS. *The Creative Encounter,* pp. 153-54.

"Going To and Fro"

CHRISTOPHER MORRIS. "The Ambivalence of Robert Lowell's 'For the Union Dead,'" *Modern Poetry Studies* 1(4), 1970, 200.

"Grandparents"

RALPH J. MILLS, JR. *Creation's Very Self,* pp. 24-26. Reprinted in: Ralph J. Mills, Jr. *Cry of the Human,* pp. 26-28.

RALPH J. MILLS, JR. *Contemporary American Poetry,* pp. 153-55.

ROBERT PHILLIPS. *The Confessional Poets,* p. 29.

"Hawthorne"

THOMAS WOODSON. "Robert Lowell's 'Hawthorne', Yvor Winters and the American Literary Tradition," *American Quarterly* 19(3), Fall 1967, 575-82.

"High Blood"

JOAN BOBBITT. "Lowell and Plath: Objectivity and the Confessional Mode," *Arizona Quarterly* 33(4), Winter 1977, 314.

"The Holy Innocents"

PETER P. REMALEY. "The Quest for Grace in Robert Lowell's *Lord Weary's Castle,*" *Renascence* 28(3), Spring 1976, 119.

"Home After Three Months Away"

CHARLES ALTIERI. "Poetry in a Prose World: Robert Lowell's 'Life Studies,'" *Modern Poetry Studies* 1(4), 1970, 192-95.

SISTER MADELINE DEFREES. "Pegasus and Six Blind Indians," *English Journal* 59(7), October 1970, 935-36.

GEORGE MCFADDEN. "'Life Studies' — Robert Lowell's Comic Breakthrough," *PMLA* 90(1), January 1975, 103-4.

ROBERT PHILLIPS. *The Confessional Poets,* pp. 35-37.

HUGH B. STAPLES. "Beyond Charles River to the Acheron: An Introduction to the Poetry," in *Poets in Progress,* pp. 34-37.

"Identification in Belfast"

ROBERT PINSKY. *The Situation of Poetry,* pp. 19-20.

"In Genesis"

DAVID KALSTONE. *Five Temperaments,* p. 73.

"In Memory of Arthur Winslow"

ALAN HOLDER. "The Flintlocks of the Fathers: Robert Lowell's Treatment of the American Past," *New England Quarterly* 44(1), March 1971, 47-48.

KENNETH JOHNSON. "The View from Lord Weary's Castle," in *The Forties*, p. 233.

JAY MARTIN. "Robert Lowell," in *Seven American Poets from MacLeish to Nemerov*, pp. 221-22.

MARJORIE PERLOFF. "Death by Water: The Winslow Elegies of Robert Lowell," *ELH* 34(1), March 1967, 117-24.

JON STALLWORTHY. "W. B. Yates and the Dynastic Theme," *Critical Quarterly* 7(3), Autumn 1965, 256-58.

"In the Cage"

DAVID BULWER LUTYENS. *The Creative Encounter*, pp. 136-37.

"Inauguration Day: January 1953"

THOMAS R. EDWARDS. *Imagination and Power*, pp. 216-21.

"It was at My Lai or Sonmy or Something"

ROBERT PINSKY. *The Situation of Poetry*, pp. 18-19.

"Jonathan Edwards in Western Massachusetts"

ALAN HOLDER. "The Flintlocks of the Fathers: Robert Lowell's Treatment of the American Past," *New England Quarterly* 44(1), March 1971, 59-60.

GEORGE S. LENSING. "Robert Lowell and Jonathan Edwards: Poetry in the Hands of an Angry God," *South Carolina Review* 6(2), April 1974, 13-15.

GABRIEL PEARSON. "Lowell's Marble Meanings," in *The Survival of Poetry*, pp. 73-75.

"July in Washington"

THOMAS R. EDWARDS. *Imagination and Power*, pp. 221-25.

"Leviathan"

PETER P. REMALEY. "The Quest for Grace in Robert Lowell's *Lord Weary's Castle*," *Renascence* 28(3), Spring 1976, 115-16.

"A Mad Negro Soldier Confined at Munich"

M. L. ROSENTHAL. *The Modern Poets*, p. 234.

"Man and Wife"

MARJORIE G. PERLOFF. "Realism and the Confessional Mode of Robert Lowell," *Contemporary Literature* 11(4), Autumn 1970, 470-87.

ROBERT PHILLIPS. *The Confessional Poets*, pp. 38-39.

"The March"

THOMAS R. EDWARDS. *Imagination and Power*, pp. 212-16.

STEPHEN C. MOORE. "Politics and the Poetry of Robert Lowell," *Georgia Review* 27(2), Summer 1973, 230.

"Marriage"

STEVEN GOULD AXELROD. "Lowell's *The Dolphin* as a 'Book of Life,'" *Contemporary Literature* 18(4), Autumn 1977, 467.

"Mary Winslow"

DAVID BULWER LUTYENS. *The Creative Encounter*, pp. 166-67.

JOHN J. MCALEER. *Explicator* 18(5), February 1960, Item 29.

"Memories of West Street and Lepke"

DAVID KALSTONE. *Five Temperaments*, pp. 52-56.

GEORGE LENSING. "'Memories of West Street and Lepke': Robert Lowell's Associative Mirror," *Concerning Poetry* 3(2), Fall 1970, 23-26.

GEORGE MCFADDEN. "'Life Studies' — Robert Lowell's Comic Breakthrough," *PMLA* 90(1), January 1975, 104.

GABRIEL PEARSON. "Lowell's Marble Meanings," in *The Survival of Poetry*, pp. 93-96.

GABRIEL PEARSON. "Robert Lowell: The Middle Years," in *Contemporary Poetry in America*, pp. 55-58.

ROBERT PHILLIPS. *The Confessional Poets*, pp. 37-38.

LOUIS SIMPSON. *A Revolution in Taste*, pp. 152-54.

"Mermaid"

STEVEN GOULD AXELROD. "Lowell's *The Dolphin* as a 'Book of Life,'" *Contemporary Literature* 18(4), Autumn 1977, 465-66.

"The Mills of the Kavanaughs"

ROGER BOWEN. "Confession and Equilibrium: Robert Lowell's Poetic Development," *Criticism* 11(1), Winter 1969, 78-93.

NEVILLE BRAYBROOKE. "The Poetry of Robert Lowell," *Catholic World* 198(1186), January 1964, 234-36.

LILLIAN FEDER. *Ancient Myth in Modern Poetry*, pp. 20-22.

DAVID BULWER LUTYENS. *The Creative Encounter*, pp. 187-88.

JAY MARTIN. "Robert Lowell," in *Seven American Poets from MacLeish to Nemerov*, p. 224.

RALPH J. MILLS, JR. *Contemporary American Poetry*, pp. 146-47.

LOUIS SIMPSON. *A Revolution in Taste*, pp. 143-45.

"Mr. Edwards and the Spider"

HARRY BROWN and JOHN MILSTEAD. *What the Poem Means*, p. 139.

DENIS DONOGHUE. *Connoisseurs of Chaos*, pp. 154-57.

GEORGE S. LENSING. "Robert Lowell and Jonathan Edwards: Poetry in the Hands of an Angry God," *South Carolina Review* 6(2), April 1974, 8-11.

GABRIEL PEARSON. "Lowell's Marble Meanings," in *The Survival of Poetry*, pp. 71-73.

LAURENCE PERRINE. *100 American Poems of the Twentieth Century*, pp. 242-44. Reprinted in: Harry J. Cargas. *Daniel Berrigan and Contemporary Protest Poetry*, p. 55.

DALLAS E. WIEBE. "Mr. Lowell and Mr. Edwards," *Wisconsin Studies in Contemporary Literature* 3(2), Spring-Summer 1962, 23-26.

"Mother Marie Therese"

STEVEN AXELROD. "Baudelaire and the Poetry of Robert Lowell," *Twentieth Century Literature* 17(4), October 1971, 260-62.

JEROME MAZZARO. "Robert Lowell's Early Politics of Apocalypse," in *Modern American Poetry*, edited by Jerome Mazzaro, pp. 343-48.

RALPH J. MILLS, JR. *Contemporary American Poetry*, p. 148.

DESALES STANDERWICK. "Notes on Robert Lowell," *Renascence* 8(2), Winter 1955, 81-82.

"The Mouth of the Hudson"

STEVEN GOULD AXELROD. "Private and Public Worlds in Lowell's *For the Union Dead*," *Bucknell Review* 22(2), Fall 1976, 170.

LOWELL, ROBERT *(Cont.)*

"The Mouth of the Hudson" *(cont.)*

> WILLIAM BEDFORD. "The Morality of Form in the Poetry of Robert Lowell," *Ariel* 9(1), January 1978, 10.

"My Last Afternoon with Uncle Devereux Winslow"

> CHARLES ALTIERI. "Poetry in a Prose World: Robert Lowell's 'Life Studies,'" *Modern Poetry Studies* 1(4), 1970, 185-86.
>
> SISTER ERIC MARIE BRUMLEVE. "Permanence and Change in the Poetry of Robert Lowell," *Texas Studies in Literature and Language* 10(1), Spring 1968, 147-48.
>
> GEORGE MCFADDEN. "'Life Studies' — Robert Lowell's Comic Breakthrough," *PMLA* 90(1), January 1975, 98-100.
>
> JAY MARTIN. "Robert Lowell," in *Seven American Poets from MacLeish to Nemerov*, pp. 232-34.
>
> MARJORIE PERLOFF. "Death by Water: The Winslow Elegies of Robert Lowell," *ELH* 34(1), March 1967, 130-36.
>
> ROBERT PHILLIPS. *The Confessional Poets*, pp. 24-27.
>
> M. L. ROSENTHAL. *Poetry and the Common Life*, pp. 76-79. (P)

"Myopia: A Night"

> STEVEN GOULD AXELROD. "Private and Public Worlds in Lowell's *For the Union Dead*," *Bucknell Review* 22(2), Fall 1976, 168-69.

"Napoleon Crosses the Berezina"

> DESALES STANDERWICK. "Notes on Robert Lowell," *Renascence* 8(2), Winter 1955, 79. Reprinted in: Harry J. Cargas. *Daniel Berrigan and Contemporary Protest Poetry*, pp. 51-52.

"Near the Ocean"

> WILLIAM BEDFORD. "The Morality of Form in the Poetry of Robert Lowell," *Ariel* 9(1), January 1978, 14-16.
>
> LILLIAN FEDER. *Ancient Myth in Modern Poetry*, pp. 408-10.

"Near the Ocean Sequence"

> STEVEN AXELROD. "Baudelaire and the Poetry of Robert Lowell," *Twentieth Century Literature* 17(4), October 1971, 271-73.

"The Neo-Classical Urn"

> JOAN BOBBITT. "Lowell and Plath: Objectivity and the Confessional Mode," *Arizona Quarterly* 33(4), Winter 1977, 313.
>
> DAVID KALSTONE. *Five Temperaments*, pp. 62-64.

"The New York Intellectual"

> STEVEN G. AXELROD. "Robert Lowell and the New York Intellectuals," *English Language Notes* 11(3), March 1974, 206-9.

"Night Sweat"

> STEVEN GOULD AXELROD. "Private and Public Worlds in Lowell's *For the Union Dead*," *Bucknell Review* 22(2), Fall 1976, 169-70.
>
> DAVID KALSTONE. *Five Temperaments*, pp. 61-64.

"91 Revere Street"

> MARJORIE G. PERLOFF. "Realism and the Confessional Mode of Robert Lowell," *Contemporary Literature* 11(4), Autumn 1970, 482-86.

"Nostalgie de la Boue"

> PAUL SCHWABER. "Robert Lowell in Mid-Career," *Western Humanities Review* 25(4), Autumn 1971, 348-54.

"Obit"

> ARTHUR OBERG. "*Lowell* Had Been Misspelled Lovel," *Iowa Review* 5(3), Summer 1974, 113-14.

"The Old Flame"

> CHRISTOPHER MORRIS. "The Ambivalence of Robert Lowell's 'For the Union Dead,'" *Modern Poetry Studies* 1(4), 1970, 202.
>
> ARTHUR OBERG. "*Lowell* Had Been Misspelled Lovel," *Iowa Review* 5(3), Summer 1974, 105-6.

"Old Hickory"

> ALAN HOLDER. "The Flintlocks of the Fathers: Robert Lowell's Treatment of the American Past," *New England Quarterly* 44(1), March 1971, 60-61.

"Our Lady of Walsingham"

> see also "The Quaker Graveyard in Nantucket"
>
> DENIS DONOGHUE. *Connoisseurs of Chaos*, pp. 153-54.
>
> DAVID BULWER LUTYENS. *The Creative Encounter*, pp. 160-63.

"The Park Street Cemetery"

> JEROME MAZZARO. "Robert Lowell's Early Politics of Apocalypse," in *Modern American Poetry*, edited by Jerome Mazzaro, pp. 333-35.

"Pilgrim's Progress"

> THOMAS VOGLER. "Robert Lowell: Payment Gat He Nane," *Iowa Review* 2(3), Summer 1971, 83.

"The Public Garden"

> RUDOLPH L. NELSON. "A Note on the Evolution of Robert Lowell's 'The Public Garden,'" *American Literature* 41(1), March 1969, 106-10.

"The Quaker Graveyard in Nantucket"

> PAUL J. DOLAN. "Lowell's *Quaker Graveyard*: Poem and Tradition," *Renascence* 21(4), Summer 1969, 171-80, 194.
>
> BERNARD DUFFEY. *Poetry in America*, p. 293.
>
> RICHARD FEIN. "Mary and Bellona: The War Poetry of Robert Lowell," *Southern Review*, n.s., 1(4), Autumn 1965, 826-32.
>
> STEPHEN FENDER. "What Really Happened to Warren Winslow?" *Journal of American Studies* 7(2), August 1973, 187-90.
>
> PHILIP FURIA. "'IS, the whited monster': Lowell's Quaker Graveyard Revisited," *Texas Studies in Literature and Language* 17(4), Winter 1976, 837-53.
>
> ALAN HOLDER. "The Flintlocks of the Fathers: Robert Lowell's Treatment of the American Past," *New England Quarterly* 44(1), March 1971, 51-54.
>
> KENNETH JOHNSON. "The View from Lord Weary's Castle," in *The Forties*, pp. 234-35.
>
> JAY MARTIN. "Robert Lowell," in *Seven American Poets from MacLeish to Nemerov*, pp. 219-20.
>
> RALPH J. MILLS, JR. *Contemporary American Poetry*, pp. 141-44.
>
> MARJORIE PERLOFF. "Death by Water: The Winslow Elegies of Robert Lowell," *ELH* 34(1), March 1967, 124-30.
>
> SISTER MARY TERESE RINK. "The Sea in Lowell's 'Quaker Graveyard in Nantucket,'" *Renascence* 20(1), Autumn 1967, 39-43.
>
> LOUIS SIMPSON. *A Revolution in Taste*, pp. 140-42.
>
> DESALES STANDERWICK. "Notes on Robert Lowell," *Renascence* 8(2), Winter 1955, 76-78.
>
> THOMAS VOGLER. "Robert Lowell: Payment Gat He Nane," *Iowa Review* 2(3), Summer 1971, 74-75.

"R. F. K."

THOMAS R. EDWARDS. *Imagination and Power*, p. 3.

"Rebellion"

ALAN HOLDER. "The Flintlocks of the Fathers: Robert Lowell's Treatment of the American Past," *New England Quarterly* 44(1), March 1971, 56-57.

DAVID KALSTONE. *Five Temperaments*, pp. 45-47.

DAVID BULWER LUTYENS. *The Creative Encounter*, pp. 170-72.

"Rembrandt"

JACK BRANSCOMB. "Robert Lowell's Painters: Two Sources," *English Language Notes* 15(2), December 1977, 119-21.

"Remembrance Day, London 1970's"

ROBERT PINSKY. *The Situation of Poetry*, pp. 19, 20.

"Robert Frost"

ANDY J. MORE. "Frost — And Lowell — At Midnight," *Southern Quarterly* 15(3), April 1977, 291-95.

"Sailing Home from Rapallo"

ALAN HOLDER. "The Flintlocks of the Fathers: Robert Lowell's Treatment of the American Past," *New England Quarterly* 44(1), March 1971, 58-59.

GEORGE MCFADDEN. "'Life Studies' — Robert Lowell's Comic Breakthrough," *PMLA* 90(1), January 1975, 101-2.

NORMA PROCOPIOW. "William Carlos Williams and the Origins of the Confessional Poem," *Ariel* 7(2), April 1976, 70-73.

"Santayana's Farewell to His Nurses"

DAVID BULWER LUTYENS. *The Creative Encounter*, pp. 172-74.

RALPH J. MILLS, JR. *Contemporary American Poetry*, p. 152.

"1790"

JEROME MAZZARO. "Robert Lowell's Early Politics of Apocalypse," in *Modern American Poetry*, edited by Jerome Mazzaro, pp. 340-41.

"The Shako"

DAVID BULWER LUTYENS. *The Creative Encounter*, pp. 154-55.

"Skunk Hour"

CHARLES ALTIERI. "Poetry in a Prose World: Robert Lowell's 'Life Studies,'" *Modern Poetry Studies* 1(4), 1970, 187-88; 195-97.

JOHN BERRYMAN. *The Freedom of the Poet*, pp. 316-22.

R. P. DICKEY. "The New Genteel Tradition in American Poetry," *Sewanee Review* 82(4), Fall 1974, 738-39.

STEVEN K. HOFFMAN. "Impersonal Personalism: The Making of a Confessional Poetic," *ELH* 45(4), Winter 1978, 702-3.

DAVID KALSTONE. *Five Temperaments*, pp. 49-52.

GEORGE MCFADDEN. "'Life Studies' — Robert Lowell's Comic Breakthrough," *PMLA* 90(1), January 1975, 105.

JAY MARTIN. "Robert Lowell," in *Seven American Poets from MacLeish to Nemerov*, pp. 234-36.

ROBERT PHILLIPS. *The Confessional Poets*, pp. 39-42.

WILLIAM H. PRITCHARD. "Wildness of Logic in Modern Lyric," in *Forms of Lyric*, pp. 145-49.

JOHN R. REED. "Going Back: The Ironic Progress of Lowell's Poetry," *Modern Poetry Studies* 1(4), 1970, 167.

JON ROSENBLATT. "The Limits of the 'Confessional Mode' in Recent American Poetry," *Genre* 9(2), Summer 1976, 156.

PAUL SCHWABER. "Robert Lowell in Mid-Career," *Western Humanities Review* 25(4), Autumn 1971, 351-52.

WALTER SUTTON. *American Free Verse*, p. 158.

RICHARD WILBUR, JOHN FREDERICK NIMS, JOHN BERRYMAN and ROBERT LOWELL. "On Robert Lowell's 'Skunk Hour,'" in *The Contemporary Poet as Artist and Critic*, pp. 82-110.

"The Slough of Despond"

THOMAS VOGLER. "Robert Lowell: Payment Gat He Nane," *Iowa Review* 2(3), Summer 1971, 82-83.

"Soft Wood"

MARJORIE PERLOFF. "Death by Water: The Winslow Elegies of Robert Lowell," *ELH* 34(1), March 1967, 136-40.

"Terminal Days at Beverly Farms"

CHARLES ALTIERI. "Poetry in a Prose World: Robert Lowell's 'Life Studies,'" *Modern Poetry Studies* 1(4), 1970, 190-92.

GEORGE MCFADDEN. "'Life Studies' — Robert Lowell's Comic Breakthrough," *PMLA* 90(1), January 1975, 101.

ROBERT PHILLIPS. *The Confessional Poets*, p. 30.

NORMA PROCOPIOW. "William Carlos Williams and the Origins of the Confessional Poem," *Ariel* 7(2), April 1976, 69-70.

ROBERT G. TWOMBLY. "The Poetics of Demur: Lowell and Frost," *College English* 38(4), December 1976, 384-87.

"To Daddy"

ARTHUR OBERG. *Modern American Lyric*, p. 25.

"To Peter Taylor on the Feast of the Epiphany"

THOMAS VOGLER. "Robert Lowell: Payment Gat He Nane," *Iowa Review* 2(3), Summer 1971, 77.

"'To Speak of Woe That Is in Marriage'"

A. L. FRENCH. "Purposive Imitation: A Skirmish with Literary Theory," *Essays in Criticism* 22(2), April 1972, 128-30. (P)

DAVID BULWER LUTYENS. *The Creative Encounter*, pp. 198-99.

GEORGE MCFADDEN. "'Life Studies' — Robert Lowell's Comic Breakthrough," *PMLA* 90(1), January 1975, 105.

ROBERT PHILLIPS. *The Confessional Poets*, p. 39.

"Vanity of Human Wishes"

PATRICIA MEYER SPACKS. "From Satire to Description," *Yale Review* 58(2), December 1968, 232-48.

"Waking Early Sunday Morning"

WILLIAM BEDFORD. "The Morality of Form in the Poetry of Robert Lowell," *Ariel* 9(1), January 1978, 13-15.

DANIEL HOFFMAN. "Robert Lowell's *Near the Ocean*: The Greatness and Horror of Empire," *Hollins Critic* 4(1), February 1967, 15-16.

EDWARD LUCIE-SMITH. "Robert Lowell," in *Criticism in Action*, pp. 164-76.

ELIZABETH LUNZ. "Robert Lowell and Wallace Stevens On Sunday Morning," *University Review* 37(4), Summer 1971, 268-72.

JAY MARTIN. "Robert Lowell," in *Seven American Poets from MacLeish to Nemerov*, pp. 240-41.

LOWELL, ROBERT *(Cont.)*

"Waking Early Sunday Morning" *(cont.)*

> LOUIS SIMPSON. *A Revolution in Taste*, pp. 159-60.

"Waking in the Blue"

> CHARLES ALTIERI. "Poetry in a Prose World: Robert Lowell's 'Life Studies,'" *Modern Poetry Studies* 1(4), 1970, 193.
>
> CLEANTH BROOKS and ROBERT PENN WARREN. *Understanding Poetry*, fourth ed., pp. 39-40.
>
> GEORGE McFADDEN. "'Life Studies' — Robert Lowell's Comic Breakthrough," *PMLA* 90(1), January 1975, 103.
>
> RALPH J. MILLS, JR. *Contemporary American Poetry*, pp. 156-58.
>
> RALPH J. MILLS, JR. *Creation's Very Self*, pp. 26-27. Reprinted in: Ralph J. Mills, Jr., *Cry of the Human*, pp. 28-29.
>
> JOHN OLIVER PERRY. *The Experience of Poems*, pp. 39-40.
>
> ROBERT PHILLIPS. *The Confessional Poets*, pp. 33-35.
>
> ROBERT G. TWOMBLY. "The Poetics of Demur: Lowell and Frost," *College English* 38(4), December 1976, 373-74.

"Water"

> CHRISTOPHER MORRIS. "The Ambivalence of Robert Lowell's 'For the Union Dead,'" *Modern Poetry Studies* 1(4), 1970, 201-2.
>
> GABRIEL PEARSON. "Lowell's Marble Meanings," in *The Survival of Poetry*, pp. 64-67.
>
> JAMES M. REID. *100 American Poems of the Twentieth Century*, pp. 247-49.

"Where the Rainbow Ends"

> RANDALL JARRELL. "From the Kingdom of Necessity," *Nation* 164(3), 18 January 1947, 74, 76. Reprinted in: *Mid-Century American Poets*, pp. 160-61. Also: *On Contemporary Literature*, pp. 405-6. Also: *Readings for Liberal Education*, revised ed., II: 279-80.
>
> DAVID BULWER LUTYENS. *The Creative Encounter*, pp. 147-49.
>
> PETER P. REMALEY. "Epic Machinery in Robert Lowell's *Lord Weary's Castle*," *Ball State University Forum* 18(2), Spring 1977, 62-63.
>
> PETER P. REMALEY. "The Quest for Grace in Robert Lowell's *Lord Weary's Castle*," *Renascence* 28(3), Spring 1976, 120-22.
>
> DeSALES STANDERWICK. "Notes on Robert Lowell," *Renascence* 8(2), Winter 1955, 80-81.

"Winter in Dunbarton"

> DAVID BULWER LUTYENS. *The Creative Encounter*, pp. 164-66.

"Words for Hart Crane"

> CHARLES ALTIERI. "Poetry in a Prose World: Robert Lowell's 'Life Studies,'" *Modern Poetry Studies* 1(4), 1970, 192-93.
>
> ARTHUR OBERG. "*Lowell* Had Been Misspelled Lovel," *Iowa Review* 5(3), Summer 1974, 109.
>
> ARTHUR OBERG. *Modern American Lyric*, pp. 25-26.

"The Worst Sinner, Jonathan Edwards' God"

> GEORGE S. LENSING. "Robert Lowell and Jonathan Edwards: Poetry in the Hands of an Angry God," *South Carolina Review* 6(2), April 1974, 15-16.

LOY, MINA

"Apology for Genius"

> KENNETH FIELDS. "The Poetry of Mina Loy," *Southern Review*, n.s., 3(3), Summer 1967, 602-5.

"Der Blinde Junge"

> KENNETH FIELDS. "The Poetry of Mina Loy," *Southern Review*, n.s., 3(3), Summer 1967, 605-7.

"Lunar Baedecker"

> KENNETH FIELDS. "The Poetry of Mina Loy," *Southern Review*, n.s., 3(3), Summer 1967, 600-2.

LUCE, G. H.

"Climb Cloud, and Pencil all the Blue"

> I. A. RICHARDS. *Practical Criticism*, pp. 131-44, *passim*.

LUCIE-SMITH, EDWARD

"Genesis"

> MARTIN DODSWORTH. "Introduction: The Survival of Poetry," in *The Survival of Poetry*, pp. 18-19.

LUX, THOMAS

"Longitude and Latitude: Hart Crane"

> NORMAN DUBIE. "You Could Be Wrong," *Iowa Review* 4(4), Fall 1973, 77-78.
>
> THOMAS LUX. "Thomas Lux's Response," *Iowa Review* 4(4), Fall 1973, 79.

"There Are Many Things That Please Me"

> NORMAN DUBIE. "You Could Be Wrong," *Iowa Review* 4(4), Fall 1973, 77.
>
> THOMAS LUX. "Thomas Lux's Response," *Iowa Review* 4(4), Fall 1973, 79.

LYDGATE, JOHN

"The Churl and the Bird"

> F. W. BROWNLOW. "The Boke Compiled by Maister Skelton, Poet Laureate, Called Speake Parrot," *English Literary Renaissance* 1(1), Winter 1971, 12.

LYLY, JOHN

"Cupid and my Campaspe play'd"

> JEROME BEATY and WILLIAM H. MATCHETT. *Poetry From Statement to Meaning*, p. 216.

LYTLE, WILLIAM HAINES

"Anthony to Cleopatra"

> ISAAC ASIMOV. *Familiar Poems, Annotated*, pp. 35-41.

M

MCARTHUR, PETER

"The Stone"

    F. W. Watt. "Peter McArthur and the Agrarian Myth," *Queens Quarterly* 67(2), Summer 1960, 245-57.

MACBETH, GEORGE

"The Blood-Woman"

    Lawrence R. Ries. *Wolf Masks*, p. 149.

"A Confession"

    Patrick J. Callahan. "Collected Poems: 1958-1970 by George MacBeth," *Saturday Review* 55(16), 15 April 1972, 71.

"A Dirge"

    Roger Garfitt. "The Group," in *British Poetry Since 1960*, pp. 29-30.

"A Light in Winter"

    Roger Garfitt. "The Group," in *British Poetry Since 1960*, pp. 38-39.

"Owl"

    Roger Garfitt. "The Group," in *British Poetry Since 1960*, pp. 41-42.

"The Son"

    Roger Garfitt. "The Group," in *British Poetry Since 1960*, p. 29.

MACCAIG, NORMAN

"Celtic Cross"

    Mary Jane W. Scott. "Neoclassical MacCaig," *Studies in Scottish Literature* 10(3), January 1973, 137-39.

"Go-Between"

    Mary Jane W. Scott. "Neoclassical MacCaig," *Studies in Scottish Literature* 10(3), January 1973, 142-43.

"No Consolation"

    George Fraser. *Essays on Twentieth-Century Poets*, pp. 213-14.

"Sense About Nonsense"

    George Fraser. *Essays on Twentieth-Century Poets*, pp. 208-11.

"Tapestry"

    George Fraser. *Essays on Twentieth-Century Poets*, pp. 205-8.

MCCRAE, JOHN

"In Flanders Fields"

    Isaac Asimov. *Familiar Poems, Annotated*, pp. 265-72.

MACDIARMID, HUGH

"The Bonnie Broukit Bairn"

    Iain Crichton Smith. "Hugh MacDiarmid: *Sangschaw* and *A Drunk Man Looks at the Thistle*," *Studies in Scottish Literature* 7(3), January 1970, 172-73.

"By Wauchopeside"

    David Craig. "Hugh MacDiarmid," in *Criticism in Action*, pp. 44-47.

"The Eemis Stane"

    David Daiches. "Hugh MacDiarmid and Scottish Poetry," *Poetry* 72(4), July 1948, 206.

    Iain Crichton Smith. "Hugh MacDiarmid: *Sangschaw* and *A Drunk Man Looks at the Thistle*," *Studies in Scottish Literature* 7(3), January 1970, 174.

"Ex Vermibus"

    Ann E. Boutelle. "Language and Vision in the Early Poetry of Hugh MacDiarmid," *Contemporary Literature* 12(4), Autumn 1971, 504-6.

"Farmer's Death"

    Ann E. Boutelle. "Language and Vision in the Early Poetry of Hugh MacDiarmid," *Contemporary Literature* 12(4), Autumn 1971, 496-99.

"First Hymn to Lenin"

    David Craig. "Hugh MacDiarmid," in *Criticism in Action*, pp. 36-44.

"Gairmscoile"

    Ann E. Boutelle. "Language and Vision in the Early Poetry of Hugh MacDiarmid," *Contemporary Literature* 12(4), Autumn 1971, 499-501.

"The Huntress and Her Dogs"

    Ann E. Boutelle. "Language and Vision in the Early Poetry of Hugh MacDiarmid," *Contemporary Literature* 12(4), Autumn 1971, 506-7.

"Moonlight among the Pines"

    Iain Crichton Smith. "Hugh MacDiarmid: *Sangschaw* and *A Drunk Man Looks at the Thistle*," *Studies in Scottish Literature* 7(3), January 1970, 171.

MACDIARMID, HUGH *(Cont.)*

"O Wha's the Bride"

> ANN E. BOUTELLE. "Language and Vision in the Early Poetry of Hugh MacDiarmid," *Contemporary Literature* 12(4), Autumn 1971, 507-8.

"The Spur of Love"

> ANN E. BOUTELLE. "Language and Vision in the Early Poetry of Hugh MacDiarmid," *Contemporary Literature* 12(4), Autumn 1971, 501-4.

"The Watergaw"

> IAIN CRICHTON SMITH. "Hugh MacDiarmid: *Sangschaw* and *A Drunk Man Looks at the Thistle,*" *Studies in Scottish Literature* 7(3), January 1970, 173-74.

MACDONALD, CYNTHIA

"Departure"

> R. L. WIDMAN. "The Poetry of Cynthia MacDonald," *Concerning Poetry* 7(1), Spring 1974, 24-26.

"Inventory"

> R. L. WIDMAN. "The Poetry of Cynthia MacDonald," *Concerning Poetry* 7(1), Spring 1974, 21-24.

"Objets d'Art"

> R. L. WIDMAN. "The Poetry of Cynthia MacDonald," *Concerning Poetry* 7(1), Spring 1974, 19-21.

"Uncovering"

> AGNES STEIN. *The Uses of Poetry,* p. 42.

MACDONALD, GEORGE

"A Manchester Poem"

> ROBERT L. CHAMBERLAIN. "George MacDonald's 'A Manchester Poem' and Hopkins' 'God's Grandeur,' " *Personalist* 44(4), Autumn 1963, 518-27.

MCGINLEY, PHYLLIS

"The Doll House"

> PHYLLIS MCGINLEY. "The Light Side of the Moon," *American Scholar* 34(4), Autumn 1965, 559-60.

"Midcentury Love Letter"

> PHYLLIS MCGINLEY. "The Light Side of the Moon," *American Scholar* 34(4), Autumn 1965, 558-59.

"Portrait of Girl with Comic Book"

> LAURENCE PERRINE. *100 American Poems of the Twentieth Century,* pp. 198-200.

MCGRATH, THOMAS

"The Buffalo Coat"

> JAY GURIAN. "The Possibility of a Western Poetics," *Colorado Quarterly* 15(1), Summer 1966, 83-84.

MCKAY, CLAUDE

"Cudjoe Fresh From De Lecture"

> SISTER MARY CONROY. "The Vagabond Motif in the Writings of Claude McKay," *Negro American Literature Forum* 5(1), Spring 1971, 21-22.

"The Harlem Dancer"

> EUGENIA W. COLLIER. "I Do Not Marvel, Countee Cullen," *CLA Journal* 11(1), September 1967, 81-83. Reprinted in: *Modern Black Poets,* pp. 77-79.

"Harlem Shadows"

> EUGENIA W. COLLIER. "The Four-Way Dilemma of Claude McKay," *CLA Journal* 15(3), March 1972, 351.

"If We Must Die"

> ROBERT A. LEE. "On Claude McKay's 'If We Must Die,' " *CLA Journal* 18(2), December 1974, 216-21.

"Like a Strong Tree"

> MARK HELBLING. "Claude McKay: Art and Politics," *Negro American Literature Forum* 7(2), Summer 1973, 50-51.

"The Lynching"

> MELVIN G. WILLIAMS. "Black Literature vs. Black Studies: Three Lynchings," *Black American Literature Forum* 11(3), Fall 1977, 106.

"Outcast"

> TODD M. LIEBER. "Ralph Ellison and the Metaphor of Invisibility in Black Literary Tradition," *American Quarterly* 24(1), March 1972, 87-88.

"Romance"

> SISTER MARY CONROY. "The Vagabond Motif in the Writings of Claude McKay," *Negro American Literature Forum* 5(1), Spring 1971, 17-18.

"White Houses"

> EUGENIA W. COLLIER. "The Four-Way Dilemma of Claude McKay," *CLA Journal* 15(3), March 1972, 349-50.

MACKENZIE, GEORGE

"Caelia's Country House and Closet"

> MICHAEL R. G. SPILLER. "The Country House Poem in Scotland: Sir George MacKenzie's *Caelia's Country House and Closet,*" *Studies in Scottish Literature* 12(2), October 1974, 110-30.

MACLEISH, ARCHIBALD

"Actfive"

> DAVID BULWER LUTYENS. *The Creative Encounter,* pp. 94-97.

> GROVER SMITH. "Archibald MacLeish," in *Seven American Poets from MacLeish to Nemerov,* pp. 45-46.

"America Was Promises"

> GROVER SMITH. "Archibald MacLeish," in *Seven American Poets from MacLeish to Nemerov,* pp. 43-44.

". . . & Forty-Second Street"

> IVAR L. MYHR. *Explicator* 3(6), April 1945, Item 47.

"Ars Poetica"

> CLEANTH BROOKS, JOHN THIBAUT PURSER, and ROBERT PENN WARREN. *An Approach to Literature,* fifth ed., pp. 401-2.

> HARRY BROWN and JOHN MILSTEAD. *What the Poem Means,* pp. 140-41.

> DAN JAFFE. "Archibald MacLeish: Mapping the Tradition," in *The Thirties,* pp. 141-42.

> VICTOR H. JONES. "Literary or Not," *South Dakota Review* 14(4), Winter 1976-77, 4-6.

> DAVID J. KRESSLER. "Resolution in 'Ars Poetica,' " *Concerning Poetry* 10(1), Spring 1977, 73. (P)

> GROVER SMITH. "Archibald MacLeish," in *Seven American Poets from MacLeish to Nemerov,* pp. 30-31.

> VICTOR P. STAUDT. " 'Ars Poetica' and the Teacher," *College English* 19(1), October 1957, 28-29.

> DONALD STAUFFER. *The Nature of Poetry,* pp. 121-25. Reprinted in: *Reading Modern Poetry,* pp. 99-101.

HARRY R. SULLIVAN. "MacLeish's 'Ars Poetica,'" *English Journal* 56(9), December 1967, 1280-83.

"Certain Poets"

VICTOR H. JONES. "Literary or Not," *South Dakota Review* 14(4), Winter 1976-77, 3-4.

"Conquistador"

DAVID BULWER LUTYENS. *The Creative Encounter*, pp. 92-94.

ALLEN TATE. "MacLeish's *Conquistador*," in his *Essays of Four Decades*, pp. 358-63.

HYATT HOWE WAGGONER. *The Heel of Elohim*, pp. 148-50.

"Dr. Sigmund Freud Discovers the Sea Shell"

LAURENCE PERRINE. *100 American Poems of the Twentieth Century*, pp. 160-62.

" 'Dover Beach' — A Note to That Poem"

JAMES R. KREUZER. *Elements of Poetry*, pp. 183-89, 191-92.

JAMES ZIGERELL. *Explicator* 17(6), March 1959, Item 38.

"Einstein"

FREDERICK J. HOFFMAN. *The Twenties*, pp. 287-88; revised ed., pp. 325-26.

DAVID BULWER LUTYENS. *The Creative Encounter*, pp. 83-89.

GROVER SMITH. "Archibald MacLeish," in *Seven American Poets from MacLeish to Nemerov*, pp. 31-33.

HYATT HOWE WAGGONER. *The Heel of Elohim*, pp. 143-46.

"Eleven"

BABETTE DEUTSCH. *Poetry in Our Time*, p. 147; second ed., p. 159.

"The Empire Builders"

HAROLD E. TOLIVER. *Pastoral Forms and Attitudes*, p. 234. (P)

"The End of the World"

ANNIS COX KOCHER. " 'The End of the World' for a New Beginning," *English Journal* 55(6), September 1966, 700-2.

JAMES M. REID. *100 American Poems of the Twentieth Century*, pp. 162-63.

HYATT H. WAGGONER. *American Poets*, p. 489.

"Epistle to Be Left in the Earth"

DAVID BULWER LUTYENS. *The Creative Encounter*, pp. 89-92.

HYATT HOWE WAGGONER. *The Heel of Elohim*, pp. 146-48.

"Geography of This Time"

JOSEPH WARREN BEACH. *Obsessive Images*, p. 205.

"The Hamlet of A. MacLeish"

LILLIAN GOTTESMAN. "*The Hamlet of A. MacLeish*," *CLA Journal* 11(2), December 1967, 157-62.

DAVID BULWER LUTYENS. *The Creative Encounter*, pp. 78-81.

GROVER SMITH. "Archibald MacLeish," in *Seven American Poets from MacLeish to Nemerov*, pp. 33-35.

HYATT HOWE WAGGONER. *The Heel of Elohim*, pp. 141-43.

"Hypocrite Auteur"

NICHOLAS JOOST. *Explicator* 11(7), May 1953, Item 47.

"Invocation to the Social Muse"

DAN JAFFE. "Archibald MacLeish: Mapping the Tradition," in *The Thirties*, pp. 143-44.

"L'An Trentiesme de Mon Eage"

RICHARD E. AMACHER. *Explicator* 6(6), April 1948, Item 42.

GROVER SMITH. "Archibald MacLeish," in *Seven American Poets from MacLeish to Nemerov*, p. 30.

"Land of the Free — U.S.A."

GROVER SMITH. "Archibald MacLeish," in *Seven American Poets from MacLeish to Nemerov*, pp. 42-43.

"Lines for an Interment"

JAMES R. KREUZER. *Elements of Poetry*, pp. 140-43.

"Memorial Rain"

CLEANTH BROOKS. *Modern Poetry and the Tradition*, pp. 122-24.

"Men"

CLEANTH BROOKS. *Modern Poetry and the Tradition*, pp. 117-18.

"Nobodaddy"

GROVER SMITH. "Archibald MacLeish," in *Seven American Poets from MacLeish to Nemerov*, pp. 23-25.

" 'Not Marble Nor the Gilded Monuments' "

JEROME BEATY and WILLIAM H. MATCHETT. *Poetry From Statement to Meaning*, pp. 187-92.

HARRY BROWN and JOHN MILSTEAD. *What the Poem Means*, p. 141.

"Pony Rock"

GERALD SANDERS. *Explicator* 2(1), October 1943, Item 8.

"The Pot of Earth"

GROVER SMITH. "Archibald MacLeish," in *Seven American Poets from MacLeish to Nemerov*, pp. 25-28.

"The Revenant"

DAVID BULWER LUTYENS. *The Creative Encounter*, pp. 76-77.

"The Silent Slain"

M. L. ROSENTHAL and A. J. M. SMITH. *Exploring Poetry*, first ed., pp. 282-83.

"Speech to a Crowd"

HARRY BROWN and JOHN MILSTEAD. *What the Poem Means*, p. 141.

"The Woman on the Stair"

GROVER SMITH. "Archibald MacLeish," in *Seven American Poets from MacLeish to Nemerov*, pp. 41-42.

"You, Andrew Marvell"

CLEANTH BROOKS. *Modern Poetry and the Tradition*, p. 122.

HARRY BROWN and JOHN MILSTEAD. *What the Poem Means*, p. 142.

ELIZABETH DREW. *Poetry*, pp. 104-5.

LAURENCE PERRINE. *Sound and Sense*, pp. 68-69; second ed., pp. 74-75; third ed., pp. 88-89; fourth ed., pp. 83-84.

JAMES M. REID. *100 American Poems of the Twentieth Century*, pp. 157-60.

HYATT H. WAGGONER. *American Poets*, p. 489.

MCMICHAEL, JAMES

"Itinerary"

    ROBERT PINSKY. *The Situation of Poetry*, pp. 156-61.

"Lady Good"

    ROBERT PINSKY. *The Situation of Poetry*, pp. 161-62.

MACNEICE, LOUIS

"After the Crash"

    T. BROWN. "Louis MacNeice and the 'Dark Conceit,' " *Ariel* 3(4), October 1972, 20-22.

"Bagpipe Music"

    JEROME BEATY and WILLIAM H. MATCHETT. *Poetry From Statement to Meaning*, pp. 282-84.

    D. E. S. MAXWELL. *The Poets of the Thirties*, pp. 177-78.

"Budgie"

    WILLIAM JAY SMITH. "The Black Clock: The Poetic Achievement of Louis MacNeice," *Hollins Critic* 4(2), April 1967, 7-9.

"The Burnt Bridge"

    T. BROWN. "Louis MacNeice and the 'Dark Conceit,' " *Ariel* 3(4), October 1972, 22-23.

"Candle"

    MOYA BRENNAN. "A Poet's Revisions: A Consideration of MacNeice's *Blind Fireworks*," *Western Humanities Review* 23(2), Spring 1969, 168.

"Childhood Unhappiness"

    MOYA BRENNAN. "A Poet's Revisions: A Consideration of MacNeice's *Blind Fireworks*," *Western Humanities Review* 23(2), Spring 1969, 161-62.

"A Classical Education"

    MOYA BRENNAN. "A Poet's Revisions: A Consideration of MacNeice's *Blind Fireworks*," *Western Humanities Review* 23(2), Spring 1969, 170-71.

"The Closing Album"

    see "The Coming of War"

"The Coming of War"

    ELTON EDWARD SMITH. *The Angry Young Men of the Thirties*, pp. 90-92.

"Corpse Carousal"

    MOYA BRENNAN. "A Poet's Revisions: A Consideration of MacNeice's *Blind Fireworks*," *Western Humanities Review* 23(2), Spring 1969, 163-64.

"Eclogue Between the Motherless"

    D. E. S. MAXWELL. *The Poets of the Thirties*, p. 176.

"An Ecologue for Christmas"

    ELTON EDWARD SMITH. *The Angry Young Men of the Thirties*, pp. 71-72, 141.

"Eclogue from Iceland"

    JOSEPH WARREN BEACH. *Obsessive Images*, pp. 152-54.

    ELTON EDWARD SMITH. *The Angry Young Men of the Thirties*, pp. 76-77.

"Epilogue for W. H. Auden"

    ELTON EDWARD SMITH. *The Angry Young Men of the Thirties*, pp. 77-78.

"Hidden Ice"

    ELTON EDWARD SMITH. *The Angry Young Men of the Thirties*, p. 82.

"Homage to Clichés"

    ELTON EDWARD SMITH. *The Angry Young Men of the Thirties*, pp. 81-82.

"Homo Sum"

    MOYA BRENNAN. "A Poet's Revisions: A Consideration of MacNeice's *Blind Fireworks*," *Western Humanities Review* 23(2), Spring 1969, 162-63.

"The Humorous Atheist"

    MOYA BRENNAN. "A Poet's Revisions: A Consideration of MacNeice's *Blind Fireworks*," *Western Humanities Review* 23(2), Spring 1969, 164-65.

"Kingdom"

    ELTON EDWARD SMITH. *The Angry Young Men of the Thirties*, p. 129.

"Leaving Barra"

    STUART GERRY BROWN. "Some Poems of Louis MacNeice," *Sewanee Review* 51(1), Winter 1943, 64-66.

"London Rain"

    ELTON EDWARD SMITH. *The Angry Young Men of the Thirties*, p. 90.

"Ode" ("Tonight is so coarse with chocolate")

    ELTON EDWARD SMITH. *The Angry Young Men of the Thirties*, p. 73.

"Order to View"

    T. BROWN. "Louis MacNeice and the 'Dark Conceit,' " *Ariel* 3(4), October 1972, 19-20. (P)

"The Pale Panther"

    WILLIAM T. MCKINNON. "MacNeice's Pale Panther: An exercise in dream logic," *Essays in Criticism* 23(4), October 1973, 388-98.

"Perseus"

    JOHN I. COPE. *Explicator* 26(6), February 1968, Item 48.

    ELIZABETH DREW and JOHN L. SWEENEY. *Directions in Modern Poetry*, pp. 87-88. (Quoting Louis MacNeice)

"Postscript to Iceland"

    see "Epilogue for W. H. Auden"

"Poussin"

    MOYA BRENNAN. "A Poet's Revisions: A Consideration of MacNeice's *Blind Fireworks*," *Western Humanities Review* 23(2), Spring 1969, 167.

"Prayer Before Birth"

    BABETTE DEUTSCH. *Poetry in Our Time*, pp. 365-66; second ed., pp. 406-7.

"River in Spate"

    MOYA BRENNAN. "A Poet's Revisions: A Consideration of MacNeice's *Blind Fireworks*," *Western Humanities Review* 23(2), Spring 1969, 167-68.

"The Riddle"

    JAMES F. DORRILL. *Explicator* 29(1), September 1970, Item 7.

"Round the Corner"

    TERENCE BROWN. "MacNeice's 'Round the Corner,' " *Notes & Queries*, n.s., 17(12), December 1970, 467-68.

"A Serene Evening"

    MOYA BRENNAN. "A Poet's Revisions: A Consideration of MacNeice's *Blind Fireworks*," *Western Humanities Review* 23(2), Spring 1969, 163.

"Snow"

> MARIE BARROFF. "What a Poem Is: For Instance 'Snow,'" *Essays in Criticism* 8(4), October 1958, 393-404.
>
> SISTER M. MARTIN BARRY. *Explicator* 16(2), November 1957, Item 10.
>
> C. B. COX and A. E. DYSON. *Modern Poetry*, pp. 85-89.
>
> R. C. CRAGG. "Mr. Cragg to Mr. Roberts," *Essays in Criticism* 4(2), April 1954, 231-36.
>
> R. C. CRAGG. "*Snow*, a Philosophical Poem: A Study in Critical Procedure," *Essays in Criticism* 3(4), October 1953, 425-33.
>
> S. W. DAWSON. "Snow," *Essays in Criticism* 4(3), July 1954, 339-40.
>
> ELIZABETH DREW. *Poetry*, pp. 226-28.
>
> M. A. M. ROBERTS. "'Snow': An Answer to Mr. Cragg," *Essays in Criticism* 4(2), April 1954, 227-31.
>
> NANCY SULLIVAN. "Perspective and the Poetic Process," *Wisconsin Studies in Contemporary Literature* 6(1), Winter-Spring 1965, 125-26.

"Sunset"

> MOYA BRENNAN. "A Poet's Revisions: A Consideration of MacNeice's *Blind Fireworks*," *Western Humanities Review* 23(2), Spring 1969, 165-66.

"The Streets of Loredo"

> JOHN T. IRWIN. "MacNeice, Auden, and the Art Ballad," *Contemporary Literature* 11(1), Winter 1970, 58-74.

"Les Sylphides"

> ELIZABETH DREW and JOHN L. SWEENEY. *Directions in Modern Poetry*, pp. 247-49.

"These Days Are Misty"

> NORMAN C. STAGEBERG and WALLACE L. ANDERSON. *Poetry as Experience*, pp. 214-21.

"You Who Will Soon Be Unrecapturable"

> STUART GERRY BROWN. "Some Poems of Louis MacNeice," *Sewanee Review* 51(1), Winter 1943, 66-67.

MADGE, CHARLES

"Delusions"

> D. E. S. MAXWELL. *The Poets of the Thirties*, pp. 52-54.

MAGEE, JOHN GILLESPIE

"High Flight"

> NORMAN C. STAGEBERG and WALLACE L. ANDERSON. *Poetry as Experience*, p. 4.

MAHONY, FRANCIS

"The Bells of Shandon"

> CLEANTH BROOKS and ROBERT PENN WARREN. *Understanding Poetry*, pp. 222-24; revised ed., pp. 114-16; third ed., pp. 135-36.

MALLOCH, DAVID

"Verses Occasioned by Dr. FRAZER's Rebuilding Part of the University of Aberdeen"

> IRMA S. LUSTIG. "'Donaus,' *Donaides*, and David Malloch: A Reply to Dr. Johnson," *Modern Philology* 76(2), November 1978, 149-62.

MANDEVILLE, BERNARD

"The Grumbling Hive"

> M. M. GOLDSMITH. "Public Virtue and Private Vices: Bernard Mandeville and English Political Ideologies in the Early Eighteenth Century," *Eighteenth Century Studies* 9(4), Summer 1976, 497-99.
>
> JAMES A. PREU. "Private Vices — Public Benefits," *English Journal* 52(9), December 1963, 654-55.

MANIFOLD, JOHN

"Fife Tune"

> M. L. ROSENTHAL and A. J. M. SMITH. *Exploring Poetry*, pp. 549-50.

MARKHAM, EDWIN

"The Man With the Hoe"

> LYNN H. HARRIS. *Explicator* 3(5), March 1945, Item 41.

MARLOWE, CHRISTOPHER

"Hero and Leander"

> HARRY BROWN and JOHN MILSTEAD. *What the Poem Means*, p. 144.
>
> PAUL M. CUBETA. "Marlowe's Poet in *Hero and Leander*," *College English* 26(7), April 1965, 500-5.
>
> ELIZABETH STORY DONNO. "The Epyllion," in *English Poetry and Prose*, ed. by Christopher Ricks, pp. 87-91.
>
> WILLIAM KEACH. "Marlowe's Hero as 'Venus Nun,'" *English Literary Renaissance* 2(3), Winter 1972, 307-20.
>
> C. S. LEWIS. "Hero and Leander," in *Elizabethan Poetry*, ed. by Paul J. Alpers, pp. 235-39.
>
> JOHN MILLS. "The Courtship Ritual of Hero and Leander," *English Literary Renaissance* 2(3), Winter 1972, 298-306.
>
> RICHARD NEUSE. "Atheism and Some Functions of Myth in Marlowe's *Hero and Leander*," *Modern Language Quarterly* 31(4), December 1970, 424-39.
>
> ERICH SEGAL. "Hero and Leander: Góngora and Marlowe," *Comparative Literature* 15(4), Fall 1963, 349-56.
>
> WILLIAM E. SHEIDLEY. "The Seduction of the Reader in Marlowe's *Hero and Leander*," *Concerning Poetry* 3(1), Spring 1970, 50-56.
>
> WILLIAM P. WALSH. "Sexual Discovery and Renaissance Morality in Marlowe's 'Hero and Leander,'" *Studies in English Literature 1500-1900* 12(1), Winter 1972, 33-54.

"The Passionate Shepherd to His Love"

> MARJORIE BOULTON. *The Anatomy of Poetry*, pp. 160-63.
>
> PETER HEIDTMANN. "The Lyrics of Fulke Greville," *Ohio University Review* 10 (1968), 29.
>
> LOUIS H. LEITER. "Deification Through Love: Marlowe's 'The Passionate Shepherd to His Love,'" *College English* 27(6), March 1966, 444-49.

MARSTON, JOHN

"The Metamorphosis of Pigmalions Image"

> JOHN SCOTT COLLEY. "'Opinion' and the Reader in John Marston's *The Metamorphosis of Pygmalions Image*," *English Literary Renaissance* 3(2), Spring 1973, 221-31.
>
> ADRIAN WEISS. "Rhetoric and Satire: New Light on John Marston's *Pigmalion* and the Satires," *Journal of English and Germanic Philology* 71(1), January 1972, 22-35.

MARTIN, ALEXANDER

"A New Scene Interesting to the Citizens of the United States of America, Additional to the Historical Play of Columbus"

> RICHARD WALSER. "Alexander Martin, Poet," *Early American Literature* 6(1), Spring 1971, 55-58.

MARVELL, ANDREW

"Ametas and Thestylis Making Hay-Ropes"

> LAURENCE LERNER. "An Essay on Pastoral," *Essays in Criticism* 20(3), July 1970, 281-83. Reprinted in: Laurence Lerner. *The Uses of Nostalgia*, pp. 17-18.

"Bermudas"

> PATRICIA BEER. *An Introduction to the Metaphysical Poets*, pp. 94-98.
> EDWIN B. BENJAMIN. "Marvell's 'Bermudas,'" *CEA Critic* 29(7), April 1967, 10, 12.
> R. M. CUMMINGS. "The Difficulty of Marvell's 'Bermudas,'" *Modern Philology* 67(4), May 1970, 331-40.
> TAY FIZDALE. "Irony in Marvell's 'Bermudas,'" *ELH* 42(2), Summer 1975, 203-13.
> WILLIAM H. HALEWOOD. *The Poetry of Grace*, 118-20, 123-24.
> TOSHIHIKO KAWASAKI. "Marvell's 'Bermudas' — A Little World, or a New World?" *ELH* 43(1), Spring 1976, 38-52.
> ANTHONY LOW. *Love's Architecture*, pp. 245-50.
> LOUIS L. MARTZ. *The Wit of Love*, pp. 175-77.
> ANNABEL PATTERSON. "*Bermudas* and *The Coronet*: Marvell's Protestant Poetics," *ELH* 44(3), Fall 1977, 478-90.
> JEFFREY B. SPENCER. *Heroic Nature*, pp. 53-56.
> LEONA SPITZ. "Process and Stasis: Aspects of Nature in Vaughan and Marvell," *Huntington Library Quarterly* 32(2), February 1969, 143-44.
> HAROLD E. TOLIVER. "Pastoral Form and Idea in Some Poems of Marvell," in *Seventeenth Century English Poetry*, revised ed., pp. 362-63.
> GEORGE WILLIAMSON. *Six Metaphysical Poets*, p. 223.

"The Character of Holland"

> RUTH NEVO. *The Dial of Virtue*, pp. 69-72.

"Clorinda and Damon"

> LAURENCE LERNER. *The Uses of Nostalgia*, pp. 189-91.
> LOUIS L. MARTZ. *The Wit of Love*, pp. 156-58.
> H. R. SWARDSON. *Poetry and the Fountain of Light*, pp. 88-91.
> HAROLD E. TOLIVER. "Pastoral Form and Idea in Some Poems of Marvell," *Texas Studies in Literature and Language* 5(1), Spring 1963, 87-89. Reprinted in: *Seventeenth Century English Poetry*, revised ed., pp. 361-62.
> GEORGE WILLIAMSON. *Six Metaphysical Poets*, pp. 225-26.

"The Coronet"

> MARGARET CARPENTER. "From Herbert to Marvell: Poetics in 'A Wreath' and 'The Coronet,'" *Journal of English and Germanic Philology* 69(1), January 1970, 50-62.
> ROSALIE L. COLIE. "Andrew Marvell: Style and Stylistics (1970)," in *The Metaphysical Poets*, pp. 219-23.
> WILLIAM N. FISHER. "*Occupatio* in Sixteenth- and Seventeenth-Century Verse," *Texas Studies in Literature and Language* 14(2), Summer 1972, 220-22.

> WILLIAM H. HALEWOOD. *The Poetry of Grace*, pp. 113-15.
> JOHN EDWARD HARDY. *The Curious Frame*, pp. 45-60.
> BRUCE KING. "A Reading of Marvell's 'The Coronet,'" *Modern Language Review* 68(4), October 1973, 741-49.
> ANNABEL PATTERSON. "*Bermudas* and *The Coronet*: Marvell's Protestant Poetics," *ELH* 44(3), Fall 1977, 490-97.
> H. R. SWARDSON. *Poetry and the Fountain of Light*, pp. 83-88.
> HAROLD E. TOLIVER. "Pastoral Form and Idea in Some Poems of Marvell," in *Seventeenth Century English Poetry*, revised ed., pp. 359-61.
> GEORGE WILLIAMSON. *Six Metaphysical Poets*, pp. 223-25.

"Damon the Mower"

> ELAINE HOFFMAN BARUCH. "Theme and Counter-themes In 'Damon the Mower,'" *Comparative Literature* 26(3), Summer 1974, 242-59.
> PETER BEREK. "The Voices of Marvell's Lyrics," *Modern Language Quarterly* 32(2), June 1971, 149-51.
> JOHN CREASER. "Marvell's Effortless Superiority," *Essays in Criticism* 20(4), October 1970, 406-8.
> DAVID KALSTONE. "Marvell and the Fictions of Pastoral," *English Literary Renaissance* 4(1), Winter 1974, 175-84.
> RUTH NEVO. "Marvell's 'Songs of Innocence and Experience,'" *Studies in English Literature 1500-1900* 5(1), Winter 1965, 18-20.
> DON PARRY NORFORD. "Marvell and the Arts of Contemplation and Action," *ELH* 41(1), Spring 1974, 67-70.
> CAROL MARKS SICHERMAN. "The Mocking Voices of Donne and Marvell," *Bucknell Review* 17(2), May 1969, 43-44.
> JEFFRY B. SPENCER. *Heroic Nature*, pp. 85-89.
> JOSEPH H. SUMMERS. "Marvell's 'Nature,'" *Journal of English Literary History* 20(2), June 1953, 128.
> HAROLD E. TOLIVER. "Pastoral Form and Idea in Some Poems of Andrew Marvell," *Texas Studies in Literature and Language* 5(1), Spring 1963, 92-95. Reprinted in: *Seventeenth Century English Poetry*, revised ed., pp. 366-69.

"Daphnis and Chloe"

> K. W. GRANSDEN. "Time, Guilt and Pleasure: A Note on Marvell's Nostalgia," *Ariel* 1(2), April 1970, 91-92.
> RUTH NEVO. "Marvell's 'Songs of Innocence and Experience,'" *Studies in English Literature 1500-1900* 5(1), Winter 1965, 15-18.
> MAREN-SOFIE RØSTVIG. "Andrew Marvell and the Caroline Poets," in *English Poetry and Prose*, ed. by Christopher Ricks, p. 243.
> WILLIAM SYLVESTER. "The Existence of a Disjunctive Principle in Poetry: A Preliminary Essay," *College English* 28(4), January 1967, 271-72.

"The Definition of Love"

> A. ALVAREZ. *The School of Donne*, English ed., pp. 114-15; American ed., pp. 122-23.
> PATRICIA BEER. *An Introduction to the Metaphysical Poets*, pp. 89-94.
> ANN EVANS BERTHOFF. "The Allegorical Metaphor: Marvell's 'The Definition of Love,'" *Review of English Studies*, n.s., 17(65), February 1966, 16-29.

CLEANTH BROOKS and ROBERT PENN WARREN. *Understanding Poetry*, pp. 437-40; revised ed., pp. 294-97; third ed., pp. 296-99; fourth ed., pp. 222-25.

DENNIS DAVISON. "Marvell's 'The Definition of Love,'" *Review of English Studies*, n.s., 6(22), April 1955, 141-46. (P)

ANGELA G. DORENKAMP. "Marvell's Geometry of Love," *English Language Notes* 9(2), December 1971, 111-15.

ELIZABETH DREW. *Poetry*, pp. 201-3.

ANNE FERRY. *All in War with Time*, pp. 239-49.

E. B. GREENWOOD. "Marvell's Impossible Love," *Essays in Criticism* 27(2), April 1977, 100-11.

KATHERINE HANLEY. "Andrew Marvell's 'The Definition of Love,'" *Concerning Poetry* 2(2), Fall 1969, 73-74.

EARL MINER. *The Metaphysical Mode from Donne to Cowley*, pp. 138-40.

EARL MINER. "Wit: Definition and Dialectic," in *Seventeenth Century English Poetry*, revised ed., pp. 60-61.

MAREN-SOFIE RØSTVIG. "Andrew Marvell and the Caroline Poets," in *English Poetry and Prose*, ed. by Christopher Ricks, pp. 224-28.

MAREN-SOFIE RØSTVIG. "Images of Perfection," in *Seventeenth-Century Imagery*, pp. 16-17.

HAROLD E. TOLIVER. "Marvell's 'Definition of Love' and Poetry of Self-Exploration," *Bucknell Review* 10(4), May 1962, 263-74.

GEOFFREY WALTON. "The Poetry of Andrew Marvell: A Summing Up," *Politics and Letters* 1(4), Summer 1948, 27-28.

GEORGE WILLIAMSON. *Six Metaphysical Poets*, pp. 234-35.

LAURIE ZWICKY. *Explicator* 22(7), March 1964, Item 52.

"A Dialogue between the Resolved Soul, and Created Pleasure"

HARRY BERGER, JR. "Marvell's 'Garden': Still Another Interpretation," *Modern Language Quarterly* 28(3), September 1967, 287.

K. W. GRANSDEN. "Time, Guilt and Pleasure: A Note on Marvell's Nostalgia," *Ariel* 1(2), April 1970, 88-89.

WILLIAM H. HALEWOOD. *The Poetry of Grace*, pp. 117-18.

FRANK KERMODE. "An Introduction to Marvell," in *The Metaphysical Poets*, p. 325.

LAURENCE LERNER. *The Uses of Nostalgia*, p. 181.

ANTHONY LOW. *Love's Architecture*, pp. 242-45.

LOUIS L. MARTZ. *The Wit of Love*, pp. 159-60.

H. R. SWARDSON. *Poetry and the Fountain of Light*, p. 92.

HAROLD E. TOLIVER. "The Strategy of Marvell's Resolve against Created Pleasure," *Studies in English Literature 1500-1900* 4(1), Winter 1964, 57-69.

GEOFFREY WALTON. "The Poetry of Andrew Marvell: A Summing Up," *Politics and Letters* 1(4), Summer 1948, 26-27.

GEORGE WILLIAMSON. *Six Metaphysical Poets*, pp. 227-29.

"A Dialogue between the Soul and Body"

T. R. BARNES. *English Verse*, pp. 86-88.

PETER BEREK. "The Voices of Marvell's Lyrics," *Modern Language Quarterly* 32(2), June 1971, 144-47.

HARRY BERGER, JR. "Marvell's 'Garden': Still Another Interpretation," *Modern Language Quarterly* 28(3), September 1967, 285-87.

WILLIAM H. HALEWOOD. *The Poetry of Grace*, pp. 116-17.

F. R. LEAVIS. "The Responsible Critic; or The Function of Criticism at Any Time," *Scrutiny* 19(3), Spring 1953, 163-70.

LAURENCE LERNER. *The Uses of Nostalgia*, pp. 195-96.

ANTHONY LOW. *Love's Architecture*, pp. 241-42.

ISABEL G. MacCAFFREY. "Some Notes on Marvell's Poetry, Suggested By a Reading of His Prose," *Modern Philology* 61(4), May 1964, 263-64.

LOUIS L. MARTZ. *The Wit of Love*, pp. 160-61.

ROSALIE OSMOND. "Body and Soul Dialogues in the Seventeenth Century," *English Literary Renaissance* 4(3), Autumn 1974, 387-89.

MAREN-SOFIE RØSTVIG. "Andrew Marvell and the Caroline Poets," in *English Poetry and Prose*, ed. by Christopher Ricks, pp. 228-29.

JOSEPH H. SUMMERS. "Andrew Marvell: Private Taste and Public Judgement," in *Metaphysical Poetry*, edited by Malcolm Bradbury and David Palmer, pp. 193-94.

H. R. SWARDSON. *Poetry and the Fountain of Light*, 93-94.

ROSEMOND TUVE. *Elizabethan and Metaphysical Imagery*, pp. 207-8.

FRANK J. WARNKE. "Play and Metamorphosis in Marvell's Poetry," *Studies in English Literature 1500-1900* 5(1), Winter 1965, 28-29. Reprinted in: *Seventeenth Century English Poetry*, revised ed., pp. 353-54.

GEORGE WILLIAMSON. *Six Metaphysical Poets*, pp. 226-27.

"A Dialogue between the Two Horses"

JAMES QUIVEY. "Rhetoric and Frame: A Study of Method in Three Satires by Marvell," *Tennessee Studies in Literature* 18 (1973), 87-89.

JAMES R. SUTHERLAND. "A Note on the Satirical Poetry of Andrew Marvell," *Philological Quarterly* 45(1), January 1966, 51-53.

"A Dialogue between Thyrsis and Dorinda"

LAURENCE LERNER. *The Uses of Nostalgia*, pp. 182-83.

H. R. SWARDSON. *Poetry and the Fountain of Light*, p. 91.

"Eyes and Tears"

WILLIAM EMPSON. *Seven Types of Ambiguity*, pp. 217-20; second ed., pp. 171-73.

"The Fair Singer"

T. R. BARNES. *English Verse*, pp. 88-9.

GEORGE WILLIAMSON. *Six Metaphysical Poets*, pp. 232-33.

"The First Anniversary of the Government under His Highness the Lord Protector"

NICHOLAS GUILD. "Marvell's 'The First Anniversary of the Government Under O.C.,'" *Papers on Language and Literature* 11(3), Summer 1975, 242-53.

CHARLES S. HENSLEY. "Wither, Waller and Marvell: Panegyrists for the Protector," *Ariel* 3(1), January 1972, 7.

GEORGE DE F. LORD. "From Contemplation to Action: Marvell's Poetical Career," *Philological Quarterly* 46(2), April 1967, 217-19.

RUTH NEVO. *The Dial of Virtue*, pp. 109-14.

ANNABEL PATTERSON. "Against Polarization: Literature and Politics in Marvell's Cromwell Poems," *English Literary Renaissance* 5(2), Spring 1975, 257-68.

MARVELL, ANDREW *(Cont.)*

"The First Anniversary of the Government under His Highness the Lord Protector" *(cont.)*

JOSEPH H. SUMMERS. "Andrew Marvell: Private Taste and Public Judgement," in *Metaphysical Poetry*, edited by Malcolm Bradbury and David Palmer, pp. 199-201. Reprinted in: Joseph H. Summers. *The Heirs of Donne and Jonson*, pp. 168-71.

HAROLD E. TOLIVER. *Pastoral Forms and Attitudes*, pp. 146-48.

JOHN M. WALLACE. "Andrew Marvell and Cromwell's Kingship: 'The First Anniversary,'" *ELH* 30(3), September 1963, 209-35.

A. J. N. WILSON. "Andrew Marvell's 'The First Anniversary of the Government Under Oliver Cromwell': The Poem and Its Frame of Reference," *Modern Language Review* 69(2), April 1974, 254-73.

STEVEN N. ZWICKER. "Models of Governance in Marvell's 'The First Anniversary,'" *Criticism* 16(1), Winter 1974, 1-12.

"Flecknoe, an English Priest at Rome"

EARL MINER. *The Restoration Mode from Milton to Dryden*, pp. 398-400.

GEORGE WILLIAMSON. *Six Metaphysical Poets*, pp. 211-13.

"The Gallery"

LOUIS L. MARTZ. *The Wit of Love*, pp. 173-75.

EDMUND MILLER. "Marvell's Pastoral Ideal in 'The Gallery,'" *Concerning Poetry* 8(1), Spring 1975, 49-50.

WINIFRED NOWOTTNY. *The Language Poets Use*, pp. 92-96.

FRANK J. WARNKE. "Play and Metamorphosis in Marvell's Poetry," *Studies in English Literature 1500-1900* 5(1), Winter 1965, 23-26. Reprinted in: Seventeenth Century English Poetry, revised ed., pp. 348-51.

FRANK J. WARNKE. "Sacred Play: Baroque Poetic Style," *Journal of Aesthetics and Art Criticism* 22(4), Summer 1964, 460.

"The Garden"

HARRY BERGER, JR. "Marvell's 'Garden': Still Another Interpretation," *Modern Language Quarterly* 28(3), September 1967, 285-304.

M. C. BRADBROOK and M. G. LLOYD THOMAS. "Marvell and the Concept of Metamorphosis," *Criterion* 18(61), January 1939, 236-44.

DAVID DAICHES and WILLIAM CHARVAT. *Poems in English*, pp. 662-63.

MARGARET ANN CARPENTER. "Marvell's 'Garden,'" *Studies in English Literature 1500-1900* 10(1), Winter 1970, 155-69.

EARL DANIELS. *The Art of Reading Poetry*, pp. 261-63.

WALLACE DOUGLAS, ROY LAMSON, and HALLETT SMITH. *The Critical Reader*, pp. 68-72.

WILLIAM EMPSON. *English Pastoral Poetry*, pp. 119-32. Reprinted in: *Criticism*, pp. 342-52. Also: *Essays in Modern Literary Criticism*, pp. 335-53. Also: *Determinations*, pp. 46-56.

WILLIAM EMPSON. "Marvell: The Garden," in *Master Poems of the English Language*, pp. 213-23.

WILLIAM EMPSON. "Marvell's 'Garden,'" *Scrutiny* 1(3), December 1932, 236-40.

ANNE FERRY. *All in War with Time*, pp. 210-19.

WILLIAM LEIGH GODSHALK. "Marvell's *Garden* and the Theologians," *Studies in Philology* 66(4), July 1969, 639-53.

K. W. GRANSDEN. "Time, Guilt and Pleasure: A Note on Marvell's Nostalgia," *Ariel* 1(2), April 1970, 83-90.

GEOFFREY H. HARTMAN. "Marvell, St. Paul, and the Body of Hope," *ELH* 31(2), June 1964, 175-94. Reprinted in: Geoffrey H. Hartman. *Beyond Formalism*, pp. 151-72.

ANTHONY HECHT. "Shades of Keats and Marvell," *Hudson Review* 15(1), Spring 1962, 51-57.

DALE HERRON. "Marvell's 'Garden' and the Landscape of Poetry," *Journal of English and Germanic Philology* 73(3), July 1974, 328-37.

LAWRENCE W. HYMAN. "Marvell's *Garden*," *Journal of English Literary History* 25(1), March 1958, 13-22.

FRANK KERMODE. "The Argument of Marvell's 'Garden,'" in *Seventeenth Century English Poetry*, pp. 290-304; revised ed., pp. 333-47.

FRANK KERMODE. "An Introduction to Marvell," in *The Metaphysical Poets*, pp. 318-20.

FRANK KERMODE and A. J. SMITH. "The Metaphysical Poets," in *English Poetry*, edited by Alan Sinfield, pp. 68-69.

MILTON KLONSKY. "A Guide Through the Garden," *Sewanee Review* 58(1), Winter 1950, 16-35.

ANTHONY LOW. *Love's Architecture*, pp. 250-57.

MICHAEL MCCANLES. *Dialectical Criticism and Renaissance Literature*, pp. 101-6.

LOUIS L. MARTZ. *The Wit of Love*, pp. 171-73.

EARL MINER. *The Metaphysical Mode from Donne to Cowley*, pp. 84-91.

JOHN M. POTTER. "Another Porker in the Garden of Epicurus: Marvell's 'Hortus' and 'The Garden,'" *Studies in English Literature 1500-1900* 11(1), Winter 1971, 137-51.

I. A. RICHARDS. *Poetries: Their Media and Ends*, pp. 95-111.

MAREN-SOFIE RØSTVIG. "Andrew Marvell and the Caroline Poets," in *English Poetry and Prose*, ed. by Christopher Ricks, pp. 235-38.

MAREN-SOFIE RØSTVIG. "Andrew Marvell's 'The Garden': A Hermetic Poem," *English Studies* 40(2), April 1959, 65-76.

NICHOLAS A. SALERNO. "Andrew Marvell and the Furor Hortensis," *Studies in English Literature 1500-1900* 8(1), Winter 1968, 116-19.

JOHN N. SERIO. "Andrew Marvell's 'The Garden': An Anagogic Reading," *Ohio University Review* 12(1), 1970, 68-76.

JAMES EDWARD SIEMON. "Generic Limits in Marvell's 'Garden,'" *Papers on Language and Literature* 8(3), Summer 1972, 261-72.

JEFFRY B. SPENCER. *Heroic Nature*, pp. 80-85, 96-98.

LEONA SPITZ. "Process and Stasis: Aspects of Nature in Vaughan and Marvell," *Huntington Library Quarterly* 32(2), February 1967, 145-47.

DANIEL STEMPEL. "*The Garden*: Marvell's Cartesian Ecstasy," *Journal of the History of Ideas* 28(1), Jan.-March 1967, 99-114.

STANLEY STEWART. *The Enclosed Garden*, pp. 150-83.

JOSEPH H. SUMMERS. "Reading Marvell's 'Garden,'" *Centennial Review* 13(1), Winter 1969, 18-37. Reprinted in: Joseph H. Summers. *The Heirs of Donne and Jonson*, pp. 135-55.

H. R. SWARDSON. *Poetry and the Fountain of Light*, pp. 99-101.

LEONARD UNGER. *The Man in the Name*, pp. 126-28.

MARK VAN DOREN. *Introduction to Poetry*, pp. 59-65.

GEOFFREY WALTON. "The Poetry of Andrew Marvell: A Summing Up," *Politics and Letters* 1(4), Summer 1948, 30-31.

GEORGE WILLIAMSON. "The Context of Marvell's 'Hortus' and 'Garden,'" *Modern Language Notes* 76(7), November 1961, 590-98. Reprinted in: George Williamson. *Milton & Others*, pp. 140-49.

GEORGE WILLIAMSON. *Six Metaphysical Poets*, pp. 238-41.

"An Horatian Ode upon Cromwell's Return from Ireland"

R. L. BRETT. "Andrew Marvell: The voice of his age," *Critical Quarterly* 20(4), Winter 1978, 5-17.

CLEANTH BROOKS. "Criticism and Literary History: Marvell's 'Horatian Ode,'" *Sewanee Review* 55(2), Spring 1947, 199-222.

CLEANTH BROOKS. "Literary Criticism," *English Institute Essays*, 1946, pp. 127-58. Reprinted in: *Explication as Criticism*, pp. 99-103. Also: *Seventeenth Century English Poetry*, first ed., pp. 321-40.

CLEANTH BROOKS. "A Note on the Limits of 'History' and the Limits of 'Criticism,'" *Sewanee Review* 61(1), Winter 1953, 129-35. Reprinted in: *Seventeenth Century English Poetry*, first ed., pp. 352-58.

CLEANTH BROOKS and ROBERT PENN WARREN. *Understanding Poetry*, revised ed., pp. 667-81.

FRANKLIN G. BURROUGHS, JR. "Marvell's Cromwell and May's Caesar: 'An Horatian Ode' and the *Continuation of the Pharsalia*," *English Language Notes* 13(2), December 1975, 115-22.

DOUGLAS BUSH. "Marvell's 'Horatian Ode,'" in *Seventeenth Century English Poetry*, first ed., pp. 341-51.

JOHN S. COOLIDGE. "Marvell and Horace," *Modern Philology* 63(2), November 1965, 111-20.

DAVID K. CORNELIUS. *Explicator* 35(3), Spring 1977, 18-19.

THOMAS R. EDWARDS. *Imagination and Power*, pp. 66-81.

K. W. GRANSDEN. "Time, Guilt and Pleasure: A Note on Marvell's Nostalgia," *Ariel* 1(2), April 1970, 86.

NICHOLAS GUILD. "The Context of Marvell's Allusion to Lucan in 'An Horatian Ode,'" *Papers on Language and Literature* 14(4), Fall 1978, 406-13.

THOMAS W. HAYES. "The Dialectic of History in Marvell's *Horatian Ode*," *Clio* 1(1), October 1971, 26-36.

FRANK KERMODE. "An Introduction to Marvell," in *The Metaphysical Poets*, pp. 310-13.

L. D. LERNER. "Andrew Marvell: An Horatian Ode upon Cromwel's Return from Ireland," in *Interpretations*, pp. 62-74.

JOSEPH ANTHONY MAZZEO. "Cromwell as Machiavellian Prince in Marvell's 'An Horatian Ode,'" *Journal of the History of Ideas* 21(1), January-March 1960, 1-17.

EARL MINER. *The Metaphysical Mode from Donne to Cowley*, pp. 208-12.

RUTH NEVO. *The Dial of Virtue*, pp. 97-109.

ANNABEL PATTERSON. "Against Polarization: Literature and Politics in Marvell's Cromwell Poems," *English Literary Renaissance* 5(2), Spring 1975, 254-56.

RAMAN SELDEN. "Historical Thought and Marvell's *Horatian Ode*," *Durham University Journal*, n.s., 34(1), December 1972, 41-53.

R. H. SYFRET. "Marvell's 'Horatian Ode,'" *Review of English Studies*, n.s., 12(46), May 1961, 160-72.

DAVID M. VIETH. "Divided Consciousness: The Trauma and Triumph of Restoration Culture," *Tennessee Studies in Literature* 22(1977), 48-49.

JOHN M. WALLACE. "Marvell's Horatian Ode," *PMLA* 77(1), March 1962, 33-45.

GEORGE WILLIAMSON. *Milton & Others*, pp. 122-39.

GEORGE WILLIAMSON. *Six Metaphysical Poets*, pp. 216-18.

A. J. N. WILSON. "Andrew Marvell: *An Horatian Ode upon Cromwel's Return from Ireland*: The thread of the poem and its use of classical allusion," *Critical Quarterly* 11(4), Winter 1969, 325-41.

"Hortus"

GEORGE WILLIAMSON. "The Context of Marvell's 'Hortus' and 'Garden,'" *Modern Language Notes* 76(7), November 1961, 590-98.

"The Last Instructions to a Painter"

DAVID FARLEY-HILLS. *The Benevolence of Laughter*, pp. 72-98.

ALAN S. FISHER. "The Augustan Marvell: *The Last Instructions to a Painter*," *ELH* 38(2), June 1971, 223-38.

MICHAEL GEARIN-TOSH. "The Structure of Marvell's 'Last Instructions to a Painter,'" *Essays in Criticism* 22(1), January 1972, 48-57.

EARL MINER. "The 'Poetic Picture, Painted Poetry' of *The Last Instructions to a Painter*," *Modern Philology* 63(4), May 1966, 288-94.

EARL MINER. *The Restoration Mode from Milton to Dryden*, pp. 400-4.

RUTH NEVO. *The Dial of Virtue*, pp. 173-78.

JAMES QUIVEY. "Rhetoric and Frame: A Study of Method in Three Satires by Marvell," *Tennessee Studies in Literature* 18 (1973), 76-83.

JOSEPH H. SUMMERS. "Andrew Marvell: Private Taste and Public Judgement," in *Metaphysical Poetry*, edited by Malcolm Bradbury and David Palmer, pp. 201-4. Reprinted in: Joseph H. Summers. *The Heirs of Donne and Jonson*, pp. 171-75.

"The Loyall Scot"

JAMES QUIVEY. "Rhetoric and Frame: A Study of Method in Three Satires by Marvell," *Tennessee Studies in Literature* 18 (1973), 83-87.

"Mourning"

PAUL DELANY. "Marvell's 'Mourning,'" *Modern Language Quarterly* 33(1), March 1972, 30-36.

GEORGE WILLIAMSON. *Six Metaphysical Poets*, pp. 233-34.

"The Mower Against Gardens"

PETER BEREK. "The Voices of Marvell's Lyrics," *Modern Language Quarterly* 32(2), June 1971, 147-49.

K. W. GRANSDEN. "Time, Guilt and Pleasure: A Note on Marvell's Nostalgia," *Ariel* 1(2), April 1970, 96.

FRANK KERMODE. "An Introduction to Marvell," in *The Metaphysical Poets*, pp. 314-17.

BRUCE KING. "'The Mower against Gardens' and the Levellers," *Huntington Library Quarterly* 33(3), May 1970, 237-42.

LAURENCE LERNER. *The Uses of Nostalgia*, pp. 187-88.

DON PARRY NORFORD. "Marvell and the Arts of Contemplation and Action," *ELH* 41(1), Spring 1974, 61-63.

NICHOLAS A. SALERNO. "Andrew Marvell and the *Furor Hortensis*," *Studies in English Literature 1500-1900* 8(1), Winter 1968, 103-13.

MARVELL, ANDREW *(Cont.)*

"The Mower Against Gardens" *(cont.)*

    CAROL MARKS SICHERMAN. "The Mocking Voices of Donne and Marvell," *Bucknell Review* 17(2), May 1969, 40-43.

    H. R. SWARDSON. *Poetry and the Fountain of Light,* pp. 94-96.

    HAROLD E. TOLIVER. "Pastoral Form and Idea in Some Poems of Marvell," in *Seventeenth Century English Poetry,* revised ed., pp. 364-65.

    GEORGE WILLIAMSON. *Six Metaphysical Poets,* p. 237.

"The Mower to the Glo-Worms"

    JOHN CREASER. "Marvell's Effortless Superiority," *Essays in Criticism* 20(4), October 1970, 409-12.

    WILLIAM LEIGH GODSHALK. *Explicator* 25(2), October 1966, Item 12.

    CHARLES MITCHELL. *Explicator* 18(8), May 1960, Item 50.

    DON PARRY NORFORD. "Marvell and the Arts of Contemplation and Action," *ELH* 41(1), Spring 1974, 63-66.

    JEFFRY B. SPENCER. *Heroic Nature,* pp. 89-93.

    H. R. SWARDSON. *Poetry and the Fountain of Light,* pp. 96-97.

    E. M. W. TILLYARD. *The Metaphysicals and Milton,* pp. 32-35.

    HAROLD E. TOLIVER. "Pastoral Form and Idea in Some Poems of Andrew Marvell," *Texas Studies in Literature and Language* 5(1), Spring 1963, 96. Reprinted in: *Seventeenth Century English Poetry,* revised ed., pp. 369-70.

    GEORGE WILLIAMSON. *Six Metaphysical Poets,* pp. 236-37.

"The Mower's Song"

    BARBARA EVERETT. "Marvell's 'The Mower's Song,'" *Critical Quarterly* 4(3), Autumn 1962, 219-24.

    ANNE FERRY. *All in War with Time,* pp. 219-28.

    GEOFFREY H. HARTMAN. "Marvell, St. Paul, and the Body of Hope," *ELH* 31(2), June 1964, 189-92. Reprinted in: Geoffrey H. Hartman. *Beyond Formalism,* pp. 166-69.

    DON PARRY NORFORD. "Marvell and the Arts of Contemplation and Action," *ELH* 41(1), Spring 1974, 66-67.

    JEFFRY B. SPENCER. *Heroic Nature,* pp. 90-91, 93-94.

    H. R. SWARDSON. *Poetry and the Fountain of Light,* pp. 97-99.

    HAROLD E. TOLIVER. "Pastoral Form and Idea in Some Poems of Marvell," *Texas Studies in Literature and Language* 5(1), Spring 1963, 96-97. Reprinted in: *Seventeenth Century English Poetry,* revised ed., pp. 370-71.

"Musicks Empire"

    JONATHAN GOLDBERG. "The Typology of 'Musicks Empire,'" *Texas Studies in Literature and Language* 13(3), Fall 1971, 421-30.

"The Nymph Complaining for the Death of Her Faun"

    DON CAMERON ALLEN. *Image and Meaning,* pp. 93-114; revised ed., pp. 165-86.

    DON CAMERON ALLEN. "Marvell's 'Nymph,'" *Journal of English Literary History* 23(2), June 1956, 93-111.

    MICHAEL J. B. ALLEN. "The Chase: The Development of a Renaissance Theme," *Comparative Literature* 20(4), Fall 1968, 308-12.

    CAROLYN ASP. "Marvell's Nymph: Unravished Bride of Quietness," *Papers on Language and Literature* 14(4), Fall 1978, 394-405.

    PETER BEREK. "The Voices of Marvell's Lyrics," *Modern Language Quarterly* 32(2), June 1971, 151-53.

    M. C. BRADBROOK and M. G. LLOYD THOMAS. "Marvell and the Concept of Metamorphosis," *Criterion* 18(61), January 1939, 252-54.

    ROSALIE L. COLIE. "Andrew Marvell: Style and Stylistics (1970)," in *The Metaphysical Poets,* pp. 230-33.

    RUEL E. FOSTER. "A Tonal Study: Marvell: 'The Nymph Complaining for the Death of Her Faun,'" *University of Kansas City Review* 22(1), Autumn 1955, 73-78.

    NICHOLAS GUILD. "Marvell's 'The Nymph Complaining for the Death of Her Faun,'" *Modern Language Quarterly* 29(4), December 1968, 385-94.

    GEOFFREY H. HARTMAN. "'The Nymph Complaining for the Death of Her Fawn': A Brief Allegory," *Essays in Criticism* 18(2), April 1968, 113-35. Reprinted in: Geoffrey H. Hartman. *Beyond Formalism,* pp. 173-92.

    EVAN JONES. *Explicator* 26(9), May 1968, Item 73.

    FRANK KERMODE. "An Introduction to Marvell," in *The Metaphysical Poets,* pp. 322-24.

    EDWARD S. LE COMTE. "Marvell's 'The Nymph Complaining for the Death of Her Faun,'" *Modern Philology* 50(2), November 1952, 97-101. Reprinted in: Edward S. Le Comte. *Poets' Riddles,* pp. 161-79.

    LAURENCE LERNER. *The Uses of Nostalgia,* pp. 192-96.

    LOUIS L. MARTZ. *The Wit of Love,* pp. 180-82.

    EARL MINER. "The Death of Innocence in Marvell's *Nymph Complaining for the Death of Her Faun,*" *Modern Philology* 65(1), August 1967, 9-16.

    EARL MINER. *The Metaphysical Mode from Donne to Cowley,* pp. 246-70.

    RUTH NEVO. "Marvell's 'Songs of Innocence and Experience,'" *Studies in English Literature 1500-1900* 5(1), Winter 1965, 5-15.

    DON PARRY NORFORD. "Marvell and the Arts of Contemplation and Action," *ELH* 41(1), Spring 1974, 56-60.

    RENÉ RAPIN. *Explicator* 28(8), April 1970, Item 71.

    LEO SPITZER. "Marvell's 'Nymph Complaining for the Death of Her Faun': Sources Versus Meaning," *Modern Language Quarterly* 19(3), September 1958, 231-43. Reprinted in: Leo Spitzer. *Essays on English and American Literature,* pp. 98-115. Also: *Seventeenth Century English Poetry,* pp. 305-20; revised ed., pp. 372-87.

    JOHN J. TEUNISSEN and EVELYN J. HINZ. "What Is the Nymph Complaining For?" *ELH* 45(3), Fall 1978, 410-28.

    T. KATHARINE THOMASON. "Marvell's Complaint Against His Nymph," *Studies in English Literature 1500-1900* 18(1), Winter 1978, 95-105.

    GEORGE WILLIAMSON. *Six Metaphysical Poets,* pp. 229-31.

"On a Drop of Dew"

    JEROME BEATY and WILLIAM H. MATCHETT. *Poetry From Statement to Meaning,* p. 56.

    WILLIAM EMPSON. *Seven Types of Ambiguity,* second and third eds., p. 80. (P)

    WILLIAM H. HALEWOOD. *The Poetry of Grace,* pp. 115-16.

    ANTHONY LOW. *Love's Architecture,* pp. 238-41.

ISABEL G. MacCAFFREY. "Some Notes on Marvell's Poetry, Suggested By a Reading of His Prose," *Modern Philology* 61(4), May 1964, 266-67.

M. B. McNAMEE. "The Ignatian Meditation Pattern in the Poetry of Gerard Manley Hopkins," *Hopkins Quarterly* 2(1), April 1975, 21-24.

LOUIS L. MARTZ. *The Wit of Love,* pp. 161-63.

RUTH NEVO. "Marvell's 'Songs of Innocence and Experience,'" *Studies in English Literature 1500-1900* 5(1), Winter 1965, 1-3.

ALFRED F. ROSA. "Andrew Marvell's 'On a Drop of Dew': A Reading and Possible Source," *Concerning Poetry* 5(1), Spring 1972, 57-59.

LEONA SPITZ. "Process and Stasis: Aspects of Nature in Vaughan and Marvell," *Huntington Library Quarterly* 32(2), February 1969, 142-43.

H. R. SWARDSON. *Poetry and the Fountain of Light,* p. 92.

HAROLD E. TOLIVER. *Pastoral Forms and Attitudes,* pp. 138-40.

GEORGE WILLIAMSON. *Six Metaphysical Poets,* pp. 237-38.

"On Blake's Victory"

RUTH NEVO. *The Dial of Virtue,* pp. 115-17.

"On Mr. Milton's *Paradise Lost*"

JUDITH SCHERER HERZ. "Milton and Marvell: The Poet as Fit Reader," *Modern Language Quarterly* 39(3), September 1978, 244-47.

HENRY F. LIPPINCOTT, JR. "Marvell's 'On Paradise Lost,'" *English Language Notes* 9(4), June 1972, 265-72.

EARL MINER. *The Metaphysical Mode from Donne to Cowley,* pp. 205-6.

JOSEPH H. SUMMERS. "Andrew Marvell: Private Taste and Public Judgement," in *Metaphysical Poetry,* edited by Malcolm Bradbury and David Palmer, pp. 206-8. Reprinted in: Joseph H. Summers. *The Heirs of Donne and Jonson,* pp. 178-81.

"The Picture of Little T. C. in a Prospect of Flowers"

PETER BEREK. "The Voices of Marvell's Lyrics," *Modern Language Quarterly* 32(2), June 1971, 154-57.

PATRICK CULLEN. "Imitation and Metamorphosis: The Golden-Age Eclogue in Spenser, Milton, and Marvell," *PMLA* 84(6), October 1969, 1568-70.

A. E. DYSON and JULIAN LOVELOCK. *Masterful Images,* pp. 37-46.

ANNE FERRY. *All in War with Time,* pp. 200-10.

LAURENCE LERNER. *An Introduction to English Poetry,* pp. 62-75.

J. L. SIMMONS. *Explicator* 22(8), April 1964, Item 62.

JEFFRY B. SPENCER. *Heroic Nature,* pp. 63-68.

JOSEPH H. SUMMERS. "Marvell's 'Nature,'" *Journal of English Literary History* 20(2), June 1953, 130-34.

E. M. W. TILLYARD. *Poetry Direct and Oblique,* pp. 203-6; revised ed., pp. 77-79.

FRANK J. WARNKE. "Play and Metamorphosis in Marvell's Poetry," *Studies in English Literature 1500-1900* 5(1), Winter 1965, 26-28. Reprinted in: *Seventeenth Century English Poetry,* revised ed., pp. 351-53.

GEORGE WILLIAMSON. *Six Metaphysical Poets,* pp. 235-36.

"A Poem on the Death of His late Highnesse the Lord Protector"

CHARLES S. HENSLEY. "Wither, Waller and Marvell: Panegyrists for the Protector," *Ariel* 3(1), January 1972, 14-15.

ANNABEL PATTERSON. "Against Polarization: Literature and Politics in Marvell's Cromwell Poems," *English Literary Renaissance* 5(2), Spring 1975, 268-72.

"The Rehearsal Transposed"

GEORGE WILLIAMSON. *Six Metaphysical Poets,* pp. 215-16.

"To His Coy Mistress"

GÉMINO H. ABAD. *A Formal Approach to Lyric Poetry,* pp. 194-95.

RUSSELL AMES. "Decadence in the Art of T. S. Eliot," *Science and Society* 16(3), Summer 1952, 193-221.

MICHAEL BAUMANN. *Explicator* 31(9), May 1973, Item 72.

JEROME BEATY and WILLIAM H. MATCHETT. *Poetry From Statement to Meaning,* pp. 119-22.

R. L. BRETT. "Andrew Marvell: The Voice of His Age," *Critical Quarterly* 20(4), Winter 1978, 7-8.

CLEANTH BROOKS, JOHN THIBAUT PURSER, and ROBERT PENN WARREN. *An Approach to Literature,* pp. 504-6; second ed., pp. 504-6; third ed., pp. 393-5; fourth ed., pp. 389-92; fifth ed., pp. 446-49.

JOHN J. CARROLL. "The Sun and the Lovers in 'To His Coy Mistress,'" *Modern Language Notes* 74(1), January 1959, 4-7. (P)

J. V. CUNNINGHAM. "Marvell: To His Coy Mistress," in *Master Poems of the English Language,* pp. 204-10.

DAVID DAICHES and WILLIAM CHARVAT. *Poems in English,* pp. 663-64.

ROBERT DANIEL. *Explicator* 1(5), March 1943, Item 37.

DAVID FARLEY-HILLS. *The Benevolence of Laughter,* pp. 147-48.

ANNE FERRY. *All in War with Time,* pp. 185-99.

K. W. GRANSDEN. "Time, Guilt and Pleasure: A Note on Marvell's Nostalgia," *Ariel* 1(2), April 1970, 89-90, 92-95.

JOAN HARTWIG. "The Principle of Measure in 'To His Coy Mistress,'" *College English* 25(8), May 1964, 572-75.

T. R. HENN. *The Apple and the Spectroscope,* pp. 25-33.

PATRICK G. HOGAN, JR. "Marvell's 'Vegetable Love,'" *Studies in Philology* 60(1), January 1963, 1-11.

LAWRENCE W. HYMAN. "Marvell's 'Coy Mistress' and Desperate Lover," *Modern Language Notes* 75(1), January 1960, 8-10.

FRANK KERMODE. "An Introduction to Marvell," in *The Metaphysical Poets,* pp. 324-25.

BRUCE KING. "Irony in Marvell's 'To His Coy Mistress,'" *Southern Review,* n.s, 5(3), Summer 1969, 689-703.

LAURENCE LERNER. *An Introduction to English Poetry,* pp. 71-74.

ANTHONY LOW and PAUL J. PIVAL. "Rhetorical Pattern in Marvell's 'To His Coy Mistress,'" *Journal of English and Germanic Philology* 68(3), July 1969, 414-21.

ARCHIBALD MacLEISH. *Poetry and Experience,* pp. 82-88.

C. N. MANLOVE. *Literature and Reality,* pp. 14-15.

LOUIS L. MARTZ. *The Wit of Love,* pp. 167-69.

MARVELL, ANDREW *(Cont.)*

"To His Coy Mistress" *(cont.)*

JOSEPH J. MOLDENHAUER. "The Voices of Seduction in 'To His Coy Mistress': A Rhetorical Analysis," *Texas Studies in Literature and Language* 10(2), Summer 1968, 189-206.

JOHN OLIVER PERRY. *The Experience of Poems*, pp. 294-96.

JOHN CROWE RANSOM. *The New Criticism*, pp. 311-13.

JOHN HAWLEY ROBERTS. *Explicator* 1(3), December 1942, Item 17. Reprinted in: *Readings for Liberal Education*, II: 516-17; revised ed., II: 60-61.

M. L. ROSENTHAL and A. J. M. SMITH. *Exploring Poetry*, p. 632; second ed., pp. 430-31.

MAREN-SOFIE RØSTVIG. "Andrew Marvell and the Caroline Poets," in *English Poetry and Prose*, ed. by Christopher Ricks, pp. 241-43.

ROBIN SKELTON. *Poetry*, pp. 65-69.

STANLEY STEWART. "Marvell and the *Ars Moriendi*," in *Seventeenth-Century Imagery*, pp. 133-50.

GEOFFREY WALTON. "The Poetry of Andrew Marvell: A Summing Up," *Politics and Letters* 1(4), Summer 1948, 28-29.

GEORGE WILLIAMSON. *Six Metaphysical Poets*, pp. 231-32.

"To his noble Friend, Mr. Richard Lovelace, upon his Poems"

GEORGE WILLIAMSON. *Six Metaphysical Poets*, pp. 213-14.

"Tom May's Death"

CHRISTINE REES. " 'Tom May's Death' and Ben Jonson's Ghost: A Study of Marvell's Satiric Method," *Modern Language Review* 71(3), July 1976, 481-88.

GEORGE WILLIAMSON. *Six Metaphysical Poets*, pp. 218-20.

"The Unfortunate Lover"

ANN EVANS BERTHOFF. "The Voice of Allegory: Marvell's 'The Unfortunate Lover,' " *Modern Language Quarterly* 27(1), March 1966, 41-50.

ELSIE DUNCAN-JONES. "A Reading of Marvell's *The Unfortunate Lover*," in *I. A. Richards: Essays in His Honor*, pp. 211-26.

ANNE FERRY. *All in War with Time*, pp. 228-39.

J. MAX PATRICK. *Explicator* 20(8), April 1962, Item 65.

PETER T. SCHWENGER. "Marvell's 'Unfortunate Lover' as Device," *Modern Language Quarterly* 35(4), December 1974, 364-75.

"Upon Appleton House"

DON CAMERON ALLEN. *Image and Meaning*, pp. 115-53; revised ed., pp. 187-225.

ROSALIE L. COLIE. "Andrew Marvell: Style and Stylistics (1970)," in *The Metaphysical Poets*, pp. 223-25.

JOHN CREASER. "Marvell's Effortless Superiority," *Essays in Criticism* 20(4), October 1970, 414-20.

DAVID EVETT. " 'Paradice's Only Map': The *Topos* of the *Locus Amoenus* and the Structure of Marvell's *Upon Appleton House*," *PMLA* 85(3), May 1970, 504-13.

JONATHAN GOLDBERG. "Hesper-Vesper: Aspects of Venus in a Seventeenth-Century Trope," *Studies in English Literature 1500-1900* 15(1), Winter 1975, 46-51.

K. W. GRANSDEN. "Time, Guilt and Pleasure: A Note on Marvell's Nostalgia," *Ariel* 1(2), April 1970, 83-90.

FRANK KERMODE. "An Introduction to Marvell," in *The Metaphysical Poets*, pp. 320-22.

LAURENCE LERNER. *The Uses of Nostalgia*, pp. 183-87.

BARBARA K. LEWALSKI. "Typology and Poetry: A Consideration of Herbert, Vaughan, and Marvell," in *Illustrious Evidence*, pp. 63-68.

GEORGE DE F. LORD. "From Contemplation to Action: Marvell's Poetical Career," *Philological Quarterly* 46(2), April 1967, 211-16.

MICHAEL MCCANLES. *Dialectical Criticism and Renaissance Literature*, pp. 106-17.

EARL MINER. *The Metaphysical Mode from Donne to Cowley*, pp. 201-4.

CHARLES MOLESWORTH. "Marvell's 'Upon Appleton House': The Persona as Historian, Philosopher, and Priest," *Studies in English Literature 1500-1900* 13(1), Winter 1973, 149-62.

DON PARRY NORFORD. "Marvell's 'Holy Mathematicks,' " *Modern Language Quarterly* 38(3), September 1977, 242-60.

H. M. RICHMOND. " 'Rural Lyricism': A Renaissance Mutation Of the Pastoral," *Comparative Literature* 16(3), Summer 1964, 208-10.

MAREN-SOFIE RØSTVIG. "Andrew Marvell and the Caroline Poets," in *English Poetry and Prose*, ed. by Christopher Ricks, pp. 239-41.

JEFFRY B. SPENCER. *Heroic Nature*, pp. 68-80.

HAROLD E. TOLIVER. *Pastoral Forms and Attitudes*, pp. 142-46.

JAMES TURNER. "Marvell's Warlike Studies," *Essays in Criticism* 28(4), October 1978, 288-301.

"Upon the Death of Lord Hastings"

WILLIAM EMPSON. *Seven Types of Ambiguity*, pp. 212-17; second and third eds., pp. 168-71.

"Upon the Hill and Grove at Bill-borow"

JEFFRY B. SPENCER. *Heroic Nature*, pp. 57-62.

A. J. WILSON. "Marvell, 'Upon the Hill and Grove at Bill-Borrow': Symbolic Form?" *Notes and Queries*, n.s., 24(2), April 1977, 126-27.

"The Wish"

GEORGE WILLIAMSON. *Milton & Others*, pp. 144-46.

MASEFIELD, JOHN

"C. L. M."

WALTER GIERASCH. *Explicator* 13(4), February 1955, Item 25.

"Cargoes"

GEORGE ARMS. *Explicator* 1(2), November 1942, Item 15.

ISAAC ASIMOV. *Familiar Poems, Annotated*, pp. 257-59.

WALTER BLAIR and JOHN C. GERBER. *Better Reading 2: Literature*, pp. 176-77.

ARTHUR DICKSON. *Explicator* 2(2), November 1943, Item 12.

ROGER P. MCCUTCHEON. *Explicator* 2(4), February 1944, Item 31.

CLIFFORD A. NAULT, JR. *Explicator* 16(5), February 1958, Item 31.

"The Everlasting Mercy"

L. HUGH MOORE, JR. "Siegfried Sassoon and Georgian Realism," *Twentieth Century Literature* 14(4), January 1969, 201-2.

"King Cole"

G. WILSON KNIGHT. *Neglected Powers*, pp. 279-81.

"The Racer"
CHARLES W. COOPER and JOHN HOLMES. *Preface to Poetry*, pp. 170-73.

"Sea Fever"
C. C. CUNNINGHAM. *Literature as a Fine Art: Analysis and Interpretation*, pp. 160-64.
FRANCIS V. LLOYD, JR. *Explicator* 3(5), March 1945, Item 36. (P)

MASTERS, EDGAR LEE

"Anne Rutledge"
ISAAC ASIMOV. *Familiar Poems, Annotated*, pp. 191-94.

"Dillard Sissman"
JOHN E. HALLWAS. *Explicator* 36(3), Spring 1978, 2-3.

"Father Malloy"
HYATT H. WAGGONER. *American Poets*, pp. 449-50.

"The Lost Orchard"
RICHARD E. AMACHER. *Explicator* 7(5), March 1949, Item 38.
MARY B. DEATON. *Explicator* 8(2), November 1949, Item 16.

"Lucinda Matlock"
AGNES STEIN. *The Uses of Poetry*, pp. 39-40.

MASTERS, MARCIA

"Childhood"
GEORGE ABBE. *You and Contemporary Poetry*, pp. 17-18; 1965 ed., pp. 19-20.

MATILDA

"On Reading the Poems of Phillis Wheatly, the African Poetess"
EUGENE L. HUDDLESTON. "Matilda's 'On Reading the Poems of Phillis Wheatly, the African Poetess,'" *Early American Literature* 5(3), Winter 1970-71, 57-61.

MAURA, SISTER

"Initiate the Heart"
SISTER MARY HESTER. "Teaching 'Initiate the Heart,'" *English Journal* 53(2), February 1964, 141-42.

MAXWELL, GAVIN

"Poem" ("The power that wheels the eagle's wing")
ROBIN SKELTON. *The Poetic Pattern*, pp. 168-72.

MELVILLE, HERMAN

"After the Pleasure Party"
DARREL ABEL. "'Laurel Twined with Thorn': The Theme of Melville's *Timoleon*," *The Personalist* 41(3), Summer 1960, 333-34.
RICHARD HARTER FOGLE. "The Themes of Melville's Later Poetry," *Tulane Studies in English* 11 (1961), 77-78.
HERSHEL PARKER. "Trafficking in Melville," *Modern Language Quarterly* 33(1), March 1972, 65.
ALLEN F. STEIN. "Hawthorne's Zenobia and Melville's Urania," *American Transcendental Quarterly* 26(Suppl.), Spring 1975, 11-14.
CHARLES N. WATSON, JR. "The Estrangement of Hawthorne and Melville," *New England Quarterly* 46(3), September 1973, 399-401.

"The Age of the Antonines"
JANE DONAHUE. "Melville's Classicism: Law and Order in His Poetry," *Papers on Language and Literature* 5(1), Winter 1969, 68-70.

"Armies of the Wilderness"
JOYCE SPARER ADLER. "Melville and the Civil War," *New Letters* 40(2), December 1973, 106-7.
VAUGHAN HUDSON. "Melville's *Battle-Pieces* and Whitman's *Drum-Taps*: A Comparison," *Walt Whitman Review* 19(3), September 1973, 87-88.

"Art"
LEO HAMALIAN. *Explicator* 8(5), March 1950, Item 40.

"Ball's Bluff"
VAUGHAN HUDSON. "Melville's *Battle-Pieces* and Whitman's *Drum-Taps*: A Comparison," *Walt Whitman Review* 19(3), September 1973, 85-86.

"The Battle for Mississippi"
JOHN P. MCWILLIAMS, JR. "'Drum Taps' and *Battle-Pieces*: The Blossom of War," *American Quarterly* 23(2), May 1971, 184.

"The Battle for the Bay"
JOYCE SPARER ADLER. "Melville and the Civil War," *New Letters* 40(2), December 1973, 108-9.

"Billy in the Darbies"
M. L. ROSENTHAL and A. J. M. SMITH. *Exploring Poetry*, pp. 373-75; second ed., pp. 150-52.
ROBERT PENN WARREN. "Melville's Poems," *Southern Review*, n.s., 3(4), Autumn 1967, 840-55.

"Bridegroom Dick"
RICHARD HARTER FOGLE. "The Themes of Melville's Later Poetry," *Tulane Studies in English* 11 (1961), 70-72.
ROBERT PENN WARREN. "Melville's Poems," *Southern Review*, n.s., 3(4), Autumn 1967, 835-37.

"Butterfly Ditty"
WILLIAM BYSSHE STEIN. "Time, History, and Religion: A Glimpse of Melville's Late Poetry," *Arizona Quarterly* 22(2), Summer 1966, 142.

"A Canticle"
JOHN P. MCWILLIAMS, JR. "'Drum Taps' and *Battle-Pieces*: The Blossom of War," *American Quarterly* 23(2), May 1971, 189.

"The College Colonel"
DENIS DONOGHUE. *Connoisseurs of Chaos*, pp. 85-86.

"Commemorative of a Naval Victory"
CLEANTH BROOKS, JOHN THIBAUT PURSER, and ROBERT PENN WARREN. *An Approach to Literature*, third ed., pp. 344-45; fourth ed., pp. 342-43; fifth ed., pp. 410-11.
CLEANTH BROOKS and ROBERT PENN WARREN. *Understanding Poetry*, fourth ed., pp. 238-39.

"The Conflict of Convictions"
DENIS DONOGHUE. *Connoisseurs of Chaos*, pp. 88-89.
RALPH E. HITT. "Melville's Poems of Civil War Controversy," *Studies in the Literary Imagination* 2(1), April 1969, 59-60.
JOHN P. MCWILLIAMS, JR. "'Drum Taps' and *Battle-Pieces*: The Blossom of War," *American Quarterly* 23(2), May 1971, 183-84.
ROBERT PENN WARREN. "Melville the Poet," *Kenyon Review* 8(2), Spring 1946, 213-14.

MELVILLE, HERMAN *(Cont.)*

"The Cumberland"

LEO B. LEVY. "Hawthorne, Melville, and the *Monitor*," *American Literature* 37(1), March 1965, 39-40.

"Donelson"

JOYCE SPARER ADLER. "Melville and the Civil War," *New Letters* 40(2), December 1973, 105-6.

"The Fall of Richmond"

JOHN P. MCWILLIAMS, JR. " 'Drum Taps' and *Battle-Pieces*: The Blossom of War," *American Quarterly* 23(2), May 1971, 185.

"The Haglets"

RICHARD HARTER FOGLE. "The Themes of Melville's Later Poetry," *Tulane Studies in English* 11 (1961), 72-73.

"The House-Top"

JOHN P. MCWILLIAMS, JR. " 'Drum Taps' and *Battle-Pieces*: The Blossom of War," *American Quarterly* 23(2), May 1971, 186-87.

"In the Desert"

RICHARD HARTER FOGLE. "The Themes of Melville's Later Poetry," *Tulane Studies in English* 11 (1961), 80-81.

"In the Turret"

LEO B. LEVY. "Hawthorne, Melville, and the *Monitor*," *American Literature* 37(1), March 1965, 38-39.

"Inscription for Marye's Heights, Fredericksburg"

CLEANTH BROOKS and ROBERT PENN WARREN. *Understanding Poetry,* fourth ed., pp. 125-26.

"John Marr"

RICHARD HARTER FOGLE. "The Themes of Melville's Later Poetry," *Tulane Studies in English* 11 (1961), 68-70.

ROBERT PENN WARREN. "Melville's Poems," *Southern Review,* n.s., 3(4), Autumn 1967, 837.

"Lee in the Capitol"

DAVID J. HIBLER. "*Drum-Taps* and *Battle-Pieces*: Melville and Whitman on the Civil War," *Personalist* 50(1), Winter 1969, 144-45.

RALPH E. HITT. "Melville's Poems of Civil War Controversy," *Studies in the Literary Imagination* 2(1), April 1969, 67-68.

JOHN P. MCWILLIAMS, JR. " 'Drum Taps' and *Battle-Pieces*: The Blossom of War," *American Quarterly* 23(2), May 1971, 191.

"The Little Good Fellows"

WILLIAM BYSSHE STEIN. "Time, History, and Religion: A Glimpse of Melville's Late Poetry," *Arizona Quarterly* 22(2), Summer 1966, 142.

"The Loiterer"

WILLIAM BYSSHE STEIN. "Time, History, and Religion: A Glimpse of Melville's Late Poetry," *Arizona Quarterly* 22(2), Summer 1966, 139-41.

"Lone Founts"

DENIS DONOGHUE. *Connoisseurs of Chaos,* pp. 94-95.

"The Maldive Shark"

HERSHEL PARKER. "Trafficking in Melville," *Modern Language Quarterly* 33(1), March 1972, 63-65.

"Malvern Hill"

DENIS DONOGHUE. *Connoisseurs of Chaos,* pp. 90-91.

"The March into Virginia"

JOYCE SPARER ADLER. "Melville and the Civil War," *New Letters* 40(2), December 1973, 103-4.

"The March to the Sea"

JOYCE SPARER ADLER. "Melville and the Civil War," *New Letters* 40(2), December 1973, 109-10.

"The Martyr"

BERNARD DUFFEY. *Poetry in America,* pp. 94-95.

"Misgivings"

VAUGHAN HUDSON. "Melville's *Battle-Pieces* and Whitman's *Drum-Taps*: A Comparison," *Walt Whitman Review* 19(3), September 1973, 82-83.

"The Night-March"

LAURENCE PERRINE. "Four Forms of Metaphor," *College English* 33(2), November 1971, 135.

LAURENCE PERRINE. "The Nature of Proof in the Interpretation of Poetry," *English Journal* 51(6), September 1962, 396-97.

"Pontoosuce"

BERNARD DUFFEY. *Poetry in America,* pp. 90-92.

"The Portent"

JERRY A. HERNDON. "Parallels in Melville and Whitman," *Walt Whitman Review* 24(3), September 1978, 98-108.

"A Rail Road Cutting Near Alexandria in 1855"

THOMAS O. MABBOTT. *Explicator* 9(8), June 1951, Item 55.

"Stockings in the Farm-House Chimney"

WILLIAM BYSSHE STEIN. "Time, History, and Religion: A Glimpse of Melville's Late Poetry," *Arizona Quarterly* 22(2), Summer 1966, 144-45.

"The Swamp Angel"

JOYCE SPARER ADLER. "Melville and the Civil War," *New Letters* 40(2), December 1973, 107-8.

"Syra (A Transmitted Reminiscence)"

JANE DONAHUE. "Melville's Classicism: Law and Order in His Poetry," *Papers on Language and Literature* 5(1), Winter 1969, 70-71.

"The Temeraire"

LEO B. LEVY. "Hawthorne, Melville, and the *Monitor*," *American Literature* 37(1), March 1965, 40.

"Timoleon"

DARREL ABEL. " 'Laurel Twined With Thorn': The Theme of Melville's *Timoleon*," *The Personalist* 41(3), Summer 1960, 331-33.

RICHARD HARTER FOGLE. "The Themes of Melville's Later Poetry," *Tulane Studies in English* 11(1961), 75-76.

"Trophies of Peace"

WILLIAM BYSSHE STEIN. "Time, History, and Religion: A Glimpse of Melville's Late Poetry," *Arizona Quarterly* 22(2), Summer 1966, 143-44.

"A Utilitarian View of the *Monitor's* Fight"

LEO B. LEVY. "Hawthorne, Melville, and the *Monitor*," *American Literature* 37(1), March 1965, 35-38.

"When Forth the Shepherd Leads the Flock"

WILLIAM BYSSHE STEIN. "Time, History, and Religion: A Glimpse of Melville's Late Poetry," *Arizona Quarterly* 22(2), Summer 1966, 141-42.

MENNIS, JOHN

"A Poet's Farewell to his Threadbare Cloak"

DAVID FARLEY-HILLS. *The Benevolence of Laughter*, p. 42.

MEREDITH, GEORGE

"A Ballad of Fair Ladies in Revolt"

WENDELL STACY JOHNSON. *Sex and Marriage in Victorian Poetry*, pp. 48-50.

"Bellerophon"

J. M. S. TOMPKINS. "Meredith's *Periander*," *Review of English Studies*, n.s., 11(43), August 1960, 292-95.

"By this he knew she wept with waking eyes" (*Modern Love*, I)

P. M. PLUNKETT. *Explicator* 28(5), January 1970, Item 42.

"The Day of the Daughter of Hades"

PATRICIA MERIVALE. "The Pan Figure in Victorian Poetry: Landor to Meredith," *Philological Quarterly* 44(2), April 1965, 274-77.

"Dirge in Woods"

NORMAN C. STAGEBERG and WALLACE L. ANDERSON. *Poetry as Experience*, pp. 9-10.

"In the Woods"

NORMAN FRIEDMAN. "The Jangled Harp: Symbolic Structure in *Modern Love*," *Modern Language Quarterly* 18(1), March 1957, 16-17.

"The Lark Ascending"

HARRY BROWN and JOHN MILSTEAD. *What the Poem Means*, p. 146.

"Love in the Valley"

WENDELL STACY JOHNSON. *Sex and Marriage in Victorian Poetry*, pp. 45-46.

"Lucifer in Starlight"

WALTER BLAIR. *Manual of Reading*, pp. 145-47.

CLEANTH BROOKS and ROBERT PENN WARREN. *Understanding Poetry*, pp. 493-99; revised ed., pp. 367-73; third ed., pp. 344-48.

M. L. ROSENTHAL and A. J. M. SMITH. *Exploring Poetry*, second ed., p. 141.

"Meditation Under Stars"

R. W. WHIDDEN and J. P. KIRBY. *Explicator* 4(3), December 1945, Item 19.

"Modern Love"

PATRICIA M. BALL. *The Heart's Events*, pp. 108-22.

ARLINE GOLDEN. " 'The Game of Sentiment': Tradition and Innovation in Meredith's *Modern Love*," *ELH* 40(2), Summer 1973, 264-84.

MICHAEL LUND. "Space and Spiritual Crisis in Meredith's *Modern Love*," *Victorian Poetry* 16(4), Winter 1978, 376-82.

ARTHUR L. SIMPSON, JR. "Meredith's Pessimistic Humanism: A New Reading of *Modern Love*," *Modern Philology* 67(4), May 1970, 341-56.

PHILLIP E. WILSON. "Affective Coherence, a Principle of Abated Action, and Meredith's *Modern Love*," *Modern Philology* 72(2), November 1974, 151-71.

"The Old Chartist"

PHYLLIS BARTLETT. *Explicator* 18(9), June 1960, Item 56. (P)

"Pass we to another land"

GERALD H. PERKUS. "Toward Disengagement: A Neglected Early Meredith Manuscript Poem," *Victorian Poetry* 8(3), Fall 1970, 268-72.

"Periander"

J. M. S. TOMPKINS. "Meredith's *Periander*," *Review of English Studies*, n.s., 11(43), August 1960, 286-95.

"Phantasy"

CARL H. KETCHAM. "Meredith and the Wilis," *Victorian Poetry* 1(4), November 1963, 241-48.

"Seed-Time"

SIDNEY CALVIN. "On Concentration and Suggestion in Poetry," in *Perspectives of Poetry*, pp. 21-23.

"Shemselnihar"

DOROTHY M. MERMIN. "Poetry as Fiction: Meredith's *Modern Love*," *ELH* 43(1), Spring 1976, 102-3.

"This golden head has wit in it. I live" (*Modern Love*, XXXI)

CARL H. KETCHAM. *Explicator* 17(1), October 1958, Item 7.

"Thus piteously love closed what he begat" (*Modern Love*, L)

C. DAY LEWIS. *The Poetic Image*, pp. 83-85.

"'Tis Christmas weather and a country house" (*Modern Love*, XXIII)

DAVID KWINN. "Meredith's Psychological Insight in Modern Love XXIII," *Victorian Poetry* 7(2), Summer 1969, 151-53.

"The Woods of Westermain"

PATRICIA CRUNDEN. " 'The Woods of Westermain,' " *Victorian Poetry* 5(4), Winter 1967, 265-82.

"Youth in Memory"

NORMAN FRIEDMAN. "The Jangled Harp: Symbolic Structure in *Modern Love*," *Modern Language Quarterly* 18(1), March 1957, 24-25.

MEREDITH, WILLIAM

"Battlewagon"

DUDLEY FITTS. "Meredith's Second Volume," *Poetry* 73(2), November 1948, 114, 116.

"The Illiterate"

MARY FRANCES CLAGGETT. " 'Afraid and Letter-proud,' " *English Journal* 53(9), December 1964, 700-1.

"The Islands of My Desire"

JOSEPH WARREN BEACH. *Obsessive Images*, p. 141.

"The Wreck of the Thresher"

ROBERT H. GLAUBER. "The Poet's Intention," *Prairie Schooner* 39(3), Fall 1965, 278-79.

MERRILL, JAMES

"After the Fire"

DAVID KALSTONE. *Five Temperaments*, pp. 111-12.

"The Broken Home"

DAVID KALSTONE. *Five Temperaments*, pp. 80-81, 99-103.

"Childlessness"

DAVID KALSTONE. *Five Temperaments*, pp. 90-93.

MERRILL, JAMES *(Cont.)*

"Days of 1935"

> DAVID KALSTONE. *Five Temperaments*, pp. 77-79.

> JUDITH MOFFETT. "Masked More and Less Than Ever: James Merrill's Braving the Elements," *Hollins Critic* 10(3), June 1973, 10.

"Days of 1971"

> DAVID KALSTONE. *Five Temperaments*, p. 99.

"18 West 11th Street"

> DAVID KALSTONE. *Five Temperaments*, pp. 112-13.

"The Friend of the Fourth Decade"

> DAVID KALSTONE. *Five Temperaments*, pp. 105-6.

"From the Cupola"

> ANDREW V. ETTIN. "On James Merrill's 'Nights and Days,'" *Perspective* 15(1), Spring 1967, 39-40, 43-44.

"The House"

> DAVID KALSTONE. *Five Temperaments*, pp. 88-89.

"Lost in Translation"

> DANIEL L. GUILLORY. "The Mystique of Childhood in American Literature," *Tulane Studies in English* 23 (1978), 243-46.

> DAVID KALSTONE. *Five Temperaments*, pp. 125-27.

"Maisie"

> ANDREW V. ETTIN. "On James Merrill's 'Nights and Days,'" *Perspective* 15(1), Spring 1967, 35-36.

"Mornings in a New House"

> DAVID KALSTONE. *Five Temperaments*, pp. 108-10.

"Nightgown"

> DAVID KALSTONE. *Five Temperaments*, pp. 97-98.

"Scenes of Childhood"

> DAVID KALSTONE. *Five Temperaments*, pp. 85-86.

"Syrinx"

> DAVID KALSTONE. *Five Temperaments*, pp. 116-18.

"The Thousand and Second Night"

> ANDREW V. ETTIN. "On James Merrill's 'Nights and Days,'" *Perspective* 15(1), Spring-Summer 1967, 33-51.

> DAVID KALSTONE. *Five Temperaments*, pp. 103-5.

"Time"

> DAVID KALSTONE. *Five Temperaments*, pp. 93-96.

"To My Greek"

> DAVID KALSTONE. *Five Temperaments*, pp. 106-7.

"Up and Down"

> DAVID KALSTONE. *Five Temperaments*, pp. 81, 113-14.

"An Urban Convalescence"

> DAVID KALSTONE. *Five Temperaments*, pp. 87-88.

"Yánnina"

> DAVID KALSTONE. "The Poet: Private," *Saturday Review of the Arts* 55(49), December 1972, 42-45.

MERTON, THOMAS

"Cargo Songs" *(The Geography of Lograire)*

> JAMES YORK GLIMM. "Thomas Merton's Last Poem: *The Geography of Lograire*," *Renascence* 26(2), Winter 1974, 100-3.

"EAST: Love of the Sultan"

> VIRGINIA F. RANDALL. "Contrapuntal Irony and Theme in Thomas Merton's *The Geography of Lograire*," *Renascence* 28(4), Summer 1976, 198-99.

"EAST II, EAST WITH MALINOWSKI"

> VIRGINIA F. RANDALL. "Contrapuntal Irony and Theme in Thomas Merton's *The Geography of Lograire*," *Renascence* 28(4), Summer 1976, 199.

"Ghost Dance: Prologue"

> WALTER SUTTON. "Thomas Merton and the American Epic Tradition: The Last Poems," *Contemporary Literature* 14(1), Winter 1973, 55-56.

"Kane Relief Expedition" *(The Geography of Lograire)*

> JAMES YORK GLIMM. "Thomas Merton's Last Poem: *The Geography of Lograire*," *Renascence* 26(2), Winter 1974, 99.

"NORTH III, THE RANTERS AND THEIR PLEADS (London)"

> VIRGINIA F. RANDALL. "Contrapuntal Irony and Theme in Thomas Merton's *The Geography of Lograire*," *Renascence* 28(4), Summer 1976, 197.

"NORTH IV, KANE RELIEF EXPEDITION"

> VIRGINIA F. RANDALL. "Contrapuntal Irony and Theme in Thomas Merton's *The Geography of Lograire*," *Renascence* 28(4), Summer 1976, 197-98.

"NORTH, PROLOGUE, WHY I HAVE A WET FOOT-PRINT ON TOP OF MY MIND"

> VIRGINIA F. RANDALL. "Contrapuntal Irony and Theme in Thomas Merton's *The Geography of Lograire*," *Renascence* 28(4), Summer 1976, 196-97.

"SOUTH V, TWO MORALITIES"

> VIRGINIA F. RANDALL. "Contrapuntal Irony and Theme in Thomas Merton's *The Geography of Lograire*," *Renascence* 28(4), Summer 1976, 192-93.

"SOUTH VII, NOTES FOR A NEW LITURGY"

> VIRGINIA F. RANDALL. "Contrapuntal Irony and Theme in Thomas Merton's *The Geography of Lograire*," *Renascence* 28(4), Summer 1976, 193-94.

"SOUTH IX, THE LADIES OF TLATILCO"

> VIRGINIA F. RANDALL. "Contrapuntal Irony and Theme in Thomas Merton's *The Geography of Lograire*," *Renascence* 28(4), Summer 1976, 194-95.

"SOUTH X, CHILAM BALAM"

> VIRGINIA F. RANDALL. "Contrapuntal Irony and Theme in Thomas Merton's *The Geography of Lograire*," *Renascence* 28(4), Summer 1976, 195-96.

"SOUTH XI, DZULES"

> VIRGINIA F. RANDALL. "Contrapuntal Irony and Theme in Thomas Merton's *The Geography of Lograire*," *Renascence* 28(4), Summer 1976, 195-96.

"WEST I, DAY SIX O'HARE TELEPHANE"

> VIRGINIA F. RANDALL. "Contrapuntal Irony and Theme in Thomas Merton's *The Geography of Lograire*," *Renascence* 28(4), Summer 1976, 200-1.

"WEST III, GHOST DANCE: PROLOGUE"

> VIRGINIA F. RANDALL. "Contrapuntal Irony and Theme in Thomas Merton's *The Geography of Lograire*," *Renascence* 28(4), Summer 1976, 201.

"WEST IV, GHOST DANCE"

> VIRGINIA F. RANDALL. "Contrapuntal Irony and Theme in Thomas Merton's *The Geography of Lograire*," *Renascence* 28(4), Summer 1976, 201-2.

MERWIN, W. S.

"Air"

> JOHN VOGELSANG. "Toward the Great Language: W. S. Merwin," *Modern Poetry Studies* 3(3), 1972, 110.

"Anabasis"
GLAUCO CAMBON. *Recent American Poetry,* pp. 17-19.

"The Annunciation"
JOHN VOGELSANG. "Toward the Great Language: W. S. Merwin," *Modern Poetry Studies* 3(3), 1972, 102-5.

"Ash"
LAURENCE LIEBERMAN. "The Church of Ash," in *Contemporary Poetry in America,* pp. 256-57.

"The Asians Dying"
CARY NELSON. "Whitman in Vietnam: Poetry and History in Contemporary America," *Massachusetts Review* 16(1), Winter 1975, 61-63.

"Beginning"
CAROL KYLE. "A Riddle for the New Year: Affirmation in W. S. Merwin," *Modern Poetry Studies* 4(3), Winter 1973, 302-3.
CARY NELSON. "The Resources of Failure: W. S. Merwin's Deconstructive Career," *Boundary 2* 5(2), Winter 1977, 589-93.

"Blue Cockerel"
ALICE N. BENSTON. "Myth in the Poetry of W. S. Merwin," in *Poets in Progress,* pp. 190-91.

"The Bones"
KENNETH ANDERSEN. "The Poetry of W. S. Merwin," *Twentieth Century Literature* 16(4), October 1970, 282.

"Canso"
ALICE N. BENSTON. "Myth in the Poetry of W. S. Merwin," in *Poets in Progress,* pp. 183-84.

"The Child"
CAROL KYLE. "A Riddle for the New Year: Affirmation in W. S. Merwin," *Modern Poetry Studies* 4(3), Winter 1973, 297.

"The Counting Houses"
CHERI COLBY DAVIS. "Time and Timelessness in the Poetry of W. S. Merwin," *Modern Poetry Studies* 6(3), Winter 1975, 225-26.

"December Among the Vanished"
CARY NELSON. "The Resources of Failure: W. S. Merwin's Deconstructive Career," *Boundary 2* 5(2), Winter 1977, 585-86.

"Dictum: For a Mask of Deluge"
GLAUCO CAMBON. *Recent American Poetry,* pp. 19-20.

"Division"
EVAN WATKINS. "W. S. Merwin: A Critical Accompaniment," *Boundary 2* 4(1), Fall 1975, 195-97.

"The Drunk in the Furnace"
ALICE N. BENSTON. "Myth in the Poetry of W. S. Merwin," in *Poets in Progress,* pp. 194-96.
CARY NELSON. "The Resources of Failure: W. S. Merwin's Deconstructive Career," *Boundary 2* 5(2), Winter 1977, 580.

"East of the Sun and West of the Moon"
ALICE N. BENSTON. "Myth in the Poetry of W. S. Merwin," in *Poets in Progress,* pp. 184-86.

"Folk Art"
CARY NELSON. "The Resources of Failure: W. S. Merwin's Deconstructive Career," *Boundary 2* 5(2), Winter 1977, 594-95.

"For a Coming Extinction"
JAN B. GORDON. "The Dwelling of Disappearance: W. S. Merwin's *The Lice,*" *Modern Poetry Studies* 3(3), 1972, 127-28.
JOHN VOGELSANG. "Toward the Great Language: W. S. Merwin," *Modern Poetry Studies* 3(3), 1972, 111.

"For Now"
JOHN VOGELSANG. "Toward the Great Language: W. S. Merwin," *Modern Poetry Studies* 3(3), 1972, 107-10.

"For the Anniversary of My Death"
JAROLD RAMSEY. "The Continuities of W. S. Merwin: 'What Has Escaped Us We Bring With Us,'" *Massachusetts Review* 14(3), Summer 1973, 588-89.

"Gift"
CARY NELSON. "The Resources of Failure: W. S. Merwin's Deconstructive Career," *Boundary 2* 5(2), Winter 1977, 595-96.

"The Gods"
LILLIAN FEDER. *Ancient Myth in Modern Poetry,* p. 415.
JAROLD RAMSEY. "The Continuities of W. S. Merwin: 'What Has Escaped Us We Bring With Us,'" *Massachusetts Review* 14(3), Summer 1973, 580.

"In a Clearing"
JOHN VOGELSANG. "Toward the Great Language: W. S. Merwin," *Modern Poetry Studies* 3(3), 1972, 111-12.

"In the Time of the Blossoms"
JOHN VOGELSANG. "Toward the Great Language: W. S. Merwin," *Modern Poetry Studies* 3(3), 1972, 113-14.

"Is That What You Are"
LAURENCE LIEBERMAN. *Unassigned Frequencies,* pp. 258-59.

"It Is March"
CAROL KYLE. "A Riddle for the New Year: Affirmation in W. S. Merwin," *Modern Poetry Studies* 4(3), Winter 1973, 298-99.

"The Judgement of Paris"
LILLIAN FEDER. *Ancient Myth in Modern Poetry,* pp. 415-16.

"Last People"
CHERI COLBY DAVIS. "Time and Timelessness in the Poetry of W. S. Merwin," *Modern Poetry Studies* 6(3), Winter 1975, 227-29.

"Learning a Dead Language"
JOHN VOGELSANG. "Toward the Great Language: W. S. Merwin," *Modern Poetry Studies* 3(3), 1972, 105-7.

"Lemuel's Blessing"
PAUL CARROLL. *The Poem In Its Skin,* pp. 142-52.

"Looking for Mushrooms at Sunrise"
CARY NELSON. "The Resources of Failure: W. S. Merwin's Deconstructive Career," *Boundary 2* 5(2), Winter 1977, 583-84.

"Memory"
CHERI COLBY DAVIS. "Merwin's Odysseus," *Concerning Poetry* 8(1), Spring 1975, 27-33.

"Memory of Spring"
JOHN VOGELSANG. "Toward the Great Language: W. S. Merwin," *Modern Poetry Studies* 3(3), 1972, 114.
EVAN WATKINS. "W. S. Merwin: A Critical Accompaniment," *Boundary 2* 4(1), Fall 1975, 190-91.

MERWIN, W. S. *(Cont.)*

"The Mountain"

ALICE N. BENSTON. "Myth in the Poetry of W. S. Merwin," in *Poets in Progress,* pp. 197-98.

ROBERT LANGBAUM. "The New Nature Poetry," in *The Modern Spirit,* pp. 121-24.

"My Brothers the Silent"

JAROLD RAMSEY. "The Continuities of W. S. Merwin: 'What Has Escaped Us We Bring With Us,'" *Massachusetts Review* 14(3), Summer 1973, 581-82.

"The Night of the Shirts"

PAUL BRESLIN. "How to Read the New Contemporary Poem," *American Scholar* 47(3), Summer 1978, 358-60.

"Odysseus"

CHERI COLBY DAVIS. "Merwin's Odysseus," *Concerning Poetry* 8(1), Spring 1975, 25-27.

LILLIAN FEDER. *Ancient Myth in Modern Poetry,* pp. 413-14.

"On the Subject of Poetry"

ALICE N. BENSTON. "Myth in the Poetry of W. S. Merwin," in *Poets in Progress,* p. 182.

"Pieces for Other Lives"

CAROL KYLE. "A Riddle for the New Year: Affirmation in W. S. Merwin," *Modern Poetry Studies* 4(3), Winter 1973, 297-98.

"The Port"

CHERI COLBY DAVIS. "Time and Timelessness in the Poetry of W. S. Merwin," *Modern Poetry Studies* 6(3), Winter 1975, 229-31.

"The Prodigal Son"

CARY NELSON. "The Resources of Failure: W. S. Merwin's Deconstructive Career," *Boundary 2* 5(2), Winter 1977, 578-79.

JOHN VOGELSANG. "Toward the Great Language: W. S. Merwin," *Modern Poetry Studies* 3(3), 1972, 99-102.

"Psalm: Our Fathers"

JOHN VOGELSANG. "Toward the Great Language: W. S. Merwin," *Modern Poetry Studies* 3(3), 1972, 116-18.

"The River of Bees"

JAROLD RAMSEY. "The Continuities of W. S. Merwin: 'What Has Escaped Us We Bring With Us,'" *Massachusetts Review* 14(3), Summer 1973, 586-87.

"A Scale in May"

RALPH J. MILLS, JR. *Creation's Very Self,* pp. 17-18. Reprinted in: Ralph J. Mills, Jr. *Cry of the Human,* pp. 18-19.

JOHN VOGELSANG. "Toward the Great Language: W. S. Merwin," *Modern Poetry Studies* 3(3), 1972, 110-11.

"The Ships Are Made Ready in Silence"

CAROL KYLE. "A Riddle for the New Year: Affirmation in W. S. Merwin," *Modern Poetry Studies* 4(3), Winter 1973, 290-91.

"Signs"

JOHN VOGELSANG. "Toward the Great Language: W. S. Merwin," *Modern Poetry Studies* 3(3), 1972, 115.

"Surf-Casting"

LAURENCE LIEBERMAN. "The Church of Ash," in *Contemporary Poetry in America,* pp. 260-62. Reprinted in: Laurence Lieberman. *Unassigned Frequencies* pp. 126-27.

EVAN WATKINS. "W. S. Merwin: A Critical Accompaniment," *Boundary 2* 4(1), Fall 1975, 191-92.

"Teachers"

CAROL KYLE. "A Riddle for the New Year: Affirmation in W. S. Merwin," *Modern Poetry Studies* 4(3), Winter 1973, 300-1.

"To the Rain"

EVAN WATKINS. "W. S. Merwin: A Critical Accompaniment," *Boundary 2* 4(1), Fall 1975, 197-98.

"Under Black Leaves"

CHERI COLBY DAVIS. "Time and Timelessness in the Poetry of W. S. Merwin," *Modern Poetry Studies* 6(3), Winter 1975, 232-35.

"Unfinished Book of Kings"

CAROL KYLE. "A Riddle for the New Year: Affirmation in W. S. Merwin," *Modern Poetry Studies* 4(3), Winter 1973, 292-94.

"The Way Ahead"

LAURENCE LIEBERMAN. "The Church of Ash," in *Contemporary Poetry in America,* pp. 262-63. Reprinted in: Laurence Lieberman. *Unassigned Frequencies,* pp. 127-29.

"The Way to the River"

HAROLD BLOOM. *Figures of Capable Imagination,* pp. 124-25.

HAROLD BLOOM. "The New Transcendentalism: The Visionary Strain in Merwin, Ashbery, and Ammons," *Chicago Review* 24(3), 1972, 26.

"When You Go Away"

JAN B. GORDON. "The Dwelling of Disappearance: W. S. Merwin's *The Lice,*" *Modern Poetry Studies* 3(3), 1972, 129-30.

"Whenever I Go There"

ROBERT PINSKY. *The Situation of Poetry,* pp. 92-95.

"White Goat, White Ram"

ALICE N. BENSTON. "Myth in the Poetry of W. S. Merwin," in *Poets in Progress,* pp. 198-201.

CARY NELSON. "The Resources of Failure: W. S. Merwin's Deconstructive Career," *Boundary 2* 5(2), Winter 1977, 577.

"You, Genoese Mariner"

CAROL KYLE. "A Riddle for the New Year: Affirmation in W. S. Merwin," *Modern Poetry Studies* 4(3), Winter 1973, 290.

MIDDLETON, CHRISTOPHER

"afloat in the window pane stuck"

BRIAN SWANN. "English Opposites: Charles Tomlinson & Christopher Middleton," *Modern Poetry Studies* 5(3), Winter 1974, 231-32.

"An Alien Town"

WALLACE D. MARTIN. "Beyond Modernism: Christopher Middleton and Geoffrey Hill," *Contemporary Literature* 12(4), Autumn 1971, 423-24.

"A Cart of Apples"

JAY PARINI. "Tradition and Experiment: Charles Causley and Christopher Middleton," *Chicago Review* 29(1), Summer 1977, 140.

"Climbing a Pebble"

BRIAN SWANN. "English Opposites: Charles Tomlinson & Christopher Middleton," *Modern Poetry Studies* 5(3), Winter 1974, 229-31.

"A Drive in the Country/Henri Toulouse-Lautrec"

JAY PARINI. "Tradition and Experiment: Charles Causley and Christopher Middleton," *Chicago Review* 29(1), Summer 1977, 140-41.

"The Gloves"

JAY PARINI. "Tradition and Experiment: Charles Causley and Christopher Middleton," *Chicago Review* 29(1), Summer 1977, 141-42.

"Male Torso"

WALLACE D. MARTIN. "Beyond Modernism: Christopher Middleton and Geoffrey Hill," *Contemporary Literature* 12(4), Autumn 1971, 422.

"Old Woman at the County Dump"

JAY PARINI. "Tradition and Experiment: Charles Causley and Christopher Middleton," *Chicago Review* 29(1), Summer 1977, 143.

"The Pogroms in Sebastopol"

JAY PARINI. "Tradition and Experiment: Charles Causley and Christopher Middleton," *Chicago Review* 29(1), Summer 1977, 143.

"Pointed Boots"

BRIAN SWANN. "English Opposites: Charles Tomlinson & Christopher Middleton," *Modern Poetry Studies* 5(3), Winter 1974, 234.

"Tanker"

M. M. CARLIN. "Torse 3," *Essays in Criticism* 13(1), January 1963, 114-17.

MILLAY, EDNA ST. VINCENT

"The Betrothal"

ELIZABETH P. PERLMUTTER. "A Doll's Heart: The Girl in the Poetry of Edna St. Vincent Millay and Louise Bogan," *Twentieth Century Literature* 23(2), May 1977, 169-70.

"Euclid Alone Has Looked on Beauty Bare"

BRADFORD A. BOOTH. *Explicator* 6(1), October 1947, Item 5.

CHARLES W. COOPER and JOHN HOLMES. *Preface to Poetry*, pp. 46-52.

ARTHUR DICKSON. *Explicator* 3(3), December 1944, Item 23.

ELIZABETH DREW and JOHN L. SWEENEY. *Directions in Modern Poetry*, pp. 207-8. Reprinted in: *The Critical Reader*, pp. 110-11.

"The Fitting"

JOHN CIARDI. *Dialogue with an Audience*, p. 73. (Quoting Norma Millay)

"I Shall Go Back"

CLEANTH BROOKS and ROBERT PENN WARREN. *Understanding Poetry*, fourth ed., pp. 327-28.

"Justice Denied in Massachusetts"

HARRY BROWN and JOHN MILSTEAD. *What the Poem Means*, p. 147.

"Love is not all"

ROBERT M. BENDER. "Millay: Five Sonnets," in *Master Poems of the English Language*, pp. 994-95.

"Memorial to D. C.: Elegy"

WALTER GIERASCH. *Explicator* 2(7), May 1944, Item 54. (P)

"Oh, oh, you will be sorry for that word"

LAURENCE PERRINE. *100 American Poems of the Twentieth Century*, pp. 165-66.

"Oh, Sleep Forever in the Latmian Cave"

JOHN CROWE RANSOM. "The Poet as Woman," *Southern Review* 2(4), Spring 1937, 788-90.

JOHN CROWE RANSOM. *The World's Body*, pp. 83-86.

"Oh, think not I am faithful to a vow!"

ROBERT M. BENDER. "Millay: Five Sonnets," in *Master Poems of the English Language*, pp. 993-94.

"On Hearing a Symphony of Beethoven"

HARRY BROWN and JOHN MILSTEAD. *What the Poem Means*, p. 148.

LAURENCE PERRINE. *100 American Poems of the Twentieth Century*, pp. 167-68.

"Passer Mortuus Est"

ELIZABETH P. PERLMUTTER. "A Doll's Heart: The Girl in the Poetry of Edna St. Vincent Millay and Louise Bogan," *Twentieth Century Literature* 23(2), May 1977, 162.

"Pity Me Not"

ABRAHAM PONEMON. "For Tomorrow, Write an Analysis," *English Journal* 54(7), October 1975, 646-47.

"Renascence"

HARRY BROWN and JOHN MILSTEAD. *What the Poem Means*, pp. 148-49.

"The Return"

JOHN CROWE RANSOM. "The Poet as Woman," *Southern Review* 2(4), Spring 1937, 804-6.

JOHN CROWE RANSOM. *The World's Body*, pp. 107-10.

"The Shroud"

ELIZABETH P. PERLMUTTER. "A Doll's Heart: The Girl in the Poetry of Edna St. Vincent Millay and Louise Bogan," *Twentieth Century Literature* 23(2), May 1977, 160-61.

"Sonnets from an Ungrafted Tree"

WALTER S. MINOT. "Millay's 'Ungrafted Tree': The Problem of the Artist as Woman," *New England Quarterly* 48(2), June 1975, 260-69.

"What lips my lips have kissed"

ROBERT M. BENDER. "Millay: Five Sonnets," in *Master Poems of the English Language*, p. 994.

HARRY BROWN and JOHN MILSTEAD. *What the Poem Means*, p. 149.

LAURENCE PERRINE. *100 American Poems of the Twentieth Century*, pp. 164-65.

"What's This of Death, from You Who Never Will Die?"

WILLIAM ELTON. *Explicator* 7(5), March 1949, Item 37.

RICHARD W. LIND. "Must the Critic be Correct?" *Journal of Aesthetics and Art Criticism* 35(4), Summer 1977, 451-55.

I. A. RICHARDS. *Practical Criticism*, pp. 63-79.

MILLER, VASSAR

"Or as Gertrude Stein Says . . ."

NORMAN FRIEDMAN. "The Wesleyan Poets — IV," *Chicago Review* 19(3), June 1967, 78.

MILTON, JOHN

"L'Allegro"

LAWRENCE BABB. "The Background of 'Il Penseroso,'" *Studies in Philology* 37(2), April 1940, 257-73.

STEPHEN C. BEHRANDT. "Bright Pilgrimmage: William Blake's Designs for *L'Allegro* and *Il Penseroso*," *Milton Studies* 8 (1975), 123-47.

MILTON, JOHN *(Cont.)*

"L'Allegro" *(cont.)*

LESLIE BRISMAN. "'All Before Them Where to Choose': 'L'Allegro' and 'Il Penseroso,'" *Journal of English and Germanic Philology* 71(2), April 1972, 226-40.

CLEANTH BROOKS. *The Well Wrought Urn*, pp. 50-66; revised ed., pp. 40-53.

NAN COOKE CARPENTER. "The Place of Music in *L'Allegro* and *Il Penseroso*," *University of Toronto Quarterly* 22(4), July 1953, 354-67.

NORMAN B. COUNCIL. "*L'Allegro, Il Penseroso* and 'The Cycle of Universal Knowledge,'" *Milton Studies* 9 (1976), 203-19.

DAVID DAICHES and WILLIAM CHARVAT. *Poems in English*, pp. 669-70.

THOMAS J. EMBRY. "Sensuality and Chastity in *L'Allegro* and *Il Penseroso*," *Journal of English and Germanic Philology* 77(4), October 1978, 504-29.

VICTOR ERLICH. "Milton's Early Poetry: Its Christian Humanism," *American Imago* 32(1), Spring 1975, 92-99.

STANLEY E. FISH. "What It's Like To Read *L'Allegro* and *Il Penseroso*," *Milton Studies* 7 (1975), 77-99.

MICHAEL FIXLER. "The Orphic Technique of 'L'Allegro' and 'Il Penseroso,'" *English Literary Renaissance* 1(2), Spring 1971, 165-77.

LOWELL EDWIN FOLSOM. "'L'Allegro' and 'Il Penseroso': The Poetics of Accelerando and Ritardando," *Studies in the Humanities* 5(1), January 1976, 39-41.

DONALD FRIEDMAN. "Harmony and the Poet's Voice in Some of Milton's Early Poems," *Modern Language Quarterly* 30(4), December 1969, 531-32.

MARJORIE B. GARBER. "Fallen Landscape: The Art of Milton and Poussin," *English Literary Renaissance* 5(1), Winter 1975, 114-15.

GEORGE L. GECKLE. "Miltonic Idealism: *L'Allegro* and *Il Penseroso*," *Texas Studies in Literature and Language* 9(4), Winter 1968, 455-73.

J. P. HARDY. *Reinterpretations*, pp. 1-27.

GEOFFREY H. HARTMAN. "False Themes and Gentle Minds," *Philological Quarterly* 47(1), January 1968, 56-61. Reprinted in: Geoffrey H. Hartman. *Beyond Formalism*, pp. 285-90.

JOHN F. HUNTLEY. "The Poet-Critic and His Poem-Culture in 'L'Allegro' and 'Il Penseroso,'" *Texas Studies in Literature and Language* 13(4), Winter 1972, 541-53.

G. WILSON KNIGHT. *The Burning Oracle*, pp. 59-63. Reprinted in: *Poets of Action*, pp. 18-23.

THOMAS LAVOIE. "The Divine Vision of the Inward Eye: The Structural Hierarchy of the 'L'Allegro-Il Penseroso' Sequence," *Thoth* 16(3), Fall 1976, 3-17.

C. N. MANLOVE. *Literature and Reality*, pp. 31-36.

DAVID M. MILLER. "From Delusion to Illumination: A Larger Structure for *L'Allegro-Il Penseroso*," *PMLA* 86(1), January 1971, 32-39.

GARY STRINGER. "The Unity of 'L'Allegro' and 'Il Penseroso,'" *Texas Studies in Literature and Language* 12(2), Summer 1970, 221-29.

KESTER SVENDSON. *Explicator* 8(7), May 1950, Item 49.

KATHLEEN M. SWAIN. "Time and Structure in *L'Allegro* and *Il Penseroso*," *Texas Studies in Literature and Language* 18(3), Fall 1976, 422-32.

ELEANOR TATE. "Milton's 'L'Allegro' and 'Il Penseroso' — Balance, Progression, or Dichotomy?" *Modern Language Notes* 76(7), November 1961, 585-90.

HAROLD E. TOLIVER. *Pastoral Forms and Attitudes*, pp. 154-57.

RICHARD WILBUR. "Milton: L'Allegro and Il Penseroso," in *Master Poems of the English Language*, pp. 191-95.

MARILYN L. WILLIAMSON. "The Myth of Orpheus in 'L'Allegro' and 'Il Penseroso,'" *Modern Language Quarterly* 32(4), December 1971, 377-86.

"Arcades"

JOHN G. DEMARAY. "'Arcades' as a Literary Entertainment," *Papers on Language and Literature* 8(1), Winter 1972, 15-26.

GEOFFREY H. HARTMAN. *Beyond Formalism*, pp. 378-82.

MARY ANN McGUIRE. "Milton's *Arcades* and the Entertainment Tradition," *Studies in Philology* 75(4), October 1978, 451-71.

HAROLD E. TOLIVER. *Pastoral Forms and Attitudes*, pp. 152-54.

"At a Solemn Music"

SHARON CUMBERLAND and LYNN VEACH SADLER. "Phantasia: A Pattern in Milton's Early Poems," *Milton Quarterly* 8(2), May 1974, 50-52.

DONALD FRIEDMAN. "Harmony and the Poet's Voice in Some of Milton's Early Poems," *Modern Language Quarterly* 30(4), December 1969, 532-34.

MOTHER M. CHRISTOPHER PECHEUX. "'At a Solemn Musick': Structure and Meaning," *Studies in Philology* 75(3), July 1978, 331-46.

JOSEPH SUMMERS. "Milton and Celebration," *Milton Quarterly* 5(1), March 1971, 4-5.

"At a Vacation Exercise in the College"

GORDON CAMPBELL. "The Satire on Aristotelian Logic in Milton's 'Vacation Exercise,'" *English Language Notes* 15(2), December 1977, 106-10. (P)

DONALD FRIEDMAN. "Harmony and the Poet's Voice in Some of Milton's Early Poems," *Modern Language Quarterly* 30(4), December 1969, 527-28.

"Avenge O Lord thy slaughtered saints"
see "On the Late Massacre in Piemont"

"Comus" ("A Mask")

FRANKLIN R. BARUCH. "Milton's *Comus*: Skill, Virtue, and Henry Lawes," *Milton Studies* 5(1973), 289-308.

JACQUES BLONDEL. "The Function of Mythology in *Comus*," *Durham University Journal*, n.s., 27(2), March 1966, 63-66.

PURVIS E. BOYETTE. "Milton's Abstracted Sublimities: The Structure of Meaning in *A Mask*," *Tulane Studies in English* 18(1970), 35-58.

BARBARA BREASTED. "*Comus* and the Castlehaven Scandal," *Milton Studies* 3(1971), 201-24.

R. L. BRETT. *Reason and Imagination*, pp. 24-26, 30-31.

JOHN BROADBENT and LORNA SAGE. "*Paradise Lost, Comus*, and *Samson Agonistes*," in *English Poetry*, edited by Alan Sinfield, pp. 83-88.

DOUGLAS BUSH. *Pagan Myth and Christian Tradition in English Poetry*, pp. 13-15.

THOMAS O. CALHOUN. "On John Milton's *A Mask at Ludlow*," *Milton Studies* 6(1974), 165-79.

GALE H. CARRITHERS, JR. "Milton's Ludlow *Mask*: From Chaos to Community," *ELH* 33(1), March 1966, 23-42.

HALE CHATFIELD. "An Additional Look at the 'Meaning' of *Comus*," *Milton Quarterly* 11(3), October 1977, 86-89.

GEORGIA B. CHRISTOPHER. "The Virginity of Faith: *Comus* as a Reformation Conceit," *ELH* 43(4), Winter 1976, 479-99.

DIANA LEE MILLS CIRTIN. "Tipsy Dance vs. Grand Dance: The Use of Dance in Milton's *Comus*," *Ball State University Forum* 17(2), Spring 1976, 23-30.

JOHN D. COX. "Poetry and History in Milton's Country Masque," *ELH* 44(4), Winter 1977, 622-40.

SHARON CUMBERLAND and LYNN VEACH SADLER. "Phantasia: A Pattern in Milton's Early Poems," *Milton Quarterly* 8(2), May 1974, 53-55.

A. E. DYSON. *Between Two Worlds,* pp. 15-40.

VICTOR ERLICH. "Milton's Early Poetry: Its Christian Humanism," *American Imago* 32(1), Spring 1975, 99-106.

STANLEY E. FISH. "Problem Solving in *Comus*," in *Illustrious Evidence,* pp. 115-31.

JONATHAN GOLDBERG. "Hesper-Vesper: Aspects of Venus in a Seventeenth-Century Trope," *Studies in English Literature 1500-1900* 15(1), Winter 1975, 37-43.

MARY ANNE HUTCHINSON. "*Comus* and Milton's Maturing Conception of Chastity," *Thoth* 14(2-3), Spring/Fall 1974, 39-52.

RICHARD KELL. "Thesis and Action in Milton's *Comus*," *Essays in Criticism* 24(1), January 1974, 48-54.

G. WILSON KNIGHT. "Milton: the Poetry," in *Poets of Action,* pp. 23-28.

TERRY KIDNER KOHN. "Landscape in the Transcendent Masque," *Milton Studies* 6 (1974), 143-64.

MARCIA LANDY. "'A Free and Open Encounter': Milton and the Modern Reader," *Milton Studies* 9 (1976), 26-28.

LAURENCE LERNER. "Farewell, Rewards and Fairies: An Essay on *Comus*," *Journal of English and Germanic Philology* 70(4), October 1971, 617-31.

LAURENCE LERNER. *The Uses of Nostalgia,* pp. 163-80.

MAYNARD MACK. *English Masterpieces,* edited by William Frost, Maynard Mack, and Leonard Dean, vol. 4: *Milton,* pp. 7-9.

C. N. MANLOVE. *Literature and Reality,* pp. 36-42.

JEANNE S. MARTIN. "Transformations in Genre in Milton's *Comus*," *Genre* 10(2), Summer 1977, 195-213.

LOUIS L. MARTZ. "The Music of Comus," in *Illustrious Evidence,* pp. 93-113.

ROSEMARY KARMELICH MUNDHENK. "Dark Scandal and The Sun-Clad Power of Chastity: The Historical Milieu of Milton's *Comus*," *Studies in English Literature 1500-1900* 15(1), Winter 1975, 141-52.

RICHARD NEUSE. "Metamorphosis and Symbolic Action in *Comus*," *ELH* 34(1), March 1967, 49-64.

PHILIP DARRAUGH ORTEGO. "Comus, Circe, and the Whole Bit," *University Review* 36(4), Summer 1970, 287-91.

ANNABEL PATTERSON. "L'Allegro, Il Penseroso and Comus: The Logic of Recombination," *Milton Quarterly* 9(3), October 1975, 75-79.

B. RAJAN. "*Comus*: The Inglorious Likeness," *University of Toronto Quarterly* 37(2), January 1968, 113-35.

B. RAJAN. "The Cunning Resemblance," *Milton Studies* 7 (1975), 33-36.

CHRISTOPHER RICKS. "Milton," in *English Poetry and Prose,* edited by Christopher Ricks, pp. 271-78.

PHILIP B. ROLLINSON. "The Central Debate in *Comus*," *Philological Quarterly* 49(4), October 1970, 481-88.

MALCOLM MACKENZIE ROSS. "Milton and the Protestant Aesthetic: The Early Poems," *University of Toronto Quarterly* 17(4), July 1948, 354-58.

J. B. SAVAGE. "*Comus* and Its Traditions," *English Literary Renaissance* 5(1), Winter 1975, 58-80.

RAYMOND G. SCHOEN. "The Hierarchy of the Senses in *A Mask*," *Milton Quarterly* 7(2), May 1973, 32-37.

ALICE-LYLE SCOUFOS. "The Mysteries in Milton's *Masque*," *Milton Studies* 6 (1974), 113-42.

HAROLD E. TOLIVER. *Pastoral Forms and Attitudes,* pp. 157-67.

ROBERT WILCHER. "Milton's masque: occasion, form and meaning," *Critical Quarterly* 20(1), Spring 1978, 3-20.

ROGER B. WILKENFELD. "The Seat at the Center: An Interpretation of *Comus*," *ELH* 33(2), June 1966, 170-97.

DAVID WILKINSON. "The Escape from Pollution: A Comment on *Comus*," *Essays in Criticism* 10(1), January 1960, 32-43.

GEORGE WILLIAMSON. *Milton & Others,* pp. 33-40.

A. S. P. WOODHOUSE. *The Poet and His Faith,* pp. 96-100.

"Elegy V"

GEORGE WILLIAMSON. *Milton & Others,* p. 30.

"An Epitaph on the Marchioness of Winchester"

DONALD FRIEDMAN. "Harmony and the Poet's Voice in Some of Milton's Early Poems," *Modern Language Quarterly* 30(4), December 1969, 530-31.

MICHAEL WEST. "The *Consolatio* in Milton's Funeral Elegies," *Huntington Library Quarterly* 34(3), May 1971, 241-42.

GAYLE EDWARD WILSON. "Decorum and Milton's 'An Epitaph On The Marchioness of Winchester,'" *Milton Quarterly* 8(1), March 1974, 11-14.

"Epitaphium Damonis"

RALPH W. CONDEE. "The Structure of Milton's 'Epitaphium Damonis,'" *Studies in Philology* 62(4), July 1965, 577-94.

WILLIAM M. JONES. "Immortality in Two of Milton's Elegies," in *Myth and Symbol,* pp. 136-40.

"Harry, whose tunefull and well measured song" (Sonnet XI)

NAN COOKE CARPENTER. "Milton and Music: Henry Lawes, Dante, and Casella," *English Literary Renaissance* 2(2), Spring 1972, 237-42.

AUDREY DAVIDSON. "Milton on the Music of Henry Lawes," *Milton Newsletter* 2(2), May 1968, 19-23. (P)

"How soon hath Time, the subtle thief of youth"

see "On His Having Arrived at the Age of Twenty-Three"

"I did but prompt the age to quit their clogs" (Sonnet XII)

LEE SHERIDAN COX. "Milton's 'I Did But Prompt,' pp. 13-14," *English Language Notes* 3(2), December 1965, 102-4. (P)

WILLIAM R. PARKER. *Explicator* 8(1), October 1949, Item 3. (P)

"Lawrence of virtuous father virtuous son" (Sonnet XX)

FRASER NIEMAN. "Milton's *Sonnet XX*," *PMLA* 54(3), June 1949, 480-83.

MARK VAN DOREN. *Introduction to Poetry,* pp. 123-25.

"Lycidas"

M. H. ABRAMS. "Five Ways of Reading Lycidas," in *Varieties of Literary Experience,* pp. 1-29.

MILTON, JOHN *(Cont.)*

"Lycidas" *(cont.)*

RICHARD P. ADAMS. "The Archetypal Pattern of Death and Rebirth in Milton's *Lycidas,*" *PMLA* 54(1), March 1949, 183-88. Reprinted in: *The Dimensions of Poetry,* pp. 262-68. Also: *Master Poems of the English Language,* pp. 177-82.

PAUL ALPERS. "The Eclogue Tradition and the Nature of Pastoral," *College English* 34(3), December 1972, 367-71.

STEWART A. BAKER. "Milton's Uncouth Swain," *Milton Studies* 3 (1971), 35-53.

BARBARA CURRIER BELL. " 'Lycidas' and the Stages of Grief," *Literature and Psychology* 25(4), 1975, 166-74.

R. L. BRETT. *Reason and Imagination,* pp. 39-50.

DOUGLAS BUSH. *Pagan Myth and Christian Tradition in English Poetry,* p. 9.

DAVID DAICHES. *A Study of Literature,* pp. 170-95.

H. NEVILLE DAVIES. "Laid artfully together: Stanzaic Design in Milton's 'On the Morning of Christ's Nativity,' " in *Fair Forms,* pp. 97-99.

VICTOR ERLICH. "Milton's Early Poetry: Its Christian Humanism," *American Imago* 32(1), Spring 1975, 106-11.

ALASTAIR FOWLER. *Silent Poetry,* pp. 170-84.

J. MILTON FRENCH. "The Digresssions in Milton's 'Lycidas,' " *Studies in Philology* 50(3), July 1953, 485-90.

ROBERTS W. FRENCH. "Voice and Structure in *Lycidas,*" *Texas Studies in Literature and Language* 12(1), Spring 1970, 15-25.

DONALD M. FRIEDMAN. "*Lycidas:* The Swain's Paideia," *Milton Studies* 3 (1971), 3-34.

NORTHROP FRYE. *Fables of Identity,* pp. 119-29.

CHRISTOPHER GROSE. "Lucky Words: Process of Speech in *Lycidas,*" *Journal of English and Germanic Philology* 70(3), July 1971, 383-403.

J. P. HARDY. *Reinterpretations,* pp. 28-49.

JOHN EDWARD HARDY. *The Curious Frame,* pp. 22-44.

JOHN EDWARD HARDY. "Reconsiderations: I. Lycidas," *Kenyon Review* 7(1), Winter 1945, 99-113.

LAWRENCE W. HYMAN. "Belief and Disbelief in *Lycidas,*" *College English* 33(5), February 1972, 532-42.

KATHERINE JONES. "A Note on Milton's 'Lycidas,' " *American Imago* 19(2), Summer 1962, 141-55.

STEPHEN T. KELLY. "Virgil and Milton: The Attempt at Natural Consolation," *Comparative Literature* 30(3), Summer 1978, 193-208.

MARCIA LANDY. "Language and Mourning in 'Lycidas,' " *American Imago* 30(3), Fall 1973, 294-312.

JON S. LAWRY. " 'Eager Thought': Dialectic in *Lycidas,*" *PMLA* 77(1), March 1962, 27-32.

JON S. LAWRY. " 'The Faithful Herdman's Art' in *Lycidas,*" *Studies in English Literature 1500-1900* 13(1), Winter 1973, 111-25.

MICHAEL LIEB. " 'Yet Once More': The Formulaic Opening of *Lycidas,*" *Milton Quarterly* 12(1), March 1978, 23-28.

MICHAEL LLOYD. "The Two Worlds of 'Lycidas,' " *Essays in Criticism* 11(4), October 1961, 390-402.

MAYNARD MACK. *English Masterpieces,* edited by William Frost, Maynard Mack, and Leonard Dean, vol. 4: *Milton,* pp. 9-11.

MICHAEL MACKLEM. "The Elegiac Theme in Housman," *Queens Quarterly* 59(1), Spring 1952, 46-47.

WILLIAM G. MADSEN. "The Voice of Michael in *Lycidas,*" *Studies in English Literature 1500-1900* 3(1), Winter 1963, 1-7.

C. N. MANLOVE. *Literature and Reality,* pp. 42-47.

EMERSON R. MARKS. *Explicator* 9(6), April 1951, Item 44.

CAROLINE W. MAYERSON. "The Orpheus Image in *Lycidas,*" *PMLA* 54(1), March 1949, 189-207.

JOSEPHINE MILES. *The Primary Language of Poetry in the 1640's,* pp. 88-90.

PAUL ELMER MORE. "How to Read 'Lycidas,' " *American Review* 7(2), May 1936, 140-58. Reprinted in: *Criticism,* pp. 539-45. Also: *Literary Opinion in America,* pp. 68-82; revised and third eds., pp. 146-56.

EUGENE PAUL NASSAR. *The Rape of Cinderella,* pp. 10-11, 16-27.

LOWRY NELSON, JR. *Baroque Lyric Poetry,* pp. 64-76; 138-52.

RICHARD NEUSE. "Milton and Spenser: The Virgilian Triad Revisited," *ELH* 45(4), Winter 1978, 626-31.

B. RAJAN. "*Lycidas:* The Shattering of the Leaves," *Studies in Philology* 64(1), January 1967, 51-64.

JOHN HENRY RALEIGH. "*Lycidas:* 'Yet once more,' " *Prairie Schooner* 42(4), Winter 1968/69, 303-18.

JOHN CROWE RANSOM. "A Poem Nearly Anonymous," *American Review* 1(2), May 1933, 179-203; 1(4), September 1933, 444-67. Reprinted in: *Criticism,* pp. 333-42. Also: John Crowe Ransom. *The World's Body,* pp. 1-28.

JOHN CROWE RANSOM. *The World's Body,* pp. 29-54.

CHRISTOPHER RICKS. "Milton," in *English Poetry and Prose,* edited by Christopher Ricks, pp. 256-68.

WILLIAM G. RIGGS. "The Plant of Fame in *Lycidas,*" *Milton Studies* 4 (1972), 151-61.

M. L. ROSENTHAL and A. J. M. SMITH. *Exploring Poetry,* pp. 502-4; second ed., pp. 356-57.

MALCOLM MACKENZIE ROSS. "Milton and the Protestant Aesthetic: The Early Poems," *University of Toronto Quarterly* 17(4), July 1948, 358-60.

J. W. SAUNDERS. "Milton, Diomede, and Amaryllis," *Journal of English Literary History* 22(4), December 1955, 255-56, 260-61.

WAYNE SHUMAKER. "Flowerets and Sounding Seas: A Study in the Affective Structure of *Lycidas,*" *PMLA* 66(4), June 1951, 485-94.

EDWARD E. SULLIVAN, JR. " 'Sweet Societies That Sing': The Voice of Saints in *Lycidas,*" *Essays in Literature* 3(1), Spring 1976, 32-40.

EDWARD W. TAYLER. "*Lycidas* Yet Once More," *Huntington Library Quarterly* 41(2), February 1978, 103-17.

WRIGHT THOMAS and STUART GERRY BROWN. *Reading Poems: An Introduction to Critical Study,* pp. 692-94.

E. M. W. TILLYARD. *Poetry Direct and Oblique,* pp. 208-13; revised ed., pp. 81-84.

HAROLD E. TOLIVER. *Pastoral Forms and Attitudes,* pp. 167-76.

EDWARD WAGENKNECHT. "Milton in 'Lycidas,' " *College English* 7(7), April 1946, 393-97.

RUTH C. WALLERSTEIN. "Rhetoric in the English Renaissance: Two Elegies," *English Institute Essays,* 1948, pp. 171-78.

GEORGE WILLIAMSON. *Seventeenth Century Contexts,* pp. 132-47.

A. S. P. WOODHOUSE. *The Poet and His Faith,* pp. 100-2.

"A Mask"
   see "Comus"

"Methought I saw my late espoused saint" (Sonnet XXIII)

JOHN J. COLACCIO. " 'A Death Like Sleep': The Christology of Milton's Twenty-Third Sonnet," *Milton Studies* 6 (1974), 181-97.

DIXON FISKE. "The Theme of Purification in Milton's Sonnet XXIII," *Milton Studies* 8 (1975), 149-63.

KURT HEINZELMAN. " 'Cold Consolation': The Art of Milton's Last Sonnet," *Milton Studies* 10 (1977), 111-25.

JOHN SPENCER HILL. " 'Alcestis from the Grave': Image and Structure in *Sonnet XXIII*," *Milton Studies* 10 (1977), 127-39.

JOHN HUNTLEY. "Milton's 23rd Sonnet," *ELH* 34(3), December 1967, 468-81.

M. L. ROSENTHAL and A. J. M. SMITH. *Exploring Poetry*, p. 453; second ed., p. 331.

LEO SPITZER. *Essays on English and American Literature*, pp. 116-31.

E. M. W. TILLYARD. *The Metaphysicals and Milton*, pp. 7-11.

JOHN C. ULREICH. "Typological Symbolism in Milton's Sonnet XXIII," *Milton Quarterly* 8(1), March 1974, 7-10.

THOMAS WHEELER. "Milton's Twenty-Third Sonnet," *Studies in Philology* 58(3), July 1961, 510-15.

MARILYN L. WILLIAMSON. "A Reading of Milton's Twenty-Third Sonnet," *Milton Studies* 4 (1972), 141-49.

"On His Blindness"

CHARLES W. COOPER and JOHN HOLMES. *Preface to Poetry*, pp. 231-34.

EARL DANIELS. *The Art of Reading Poetry*, pp. 34-36. Reprinted in: *The Case for Poetry*, pp. 273-74; second ed., pp. 220-21.

DONALD C. DORIAN. *Explicator* 10(3), December 1951, Item 16. Abridged in: *The Case for Poetry*, p. 274; second ed., p. 221.

DIXON FISKE. "Milton in the Middle of Life: Sonnet XIX," *ELH* 41(1), Spring 1974, 37-49.

NIGEL FOXELL. *Ten Poems Analyzed*, pp. 13-22.

ROBERTS W. FRENCH. "Reading a Poem: Two Sonnets by Milton," *Concerning Poetry* 2(2), Fall 1969, 11-16.

JOHN J. GLAVIN. " 'The Exercise of Saints': Hopkins, Milton, and Patience," *Texas Studies in Literature and Language* 20(2), Summer 1978, 139-52.

PAUL GOODMAN. *The Structure of Literature*, pp. 204-15.

ANN GOSSMAN and GEORGE W. WHITING. "Milton's First Sonnet on his Blindness," with a reply by Fitzroy Pyle, *Review of English Studies*, n.s., 12(48), November 1961, 364-72.

DALE HERRON. "Poetic Vision in Two Sonnets of Milton," *Milton Newsletter* 2(2), May 1968, 25-27.

JOHN F. HUNTLEY. "The Ecology and Anatomy of Criticism: Milton's Sonnet 19 and the Bee Simile in 'Paradise Lost,' I. 768-76," *Journal of Aesthetics and Art Criticism* 24(3), Spring 1966, 386-88.

JAMES L. JACKSON and WALTER E. WEESE. " '. . .Who Only Stand and Wait': Milton's Sonnet 'On His Blindness,' " *Modern Language Notes* 72(2), February 1957, 91-93. (P)

LAURENCE LERNER. *An Introduction to English Poetry*, pp. 76-86.

GEORGE MONTEIRO. *Explicator* 24(8), April 1966, Item 67.

JOSEPH PEQUIGNEY. "Milton's Sonnet XIX Reconsidered," *Texas Studies in Literature and Language* 8(4), Winter 1967, 485-98.

HARRY F. ROBINS. "Milton's First Sonnet on His Blindness," *Review of English Studies*, n.s., 7(28), October 1956, 360-66.

ROGER L. SLAKELY. "Milton's Sonnet 'On His Blindness,' " *ELH* 27(2), June 1960, 122-30.

GARY A. STRINGER. "Milton's 'Thorn in the Flesh': Pauline Didacticism in *Sonnet XIX*," *Milton Studies* 10 (1977), 141-54.

THOMAS B. STROUP. " 'When I Consider': Milton's Sonnet XIX," *Studies in Philology* 69(2), April 1972, 242-58.

STEPHEN WIGLER. "Outrageous Noise and the Sovereign Voice: Satan, Sin, and Syntax in *Sonnet XIX* and Book VI of *Paradise Lost*," *Milton Studies* 10 (1977), 155-57.

"On His Deceased Wife"
   see "Methought I saw my late espoused saint"

"On His Having Arrived at the Age of Twenty-Three"

DONALD C. DORIAN. *Explicator* 8(2), November 1949, Item 10.

ROBERTS W. FRENCH. "Reading a Poem: Two Sonnets by Milton," *Concerning Poetry* 2(2), Fall 1969, 11-16.

JOHN SPENCER HILL. "Poet-Priest: Vocational Tension in Milton's Early Development," *Milton Studies* 8 (1975), 44-46.

SAMUEL S. STOLLMAN. "Analogues and Sources for Milton's 'Great Task-Master,' " *Milton Quarterly* 6(2), May 1972, 27-32.

KESTER SVENDSEN. *Explicator* 7(7), May 1949, Item 53. (P)

A. S. P. WOODHOUSE. *The Poet and His Faith*, p. 95.

"On the Death of a Fair Infant Dying of a Cough"

JACKSON I. COPE. "Fortunate Falls as Form in Milton's 'Fair Infant,' " *Journal of English and Germanic Philology* 63(4), October 1964, 660-74.

VICTOR ERLICH. "Milton's Early Poetry: Its Christian Humanism," *American Imago* 32(1), Spring 1975, 77-86.

DONALD FRIEDMAN. "Harmony and the Poet's Voice in Some of Milton's Early Poems," *Modern Language Quarterly* 30(4), December 1969, 526-27.

WILLIAM M. JONES. "Immortality in Two of Milton's Elegies," in *Myth and Symbol*, pp. 133-36.

WILLIAM KERRIGAN. "The Heretical Milton: From Assumption to Mortalism," *English Literary Renaissance* 5(1), Winter 1975, 130-33.

HUGH N. MACLEAN. "Milton's *Fair Infant*," *Journal of English Literary History* 24(4), December 1957, 296-305.

MICHAEL WEST. "The *Consolatio* in Milton's Funeral Elegies," *Huntington Library Quarterly* 34(3), May 1971, 239-41.

"On the Late Massacre in Piemont"

ISAAC ASIMOV. *Familiar Poems, Annotated*, pp. 121-24.

DAVID S. BERKELEY. *Explicator* 15(9), June 1957, Item 58.

SHEILA BLANCHARD. "Milton's Foothill: Pattern in the Piedmont Sonnet," *Genre* 4(1), March 1971, 39-44.

SANFORD BUDICK. *Poetry of Civilization*, pp. 42-45.

MILTON, JOHN *(Cont.)*

"On the Late Massacre in Piemont" *(cont.)*

JESSE FRANKS. "Linguistic Awareness in the Teaching of Poetry," *Ball State University Forum* 9(1), Winter 1968, 53-56.

ALLEN GROSSMAN. "Milton's sonnet 'On the late massacre in Piemont': a note on the vulnerability of persons in a revolutionary situation," in *Literature in Revolution,* pp. 283-301.

DALE HERRON. "Poetic Vision in Two Sonnets of Milton," *Milton Newsletter* 2(2), May 1968, 23-25.

LAWRENCE W. HYMAN. "Milton's 'On the Late Massacre in Piedmont," *English Language Notes* 3(1), September 1965, 26-29.

NICHOLAS R. JONES. "The Education of the Faithful in Milton's Piedmontese Sonnet," *Milton Studies* 10 (1977), 167-76.

KESTER SVENDSON. "Milton's Sonnet on the Massacre in Piedmont," *Shakespeare Association Bulletin* 20(4), October 1945, 147-55.

MARK VAN DOREN. *Introduction to Poetry,* pp. 120-23.

"On the Morning of Christ's Nativity"

DOUGLAS BUSH. *Pagan Myth and Christian Tradition in English Poetry,* pp. 6-9.

PATRICK CULLEN. "Imitation and Metamorphosis: The Golden-Age Eclogue in Spenser, Milton, and Marvell," *PMLA* 84(6), October 1969, 1565-68.

SHARON CUMBERLAND and LYNN VEACH SADLER. "Phantasia: A Pattern in Milton's Early Poems," *Milton Quarterly* 8(2), May 1974, 50-52.

DAVID DAICHES and WILLIAM CHARVAT. *Poems in English,* pp. 665-69.

H. NEVILLE DAVIES. "Laid artfully together: Stanzaic Design in Milton's 'On the Morning of Christ's Nativity,'" in *Fair Forms,* pp. 85-116.

VICTOR ERLICH. "Milton's Early Poetry: Its Christian Humanism," *American Imago* 32(1), Spring 1975, 87-92.

DONALD FRIEDMAN. "Harmony and the Poet's Voice in Some of Milton's Early Poems," *Modern Language Quarterly* 30(4), December 1969, 528-30.

JONATHAN GOLDBERG. "Hesper-Vesper: Aspects of Venus in a Seventeenth-Century Trope," *Studies in English Literature 1500-1900* 15(1), Winter 1975, 43-45.

LAWRENCE W. HYMAN. "Christ's Nativity and the Pagan Deities," *Milton Studies* 2 (1970), 103-12.

LAURENCE H. JACOBS. "'Unexpressive Notes': The Decorum of Milton's Nativity Ode," *Essays in Literature* 1(2), Fall 1974, 166-77.

LAWRENCE W. KINGSLEY. "Mythic Dialectic in the Nativity Ode," *Milton Studies* 4 (1972), 163-76.

G. WILSON KNIGHT. *The Burning Oracle,* pp. 59, 61.

G. WILSON KNIGHT. *Poets of Action,* p. 20.

MAYNARD MACK. *English Masterpieces,* edited by William Frost, Maynard Mack, and Leonard Dean, vol. 4: *Milton,* pp. 5-7.

LOUIS L. MARTZ. *The Poetry of Meditation,* revised ed., pp. 164-67.

JACKSON MATTHEWS. "Milton: On the Morning of Christ's Nativity," in *Master Poems of the English Language,* pp. 168-71.

T. K. MEIER. "Milton's 'Nativity Ode': Sectarian Discord," *Modern Language Review* 65(1), January 1970, 7-10.

DAVID B. MORRIS. "Drama and Stasis in Milton's 'Ode on the Morning of Christ's Nativity,'" *Studies in Philology* 68(2), April 1971, 207-22.

LOWRY NELSON, JR. *Baroque Lyric Poetry,* pp. 32-33, 41-52.

MOTHER M. CHRISTOPHER PECHEUX. "The Image of the Sun in Milton's 'Nativity Ode,'" *Huntington Library Quarterly* 38(4), August 1975, 315-33.

CHRISTOPHER RICKS. "Milton," in *English Poetry and Prose,* edited by Christopher Ricks, pp. 268-71.

PHILIP ROLLINSON. "Milton's Nativity Poem and the Decorum of Genre," *Milton Studies* 7 (1975), 165-88.

WILLIAM JOHN ROSCELLI. "The Metaphysical Milton (1625-1631)," *Texas Studies in Literature and Language* 8(4), Winter 1967, 477-83.

MALCOLM MACKENZIE ROSS. "Milton and the Protestant Aesthetic: The Early Poems," *University of Toronto Quarterly* 17(4), July 1948, 349-52.

MAREN-SOFIE RØSTVIG. "Elaborate Song: Conceptual Structure in Milton's 'On the Morning of Christ's Nativity,'" in *Fair Forms,* pp. 62-72.

LYNN VEACH SADLER. "Magic and the Temporal Scheme in 'On the Morning of Christ's Nativity,'" *Ball State University Forum* 17(2), Spring 1976, 3-9.

GEORGE WILLIAM SMITH, JR. "Milton's Method of Mistakes in the Nativity Ode," *Studies in English Literature 1500-1900* 18(1), Winter 1978, 107-23.

E. M. W. TILLYARD. *The Metaphysicals and Milton,* pp. 42-44.

JOAN WEBBER. "The Son of God and Power of Life in Three Poems by Milton," *ELH* 37(2), June 1970, 175-80.

A. S. P. WOODHOUSE. *The Poet and His Faith,* pp. 51-53.

"On the University Carrier"

JOAN OZARK HOLMER. "Milton's Hobson Poems: Rhetorical Manifestation of Wit," *Milton Quarterly* 11(1), March 1977, 16-21.

"On Time"

O. B. HARDISON, JR. "Milton's 'On Time' and Its Scholastic Background," *Texas Studies in Literature and Language* 3(1), Spring 1961, 107-22.

ANNE B. LONG. "Coping with Milton's Power," *CEA Critic* 35(3), March 1973, 33-35.

R. DARBY WILLIAMS. "Two Baroque Game Poems on Grace: Herbert's 'Paradise' and Milton's 'On Time,'" *Criticism* 12(3), Summer 1970, 186-92.

"The Passion"

SHARON CUMBERLAND and LYNN VEACH SADLER. "Phantasia: A Pattern in Milton's Early Poems," *Milton Quarterly* 8(2), May 1974, 52-53.

PHILIP J. GALLAGHER. "Milton's 'The Passion': Inspired Mediocrity," *Milton Quarterly* 19(2), May 1977, 44-50.

JOHN A. VIA. "Milton's *The Passion*: A Successful Failure," *Milton Quarterly* 5(2), May 1971, 35-38.

"Il Penseroso"

LAWRENCE BABB. "The Background of 'Il Penseroso,'" *Studies in Philology* 37(2), April 1940, 257-73.

STEPHEN C. BEHRANDT. "Bright Pilgrimage: William Blake's Designs for *L'Allegro* and *Il Penseroso*," *Milton Studies* 8 (1975), 123-47.

LESLIE BRISMAN. "'All Before Them Where to Choose': 'L'Allegro' and 'Il Penseroso,'" *Journal of English and Germanic Philology* 71(2), April 1972, 226-40.

CLEANTH BROOKS. *The Well Wrought Urn*, pp. 50-66; revised ed., pp. 40-53.

NAN COOKE CARPENTER. "The Place of Music in *L'Allegro* and *Il Penseroso*," *University of Toronto Quarterly* 22(4), July 1953, 354-67.

NORMAN B. COUNCIL. "*L'Allegro, Il Penseroso* and 'The Cycle of Universal Knowledge,'" *Milton Studies* 9 (1976), 203-19.

DAVID DAICHES and WILLIAM CHARVAT. *Poems in English*, pp. 670-71.

THOMAS J. EMBRY. "Sensuality and Chastity in *L'Allegro* and *Il Penseroso*," *Journal of English and Germanic Philology* 77(4), October 1978, 504-29.

VICTOR ERLICH. "Milton's Early Poetry: Its Christian Humanism," *American Imago* 32(1), Spring 1975, 92-99.

STANLEY E. FISH. "What It's Like To Read *L'Allegro* and *Il Penseroso*," *Milton Studies* 7 (1975), 77-99.

MICHAEL FIXLER. "The Orphic Technique of 'L'Allegro' and 'Il Penseroso,'" *English Literary Renaissance* 1(2), Spring 1971, 165-77.

LOWELL EDWIN FOLSOM. "'L'Allegro' and 'Il Penseroso': The Poetics of Accelerando and Ritardando," *Studies in the Humanities* 5(1), January 1976, 39-41.

DONALD FRIEDMAN. "Harmony and the Poet's Voice in Some of Milton's Early Poems," *Modern Language Quarterly* 30(4), December 1969, 531-32.

MARJORIE B. GARBER. "Fallen Landscape: The Art of Milton and Poussin," *English Literary Renaissance* 5(1), Winter 1975, 114-15.

GEORGE L. GECKLE. "Miltonic Idealism: *L'Allegro* and *Il Penseroso*," *Texas Studies in Literature and Language* 9(4), Winter 1968, 455-73.

J. P. HARDY. *Reinterpretations*, pp. 1-27.

GEOFFREY H. HARTMAN. "False Themes and Gentle Minds," *Philological Quarterly* 47(1), January 1968, 56-61. Reprinted in: Geoffrey H. Hartman. *Beyond Formalism*, pp. 285-90.

JOHN F. HUNTLEY. "The Poet-Critic and His Poem-Culture in 'L'Allegro' and 'Il Penseroso,'" *Texas Studies in Literature and Language* 13(4), Winter 1972, 541-53.

G. WILSON KNIGHT. *The Burning Oracle*, pp. 59-63. Reprinted in: *Poets of Action*, pp. 18-23.

THOMAS LAVOIE. "The Divine Vision of the Inward Eye: The Structural Hierarchy of the 'L'Allegro-Il Penseroso' Sequence," *Thoth* 16(3), Fall 1976, 3-17.

C. N. MANLOVE. *Literature and Reality*, pp. 31-36.

DAVID M. MILLER. "From Delusion to Illumination: A Larger Structure for *L'Allegro-Il Penseroso*," *PMLA* 86(1), January 1971, 32-39.

GARY STRINGER. "The Unity of 'L'Allegro' and 'Il Penseroso,'" *Texas Studies in Literature and Language* 12(2), Summer 1970, 221-29.

KESTER SVENDSON. *Explicator* 8(7), May 1950, Item 49.

KATHLEEN M. SWAIN. "Time and Structure in *L'Allegro* and *Il Penseroso*," *Texas Studies in Literature and Language* 18(3), Fall 1976, 422-32.

ELEANOR TATE. "Milton's 'L'Allegro' and 'Il Penseroso' — Balance Progression, or Dichotomy?" *Modern Language Notes* 76(7), November 1961, 585-90.

HAROLD E. TOLIVER. *Pastoral Forms and Attitudes*, pp. 154-57.

RICHARD WILBUR. "Milton: L'Allegro and Il Penseroso," in *Master Poems of the English Language*, pp. 191-95.

MARILYN L. WILLIAMSON. "The Myth of Orpheus in 'L'Allegro' and 'Il Penseroso,'" *Modern Language Quarterly* 32(4), December 1971, 377-86.

"A Psalm, A Song. For the Sabbath Day"

CAROLE S. KESSNER. "Psalm 92 and Milton's Sabbath Hymn," *Milton Quarterly* 10(3), October 1976, 75-77.

"Sonnet VII"
see "On His Having Arrived at the Age of Twenty-Three"

"Sonnet XI"
see "Harry, whose tunefull and well measured song"

"Sonnet XII"
see "I did but prompt the age to quit their clogs"

"Sonnet XVIII"
see "On the Late Massacre in Piemont"

"Sonnet XIX"
see "On His Blindness"

"Sonnet XXIII"
see "Methought I saw my late espoused saint"

"To Mr. H. Lawes on His Airs"
see "Harry, whose tunefull and well measured song"

"To the Lord General Cromwell" (Sonnet XVI)

GEORGE WILLIAMSON. *Milton & Others*, pp. 129-32.

"To the Lord General Fairfax at the Siege of Colchester" (Sonnet XV)

JOHN T. SHAWCROSS. "Milton's 'Fairfax' Sonnet," *Notes and Queries*, n.s., 2(5), May 1955, 195-96. (P)

"Upon the Circumcision"

A. B. CHAMBERS. "Milton's 'Upon the Circumcision': Backgrounds and Meanings," *Texas Studies in Literature and Language* 17(3), Fall 1975, 687-97.

"When I consider how my light is spent"
see "On His Blindness"

MOFFITT, JOHN

"Along the Curb"

JUDSON JEROME. "A Moffitt Sampler," *Antioch Review* 24(2), Summer 1964, 220-21.

MOMADAY, N. SCOTT

"Angle of Geese"

ROGER DICKINSON-BROWN. "The Art and Importance of N. Scott Momaday," *Southern Review*, n.s., 14(1), Winter 1978, 42-45.

KENNETH FIELDS. "More Than Language Means: A Review of N. Scott Momaday's *The Way to Rainy Mountain*," *Southern Review*, n.s., 6(1), Winter 1970, 197-99.

"Plainview: 2"

ROGER DICKINSON-BROWN. "The Art and Importance of N. Scott Momaday," *Southern Review*, n.s., 14(1), Winter 1978, 35-37.

MONRO, HAROLD

"The Garden"

STEPHEN SPENDER. "The Collected Poems of Harold Monro," *Criterion* 12(49), July 1933, 681-82.

"Trees"

ROBIN SKELTON. *The Poetic Pattern*, pp. 122-28.

MONTAGUE, MARY WORTLEY
"Epistle from Mrs. Y — — to Her Husband. 1724"
>   ISOBEL GRUNDY. "Ovid and Eighteenth-Century Divorce: An Unpublished Poem by Lady Mary Wortley Montague," *Review of English Studies*, n.s., 23(92), November 1972, 417-28.

MONTGOMERIE, ALEXANDER
"Against the Calvinist Ministers"
>   HELENA M. SHIRE. "Alexander Montgomerie: The oppositione of the court to conscience. 'Court and Conscience walis not weill,'" *Studies in Scottish Literature* 3(3), January 1966, 146.

"Another of the same"
>   HELENA M. SHIRE. "Alexander Montgomerie: The oppositione of the court to conscience. 'Court and Conscience walis not weill,'" *Studies in Scottish Literature* 3(3), January 1966, 145-46.

"Another of the same: epigram"
>   HELENA M. SHIRE. "Alexander Montgomerie: The oppositione of the court to conscience. 'Court and Conscience walis not weill,'" *Studies in Scottish Literature* 3(3), January 1966, 146.

"A funeral song"
>   HELENA M. SHIRE. "Alexander Montgomerie: The oppositione of the court to conscience. 'Court and Conscience walis not weill,'" *Studies in Scottish Literature* 3(3), January 1966, 145.

MONTOYA, JOSÉ
"Resonant Valley"
>   FRANK PINO. "Chicano Poetry: A Popular Manifesto," *Journal of Popular Culture* 6(4), Spring 1973, 724-26.

MOODY, WILLIAM VAUGHAN
"Gloucester Moors"
>   HYATT H. WAGGONER. *American Poets*, pp. 251-54.

"An Ode in Time of Hesitation"
>   STEVEN AXELROD. "Colonel Shaw in American Poetry: 'For the Union Dead' and its Precursors," *American Quarterly* 24(4), October 1972, 530-34.
>   R. P. BLACKMUR. "Moody in Retrospect," *Poetry* 38(6), September 1931, 334-35.

MOORE, CLEMENT CLARKE
"A Visit from St. Nicholas"
>   ISAAC ASIMOV. *Familiar Poems, Annotated*, pp. 177-82.
>   DERMAN THOMAS. "Not Even A Mouse: An Explication," *CEA Critic* 29(5), February 1967, 1, 5.

MOORE, MARIANNE
"Apparition of Splendor"
>   REBECCA PRICE PARKIN. "Certain Difficulties in Reading Marianne Moore: Exemplified in her 'Apparition of Splendor,'" *PMLA* 81(3), June 1966, 167-72.
>   REBECCA PRICE PARKIN. "Some Characteristics of Marianne Moore's Humor," *College English* 27(5), February 1966, 406-7.

"Bird-Witted"
>   LLOYD FRANKENBERG. "The Imaginary Garden," *Quarterly Review of Literature* 4(2), 1948, 210-12.
>   LLOYD FRANKENBERG. *Pleasure Dome*, pp. 142-43.

"Black Earth"
>   R. P. BLACKMUR. *The Double Agent*, pp. 150-54.
>   CHARLES TOMLINSON. "Abundance, Not Too Much: The Poetry of Marianne Moore," *Sewanee Review* 65(4), Autumn 1957, 677-82.

"By Disposition of Angels"
>   L. S. DEMBO. *Conceptions of Reality in Modern American Poetry*, p. 110.

"A Carriage from Sweden"
>   JAMES M. REID. *100 American Poems of the Twentieth Century*, pp. 95-98.

"Critics and Connoisseurs"
>   JAMES M. REID. *100 American Poems of the Twentieth Century*, pp. 98-100.

"An Egyptian Pulled Glass Bottle in the Shape of a Fish"
>   SUZANNE JUHASZ. *Naked and Fiery Forms*, pp. 41-42.

"Elephants"
>   CLEANTH BROOKS. "Miss Marianne Moore's Zoo," *Quarterly Review of Literature* 4(2), 1948, 179-80.
>   WALLACE FOWLIE. "Under the Equanimity of Language," *Quarterly Review of Literature* 4(2), 1948, 175-76.

"A Face"
>   BERNARD F. ENGEL. *Explicator* 34(4), December 1975, Item 29.

"The Fish"
>   KENNETH BURKE. "Motives and Motifs in the Poetry of Marianne Moore," in *Modern Poetry* pp. 208-9.
>   MORTON DAUWEN. "A Literalist of the Imagination," in *Literary Opinion in America*, pp. 433-34; revised and third eds., pp. 390-91.
>   VIVIENNE KOCH. "The Peaceable Kingdom of Marianne Moore," *Quarterly Review of Literature* 4(2), 1948, 163-64. Reprinted in: Norman C. Stageberg and Wallace L. Anderson. *Poetry as Experience*, p. 499.
>   SUE RENICK. *Explicator* 21(1), September 1962, Item 7.
>   WALTER SUTTON. *American Free Verse*, pp. 111-13.
>   WILLIAM A. SYLVESTER. *Explicator* 7(4), February 1949, Item 30.

"Granite and Steel"
>   DANIEL L. GUILLORY. "Hart Crane, Marianne Moore and the Brooklyn Bridge," *Ball State University Forum* 15(3), Summer 1974, 48-49.

"A Grave"
>   NANCY SULLIVAN. "Perspective and the Poetic Process," *Wisconsin Studies in Contemporary Literature* 6(1), Winter-Spring 1965, 117-21.

"He 'Digesteth Harde Yron'"
>   WALLACE STEVENS. "About One of Marianne Moore's Poems," *Quarterly Review of Literature* 4(2), 1948, 143-47.
>   WALLACE STEVENS. *The Necessary Angel*, pp. 93-103.
>   JOHN CROWE RANSOM. "On Being Modern with Distinction," *Quarterly Review of Literature* 4(2), 1948, 140-41.
>   WALTER SUTTON. *American Free Verse*, pp. 105-6.

"The Hero"
>   JOSEPH WARREN BEACH. *Obsessive Images*, pp. 213-15.
>   R. P. BLACKMUR. *The Double Agent*, pp. 162-63. (P)

"His Shield"
>   SUZANNE JUHASZ. *Naked and Fiery Forms*, pp. 42-46.

"The Icosasphere"

MARIE BORROFF. *Explicator* 16(4), January 1958, Item 21.

L. S. DEMBO. *Conceptions of Reality in Modern American Poetry*, pp. 113-14.

"In a Public Garden"

A. K. WEATHERHEAD. "Two Kinds of Vision in Marianne Moore," *ELH* 31(4), December 1964, 488-91.

"In Distrust of Merits"

MARCIA EPSTEIN ALLENTUCK. *Explicator* 10(6), April 1952, Item 42.

HARRY BROWN and JOHN MILSTEAD. *What the Poem Means*, p. 152.

WALLACE FOWLIE. "Under the Equanimity of Language," *Quarterly Review of Literature* 4(2), 1948, 176-77.

LLOYD FRANKENBERG. "The Imaginary Garden," *Quarterly Review of Literature* 4(2), 1948, 221-22.

LLOYD FRANKENBERG. *Pleasure Dome*, pp. 153-55.

DAN JAFFE. "Poets in the Inferno: Civilians, C.O.'s and Combatants," in *The Forties*, pp. 36-37.

"The Jerboa"

CLEANTH BROOKS. "Miss Marianne Moore's Zoo," *Quarterly Review of Literature* 4(2), 1948, 182-83.

LLOYD FRANKENBERG. "The Imaginary Garden," *Quarterly Review of Literature* 4(2), 1948, 202-3.

KIMON FRIAR and JOHN MALCOLM BRINNIN. *Modern Poetry*, pp. 523-24.

PHILIP FERGUSON LEGLER. "Marianne Moore and the Idea of Freedom," *Poetry* 83(3), December 1953, 158-67.

"The Labours of Hercules"

JEAN GARRIGUE. "Marianne Moore," in *Six American Poets from Emily Dickinson to the Present*, pp. 96-97.

"Love in America"

WALTER SUTTON. *American Free Verse*, pp. 115-16.

"Marriage"

JEAN GARRIGUE. "Marianne Moore," in *Six American Poets from Emily Dickinson to the Present*, pp. 91-93.

MILDRED E. HARTSOCK. "Marianne Moore: A 'Salvo of Barks,'" *Bucknell Review* 11(1), December 1962, 32-34.

VIVIENNE KOCH. "The Peaceable Kingdom of Marianne Moore," *Quarterly Review of Literature* 4(2), 1948, 167.

MARGARET NEWLIN. "'Unhelpful Hymen!': Marianne Moore and Hilda Doolittle," *Essays in Criticism* 27(3), July 1977, 224-26.

"Melancthon"

L. S. DEMBO. *Conceptions of Reality in Modern American Poetry*, pp. 116-17.

"The Mind Is an Enchanting Thing"

LLOYD FRANKENBERG. *Invitation to Poetry*, pp. 388-90.

"The Monkey Puzzle"

JEAN GARRIGUE. "Marianne Moore," in *Six American Poets from Emily Dickinson to the Present*, p. 105.

"The Monkeys"

R. P. BLACKMUR. *The Double Agent*, pp. 166-67. Reprinted in: R. P. Blackmur. *Language as Gesture*, p. 281.

LOIS MILLER. "I Went to the Animal Fair: An analysis of Marianne Moore's 'The Monkeys,'" *English Journal* 52(1), January 1963, 66-67.

"Nevertheless"

LLOYD FRANKENBERG. "The Imaginary Garden," *Quarterly Review of Literature* 4(2), 1948, 195-96.

LLOYD FRANKENBERG. *Pleasure Dome*, p. 126.

"New York"

JEAN GARRIGUE. "Marianne Moore," in *Six American Poets from Emily Dickinson to the Present*, pp. 103-4.

"No Swan So Fine"

SUZANNE JUHASZ. *Naked and Fiery Forms*, pp. 47-48.

REBECCA PRICE PARKIN. "Some Characteristics of Marianne Moore's Humor," *College English* 27(5), February 1966, 407.

ROY HARVEY PEARCE. *The Continuity of American Poetry*, pp. 370-71.

"Novices"

R. P. BLACKMUR. *Form and Value in Modern Poetry*, pp. 228-30.

JEAN GARRIGUE. "Marianne Moore," in *Six American Poets from Emily Dickinson to the Present*, pp. 94-95.

"O to Be a Dragon"

SUZANNE JUHASZ. *Naked and Fiery Forms*, pp. 53-54.

REBECCA PRICE PARKIN. "Some Characteristics of Marianne Moore's Humor," *College English* 27(5), February 1966, 406.

"An Octopus"

L. S. DEMBO. *Conceptions of Reality in Modern American Poetry*, pp. 114-15.

MARTIN DODSWORTH. "Marianne Moore," in *The Modern Poet*, edited by Ian Hamilton, p. 130.

JEAN GARRIGUE. "Marianne Moore," in *Six American Poets from Emily Dickinson to the Present*, pp. 106-7.

MILDRED E. HARTSOCK. "Marianne Moore: A 'Salvo of Barks,'" *Bucknell Review* 11(1), December 1962, 31-32.

A. K. WEATHERHEAD. "Two Kinds of Vision in Marianne Moore," *ELH* 31(4), December 1964, 491-94.

"The Pangolin"

L. S. DEMBO. *Conceptions of Reality in Modern American Poetry*, p. 116.

DENIS DONOGHUE. *The Ordinary Universe*, pp. 47-49.

REBECCA PRICE PARKIN. "Some Characteristics of Marianne Moore's Humor," *College English* 27(5), February 1966, 403-6.

WALTER SUTTON. *American Free Verse*, pp. 106-7.

"The Paper Nautilus"

WALTER SUTTON. *American Free Verse*, pp. 107-8.

"The Past Is the Present"

R. P. BLACKMUR. *The Double Agent*, pp. 142-49.

JEAN GARRIGUE. "Marianne Moore," in *Six American Poets from Emily Dickinson to the Present*, pp. 93-94.

"The Plumet Basilisk"

ROBERT LANGBAUM. "The New Nature Poetry," in *The Modern Spirit*, pp. 119-20.

"Poetry"

R. P. BLACKMUR. *Form and Value in Modern Poetry*, pp. 233-36.

LLOYD FRANKENBERG. "The Imaginary Garden," *Quarterly Review of Literature* 4(2), 1948, 207-9.

LLOYD FRANKENBERG. *Pleasure Dome*, pp. 137-41.

JEAN GARRIGUE. "Marianne Moore," in *Six American Poets from Emily Dickinson to the Present*, pp. 101-3.

MOORE, MARIANNE *(Cont.)*

"Poetry" *(cont.)*

    SUZANNE JUHASZ. *Naked and Fiery Forms*, pp. 49-51.

    AGNES STEIN. *The Uses of Poetry*, p. 148.

    HYATT H. WAGGONER. *American Poets*, pp. 365-66.

"Roses Only"

    REUBEN ARTHUR BROWER. *The Fields of Light*, pp. 48-50.

"St. Nicholas"

    A. KINGSLEY WEATHERHEAD. "Imagination and Fancy: Robert Lowell and Marianne Moore," *Texas Studies in Literature and Language* 6(2), Summer 1964, 197-98.

"Sea Unicorns and Land Unicorns"

    JEAN GARRIGUE. "Marianne Moore," in *Six American Poets from Emily Dickinson to the Present*, p. 98.

"See in the Midst of Fair Leaves"

    DAN G. HOFFMAN. *Explicator* 10(5), March 1952, Item 34. Reprinted in: *Readings for Liberal Education*, third ed., II: 203-4; fourth ed., II: 204-5; fifth ed., II: 187-88.

"Silence"

    R. P. BLACKMUR. *The Double Agent*, pp. 154-60. Reprinted in: R. P. Blackmur. *Language as Gesture*, pp. 271-76.

"Snakes, Mongooses, Snake-Charmer and the Like"

    M. L. ROSENTHAL and A. J. M. SMITH. *Exploring Poetry*, pp. 250-51; second ed., pp. 214-15.

"Spenser's Ireland"

    KENNETH BURKE. "Motives and Motifs in the Poetry of Marianne Moore," in *Modern Poetry*, pp. 205-6.

    JOSEPHINE MILES. "Moore: Spenser's Ireland," in *Master Poems of the English Language*, pp. 938-41.

    MAURICE J. O'SULLIVAN, JR. "Native Genius for Disunion: Marianne Moore's 'Spenser's Ireland,'" *Concerning Poetry* 7(2), Fall 1974, 42-47.

"The Steeple-Jack"

    LOUISE BOGAN. "Reading Contemporary Poetry," *College English* 14(5), February 1953, 257-58.

    HARRY BROWN and JOHN MILSTEAD. *What the Poem Means*, p. 153.

    DANIEL HOFFMAN. *Barbarous Knowledge*, p. 3.

    SUZANNE JUHASZ. *Naked and Fiery Forms*, pp. 47-48.

    WALTER SUTTON. *American Free Verse*, pp. 110-11.

    CHARLES TOMLINSON. "Abundance, Not Too Much: The Poetry of Marianne Moore," *Sewanee Review* 65(4), Autumn 1957, 682-84.

    A. K. WEATHERHEAD. "Two Kinds of Vision in Marianne Moore," *ELH* 31(4), December 1964, 482-84.

"Tell Me, Tell Me"

    REBECCA PRICE PARKIN. "Some Characteristics of Marianne Moore's Humor," *College English* 27(5), February 1966, 407.

"Then the Ermine"

    REBECCA PRICE PARKIN. "Some Characteristics of Marianne Moore's Humor," *College English* 27(5), February 1966, 407.

"Those Various Scalpels"

    JEAN GARRIGUE. "Marianne Moore," in *Six American Poets from Emily Dickinson to the Present*, pp. 97-98.

"To a Snail"

    FRANCIS W. WARLOW. *Explicator* 26(6), February 1968, Item 51.

"To a Steam Roller"

    KENNETH BURKE. "Motives and Motifs in the Poetry of Marianne Moore," in *Modern Poetry*, p. 217.

"Tom Fool at Jamaica"

    MARIE BORROFF. "'Tom Fool at Jamaica' by Marianne Moore: Meaning and Structure," *College English* 17(8), May 1965, 466-69.

    ELDER OLSON. "The Poetry of Marianne Moore," *Chicago Review* 11(1), Spring 1957, 103-4.

    A. K. WEATHERHEAD. "Two Kinds of Vision in Marianne Moore," *ELH* 31(4), December 1964, 486-87.

"What Are Years?"

    HARRY BROWN and JOHN MILSTEAD. *What the Poem Means*, p. 153.

    KENNETH BURKE. "Motives and Motifs in the Poetry of Marianne Moore," in *Modern Poetry*, 206-7.

    LLOYD FRANKENBERG. "Meaning in Modern Poetry," *Saturday Review of Literature* 29(12), 23 March 1946, 5.

    WILLIAM VAN O'CONNOR. *Sense and Sensibility in Modern Poetry*, pp. 229-30.

    JAMES M. REID. *100 American Poems of the Twentieth Century*, pp. 101-2.

"The Wood-Weasel"

    CLEANTH BROOKS. "Miss Marianne Moore's Zoo," *Quarterly Review of Literature* 4(2), 1948, 182.

    SUZANNE JUHASZ. *Naked and Fiery Forms*, pp. 51-52.

MOORE, MERRILL

"Granny Weeks"

    DUDLEY FITTS. "The Sonnets of Merrill Moore," *Sewanee Review* 47(2), April-June 1939, 278-79.

"The Gun Barrel Looked at Him With Love in Its Single Eyehole"

    DUDLEY FITTS. "The Sonnets of Merrill Moore," *Sewanee Review* 47(2), April-June 1939, 274-75.

"The Sound of Time Hangs Heavy in My Ears"

    DUDLEY FITTS. "The Sonnets of Merrill Moore," *Sewanee Review* 47(2), April-June 1939, 291-92.

MOORE, T. STURGE

"From Titian"

    YVOR WINTERS. "The Poetry of T. Sturge Moore," *Southern Review*, n.s., 2(1), Winter 1966, 13-15.

"Love's Faintness Accepted"

    FREDERICK L. GWYNN. *Explicator* 7(6), April 1949, Item 45.

"Sicilian Idyll"

    "'The New Poetry,' Arthur Waugh, 'Quarterly Review,'" in *Georgian Poetry*, pp. 148-49.

"Silence"

    YVOR WINTERS. "The Poetry of T. Sturge Moore," *Southern Review*, n.s., 2(1), Winter 1966, 12-13.

"To Silence"

    YVOR WINTERS. "The Poetry of T. Sturge Moore," *Southern Review*, n.s., 2(1), Winter 1966, 9-12.

    YVOR WINTERS. *Primitivism and Decadence*, pp. 86-89. Reprinted in: Yvor Winters. *In Defense of Reason*, pp. 96-99. Also: *Essays in Modern Literary Criticism*, pp. 223-25.

MOORE, THOMAS

"The Last Rose of Summer"

JAMES R. KREUZER. *Elements of Poetry*, pp. 196-98.

"The Song of Fionnuala"

BRENDAN P. O. HEHIR. *Explicator* 15(4), January 1957, Item 23.

MORGAN, FREDERICK

"The Smile"

LAURENCE LIEBERMAN. *Unassigned Frequencies*, p. 281.

MORGAN, ROBIN

"The Network of the Imaginary Mother"

CYNTHIA A. DAVIS. "Weaving Poetry: Robin Morgan's 'The Network of the Imaginary Mother,'" *Concerning Poetry* 11(2), Fall 1978, 5-10.

MORRIS, WILLIAM

"The Blue Closet"

MARGARET A. LOURIE. "The Embodiment of Dreams: William Morris' 'Blue Closet' Group," *Victorian Poetry* 15(3), Autumn 1977, 195-201.

"The Chapel in Lyoness"

CURTIS DAHL. "Morris's 'The Chapel in Lyoness': An Interpretation," *Studies in Philology* 51(3), July 1954, 482-91.

MEREDITH B. RAYMOND. "The Arthurian Group in *The Defence of Guenevere and Other Poems*," *Victorian Poetry* 4(3), Summer 1966, 213-18.

DAVID STAINES. "Morris' Treatment of His Medieval Sources in *The Defense of Guenevere and Other Poems*,'" *Studies in Philology* 70(4), October 1973, 449-50.

"Concerning Geffray Teste Noire"

PATRICK BRANTLINGER. "A Reading of Morris' *The Defence of Guenevere and Other Poems*," *Victorian Newsletter* 44 (Fall 1973), 19-20.

MARGARET GENT. "'To Flinch From Modern Varnish': The Appeal of the Past to the Victorian Imagination," in *Victorian Poetry*, pp. 23-32.

DIANNE F. SADOFF. "Erotic Murders: Structural and Rhetorical Irony in William Morris' Froissart Poems," *Victorian Poetry* 13(3-4), Fall-Winter 1975, 11-26.

DAVID STAINES. "Morris' Treatment of His Medieval Sources in *The Defence of Guenevere and Other Poems*," *Studies in Philology* 70(4), October 1973, 452-54.

"The Defence of Guenevere"

DENIS R. BALCH. "Guenevere's Fidelity to Arthur in 'The Defence of Guenevere' and 'King Arthur's Tomb,'" *Victorian Poetry* 13(3-4), Fall-Winter 1975, 61-70.

HARRY BROWN and JOHN MILSTEAD. *What the Poem Means*, p. 154.

AUBREY E. GALYON. "William Morris: The Past as Standard," *Philological Quarterly* 56(2), Spring 1977, 246-48.

JOHN HOLLOW. "William Morris and the Judgment of God," *PMLA* 86(3), May 1971, 447-49.

LAURENCE PERRINE. "Morris's Guenevere: An Interpretation," *Philological Quarterly* 39(2), April 1960, 234-41.

MEREDITH B. RAYMOND. "The Arthurian Group in *The Defence of Guenevere and Other Poems*," *Victorian Poetry* 4(3), Summer 1966, 213-18.

CAROLE G. SILVER. "'The Defence of Guenevere': A Further Interpretation," *Studies in English Literature 1500-1900* 9(4), Autumn 1969, 695-702.

HARTLEY S. SPATT. "William Morris and the Uses of the Past," *Victorian Poetry* 13(3-4), Fall-Winter 1975, 5-7.

DAVID STAINES. "Morris' Treatment of His Medieval Sources in *The Defense of Guenevere and Other Poems*," *Studies in Philology* 70(4), October 1973, 441-45.

ROBERT L. STALLMAN. "The Lovers' Progress: An Investigation of William Morris' 'The Defence of Guenevere' and 'King Arthur's Tomb,'" *Studies in English Literature 1500-1900* 15(4), Autumn 1975, 658-65.

"The Doom of King Acrisius"

JEROME J. MCGANN. "The Beauty of the Medusa: A Study in Romantic Literary Iconology," *Studies in Romanticism* 11(1), Winter 1972, 17-21.

"The Eve of Crecy"

DAVID STAINES. "Morris' Treatment of His Medieval Sources in *The Defence of Guenevere and Other Poems*," *Studies in Philology* 70(4), October 1973, 456-57.

"Golden Wings"

PATRICK BRANTLINGER. "A Reading of Morris' *The Defence of Guenevere and Other Poems*," *Victorian Newsletter* 44 (Fall 1973), 22.

"The Haystack in the Floods"

R. C. ELLISON. "'The Undying Glory of Dreams': William Morris and the 'Northland of Old,'" in *Victorian Poetry*, pp. 147-48.

MARGARET GENT. "'To Flinch From Modern Varnish': The Appeal of the Past to the Victorian Imagination," in *Victorian Poetry*, pp. 33-35.

DIANNE F. SADOFF. "Erotic Murders: Structural and Rhetorical Irony in William Morris' Froissart Poems," *Victorian Poetry* 13(3-4), Fall-Winter 1975, 11-26.

DAVID STAINES. "Morris' Treatment of His Medieval Sources in *The Defence of Guenevere and Other Poems*," *Studies in Philology* 70(4), October 1973, 456.

"The Hill of Venus"

BARBARA FASS. "William Morris and the Tannhäuser Legend: A Gloss on the Earthly Paradise Motif," *Victorian Newsletter* 40 (Fall 1971), 22-26.

"The Judgment of God"

JOHN HOLLOW. "William Morris and the Judgment of God," *PMLA* 86(3), May 1971, 446-47.

"King Arthur's Tomb"

DENNIS R. BALCH. "Guenevere's Fidelity to Arthur in 'The Defence of Guenevere' and 'King Arthur's Tomb,'" *Victorian Poetry* 13(3-4), Fall-Winter 1975, 61-70.

AUBREY E. GALYON. "William Morris: The Past as Standard," *Philological Quarterly* 56(2), Spring 1977, 248-49.

JOHN HOLLOW. "William Morris and the Judgment of God," *PMLA* 86(3), May 1971, 449-51.

MEREDITH B. RAYMOND. "The Arthurian Group in *The Defence of Guenevere and Other Poems*," *Victorian Poetry* 4(3), Summer 1966, 213-18.

MORRIS, WILLIAM *(Cont.)*

"King Arthur's Tomb" *(cont.)*

DAVID ROBINSON. "The Thematic Ambiguity of William Morris' 'King Arthur's Tomb,'" *Concerning Poetry* 9(1), Spring 1976, 41-44.

HARTLEY S. SPATT. "William Morris and the Uses of the Past," *Victorian Poetry* 13(3-4), Fall-Winter 1975, 7-9.

DAVID STAINES. "Morris' Treatment of His Medieval Sources in *The Defence of Guenevere and Other Poems*," *Studies in Philology* 70(4), October 1973, 445-47.

ROBERT L. STALLMAN. "The Lovers' Progress: An Investigation of William Morris' 'The Defence of Guenevere' and 'King Arthur's Tomb,'" *Studies in English Literature 1500-1900* 15(4), Autumn 1975, 665-69.

"Lonely Love and Loveless Death"

DAVID J. DELAURA. "An Unpublished Poem of William Morris," *Modern Philology* 62(4), May 1965, 340-41.

"The Lovers of Gudrun"

R. C. ELLISON. "'The Undying Glory of Dreams': William Morris and the 'Northland of Old,'" in *Victorian Poetry*, pp. 158-66.

"The Nymph's Song to Hylas" (*The Life and Death of Jason*)

PAUL F. JAMIESON. *Explicator* 14(6), March 1956, Item 36.

ANDREW RUTHERFORD. *Explicator* 14(6), March 1956, Item 36.

"Rapunzel"

MICHAEL O. REED. "Morris' 'Rapunzel' as an Oedipal Fantasy," *American Imago* 30(3), Fall 1973, 313-22.

DIANNE F. SADOFF. "Imaginative Transformation in William Morris' 'Rapunzel,'" *Victorian Poetry* 12(2), Summer 1974, 153-64.

"Sir Galahad, A Christmas Mystery"

MEREDITH B. RAYMOND. "The Arthurian Group in *The Defence of Guenevere and Other Poems*," *Victorian Poetry* 4(3), Summer 1966, 213-18.

DAVID STAINES. "Morris' Treatment of His Medieval Sources in *The Defence of Guenevere and Other Poems*," *Studies in Philology* 70(4), October 1973, 448-49.

"The Story of the Unknown Church"

HARTLEY S. SPATT. "William Morris and the Uses of the Past," *Victorian Poetry* 13(3-4), Fall-Winter 1975, 2-4.

"The Three Flowers"

JOHN LEBOURGEOIS. "The Love and Marriage of William Morris: A New Interpretation," *South Carolina Review* 9(2), April 1977, 45-48.

"The Tune of Seven Towers"

PATRICK BRANTLINGER. "A Reading of Morris' *The Defence of Guenevere and Other Poems*," *Victorian Newsletter* 44 (Fall 1973), 22-23.

MOSES, W. R.

"One Time on One River"

LAURENCE LIEBERMAN. *Unassigned Frequencies*, pp. 224-25.

MOSS, HOWARD

"Ménage à Trois"

LAURENCE LIEBERMAN. *Unassigned Frequencies*, pp. 137-38.

"Water Island"

LAURENCE LIEBERMAN. *Unassigned Frequencies*, p. 134.

MOTHER GOOSE

"Georgie Porgie"

H. ALAN WYCHERLEY. "'Georgie Porgie,'" *CEA Critic* 32(7), April 1970, 16.

"Goosey-Goosey-Gander"

ROBERT GRAVES. "Mother Goose's Lost Goslings," *Hudson Review* 4(4), Winter 1952, 590-91.

"The Grand Old Duke of York"

ROBERT GRAVES. "Mother Goose's Lost Goslings," *Hudson Review* 4(4), Winter 1952, 587.

"Hickory, Dickory, Dock"

AGNES STEIN. *The Uses of Poetry*, pp. 72-73.

"Humpty Dumpty"

BERNARD M. KNIEGER. "Humpty Dumpty and Symbolism," in *The Creative Reader*, second ed., pp. 901-2.

"The Lion and the Unicorn"

ROBERT GRAVES. "Mother Goose's Lost Goslings," *Hudson Review* 4(4), Winter 1952, 591-92.

"Little Jack Horner"

ROBERT GRAVES. "Mother Goose's Lost Goslings," *Hudson Review* 4(4), Winter 1952, 588.

"Little Miss Muffet"

EARL DANIELS. *The Art of Reading Poetry*, pp. 77-80.

MUIR, EDWIN

"Adam's Dream"

BRIAN KEEBLE. "In Time's Despite: On the Poetry of Edwin Muir," *Sewanee Review* 81(3), Summer 1973, 643-45.

"The Animals"

JANET EMIG. "The Articulate Breath," *English Journal* 52(7), October 1963, 540-41.

RALPH J. MILLS, JR. "Eden's Gate: The Later Poetry of Edwin Muir," *Personalist* 44(1), Winter 1963, 65-66.

"The Ballad of Everyman"

RALPH J. MILLS, JR. "Eden's Gate: The Later Poetry of Edwin Muir," *Personalist* 44(1), Winter 1963, 75-76.

"The Ballad of Hector in Hades"

LILLIAN FEDER. *Ancient Myth in Modern Poetry*, pp. 370-72.

DANIEL HOFFMAN. *Barbarous Knowledge*, pp. 247-50.

DANIEL HOFFMAN. "Edwin Muir: The Story and the Fable," *Yale Review* 55(3), March 1966, 419-21.

"Ballad of the Flood"

DANIEL HOFFMAN. *Barbarous Knowledge*, pp. 241-42.

DANIEL HOFFMAN. "Edwin Muir: The Story and the Fable," *Yale Review* 55(3), March 1966, 414-16.

"The Brothers"

RALPH J. MILLS, JR. "Eden's Gate: The Later Poetry of Edwin Muir," *Personalist* 44(1), Winter 1963, 68-70.

"The Combat"

DANIEL HOFFMAN. *Barbarous Knowledge*, pp. 244-46.

DANIEL HOFFMAN. "Edwin Muir: The Story and the Fable," *Yale Review* 55(3), March 1966, 417-19.

GEOFFREY THURLEY. *The Ironic Harvest*, pp. 132-33.

"Comfort in Self-Despite"

SISTER M. JOSELYN. "Herbert and Muir: Pilgrims of Their Age," *Renascence* 15(3), Spring 1963, 129.

"The Covenant"

FREDERICK GARBER. "Edwin Muir's Heraldic Mode," *Twentieth Century Literature* 12(2), July 1966, 96-97.

"The Day"

RAYMOND TSCHUMI. *Thought in Twentieth-Century English Poetry*, pp. 96-97.

"The Days"

RALPH J. MILLS, JR. "Eden's Gate: The Later Poetry of Edwin Muir," *Personalist* 44(1), Winter 1963, 65-68.

RALPH J. MILLS, JR. "Edwin Muir: A Speech from Darkness Grown," *Accent* 19(1), Winter 1959, 66-67.

"Dialogue"

RAYMOND TSCHUMI. *Thought in Twentieth-Century English Poetry*, pp. 113-14.

"The Enchanted Knight"

R. P. BLACKMUR. "Edwin Muir: Between the Tiger's Paws," in *Four Poets on Poetry*, pp. 36-37.

"The Fathers"

RAYMOND TSCHUMI. *Thought in Twentieth-Century English Poetry*, pp. 100-1.

"The Gate"

KIMON FRIAR. "The Circular Route," *Poetry* 84(1), April 1954, 29.

ELIZABETH HUBERMAN. "Initiation and Tragedy: A New Look at Edwin Muir's 'The Gate,'" *PMLA* 87(1), January 1972, 75-79.

"The Good Man in Hell"

SISTER M. JOSELYN. "Herbert and Muir: Pilgrims of Their Age," *Renascence* 15(3), Spring 1963, 128.

RAYMOND TSCHUMI. *Thought in Twentieth-Century English Poetry*, p. 109.

"The Grove"

FREDERICK GARBER. "Edwin Muir's Heraldic Mode," *Twentieth Century Literature* 12(2), July 1966, 102.

RALPH J. MILLS, JR. "Edwin Muir: A Speech from Darkness Grown," *Accent* 19(1), Winter 1959, 60-62.

"Hölderlin's Journey"

DANIEL HOFFMAN. *Barbarous Knowledge*, p. 228.

"The Horses"

C. B. COX and A. E. DYSON. *Modern Poetry*, pp. 128-32.

LILLIAN FEDER. *Ancient Myth in Modern Poetry*, pp. 376-77.

RALPH J. MILLS, JR. "Edwin Muir: A Speech from Darkness Grown," *Accent* 19(1), Winter 1959, 68-69.

"The Human Fold"

RAYMOND TSCHUMI. *Thought in Twentieth-Century English Poetry*, pp. 105-6.

"'I Have Been Taught'"

LILLIAN FEDER. *Ancient Myth in Modern Poetry*, p. 377.

"The Interceptor"

SISTER M. JOSELYN. "Herbert and Muir: Pilgrims of Their Age," *Renascence* 15(3), Spring 1963, 131.

"The Interrogation"

DANIEL HOFFMAN. *Barbarous Knowledge*, pp. 246-47.

"Isaiah"

RAYMOND TSCHUMI. *Thought in Twentieth-Century English Poetry*, pp. 94-95.

"The Island"

R. P. BLACKMUR. "Edwin Muir: Between the Tiger's Paws," in *Four Poets on Poetry*, pp. 37-38.

"The Killing"

LILLIAN FEDER. *Ancient Myth in Modern Poetry*, p. 375.

"The Labyrinth"

LILLIAN FEDER. *Ancient Myth in Modern Poetry*, pp. 373-75.

RALPH J. MILLS, JR. "Edwin Muir: A Speech from Darkness Grown," *Accent* 19(1), Winter 1959, 64-65.

CHRISTOPHER WISEMAN. "Edwin Muir's 'The Labyrinth': A Study of Symbol and Structure," *Studies in Scottish Literature* 10(2), October 1972, 67-78.

"The Law"

SISTER M. JOSELYN. "Herbert and Muir: Pilgrims of Their Age," *Renascence* 15(3), Spring 1963, 132.

"The Little General"

FREDERICK GARBER. "Edwin Muir's Heraldic Mode," *Twentieth Century Literature* 12(2), July 1966, 98.

"Merlin"

DANIEL HOFFMAN. *Barbarous Knowledge*, pp. 234-35.

"The Mythical Journey"

DANIEL HOFFMAN. *Barbarous Knowledge*, pp. 252-53.

DANIEL HOFFMAN. "Edwin Muir: The Story and the Fable," *Yale Review* 55(3), March 1966, 423-24.

"The Narrow Place"

RAYMOND TSCHUMI. *Thought in Twentieth-Century English Poetry*, pp. 106-7.

"The Old Gods"

RAYMOND TSCHUMI. *Barbarous Knowledge*, pp. 235-36.

"The Other Oedipus"

RALPH J. MILLS, JR. "Eden's Gate: The Later Poetry of Edwin Muir," *Personalist* 44(1), Winter 1963, 70.

"Outside Eden"

RALPH J. MILLS, JR. "Eden's Gate: The Later Poetry of Edwin Muir," *Personalist* 44(1), Winter 1963, 70-72.

RALPH J. MILLS, JR. "Edwin Muir: A Speech from Darkness Grown," *Accent* 19(1), Winter 1959, 67-68.

"The Poet"

DANIEL HOFFMAN. *Barbarous Knowledge*, pp. 8-9.

"The Prize"

SISTER M. JOSELYN. "Herbert and Muir: Pilgrims of Their Age," *Renascence* 15(3), Spring 1963, 127-28.

"The Recurrence"

KIMON FRIAR and JOHN MALCOLM BRINNIN. *Modern Poetry*, pp. 524-25. (Quoting Edwin Muir)

FREDERICK GARBER. "Edwin Muir's Heraldic Mode," *Twentieth Century Literature* 12(2), July 1966, 101-2.

RAYMOND TSCHUMI. *Thought in Twentieth-Century English Poetry*, pp. 107-8.

"The Refugees"

RAYMOND TSCHUMI. *Thought in Twentieth-Century English Poetry*, pp. 89-90.

MUIR, EDWIN (*Cont.*)

"The Return"

R. P. BLACKMUR. "Edwin Muir: Between the Tiger's Paws," in *Four Poets on Poetry,* pp. 30-31.

"The Rider Victory"

RAYMOND TSCHUMI. *Thought in Twentieth-Century English Poetry,* pp. 92-93.

"The River"

RAYMOND TSCHUMI. *Thought in Twentieth-Century English Poetry,* pp. 102-3.

"The Road"

FREDERICK GARBER. "Edwin Muir's Heraldic Mode," *Twentieth Century Literature* 12(2), July 1966, 100-1.

"Scotland 1941"

RAYMOND TSCHUMI. *Thought in Twentieth-Century English Poetry,* pp. 88-89.

"Song of Patience"

RAYMOND TSCHUMI. *Thought in Twentieth-Century English Poetry,* p. 102.

"Sorrow"

SISTER M. JOSELYN. "Herbert and Muir: Pilgrims of Their Age," *Renascence* 15(3), Spring 1963, 129-30.

"Thought and Image"

RAYMOND TSCHUMI. *Thought in Twentieth-Century English Poetry,* p. 97.

"The Three Mirrors"

RAYMOND TSCHUMI. *Thought in Twentieth-Century English Poetry,* pp. 115-18.

"T. J. F. H."

RAYMOND TSCHUMI. *Thought in Twentieth-Century English Poetry,* pp. 98-100.

"The Toy Horse"

K. L. GOODWIN. *Explicator* 23(1), September 1964, Item 6.

T. S. K. SCOTT-CRAIG. *Explicator* 24(7), March 1966, Item 62.

"The Transfiguration"

BRIAN KEEBLE. "In Time's Despite: On the Poetry of Edwin Muir," *Sewanee Review* 81(3), Summer 1973, 646-50.

RALPH J. MILLS, JR. "Eden's Gate: The Later Poetry of Edwin Muir," *Personalist* 44(1), Winter 1963, 61-63.

ANNE RIDLER. "Muir: The Transfiguration," in *Master Poems of the English Language,* pp. 931-34.

"Troy"

EDWIN MORGAN. "Edwin Muir," in *The Modern Poet,* edited by Ian Hamilton, p. 46.

"Twice-Done, Once-Done"

SISTER M. JOSELYN. "Herbert and Muir: Pilgrims of Their Age," *Renascence* 15(3), Spring 1963, 130-31.

RAYMOND TSCHUMI. *Thought in Twentieth-Century English Poetry,* pp. 111-13.

"Variations on a Time Theme"

see also "Who curbed the lion long ago?"

RALPH J. MILLS, JR. "Edwin Muir: A Speech from Darkness Grown," *Accent* 19(1), Winter 1959, 54-56.

RAYMOND TSCHUMI. *Thought in Twentieth-Century English Poetry,* pp. 32-34.

J. R. WATSON. "Edwin Muir and the Problem of Evil," *Critical Quarterly* 6(3), Autumn 1964, 234-37.

"The Voyage"

RALPH J. MILLS, JR. "Edwin Muir: A Speech from Darkness Grown," *Accent* 19(1), Winter 1959, 62-64.

RAYMOND TSCHUMI. *Thought in Twentieth-Century English Poetry,* pp. 104-5.

"The Way"

SISTER M. JOSELYN. "Herbert and Muir: Pilgrims of Their Age," *Renascence* 15(3), Spring 1963, 131.

"The Wayside Station"

RAYMOND TSCHUMI. *Thought in Twentieth-Century English Poetry,* pp. 93-94.

"The Wheel"

RAYMOND TSCHUMI. *Thought in Twentieth-Century English Poetry,* pp. 109-11.

"Who curbed the lion long ago?"

see also "Variations on a Time Theme"

FREDERICK GARBER. "Edwin Muir's Heraldic Mode," *Twentieth Century Literature* 12(2), July 1966, 96-97.

"The Window"

KIMON FRIAR. "The Circular Route," *Poetry* 84(1), April 1954, 28.

RAYMOND TSCHUMI. *Thought in Twentieth-Century English Poetry,* pp. 114-15.

MUNDAY, ANTHONY

"I serve a Mistres whiter than the snowe"

JEROME BEATY and WILLIAM H. MATCHETT. *Poetry From Statement to Meaning,* pp. 199-200.

MUNRO, ROBIN

"Ancestors"

EDWARD BRUNNER. "Uncomely Relations," *Iowa Review* 6(3-4), Summer-Fall 1975, 242-43.

MURPHY, RICHARD

"The Poet on the Island"

DONALD T. TORCHIANA. "Contemporary Irish Poetry," *Chicago Review* 17(2-3), 1964, 155-56.

MYERS, JACK

"The Family War"

JAMES WELCH. "TNT," *Iowa Review* 4(4), Fall 1973, 82-83.

N

NABOKOV, VLADIMIR

"Pale Fire"

    PHYLLIS A. ROTH. "The Psychology of the Double in Nabokov's *Pale Fire*," *Essays in Literature* 2(2), Fall 1975, 209-29.

NASH, OGDEN

"Literary Reflection"

    WARREN BECK. "Boundaries of Poetry," *College English* 4(7), March 1943, 347.

"Portrait of the Artist as a Prematurely Old Man"

    LAURENCE PERRINE. *100 American Poems of the Twentieth Century*, pp. 186-88.

"The Turtle"

    LAURENCE PERRINE. *Sound and Sense*, pp. 135-36; second ed., pp. 148-49; third ed., pp. 178-79; fourth ed., pp. 167-68.

NASHE, THOMAS

"Adieu, Farewell, Earth's Bliss"

    JUDITH LITTLE. *Explicator* 30(3), November 1971, Item 19.

    WESLEY TRIMPI. "The Practice of Historical Interpretation and Nashe's 'Brightnesse Falls From the Ayre,' " *Journal of English and Germanic Philology* 66(4), October 1967, 501-18.

"Choise of Valentines"

    DAVID O. FRANTZ. " 'Leud Priapians' and Renaissance Pornography," *Studies in English Literature 1500-1900* 12(1), Winter 1972, 168-70.

"Spring"

    JEROME BEATY and WILLIAM H. MATCHETT. *Poetry From Statement to Meaning*, pp. 195-96.

    BARBARA HARDY. *The Advantage of Lyric*, pp. 10-11.

"Summer's Last Will and Testament"

    WILLIAM EMPSON. *Seven Types of Ambiguity*, pp. 32-35, 145-47; second and third eds., pp. 25-27, 115-16.

NEIHARDT, JOHN G.

"The Song of the Indian Wars"

    JOHN T. FLANAGAN. "John G. Neihardt, Chronicler of the West," *Arizona Quarterly* 21(1), Spring 1965, 13-14.

"The Song of the Messiah"

    JOHN T. FLANAGAN. "John G. Neihardt, Chronicler of the West," *Arizona Quarterly* 21(1), Spring 1965, 13.

NEMEROV, HOWARD

"The Beekeeper Speaks . . . And Is Silent"

    ROBERT BOYERS. *Excursions*, pp. 223-26.

"Beginner's Guide"

    ROBERT BOYERS. *Excursions*, pp. 240-41.

"The Blue Swallows"

    ROBERT BOYERS. *Excursions*, pp. 229-31.

    JOYCE CAROL OATES. "The Death Throes of Romanticism: The Poems of Sylvia Plath," in *Contemporary Poetry in America*, pp. 149-50.

    RAYMOND SMITH. "Nemerov and Nature: 'The Stillness In Moving Things,' " *Southern Review*, n.s., 10(1), Winter 1974, 168-69.

"Brainstorm"

    ROBERT D. HARVEY. "A Prophet Armed: An Introduction to the Poetry of Howard Nemerov," in *Poets in Progress*, pp. 129-30.

    JAMES M. KIEHL. "The Poems of Howard Nemerov: Where Loveliness Adorns Intelligible Things," *Salmagundi* 22-23 (Spring-Summer 1973), 236. Reprinted in: *Contemporary Poetry in America*, p. 281.

"The Breaking of Rainbows"

    ROBERT BOYERS. *Excursions*, pp. 233-34.

"The Cherry Tree"

    JAMES M. KIEHL. "The Poems of Howard Nemerov: Where Loveliness Adorns Intelligible Things," *Salmagundi* 22-23 (Spring-Summer 1973), 255-56. Reprinted in: *Contemporary Poetry in America*, pp. 300-1.

"A Day on the Big Branch"

    PETER MEINKE. "Howard Nemerov," in *Seven American Poets from MacLeish to Nemerov*, pp. 265-66.

    M. L. ROSENTHAL. *The Modern Poets*, pp. 259-60.

"Deep Woods"

    ROBERT BOYERS. *Excursions*, pp. 236-39.

    PETER MEINKE. "Howard Nemerov," in *Seven American Poets from MacLeish to Nemerov*, pp. 263-64.

"History of a Literary Movement"

    JAMES M. KIEHL. "The Poems of Howard Nemerov: Where Loveliness Adorns Intelligible Things," *Salmagundi* 22-23 (Spring-Summer 1973), 252. Reprinted in: *Contemporary Poetry in America*, p. 297.

NEMEROV, HOWARD *(Cont.)*

"Holding the Mirror up to Nature"
> PETER MEINKE. "Howard Nemerov," in *Seven American Poets from MacLeish to Nemerov*, pp. 266-67.

"The Human Condition"
> RAYMOND SMITH. "Nemerov and Nature: 'The Stillness In Moving Things,'" *Southern Review* n.s., 10(1), Winter 1974, 161.

"I Only Am Escaped Alone to Tell Thee"
> PETER MEINKE. "Howard Nemerov," in *Seven American Poets from MacLeish to Nemerov*, pp. 261-62.

"The Junction, on a Warm Afternoon"
> JAMES M. KIEHL. "The Poems of Howard Nemerov: Where Loveliness Adorns Intelligible Things," *Salmagundi* 22-23 (Spring-Summer 1973), 248. Reprinted in: *Contemporary Poetry in America*, p. 293.

"Landscape with Figures"
> JAMES M. KIEHL. "The Poems of Howard Nemerov: Where Loveliness Adorns Intelligible Things," *Salmagundi* 22-23 (Spring-Summer 1973), 252-53. Reprinted in: *Contemporary Poetry in America*, p. 297-98.

"Lines and Circularities"
> JAMES K. ROBINSON. "Sailing Close-hauled and Diving into the Wreck: From Nemerov to Rich," *Southern Review*, n.s., 11(3), Summer 1975, 670-71.

"Lore"
> M. L. ROSENTHAL. *The Modern Poets*, p. 259.

"Mrs. Mandrill"
> PETER MEINKE. "Howard Nemerov," in *Seven American Poets from MacLeish to Nemerov*, p. 270.

"The Mud Turtle"
> ROBERT BOYERS. *Excursions*, pp. 227-29.

"One Forever Alien"
> JAMES M. KIEHL. "The Poems of Howard Nemerov: Where Loveliness Adorns Intelligible Things," *Salmagundi* 22-23 (Spring-Summer 1973), 250-51. Reprinted in: *Contemporary Poetry in America*, p. 295-96.

"Painting a Mountain Stream"
> RAYMOND SMITH. "Nemerov and Nature: 'The Stillness in Moving Things,'" *Southern Review*, n.s., 10(1), Winter 1974, 155-58.

"Polonius Passing Through a Stage"
> HOWARD NEMEROV. *Reflexions on Poetry and Poetics*, pp. 153-58.

"Redeployment"
> ROBERT D. HARVEY. "A Prophet Armed: An Introduction to the Poetry of Howard Nemerov," in *Poets in Progress*, pp. 117-19.
> JAMES M. KIEHL. "The Poems of Howard Nemerov: Where Loveliness Adorns Intelligible Things," *Salmagundi* 22-23 (Spring-Summer 1973), 251-52. Reprinted in: *Contemporary Poetry in America*, p. 296-97.

"The Rope's End"
> JAMES M. KIEHL. "The Poems of Howard Nemerov: Where Loveliness Adorns Intelligible Things," *Salmagundi* 22-23 (Spring-Summer 1973), 256. Reprinted in: *Contemporary Poetry in America*, p. 301.

"Runes"
> RAYMOND BENOIT. *Single Nature's Double Name*, pp. 136-38.

> PETER MEINKE. "Howard Nemerov," in *Seven American Poets from MacLeish to Nemerov*, pp. 267-69.
> RAYMOND SMITH. "Nemerov and Nature: 'The Stillness In Moving Things,'" *Southern Review*, n.s., 10(1), Winter 1974, 163-68.

"The Salt Garden"
> ROBERT D. HARVEY. "A Prophet Armed: An Introduction to the Poetry of Howard Nemerov," in *Poets in Progress*, pp. 120-22.
> PETER MEINKE. "Howard Nemerov," in *Seven American Poets from MacLeish to Nemerov*, p. 260.

"The Sanctuary"
> RAYMOND SMITH. "Nemerov and Nature: 'The Stillness In Moving Things,'" *Southern Review*, n.s., 10(1), Winter 1974, 159-60.

"Santa Claus"
> LAURENCE PERRINE. *100 American Poems of the Twentieth Century*, pp. 252-53.

"The Scales of the Eyes"
> JAMES DICKEY. *Babel to Byzantium*, pp. 37-38.
> PETER MEINKE. "Howard Nemerov," in *Seven American Poets from MacLeish to Nemerov*, pp. 260-61.

"September, the First Day of School"
> ROBERT BOYERS. *Excursions*, pp. 234-35.

"Shells"
> ROBERT BOYERS. *Excursions*, p. 236.

"The Sweeper of Ways"
> HOWARD NEMEROV. *Reflexions on Poetry and Poetics*, pp. 159-63.

"Thirteenth Anniversary Report of the Class of '41"
> ROBERT BOYERS. *Excursions*, pp. 218-19.

"To Lu Chi"
> RAYMOND BENOIT. *Single Nature's Double Name*, pp. 133-35.

"The Town Dump"
> ROBERT D. HARVEY. "A Prophet Armed: An Introduction to the Poetry of Howard Nemerov," in *Poets in Progress*, pp. 122-25.
> M. L. ROSENTHAL. *The Modern Poets*, p. 260.

"Trees"
> RAYMOND BENOIT. *Single Nature's Double Name*, pp. 135-36.

"Unscientific Postscript"
> JOSEPH WARREN BEACH. *Obsessive Images*, p. 102.

"Vermeer"
> PETER MEINKE. "Howard Nemerov," in *Seven American Poets from MacLeish to Nemerov*, p. 273.

"The View"
> RAYMOND SMITH. "Nemerov and Nature: 'The Stillness In Moving Things,'" *Southern Review*, n.s., 10(1), Winter 1974, 161-63.

"Writing"
> ROBERT BOYERS. *Excursions*, pp. 232-33.

NEWMAN, JOHN HENRY

"Lead, Kindly Light"
> see "The Pillar of the Cloud"

"The Pillar of the Cloud"
> PAULL F. BAUM. "The Road to Palermo," *South Atlantic Quarterly* 55(2), April 1956, 192-97.

CHARLES W. COOPER and JOHN HOLMES. *Preface to Poetry*, pp. 278-81.

NICCOLS, RICHARD

"A Winter Night's Vision"

ALAN T. BRADFORD. "Mirrors of Mutability: Winter Landscapes in Tudor Poetry," *English Literary Renaissance* 4(1), Winter 1974, 36-39.

NICHOLSON, NORMAN

"Across the Estuary"

K. MORGAN. "Some Christian Themes in the Poetry of Norman Nicholson," *Review of English Literature* 5(3), July 1964, 74-75.

"Cleator Moor"

BABETTE DEUTSCH. *Poetry in Our Time*, pp. 15-16; second ed., pp. 16-17.

PHILIP GARDNER. "The Provincial Poetry of Norman Nicholson," *University of Toronto Quarterly* 36(3), April 1967, 278.

"Egremont"

PHILIP GARDNER. "The Provincial Poetry of Norman Nicholson," *University of Toronto Quarterly* 36(3), April 1967, 277.

"The Evacuees"

PHILIP GARDNER. "The Provincial Poetry of Norman Nicholson," *University of Toronto Quarterly* 36(3), April 1967, 279-80.

"From Walney Island"

PHILIP GARDNER. "The Provincial Poetry of Norman Nicholson," *University of Toronto Quarterly* 36(3), April 1967, 287-88.

"Near Widnes"

PHILIP GARDNER. "The Provincial Poetry of Norman Nicholson," *University of Toronto Quarterly* 36(3), April 1967, 289.

"Old Main Street, Holborn Hill, Millom"

PHILIP GARDNER. "The Provincial Poetry of Norman Nicholson," *University of Toronto Quarterly* 36(3), April 1967, 289-90.

"The Pot Geranium"

PHILIP GARDNER. "The Provincial Poetry of Norman Nicholson," *University of Toronto Quarterly* 36(3), April 1967, 286.

"Rockferns"

GÉMINO H. ABAD. *A Formal Approach to Lyric Poetry*, p. 269.

"The Seven Rocks"

PHILIP GARDNER. "The Provincial Poetry of Norman Nicholson," *University of Toronto Quarterly* 36(3), April 1967, 290-91.

"Silecroft Shore"

PHILIP GARDNER. "The Provincial Poetry of Norman Nicholson," *University of Toronto Quarterly* 36(3), April 1967, 283-84.

"To the River Duddon"

PHILIP GARDNER. "The Provincial Poetry of Norman Nicholson," *University of Toronto Quarterly* 36(3), April 1967, 280-82.

"A Turn for the Better"

ROBIN SKELTON. *Poetry*, pp. 62-64.

NICHOLSON, SAMUEL

"Acolastus"

J. M. BEMROSE. "A Critical Examination of the Borrowings from *Venus and Adonis* and *Lucrece* in Samuel Nicholson's *Acolastus*," *Shakespeare Quarterly* 15(1), Winter 1964, 86-89.

NIMS, JOHN FREDERICK

"Love Poem"

LAURENCE PERRINE. *100 American Poems of the Twentieth Century*, pp. 233-35.

"Penny Arcade"

ROBERT SHELLEY. "A Palmtree of Steel," *Western Review* 15(2), Winter 1951, 141-42.

"Winter in the Park"

ROBERT SHELLEY. "A Palmtree of Steel," *Western Review* 15(2), Winter 1951, 140. (P)

NOLL, BINK

"Quaker Hero, Burning"

HARRY M. CAMPBELL. *Explicator* 29(9), May 1971, Item 75.

NORTON, CAROLINE

"A Voice from the Factories"

MICHAEL D. WHEELER. "The Writer as Reader in *Mary Barton*," *Durham University Journal*, n.s., 36(1), December 1974, 96.

NOYES, ALFRED

"For the Eightieth Birthday of George Meredith"

I. A. RICHARDS. *Practical Criticism*, pp. 119-29.

NYERGES, ANTON N.

"Ascents"

H. H. HALL. "Anton N. Nyerges: The Graceful Hunter," *Modern Poetry Studies* 1(5), 1970, 259-60.

"The Homonym"

H. H. HALL. "Anton N. Nyerges: The Graceful Hunter," *Modern Poetry Studies* 1(5), 1970, 261-62.

"Montage"

H. H. HALL. "Anton N. Nyerges: The Graceful Hunter," *Modern Poetry Studies* 1(5), 1970, 258.

"Outskirts"

H. H. HALL. "Anton N. Nyerges: The Graceful Hunter," *Modern Poetry Studies* 1(5), 1970, 264-65.

"The Smugglers"

H. H. HALL. "Anton N. Nyerges: The Graceful Hunter," *Modern Poetry Studies* 1(5), 1970, 257.

"The Touch"

H. H. HALL. "Anton N. Nyerges: The Graceful Hunter," *Modern Poetry Studies* 1(5), 1970, 260-61.

O

OAKES, URIAN

"An Elegie upon That Reverend, Learned, Eminently Pious and Singularly Accomplished Divine, My Ever Honoured Brother Mr. Thomas Shepard"

> T. G. HAHN. "Urian Oakes's *Elegie* on Thomas Shepard and Puritan Poetics," *American Literature* 45(2), May 1973, 163-81.

> ROY HARVEY PEARCE. *The Continuity of American Poetry*, pp. 26-28.

> WILLIAM J. SCHEICK. "Standing in the Gap: Urian Oakes's Elegy on Thomas Shepard," *Early American Literature* 9(3), Winter 1975, 301-6.

O'DONNELL, GEORGE MARION

"Return"

> JOHN CROWE RANSOM. "The Making of a Modern: The Poetry of George Marion O'Donnell," *Southern Review* 1(4), Spring 1936, 869-70.

O'GORMAN, NED

"Adjectives Toward the Description of a Crucifix"

> RICHARD KELLY. "In Praise of Beauty: Ned O'Gorman," *Renascence* 17(4), Summer 1965, 176-77.

"Beauty"

> RICHARD KELLY. "In Praise of Beauty: Ned O'Gorman," *Renascence* 17(4), Summer 1965, 173-75.

"A Description of the Sea for Lina Lenzi Who Has Never Seen It"

> RICHARD KELLY. "In Praise of Beauty: Ned O'Gorman," *Renascence* 17(4), Summer 1965, 175-76.

"A Rectification of the Lyric"

> RICHARD KELLY. "In Praise of Beauty: Ned O'Gorman," *Renascence* 17(4), Summer 1965, 177-78.

O'HARA, FRANK

"Adieu to Norman, Bon Jour To Joan and Jean-Paul"

> CHARLES ALTIERI. "The Significance of Frank O'Hara," *Iowa Review* 4(1), Winter 1973, 96-98.

"The Day Lady Died"

> CHARLES ALTIERI. "The Significance of Frank O'Hara," *Iowa Review* 4(1), Winter 1973, 102-4.

> PAUL CARROLL. *The Poem in Its Skin*, pp. 157-64.

> RALPH J. MILLS, JR. *Creation's Very Self*, pp. 16-17. Reprinted in: Ralph J. Mills, Jr. *Cry of the Human*, pp. 17-18.

> ROBERT PINSKY. *The Situation of Poetry*, pp. 102-3.

> LOUIS UNTERMEYER. "The Law of Order, The Promise of Poetry," *Saturday Review* 54(12), 20 March 1971, 19-20.

"Early on Sunday"

> MARJORIE G. PERLOFF. "New Thresholds, Old Anatomies: Contemporary Poetry and the Limits of Exegesis," *Iowa Review* 5(1), Winter 1974, 98-99.

"Easter"

> ANTHONY LIBBY. "O'Hara on the Silver Range," *Contemporary Literature* 17(2), Spring 1976, 249-50.

"Essay on Style"

> MARJORIE G. PERLOFF. "New Thresholds, Old Anatomies: Contemporary Poetry and the Limits of Exegesis," *Iowa Review* 5(1), Winter 1974, 91-95.

"Fantasy"

> CHARLES ALTIERI. "The Significance of Frank O'Hara," *Iowa Review* 4(1), Winter 1973, 91-92.

"The Hunter"

> ANTHONY LIBBY. "O'Hara on the Silver Range," *Contemporary Literature* 17(2), Spring 1976, 248-49.

"In Memory of My Feelings"

> MICHAEL DAVIDSON. "Languages of Post-Modernism," *Chicago Review* 27(1), Summer 1975, 13-15.

> ANTHONY LIBBY. "O'Hara on the Silver Range," *Contemporary Literature* 17(2), Spring 1976, 259.

"Music"

> MARJORIE PERLOFF. "Frank O'Hara and the Aesthetics of Attention," *Boundary 2* 4(3), Spring 1976, 782-86.

"Poem" ("At night Chinamen jump")

> ANTHONY LIBBY. "O'Hara on the Silver Range," *Contemporary Literature* 17(2), Spring 1976, 254-55.

"Poem" ("The eager note on my door said 'Call me' ")

> ROBERT PINSKY. *The Situation of Poetry*, pp. 99-101.

"2 Poems from the Ohara Monogatari," #2

> CHARLES ALTIERI. "The Significance of Frank O'Hara," *Iowa Review* 4(1), Winter 1973, 100.

OLDHAM, JOHN

"Garnet's Ghost Addressing to the Jesuits" (*Satyrs Upon the Jesuits,* I)

> COOPER R. MACKIN. "The Satiric Technique of John Oldham's *Satyrs Upon the Jesuits*," *Studies in Philology* 62(1), January 1965, 79-85.

"Sardanapalus"

JOHN H. O'NEILL. "Oldham's 'Sardanapalus': A Restoration Mock-Encomium and its Topical Implications," *Clio* 5(2), Winter 1976, 193-210.

"Satyr Addressed to a Friend"

EARL MINER. *The Restoration Mode from Milton to Dryden*, pp. 429-30.

"Satyr II" (*Satyrs Upon the Jesuits*)

COOPER R. MACKIN. "The Satiric Technique of John Oldham's *Satyrs Upon the Jesuits*," *Studies in Philology* 62(1), January 1965, 85-89.

OLSON, CHARLES

"Anecdotes of the Late War"

ROBERT J. BERTHOLF. "Righting the Balance: Olson's *The Distances*," *Boundary 2* 2(1-2), Fall 1973-Winter 1974, 240-41.

"April Today Main Street" (*Maximus Poems*)

FRANK DAVEY. "Six Readings of Olson's *Maximus*," *Boundary 2* 2(1-2), Fall 1973-Winter 1974, 307-8.

SHERMAN PAUL. "In and About the Maximus Poems," *Iowa Review* 6(3-4), Summer-Fall 1975, 94-95.

"As the Dead Prey Upon Us"

ROBERT J. BERTHOLF. "Righting the Balance: Olson's *The Distances*," *Boundary 2* 2(1-2), Fall 1973-Winter 1974, 244-45.

"Capt. Christopher Levett (of York)"

J. B. PHILIP. "Charles Olson Reconsidered," *Journal of American Studies* 5(3), December 1971, 295-96.

"The Death of Europe"

ROBERT J. BERTHOLF. "Righting the Balance: Olson's *The Distances*," *Boundary 2* 2(1-2), Fall 1973-Winter 1974, 242-43.

PHILIP E. SMITH II. "Descent into Polis: Charles Olson's Search for Community," *Modern Poetry Studies* 8(1), Spring 1977, 17-21.

"Fact 2"

MARTIN L. POPS. "Melville: To Him, Olson," *Boundary 2* 2(1-2), Fall 1973-Winter 1974, 59-60.

"Gloucester can view/those men"

SHERMAN PAUL. "In and About the Maximus Poems," *Iowa Review* 6(3-4), Summer-Fall 1975, 84-85.

"Gravel Hill"

JOHN SCOGGAN. " 'Gravel Hill,' " *Boundary 2* 2(1-2), Fall 1973-Winter 1974, 333-39.

"History is the Memory of Time"

ROBERT VON HALLBERG. "Olson's Relation to Pound and Williams," *Contemporary Literature* 15(1), Winter 1974, 26-28.

"I, Mencius, Pupil of the Master"

ROBERT J. BERTHOLF. "Righting the Balance: Olson's *The Distances*," *Boundary 2* 2(1-2), Fall 1973-Winter 1974, 241-42.

"In Cold Hell, In Thicket"

ROBERT J. BERTHOLF. "Righting the Balance: Olson's *The Distances*," *Boundary 2* 2(1-2), Fall 1973-Winter 1974, 234-36.

"The Kingfishers"

ROBERT J. BERTHOLF. "Righting the Balance: Olson's *The Distances*," *Boundary 2* 2(1-2), Fall 1973-Winter 1974, 230-31.

GUY DAVENPORT. "Scholia and Conjectures for Olson's 'The Kingfishers,' " *Boundary 2* 2(1-2), Fall 1973-Winter 1974, 250-62.

THOMAS F. MERRILL. " 'The Kingfishers': Charles Olson's 'Marvelous Maneuver,' " *Contemporary Literature* 17(4), Autumn 1976, 506-28.

"Letter 1" (*Maximus Poems*)

FRANK DAVEY. "Six Readings of Olson's *Maximus*," *Boundary 2* 2(1-2), Fall 1973-Winter 1974, 297-99.

"Letter 5" (*Maximus Poems*)

FRANK DAVEY. "Six Readings of Olson's *Maximus*," *Boundary 2* 2(1-2), Fall 1973-Winter 1974, 313-14.

"Letter 7" (*Maximus Poems*)

SAMUEL CHARTERS. *Some Poems/Poets*, pp. 27-35.

"Letter 9" (*Maximus Poems*)

SHERMAN PAUL. "In and About the Maximus Poems," *Iowa Review* 6(1), Winter 1975, 128-29.

"Letter 10" (*Maximus Poems*)

SHERMAN PAUL. "In and About the Maximus Poems," *Iowa Review* 6(1), Winter 1975, 129-30.

"Letter 11" (*Maximus Poems*)

SHERMAN PAUL. "In and About the Maximus Poems," *Iowa Review* 6(3-4), Summer-Fall 1975, 75-77.

"Letter 12" (*Maximus Poems*)

SHERMAN PAUL. "In and About the Maximus Poems," *Iowa Review* 6(3-4), Summer-Fall 1975, 77-78.

"Letter 13" (*Maximus Poems*)

SHERMAN PAUL. "In and About the Maximus Poems," *Iowa Review* 6(3-4), Summer-Fall 1975, 78.

"Letter 18" (*Maximus Poems*)

see "The Twist"

"Letter 19 (A Pastoral Letter)" (*Maximus Poems*)

CATHERINE R. STIMPSON. "Charles Olson: Preliminary Images," *Boundary 2* 2(1-2), Fall 1973-Winter 1974, 166-67.

"Letter 20: not a pastoral letter" (*Maximus Poems*)

ROBERT VON HALLBERG. "Olson's Relation to Pound and Williams," *Contemporary Literature* 15(1), Winter 1974, 33-34.

"Letter 24" (*Maximus Poems*)

see "A Plantation, a beginning"

"Letter 25" (*Maximus Poems*)

SHERMAN PAUL. "In and About the Maximus Poems," *Iowa Review* 6(3-4), Summer-Fall 1975, 83-84.

"Letter 30" (*Maximus Poems*)

SHERMAN PAUL. "In and About the Maximus Poems," *Iowa Review* 6(3-4), Summer-Fall 1975, 86-87.

"Letter 35" (*Maximus Poems*)

SHERMAN PAUL. "In and About the Maximus Poems," *Iowa Review* 6(3-4), Summer-Fall 1975, 89-91.

"Letter 36" (*Maximus Poems*)

see "Maximus, to Gloucester, Sunday, July 19"

"Letter for Melville 1951"

ROBERT J. BERTHOLF. "Righting the Balance: Olson's *The Distances*," *Boundary 2* 2(1-2), Fall 1973-Winter 1974, 240.

"The Librarian"

ROBERT J. BERTHOLF. "Righting the Balance: Olson's *The Distances*," *Boundary 2* 2(1-2), Fall 1973-Winter 1974, 247.

OLSON, CHARLES *(Cont.)*

"The Librarian" *(cont.)*

ANN CHARTERS. "I, Maximus: Charles Olson as Mythologist," *Modern Poetry Studies* 2(2), 1971, 56-57.

"Maximus from Dogtown 1" *(Maximus Poems)*

FRANK DAVEY. "Six Readings of Olson's *Maximus*," *Boundary 2* 2(1-2), Fall 1973-Winter 1974, 315-20.

"Maximus letter # whatever" *(Maximus Poems)*

CORY R. GREENSPAN. "Charles Olson: Language, Time and Person," *Boundary 2* 2(1-2), Fall 1973-Winter 1974, 351-53.

"Maximus to Gloucester, Letter 27"

J. B. PHILIP. "Charles Olson Reconsidered," *Journal of American Studies* 5(3), December 1971, 298-302.

"Maximus, to Gloucester, Sunday, July 19"

SHERMAN PAUL. "In and About the Maximus Poems," *Iowa Review* 6(3-4), Summer-Fall 1975, 91-94.

"Maximus to Himself" *(Maximus Poems)*

ANN CHARTERS. "I, Maximus: Charles Olson as Mythologist," *Modern Poetry Studies* 2(2), 1971, 59.

CORY R. GREENSPAN. "Charles Olson: Language, Time and Person," *Boundary 2* 2(1-2), Fall 1973-Winter 1974, 340-43.

"The Moon is the Number 18"

ROBERT J. BERTHOLF. "Righting the Balance: Olson's *The Distances*," *Boundary 2* 2(1-2), Fall 1973-Winter 1974, 236-37.

RICHARD G. INGBER. "Number, Image, Sortilege: A Short Analysis of 'The Moon is the Number 18,' " *Boundary 2* 2(1-2), Fall 1973-Winter 1974, 269-72.

"Moonset, Gloucester, December 1, 1957, 1:58 AM"

ROBERT J. BERTHOLF. "Righting the Balance: Olson's *The Distances*," *Boundary 2* 2(1-2), Fall 1973-Winter 1974, 247-48.

"On First Looking Out through Juan de la Cosa's Eyes"

STEVE BALLEW. "History as Animated Metaphor in the *Maximus Poems*," *New England Quarterly* 47(1), March 1974, 61-62.

DANIEL G. HISE. "Noticing Juan De La Cosa," *Boundary 2* 2(1-2), Fall 1973-Winter 1974, 323-32.

ROSEMARIE WALDROP. "Charles Olson: Process and Relationship," *Twentieth Century Literature* 23(4), December 1977, 477.

"A Plantation, a beginning"

DON BYRD. "The Possibility of Measure in Olson's *Maximus*," *Boundary 2* 2(1-2), Fall 1973-Winter 1974, 51-52.

SHERMAN PAUL. "In and About the Maximus Poems," *Iowa Review* 6(3-4), Summer-Fall 1975, 83.

"The Praises"

MAXINE ASPEL. " 'The Praises,' " *Boundary 2* 2(1-2), Fall 1973-Winter 1974, 263-68.

"The Record" *(Maximus Poems)*

CORY R. GREENSPAN. "Charles Olson: Language, Time and Person," *Boundary 2* 2(1-2), Fall 1973-Winter 1974, 345.

"The Song of Ullikummi"

ROSEMARIE WALDROP. "Charles Olson: Process and Relationship," *Twentieth Century Literature* 23(4), December 1977, 477.

"Stiffening in the Master Founders' Wills"

ROBERT VON HALLBERG. "Olson, Whitehead, and the Objectivists," *Boundary 2* 2(1-21), Fall 1973-Winter 1974, 96-97.

"To Gerhardt, There Among Europe's Things of Which He Has Written Us in His 'Brief an Creeley und Olson' "

ROBERT J. BERTHOLF. "Righting the Balance: Olson's *The Distances*," *Boundary 2* 2(1-2), Fall 1973-Winter 1974, 238-39.

PHILIP E. SMITH II. "Descent Into Polis: Charles Olson's Search for Community," *Modern Poetry Studies* 8(1), Spring 1977, 13-17.

"The Twist"

SHERMAN PAUL. "In and About the Maximus Poems," *Iowa Review* 6(3-4), Summer-Fall 1975, 79-80.

"Tyrian Business"

L. S. DEMBO. "Olson's *Maximus* and the Way to Knowledge," *Boundary 2* 2(1-2), Fall 1973-Winter 1974, 283-89.

SHERMAN PAUL. "In and About the Maximus Poems," *Iowa Review* 6(1), Winter 1975, 127-28.

ROSEMARIE WALDROP. "Charles Olson: Process and Relationship," *Twentieth Century Literature* 23(4), December 1977, 483-84.

"Variations Done for Gerald Van de Wiele"

CHARLES ALTIERI. "Olson's Poetics and the Tradition," *Boundary 2* 2(1-2), Fall 1973-Winter 1974, 183-88.

ROBERT J. BERTHOLF. "Righting the Balance: Olson's *The Distances*," *Boundary 2* 2(1-2), Fall 1973-Winter 1974, 245-46.

OLSON, LAWRENCE

"Great Abaco"

MACHA ROSENTHAL. "Sailing for Great Abaco," *Poetry* 72(1), April 1948, 52-53.

OPPEN, GEORGE

"Giovanni's *Rape of the Sabine Women* at Wildenstein's"

L. S. DEMBO. "The Existential World of George Oppen," *Iowa Review* 3(1), Winter 1972, 83-85.

"Image of the Engine"

L. S. DEMBO. "The Existential World of George Oppen," *Iowa Review* 3(1), Winter 1972, 77-79.

"Myself I Sing"

L. S. DEMBO. "The Existential World of George Oppen," *Iowa Review* 3(1), Winter 1972, 73-74.

"Of What, Maud Blessingbourne it was"

L. S. DEMBO. "The Existential World of George Oppen," *Iowa Review* 3(1), Winter 1972, 70.

"Party on Shipboard"

L. S. DEMBO. "The Existential World of George Oppen," *Iowa Review* 3(1), Winter 1972, 68-69.

"Return"

L. S. DEMBO. "The Existential World of George Oppen," *Iowa Review* 3(1), Winter 1972, 71-73.

"Route"

L. S. DEMBO. "The Existential World of George Oppen," *Iowa Review* 3(1), Winter 1972, 88-90.

"Town, a Town"

L. S. DEMBO. "The Existential World of George Oppen," *Iowa Review* 3(1), Winter 1972, 69.

"Vulcan"

L. S. DEMBO. "The Existential World of George Oppen," *Iowa Review* 3(1), Winter 1972, 76-77.

O'REILLY, JOHN BOYLE

"A White Rose"

LAURENCE PERRINE. *Sound and Sense*, p. 65; second ed., p. 71; third ed., pp. 85-86; fourth ed., pp. 80-81.

LAURENCE PERRINE. "The Untranslatable Language," *English Journal* 60(1), January 1971, 60.

ORR, GREGORY

"Poem" ("Before he passes")

LOUISE GLÜCK. "On Gregory Orr's Poems," *Iowa Review* 4(4), Fall 1973, 87.

"Some Things"

GREGORY ORR. "Gregory Orr's Response," *Iowa Review* 4(4), Fall 1973, 88-89.

O'SULLIVAN, SEUMAS

"Birds"

DAVID RIDGLEY CLARK. *Lyric Resonance*, pp. 79-82.

"Nelson Street"

DAVID RIDGLEY CLARK. *Lyric Resonance*, pp. 77-79.

"The Sheep"

DAVID RIDGLEY CLARK. *Lyric Resonance*, pp. 82-84.

OWEN, WILFRED

"Anthem for Doomed Youth"

EDWARD A. BLOOM, CHARLES H. PHILBRICK, and ELMER M. BLISTEIN. *The Order of Poetry*, pp. 134-38.

CHRISTOPHER GILLIE. *Movements in English Literature*, pp. 71-72.

SAMUEL J. HAZO. "The Passion of Wilfred Owen," *Renascence* 11(4), Summer 1959, 205-6.

HORACE G. POSEY, JR. "Muted Satire in 'Anthem for Doomed Youth,'" *Essays in Criticism* 21(4), October 1971, 377-81.

JON SILKIN. *Out of Battle*, pp. 210-11.

"Apologia pro Poemate Meo"

ROSEMARY FREEMAN. "Parody as a Literary Form: George Herbert and Wilfred Owen," *Essays in Criticism* 13(4), October 1963, 316-17.

TIMOTHY O'KEEFFE. "Ironic Allusion in the Poetry of Wilfred Owen," *Ariel* 3(4), October 1972, 75.

"Arms and the Boy"

JOHN CLARK PRATT. *The Meaning of Modern Poetry*, 28-29, 37, 31.

"Asleep"

JON SILKIN. *Out of Battle*, pp. 211-13.

"At a Calvary near the Ancre"

TIMOTHY O'KEEFFE. "Ironic Allusion in the Poetry of Wilfred Owen," *Ariel* 3(4), October 1972, 79.

JON SILKIN. *Out of Battle*, pp. 231-33.

"Le Christianisme"

JON SILKIN. *Out of Battle*, pp. 231-33.

"The Dead-Beat"

JON SILKIN. *Out of Battle*, pp. 221-23.

"Disabled"

EDMUND FARRELL. "Owen's 'Disabled': A Remembrance of Things Present," *English Journal* 51(7), October 1962, 495-97.

JON SILKIN. *Out of Battle*, pp. 226-27.

"Dulce et Decorum Est"

CLEANTH BROOKS and ROBERT PENN WARREN. *Understanding Poetry*, fourth ed., p. 129.

HARRY BROWN and JOHN MILSTEAD. *What the Poem Means*, p. 157.

SAMUEL J. HAZO. "The Passion of Wilfred Owen," *Renascence* 11(4), Summer 1959, 202.

TIMOTHY O'KEEFFE. "Ironic Allusion in the Poetry of Wilfred Owen," *Ariel* 3(4), October 1972, 73-74.

JON SILKIN. *Out of Battle*, pp. 220-21.

JON STALLWORTHY. "W. B. Yeats and Wilfred Owen," *Critical Quarterly* 11(3), Autumn 1969, 207-9.

"Exposure"

JON SILKIN. *Out of Battle*, pp. 202-6.

"Fragment: Cramped in that Funnelled Hole"

JENNIFER BREEN. "Wilfred Owen: 'Greater Love' and Late Romanticism," *English Literature in Transition* 17(3), 1974, 181.

"Futility"

T. R. BARNES. *English Verse*, p. 276.

BERNARD BERGONZI. *Heroes' Twilight*, pp. 129-30.

C. B. COX and A. E. DYSON. *Modern Poetry*, pp. 52-56.

JON SILKIN. *Out of Battle*, pp. 217-19.

"Greater Love"

BERNARD BERGONZI. *Heroes' Twilight*, p. 130.

ROLAND BARTEL. "Teaching Wilfred Owen's War Poems and the Bible," *English Journal* 61(1), January 1972, 39-40.

JENNIFER BREEN. "Wilfred Owen: 'Greater Love' and Late Romanticism," *English Literature in Transition* 17(3), 1974, 177-81.

HARRY BROWN and JOHN MILSTEAD. *What the Poem Means*, pp. 157-58.

CHARLES CAUSLEY. "Owen: Greater Love," in *Master Poems of the English Language*, pp. 998-1001.

JOSEPH COHEN. "Owen Agonistes," *English Literature in Transition* 8(5), 1965, 264-65.

ROSEMARY FREEMAN. "Parody as a Literary Form: George Herbert and Wilfred Owen," *Essays in Criticism* 13(4), October 1963, 318-22.

SAMUEL J. HAZO. "The Passion of Wilfred Owen," *Renascence* 11(4), Summer 1959, 204-5.

JAMES J. HILL, JR. "Wilfred Owen's 'Greater Love,'" *Essays in Criticism* 15(4), October 1965, 476-77.

TIMOTHY O'KEEFFE. "Ironic Allusion in the Poetry of Wilfred Owen," *Ariel* 3(4), October 1972, 78.

JON SILKIN. *Out of Battle*, pp. 234-36.

"Happiness"

JOSEPH COHEN. "Owen Agonistes," *English Literature in Transition* 8(5), 1965, 260-61.

"Hospital Barge at Cérisy"

T. R. BARNES. *English Verse*, p. 277.

"Insensibility"

M. L. ROSENTHAL. *Poetry and the Common Life*, pp. 90-92.

JON SILKIN. *Out of Battle*, pp. 244-45.

OWEN, WILFRED *(Cont.)*

"Inspection"

TIMOTHY O'KEEFFE. "Ironic Allusion in the Poetry of Wilfred Owen," *Ariel* 3(4), October 1972, 76.

"Miners"

JENNIFER BREEN. "The Dating and Sources of Wilfred Owen's 'Miners,'" *Notes & Queries,* n.s., 21(10), October 1974, 366-70.

JON SILKIN. *Out of Battle,* pp. 216-17.

"The Parable of the Old Man and the Young"

ROLAND BARTEL. "Teaching Wilfred Owen's War Poems and the Bible," *English Journal* 61(1), January 1972, 36-39.

ROSEMARY FREEMAN. "Parody as a Literary Form: George Herbert and Wilfred Owen," *Essays in Criticism* 13(4), October 1963, 315-16.

TIMOTHY O'KEEFFE. "Ironic Allusion in the Poetry of Wilfred Owen," *Ariel* 3(4), October 1972, 79-80.

JON SILKIN. *Out of Battle,* p. 230.

"The Show"

JOSEPH COHEN. *Explicator* 16(2), November 1957, Item 8.

BABETTE DEUTSCH. *Poetry in Our Time,* pp. 349-51; second ed., pp. 390-92.

JON SILKIN. *Out of Battle,* pp. 213-15.

JON STALLWORTHY. "W. B. Yeats and Wilfred Owen," *Critical Quarterly* 11(3), Autumn 1969, 203.

"Smile, Smile, Smile"

TIMOTHY O'KEEFFE. "Ironic Allusion in the Poetry of Wilfred Owen," *Ariel* 3(4), October 1972, 80.

JON SILKIN. *Out of Battle,* pp. 228-29.

"Soldier's Dream"

JOSEPH COHEN. "Owen Agonistes," *English Literature in Transition* 8(5), 1965, 260.

TIMOTHY O'KEEFFE. "Ironic Allusion in the Poetry of Wilfred Owen," *Ariel* 3(4), October 1972, 76-77.

"Spring Offensive"

DOMINIC HIBBERD. "Images of Darkness in the Poems of Wilfred Owen," *Durham University Journal,* n.s., 35(2), March 1974, 162.

JON SILKIN. *Out of Battle,* pp. 215-16.

"Strange Meeting"

ROLAND BARTEL. "Teaching Wilfred Owen's War Poems and the Bible," *English Journal* 61(1), January 1972, 41-42.

BERNARD BERGONZI. *Heroes' Twilight,* pp. 132-34.

ELLIOTT B. GOSE, JR. "Digging In: An Interpretation of Wilfred Owen's 'Strange Meeting,'" *College English* 22(6), March 1961, 417-19.

SAMUEL J. HAZO. "The Passion of Wilfred Owen," *Renascence* 11(4), Summer 1959, 206-8.

TIMOTHY O'KEEFFE. "Ironic Allusion in the Poetry of Wilfred Owen," *Ariel* 3(4), October 1972, 74-75.

M. L. ROSENTHAL and A. J. M. SMITH. *Exploring Poetry,* pp. 546-47; second ed., pp. 352-53.

D. S. SAVAGE. "Two Prophetic Poems," *Western Review* 13(2), Winter 1949, 67-78.

JON SILKIN. *Out of Battle,* pp. 236-43.

ROBIN SKELTON. *The Poetic Pattern,* pp. 113-14.

"A Terre"

TIMOTHY O'KEEFFE. "Ironic Allusion in the Poetry of Wilfred Owen," *Ariel* 3(4), October 1972, 75-76.

JON SILKIN. *Out of Battle,* pp. 223-26.

"Wild with all Regrets"

JON SILKIN. *Out of Battle,* pp. 223-26.

P

PAIN, PHILIP

"Alas, what is the World? a sea Glass" (Meditation 10)

> DONALD E. STANFORD. "The Imagination of Death in the Poetry of Philip Pain, Edward Taylor, and George Herbert," *Studies in the Literary Imagination* 9(2), Fall 1976, 56.

"The damned now in Hell, there do ly" (Meditation 32)

> DONALD E. STANFORD. "The Imagination of Death in the Poetry of Philip Pain, Edward Taylor, and George Herbert," *Studies in the Literary Imagination* 9(2), Fall 1976, 54-55.

"Scarce do I pass a day, but that I hear" (Meditation 8)

> DONALD E. STANFORD. "The Imagination of Death in the Poetry of Philip Pain, Edward Taylor, and George Herbert," *Studies in the Literary Imagination* 9(2), Fall 1976, 56-57.

"Sure every soul in this world hath its day" (Meditation 30)

> DONALD E. STANFORD. "The Imagination of Death in the Poetry of Philip Pain, Edward Taylor, and George Herbert," *Studies in the Literary Imagination* 9(2), Fall 1976, 54-55.

"We have no License from our God to waste" (Meditation 31)

> DONALD E. STANFORD. "The Imagination of Death in the Poetry of Philip Pain, Edward Taylor, and George Herbert," *Studies in the Literary Imagination* 9(2), Fall 1976, 60.

PARKER, DOROTHY

"The Actress"

> EARL DANIELS. *The Art of Reading Poetry,* pp. 353-54.

PARNELL, THOMAS

"Hymn to Contentment"

> RAYMOND D. HAVENS. "Parnell's 'Hymn to Contentment,'" *Modern Language Notes* 59(5), May 1944, 329-31.

PARRISH, WENDY

"Conversations in the Gallery"

> E(RIC) H(ORSTING). "Poems by Wendy Parrish," *Antioch Review* 32(4), 1973, 640-41.

PATCHEN, KENNETH

"Moon, Sun, Sleep, Birds, Live"

> JOHN FREDERICK NIMS. *Western Wind,* p. 146.

PATMORE, COVENTRY

"The Azalea"

> PATRICIA M. BALL. *The Heart's Events,* pp. 68-71.

"The Day After Tomorrow"

> PATRICIA M. BALL. *The Heart's Events,* pp. 62-65.

"Departure"

> PATRICIA M. BALL. *The Heart's Events,* pp. 71-74.

"Eurydice"

> PATRICIA M. BALL. *The Heart's Events,* pp. 74-76.

"A Farewell"

> PATRICIA M. BALL. *The Heart's Events,* pp. 83-84.

"If I Were Dead"

> PATRICIA M. BALL. *The Heart's Events,* pp. 82-83.

"Love at Large"

> WILLIAM CUDBURY. "The Structure of Feeling in a Poem by Patmore: Meter, Phonology, Form," *Victorian Poetry* 4(4), Autumn 1966, 239-51.

"Tired Memory"

> PATRICIA M. BALL. *The Heart's Events,* pp. 77-82.

"The Toys"

> PATRICIA M. BALL. *The Heart's Events,* pp. 76-77.

"Tristitia"

> PATRICIA M. BALL. *The Heart's Events,* pp. 65-68.

PATTEN, BRIAN

"Ode on Celestial Music (or: It's The Girl in the Bathroom Singing)"

> DAVID HOLBROOK. *Lost Bearings in English Poetry,* pp. 174-77.

"Portrait of a Young Girl Raped at a Suburban Party"

> DAVID HOLBROOK. *Lost Bearings in English Poetry,* pp. 177-80.

PEACOCK, THOMAS LOVE

"Rhododaphne, or the Thessalian Spell"

> WILLIAM E. HARROLD. "Keats's 'Lamia' and Peacock's 'Rhododaphne,'" *Modern Language Review* 61(4), October 1966, 579-84.

"War Song"

> WILLIAM EMPSON. *Seven Types of Ambiguity,* pp. 28-30; second and third eds., p. 22.

PECK, JOHN

"Cider and Vesalius"

LAURENCE LIEBERMAN. *Unassigned Frequencies*, pp. 228-29.

PEELE, GEORGE

"Bathsheba's Song"

MARK VAN DOREN. *Introduction to Poetry*, pp. 31-33.

PELLEW, J. D. C.

"The Temple"

I. A. RICHARDS. *Practical Criticism*, pp. 93-102, 212-13.

PEMBROKE, MARY SIDNEY HERBERT, COUNTESS OF

"A Dialogue Between Two Shepherds, Thenot and Piers, In Praise of Astrea"

G. F. WALLER. "Mary Sidney's . . . 'Two Shepherds,'" *American Notes and Queries*, n.s., 9(7), March 1971, 100-2.

PEMBROKE, WILLIAM, EARL OF

"A Song" ("Soules joy, now I am gone")

ROSAMOND TUVE. "Sacred 'Parody' of Love Poetry, and Herbert," *Studies in the Renaissance* 8 (1961), 249-90.

PERCY, WILL

"Enzio's Kingdom"

RICHARD H. KING. "Mourning and Melancholia: Will Percy and the Southern Tradition," *Virginia Quarterly Review* 53(2), Spring 1977, 261-62.

PETT, PETER

"Time's Journey to seeke his Daughter Truth"

SOJI IWASAKI. "*Veritas Filia Temporis* and Shakespeare," *English Literary Renaissance* 3(2), Spring 1973, 249-63.

PHILLIPS, JOHN

"Satyr against Hypocrites"

RUTH NEVO. *The Dial of Virtue*, pp. 66-69.

PIERCE, BILLIE

"Married Man Blues"

SHERLEY A. WILLIAMS. "The Blues Roots of Contemporary Afro-American Poetry," *Massachusetts Review* 18(3), Autumn 1977, 548-49.

PIERCY, MARGE

"Barbie doll"

JEAN ROSENBAUM. "You Are Your Own Magician: A Vision of Integrity in the Poetry of Marge Piercy," *Modern Poetry Studies* 8(3), Winter 1977, 194-95.

"Breaking Camp"

VICTOR CONTOSKI. "Marge Piercy: A Vision of the Peaceable Kingdom," *Modern Poetry Studies* 8(3), Winter 1977, 210.

"The crippling"

JEAN ROSENBAUM. "You Are Your Own Magician: A Vision of Integrity in the Poetry of Marge Piercy," *Modern Poetry Studies* 8(3), Winter 1977, 195.

"In the men's room(s)"

JEAN ROSENBAUM. "You Are Your Own Magician: A Vision of Integrity in the Poetry of Marge Piercy," *Modern Poetry Studies* 8(3), Winter 1977, 201-2.

"The morning half-life blues"

JEAN ROSENBAUM. "You Are Your Own Magician: A Vision of Integrity in the Poetry of Marge Piercy," *Modern Poetry Studies* 8(3), Winter 1977, 196-97.

"The Peaceable Kingdom"

VICTOR CONTOSKI. "Marge Piercy: A Vision of the Peaceable Kingdom," *Modern Poetry Studies* 8(3), Winter 1977, 206-7.

"The Simplification"

VICTOR CONTOSKI. "Marge Piercy: A Vision of the Peaceable Kingdom," *Modern Poetry Studies* 8(3), Winter 1977, 209.

"Visiting a Dead Man on a Summer Day"

VICTOR CONTOSKI. "Marge Piercy: A Vision of the Peaceable Kingdom," *Modern Poetry Studies* 8(3), Winter 1977, 207-8.

"Walking into Love"

VICTOR CONTOSKI. "Marge Piercy: A Vision of the Peaceable Kingdom," *Modern Poetry Studies* 8(3), Winter 1977, 210-11.

"A work of artifice"

JEAN ROSENBAUM. "You Are Your Own Magician: A Vision of Integrity in the Poetry of Marge Piercy," *Modern Poetry Studies* 8(3), Winter 1977, 195.

PILLIN, WILLIAM

"Folk Song"

GEORGE ABBE. *You and Contemporary Poetry*, pp. 66-68; 1965 ed., pp. 91-93.

PLATH, SYLVIA

"Aftermath"

JOHN F. LYNEN. "Forms of Time in Modern Poetry," *Queen's Quarterly* 82(3), Autumn 1975, 349-50.

"All the Dead Dears"

BARBARA HARDY. *The Advantage of Lyric*, pp. 129-30.

BARBARA HARDY. "The Poetry of Sylvia Plath: Enlargement or Derangement?" in *The Survival of Poetry*, pp. 174-76.

LAWRENCE R. RIES. *Wolf Masks*, pp. 41-42.

"The Applicant"

JOAN BOBBITT. "Lowell and Plath: Objectivity and the Confessional Mode," *Arizona Quarterly* 33(4), Winter 1977, 314.

PETER COOLEY. "Autism, Autoeroticism, Auto-da-fe: The Tragic Poetry of Sylvia Plath," *Hollins Critic* 10(1), February 1973, 7-8.

BARBARA HARDY. *The Advantage of Lyric*, pp. 136-38.

BARBARA HARDY. "The Poetry of Sylvia Plath: Enlargement or Derangement?" in *The Survival of Poetry*, pp. 181-83.

ARTHUR OBERG. *Modern American Lyric*, pp. 143-46.

LAWRENCE R. RIES. *Wolf Masks*, p. 56.

AGNES STEIN. *The Uses of Poetry*, pp. 110-11.

M. D. UROFF. "Sylvia Plath and Confessional Poetry: A Reconsideration," *Iowa Review* 8(1), Winter 1977, 109-11.

"Ariel"

> A. ALVAREZ. "Sylvia Plath," in *The Modern Poet*, edited by Ian Hamilton, p. 78.
>
> WILLIAM V. DAVIS. "Sylvia Plath's 'Ariel,'" *Modern Poetry Studies* 3(4), 1972, 176-84.
>
> D. F. MCKAY. "Aspects of Energy in the Poetry of Dylan Thomas and Sylvia Plath," *Critical Quarterly* 16(1), Spring 1974, 54-56.
>
> LINDA MIZEJEWSKI. "Sappho to Sexton: Womanhood Uncontained," *College English* 35(3), December 1973, 341-42.
>
> MARJORIE PERLOFF. "*Angst* and Animism in the Poetry of Sylvia Plath," *Journal of Modern Literature* 1(1), 1970, 66-67.
>
> ROBERT PHILLIPS. *The Confessional Poets*, p. 147.
>
> ROBERT PHILLIPS. "The Dark Funnel: A Reading of Sylvia Plath," *Modern Poetry Studies* 3(2), 1972, 69.
>
> WALTER SUTTON. *American Free Verse*, pp. 191-92.
>
> LINDA WAGNER. "Plath's 'Ariel': 'Auspicious Gales,'" *Concerning Poetry* 10(2), Fall 1977, 5-7.

"The Arrival of the Bee Box"

> BARBARA HARDY. "The Poetry of Sylvia Plath: Enlargement or Derangement?" in *The Survival of Poetry*, pp. 179-80.
>
> JAMES F. HOYLE. "Sylvia Plath: A Poetry of Suicidal Mania," *Literature and Psychology* 18(4), 1968, 197.
>
> LAWRENCE R. RIES. *Wolf Masks*, pp. 43-44.

"Balloons"

> JAN B. GORDON. "'Who Is Sylvia?' The Art of Sylvia Plath," *Modern Poetry Studies* 1(1), 1970, 30.

"The Bee Meeting"

> JAMES F. HOYLE. "Sylvia Plath: A Poetry of Suicidal Mania," *Literature and Psychology* 18(4), 1968, 197.
>
> ROBERT PHILLIPS. *The Confessional Poets*, pp. 149-50.
>
> ROBERT PHILLIPS. "The Dark Funnel: A Reading of Sylvia Plath," *Modern Poetry Studies* 3(2), 1972, 72.
>
> LOUIS SIMPSON. *A Revolution in Taste*, pp. 124-26.

"The Beekeeper's Daughter"

> ROBERT PHILLIPS. *The Confessional Poets*, pp. 138-39.
>
> ROBERT PHILLIPS. "The Dark Funnel: A Reading of Sylvia Plath," *Modern Poetry Studies* 3(2), 1972, 60.
>
> PAMELA SMITH. "Architectonics: Sylvia Plath's Colossus," *Ariel* 4(1), January 1973, 9-10.

"A Birthday Present"

> JAN B. GORDON. "'Who Is Sylvia?' The Art of Sylvia Plath," *Modern Poetry Studies* 1(1), 1970, 26.
>
> BARBARA HARDY. *The Advantage of Lyric*, pp. 139-40.
>
> BARBARA HARDY. "The Poetry of Sylvia Plath: Enlargement or Derangement?" in *The Survival of Poetry*, p. 186.
>
> MARGARET NEWLIN. "The Suicide Bandwagon," *Critical Quarterly* 14(4), Winter 1972, 372.
>
> ARTHUR OBERG. *Modern American Lyric*, pp. 139-43.

"Blue Moles"

> MARJORIE PERLOFF. "*Angst* and Animism in the Poetry of Sylvia Plath," *Journal of Modern Literature* 1(1), 1970, 65-66.
>
> LAWRENCE R. RIES. *Wolf Masks*, pp. 55-56.

"The Bull of Bendylaw"

> ROBERT PHILLIPS. *The Confessional Poets*, pp. 135-36.
>
> ROBERT PHILLIPS. "The Dark Funnel: A Reading of Sylvia Plath," *Modern Poetry Studies* 3(2), 1972, 57-58.
>
> LAWRENCE R. RIES. *Wolf Masks*, pp. 39-40.

"Childless Woman"

> ARTHUR OBERG. *Modern American Lyric*, pp. 148-50.

"The Colossus"

> SUZANNE JUHASZ. *Naked and Fiery Forms*, pp. 94-95.
>
> ROBERT PHILLIPS. *The Confessional Poets*, p. 135.

"The Couriers"

> JON ROSENBLATT. *Explicator* 34(4), December 1975, Item 28.

"Crossing the Water"

> MARJORIE G. PERLOFF. "On the Road to *Ariel*: The 'Transitional' Poetry of Sylvia Plath," *Iowa Review* 4(2), Spring 1973, 106.

"Cut"

> JOAN BOBBITT. "Lowell and Plath: Objectivity and the Confessional Mode," *Arizona Quarterly* 33(4), Winter 1977, 315.
>
> ROBERT BOYERS. "Sylvia Plath: The Trepanned Veteran," *Centennial Review* 13(2), Spring 1969, 142-46. Reprinted in: Robert Boyers. *Excursions*, pp. 159-62.
>
> JAMES F. HOYLE. "Sylvia Plath: A Poetry of Suicidal Mania," *Literature and Psychology* 18(4), 1968, 190-91.
>
> MARJORIE PERLOFF. "*Angst* and Animism in the Poetry of Sylvia Plath," *Journal of Modern Literature* 1(1), 1970, 70-72.
>
> R. J. SPENDAL. "Sylvia Plath's 'Cut,'" *Modern Poetry Studies* 6(2), Autumn 1975, 128-34.

"Daddy"

> A. ALVAREZ. "Sylvia Plath," in *The Modern Poet*, edited by Ian Hamilton, pp. 81-82.
>
> ROBERT BOYERS. "Sylvia Plath: The Trepanned Veteran," *Centennial Review* 13(2), Spring 1969, 150-52. Reprinted in: Robert Boyers. *Excursions*, pp. 164-67.
>
> PETER COOLEY. "Autism, Autoeroticism, Auto-da-fe: The Tragic Poetry of Sylvia Plath," *Hollins Critic* 10(1), February 1973, 8-9.
>
> C. B. COX and A. R. JONES. "After the Tranquillized Fifties: Notes on Sylvia Plath and James Baldwin," *Critical Quarterly* 6(2), Summer 1964, 108-12.
>
> JUDITH B. HERMAN. "Plath's 'Daddy' and the Myth of Tereus and Philomela," *Notes on Contemporary Literature* 7(1), January 1977, 9-10.
>
> PHILIP HOBSBAUM. "The Temptation of Giant Despair," *Hudson Review* 25(4), Winter 1972-73, 605-8.
>
> JAMES F. HOYLE. "Sylvia Plath: A Poetry of Suicidal Mania," *Literature and Psychology* 18(4), 1968, 192-93.
>
> D. F. MCKAY. "Aspects of Energy in the Poetry of Dylan Thomas and Sylvia Plath," *Critical Quarterly* 16(1), Spring 1974, 65.
>
> GUINEVARA A. NANCE and JUDITH P. JONES. "Doing Away with Daddy: Exorcism and Sympathetic Magic in Plath's Poetry," *Concerning Poetry* 11(1), Spring 1978, 75-81.
>
> ARTHUR OBERG. *Modern American Lyric*, pp. 143-48.
>
> ROBERT PHILLIPS. *The Confessional Poets*, pp. 148-49.
>
> ROBERT PHILLIPS. "The Dark Funnel: A Reading of Sylvia Plath," *Modern Poetry Studies* 3(2), 1972, 70-71.
>
> LAWRENCE R. RIES. *Wolf Masks*, pp. 11, 48-50.
>
> M. L. ROSENTHAL and A. J. M. SMITH. *Exploring Poetry*, second ed., pp. 9, 11.
>
> LOUIS UNTERMEYER. *50 Modern American & British Poets*, pp. 342-43.

PLATH, SYLVIA *(Cont.)*

"Daddy" *(cont.)*

M. D. UROFF. "Sylvia Plath and Confessional Poetry: A Reconsideration," *Iowa Review* 8(1), Winter 1977, 113-15.

"The Disquieting Muses"

SUZANNE JUHASZ. *Naked and Fiery Forms*, pp. 95-98.

"Dream With Clam-Diggers"

JAN B. GORDON. "'Who Is Sylvia?' The Art of Sylvia Plath," *Modern Poetry Studies* 1(1), 1970, 12-13.

"Edge"

SUZANNE JUHASZ. *Naked and Fiery Forms*, pp. 112-14.

MARGARET NEWLIN. "The Suicide Bandwagon," *Critical Quarterly* 14(4), Winter 1972, 369-70.

ARTHUR OBERG. *Modern American Lyric*, pp. 158-61.

JOHN ROMANO. "Sylvia Plath Reconsidered," *Commentary* 57(4), April 1974, 51-52.

CONSTANCE SCHEERER. "The Deadly Paradise of Sylvia Plath," *Antioch Review* 34(4), Summer 1976, 480.

"Electra on Azalea Path"

JAN B. GORDON. "'Who Is Sylvia?' The Art of Sylvia Plath," *Modern Poetry Studies* 1(1), 1970, 17-18.

"Event"

M. D. UROFF. "Sylvia Plath's Women," *Concerning Poetry* 7(1), Spring 1974, 50.

"Face Lift"

MARJORIE G. PERLOFF. "On the Road to *Ariel*: The 'Transitional' Poetry of Sylvia Plath," *Iowa Review* 4(2), Spring 1973, 104-5.

"Fever 103°"

A. ALVAREZ. "Sylvia Plath," in *The Modern Poet*, edited by Ian Hamilton, pp. 79-80.

M. D. UROFF. "Sylvia Plath's Women," *Concerning Poetry* 7(1), Spring 1974, 52.

"Flute Notes from a Reedy Pond"

PAMELA SMITH. "Architectonics: Sylvia Plath's Colossus," *Ariel* 4(1), January 1973, 11.

"For a Fatherless Son"

JOYCE CAROL OATES. "The Death Throes of Romanticism: The Poetry of Sylvia Plath," *Southern Review*, n.s., 9(3), Summer 1973, 518. Reprinted in: *Contemporary Poetry in America*, p. 153.

"Full Fathom Five"

ROBERT PHILLIPS. *The Confessional Poets*, p. 137.

PAMELA SMITH. "Architectonics: Sylvia Plath's Colossus," *Ariel* 4(1), January 1973, 13-14.

"Getting There"

BARBARA HARDY. "The Poetry of Sylvia Plath: Enlargement or Derangement?" in *The Survival of Poetry*, pp. 183-84.

RALPH J. MILLS, JR. *Creation's Very Self*, pp. 34-36. Reprinted in: Ralph J. Mills, Jr. *Cry of the Human*, pp. 37-39.

"Gigolo"

ROBERT PHILLIPS. *The Confessional Poets*, p. 143.

ROBERT PHILLIPS. "The Dark Funnel: A Reading of Sylvia Plath," *Modern Poetry Studies* 3(2), 1972, 65.

"Go Get the Goodly Squab"

JAN B. GORDON. "'Who Is Sylvia?' The Art of Sylvia Plath," *Modern Poetry Studies* 1(1), 1970, 13-14.

"The Goring"

LAWRENCE R. RIES. *Wolf Masks*, pp. 40-41.

"Gulliver"

LAWRENCE R. RIES. *Wolf Masks*, pp. 46-47.

"Hardcastle Crags"

MARJORIE PERLOFF. "*Angst* and Animism in the Poetry of Sylvia Plath," *Journal of Modern Literature* 1(1), 1970, 62-63.

"I Am Vertical"

ROBERT PHILLIPS. *The Confessional Poets*, p. 140.

ROBERT PHILLIPS. "The Dark Funnel: A Reading of Sylvia Plath," *Modern Poetry Studies* 3(2), 1972, 61-62.

NORMA PROCOPIOW. "Sylvia Plath and the New England Mind," *Thoth* 13(3), Fall 1973, 9-15.

"In Plaster"

BARBARA HARDY. "The Poetry of Sylvia Plath: Enlargement or Derangement?" in *The Survival of Poetry*, pp. 176-77.

A. R. JONES. "Necessity and Freedom: The Poetry of Robert Lowell, Sylvia Plath and Anne Sexton," *Critical Quarterly* 7(1), Spring 1965, 22-23.

SUZANNE JUHASZ. *Naked and Fiery Forms*, pp. 99-101.

LAWRENCE R. RIES. *Wolf Masks*, p. 52.

"Kindness"

ARTHUR OBERG. *Modern American Lyric*, pp. 158-61.

"Lady Lazarus"

A. ALVAREZ. "Sylvia Plath," in *The Modern Poet*, edited by Ian Hamilton, pp. 80-81.

JOAN BOBBITT. "Lowell and Plath: Objectivity and the Confessional Mode," *Arizona Quarterly* 33(4), Winter 1977, 315-16.

ROBERT BOYERS. *Excursions*, pp. 162-63.

FREDERICK BUELL. "Sylvia Plath's Traditionalism," *Boundary 2* 5(1), Fall 1976, 207-8.

PETER COOLEY. "Autism, Autoeroticism, Auto-da-fe: The Tragic Poetry of Sylvia Plath," *Hollins Critic* 10(1), February 1973, 10.

BARBARA HARDY. *The Advantage of Lyric*, pp. 135-36.

BARBARA HARDY. "The Poetry of Sylvia Plath: Enlargement or Derangement?" in *The Survival of Poetry*, pp. 180-81.

NANCY JO HOFFMAN. "Reading Women's Poetry: The Meaning and Our Lives," *College English* 34(1), October 1972, 52-56.

JAMES F. HOYLE. "Sylvia Plath: A Poetry of Suicidal Mania," *Literature and Psychology* 18(4), 1968, 192.

ARTHUR OBERG. *Modern American Lyric*, pp. 143-48.

LAWRENCE R. RIES. *Wolf Masks*, pp. 50-51.

JOHN ROMANO. "Sylvia Plath Reconsidered," *Commentary* 57(4), April 1974, 48.

JEFFREY STEINBRINK. "Emily Dickinson and Sylvia Plath: The Values of Mortality," *Women & Literature* 4(1), Spring 1976, 47-48.

M. D. UROFF. "Sylvia Plath and Confessional Poetry: A Reconsideration," *Iowa Review* 8(1), Winter 1977, 111-13.

"Last Words"

ARTHUR OBERG. *Modern American Lyric*, pp. 168-70.

"Leaving Early"

MARJORIE G. PERLOFF. "On the Road to *Ariel*: The 'Transitional' Poetry of Sylvia Plath," *Iowa Review* 4(2), Spring 1973, 103.

Constance Scheerer. "The Deathly Paradise of Sylvia Plath," *Antioch Review* 34(4), Summer 1976, 475-76.

M. D. Uroff. "Sylvia Plath's Women," *Concerning Poetry* 7(1), Spring 1974, 49-50.

"Lesbos"

Marjorie G. Perloff. "On the Road to *Ariel*: The 'Transitional' Poetry of Sylvia Plath," *Iowa Review* 4(2), Spring 1973, 103-4.

Laurin K. Roland. "Sylvia Plath's 'Lesbos': A Self Divided," *Concerning Poetry* 9(2), Fall 1976, 61-65.

"Little Fugue"

Marjorie G. Perloff. "On the Road to *Ariel*: The 'Transitional' Poetry of Sylvia Plath," *Iowa Review* 4(2), Spring 1973, 99-102.

"Lorelei"

Barbara Hardy. *The Advantage of Lyric*, pp. 129-30.

Barbara Hardy. "The Poetry of Sylvia Plath: Enlargement or Derangement?" in *The Survival of Poetry*, pp. 174-76.

Pamela Smith. "Architectonics: Sylvia Plath's Colossus," *Ariel* 4(1), January 1973, 14-15.

"Love Letter"

M. D. Uroff. "Sylvia Plath's Women," *Concerning Poetry* 7(1), Spring 1974, 50-51.

"Maenad"

Anthony Libby. "God's Lioness and the Priest of Sycorax: Plath and Hughes," *Contemporary Literature* 15(3), Summer 1974, 396.

"Magi"

Joyce Carol Oates. "The Death Throes of Romanticism: The Poetry of Sylvia Plath," *Southern Review*, n.s., 9(3), Summer 1973, 506-8.

"Man in Black"

Suzanne Juhasz. *Naked and Fiery Forms*, pp. 92-93.

Pamela Smith. "Architectonics: Sylvia Plath's Colossus," *Ariel* 4(1), January 1973, 12-13.

"Manor Garden"

Jerome F. Megna. *Explicator* 30(7), March 1972, Item 58.

"Mary's Song"

Lawrence R. Ries. *Wolf Masks*, p. 43.

"Medallion"

Arthur Oberg. *Modern American Lyric*, pp. 133-38.

"Medusa"

Anthony Libby. "God's Lioness and the Priest of Sycorax: Plath and Hughes," *Contemporary Literature* 15(3), Summer 1974, 397.

"Miss Drake Proceeds to Supper"

M. D. Uroff. "Sylvia Plath and Confessional Poetry: A Reconsideration," *Iowa Review* 8(1), Winter 1977, 106-7.

"The Moon and the Yew Tree"

Barbara Hardy. *The Advantage of Lyric*, pp. 138-39.

Barbara Hardy. "The Poetry of Sylvia Plath: Enlargement or Derangement?" in *The Survival of Poetry*, pp. 184-86.

Robert Phillips. *The Confessional Poets*, pp. 147-48.

Robert Phillips. "The Dark Funnel: A Reading of Sylvia Plath," *Modern Poetry Studies* 3(2), 1972, 69-70.

Lawrence R. Ries. *Wolf Masks*, pp. 56-57.

"Moonrise"

Pamela Smith. "Architectonics: Sylvia Plath's Colossus," *Ariel* 4(1), January 1973, 10-11.

"Morning Song"

Marjorie Perloff. "*Angst* and Animism in the Poetry of Sylvia Plath," *Journal of Modern Literature* 1(1), 1970, 68-69.

"The Munich Mannequins"

Sandra M. Gilbert. " 'A Fine, White Flying Myth': Confessions of a Plath Addict," *Massachusetts Review* 19(3), Autumn 1978, 596-97.

Jan B. Gordon. " 'Who Is Sylvia?' The Art of Sylvia Plath," *Modern Poetry Studies* 1(1), 1970, 23-24.

"Mussel Hunter at Rock Harbor"

Barbara Hardy. "The Poetry of Sylvia Plath: Enlargement or Derangement?" in *The Survival of Poetry*, pp. 174-76.

"Mystic"

Joyce Carol Oates. "The Death Throes of Romanticism: The Poetry of Sylvia Plath," *Southern Review*, n.s., 9(3), Summer 1973, 520. Reprinted in: *Contemporary Poetry in America*, p. 155.

"Nick and the Candlestick"

Barbara Hardy. *The Advantage of Lyric*, pp. 122-27.

Barbara Hardy. "The Poetry of Sylvia Plath: Enlargement or Derangement?" in *The Survival of Poetry*, pp. 166-70.

"Night Shift"

Lawrence R. Ries. *Wolf Masks*, pp. 52-53.

"Parliament Hill Fields"

Marjorie G. Perloff. "On the Road to *Ariel*: The 'Transitional' Poetry of Sylvia Plath," *Iowa Review* 4(2), Spring 1973, 96-99.

"Poem for Three Voices"

Robert Phillips. *The Confessional Poets*, pp. 144-45.

Robert Phillips. "The Dark Funnel: A Reading of Sylvia Plath," *Modern Poetry Studies* 3(2), 1972, 66-67.

"Poppies in July"

Robert Boyers. "Sylvia Plath: The Trepanned Veteran," *Centennial Review* 13(2), Spring 1969, 141-42. Reprinted in: Robert Boyers. *Excursions*, pp. 158-59.

Robert Pinsky. *The Situation of Poetry*, pp. 129-31.

"Poppies in October"

A. Alvarez. "Sylvia Plath," in *The Modern Poet*, edited by Ian Hamilton, pp. 77-78.

"Private Ground"

Robert N. Mollinger. "Sylvia Plath's 'Private Ground,' " *Notes on Contemporary Literature* 5(2), March 1975, 14-15.

"The Pursuit"

Jan B. Gordon. " 'Who Is Sylvia?' The Art of Sylvia Plath," *Modern Poetry Studies* 1(1), 1970, 15-16.

Lawrence R. Ries. *Wolf Masks*, pp. 38-39.

"The Rabbit Catcher"

Robert Phillips. *The Confessional Poets*, p. 143.

Robert Phillips. "The Dark Funnel: A Reading of Sylvia Plath," *Modern Poetry Studies* 3(2), 1972, 65.

"Sheep In Fog"

Jon Rosenblatt. "The Limits of the 'Confessional Mode' in Recent American Poetry," *Genre* 9(2), Summer 1976, 157-58.

PLATH, SYLVIA (*Cont.*)

"Snakecharmer"

CONSTANCE SCHEERER. "The Deathly Paradise of Sylvia Plath," *Antioch Review* 34(4), Summer 1976, 471-72.

"The Snowman on the Moor"

MARJORIE PERLOFF. "*Angst* and Animism in the Poetry of Sylvia Plath," *Journal of Modern Literature* 1(1), 1970, 63-64.

"Spinster"

ROBERT PHILLIPS. *The Confessional Poets*, p. 138.

LAWRENCE R. RIES. *Wolf Masks*, pp. 57-58.

"Stings"

ROBERT PHILLIPS. *The Confessional Poets*, pp. 150-51.

"The Stones"

ROBERT PHILLIPS. *The Confessional Poets*, p. 139.

ROBERT PHILLIPS. "The Dark Funnel: A Reading of Sylvia Plath," *Modern Poetry Studies* 3(2), 1972, 60-61.

"Suicide off Egg Rock"

LAWRENCE R. RIES. *Wolf Masks*, p. 53.

"The Surgeon at 2 A.M."

JOAN BOBBITT. "Lowell and Plath: Objectivity and the Confessional Mode," *Arizona Quarterly* 33(4), Winter 1977, 316-17.

CONSTANCE SCHEERER. "The Deathly Paradise of Sylvia Plath," *Antioch Review* 34(4), Summer 1976, 473-75.

"The Swarm"

ARTHUR OBERG. *Modern American Lyric*, pp. 139-43.

"Thalidomide"

ARTHUR OBERG. *Modern American Lyric*, pp. 148-50.

"The Tour"

M. D. UROFF. "Sylvia Plath and Confessional Poetry: A Reconsideration," *Iowa Review* 8(1), Winter 1977, 108-9.

"Tulips"

BARBARA HARDY. *The Advantage of Lyric*, pp. 132-33.

BARBARA HARDY. "The Poetry of Sylvia Plath: Enlargement or Derangement?" in *The Survival of Poetry*, pp. 176-79.

SUZANNE JUHASZ. *Naked and Fiery Forms*, pp. 107-9.

CHARLES MOLESWORTH. " 'With Your Own Face On': The Origins and Consequences of Confessional Poetry," *Twentieth Century Literature* 22(2), May 1976, 166.

D. F. MCKAY. "Aspects of Energy in the Poetry of Dylan Thomas and Sylvia Plath," *Critical Quarterly* 16(1), Spring 1974, 62-63.

ARTHUR OBERG. *Modern American Lyric*, pp. 139-43.

MARJORIE PERLOFF. "*Angst* and Animism in the Poetry of Sylvia Plath," *Journal of Modern Literature* 1(1), 1970, 69-70.

CONSTANCE SCHEERER. "The Deathly Paradise of Sylvia Plath," *Antioch Review* 34(4), Summer 1976, 476.

JEFFREY STEINBRINK. "Emily Dickinson and Sylvia Plath: The Values of Mortality," *Women & Literature* 4(1), Spring 1976, 47.

M. D. UROFF. "Sylvia Plath and Confessional Poetry: A Reconsideration," *Iowa Review* 8(1), Winter 1977, 107-8.

M. D. UROFF. "Sylvia Plath's Women," *Concerning Poetry* 7(1), Spring 1974, 51-52.

"Two Campers in Cloud Country"

ROBERT BOYERS. "On Sylvia Plath," *Salmagundi* 21 (Winter 1973), 101. Reprinted in: Robert Boyers. *Excursions*, p. 173.

"Two Sisters of Persephone"

SANDRA M. GILBERT. " 'A Fine, White Flying Myth': Confessions of a Plath Addict," *Massachusetts Review* 19(3), Autumn 1978, 597.

"Two Views of a Cadaver Room"

SUZANNE JUHASZ. *Naked and Fiery Forms*, pp. 93-94.

MARJORIE PERLOFF. "*Angst* and Animism in the Poetry of Sylvia Plath," *Journal of Modern Literature* 1(1), 1970, 64-65.

LAWRENCE R. RIES. *Wolf Masks*, p. 56.

LOUIS SIMPSON. *A Revolution in Taste*, pp. 100-1.

PAMELA SMITH. "Architectonics: Sylvia Plath's Colossus," *Ariel* 4(1), January 1973, 8-9.

"Whitsun"

M. D. UROFF. "Sylvia Plath's Women," *Concerning Poetry* 7(1), Spring 1974, 47-48.

"Who"

ANTHONY LIBBY. "God's Lioness and the Priest of Sycorax: Plath and Hughes," *Contemporary Literature* 15(3), Summer 1974, 395-96.

"Widow"

ROBERT BOYERS. "On Sylvia Plath," *Salmagundi* 21 (Winter 1973), 99-101. Reprinted in: Robert Boyers. *Excursions*, pp. 171-72.

"Winter Trees"

ROBERT PHILLIPS. *The Confessional Poets*, pp. 142-43.

ROBERT PHILLIPS. "The Dark Funnel: A Reading of Sylvia Plath," *Modern Poetry Studies* 3(2), 1972, 64.

"Witch Burning"

VINCENT D. BALITAS. "On Becoming a Witch: A Reading of Sylvia Plath's 'Witch Burning,' " *Studies in the Humanities* 4(2), February 1975, 27-30.

"Words"

WALTER SUTTON. *American Free Verse*, pp. 192-93.

"Wreath for a Bridal"

M. D. UROFF. "Sylvia Plath's Women," *Concerning Poetry* 7(1), Spring 1974, 47.

"Wuthering Heights"

MARJORIE G. PERLOFF. "On the Road to *Ariel*: The 'Transitional' Poetry of Sylvia Plath," *Iowa Review* 4(2), Spring 1973, 105-6.

"Years"

WILLIAM V. DAVIS. "Sylvia Plath's 'Ariel,' " *Modern Poetry Studies* 3(4), 1972, 182-83.

D. F. MCKAY. "Aspects of Energy in the Poetry of Dylan Thomas and Sylvia Plath," *Critical Quarterly* 16(1), Spring 1974, 63-64.

"You're"

CHARLES MOLESWORTH. " 'With Your Own Face On': The Origins and Consequences of Confessional Poetry," *Twentieth Century Literature* 22(2), May 1976, 172-73.

"Zoo Keeper's Wife"

ROBERT PHILLIPS. *The Confessional Poets*, p. 142.

ROBERT PHILLIPS. "The Dark Funnel: A Reading of Sylvia Plath," *Modern Poetry Studies* 3(2), 1972, 63-64.

M. D. UROFF. "Sylvia Plath and Confessional Poetry: A Reconsideration," *Iowa Review* 8(1), Winter 1977, 107.

M. D. UROFF. "Sylvia Plath's Women," *Concerning Poetry* 7(1), Spring 1974, 48-49.

PLUMLY, STANLEY

"In Sleep"

MAURA STANTON. "On Stanley Plumly's Poems," *Iowa Review* 4(4), Fall 1973, 92-93.

"Light"

MAURA STANTON. "On Stanley Plumly's Poems," *Iowa Review* 4(4), Fall 1973, 92-93.

PLUTZIK, HYAM

"For T. S. E. Only"

NORMAN FRIEDMAN. "The Wesleyan Poets — IV," *Chicago Review* 19(3), June 1967, 83-84.

"I Am Disquieted When I See Many Hills"

THOMAS FRIEDMANN. "Time for Hyam Plutzik: A Critique and Checklist of Criticism," *Thoth* 11(2), Winter 1971, 38.

"A Philosopher on a Mountain in Scythia"

THOMAS FRIEDMANN. "Time for Hyam Plutzik: A Critique and Checklist of Criticism," *Thoth* 11(2), Winter 1971, 38-39.

"Portrait"

THOMAS FRIEDMANN. "Time for Hyam Plutzik: A Critique and Checklist of Criticism," *Thoth* 11(2), Winter 1971, 39.

"The Priest Ekranath"

THOMAS FRIEDMANN. "Time for Hyam Plutzik: A Critique and Checklist of Criticism," *Thoth* 11(2), Winter 1971, 39-41.

NORMAN FRIEDMAN. "The Wesleyan Poets — IV," *Chicago Review* 19(3), June 1967, 81-83.

"The Shepherd"

NORMAN FRIEDMAN. "The Wesleyan Poets — IV," *Chicago Review* 19(3), June 1967, 84.

POE, EDGAR ALLAN

"Al Aaraaf"

RICHARD CAMPBELL and MARIE MORGAN PETTIGREW. "A Reply to Floyd Stovall's Interpretation of 'Al Aaraaf,' " *American Literature* 8(4), January 1937, 439-45.

ROBERT D. JACOBS. "The Self and the World: Poe's Early Poems," *Georgia Review* 31(3), Fall 1977, 653-54.

E. SAN JUAN, JR. "The Form of Experience in the Poems of Edgar Allan Poe," *Georgia Review* 21(1), Spring 1967, 78-79.

FLOYD STOVALL. "An Interpretation of Poe's 'Al Aaraaf,' " *Texas Studies in English* 9 (1929), 106-33.

"Annabel Lee"

GÉMINO H. ABAD. *A Formal Approach to Lyric Poetry,* pp. 295-96.

BRADFORD A. BOOTH. "The Identity of Annabel Lee," *College English* 7(1), October 1945, 17-19.

WALLACE C. BROWN. "The English Professor's Dilemma," *College English* 5(7), April 1944, 380-82.

JULIENNE H. EMPRIC. "A Note on 'Annabel Lee,' " *Poe Studies* 6(1), June 1973, 26.

E. SAN JUAN, JR. "The Form of Experience in the Poems of Edgar Allan Poe," *Georgia Review* 21(1), Spring 1967, 74.

"The Bells"

ARTHUR E. DU BOIS. "The Jazz Bells of Poe," *College English* 2(3), December 1940, 240-44.

PAUL O. WILLIAMS. "A Reading of Poe's 'The Bells,' " *Poe Newsletter* 1(2), October 1968, 24-25.

"The City in the Sea"

RICHARD E. AMACHER. *Explicator* 19(8), May 1961, Item 60.

ROY P. BASLER. *Explicator* 4(4), February 1946, Item 30.

ROY P. BASLER. *Sex, Symbolism, and Psychology in Literature,* pp. 192-95.

C. M. BOWRA. *The Romantic Imagination,* pp. 183-84.

HARRY BROWN and JOHN MILSTEAD. *What the Poem Means,* p. 160.

DAVID DAICHES and WILLIAM CHARVAT. *Poems in English,* p. 709.

ROBERT D. JACOBS. "The Self and the World: Poe's Early Poems," *Georgia Review* 31(3), Fall 1977, 662.

T. FREDERICK KEEFER. " 'The City in the Sea': A Reexamination," *College English* 25(6), March 1964, 436-39.

T. O. MABBOTT. *Explicator* 4(1), October 1945, Item 1.

E. SAN JUAN, JR. "The Form of Experience in the Poems of Edgar Allan Poe," *Georgia Review* 21(1), Spring 1967, 72-73.

ERIC W. STOCKTON. "Celestial Inferno: Poe's 'The City in the Sea,' " *Tennessee Studies in Literature* 8 (1963), 99-106.

ALLEN TATE. "The Poetry of Edgar Allan Poe," *Sewanee Review* 76(2), Spring 1968, 224-25.

HYATT H. WAGGONER. *American Poets,* pp. 142-43.

"The Coliseum"

PATRICIA C. SMITH. "Poe's Arabesque," *Poe Studies* 7(2), December 1974, 44.

"The Conqueror Worm"

KLAUS LUBBERS. "Poe's 'The Conqueror Worm,' " *American Literature* 39(3), November 1967, 375-79.

J. REA. "Classicism and Romanticism in Poe's 'Ligeia,' " *Ball State University Forum* 8(1), Winter 1967, 27-28.

DONALD R. SWANSON. *Explicator* 19(7), April 1961, Item 52.

MICHAEL TRITT. " 'Ligeia' and 'The Conqueror Worm,' " *Poe Studies* 9(1), June 1976, 21-22.

"A Dream"

ROBERT D. JACOBS. "The Self and the World: Poe's Early Poems," *Georgia Review* 31(3), Fall 1977, 644.

"Dream-Land"

J. O. BAILEY. "The Geography of Poe's 'Dream-Land' and 'Ulalume,' " *Studies in Philology* 45(3), July 1948, 517-18.

DENNIS W. EDDINGS. "Poe's 'Dream-Land': Nightmare or Sublime Vision?" *Poe Studies* 8(1), June 1974, 5-8.

E. SAN JUAN, JR. "The Form of Experience in the Poems of Edgar Allan Poe," *Georgia Review* 21(1), Spring 1967, 73.

"A Dream within a Dream"

ROBERT D. JACOBS. "The Self and the World: Poe's Early Poems," *Georgia Review* 31(3), Fall 1977, 643.

E. SAN JUAN, JR. "The Form of Experience in the Poems of Edgar Allan Poe," *Georgia Review* 21(1), Spring 1967, 70.

HYATT A. WAGGONER. *American Poets,* pp. 143-45.

POE, EDGAR ALLAN *(Cont.)*

"Dreams"

ROY HARVEY PEARCE. *The Continuity of American Poetry*, pp. 150-51.

"Eldorado"

HARRY BROWN and JOHN MILSTEAD. *What the Poem Means*, p. 159.

ERIC W. CARLSON. "Poe's 'Eldorado,'" *Modern Language Notes* 76(3), March 1961, 232-33.

ORAL SUMMER COAD. "The Meaning of Poe's 'Eldorado,'" *Modern Language Notes* 59(1), January 1944, 59-61.

THOMAS OLLIVE MABBOTT. "The Sources of Poe's 'Eldorado,'" *Modern Language Notes* 60(5), May 1945, 312-14.

W. STEPHEN SANDERLIN, JR. "Poe's 'Eldorado' Again," *Modern Langage Notes* 71(3), March 1956, 189-92.

"Eureka: A Prose Poem"

ALBERT GELPI. *The Tenth Muse*, pp. 140-43.

"Evening Star"

PATRICK E. KILBURN. *Explicator* 28(9), May 1970, Item 76.

"Fairyland"

ROBERT D. JACOBS. "The Self and the World: Poe's Early Poems," *Georgia Review* 31(3), Fall 1977, 656-58.

"For Annie"

J. M. ARMISTEAD. "Poe and Lyric Conventions: The Example of 'For Annie,'" *Poe Studies* 8(1), June 1975, 1-5.

C. M. BOWRA. *The Romantic Imagination*, pp. 188-89.

JAMES M. KIEHL. "The Valley of Unrest: A Major Metaphor in the Poetry of Edgar Allan Poe," *Thoth* 5(1), Winter 1964, 45-46.

"The Haunted Palace"

ALBERT GELPI. *The Tenth Muse*, pp. 147-49.

MICHAEL J. HOFFMAN. *The Subversive Vision*, pp. 21-22.

JAMES M. KIEHL. "The Valley of Unrest: A Major Metaphor in the Poetry of Edgar Allan Poe," *Thoth* 5(1), Winter 1964, 46-47.

RICHARD WILBUR. "The House of Poe," in *Anniversary Lectures 1959*, pp. 26-28.

"Israfel"

HARRY BROWN and JOHN MILSTEAD. *What the Poem Means*, p. 159.

ROBERT D. JACOBS. "The Self and the World: Poe's Early Poems," *Georgia Review* 31(3), Fall 1977, 659-60.

THOMAS OLLIVE MABBOTT. *Explicator* 2(8), June 1944, Item 57.

E. SAN JUAN, JR. "The Form of Experience in the Poems of Edgar Allan Poe," *Georgia Review* 21(1), Spring 1967, 77-78.

HYATT H. WAGGONER. *American Poets*, pp. 141-42.

"The Lake: To — "

ROBERT D. JACOBS. "The Self and the World: Poe's Early Poems," *Georgia Review* 31(3), Fall 1977, 644-45.

"Lenore"

JOHN C. BRODERICK. "Poe's Revisions of 'Lenore,'" *American Literature* 35(4), January 1964, 504-10.

"The Raven"

NED J. DAVISON. "'The Raven' and 'Out of the Cradle Endlessly Rocking,'" *Poe Newsletter* 1(1), April 1968, 5-6.

EDWIN FUSSELL. *Lucifer in Harness*, pp. 59-60.

BYRD HOWELL GRANGER. "Devil Lore in 'The Raven,'" *Poe Studies* 5(2), December 1972, 53-54.

HOWARD MUMFORD JONES. "Poe, 'The Raven,' and the Anonymous Young Man," *Western Humanities Review* 9(2), Spring 1955, 132-38.

KENT LJUNGQUIST. "Poe's Raven and Bryant's *Mythology*," *American Transcendental Quarterly* 29(1), Winter 1976, 28-30.

EDGAR ALLAN POE. "The Philosophy of Composition," in *Poems in the Making*, pp. 159-68. Also in: *Prose Keys to Modern Poetry*, pp. 3-13.

BARTON LEVI ST. ARMAND. "Poe's Emblematic Raven: A Pictorial Approach," *ESQ* 22(4), Fourth Quarter 1976, 191-210.

E. SAN JUAN, JR. "The Form of Experience in the Poems of Edgar Allan Poe," *Georgia Review* 21(1), Spring 1967, 66-69.

"Romance"

ROBERT D. JACOBS. "The Self and the World: Poe's Early Poems," *Georgia Review* 31(3), Fall 1977, 655-56.

HYATT H. WAGGONER. *American Poets*, pp. 139-40.

"Silence: A Fable"

JAMES M. KIEHL. "The Valley of Unrest: A Major Metaphor in the Poetry of Edgar Allan Poe," *Thoth* 5(1), Winter 1964, 43-44.

"The Sleeper"

ROBERT D. JACOBS. "The Self and the World: Poe's Early Poems," *Georgia Review* 31(3), Fall 1977, 663-65.

JAMES M. KIEHL. "The Valley of Unrest: A Major Metaphor in the Poetry of Edgar Allan Poe," *Thoth* 5(1), Winter 1964, 44-45.

THOMAS O. MABBOTT. "Poe's 'The Sleeper' Again," *American Literature* 21(3), November 1949, 339-40. (P)

E. SAN JUAN, JR. "The Form of Experience in the Poems of Edgar Allan Poe," *Georgia Review* 21(1), Spring 1967, 73-74.

"Sonnet — Silence"

ALBERT GELPI. *The Tenth Muse*, p. 122.

"Sonnet — To Science"

ROBERT D. JACOBS. "The Self and the World: Poe's Early Poems," *Georgia Review* 31(3), Fall 1977, 654-55.

HYATT H. WAGGONER. *American Poets*, pp. 138-39.

"Spirits of the Dead"

ROBERT D. JACOBS. "The Self and the World: Poe's Early Poems," *Georgia Review* 31(3), Fall 1977, 646.

"Stanzas"

MICHAEL HINDEN. "Poe's Debt to Wordsworth: A Reading of 'Stanzas,'" *Studies in Romanticism* 8(2), Winter 1969, 109-20.

"Tamerlane"

ROBERT D. JACOBS. "The Self and the World: Poe's Early Poems," *Georgia Review* 31(3), Fall 1977, 647-52.

"To — — — — " ("Not long ago the writer of these lines")

ROY HARVEY PEARCE. *The Continuity of American Poetry*, pp. 151-52.

"To Helen"

ISAAC ASIMOV. *Familiar Poems, Annotated*, pp. 187-90.

C. M. BOWRA. *The Romantic Imagination*, pp. 185-86, 192.

WALLACE C. BROWN. "The English Professor's Dilemma," *College English* 5(7), April 1944, 382-85.

ROBERT A. COLBY. "Poe's Philosophy of Composition," *University of Kansas City Review* 20(3), Spring 1954, 211-14.

ELIZABETH DREW. *Poetry*, p. 209.

RICHARD EBERHART. "Will and Psyche in Poetry," in *The Moment of Poetry*, pp. 55-59.

JAMES W. GARGANO. "Poe's 'To Helen,'" *Modern Language Notes* 75(8), December 1960, 652-53.

ROBERT D. JACOBS. "The Self and the World: Poe's Early Poems," *Georgia Review* 31(3), Fall 1977, 659.

T. O. MABBOTT. *Explicator* 1(8), June 1943, Item 60. Reprinted in: *Readings for Liberal Education*, first ed., II: 209-10.

J. M. PEMBERTON. "Poe's 'To Helen': Functional Wordplay and A Possible Source," *Poe Newsletter* 3(1), June 1970, 6-7.

M. L. ROSENTHAL and A. J. M. SMITH. *Exploring Poetry*, pp. 603-4; second ed., pp. 406-7.

E. SAN JUAN, JR. "The Form of Experience in the Poems of Edgar Allan Poe," *Georgia Review* 21(1), Spring 1967, 75-76.

ARTHUR SCHWARTZ. "The Transport: A Matter of Time and Space," *CEA Critic* 31(3), December 1968, 14-15.

ALLEN TATE. "The Poetry of Edgar Allan Poe," *Sewanee Review* 76(2), Spring 1968, 221-22.

HYATT H. WAGGONER. *American Poets*, pp. 140-41.

"To One in Paradise"

ROY P. BASLER. "Byronism in Poe's 'To One in Paradise,'" *American Literature* 9(2), May 1937, 232-36.

ALBERT GELPI. *The Tenth Muse*, pp. 122-23.

E. SAN JUAN, JR. "The Form of Experience in the Poems of Edgar Allan Poe," *Georgia Review* 21(1), Spring 1967, 75.

"Ulalume"

J. O. BAILEY. "The Geography of Poe's 'Dream-Land' and 'Ulalume,'" *Studies in Philology* 45(3), July 1948, 518-23.

ROY P. BASLER. *Explicator* 2(7), May 1944, Item 49.

ROY P. BASLER. *Sex, Symbolism, and Psychology in Literature*, pp. 184-87. Reprinted in: *The Creative Reader*, pp. 861-62.

CLEANTH BROOKS and ROBERT PENN WARREN. *Understanding Poetry*, pp. 358-59; revised ed., pp. 197-201; third ed., pp. 228-33.

ERIC W. CARLSON. "Symbol and Sense in Poe's 'Ulalume,'" *American Literature* 35(1), March 1963, 22-37.

THOMAS E. CONNOLLY. *Explicator* 22(1), September 1963, Item 4.

JAMES M. KIEHL. "The Valley of Unrest: A Major Metaphor in the Poetry of Edgar Allan Poe," *Thoth* 5(1), Winter 1964, 47-51.

LOU ANN KRIEGISCH. "'Ulalume' — A Platonic Profanation of Beauty and Love," *Poe Studies* 11(2), December 1978, 29-31.

T. O. MABBOTT. *Explicator* 1(4), February 1948, Item 25. Reprinted in: *The Creative Reader*, pp. 860-61.

JAMES E. MILLER, JR. "'Ulalume' Resurrected," *Philological Quarterly* 34(2), April 1955, 197-205. Reprinted in: James E. Miller, Jr. *Quests Surd and Absurd*, pp. 239-48.

JAMES E. MULQUEEN. "The Meaning of Poe's 'Ulalume,'" *American Transcendental Quarterly* 1(1), First Quarter 1969, 27-30.

DAVID ROBINSON. "The Romantic Quest in Poe and Emerson: 'Ulalume' and 'The Sphinx,'" *American Transcendental Quarterly* 26(Suppl.), Spring 1975, 26-30.

DAVID ROBINSON. "'Ulalume' — The Ghouls and the Critics," *Poe Studies* 8(1), June 1974, 8-10.

LEONARD UNGER and WILLIAM VAN O'CONNOR. *Poems for Study*, pp. 468-72.

YVOR WINTERS. "A Crisis in the History of American Obscurantism," *American Literature* 8(4), January 1937, 394-95. Reprinted in: Yvor Winters. *In Defense of Reason*, pp. 252-53. Also: Yvor Winters. *Maule's Curse*, pp. 112-13.

"The Valley of Unrest"

ROY P. BASLER. *Explicator* 5(3), December 1946, Item 25. Reprinted in: Roy P. Basler. *Sex, Symbolism, and Psychology in Literature*, pp. 197-200. Also: *Readings for Liberal Education*, revised ed., II: 127-28; third ed., II: 121-22; fourth ed., II: 120-21; fifth ed., II: 111-12.

JAMES M. KIEHL. "The Valley of Unrest: A Major Metaphor in the Poetry of Edgar Allan Poe," *Thoth* 5(1), Winter 1964, 42-43.

E. SAN JUAN, JR. "The Form of Experience in the Poems of Edgar Allan Poe," *Georgia Review* 21(1), Spring 1967, 71-72.

POMFRET, JOHN

"The Choice"

DAVID DAICHES and WILLIAM CHARVAT. *Poems in English*, p. 676.

POPE, ALEXANDER

"Autumn"

see also "Pastorals"

JEFFRY B. SPENCER. *Heroic Nature*, pp. 203-4.

"Elegy to the Memory of an Unfortunate Lady"

CHRISTOPHER GILLIE. "Alexander Pope: Elegy to the Memory of an Unfortunate Lady," in *Interpretations*, pp. 75-85.

F. R. LEAVIS. "Revaluations (II): The Poetry of Pope," *Scrutiny* 2(3), December 1933, 269-77. Reprinted in: F. R. Leavis. *Revaluation*, pp. 69-73, 80-81.

DONALD C. MELL, JR. "Pope's Idea of the Imagination and the Design of 'Elegy to the Memory of an Unfortunate Lady,'" *Modern Language Quarterly* 29(4), December 1968, 395-406.

EDWIN NIERENBERG. "Pope and God at Twickenham," *Personalist* 44(4), Autumn 1963, 485-87.

HOWARD D. WEINBROT. "Pope's 'Elegy to the Memory of an Unfortunate Lady,'" *Modern Language Quarterly* 32(3), September 1971, 255-67.

"Eloisa to Abelard"

EDWARD E. FOSTER. "Rhetorical Control in Pope's *Eloisa to Abelard*," *Tennessee Studies in Literature* 13 (1968), 63-74.

POPE, ALEXANDER *(Cont.)*

"Eloisa to Abelard" *(cont.)*

EVELYN HOOVEN. "Racine and Pope's Eloisa," *Essays in Criticism* 24(4), October 1974, 368-74.

DAVID K. JEFFREY. "A 'Strange Itch in the Flesh of a Nun': The Dramatic Movement and the Imagery of Pope's 'Eloisa to Abelard,' " *Ball State University Forum* 16(4), Autumn 1975, 28-35.

ROBERT P. KALMEY. "Rhetoric, Language, and Structure in *Eloisa to Abelard*," *Eighteenth Century Studies* 5(2), Winter 1971-72, 315-18.

G. WILSON KNIGHT. *The Burning Oracle*, pp. 148-55.

MURRAY KRIEGER. *The Classic Vision*, pp. 83-103.

MURRAY KRIEGER. " 'Eloisa to Abelard': The Escape from Body or the Embrace of Body," *Eighteenth Century Studies* 3(1), Fall 1969, 28-47.

ROBERT LANGBAUM. *The Poetry of Experience*, pp. 146-48.

BARRETT JOHN MANDEL. "Pope's 'Eloisa to Abelard,' " *Texas Studies in Literature and Language* 9(1), Spring 1967, 57-68.

DAVID B. MORRIS. " 'The Visionary Maid': Tragic Passion and Redemptive Sympathy in Pope's 'Eloisa to Abelard,' " *Modern Language Quarterly* 34(3), September 1973, 247-71.

HENRY PETTIT. "Pope's *Eloisa to Abelard*: An Interpretation," *University of Colorado Studies, Series in Language and Literature*, #4 (July 1953), 67-74.

JAMES QUIVEY. "Pope's *Eloisa to Abelard*: A Study in Irony," *Studies in the Humanities* 2(2), Summer 1971, 14-22.

"Epilogue to the Satires"

JOHN M. ADEN. "Pope and the Satiric Adversary," *Studies in English Literature 1500-1900* 2(3), Summer 1962, 280-86.

SANFORD BUDICK. *Poetry of Civilization*, pp. 126-30.

THOMAS R. EDWARDS, JR. "Heroic Folly: Pope's Satiric Identity," in *In Defense of Reading*, pp. 191-205. Reprinted in: Thomas R. Edwards. *Imagination and Power*, pp. 106-18.

DONALD J. GREENE. " 'Dramatic Texture' in Pope," in *From Sensibility to Romanticism*, pp. 42-47.

MALCOLM KELSALL. "Augustus and Pope," *Huntington Library Quarterly* 39(2), February 1976, 117-31.

"Epilogue to the Satires, Dialogue I"

MAYNARD MACK. *English Masterpieces*, edited by William Frost, Maynard Mack, and Leonard Dean, vol. 5: *The Augustans*, pp. 32-34.

HANS OSTROM. *Explicator* 36(4), Summer 1978, 11-14.

REBECCA PRICE PARKIN. "The Quality of Alexander Pope's Humor," *College English* 14(4), January 1953, 200-1.

"Epistle to a Lady"

WALLACE DOUGLAS, ROY LAMSON, and HALLETT SMITH. *The Critical Reader*, pp. 25-31. Reprinted in: *Readings for Liberal Education*, revised ed., II: 76-80; third ed., II: 68-72; fourth ed., II: 63-67; fifth ed., II: 64-68.

JAY ARNOLD LEVINE. "The Status of the Verse Epistle Before Pope," *Studies in Philology* 59(4), October 1962, 665-67.

MAYNARD MACK. *English Masterpieces*, edited by William Frost, Maynard Mack, and Leonard Dean, vol. 5: *The Augustans*, pp. 29-30.

FELICITY A. NUSSBAUM. "Pope's 'To a Lady' and the Eighteenth-Century Woman," *Philological Quarterly* 54(2), Spring 1975, 444-56.

REBECCA P. PARKIN. "The Role of Time in Alexander Pope's *Epistle to a Lady*," *ELH* 32(4), December 1965, 490-501.

LEONARD UNGER and WILLIAM VAN O'CONNOR. *Poems for Study*, pp. 254-62.

"Epistle to Addison"

THOMAS O. MABBOTT. *Explicator* 10(2), November 1951, Item 11.

"Epistle to Augustus"

MALCOLM KELSALL. "Augustus and Pope," *Huntington Library Quarterly* 39(2), February 1976, 117-31.

JAY ARNOLD LEVINE. "Pope's *Epistle to Augustus*, Lines 1-30," *Studies in English Literature 1500-1900* 7(3), Summer 1967, 427-51. (P)

MANUEL SCHONHORN. "The Audacious Contemporaneity of Pope's *Epistle to Augustus*," *Studies in English Literature 1500-1900* 8(3), Summer 1968, 431-43.

MANUEL SCHONHORN. "Pope's *Epistle to Augustus*: Notes Toward a Mythology," *Tennessee Studies in Literature* 16 (1971), 15-33.

"Epistle to Bathurst"

VINCENT CARRETTA. "Pope's *Epistle to Bathurst* and the South Sea Bubble," *Journal of English and Germanic Philology* 77(2), April 1978, 212-31.

THOMAS R. EDWARDS, JR. " 'Reconcil'd Extremes:' Pope's *Epistle to Bathurst*," *Essays in Criticism* 11(3), July 1961, 290-308.

MAYNARD MACK. "On Reading Pope," *College English* 7(5), February 1946, 269-71. (P)

C. N. MANLOVE. *Literature and Reality*, pp. 84-85, 89-90.

JEFFRY B. SPENCER. *Heroic Nature*, pp. 216-17.

"Epistle to Bolingbroke"

BARBARA LAUREN. "Pope's *Epistle to Bolingbroke*: Satire from the Vantage of Retirement," *Studies in English Literature 1500-1900* 15(3), Summer 1975, 419-30.

"Epistle to Burlington"

REUBEN ARTHUR BROWER. *The Fields of Light*, pp. 144-63.

WILLIAM A. GIBSON. "Three Principles of Renaissance Architectural Theory in Pope's *Epistle to Burlington*," *Studies in English Literature 1500-1900* 11(3), Summer 1971, 487-505.

F. R. LEAVIS. *Revaluation*, pp. 77-80, 92-100.

F. R. LEAVIS. "Revaluations (II): The Poetry of Pope," *Scrutiny* 2(3), December 1933, 274-76. (P)

C. N. MANLOVE. *Literature and Reality*, pp. 85-89.

PETER E. MARTIN. "The Garden and Pope's Vision of Order in the 'Epistle to Burlington,' " *Durham University Journal*, n.s., 34(3), June 1973, 248-59.

PATRICIA MEYER SPACKS. "Pope's Satiric Use of Nature," *Studies in the Literary Imagination* 5(2), October 1972, 42-50.

JEFFRY B. SPENCER. *Heroic Nature*, pp. 217-19.

"Epistle to Cobham"

C. N. MANLOVE. *Literature and Reality*, pp. 83-84.

JOHN E. SITTER. "The Argument of Pope's *Epistle to Cobham*," *Studies in English Literature 1500-1900* 17(3), Summer 1977, 435-49.

"Epistle to Dr. Arbuthnot"

JOHN M. ADEN. "Pope and the Satiric Adversary," *Studies in English Literature* 2(3), Summer 1962, 276-80.

ALWYN BERLAND. "Some Techniques of Fiction in Poetry," *Essays in Criticism* 4(4), October 1954, 373-76.

WALLACE C. BROWN. "Dramatic Tension in Neoclassic Satire," *College English* 6(5), February 1945, 265-66.

DAVID DAICHES and WILLIAM CHARVAT. *Poems in English*, pp. 680-82.

LAWRENCE LEE DAVIDOW. "Pope's Verse Epistles: Friendship and the Private Sphere of Life," *Huntington Library Quarterly* 40(2), February 1977, 161-68.

RICHARD H. DOUGLASS. "More on the Rhetoric and Imagery of Pope's *Arbuthnot*," *Studies in English Literature 1500-1900* 13(3), Summer 1973, 488-502.

NIGEL FOXELL. *Ten Poems Analyzed*, pp. 41-101.

DONALD J. GREENE. "'Dramatic Texture' in Pope," in *From Sensibility to Romanticism*, pp. 38-41.

J. P. HARDY. *Reinterpretations*, pp. 81-102.

RIPLEY HOTCH. "The Dilemma of an Obedient Son: Pope's *Epistle to Dr. Arbuthnot*," *Essays in Literature* 1(1), Spring 1974, 37-45.

J. PAUL HUNTER. "Satiric Apology as Satiric Instance: Pope's *Arbuthnot*," *Journal of English and Germanic Philology* 68(4), October 1969, 625-47.

U. C. KNOEPFLMACHER. "The Poet as Physician: Pope's *Epistle to Dr. Arbuthnot*," *Modern Language Quarterly* 31(4), December 1970, 440-49.

MAYNARD MACK. *English Masterpieces*, edited by William Frost, Maynard Mack, and Leonard Dean, vol. 5: *The Augustans*, pp. 30-32.

C. N. MANLOVE. *Literature and Reality*, pp. 90-98.

ELDER OLSON. "Rhetoric and the Appreciation of Pope," *Modern Philology* 37(1), August 1939, 21-33.

PATRICIA MEYER SPACKS. "In Search of Sincerity," *College English* 29(8), May 1968, 596-98.

"Epistle to Miss Blount, On Her Leaving the Town, After the Coronation"

JOHN D. BOYD. *Explicator* 36(1), Fall 1977, 21-23.

C. N. MANLOVE. *Literature and Reality*, pp. 78-82.

"An Essay on Criticism"

JOHN M. ADEN. "The Doctrinal Design of *An Essay on Criticism*," *College English* 22(5), February 1961, 311-15.

JOHN M. ADEN. "'First Follow Nature': Strategy and Stratification in *An Essay on Criticism*," *Journal of English and Germanic Philology* 55(4), October 1956, 604-17.

HARRY BROWN and JOHN MILSTEAD. *What the Poem Means*, pp. 161-65.

WILLIAM EMPSON. *The Structure of Complex Words*, pp. 84-100.

WILLIAM EMPSON. "Wit in the Essay on Criticism," *Hudson Review* 2(4), Winter 1950, 559-77.

ARTHUR FENNER, JR. "The Unity of Pope's *Essay on Criticism*," *Philological Quarterly* 39(4), October 1960, 435-46.

ALAN S. FISHER. "Cheerful Noonday, 'Gloomy' Twilight: Pope's *Essay on Criticism*," *Philological Quarterly* 51(4), October 1972, 832-44.

RIPLEY HOTCH. "Pope Surveys His Kingdom: *An Essay on Criticism*," *Studies in English Literature 1500-1900* 13(3), Summer 1973, 474-87.

MARTIN KALLICH. "Image and Theme in Pope's *Essay on Criticism*," *Ball State University Forum* 8(3), Summer 1967, 54-60.

MARTIN KALLICH. "Pegasus on the Seesaw: Balance and Antithesis in Pope's *Essay on Criticism*," *Tennessee Studies in Literature* 12 (1967), 57-68.

G. WILSON KNIGHT. *The Burning Oracle*, pp. 155-59.

MAYNARD MACK. *English Masterpieces*, edited by William Frost, Maynard Mack, and Leonard Dean, vol. 5: *The Augustans*, pp. 20-23.

DOUGLAS B. PARK. "'At Once the *Source*, and *End*': Nature's Defining Pattern in *An Essay on Criticism*," *PMLA* 90(5), October 1975, 861-73.

HUGO M. REICHARD. "Pope's Exacting Course in Criticism," *South Atlantic Quarterly* 75(4), Autumn 1976, 470-82.

WILLIAM BYSSHE STEIN. "Pope's 'An Essay on Criticism': The Play of Sophia," *Bucknell Review* 13(3), December 1965, 75-86.

"The First Book of Statius his Thebais"

JOHN M. ADEN. "'The Change of Scepters, and impending Woe': Political Allusion in Pope's Statius," *Philological Quarterly* 52(4), October 1973, 728-38.

"The First Epistle of the First Book of Horace Imitated"
see "Epistle to Bolingbroke"

"The First Epistle of the Second Book of Horace Imitated"
see "Epistle to Augustus"

"The First Ode of the Fourth Book of Horace Imitated"

ROBERT F. FLEISSNER. *Explicator* 34(6), February 1976, Item 42.

"The First Satire of the Second Book of Horace Imitated"

JOHN M. ADEN. "Pope and the Satiric Adversary," *Studies in English Literature 1500-1900* 2(3), Summer 1962, 270-75.

G. K. HUNTER. "The 'Romanticism' of Pope's Horace," *Essays in Criticism* 10(4), October 1960, 390-404.

MALCOLM KELSALL. "Augustus and Pope," *Huntington Library Quarterly* 39(2), February 1976, 117-31.

LAURENCE LERNER. *An Introduction to English Poetry*, pp. 87-105.

THOMAS E. MARESCA. "Pope's Defense of Satire: The First Satire of the Second Book of Horace, Imitated," *ELH* 31(4), December 1964, 366-94.

PHILIP PINKUS. "The New Satire of Augustan England," *University of Toronto Quarterly* 38(2), January 1969, 146-48.

CEDRIC D. REVERAND III. "*Ut pictura poesis*, and Pope's 'Satire II, i,'" *Eighteenth Century Studies* 9(4), Summer 1976, 553-68.

FREDERICK S. TROY. "Pope's Images of Man," *Massachusetts Review* 1(2), Winter 1960, 376-81.

"I am His Highness' dog at Kew"

HOWARD NEMEROV. "Bottom's Dream: The Likeness of Poems and Jokes," *Virginia Quarterly Review* 42(4), Autumn 1966, 566-67. Reprinted in: Howard Nemerov. *Reflexions on Poetry & Poetics*, p. 12.

W. K. THOMAS. "His Highness' Dog at Kew," *College English* 30(7), April 1969, 581-82.

"Messiah"

JEFFRY B. SPENCER. *Heroic Nature*, pp. 207-11.

"Moral Essays"

see "Epistle to a Lady," "Epistle to Addison," "Epistle to Bathurst," "Epistle to Burlington," and "Epistle to Cobham"

POPE, ALEXANDER *(Cont.)*

"Ode for Music on St. Cecilia's Day"

EARL R. WASSERMAN. "Pope's *Ode for Musick*," *ELH* 28(2), June 1961, 169-86.

"Ode on Solitude"

DUSTIN GRIFFIN. "Revisions in Pope's 'Ode on Solitude,' " *Modern Language Quarterly* 36(4), December 1975, 369-75.

DONALD STAUFFER. *The Nature of Poetry*, pp. 160-62.

"Pastorals"

see also "Autumn," "Spring," and "Winter"

MARTIN C. BATTESTIN. "The Transforming Power: Nature and Art in Pope's Pastorals," *Eighteenth Century Studies* 2(3), Spring 1969, 183-204.

DAVID S. DURANT. "Man and Nature in Alexander Pope's *Pastorals*," *Studies in English Literature 1500-1900* 11(3), Summer 1971, 469-85.

"The Rape of the Lock"

KENT BEYETTE. "Milton and Pope's *The Rape of the Lock*," *Studies in English Literature 1500-1900* 16(3), Summer 1976, 421-36.

CLEANTH BROOKS. "The Case of Miss Arabella Fermor: A Re-Examination," *Sewanee Review* 51(4), Autumn 1943, 505-24.

CLEANTH BROOKS. *The Well Wrought Urn*, pp. 80-104; revised ed., pp. 65-84.

HARRY BROWN and JOHN MILSTEAD. *What the Poem Means*, pp. 168-71.

W. B. CARNOCHAN. *Explicator* 22(6), February 1964, Item 45.

MURRAY COHEN. "Versions of the Lock: Readers of 'The Rape of the Lock,' " *ELH* 43(1), Spring 1976, 53-73.

RALPH COHEN. "Transformation in *The Rape of the Lock*," *Eighteenth Century Studies* 2(3), Spring 1969, 205-24.

RICHARD I. COOK. "Garth's *Dispensary* and Pope's *Rape of the Lock*," *CLA Journal* 6(2), December 1962, 107-16.

MICHAEL G. COOKE. *The Romantic Will*, pp. 70-76.

A. E. DYSON and JULIAN LOVELOCK. *Masterful Images*, pp. 97-123.

ROBERT FOLKENFLIK. "Metamorphosis in *The Rape of the Lock*," *Ariel* 5(2), April 1974, 27-36.

J. P. HARDY. *Reinterpretations*, pp. 50-80.

STANLEY EDGAR HYMAN. "The Rape of the Lock," *Hudson Review* 13(3), Autumn 1960, 406-12.

G. WILSON KNIGHT. *The Burning Oracle*, pp. 136-48.

MURRAY KRIEGER. *The Classic Vision*, pp. 105-24.

MURRAY KRIEGER. "The 'Frail China Jar' and the Rude Hand of Chaos," *Centennial Review* 5(2), Spring 1961, 176-94.

BARRY M. KROLL. "The Relationship of the Supernatural Machinery to Humoral Doctrine in *The Rape of the Lock* (1714)," *Thoth* 14(1), Winter 1973-74, 45-50.

MAYNARD MACK. *English Masterpieces*, edited by William Frost, Maynard Mack, and Leonard Dean, vol. 5: *The Augustans*, pp. 23-26.

JOHN B. McKEE. "The 'Outside World' and the Game of Omber in Pope's *The Rape of the Lock*: An Experiment in the Use of Evolutionary Evidence," *Concerning Poetry* 9(2), Fall 1976, 47-52.

JEFFREY MEYERS. "The Personality of Belinda's Baron: Pope's 'The Rape of the Lock,' " *American Imago* 26(1), Spring 1969, 71-77.

REBECCA PRICE PARKIN. "The Quality of Alexander Pope's Huron," *College English* 14(4), January 1953, 199.

JOHN PRESTON. " 'Th' Informing Soul': Creative Irony in *The Rape of the Lock*," *Durham University Journal*, n.s., 27(3), June 1966, 125-30.

RICARDO QUINTANA. " 'The Rape of the Lock' as a Comedy of Continuity," *Review of English Literature* 7(2), April 1966, 9-19.

HUGO M. REICHARD. "The Love Affair in Pope's *Rape of the Lock*," *PMLA* 69(4), September 1954, 887-902.

PAT ROGERS. "Faery Lore and *The Rape of the Lock*," *Review of English Studies*, n.s., 25(97), February 1974, 25-38.

PAT ROGERS. "Wit and Grammar in *The Rape of the Lock*," *Journal of English and Germanic Philology* 72(1), January 1973, 17-31.

WOLFGANG E. H. RUDAT. "Another Look at the Limits of Allusion: Pope's *Rape of the Lock* and the Virgilian Tradition," *Durham University Journal*, n.s., 40(1), December 1978, 27-34.

A. J. M. SMITH. "Pope: The Rape of the Lock," in *Master Poems of the English Language*, pp. 285-89.

PATRICIA MEYER SPACKS. "Pope's Satiric Use of Nature," *Studies in the Literary Imagination* 5(2), October 1972, 41-42.

HAROLD TOLIVER. "The Augustan Balance of Nature and Art in 'The Rape of the Lock,' " *Concerning Poetry* 1(1), Spring 1968, 58-69.

HAROLD E. TOLIVER. *Pastoral Forms and Attitudes*, pp. 177-89.

AUSTIN WARREN. "The Mask of Pope," *Sewanee Review* 54(1), Winter 1946, 27-29.

AUSTIN WARREN. *Rage for Order*, pp. 46-49. Reprinted in: *Modern Literary Criticism*, pp. 333-35. Also: *Essays in Modern Literary Criticism*, pp. 371-73.

EARL R. WASSERMAN. "The Limits of Allusion in *The Rape of the Lock*," *Journal of English and Germanic Philology* 65(3), July 1966, 425-44.

W. K. WIMSATT. *Day of the Leopards*, pp. 99-116.

"The Second Epistle of the Second Book of Horace Imitated"

AUBREY L. WILLIAMS. "Pope and Horace: *The Second Epistle of the Second Book*," in *Restoration and Eighteenth-Century Literature*, pp. 309-21.

"The Second Satire of the Second Book of Horace Imitated"

DONALD J. GREENE. " 'Dramatic Texture' in Pope," in *From Sensibility to Romanticism*, pp. 32-37.

PHILIP PINKUS. "The New Satire of Augustan England," *University of Toronto Quarterly* 38(2), January 1969, 148-49.

"Spring"

see also "Pastorals"

JEFFRY B. SPENCER. *Heroic Nature*, pp. 199-202.

"Well, if it be my time to quit the Stage" (*The Satires of Dr. John Donne*, IV)

WILLIAM YOUNGREN. "Generality in Augustan Satire," in *In Defense of Reading*, pp. 207-17.

"Windsor-Forest"

SANFORD BUDICK. *Poetry of Civilization*, pp. 111-24.

FRANCES M. CLEMENTS. "Landsdowne, Pope, and the Unity of *Windsor-Forest*," *Modern Language Quarterly* 33(1), March 1972, 44-53.

DAVID R. HAUSER. "Pope's London and the Uses of Mythology," *Studies in English Literature 1500-1900* 6(3), Summer 1966, 465-82.

JAMES M. KIEHL. "*Windsor-Forest* as Epical Counterpart," *Thoth* 7(2), Spring 1966, 53-67.

G. WILSON KNIGHT. *The Burning Oracle*, pp. 131-36.

MAYNARD MACK. "On Reading Pope," *College English* 7(5), February 1946, 264-68.

DAVID B. MORRIS. "Virgilian Attitudes in Pope's *Windsor-Forest*," *Texas Studies in Literature and Language* 15(2), Summer 1973, 231-50.

FREDERICK A. POTTLE. *The Idiom of Poetry*, pp. 113-22; second ed., pp. 121-29.

JEFFRY B. SPENCER. *Heroic Nature*, pp. 211-16.

A. J. VARNEY. "The Composition of Pope's *Windsor Forest*," *Durham University Journal*, n.s., 36(1), December 1974, 57-67.

EARL R. WASSERMAN. *The Subtler Language*, pp. 101-68.

"Winter"

see also "Pastorals"

GARY A. BOIRE. "The Context of Allusion and Pope's 'Winter' Pastoral," *Concerning Poetry* 10(1), Spring 1977, 79-84.

JEFFRY B. SPENCER. *Heroic Nature*, pp. 204-7.

PORTER, PETER

"Annotations of Auschwitz"

LAWRENCE R. RIES. *Wolf Masks*, pp. 147-48.

"Last Days"

ROGER GARFITT. "The Group," in *British Poetry Since 1960*, pp. 53-54.

"What A Lying Lot the Writers Are"

DAVID HOLBROOK. *Lost Bearings in English Poetry*, pp. 189-90.

POUND, EZRA

"Addendum for Canto C"

FRED MORAMARCO. "Concluding an Epic: The Drafts and Fragments of *The Cantos*," *American Literature* 49(3), November 1977, 324.

"The Alchemist"

M. L. ROSENTHAL. *The Modern Poets*, p. 53. Reprinted in: *Modern American Poetry*, edited by Jerome Mazzaro, pp. 159-60.

"The Ballad of the Goodly Fere"

GÉMINO H. ABAD. *A Formal Approach to Lyric Poetry*, pp. 172-73, 175-76.

GÉMINO H. ABAD. *In Another Light*, pp. 170-71.

HARRY BROWN and JOHN MILSTEAD. *What the Poem Means*, p. 172.

LAURA RIDING and ROBERT GRAVES. *A Survey of Modernist Poetry*, pp. 140-41.

"Ballatetta"

M. L. ROSENTHAL. "Ezra Pound and T. S. Eliot," in *English Poetry*, edited by Alan Sinfield, p. 189.

"Canto I"

HARRY BROWN and JOHN MILSTEAD. *What the Poem Means*, pp. 172-73.

MAX HALPEREN. "How to Read a Canto," in *The Twenties*, edited by Richard E. Langford and William E. Taylor, pp. 7-8. Reprinted in: *The Twenties*, edited by Warren French, pp. 337-39.

WILLIAM VAN O'CONNOR. "Ezra Pound," in *Seven Modern American Poets*, pp. 142-43.

WALTER SUTTON. *American Free Verse*, pp. 68-69.

"Canto II"

GUY DAVENPORT. "Ezra Pound's Radiant Gists: A Reading of Cantos II and IV," *Wisconsin Studies in Contemporary Literature* 3(2), Spring-Summer 1962, 50-56.

BABETTE DEUTSCH. *Poetry in Our Time*, p. 134; second ed., p. 144.

JOHN L. FOSTER. "Pound's Revision of Cantos I-III," *Modern Philology* 63(3), February 1966, 242-44.

MAX HALPEREN. "How to Read a Canto," in *The Twenties*, edited by Richard E. Langford and William E. Taylor, pp. 8-10. Reprinted in: *The Twenties*, edited by Warren French, pp. 339-43.

WALTER SUTTON. *American Free Verse*, pp. 69-70.

"Canto III"

MAX HALPEREN. "How to Read a Canto," in *The Twenties*, edited by Richard E. Langford and William E. Taylor, p. 10. Reprinted in: *The Twenties*, edited by Warren French, pp. 343-44.

"Canto IV"

GAY DAVENPORT. "Ezra Pound's Radiant Gists: A Reading of Cantos II and IV," *Wisconsin Studies in Contemporary Literature* 3(2), Spring-Summer 1962, 56-64.

MAX HALPEREN. "How to Read a Canto," in *The Twenties*, edited by Richard E. Langford and William E. Taylor, pp. 10-11. Reprinted in: *The Twenties*, edited by Warren French, pp. 344-46.

MARJORIE G. PERLOFF. "Pound and Rimbaud: The Retreat from Symbolism," *Iowa Review* 6(1), Winter 1975, 103-4.

"Canto VI"

MAX HALPEREN. "How to Read a Canto," in *The Twenties*, edited by Richard E. Langford and William E. Taylor, pp. 11-12. Reprinted in: *The Twenties*, edited by Warren French, pp. 346-49.

"Canto VIII"

MARJORIE G. PERLOFF. "Pound and Rimbaud: The Retreat from Symbolism," *Iowa Review* 6(1), Winter 1975, 107-10.

"Canto IX"

MARJORIE G. PERLOFF. "Pound and Rimbaud: The Retreat from Symbolism," *Iowa Review* 6(1), Winter 1975, 106-11.

"Canto XIII"

M. L. ROSENTHAL. *The Modern Poets*, p. 68.

"Canto XVI"

KIMON FRIAR and JOHN MALCOLM BRINNIN. *Modern Poetry*, p. 525.

"Canto XX"

KIMON FRIAR and JOHN MALCOLM BRINNIN. *Modern Poetry*, p. 526.

"Canto XXI"

KIMON FRIAR and JOHN MALCOLM BRINNIN. *Modern Poetry*, pp. 526-27.

P. L. SURETTE. "The City of Dioce, U.S.A.: Pound and America," *Bucknell Review* 20(2), Fall 1972, 25-26.

"Canto XXIX"

M. L. ROSENTHAL. *Sailing into the Unknown*, pp. 88-94.

"Canto XXXVII"

RON BAAR. "Ezra Pound: Poet as Historian," *American Literature* 42(4), January 1971, 531-43.

POUND, EZRA *(Cont.)*

"Canto XXXIX"

> LILLIAN FEDER. *Ancient Myth in Modern Poetry*, pp. 111-12, 201-2.

"Canto XLI"

> JOHN LAUBER. "Pound's *Cantos*: A Fascist Epic," *Journal of American Studies* 12(1), April 1978, 5.

"Canto XLV"

> HARRY BROWN and JOHN MILSTEAD. *What the Poem Means*, p. 173.
>
> KIMON FRIAR and JOHN MALCOLM BRINNIN. *Modern Poetry*, p. 561.
>
> WALTER SUTTON. *American Free Verse*, pp. 73-74.

"Canto XLVI"

> BABETTE DEUTSCH. *Poetry in Our Time*, pp. 134-35; second ed., pp. 145-46.

"Canto XLVII"

> LILLIAN FEDER. *Ancient Myth in Modern Poetry*, pp. 114-15, 204-5.
>
> KIMON FRIAR and JOHN MALCOLM BRINNIN. *Modern Poetry*, p. 527.
>
> M. L. ROSENTHAL. *Sailing into the Unknown*, pp. 12-25.

"Canto XLVIII"

> LILLIAN FEDER. *Ancient Myth in Modern Poetry*, pp. 206-7.

"Canto LXXIII"

> JOHN LAUBER. "Pound's *Cantos*: A Fascist Epic," *Journal of American Studies* 12(1), April 1978, 19-20.

"Canto LXXIV"

> FRED MORAMARCO. "Thirty Years with The Pisan Cantos: A Reading," *Modern Poetry Studies* 9(1), Spring 1978, 4-8.
>
> M. L. ROSENTHAL. *Sailing into the Unknown*, pp. 101-4, 106-9. (P)
>
> WALTER SUTTON. *American Free Verse*, pp. 77-78.

"Canto LXXV"

> LOISANN OAKES. "An Explication of 'Canto LXXV' by Ezra Pound," *Wisconsin Studies in Contemporary Literature* 5(2), Summer 1964, 105-9.

"Canto LXXVI"

> FRED MORAMARCO. "Thirty Years with The Pisan Cantos: A Reading," *Modern Poetry Studies* 9(1), Spring 1978, 8-9.

"Canto LXXVII"

> FRED MORAMARCO. "Thirty Years with The Pisan Cantos: A Reading," *Modern Poetry Studies* 9(1), Spring 1978, 9-10.

"Canto LXXVIII"

> JOHN LAUBER. "Pound's *Cantos*: A Fascist Epic," *Journal of American Studies* 12(1), April 1978, 7.
>
> FRED MORAMARCO. "Thirty Years with The Pisan Cantos: A Reading," *Modern Poetry Studies* 9(1), Spring 1978, 10-11.

"Canto LXXIX"

> FRED MORAMARCO. "Thirty Years with The Pisan Cantos: A Reading," *Modern Poetry Studies* 9(1), Spring 1978, 11-12.

"Canto LXXX"

> FRED MORAMARCO. "Thirty Years with The Pisan Cantos: A Reading," *Modern Poetry Studies* 9(1), Spring 1978, 12-13.

"Canto LXXXI"

> FRED MORAMARCO. "Thirty Years with The Pisan Cantos: A Reading," *Modern Poetry Studies* 9(1), Spring 1978, 13-14.

"Canto LXXXII"

> FRED MORAMARCO. "Thirty Years with The Pisan Cantos: A Reading," *Modern Poetry Studies* 9(1), Spring 1978, 14-15.
>
> ROY HARVEY PEARCE. *The Continuity of American Poetry*, pp. 84-88.

"Canto LXXXIII"

> FRED MORAMARCO. "Thirty Years with The Pisan Cantos: A Reading," *Modern Poetry Studies* 9(1), Spring 1978, 15-16.

"Canto LXXXIV"

> FRED MORAMARCO. "Thirty Years with The Pisan Cantos: A Reading," *Modern Poetry Studies* 9(1), Spring 1978, 16-17.

"Canto LXXXVII"

> DONALD DAVIE. "The Rock-Drill Cantos," in *Modern Poetry*, pp. 455-56.

"Canto LXXXVIII"

> RON BAAR. "Ezra Pound: Poet as Historian," *American Literature* 42(4), January 1971, 531-43.
>
> JAMES J. WILHELM. "The Dragon and the Duel: A Defense of Pound's Canto 88," *Twentieth Century Literature* 20(2), April 1974, 114-25.

"Canto LXXXIX"

> RON BAAR. "Ezra Pound: Poet as Historian," *American Literature* 42(4), January 1971, 531-43.

"Canto XC"

> DONALD DAVIE. "The Rock-Drill Cantos," in *Modern Poetry*, pp. 451-59.

"Canto XCI"

> DONALD DAVIE. "The Rock-Drill Cantos," in *Modern Poetry*, pp. 461-68.

"Canto CX"

> FRED MORAMARCO. "Concluding an Epic: The Drafts and Fragments of *The Cantos*," *American Literature* 49(3), November 1977, 310-14.

"Canto CXII"

> FRED MORAMARCO. "Concluding an Epic: The Drafts and Fragments of *The Cantos*," *American Literature* 49(3), November 1977, 315-16.

"Canto CXIII"

> FRED MORAMARCO. "Concluding an Epic: The Drafts and Fragments of *The Cantos*," *American Literature* 49(3), November 1977, 316-18.

"Canto CXIV"

> FRED MORAMARCO. "Concluding an Epic: The Drafts and Fragments of *The Cantos*," *American Literature* 49(3), November 1977, 318-21.

"Canto CXV"

> FRED MORAMARCO. "Concluding an Epic: The Drafts and Fragments of *The Cantos*," *American Literature* 49(3), November 1977, 322.

"Canto CXVI"

> DAVID HOLBROOK. *Lost Bearings in English Poetry*, pp. 61-63.
>
> FRED MORAMARCO. "Concluding an Epic: The Drafts and Fragments of *The Cantos*," *American Literature* 49(3), November 1977, 322-23.

"Canto CXX"

FRED MORAMARCO. "Concluding an Epic: The Drafts and Fragments of *The Cantos*," *American Literature* 49(3), November 1977, 325-26.

"Donzella Beata"

RON D. K. BANERJEE. "Dante Through the Looking Glass: Rossetti, Pound and Eliot," *Comparative Literature* 24(2), Spring 1972, 140-43.

"Fan Piece for Her Imperial Lord"

EARL MINER. "Pound, *Haiku* and the Image," *Hudson Review* 9(4), Winter 1956-57, 580-81.

RICHARD EUGENE SMITH. "Ezra Pound and the Haiku," *College English* 26(7), April 1965, 525-26.

"La Fraisne"

L. S. DEMBO. *Conceptions of Reality in Modern American Poetry*, pp. 160-61.

"Francesca"

AGNES STEIN. *The Uses of Poetry*, pp. 143-44.

"The Garden"

HARRY BROWN and JOHN MILSTEAD. *What the Poem Means*, p. 176.

MARK VAN DOREN. *Introduction to Poetry*, pp. 46-49.

"Greek Epigram"

SHARON J. WIGGS. "Pound's 'Greek Epigram': Indictment and Sentence for Inconstancy," *Studies in the Humanities* 7(1), December 1978, 48-50.

"Homage to Sextus Propertius"

RICHARD P. BLACKMUR. "Masks of Ezra Pound," *Hound and Horn* 7(2), January-March 1934, 184-91. Reprinted in: R. P. Blackmur. *Language as Gesture*, pp. 130-36. Also: R. P. Blackmur. *Form and Value in Modern Poetry*, pp. 85-92.

L. S. DEMBO. *Conceptions of Reality in Modern American Poetry*, pp. 163-64.

LILLIAN FEDER. *Ancient Myth in Modern Poetry*, pp. 92-99.

VINCENT E. MILLER. "The Serious Wit of Pound's *Homage to Sextus Propertius*," *Contemporary Literature* 16(4), Autumn 1975, 452-62.

M. L. ROSENTHAL. *The Modern Poets*, pp. 55-58. Reprinted in: *Modern American Poetry*, edited by Jerome Mazzaro, pp. 161-64.

JOHN SPEIRS. "Mr. Pound's Propertius," *Scrutiny* 3(4), March 1935, 409-18.

J. P. SULLIVAN. "Pound's *Homage to Propertius*: The Structure of a Mask," *Essays in Criticism* 10(3), July 1960, 239-49.

"Hugh Selwyn Mauberley"

RICHARD P. BLACKMUR. "Masks of Ezra Pound," *Hound and Horn* 7(2), January-March 1934, 180-84. Reprinted in: R. P. Blackmur. *Language as Gesture*, pp. 126-30. Reprinted in: R. P. Blackmur. *Form and Value in Modern Poetry*, pp. 81-85.

HARRY BROWN and JOHN MILSTEAD. *What the Poem Means*, pp. 173-75.

THOMAS E. CONNOLLY. "Further Notes on Mauberley," *Accent* 16(1), Winter 1965, 59-67.

DONALD DAVIE. *The Poet in the Imaginary Museum*, pp. 81-92.

L. S. DEMBO. *Conceptions of Reality in Modern American Poetry*, pp. 164-67.

BABETTE DEUTSCH. *This Modern Poetry*, pp. 115-18.

BERNARD DUFFEY. *Poetry in America*, pp. 298-301.

LILLIAN FEDER. *Ancient Myth in Modern Poetry*, pp. 99-105.

A. L. FRENCH. " 'Olympian Apathein': Pound's *Hugh Selwyn Mauberley* and Modern Poetry," *Essays in Criticism* 15(4), October 1965, 428-45.

KIMON FRIAR and JOHN MALCOLM BRINNIN. *Modern Poetry*, pp. 527-31.

FREDERICK J. HOFFMAN. *The Twenties*, pp. 37-46; revised ed., pp. 56-66.

DAVID HOLBROOK. *Lost Bearings in English Poetry*, pp. 58-91.

F. R. LEAVIS. *New Bearings on English Poetry*, pp. 138-51.

RICHARD A. LONG. *Explicator* 10(8), June 1952, Item 56.

KARL MALKOFF. "Allusion as Irony: Pound's Use of Dante in *Hugh Selwyn Mauberley*," *Minnesota Review* 7(1), 1967, 81-88.

WILLIAM VAN O'CONNOR. "Pound: Hugh Selwyn Mauberley," in *Master Poems of the English Language*, pp. 924-27.

CHRISTOPHER REISS. "In Defence of *Mauberley*," *Essays in Criticism* 16(3), July 1966, 351-55.

M. L. ROSENTHAL. *The Modern Poets*, pp. 61-66. Reprinted in: *Modern American Poetry*, edited by Jerome Mazzaro, pp. 167-72.

WALTER SUTTON. *American Free Verse*, pp. 57-64.

"In a Station of the Metro"

GÉMINO H. ABAD. *In Another Light*, pp. 134-39.

WARREN BECK. "Boundaries of Poetry," *College English* 4(6), March 1943, 346.

CLEANTH BROOKS and ROBERT PENN WARREN. *Understanding Poetry*, pp. 175-76; revised ed., pp. 78-80; third ed., pp. 89-90; fourth ed., pp. 71-73.

JOHN J. ESPEY. *Explicator* 11(8), June 1953, Item 59. Abridged in: *The Case for Poetry*, p. 287; second ed., pp. 231-32.

JOSEPH H. FRIEND. "Teaching the 'Grammar of Poetry,' " *College English* 27(5), February 1966, 362-63.

THOMAS A. HANZO. *Explicator* 11(4), February 1953, Item 26. Abridged in: *The Case for Poetry*, p. 287; second ed., p. 231.

YOSHIYUKI IWAMOTO. *Explicator* 19(5), February 1961, Item 30.

MICHAEL L. LASSER. *Explicator* 19(5), February 1961, Item 30.

LARRY OAKNER. "Going Down with Williams: A De/Structural Study of *Kora in Hell: Improvisations*," *Thoth* 16(1), Winter 1975-76, 30-31.

JOHN OLIVER PERRY. *The Experience of Poems*, pp. 265-66.

M. L. ROSENTHAL and A. J. M. SMITH. *Exploring Poetry*, pp. 157-58; second ed., p. 68.

"In Exitum Cuiusdam"

M. L. ROSENTHAL. *Sailing into the Unknown*, pp. 69-72.

"Lament of the Frontier Guard"

BABETTE DEUTSCH. *Poetry in Our Time*, pp. 131-32; second ed., pp. 141-42.

"Near Perigord"

THOMAS E. CONNOLLY. "Ezra Pound's 'Near Perigord': The Background of a Poem," *Comparative Literature* 8(2), Spring 1956, 110-16.

POUND, EZRA *(Cont.)*

"A Pact"

MARIO L. D'AVANZO. *Explicator* 24(6), February 1966, Item 51.

DONALD B. GIBSON. "The Good Black Poet and the Good Gray Poet: The Poetry of Hughes and Whitman," in *Modern Black Poets*, p. 53.

"Papyrus"

CHRISTOPHER M. DAWSON. *Explicator* 9(4), February 1951, Item 30.

GILBERT HIGHET. *The Classical Tradition*, p. 517.

"Portrait d'une Femme"

HARRY BROWN and JOHN MILSTEAD. *What the Poem Means*, p. 175.

BABETTE DEUTSCH. *Poetry in Our Time*, p. 127; second ed., p. 137.

RICHARD J. GIANNONE. "Eliot's 'Portrait of a Lady' and Pound's 'Portrait d'une Femme,'" *Twentieth Century Literature* 5(3), October 1959, 131-34.

LAURENCE PERRINE. *100 American Poems of the Twentieth Century*, pp. 81-83.

HYATT H. WAGGONER. *American Poets*, pp. 418-19.

"The Return"

BABETTE DEUTSCH. *Poetry in Our Time*, pp. 124-25; second ed., pp. 134-35.

M. L. ROSENTHAL. "Ezra Pound and T. S. Eliot," in *English Poetry*, edited by Alan Sinfield, p. 190.

M. L. ROSENTHAL. *The Modern Poets*, pp. 51-53. Reprinted in: *Modern American Poetry*, edited by Jerome Mazzaro, pp. 157-58.

WALTER SUTTON. *American Free Verse*, pp. 51-52.

"The River-Merchant's Wife: A Letter"

JOHN OLIVER PERRY. *The Experience of Poems*, pp. 69-71.

"The Seafarer"

VILAS SARANG. "Pound's *Seafarer*," *Concerning Poetry* 6(2), Fall 1973, 5-11.

WALTER SUTTON. *American Free Verse*, pp. 52-53.

"Sestina: Altaforte"

HARRY BROWN and JOHN MILSTEAD. *What the Poem Means*, p. 176.

PAUL CUMMINS. "The Sestina in the 20th Century," *Concerning Poetry* 11(1), Spring 1978, 16-17.

"Song of the Bowmen of Shu"

WALTER SUTTON. *American Free Verse*, pp. 55-56.

"The Study in Aesthetics"

M. L. ROSENTHAL. "Ezra Pound and T. S. Eliot," in *English Poetry*, edited by Alan Sinfield, pp. 187-89.

"The tea-rose tea gown, etc." (Hugh Selwyn Mauberly, 3)

ARCHIBALD MacLEISH. *Poetry and Experience*, pp. 39-41.

MARJORIE G. PERLOFF. "Pound and Rimbaud: The Retreat from Symbolism," *Iowa Review* 6(1), Winter 1975, 100-1.

"Villanelle: The Psychological Hour"

M. L. ROSENTHAL. *Sailing into the Unknown*, pp. 72-76.

"A Virginal"

HARRY BROWN and JOHN MILSTEAD. *What the Poem Means*, p. 172.

POWYS, JOHN COWPER

"The Castle of Gathore"

G. WILSON KNIGHT. *Neglected Powers*, pp. 208-9.

"The Classic Touch"

G. WILSON KNIGHT. *Neglected Powers*, pp. 206-7.

"The *Disaster*"

G. WILSON KNIGHT. *Neglected Powers*, p. 210.

"The Face"

G. WILSON KNIGHT. *Neglected Powers*, p. 209.

"The Rider"

G. WILSON KNIGHT. *Neglected Powers*, p. 222.

"Saturn"

G. WILSON KNIGHT. *Neglected Powers*, pp. 204-5.

"The Saturnian"

G. WILSON KNIGHT. *Neglected Powers*, p. 203.

"The Ship"

G. WILSON KNIGHT. *Neglected Powers*, pp. 222-25.

"The Ultimate"

G. WILSON KNIGHT. *Neglected Powers*, pp. 210-12.

"Whiteness"

G. WILSON KNIGHT. *Neglected Powers*, p. 201.

PRINCE, FRANK

"The Old Age of Michelangelo"

MICHAEL BLACK. "Frank Prince," in *Criticism in Action*, pp. 144-62.

"Soldiers Bathing"

VERNON SCANNELL. *Not Without Glory*, pp. 153-55.

PRIOR, MATTHEW

"Answer to Chloe Jealous, in the same Stile. The Author sick"

RONALD ROWER. "Pastoral Wars: Matthew Prior's Poems to Chloe," *Ball State University Forum* 19(2), Spring 1978, 48.

"A Better Answer"

RONALD ROWER. "Pastoral Wars: Matthew Prior's Poems to Chloe," *Ball State University Forum* 19(2), Spring 1978, 48-49.

"Chloe Jealous"

RONALD ROWER. "Pastoral Wars: Matthew Prior's Poems to Chloe," *Ball State University Forum* 19(2), Spring 1978, 47-48.

"Epistle to Fleetwood Shephard"

JAY ARNOLD LEVINE. "The Status of the Verse Epistle Before Pope," *Studies in Philology* 59(4), October 1962, 662-64.

"The Garland"

RONALD ROWER. "Pastoral Wars: Matthew Prior's Poems to Chloe," *Ball State University Forum* 19(2), Spring 1978, 46-47.

"Henry and Emma"

KARL KROEBER. *Romantic Narrative Art*, pp. 13-19.

"The Lady Who Offers Her Looking Glass to Venus"

F. W. BATESON. *English Poetry*, pp. 83-84.

RONALD ROWER. "Pastoral Wars: Matthew Prior's Poems to Chloe," *Ball State University Forum* 19(2), Spring 1978, 47.

"Lisetta's Reply"

RONALD ROWER. "Pastoral Wars: Matthew Prior's Poems to Chloe," *Ball State University Forum* 19(2), Spring 1978, 46.

"A Lover's Anger"

RONALD ROWER. "Pastoral Wars: Matthew Prior's Poems to Chloe," *Ball State University Forum* 19(2), Spring 1978, 44-45.

"The Merchant to Secure"

RONALD ROWER. "Pastoral Wars: Matthew Prior's Poems to Chloe," *Ball State University Forum* 19(2), Spring 1978, 41-42.

"An Ode"

MARK VAN DOREN. *Introduction to Poetry*, pp. 17-21.

"On Beauty. A Riddle"

RONALD ROWER. "Pastoral Wars: Matthew Prior's Poems to Chloe," *Ball State University Forum* 19(2), Spring 1978, 45-46.

"The Question, to Lisetta"

RONALD ROWER. "Pastoral Wars: Matthew Prior's Poems to Chloe," *Ball State University Forum* 19(2), Spring 1978, 46.

"Satyr on the Poets"

LEONARD A. MOSKOVIT. "Pope and the Tradition of the Neoclassical Imitation," *Studies in English Literature 1500-1900* 8(3), Summer 1968, 454-55.

"To a Child of Quality"

LAURENCE LERNER. *An Introduction to English Poetry*, pp. 68-69.

"To the Honourable Charles Montague, esq."

LEONARD E. HELD, JR. *Explicator* 28(9), May 1970, Item 75.

"Written in the Beginning of Mezeray's History of France"

DAVID DAICHES. *A Study of Literature*, pp. 168-70.

LEONARD UNGER and WILLIAM VAN O'CONNOR. *Poems for Study*, pp. 15-16.

PROCTOR, ADELAIDE ANNE

"The Pilgrims"

CLEANTH BROOKS and ROBERT PENN WARREN. *Understanding Poetry*, pp. 334-36; revised ed., pp. 181-83; third ed., pp. 223-25.

PROKOSCH, FREDERIC

"Elegy"

JOSEPH WARREN BEACH. *Obsessive Images*, pp. 318-19.

"Going into Exile"

JOSEPH WARREN BEACH. *Obsessive Images*, p. 160.

"The Sacred Wood"

JOSEPH WARREN BEACH. *Obsessive Images*, pp. 130-31.

PUTNAM, PHELPS

"Ballad of a Strange Thing"

F. O. MATTHIESSEN. "Phelps Putnam (1894-1948)," *Kenyon Review* 11(1), Winter 1949, 80-82. Reprinted in: F. O. Matthiessen. *The Responsibilities of the Critic*, pp. 274-76.

"The Five Seasons"

MORTON D. ZABEL. "Phelps Putnam and America," *Poetry* 40(6), September 1932, 335-44.

"Hasbrouck and the Rose"

F. O. MATTHIESSEN. "Phelps Putnam (1894-1948)," *Kenyon Review* 11(1), Winter 1949, 78-80. Reprinted in: F. O. Matthiessen. *The Responsibilities of the Critic*, pp. 273-74.

PYBUS, RODNEY

"Anne Frank's House"

EDWARD BRUNNER. "Uncomely Relations," *Iowa Review* 6(3-4), Summer-Fall 1975, 237.

"Marketing"

EDWARD BRUNNER. "Uncomely Relations," *Iowa Review* 6(3-4), Summer-Fall 1975, 237-38.

ANDREW WATERMAN. "Andrew Waterman on Rodney Pybus," *Iowa Review* 6(3-4), Summer-Fall 1975, 211-12.

PYNCHON, THOMAS

"Every night is Christmas Eve on Old East Main" (*V*)

WILLIAM VESTERMAN. "Pynchon's Poetry," *Twentieth Century Literature* 21(2), May 1975, 214-15.

"There is a Hand to turn the time" (*Gravity's Rainbow*)

WILLIAM VESTERMAN. "Pynchon's Poetry," *Twentieth Century Literature* 21(2), May 1975, 218-19.

Q

QUARLES, FRANCIS

"O fetch me Apples from Loves fruitfull Grove"
  STANLEY STEWART. *The Enclosed Garden*, pp. 88-90.

"On Zacheus (I)"
  STANLEY STEWART. *The Enclosed Garden*, p. 91.

R

RAFFEL, BURTON

"Further Reflections on Existence, Manner, Mode, and Function"

> JOHN MILES FOLEY. "Singer of His Own Songs: The Poems of Burton Raffel," *Modern Poetry Studies* 9(2), Autumn 1978, 143-45.

"Knight's Hall, Acre"

> JOHN MILES FOLEY. "Singer of His Own Songs: The Poems of Burton Raffel," *Modern Poetry Studies* 9(2), Autumn 1978, 142-43.

"Moving Day"

> JOHN MILES FOLEY. "Singer of His Own Songs: The Poems of Burton Raffel," *Modern Poetry Studies* 9(2), Autumn 1978, 145-47.

"Old Friends Re-Seen"

> JOHN MILES FOLEY. "Singer of His Own Songs: The Poems of Burton Raffel," *Modern Poetry Studies* 9(2), Autumn 1978, 137-40.

RAINE, KATHLEEN

"Air"

> RALPH J. MILLS, JR. "The Visionary Poetry of Kathleen Raine," *Renascence* 14(3), Spring 1962, 149.

"The Hyacinth"

> RALPH J. MILLS, JR. "The Visionary Poetry of Kathleen Raine," *Renascence* 14(3), Spring 1962, 146-47.

"Isis Wandered"

> RALPH J. MILLS, JR. "The Visionary Poetry of Kathleen Raine," *Renascence* 14(3), Spring 1962, 153.

"Love Spell"

> RALPH J. MILLS, JR. "The Visionary Poetry of Kathleen Raine," *Renascence* 14(3), Spring 1962, 152.

"Lyric" (*Stone and Flower*)

> RALPH J. MILLS, JR. "The Visionary Poetry of Kathleen Raine," *Renascence* 14(3), Spring 1962, 139-40.

"Message"

> RALPH J. MILLS, JR. "The Visionary Poetry of Kathleen Raine," *Renascence* 14(3), Spring 1962, 152-53.

"Not upon earth, as you suppose"

> RALPH J. MILLS, JR. "The Visionary Poetry of Kathleen Raine," *Renascence* 14(3), Spring 1962, 144-45.

"Self"

> RALPH J. MILLS, JR. "The Visionary Poetry of Kathleen Raine," *Renascence* 14(3), Spring 1962, 150.

"The Transit of the Gods"

> LILLIAN FEDER. *Ancient Myth in Modern Poetry*, pp. 18-20.

"The Tree of Heaven"

> RALPH J. MILLS, JR. "The Visionary Poetry of Kathleen Raine," *Renascence* 14(3), Spring 1962, 148.

"Yours is the face that the earth turns to me"

> RALPH J. MILLS, JR. "The Visionary Poetry of Kathleen Raine," *Renascence* 14(3), Spring 1962, 143.

RAINOLDS, HENRY

"A Blackmore Mayd wooing a faire Boy: sent to the Author by Mr. Hen. Rainolds"

> ELLIOT H. TOKSON. "The Image of the Negro in Four Seventeenth-Century Love Poems," *Modern Language Quarterly* 30(4), December 1969, 510-16.

RAKOSI, CARL

"A Journey Away"

> L. S. DEMBO. "The Poetry of Carl Rakosi," *Iowa Review* 2(1), Winter 1971, 74-76.

"Time to Kill"

> L. S. DEMBO. "The Poetry of Carl Rakosi," *Iowa Review* 2(1), Winter 1971, 78-79.

"Young Girl"

> L. S. DEMBO. "The Poetry of Carl Rakosi," *Iowa Review* 2(1), Winter 1971, 77-78.

RALEGH, WALTER

"A Description of Love"

> MICHAEL WEST. "Raleigh's Disputed Authorship of 'A Description of Love,'" *English Language Notes* 10(2), December 1972, 92-99.

"Farewell to the Court"

> EDITH WHITEHURST WILLIAMS. "The Anglo-Saxon Theme of Exile in Renaissance Lyrics: A Perspective on Two Sonnets of Sir Walter Ralegh," *ELH* 42(2), Summer 1975, 171-80.

"The Lie"

> GEORGE ARMS and R. W. WHIDDEN. *Explicator* 3(6), April 1945, Item 50.

> JOSEPH BENNETT. "Raleigh: The Lie," in *Master Poems of the English Language*, pp. 10-12.

RALEGH, WALTER (*Cont.*)

"The Lie" (*cont.*)

> HARRY BROWN and JOHN MILSTEAD. *What the Poem Means*, p. 177.

> LAURENCE LERNER. *An Introduction to English Poetry*, pp. 28-35.

> LEONARD UNGER and WILLIAM VAN O'CONNOR. *Poems for Study*, pp. 99-100.

"Like to a Hermit"

> EDITH WHITEHURST WILLIAMS. "The Anglo-Saxon Theme of Exile in Renaissance Lyrics: A Perspective on Two Sonnets of Sir Walter Ralegh," *ELH* 42(2), Summer 1975, 180-86.

"Methought I saw the grave, where *Laura* lay"

> PETER URE. "The Poetry of Sir Walter Ralegh," *Review of English Literature* 1(3), July 1960, 22-23.

"The Ocean to Cynthia"

> JOYCE HORNER. "The Large Landscape: A Study of Certain Images in Ralegh," *Essays in Criticism* 5(3), July 1955, 199-207.

"The Ocean's Love to Cynthia"

> MICHAEL L. JOHNSON. "Some Problems of Unity in Sir Walter Ralegh's *The Ocean's Love to Cynthia*," *Studies in English Literature 1500-1900* 14(1), Winter 1974, 17-30.

"The Passionate Man's Pilgrimage"

> MELVIN W. ASKEW. *Explicator* 13(2), November 1954, Item 9.

> PHILIP EDWARDS. "Who Wrote *The Passionate Man's Pilgrimage?*" *English Literary Renaissance* 4(1), Winter 1974, 83-97.

> HARRY MORRIS. "*In Articulo Mortis*," *Tulane Studies in English* 11(1961), 32-33.

"Sir Walter Ralegh to his sonne"

> JAMES REEVES and MARTIN-SEYMOUR SMITH. *Inside Poetry*, pp. 68-70.

"Walsingham"

> O. C. WILLIAMS. *Explicator* 9(4), February 1951, Item 27.

"What is our life? A play of passion"

> T. R. BARNES. *English Verse*, pp. 24-25.

RANDALL, JAMES RYDER

"Maryland, My Maryland"

> ISAAC ASIMOV. *Familiar Poems, Annotated*, pp. 202-8.

RANDALL, MARGARET

"Written While It Rains Everyday"

> JAMES G. KENNEDY. "The Two European Cultures and the Necessary New Sense of Literature," *College English* 31(6), March 1970, 583.

RANDOLPH, THOMAS

"A Gratulatory to Mr. Ben Johnson for His Adopting of Him to Be His Son"

> EARL MINER. *The Cavalier Mode from Jonson to Cotton*, pp. 267-68.

RANSOM, JOHN CROWE

"The Address to the Scholars of New England"

> GUY OWEN. "John Crowe Ransom: The Evolution of His Style," in *The Twenties*, edited by Richard E. Langford and William E. Taylor, p. 51. Reprinted in: *Modern American Poetry*, edited by Guy Owen, p. 162.

"Amphibious Crocodile"

> RICHMOND CROOM BEATTY. "John Crowe Ransom as Poet," *Sewanee Review* 52(2), Summer 1944, 362-63.

> LOUIS D. RUBIN, JR. "The Wary Fugitive: John Crowe Ransom," *Sewanee Review* 82(4), Fall 1974, 615-18.

"Antique Harvesters"

> RICHARD GRAY. "The 'Compleat Gentleman': An Approach to John Crowe Ransom," *Southern Review*, n.s., 12(3), Summer 1976, 628-31.

> KARL F. KNIGHT. "Love As Symbol in the Poetry of Ransom," *Mississippi Quarterly* 13(3), Summer 1960, 136.

> VIVIENNE KOCH. "The Achievement of John Crowe Ransom," *Sewanee Review* 58(2), Spring 1950, 252-55.

> VIVIENNE KOCH. "The Poetry of John Crowe Ransom," in *Modern American Poetry*, edited by B. Rajan, pp. 58-61.

> JANE MARSTON. "Persona and Perspective in John Crowe Ransom's Poetry," *Mississippi Quarterly* 30(1), Winter 1976-77, 65-66.

> F. O. MATTHIESSEN. "Primarily Language," *Sewanee Review* 56(3), Summer 1948, 394-95. Reprinted in: F. O. Matthiessen. *The Responsibilities of the Critic*, pp. 43-44.

> LOUIS D. RUBIN, JR. "The Concept of Nature in Modern Southern Poetry," *American Quarterly* 9(1), Spring 1957, 69-70.

> LOUIS D. RUBIN, JR. "The Wary Fugitive: John Crowe Ransom," *Sewanee Review* 82(4), Fall 1974, 602-5.

> HYATT H. WAGGONER. *American Poets*, pp. 534-37.

"Armageddon"

> LOUIS D. RUBIN, JR. "The Wary Fugitive: John Crowe Ransom," *Sewanee Review* 82(4), Fall 1974, 601-2.

> JOHN L. STEWART. "John Crowe Ransom," in *Seven Modern American Poets*, pp. 169-71.

"The Bachelor"

> LOUISE COWAN. "The Communal World of Southern Literature," *Georgia Review* 14(3), Fall 1960, 251-52.

"Bells for John Whiteside's Daughter"

> M. E. BRADFORD. "A Modern Elegy: Ransom's 'Bells for John Whiteside's Daughter,'" *Mississippi Quarterly* 21(1), Winter 1967-68, 43-47.

> CLEANTH BROOKS, JOHN THIBAUT PURSER, and ROBERT PENN WARREN. *An Approach to Literature*, fifth ed., pp. 383-84.

> CLEANTH BROOKS and ROBERT PENN WARREN. *Understanding Poetry*, third ed., pp. 236-38.

> ROBERT B. HEILMAN. "Poetic and Prosaic: Program Notes on Opposite Numbers," *Pacific Spectator* 5 (Autumn 1951), 458-60. Reprinted in: *The Case for Poetry*, p. 293; second ed., p. 236.

> VIVIENNE KOCH. "The Poetry of John Crowe Ransom," in *Modern American Poetry*, edited by B. Rajan, pp. 43-44.

> MARION MONTGOMERY. "Bells for John Stewart's Burden: A Sermon upon the Desirable Death of the 'New Provincialism' Here Typified," *Georgia Review* 20(2), Summer 1966, 173-79.

> JOHN FREDERICK NIMS. *Western Wind*, p. 131.

> THORNTON H. PARSONS. "The Civilized Poetry of John Crowe Ransom," *Perspective* 13(4), Autumn 1964, 257-58.

> ELIAS SCHWARTZ. "Ransom's 'Bells for John Whiteside's Daughter,'" *English Language Notes* 1(4), June 1964, 284-85.

CHAD WALSH. *Doors into Poetry*, pp. 27-28.

ROBERT PENN WARREN. "John Crowe Ransom: A Study in Irony," *Virginia Quarterly Review* 11(1), January 1935, 105-6. Abridged in: *The Case for Poetry*, p. 293; second ed., pp. 235-36.

ROBERT PENN WARREN. "Pure and Impure Poetry," *Kenyon Review* 5(2), Spring 1943, 237-40. Reprinted in: *Criticism*, pp. 370-72. Also: *Reading Modern Poetry*, pp. 69-71; revised ed., pp. 42-44. Also: *The Kenyon Critics*, pp. 26-29. Also: *Critiques and Essays in Criticism*, pp. 92-94. Also: *Essays in Modern Literary Criticism*, pp. 253-55.

"Birthday of an Aging Seer"

ROBERT BUFFINGTON. "The Poetry of the Master's Old Age," *Georgia Review* 25(1), Spring 1971, 11-12.

"Blackberry Winter"

G. R. WASSERMAN. "The Irony of John Crowe Ransom," *University of Kansas City Review* 23(2), Winter 1956, 154-55.

"Blue Girls"

JOHN CIARDI. *How Does a Poem Mean?* first ed., pp. 802-3.

VIVIENNE KOCH. "The Achievement of John Crowe Ransom," *Sewanee Review* 58(2), Spring 1950, 250-52.

VIVIENNE KOCH. "The Poetry of John Crowe Ransom," in *Modern American Poetry*, edited by B. Rajan, pp. 56-58.

HOWARD NEMEROV. "Summer's Flare and Winter's Flaw," *Sewanee Review* 56(3), Summer 1948, 418. Reprinted in: Howard Nemerov, *Poetry and Fiction*, pp. 94-95.

SCOTT C. OSBORN. *Explicator* 21(3), November 1962, Item 22.

WILLIAM R. OSBORNE. *Explicator* 19(8), May 1961, Item 53.

JAMES M. REID. *100 American Poems of the Twentieth Century*, pp. 137-38.

HYATT H. WAGGONER. *Explicator* 18(1), October 1959, Item 6.

"Captain Carpenter"

JOHN BERRYMAN. "Ransom: Captain Carpenter," in *Master Poems of the English Language*, pp. 985-87.

JOHN BERRYMAN. "The Sorrows of Captain Carpenter," in *The Freedom of the Poet*, pp. 279-81.

CLEANTH BROOKS. *Modern Poetry and the Tradition*, pp. 35-37.

VERNON HALL. *Explicator* 26(3), November 1967, Item 28.

RICHARD KELLY. "Captain Carpenter's Inverted Ancestor," *American Notes & Queries*, n.s., 7(1), September 1968, 6-7.

RICHARD KELLY. *Explicator* 25(7), March 1967, Item 57.

JANE MARSTON. "Persona and Perspective in John Crowe Ransom's Poetry," *Mississippi Quarterly* 30(1), Winter 1976-77, 69.

LAURA RIDING and ROBERT GRAVES. *A Survey of Modernist Poetry*, pp. 103-9.

JOHN L. STEWART. "John Crowe Ransom," in *Seven Modern American Poets*, pp. 173-74.

JOHN WAIN. *Professing Poetry*, pp. 260-63.

"Conrad in Twilight"

NAT HENRY. *Explicator* 34(8), April 1976, Item 62.

LOUIS D. RUBIN, JR. "The Wary Fugitive: John Crowe Ransom," *Sewanee Review* 82(4), Fall 1974, 614-15.

DELMORE SCHWARTZ. "Instructed of Much Mortality: A Note on the Poetry of John Crowe Ransom," *Sewanee Review* 54(3), Summer 1946, 445-46.

DELMORE SCHWARTZ. *Selected Essays of Delmore Schwartz*, pp. 178-79.

"Dead Boy"

CHRISTOPHER CLAUSEN. "Grecian Thoughts in the Home Fields: Reflections on Southern Poetry," *Georgia Review* 32(2), Summer 1978, 287-88.

RICHARD GRAY. "The 'Compleat Gentleman': An Approach to John Crowe Ransom," *Southern Review*, n.s., 12(3), Summer 1976, 626-27.

VIVIENNE KOCH. "The Achievement of John Crowe Ransom," *Sewanee Review* 58(2), Spring 1950, 238-39.

VIVIENNE KOCH. "The Poetry of John Crowe Ransom," in *Modern American Poetry*, edited by B. Rajan, p. 46.

JANE MARSTON. "Persona and Perspective in John Crowe Ransom's Poetry," *Mississippi Quarterly* 30(1), Winter 1976-77, 63-64.

F. O. MATTHIESSEN. "Primarily Language," *Sewanee Review* 56(3), Summer 1948, 398-400. Reprinted in: F. O. Matthiessen. *The Responsibilities of the Critic*, pp. 47-49.

THORNTON H. PARSONS. "The Civilized Poetry of John Crowe Ransom," *Perspective* 13(4), Autumn 1964, 254-57.

NORMAN C. STAGEBERG and WALLACE L. ANDERSON. *Poetry as Experience*, pp. 26-27.

HYATT H. WAGGONER. *American Poets*, pp. 533-34.

ROBERT PENN WARREN. "Notes on the Poetry of John Crowe Ransom At His Eightieth Birthday," *Kenyon Review* 30(3), 1968, 337-38.

G. R. WASSERMAN. "The Irony of John Crowe Ransom," *University of Kansas City Review* 23(2), Winter 1956, 157-58.

"Ego"

LOUIS D. RUBIN, JR. "The Wary Fugitive: John Crowe Ransom," *Sewanee Review* 82(4), Fall 1974, 592-93.

"Emily Hardcastle, Spinster"

JANE MARSTON. "Persona and Perspective in John Crowe Ransom's Poetry," *Mississippi Quarterly* 30(1), Winter 1976-77, 64-65.

THORNTON H. PARSONS. "The Civilized Poetry of John Crowe Ransom," *Perspective* 13(4), Autumn 1964, 251-53.

"The Equilibrists"

RICHMOND CROOM BEATTY. "John Crowe Ransom as Poet," *Sewanee Review* 52(2), Summer 1944, 359-60.

BERNARD BERGONZI. "A Poem about the History of Love," *Critical Quarterly* 4(2), Summer 1962, 127-37.

HARRY BROWN and JOHN MILSTEAD. *What the Poem Means*, p. 180.

ELIZABETH DREW and JOHN L. SWEENEY. *Directions in Modern Poetry*, pp. 208-11.

JANE MARSTON. "Persona and Perspective in John Crowe Ransom's Poetry," *Mississippi Quarterly* 30(1), Winter 1976-77, 66-68.

HOWARD NEMEROV. "Summer's Flare and Winter's Flaw," *Sewanee Review* 56(3), Summer 1948, 419-20. Reprinted in: Howard Nemerov. *Poetry and Fiction*, p. 96.

THORNTON H. PARSONS. "Ransom and the Poetics of Monastic Ecstasy," *Modern Language Quarterly* 26(4), December 1965, 575-81.

RANSOM, JOHN CROWE *(Cont.)*

"The Equilibrists" *(cont.)*

JAMES M. REID. *100 American Poems of the Twentieth Century*, pp. 135-37.

LOUIS D. RUBIN, JR. "The Wary Fugitive: John Crowe Ransom," *Sewanee Review* 82(4), Fall 1974, 599-600.

JOHN L. STEWART. "John Crowe Ransom," in *Seven Modern American Poets*, p. 171.

G. R. WASSERMAN. "The Irony of John Crowe Ransom," *University of Kansas City Review* 23(2), Winter 1956, 158-59.

G. R. WILSON, JR. "Marvellian Analogues in Ransom's 'The Equilibrists,'" *Notes on Modern American Literature* 1(3), Summer 1977, Item 21.

"The First Travels of Max"

VIVIENNE KOCH. "The Achievement of John Crowe Ransom," *Sewanee Review* 58(2), Spring 1950, 237.

VIVIENNE KOCH. "The Poetry of John Crowe Ransom," in *Modern American Poetry*, edited by B. Rajan, pp. 44-45.

JOHN L. STEWART. "John Crowe Ransom," in *Seven Modern American Poets*, p. 172.

"Geometry"

RICHMOND CROOM BEATTY. "John Crowe Ransom as Poet," *Sewanee Review* 52(3), Summer 1944, 348.

"Grace"

RICHMOND CROOM BEATTY. "John Crowe Ransom as Poet," *Sewanee Review* 52(2), Summer 1944, 347-48.

G. R. WASSERMAN. "The Irony of John Crowe Ransom," *University of Kansas City Review* 23(2), Winter 1956, 152-53.

"Here Lies a Lady"

WILLIAM BLEIFUSS. *Explicator* 11(7), May 1953, Item 51.

ELLSWORTH MASON. *Explicator* 8(1), October 1949, Item 1. Reprinted in: *Readings for Liberal Education*, revised ed., II: 234-35.

ROBERT BUFFINGTON. "The Poetry of the Master's Old Age," *Georgia Review* 25(1), Spring 1971, 14-16.

CLYDE S. KILBY. *Poetry and Life*, pp. 16-17.

THORNTON H. PARSONS. "The Civilized Poetry of John Crowe Ransom," *Perspective* 13(4), Autumn 1964, 249-51.

RENATO POGGIOLI. "Decadence in Miniature," *Massachusetts Review* 4(3), Spring 1963, 561-62.

FRED H. STOCKING. *Explicator* 8(1), October 1949, Item 1. Reprinted in: *Readings for Liberal Education*, revised ed., II: 233-34.

"Janet Waking"

CLEANTH BROOKS. *Modern Poetry and the Tradition*, pp. 92-93. Reprinted in: *Modern Poetry*, pp. 124-25.

BABETTE DEUTSCH. *Poetry in Our Time*, pp. 206-7; second ed., pp. 223-24.

VIVIENNE KOCH. "The Achievement of John Crowe Ransom," *Sewanee Review* 58(2), Spring 1950, 249-50.

VIVIENNE KOCH. "The Poetry of John Crowe Ransom," in *Modern American Poetry*, edited by B. Rajan, pp. 55-56.

WILLIAM VAN O'CONNOR. *Sense and Sensibility in Modern Poetry*, pp. 140-41.

THORNTON H. PARSONS. "The Civilized Poetry of John Crowe Ransom," *Perspective* 13(4), Autumn 1964, 248-49.

M. L. ROSENTHAL and A. J. M. SMITH. *Exploring Poetry*, pp. 7-8; second ed., pp. 6-8.

JOHN L. STEWART. "John Crowe Ransom," in *Seven Modern American Poets*, pp. 172-73.

G. R. WASSERMAN. "The Irony of John Crowe Ransom," *University of Kansas City Review* 23(2), Winter 1956, 155-56.

"Lady Lost"

VIVIENNE KOCH. "The Achievement of John Crowe Ransom," *Sewanee Review* 58(2), Spring 1950, 247-49.

VIVIENNE KOCH. "The Poetry of John Crowe Ransom," in *Modern American Poetry*, edited by B. Rajan, pp. 54-55.

"Little Boy Blue"

CHARLES MITCHELL. *Explicator* 22(1), September 1963, Item 5.

"Master's in the Garden Again"

W. D. SNODGRASS, LEONIE ADAMS, MURIEL RUKEYSER and JOHN CROWE RANSOM. "On John Crowe Ransom's 'Master's in the Garden Again,'" in *The Contemporary Poet as Artist and Critic*, pp. 112-40.

"Miller's Daughter"

RICHMOND CROOM BEATTY. "John Crowe Ransom as Poet," *Sewanee Review* 52(2), Summer 1944, 357-58.

"Miriam Tazewell"

ROBERT FLYNN. *Explicator* 12(7), May 1954, Item 45.

VIVIENNE KOCH. "The Achievement of John Crowe Ransom," *Sewanee Review* 58(2), Spring 1950, 239-40.

VIVIENNE KOCH. "The Poetry of John Crowe Ransom," in *Modern American Poetry*, edited by B. Rajan, pp. 46-47.

JANE MARSTON. "Persona and Perspective in John Crowe Ransom's Poetry," *Mississippi Quarterly* 30(1), Winter 1976-77, 62-63.

G. R. WASSERMAN. "The Irony of John Crowe Ransom," *University of Kansas City Review* 23(2), Winter 1956, 156-57.

"Necrological"

KARL F. KNIGHT. "Love As Symbol in the Poetry of Ransom," *Mississippi Quarterly* 13(3), Summer 1960, 133-34.

JANE MARSTON. "Persona and Perspective in John Crowe Ransom's Poetry," *Mississippi Quarterly* 30(1), Winter 1976-77, 66.

THORNTON H. PARSONS. "The Civilized Poetry of John Crowe Ransom," *Perspective* 13(4), Autumn 1964, 246-48.

JAMES REEVES and MARTIN SEYMOUR-SMITH. *Inside Poetry*, pp. 74-77.

JOHN L. STEWART. "John Crowe Ransom," in *Seven Modern American Poets*, pp. 164-69.

"Night Voices"

RICHMOND CROOM BEATTY. "John Crowe Ransom as Poet," *Sewanee Review* 52(2), Summer 1944, 354-55.

"Noonday Grace"

RICHMOND CROOM BEATTY. "John Crowe Ransom as Poet," *Sewanee Review* 52(2), Summer 1944, 345-46.

LOUIS D. RUBIN, JR. "The Wary Fugitive: John Crowe Ransom," *Sewanee Review* 82(4), Fall 1974, 587.

"Old Mansion"

ASHLEY BROWN. "Landscape into Art: Henry James and John Crowe Ransom," *Sewanee Review* 79(2), Spring 1971, 206-12. (P)

CHRISTOPHER CLAUSEN. "Grecian Thoughts in the Home Fields: Reflections on Southern Poetry," *Georgia Review* 32(2), Summer 1978, 288-89.

VIVIENNE KOCH. "The Achievement of John Crowe Ransom," *Sewanee Review* 58(2), Spring 1950, 245-47.

VIVIENNE KOCH. "The Poetry of John Crowe Ransom," in *Modern American Poetry*, ed. by B. Rajan, pp. 52-53.

"One Who Rejected Christ"

HYATT H. WAGGONER. *American Poets*, p. 531.

"Painted Head"

RICHMOND CROOM BEATTY. "John Crowe Ransom as Poet," *Sewanee Review* 52(2), Summer 1944, 365-66.

JOHN M. BRADBURY. "Ransom as Poet," *Accent* 11(1), Winter 1951, 55-56.

CLEANTH BROOKS. *Modern Poetry and the Tradition*, pp. 94-95. Reprinted in: *Modern Poetry*, p. 126.

KIMON FRIAR and JOHN MALCOLM BRINNIN. *Modern Poetry*, p. 532.

VIVIENNE KOCH. "The Poetry of John Crowe Ransom," in *Modern American Poetry*, edited by B. Rajan, pp. 62-64.

SAMUEL H. McMILLAN. "John Crowe Ransom's 'Painted Head,'" *Georgia Review* 22(2), Summer 1968, 194-97.

CHARLES MOORMAN. *Explicator* 10(3), December 1951, Item 15.

JOHN L. STEWART. "John Crowe Ransom," in *Seven Modern American Poets*, pp. 178-79.

VIRGINIA WALLACH. *Explicator* 14(7), April 1956, Item 45.

"Parting, Without a Sequel"

HARRY BROWN and JOHN MILSTEAD. *What the Poem Means*, p. 179.

LAURENCE PERRINE. *100 American Poems of the Twentieth Century*, pp. 139-41.

"Persistent Explorer"

CLEANTH BROOKS. *Modern Poetry and the Tradition*, pp. 90-91. Reprinted in: *Modern Poetry*, pp. 122-23.

HYATT H. WAGGONER. *American Poets*, pp. 532-33.

"Philomela"

LOUIS D. RUBIN, JR. "The Wary Fugitive: John Crowe Ransom," *Sewanee Review* 82(4), Fall 1974, 593-94.

DELMORE SCHWARTZ. "Instructed of Much Mortality: A Note on the Poetry of John Crowe Ransom," *Sewanee Review* 54(3), Summer 1946, 443-44.

SAMUEL H. WOODS, JR. "'Philomela': John Crowe Ransom's *Ars Poetica*," *College English* 27(5), February 1966, 408-13.

"Piazza Piece"

THORNTON H. PARSONS. "The Civilized Poetry of John Crowe Ransom," *Perspective* 13(4), Autumn 1964, 246.

"Plea in Mitigation"

VIVIENNE KOCH. "The Poetry of John Crowe Ransom," in *Modern American Poetry*, edited by B. Rajan, pp. 42-43.

"Prelude to an Evening"

CLEANTH BROOKS. "The Doric Delicacy," *Sewanee Review* 56(3), Summer 1948, 412-14.

DENIS DONOGHUE. *The Ordinary Universe*, pp. 174-79.

LILLIAN FEDER. *Ancient Myth in Modern Poetry*, pp. 396-97.

KARL F. KNIGHT. "Love As Symbol In the Poetry of Ransom," *Mississippi Quarterly* 13(3), Summer 1960, 138.

VIVIENNE KOCH. "The Poetry of John Crowe Ransom," in *Modern American Poetry*, edited by B. Rajan, pp. 62-64.

GUY OWEN. "John Crowe Ransom: The Evolution of His Style," in *The Twenties*, edited by Richard E. Langford and William E. Taylor, pp. 51-52. Reprinted in: *Modern American Poetry*, edited by Guy Owen, pp. 162-63.

VIRGINIA L. PECK. *Explicator* 20(5), January 1962, Item 41.

JOHN CROWE RANSOM. "Prelude to an Evening: A Poem Revised and Explicated," *Kenyon Review* 25(1), Winter 1963, 70-80.

"Prometheus in Straits"

LILLIAN FEDER. *Ancient Myth in Modern Poetry*, p. 395.

"Puncture"

THORNTON H. PARSONS. "The Civilized Poetry of John Crowe Ransom," *Perspective* 12(4), Autumn 1964, 259-62.

"The School"

RICHMOND CROOM BEATTY. "John Crowe Ransom as Poet," *Sewanee Review* 52(2), Summer 1944, 350.

LOUISE COWAN. "The Communal World of Southern Literature," *Georgia Review* 14(3), Fall 1960, 253-54.

"Spectral Lovers"

CLEANTH BROOKS. "The Doric Delicacy," *Sewanee Review* 56(3), Summer 1948, 410-12.

KARL F. KNIGHT. "Love As Symbol in the Poetry of Ransom," *Mississippi Quarterly* 13(3), Summer 1960, 134.

VIVIENNE KOCH. "The Achievement of John Crowe Ransom," *Sewanee Review* 58(2), Spring 1950, 240-43.

VIVIENNE KOCH. "The Poetry of John Crowe Ransom," in *Modern American Poetry*, edited by B. Rajan, pp. 47-50.

JANE MARSTON. "Persona and Perspective in John Crowe Ransom's Poetry," *Mississippi Quarterly* 30(1), Winter 1976-77, 68.

THORNTON H. PARSONS. "Ransom and the Poetics of Monastic Ecstasy," *Modern Language Quarterly* 26(4), December 1965, 572-75.

"Spiel of the Three Mountebanks"

HOWARD NEMEROV. "Summer's Flare and Winter's Flaw," *Sewanee Review* 56(3), Summer 1948, 422.

"The Swimmer"

RICHMOND CROOM BEATTY. "John Crowe Ransom as Poet," *Sewanee Review* 52(2), Summer 1944, 345.

LOUISE COWAN. "The Communal World of Southern Literature," *Georgia Review* 14(3), Fall 1960, 252-53.

"The Tall Girl"

VIVIENNE KOCH. "The Poetry of John Crowe Ransom," in *Modern American Poetry*, edited by B. Rajan, pp. 51-52.

RANSOM, JOHN CROWE (*Cont.*)

"Tom, Tom, the Piper's Son"

> VIVIENNE KOCH. "The Poetry of John Crowe Ransom," in *Modern American Poetry*, edited by B. Rajan, p. 42.

"Two Gentlemen in Bonds"

> BABETTE DEUTSCH. *Poetry in Our Time*, p. 207; second ed., p. 225.

"Two in August"

> RICHMOND CROOM BEATTY. "John Crowe Ransom as Poet," *Sewanee Review* 52(2), Summer 1944, 359.
>
> KATHERINE W. SNIPES. *Explicator* 26(2), October 1967, Item 15.

"Vaunting Oak"

> CLEANTH BROOKS. "The Doric Delicacy," *Sewanee Review* 56(3), Summer 1948, 406-8.
>
> F. O. MATTHIESSEN. "Primarily Language," *Sewanee Review* 56(3), Summer 1948, 395-97. Reprinted in: F. O. Matthiessen. *The Responsibilities of the Critic*, pp. 45-46.

"Vision by Sweetwater"

> JANE MARSTON. "Persona and Perspective in John Crowe Ransom's Poetry," *Mississippi Quarterly* 30(1), Winter 1976-77, 69.
>
> ROBERT PENN WARREN. "Notes on the Poetry of John Crowe Ransom At His Eightieth Birthday," *Kenyon Review* 30(3), 1968, 341-42. (P)

"Winter Remembered"

> EDWARD A. BLOOM, CHARLES H. PHILBRICK, and ELMER M. BLISTEIN. *The Order of Poetry*, pp. 100-4.
>
> JANE MARSTON. "Persona and Perspective in John Crowe Ransom's Poetry," *Mississippi Quarterly* 30(1), Winter 1976-77, 60-61.
>
> THORNTON H. PARSONS. "Ransom and the Poetics of Monastic Ecstasy," *Modern Language Quarterly* 26(4), December 1965, 582-85.
>
> LAURA RIDING and ROBERT GRAVES. *A Survey of Modernist Poetry*, pp. 229-30.

RATTI, JOHN

"The Master's Eye: Eakins' Photograph of Bill Duckett"

> ROBERT PINSKY. *The Situation of Poetry*, pp. 106-8.

RAVENAL DE LA COSTE, MARIE

"Somebody's Darling"

> CLEANTH BROOKS and ROBERT PENN WARREN. *Understanding Poetry*, fourth ed., pp. 123-25.

READ, HERBERT

"The Analysis of Love"

> RAYMOND TSCHUMI. *Thought in Twentieth-Century English Poetry*, pp. 181-82.

"Beata l'Alma"

> RAYMOND TSCHUMI. *Thought in Twentieth-Century English Poetry*, pp. 182-83.

"The Contrary Experience"

> RAYMOND TSCHUMI. *Thought in Twentieth-Century English Poetry*, p. 171.

"The End of a War"

> BERNARD BERGONZI. *Heroes' Twilight*, pp. 75-79.
>
> JON SILKIN. *Out of Battle*, pp. 177-86.
>
> RAYMOND TSCHUMI. *Thought in Twentieth-Century English Poetry*, pp. 169-70.

"Equation a + b + c = x"

> RAYMOND TSCHUMI. *Thought in Twentieth-Century English Poetry*, p. 175.

"The Execution of Cornelius Vane"

> JON SILKIN. *Out of Battle*, pp. 176-77.

"The Falcon and the Dove"

> RAYMOND TSCHUMI. *Thought in Twentieth-Century English Poetry*, pp. 177-78.

"Fear"

> BERNARD BERGONZI. *Heroes' Twilight*, p. 74.

"The Happy Warrior"

> JOHN SILKIN. *Out of Battle*, pp. 171-73.

"John Donne Declines a Benefice"

> RAYMOND TSCHUMI. *Thought in Twentieth-Century English Poetry*, pp. 179-80.

"Kneeshaw Goes to War"

> JON SILKIN. *Out of Battle*, pp. 173-75.

"The Lament of St. Denis"

> RAYMOND TSCHUMI. *Thought in Twentieth-Century English Poetry*, pp. 190-92.

"Love and Death"

> ROBIN SKELTON. *The Poetic Pattern*, pp. 146-50.

"Meditation of the Dying German Officer"

> JON SILKIN. *Out of Battle*, pp. 179-83.

"Mutations of the Phoenix"

> RAYMOND TSCHUMI. *Thought in Twentieth-Century English Poetry*, pp. 186-90.

"My Company"

> JON SILKIN. *Out of Battle*, pp. 175-76.

"Naming of Parts"

> RICHARD A. CONDON. *Explicator* 12(8), June 1954, Item 54.
>
> IAN HAMILTON. *A Poetry Chronicle*, pp. 68-70.

"The Narrow Labyrinth Has Light"

> HERBERT READ. "Surrealism and the Romantic Principle," in *Criticism*, pp. 110-12.

"Nuncio"

> RAYMOND TSCHUMI. *Thought in Twentieth-Century English Poetry*, pp. 192-93.

"Ode Written during the Battle of Dunkirk, May, 1940"

> RAYMOND TSCHUMI. *Thought in Twentieth-Century English Poetry*, pp. 171-72.

"The Retreat"

> RAYMOND TSCHUMI. *Thought in Twentieth-Century English Poetry*, pp. 183-85.

"A World Within a War"

> KIMON FRIAR and JOHN MALCOLM BRINNIN. *Modern Poetry*, p. 533. (Quoting Herbert Read)
>
> RAYMOND TSCHUMI. *Thought in Twentieth-Century English Poetry*, pp. 173-74.

REDDY, T. J.

"Running Upon a Wall"

> H. BRUCE FRANKLIN. "The Literature of the American Prison," *Massachusetts Review* 18(1), Spring 1977, 72.

REDGROVE, PETER

"Bedtime Story for my Son"

> G. S. FRASER. *Vision and Rhetoric*, pp. 265-67.

REED, HENRY

"Judging Distances"

IAN HAMILTON. *A Poetry Chronicle*, pp. 68-70.
VERNON SCANNELL. *Not Without Glory*, pp. 135-37.

"Unarmed Combat"

VERNON SCANNELL. *Not Without Glory*, pp. 138-41.

REED, ISHMAEL

"Dualism"

CHESTER J. FONTENAT. "Ishmael Reed and the Politics of Aesthetics, or Shake Hands and Come Out Conjuring," *Black American Literature Forum* 12(1), Spring 1978, 22-23.

"I Am a Cowboy in the Boat of Ra"

ROBERT H. ABEL. *Explicator* 30(9), May 1972, 81.
MADGE AMBLER. "Ishmael Reed: Whose Radio Broke Down?" *Negro American Literature Forum* 6(4), Winter 1972, 125-26.
CHESTER J. FONTENAT. "Ishmael Reed and the Politics of Aesthetics, or Shake Hands and Come Out Conjuring," *Black American Literature Forum* 12(1), Spring 1978, 21-22.

"The Neo-HooDoo Aesthetic"

CHESTER J. FONTENAT. "Ishmael Reed and the Politics of Aesthetics, or Shake Hands and Come Out Conjuring," *Black American Literature Forum* 12(1), Spring 1978, 22.

"Railroad Bill, A Conjure Man"

CHESTER J. FONTENAT. "Ishmael Reed and the Politics of Aesthetics, or Shake Hands and Come Out Conjuring," *Black American Literature Forum* 12(1), Spring 1978, 20.

"Why I Often Allude to Osiris"

CHESTER J. FONTENAT. "Ishmael Reed and the Politics of Aesthetics, or Shake Hands and C ome Out Conjuring," *Black American Literature Forum* 12(1), Spring 1978, 22.

REVETT, ELDRED

"Elegy on Richard Lovelace"

AVON JACK MURPHY. "The Critical Elegy of Earlier Seventeenth-Century England," *Genre* 5(1), March 1972, 79-80.

REXROTH, KENNETH

"The Dragon and the Unicorn"

JOSEPH WARREN BEACH. *Obsessive Images*, pp. 357-59.

"The Homestead Called Damascus"

LAWRENCE LIPTON. "Notes Toward an Understanding of Kenneth Rexroth with Special Attention to 'The Homestead Called Damascus,' " *Quarterly Review of Literature* 9(2), 1957, 37-46.

"Now, on this day of the first hundred flowers"

THOMAS PARKINSON. "Kenneth Rexroth, Poet," *Ohio Review* 17(2), Winter 1976, 59-60.

"Our Home Is in the Rocks"

M. L. ROSENTHAL. *The Modern Poets*, pp. 265-66.

"The Phoenix and the Tortoise"

JOSEPH WARREN BEACH. *Obsessive Images*, pp. 353-55.
THOMAS PARKINSON. "Kenneth Rexroth, Poet," *Ohio Review* 17(2), Winter 1976, 62-66.

RICH, ADRIENNE

"After Dark"

ROBERT BOYERS. "On Adrienne Rich: Intelligence and Will," *Salmagundi* 22-23 (Spring-Summer 1973), 134-37. Reprinted in: *Contemporary Poetry in America*, pp. 159-62. Also: Robert Boyers. *Excursions*, pp. 203-6.

"Antinöus: The Diaries"

SUSAN R. VAN DYNE. "The Mirrored Vision of Adrienne Rich," *Modern Poetry Studies* 8(2), Autumn 1977, 164-65.

"Boundary"

SUZANNE JUHASZ. *Naked and Fiery Forms*, pp. 187-88.

"The Burning of Paper Instead of Children"

DAVID KALSTONE. *Five Temperaments*, pp. 133-37.

"Cartographies of Silence"

DAVID KALSTONE. *Five Temperaments*, pp. 168-69.

"Diving into the Wreck"

GALE FLYNN. "The Radicalization of Adrienne Rich," *Hollins Critic* 11(4), October 1974, 12, 15.

"Face to Face"

DAVID KALSTONE. *Five Temperaments*, pp. 138-39.

"From an Old House in America"

DAVID KALSTONE. *Five Temperaments*, pp. 139-41.

"Halfway"

DAVID KALSTONE. *Five Temperaments*, pp. 153-54.

"Implosions"

SUZANNE JUHASZ. *Naked and Fiery Forms*, pp. 192-93.

"Like This Together"

ROBERT BOYERS. "On Adrienne Rich: Intelligence and Will," *Salmagundi* 22-23 (Spring-Summer 1973), 140-42. Reprinted in: *Contemporary Poetry in America*, pp. 165-67. Also: Robert Boyers. *Excursions*, pp. 209-11.

"A Marriage in the Sixties"

SUZANNE JUHASZ. *Naked and Fiery Forms*, pp. 188-89.

"Meditations for a Savage Child"

DAVID KALSTONE. *Five Temperaments*, pp. 165-68.

"The Middle-aged"

SUSAN R. VAN DYNE. "The Mirrored Vision of Adrienne Rich," *Modern Poetry Studies* 8(2), Autumn 1977, 147-48.

"The Mirror in Which Two Are Seen as One"

SUSAN R. VAN DYNE. "The Mirrored Vision of Adrienne Rich," *Modern Poetry Studies* 8(2), Autumn 1977, 161-66.

"Mourning Picture"

SUSAN R. VAN DYNE. "The Mirrored Vision of Adrienne Rich," *Modern Poetry Studies* 8(2), Autumn 1977, 157-58.

"(Newsreel)"

CARY NELSON. "Whitman in Vietnam: Poetry and History in Contemporary America," *Massachusetts Review* 16(1), Winter 1975, 69-71.

"Not Like That"

ROBERT BOYERS. "On Adrienne Rich: Intelligence and Will," *Salmagundi* 22-23 (Spring-Summer 1973), 138-39. Reprinted in: *Contemporary Poetry in America*, pp. 163-64. Also: Robert Boyers. *Excursions*, p. 208.

RICH, ADRIENNE *(Cont.)*

"Novella"
> SUZANNE JUHASZ. *Naked and Fiery Forms,* pp. 189-90.

"The Observer"
> DAVID KALSTONE. *Five Temperaments,* pp. 156-57.
> SUSAN R. VAN DYNE. "The Mirrored Vision of Adrienne Rich," *Modern Poetry Studies* 8(2), Autumn 1977, 155.

"Open-Air Museum"
> ROBERT BOYERS. "On Adrienne Rich: Intelligence and Will," *Salmagundi* 22-23 (Spring-Summer 1973), 140. Reprinted in: *Contemporary Poetry in America,* p. 165. Also: Robert Boyers. *Excursions,* p. 209.

"Our Whole Life"
> SUZANNE JUHASZ. *Naked and Fiery Forms,* p. 196.

"The Photograph of the Unmade Bed"
> DAVID KALSTONE. *Five Temperaments,* pp. 157-58.

"Planetarium"
> LOUIS UNTERMEYER. *50 Modern American & British Poets,* p. 336.

"A Primary Ground"
> SUSAN R. VAN DYNE. "The Mirrored Vision of Adrienne Rich," *Modern Poetry Studies* 8(2), Autumn 1977, 167.

"Readings of History"
> SUSAN R. VAN DYNE. "The Mirrored Vision of Adrienne Rich," *Modern Poetry Studies* 8(2), Autumn 1977, 150-53.

"The Roofwalker"
> SUSAN R. VAN DYNE. "The Mirrored Vision of Adrienne Rich," *Modern Poetry Studies* 8(2), Autumn 1977, 153-54.

"Shooting Script"
> DAVID KALSTONE. *Five Temperaments,* pp. 159-62.

"Side by Side"
> ROBERT BOYERS. "On Adrienne Rich: Intelligence and Will," *Salmagundi* 22-23 (Spring-Summer 1973), 137-38. Reprinted in: *Contemporary Poetry in America,* pp. 162-63. Also: Robert Boyers. *Excursions,* pp. 206-7.

"Stepping Backward"
> SUSAN R. VAN DYNE. "The Mirrored Vision of Adrienne Rich," *Modern Poetry Studies* 8(2), Autumn 1977, 146.

"Translations"
> DAVID KALSTONE. *Five Temperaments,* pp. 162-63.

"The Trees"
> SUSAN R. VAN DYNE. "The Mirrored Vision of Adrienne Rich," *Modern Poetry Studies* 8(2), Autumn 1977, 156-57.

"Two Songs"
> SUZANNE JUHASZ. *Naked and Fiery Forms,* pp. 191-92.

"A Valediction Forbidding Mourning"
> CAROL BERE. "A Reading of Adrienne Rich's 'A Valediction Forbidding Mourning,'" *Concerning Poetry* 11(2), Fall 1978, 33-38.

"The Well"
> SUZANNE JUHASZ. *Naked and Fiery Forms,* pp. 190-91.

RICHARDS, I. A.

"Harvard Yard in April April in Harvard Yard"
> I. A. RICHARDS. "Poetic Process and Literary Analysis," in *Poems in the Making,* pp. 231-36.

"Not No"
> "The Poems of a Sage," *Times Literary Supplement,* 1 May 1959, p. 256.

RICKWORD, EDGELL

"Birthday Ruminations"
> DAVID HOLBROOK. "The Poetic Mind of Edgell Rickword," *Essays in Criticism* 12(3), July 1962, 280-81.

"Obsession"
> DAVID HOLBROOK. "The Poetic Mind of Edgell Rickword," *Essays in Criticism* 12(3), July 1962, 282.

"Ode to a Train-de-luxe"
> DAVID HOLBROOK. "The Poetic Mind of Edgell Rickword," *Essays in Criticism* 12(3), July 1962, 285-86.

"Ode to the Wife of a Non-interventionist Statesman"
> DAVID HOLBROOK. "The Poetic Mind of Edgell Rickword," *Essays in Criticism* 12(3), July 1962, 288-89.

"The Soldier Addresses His Body"
> DAVID HOLBROOK. "The Poetic Mind of Edgell Rickword," *Essays in Criticism* 12(3), July 1962, 278-80.

"To the Sun and Another Dancer"
> DAVID HOLBROOK. "The Poetic Mind of Edgell Rickword," *Essays in Criticism* 12(3), July 1962, 275-78.

"Twittingpan"
> DAVID HOLBROOK. "The Poetic Mind of Edgell Rickword," *Essays in Criticism* 12(3), July 1962, 287-88.

RIDING, LAURA

"Afternoon"
> DONALD DAVIE. *The Poet in the Imaginary Museum,* pp. 250-52.

"The Dilemmist"
> MICHAEL KIRKHAM. "Robert Graves's Debt to Laura Riding," *Focus on Robert Graves* 3 (December 1973), 41-42.

"Earth"
> MICHAEL KIRKHAM. "Robert Graves's Debt to Laura Riding," *Focus on Robert Graves* 3 (December 1973), 42.

"World's End"
> MICHAEL KIRKHAM. "Robert Graves's Debt to Laura Riding," *Focus on Robert Graves* 3 (December 1973), 39-41.

RIVERA, TOMAS

"Odio"
> FRANK PINO. "Chicano Poetry: A Popular Manifesto," *Journal of Popular Culture* 6(4), Spring 1973, 728-29.

ROBERTS, MICHAEL

"Poem for Elsa"
> C. B. COX and A. E. DYSON. *Modern Poetry,* pp. 109-15.

"The World's End"
> SAMUEL HYNES. "Michael Roberts' Tragic View," *Contemporary Literature* 12(3), Autumn 1971, 449-50.

ROBINSON, EDWIN ARLINGTON

"Aaron Stark"
> H. R. WOLF. "E. A. Robinson and the Integration of Self," in *Modern American Poetry,* edited by Jerome Mazzaro, p. 56.

"Amaryllis"
> WILLIAM C. CHILDERS. *Explicator* 14(5), February 1956, Item 34.

"Annandale Again"
> H. R. WOLF. "E. A. Robinson and the Integration of Self," in *Modern American Poetry,* edited by Jerome Mazzaro, pp. 50-51.

"Archibald's Example"
> PAUL ZIETLOW. "The Meaning of Tilbury Town: Robinson as a Regional Poet," *New England Quarterly* 40(2), June 1967, 190-91.

"Aunt Imogen"
> WILLIAM J. FREE. "E. A. Robinson's Use of Emerson," *American Literature* 38(1), March 1966, 79-80.
> H. R. WOLF. "E. A. Robinson and the Integration of Self," in *Modern American Poetry,* edited by Jerome Mazzaro, pp. 52-53.

"Battle After War"
> DEAN SHERMAN. *Explicator* 27(8), April 1969, Item 64.

"Ben Jonson Entertains a Man from Stratford"
> RICHARD P. ADAMS. "The Failure of Edwin Arlington Robinson," *Tulane Studies in English* 11 (1961), 114-15.
> WILLIAM J. FREE. "E. A. Robinson's Use of Emerson," *American Literature* 38(1), March 1966, 81-82.

"The Book of Annandale"
> RICHARD P. ADAMS. "The Failure of Edwin Arlington Robinson," *Tulane Studies in English* 11 (1961), 120-22.
> WILLIAM H. PRITCHARD. "Edwin Arlington Robinson: The Prince of Heartachers," *American Scholar* 48(1), Winter 1978/79, 91-92.
> H. R. WOLF. "E. A. Robinson and the Integration of Self," in *Modern American Poetry,* edited by Jerome Mazzaro, pp. 49-50.

"Calverly's"
> JAMES DICKEY. *Babel to Byzantium,* pp. 211-13.
> JAMES DICKEY. "Edwin Arlington Robinson: The Many Truths," in *Modern American Poetry,* edited by Guy Owen, pp. 3-4.

"Cassandra"
> DAVID H. BURTON. "Theodore Roosevelt and Edwin Arlington Robinson: A Common Vision," *Personalist* 49(3), Summer 1968, 339-40.
> YVOR WINTERS. "Religious and Social Ideas in the Didactic Work of E. A. Robinson," *Arizona Quarterly* 1(1), Spring 1945, 79-80.

"Charles Carville's Eyes"
> M. L. ROSENTHAL. *The Modern Poets,* p. 106.

"The Clerks"
> LOUIS O. COXE. "E. A. Robinson: The Lost Tradition," *Sewanee Review* 62(2), Spring 1954, 259-61. Reprinted in: Louis Coxe. *Enabling Acts,* pp. 19-20.
> LOUIS COXE. "Edwin Arlington Robinson," in *Six American Poets from Emily Dickinson to the Present,* pp. 69-71.

"Cliff Klingenhagen"
> WILLIAM J. FREE. "E. A. Robinson's Use of Emerson," *American Literature* 38(1), March 1966, 79.

"Credo"
> RICHARD P. ADAMS. "The Failure of Edwin Arlington Robinson," *Tulane Studies in English* 11 (1961), 107-9.

"The Dark Hills"
> LAURENCE PERRINE. *100 American Poems of the Twentieth Century,* pp. 22-23.
> G. THOMAS TANSELLE. "Robinson's 'Dark Hills,'" *CEA Critic* 26(5), February 1964, 8-10.
> HYATT H. WAGGONER. *American Poets,* p. 281.

"Demos"
> DAVID H. BURTON. "Theodore Roosevelt and Edwin Arlington Robinson: A Common Vision," *Personalist* 49(3), Summer 1968, 344.
> YVOR WINTERS. "Religious and Social Ideas in the Didactic Work of E. A. Robinson," *Arizona Quarterly* 1(1), Spring 1945, 80-81.

"Demos and Dionysius"
> RICHARD P. ADAMS. "The Failure of Edwin Arlington Robinson," *Tulane Studies in English* 11 (1961), 117-18.
> DAVID H. BURTON. "Theodore Roosevelt and Edwin Arlington Robinson: A Common Vision," *Personalist* 49(3), Summer 1968, 344-47.
> DENIS DONOGHUE. *Connoisseurs of Chaos,* pp. 139-40.

"Dionysius in Doubt"
> DAVID H. BURTON. "Theodore Roosevelt and Edwin Arlington Robinson: A Common Vision," *Personalist* 49(3), Summer 1968, 344-46.
> YVOR WINTERS. "Religious and Social Ideas in the Didactic Work of E. A. Robinson," *Arizona Quarterly* 1(1), Spring 1945, 82-84.

"En Passant"
> BERNICE SLOTE. *Explicator* 15(5), February 1957, Item 27.

"Erasmus"
> HYATT H. WAGGONER. *American Poets,* pp. 274-77.

"Eros Turannos"
> RICHARD P. ADAMS. "The Failure of Edwin Arlington Robinson," *Tulane Studies in English* 11 (1961), 145-51.
> LOUIS O. COXE. "E. A. Robinson: The Lost Tradition," *Sewanee Review* 62(2), Spring 1954, 252-57, 259. Reprinted in: Louis Coxe. *Enabling Acts,* pp. 12-18.
> LOUIS O. COXE. "Edwin Arlington Robinson," in *Six American Poets from Emily Dickinson to the Present,* pp. 63-69.
> DAVID DAICHES and WILLIAM CHARVAT. *Poems in English,* pp. 730-31.
> BENJAMIN W. GRIFFITH. "A Note on Robinson's Use of Turannos," *Concerning Poetry* 4(1), Spring 1971, 39.
> ROY HARVEY PEARCE. *The Continuity of American Poetry,* pp. 261-64.
> LAURENCE PERRINE. *Explicator* 8(3), December 1949, Item 20.

"The Field of Glory"
> RICHARD CROWDER. *Explicator* 8(4), February 1950, Item 31.

ROBINSON, EDWIN ARLINGTON *(Cont.)*

"Firelight"

> JAMES D. BARRY. *Explicator* 22(3), November 1963, Item 21.

"Flammonde"

> HILTON ANDERSON. "Robinson's 'Flammonde,'" *Southern Quarterly* 7(2), January 1969, 179-83.
>
> FRED B. MILLETT. *Reading Poetry*, p. 64; second ed., pp. 80-81.
>
> MARK STRAND. "Robinson: Richard Cory," in *Master Poems of the English Language*, pp. 866-67.

"The Flying Dutchman"

> H. R. WOLF. "E. A. Robinson and the Integration of Self," in *Modern American Poetry*, edited by Jerome Mazzaro, pp. 55-56.

"For a Dead Lady"

> RICHARD P. ADAMS. "The Failure of Edwin Arlington Robinson," *Tulane Studies in English* 11 (1961), 141-44.
>
> RICHARD CROWDER. *Explicator* 5(3), December 1946, Item 19. (P)
>
> W. H. FRENCH. *Explicator* 10(7), May 1952, Item 51.
>
> R. H. SUPER. *Explicator* 5(8), June 1947, Item 60.

"The Gift of God"

> LOUIS O. COXE. "E. A. Robinson: The Lost Tradition," *Sewanee Review* 62(2), Spring 1954, 261-65. Reprinted in: Louis Coxe. *Enabling Acts*, pp. 20-25.
>
> LOUIS COXE. "Edwin Arlington Robinson," in *Six American Poets from Emily Dickinson to the Present*, pp. 71-75.
>
> WILLIAM H. PRITCHARD. "Edwin Arlington Robinson: The Prince of Heartachers," *American Scholar* 48(1), Winter 1978-79, 98.
>
> H. R. WOLF. "E. A. Robinson and the Integration of Self," in *Modern American Poetry*, edited by Jerome Mazzaro, pp. 53-54.

"The Glory of the Nightingales"

> CHARLES T. DAVIS. "Image Patterns in the Poetry of Edwin Arlington Robinson," *College English* 22(6), March 1961, 385-86.

"Hillcrest"

> GLAUCO CAMBON. *The Inclusive Flame*, pp. 63-65.
>
> GERALD E. GRAFF. "Statement and Poetry," *Southern Review*, n.s., 2(3), Summer 1966, 503-11.

"Isaac and Archibald"

> RICHARD P. ADAMS. "The Failure of Edwin Arlington Robinson," *Tulane Studies in English* 11 (1961), 111-13.
>
> JAMES DICKEY. *Babel to Byzantium*, pp. 223-25.
>
> JAMES DICKEY. "Edwin Arlington Robinson: The Many Truths," in *Modern American Poetry*, ed. by Guy Owen, pp. 13-15.
>
> J. C. LEVENSON. "Robinson's Modernity," *Virginia Quarterly Review* 44(4), Autumn 1968, 606-10.
>
> LAURENCE PERRINE. *100 American Poems of the Twentieth Century*, pp. 9-22.
>
> PAUL ZIETLOW. "The Meaning of Tilbury Town: Robinson as a Regional Poet," *New England Quarterly* 40(2), June 1967, 208-10.

"Llewellyn and the Tree"

> PAUL ZIETLOW. "The Meaning of Tilbury Town: Robinson as a Regional Poet," *New England Quarterly* 40(2), June 1967, 200-3.

"Lost Anchors"

> S. A. COWAN. *Explicator* 24(8), April 1966, Item 68.
>
> JAMES GRIMSHAW. *Explicator* 30(4), December 1971, Item 36.
>
> RALPH E. JENKINS. *Explicator* 23(8), April 1965, Item 64.
>
> CELESTE TURNER WRIGHT. *Explicator* 11(8), June 1953, Item 57.

"Luke Havergal"

> RICHARD P. ADAMS. "The Failure of Edwin Arlington Robinson," *Tulane Studies in English* 11 (1961), 129-36.
>
> WALTON BEACHAM. *The Meaning of Poetry*, pp. 259-79.
>
> WALTER GIERASCH. *Explicator* 3(1), October 1944, Item 8. Abridged in: *The Case for Poetry*, p. 297; second ed., p. 240.
>
> JAMES G. HEPBURN. "E. A. Robinson's System of Opposites," *PMLA* 80(3), June 1965, 269-72.
>
> MATHILDE M. PARLETT. *Explicator* 3(8), June 1945, Item 57.
>
> A. A. RAVEN. *Explicator* 3(3), December 1944, Item 24.
>
> H. R. WOLF. "E. A. Robinson and the Integration of Self," in *Modern American Poetry*, edited by Jerome Mazzaro, pp. 55-56.

"The Man against the Sky"

> RICHARD P. ADAMS. "The Failure of Edwin Arlington Robinson," *Tulane Studies in English* 11 (1961), 136-41.
>
> RICHARD CROWDER. "'Man Against the Sky,'" *College English* 14(5), February 1953, 269-76.
>
> JAMES DICKEY. *Babel to Byzantium*, pp. 227-29.
>
> JAMES DICKEY. "Edwin Arlington Robinson: The Many Truths," in *Modern American Poetry*, ed. by Guy Owen, pp. 16-18.
>
> J. C. LEVENSON. "Robinson's Modernity," *Virginia Quarterly Review* 44(4), Autumn 1968, 590-91.
>
> ROY HARVEY PEARCE. *The Continuity of American Poetry*, pp. 265-67.
>
> WINIFIELD TOWNLEY SCOTT. "To See Robinson," *New Mexico Quarterly Review* 26(2), Summer 1956, 169.
>
> HYATT HOWE WAGGONER. *The Heel of Elohim*, pp. 29-36.
>
> YVOR WINTERS. "Religious and Social Ideas in the Didactic Work of E. A. Robinson," *Arizona Quarterly* 1(1), Spring 1945, 74-75.

"The Man Who Died Twice"

> RICHARD P. ADAMS. "The Failure of Edwin Arlington Robinson," *Tulane Studies in English* 11 (1961), 127-28.
>
> RICHARD CROWDER. "E. A. Robinson's Symphony: 'The Man Who Died Twice,'" *College English* 11(3), December 1949, 141-44.

"Maya"

> DENIS DONOGHUE. *Connoisseurs of Chaos*, p. 140.

"Miniver Cheevy"

> GÉMINO H. ABAD. *A Formal Approach to Lyric Poetry*, pp. 172-73, 175-76.
>
> GÉMINO H. ABAD. *In Another Light*, pp. 164-65.
>
> RICHARD P. ADAMS. "The Failure of Edwin Arlington Robinson," *Tulane Studies in English* 11 (1961), 113-14.
>
> ISAAC ASIMOV. *Familiar Poems, Annotated*, pp. 260-64.
>
> LAURENCE PERRINE. *100 American Poems of the Twentieth Century*, pp. 3-5.

Hyatt H. Waggoner. *American Poets,* pp. 282-84.

"Mr. Flood's Party"

James L. Allen, Jr. "Symbol and Theme in 'Mr. Flood's Party,'" *Mississippi Quarterly* 15(4), Fall 1962, 139-43.

Cleanth Brooks and Robert Penn Warren. *Understanding Poetry,* third ed., pp. 213-17.

John Ciardi. *How Does a Poem Mean?* p. 712; second ed., p. 51.

Willis D. Jacobs. "E. A. Robinson's 'Mr. Flood's Party,'" *College English* 12(2), November 1950, 110.

John E. Parish. "The Rehabilitation of Eben Flood," *English Journal* 55(6), September 1966, 696-99.

Laurence Perrine. *100 American Poems of the Twentieth Century,* pp. 5-8.

Chad Walsh. *Doors into Poetry,* pp. 108-11.

H. R. Wolf. "E. A. Robinson and the Integration of Self," in *Modern American Poetry,* edited by Jerome Mazzaro, pp. 47-49.

"Mortmain"

H. R. Wolf. "E. A. Robinson and the Integration of Self," in *Modern American Poetry,* edited by Jerome Mazzaro, p. 58.

"New England"

Richard E. Amacher. *Explicator* 10(5), March 1952, Item 33.

Denis Donoghue. *Connoisseurs of Chaos,* pp. 140-42.

H. H. Waggoner. *Explicator* 10(5), March 1952, Item 33.

Paul Zietlow. "The Meaning of Tilbury Town: Robinson as a Regional Poet," *New England Quarterly* 40(2), June 1967, 194-95.

"The Night Before"

James G. Hepburn. "E. A. Robinson's System of Opposites," *PMLA* 80(3), June 1965, 266-67.

"Nimmo"

Paul Zietlow. "The Meaning of Tilbury Town: Robinson as a Regional Poet," *New England Quarterly* 40(2), June 1967, 196-97.

"Octaves"

Hyatt H. Waggoner. *American Poets,* pp. 272-74.

"Oh for a poet — for a beacon bright"

M. N. O. *Explicator* 5(7), May 1947, Q21.

"An Old Story"

Richard Crowder. *Explicator* 4(3), December 1945, Item 22. (P)

"Old Trails"

Paul Zietlow. "The Meaning of Tilbury Town: Robinson as a Regional Poet," *New England Quarterly* 40(2), June 1967, 203-4.

"On The Way"

David H. Burton. "Theodore Roosevelt and Edwin Arlington Robinson: A Common Vision," *Personalist* 49(3), Summer 1968, 342-43.

"Rembrandt to Rembrandt"

Richard P. Adams. "The Failure of Edwin Arlington Robinson," *Tulane Studies in English* 11 (1961), 115-16.

"Reuben Bright"

H. R. Wolf. "E. A. Robinson and the Integration of Self," in *Modern American Poetry,* edited by Jerome Mazzaro, p. 57.

"The Revealer"

David H. Burton. "Theodore Roosevelt and Edwin Arlington Robinson: A Common Vision," *Personalist* 49(3), Summer 1968, 343-44.

"Richard Cory"

Charles Burkhart. *Explicator* 19(2), November 1960, Item 9.

William J. Free. "E. A. Robinson's Use of Emerson," *American Literature* 38(1), March 1966, 77-79.

Harry R. Gavin. "'Comprehensive Criticism': A Humanistic Discipline," *Bucknell Review* 10(4), May 1962, 313-21.

Sister Marie Jerome. "'Not By Bread Alone,'" *English Journal* 53(7), October 1964, 517-18.

J. C. Levenson. "Robinson's Modernity," *Virginia Quarterly Review* 44(4), Autumn 1968, 602-3.

Charles R. Morris. *Explicator* 23(7), March 1965, Item 52.

Laurence Perrine. *100 American Poems of the Twentieth Century,* pp. 1-2.

David M. Rein. "The Appeal of 'Richard Cory,'" *CEA Critic* 26(2), November 1963, 6.

Norman C. Stageberg and Wallace L. Anderson. *Poetry as Experience,* pp. 188-92.

Agnes Stein. *The Uses of Poetry,* p. 38.

Mark Strand. "Robinson: Richard Cory," in *Master Poems of the English Language,* pp. 866-67.

Paul Zietlow. "The Meaning of Tilbury Town: Robinson as a Regional Poet," *New England Quarterly* 40(2), June 1967, 192.

"The Sage"

Hyatt H. Waggoner. *American Poets,* pp. 274-75.

"The Sheaves"

Richard Crowder. *Explicator* 4(5), March 1946, Item 38.

Mary S. Mattfield. "Edwin Arlington Robinson's 'The Sheaves,'" *CEA Critic* 31(2), November 1968, 10.

"The Three Taverns"

Louis Coxe. "Edwin Arlington Robinson," in *Six American Poets from Emily Dickinson to the Present,* pp. 76-77.

"The Tree in Pamela's Garden"

Marvin Klotz. *Explicator* 20(5), January 1962, Item 42.

Laurence Perrine. *Explicator* 30(3), November 1971, Item 18.

Elizabeth Wright. *Explicator* 21(6), February 1963, Item 47.

"Two Sonnets"

Hyatt W. Waggoner. *American Poets,* pp. 270-71.

"Uncle Ananias"

Paul Zietlow. "The Meaning of Tilbury Town: Robinson as a Regional Poet," *New England Quarterly* 40(2), June 1967, 199-200.

"The Unforgiven"

Denis Donoghue. *Connoisseurs of Chaos,* pp. 134-36.

"Veteran Sirens"

Brian M. Barbour. *Explicator* 28(3), November 1969, Item 20.

Louis Coxe. *Enabling Acts,* pp. 10-11.

Laurence Perrine. *Explicator* 6(2), November 1947, Item 13.

ROBINSON, EDWIN ARLINGTON *(Cont.)*

"Walt Whitman"

ROY HARVEY PEARCE. *The Continuity of American Poetry,* p. 257.

"The Wandering Jew"

DONALD E. STANFORD. "Edwin Arlington Robinson's 'The Wandering Jew,'" *Tulane Studies in English* 23 (1978), 95-108.

PAUL ZIETLOW. "The Meaning of Tilbury Town: Robinson as a Regional Poet," *New England Quarterly* 40(2), June 1967, 207-8.

"The Whip"

HENRY PETTIT. *Explicator* 1(6), April 1943, Item 50.

ROCHESTER, JOHN WILMOT, EARL OF

"The Advice"

JEREMY TREGLOWN. "The Satirical Inversion of Some English Sources in Rochester's Poetry," *Review of English Studies,* n.s., 24(93), February 1973, 45.

"An Allusion to Horace"

JOS. A. JOHNSON, JR. "'An Allusion to Horace': The Poetics of John Wilmot, Earl of Rochester," *Durham University Journal,* n.s., 35(1), December 1973, 52-59.

EARL MINER. *The Restoration Mode from Milton to Dryden,* pp. 415-17.

LEONARD A. MOSKOVIT. "Pope and the Tradition of the Neoclassical Imitation," *Studies in English Literature 1500-1900* 8(3), Summer 1968, 451-53.

HOWARD D. WEINBROT. "The 'Allusion to Horace': Rochester's Imitative Mode," *Studies in Philology* 69(3), July 1972, 348-68.

"The Disabled Debauchee"

see "The Maim'd Debauchee"

"Epitaph on Charles II"

CHARLES W. COOPER and JOHN HOLMES. *Preface to Poetry,* pp. 169-70.

"Fair Chloris in a pigsty lay"

see "A Song to Chloris"

"The Fall"

CAROL FABRICANT. "Rochester's World of Imperfect Enjoyment," *Journal of English and Germanic Philology* 73(3), July 1974, 339-40.

DAVID FARLEY-HILLS. *The Benevolence of Laughter,* pp. 141-45.

A. J. SMITH. "The Failure of Love: Love Lyrics after Donne," in *Metaphysical Poetry,* edited by Malcolm Bradbury and David Palmer, p. 67.

"The Imperfect Enjoyment"

DAVID FARLEY-HILLS. *The Benevolence of Laughter,* pp. 148-51.

REBA WILCOXON. "Pornography, Obscenity, and Rochester's 'The Imperfect Enjoyment,'" *Studies in English Literature 1500-1900* 15(3), Summer 1975, 375-90.

"A Letter from Artemisia in the Town, to Chloe in the Country"

PAUL C. DAVIES. "Rochester: Augustan and Explorer," *Durham University Journal,* n.s., 30(2), March 1969, 61-64.

CAROL FABRICANT. "The Writer as Hero and Whore: Rochester's *Letter from Artemisia to Chloe,*" *Essays in Literature* 3(2), Fall 1976, 152-66.

DAVID FARLEY-HILLS. *The Benevolence of Laughter,* pp. 177-83.

EARL MINER. *The Restoration Mode from Milton to Dryden,* pp. 413-15.

JOHN E. SITTER. "Rochester's Reader and the Problem of Satiric Audience," *Papers on Language and Literature* 12(3), Summer 1976, 293-98.

HOWARD D. WEINBROT. "The Swelling Volume: The Apocalyptic Satire of Rochester's *Letter From Artemisia In The Town To Chloe In The Country,*" *Studies in the Literary Imagination* 5(2), October 1972, 19-37.

"Love and Life"

DAVID FARLEY-HILLS. *The Benevolence of Laughter,* pp. 147-48.

A. J. SMITH. "The Failure of Love: Love Lyrics after Donne," in *Metaphysical Poetry,* edited by Malcolm Bradbury and David Palmer, pp. 67-68.

REBA WILCOXON. "Rochester's Philosophical Premises: A Case for Consistency," *Eighteenth Century Studies* 8(2), Winter 1974/75, 198-200.

"The Maim'd Debauchee"

GÉMINO H. ABAD. *A Formal Approach to Lyric Poetry,* p. 245.

VIVIAN DE S. PINTO. "John Wilmot, Earl of Rochester, and the Right Veine of Satire," in *Seventeenth Century English Poetry,* pp. 367-68; revised ed., pp. 482-83.

CAROL FABRICANT. "Rochester's World of Imperfect Enjoyment," *Journal of English and Germanic Philology* 73(3), July 1974, 342, 350.

DAVID FARLEY-HILLS. *The Benevolence of Laughter,* pp. 139-41.

"The Mistress"

EARL MINER. *The Restoration Mode from Milton to Dryden,* pp. 373-74.

"Mock Song"

REBA WILCOXON. "The Rhetoric of Sex in Rochester's Burlesque," *Papers on Language and Literature* 12(3), Summer 1976, 276-77.

"The Platonic Lady"

EARL MINER. *The Cavalier Mode from Jonson to Cotton,* pp. 238-39.

"A Ramble in St. James's Park"

DAVID FARLEY-HILLS. *The Benevolence of Laughter,* pp. 148-51.

JOHN E. SITTER. "Rochester's Reader and the Problem of Satiric Audience," *Papers on Language and Literature* 12(3), Summer 1976, 291-92.

REBA WILCOXON. "The Rhetoric of Sex in Rochester's Burlesque," *Papers on Language and Literature* 12(3), Summer 1976, 279-84.

"A Satyr against Mankind"

ROBERT M. BENDER. "Wilmot: A Satire Against Mankind," in *Master Poems of the English Language,* pp. 245-48.

PAUL C. DAVIES. "Rochester: Augustan and Explorer," *Durham University Journal,* n.s., 30(2), March 1969, 60.

VIVIAN DE S. PINTO. "John Wilmot, Earl of Rochester, and the Right Veine of Satire," in *Seventeenth Century English Poetry,* pp. 370-72; revised ed., pp. 485-87.

DAVID FARLEY-HILLS. *The Benevolence of Laughter,* pp. 168-77.

THOMAS H. FIJIMURA. "Rochester's 'Satyr Against Mankind': An Analysis," *Studies in Philology* 55(4), October 1958, 578-90.

RONALD W. JOHNSON. "Rhetoric and Drama in Rochester's 'Satyr against Reason and Mankind,'" *Studies in English Literature 1500-1900* 15(3), Summer 1975, 365-73.

CHARLES A. KNIGHT. "The Paradox of Reason: Argument in Rochester's 'Satyr Against Mankind,'" *Modern Languages Review* 65(2), April 1970, 254-60.

EARL MINER. *The Restoration Mode from Milton to Dryden*, pp. 419-22.

KRISTOFFER F. PAULSON. "The Reverend Edward Stillingfleet and the 'Epilogue' to Rochester's *A Satyr against Reason and Mankind*," *Philological Quarterly* 50(4), October 1971, 657-63.

REBA WILCOXON. "Rochester's Philosophical Premises: A Case for Consistency," *Eighteenth Century Studies* 8(2), Winter 1974/75, 189-98.

GEORGE WILLIAMSON. *Six Metaphysical Poets*, pp. 251-53.

"The Song of a Young Lady to Her Ancient Lover"

CAROLE FABRICANT. "Rochester's World of Imperfect Enjoyment," *Journal of English and Germanic Philology* 73(3), July 1974, 343-44.

DAVID FARLEY-HILLS. *The Benevolence of Laughter*, pp. 137-39.

"A Song to Chloris"

DAVID FARLEY-HILLS. *The Benevolence of Laughter*, pp. 145-47.

EARL MINER. *The Restoration Mode from Milton to Dryden*, p. 375.

REBA WILCOXON. "The Rhetoric of Sex in Rochester's Burlesque," *Papers on Language and Literature* 12(3), Summer 1976, 274-75.

"Timon"

DAVID FARLEY-HILLS. *The Benevolence of Laughter*, pp. 158-64.

"Tunbridge-Wells"

DAVID FARLEY-HILLS. *The Benevolence of Laughter*, pp. 164-68.

EARL MINER. *The Restoration Mode from Milton to Dryden*, pp. 412-13.

"Upon Nothing"

VIVIAN DE S. PINTO. "John Wilmot, Earl of Rochester and the Right Veine of Satire," in *Seventeenth Century English Poetry*, p. 367; revised ed., p. 482.

KRISTOFFER F. PAULSON. "Pun Intended: Rochester's *Upon Nothing*," *English Language Notes* 9(2), December 1971, 118-21.

DAVID M. VIETH. "Divided Consciousness: The Trauma and Triumph of Restoration Culture," *Tennessee Studies in Literature* 22(1977), 54.

REBA WILCOXON. "Rochester's Philosophical Premises: A Case for Consistency," *Eighteenth Century Studies* 8(2), Winter 1974/75, 183-89.

GEORGE WILLIAMSON. *Six Metaphysical Poets*, pp. 253-56.

"A very Heroical Epistle in Answer to Ephelia"

DAVID FARLEY-HILLS. *The Benevolence of Laughter*, pp. 152-54.

RODGERS, W. R.

"Lent"

W. R. RODGERS. "W. R. Rodgers," in *The Poet Speaks*, pp. 208-9.

ROETHKE, THEODORE

"The Abyss"

see also "Mixed Sequence"

WILLIAM HEYEN. "The Divine Abyss: Theodore Roethke's Mysticism," *Texas Studies in Literature and Language* 11(2), Summer 1969, 1051-68.

DONALD WESLING. "The Inevitable Ear: Freedom and Necessity in Lyric Form, Wordsworth and After," in *Forms of Lyric*, pp. 124-25.

"The Auction"

JAMES MCMICHAEL. "The Poetry of Theodore Roethke," *Southern Review*, n.s., 5(1), Winter 1969, 4-5.

"Big Wind"

see also "Greenhouse Sequence"

JOHN D. BOYD. "Texture and Form in Theodore Roethke's Greenhouse Poems," *Modern Language Quarterly* 32(4), December 1971, 415-18.

KENNETH BURKE. "The Vegetal Radicalism of Theodore Roethke," *Sewanee Review* 58(1), Winter 1950, 69-71.

ROBERT PHILLIPS. *The Confessional Poets*, p. 114.

"The Boy and the Bush"

DEL IVAN JANIK. *Explicator* 32(3), November 1973, Item 20.

"Bring the Day!"

RALPH J. MILLS, JR. "Theodore Roethke," in *Seven American Poets from MacLeish to Nemerov*, p. 108.

JOHN VERNON. *The Garden and the Map*, pp. 177-79.

JOHN VERNON. "Theodore Roethke's *Praise to the End!* Poems," *Iowa Review* 2(4), Fall 1971, 71-72.

"Carnations"

see "Greenhouse Sequence"

"Child on Top of a Greenhouse"

see also "Greenhouse Sequence"

ROBERT PHILLIPS. *The Confessional Poets*, p. 115.

"Cuttings"

see also "Greenhouse Sequence"

ROBERT PHILLIPS. *The Confessional Poets*, p. 111.

"Cuttings (later)"

see also "Greenhouse Sequence"

JOHN D. BOYD. "Texture and Form in Theodore Roethke's Greenhouse Poems," *Modern Language Quarterly* 32(4), December 1971, 422-24.

ROBERT PHILLIPS. *The Confessional Poets*, p. 111.

"The Cycle"

WILLIAM HEYEN. "Theodore Roethke's Minimals," *Minnesota Review* 8(4), 1968, 366-67.

ROY HARVEY PEARCE. *Historicism Once More*, pp. 304-5.

"The Dance"

see also "Four for Sir John Davies"

CARROLL ARNETT. "Minimal to Maximal: Theodore Roethke's Dialectic," *College English* 18(8), May 1957, 415-16.

"The Decision"

see also "Sequence, Sometimes Metaphysical"

ROETHKE, THEODORE *(Cont.)*

"The Decision" *(cont.)*

RICHARD A. BLESSING. "Theodore Roethke's Sometimes Metaphysical Motion," *Texas Studies in Literature and Language* 14(4), Winter 1973, 141-42.

"Dolor"

ROBERT PHILLIPS. *The Confessional Poets,* pp. 117-18.

"The Dream"

JENIJOY LA BELLE. "Martyr to a Motion Not His Own: Theodore Roethke's *Love Poems,*" *Ball State University Forum* 16(2), Spring 1975, 72-73.

"The Dying Man"

see also "The Wall"

WILLIAM HEYEN. "The Yeats Influence: Roethke's Formal Lyrics of the Fifties," *John Berryman Studies* 3(4), Fall 1977, 56-59.

RALPH J. MILLS, JR. "Theodore Roethke," in *Seven American Poets from MacLeish to Nemerov,* pp. 121-23.

"Elegy" ("Should every creature be as I have been")

RICHARD A. BLESSING. "Theodore Roethke: A Celebration," *Tulane Studies in English* 20 (1972), 176-79.

"Elegy for Jane"

RICHARD A. BLESSING. "Theodore Roethke: A Celebration," *Tulane Studies in English* 20 (1972), 173-74.

JAMES M. REID. *100 American Poems of the Twentieth Century,* pp. 204-6.

EVELYN M. ROMIG. "An Achievement of H. D. and Theodore Roethke: Psychoanalysis and the Poetics of Teaching," *Literature and Psychology* 28(3-4), 1978, 107-8.

"The Far Field"

see also "North American Sequence"

DENIS DONOGHUE. *Connoisseurs of Chaos,* pp. 242-44.

JAMES MCMICHAEL. "The Poetry of Theodore Roethke," *Southern Review,* n.s., 5(1), Winter 1969, 20-22.

HUGH B. STAPLES. "The Rose in the Sea-Wind: A Reading of Theodore Roethke's 'North American Sequence,'" *American Literature* 36(2), May 1964, 201-2.

ROSEMARY SULLIVAN. "A Still Center: A Reading of Theodore Roethke's 'North American Sequence,'" *Texas Studies in Literature and Language* 16(4), Winter 1975, 775-77.

"A Field of Light"

KENNETH BURKE. "The Vegetal Radicalism of Theodore Roethke," *Sewanee Review* 58(1), Winter 1950, 94-95.

ROBERT PHILLIPS. *The Confessional Poets,* pp. 124-25.

C. W. TRUESDALE. "Theodore Roethke and the Landscape of American Poetry," *Minnesota Review* 8(4), 1968, 355-56.

"Flower Dump"

see also "Greenhouse Sequence"

ROBERT PHILLIPS. *The Confessional Poets,* p. 115.

"Forcing House"

see also "Greenhouse Sequence"

ROBERT PHILLIPS. *The Confessional Poets,* pp. 111-12.

"Four for Sir John Davies"

see also "The Dance"

HARRY BROWN and JOHN MILSTEAD. *What the Poem Means,* p. 183.

WILLIAM HEYEN. "The Yeats Influence: Roethke's Formal Lyrics of the Fifties," *John Berryman Studies* 3(4), Fall 1977, 34-39.

FREDERICK J. HOFFMAN. "Theodore Roethke: The Poetic Shape of Death," in *Modern American Poetry,* edited by Jerome Mazzaro, pp. 309-11.

JENIJOY LA BELLE. "Theodore Roethke's Dancing Masters in 'Four for Sir John Davies,'" *Concerning Poetry* 8(2), Fall 1975, 29-35.

JAMES MCMICHAEL. "The Poetry of Theodore Roethke," *Southern Review,* n.s., 5(1), Winter 1969, 13-14.

RALPH J. MILLS, JR. *Contemporary American Poetry,* pp. 61-62.

RALPH J. MILLS, JR. "Theodore Roethke," in *Seven American Poets from MacLeish to Nemerov,* pp. 116-19.

RALPH J. MILLS, JR. "Theodore Roethke: The Lyric of the Self," in *Poets in Progress,* pp. 17-19.

C. J. RAWSON. "Nature's Dance of Death: Part I: Urbanity and Strain in Fielding, Swift, and Pope," *Eighteenth Century Studies* 3(3), Spring 1970, 312-13.

"Frau Bauman, Frau Schmidt, and Frau Schwartze"

see also "Greenhouse Sequence"

RICHARD A. BLESSING. "Theodore Roethke: A Celebration," *Tulane Studies in English* 20 (1972), 174-76.

ROBERT PHILLIPS. *The Confessional Poets,* pp. 115-16.

"The Gentle"

D. L. COLUSSI. *Explicator* 27(9), May 1969, Item 73.

"Give Way, Ye Gates"

see also "Praise to the End"

HILTON KRAMER. "The Poetry of Theodore Roethke," *Western Review* 18(2), Winter 1954, 138.

M. L. ROSENTHAL. *The Modern Poets,* pp. 241-42.

JOHN VERNON. *The Garden and the Map,* pp. 179-81.

JOHN VERNON. "Theodore Roethke's *Praise to the End!* Poems," *Iowa Review* 2(4), Fall 1971, 72-74.

"Greenhouse Sequence"

see also individual titles in the sequence

JOHN D. BOYD. "Texture and Form in Theodore Roethke's Greenhouse Poems," *Modern Language Quarterly* 32(4), December 1971, 409-24.

WILLIAM HEYEN. "Theodore Roethke's Minimals," *Minnesota Review* 8(4), 1968, 361-63.

LOUIS L. MARTZ. *The Poem of the Mind,* pp. 170-76.

RALPH J. MILLS, JR. "Theodore Roethke," in *Seven American Poets from MacLeish to Nemerov,* pp. 98-101.

ROY HARVEY PEARCE. *Historicism Once More,* pp. 302-4.

ROBERT PHILLIPS. *The Confessional Poets,* pp. 110-16.

JAROLD RAMSEY. "Roethke in the Greenhouse," *Western Humanities Review* 26(1), Winter 1972, 35-47.

"I Knew a Woman"

DENNIS E. BROWN. "Theodore Roethke's 'Self-World' and the Modernist Position," *Journal of Modern Literature* 3(5), July 1974, 1249.

HELEN T. BUTTEL. *Explicator* 24(9), May 1966, Item 78.

NAT HENRY. *Explicator* 27(5), January 1969, Item 31.

JENIJOY LA BELLE. *Explicator* 32(2), October 1973, Item 15.

VIRGINIA L. PECK. *Explicator* 22(8), April 1964, Item 66.

"I Need, I Need"
see also "Praise to the End"
RALPH J. MILLS, JR. "Theodore Roethke," in *Seven American Poets from MacLeish to Nemerov*, pp. 106-8.
JOHN VERNON. *The Garden and the Map*, pp. 175-77.
JOHN VERNON. "Theodore Roethke's *Praise to the End!* Poems," *Iowa Review* 2(4), Fall 1971, 70-71.

"I Waited"
see also "Sequence, Sometimes Metaphysical"
RICHARD A. BLESSING. "Theodore Roethke's Sometimes Metaphysical Motion," *Texas Studies in Literature and Language* 14(4), Winter 1973, 743-44.

"In a Dark Time"
see also "Sequence, Sometimes Metaphysical"
RICHARD A. BLESSING. "Theodore Roethke's Sometimes Metaphysical Motion," *Texas Studies in Literature and Language* 14(4), Winter 1973, 732-35.
JOHN HOBBS. "The Poet as His Own Interpreter: Roethke on 'In a Dark Time,'" *College English* 33(1), October 1971, 55-66.
FREDERICK J. HOFFMAN. "Theodore Roethke: The Poetic Shape of Death," in *Modern American Poetry*, edited by Jerome Mazzaro, pp. 316-19.
J. D. McCLATCHY. "Sweating Light from a Stone: Identifying Theodore Roethke," *Modern Poetry Studies* 3(1), 1972, 22-23.
RALPH J. MILLS, JR. *Creation's Very Self*, pp. 12-13. Reprinted in: Ralph J. Mills, Jr. *Cry of the Human*, pp. 12-13.
JOHN CROWE RANSOM, BABETTE DEUTSCH, STANLEY KUNITZ and THEODORE ROETHKE. "On Theodore Roethke's 'In a Dark Time,'" in *The Contemporary Poet as Artist and Critic*, pp. 24-53.
AGNES STEIN. *The Uses of Poetry*, pp. 355-56.
LOUIS UNTERMEYER. *50 Modern American & British Poets*, pp. 278-79.

"In Evening Air"
see also "Sequence, Sometimes Metaphysical"
RICHARD A. BLESSING. "Theodore Roethke's Sometimes Metaphysical Motion," *Texas Studies in Literature and Language* 14(4), Winter 1973, 735-37.

"Infirmity"
see also "Sequence, Sometimes Metaphysical"
RICHARD A. BLESSING. "Theodore Roethke's Sometimes Metaphysical Motion," *Texas Studies in Literature and Language* 14(4), Winter 1973, 740-41.

"Interlude"
C. E. NICHOLSON and W. H. WASILEWSKI. *Explicator* 36(3), Spring 1978, 26-27.
LAURENCE PERRINE. "The Theme of Theodore Roethke's 'Interlude,'" *Notes on Modern American Literature* 1(3), Summer 1977, Item 23.

"Journey to the Interior"
see also "North American Sequence"
JAMES McMICHAEL. "The Poetry of Theodore Roethke," *Southern Review*, n.s., 5(1), Winter 1969, 18-20.
HUGH B. STAPLES. "The Rose in the Sea-Wind: A Reading of Theodore Roethke's 'North American Sequence,'" *American Literature* 36(2), May 1964, 198-200.

"Judge Not"
ROBERT PHILLIPS. *The Confessional Poets*, p. 118.

"The Long Alley"
KENNETH BURKE. "The Vegetal Radicalism of Theodore Roethke," *Sewanee Review* 58(1), Winter 1950, 85-86, 93-94.
BRENDAN GALVIN. "Theodore Roethke's Proverbs," *Concerning Poetry* 5(1), Spring 1972, 38-39.
ROBERT PHILLIPS. *The Confessional Poets*, pp. 122-24.

"The Long Waters"
see also "North American Sequence"
JAMES McMICHAEL. "The Poetry of Theodore Roethke," *Southern Review*, n.s., 5(1), Winter 1969, 20.
HUGH B. STAPLES. "The Rose in the Sea-Wind: A Reading of Theodore Roethke's 'North American Sequence,'" *American Literature* 36(2), May 1964, 200-1.

"The Longing"
see also "North American Sequence"
JAMES McMICHAEL. "The Poetry of Theodore Roethke," *Southern Review*, n.s., 5(1), Winter 1969, 15-16.
HUGH B. STAPLES. "The Rose in the Sea-Wind: A Reading of Theodore Roethke's 'North American Sequence,'" *American Literature* 36(2), May 1964, 193-95.

"The Lost Son"
CARROLL ARNETT. "Minimal to Maximal: Theodore Roethke's Dialectic," *College English* 18(8), May 1957, 415.
KENNETH BURKE. "The Vegetal Radicalism of Theodore Roethke," *Sewanee Review* 58(1), Winter 1950, 87-93.
BABETTE DEUTSCH. *Poetry in Our Time*, pp. 184-85; second ed., pp. 198-99.
HILTON KRAMER. "The Poetry of Theodore Roethke," *Western Review* 18(2), Winter 1954, 138-41.
JENIJOY LA BELLE. "Theodore Roethke's 'The Lost Son': From Archetypes to Literary History," *Modern Language Quarterly* 37(2), June 1976, 179-95.
J. D. McCLATCHY. "Sweating Light from a Stone: Identifying Theodore Roethke," *Modern Poetry Studies* 3(1), 1972, 10-12.
RALPH J. MILLS, JR. *Contemporary American Poetry*, pp. 56-60.
RALPH J. MILLS, JR. "Theodore Roethke," in *Modern American Poetry*, edited by Guy Owen, pp. 192-95.
RALPH J. MILLS, JR. "Theodore Roethke," in *Seven American Poets from MacLeish to Nemerov*, pp. 109-13.
RALPH J. MILLS, JR. "Theodore Roethke: The Lyric of the Self," in *Poets in Progress*, pp. 12-16.
ROY HARVEY PEARCE. *Historicism Once More*, pp. 310-11.
ROBERT PHILLIPS. *The Confessional Poets*, pp. 119-21.
THEODORE ROETHKE. "Open Letter," in *Mid-Century American Poets*, pp. 68-72.
C. W. TRUESDALE. "Theodore Roethke and the Landscape of American Poetry," *Minnesota Review* 8(4), 1968, 353-54.
JOHN VERNON. *The Garden and the Map*, pp. 185-90.

"Love Poems"
JAMES G. SOUTHWORTH. "Theodore Roethke: *The Far Field*," *College English* 27(5), February 1966, 416.

"The Marrow"
see also "Sequence, Sometimes Metaphysical"

ROETHKE, THEODORE *(Cont.)*

"The Marrow" *(cont.)*

RICHARD A. BLESSING. "Theodore Roethke's Sometimes Metaphysical Motion," *Texas Studies in Literature and Language* 14(4), Winter 1973, 742-43.

DENIS DONOGHUE. *Connoisseurs of Chaos*, pp. 233-34.

JAMES MCMICHAEL. "The Poetry of Theodore Roethke," *Southern Review*, n.s., 5(1), Winter 1969, 5.

"Meditation at Oyster River"

see also "North American Sequence"

J. D. MCCLATCHY. "Sweating Light from a Stone: Identifying Theodore Roethke," *Modern Poetry Studies* 3(1), 1972, 20-21.

JAMES MCMICHAEL. "The Poetry of Theodore Roethke," *Southern Review*, n.s., 5(1), Winter 1969, 17-18.

HUGH B. STAPLES. "The Rose in the Sea-Wind: A Reading of Theodore Roethke's 'North American Sequence,'" *American Literature* 36(2), May 1964, 196-98.

"Meditations of an Old Woman"

WILLIAM HEYEN. "Theodore Roethke's Minimals," *Minnesota Review* 8(4), 1968, 367-75.

FREDERICK J. HOFFMAN. "Theodore Roethke: The Poetic Shape of Death," in *Modern American Poetry*, edited by Jerome Mazzaro, pp. 313-14.

RALPH J. MILLS, JR. *Contemporary American Poetry*, pp. 63-66.

RALPH J. MILLS, JR. "Theodore Roethke," in *Modern American Poetry*, ed. by Guy Owen, pp. 198-200.

RALPH J. MILLS, JR. "Theodore Roethke," in *Seven American Poets from MacLeish to Nemerov*, pp. 123-28.

RALPH J. MILLS, JR. "Theodore Roethke: The Lyric of the Self," in *Poets in Progress*, pp. 20-23.

JOHN CROWE RANSOM. "On Theodore Roethke's 'In a Dark Time,'" in *The Contemporary Poet as Artist and Critic*, pp. 32-33.

"Mixed Sequence"

ROBERT G. SOUTHWORTH. "Theodore Roethke: *The Far Field*," *College English* 27(5), February 1966, 416-17.

"The Moment"

see also "Mixed Sequence"

JERRALD RANTA. "Geometry, Vision, and Poetic Form," *College English* 39(6), February 1978, 711-12.

"Moss-Gathering"

see also "Greenhouse Sequence"

ROBERT PHILLIPS. *The Confessional Poets*, pp. 113-14.

"The Motion"

see also "Sequence, Sometimes Metaphysical"

RICHARD A. BLESSING. "Theodore Roethke's Sometimes Metaphysical Motion," *Texas Studies in Literature and Language* 14(4), Winter 1973, 739.

"My Papa's Waltz"

JEROME BEATY and WILLIAM H. MATCHETT. *Poetry From Statement to Meaning*, pp. 225-26.

JOHN CIARDI. *How Does a Poem Mean?* pp. 1003-4; second ed., pp. 369-70.

ROBERT PHILLIPS. *The Confessional Poets*, pp. 116-17.

JAMES M. REID. *100 American Poems of the Twentieth Century*, pp. 206-7.

"Night Crow"

WILLIAM HEYEN. "Theodore Roethke's Minimals," *Minnesota Review* 8(4), 1968, 365-66.

"North American Sequence"

see also individual titles in the sequence

DENNIS E. BROWN. "Theodore Roethke's 'Self-World' and the Modernist Position," *Journal of Modern Literature* 3(5), July 1974, 1252-54.

WILLIAM V. DAVIS. "The Escape into Time: Theodore Roethke's 'The Waking,'" *Notes on Contemporary Literature* 5(2), March 1975, 3-4.

STANLEY KUNITZ. "Roethke: Poet of Transformations," in *Contemporary Poetry in America*, pp. 107-8.

J. D. MCCLATCHY. "Sweating Light from a Stone: Identifying Theodore Roethke," *Modern Poetry Studies* 3(1), 1972, 19-21.

JAMES MCMICHAEL. "The Poetry of Theodore Roethke," *Southern Review*, n.s., 5(1), Winter 1969, 15-25.

LOUIS L. MARTZ. *The Poem of the Mind*, pp. 162-65.

ROY HARVEY PEARCE. *Historicism Once More*, pp. 319-21.

JAMES G. SOUTHWORTH. "Theodore Roethke: *The Far Field*," *College English* 27(5), February 1966, 413-16.

HUGH B. STAPLES. "The Rose in the Sea-Wind: A Reading of Theodore Roethke's 'North American Sequence,'" *American Literature* 36(2), May 1964, 189-203.

ROSEMARY SULLIVAN. "A Still Center: A Reading of Theodore Roethke's 'North American Sequence,'" *Texas Studies in Literature and Language* 16(4), Winter 1975, 765-83.

"O Lull Me, Lull Me"

see also "Praise to the End"

JOHN VERNON. *The Garden and the Map*, pp. 183-84.

"O, Thou Opening, O"

BRENDAN GALVIN. "Theodore Roethke's Proverbs," *Concerning Poetry* 5(1), Spring 1972, 42-45.

"Old Florist"

see "Greenhouse Sequence"

"Once More, the Round"

see also "Sequence, Sometimes Metaphysical"

RICHARD A. BLESSING. "Theodore Roethke's Sometimes Metaphysical Motion," *Texas Studies in Literature and Language* 14(4), Winter 1973, 748.

"Open House"

GERALD M. GARMON. *Explicator* 28(3), November 1969, Item 27.

"Orchids"

see also "Greenhouse Sequence"

JOHN D. BOYD. "Texture and Form in Theodore Roethke's Greenhouse Poems," *Modern Language Quarterly* 32(4), December 1971, 419-21.

ROBERT PHILLIPS. *The Confessional Poets*, p. 113.

ROBERT PINSKY. *The Situation of Poetry*, pp. 124-29.

"Pickle Belt"

ROBERT PHILLIPS. *The Confessional Poets*, p. 117.

"Praise to the End!"

see also individual titles in the sequence

HILTON KRAMER. "The Poetry of Theodore Roethke," *Western Review* 18(2), Winter 1954, 134-42.

ROY HARVEY PEARCE. *Historicism Once More*, pp. 305-12.

C. W. TRUESDALE. "Theodore Roethke and the Landscape of American Poetry," *Minnesota Review* 8(4), 1968, 356-57.

JOHN VERNON. "Theodore Roethke's *Praise to the End! Poems*," *Iowa Review* 2(4), Fall 1971, 60-79.

"The Pure Fury"

PAUL J. SCHUMACHER. "The Unity of Being: A Study of Theodore Roethke's Poetry," *Ohio University Review* 12(1), 1970, 32-34.

"The Restored"

see "Sequence, Sometimes Metaphysical"

"The Return"

ROY HARVEY PEARCE. *Historicism Once More*, pp. 297-98.

"The Right Thing"

see also "Sequence, Sometimes Metaphysical"

RICHARD A. BLESSING. "Theodore Roethke's Sometimes Metaphysical Motion," *Texas Studies in Literature and Language* 14(4), Winter 1973, 746-47.

"Root Cellar"

see also "Greenhouse Sequence"

ROBERT PHILLIPS. *The Confessional Poets*, p. 111.

GEORGE WOLFF. *Explicator* 29(6), February 1971, Item 47.

"The Rose"

see also "North American Sequence"

JAMES MCMICHAEL. "The Poetry of Theodore Roethke," *Southern Review*, n.s., 5(1), Winter 1969, 22-25.

HUGH B. STAPLES. "The Rose in the Sea-Wind: A Reading of Theodore Roethke's 'North American Sequence,'" *American Literature* 36(2), May 1964, 202-3.

"Sensibility! O La!"

see also "Praise to the End"

JOHN VERNON. *The Garden and the Map*, pp. 184-85.

"The Sequel"

see also "Sequence, Sometimes Metaphysical"

RICHARD A. BLESSING. "Theodore Roethke's Sometimes Metaphysical Motion," *Texas Studies in Literature and Language* 14(4), Winter 1973, 737-39.

"Sequence, Sometimes Metaphysical"

see also individual titles in the sequence

RICHARD A. BLESSING. "Theodore Roethke's Sometimes Metaphysical Motion," *Texas Studies in Literature and Language* 14(4), Winter 1973, 731-49.

STANLEY KUNITZ. "Roethke: Poet of Transformations," in *Contemporary Poetry in America*, pp. 108-9.

RALPH J. MILLS, JR. *Contemporary American Poetry*, pp. 62-63.

RALPH J. MILLS, JR. "Theodore Roethke," in *Seven American Poets from MacLeish to Nemerov*, p. 129.

ROY HARVEY PEARCE. *Historicism Once More*, pp. 321-23.

ROBERT G. SOUTHWORTH. "Theodore Roethke: *The Far Field*," *College English* 27(5), February 1966, 417-18.

"The Shape of Fire"

KENNETH BURKE. "The Vegetal Radicalism of Theodore Roethke," *Sewanee Review* 58(1), Winter 1950, 95-97.

DAN JAFFE. "Theodore Roethke: 'In a Slow Up-Sway,'" in *The Fifties*, p. 205.

HILTON KRAMER. "The Poetry of Theodore Roethke," *Western Review* 18(2), Winter 1954, 141-42.

ROBERT PHILLIPS. *The Confessional Poets*, pp. 125-6, 127.

M. L. ROSENTHAL. *The Modern Poets*, pp. 242-43.

"The Song" ("I met a ragged man")

WILLIAM R. SLAUGHTER. "Roethke's 'Song,'" *Minnesota Review* 8(4), 1968, 342-44.

"Transplanting"

see also "Greenhouse Sequence"

RALPH J. MILLS, JR. *Contemporary American Poetry*, pp. 52-53.

ROBERT PHILLIPS. *The Confessional Poets*, pp. 114-15.

"The Tree, the Bird"

see also "Sequence, Sometimes Metaphysical"

RICHARD A. BLESSING. "Theodore Roethke's Sometimes Metaphysical Motion," *Texas Studies in Literature and Language* 14(4), Winter 1973, 744-45.

"The Visitant"

KENNETH BURKE. "The Vegetal Radicalism of Theodore Roethke," *Sewanee Review* 58(1), Winter 1950, 71-72.

"The Waking"

RICHARD A. BLESSING. "The Shaking That Steadies: Theodore Roethke's 'The Waking,'" *Ball State University Forum* 12(4), Autumn 1971, 17-19.

WILLIAM V. DAVIS. "The Escape into Time: Theodore Roethke's 'The Waking,'" *Notes on Contemporary Literature* 5(2), March 1975, 2-10.

ROBERT ELY. *Explicator* 34(7), March 1976, Item 54.

WILLIAM HEYEN. "Theodore Roethke's Minimals," *Minnesota Review* 8(4), 1968, 366.

"A Walk in Late Summer"

JAMES MCMICHAEL. "The Poetry of Theodore Roethke," *Southern Review*, n.s., 5(1), Winter 1969, 5-7.

"The Wall"

see also "The Dying Man"

JOHN CROWE RANSOM. "On Theodore Roethke's 'In a Dark Time,'" in *The Contemporary Poet as Artist and Critic*, pp. 31-32.

"Weed Puller"

see also "Greenhouse Sequence"

DENNIS E. BROWN. "Theodore Roethke's 'Self-World' and the Modernist Position," *Journal of Modern Literature* 3(5), July 1974, 1245.

ROBERT PHILLIPS. *The Confessional Poets*, pp. 112-13.

"Where Knock Is Open Wide"

see also "Praise to the End"

KENNETH BURKE. "The Vegetal Radicalism of Theodore Roethke," *Sewanee Review* 58(1), Winter 1950, 105-7.

HILTON KRAMER. "The Poetry of Theodore Roethke," *Western Review* 18(2), Winter 1954, 135-36.

RALPH J. MILLS, JR. "Theodore Roethke," in *Seven American Poets from MacLeish to Nemerov*, p. 103-6.

ROY HARVEY PEARCE. *Historicism Once More*, pp. 307-9.

JOHN VERNON. *The Garden and the Map*, pp. 164-75.

JOHN VERNON. "Theodore Roethke's *Praise to the End! Poems*," *Iowa Review* 2(4), Fall 1971, 62-70.

"Where Knock is Open Wide, Part 1"

RONALD REICHERTZ. *Explicator* 26(4), December 1967, Item 34.

ROETHKE, THEODORE *(Cont.)*

"Words for the Wind"

RALPH J. MILLS, JR. "Theodore Roethke," in *Seven American Poets from MacLeish to Nemerov*, pp. 119-21.

ROLLE, RICHARD

"Luf es lyf Pat lastes ay"

STEPHEN MANNING. *Wisdom and Number*, pp. 58-59.

ROSENBERG, ISAAC

"The Amulet"

JON SILKIN. *Out of Battle*, pp. 307-11.

"Break of Day in the Trenches"

BERNARD BERGONZI. *Heroes' Twilight*, pp. 115-16.

MARIUS BEWLEY. *Masks & Mirrors*, p. 298.

CHRISTOPHER GILLIE. *Movements in English Literature*, pp. 72-73.

DAVID HOLBROOK. *Lost Bearings in English Poetry*, pp. 191-93.

JON SILKIN. *Out of Battle*, pp. 276-81.

"The Burning of the Temple"

JON SILKIN. *Out of Battle*, pp. 299, 301.

"Chagrin"

PHILIP HOBSBAUM. "Isaac Rosenberg," in *Criticism in Action*, pp. 29-34.

"Daughters of War"

D. W. HARDING. *Experience Into Words*, p. 96.

JON SILKIN. *Out of Battle*, pp. 289-91.

"Dead Man's Dump"

BERNARD BERGONZI. *Heroes' Twilight*, pp. 116-19.

JON SILKIN. *Out of Battle*, pp. 281-89.

"The Destruction of Jerusalem by the Babylonian Hordes"

JON SILKIN. *Out of Battle*, pp. 299-301.

"Girl to Soldier on Leave"

JON SILKIN. *Out of Battle*, pp. 295-98.

"God"

JON SILKIN. *Out of Battle*, pp. 267-70.

"God Made Blind"

JON SILKIN. *Out of Battle*, pp. 266-67.

"Louse-Hunting"

JON SILKIN. *Out of Battle*, pp. 298-99.

"Marching"

BERNARD BERGONZI. *Heroes' Twilight*, pp. 114-15.

"On Receiving News of the War"

JON SILKIN. *Out of Battle*, pp. 274-75.

"The One Lost"

JON SILKIN. *Out of Battle*, pp. 266-67.

"Returning We Hear the Larks"

MARIUS BEWLEY. *Masks & Mirrors*, pp. 295-98.

PHILIP HOBSBAUM. "Isaac Rosenberg," in *Criticism in Action*, pp. 24-29.

JON SILKIN. *Out of Battle*, pp. 292-94.

"Soldier: Twentieth Century"

JON SILKIN. *Out of Battle*, pp. 294-95.

ROSENTHAL, M. L.

"Beyond Power: A Sequence"

SALLY M. GALL. " 'Wild with the Morning': The Poetry of M. L. Rosenthal," *Modern Poetry Studies* 8(2), Autumn 1977, 123-24.

"His Present Discontents"

SALLY M. GALL. " 'Wild with the Morning': The Poetry of M. L. Rosenthal," *Modern Poetry Studies* 8(2), Autumn 1977, 125-26.

"Late at Night"

SALLY M. GALL. " 'Wild with the Morning': The Poetry of M. L. Rosenthal," *Modern Poetry Studies* 8(2), Autumn 1977, 127.

"Through Streets Where Smiling Children"

SALLY M. GALL. " 'Wild with the Morning': The Poetry of M. L. Rosenthal," *Modern Poetry Studies* 8(2), Autumn 1977, 133.

ROSS, ALAN

"J. W. 51B A Convoy"

VERNON SCANNELL. *Not Without Glory*, pp. 122-26.

"Night Train Images"

VERNON SCANNELL. *Not Without Glory*, pp. 119-20.

"Radar"

LAURENCE PERRINE. *100 American Poems of the Twentieth Century*, pp. 281-82.

ROSSETTI, CHRISTINA

"Acme"

K. E. JANOWITZ. "The Antipodes of Self: Three Poems by Christina Rossetti," *Victorian Poetry* 11(3), Autumn 1973, 203-5.

"Advent"

JOHN O. WILDER. "Christ's Second Coming: Christina Rossetti and the Premillennialist William Dodsworth," *New York Public Library Bulletin* 73(7), September 1969, 474-76.

"Amor Mundi"

EUGENE J. BRZENK. " 'Up-Hill' and 'Down-' by Christina Rossetti," *Victorian Poetry* 10(4), Winter 1972, 367-71.

"A Birthday"

CONRAD FESTA. "Symbol and Meaning in 'A Birthday,' " *English Language Notes* 11(1), September 1973, 50-56.

RICHARD D. LYNDE. "A Note on the Imagery in Christina Rossetti's 'A Birthday,' " *Victorian Poetry* 3(4), Autumn 1965, 261-63.

AGNES STEIN. *The Uses of Poetry*, pp. 8-10.

"The Convent Threshold"

FLORENCE K. RIDDLE. "Hopkins' Dramatic Monologues," *Hopkins Quarterly* 2(2), July 1975, 58.

WILLIAM STAFFORD. "C. Rossetti: The Convent Threshold," in *Master Poems of the English Language*, pp. 742-47.

"Eve"

C. M. BOWRA. *The Romantic Imagination*, pp. 251-54.

"From House to Home"

JOHN O. WALLER. "Christ's Second Coming: Christina Rossetti and the Premillennialist William Dodsworth," *New York Public Library Bulletin* 73(7), September 1969, 473-74.

"Goblin Market"

> HARRY BROWN and JOHN MILSTEAD. *What the Poem Means*, p. 185.

> A. A. DEVITIS. "*Goblin Market*: Fairy Tale and Reality," *Journal of Popular Culture* 1(4), Spring 1968, 418-26.

> ELLEN GOLUB. "Untying Goblin Apron Strings: A Psychoanalytic Reading of 'Goblin Market,' " *Literature and Psychology* 25(4), 1974, 158-65.

> WARREN HERENDEEN. "The Midsummer Eves of Shakespeare and Christina Rossetti," *Victorian Newsletter* 41 (Spring 1972), 24-26.

> WENDELL STACY JOHNSON. "Some Functions of Poetic Form," *Journal of Aesthetics and Art Criticism* 13(4), June 1955, 504-5.

> LONA MOSK PACKER. "Symbol and Reality in Christina Rossetti's *Goblin Market*," *PMLA* 73(4), September 1958, 375-85.

> WINSTON WEATHERS. "Christina Rossetti: The Sisterhood of Self," *Victorian Poetry* 3(2), Spring 1965, 82-84.

"Maiden-Song"

> WINSTON WEATHERS. "Christina Rossetti: The Sisterhood of Self," *Victorian Poetry* 3(2), Spring 1965, 87.

"Noble Sisters"

> WINSTON WEATHERS. "Christina Rossetti: The Sisterhood of Self," *Victorian Poetry* 3(2), Spring 1965, 86-87.

"Passing away (saith the World) passing Away"

> JOHN O. WALLER. "Christ's Second Coming: Christina Rossetti and the Premillennialist William Dodsworth," *New York Public Library Bulletin* 73(7), September 1969, 474.

"Rest"

> JAMES R. KREUTZER. *Elements of Poetry*, pp. 17-18.

> WRIGHT THOMAS and STUART GERRY BROWN. *Reading Poems: An Introduction to Critical Study*, pp. 638-69.

"Restive"

> K. E. JANOWITZ. "The Antipodes of Self: Three Poems by Christina Rossetti," *Victorian Poetry* 11(3), Autumn 1973, 198-203.

"Sister Maude"

> WINSTON WEATHERS. "Christina Rossetti: The Sisterhood of Self," *Victorian Poetry* 3(2), Spring 1965, 86.

"Spring"

> K. E. JANOWITZ. "The Antipodes of Self: Three Poems by Christina Rossetti," *Victorian Poetry* 11(3), Autumn 1973, 196-98.

"Spring Quiet"

> I. A. RICHARDS. *Practical Criticism*, pp. 32-41, *passim*.

"A Triad"

> WINSTON WEATHERS. "Christina Rossetti: The Sisterhood of Self," *Victorian Poetry* 3(2), Spring 1965, 84-85.

"Up-Hill"

> EUGENE J. BRZENK. " 'Up-Hill' and 'Down-' by Christina Rossetti," *Victorian Poetry* 10(4), Winter 1972, 367-71.

> ELIZABETH DREW. *Poetry*, p. 243.

ROSSETTI, DANTE GABRIEL

"Aspecta Medusa"

> JEROME J. MCGANN. "The Beauty of the Medusa: A Study in Romantic Literary Iconology," *Studies in Romanticism* 11(1), Winter 1972, 21-22.

KENT PATTERSON. "A Terrible Beauty: Medusa in Three Victorian Poets," *Tennessee Studies in Literature* 17 (1972), 113-15.

"Ave"

> D. M. R. BENTLEY. "Rossetti's 'Ave' and Related Pictures," *Victorian Poetry* 15(1), Spring 1977, 21-35.

"Barren Spring"

> GEORGE P. LANDOW. " 'Life touching lips with immortality': Rossetti's Typological Structures," *Studies in Romanticism* 17(3), Summer 1973, 263-64.

"The Blessed Damozel"

> RON D. K. BANERJEE. "Dante Through the Looking Glass: Rossetti, Pound and Eliot," *Comparative Literature* 24(2), Spring 1972, 140-41.

> HARRY BROWN and JOHN MILSTEAD. *What the Poem Means*, pp. 186-87.

> THOMAS H. BROWN. "The Quest of Dante Gabriel Rossetti in 'The Blessed Damozel,' " *Victorian Poetry* 10(3), Autumn 1972, 273-77.

> C. C. CUNNINGHAM. *Literature as a Fine Art: Analysis and Interpretation*, pp. 142-47.

> DAVID DAICHES. "D. G. Rossetti: The Blessed Damozel," in *Master Poems of the English Language*, pp. 733-36.

> BARBARA CHARLESWORTH GELPI. "The Image of the Anima in the Work of Dante Gabriel Rossetti," *Victorian Newsletter* 45(Spring 1974), 3-4.

> STANLEY M. HOLBERG. "Rossetti and the Trance," *Victorian Poetry* 8(4), Winter 1970, 311-14.

> K. L. KNICKERBOCKER. "Rossetti's 'The Blessed Damozel,' " *Studies in Philology* 29(3), July 1932, 485-504.

> JEROME J. MCGANN. "Rossetti's Significant Details," *Victorian Poetry* 7(1), Spring 1969, 48-54.

> HELENE E. ROBERTS. "The Dream World of Dante Gabriel Rossetti," *Victorian Studies* 17(4), June 1974, 387-88.

> STEPHEN J. SPECTOR. "Love, Unity, and Desire in the Poetry of Dante Gabriel Rossetti," *ELH* 38(3), September 1971, 435.

> RICHARD L. STEIN. "Dante Gabriel Rossetti: Painting and the Problem of Poetic Form," *Studies in English Literature 1500-1900* 10(4), Autumn 1970, 780-81.

"Bridal Birth"

> HELEN BUTTEL. *Explicator* 23(3), November 1964, Item 22.

> RICHARD L. STEIN. "Dante Gabriel Rossetti: Painting and the Problem of Poetic Form," *Studies in English Literature 1500-1900* 10(4), Autumn 1970, 786-87.

"The Bride's Prelude"

> STANLEY M. HOLBERG. "Rossetti and the Trance," *Victorian Poetry* 8(4), Winter 1970, 304-8.

"The Burden of Ninevah"

> HARRY BROWN and JOHN MILSTEAD. *What the Poem Means*, p. 187.

> JEROME H. BUCKLEY. "Pre-Raphaelite Past and Present: The Poetry of the Rossettis," in *Victorian Poetry*, pp. 133-34.

> GEORGE P. LANDOW. " 'Life touching lips with immortality': Rossetti's Typological Structures," *Studies in Romanticism* 17(3), Summer 1978, 254-56.

> JOHN R. REED. "Mixing Memory and Desire in Late Victorian Literature," *English Literature in Transition* 14(1), 1971, 10.

ROSSETTI, DANTE GABRIEL *(Cont.)*

"The Card Dealer"

STANLEY M. HOLBERG. "Rossetti and the Trance," *Victorian Poetry* 8(4), Winter 1970, 309-10.

"The Cloud Confines"

STEPHEN J. SPECTOR. "Love, Unity, and Desire in the Poetry of Dante Gabriel Rossetti," *ELH* 38(3), September 1971, 439-41.

"The Dark Glass"

JEFFREY R. PRINCE. "D. G. Rossetti and the Pre-Raphaelite Conception of the Special Moment," *Modern Language Quarterly* 37(4), December 1976, 357.

"Death-in-Love"

MICHAEL E. GREENE. "The Severed Self: The Dramatic Impulse in *The House of Life*," *Ball State University Forum* 14(4), Autumn 1973, 51.

"Death's Songsters"

JOSEPH F. VOGEL. *Explicator* 21(8), April 1963, Item 64.

"Eden Bower"

PHILIP McM. PITTMAN. "The Strumpet and the Snake: Rossetti's Treatment of Sex as Original Sin," *Victorian Poetry* 12(1), Spring 1974, 45-54.

"For a Venetian Pastoral"

GEORGE P. LANDOW. " 'Life touching lips with immortality': Rossetti's Typological Structures," *Studies in Romanticism* 17(3), Summer 1978, 257-58.

JEFFREY R. PRINCE. "The Iconic Poem and the Aesthetic Tradition," *ELH* 43(4), Winter 1976, 568-71.

"Hand and Soul"

BARBARA CHARLESWORTH GELPI. "The Image of the Anima in the Work of Dante Gabriel Rossetti," *Victorian Newsletter* 45 (Spring 1974), 1.

"Heart's Hope"

RICHARD L. STEIN. "Dante Gabriel Rossetti: Painting and the Problem of Poetic Form," *Studies in English Literature 1500-1900* 10(4), Autumn 1970, 787-89.

"The Hill Summit"

FRANCES NOEL LEES. "The Keys Are at the Palace: A Note on Criticism and Biography," *College English* 28(2), November 1966, 101-8.

"The Holy Family"

GEORGE P. LANDOW. " 'Life touching lips with immortality': Rossetti's Typological Structures," *Studies in Romanticism* 17(3), Summer 1978, 250-51.

"The Husbandmen"

D. M. R. BENTLEY. "Rossetti's Pre-Raphaelite Manifesto: The 'Old and New Art' Sonnets," *English Language Notes* 15(3), March 1978, 201-2.

"Jenny"

ROBERT N. KEANE. "Rossetti's 'Jenny': Moral Ambiguity and the '*Inner* Standing Point,' " *Papers on Language and Literature* 9(3), Summer 1973, 271-80.

JAMES G. NELSON. "The Rejected Harlot: A Reading of Rossetti's 'A Last Confession' and 'Jenny,' " *Victorian Poetry* 10(2), Summer 1972, 126-29.

JULES PAUL SEIGEL. "*Jenny*: The Divided Sensibility of a Young and Thoughtful Man of the World," *Studies in English Literature 1500-1900* 9(4), Autumn 1969, 677-93.

STEPHEN J. SPECTOR. "Love, Unity, and Desire in the Poetry of Dante Gabriel Rossetti," *ELH* 38(3), September 1971, 435-36.

"A Last Confession"

RONNALIE ROPER HOWARD. "Rossetti's *A Last Confession*: A Dramatic Monologue," *Victorian Poetry* 5(1), Spring 1967, 21-29.

JAMES G. NELSON. "The Rejected Harlot: A Reading of Rossetti's 'A Last Confession' and 'Jenny,' " *Victorian Poetry* 10(2), Summer 1972, 123-26.

CARL A. PETERSON. "Rossetti's *A Last Confession* as Dramatic Monologue," *Victorian Poetry* 11(2), Summer 1973, 127-42.

"Last Fire"

GEORGE P. LANDOW. " 'Life touching lips with immortality': Rossetti's Typological Structures," *Studies in Romanticism* 17(3), Summer 1978, 261-62.

"Life-in-Love"

BARBARA CHARLESWORTH GELPI. "The Image of the Anima in the Work of Dante Gabriel Rossetti," *Victorian Newsletter* 45 (Spring 1974), 5.

CLYDE DE L. RYALS. "The Narrative Unity of *The House of Life*," *Journal of English and Germanic Philology* 69(2), April 1970, 248-49.

"The lilies stand before her like a screen"

D. M. R. BENTLEY. "Light, Architecture, and Awe in Rossetti's Early Annunciations," *Ariel* 7(2), April 1976, 22-24.

"Lost on Both Sides"

MICHAEL E. GREENE. "The Severed Self: The Dramatic Impulse in *The House of Life*," *Ball State University Forum* 14(4), Autumn 1973, 52.

"Love and Hope"

GEORGE P. LANDOW. " 'Life touching lips with immortality': Rossetti's Typological Structures," *Studies in Romanticism* 17(3), Summer 1978, 263.

"The Lovers' Walk"

STEPHEN J. SPECTOR. "Love, Unity, and Desire in the Poetry of Dante Gabriel Rossetti," *ELH* 38(3), September 1971, 450-52.

"Love's Fatality"

MICHAEL E. GREENE. "The Severed Self: The Dramatic Impulse in *The House of Life*," *Ball State University Forum* 14(4), Autumn 1973, 51.

"Memorial Thresholds"

JOSEPH F. VOGEL. *Explicator* 23(4), December 1964, Item 29.

"The Monochord"

STEPHEN J. SPECTOR. "Love, Unity, and Desire in the Poetry of Dante Gabriel Rossetti," *ELH* 38(3), September 1971, 452-54.

"My Sister's Sleep"

STANLEY M. HOLBERG. "Rossetti and the Trance," *Victorian Poetry* 8(4), Winter 1970, 302-4.

JEROME J. McGANN. "Rossetti's Significant Details," *Victorian Poetry* 7(1), Spring 1969, 42-45.

JAMES G. NELSON. "Aesthetic Experience and Rossetti's 'My Sister's Sleep,' " *Victorian Poetry* 7(2), Summer 1969, 154-58.

JAMES G. NELSON. "The Nature of Aesthetic Experience in the Poetry of the Nineties: Ernest Dowson, Lionel Johnson, and John Gray," *English Literature in Transition* 17(4), 1974, 224.

HERBERT SUSSMAN. "Rossetti's Changing Style: The Revisions of 'My Sister's Sleep,' " *Victorian Newsletter* 41 (Spring 1972), 6-8.

"Not As These"

D. M. R. BENTLEY. "Rossetti's Pre-Raphaelite Manifesto: The 'Old and New Art' Sonnets," *English Language Notes* 15(3), March 1978, 199-201.

"Nuptial Sleep"

C. M. BOWRA. *The Romantic Imagination,* pp. 212-13.

"On Mary's Portrait Which I Painted Six Years Ago"

BARBARA CHARLESWORTH GELPI. "The Image of the Anima in the Work of Dante Gabriel Rossetti," *Victorian Newsletter* 45 (Spring 1974), 1-3.

STANLEY M. HOLBERG. "Rossetti and the Trance," *Victorian Poetry* 8(4), Winter 1970, 308-9.

"The One Hope"

JOHN LINDBERG. "Rossetti's Cumaean Oracle," *Victorian Newsletter* 22 (Fall 1962), 20-21.

"The Paris Railway-Station"

JEROME J. McGANN. "Rossetti's Significant Details," *Victorian Poetry* 7(1), Spring 1969, 46-48.

"The Passover in the Holy Family"

GEORGE P. LANDOW. " 'Life touching lips with immortality': Rossetti's Typological Structures," *Studies in Romanticism* 17(3), Summer 1978, 249-50.

"The Portrait"

ROBERT N. KEANE. "Rossetti: The Artist and 'The Portrait,' " *English Language Notes* 12(2), December 1974, 96-102.

"Rose Mary"

CLYDE K. HYDER. "Rossetti's *Rose Mary*: A Study in the Occult," *Victorian Poetry* 1(3), August 1963, 197-207.

"St. Luke the Painter"

D. M. R. BENTLEY. "Rossetti's Pre-Raphaelite Manifesto: The 'Old and New Art' Sonnets," *English Language Notes* 15(3), March 1978, 197-99.

RICHARD L. STEIN. "Dante Gabriel Rossetti: Painting and the Problem of Poetic Form," *Studies in English Literature 1500-1900* 10(4), Autumn 1970, 777-80.

"The Sea-Limits"

STEPHEN J. SPECTOR. "Love, Unity, and Desire in the Poetry of Dante Gabriel Rossetti," *ELH* 38(3), September 1971, 449-50.

"Silent Noon"

GEORGE P. LANDOW. " 'Life touching lips with immortality': Rossetti's Typological Structures," *Studies in Romanticism* 17(3), Summer 1978, 260-61.

JEFFREY R. PRINCE. "D. G. Rossetti and the Pre-Raphaelite Conception of the Special Moment," *Modern Language Quarterly* 37(4), December 1976, 355-59.

STEPHEN J. SPECTOR. "Rossetti's Self-Destroying 'Moment's Monument': Silent Noon," *Victorian Poetry* 14(1), Spring 1976, 54-58.

"Sister Helen"

STEPHEN J. SPECTOR. "Love, Unity, and Desire in the Poetry of Dante Gabriel Rossetti," *ELH* 38(3), September 1971, 436-37.

"The Song-Throe"

D. M. R. BENTLEY. " 'The Song-Throe' by D. G. Rossetti," *Notes & Queries,* n.s., 24(5), October 1977, 421-22.

"The Sonnet" (*The House of Life*)

HARRY BROWN and JOHN MILSTEAD. *What the Poem Means,* p. 188.

DONALD STAUFFER. *The Nature of Poetry,* pp. 236-37.

"Stillborn Love"

GEORGE P. LANDOW. " 'Life touching lips with immortality': Rossetti's Typological Structures," *Studies in Romanticism* 17(3), Summer 1978, 263.

"The Stream's Secret"

JOHN N. HOBBS. "Love and Time in Rossetti's 'The Stream's Secret,' " *Victorian Poetry* 9(4), Winter 1971, 395-404.

JEFFREY R. PRINCE. "D. G. Rossetti and the Pre-Raphaelite Conception of the Special Moment," *Modern Language Quarterly* 37(4), December 1976, 363-67.

STEPHEN J. SPECTOR. "Love, Unity, and Desire in the Poetry of Dante Gabriel Rossetti," *ELH* 38(3), September 1971, 445-47, *passim.*

"Sunset Wings"

D. M. R. BENTLEY. *Explicator* 37(1), Fall 1978, 39.

"Troy Town"

GEORGE P. LANDOW. " 'Life touching lips with immortality': Rossetti's Typological Structures," *Studies in Romanticism* 17(3), Summer 1978, 256-57.

"The Vase of Life"

RICHARD L. STEIN. "Dante Gabriel Rossetti: Painting and the Problem of Poetic Form," *Studies in English Literature 1500-1900* 10(4), Autumn 1970, 785-87.

"William and Marie"

BENJAMIN FRANKLIN FISHER IV. "Rossetti's 'William and Marie': Hints of the Future," *English Language Notes* 9(2), December 1971, 121-29.

"Willowood Sequence"

STEPHEN J. SPECTOR. "Love, Unity, and Desire in the Poetry of Dante Gabriel Rossetti," *ELH* 38(3), September 1971, 455-57.

"The Woodspurge"

STANLEY M. HOLBERG. "Rossetti and the Trance," *Victorian Poetry* 8(4), Winter 1970, 301-2.

JEROME J. McGANN. "Rossetti's Significant Details," *Victorian Poetry* 7(1), Spring 1969, 45-46.

ROSSETTI, WILLIAM MICHAEL

"Socialism"

LEONID M. ARINSHTEIN WITH WILLIAM E. FREDEMAN. "William Michael Rossetti's 'Democratic Sonnets,' " *Victorian Studies* 14(3), March 1971, 259.

"The Transvaal"

LEONID M. ARINSHTEIN WITH WILLIAM E. FREDEMAN. "William Michael Rossetti's 'Democratic Sonnets,' " *Victorian Studies* 14(3), March 1971, 256-57.

RUKEYSER, MURIEL

"Boy with His Hair Cut Short"

M. L. ROSENTHAL and A. J. M. SMITH. *Exploring Poetry,* pp. 285-87.

"Breaking Open"

M. L. ROSENTHAL. *Poetry and the Common Life,* pp. 117-18.

"The Disease"

ESTELLE GERSHGOREN NOVAK. "The Dynamo School of Poets," *Contemporary Literature* 11(4), Autumn 1970, 536.

RUKEYSER, MURIEL *(Cont.)*

"Effort at Speech Between Two People"

> JAMES M. REID. *100 American Poems of the Twentieth Century*, pp. 216-17.

"First Elegy: Rotten Lake"

> ESTELLE GERSHGOREN NOVAK. "The Dynamo School of Poets," *Contemporary Literature* 11(4), Autumn 1970, 538.

"Gauley Bridge"

> ESTELLE GERSHGOREN NOVAK. "The Dynamo School of Poets," *Contemporary Literature* 11(4), Autumn 1970, 536-37.

"Ryder"

> ESTELLE GERSHGOREN NOVAK. "The Dynamo School of Poets," *Contemporary Literature* 11(4), Autumn 1970, 537-38.

"Second Elegy. Age of Magicians"

> DAN JAFFE. "Poets in the Inferno: Civilians, C.O.'s and Combatants," in *The Forties*, p. 41.

RUNT, HARRIE

"Maroccus Extaticus"

> EJNER J. JENSON. "The Wit of Renaissance Satire," *Philological Quarterly* 51(2), April 1972, 400-1.

RUSKIN, JOHN

"A Walk in Chamouni"

> GERALD LEVIN. "The Imagery of Ruskin's 'A Walk in Chamouni,'" *Victorian Poetry* 5(4), Winter 1967, 283-90.

RUTSALA, VERN

"The Adventurer"

> NORMAN FRIEDMAN. "The Wesleyan Poets — IV," *Chicago Review* 19(3), June 1967, 89-90.

"Nightfall"

> NORMAN FRIEDMAN. "The Wesleyan Poets — IV," *Chicago Review* 19(3), June 1967, 87-88.

S

SABIE, FRANCES

"The Fisherman's Tale"
> STANLEY R. MAVEETY. "High Style, Strange Words, and the Answer to an Old Problem," *English Language Notes* 5(3), March 1968, 159-63.

SANDBURG, CARL

"Ashes and Dreams"
> JOHN E. HALLWAS. "Sandburg's 'Ashes and Dreams': An Uncollected Poem," *Notes on Modern American Literature* 2(3), Summer 1978, Item 24.

"Broken-Face Gargoyles"
> BERNARD S. OLDSEY. *Explicator* 7(7), May 1949, Item 50.

"Caboose Thoughts"
> RICHARD CROWDER. *Explicator* 4(7), May 1946, Item 52.

"Chicago"
> WALTER BLAIR. *Literature of the United States*, II: 962.
> JAMES M. REID. *100 American Poems of the Twentieth Century*, pp. 52-54.

"Cool Tombs"
> HARRY BROWN and JOHN MILSTEAD. *What the Poem Means*, p. 193.
> DANIEL G. HOFFMAN. *Explicator* 9(7), May 1951, Item 46.

"Early Lynching"
> RALPH P. BOAS. *Explicator* 1(7), June 1943, Item 67.

"A Fence"
> SELMA WAGNER. *Explicator* 27(6), February 1969, Item 42.

"Fire Flowers"
> JOHN E. HALLWAS. " 'Fire Flowers': An Uncollected Poem by Carl Sandburg," *Notes on Modern American Literature* 1(3), Summer 1977, Item 16.

"Fog"
> WRIGHT THOMAS and STUART GERRY BROWN. *Reading Poems: An Introduction to Critical Study*, pp. 646-47. (P)

"Four Preludes on Playthings of the Wind"
> CLEANTH BROOKS. *Modern Poetry and the Tradition*, pp. 97-98.
> HARRY BROWN and JOHN MILSTEAD. *What the Poem Means*, p. 194.

"Limited"
> JOHN CLARK PRATT. *The Meaning of Modern Poetry*, pp. 178, 181, 184.

"Lost"
> ARCHIBALD A. HILL. *Constituent and Pattern in Poetry*, pp. 49-50.

"To the Ghost of John Milton"
> PAUL ENGLE. *Reading Modern Poetry*, pp. 32-34; revised ed., pp. 17-19.

"Wind Song"
> JAMES M. REID. *100 American Poems of the Twentieth Century*, pp. 54-55.

SANTAYANA, GEORGE

"Above the battlements of heaven rise" (Sonnet XIX)
> LOIS HUGHSON. "The Uses of Despair: The Sources of Creative Energy in George Santayana," *American Quarterly* 23(5), December 1971, 731-32.

"Athletic Code"
> EDWARD L. SHAUGHNESSY. "Santayana on Athletics," *Journal of American Studies* 10(2), August 1976, 177-78.

"But is this love, that in my hollow breast" (Sonnet XXIII)
> LOIS HUGHSON. "The Uses of Despair: The Sources of Creative Energy in George Santayana," *American Quarterly* 23(5), December 1971, 735-36.

"I sought on earth a garden of delight" (Sonnet I)
> PHILIP BLAIR RICE. "George Santayana: The Philosopher as Poet," *Kenyon Review* 2(4), Autumn 1940, 469-71.

"The Judgement of Paris or How the First-Ten Man Chooses a Club"
> WILLIAM G. HOLZBERGER. "The Unpublished Poems of George Santayana: Some Critical And Textual Considerations," *Southern Review*, n.s., 11(1), Winter 1975, 148-50.

"Let my lips touch thy lips, and my desire" (Sonnet XXX)
> LOIS HUGHSON. "The Uses of Despair: The Sources of Creative Energy in George Santayana," *American Quarterly* 23(5), December 1971, 736-37.

"Lines Read at the Inauguration of the New Clubhouse"
> JOEL PORTE. "Santayana at the 'Gas House,' " *New England Quarterly* 35(3), September 1962, 341-44.

SANTAYANA, GEORGE *(Cont.)*

"On a Volume of Scholastic Philosophy"

GÉMINO H. ABAD. *A Formal Approach to Lyric Poetry*, pp. 316-17.

"The Power of Art"

MAURICE F. BROWN. "Santayana's Necessary Angel," *New England Quarterly* 36(4), December 1963, 441-42.

"To W. P."

DOUGLAS L. WILSON. "Santayana's *Metanoia*: The Second Sonnet Sequence," *New England Quarterly* 39(1), March 1966, 8-10.

SARETT, LEW

"Requiem for a Modern Croesus"

C. C. CUNNINGHAM. *Literature as a Fine Art*, pp. 249-51.

SARGENT, ELIZABETH

"A Sailor at Midnight"

ELAINE SHOWALTER. "Killing the Angel in the House: The Autonomy of Women Writers," *Antioch Review* 32(3), 1973, 349.

SARGENT, ROBERT

"Pharaoh"

JUDSON JEROME and ROBERT SARGENT. "The Moses Poems of Robert Sargent," *Antioch Review* 23(3), Fall 1963, 294-95.

"Zipporah at Bethpeor"

JUDSON JEROME and ROBERT SARGENT. "The Moses Poems of Robert Sargent," *Antioch Review* 23(3), Fall 1963, 294-97.

SAROYAN, ARAM

"wake/walk"

ALICIA OSTRIKER. "Poem Objects," *Partisan Review* 40(1), Winter 1973, 105.

"wire air"

PETER D. HERTZ. "Minimal Poetry," *Western Humanities Review* 24(1), Winter 1970, 39-40.

SARTON, MAY

"A Divorce of Lovers"

HENRY TAYLOR. "Home To a Place Beyond Exile: The Collected Poems of May Sarton," *Hollins Critic* 11(3), June 1974, 12-13.

"Lifting Stone"

MAY SARTON. "The School of Babylon," in *The Moment of Poetry*, pp. 45-47.

"Poet in Residence"

HENRY TAYLOR. "Home To a Place Beyond Exile: The Collected Poems of May Sarton," *Hollins Critic* 11(3), June 1974, 5-6.

"The Second Spring"

HENRY TAYLOR. "Home To a Place Beyond Exile: The Collected Poems of May Sarton," *Hollins Critic* 11(3), June 1974, 10.

"She Shall Be Called Woman"

HENRY TAYLOR. "Home To a Place Beyond Exile: The Collected Poems of May Sarton," *Hollins Critic* 11(3), June 1974, 3-4.

"These Images Remain"

HENRY TAYLOR. "Home To a Place Beyond Exile: The Collected Poems of May Sarton," *Hollins Critic* 11(3), June 1974, 11-12.

SASSOON, SIEGFRIED

"Acceptance"

C. E. MAGUIRE. "Harmony Unheard: The Poetry of Siegfried Sassoon," *Renascence* 11(3), Spring 1959, 122.

"Base Details"

JON SILKIN. *Out of Battle*, pp. 159-60.

"Counter-Attack"

BERNARD BERGONZI. *Heroes' Twilight*, pp. 102-3.

JON SILKIN. *Out of Battle*, pp. 155-58.

"The Daffodil Murderer"

L. HUGH MOORE, JR. "Siegfried Sassoon and Georgian Realism," *Twentieth Century Literature* 14(4), January 1969, 202-4.

"Everyone Sang"

LLOYD FRANKENBERG. *Invitation to Poetry*, pp. 185-86.

ROBIN SKELTON. *The Poetic Pattern*, p. 142.

"Fight to a Finish"

JON SILKIN. *Out of Battle*, pp. 160-61.

"The General"

JON SILKIN. *Out of Battle*, p. 160.

"Glory of Women"

JON SILKIN. *Out of Battle*, pp. 161-62.

"The Hero"

JON SILKIN. *Out of Battle*, pp. 142-43.

"The Imperfect Lover"

C. E. MAGUIRE. "Harmony Unheard: The Poetry of Siegfried Sassoon," *Renascence* 11(3), Spring 1959, 119.

"The Last Meeting"

JON SILKIN. *Out of Battle*, pp. 143-46.

"The Messenger"

C. E. MAGUIRE. "Harmony Unheard: The Poetry of Siegfried Sassoon," *Renascence* 11(3), Spring 1959, 122-23.

"Morning Express"

L. HUGH MOORE, JR. "Siegfried Sassoon and Georgian Realism," *Twentieth Century Literature* 14(4), January 1969, 204-5.

"The Old Huntsman"

L. HUGH MOORE, JR. "Siegfried Sassoon and Georgian Realism," *Twentieth Century Literature* 14(4), January 1969, 204.

"The Redeemer"

JON SILKIN. *Out of Battle*, pp. 137-39.

"Repression of War Experience"

M. L. ROSENTHAL. *Poetry and the Common Life*, pp. 88-89. (P)

JON SILKIN. *Out of Battle*, pp. 163-66.

"Stand-to: Good Friday Morning"

JON SILKIN. *Out of Battle*, pp. 141-42.

"Their Frailty"

JON SILKIN. *Out of Battle*, pp. 161-62.

"They"
JON SILKIN. *Out of Battle,* pp. 139-41.

"To any Dead Officer"
JON SILKIN. *Out of Battle,* pp. 162-63.

"To Victory"
JON SILKIN. *Out of Battle,* pp. 135-36.

SCHOTT, PENELOPE SCAMBLY

"Before Visiting My Grandmother"
PENELOPE SCAMBLY SCHOTT. "For my mother, again," *Women's Studies* 4(1), 1976, 3-9.

"Dream of a Vigil in My Grandparents' Old House"
PENELOPE SCAMBLY SCHOTT. "For my mother, again," *Women's Studies* 4(1), 1976, 3-9.

SCHWARTZ, DELMORE

"Abraham and Orpheus, Be With Me Now"
JAMES F. KNAPP. "Delmore Schwartz: Poet of the Orphic Journey," *Sewanee Review* 78(3), Summer 1970, 507-8.

"Aubade"
LILA LEE VALENTI. "The Apprenticeship of Delmore Schwartz," *Twentieth Century Literature* 20(3), July 1974, 214-15.

"The blueness of the sky is overhead" (Song VI)
LILA LEE VALENTI. "The Apprenticeship of Delmore Schwartz," *Twentieth Century Literature* 20(3), July 1974, 207-9.

"Cupid's Chant"
JAMES F. KNAPP. "Delmore Schwartz: Poet of the Orphic Journey," *Sewanee Review* 78(3), Summer 1970, 515-16.

"A Dog Named Ego"
STANLEY POSS. "Frost, Freud, and Delmore Schwartz," *CEA Critic* 30(7), April 1968, 6-7.

"Father and Son"
R. H. DEUTSCH. "Poetry and Belief in Delmore Schwartz," *Sewanee Review* 74(4), Autumn 1966, 918-19.
JAMES F. KNAPP. "Delmore Schwartz: Poet of the Orphic Journey," *Sewanee Review* 78(3), Summer 1970, 510-11.

"Genesis, Book One"
JAMES F. KNAPP. "Delmore Schwartz: Poet of the Orphic Journey," *Sewanee Review* 78(3), Summer 1970, 512-14.

"The Heavy Bear"
SISTER M. HILDA BONHAM. "Delmore Schwartz: An Idea of the World," *Renascence* 13(3), Spring 1961, 132-35.
JAMES F. KNAPP. "Delmore Schwartz: Poet of the Orphic Journey," *Sewanee Review* 78(3), Summer 1970, 511-12.
JAMES M. REID. *100 American Poems of the Twentieth Century,* pp. 218-19.

"The Masters of the Heart Touched the Unknown"
JAMES F. KNAPP. "Delmore Schwartz: Poet of the Orphic Journey," *Sewanee Review* 78(3), Summer 1970, 508-9.

"Once and For All"
JAMES F. KNAPP. "Delmore Schwartz: Poet of the Orphic Journey," *Sewanee Review* 78(3), Summer 1970, 514-15.

"The Self Betrayal Which Is Nothing New"
R. H. DEUTSCH. "Delmore Schwartz: Middle Poems," *Concerning Poetry* 2(2), Fall 1969, 25-26.

"The self is unlike music"
LILA LEE VALENTI. "The Apprenticeship of Delmore Schwartz," *Twentieth Century Literature* 20(3), July 1974, 205.

"Seurat's Sunday Afternoon along the Seine"
R. K. MEINERS. "The Way Out: The Poetry of Delmore Schwartz and Others," *Southern Review,* n.s., 7(1), Winter 1970, 332-33.

"Someone Is Harshly Coughing As Before"
JAMES F. KNAPP. "Delmore Schwartz: Poet of the Orphic Journey," *Sewanee Review* 78(3), Summer 1970, 507.

"Starlight life Intuition Pierced the Twelve"
R. H. DEUTSCH. "Poetry and Belief in Delmore Schwartz," *Sewanee Review* 74(4), Autumn 1966, 922-24.

"Tired and unhappy, you think of houses"
RICHARD WILBUR. "Poetry's Debt to Poetry," *Hudson Review* 26(2), Summer 1973, 290-92. Reprinted in: Richard Wilbur. *Responses,* pp. 179-82.

"The Winter Twilight Glowing Black and Gold"
R. H. DEUTSCH. "Delmore Schwartz: Middle Poems," *Concerning Poetry* 2(2), Fall 1969, 26-27.

SCOTT, ALEXANDER

"Justing and Debait up at the Drum betuix William Adamsone and Johine Sym"
ALLAN H. MACLAINE. "The *Christis Kirk* Tradition: Its Evolution in Scots Poetry to Burns," *Studies in Scottish Literature* 2(2), October 1964, 112-14.

SCOTT, TOM

"The Arrival"
ROBIN SKELTON. *The Poetic Pattern,* pp. 162-63.

"The Bride"
ROBIN SKELTON. *The Poetic Pattern,* pp. 159-62.

SCOTT, WALTER

"County Guy"
DON A. KEISTER. *Explicator* 4(7), May 1946, Item 49.

"Dark on their journey frowned the gloomy day"
I. A. RICHARDS. *Poetries: Their Media and Ends,* p. 62.

"The Lady of the Lake"
KARL KROEBER. *Romantic Narrative Art,* pp. 172-75.

"Proud Maisie"
I. A. RICHARDS. *Poetries: Their Media and Ends,* pp. 61-62.

"Rokeby"
KARL KROEBER. *Romantic Narrative Art,* pp. 175-77.

SCOTT, WINFIELD TOWNLEY

"The U.S. Sailor with the Japanese Skull"
GEORGE ABBE. *You and Contemporary Poetry,* pp. 65-66; second ed., pp. 89-90.
DAN JAFFE. "Poets in the Inferno: Civilians, C.O.'s, and Combatants," in *The Forties,* pp. 37-38.
JAMES M. REID *100 American Poems of the Twentieth Century,* pp. 207-10.

SCULLY, JAMES

"Midsummer"

> JAMES M. REID. *100 American Poems of the Twentieth Century*, pp. 270-72.

SEARS, EDMUND HAMILTON

"The Angels' Song"

> ISAAC ASIMOV. *Familiar Poems, Annotated*, pp. 42-47.

SEAY, JAMES

"It All Comes Together Outside the Restroom in Hogansville"

> DAVID BOTTOMS. "Note on the Structure of James Seay's 'It All Comes Together Outside the Restroom in Hogansville,'" *Notes on Contemporary Literature* 7(4), September 1977, 6-7.

SEDLEY, SIR CHARLES

"Child and Maiden"

> DENIS DONOGHUE. "Notes Towards a Critical Method: Language as Order," *Studies* 44(174), Summer 1955, 182-83.

SEEGER, ALAN

"I have a rendezvous with Death"

> EDWARD A. BLOOM, CHARLES H. PHILBRICK, and ELMER M. BLISTEIN. *The Order of Poetry*, pp. viii-x.

SEWARD, ANNA B.

"Monody on Major André"

> ROBERT D. ARNER. "The Death of Major André: Some Eighteenth-Century Views," *Early American Literature* 11(1), Spring 1976, 57-58.

SEXTON, ANNE

"The Addict"

> PAUL A. LACEY. *The Inner War*, p. 28.

"All My Pretty Ones"

> PAUL A. LACEY. *The Inner War*, pp. 18-19.

"The Bells"

> BEVERLY FIELDS. "The Poetry of Anne Sexton," in *Poets in Progress*, second ed., pp. 263-65.

"The Black Art"

> PAUL A. LACEY. *The Inner War*, p. 17.

"The Break"

> ROBERT PHILLIPS. *The Confessional Poets*, pp. 85-86.

"Cinderella"

> ROBERT PHILLIPS. *The Confessional Poets*, p. 90.

"Dearest"

> BEVERLY FIELDS. "The Poetry of Anne Sexton," in *Poets in Progress*, second ed., pp. 282-85.

"The Death Baby"

> SUZANNE JUHASZ. *Naked and Fiery Forms*, pp. 134-38.

"The Death of the Fathers"

> J. D. McCLATCHY. "Anne Sexton: Somehow to Endure," *Centennial Review* 19(2), Spring 1975, 28-31.

"December 9th"

> ROBERT PHILLIPS. *The Confessional Poets*, p. 87.

"December 12th"

> ROBERT PHILLIPS. *The Confessional Poets*, pp. 83-84.

"The Division of Parts"

> BEVERLY FIELDS. "The Poetry of Anne Sexton," in *Poets in Progress*, second ed., pp. 274-75.
>
> PAUL A. LACEY. *The Inner War*, pp. 19-21.
>
> J. D. McCLATCHY. "Anne Sexton: Somehow to Endure," *Centennial Review* 19(2), Spring 1975, 11-12.
>
> RALPH J. MILLS, JR. *Contemporary American Poetry* pp. 230-31.
>
> ROBERT PHILLIPS. *The Confessional Poets*, pp. 79-80.
>
> JON STALLWORTHY. "W. B. Yeats and the Dynastic Theme," *Critical Quarterly* 7(3), Autumn 1965, 260-61.

"The Double Image"

> RISE B. AXELROD. "The Transforming Art of Anne Sexton," *Concerning Poetry* 7(1), Spring 1974, 7-8.
>
> BEVERLY FIELDS. "The Poetry of Anne Sexton," in *Poets in Progress*, second ed., pp. 269-73.
>
> SUZANNE JUHASZ. *Naked and Fiery Forms*, pp. 120-24.
>
> J. D. McCLATCHY. "Anne Sexton: Somehow to Endure," *Centennial Review* 19(2), Spring 1975, 9-11.
>
> ROBERT PHILLIPS. *The Confessional Poets*, p. 78.
>
> JON STALLWORTHY. "W. B. Yeats and the Dynastic Theme," *Critical Quarterly* 7(3), Autumn 1965, 260-61.

"Flight"

> A. R. JONES. "Necessity and Freedom: The Poetry of Robert Lowell, Sylvia Plath and Anne Sexton," *Critical Quarterly* 7(1), Spring 1965, 26-27.

"For God While Sleeping"

> RALPH J. MILLS, JR. *Contemporary American Poetry*, pp. 232-33.

"For John, Who Begs Me Not to Enquire Further"

> RISE B. AXELROD. "The Transforming Art of Anne Sexton," *Concerning Poetry* 7(1), Spring 1974, 6-7.
>
> BEVERLY FIELDS. "The Poetry of Anne Sexton," in *Poets in Progress*, second ed., pp. 258-60.
>
> SUZANNE JUHASZ. *Naked and Fiery Forms*, pp. 125-26.
>
> ROBERT PHILLIPS. *The Confessional Poets*, p. 78.

"For Johnny Pole on the Forgotten Beach"

> BEVERLY FIELDS. "The Poetry of Anne Sexton," in *Poets in Progress*, second ed., pp. 260-61.
>
> RALPH J. MILLS, JR. *Contemporary American Poetry*, pp. 221-23.

"For My Lover, Returning to His Wife"

> IRA SHOR. "Anne Sexton's 'For My Lover . . .': Feminism in the Classroom," *College English* 34(8), May 1973, 1082-90.

"For the Year of the Insane"

> PAUL A. LACEY. *The Inner War*, pp. 26-27.
>
> RALPH J. MILLS, JR. *Creation's Very Self*, pp. 33-34. Reprinted in: Ralph J. Mills, Jr. *Cry of the Human*, pp. 35-36.

"The Fortress"

> JAMES M. REID. *100 American Poems of the Twentieth Century*, pp. 275-77.

"The House"

> J. D. McCLATCHY. "Anne Sexton: Somehow to Endure," *Centennial Review* 19(2), Spring 1975, 15-16.

"In Celebration of My Uterus"

> MYRA STARK. "Walt Whitman and Anne Sexton: A Note on the Uses of Tradition," *Notes on Contemporary Literature* 8(4), September 1978, 7-8.

"In the Deep Museum"
>   BEVERLY FIELDS. "The Poetry of Anne Sexton," in *Poets in Progress*, second ed., pp. 279-80.

"Little Girl, My String Bean, My Lovely Woman"
>   PAUL A. LACEY. *The Inner War*, pp. 23-24.

"Live"
>   NANCY JO HOFFMAN. "Reading Women's Poetry: The Meaning and Our Lives," *College English* 34(1), October 1972, 52-56.

"The Lost Ingredient"
>   PAUL A. LACEY. *The Inner War*, p. 23.

"Loving the Killer"
>   ROBERT PHILLIPS. *The Confessional Poets*, p. 86.

"The Moss of His Skin"
>   BEVERLY FIELDS. "The Poetry of Anne Sexton," in *Poets in Progress*, pp. 252-54.

"Music Swims Back to Me"
>   BEVERLY FIELDS. "The Poetry of Anne Sexton," in *Poets in Progress*, second ed., pp. 261-63.

"Old Dwarf Heart"
>   BEVERLY FIELDS. "The Poetry of Anne Sexton," in *Poets in Progress*, second ed., pp. 281-82.

"The Operation"
>   A. R. JONES. "Necessity and Freedom: The Poetry of Robert Lowell, Sylvia Plath and Anne Sexton," *Critical Quarterly* 7(1), Spring 1965, 27-28.
>   RALPH J. MILLS, JR. *Contemporary American Poetry*, pp. 228-30.

"Pain for a Daughter"
>   PAUL A. LACEY. *The Inner War*, pp. 24-25.

"Portrait of an Old Woman on the College Tavern Wall"
>   BEVERLY FIELDS. "The Poetry of Anne Sexton," in *Poets in Progress*, second ed., pp. 255-56.

"Rapunzel"
>   SUZANNE JUHASZ. *Naked and Fiery Forms*, pp. 130-32.

"Said the Poet to the Analyst"
>   BEVERLY FIELDS. "The Poetry of Anne Sexton," in *Poets in Progress*, second ed., pp. 265-67.

"Some Foreign Letters"
>   J. D. MCCLATCHY. "Anne Sexton: Somehow to Endure," *Centennial Review* 19(2), Spring 1975, 7-9.
>   RALPH J. MILLS, JR. *Contemporary American Poetry*, pp. 224-27.
>   ROBERT PHILLIPS. *The Confessional Poets*, p. 77.

"The Starry Night"
>   LINDA MIZEJEWSKI. "Sappho to Sexton: Womanhood Uncontained," *College English* 35(3), December 1973, 342.

"Those Times"
>   PAUL A. LACEY. *The Inner War*, pp. 22-23.

"To a Friend Whose Work Has Come to Triumph"
>   LAURENCE PERRINE. "Theme and Tone in Anne Sexton's 'To a Friend Whose Work Has Come to Triumph,'" *Notes on Contemporary Literature* 7(3), May 1977, 2-3.

"The Touch"
>   RISE B. AXELROD. "The Transforming Art of Anne Sexton," *Concerning Poetry* 7(1), Spring 1974, 10-11.
>   GREGORY FITZ GERALD. "The Choir from the Soul: A Conversation with Anne Sexton," *Massachusetts Review* 19(1), Spring 1978, 80.

"The Truth the Dead Know"
>   BEVERLY FIELDS. "The Poetry of Anne Sexton," in *Poets in Progress*, second ed., pp. 275-77.
>   RALPH J. MILLS, JR. *Contemporary American Poetry*, pp. 227-28.

"Unknown Girl in the Maternity Ward"
>   BEVERLY FIELDS. "The Poetry of Anne Sexton," in *Poets in Progress*, second ed., pp. 256-57.

"Where I Live in This Honorable House of the Laurel Tree"
>   BEVERLY FIELDS. "The Poetry of Anne Sexton," in *Poets in Progress*, second ed., pp. 254-55.

"With Mercy for the Greedy"
>   A. R. JONES. "Necessity and Freedom: The Poetry of Robert Lowell, Sylvia Plath and Anne Sexton," *Critical Quarterly* 7(1), Spring 1965, 29.
>   PAUL A. LACEY. *The Inner War*, pp. 25-26.

"You, Doctor Martin"
>   BEVERLY FIELDS. "The Poetry of Anne Sexton," in *Poets in Progress*, second ed., pp. 267-68.
>   PAUL A. LACEY. *The Inner War*, p. 16.

SEYMOUR-SMITH, MARTIN

"The Punishment"
>   G. S. FRASER. *Vision and Rhetoric*, pp. 268-70.

SHADWELL, THOMAS

"A Song for St. Cecilia's Day, 1690"
>   H. NEVILLE DAVIES. "The Structure of Shadwell's *A Song for St. Cecilia's Day, 1690*," in *Silent Poetry*, edited by Alastair Fowler, pp. 201-33.

SHAKESPEARE, WILLIAM

"But When I Came Alas to Wive" (*Twelfth Night*)
>   J. DOVER WILSON. "'Twelfth Night,'" *Times Literary Supplement*, 26 July 1947, p. 379. (P)

"Doubt Thou the Stars are Fire" (*Hamlet*)
>   FRANK DOGGETT. *Explicator* 16(4), January 1958, Item 25.

"Fear No More the Heat o' the Sun" (*Cymbeline*)
>   W. W. MAIN. *Explicator* 9(5), March 1951, Item 36. (P)
>   EDWARD F. NOLAN. *Explicator* 11(1), October 1952, Item 4.
>   GEORGE L. PHILLIPS. *Explicator* 12(1), October 1953, Item 2.

"Full fathom five"
>   JEROME BEATY and WILLIAM H. MATCHETT. *Poetry From Statement to Meaning*, pp. 229-31.
>   JOHN TYREE FAIN. "Some Notes on Ariel's Song," *Shakespeare Quarterly* 19(4), Autumn 1968, 329-32.
>   ABBY JANE DUBMAN HANSEN. "Shakespeare's The Tempest (Coral in Full Fadom Five)," *Explicator* 35(1), Fall 1976, 19-20.

"The Phoenix and Turtle"
>   A. ALVAREZ. "William Shakespeare: The Phoenix and the Turtle," in *Interpretations*, pp. 1-16.
>   RONALD BATES. "Shakespeare's 'The Phoenix and Turtle,'" *Shakespeare Quarterly* 6(1), Winter 1955, 19-30.
>   S. M. BONAVENTURE. "The Phoenix Renewed," *Ball State Teachers College Forum* 5(3), Autumn 1964, 72-76.
>   M. C. BRADBROOK. "'The Phoenix and the Turtle,'" *Shakespeare Quarterly* 6(3), Summer 1955, 356-58.

SHAKESPEARE, WILLIAM *(Cont.)*

"The Phoenix and Turtle" *(cont.)*

CLEANTH BROOKS. *The Well Wrought Urn*, pp. 19-20; revised ed., pp. 14-15. Reprinted in: *Criticism*, pp. 365-66. Also: *Critiques and Essays in Criticism*, pp. 76-78. Also: *The Language of Paradox*, pp. 59-61. Also: *American Literary Criticism*, pp. 529-31. Also: *The Study of Literature*, pp. 186-88.

MURRAY COPLAND. "The Dead Phoenix," *Essays in Criticism* 15(3), July 1965, 279-87.

J. V. CUNNINGHAM. " 'Essence' and the *Phoenix and the Turtle*," *Journal of English Literary History* 19(4), December 1952, 265-76.

ROBERT ELLRODT. "An Anatomy of 'The Phoenix and the Turtle,' " *Shakespeare Survey* 15 (1962), 99-110.

WILLIAM EMPSON. "Shakespeare: The Phoenix and the Turtle," in *Master Poems of the English Language*, pp. 41-46.

FRANK KERMODE. *Shakespeare, Spenser, Donne*, pp. 193-99.

W. J. ONG. "Metaphor and the Twinned Vision (*The Phoenix and the Turtle*)," *Sewanee Review* 63(2), Spring 1955, 199-201.

VINCENT F. PETRONELLA. "Shakespeare's *The Phoenix and the Turtle* and the Defunctive Music of Ecstasy," *Shakespeare Studies* 8 (1975), 311-31.

I. A. RICHARDS. *Poetries: Their Media and Ends*, pp. 50-58.

ELIAS SCHWARTZ. "Shakespeare's Dead Phoenix," *English Language Notes* 7(1), September 1969, 25-32.

DANIEL SELTZER. " 'Their Tragic Scene': The Phoenix and Turtle and Shakespeare's Love Tragedies," *Shakespeare Quarterly* 12(2), Spring 1961, 91-101.

RICHARD WILBUR. *Responses*, pp. 89-90.

"Sonnet III" ("Look in thy glass, and tell the face thou viewest")

ANNE FERRY. *All in War with Time*, pp. 60-62.

DAVID PARKER. "Verbal Moods in Shakespeare's Sonnets," *Modern Language Quarterly* 30(3), September 1969, 332-35.

"Sonnet IV" ("Unthrifty loveliness, why dost thou spend")

WINIFRED M. T. NOWOTTNY. "Formal Elements in Shakespeare's Sonnets: Sonnets I-VI," *Essays in Criticism* 2(1), January 1952, 78-81.

"Sonnet V" ("Those hours that with gentle work did frame")

PAUL ELMEN. "Shakespeare's Gentle Hours," *Shakespeare Quarterly* 4(3), July 1953, 301-9.

WINIFRED M. T. NOWOTTNY. "Formal Elements in Shakespeare's Sonnets: Sonnets I-VI," *Essays in Criticism* 2(1), January 1952, 81-83.

"Sonnet VII" ("Lo, in the orient when the gracious light")

ANNE FERRY. *All in War with Time*, pp. 22-23.

"Sonnet VIII" ("Music to hear, why hear'st thou music sadly?")

THEODORE H. BANKS. "Shakespeare's Sonnet No. 8," *Modern Language Notes* 63(8), December 1948, 541-42.

DOUGLAS L. PETERSON. *The English Lyric from Wyatt to Donne*, pp. 232-33.

"Sonnet XII" ("When I do count the clock that tells the time")

J. WILKES BERRY. *Explicator* 27(2), October 1968, Item 13.

S. H. BURTON. *The Criticism of Poetry*, pp. 55-56.

"Sonnet XV" ("When I consider everything that grows")

ANNE FERRY. *All in War with Time*, pp. 3-10.

RICHARD RAY KIRK and ROGER PHILIP MCCUTCHEON. *An Introduction to the Study of Poetry*, pp. 39-41.

RAYMOND B. WADDINGTON. "Shakespeare's Sonnet 15 and the Art of Memory," in *The Rhetoric of Renaissance Poetry*, pp. 96-122.

"Sonnet XVI" ("But wherefore do you not a mightier way")

WILLIAM EMPSON. *Seven Types of Ambiguity*, pp. 70-73; second and third eds., pp. 54-57.

"Sonnet XVIII" ("Shall I compare thee to a summer's day?")

ANNE FERRY. *All in War with Time*, pp. 10-13.

HALLETT SMITH. *Elizabethan Poetry*, p. 178.

FRED H. STOCKING. "A Well-Tempered Sonnet," *Shakespeare Newsletter* 21(4), September 1971, 48.

"Sonnet XIX" ("Devouring Time, blunt thou the lion's paws")

ANNE FERRY. *All in War with Time*, pp. 13-15.

MICHAEL HANCHER. "Understanding Poetic Speech Acts," *College English* 36(6), February 1975, 632-36.

"Sonnet XX" ("A woman's face, with Nature's own hand painted")

PURVIS E. BOYETTE. "Shakespeare's *Sonnets*: Homosexuality and the Critics," *Tulane Studies in English* 21 (1974), 36-37.

MARTIN B. FRIEDMAN. "Shakespeare's 'Master Mistris': Image and Tone in Sonnet 20," *Shakespeare Quarterly* 22(2), Spring 1971, 189-91.

"Sonnet XXI" ("So it is not with me as with that Muse")

JACQUELINE E. M. LATHAM. "Shakespeare's Sonnet 21," *Notes & Queries*, n.s., 25(2), April 1978, 110-12.

DOUGLAS L. PETERSON. *The English Lyric from Wyatt to Donne*, pp. 214-15.

"Sonnet XXIV" ("Mine eye hath played the painter and hath stelled")

LINWOOD E. ORANGE. "Shakespeare's Sonnet 24," *Southern Quarterly* 4(4), July 1966, 409-10.

"Sonnet XXIX" ("When in disgrace with Fortune and men's eyes")

GÉMINO H. ABAD. *A Formal Approach to Lyric Poetry*, pp. 124-27.

MALCOLM BROWN. "The Sweet Crystalline Cry," *Western Review* 16(4), Summer 1952, 264-65.

ANNE FERRY. *All in War with Time*, pp. 54-55.

LLOYD FRANKENBERG. *Invitation to Poetry*, pp. 238-39.

NEAL L. GOLDSTEIN. "Money and Love in Shakespeare's Sonnets," *Bucknell Review* 17(3), December 1969, 99.

"Sonnet XXX" ("When to the sessions of sweet silent thought")

LEONARD DEAN. *English Masterpieces*, edited by William Frost, Maynard Mack, and Leonard Dean, vol. 3: *Renaissance Poetry*, p. 9.

ANNE FERRY. *All in War with Time*, pp. 20-22.

L. C. KNIGHTS. *Explorations*, pp. 74-75.

L. C. KNIGHTS. "Revaluations (V): Shakespeare's Sonnets," *Scrutiny* 3(2), September 1934, 153.

L. C. KNIGHTS. "Shakespeare's Sonnets," in *Elizabethan Poetry*, edited by Paul J. Alpers, p. 292.

JAMES R. KREUZER. *Elements of Poetry*, pp. 67-70.

STEPHEN C. PEPPER. *The Basis of Criticism in the Arts,* pp. 115-27. Abridged in: *The Case for Poetry,* pp. 307-9; second ed., pp. 248-50.

CHARLES LAMAR THOMPSON and CHARLES WEINER. "An Approach to Poetry Through Transformational Processes," *English Journal* 61(3), March 1972, 372-73.

"Sonnet XXXI" ("Thy bosom is endeared with all hearts")

H. W. PIPER. "Shakespeare's Thirty-First Sonnet," *Times Literary Supplement,* 13 April 1951, p. 229.

"Sonnet XXXIII" ("Full many a glorious morning have I seen")

LEONARD DEAN. *English Masterpieces,* edited by William Frost, Maynard Mack, and Leonard Dean, vol. 3: *Renaissance Poetry,* p. 10.

M. M. MAHOOD. "Love's Confined Doom," *Shakespeare Survey* 15 (1962), 50-53.

JOHN CROWE RANSOM. *The World's Body,* pp. 279-80.

"Sonnet XXXIV" ("Why didst thou promise such a beauteous day")

LAURENCE LERNER. *An Introduction to English Poetry,* pp. 17-27.

RICHARD LEVIN. *Explicator* 29(6), February 1971, Item 49.

"Sonnet XXXV" ("No more be grieved at that which thou hast done")

L. C. KNIGHTS. *Explorations,* pp. 64-66.

L. C. KNIGHTS. "Revaluations (V): Shakespeare's Sonnets," *Scrutiny* 3(2), September 1934, 142-43. Reprinted in: Cleanth Brooks and Robert Penn Warren. *Understanding Poetry,* pp. 292-93; revised ed., pp. 152-53; third ed., pp. 166-67; fourth ed., pp. 540-41.

L. C. KNIGHTS. "Shakespeare's Sonnets," in *Elizabethan Poetry,* edited by Paul J. Alpers, pp. 282-83.

DOUGLAS L. PETERSON. *The English Lyric from Wyatt to Donne,* pp. 238-40.

"Sonnet XXXVI" ("Let me confess that we two must be twain")

DAVID K. WEISER. "'I' and 'Thou' in Shakespeare's Sonnets," *Journal of English and Germanic Philology* 76(4), October 1977, 517-20.

"Sonnet XLVI" ("Mine eye and heart are at a mortal war")

PAUL S. CLARKSON and CLYDE T. WARREN. "Pleading and Practice in Shakespeare's Sonnet XLVI," *Modern Language Notes* 62(2), February 1947, 102-10.

"Sonnet LI" ("Thus can my love excuse the slow offense")

A. DAVENPORT. "Shakespeare's Sonnet 51 Again," *Notes & Queries* 198(1), January 1953, 15-16. (P)

"Sonnet LII" ("So am I as the rich whose blessed key")

DAVID K. WEISER. "'I' and 'Thou' in Shakespeare's Sonnets," *Journal of English and Germanic Philology* 76(4), October 1977, 514-15.

"Sonnet LIV" ("O, how much more doth beauty beauteous seem")

HARRY BROWN and JOHN MILSTEAD. *What the Poem Means,* p. 197.

ANNE FERRY. *All in War with Time,* pp. 29-35.

"Sonnet LV" ("Not marble nor the gilded monuments")

HALLETT SMITH. *Elizabethan Poetry,* pp. 178-81. Reprinted in: *The Dimensions of Poetry,* pp. 199-201.

"Sonnet LX" ("Like as the waves make towards the pebbled shore")

HARRY BROWN and JOHN MILSTEAD. *What the Poem Means,* p. 198.

WALLACE DOUGLAS, ROY LAMSON, and HALLETT SMITH. *The Critical Reader,* pp. 56-59.

DAVID KAULA. "'In War With Time': Temporal Perspectives in Shakespeare's Sonnets," *Studies in English Literature 1500-1900* 3(1), Winter 1963, 51.

JOHN OLIVER PERRY. *The Experience of Poems,* pp. 183-84.

JOHN CROWE RANSOM. "Shakespeare at Sonnets," *Southern Review* 3(3), Winter 1938, 548-49.

JOHN CROWE RANSOM. *The World's Body,* pp. 296-97. Reprinted in: *Poems and Critics,* pp. 39-40.

"Sonnet LXI" ("Is it thy will thy image should keep open")

DAVID K. WEISER. "'I' and 'Thou' in Shakespeare's Sonnets," *Journal of English and Germanic Philology* 76(4), October 1977, 521-22.

"Sonnet LXII" ("Sin of self-love possesseth all mine eye")

ELIOT SLATER. "Sinne of Self-Love," *Notes & Queries,* n.s., 23(4), April 1976, 155-56.

"Sonnet LXXIII" ("That time of year thou mayst in me behold")

WINIFRED NOWOTTNY. *The Language Poets Use,* pp. 76-86.

"Sonnet LXIV" ("When I have seen by Time's fell hand defaced")

HARRY BROWN and JOHN MILSTEAD. *What the Poem Means,* pp. 198-99.

JAMES R. CALDWELL. "States of Mind: States of Consciousness," *Essays in Criticism* 4(2), April 1954, 174-78.

ANNE FERRY. *All in War with Time,* pp. 25-28.

JAMES GRIMSHAW. "Amphibology in Shakespeare's Sonnet 64," *Shakespeare Quarterly* 25(1), Winter 1974, 127-29.

RICHARD LEVIN. *Explicator* 24(4), December 1965, Item 39.

DOUGLAS L. PETERSON. *The English Lyric from Wyatt to Donne,* pp. 225-26.

WILLIAM BOWMAN PIPER. "A Poem Turned in Process," *ELH* 43(4), Winter 1976, 446-47.

MARK VAN DOREN. *Introduction to Poetry,* pp. 116-20.

"Sonnet LXV" ("Since brass, nor stone, nor earth, nor boundless sea")

ANNE FERRY. *All in War with Time,* pp. 15-19.

FRED B. MILLETT. *Reading Poetry,* pp. 59-61; second ed., pp. 72-74.

"Sonnet LXVI" ("Tired with all these, for restful death I cry")

RICHARD LEVIN. *Explicator* 22(5), January 1964, Item 36.

"Sonnet LXXI" ("No longer mourn for me when I am dead")

JACK M. DAVIS and J. E. GRANT. "A Critical Dialogue on Shakespeare's Sonnet 71," *Texas Studies in Literature and Language* 1(2), Summer 1959, 214-32.

JAMES R. KREUZER. *Elements of Poetry,* pp. 167-68.

MARK VAN DOREN. *Introduction to Poetry,* pp. 116-18, 120.

"Sonnet LXXIII" ("That time of year thou mayst in me behold")

MELVIN W. ASKEW. "Form and Process in Lyric Poetry," *Sewanee Review* 72(2), Spring 1964, 285-88.

ROBERT BERKELMAN. "The Drama in Shakespeare's Sonnets," *College English* 10(3), December 1948, 139.

SHAKESPEARE, WILLIAM *(Cont.)*

"Sonnet LXXIII" ("That time of year thou mayst in me behold") *(cont.)*

CLEANTH BROOKS and ROBERT PENN WARREN. *Understanding Poetry*, fourth ed., p. 5.

HARRY BROWN and JOHN MILSTEAD. *What the Poem Means*, p. 199.

I. R. W. COOK. "William Hervey and Shakespeare's Sonnets," *Shakespeare Survey* 21(1968), 104-5.

FRED M. FETROW. "Strata and Structure: A Reading of Shakespeare's Sonnet 73," *Concerning Poetry* 9(2), Fall 1976, 23-25.

ROBERT HAWKINS. *Preface to Poetry*, pp. 96-97.

RICHARD B. HOVEY. "Sonnet 73," *College English* 23(8), May 1962, 672-73.

J. G. KEOGH. *Explicator* 28(1), September 1969, Item 6.

R. M. LUMIANSKY. *Explicator* 6(8), June 1948, Item 55.

WINIFRED LYNSKEY. "A Critic in Action: Mr. Ransom," *College English* 5(5), February 1944, 244-46.

CARLISLE MOORE. *Explicator* 8(1), October 1949, Item 2.

DOUGLAS L. PETERSON. *The English Lyric from Wyatt to Donne*, pp. 223-25.

WILLIAM BOWMAN PIPER. "A Poem Turned in Process," *ELH* 43(4), Winter 1976, 447-49.

JOHN CROWE RANSOM. *The World's Body*, pp. 297-98.

RENÉ RAPIN. *Explicator* 30(1), September 1971, Item 3.

THOMAS P. ROCHE. "Shakespeare and the Sonnet Sequence," in *English Poetry and Prose*, edited by Christopher Ricks, pp. 112-14.

M. L. ROSENTHAL and A. J. M. SMITH. *Exploring Poetry*, pp. 91-94; second ed., pp. 347-48.

JAMES SCHROETER. "Shakespeare's Not 'To-Be-Pitied Lover,'" *College English* 23(4), January 1962, 250-55.

KENNETH SEIB. "Shakespeare's 'Well': A Note on Sonnet 73," *Shakespeare Newsletter* 17(6), December 1967, 55.

HALLETT SMITH. *Elizabethan Poetry*, pp. 182-85.

WRIGHT THOMAS and STUART GERRY BROWN. *Reading Poems: An Introduction to Critical Study*, pp. 744-48.

ROBERT L. WHITE. "Sonnet 73 Again — A Rebuttal and New Reading," *CLA Journal* 6(2), December 1962, 125-32.

"Sonnet LXXIV" ("But he contented: when that fell arrest")

LONGWORTH CHAMBRUN. "The Rival Poet," *Times Literary Supplement*, 2 February 1951, p. 69. (P)

"Sonnet LXXVII" ("Thy glass will show thee how thy beauties wear")

YVOR WINTERS. "Poetic Styles, Old and New," in *Four Poets on Poetry*, pp. 58-60.

YVOR WINTERS. "The 16th Century Lyric in England: A Critical and Historical Reinterpretation: Part III," *Poetry* 54(1), April 1939, 49-51. Reprinted in: *Elizabethan Poetry*, edited by Paul J. Alpers, pp. 121-22.

"Sonnet LXXXI" ("Or shall I live your epitaph to make")

WILLIAM EMPSON. *Seven Types of Ambiguity*, pp. 69-70; second and third eds., pp. 53-54. (P)

"Sonnet LXXXIII" ("I never saw that you did painting need")

WILLIAM EMPSON. *Seven Types of Ambiguity*, pp. 167-75; second and third eds., pp. 133-39. Reprinted in: *The Modern Critical Spectrum*, pp. 92-97.

ANNE FERRY. *All in War with Time*, pp. 52-54.

"Sonnet LXXXVI" ("Was it the proud full sail of his great verse")

LLOYD FRANKENBERG. *Invitation to Poetry*, pp. 94-95.

"Sonnet LXXXVII" ("Farewell: thou art too dear for my possessing")

HARRY BROWN and JOHN MILSTEAD. *What the Poem Means*, p. 200.

EARL DANIELS. *The Art of Reading Poetry*, p. 212.

"Sonnet LXXXVIII" ("When thou shalt be disposed to set me light")

RICHARD P. WHEELER. "Poetry and Fantasy in Shakespeare's Sonnets 88-96," *Literature and Psychology* 22(3), 1972, 154-58.

"Sonnet LXXXIX" ("Say that thou didst forsake me for some fault")

RICHARD P. WHEELER. "Poetry and Fantasy in Shakespeare's Sonnets 88-96," *Literature and Psychology* 22(3), 1972, 154-58.

"Sonnet XC" ("Then hate me when thou wilt; if ever, now")

VIRGINIA JORGENSEN. "Of Love and Hate," *English Journal* 53(6), September 1964, 459-61.

RICHARD P. WHEELER. "Poetry and Fantasy in Shakespeare's Sonnets 88-96," *Literature and Psychology* 22(3), 1972, 154-58.

"Sonnet XCI" ("Some glory in their birth, some in their skill")

RICHARD P. WHEELER. "Poetry and Fantasy in Shakespeare's Sonnets 88-96," *Literature and Psychology* 22(3), 1972, 154-58.

"Sonnet XCII" ("But do thou worst to steal thyself away")

RICHARD P. WHEELER. "Poetry and Fantasy in Shakespeare's Sonnets 88-96," *Literature and Psychology* 22(3), 1972, 154-58.

"Sonnet XCIII" ("So shall I live, supposing thou art true")

WILLIAM EMPSON. *English Pastoral Poetry*, pp. 90-91.

RICHARD P. WHEELER. "Poetry and Fantasy in Shakespeare's Sonnets 88-96," *Literature and Psychology* 22(3), 1972, 158.

"Sonnet XCIV" ("They that have pow'r to hurt and will do none")

WILLIAM EMPSON. *English Pastoral Poetry*, pp. 89-101.

WILLIAM EMPSON. "Shakespeare: They That Have Pow'r to Hurt and Will Do None," in *Master Poems of the English Language*, pp. 63-71.

L. C. KNIGHTS. *Explorations*, pp. 69-70.

L. C. KNIGHTS. "Revaluations (V): Shakespeare's Sonnets," *Scrutiny* 3(2), September 1934, 147-48. Reprinted in: *Elizabethan Poetry*, edited by Paul J. Alpers, pp. 286-87.

CAROL THOMAS NEELY. "Detachment and Engagement in Shakespeare's Sonnets: 94, 116, and 129," *PMLA* 92(1), January 1977, 83-87.

ELIAS SCHWARTZ. "Shakespeare's Sonnet XCIV," *Shakespeare Quarterly* 22(4), Autumn 1971, 397-99.

HALLETT SMITH. *Elizabethan Poetry*, pp. 188-91.

LORENA STOOKEY and ROBERT MERRILL. "Shakespeare's Fearful Meditation: Sonnet 94," *Modern Language Quarterly* 39(1), March 1978, 27-37.

RICHARD P. WHEELER. "Poetry and Fantasy in Shakespeare's Sonnets 88-96," *Literature and Psychology* 22(3), 1972, 159-60.

"Sonnet XCV" ("How sweet and lovely dost thou make the shame")

RICHARD P. WHEELER. "Poetry and Fantasy in Shakespeare's Sonnets 88-96," *Literature and Psychology* 22(3), 1972, 160.

"Sonnet XCVI" ("Some say thy fault is youth, some wantonness")

RICHARD P. WHEELER. "Poetry and Fantasy in Shakespeare's Sonnets 88-96," *Literature and Psychology* 22(3), 1972, 160-61.

"Sonnet XCVII" ("How like a winter hath my absence been")

E. C. EVANS. "Shakespeare's Sonnet 97," *Review of English Studies*, n.s., 14(56), November 1963, 379-80.

ALISTAIR FOWLER. *Conceitful Thought*, pp. 109-13.

JAMES R. KREUZER. *Elements of Poetry*, pp. 10-11.

DOUGLAS L. PETERSON. *The English Lyric from Wyatt to Donne*, pp. 222-23.

RICHARD P. WHEELER. "Poetry and Fantasy in Shakespeare's Sonnets 88-96," *Literature and Psychology* 22(3), 1972, 161.

"Sonnet XCVIII" ("From you have I been absent in the Spring")

HARRY BROWN and JOHN MILSTEAD. *What the Poem Means*, p. 200.

"Sonnet C" ("Where art thou, Muse, that thou forget'st so long")

ANNE FERRY. *All in War with Time*, pp. 37-39.

"Sonnet CI" ("Oh truant Muse what shall be thy amends")

ANNE FERRY. *All in War with Time*, pp. 36-37.

"Sonnet CIV" ("To me, fair friend, you never can be old")

ANNE FERRY. *All in War with Time*, pp. 41-47.

BARBARA HARDY. *The Advantage of Lyric*, pp. 1-3.

WILLIAM BOWMAN PIPER. "A Poem Turned in Process," *ELH* 43(4), Winter 1976, 444-60.

"Sonnet CVI" ("When in the chronicle of wasted time")

LOUIS F. MAY, JR. "The *Figura* in Sonnet 106," *Shakespeare Quarterly* 11(1), Winter 1960, 93-94.

"Sonnet CVII" ("Not mine own fears, nor the prophetic soul")

HARRY BROWN and JOHN MILSTEAD. *What the Poem Means*, p. 201.

LAURENCE MICHEL. "Shakespeare's Sonnet CVII," *Journal of English and Germanic Philology* 54(2), April 1955, 301-5. (P)

JOHN CROWE RANSOM. *The World's Body*, pp. 298-99.

YVOR WINTERS. "Poetic Styles, Old and New," in *Four Poets on Poetry*, pp. 52-55.

"Sonnet CVIII" ("What's in the brain that ink may character")

ANNE FERRY. *All in War with Time*, pp. 47-49.

"Sonnet CIX" ("O, never say that I was false of heart")

RUDOLF GERMER. "The Well Wrought Sonnet," *Shakespeare Newsletter* 16(3), May 1966, 27.

"Sonnet CX" ("Alas 'tis true I have gone here and there")

VIRGINIA L. RADLEY and DAVID C. REDDING. "Shakespeare: Sonnet 110, a New Look," *Shakespeare Quarterly* 12(4), Autumn 1961, 462-63.

"Sonnet CXI" ("O, for my sake do you with Fortune chide")

DOUGLAS L. PETERSON. *The English Lyric from Wyatt to Donne*, pp. 247-48.

"Sonnet CXIII" ("Since I left you, mine eye is in my mind")

DONIPHAN LOUTHAN. "Sonnet 113," *Times Literary Supplement*, 6 July 1951, p. 421. (P)

"Sonnet CXV" ("Those lines that I before have writ do lie")

HILTON LANDRY. "The Marriage of True Minds: Truth and Error in Sonnet 116," *Shakespeare Studies* 3 (1967), 100.

"Sonnet CXVI" ("Let me not to the marriage of true minds")

GÉMINO H. ABAD. *A Formal Approach to Lyric Poetry*, pp. 124-27.

HARRY BROWN and JOHN MILSTEAD. *What the Poem Means*, p. 201.

SIGURD BURCKHARDT. "The Poet as Fool and Priest," *Journal of English Literary History* 23(4), December 1956, 289-97.

SEYMOUR CHATMAN. "Reading Literature as Problem-Solving," *English Journal* 52(5), May 1963, 351-52.

JOHN DOEBLER. "A Submerged Emblem in Sonnet 116," *Shakespeare Quarterly* 15(1), Winter 1964, 109-10.

ELIZABETH DREW. *Poetry*, pp. 213-14.

LLOYD FRANKENBERG. *Invitation to Poetry*, pp. 398-99.

HILTON LANDRY. "The Marriage of True Minds: Truth and Error in Sonnet 116," *Shakespeare Studies* 3 (1967), 98-110.

ARCHIBALD MACLEISH. *Poetry and Experience*, pp. 33-36.

CHARLES MATTHEWS and MARGARET M. BLUM. "To the Student of Poetry: An Essay on Essays," *CEA Critic* 35(2), January 1973, 24-27.

CAROL THOMAS NEELY. "Detachment and Engagement in Shakespeare's Sonnets: 94, 116, and 129," *PMLA* 92(1), January 1977, 88-90.

DOUGLAS L. PETERSON. *The English Lyric from Wyatt to Donne*, pp. 244-46.

HALLETT SMITH. *Exploring Poetry*, pp. 172-76.

C. F. WILLIAMSON. "Themes and Patterns in Shakespeare's Sonnets," *Essays in Criticism* 26(3), July 1976, 199-200.

YVOR WINTERS. "Poetic Styles, Old and New," in *Four Poets on Poetry*, pp. 50-52.

"Sonnet CXVII" ("Accuse me thus, that I have scanted all")

HILTON LANDRY. "The Marriage of True Minds: Truth and Error in Sonnet 116," *Shakespeare Studies* 3 (1967), 100-2.

"Sonnet CXX" ("That you were once unkind befriends me now")

ANNE FERRY. *All in War with Time*, pp. 55-57.

HILTON LANDRY. "The Marriage of True Minds: Truth and Error in Sonnet 116," *Shakespeare Studies* 3 (1967), 102.

DAVID K. WEISER. "'I' and 'Thou' in Shakespeare's Sonnets," *Journal of English and Germanic Philology* 76(4), October 1977, 523-24.

"Sonnet CXXI" ("'Tis better to be vile than vile esteemed")

L. C. KNIGHTS. "Revaluations (V): Shakespeare's Sonnets," *Scrutiny* 3(2), September 1934, 155-56.

DAVID PARKER. "Verbal Moods in Shakespeare's Sonnets," *Modern Language Quarterly* 30(3), September 1969, 337-38.

DAVID K. WEISER. "Theme and Structure in Shakespeare's Sonnet 121," *Studies in Philology* 75(2), April 1978, 142-62.

SHAKESPEARE, WILLIAM *(Cont.)*

"Sonnet CXXII" ("Thy gift, thy tables, are within my brain")

> ANNE FERRY. *All in War with Time,* pp. 49-50.

"Sonnet CXXIII" ("No Time, thou shalt not boast that I do change")

> ANNE FERRY. *All in War with Time,* pp. 50-52.
>
> L. C. KNIGHTS. *Explorations,* pp. 79-80.
>
> L. C. KNIGHTS. "Revaluations (V): Shakespeare's Sonnets," *Scrutiny* 3(2), September 1934, 158-60. Reprinted in: *Elizabethan Poetry,* edited by Paul J. Alpers, pp. 296-97.

"Sonnet CXXIV" ("If my dear love were but the child of state")

> ARTHUR MIZENER. "The Structure of Figurative Language in Shakespeare's Sonnets," *Southern Review* 5(4), Spring 1940, 734-47.

"Sonnet CXXVI" ("O thou, my lovely boy, who in thy power")

> MICHAEL J. B. ALLEN. "Shakespeare's Man Descending a Staircase: Sonnets 126 to 154," *Shakespeare Survey* 31 (1978), 134-36.
>
> ANNE FERRY. *All in War with Time,* pp. 59-62.

"Sonnet CXXVII" ("In the old age black was not counted fair")

> C. F. WILLIAMSON. "Themes and Patterns in Shakespeare's Sonnets," *Essays in Criticism* 26(3), July 1976, 202-3.

"Sonnet CXXVIII" ("How oft, when thou, my music, music play'st")

> RICHARD PURDUM. "Shakespeare's Sonnet 128," *Journal of English and Germanic Philology* 63(2), April 1964, 235-39.

"Sonnet CXXIX" ("Th' expense of spirit in a waste of shame")

> J. BUNSELMEYER. "Appearances and Verbal Paradox: Sonnets 129 and 138," *Shakespeare Quarterly* 25(1), Winter 1974, 104-5.
>
> C. W. M. JOHNSON. *Explicator* 7(6), April 1949, Item 41.
>
> RICHARD LEVIN. "Sonnet CXXIX as a 'Dramatic' Poem," *Shakespeare Quarterly* 16(2), Spring 1965, 175-81.
>
> CAROL THOMAS NEELY. "Detachment and Engagement in Shakespeare's Sonnets: 94, 116, and 129," *PMLA* 92(1), January 1977, 90-92.
>
> EDWARD F. NOLAN. *Explicator* 7(2), November 1948, Item 13.
>
> LAURA RIDING and ROBERT GRAVES. *A Survey of Modernist Poetry,* pp. 63-75, 78-80.
>
> B. F. SKINNER. "Reflections on Meaning and Structure," in *I. A. Richards: Essays in His Honor,* pp. 199-209.
>
> HALLETT SMITH. *Elizabethan Poetry,* pp. 187-88.
>
> KARL F. THOMPSON. *Explicator* 7(4), February 1949, Item 27.
>
> HELEN VENDLER. "Jakobson, Richards, and Shakespeare's Sonnet CXXIX," in *I. A. Richards: Essays in His Honor,* pp. 179-98.

"Sonnet CXXX" ("My mistress' eyes are nothing like the sun")

> JOSEPH H. FRIEND. "Teaching the 'Grammar of Poetry,' " *College English* 27(5), February 1966, 365-66.
>
> DAVID PARKER. "Verbal Moods in Shakespeare's Sonnets," *Modern Language Quarterly* 30(3), September 1969, 336-37.

"Sonnet CXXXI" ("Thou art as tyrannous, so as thou art")

> DOUGLAS L. PETERSON. *The English Lyric from Wyatt to Donne,* pp. 212-13.

"Sonnet CXXXII" ("Thine eyes I love, and they as pitying me")

> DOUGLAS L. PETERSON. *The English Lyric from Wyatt to Donne,* pp. 213-14.

"Sonnet CXXVII" ("Thou blind fool, Love, what dost thou to mine eyes")

> ROBERT F. FLEISSNER. *Explicator* 35(3), Spring 1977, 21-22.

"Sonnet CXXXVIII" ("When my love swears that she is made of truth")

> MICHAEL J. B. ALLEN. "Shakespeare's Man Descending a Staircase: Sonnets 126 to 154," *Shakespeare Survey* 31 (1978), 130-31.
>
> J. BUNSELMEYER. "Appearances and Verbal Paradox: Sonnets 129 and 138," *Shakespeare Quarterly* 25(1), Winter 1974, 105-6.
>
> C. R. B. COMBELLACK. *Explicator* 30(4), December 1971, Item 33.
>
> RICHARD HELGERSON. *Explicator* 28(6), February 1970, Item 48.
>
> SAMUEL HUX. *Explicator* 25(5), January 1967, Item 45.
>
> RICHARD LEVIN. *Explicator* 36(3), Spring 1978, 28-29.

"Sonnet CXXXIX" ("O, call me not to justify the wrong")

> MICHAEL J. B. ALLEN. "Shakespeare's Man Descending a Staircase: Sonnets 126 to 154," *Shakespeare Survey* 31 (1978), 131.

"Sonnet CXLII" ("Love is my sin, and thy dear virtue hate")

> T. WALTER HERBERT. *Explicator* 13(6), April 1955, Item 38.

"Sonnet CXLIV" ("Two loves I have, of comfort and despair")

> PAUL RAMSEY. "A Question of Judgement: Wimsatt on Intent," *Essays in Criticism* 22(4), October 1972, 408-9. (P)
>
> JOHN M. STEADMAN. " 'Like Two Spirits': Shakespeare and Ficino," *Shakespeare Quarterly* 10(2), Spring 1959, 244-46.

"Sonnet CXLV" ("Those lips that Love's own hand did make")

> ANDREW GURR. "Shakespeare's First Poem: Sonnet 145," *Essays in Criticism* 21(3), July 1971, 221-26.

"Sonnet CXLVI" ("Poor soul, the center of my sinful earth")

> ROBERT BERKELMAN. "The Drama in Shakespeare's Sonnets," *College English* 10(3), December 1948, 139-41.
>
> CLEANTH BROOKS, JOHN THIBAUT PURSER, and ROBERT PENN WARREN. *An Approach to Literature,* fourth ed., p. 393; fifth ed., pp. 457-58.
>
> ROBERT HILLIS GOLDSMITH. "Shakespeare's Christian Sonnet, Number 146," *Studies in the Literary Imagination* 11(1), Spring 1978, 99-106.
>
> CHARLES A. HUTTAR. "The Christian Basis of Shakespeare's Sonnet 146," *Shakespeare Quarterly* 19(4), Autumn 1968, 355-65.
>
> JAMES R. KREUZER. *Elements of Poetry,* pp. 91-92.
>
> THOMAS P. ROCHE. "Shakespeare and the Sonnet Sequence," in *English Poetry and Prose,* edited by Christopher Ricks, pp. 111-12.

B. C. SOUTHAM. "Shakespeare's Christian Sonnet? Number 146," *Shakespeare Quarterly* 11(1), Winter 1960, 67-71.

DONALD A. STAUFFER, et al. "Critical Principles and a Sonnet," *American Scholar* 12(1), Winter 1942-43, 52-62. Abridged in: *The Case for Poetry*, pp. 317-19; second ed., pp. 256-59.

MICHAEL WEST. "The Internal Dialogue of Shakespeare's Sonnet 146," *Shakespeare Quarterly* 25(1), Winter 1974, 109-22.

"Sonnet CXLVII" ("My love is a fever, longing still")

MICHAEL J. B. ALLEN. "Shakespeare's Man Descending a Staircase: Sonnets 126 to 154," *Shakespeare Survey* 31 (1978), 133-34.

HALLETT SMITH. *Elizabethan Poetry*, pp. 186-87.

"Sonnet CLII" ("In loving thee thou know'st I am forsworn")

MICHAEL J. B. ALLEN. "Shakespeare's Man Descending a Staircase: Sonnets 126 to 154," *Shakespeare Survey* 31 (1978), 136-37.

"Sonnet CLIII" ("Cupid laid by his brand and fell asleep")

MICHAEL J. B. ALLEN. "Shakespeare's Man Descending a Staircase: Sonnets 126 to 154," *Shakespeare Survey* 31 (1978), 136-37.

"Spring"

BERTRAND H. BRONSON. "Daisies Pied and Icicles," *Modern Language Notes* 63(1), January 1948, 35-38.

CLEANTH BROOKS and ROBERT PENN WARREN. *Understanding Poetry*, fourth ed., pp. 85-86.

LAURENCE PERRINE. "The Art of Total Relevance," *CEA Critic* 36(1), November 1973, 10-12.

JOHN M. WARNER. "Shakespeare's 'Winter' and 'Spring' and the Radical Teaching of Poetry," *CEA Critic* 34(3), March 1972, 18-19.

"Take Oh Take Those Lips Away" (*Measure for Measure*)

WILLIAM EMPSON. *Seven Types of Ambiguity*, pp. 229-30; second and third eds., pp. 180-82.

DONALD STAUFFER. *The Nature of Poetry*, p. 107.

"Tell me where is fancie bred" (*Merchant of Venice*)

ARCHIBALD A. HILL. *Constituent and Pattern in Poetry*, pp. 19-22.

"Under the Greenwood Tree" (*As You Like It*)

CLEANTH BROOKS and ROBERT PENN WARREN. *Understanding Poetry*, fourth ed., pp. 282-83.

"What Shall He Have That Kill'd the Deer?" (*As You Like It*)

PETER J. SENG. "The Foresters' Song in *As You Like It*," *Shakespeare Quarterly* 10(2), Spring 1959, 246-49.

"When daisies pied and violets blue"
see "Spring"

"When icicles hang by the wall"
see "Winter"

"Who Is Silvia?" (*The Two Gentlemen of Verona*)

CLEANTH BROOKS. "Irony and 'Ironic' Poetry," *English Journal* 37(2), February 1948, 60-61. Reprinted in: *College English* 9(5), February 1948, 234-35. Also: *Literary Opinion in America*, revised and third eds., pp. 733-34.

PAUL R. SULLIVAN. "Untheological Grace," *College English* 10(3), December 1948, 164-65.

"Winter"

BERTRAND H. BRONSON. "Daisies Pied and Icicles," *Modern Language Notes* 63(1), January 1948, 35-38.

EARL DANIELS. *The Art of Reading Poetry*, pp. 50-51.

LAURENCE PERRINE. *Sound and Sense*, pp. 7-8.

JOHN M. WARNER. "Shakespeare's 'Winter' and 'Spring' and the Radical Teaching of Poetry," *CEA Critic* 34(3), March 1972, 16-17.

SHAPIRO, KARL

"Adam and Eve"

RICHARD SLOTKIN. "The Contextual Symbol: Karl Shapiro's Image of 'The Jew,'" *American Quarterly* 18(2), Summer 1966, 223-24.

"The Alphabet"

KARL MALKOFF. "The Self in the Modern World: Karl Shapiro's Jewish Poems," in *Contemporary American-Jewish Literature*, pp. 215-16.

"Auto Wreck"

EDWARD A. BLOOM, CHARLES H. PHILBRICK, and ELMER M. BLISTEIN. *The Order of Poetry*, pp. 23-28.

ALICE COLEMAN. "'Doors Leap Open,'" *English Journal* 53(8), November 1964, 631-33.

J. M. LINEBARGER and SHELLY ANGEL. "The Argument of 'Auto Wreck,'" *Notes on Modern American Literature* 2(1), Winter 1977, Item 2.

RALPH J. MILLS, JR. *Contemporary American Poetry*, pp. 110-13.

JAMES M. REID. *100 American Poems of the Twentieth Century*, pp. 224-25.

"The bourgeois poet closes the door of his study . . ." (*The Bourgeois Poet*, 15)

DONALD JUSTICE. "On Karl Shapiro's The Bourgeois Poet," in *The Contemporary Poet as Artist and Critic*, pp. 199-200.

"Christmas Eve: Australia"

DAVID DAICHES. "The Poetry of Karl Shapiro," *Poetry* 66(5), August 1945, 267-69. Reprinted in: *Reading Modern Poetry*, pp. 250-51.

"Condemned to write a long bad poem . . ." (*The Bourgeois Poet*, 16)

DONALD JUSTICE. "On Karl Shapiro's The Bourgeois Poet," in *The Contemporary Poet as Artist and Critic*, pp. 201-4.

"The Conscientious Objector"

HARRY J. CARGAS. *Daniel Berrigan and Contemporary Protest Poetry*, p. 35.

"The Dirty Word"

KARL MALKOFF. "The Self in the Modern World: Karl Shapiro's Jewish Poems," in *Contemporary American-Jewish Literature*, pp. 218-19.

"The Dome of Sunday"

EDWIN FUSSELL. "Karl Shapiro: The Paradox of Prose and Poetry," *Western Review* 18(3), Spring 1954, 240-42.

"Drug Store"

LAURENCE PERRINE. *100 American Poems of the Twentieth Century*, pp. 225-27.

"Elegy for a Dead Soldier"

BABETTE DEUTSCH. *Poetry in Our Time*, p. 375; second ed., pp. 418-19.

PAUL ENGLE. "Five Years of Pulitzer Poets," *English Journal* 38(2), February 1949, 62-63.

SHAPIRO, KARL *(Cont.)*

"Elegy for a Dead Soldier" *(cont.)*

DAN JAFFE. "Poets in the Inferno: Civilians, C.O.'s and Combatants," in *The Forties*, pp. 54-55.

VERNON SCANNELL. *Not Without Glory*, pp. 204-6.

WALTER SUTTON. *American Free Verse*, pp. 160-61.

"The First Time"

KARL MALKOFF. "The Self in the Modern World: Karl Shapiro's Jewish Poems," in *Contemporary American-Jewish Literature*, pp. 219-20.

"The Fly"

HARRY J. CARGAS. *Daniel Berrigan and Contemporary Protest Poetry*, p. 38.

BABETTE DEUTSCH. *Poetry in Our Time*, p. 373; second ed., p. 417.

"The Gun"

VERNON SCANNELL. *Not Without Glory*, pp. 200-1.

"Homecoming"

JOSEPH WARREN BEACH. *Obsessive Images*, pp. 163-64.

"The Intellectual"

HARRY BROWN and JOHN MILSTEAD. *What the Poem Means*, p. 204.

"The Interlude, II"

BABETTE DEUTSCH. *Poetry in Our Time*, p. 374; second ed., pp. 417-18. (P)

"The Leg"

KARL MALKOFF. "The Self in the Modern World: Karl Shapiro's Jewish Poems," in *Contemporary American-Jewish Literature*, pp. 220-23.

RALPH J. MILLS, JR. *Contemporary American Poetry*, pp. 113-15.

"Messias"

RICHARD SLOTKIN. "The Contextual Symbol: Karl Shapiro's Image of 'The Jew,'" *American Quarterly* 18(2), Summer 1966, 223.

"Mongolian Idiot"

RICHARD SLOTKIN. "The Contextual Symbol: Karl Shapiro's Image of 'The Jew,'" *American Quarterly* 18(2), Summer 1966, 225.

"Poet"

MICHEL VINAVERT. *Explicator* 4(3), December 1945, Item 23.

"The Progress of Faust"

LAURENCE PERRINE. *100 American Poems of the Twentieth Century*, pp. 220-23.

"Scyros"

HARRY J. CARGAS. *Daniel Berrigan and Contemporary Protest Poetry*, pp. 33-34.

"The Synagogue"

KARL MALKOFF. "The Self in the Modern World: Karl Shapiro's Jewish Poems," in *Contemporary American-Jewish Literature*, pp. 217-18.

RICHARD SLOTKIN. "The Contextual Symbol: Karl Shapiro's Image of 'The Jew,'" *American Quarterly* 18(2), Summer 1966, 221-22.

"They held a celebration for you" (*The Bourgeois Poet*, 14)

DONALD JUSTICE. "On Karl Shapiro's The Bourgeois Poet," in *The Contemporary Poet as Artist and Critic*, pp. 196-99.

"University"

HARRY BROWN and JOHN MILSTEAD. *What the Poem Means*, p. 204.

KARL MALKOFF. "The Self in the Modern World: Karl Shapiro's Jewish Poems," in *Contemporary American-Jewish Literature*, pp. 216-17.

RALPH J. MILLS, JR. *Contemporary American Poetry*, pp. 106-8.

"V-Letter"

RICHARD SLOTKIN. "The Contextual Symbol: Karl Shapiro's Image of 'The Jew,'" *American Quarterly* 18(2), Summer 1966, 224-25.

SHAPIRO, HARVEY

"The Way"

HAROLD BLOOM. *Figures of Capable Imagination*, pp. 255-56.

SHAW, CARLETON F.

"Arena"

JOSEPHINE MILES. *Poetry and Change*, p. 171.

SHELLEY, PERCY B.

"Adonais"

CARLOS BAKER. "Shelley: Adonais," in *Master Poems of the English Language*, pp. 543-46.

JAMES BENZIGER. *Images of Eternity*, pp. 92-95.

HAROLD BLOOM. "The Unpastured Sea: An Introduction to Shelley," in *Romanticism and Consciousness*, pp. 396-98.

HAROLD BLOOM. *The Visionary Company*, pp. 333-41.

EDWARD E. BOSTETTER. *The Romantic Ventriloquists*, pp. 224-29.

HARRY BROWN and JOHN MILSTEAD. *What the Poem Means*, pp. 205-6.

DEREK COLVILLE. *Victorian Poetry and the Romantic Religion*, pp. 37-38.

DAVID DAICHES and WILLIAM CHARVAT. *Poems in English*, pp. 703-5.

JAMES C. EVANS. "Masks of the Poet: A Study of Self-Confrontation in Shelley's Poetry," *Keats-Shelley Journal* 24 (1975), 83-84.

D. W. HARDING. *Experience Into Words*, pp. 187-91. (P)

EDWIN HONIG. "Shelley: Adonais," in *Master Poems of the English Language*, pp. 540-42.

EDWARD B. HUNGERFORD. *Shores of Darkness*, pp. 216-39.

JEROME J. MCGANN. "Shelley's Veils: A Thousand Images of Loveliness," in *Romantic and Victorian*, pp. 212-14.

MICHAEL MACKLEM. "The Elegiac Theme in Housman," *Queens Quarterly* 59(1), Spring 1952, 47-48.

GEORGE D. RICHARDS. "Shelley's Urn of Bitter Prophecy," *Keats-Shelley Journal* 21-22 (1972-1973), 123-24.

E. M. W. TILLYARD. *Poetry Direct and Oblique*, pp. 172-73.

EARL R. WASSERMAN. "*Adonais*: Progressive Revelation as a Poetic Mode," *Journal of English Literary History* 21(4), December 1954, 274-326.

EARL R. WASSERMAN. *The Subtler Language*, pp. 305-61.

R. G. WOODMAN. "Shelley's Urania," *Studies in Romanticism* 17(1), Winter 1978, 61-75.

"Alastor"

JOHN C. BEAN. "The Poet Borne Darkly: The Dream-Voyage Allegory in Shelley's *Alastor*," *Keats-Shelley Journal* 23 (1974), 60-76.

FREDERICK L. BEATY. *Light from Heaven*, pp. 165-68.

JAMES BENZIGER. *Images of Eternity*, pp. 88-91.

HAROLD BLOOM. "The Unpastured Sea: An Introduction to Shelley," in *Romanticism and Consciousness*, pp. 378-79.

HAROLD BLOOM. *The Visionary Company*, pp. 277-82.

LESLIE BRISMAN. *Romantic Origins*, pp. 138-46.

LEONARD BROWN. "The Genesis, Growth, and Meaning of *Endymion*," *Studies in Philology* 30(4), October 1933, 623-28.

KENNETH NEILL CAMERON. "*Rasselas* and *Alastor*: A Study in Transmutation," *Studies in Philology* 40(1), January 1943, 58-78.

DEREK COLVILLE. *Victorian Poetry and the Romantic Religion*, pp. 39-40.

BRYAN COOPER. "Shelley's *Alastor*: The Quest for a Vision," *Keats-Shelley Journal* 19 (1970), 63-76.

JEAN L. DE PALACIO. "Music and Musical Themes in Shelley's Poetry," *Modern Language Review* 59(3), July 1964, 345-48.

ARTHUR E. DUBOIS. "Alastor: The Spirit of Solitude," *Journal of English and Germanic Philology* 35(4), October 1936, 530-45.

JAMES C. EVANS. "Masks of the Poet: A Study of Self-Confrontation in Shelley's Poetry," *Keats-Shelley Journal* 24 (1975), 71-75.

ALBERT GERARD. "*Alastor*, or the Spirit of Solipsism," *Philological Quarterly* 33(2), April 1954, 164-77.

EVAN K. GIBSON. "*Alastor*: A Reinterpretation," *PMLA* 62(4), December 1947, 1022-45.

RAYMOND D. HAVENS. "Shelley's *Alastor*," *PMLA* 45(4), December 1930, 1098-1115.

W. H. HILDEBRAND. "Shelley's Early Vision Poems," *Studies in Romanticism* 8(4), Summer 1969, 207-15.

A. M. D. HUGHES. " 'Alastor, or the Spirit of Solitude,' " *Modern Language Review* 43(4), October 1948, 465-70.

FREDERICK L. JONES. "The Inconsistency of Shelley's *Alastor*," *English Literary History* 13(4), December 1946, 291-98.

FREDERICK L. JONES. "The Vision Theme in Shelley's *Alastor* and Related Works," *Studies in Philology* 44(1), January 1947, 108-25.

WILLIAM KEACH. "Reflexive Imagery in Shelley," *Keats-Shelley Journal* 24 (1975), 50-57.

MARCEL KESSEL, PAUL MUESCHKE and EARL LESLIE GRIGGS. "The Poet in Shelley's *Alastor*: A Criticism and a Reply," *PMLA* 51(1), March 1936, 302-12.

G. WILSON KNIGHT. *The Starlit Dome*, pp. 185-88.

C. S. LEWIS. "Shelley, Dryden, and Mr. Eliot," in *English Romantic Poets*, p. 259.

GEORGE D. RICHARDS. "Shelley's Urn of Bitter Prophecy," *Keats-Shelley Journal* 21-22 (1972-1973), 114-15.

ALLAN RODWAY. *The Romantic Conflict*, pp. 184-85.

LISA M. STEINMAN. "Shelley's Skepticism: Allegory in 'Alastor,' " *ELH* 45(2), Summer 1978, 255-69.

NORMAN THURSTON. "Author, Narrator, and Hero in Shelley's *Alastor*," *Studies in Romanticism* 14(2), Spring 1975, 119-31.

E. M. W. TILLYARD. *Poetry Direct and Oblique*, pp. 124-28; second ed., pp. 29-32.

"The Cloud"

CLEANTH BROOKS, JOHN THIBAUT PURSER, and ROBERT PENN WARREN. *An Approach to Literature*, first and second eds., pp. 471-73.

DONALD DAVIE. "Shelley's Urbanity," in *English Romantic Poets*, pp. 308-9.

MIGNONETTE E. HARRISON. *Explicator* 12(2), November 1953, Item 10.

PARKS C. HUNTER, JR. "Undercurrents of Anacreontics in Shelley's 'To a Skylark' and 'The Cloud,' " *Studies in Philology* 65(4), July 1968, 677-82, 687-91.

G. WILSON KNIGHT. *The Starlit Dome*, pp. 198-99.

ALLAN H. MACLAINE. "Shelley's 'The Cloud' and Pope's 'Rape of the Lock': An Unsuspected Link," *Keats-Shelley Journal* 8(1), Winter 1959, 14-16.

DONALD PEARCE. "The Riddle of Shelley's Cloud," *Yale Review* 62(2), December 1972, 202-20.

STELLA P. REVARD. "Shelley and Aristophanes: 'The Cloud' and *Clouds*, 269-290," *English Language Notes* 15(3), March 1978, 188-92.

"Dedication" (*The Revolt of Islam*)

HAROLD BLOOM. *A Map of Misreading*, pp. 11-12.

"A Dream of the Unknown"

T. R. BARNES. *English Verse*, pp. 205-7.

"Epipsychidion"

FREDERICK L. BEATY. *Light from Heaven*, pp. 170-74.

HAROLD BLOOM. "The Unpastured Sea: An Introduction to Shelley," in *Romanticism and Consciousness*, pp. 394-96.

HAROLD BLOOM. *The Visionary Company*, pp. 327-33.

EDWARD E. BOSTETTER. *The Romantic Ventriloquists*, pp. 198-216.

LESLIE BRISMAN. *Romantic Origins*, pp. 159-69.

RICHARD E. BROWN. "The Role of Dante In *Epipsychidion*," *Comparative Literature* 30(3), Summer 1978, 223-35.

JAMES C. EVANS. "Masks of the Poet: A Study of Self-Confrontation in Shelley's Poetry," *Keats-Shelley Journal* 24 (1975), 81-83.

D. J. HUGHES. "Coherence and Collapse in Shelley, with Particular Reference to *Epipsychidion*," *ELH* 28(3), September 1961, 260-83.

G. WILSON KNIGHT. *The Starlit Dome*, pp. 234-42.

LAURENCE LERNER. *The Uses of Nostalgia*, pp. 35-37.

FRANK D. MCCONNELL. "Shelleyan 'Allegory': *Epipsychidion*," *Keats-Shelley Journal* 20 (1971), 100-12.

JEROME J. MCGANN. "Shelley's Veils: A Thousand Images of Loveliness," in *Romantic and Victorian*, pp. 207-12, 214-15.

GEORGE D. RICHARDS. "Shelley's Urn of Bitter Prophecy," *Keats-Shelley Journal* 21-22 (1972-1973), 121-23.

JOHN HAWLEY ROBERTS. *Explicator* 1(6), April 1943, Item 49.

EDWARD J. ROSE. "Shelley Recommended Plain," *Bucknell Review* 14(2), May 1966, 59-63.

JOHN F. SLATER. "Self-Concealment and Self-Revelation in Shelley's 'Epipsychidion,' " *Papers on Language and Literature* 11(3), Summer 1975, 279-92.

LEONE VIVANTE. *English Poetry*, pp. 174-77.

"Fragment Supposed to be an Epithalamium of Francis Ravaillac and Charlotte Corday"

W. H. HILDEBRAND. "Shelley's Early Vision Poems," *Studies in Romanticism* 8(4), Summer 1969, 198-200.

SHELLEY, PERCY B. *(Cont.)*

"Ginevra"

BEN W. GRIFFITH, JR. "Shelley's 'Ginevra,'" *Times Literary Supplement*, 15 January 1954, p. 41.

"Hymn to Intellectual Beauty"

FREDERICK L. BEATY. *Light from Heaven*, pp. 168-69.

HAROLD BLOOM. "The Unpastured Sea: An Introduction to Shelley," in *Romanticism and Consciousness*, p. 377.

HAROLD BLOOM. *The Visionary Company*, pp. 283-85.

HARRY BROWN and JOHN MILSTEAD. *What the Poem Means*, p. 206.

DEREK COLVILLE. *Victorian Poetry and the Romantic Religion*, pp. 35-36.

BARBARA FASS. "Shelley and St. Paul," *Concerning Poetry* 4(1), Spring 1971, 23-24.

W. H. HILDEBRAND. "Shelley's Early Vision Poems," *Studies in Romanticism* 8(4), Summer 1969, 211-14.

PASQUALE JANNACCONE. "The Aesthetics of Edgar Poe," trans. by Peter Metilineos, *Poe Studies* 7(1), June 1974, 10.

FREDERICK L. JONES. "Shelley's *On Life*," *PMLA* 62(3), September 1947, 775-78.

GERALD MCNIECE. "The Poet as Ironist in 'Mont Blanc' and 'Hymn to Intellectual Beauty,'" *Studies in Romanticism* 14(4), Fall 1975, 327-36.

ELIZABETH NITCHIE. "Shelley's 'Hymn to Intellectual Beauty,'" *PMLA* 63(2), June 1948, 752-53.

GEORGE D. RICHARDS. "Shelley's Urn of Bitter Prophecy," *Keats-Shelley Journal* 21-22 (1972-1973), 116.

"Hymn to Mercury"

TIMOTHY WEBB. "Shelley and the Religion of Joy," *Studies in Romanticism* 15(3), Summer 1976, 378-81.

"The Indian Serenade"

EDWARD E. BOSTETTER. *The Romantic Ventriloquists*, p. 215.

CLEANTH BROOKS and ROBERT PENN WARREN. *Understanding Poetry*, pp. 320-23; revised ed., pp. 174-76.

RICHARD LEVIN. "Shelley's 'Indian Serenade': A Re-Revaluation," *College English* 24(4), January 1963, 305-7.

B. A. PARK. "The Indian Elements of the 'Indian Serenade,'" *Keats-Shelley Journal* 10 (Winter 1961), 8-12.

"Julian and Maddalo"

CARLOS BAKER. "Shelley's Ferrarese Maniac," *English Institute Essays*, 1946, pp. 41-73.

PATRICIA M. BALL. *The Central Self*, pp. 133-39.

LESLIE BRISMAN. *Romantic Origins*, pp. 149-52.

JAMES L. HILL. "Dramatic Structure in Shelley's *Julian and Maddalo*," *ELH* 35(1), March 1968, 84-93.

BERNARD A. HIRSCH. "'A Want of That True Theory': *Julian and Maddalo* as Dramatic Monologue," *Studies in Romanticism* 17(1), Winter 1978, 13-34.

NORMAN THURSTON. "Shelley and the Duty of Hope," *Keats-Shelley Journal* 26 (1977), 24-25.

"Laon and Cyntha"

FREDERICK L. BEATY. *Light from Heaven*, pp. 138-39.

"Lines: When the Lamp is Shattered"

JOSEPH WARREN BEACH. *A Romantic View of Poetry*, pp. 76-77, 80-81.

LOUISE SHUTZ BOAS. *Explicator* 1(6), April 1943, Item 48. (P)

HARRY BROWN and JOHN MILSTEAD. *What the Poem Means*, pp. 206-7.

RICHARD H. FOGLE. "Romantic Bards and Metaphysical Reviewers," *English Literary History* 12(3), September 1945, 234-35. (P)

DANIEL GIBSON, F. A. PHILBRICK, and GILBERT MACBETH. *Explicator* 1(7), May 1943, Item 51.

F. R. LEAVIS. "Revaluations (VIII): Shelley," *Scrutiny* 4(2), September 1935, 168-71. Reprinted in: F. R. Leavis. *Revaluation*, pp. 216-20. Also: *Critiques and Essays in Criticism*, pp. 169-72.

F. R. LEAVIS. "Shelley," in *English Romantic Poets*, pp. 276-79.

NORMAN NATHAN. "Shelley's 'Eagle Home,'" *Notes & Queries*, n.s., 1(1), January 1954, 30. (P)

FREDERICK A. POTTLE. "The Case of Shelley," in *English Romantic Poets*, pp. 302-5.

ALLEN TATE. "Understanding Modern Poetry," *College English* 1(7), April 1940, 570-71. (P) Reprinted in: Allen Tate. *On the Limits of Poetry*, pp. 126-27. Also: Allen Tate. *Reason in Madness*, pp. 96-97.

RENE WELLEK. "Literary Criticism and Philosophy," *Scrutiny* 5(4), March 1937, 381-82. (P) Reprinted in: *The Importance of Scrutiny*, p. 28.

"Lines Written Among the Euganean Hills"

JAMES BENZIGER. *Images of Eternity*, pp. 83-86.

LOUISE SCHUTZ BOAS. *Explicator* 3(2), November 1944, Item 14.

J. P. KIRBY. *Explicator* 1(1), October 1942, Item 5. (P)

KARL KROEBER. "Experience as History: Shelley's Venice, Turner's Carthage," *ELH* 41(3), Fall 1974, 321-39.

DONALD H. REIMAN. "Structure, Symbol, and Theme in 'Lines Written Among the Euganean Hills,'" *PMLA* 77(4), September 1962, 404-13.

GEORGE D. RICHARDS. "Shelley's Urn of Bitter Prophecy," *Keats-Shelley Journal* 21-22 (1972-1973), 116-17.

"Lines Written in the Bay of Lerici"

HAROLD BLOOM. *The Visionary Company*, pp. 342-43.

"Love's Philosophy"

GILBERT HIGHET. *The Powers of Poetry*, pp. 180-81.

"Marrianne's Dream"

ALLAN RODWAY. *The Romantic Conflict*, p. 185.

"The Mask of Anarchy"

THOMAS R. EDWARDS. *Imagination and Power*, pp. 160-68.

STANLEY G. ESKIN. "Revolution and Poetry: Some Political Patterns in the Romantic Tradition and After," *CLA Journal* 11(3), March 1968, 192.

RICHARD HENDRIX. "The Necessity of Response: How Shelley's Radical Poetry Works," *Keats-Shelley Journal* 27 (1978), 45-69.

ALLAN RODWAY. *The Romantic Conflict*, pp. 192-94.

"Mont Blanc"

JAMES BENZIGER. *Images of Eternity*, pp. 74-77.

HAROLD BLOOM. "The Unpastured Sea: An Introduction to Shelley," in *Romanticism and Consciousness*, p. 377.

HAROLD BLOOM. *The Visionary Company*, pp. 285-89.

LESLIE BRISMAN. *Romantic Origins*, pp. 147-49, 379-83.

DEREK COLVILLE. *Victorian Poetry and the Romantic Religion*, pp. 36-37.

SPENCER HALL. "Shelley's 'Mont Blanc,'" *Studies in Philology* 70(2), April 1973, 199-221.

I. J. KAPSTEIN. "The Meaning of Shelley's 'Mont Blanc,'" *PMLA* 62(4), December 1947, 1046-60.

F. R. LEAVIS. *Revaluation*, pp. 212-14. Reprinted in: *Critiques and Essays in Criticism*, pp. 167-68.

F. R. LEAVIS. "Shelley," in *English Romantic Poets*, pp. 273-75.

GERALD MCNIECE. "The Poet as Ironist in 'Mont Blanc' and 'Hymn to Intellectual Beauty,'" *Studies in Romanticism* 14(4), Fall 1975, 313-27, 334-36.

PETER MORTENSON. "Image and Structure in Shelley's Longer Lyrics," *Studies in Romanticism* 4(2), Winter 1965, 104-6.

JOAN REES. "'But For Such Faith': A Shelley Crux," *Review of English Studies*, n.s., 15(58), May 1964, 185-86.

GEORGE D. RICHARDS. "Shelley's Urn of Bitter Prophecy," *Keats-Shelley Journal* 21-22 (1972-1973), 115.

EARL R. WASSERMAN. *The Subtler Language*, pp. 195-240.

W. B. YEATS. *Essays*, pp. 104-7.

"Music, When Soft Voices Die"

MARJORIE BOULTON. *The Anatomy of Poetry*, pp. 123-25.

JOHN CROSSETT. *Explicator* 14(5), February 1956, Item 32.

BEN W. GRIFFITH, JR. *Explicator* 15(4), January 1957, Item 26.

WILLIAM HOWARD. *Explicator* 15(4), January 1957, Item 26.

F. R. LEAVIS. "'Thought' and Emotional Quality: Notes in the Analysis of Poetry," *Scrutiny* 13(1), Spring 1945, 66-67.

IRVING MASSEY. "Shelley's 'Music, When Soft Voices Die': Text and Meaning," *Journal of English and Germanic Philology* 59(3), July 1960, 430-38.

JOHN UNTERECKER. *Explicator* 15(4), January 1957, Item 26.

"Mutability"

JUDITH CHERNAIK. "Textual Emendations for Three Poems by Shelley," *Keats-Shelley Journal* 19 (1970), 41-43.

"Ode to the West Wind"

MELVIN W. ASKEW. "Form and Process in Lyric Poetry," *Sewanee Review* 72(2), Spring 1964, 292-93.

PATRICIA M. BALL. *The Central Self*, pp. 139-40.

T. R. BARNES. *English Verse*, pp. 207-11.

EBEN BASS. "The Fourth Element in 'Ode to the West Wind,'" *Papers on Language and Literature* 3(4), Fall 1967, 327-38.

F. W. BATESON. *English Poetry*, pp. 213-17. Abridged in: *The Case for Poetry*, pp. 325, 327; second ed., p. 264.

HAROLD BLOOM. *A Map of Misreading*, pp. 149-52.

HAROLD BLOOM. "The Unpastured Sea: An Introduction to Shelley," in *Romanticism and Consciousness*, pp. 387-88.

HAROLD BLOOM. *The Visionary Company*, pp. 289-94. Abridged in: *The Case for Poetry*, second ed., pp. 264-65.

REUBEN ARTHUR BROWER. "The Speaking Voice," in *The Study of Literature*, pp. 161-62.

HARRY BROWN and JOHN MILSTEAD. *What the Poem Means*, p. 207.

IRENE H. CHAYES. "Rhetoric as Drama: An Approach to the Romantic Ode," *PMLA* 79(1), March 1964, 71-74.

C. C. CUNNINGHAM. *Literature as a Fine Art*, pp. 121-22.

DAVID DAICHES and WILLIAM CHARVAT. *Poems in English*, p. 702.

A. E. DYSON and JULIAN LOVELOCK. *Masterful Images*, pp. 193-203.

STANLEY G. ESKIN. "Revolution and Poetry: Some Political Patterns in the Romantic Tradition and After," *CLA Journal* 11(3), March 1968, 191.

RICHARD HARTER FOGLE. *Explicator* 6(1), October 1947, Item 1.

RICHARD HARTER FOGLE. "The Imaginal Design of Shelley's 'Ode to the West Wind,'" *English Literary History* 15(3), September 1948, 219-26. Reprinted in: *British Romantic Poets*, pp. 202-9. Abridged in: *The Case for Poetry*, pp. 323, 325; second ed., p. 264.

RICHARD H. FOGLE. "Romantic Bards and Metaphysical Reviewers," *English Literary History* 12(3), September 1945, 236-38, 249-50. (P)

I. J. KAPSTEIN. "The Symbolism of the Wind and Leaves in Shelley's 'Ode to the West Wind,'" *PMLA* 51(4), December 1936, 1069-79.

G. WILSON KNIGHT. *The Starlit Dome*, pp. 200-1. Reprinted in: *Poems and Critics*, pp. 184-85.

F. R. LEAVIS. "Revaluations (VIII): Shelley," *Scrutiny* 4(2), September 1935, 159-61. Reprinted in: F. R. Leavis. *Revaluation*, pp. 204-6. Also: *English Romantic Poets*, pp. 269-71, 279-80.

DOUGLASS S. MEAD. *Explicator* 5(7), May 1947, Q20.

COLEMAN O. PARSONS. "Shelley's Prayer to the West Wind," *Keats-Shelley Journal* 11(Winter 1962), 31-37.

WILLIAM I. THOMPSON. "Collapsed Universe and Structured Poem: An Essay in Whiteadian Criticism," *College English* 28(1), October 1966, 32-33.

LEONE VIVANTE. *English Poetry*, pp. 164-69.

RENE WELLEK. "Literary Criticism and Philosophy," *Scrutiny* 5(4), March 1937, 380. Reprinted in: *The Importance of Scrutiny*, pp. 26-27.

STEWART C. WILCOX. "Imagery, Ideas, and Design in Shelley's *Ode to the West Wind*," *Studies in Philology* 47(4), October 1950, 634-49. Abridged in: *The Case for Poetry*, first ed., p. 325.

ARTHUR WORMHOUDT. *Explicator* 6(1), October 1947, Item 1.

"On the Medusa of Leonardo da Vinci in the Florentine Gallery"

DANIEL HUGHES. "Shelley, Leonardo, and the Monsters of Thought," *Criticism* 12(3), Summer 1970, 201-6.

JEROME J. MCGANN. "The Beauty of the Medusa: A Study in Romantic Literary Iconology," *Studies in Romanticism* 11(1), Winter 1972, 4-10.

KENT PATTERSON. "A Terrible Beauty: Medusa in Three Victorian Poets," *Tennessee Studies in Literature* 17 (1972), 113.

"Ozymandias"

GÉMINO H. ABAD. *A Formal Approach to Lyric Poetry*, p. 227.

ISAAC ASIMOV. *Familiar Poems, Annotated*, pp. 1-4.

WILLIAM B. BACHE. "Vanity and Art in 'Ozymandias,'" *CEA Critic* 31(5), February 1969, 20.

WALTON BEACHAM. *The Meaning of Poetry*, pp. 26-28.

M. K. BEQUETTE. "Shelley and Smith: Two Sonnets on Ozymandias," *Keats-Shelley Journal* 26 (1977), 29-31.

SHELLEY, PERCY B. *(Cont.)*

"Ozymandias" *(cont.)*

CHARLES W. COOPER and JOHN HOLMES. *Preface to Poetry*, pp. 202-4.

ROBERT B. HEILMAN. "Poetic and Prosaic: Program Notes on Opposite Numbers," *Pacific Spectator* 5 (Autumn 1951), 456-57.

JOHN GARLAND KENYON. "A New Approach to Teaching Explication," *English Journal* 53(6), September 1964, 428-30.

RICHARD RAY KIRK and ROGER PHILIP MCCUTCHEON. *An Introduction to the Study of Poetry*, pp. 37-39. Reprinted in: *Readings for Liberal Education*, first ed., II: 309-10.

M. L. ROSENTHAL and A. J. M. SMITH. *Exploring Poetry*, p. 576; second ed., p. 385.

WILLIAM V. SPANOS. "Shelley's 'Ozymandias' and the Problem of the Persona," *CEA Critic* 30(4), January 1968, 14-15.

E. M. W. TILLYARD. *Essays, Literary & Educational*, pp. 108-13.

"Peter Bell the Third"

ALLAN RODWAY. *The Romantic Conflict*, pp. 190-92.

"A Retrospect of Times of Old"

WILLIAM ROYCE CAMPBELL. "Shelley's Philosophy of History: A Reconsideration," *Keats-Shelley Journal* 21-22 (1972-1973), 45-46.

"The Sensitive Plant"

FREDERICK L. BEATY. *Light from Heaven*, p. 169.

HAROLD BLOOM. "The Unpastured Sea: An Introduction to Shelley," in *Romanticism and Consciousness*, pp. 392-93.

RICHARD S. CALDWELL. "'The Sensitive Plant' as Original Fantasy," *Studies in Romanticism* 15(2), Spring 1976, 221-52.

DONALD DAVIE. "Shelley's Urbanity," in *English Romantic Poets*, pp. 319-22.

FREDERICK L. JONES. "Shelley and Spenser," *Studies in Philology* 39(4), October 1942, 667-69.

ROBERT M. MANIQUIS. "The Puzzling *Mimosa*: Sensitivity and Plant Symbols in Romanticism," *Studies in Romanticism* 8(3), Spring 1969, 144-50.

ELIZABETH NITCHIE. *Explicator* 15(3), December 1956, Item 15.

WILLIAM H. PIXTON. "*The Sensitive Plant*: Shelley's Acquiescence to Agnosticism," *Ball State University Forum* 14(4), Autumn 1973, 35-44.

EARL R. WASSERMAN. *The Subtler Language*, pp. 251-84.

"Song to the Men of England"

RICHARD HENDRIX. "The Necessity of Response: How Shelley's Radical Poetry Works," *Keats-Shelley Journal* 27 (1978), 50-51.

"Stanzas Written in Dejection, near Naples"

LAURENCE LERNER. *An Introduction to English Poetry*, pp. 145-51.

THOMAS PARKINSON. "The Art of Loneliness," *Ohio Review* 18(2), Spring/Summer 1977, 13-14.

"Summer and Winter"

GÉMINO H. ABAD. *A Formal Approach to Lyric Poetry*, pp. 262-63.

"To a Skylark"

JAMES V. BAKER. "The Lark in English Poetry," *Prairie Schooner* 24(1), Spring 1950, 71-74.

HAROLD BLOOM. *The Visionary Company*, pp. 294-97.

HARRY BROWN and JOHN MILSTEAD. *What the Poem Means*, p. 211.

FRANK DOGGETT. "Romanticism's Singing Bird," *Studies in English Literature 1500-1900* 14(4), Autumn 1974, 552-53.

WILLIAM EMPSON. *Seven Types of Ambiguity*, pp. 197-201; second and third eds., pp. 156-59.

NIGEL FOXELL. *Ten Poems Analyzed*, pp. 143-63.

LLOYD FRANKENBERG. *Invitation to Poetry*, pp. 82-83.

PARKS C. HUNTER, JR. "Undercurrents of Anacreontics in Shelley's 'To a Skylark' and 'The Cloud,'" *Studies in Philology* 65(4), July 1968, 677-687.

G. WILSON KNIGHT. *The Starlit Dome*, pp. 199-200.

E. WAYNE MARJARUM. "The Symbolism of Shelley's 'To a Skylark,'" *PMLA* 52(3), September 1937, 911-13.

KATHLEEN RAINE. "A Defense of Shelley's Poetry," *Southern Review*, n.s., 3(4), Autumn 1967, 863-67. Reprinted in: Kathleen Raine. *Defending Ancient Springs*, pp. 146-50.

E. M. W. TILLYARD. *Poetry Direct and Oblique*, pp. 163-66.

LEONE VIVANTE. *English Poetry*, pp. 169-74.

STEWART C. WILCOX. "The Sources, Symbolism, and Unity of Shelley's *Skylark*," *Studies in Philology* 46(4), October 1949, 560-76. Reprinted in: *British Romantic Poets*, pp. 239-56.

"To Ianthe"

CLEANTH BROOKS, JOHN THIBAUT PURSER, and ROBERT PENN WARREN. *An Approach to Literature*, p. 463; second ed., p. 463; third ed., pp. 333-34; fourth ed., pp. 330-31; fifth ed., p. 383.

"To Jane: The Invitation"

JEROME J. McGANN. "The Secrets of an Elder Day: Shelley After *Hellas*," *Keats-Shelley Journal* 15 (Winter 1966), 32-33.

"To Jane: The Recollection"

JEROME J. McGANN. "The Secrets of an Elder Day: Shelley After *Hellas*," *Keats-Shelley Journal* 15 (Winter 1966), 34.

KATHLEEN RAINE. *Defending Ancient Springs*, pp. 150-51.

LEONE VIVANTE. *English Poetry*, pp. 177-81.

"To Mary Shelley"

JUDITH CHERNAIK. "Textual Emendations for Three Poems by Shelley," *Keats-Shelley Journal* 19 (1970), 43-44.

"To Night"

EARL DANIELS. *The Art of Reading Poetry*, pp. 354-58.

"The Triumph of Life"

LLOYD ABBEY. "Apocalyptic Scepticism: The Imagery of Shelley's 'The Triumph of Life,'" *Keats-Shelley Journal* 27 (1978), 70-86.

CARLOS BAKER. "Shelley: The Triumph of Life," in *Master Poems of the English Language*, pp. 562-65.

FREDERICK L. BEATY. *Light from Heaven*, pp. 175-76.

HAROLD BLOOM. *Poetry and Repression*, pp. 98-111.

HAROLD BLOOM. "The Unpastured Sea: An Introduction to Shelley," in *Romanticism and Consciousness*, pp. 398-400.

HAROLD BLOOM. *The Visionary Company*, pp. 344-53.

EDWARD E. BOSTETTER. *The Romantic Ventriloquists*, pp. 181-92, 237-40.

LESLIE BRISMAN. *Romantic Origins*, pp. 169-82.

P. H. BUTTER. "Sun and Shape in Shelley's *The Triumph of Life*," *Review of English Studies*, n.s., 13(49), February 1962, 40-51.

WILLIAM CHERUBINI. "Shelley's '*Own Symposium*': *The Triumph of Life*," *Studies in Philology* 39(3), July 1942, 559-70.

DEREK COLVILLE. *Victorian Poetry and the Romantic Religion*, pp. 40-41.

DAVID EGGENSCHWILER. "Sexual Parody in 'The Triumph of Life,'" *Concerning Poetry* 5(2), Fall 1972, 28-36.

JAMES C. EVANS. "Masks of the Poet: A Study of Self-Confrontation in Shelley's Poetry," *Keats-Shelley Journal* 24 (1975), 84-86.

JOHN A. HODGSON. "The World's Mysterious Doom: Shelley's *The Triumph of Life*," *ELH* 42(4), Winter 1975, 595-622.

DANIEL HUGHES. "Kindling and Dwindling: The Poetic Process in Shelley," *Keats-Shelley Journal* 13 (Winter 1964), 23-24.

G. WILSON KNIGHT. *The Starlit Dome*, pp. 251-56.

JEROME J. McGANN. "The Secrets of an Elder Day: Shelley After *Hellas*," *Keats-Shelley Journal* 15 (Winter 1966), 35-41.

ALLAN RODWAY. *The Romantic Conflict*, p. 194.

W. B. YEATS. *Essays*, pp. 92-94.

"The Two Spirits: An Allegory"

HAROLD BLOOM. *The Visionary Company*, pp. 315-17.

"A Vision of the Sea"

CARL H. KETCHAM. "Shelley's 'A Vision of the Sea,'" *Studies in Romanticism* 17(1), Winter 1978, 51-59.

KARL KROEBER. *Romantic Narrative Art*, pp. 53-54.

"A widow bird sate mourning" (*Charles the First*)

AGNES STEIN. *The Uses of Poetry*, pp. 220-21.

"The Witch of Atlas"

FREDERICK L. BEATY. *Light from Heaven*, pp. 169-70.

HAROLD BLOOM. "The Unpastured Sea: An Introduction to Shelley," in *Romanticism and Consciousness*, pp. 393-94.

HAROLD BLOOM. *The Visionary Company*, pp. 318-27.

FREDERIC S. COLWELL. "Shelley's 'Witch of Atlas' and the Mythic Geography of the Nile," *ELH* 45(1), Spring 1978, 69-92.

RICHARD CRONIN. "Shelley's Witch of Atlas," *Keats-Shelley Journal* 26 (1977), 88-100.

G. WILSON KNIGHT. *The Starlit Dome*, pp. 224-34.

JEAN WATSON ROSENBAUM. "Shelley's Witch: The Naked Conception," *Concerning Poetry* 10(1), Spring 1977, 33-43.

DAVID RUBIN. "A Study of Antinomies in Shelley's *The Witch of Atlas*," *Studies in Romanticism* 8(4), Summer 1969, 216-28.

"With a Guitar, to Jane"

JEROME J. McGANN. "The Secrets of an Elder Day: Shelley After *Hellas*," *Keats-Shelley Journal* 15 (Winter 1966), 31-32.

"The World's Great Age Begins Anew"

WILLIAM EMPSON. *Seven Types of Ambiguity*, second and third eds., pp. 159-60. (P)

LAURENCE LERNER. *The Uses of Nostalgia*, pp. 74-76.

M. L. ROSENTHAL. *Poetry and the Common Life*, pp. 105-7.

SHIRLEY, JAMES

"The Glories of Our Blood and State"

MARJORIE BOULTON. *The Anatomy of Poetry*, pp. 165-67.

LAURENCE LERNER. *The Uses of Nostalgia*, pp. 124-25.

E. SYDNOR OWNBEY. *Explicator* 10(4), February 1952, Item 30.

SIDNEY, PHILIP

"Alas have I not paine enough my friend" (*Astrophil and Stella*, 14)

ROBERT EMMET FINNEGAN. *Explicator* 35(2), Winter 1976, 22-23.

LELAND RYKEN. "The Drama of Choice in Sidney's *Astrophel and Stella*," *Journal of English and Germanic Philology* 68(4), October 1969, 651.

ALAN SINFIELD. "Sexual Puns in *Astrophil and Stella*," *Essays in Criticism* 24(4), October 1974, 344-46.

"And have I heard her say, 'O cruell paine!'" (*Certain Sonnets*, 11)

PAUL K. DEMPSEY. *Explicator* 25(6), February 1967, Item 51.

"As good to write as for to lie and grone" (*Astrophil and Stella*, 40)

JAMES F. COTTER. *Explicator* 27(7), March 1969, Item 51.

"Because I oft in darke abstracted guise" (*Astrophil and Stella*, 27)

ROSEMOND TUVE. *Elizabethan and Metaphysical Imagery*, p. 320.

"Come let me write, 'And to what end?' To ease" (*Astrophil and Stella*, 34)

RICHARD A. LANHAM. "*Astrophil and Stella*: Pure and Impure Persuasion," *English Literary Renaissance* 2(1), Winter 1972, 114-15.

"*Cupid*, because thou shin'st in *Stella's* eyes" (*Astrophil and Stella*, 12)

ROBERT S. KINSMAN. *Explicator* 8(8), June 1950, Item 56. (P)

"Deare, why make you more of a dog than me?" (*Astrophil and Stella*, 59)

ROSEMOND TUVE. *Elizabethan and Metaphysical Imagery*, p. 321.

"Desire"

see "Thou blind man's marke, thou foole's selfe chosen snare"

"Doubt you to whom my Muse these notes entendeth" (*Astrophil and Stella*, "First Song")

JAMES FINN COTTER. "The Songs in *Astrophil and Stella*," *Studies in Philology* 67(2), April 1970, 180-81.

"Go my flocke, go get you hence" (*Astrophil and Stella*, "Ninth Song")

JAMES FINN COTTER. "The Songs in *Astrophil and Stella*," *Studies in Philology* 67(2), April 1970, 195-96.

"Good brother *Philip*, I have borne you long" (*Astrophil and Stella*, 83)

JAMES FINN COTTER. "The 'Baiser' Group in Sidney's *Astrophil and Stella*," *Texas Studies in Literature and Language* 12(3), Fall 1970, 400.

"Have I caught my heav'nly jewell" (*Astrophil and Stella*, "Second Song")

JAMES FINN COTTER. "The Songs in *Astrophil and Stella*," *Studies in Philology* 67(2), April 1970, 181-83.

SIDNEY, PHILIP *(Cont.)*

"Having this day my horse, my hand, my launce" *(Astrophil and Stella,* 41)

 RICHARD B. YOUNG. "English Petrarke: A Study of Sidney's *Astrophel and Stella*," in *Three Studies in the Renaissance,* pp. 15-16.

"Highway since you my chiefe Pernassus be" *(Astrophil and Stella,* 84)

 CURTIS DAHL. *Explicator* 6(7), May 1948, Item 46.

 MARIANN S. REGAN. "Astrophel: Full of Desire, Emptie of Wit," *English Language Notes* 14(4), June 1977, 254.

 YVOR WINTERS. "The 16th Century Lyric in England: A Critical and Historical Reinterpreation: Part II," *Poetry* 53(6), March 1939, 328-29. Reprinted in: *Elizabethan Poetry,* edited by Paul J. Alpers, pp. 107-8.

"I might, unhappie word, o me, I might" *(Astrophil and Stella,* 33)

 A. C. HAMILTON. "The Modern Study of Renaissance English Literature: A Critical Survey," *Modern Language Quarterly* 26(1), March 1965, 180-81.

"I never dranke of *Aganippe* well" *(Astrophil and Stella,* 74)

 JAMES FINN COTTER. "The 'Baiser' Group in Sidney's *Astrophil and Stella*," *Texas Studies in Literature and Language* 12(3), Fall 1970, 392-93.

"If Orpheus' voyce had force to breathe such musicke's love" *(Astrophil and Stella,* "Third Song")

 JAMES FINN COTTER. "The Songs in *Astrophil and Stella*," *Studies in Philology* 67(2), April 1970, 183-85.

"In a grove most rich of shade" *(Astrophil and Stella,* "Eighth Song")

 JAMES FINN COTTER. "The Songs in *Astrophil and Stella*," *Studies in Philology* 67(2), April 1970, 192-95.

 MARIANN S. REGAN. "Astrophel: Full of Desire, Emptie of Wit," *English Language Notes* 14(4), June 1977, 255-56.

 ANDREW D. WEINER. " 'In a grove most rich of shade': A Figurative Reading of the Eighth Song of *Astrophil and Stella*," *Texas Studies in Literature and Language* 18(3), Fall 1976, 345-61.

 GEORGE WILLIAMSON. *Seventeenth Century Contexts,* pp. 65-66.

"In highest way of heav'n the Sunne did ride" *(Astrophil and Stella,* 22)

 ALAN SINFIELD. "Sexual Puns in 'Astrophil and Stella,' " *Essays in Criticism* 24(4), October 1974, 350-52.

"It is most true, that eyes are form'd to serve" *(Astrophil and Stella,* 5)

 ODETTE DE MOURGUES. *Metaphysical Baroque & Precieux Poetry,* pp. 14-15.

 ROBERT L. MONTGOMERY, JR. "Reason, Passion, and Introspection In *Astrophel and Stella*," *Texas University Studies in English* 36 (1957), 132-33.

 DOUGLAS L. PETERSON. *The English Lyric from Wyatt to Donne,* pp. 194-96.

 JAMES J. SCANLON. "Sidney's *Astrophil and Stella*: 'See what it is to Love' Sensually!" *Studies in English Literature 1500-1900* 16(1), Winter 1976, 66-67.

 ANDREW D. WEINER. "Structure and 'Fore Conceit' in *Astrophil and Stella*," *Texas Studies in Literature and Language* 16(1), Spring 1974, 7-8.

"Lamon's Tale"

 ALISTAIR FOWLER. *Conceitful Thought,* pp. 52-56.

"Leave me O Love, which reachest but to dust" *(Certain Sonnets,* 32)

 DAVID DAICHES and WILLIAM CHARVAT. *Poems in English,* p. 647.

 W. K. THOMAS. *Explicator* 28(5), January 1970, Item 45.

 HAROLD S. WILSON. *Explicator* 2(6), April 1944, Item 47. Reprinted in: *Readings for Liberal Education,* revised ed., II: 22-23; third ed., II: 23-24.

"Let daintie wits crie on the Sisters nine" *(Astrophil and Stella,* 3)

 ANDREW D. WEINER. "Structure and 'Fore Conceit' in *Astrophil and Stella*," *Texas Studies in Literature and Language* 16(1), Spring 1974, 5-6.

"Like some weake Lords, neighbord by mighty kings" *(Astrophil and Stella,* 29)

 SUSAN M. LUTHER. *Explicator* 33(5), January 1975, Item 40.

 DOUGLAS L. PETERSON. *The English Lyric from Wyatt to Donne,* pp. 189-90.

"A Litany"

 CLEANTH BROOKS and ROBERT PENN WARREN. *Understanding Poetry,* pp. 342-45; revised ed., pp. 206-10; third ed., pp. 251-55; fourth ed., pp. 185-87.

"Love by sure proofe I may call thee unkind" *(Astrophil and Stella,* 65)

 RICHARD B. YOUNG. "English Petrarke: A Study of Sidney's *Astrophel and Stella*," in *Three Studies in the Renaissance,* pp. 18-20.

"Loving in truth, and faine in verse my love to show" *(Astrophil and Stella,* 1)

 ROBERT M. ADAMS. *Strains of Discord,* pp. 4-6.

 EARLE BIRNEY. "Sidney: Loving in Truth," in *Master Poems of the English Language,* pp. 31-34.

 ARTHUR DICKSON. *Explicator* 3(1), October 1944, Item 3.

 ALISTAIR FOWLER. *Conceitful Thought,* pp. 100-1.

 DAVID KALSTONE. "Sir Philip Sidney and 'Poore *Petrarchs* Long Deceased Woes,' " *Journal of English and Germanic Philology* 63(1), January 1964, 30-31.

 RICHARD A. LANHAM. "*Astrophil and Stella*: Pure and Impure Persuasion," *English Literary Renaissance* 2(1), Winter 1972, 100-2.

 DOUGLAS L. PETERSON. *The English Lyric from Wyatt to Donne,* pp. 191-92.

 GERALD SANDERS. 1(4), February 1943, Item 26.

 THOMAS O. SLOAN. "The Crossing of Rhetoric and Poetry in the English Renaissance," in *The Rhetoric of Renaissance Poetry,* pp. 226-36.

 ANDREW D. WEINER. "Structure and 'Fore Conceit' in *Astrophil and Stella*," *Texas Studies in Literature and Language* 16(1), Spring 1974, 3-4.

"My mouth doth water, and my breast doth swell" *(Astrophil and Stella,* 37)

 A. C. HAMILTON. "The Modern Study of Renaissance English Literature: A Critical Survey," *Modern Language Quarterly* 26(1), March 1965, 177-78.

"My words I know do well set forth my mind" *(Astrophil and Stella,* 44)

 ALAN SINFIELD. "Astrophil's Self-Deception," *Essays in Criticism* 28(1), January 1978, 6-7.

"No more, my deare, no more these counsels trie" *(Astrophil and Stella,* 64)

 ROBERT L. MONTGOMERY, JR. "Reason, Passion, and Introspection in *Astrophel and Stella*," *Texas University Studies in English* 36 (1957), 137.

"Not at first sight, nor with a dribbed shot" (*Astrophil and Stella*, 2)

> Douglas L. Peterson. *The English Lyric from Wyatt to Donne*, pp. 192-93.
>
> Leland Ryken. "The Drama of Choice in Sidney's *Astrophel and Stella*," *Journal of English and Germanic Philology* 68(4), October 1969, 649.
>
> Andrew D. Weiner. "Structure and 'Fore Conceit' in *Astrophil and Stella*," *Texas Studies in Literature and Language* 16(1), Spring 1974, 4-5.

"Nymph of the gard'n, where all beauties be" (*Astrophil and Stella*, 82)

> James Finn Cotter. "The 'Baiser' Group in Sidney's *Astrophil and Stella*," *Texas Studies in Literature and Language* 12(3), Fall 1970, 399-400.

"O deare life, when shall it be" (*Astrophil and Stella*, "Tenth Song")

> James Finn Cotter. "The Songs in *Astrophil and Stella*," *Studies in Philology* 67(2), April 1970, 197-98.
>
> Alan Sinfield. "Sexual Puns in 'Astrophil and Stella,'" *Essays in Criticism* 24(4), October 1974, 353-55.

"O how the pleasant aires of true love be" (*Astrophil and Stella*, 78)

> James Finn Cotter. "The 'Baiser' Group in Sidney's *Astrophil and Stella*," *Texas Studies in Literature and Language* 12(3), Fall 1970, 395-96.
>
> Harold S. Wilson. *Explicator* 2(2), November 1943, Item 17.

"O kisse, which doest those ruddie gemmes impart" (*Astrophil and Stella*, 81)

> James Finn Cotter. "The 'Baiser' Group in Sidney's *Astrophil and Stella*," *Texas Studies in Literature and Language* 12(3), Fall 1970, 398-99.

"O you that heare this voice" (*Astrophil and Stella*, "Sixth Song")

> James Finn Cotter. "The Songs in *Astrophil and Stella*," *Studies in Philology* 67(2), April 1970, 188-90.

"Of all the kings that ever here did raigne" (*Astrophil and Stella*, 75)

> James Finn Cotter. "The 'Baiser' Group in Sidney's *Astrophil and Stella*," *Texas Studies in Literature and Language* 12(3), Fall 1970, 393.
>
> James Finn Cotter. *Explicator* 27(9), May 1969, Item 70. (P)

"Onely joy, now here you are" (*Astrophil and Stella*, "Fourth Song")

> Russell M. Brown. *Explicator* 29(6), February 1971, Item 48.
>
> James Finn Cotter. "The Songs in *Astrophil and Stella*," *Studies in Philology* 67(2), April 1970, 185-86.

"*Phoebus* was Judge betweene *Jove, Mars,* and *Love*" (*Astrophil and Stella*, 13)

> Richard B. Young. "English Petrarke: A Study of Sidney's *Astrophel and Stella*," in *Three Studies in the Renaissance*, pp. 20-22.

"Queen *Vertue's* court, which some call *Stella's* face" (*Astrophil and Stella*, 9)

> Alistair Fowler. *Conceitful Thought*, pp. 98-100.
>
> Douglas L. Peterson. *The English Lyric from Wyatt to Donne*, pp. 188-89.
>
> Max Putzel. *Explicator* 19(4), January 1961, Item 25.
>
> Richard B. Young. "English Petrarke: A Study of Sidney's *Astrophel and Stella*," in *Three Studies in the Renaissance*, p. 11.

"Reason, in faith thou art well serv'd, that still" (*Astrophil and Stella*, 10)

> Leland Ryken. "The Drama of Choice in Sidney's *Astrophel and Stella*," *Journal of English and Germanic Philology* 68(4), October 1969, 650-51.

"Rich fooles there be, whose base and filthy hart" (*Astrophil and Stella*, 24)

> Alan Sinfield. "Sexual Puns in 'Astrophil and Stella,'" *Essays in Criticism* 24(4), October 1974, 349-50.
>
> Richard B. Young. "English Petrarke: A Study of Sidney's *Astrophel and Stella*," in *Three Studies in the Renaissance*, pp. 29-30.

"Ring out your belles, let mourning shewes be spread"

> Patricia Thomson. *Elizabethan Lyrical Poets*, p. 159.

"She comes, and streight therewith her shining twins do move" (*Astrophil and Stella*, 76)

> James Finn Cotter. "The 'Baiser' Group in Sidney's *Astrophil and Stella*," *Texas Studies in Literature and Language* 12(3), Fall 1970, 393-94.

"*Stella*, the onely Planet of my light" (*Astrophil and Stella*, 68)

> Richard B. Young. "English Petrarke: A Study of Sidney's *Astrophel and Stella*," in *Three Studies in the Renaissance*, pp. 35-36.

"A strife is growne betweene Vertue and Love" (*Astrophil and Stella*, 52)

> Douglas L. Peterson. *The English Lyric from Wyatt to Donne*, pp. 196-97.

"Sweet kisse, thy sweets I faine would sweetly endite" (*Astrophil and Stella*, 79)

> James Finn Cotter. "The 'Baiser' Group in Sidney's *Astrophil and Stella*," *Texas Studies in Literature and Language* 12(3), Fall 1970, 396-97.

"Sweet swelling lip, well maist thou swell in pride" (*Astrophil and Stella*, 80)

> James Finn Cotter. "The 'Baiser' Group in Sidney's *Astrophil and Stella*," *Texas Studies in Literature and Language* 12(3), Fall 1970, 397-98.

"Those lookes, whose beames be joy, whose motion is delight" (*Astrophil and Stella*, 77)

> James Finn Cotter. "The 'Baiser' Group in Sidney's *Astrophil and Stella*," *Texas Studies in Literature and Language* 12(3), Fall 1970, 394-95.

"Thou blind man's marke, thou foole's selfe chosen snare" (*Certain Sonnets*, 31)

> Elizabeth Drew. *Poetry*, pp. 204-5.
>
> Dan G. Hoffman. *Explicator* 8(4), February 1950, Item 29.
>
> Walter James Miller. "Sidney: Desire," in *Master Poems of the English Language*, pp. 36-37.
>
> Douglas L. Peterson. *The English Lyric from Wyatt to Donne*, pp. 199-201.

"Vertue alas, now let me take some rest" (*Astrophil and Stella*, 4)

> Douglas L. Peterson. *The English Lyric from Wyatt to Donne*, pp. 193-94.
>
> Leland Ryken. "The Drama of Choice in Sidney's *Astrophel and Stella*," *Journal of English and Germanic Philology* 68(4), October 1969, 649-50.
>
> James J. Scanlon. "Sidney's *Astrophil and Stella*: 'See what it is to Love' Sensually!" *Studies in English Literature 1500-1900* 16(1), Winter 1976, 68-69.
>
> Andrew D. Weiner. "Structure and 'Fore Conceit' in *Astrophil and Stella*," *Texas Studies in Literature and Language* 16(1), Spring 1974, 6.

SIDNEY, PHILIP *(Cont.)*

"Vertue alas, now let me take some rest" *(cont.)*

> RICHARD B. YOUNG. "English Petrarke: A Study of Sidney's *Astrophel and Stella*," in *Three Studies in the Renaissance*, pp. 33-34.

"What, have I thus betrayed my libertie?" *(Astrophil and Stella*, 47)

> RICHARD A. LANHAM. "*Astrophil and Stella*: Pure and Impure Persuasion," *English Literary Renaissance* 2(1), Winter 1972, 106-7.
>
> ROBERT L. MONTGOMERY, JR. "Reason, Passion, and Introspection In *Astrophel and Stella*," *Texas University Studies in English* 36 (1957), 136-37.
>
> RICHARD B. YOUNG. "English Petrarke: A Study of Sidney's *Astrophel and Stella*," in *Three Studies in the Renaissance*, pp. 23-24.

"What may words say, or what may words not say" *(Astrophil and Stella*, 35)

> MURRAY KRIEGER. *The Classic Vision*, pp. 59-62.
>
> MURRAY KRIEGER. "The Continuing Need for Criticism," *Concerning Poetry* 1(1), Spring 1968, 18-19.

"What tongue can her perfections tell"

> DOROTHY JONES. "Sidney's Erotic Pen: An Interpretation of One of the *Arcadia* Poems," *Journal of English and Germanic Philology* 73(1), January 1974, 32-47.

"When far spent night perswades each mortall eye" *(Astrophil and Stella*, 99)

> RICHARD B. YOUNG. "English Petrarke: A Study of Sidney's *Astrophel and Stella*," in *Three Studies in the Renaissance*, p. 85.

"When my good Angell guides me to the place" *(Astrophil and Stella*, 60)

> ODETTE DE MORGUES. *Metaphysical Baroque & Precieux Poetry*, pp. 15-16.

"When Nature made her chiefe worke, Stella's eyes" *(Astrophil and Stella*, 7)

> LEONORA LEET BRODWIN. "The Structure of Sidney's *Astrophel and Stella*," *Modern Philology* 67(1), August 1969, 27.

"When sorrow (using mine owne fier's might)" *(Astrophil and Stella*, 108)

> DOUGLAS L. PETERSON. *The English Lyric from Wyatt to Donne*, pp. 198-99.

"Whence has thou Ivorie, Rubies, pearle and gold" *(Astrophil and Stella*, 32)

> DAVID KALSTONE. "Sir Philip Sidney: The Petrarchan Vision," in *Elizabethan Poetry*, edited by Paul J. Alpers, pp. 203-5.

"Whether the Turkish new-moone minded be" *(Astrophil and Stella*, 30)

> JACQUELINE E. M. LATHAM. *Explicator* 33(6), February 1975, Item 47.

"While favour fed my hope, delight with hope was brought" *(Astrophil and Stella*, "Fifth Song")

> JAMES FINN COTTER. "The Songs in *Astrophil and Stella*," *Studies in Philology* 67(2), April 1970, 186-88.

" 'Who is it that this dark night' " *(Astrophil and Stella*, "Eleventh Song")

> JAMES FINN COTTER. "The Songs in *Astrophil and Stella*," *Studies in Philology* 67(2), April 1970, 198-200.

"Who will in fairest booke of Nature know" *(Astrophil and Stella*, 71)

> DAVID KALSTONE. "Sir Philip Sidney and 'Poore *Petrarchs* Long Deceased Woes,' " *Journal of English and Germanic Philology* 63(1), January 1964, 26-29.
>
> DAVID KALSTONE. "Sir Philip Sidney: The Petrarchan Vision," in *Elizabethan Poetry*, edited by Paul J. Alpers, pp. 197-201.

"Whose senses in so evill consort, their stepdame Nature laies" *(Astrophil and Stella*, "Seventh Song")

> JAMES FINN COTTER. "The Songs in *Astrophil and Stella*," *Studies in Philology* 67(2), April 1970, 190-92.

"With how sad steps, O Moone, thou climb'st the skies" *(Astrophil and Stella*, 31)

> CLINTON S. BURHANS, JR. *Explicator* 18(4), January 1960, Item 26. (P)
>
> DAVID DAICHES and WILLIAM CHARVAT. *Poems in English*, p. 647.
>
> KENNETH MUIR. " 'Astrophel and Stella', XXXI," *Notes & Queries*, n.s., 7(2), February 1960, 51-52.
>
> ANDREW D. WEINER. "Structure and 'Fore Conceit' in *Astrophil and Stella*," *Texas Studies in Literature and Language* 16(1), Spring 1974, 12-13.
>
> RICHARD B. YOUNG. "English Petrarke: A Study of Sidney's *Astrophel and Stella*," in *Three Studies in the Renaissance*, pp. 49-50.

"With what sharpe checkes I in my selfe am shent" *(Astrophil and Stella*, 18)

> RICHARD A. LANHAM. "*Astrophil and Stella*: Pure and Impure Persuasion," *English Literary Renaissance* 2(1), Winter 1972, 105-6.
>
> ALAN SINFIELD. "Sexual Puns in 'Astrophil and Stella,' " *Essays in Criticism* 24(4), October 1974, 347-49.

"Yee Gote-heard Gods, that love the grassie mountaines"

> WILLIAM EMPSON. *Seven Types of Ambiguity*, pp. 45-50; second and third eds., pp. 34-38.
>
> ALISTAIR FOWLER. *Conceitful Thought*, pp. 38-52.
>
> DAVID KALSTONE. "The Transformation of Arcadia: Sannazaro and Sir Philip Sidney," *Comparative Literature* 15(3), Summer 1963, 245-49.
>
> GARY L. LITT. "Characterization and Rhetoric in Sidney's 'Ye Goatherd Gods,' " *Studies in the Literary Imagination* 11(1), Spring 1978, 115-24.
>
> JOHN CROWE RANSOM. *The New Criticism*, pp. 108-14.

"You that do search for every purling spring" *(Astrophil and Stella*, 15)

> T. R. BARNES. *English Verse*, pp. 19-20.
>
> LAURENCE LERNER. *An Introduction to English Poetry*, pp. 20-22.

SIDNEY, ROBERT

"Yow that take pleasure in yowr cruelty"

> G. F. WALLER. " 'My wants and yowr perfections': Elizabethan England's Newest Poet," *Ariel* 8(2), April 1977, 8-10.

SILKIN, JON

"Amana Grass"

> MERLE E. BROWN. "On Jon Silkin's 'Amana Grass,' " *Iowa Review* 1(1), Winter 1970, 115-25.

"Brought up with Grass"

> MERLE BROWN. "Stress in Silkin's Poetry and the Healing Emptiness of America," *Contemporary Literature* 18(3), Summer 1977, 376-79.

"Carved"

MERLE BROWN. "Stress in Silkin's Poetry and the Healing Emptiness of America," *Contemporary Literature* 18(3), Summer 1977, 367-68.

"Death of a Son"

MERLE BROWN. "Stress in Silkin's Poetry and the Healing Emptiness of America," *Contemporary Literature* 18(3), Summer 1977, 368-72.

"A Death to Us"

MERLE BROWN. "Stress in Silkin's Poetry and the Healing Emptiness of America," *Contemporary Literature* 18(3), Summer 1977, 364-66.

"From the road . . ."

MERLE BROWN. "Stress in Silkin's Poetry and the Healing Emptiness of America," *Contemporary Literature* 18(3), Summer 1977, 381-83.

"Killhope Wheel"

MERLE BROWN. "Stress in Silkin's Poetry and the Healing Emptiness of America," *Contemporary Literature* 18(3), Summer 1977, 383-90.

"Nature with Man"

MERLE BROWN. "Stress in Silkin's Poetry and the Healing Emptiness of America," *Contemporary Literature* 18(3), Summer 1977, 374-76.

"Night"

ANNE CLUYSENAAR. "Alone in a Mine of Reality: A Matrix in the Poetry of Jon Silkin," in *British Poetry Since 1960*, p. 165.

"Something has been Teased from Me"

ANNE CLUYSENAAR. "Alone in a Mine of Reality: A Matrix in the Poetry of Jon Silkin," in *British Poetry Since 1960*, p. 170.

"Violet"

TERRY EAGLETON. "Jon Silkin," in *Criticism in Action*, pp. 80-84.

"Worm"

MERLE BROWN. "Stress in Silkin's Poetry and the Healing Emptiness of America," *Contemporary Literature* 18(3), Summer 1977, 379.

TERRY EAGLETON. "Jon Silkin," in *Criticism in Action*, pp. 76-80.

SIMIC, CHARLES

"The Bird"

VICTOR CONTOSKI. "Charles Simic: Language at the Stone's Heart," *Chicago Review* 28(4), Spring 1977, 154.

"Charles Simic is a sentence"

VICTOR CONTOSKI. "Charles Simic: Language at the Stone's Heart," *Chicago Review* 28(4), Spring 1977, 156.

"Dismantling the Silence"

VICTOR CONTOSKI. "Charles Simic: Language at the Stone's Heart," *Chicago Review* 28(4), Spring 1977, 149-50.

"Eating Out the Angel of Death"

VICTOR CONTOSKI. "Charles Simic: Language at the Stone's Heart," *Chicago Review* 28(4), Spring 1977, 151-52.

"The Knife"

PAUL BRESLIN. "How to Read the New Contemporary Poem," *American Scholar* 47(3), Summer 1978, 361.

"The Point"

VICTOR CONTOSKI. "Charles Simic: Language at the Stone's Heart," *Chicago Review* 28(4), Spring 1977, 155-56.

"Stone Inside a Stone"

VICTOR CONTOSKI. "Charles Simic: Language at the Stone's Heart," *Chicago Review* 28(4), Spring 1977, 149.

"Summer Morning"

VICTOR CONTOSKI. "Charles Simic: Language at the Stone's Heart," *Chicago Review* 28(4), Spring 1977, 146-48.

"Travelling"

VICTOR CONTOSKI. "Charles Simic: Language at the Stone's Heart," *Chicago Review* 28(4), Spring 1977, 155.

"The Wind"

VICTOR CONTOSKI. "Charles Simic: Language at the Stone's Heart," *Chicago Review* 28(4), Spring 1977, 150.

SIMON, PAUL

"Richard Cory"

AGNES STEIN. *The Uses of Poetry*, p. 38.

SIMPSON, LOUIS

"Adam Yankev"

GEORGE S. LENSING and RONALD MORAN. *Four Poets and the Emotive Imagination*, p. 144.

"After Midnight"

GEORGE LENSING. "The Lyric Plenitude: A Time of Rediscovery," *Southern Review*, n.s., 3(1), Winter 1967, 204-5.

"American Poetry"

GEORGE S. LENSING and RONALD MORAN. *Four Poets and the Emotive Imagination*, p. 147.

"Arm in Arm"

YOHMA GRAY. "The Poetry of Louis Simpson," in *Poets in Progress*, second ed., pp. 232-33.

GEORGE S. LENSING and RONALD MORAN. *Four Poets and the Emotive Imagination*, pp. 149-50.

"The Ash and the Oak"

GEORGE S. LENSING and RONALD MORAN. *Four Poets and the Emotive Imagination*, p. 152.

"The Battle"

VERNON SCANNELL. *Not Without Glory*, pp. 207-8.

"Carentan O Carentan"

C. B. COX. "The Poetry of Louis Simpson," *Critical Quarterly* 8(1), Spring 1966, 73.

GEORGE S. LENSING and RONALD MORAN. *Four Poets and the Emotive Imagination*, pp. 149-50.

"Confessions of an American Poet"

C. B. COX. "The Poetry of Louis Simpson," *Critical Quarterly* 8(1), Spring 1966, 75.

"Good News of Death"

C. B. COX. "The Poetry of Louis Simpson," *Critical Quarterly* 8(1), Spring 1966, 77-78.

"The Green Shepherd"

LAURENCE PERRINE. *100 American Poems of the Twentieth Century*, pp. 264-67.

SIMPSON, LOUIS (*Cont.*)

"Indian Country"

> LOUIS SIMPSON. "Indian Country," *American Scholar* 37(1), Winter 1967/68, 80-84.

"The Inner Part"

> YOHMA GRAY. "The Poetry of Louis Simpson," in *Poets in Progress,* second ed., pp. 236-37.

"The Lady Sings"

> YOHMA GRAY. "The Poetry of Louis Simpson," in *Poets in Progress,* second ed., pp. 231-32.

"Lines Written Near San Francisco"

> GEORGE S. LENSING and RONALD MORAN. *Four Poets and the Emotive Imagination,* pp. 166-68.

"Mediterranean"

> GEORGE S. LENSING and RONALD MORAN. *Four Poets and the Emotive Imagination,* pp. 162-63.

"Memories of the Last War"

> VERNON SCANNELL. *Not Without Glory,* pp. 208-9.

"The Morning Light"

> RALPH J. MILLS, JR. *Creation's Very Self,* pp. 19-20. Reprinted in: Ralph J. Mills, Jr. *Cry of the Human,* pp. 20-21.

"Moving the Walls"

> C. B. COX. "The Poetry of Louis Simpson," *Critical Quarterly* 8(1), Spring 1966, 78-83.

"My Father in the Night Commanding No"

> C. B. COX. "The Poetry of Louis Simpson," *Critical Quarterly* 8(1), Spring 1966, 74-75.

"Orpheus in the Underworld"

> C. B. COX. "The Poetry of Louis Simpson," *Critical Quarterly* 8(1), Spring 1966, 77.

"The Runner"

> GEORGE S. LENSING and RONALD MORAN. *Four Poets and the Emotive Imagination,* pp. 152-53.
>
> VERNON SCANNELL. *Not Without Glory,* pp. 210-19.

"Summer Morning"

> PETER STITT. "North of Jamaica into the Self: Louis Simpson and Ronald Moran," *Southern Review,* n.s., 10(2), Spring 1974, 523.

"Things"

> C. B. COX. "The Poetry of Louis Simpson," *Critical Quarterly* 8(1), Spring 1966, 83.

"Walt Whitman at Bear Mountain"

> GEORGE S. LENSING and RONALD MORAN. *Four Poets and the Emotive Imagination,* pp. 166-68.
>
> RONALD MORAN. " 'Walt Whitman at Bear Mountain' and the American Illusion," *Concerning Poetry* 2(1), Spring 1969, 5-9.

"A Woman Too Well Remembered"

> JOHN CLARK PRATT. *The Meaning of Modern Poetry,* pp. 77, 80-81, 84-85, 88.

SITWELL, EDITH

"Aubade"

> MAX EASTMAN. *The Literary Mind,* pp. 73-76. (Quoting Edith Sitwell)
>
> NORMAN C. STAGEBERG and WALLACE L. ANDERSON. *Poetry as Experience,* pp. 497-98. (Quoting Edith Sitwell)

"Elegy on Dead Fashion"

> JOHN OWER. "A Golden Labyrinth: Edith Sitwell and the Theme of Time," *Renascence* 26(4), Summer 1974, 211-13.

"Fantasia for Mouth Organ"

> LAURA RIDING and ROBERT GRAVES. *A Survey of Modernist Poetry,* pp. 247-49.

"Gold Coast Customs"

> KEITH D. CUFFEL. "The Shadow of Cain: Themes in Dame Edith Sitwell's Later Poetry," *Personalist* 46(4), Autumn 1965, 518-19.
>
> BABETTE DEUTSCH. *Poetry in Our Time,* pp. 222-23; second ed., pp. 245-46.
>
> RALPH J. MILLS, JR. "The Poetic Roles of Edith Sitwell," *Chicago Review* 14(4), Spring 1961, 46-53.

"Metamorphosis"

> DAVID V. HARRINGTON. "The 'Metamorphosis' of Edith Sitwell," *Criticism* 9(1), Winter 1967, 80-91.
>
> JOHN OWER. "A Golden Labyrinth: Edith Sitwell and the Theme of Time," *Renascence* 26(4), Summer 1974, 213-17.

"The Poet Laments the Coming of Old Age"

> BABETTE DEUTSCH. *Poetry in Our Time,* p. 226; second ed., p. 249.

"The Shadow of Cain"

> SISTER M. JEREMY. "Clown and Canticle: The Achievement of Edith Sitwell," *Renascence* 3(2), Spring 1951, 135-36.
>
> JACK LINDSAY. "The Poetry of Edith Sitwell," *Life and Letters* 64(1), January 1950, 51-52.

"The Sleeping Beauty"

> BABETTE DEUTSCH. *Poetry in Our Time,* pp. 223-24; second ed., pp. 246-47.
>
> JOHN OWER. "A Golden Labyrinth: Edith Sitwell and the Theme of Time," *Renascence* 26(4), Summer 1974, 208-10.

"Spring Morning"

> SISTER M. JEREMY. "Clown and Canticle: The Achievement of Edith Sitwell," *Renascence* 3(2), Spring 1951, 136-37. (P)

"Still Falls the Rain"

> JAMES BROPHY. *Explicator* 29(4), December 1970, Item 36.

"Tears"

> KIMON FRIAR and JOHN MALCOLM BRINNIN. *Modern Poetry,* p. 534.

"Three Poems of the Atomic Age"

> KEITH D. CUFFEL. "The Shadow of Cain: Themes in Dame Edith Sitwell's Later Poetry," *Personalist* 46(4), Autumn 1965, 520-25.

"When Sir Beelzebub"

> EARL DANIELS. *The Art of Reading Poetry,* pp. 400-1.

"The Winds Bastinado Whipt on the Calico"

> LAURA RIDING and ROBERT GRAVES. *A Survey of Modernist Poetry,* pp. 231-33.

SITWELL, SACHEVERALL

"The Lady and the Rooks"

> JOSEPH WARREN BEACH. "Rococo: The Poetry of Sacheverell Sitwell," *Poetry* 74(4), July 1949, 229-31.

"New Water Music"

> JOSEPH WARREN BEACH. "Rococo: The Poetry of Sacheverell Sitwell," *Poetry* 74(4), July 1949, 227.

SKELTON, JOHN

"The Bowge of Courte"

> JUDITH SWEITZER LARSON. "What Is *The Bowge of Courte?*" *Journal of English and Germanic Philology* 61(2), April 1962, 288-95.
>
> A. C. SPEARING. *Medieval Dream-Poetry*, pp. 197-202.

"Manerly Margery Mylk and Ale"

> DAVID V. HARRINGTON. *Explicator* 25(5), January 1967, Item 42.

"Speke, Parrot"

> F. W. BROWNLOW. "The Boke Compiled by Maister Skelton, Poet Laureate, Called Speake Parrot," *English Literary Renaissance* 1(1), Winter 1971, 3-26.
>
> F. W. BROWNLOW. "*Speke, Parrot*: Skelton's Allegorical Denunciation of Cardinal Wolsey," *Studies in Philology* 65(2), April 1968, 124-39.
>
> WILLIAM NELSON. "Skelton's *Speak, Parrot*," *PMLA* 51(1), March 1936, 59-82.

"The Tunning of Elinour Rumming"

> RICHARD H. HAWKINS. "Structure through Irony in *The Tunning of Elinour Rumming*," *University Review* 34(3), Spring 1968, 199-203.
>
> LEONARD UNGER and WILLIAM VAN O'CONNOR. *Poems for Study*, pp. 46-49.

SKELTON, ROBIN

"The Shell"

> ROBIN SKELTON. *The Poetic Pattern*, pp. 152-53.

"Temple Flower"

> ROBIN SKELTON. *The Poetic Pattern*, pp. 150-52.

"Under the rock is an iron ball"

> ROBIN SKELTON. *Poetry*, pp. 19-25.

SKINNER, JOHN

"The Monymusk Christmas Ba'ing"

> ALLAN H. MACLAINE. "The *Christis Kirk* Tradition: Its Evolution in Scots Poetry To Burns," *Studies in Scottish Literature* 2(3), 1965, 170-71.

SMART, CHRISTOPHER

"The Author Apologizes to a Lady for His Being a Little Man"

> PATRICIA MEYER SPACKS. *The Poetry of Vision*, pp. 151-52.

"The Circumcision"

> KARINA WILLIAMSON. "Christopher Smart's *Hymns and Spiritual Songs*," *Philological Quarterly* 38(4), October 1959, 416-17. (P)

"Easter Day"

> PATRICIA MEYER SPACKS. *The Poetry of Vision*, pp. 159-60. (P)

"Epiphany"

> JEAN WILKINSON. "Three Sets of Religious Poems," *Huntington Library Quarterly* 36(3), May 1973, 219-22.

"The Hop-Garden"

> PATRICIA MEYER SPACKS. *The Poetry of Vision*, pp. 153-56.

"Hymn on the Nativity"

> DONALD DAVIE. "Christopher Smart: Some Neglected Poems," *Eighteenth Century Studies* 3(2), Winter 1969, 250-53.

"Jubilate Agno"

> FRANCIS D. ADAMS. "*Jubilate Agno* and the 'Theme of Gratitude,'" *Papers on Language and Literature* 3(3), Summer 1967, 195-209.
>
> JOHN BLOCK FRIEDMAN. "The Cosmology of Praise: Smart's *Jubilate Agno*," *PMLA* 82(2), May 1967, 250-56.
>
> GEOFFREY H. HARTMAN. "Christopher Smart's *Magnificat*: Toward a Theory of Representation," *ELH* 41(3), Fall 1974, 429-54.
>
> BRUCE HUNSBERGER. "Kit Smart's *Howl*," *Wisconsin Studies in Contemporary Literature* 6(1), Winter-Spring 1965, 34-44.
>
> ALBERT J. KUHN. "Christopher Smart: The Poet as Patriot of the Lord," *ELH* 30(2), June 1963, 121-36.
>
> ALLAN RODWAY. *The Romantic Conflict*, pp. 83-87.
>
> PATRICIA MEYER SPACKS. *The Poetry of Vision*, pp. 140-50.

"Munificence and Modesty"

> LYNA LEE MONTGOMERY. "The Phoenix: Its Use as a Literary Device in English From the Seventeenth Century to the Twentieth Century," *D. H. Lawrence Review* 5(3), Fall 1972, 292.

"My Cat Jeoffrey"

> MAX KEITH SUTTON. "Smart's 'Compleat Cat,'" *College English* 24(4), January 1963, 302-4.

"A Noon-Piece, or, The Mowers at Dinner"

> PATRICIA MEYER SPACKS. *The Poetry of Vision*, pp. 150-51.

"On a Bed of Guernsey Lilies"

> JEAN WILKINSON. "Three Sets of Religious Poems," *Huntington Library Quarterly* 36(3), May 1973, 216-17. (P)

"The Presentation of Christ in the Temple"

> PATRICIA MEYER SPACKS. *The Poetry of Vision*, pp. 158-59.

"St. Barnabas"

> PATRICIA MEYER SPACKS. *The Poetry of Vision*, p. 162.

"St. Philip and St. James"

> PATRICIA MEYER SPACKS. *The Poetry of Vision*, pp. 162-63.

"A Song to David"

> CHRISTOPHER M. DENNIS. "A Structural Conceit in Smart's *Song to David*," *Review of English Studies*, n.s., 29(115), August 1978, 257-66.
>
> JAMES DICKEY. "Christopher Smart: A Song to David," in *Babel to Byzantium*, pp. 233-35.
>
> JAMES DICKEY. "Smart: A Song to David," in *Master Poems of the English Language*, pp. 339-40.
>
> RAYMOND D. HAVENS. "The Structure of Smart's *Song to David*," *Review of English Studies* 14(54), April 1938, 178-82.
>
> CLIFFORD LEECH. "When writing becomes absurd," *Colorado Quarterly* 13(1), Summer 1964, 13-14.
>
> ALLAN RODWAY. *The Romantic Conflict*, pp. 87-90.
>
> PATRICIA MEYER SPACKS. *The Poetry of Vision*, pp. 119-39.

SMART, CHRISTOPHER *(Cont.)*

"Taste"

> Donald Davie. "Christopher Smart: Some Neglected Poems," *Eighteenth Century Studies* 3(2), Winter 1969, 263-64.

SMITH, A. J. M.

"The Archer"

> A. J. M. Smith. "The Poetic Process: Of the Making of Poems," *Centennial Review* 8(4), Fall 1964, 361-66.

SMITH, CHARLOTTE

"To the River Arun"

> Bishop C. Hunt, Jr. "Wordsworth and Charlotte Smith," *Wordsworth Circle* 1(3), Summer 1970, 89-90.

SMITH, EBENEZER

"A Brief Hint of the Mischief of Envy"

> William G. McLoughlin, editor. "Ebenezer Smith's Ballad of the Ashfield Baptists, 1772," *New England Quarterly* 47(1), March 1974, 97-108.

SMITH, HORACE

"Ozymandias"

> M. K. Bequette. "Shelley and Smith: Two Sonnets on Ozymandias," *Keats-Shelley Journal* 26 (1977), 29-31.

SMITH, LANGDON

"Evolution"

> Martin Gardner. "When You Were a Tadpole and I Was a Fish," *Antioch Review* 22(3), Fall 1962, 332-40.

SMITH, STEVIE

"Fafnir and the Knights"

> Calvin Bedient. *Eight Contemporary Poets*, pp. 147-50.

"The Frog Prince"

> Calvin Bedient. *Eight Contemporary Poets*, pp. 154-56.

"I had a dream . . ."

> Calvin Bedient. *Eight Contemporary Poets*, pp. 156-58.

"The Lady of the Well-Spring"

> Calvin Bedient. *Eight Contemporary Poets*, pp. 152-53.

"Pretty"

> Calvin Bedient. *Eight Contemporary Poets*, pp. 145-47.

SMITH, SYDNEY GOODSIR

"The Grace of God and the Meth-Drinker"

> Thomas Crawford. "The Poetry of Sydney Goodsir Smith," *Studies in Scottish Literature* 7(1-2), July-October 1969, 53-54.

"Kynd Kittock's Land"

> Thomas Crawford. "The Poetry of Sydney Goodsir Smith," *Studies in Scottish Literature* 7(1-2), July-October 1969, 54-56.

SMITH, WILLIAM

"Copy of Verses, Addressed to the Gentlemen of the House of Representatives"

> William D. Andrews. "William Smith and the Rising Glory of America," *Early American Literature* 8(1), Spring 1973, 33-43.

SMITH, WILLIAM JAY

"American Primitive"

> C. F. Burgess. "William Jay Smith's 'American Primitive': Toward a Reading," *Arizona Quarterly* 26(1), Spring 1970, 71-75.

"At the Tombs of the House of Sway"

> Josephine Jacobsen. "The Dark Train and the Green Place: The Poetry of William Jay Smith," *Hollins Critic* 12(1), February 1975, 9-11.

"Persian Miniature"

> Josephine Jacobsen. "The Dark Train and the Green Place: The Poetry of William Jay Smith," *Hollins Critic* 12(1), February 1975, 8-11.

SMOLLETT, TOBIAS

"Advice"

> Donald M. Korte. "Smollett's 'Advice' and 'Reproof': Apprenticeship in Satire," *Studies in Scottish Literature* 8(4), April 1971, 239-52.
>
> Donald M. Korte. "Tobias Smollett's 'Advice' and 'Reproof,' " *Thoth* 8(2), Spring 1967, 45-57.

"Reproof"

> Donald M. Korte. "Smollett's 'Advice' and 'Reproof': Apprenticeship in Satire," *Studies in Scottish Literature* 8(4), April 1971, 239-52.
>
> Donald M. Korte. "Tobias Smollett's 'Advice' and 'Reproof,' " *Thoth* 8(2), Spring 1967, 45-46, 58-65.

SNODGRASS, W. D.

"April Inventory"

> Paul Carroll. *The Poem In Its Skin*, pp. 174-85.
>
> Robert Phillips. *The Confessional Poets*, p. 56.
>
> Donald T. Torchiana. "Heart's Needle: Snodgrass Strides Through the Universe," in *Poets in Progress*, p. 104.

"The Campus on the Hill"

> J. D. McClatchy. "W. D. Snodgrass: The Mild, Reflective Art," *Massachusetts Review* 16(2), Spring 1975, 294-95.
>
> Robert Phillips. *The Confessional Poets*, pp. 55-56.

"A Cardinal"

> J. D. McClatchy. "W. D. Snodgrass: The Mild, Reflective Art," *Massachusetts Review* 16(2), Spring 1975, 292-93.
>
> Robert Phillips. *The Confessional Poets*, pp. 54-55.
>
> Donald T. Torchiana. "Heart's Needle: Snodgrass Strides Through the Universe," in *Poets in Progress*, pp. 106-7.

"Diplomacy: The Father"

> J. D. McClatchy. "W. D. Snodgrass: The Mild, Reflective Art," *Massachusetts Review* 16(2), Spring 1975, 303-5.

"The Examination"

> Robert Phillips. *The Confessional Poets*, pp. 67-68.
>
> Chad Walsh. *Doors into Poetry*, pp. 121-24.

"The First Leaf"

> Robert Phillips. *The Confessional Poets*, pp. 63-64.

"A Flat One"

> Laurence Lieberman. *Unassigned Frequencies*, pp. 235-36.
>
> J. D. McClatchy. "W. D. Snodgrass: The Mild, Reflective Art," *Massachusetts Review* 16(2), Spring 1975, 313-14.

"Fourth of July"

J. D. McClatchy. "W. D. Snodgrass: The Mild, Reflective Art," *Massachusetts Review* 16(2), Spring 1975, 306-7.

"Heart's Needle"

Glauco Cambon. *Recent American Poetry*, pp. 25-29.

David Farrelly. "Heart's Fling: The Poetry of W. D. Snodgrass," *Perspective* 13(3), Winter 1964, 192-99.

William Heyen. "Fishing the Swamp: The Poetry of W. D. Snodgrass," in *Modern American Poetry*, edited by Jerome Mazzaro, pp. 355-61.

J. D. McClatchy. "W. D. Snodgrass: The Mild, Reflective Art," *Massachusetts Review* 16(2), Spring 1975, 296-303.

Robert Phillips. *The Confessional Poets*, pp. 57-62.

Donald T. Torchiana. "Heart's Needle: Snodgrass Strides Through the Universe," in *Poets in Progress*, pp. 109-14.

"Home Town"

Donald T. Torchiana. "Heart's Needle: Snodgrass Strides Through the Universe," in *Poets in Progress*, p. 98.

"Leaving Ithaca"

J. D. McClatchy. "W. D. Snodgrass: The Mild, Reflective Art," *Massachusetts Review* 16(2), Spring 1975, 313.

"The Marsh"

Robert Phillips. *The Confessional Poets*, p. 51.

Donald T. Torchiana. "Heart's Needle: Snodgrass Strides Through the Universe," in *Poets in Progress*, pp. 99-100.

"Mementos 1"

J. D. McClatchy. "W. D. Snodgrass: The Mild, Reflective Art," *Massachusetts Review* 16(2), Spring 1975, 312.

"Mementos 2"

J. D. McClatchy. "W. D. Snodgrass: The Mild, Reflective Art," *Massachusetts Review* 16(2), Spring 1975, 312.

"MHTIS . . . OUTIS"

Robert Phillips. *The Confessional Poets*, p. 50.

Donald T. Torchiana. "Heart's Needle: Snodgrass Strides Through the Universe," in *Poets in Progress*, p. 98.

"The Mother"

J. D. McClatchy. "W. D. Snodgrass: The Mild, Reflective Art," *Massachusetts Review* 16(2), Spring 1975, 303-4.

"The Operation"

Robert Phillips. *The Confessional Poets*, pp. 52-53.

Donald T. Torchiana. "Heart's Needle: Snodgrass Strides Through the Universe," in *Poets in Progress*, pp. 101-2.

"Orpheus"

J. D. McClatchy. "W. D. Snodgrass: The Mild, Reflective Art," *Massachusetts Review* 16(2), Spring 1975, 291.

Robert Phillips. *The Confessional Poets*, pp. 50-51.

Donald T. Torchiana. "Heart's Needle: Snodgrass Strides Through the Universe," in *Poets in Progress*, p. 99.

"Papageno"

J. D. McClatchy. "W. D. Snodgrass: The Mild, Reflective Art," *Massachusetts Review* 16(2), Spring 1975, 291.

Robert Phillips. *The Confessional Poets*, p. 51.

"Powwow"

Laurence Perrine. *100 American Poems of the Twentieth Century*, pp. 267-70.

Robert Phillips. *The Confessional Poets*, pp. 65-66.

"Reconstructions"

Robert Phillips. *The Confessional Poets*, p. 63.

"Remains"

Robert Phillips. *The Confessional Poets*, pp. 68-72.

"Returned to Frisco, 1946"

Robert Phillips. *The Confessional Poets*, p. 50.

Donald T. Torchiana. "Heart's Needle: Snodgrass Strides Through the Universe," in *Poets in Progress*, pp. 97-98.

"September in the Park"

Robert Phillips. *The Confessional Poets*, pp. 51-52.

"Songs of a Wayfarer"

David Farrelly. "Heart's Fling: The Poetry of W. D. Snodgrass," *Perspective* 13(3), Winter 1964, 190-92.

"Ten Days Leave"

J. D. McClatchy. "W. D. Snodgrass: The Mild, Reflective Art," *Massachusetts Review* 16(2), Spring 1975, 289.

Robert Phillips. *The Confessional Poets*, pp. 49-50.

"To a Child"

Robert Phillips. *The Confessional Poets*, pp. 71-72.

"Viewing the Body"

Robert Phillips. *The Confessional Poets*, p. 70.

"What We Said"

Louis Untermeyer. *50 Modern American & British Poets*, p. 320.

"Winter Bouquet"

Robert Phillips. *The Confessional Poets*, pp. 53-54.

SNYDER, GARY

"After Work"

Anthony Hunt. *Explicator* 32(8), April 1974, Item 61.

Sherman Paul. "From Lookout to Ashram: The Way of Gary Snyder," *Iowa Review* 1(4), Fall 1970, 79-80.

"February"

Robert Kern. "Recipes, Catalogues, Open Form Poetics: Gary Snyder's Archetypal Voice," *Contemporary Literature* 18(2), Spring 1977, 187-89.

"For George Leigh-Mallory"

Robert Ian Scott. "Gary Snyder's Early Uncollected Mallory Poem," *Concerning Poetry* 2(1), Spring 1969, 33-37.

"For the Boy Who Was Dodger Point Lookout Fifteen Years Ago"

Sherman Paul. "From Lookout to Ashram: The Way of Gary Snyder," *Iowa Review* 1(4), Fall 1970, 80.

"Front-Lines"

Charles Altieri. "Gary Snyder's *Turtle Island*: The Problem of Reconciling the Roles of Seer and Prophet," *Boundary 2* 4(3), Spring 1976, 773-74.

SNYDER, GARY *(Cont.)*

"Hay for the Horses"
>   AGNES STEIN. *The Uses of Poetry,* pp. 41-42.

"How To Make Stew in the Pinacarte Desert Recipe for Locke and Drum"
>   SAMUEL CHARTERS. *Some Poems/Poets,* pp. 57-63.
>   ROBERT KERN. "Recipes, Catalogues, Open Form Poetics: Gary Snyder's Archetypal Voice," *Contemporary Literature* 18(2), Spring 1977, 189-90.

"Lookout's Journal"
>   SHERMAN PAUL. "From Lookout to Ashram: The Way of Gary Snyder," *Iowa Review* 1(3), Summer 1970, 81-86.

"Marin-An"
>   CHENG LOK CHUA and N. SASAKI. "Zen and the Title of Gary Snyder's 'Marin-An,' " *Notes on Contemporary Literature* 8(3), May 1978, 2-3.

"Mid-August at Sour-dough Mountain Lookout"
>   ROBERT KERN. "Toward a New Nature Poetry," *Centennial Review* 19(3), Summer 1975, 212-16.

"Milton by Firelight"
>   RAYMOND BENOIT. *Single Nature's Double Name,* pp. 124-25.

"Nooksack Valley"
>   SHERMAN PAUL. "From Lookout to Ashram: The Way of Gary Snyder," *Iowa Review* 1(4), Fall 1970, 71-72.

"Piute Creek"
>   ROBERT KERN. "Clearing the Ground: Gary Snyder and the Modernist Imperative," *Criticism* 19(2), Spring 1977, 168-70.
>   ROBERT PINSKY. *The Situation of Poetry,* pp. 70-71.

"Prayer for the Great Family"
>   CHARLES ALTIERI. "Gary Snyder's *Turtle Island*: The Problem of Reconciling the Roles of Seer and Prophet," *Boundary 2* 4(3), Spring 1976, 766-68.

"A Stone Garden"
>   SHERMAN PAUL. "From Lookout to Ashram: The Way of Gary Snyder," *Iowa Review* 1(4), Fall 1970, 72-73.

"Straight-Creek-Great Burn"
>   CHARLES ALTIERI. "Gary Snyder's *Turtle Island*: The Problem of Reconciling the Roles of Seer and Prophet," *Boundary 2* 4(3), Spring 1976, 764-65.

"Thin Ice"
>   ROBERT KERN. "Clearing the Ground: Gary Snyder and the Modernist Imperative," *Criticism* 19(2), Spring 1977, 170-2.

"Three Worlds: Three Realms: Six Roads"
>   ROBERT KERN. "Recipes, Catalogues, Open Form Poetics: Gary Snyder's Archetypal Voice," *Contemporary Literature* 18(2), Spring 1977, 190-95.

SOMERVILE, WILLIAM

"The Officious Messenger"
>   WALLACE SHUGG. "The Cartesian Beast-Machine in English Literature (1663-1750)," *Journal of the History of Ideas* 29(2), Apr.-June 1968, 290-91.

SORLEY, CHARLES

"All the Hills and Vales Along"
>   BERNARD BERGONZI. *Heroes' Twilight,* pp. 57-58.
>   JON SILKIN. *Out of Battle,* pp. 83-84.

"To Poets"
>   JON SILKIN. *Out of Battle,* pp. 246-47.

SOUTHEY, ROBERT

"The Battle of Blenheim"
>   MARY JACOBUS. "Southey's Debt to *Lyrical Ballads* (1798)," *Review of English Studies,* n.s., 22(85), February 1971, 29-30.

"God's Judgment on a Bishop"
>   WARREN U. OBER and KENNETH H. OBER. "Žukovskij and Southey's Ballads: The Translator as Rival," *Wordsworth Circle* 5(2), Spring 1974, 77-78.

"His Books"
>   CLEANTH BROOKS, JOHN THIBAUT PURSER, and ROBERT PENN WARREN. *An Approach to Literature,* pp. 464-67; second ed., pp. 464-67; third ed., pp. 336-40; fourth ed., pp. 334-38.

"The Idiot"
>   ELIZABETH DUTHIE. "A Fresh Comparison of 'The Idiot Boy' and 'The Idiot,' " *Notes & Queries,* n.s., 25(3), June 1978, 219-20.
>   MARY JACOBUS. "Southey's Debt to *Lyrical Ballads* (1798)," *Review of English Studies,* n.s., 22(85), February 1971, 24-25.

"Jaspar"
>   WARREN U. OBER and KENNETH H. OBER. "Žukovskij and Southey's Ballads: The Translator as Rival," *Wordsworth Circle* 5(2), Spring 1974, 83-84.

"The Mad Woman"
>   MARY JACOBUS. "Southey's Debt to *Lyrical Ballads* (1798)," *Review of English Studies,* n.s., 22(85), February 1971, 25-27.

"Mary the Maid of the Inn"
>   WARREN U. OBER and KENNETH H. OBER. "Žukovskij and Southey's Ballads: The Translator as Rival," *Wordsworth Circle* 5(2), Spring 1974, 83.

"The Sailor, who had served in the Slave Trade"
>   MARY JACOBUS. "Southey's Debt to *Lyrical Ballads* (1798)," *Review of English Studies,* n.s., 22(85), February 1971, 30-32.

"The Secret Expedition"
>   MARY JACOBUS. "Southey's Debt to *Lyrical Ballads* (1798)," *Review of English Studies,* n.s., 22(85), February 1971, 33-35.

SOUTHWELL, ROBERT

"At Home in Heaven"
>   LOUIS L. MARTZ. *The Poetry of Meditation,* pp. 188-89.

"David's Peccavi"
>   ANTHONY RASPA. "Crashaw and the Jesuit Poetic," *University of Toronto Quarterly* 36(1), October 1966, 49-50.

"A Fancy Turned to a Sinners' Complaint"
>   LOUIS L. MARTZ. *The Poetry of Meditation,* pp. 189-91.

"I Die Alive"
>   HARRY MORRIS. "*In Articulo Mortis*," *Tulane Studies in English* 11 (1961), 21-28.

"Lewd love is losse"
>   STANLEY STEWART. *The Enclosed Garden,* pp. 125-26.

"Life Is But Losse"
>   HARRY MORRIS. "*In Articulo Mortis*," *Tulane Studies in English* 11(1961), 28-29.

"Life's Death, Love's Life"

> HARRY MORRIS. "*In Articulo Mortis*," *Tulane Studies in English* 11(1961), 29.

"Loves Garden griefe"

> STANLEY STEWART. *The Enclosed Garden*, p. 125.

"Man To The Wound in Christ's Side"

> HARRY MORRIS. "*In Articulo Mortis*," *Tulane Studies in English* 11 (1961), 30-32.

"Mary Magdalen's Complaint at Christ's Death"

> LOUIS L. MARTZ. *The Poetry of Meditation*, pp. 191-93.

"Saint Peter's Complaint"

> NANCY POLLARD BROWN. "The Structure of Southwell's 'Saint Peter's Complaint,' " *Modern Language Review* 61(1), January 1966, 3-11.

> LOUIS L. MARTZ. *The Poetry of Meditation*, pp. 193-97.

> HELEN C. WHITE. "Southwell: Metaphysical and Baroque," *Modern Philology* 61(3), February 1964, 164-67.

"A Vale of Tears"

> LOUIS L. MARTZ. *The Poetry of Meditation*, pp. 207-10.

SPENCER, BERNARD

"Aegean Islands 1940-41"

> MARTIN DODSWORTH. "Bernard Spencer," in *The Modern Poet*, edited by Ian Hamilton, pp. 96-97.

"Allotments: April"

> MARTIN DODSWORTH. "Bernard Spencer," in *The Modern Poet*, edited by Ian Hamilton, pp. 90-92, 95.

"Delicate Grasses"

> MARTIN DODSWORTH. "Bernard Spencer," in *The Modern Poet*, edited by Ian Hamilton, pp. 98-99.

"Fluted Armour"

> MARTIN DODSWORTH. "Bernard Spencer," in *The Modern Poet*, edited by Ian Hamilton, p. 98.

SPENCER, THEODORE

"The Circus; or One View of It"

> JAMES M. REID. *100 American Poems of the Twentieth Century*, pp. 188-90.

"The Inflatable Globe"

> ROBIN SKELTON. *Poetry*, pp. 70-71.

SPENDER, STEPHEN

"Abrupt and Charming Mover"

> RUDOLF ARNHEIM. "Psychological Notes on the Poetical Process," in *Poets at Work*, pp. 148-50, 158-59.

"Air Raid across the Bay of Plymouth"

> GEOFFREY THURLEY. *The Ironic Harvest*, p. 96.

"Awaking"

> BERNARD KNIEGER. *Explicator* 12(5), March 1954, Item 30.

"The Bombed Happiness"

> ELTON EDWARD SMITH. *The Angry Young Men of the Thirties*, pp. 50-51.

"Dark and Light"

> A. K. WEATHERHEAD. "Stephen Spender: Lyric Impulse and Will," *Contemporary Literature* 12(4), Autumn 1971, 453-54.

"An Elementary School Class Room in a Slum"

> PHYLLIS BARTLETT. *Poems in Progress*, pp. 217-19.

"Exiles from Their Land, History Their Domicile"

> JOSEPH WARREN BEACH. *Obsessive Images*, pp. 148-52.

"The Express"

> RICHARD C. BLAKESLEE. "Three Ways Past Edinburgh: Stephen Spender's 'The Express,' " *College English* 26(7), April 1965, 556-58.

> WALLACE DOUGLAS, ROY LAMSON, and HALLETT SMITH. *The Critical Reader*, pp. 134-36.

> MORDECAI MARCUS. "*Walden* as a Possible Source for Stephen Spender's 'The Express,' " *Thoreau Society Bulletin* 75 (Spring 1961), 1.

> KARL SHAPIRO. "The Meaning of the Discarded Poem," in *Poets at Work*, pp. 94-101. Reprinted in: *Poems in the Making*, pp. 62-68.

"The Fates"

> RONALD B. HERZMAN. "Stephen Spender: The Critic as Poet," *Notes on Contemporary Literature* 3(5), November 1973, 6-7.

"The Funeral"

> WILLIS D. JACOBS. "The Moderate Poetical Success of Stephen Spender," *College English* 17(7), April 1956, 376.

> KARL SHAPIRO. "The Meaning of the Discarded Poem," in *Poets at Work*, pp. 101-5. Reprinted in: Walker Gibson. *Poems in the Making*, pp. 68-72.

> ELTON EDWARD SMITH. *The Angry Young Men of the Thirties*, pp. 42-43.

"He Will Watch the Hawk With an Indifferent Eye"

> S. A. COWAN. *Explicator* 28(8), April 1970, Item 67.

"How Strangely This Sun Reminds Me of My Love!"

> ELTON EDWARD SMITH. *The Angry Young Men of the Thirties*, p. 65.

"I Think Continually of Those Who Were Truly Great"

> HARRY BROWN and JOHN MILSTEAD. *What the Poem Means*, p. 213.

> DONALD A. STAUFFER. "Genesis, of the Poet as Maker," in *Poets at Work*, pp. 76-80.

> A. K. WEATHERHEAD. "Stephen Spender: Lyric Impulse and Will," *Contemporary Literature* 12(4), Autumn 1971, 459-60.

"In 1929"

> D. E. S. MAXWELL. *The Poets of the Thirties*, p. 196.

> ELTON EDWARD SMITH. *The Angry Young Men of the Thirties*, p. 44.

"Judas Iscariot"

> LESLIE M. THOMPSON. "Spender's 'Judas Iscariot,' " *English Language Notes* 8(2), December 1970, 126-30.

"The Landscape Near an Aerodrome"

> HARRY BROWN and JOHN MILSTEAD. *What the Poem Means*, p. 214.

> C. B. COX and A. E. DYSON. *Modern Poetry*, pp. 80-84.

> WILLIS D. JACOBS. "The Moderate Poetical Success of Stephen Spender," *College English* 17(7), April 1956, 375-76.

> GEOFFREY THURLEY. *The Ironic Harvest*, pp. 93-94.

> CHARLES C. WALCUTT. *Explicator* 5(5), March 1947, Item 37. Reprinted in: *Reading Modern Poetry*, pp. 85-86.

"Moving through the silent crowd"

> GEOFFREY THURLEY. *The Ironic Harvest*, pp. 92-93.

SPENDER, STEPHEN *(Cont.)*

"Never being, but always at the edge of Being"
A. K. WEATHERHEAD. "Stephen Spender: Lyric Impulse and Will," *Contemporary Literature* 12(4), Autumn 1971, 464-65.

"Not Palaces, an Era's Crown"
HARRY BROWN and JOHN MILSTEAD. *What the Poem Means*, p. 213.
WILLIS D. JACOBS. "The Moderate Poetical Success of Stephen Spender," *College English* 17(7), April 1956, 376-77.
M. L. ROSENTHAL. *The Modern Poets*, p. 198.
A. K. WEATHERHEAD. "Stephen Spender: Lyric Impulse and Will," *Contemporary Literature* 12(4), Autumn 1971, 451-53.

"Oh What Is the Use Now of Our Meeting and Speaking"
RUDOLF ARNHEIM. "Psychological Notes on the Poetical Process," in *Poets at Work*, pp. 146-47. (P)

"The Pylons"
CHARLES D. ABBOTT. "Poetry in the Making," *Poetry* 55(5), February 1940, 262-66.

"Rejoice in the Abyss"
GEOFFREY THURLEY. *The Ironic Harvest*, pp. 90-91.

"Responsibility: The Pilots Who Destroyed Germany, Spring, 1945"
A. K. WEATHERHEAD. "Stephen Spender: Lyric Impulse and Will," *Contemporary Literature* 12(4), Autumn 1971, 462-63.

"Returning to Vienna"
ELTON EDWARD SMITH. *The Angry Young Men of the Thirties*, p. 44.

"Rolled Over on Europe"
EARL DANIELS. *The Art of Reading Poetry*, p. 293.

"Seascape"
BARBARA GIBBS. " 'Where Thoughts Lash Tail and Fin,' " *Poetry* 86(4), July 1956, 239-40. (P)
C. DAY LEWIS. *The Poetic Image*, pp. 136-40.
STEPHEN SPENDER. "The Making of a Poem," *Partisan Review* 13(3), Summer 1946, 297-300. Reprinted in: *Critiques and Essays in Criticism*, pp. 20-22. Also: *Criticism*, pp. 189-90. Also: Walker Gibson. *Poems in the Making*, pp. 78-80.

"Spiritual Explorations"
RAYMOND TSCHUMI. *Thought in Twentieth-Century English Poetry*, pp. 276-78.

"To a Spanish Poet"
ELTON EDWARD SMITH. *The Angry Young Men of the Thirties*, pp. 47-48.

"Tom's A Cold"
BABETTE DEUTSCH. *Poetry in Our Time*, pp. 1-2.

"Ultima Ratio Regum"
HARRY BROWN and JOHN MILSTEAD. *What the Poem Means*, pp. 214-15.

"Vienna"
D. E. S. MAXWELL. *The Poets of the Thirties*, pp. 197-99.

"Your body is stars whose million glitter here"
GEOFFREY THURLEY. *The Ironic Harvest*, pp. 85-86.

SPENSER, EDMUND

"Anacreontic IV"
CAROL V. KASKE. "*Spenser's Amoretti and Epithalamion* of 1595: Structure, Genre, and Numerology," *English Literary Renaissance* 8(3), Autumn 1978, 277-80.

"April"
THOMAS H. CAIN. "The Strategy of Praise in Spenser's 'Aprill,' " *Studies in English Literature 1500-1900* 8(1), Winter 1968, 45-58.
PATRICK CULLEN. "Imitation and Metamorphosis: The Golden-Age Eclogue in Spenser, Milton, and Marvell," *PMLA* 84(6), October 1969, 1562-65.
WALTER F. STATON, JR. "Spenser's 'April' lay as a Dramatic Chorus," *Studies in Philology* 59(2, pt. 1), April 1962, 111-18.

"Astrophel"
MICHAEL O'CONNELL. "*Astrophel*: Spenser's Double Elegy," *Studies in English Literature 1500-1900* 11(1), Winter 1971, 27-35.
LEONARD D. TOURNEY. "Spenser's *Astrophel*: Myth and the Critique of Values," *Essays in Literature* 3(2), Fall 1976, 145-51.

"Be nought dismayd that her unmoved mind" *(Amoretti, VI)*
ALISTAIR FOWLER. *Conceitful Thought*, pp. 89-91.
WILLIAM C. JOHNSON. *Explicator* 29(5), January 1971, Item 38.

"Colin Clouts Come Home Again"
DAVID W. BURCHMORE. "The Image of the Centre in *Colin Clouts Come Home Againe*," *Review of English Studies*, n.s., 28(112), November 1977, 393-406.
TERRY COMITO. "The Lady in the Landscape and the Poetics of Elizabethan Pastoral," *University of Toronto Quarterly* 41(3), Spring 1972, 204-10.
THOMAS R. EDWARDS. *Imagination and Power*, pp. 48-63.
MILLAR MACLURE. "Spenser," in *English Poetry and Prose*, ed. by Christopher Ricks, pp. 69-70.
SAM MEYER. "The Figures of Rhetoric in Spenser's *Colin Clout*," *PMLA* 79(3), June 1964, 206-18.

"Comming to kisse her lyps, (such grace I found)" *(Amoretti, LXIV)*
ALISTAIR FOWLER. *Conceitful Thought*, pp. 96-97.

"December"
HALLETT SMITH. "*The Shepheardes Calender* and Pastoral Poetry," in *Elizabethan Poetry*, edited by Paul J. Alpers, pp. 176-77.

"Epithalamion"
HARRY BROWN and JOHN MILSTEAD. *What the Poem Means*, pp. 219-20.
A. R. CIRILLO. "Spenser's *Epithalamion*: The Harmonious Universe of Love," *Studies in English Literature 1500-1900* 8(1), Winter 1968, 19-34.
WOLFGANG CLEMEN. "The Uniqueness of Spenser's 'Epithalamion,' " in *The Poetic Tradition*, pp. 81-98.
WILLIAM V. DAVIS. "Edmund Spenser's 'Epithalamion,' " *American Notes & Queries*, n.s., 7(6), February 1969, 84-85.
J. C. EADE. "The Pattern in the Astronomy of Spenser's *Epithalamion*," *Review of English Studies*, n.s., 23(90), May 1972, 173-78.
WILLIAM HEYEN. "Narration in Spenser's 'Epithalamion,' " *Ball State University Forum* 6(3), Autumn 1965, 51-54.

CAROL V. KASKE. "Spenser's *Amoretti and Epithalamion* of 1595: Structure, Genre, and Numerology," *English Literary Renaissance* 8(3), Autumn 1978, 285-95.

WALTER JAMES MILLER. "Spenser: Epithalamion," in *Master Poems of the English Language*, pp. 25-28.

RICHARD NEUSE. "The Triumph Over Hasty Accidents: A Note on the Symbolic Mode of the 'Epithalamion,' " *Modern Language Review* 61(2), April 1966, 163-74.

W. H. STEVENSON. "The Spaciousness of Spenser's 'Epithalamion,' " *Review of English Literature* 5(3), July 1964, 61-69.

MAX A. WICKERT. "Structure and Ceremony in Spenser's *Epithalamion*," *ELH* 35(2), June 1968, 135-57.

"Fayre ye be sure, but cruell and unkind" (*Amoretti*, LVI)

WINIFRED LYNSKEY. "A Critic in Action: Mr. Ransom," *College English* 5(5), February 1944, 244.

"Fresh Spring, the herald of loves mighty king" (*Amoretti*, LXX)

JUDITH KALIL. " 'Mask in Myrth Lyke to a Comedy': Spenser's Persona in the *Amoretti*," *Thoth* 13(2), Spring 1973, 24.

"Happy ye leaves! when as those lilly hands" (*Amoretti*, I)

ALISTAIR FOWLER. *Conceitful Thought*, pp. 92-95.

JOHN T. SHAWCROSS. "The Poet as Orator: One Phase in His Judicial Pose," in *The Rhetoric of Renaissance Poetry*, pp. 21-22.

"An Hymne in Honour of Beautie"

EINAR BJORVAND. "Spenser's defense of poetry: Some Structural Aspects of the *Fowre Hymnes*," in *Fair Forms*, pp. 13-46.

HARRY BROWN and JOHN MILSTEAD. *What the Poem Means*, pp. 215-16.

TERRY COMITO. "A Dialectic of Images in Spenser's *Fowre Hymnes*," *Studies in Philology* 74(3), July 1977, 301-21.

G. WILSON KNIGHT. "The Spenserian Fluidity," in *Poets in Action*, pp. 3-4.

PHILIP B. ROLLINSON. "A Generic View of Spenser's *Four Hymns*," *Studies in Philology* 68(3), July 1971, 292-304.

"An Hymne in Honour of Love"

EINER BJORVAND. "Spenser's defense of poetry: Some Structural Aspects of the *Fowre Hymnes*," in *Fair Forms*, pp. 13-46.

HARRY BROWN and JOHN MILSTEAD. *What the Poem Means*, p. 216.

TERRY COMITO. "A Dialectic of Images in Spenser's *Fowre Hymnes*," *Studies in Philology* 74(3), July 1977, 301-21.

G. WILSON KNIGHT. "The Spenserian Fluidity," in *Poets of Action*, pp. 2-3.

PHILIP B. ROLLINSON. "A Generic View of Spenser's *Four Hymns*," *Studies in Philology* 68(3), July 1971, 292-304.

"An Hymne of Heavenly Beautie"

EINAR BJORVAND. "Spenser's defense of poetry: Some Structural Aspects of the *Fowre Hymnes*," in *Fair Forms*, pp. 13-46.

HARRY BROWN and JOHN MILSTEAD. *What the Poem Means*, pp. 217-18.

TERRY COMITO. "A Dialectic of Images in Spenser's *Fowre Hymnes*," *Studies in Philology* 74(3), July 1977, 301-21.

G. WILSON KNIGHT. "The Spenserian Fluidity," in *Poets of Action*, pp. 5-6.

JON A. QUITSLUND. "Spenser's Image of Sapience," *Studies in the Renaissance* 16 (1969), 181-213.

PHILIP B. ROLLINSON. "A Generic View of Spenser's *Four Hymns*," *Studies in Philology* 68(3), July 1971, 292-304.

IAN SOWTON. "Hidden Persuaders as a Means of Literary Grace: Sixteenth-Century Poetics and Rhetoric in England," *University of Toronto Quarterly* 32(1), October 1962, 60-64.

A. S. P. WOODHOUSE. *The Poet and His Faith*, pp. 28-32.

"An Hymne of Heavenly Love"

EINAR BJORVAND. "Spenser's Defense of Poetry: Some Structural Aspects of the *Fowre Hymnes*," in *Fair Forms*, pp. 13-46.

HARRY BROWN and JOHN MILSTEAD. *What the Poem Means*, pp. 218-19.

TERRY COMITO. "A Dialectic of Images in Spenser's *Fowre Hymnes*," *Studies in Philology* 74(3), July 1977, 301-21.

G. WILSON KNIGHT. "The Spenserian Fluidity," in *Poets of Action*, pp. 4-5.

PHILIP B. ROLLINSON. "A Generic View of Spenser's *Four Hymns*," *Studies in Philology* 68(3), July 1971, 292-304.

A. S. P. WOODHOUSE. *The Poet and His Faith*, pp. 28-32.

"Is it her nature, or is it her will" (*Amoretti*, XLI)

ROSEMOND TUVE. *Elizabethan and Metaphysical Imagery*, pp. 63-64.

"January"

JOHN W. MOORE, JR. "Colin Breaks His Pipe: A Reading of the 'January' Eclogue," *English Literary Renaissance* 5(1), Winter 1975, 3-24.

HALLETT SMITH. "*The Shepheardes Calender* and Pastoral Poetry," in *Elizabethan Poetry*, edited by Paul J. Alpers, pp. 172-73.

"June"

HALLETT SMITH. "*The Shepheardes Calender* and Pastoral Poetry," in *Elizabethan Poetry*, edited by Paul J. Alpers, pp. 173-75.

"Leave, lady, in your glasse of christall clene" (*Amoretti*, XLV)

DOUGLAS L. PETERSON. *The English Lyric from Wyatt to Donne*, pp. 208-9.

"Lyke as a huntsman, after weary chace" (*Amoretti*, LXVII)

MURRAY KRIEGER. *The Classic Vision*, pp. 66-67.

WILLIAM BOWMAN PIPER. "Spenser's 'Lyke as a Huntsman,' " *College English* 22(6), March 1961, 405.

"Lyke as a ship, that through the ocean wyde" (*Amoretti*, XXXIV)

LEONARD UNGER and WILLIAM VAN O'CONNOR. *Poems for Study*, pp. 60-62.

"March"

DON CAMERON ALLEN. *Image and Meaning*, pp. 1-19.

"Mark when she smiles with amiable cheare" (*Amoretti*, XL)

JUDITH KALIL. " 'Mask in Myrth Lyke to a Comedy': Spenser's Persona in the *Amoretti*," *Thoth* 13(2), Spring 1972, 23.

SPENSER, EDMUND *(Cont.)*

"May"

HALLETT SMITH. *"The Shepheardes Calender* and Pastoral Poetry," in *Elizabethan Poetry,* edited by Paul J. Alpers, pp. 178-79.

"Men call you fayre, and you do credit it" *(Amoretti,* LXXIX)

DOUGLAS L. PETERSON. *The English Lyric from Wyatt to Donne,* pp. 209-10.

"Most glorious Lord of lyfe, that on this day" *(Amoretti,* LXVIII)

JUDITH KALIL. " 'Mask in Myrth Lyke to a Comedy': Spenser's Persona in the *Amoretti," Thoth* 13(2), Spring 1973, 23.

"Muiopotmos"

DON CAMERON ALLEN. "On Spenser's *Muiopotmos," Studies in Philology* 53(2), April 1956, 141-58. Reprinted in: Don Cameron Allen. *Image and Meaning,* pp. 20-41.

FRANKLIN E. COURT. "The Theme and Structure of Spenser's *Muiopotmos," Studies in English Literature 1500-1900* 10(1), Winter 1970, 1-15.

"My hungry eyes, through greedy covetize" *(Amoretti,* XXXV)

CALVIN R. EDWARDS. "The Narcissus Myth in Spenser's Poetry," *Studies in Philology* 74(1), January 1977, 70-75.

"New Yeare, forth looking out of Janus gate" *(Amoretti,* IV)

JUDITH KALIL. " 'Mask in Myrth Lyke to a Comedy': Spenser's Persona in the *Amoretti," Thoth* 13(2), Spring 1973, 24.

"November"

HALLETT SMITH. *"The Shepheardes Calender* and Pastoral Poetry," in *Elizabethan Poetry,* edited by Paul J. Alpers, pp. 175-76.

"October"

MICHAEL F. DIXON. "Rhetorical Patterns and Methods of Advocacy in Spenser's *Shepheardes Calender," English Literary Renaissance* 7(2), Spring 1977, 149-51.

RICHARD F. HARDIN. "The Resolved Debate of Spenser's 'October,' " *Modern Philology* 73(3), February 1976, 257-63.

HALLETT SMITH. *"The Shepheardes Calender* and Pastoral Poetry," in *Elizabethan Poetry,* edited by Paul J. Alpers, pp. 180-81.

"Of this worlds theatre in which we stay" *(Amoretti,* LIV)

JUDITH KALIL. " 'Mask in Myrth Lyke to a Comedy': Spenser's Persona in the *Amoretti," Thoth* 13(2), Spring 1973, 25.

"Oft when my spirit doth spred her bolder winges" *(Amoretti,* LXXI)

W. B. C. WATKINS. "The Kingdom of Our Language," *Hudson Review* 2(3), Autumn 1949, 343-44. Reprinted in: *Readings for Liberal Education,* revised ed., II: 20-21.

"One day I wrote her name upon the strand" *(Amoretti,* LXXV)

JUDITH KALIL. " 'Mask in Myrth Lyke to a Comedy': Spenser's Persona in the *Amoretti," Thoth* 13(2), Spring 1973, 21-22.

"Penelope, for her Ulisses sake" *(Amoretti,* XXIII)

JAMES R. KREUZER. *Elements of Poetry,* pp. 83-84.

"Prothalamion"

GEORGE ARMS. *Explicator* 1(5), March 1943, Item 36.

HARRY BERGER. "Spenser's *Prothalamion*: an Interpretation," *Essays in Criticism,* 15(4), October 1965, 363-80.

DAVID DAICHES and WILLIAM CHARVAT. *Poems in English,* pp. 650-52.

ALISTAIR FOWLER. *Conceitful Thought,* pp. 59-86.

JAY L. HALIO. " 'Prothalamion,' 'Ulysses,' and Intention in Poetry," *College English* 22(6), March 1961, 390-92.

DAN S. NORTON. "Queen Elizabeth's 'Brydale Day,' " *Modern Language Quarterly* 5(2), June 1944, 149-54. (P)

WILLIAM ELFORD ROGERS. "Proserpina in the *Prothalamion," American Notes & Queries,* n.s., 15(9), May 1977, 131-34.

M. L. WINE. "Spenser's 'Sweete *Themmes* Of Time and the River,' " *Studies in English Litrature* 2(1), Winter 1962, 111-17.

DANIEL H. WOODWARD. "Some Themes in Spenser's 'Prothalamion,' " *ELH* 29(1), March 1962, 34-46.

"The Ruines of Time"

LAURENCE GOLDSTEIN. "Immortal Longings and 'The Ruines of Time,' " *Journal of English and Germanic Philology* 75(3), July 1976, 337-51.

"September"

LAURENCE LERNER. *The Uses of Nostalgia,* pp. 130-33.

HALLETT SMITH. *"The Shepheardes Calender* and Pastoral Poetry," in *Elizabethan Poetry,* edited by Paul J. Alpers, pp. 180-81.

"The Teares of the Muses"

GERALD SNARE. "The Muses on Poetry: Spenser's *The Teares of the Muses," Tulane Studies in English* 17 (1969), 31-52.

"This holy season, fit to fast and pray" *(Amoretti,* XXII)

JUDITH KALIL. " 'Mask in Myrth Lyke to a Comedy': Spenser's Persona in the *Amoretti," Thoth* 13(2), Spring 1973, 22.

"Thrise happy she that is so well assured" *(Amoretti,* LIX)

F. W. BATESON. *English Poetry and the English Language,* pp. 32-33.

"When my abodes prefixed time is spent" *(Amoretti,* XLVI)

ROSEMOND TUVE. *Elizabethan and Metaphysical Imagery,* pp. 325-27.

"Ye tradefull merchants, that with weary toyle" *(Amoretti,* XV)

ALISTAIR FOWLER. *Conceitful Thought,* pp. 95-96.

ROSEMOND TUVE. *Elizabethan and Metaphysical Imagery,* pp. 64-65.

SPICER, JACK

" 'Arf,' says Sandy" ("Love Poem," III)

LARRY OAKNER. "Going Down With Williams: A De/ Structural Study of *Kora in Hell: Improvisations," Thoth* 16(1), Winter 1975-76, 29-30.

"Billy the Kid"

FRANK SADLER. "The Frontier in Jack Spicer's 'Billy the Kid,' " *Concerning Poetry* 9(2), Fall 1976, 15-21.

"The Book of Galahad"

PETER RILEY. "The Narratives of *The Holy Grail," Boundary 2* 6(1), Fall 1977, 183-85.

"The Book of Gawain"
  PETER RILEY. "The Narratives of *The Holy Grail*," *Boundary 2* 6(1), Fall 1977, 169-72.
"The Book of Gwenivere"
  PETER RILEY. "The Narratives of *The Holy Grail*," *Boundary 2* 6(1), Fall 1977, 176-80.
"The Book of Lancelot"
  PETER RILEY. "The Narratives of *The Holy Grail*," *Boundary 2* 6(1), Fall 1977, 175-76.
"The Book of Merlin"
  PETER RILEY. "The Narratives of *The Holy Grail*," *Boundary 2* 6(1), Fall 1977, 180-83.
"The Book of Percival"
  PETER RILEY. "The Narratives of *The Holy Grail*," *Boundary 2* 6(1), Fall 1977, 172-75.
"The Book of the Death of Arthur"
  PETER RILEY. "The Narratives of *The Holy Grail*," *Boundary 2* 6(1), Fall 1977, 185-89.
"Dash"
  MICHAEL DAVIDSON. "Incarnations of Jack Spicer: *Heads of the Town up to the Aether*," *Boundary 2* 6(1), Fall 1977, 110-11.
"Downbeat"
  JAMES LIDDY. "A Problem with Sparrows: Spicer's Last Stance," *Boundary 2* 6(1), Fall 1977, 265-66.
"Imaginary Elegy, I"
  SAMUEL CHARTERS. *Some Poems/Poets*, pp. 38-39.
"Imaginary Elegy, II"
  SAMUEL CHARTERS. *Some Poems/Poets*, pp. 39-41.
"Imaginary Elegy, III"
  SAMUEL CHARTERS. *Some Poems/Poets*, pp. 42-44.
"Imaginary Elegy, IV"
  SAMUEL CHARTERS. *Some Poems/Poets*, pp. 44-45.
"Mummer"
  JED RASULA. "Spicer's Orpheus and the Emancipation of Pronouns," *Boundary 2* 6(1), Fall 1977, 75-76.
"The Poem Rimbaud Wrote on October 20, 1869"
  MICHAEL DAVIDSON. "Incarnations of Jack Spicer: *Heads of the Town Up to the Aether*," *Boundary 2* 6(1), Fall 1977, 121-22.
"Poetry"
  JAMES LIDDY. "A Problem with Sparrows: Spicer's Last Stance," *Boundary 2* 6(1), Fall 1977, 262-63.
"Ramparts"
  JAMES LIDDY. "A Problem with Sparrows: Spicer's Last Stance," *Boundary 2* 6(1), Fall 1977, 264.
"A Red Wheelbarrow"
  JED RASULA. "Spicer's Orpheus and the Emancipation of Pronouns," *Boundary 2* 6(1), Fall 1977, 83-84.
"The St. Louis Sporting News"
  JAMES LIDDY. "A Problem with Sparrows: Spicer's Last Stance," *Boundary 2* 6(1), Fall 1977, 264-65.
"Sheep Trails Are Fateful to Strangers"
  MICHAEL DAVIDSON. "Incarnations of Jack Spicer: *Heads of the Town up to the Aether*," *Boundary 2* 6(1), Fall 1977, 116-17.
"The Territory Is Not the Map"
  MICHAEL DAVIDSON. "Incarnations of Jack Spicer: *Heads of the Town up to the Aether*," *Boundary 2* 6(1), Fall 1977, 115.

"A Textbook of Poetry"
  JED RASULA. "Spicer's Orpheus and the Emancipation of Pronouns," *Boundary 2* 6(1), Fall 1977, 58-59.
"Tish"
  JAMES LIDDY. "A Problem with Sparrows: Spicer's Last Stance," *Boundary 2* 6(1), Fall 1977, 263-64.
"Vancouver Festival"
  JAMES LIDDY. "A Problem with Sparrows: Spicer's Last Stance," *Boundary 2* 6(1), Fall 1977, 265.
"Wrong Turn"
  MICHAEL DAVIDSON. "Incarnations of Jack Spicer: *Heads of the Town Up to the Aether*," *Boundary 2* 6(1), Fall 1977, 117-18.

SPITZER, LEO

"Blow, Northern Wind"
  LEO SPITZER. *Essays on English and American Literature*, pp. 195-216.

STAFFORD, WILLIAM

"At Cove on the Crooked River"
  JOHN LAUBER. "World's Guest — William Stafford," *Iowa Review* 5(2), Spring 1974, 91-92.
"Boone Children"
  GEORGE S. LENSING and RONALD MORAN. *Four Poets and the Emotive Imagination*, p. 192.
"The Concealment: Ishi, the Last Wild Indian"
  JOHN LAUBER. "World's Guest — William Stafford," *Iowa Review* 5(2), Spring 1974, 89.
"Connections"
  GEORGE S. LENSING. "William Stafford, Mythmaker," *Modern Poetry Studies* 6(1), Spring 1975, 7-9.
  GEORGE S. LENSING and RONALD MORAN. *Four Poets and the Emotive Imagination*, pp. 205-7.
"A Documentary from America"
  GEORGE S. LENSING and RONALD MORAN. *Four Poets and the Emotive Imagination*, p. 201.
"Father and Son"
  LAURENCE LIEBERMAN. *Unassigned Frequencies*, p. 274.
"Fifteen"
  DENNIS DALEY LYNCH. "Journeys in Search of Oneself: The Metaphor of the Road in William Stafford's Traveling Through the Dark and The Rescued Year," *Modern Poetry Studies* 7(2), Autumn 1976, 129-30.
"Glimpse Between Buildings"
  ALBERTA T. TURNER. "William Stafford and the Surprise Cliché," *South Carolina Review* 7(2), April 1975, 28-30.
"Glimpses in the Woods"
  GEORGE S. LENSING and RONALD MORAN. *Four Poets and the Emotive Imagination*, p. 213.
"In California"
  JOHN LAUBER. "World's Guest — William Stafford," *Iowa Review* 5(2), Spring 1974, 94.
"In Fog"
  GEORGE S. LENSING and RONALD MORAN. *Four Poets and the Emotive Imagination*, pp. 182-83.
"Montana Eclogue"
  WILLIAM HEYEN. "William Stafford's Allegiances," *Modern Poetry Studies* 1(6), 1970, 311-13.

STAFFORD, WILLIAM *(Cont.)*

"The Move to California"

> JOHN LAUBER. "World's Guest — William Stafford," *Iowa Review* 5(2), Spring 1974, 92-93.
>
> DENNIS DALEY LYNCH. "Journeys in Search of Oneself: The Metaphor of the Road in William Stafford's Traveling Through the Dark and The Rescued Year," *Modern Poetry Studies* 7(2), Autumn 1976, 126.

"One Home"

> JOHN LAUBER. "World's Guest — William Stafford," *Iowa Review* 5(2), Spring 1974, 90-91.

"Parentage"

> GEORGE S. LENSING and RONALD MORAN. *Four Poets and the Emotive Imagination*, p. 189.

"Representing Far Places"

> RAYMOND BENOIT. *Single Nature's Double Name*, p. 127.

"Returned to Say"

> GEORGE S. LENSING and RONALD MORAN. *Four Poets and the Emotive Imagination*, pp. 193-94.

"Shadows"

> GEORGE S. LENSING. "William Stafford, Mythmaker," *Modern Poetry Studies* 6(1), Spring 1975, 9-13.

"Sophocles Says"

> ALBERTA T. TURNER. "William Stafford and the Surprise Cliché," *South Carolina Review* 7(2), April 1975, 30-32.

"Summer Will Rise"

> JOHN LAUBER. "World's Guest — William Stafford," *Iowa Review* 5(2), Spring 1974, 96.

"Traveling Through the Dark"

> CHARLES F. GREINER. "Stafford's 'Traveling Through the Dark': A Discussion of Style," *English Journal* 55(8), November 1966, 1015-18.
>
> GEORGE S. LENSING and RONALD MORAN. *Four Poets and the Emotive Imagination*, pp. 198-200.
>
> LAURENCE LIEBERMAN. "Robert Sward: A Mysticism of Objects," *Carleton Miscellany* 8(2), Spring 1967, 20-28.
>
> DENNIS DALEY LYNCH. "Journeys in Search of Oneself: The Metaphor of the Road in William Stafford's Traveling Through the Dark and The Rescued Year," *Modern Poetry Studies* 7(2), Autumn 1976, 128-29.

"Watching the Jet Planes Dive"

> GEORGE S. LENSING and RONALD MORAN. *Four Poets and the Emotive Imagination*, p. 212.

STANLEY, THOMAS

"The Idolator"

> A. J. SMITH. "The Failure of Love: Love Lyrics after Donne," in *Metaphysical Poetry*, edited by Malcolm Bradbury and David Palmer, p. 44.

"On a Violet in her Breast"

> A. J. SMITH. "The Failure of Love: Love Lyrics after Donne," in *Metaphysical Poetry*, edited by Malcolm Bradbury and David Palmer, pp. 45-46.

"To Mr. W. Hammond"

> EARL MINER. *The Cavalier Mode from Jonson to Cotton*, p. 253.

STANTON, MAURA

"Crabs"

> GREGORY ORR. "On Maura Stanton's Poems," *Iowa Review* 4(4), Fall 1973, 97-99.

"The First Child"

> GREGORY ORR. "On Maura Stanton's Poems," *Iowa Review* 4(4), Fall 1973, 97-99.

STANTON, WILL

"Dandelions"

> LAURENCE PERRINE. *100 American Poems of the Twentieth Century*, pp. 282-84.

STEERE, RICHARD

"Earth Felicities, Heavens Allowances"

> ROBERT DALY. *God's Altar*, pp. 12-20.

"Monumental Memorial of Marine Mercy & c."

> ROBERT DALY. *God's Altar*, pp. 145-47.
>
> ROGER B. STEIN. "Seascape and the American Imagination: The Puritan Seventeenth Century," *Early American Literature* 7(1), Spring 1972, 31-33.

STEFANILE, FELIX N.

"That Underground Sun"

> GEORGE ABBE. *You and Contemporary Poetry*, pp. 22-24; second ed., pp. 29-32.

STEIN, GERTRUDE

"A Box"

> JONATHAN C. GEORGE. *Explicator* 31(6), February 1973, Item 42.

"Guillaume Apollinaire"

> MICHAEL J. HOFFMAN. "Gertrude Stein's 'Portraits,' " *Twentieth Century Literature* 11(3), October 1965, 120-21.

"Irma"

> MICHAEL J. HOFFMAN. "Gertrude Stein's 'Portraits,' " *Twentieth Century Literature* 11(3), October 1965, 120.

"Lipschitz"

> HARRY R. GARVIN. *Explicator* 14(3), December 1955, Item 18.

"A Long Dress"

> RUTH H. BRADY. *Explicator* 34(6), February 1976, Item 47.

"This Is This Dress, Aider"

> NEIL SCHMITZ. "Gertrude Stein as Post-Modernist: The Rhetoric of *Tender Buttons*," *Journal of Modern Literature* 3(5), July 1974, 1211-12.

STEINGASS, DAVID

"Japanese TV"

> ROBERT PINSKY. *The Situation of Poetry*, pp. 108-9.

STEPHENS, ALAN

"The Death of a Buffalo"

> ROBERT PINSKY. *The Situation of Poetry*, pp. 55-56.

"Desert"

> DONALD W. MARKOS. "Alan Stephens: The Lineaments of the Real," *Southern Review*, n.s., 11(2), Spring 1975, 348.

"The dragon of things"
DONALD W. MARKOS. "Alan Stephens: The Lineaments of the Real," *Southern Review*, n.s., 11(2), Spring 1975, 346-47.

"Epilogue: The Heresies"
DONALD W. MARKOS. "Alan Stephens: The Lineaments of the Real," *Southern Review*, n.s., 11(2), Spring 1975, 342-43.

"First twenty-four hours"
DONALD W. MARKOS. "Alan Stephens: The Lineaments of the Real," *Southern Review*, n.s., 11(2), Spring 1975, 351-53.

"The Green Cape with Voices"
DONALD W. MARKOS. "Alan Stephens: The Lineaments of the Real," *Southern Review*, n.s., 11(2), Spring 1975, 349-51.

"Homily"
DONALD W. MARKOS. "Alan Stephens: The Lineaments of the Real," *Southern Review*, n.s., 11(2), Spring 1975, 335-36.

"Lore"
DONALD W. MARKOS. "Alan Stephens: The Lineaments of the Real," *Southern Review*, n.s., 11(2), Spring 1975, 348-49.

"The open world"
DONALD W. MARKOS. "Alan Stephens: The Lineaments of the Real," *Southern Review*, n.s., 11(2), Spring 1975, 338-41.

"The Three Sisters"
DONALD W. MARKOS. "Alan Stephens: The Lineaments of the Real," *Southern Review*, n.s., 11(2), Spring 1975, 347-48.

"Tree Meditation"
DONALD W. MARKOS. "Alan Stephens: The Lineaments of the Real," *Southern Review*, n.s., 11(2), Spring 1975, 353-55.

"Viatic"
DONALD W. MARKOS. "Alan Stephens: The Lineaments of the Real," *Southern Review*, n.s., 11(2), Spring 1975, 336-37.

"A Walk in the Void"
DONALD W. MARKOS. "Alan Stephens: The Lineaments of the Real," *Southern Review*, n.s., 11(2), Spring 1975, 333-35.

"What I will think of as the white dog truth"
DONALD W. MARKOS. "Alan Stephens: The Lineaments of the Real," *Southern Review*, n.s., 11(2), Spring 1975, 345-46.

STEPHENS, JAMES

"The Autumn in Ireland: 1915"
BARTON R. FRIEDMAN. "Returning to Ireland's Fountains: Nationalism and James Stephens," *Arizona Quarterly* 22(3), Autumn 1966, 236-39.

"The Goat Paths"
CLEANTH BROOKS and ROBERT PENN WARREN. *Understanding Poetry*, third ed., pp. 282-83.
GEOFFREY THURLEY. *The Ironic Harvest*, pp. 179-80.

"Inis Fál"
BARTON R. FRIEDMAN. "Returning to Ireland's Fountains: Nationalism and James Stephens," *Arizona Quarterly* 22(3), Autumn 1966, 244-45.

"Little Things"
NAT HENRY. *Explicator* 9(3), December 1950, Item 20.
LYSANDER KEMP. *Explicator* 8(7), May 1950, Item 50. (P)

"The Main-Deep"
CLEANTH BROOKS and ROBERT PENN WARREN. *Understanding Poetry*, pp. 170-73; revised ed., pp. 74-77; third ed., pp. 83-86.
FRED B. MILLETT, ARTHUR W. HOFFMAN and DAVID R. CLARK. *Reading Poetry*, second ed., pp. 12-13.

"Odell"
BARTON R. FRIEDMAN. "Returning to Ireland's Fountains: Nationalism and James Stephens," *Arizona Quarterly* 22(3), Autumn 1966, 245-47.

"The Rivals"
LLOYD FRANKENBERG. *Invitation to Poetry*, pp. 57-58.

"The Spring in Ireland: 1916"
BARTON R. FRIEDMAN. "Returning to Ireland's Fountains: Nationalism and James Stephens," *Arizona Quarterly* 22(3), Autumn 1966, 235-42.

STEVENS, WALLACE

"Academic Discourse at Havana"
KIMON FRIAR and JOHN MALCOLM BRINNIN. *Modern Poetry*, p. 537.

"All the Preludes to Felicity"
THOMAS B. WHITBREAD. "The Poet-Readers of Wallace Stevens," in *In Defense of Reading*, pp. 97-99.

"The American Sublime"
HELEN VENDLER. "Wallace Stevens: The False and True Sublime," *Southern Review*, n.s., 7(3), Summer 1971, 683-84.

"Americana"
DWIGHT EDDINS. "Wallace Stevens: America the Primordial," *Modern Language Quarterly* 32(1), March 1971, 79-80.

"Analysis of a Theme"
KATHLEEN A. DALE. "Extensions: Beyond Resemblance and the Pleasure Principle in Wallace Stevens' Supreme Fiction," *Boundary 2* 4(1), Fall 1975, 268-70.
MONROE K. SPEARS. *Space Against Time in Modern American Poetry*, pp. 20-21.

"Anatomy of Monotony"
FRANK DOGGETT. "Our Number is Her Nature," in *The Twenties*, edited by Richard E. Langford and William E. Taylor, p. 41.

"Anecdote of Men by the Thousand"
SISTER M. BERNETTA QUINN. *The Metamorphic Tradition*, p. 77.

"Anecdote of the Abnormal"
SAMUEL FRENCH MORSE. "Wallace Stevens, Bergson, Pater," *ELH* 31(1), March 1964, 16-17.

"Anecdote of the Jar"
GÉMINO H. ABAD. *A Formal Approach to Lyric Poetry*, pp. 145-47.
HOWARD BAKER. "Wallace Stevens and Other Poets," *Southern Review* 1(2), Autumn 1935, 376-77.
HAROLD BLOOM. "The Necessity of Misreading," *Georgia Review* 29(2), Summer 1975, 277-78.
JOHN WILLIAM CORRINGTON. "Wallace Stevens and the Problem of Order: A Study of Three Poems," *Arlington Quarterly* 1(4), Summer 1968, 56-61.

STEVENS, WALLACE *(Cont.)*

"Anecdote of the Jar" *(cont.)*

SISTER MADELINE DEFREES. "Pegasus and Six Blind Indians," *English Journal* 59(7), October 1970, 935.

DON GEIGER. "Wallace Stevens' Wealth," *Perspective* 7(3), Autumn 1954, 160.

ROBERT HASS. "Wendell Berry: Finding the Land," *Modern Poetry Studies* 2(1), 1971, 32-33.

SAMUEL JAY KEYSER. "Wallace Stevens: Form and Meaning in Four Poems," *College English* 37(6), February 1976, 585-89.

J. P. KIRBY. *Explicator* 3(2), November 1944, Item 16.

MURRAY KRIEGER. "*Ekphrasis* and the Still Movement of Poetry; or *Laokoön* Revisited," in *The Poet as Critic,* pp. 24-25.

PATRICIA MERIVALE. "Wallace Stevens' 'Jar': The Absurd Detritus of Romantic Myth," *College English* 26(7), April 1965, 527-32.

MARGARET PETERSON. "*Harmonium* and William James," *Southern Review,* n.s., 7(3), Summer 1971, 676-77.

M. L. ROSENTHAL. *The Modern Poets,* pp. 125-26.

GEORGE STEINER. "On Difficulty," *Journal of Aesthetics and Art Criticism* 36(3), Spring 1978, 272-73.

WILLIAM C. STEPHENSON and WARWICK WADLINGTON. " 'Deep Within The Reader's Eye' With Wallace Stevens," *Wallace Stevens Journal* 2(3-4), Fall 1978, 21-33.

NANCY SULLIVAN. "Perspective and the Poetic Process," *Wisconsin Studies in Contemporary Literature* 6(1), Winter-Spring 1965, 124-25.

WILLIAM YORK TINDALL. "Wallace Stevens," in *Seven Modern American Poets,* pp. 62-63.

CHARLES CHILD WALCUTT. "Interpreting the Symbol," *College English* 14(8), May 1953, 447-49.

YVOR WINTERS. *Anatomy of Nonsense,* pp. 93-95. Reprinted in: Yvor Winters. *In Defense of Reason,* pp. 435-37.

"Annual Gaiety"

JUSTUS GEORGE LAWLER. *The Christian Image,* pp. 111-15.

"The Apostrophe to Vincentine"

FRANK DOGGETT. "Wallace Stevens and the World We Know," *English Journal* 48(7), October 1959, 369-70.

SISTER M. BERNETTA QUINN. *The Metamorphic Tradition,* pp. 75-76.

SISTER M. BERNETTA QUINN. "Metamorphosis in Wallace Stevens," *Sewanee Review* 60(2), Spring 1952, 243-44.

"Arcades of Philadelphia the Past"

R. D. ACKERMAN. *Explicator* 24(9), May 1966, Item 80.

PAUL SANDERS. *Explicator* 25(9), May 1967, Item 72.

"Arrival at the Waldorf"

ROBERT MOLLINGER. *Explicator* 31(5), January 1973, Item 40.

"Artificial Populations"

ROY HARVEY PEARCE. *Historicism Once More,* pp. 284-85.

"As You Leave the Room"

ROY HARVEY PEARCE. "Wallace Stevens: The Last Lesson of the Master," *ELH* 31(1), March 1964, 75-77. Reprinted in: Roy Harvey Pearce. *Historicism Once More,* pp. 280-83.

FRED MILLER ROBINSON. "Poems That Took the Place of Mountains: Realization in Stevens and Cézanne," *Centennial Review* 22(3), Summer 1978, 295-96.

"Asides on the Oboe"

MERLE E. BROWN. "A Critical Performance of 'Asides on the Oboe,' " *Journal of Aesthetics and Art Criticism* 29(1), Fall 1970, 121-28.

JUSTUS GEORGE LAWLER. *The Christian Image,* pp. 122-30.

JOHN F. LYNEN. "Forms of Time in Modern Poetry," *Queen's Quarterly* 82(3), Autumn 1975, 348-49.

ROBERT N. MOLLINGER. "Wallace Stevens' Search for the Central Man," *Tennessee Studies in Literature* 21 (1976), 72-74.

GROSVENOR E. POWELL. "Of Heroes and Nobility: The Personae of Wallace Stevens," *Southern Review,* n.s., 7(3), Summer 1971, 739-41.

HI SIMONS. "The Genre of Wallace Stevens," *Sewanee Review* 53(4), Autumn 1945, 570-79.

KARL P. WENTERSDORF. "Wallace Stevens, Dante Alighieri, and the Emperor," *Twentieth Century Literature* 13(4), January 1968, 198-99.

"The Auroras of Autumn"

JOSEPH WARREN BEACH. *Obsessive Images,* pp. 338-40.

MICHAEL T. BEEHLER. "Inversion/Subversion: Strategy in Stevens' 'The Auroras of Autumn,' " *Genre* 11(4), Winter 1978, 627-51.

ROBERT J. BERTHOLF. "Renewing the Set: Wallace Stevens' 'The Auroras of Autumn,' " *Ball State University Forum* 17(2), Spring 1976, 37-45.

HAROLD BLOOM. "The Central Man: Emerson, Whitman, Wallace Stevens," *Massachusetts Review* 7(1), Winter 1966, 38-41.

HAROLD BLOOM. *A Map of Misreading,* pp. 186-92.

PETER L. MCNAMARA. "Wallace Stevens' Autumnal Doctrine," *Renascence* 26(2), Winter 1974, 72-82.

ROBERT PACK. "Wallace Stevens' Sufficient Muse," *Southern Review,* n.s., 11(4), Autumn 1975, 770.

RICHARD F. PATTESON. "The Failure of Consolation in *The Auroras of Autumn,*" *Concerning Poetry* 8(2), Fall 1975, 37-46.

JOSEPH N. RIDDEL. "Wallace Stevens' 'Visibility of Thought,' " *PMLA* 77(4), September 1962, 486-88.

"The Auroras of Autumn, II"

FRANK DOGGETT. "The Poet of the Earth: Wallace Stevens," *College English* 22(6), March 1961, 378-80.

"Autumn Refrain"

TERRANCE KING. *Explicator* 36(4), Summer 1978, 19-20.

ROBERT PACK. "Wallace Stevens' Sufficient Muse," *Southern Review,* n.s., 11(4), Autumn 1975, 771-73.

"Ballade of the Pink Parasol"

ROBERT BUTTEL. "Wallace Stevens at Harvard: Some Origins of His Theme and Style," *ELH* 29(1), March 1962, 113-18.

"Bantams in Pine-Woods"

MARIUS BEWLEY. "The Poetry of Wallace Stevens," *Partisan Review* 16(9), September 1949, 898-905.

MARIO L. D'AVANZO. "Emerson and Shakespeare in Stevens's 'Bantams in Pine-Woods,' " *American Literature* 49(1), March 1977, 103-7.

RICHARD M. GOLLIN. "Wallace Stevens: the poet in society," *Colorado Quarterly* 9(1), Summer 1960, 52-53.

MILDRED E. HARTSOCK. *Explicator* 18(6), March 1960, Item 33.

MILDRED E. HARTSOCK. "Image and Idea in the Poetry of Stevens," *Twentieth Century Litrature* 7(1), April 1961, 16.

WILLIAM VAN O'CONNOR. "Wallace Stevens on 'The Poems of Our Climate,'" *University of Kansas City Review* 15(2), Winter 1948, 106-7.

FRED H. STOCKING. *Explicator* 3(6), April 1945, Item 45.

HAROLD E. TOLIVER. *Pastoral Forms and Attitudes,* p. 308.

"The Bed of Old John Zeller"

JOSEPH N. RIDDEL. "The Metaphysical Changes of Stevens' 'Esthétique du Mal,'" *Twentieth Century Literature* 7(2), July 1961, 65-66.

JOY M. SEMEL. "Pennsylvania Dutch Country: Stevens' World as Meditation," *Contemporary Literature* 14(3), Summer 1973, 317-18.

"Bethou me, said sparrow, to the crackled blade" (Notes Toward a Supreme Fiction, "It Must Change," VI)

FRANK DOGGETT. *Explicator* 15(5), February 1957, Item 30.

"The Bird with the Coppery, Keen Claws"

LOUIS H. LEITER. "Sense in Nonsense: Wallace Stevens' 'The Bird with the Coppery, Keen Claws,'" *College English* 26(7), April 1965, 551-54.

MARGARET PETERSON. "*Harmonium* and William James," *Southern Review,* n.s., 7(3), Summer 1971, 664-67.

"Blanche McCarthy"

HAROLD BLOOM. *A Map of Misreading,* p. 25.

HAROLD BLOOM. "Poetic Crossing, II: American Stances," *Georgia Review* 30(4), Winter 1976, 790-92.

"The Bouquet"

STEVEN FOSTER. "The *Gestalt* Configurations of Wallace Stevens," *Modern Language Quarterly* 28(1), March 1967, 75-76.

GEORGE McFADDEN. "Poet, Nature, and Society in Wallace Stevens," *Modern Language Quarterly* 23(3), September 1962, 269-70.

"Bouquet of Roses in Sunlight"

KATHLEEN A. DALE. "Extensions: Beyond Resemblance and the Pleasure Principle in Wallace Stevens' Supreme Fiction," *Boundary 2* 4(1), Fall 1975, 265-66.

"Certain Phenomena of Sound"

WILLIAM H. HEATH. *Explicator* 12(3), December 1953, Item 16.

TERRANCE J. KING. "'Certain Phenomena of Sound': An Illustration of Wallace Stevens' Poetry of Words," *Texas Studies in Literature and Language* 20(4), Winter 1978, 599-614.

"A Child Asleep in Its Own Life"

ROY HARVEY PEARCE. *The Continuity of American Poetry,* p. 419.

"Chocorua to Its Neighbor"

JAMES E. MULQUEEN. "Man and Cosmic Man in the Poetry of Wallace Stevens," *South Dakota Review* 11(2), Summer 1973, 17-19.

ROBERT PACK. "The Abstracting Imagination of Wallace Stevens: Nothingness and the Hero," *Arizona Quarterly* 11(3), Autumn 1955, 206-9.

ROY HARVEY PEARCE. *The Continuity of American Poetry,* p. 393.

"A Clear Day and No Memories"

WILLIAM BEVIS. "Stevens' Toneless Poetry," *ELH* 41(2), Summer 1974, 269-70.

RICHARD BLESSING. "Wallace Stevens and the Necessary Reader: A Technique of Dynamism," *Twentieth Century Literature* 18(4), October 1972, 255-56.

"The Comedian as the Letter C"

RICHARD P. ADAMS. "'The Comedian as the Letter C': A Somewhat Literal Reading," *Tulane Studies in English* 18 (1970), 95-114.

HOWARD BAKER. "Wallace Stevens and Other Poets," *Southern Review* 1(2), Autumn 1955, 377-78.

JAMES BENZIGER. *Images of Eternity,* pp. 236-37.

R. P. BLACKMUR. "Examples of Wallace Stevens," *Hound and Horn* 5(2), January-March 1932, 248-55. Reprinted in: R. P. Blackmur. *Language as Gesture,* pp. 243-49. Also: R. P. Blackmur. *The Double Agent,* pp. 94-102. Also: R. P. Blackmur. *Form and Value in Modern Poetry,* pp. 206-12.

ELEANOR COOK. "Wallace Stevens: *The Comedian as the Letter C,*" *American Literature* 49(2), May 1977, 192-205.

J. V. CUNNINGHAM. "The Poetry of Wallace Stevens," *Poetry* 75(3), December 1949, 154-59. Reprinted in: *Modern Literary Criticism,* pp. 356-60.

GUY DAVENPORT. "Spinoza's Tulips: A Commentary on 'The Comedian as the Letter C,'" *Perspective* 7(3), Autumn 1954, 147-54.

L. S. DEMBO. *Conceptions of Reality in Modern American Poetry,* pp. 87-90.

FRANK DOGGETT. "Our Number is Her Nature," in *The Twenties,* edited by Richard E. Langford and William E. Taylor, pp. 39-40.

DENIS DONOGHUE. *Connoisseurs of Chaos,* pp. 204-5.

BERNARD DUFFEY. *Poetry in America,* pp. 318-20.

JOHN J. ENCK. "Stevens' Crispin as the Clown," *Texas Studies in Literature and Language* 3(3), Autumn 1961, 389-98.

LLOYD FRANKENBERG. *Pleasure Dome,* pp. 210-15.

PHILIP FURIA and MARTIN ROTH. "Stevens' Fusky Alphabet," *PMLA* 93(1), January 1978, 72-76.

DON GEIGER. "Wallace Stevens' Wealth," *Perspective* 7(3), Autumn 1954, 165.

EDWARD GUERESCHI. "'The Comedian as the Letter C': Wallace Stevens' Anti-Mythological Poem," *Centennial Review* 8(4), Fall 1964, 465-77.

FREDERICK J. HOFFMAN. *The Twenties,* pp. 183-85; revised ed., pp. 213-16.

GRAHAM HOUGH. "The Poetry of Wallace Stevens," *Critical Quarterly* 2(3), Autumn 1960, 209-10.

R. W. B. LEWIS. "Hart Crane and the Clown Tradition," *Massachusetts Review* 4(4), Summer 1963, 761-62.

J. HILLIS MILLER. *Poets of Reality,* p. 221.

ROBERT N. MOLLINGER. "Wallace Stevens' Search for the Central Man," *Tennessee Studies in Literature* 21 (1976), 67-69.

SAMUEL FRENCH MORSE. "Wallace Stevens, Bergson, Pater," *ELH* 31(1), March 1964, 23-34.

FRANCIS MURPHY. "'The Comedian as the Letter C,'" *Wisconsin Studies in Contemporary Literature* 3(2), Spring-Summer 1962, 79-99.

WILLIAM VAN O'CONNOR. *Sense and Sensibility in Modern Poetry,* pp. 141-42.

WILLIAM VAN O'CONNOR. "Wallace Stevens on 'The Poems of Our Climate,'" *University of Kansas City Review* 15(2), Winter 1948, 109.

STEVENS, WALLACE (*Cont.*)

"The Comedian as the Letter C" (*cont.*)

ROY HARVEY PEARCE. *The Continuity of American Poetry*, pp. 387-89, 424-26.

A. POULIN, JR. "Crispin as Everyman as Adam: 'The Comedian as the Letter C,' " *Concerning Poetry* 5(1), Spring 1972, 5-23.

JOHN N. SERIO. " 'The Comedian' as the Idea of Order in *Harmonium*," *Papers on Language and Literature* 12(1), Winter 1976, 87-104.

JOHN N. SERIO. "Stevens' 'Affair of Places,' " *Wallace Stevens Journal* 2(1-2), Spring 1978, 26-29.

HI SIMONS. " 'The Comedian as the Letter C': Its Sense and Its Significance," *Southern Review* 5(3), Winter 1940, 453-68.

FRED H. STOCKING. *Explicator* 3(5), March 1945, Item 43.

WILLIAM YORK TINDALL. "Wallace Stevens," in *Seven Modern American Poets*, pp. 63-65.

HYATT H. WAGGONER. *American Poets*, pp. 432-33.

YVOR WINTERS. *Anatomy of Nonsense*, pp. 98-103. Reprinted in: Yvor Winters. *In Defense of Reason*, pp. 439-44.

"A Completely New Set of Objects"

FRANK DOGGETT. "Stevens on the Genesis of a Poem," *Contemporary Literature* 16(4), Autumn 1975, 469-70.

LAWRENCE KRAMER. " 'A Completely New Set of Objects': Wallace Stevens and Charles Ives," *Wallace Stevens Journal* 2(3-4), Fall 1978, 6-7.

JOY M. SEMEL. "Pennsylvania Dutch Country: Stevens' World as Meditation," *Contemporary Literature* 14(3), Summer 1973, 316-17.

"Connoisseur of Chaos"

GÉMINO H. ABAD. *A Formal Approach to Lyric Poetry*, pp. 148-51.

DENIS DONOGHUE. *Connoisseurs of Chaos*, p. 23.

KIMON FRIAR and JOHN MALCOLM BRINNIN. *Modern Poetry*, pp. 536-37.

PHILIP FURIA and MARTIN ROTH. "Stevens' Fusky Alphabet," *PMLA* 93(1), January 1978, 72.

HOWARD NEMEROV. *Poetry and Fiction*, pp. 77-78.

LISA STEINMAN. "Figure and Figuration in Stevens' Long Poems," *Wallace Stevens Journal* 1(1), Spring 1977, 11-13.

"Conversation with Three Women of New England"

ROY HARVEY PEARCE. "Wallace Stevens: The Last Lesson of the Master," *ELH* 31(1), March 1964, 77-79.

"Cortège for Rosenbloom"

RICHARD ELLMANN. "Wallace Stevens' Ice-Cream," *Kenyon Review* 19(1), Winter 1957, 90-92. Reprinted in: *Aspects of American Poetry*, pp. 205-7.

"The Course of a Particular"

WILLIAM BEVIS. "Stevens' Toneless Poetry," *ELH* 41(2), Summer 1974, 273-75.

RICHARD BLESSING. "Wallace Stevens and the Necessary Reader: A Technique of Dynamism," *Twentieth Century Literature* 18(4), October 1972, 256.

SIGURD BURCKHARDT. "Poetry, Language, and the Condition of Modern Man," *Centennial Review* 4(1), Winter 1960, 9-13.

KENNETH FIELDS. "Postures of the Nerves: Reflections of the Nineteenth Century in the Poems of Wallace Stevens," *Southern Review*, n.s., 7(3), Summer 1971, 807, 809-10.

ROBERT PACK. "The Abstracting Imagination of Wallace Stevens: Nothingness and the Hero," *Arizona Quarterly* 11(3), Autumn 1955, 198-99. (P)

JOHN N. SERIO. "Stevens as a Connoisseur of Chaos," *Notes on Modern American Literature* 2(3), Summer 1978, Item 21.

"The Creations of Sound"

FRANK DOGGETT. "Stevens on the Genesis of a Poem," *Contemporary Literature* 16(4), Autumn 1975, 467, 473-75.

"Credences of Summer"

ROBERT J. BERTHOLF. "The Revolving Toward Myth: Stevens' 'Credences of Summer,' " *Bucknell Review* 22(2), Fall 1976, 216-29.

SANDY COHEN. "A Calculus of the Cycle: Wallace Stevens' 'Credences of Summer,' an Alternate View," *Ball State University Forum* 17(2), Spring 1976, 31-36.

BERNARD HERINGMAN. "The Poetry of Synthesis," *Perspective* 7(3), Autumn 1954, 171-74.

J. DENNIS HUSTON. "*Credences of Summer*: An Analysis," *Modern Philology* 67(3), February 1970, 263-72.

GEORGE S. LENSING. " 'Credences of Summer': Wallace Stevens' Secular Mysticism," *Wallace Stevens Journal* 1(1), Spring 1977, 3-9.

ISABEL G. MACCAFFREY. "The Other Side of Silence: 'Credences of Summer' as an Example," *Modern Language Quarterly* 30(3), September 1969, 417-38.

RALPH J. MILLS, JR. "Wallace Stevens: The Image of the Rock," *Accent* 18(2), Spring 1958, 77-78, 81-82.

JOHN N. SERIO. "Stevens' 'Affair of Places,' " *Wallace Stevens Journal* 2(1-2), Spring 1978, 29-31.

WILLIAM YORK TINDALL. "Wallace Stevens," in *Seven Modern American Poets*, pp. 79-80.

HAROLD H. WATTS. "Wallace Stevens and the Rock of Summer," *Kenyon Review* 14(1), Winter 1952, 122-24. (P)

JUDITH WEISSMAN. "Stevens's war poems: 'And is their logic to outweigh McDonagh's bony thumb?' " *Critical Quarterly* 20(2), Summer 1978, 52-55.

"The Curtains in the House of the Metaphysician"

ARTHUR C. MCGILL. *The Celebration of Flesh*, pp. 152-54.

"Dance of the Macabre Mice"

JAMES REEVES and MARTIN SEYMOUR-SMITH. *Inside Poetry*, pp. 53-54.

"The Death of a Soldier"

R. P. BLACKMUR. "Examples of Wallace Stevens," *Hound and Horn* 5(2), January-March 1932, 229-30. (P) Reprinted in: R. P. Blackmur. *The Double Agent*, pp. 74-75.

SAMUEL JAY KEYSER. "Wallace Stevens: Form and Meaning in Four Poems," *College English* 37(6), February 1976, 578-84.

JAMES MCMICHAEL. "The Wallace Stevens Vulgates," *Southern Review*, n.s., 7(3), Summer 1971, 701-4.

"Depression Before Spring"

ROBERT J. BERTHOLF. "The Revolving Toward Myth: Stevens' 'Credences of Summer,' " *Bucknell Review* 22(2), Fall 1976, 210-11.

"Description without Place"

MICHAEL T. BEEHLER. "Meteoric Poetry: Wallace Stevens' 'Description Without Place,' " *Criticism* 19(3), Summer 1977, 241-59.

THOMAS J. HINES. "Stevens' Poetry of Being in 'Description without Place,' " *Wallace Stevens Journal* 1(2), Summer 1977, 57-63.

ROBERT PACK. "The Abstracting Imagination of Wallace Stevens: Nothingness and the Hero," *Arizona Quarterly* 11(3), Autumn 1955, 199-200.

GROSVENOR E. POWELL. "Of Heroes and Nobility: The Personae of Wallace Stevens," *Southern Review,* n.s., 7(3), Summer 1971, 746-47. (P)

"Disillusionment of Ten O'Clock"

JOHN WILLIAM CORRINGTON. "Wallace Stevens and the Problem of Order: A Study of Three Poems," *Arlington Quarterly* 1(4), Summer 1968, 52-54.

MORRIS GREENHUT. "Sources of Obscurity in Modern Poetry: The Examples of Eliot, Stevens, and Tate," *Centennial Review* 7(2), Spring 1963, 179-81.

MARGARET PETERSON. "*Harmonium* and William James," *Southern Review,* n.s., 7(3), Summer 1971, 669-72.

"The Doctor of Geneva"

MARGARET PETERSON. "*Harmonium* and William James," *Southern Review,* n.s., 7(3), Summer 1971, 667.

"Domination of Black"

HAROLD BLOOM. "Poetic Crossing: Rhetoric and Psychology," *Georgia Review* 30(3), Fall 1976, 495-524.

FRANK DOGGETT. "Our Number is Her Nature," in *The Twenties,* edited by Richard E. Langford and William E. Taylor, p. 36.

JAMES MCMICHAEL. "The Wallace Stevens Vulgates," *Southern Review,* n.s., 7(3), Summer 1971, 706-12.

DOROTHY PETITT. " 'Domination of Black': A Study in Involvement," *English Journal* 51(5), May 1962, 347-48.

WILLIAM JOSEPH ROONEY. " 'Spelt from Sibyl's Leaves' — A Study in Contrasting Methods of Evaluation," *Journal of Aesthetics and Art Criticism* 13(4), June 1955, 511-14.

"Dry loaf"

JUDITH WEISSMAN. "Stevens's war poems: 'And is their logic to outweigh McDonagh's bony thumb?' " *Critical Quarterly* 20(2), Summer 1978, 40.

"A Duck for Dinner"

DONALD SHEEHAN. "Wallace Stevens in the 30s: Gaudy Bosh and the Gesture's Whim," in *The Thirties,* pp. 153-54.

"Dutch Graves in Bucks Country"

JOY M. SEMEL. "Pennsylvania Dutch Country: Stevens' World as Meditation," *Contemporary Literature* 14(3), Summer 1973, 318-19.

"The Dwarf"

ROBERT J. BERTHOLF. "The Revolving Toward Myth: Stevens' 'Credences of Summer,' " *Bucknell Review* 22(2), Fall 1976, 212-14.

ROBERT PACK. "The Abstracting Imagination of Wallace Stevens: Nothingness and the Hero," *Arizona Quarterly* 11(3), Autumn 1955, 197-98.

"Earthy Anecdote"

GEORGE BETAR. *Explicator* 22(6), February 1964, Item 43.

LLOYD FRANKENBERG. *Pleasure Dome,* pp. 198-99.

J. HILLIS MILLER. *Poets of Reality,* pp. 234-35.

HUGH L. SMITH. *Explicator* 24(4), December 1965, Item 37.

HYATT H. WAGGONER. *American Poets,* p. 432.

"The Emperor of Ice-Cream"

R. P. BLACKMUR. "Examples of Wallace Stevens," *Hound and Horn* 5(2), January-March 1932, 230-32. Reprinted in: R. P. Blackmur. *The Double Agent,* pp. 75-77. Also: R. P. Blackmur. *Language as Gesture,* pp. 227-29. Also: R. P. Blackmur. *Form and Value in Modern Poetry,* pp. 190-91. Also: Chad and Eva T. Walsh. *Twice Ten,* pp. 224-25.

HARRY BROWN and JOHN MILSTEAD. *What the Poem Means,* pp. 224-25.

TAYLOR CULBERT and JOHN M. VIOLETTE. "Wallace Stevens' Emperor," *Criticism* 2(1), Winter 1960, 38-47.

SISTER MADELINE DEFREES. "Pegasus and Six Blind Indians," *English Journal* 59(7), October 1970, 933-34.

ELIZABETH DREW and JOHN L. SWEENEY. *Directions in Modern Poetry,* pp. 227-31. Abridged in: *The Case for Poetry,* p. 341.

RICHARD ELLMANN. "Wallace Stevens' Ice-Cream," *Kenyon Review* 19(1), Winter 1957, 92-95. Reprinted in: *Aspects of American Poetry,* pp. 207-10.

KIMON FRIAR and JOHN MALCOLM BRINNIN. *Modern Poetry,* p. 538.

KENNETH LASH. *Explicator* 6(6), April 1948, Item 36.

EDWARD NEILL. "The Melting Moment: Stevens' Rehabilitation of Ice Cream," *Ariel* 4(1), January 1973, 88-96.

ELDER OLSON. "The Poetry of Wallace Stevens," *College English* 16(7), April 1955, 397-98.

MARGARET PETERSON. "*Harmonium* and William James," *Southern Review,* n.s., 7(3), Summer 1971, 669-71.

JAMES REEVES and MARTIN SEYMOUR-SMITH. *Inside Poetry,* pp. 84-88.

M. L. ROSENTHAL. *The Modern Poets,* pp. 129-30.

STUART SILVERMAN. "The Emperor of Ice Cream," *Western Humanities Review* 26(2), Spring 1972, 165-68.

WILLIAM BYSSHE STEIN. "Stevens' '*The Emperor of Ice-Cream*': The Requiem of the Romantic Muse," *Notes on Modern American Literature* 1(2), Spring 1977, Item 9.

ROBERT THACKABERRY. *Explicator* 6(6), April 1948, Item 36. Abridged in: *The Case for Poetry,* p. 342.

WILLIAM YORK TINDALL. "Wallace Stevens," in *Seven Modern American Poets,* pp. 57-58.

HAROLD E. TOLIVER. *Pastoral Forms and Attitudes,* pp. 306-7.

KARL P. WENTERSDORF. "Wallace Stevens, Dante Alighieri, and the Emperor," *Twentieth Century Literature* 13(4), January 1968, 199-203.

MICHAEL ZIMMERMAN. "Wallace Stevens' Emperor," *English Language Notes* 4(2), December 1966, 119-23.

"Esthétique du Mal"

ROBERT J. BERTHOLF. "Parables and Wallace Stevens' 'Esthétique du Mal,' " *ELH* 42(4), Winter 1975, 669-89.

FRANK DOGGETT. "The Poet of the Earth: Wallace Stevens," *College English* 22(6), March 1961, 376-77.

DENIS DONOGHUE. *Connoisseurs of Chaos,* pp. 206-7.

BERNARD DUFFEY. *Poetry in America,* pp. 323-26.

RICHARD ELLMANN. "Wallace Stevens' Ice-Cream," *Kenyon Review* 19(1), Winter 1957, 100-1. Reprinted in: *Aspects of American Poetry,* pp. 215-17.

STEVENS, WALLACE *(Cont.)*

"Esthétique du Mal" *(cont.)*

    LLOYD FRANKENBERG. *Pleasure Dome,* pp. 249-51.

    RICHARD GUSTAFSON. "The Practick of the Maker in Wallace Stevens," *Twentieth Century Literature* 9(2), July 1963, 87.

    ELLWOOD JOHNSON. "Title and Substance of Wallace Stevens' 'Esthétique du Mal,' " *Notes on Contemporary Literature* 8(5), November 1978, 2-3.

    JOSEPH N. RIDDEL. "The Metaphysical Changes of Stevens' 'Esthétique du Mal,' " *Twentieth Century Literature* 7(2), July 1961, 64-80.

    WYLIE SYPHER. "Connoisseur of Chaos: Wallace Stevens," *Partisan Review* 13(1), Winter 1946, 84-86.

    JUDITH WEISSMAN. "Stevens's war poems: 'And is their logic to outweigh McDonagh's bony thumb?' " *Critical Quarterly* 20(2), Summer 1978, 47-51.

"Evening Without Angels"

    KIMON FRIAR and JOHN MALCOLM BRINNIN. *Modern Poetry,* p. 537.

    HAROLD E. TOLIVER. *Pastoral Forms and Attitudes,* p. 309.

    CHAD and EVA T. WALSH. *Twice Ten,* pp. 226-28.

"Examination of the Hero in a Time of War"

    JOSEPH WARREN BEACH. *Obsessive Images,* pp. 209-11.

    ROBERT N. MOLLINGER. "Wallace Stevens' Search for the Central Man," *Tennessee Studies in Literature* 21 (1976), 74-75.

    JAMES E. MULQUEEN. "Man and Cosmic Man in the Poetry of Wallace Stevens," *South Dakota Review* 11(2), Summer 1973, 22-26.

    GROSVENOR E. POWELL. "Of Heroes and Nobility: The Personae of Wallace Stevens," *Southern Review,* n.s., 7(3), Summer 1971, 734-39.

    SISTER M. BERNETTA QUINN. *The Metamorphic Tradition,* p. 82.

    JUDITH WEISSMAN. "Stevens's war poems: 'And is their logic to outweigh McDonagh's bony thumb?' " *Critical Quarterly* 20(2), Summer 1978, 43-45.

"Explanation"

    MARGARET PETERSON. "*Harmonium* and William James," *Southern Review,* n.s., 7(3), Summer 1971, 668-69.

"Extracts from Addresses to the Academy of Fine Ideas"

    DANIEL P. TOMPKINS. " 'To Abstract Reality': Abstract Language and the Intrusion of Consciousness in Wallace Stevens," *American Literature* 45(1), March 1973, 89-90.

"Extraordinary References"

    DWIGHT EDDINS. "Wallace Stevens: America the Primordial," *Modern Language Quarterly* 32(1), March 1971, 86-87.

"The Figure of the Youth as a Virile Poet"

    MONTGOMERY W. KING. "The Two Worlds of Wallace Stevens," *CLA Journal* 8(2), December 1964, 147.

"Final Soliloquy of the Interior Paramour"

    CHARLES ALTIERI. "The Poem as Act: A Way to Reconcile Presentational and Mimetic Theories," *Iowa Review* 6(3-4), Summer-Fall 1975, 116-22.

    SHARON CAMERON. " 'The Sense Against Calamity': Ideas of a Self in Three Poems by Wallace Stevens," *ELH* 43(4), Winter 1976, 593-602.

    DORIS L. EDER. "The Meaning of Wallace Stevens' Two Themes," *Critical Quarterly* 11(2), Summer 1969, 189-90.

"Floral Decorations for Bananas"

    JAN PINKERTON. "Wallace Stevens in the Tropics: A Conservative Protest," *Yale Review* 60(2), December 1970, 225.

"Flyer's Fall"

    HAROLD H. WATTS. "Wallace Stevens and the Rock of Summer," *Kenyon Review* 14(1), Winter 1952, 133-34. (P)

    THOMAS WHITBREAD. "Wallace Stevens' 'Highest Candle,' " *Texas Studies in Literature and Language* 4(4), Winter 1963, 469-70.

"For an Old Woman in a Wig"

    HAROLD BLOOM. "Poetic Crossing, II: American Stances," *Georgia Review* 30(4), Winter 1976, 793-94.

"Frogs Eat Butterflies. Snakes Eat Frogs. Hogs Eat Snakes. Men Eat Hogs."

    DON GEIGER. "Wallace Stevens' Wealth," *Perspective* 7(3), Autumn 1954, 158-60.

    ROBERT MCILVAINE. *Explicator* 33(2), October 1974, Item 14.

    C. J. RAWSON. " 'Tis only infinite below': Speculations on Swift, Wallace Stevens, R. D. Laing and others," *Essays in Criticism* 22(2), April 1972, 161.

    JOHN N. SERIO. " 'The Comedian' as the Idea of Order in *Harmonium,*" *Papers on Language and Literature* 12(2), Spring 1976, 102-3.

"From the Packet of Anacharsis"

    MICHAEL D. CHANNING. " 'From the Packet of Anacharsis': A Tentative Identification," *English Language Notes* 16(1), September 1978, 51-54.

"Gallant Chateau"

    HARRY BROWN and JOHN MILSTEAD. *What the Poem Means,* p. 222.

"Girl in a Nightgown"

    ARTHUR C. MCGILL. *The Celebration of Flesh,* p. 157.

"The Glass of Water"

    HARRY BROWN and JOHN MILSTEAD. *What the Poem Means,* p. 225.

    WARREN G. FRENCH. *Explicator* 19(4), January 1961, Item 23.

    DAVID H. OWEN. " 'The Glass of Water,' " *Perspective* 7(3), Autumn 1954, 175-83.

    ERIC SELLIN. *Explicator* 17(4), January 1959, Item 28.

    SISTER THERESE. *Explicator* 21(7), March 1963, Item 56.

    HYATT H. WAGGONER. *American Poets,* pp. 438-39.

"God is Good. It is a Beautiful Night"

    FRANK DOGGETT. "Stevens on the Genesis of a Poem," *Contemporary Literature* 16(4), Autumn 1975, 467.

    THOMAS B. WHITBREAD. "The Poet-Readers of Wallace Stevens," in *In Defense of Reading,* pp. 103-6.

"The Good Man Has No Shape"

    RICHARD GUSTAFSON. "The Practick of the Maker in Wallace Stevens," *Twentieth Century Literature* 9(2), July 1963, 87-88.

    JANET MCCANN. "Wallace Stevens' 'The Good Man Has No Shape,' " *Notes on Contemporary Literature* 6(2), March 1976, 9-10.

"The Green Plant"

    MARJORIE PERLOFF. "Irony in Wallace Stevens' *The Rock,*" *American Literature* 36(3), November 1964, 335-36.

"Gubbinal"

J. M. LINEBARGER. "Wallace Stevens' 'Gubbinal,' " *Wallace Stevens Newsletter* 2(2), April 1971, 25.

"The Hermitage at the Center"

ISABEL G. MACCAFFREY. "A Point of Central Arrival: Stevens' *The Rock*," *ELH* 40(4), Winter 1973, 628-29.

MARJORIE PERLOFF. "Irony in Wallace Stevens' *The Rock*," *American Literature* 36(3), November 1964, 338-39.

"Hibiscus on the Sleeping Shores"

JACK HARDIE. "Hibiscus and the Spaniard of the Rose: Williams' Dialogue with Wallace Stevens," *William Carlos Williams Newsletter* 4(2), Fall 1978, 20-24.

"A High-Toned Old Christian Woman"

HARRY BROWN and JOHN MILSTEAD. *What the Poem Means*, p. 221.

WILLIAM VAN O'CONNOR. "Wallace Stevens on 'The Poems of Our Climate,' " *University of Kansas City Review* 15(2), Winter 1948, 110.

LAURENCE PERRINE. *100 American Poems of the Twentieth Century*, pp. 71-73.

ARTHUR E. WATERMAN. "Poetry as Play," *CEA Critic* 26(4), January 1964, 7.

"Holiday in Reality"

BERNARD HERINGMAN. "The Poetry of Synthesis," *Perspective* 7(3), Autumn 1954, 169-71.

"Homunculus et la Belle Étoile"

KATHLEEN A. DALE. "Extensions: Beyond Resemblance and the Pleasure Principle in Wallace Stevens' Supreme Fiction," *Boundary 2* 4(1), Fall 1975, 261-63.

JUSTUS GEORGE LAWLER. *The Christian Image*, pp. 115-22.

NORMAN SILVERSTEIN. *Explicator* 13(7), May 1955, Item 40.

"The House Was Quiet and the World Was Calm"

KENNETH FIELDS. "Postures of the Nerves: Reflections of the Nineteenth Century In the Poems of Wallace Stevens," *Southern Review*, n.s., 7(3), Summer 1971, 810-14.

LAURENCE LERNER. *An Introduction to English Poetry*, pp. 195-96.

ARTHUR C. MCGILL. *The Celebration of Flesh*, pp. 158-59.

SISTER M. BERNETTA QUINN. *The Metamorphic Tradition*, p. 76.

THOMAS R. WHITBREAD. "The Poet-Readers of Wallace Stevens," in *In Defense of Reading*, pp. 95-96.

"How to Live, What to Do"

RALPH J. MILLS, JR. "Wallace Stevens: The Image of the Rock," *Accent* 18(2), Spring 1958, 76-77.

"Human Arrangement"

JOHN N. SERIO. "Stevens' 'Human Arrangement,' " *Wallace Stevens Journal* 1(1), Spring 1977, 25-26.

"The Idea of Order at Key West"

HARRY BROWN and JOHN MILSTEAD. *What the Poem Means*, pp. 225-26.

L. S. DEMBO. *Conceptions of Reality in Modern American Poetry*, pp. 90-92.

BABETTE DEUTSCH. *Poetry in Our Time*, pp. 247-50; second ed., p. 285.

FRANK DOGGETT. "Wallace Stevens and the World We Know," *English Journal* 48(7), October 1959, 370-71.

DENIS DONOGHUE. *Connoisseurs of Chaos*, pp. 190-91, 210-11.

ELIZABETH DREW. *Poetry*, pp. 261-62.

RICHARD GUSTAFSON. "The Practick of the Maker in Wallace Stevens," *Twentieth Century Literature* 9(2), July 1963, 84.

GRAHAM HOUGH. "The Poetry of Wallace Stevens," *Critical Quarterly* 2(3), Autumn 1960, 204-5.

TODD M. LIEBER. "Robert Frost and Wallace Stevens: 'What to Make of a Diminished Thing,' " *American Literature* 47(1), March 1975, 71-73.

JAMES MCMICHAEL. "The Wallace Stevens Vulgates," *Southern Review*, n.s., 7(3), Summer 1971, 718-20.

LOUIS L. MARTZ. *The Poem of the Mind*, pp. 191-93.

LOUIS L. MARTZ. "The World of Wallace Stevens," in *Modern American Poetry*, edited by B. Rajan, pp. 101-3.

JOSEPH N. RIDDEL. "Wallace Stevens' *Ideas of Order*: The Rhetoric of Politics and the Rhetoric of Poetry," *New England Quarterly* 34(3), September 1961, 346-51.

GORDON WILLIAM ROCKETT. "The Humanities and the University Revolution," *College English* 29(1), October 1967, 20-22.

HYATT H. WAGGONER. *American Poets*, pp. 434-35.

KENNETH WALKER. *Explicator* 32(8), April 1974, Item 59.

THOMAS R. WHITAKER. "Voices in the Open: Wordsworth, Eliot, and Stevens," *Iowa Review* 2(3), Summer 1971, 105-6.

"In a Bad Time"

C. ROLAND WAGNER. "The Idea of Nothingness in Wallace Stevens," *Accent* 12(2), Spring 1952, 119.

"Infanta Marina"

MARIUS BEWLEY. "The Poetry of Wallace Stevens," *Partisan Review* 16(9), September 1949, 906.

"The Irish Cliffs of Moher"

JUDITH MCDANIEL. "Wallace Stevens and the Scientific Imagination," *Contemporary Literature* 15(2), Spring 1974, 227-28.

"July Mountain"

ROY HARVEY PEARCE. *Historicism Once More*, pp. 285-86.

"Landscape with Boat"

TODD M. LIEBER. "Robert Frost and Wallace Stevens: 'What to Make of a Diminished Thing,' " *American Literature* 47(1), March 1975, 74-77.

J. HILLIS MILLER. *Poets of Reality*, pp. 254-55.

HAROLD H. WATTS. *Hound and Quarry*, pp. 48-49.

HAROLD H. WATTS. "Wallace Stevens and the Rock of Summer," *Kenyon Review* 14(1), Winter 1952, 128-29.

"Large Red Man Reading"

FRANK DOGGETT. "Wallace Stevens and the World We Know," *English Journal* 48(7), October 1959, 371-73.

THOMAS B. WHITBREAD. "The Poet-Readers of Wallace Stevens," in *In Defense of Reading*, pp. 106-8.

"Last Looks at the Lilacs"

FRANK DOGGETT. "Our Number is Her Nature," in *The Twenties*, edited by Richard E. Langford and William E. Taylor, p. 38.

"Late Hymn from the Myrrh-Mountain"

ARTHUR C. MCGILL. *The Celebration of Flesh*, pp. 143-46.

STEVENS, WALLACE *(Cont.)*
"Late Hymn from the Myrrh-Mountain" *(cont.)*

> JOY M. SEMEL. "Pennsylvania Dutch Country: Stevens' World as Meditation," *Contemporary Literature* 14(3), Summer 1973, 316.

"Lebensweisheitspielerei"

> JUDITH MCDANIEL. "Wallace Stevens and the Scientific Imagination," *Contemporary Literature* 15(2), Spring 1974, 229.

"Less and Less Human, O Savage Spirit"

> C. ROLAND WAGNER. "The Idea of Nothingness in Wallace Stevens," *Accent* 12(2), Spring 1952, 113-14.

"Life is Motion"

> ELDER OLSON. "The Poetry of Wallace Stevens," *College English* 16(7), April 1955, 396-97.
> MARGARET PETERSON. "*Harmonium* and William James," *Southern Review,* n.s., 7(3), Summer 1971, 678-79.
> HUGH L. SMITH, JR. *Explicator* 19(7), April 1961, Item 48.
> NANCY SULLIVAN. "Perspective and the Poetic Process," *Wisconsin Studies in Contemporary Literature* 6(1), Winter-Spring 1965, 123-24.

"Life on a Battleship"

> LLOYD FRANKENBERG. *Pleasure Dome,* pp. 240-42.
> WILLIAM VAN O'CONNOR. "The Politics of a Poet," *Perspective* 1 (Summer 1948), 206-7.

"Like Decorations in a Nigger Cemetery"

> ARDYTH BRADLEY. "Wallace Stevens' Decorations," *Twentieth Century Literature* 7(3), October 1961, 114-17.
> PAUL MCBREARTY. "Wallace Stevens's 'Like Decorations in a Nigger Cemetery': Notes toward an Explication," *Texas Studies in Literature and Language* 15(2), Summer 1973, 341-56.
> HELEN HENNESSY VENDLER. "Stevens' 'Like Decorations in a Nigger Cemetery,' " *Massachusetts Review* 7(1), Winter 1966, 136-46. Reprinted in: *Modern Poetry,* pp. 473-84.

"Lions in Sweden"

> RAMON GUTHRIE. *Explicator* 20(4), December 1961, Item 32. (P)
> WILLIAM YORK TINDALL. "Wallace Stevens," in *Seven Modern American Poets,* p. 56. (P)

"The Load of Sugar-Cane"

> DON GEIGER. "Wallace Stevens' Wealth," *Perspective* 7(3), Autumn 1954, 157-58.

"Loneliness in Jersey City"

> DWIGHT EDDINS. "Wallace Stevens: America the Primordial," *Modern Language Quarterly* 32(1), March 1971, 78-79.

"Long and Sluggish Lines"

> MARJORIE PERLOFF. "Irony in Wallace Stevens' *The Rock,*" *American Literature* 36(3), November 1964, 337-38.

"Looking Across the Fields and Watching the Birds Fly"

> MARIUS BEWLEY. "The Poetry of Wallace Stevens," *Commonweal* 62(25), September 23, 1955, 620.
> ISABEL G. MACCAFFREY. "A Point of Central Arrival: Stevens' The Rock," *ELH* 40(4), Winter 1973, 629-31.
> MARJORIE PERLOFF. "Irony in Wallace Stevens' *The Rock,*" *American Literature* 36(3), November 1964, 334-35.

"Madame La Fleurie"

> HAROLD BLOOM. *A Map of Misreading,* p. 26.
> JUDITH MCDANIEL. "Wallace Stevens and the Scientific Imagination," *Contemporary Literature* 15(2), Spring 1974, 232-34.

"The Man on the Dump"

> J. HILLIS MILLER. *Poets of Reality,* p. 246.
> HAROLD E. TOLIVER. *Pastoral Forms and Attitudes,* pp. 310-12.

"The Man Whose Pharynx Was Bad"

> MARIUS BEWLEY. "The Poetry of Wallace Stevens," *Partisan Review* 16(9), September 1949, 908-10.

"The Man with the Blue Guitar"

> RICHARD P. ADAMS. "Wallace Stevens and Schopenhauer's *The World as Will and Idea,*" *Tulane Studies in English* 20 (1972), 143-51.
> MERLE E. BROWN. "Concordia Discors in the Poetry of Wallace Stevens," *American Literature* 34(2), May 1962, 249-54.
> DAVID CAVITCH. *Explicator* 27(4), December 1968, Item 30.
> LLOYD FRANKENBERG. *Pleasure Dome,* pp. 222-27.
> GRAHAM HOUGH. "The Poetry of Wallace Stevens," *Critical Quarterly* 2(3), Autumn 1960, 210-12.
> LOUIS MARTZ. "Wallace Stevens: The World as Meditation," in *Modern American Poetry,* ed. by Guy Owen, pp. 47-49.
> JAMES E. MULQUEEN. "Man and Cosmic Man in the Poetry of Wallace Stevens," *South Dakota Review* 11(2), Summer 1973, 19-21.
> ROY HARVEY PEARCE. "Wallace Stevens: The Last Lesson of the Master," *ELH* 31(1), March 1964, 72.
> DONALD SHEEHAN. "Wallace Stevens in the 30s: Gaudy Bosh and the Gesture's Whim," in *The Thirties,* pp. 155-56.
> WALTER SUTTON. *American Free Verse,* p. 42.
> WILLIAM YORK TINDALL. "Wallace Stevens," in *Seven Modern American Poets,* pp. 65-68.
> JUDITH WEISSMAN. "Stevens's war poems: 'And is their logic to outweigh McDonagh's bony thumb?' " *Critical Quarterly* 20(2), Summer 1978, 39.

"Martial Cadenza"

> MARJORIE PERLOFF. "Irony in Wallace Stevens' *The Rock,*" *American Literature* 36(3), November 1964, 331-32.

"Meditation Celestial & Terrestrial"

> ROBERT J. BERTHOLF. "The Revolving Toward Myth: Stevens' 'Credences of Summer,' " *Bucknell Review* 22(2), Fall 1976, 211-12.

"Memorandum"

> DWIGHT EDDINS. "Wallace Stevens: America the Primordial," *Modern Language Quarterly* 32(1), March 1971, 77-78.

"The Men That Are Falling"

> CLARK GRIFFITH. *Explicator* 23(5), January 1965, Item 41.
> RALPH J. MILLS, JR. "Wallace Stevens: The Image of the Rock," *Accent* 18(2), Spring 1958, 78-79.

"Metamorphosis"

> SISTER M. BERNETTA QUINN. *The Metamorphic Tradition,* pp. 57-58.
> SISTER M. BERNETTA QUINN. "Metamorphosis in Wallace Stevens," *Sewanee Review* 60(2), Spring 1952, 235-36.

"Metaphor as Degeneration"

HYATT H. WAGGONER. *American Poets*, pp. 439-40.

"Metaphors of a Magnifico"

MARIUS BEWLEY. "The Poetry of Wallace Stevens," *Partisan Review* 16(9), September 1949, 903-4.

C. D. CECIL. "An Audience for Wallace Stevens," *Essays in Criticism*, 15(2), April 1965, 201-3.

DORIS L. EDER. "Wallace Stevens: The War Between Mind and Eye," *Southern Review*, n.s., 7(3), Summer 1971, 755.

DON GEIGER. "Wallace Stevens' Wealth," *Perspective* 7(3), Autumn 1954, 156.

ALEXANDER S. LIDDIE. *Explicator* 21(2), October 1962, Item 15.

MARGARET PETERSON. "*Harmonium* and William James," *Southern Review*, n.s., 7(3), Summer 1971, 672-75.

SISTER M. BERNETTA QUINN. *The Metamorphic Tradition*, pp. 50-51.

WILLIAM YORK TINDALL. "Wallace Stevens," in *Seven Modern American Poets*, p. 77.

"Mr. Burnshaw and the Statue"

DONALD SHEEHAN. "Wallace Stevens in the 30s: Gaudy Bosh and the Gesture's Whim," in *The Thirties*, p. 153.

"Mrs. Alfred Uruguay"

RICHARD P. ADAMS. "Wallace Stevens and Schopenhauer's *The World as Will and Idea*," *Tulane Studies in English* 20 (1972), 152.

KIMON FRIAR and JOHN MALCOLM BRINNIN. *Modern Poetry*, p. 536.

J. HILLIS MILLER. *Poets of Reality*, pp. 254-55.

"Le Monocle de Mon Oncle"

R. P. BLACKMUR. "Examples of Wallace Stevens," *Hound and Horn* 5(2), January-March 1932, 232-33, 245-46. (P) Reprinted in: R. P. Blackmur. *The Double Agent*, pp. 77-78, 91-93. Also: R. P. Blackmur. *Language as Gesture*, pp. 229-30.

DONALD DAVIE. " 'Essential Gaudiness': The Poems of Wallace Stevens," *Twentieth Century* 153(916), June 1953, 455-62.

DONALD DAVIE. *The Poet in the Imaginary Museum*, pp. 11-12, 16-17.

FRANK DOGGETT. "Our Number is Her Nature," in *The Twenties*, edited by Richard E. Langford and William E. Taylor, pp. 38-39.

BERNARD DUFFEY. *Poetry in America*, p. 220.

RICHARD ELLMANN. "Wallace Stevens' Ice-Cream," *Kenyon Review* 19(1), Winter 1957, 97-99. Reprinted in: *Aspects of American Poetry*, pp. 212-15.

WILLIAM A. FAHEY. *Explicator* 15(3), December 1956, Item 16.

LLOYD FRANKENBERG. *Pleasure Dome*, pp. 205-7.

R. M. GAY. *Explicator* 6(4), February 1948, Item 27.

RICHARD GUSTAFSON. "The Practick of the Maker in Wallace Stevens," *Twentieth Century Literature* 9(2), July 1963, 87.

EARL ROY MINER. *Explicator* 13(5), March 1955, Item 28.

ROBERT PACK. "Wallace Stevens: The Secular Mystery and the Comic Spirit," *Western Review* 20(1), Autumn 1955, 57-59.

MARGARET PETERSON. "*Harmonium* and William James," *Southern Review*, n.s., 7(3), Summer 1971, 680.

DELMORE SCHWARTZ. "In the Orchards of Imagination," *New Republic* 131(18), November 1, 1954, 17.

WILLIAM YORK TINDALL. "Wallace Stevens," in *Seven Modern American Poets*, pp. 53-54.

"Montrachet-le-Jardin"

GROSVENOR E. POWELL. "Of Heroes and Nobility: The Personae of Wallace Stevens," *Southern Review*, n.s., 7(3), Summer 1971, 733-34.

"The Motive for Metaphor"

HARRY BROWN and JOHN MILSTEAD. *What the Poem Means*, p. 226.

JOHN CROWE RANSOM. "The Concrete Universal: Observations on the Understanding of Poetry, II," *Kenyon Review* 17(3), Summer 1955, 400-2.

"Mountains Covered with Cats"

KATHLEEN A. DALE. "Extensions: Beyond Resemblance and the Pleasure Principle in Wallace Stevens' Supreme Fiction," *Boundary 2* 4(1), Fall 1975, 256-57.

"Mystic Garden & Middling Beast"

JAMES E. MULQUEEN. "Man and Cosmic Man in the Poetry of Wallace Stevens," *South Dakota Review* 11(2), Summer 1973, 21-22.

"Negation"

MARGARET PETERSON. "*Harmonium* and William James," *Southern Review*, n.s., 7(3), Summer 1971, 661-63.

"No Possum, No Sop, No Taters"

MERLE E. BROWN. "Concordia Discors in the Poetry of Wallace Stevens," *American Literature* 34(2), May 1962, 247-49.

BABETTE DEUTSCH. *Poetry in Our Time*, p. 245; second ed., p. 275.

GEORGE LENSING. "Wallace Stevens and the State of Winter Simplicity," *Southern Review*, n.s., 7(3), Summer 1971, 773-74.

ARTHUR C. MCGILL. *The Celebration of Flesh*, pp. 156-57.

KARL P. WENTERSDORF. "Wallace Stevens, Dante Alighieri, and the Emperor," *Twentieth Century Literature* 13(4), January 1968, 197-98.

"Nomad Exquisite"

DWIGHT EDDINS. "Wallace Stevens: America the Primordial," *Modern Language Quarterly* 32(1), March 1971, 84.

JAN PINKERTON. "Wallace Stevens in the Tropics: A Conservative Protest," *Yale Review* 60(2), December 1970, 223.

"Not Ideas about the Thing but the Thing Itself"

RICHARD P. ADAMS. "Wallace Stevens and Schopenhauer's *The World as Will and Idea*," *Tulane Studies in English* 20 (1972), 136-37.

JAMES BENZIGER. *Images of Eternity*, pp. 241-43.

WILLIAM BEVIS. "Stevens' Toneless Poetry," *ELH* 41(2), Summer 1974, 280-82.

JANET MCCANN. "Wallace Stevens' '*Not Ideas About the Thing But the Thing Itself*,' " *Notes on Modern American Literature* 1(4), Fall 1977, Item 32.

ROY HARVEY PEARCE. "Wallace Stevens: The Last Lesson of the Master," *ELH* 31(1), March 1964, 67-69. Reprinted in: Roy Harvey Pearce. *Historicism Once More*, pp. 270-72.

MARJORIE PERLOFF. "Irony in Wallace Stevens' *The Rock*," *American Literature* 36(3), November 1964, 339-40.

STEVENS, WALLACE *(Cont.)*

"Not Ideas about the Thing but the Thing Itself" *(cont.)*

> JOHN N. SERIO. "Stevens as a Connoisseur of Chaos," *Notes on Modern American Literature* 2(3), Summer 1978, Item 21.

> JOHN N. SERIO. "The Ultimate Music Is Abstract: Charles Ives and Wallace Stevens," *Bucknell Review* 24(2), Fall 1978, 129-30.

> HAROLD E. TOLIVER. *Pastoral Forms and Attitudes*, pp. 320-22.

"Note on Moonlight"

> ROBERT PACK. "Wallace Stevens' Sufficient Muse," *Southern Review*, n.s., 11(4), Autumn 1975, 778.

"Notes Toward a Supreme Fiction"

> RICHARD P. ADAMS. "Wallace Stevens and Schopenhauer's *The World as Will and Idea*," *Tulane Studies in English* 20 (1972), 153-67.

> HAROLD BLOOM. *Poetry and Repression*, pp. 286-93.

> GEORGE BORNSTEIN. "Provisional Romanticism in 'Notes toward a Supreme Fiction,' " *Wallace Stevens Journal* 1(1), Spring 1977, 17-24.

> MERLE E. BROWN. "Concordia Discors in the Poetry of Wallace Stevens," *American Literature* 34(2), May 1962, 254-62.

> GLAUCO CAMBON. *The Inclusive Flame*, pp. 79-119.

> L. S. DEMBO. *Conceptions of Reality in Modern American Poetry*, pp. 98-103.

> BABETTE DEUTSCH. *Poetry in Our Time*, pp. 251-52; second ed., p. 283.

> FRANK DOGGETT. "This Invented World: Stevens' 'Notes Toward a Supreme Fiction,' " *ELH* 28(3), September 1961, 284-99.

> DENIS DONOGHUE. *The Ordinary Universe*, pp. 267-90.

> BERNARD DUFFEY. *Poetry in America*, pp. 320-23.

> LLOYD FRANKENBERG. *Pleasure Dome*, pp. 257-67.

> RALPH FREEDMAN. "Wallace Stevens and Rainer Maria Rilke: Two Versions of a Poetic," in *The Poet as Critic*, pp. 69-70.

> KIMON FRIAR and JOHN MALCOLM BRINNIN. *Modern Poetry*, pp. 535-36.

> BERNARD HERINGMAN. "The Poetry of Synthesis," *Perspective* 7(3), Autumn 1954, 167-68.

> LOUIS L. MARTZ. "The World of Wallace Stevens," in *Modern American Poetry*, edited by B. Rajan, pp. 98-101.

> ROY HARVEY PEARCE. *The Continuity of American Poetry*, pp. 395-404.

> JOSEPH N. RIDDEL. "Wallace Stevens — 'It Must Be Human,' " *English Journal* 56(4), April 1967, 527-30.

> JOSEPH N. RIDDEL. "Wallace Stevens' 'Notes Toward a Supreme Fiction,' " *Wisconsin Studies in Contemporary Literature* 2(2), Spring-Summer 1961, 20-42.

> DONALD SHEEHAN. "The Ultimate Plato: A Reading of Wallace Stevens' 'Notes Toward a Supreme Fiction,' " in *The Forties*, pp. 165-77.

> WILLIAM YORK TINDALL. "Wallace Stevens," in *Seven Modern American Poets*, pp. 68-72.

> HAROLD E. TOLIVER. *Pastoral Forms and Attitudes*, pp. 313-16.

"The Novel"

> ROY HARVEY PEARCE. "Wallace Stevens: The Last Lesson of the Master," *ELH* 31(1), March 1964, 65-66. Reprinted in: Roy Harvey Pearce. *Historicism Once More*, pp. 262-63.

"Nuances of a Theme by Williams"

> DORIS L. EDER. "The Meaning of Wallace Stevens' Two Themes," *Critical Quarterly* 11(2), Summer 1969, 188-89.

> M. L. ROSENTHAL. *The Modern Poets*, pp. 121-22.

"O Florida, Venereal Soil"

> FRANK DOGGETT. "Our Number is Her Nature," in *The Twenties*, edited by Richard E. Langford and William E. Taylor, p. 38.

> DWIGHT EDDINS. "Wallace Stevens: America the Primordial," *Modern Language Quarterly* 32(1), March 1971, 83.

"Oak Leaves Are Hands"

> SISTER M. BERNETTA QUINN. *The Metamorphic Tradition*, p. 85.

> SISTER M. BERNETTA QUINN. "Metamorphosis in Wallace Stevens," *Sewanee Review* 60(2), Spring 1952, 250-51.

"Of Bright & Blue Birds & the Gala Sun"

> RICHARD P. ADAMS. "Wallace Stevens and Schopenhauer's *The World as Will and Idea*," *Tulane Studies in English* 20(1972), 151-52.

> KATHLEEN A. DALE. "Extensions: Beyond Resemblance and the Pleasure Principle in Wallace Stevens' Supreme Fiction," *Boundary 2* 4(1), Fall 1975, 263-64.

"Of Hartford in a Purple Light"

> NORMAN SILVERSTEIN. *Explicator* 18(3), December 1959, Item 20.

"Of Heaven Considered as a Tomb"

> LAURENCE LERNER. "Reading Modern Poetry," in *English Poetry*, edited by Alan Sinfield, pp. 165-68.

> JAMES MCMICHAEL. "The Wallace Stevens Vulgates," *Southern Review*, n.s., 7(3), Summer 1971, 704-6.

"Of Mere Being"

> WILLIAM BEVIS. "Stevens' Toneless Poetry," *ELH* 41(2), Summer 1974, 279-80.

> FRANK DOGGETT. "The Poet of the Earth: Wallace Stevens," *College English* 22(6), March 1961, 374.

> JOHN N. SERIO. "Stevens as a Connoisseur of Chaos," *Notes on Modern American Literature* 2(3), Summer 1978, Item 21.

"Of Modern Poetry"

> LOUIS MARTZ. "Wallace Stevens: The World as Meditation," in *Modern American Poetry*, ed. by Guy Owen, pp. 49-50.

> ARTHUR OBERG. "The Modern British and American Lyric: What Will Suffice," *Papers on Language and Literature* 8(1), Winter 1972, 72-74.

> WILLIAM VAN O'CONNOR. "Wallace Stevens on 'The Poems of Our Climate,' " *University of Kansas City Review* 15(2), Winter 1948, 108-9.

"Of the Surface of Things"

> L. S. DEMBO. *Conceptions of Reality in Modern American Poetry*, p. 84.

"An Old Man Asleep"

> ISABEL G. MACCAFFREY. "A Point of Central Arrival: Stevens' *The Rock*," *ELH* 40(4), Winter 1973, 608-9.

"The Old Woman and the Statue"

> DONALD SHEEHAN. "Wallace Stevens in the 30s: Gaudy Bosh and the Gesture's Whim," in *The Thirties*, pp. 152-53.

"On the Road Home"

DORIS L. EDER. "Wallace Stevens: The War Between Mind and Eye," *Southern Review*, n.s., 7(3), Summer 1971, 759-60.

GRAHAM HOUGH. "The Poetry of Wallace Stevens," *Critical Quarterly* 2(3), Autumn 1960, 215-16.

SISTER M. BERNETTA QUINN. *The Metamorphic Tradition*, p. 83.

"On the Way to the Bus"

C. D. CECIL. "An Audience for Wallace Stevens," *Essays in Criticism* 15(2), April 1965, 205-6.

"One of the Inhabitants of the West"

MARJORIE PERLOFF. "Irony in Wallace Stevens' *The Rock*," *American Literature* 36(3), November 1964, 331-32.

"An Ordinary Evening in New Haven"

HAROLD BLOOM. *Poetry and Repression*, pp. 273-77.

MERLE E. BROWN. "Concordia Discors in the Poetry of Wallace Stevens," *American Literature* 34(2), May 1962, 262-69.

PHILIP FURIA and MARTIN ROTH. "Stevens' Fusky Alphabet," *PMLA* 93(1), January 1978, 70-71.

JAMES E. MULQUEEN. "A Reading of Wallace Stevens' 'An Ordinary Evening in New Haven,'" *Perspective* 17(4), Spring 1975, 268-77.

JOSEPH N. RIDDEL. "Wallace Stevens' 'Visibility of Thought,'" *PMLA* 77(4), September 1962, 493-97.

WILLIAM YORK TINDALL. "Wallace Stevens," in *Seven Modern American Poets*, pp. 75-77.

LEWIS TURCO. "The Agonism and the Existentity: Stevens," *Concerning Poetry* 6(1), Spring 1973, 32-44.

C. ROLAND WAGNER. "The Idea of Nothingness in Wallace Stevens," *Accent* 12(2), Spring 1952, 120-21. (P)

"The Ordinary Women"

DON GEIGER. "Wallace Stevens' Wealth," *Perspective* 7(3), Autumn 1954, 160-63.

FRED H. STOCKING. *Explicator* 4(1), October 1945, Item 4.

"Our Stars Come From Ireland"

LAWRENCE KRAMER. "'A Completely New Set of Objects': Wallace Stevens and Charles Ives," *Wallace Stevens Journal* 2(3-4), Fall 1978, 12-14.

"The Owl in the Sarcophagus"

HAROLD BLOOM. *Figures of Capable Imagination*, pp. 100-2.

J. HILLIS MILLER. *Poets of Reality*, pp. 268-70.

J. HILLIS MILLER. "Wallace Stevens' Poetry of Being," *ELH* 31(1), March 1964, 95-96. Reprinted in: *Modern American Poetry*, edited by Jerome Mazzaro, pp. 103-5.

RALPH J. MILLS, JR. "Wallace Stevens: The Image of the Rock," *Accent* 18(2), Spring 1958, 83.

JOSEPH N. RIDDEL. "Wallace Stevens' 'Visibility of Thought,'" *PMLA* 77(4), September 1962, 488.

C. ROLAND WAGNER. "The Idea of Nothingness in Wallace Stevens," *Accent* 12(2), Spring 1952, 115-16. (P)

THOMAS WHITBREAD. "Wallace Stevens' 'Highest Candle,'" *Texas Studies in Literature and Language* 4(4), Winter 1963, 470-78.

"Owl's Clover"

LLOYD FRANKENBERG. *Pleasure Dome*, pp. 227-31.

"Page from a Tale"

ARTHUR C. MCGILL. *The Celebration of Flesh*, p. 172.

"The Paltry Nude"

HAROLD BLOOM. "Poetic Crossing, II: American Stances," *Georgia Review* 30(4), Winter 1976, 795-96.

"A Pastoral Nun"

KATHLEEN A. DALE. "Extensions: Beyond Resemblance and the Pleasure Principle in Wallace Stevens' Supreme Fiction," *Boundary 2* 4(1), Fall 1975, 260.

"Peter Quince at the Clavier"

HARRY BROWN and JOHN MILSTEAD. *What the Poem Means*, pp. 223-24.

CHARLES W. COOPER and JOHN HOLMES. *Preface to Poetry*, p. 63.

CAROL FLAKE. "Wallace Stevens' 'Peter Quince at the Clavier': Sources and Structure," *English Language Notes* 12(2), December 1974, 116-20.

NEWELL F. FORD. "Peter Quince's Orchestra," *Modern Language Notes* 75(5), May 1960, 405-11.

WENDELL STACY JOHNSON. "Some Functions of Poetic Form," *Journal of Aesthetics and Art Criticism* 13(4), June 1955, 501-3.

EUGENE NASSAR. "Wallace Stevens: 'Peter Quince at the Clavier,'" *College English* 26(7), April 1965, 549-51.

PHYLLIS E. NELSON. *Explicator* 24(6), February 1966, Item 52.

WILLIAM VAN O'CONNOR. *Sense and Sensibility in Modern Poetry*, pp. 149-50.

WILLIAM VAN O'CONNOR. "Tension and Structure of Poetry," *Sewanee Review* 51(4), Autumn 1943, 559.

LAURENCE PERRINE. *100 American Poems of the Twentieth Century*, pp. 66-70.

LAURENCE PERRINE. "'Peter Quince at the Clavier': A Protest," *College English* 27(5), February 1966, 430.

JOSEPH N. RIDDEL. "Stevens' 'Peter Quince at the Clavier': Immortality as Form," *College English* 23(4), January 1962, 307-9.

M. L. ROSENTHAL. *The Modern Poets*, pp. 126-28.

JOHN N. SERIO. "'The Comedian' as the Idea of Order in *Harmonium*," *Papers on Language and Literature* 12(2), Spring 1976, 97-98.

FRED H. STOCKING. *Explicator* 5(7), May 1947, Item 47.

MARY JANE STORM. *Explicator* 14(2), November 1955, Item 9.

WILLIAM YORK TINDALL. "Wallace Stevens," in *Seven Modern American Poets*, p. 59.

CHAD WALSH. *Doors into Poetry*, pp. 115-20.

CHARLES WOLFE. *Explicator* 33(6), February 1975, Item 43.

"Phosphor Reading by His Own Light"

THOMAS B. WHITBREAD. "The Poet-Readers of Wallace Stevens," in *In Defense of Reading*, pp. 100-3.

"The Plain Sense of Things"

WILLIAM BEVIS. "Stevens' Toneless Poetry," *ELH* 41(2), Summer 1974, 282-83.

STEVENS, WALLACE *(Cont.)*

"The Plain Sense of Things" *(cont.)*

JUDITH MCDANIEL. "Wallace Stevens and the Scientific Imagination," *Contemporary Literature* 15(2), Spring 1974, 228-29.

ROBERT PACK. "Wallace Stevens' Sufficient Muse," *Southern Review*, n.s., 11(4), Autumn 1975, 773-76.

"The Pleasures of Merely Circulating"

CHAD and EVA T. WALSH. *Twice Ten*, pp. 225-26.

"The Plot Against the Giant"

LLOYD FRANKENBERG. *Pleasure Dome*, p. 201.

ALBERT WILLIAM LEVI. "A Note on Wallace Stevens and the Poem of Perspective," *Perspective* 7(3), Autumn 1954, 138-39.

M. L. ROSENTHAL. *The Modern Poets*, p. 123.

"The Poem That Took the Place of a Mountain"

FRED MILLER ROBINSON. "Poems That Took the Place of Mountains: Realization in Stevens and Cézanne," *Centennial Review* 22(3), Summer 1978, 296-97.

THOMAS WHITBREAD. "Wallace Stevens' 'Highest Candle,'" *Texas Studies in Literature and Language* 4(4), Winter 1963, 466-69.

"Poems from 'Primordia'"

DWIGHT EDDINS. "Wallace Stevens: America the Primordial," *Modern Language Quarterly* 32(1), March 1971, 80-81. (P)

"The Poems of Our Climate"

GEORGE LENSING. "Wallace Stevens and the State of Winter Simplicity," *Southern Review*, n.s., 7(3), Summer 1971, 770-72.

SISTER MARY NOËL. "'In This Bitterness, Delight,'" *English Journal* 54(8), November 1965, 763-64.

ROY HARVEY PEARCE. *Historicism Once More*, pp. 267-68.

LOUIS UNTERMEYER. *50 Modern American & British Poets*, p. 231.

HYATT H. WAGGONER. *American Poets*, p. 435.

"Poetry Is a Destructive Force"

EMILIE BUCHWALD. "Wallace Stevens: The Delicatest Eye of the Mind," *American Quarterly* 14(2), Summer 1962, 187.

SAMUEL JAY KEYSER. "Wallace Stevens: Form and Meaning in Four Poems," *College English* 37(6), February 1976, 584-85.

J. HILLIS MILLER. *Poets of Reality*, p. 220.

"A Postcard from the Volcano"

JEROME BEATY and WILLIAM H. MATCHETT. *Poetry From Statement to Meaning*, pp. 204-5.

"A Primitive Like an Orb"

JAMES E. MULQUEEN. "Man and Cosmic Man in the Poetry of Wallace Stevens," *South Dakota Review* 11(2), Summer 1973, 16-17.

LISA STEINMAN. "Figure and Figuration in Stevens' Long Poems," *Wallace Stevens Journal* 1(1), Spring 1977, 13-15.

HAROLD H. WATTS. *Hound and Quarry*, pp. 54-55. (P)

"Prologues to What Is Possible"

JANET MCCANN. "'Prologues to What Is Possible': Wallace Stevens and Jung," *Ball State University Forum* 17(2), Spring 1976, 46-50.

JUDITH MCDANIEL. "Wallace Stevens and the Scientific Imagination," *Contemporary Literature* 15(2), Spring 1974, 231-32.

MARJORIE PERLOFF. "Irony in Wallace Stevens' *The Rock*," *American Literature* 36(3), November 1964, 332-34.

JOSEPH N. RIDDEL. "Wallace Stevens — 'It Must Be Human,'" *English Journal* 56(4), April 1967, 532-33.

"A Rabbit As King of the Ghosts"

KENNETH FIELDS. "Postures of the Nerves: Reflections of the Nineteenth Century In the Poems of Wallace Stevens," *Southern Review*, n.s., 7(3), Summer 1971, 810-12.

JAMES E. MULQUEEN. "Man and Cosmic Man in the Poetry of Wallace Stevens," *South Dakota Review* 11(2), Summer 1973. 19.

"The Reader"

JUDITH MCDANIEL. "Wallace Stevens and the Scientific Imagination," *Contemporary Literature* 15(2), Spring 1974, 228.

"Reality Is an Activity of the Most August Imagination"

RICHARD BLESSING. "Wallace Stevens and the Necessary Reader: A Technique of Dynamism," *Twentieth Century Literature* 18(4), October 1972, 257.

C. D. CECIL. "An Audience for Wallace Stevens," *Essays in Criticism* 15(2), April 1965, 199-201.

"The Region November"

ROY HARVEY PEARCE. "Wallace Stevens: The Last Lesson of the Master," *ELH* 31(1), March 1964, 73-75. Reprinted in: Roy Harvey Pearce. *Historicism Once More*, pp. 278-80.

"Repetitions of a Young Captain"

BERNARD HERINGMAN. "The Poetry of Synthesis," *Perspective* 7(3), Autumn 1954, 168-69. (P)

"Re-statement of Romance"

ROBERT J. BERTHOLF. "The Revolving Toward Myth: Stevens' 'Credences of Summer,'" *Bucknell Review* 22(2), Fall 1976, 215.

HAROLD H. WATTS. *Hound and Quarry*, pp. 52-53.

"The River of Rivers in Connecticut"

DENIS DONOGHUE. *Connoisseurs of Chaos*, pp. 211-14.

LAWRENCE KRAMER. "'A Completely New Set of Objects': Wallace Stevens and Charles Ives," *Wallace Stevens Journal* 2(3-4), Fall 1978, 11-12.

"The Rock"

PHILIP FURIA and MARTIN ROTH. "Stevens' Fusky Alphabet," *PMLA* 93(1), January 1978, 68-69.

MILDRED E. HARTSOCK. "Wallace Stevens and the 'Rock,'" *The Personalist* 42(1), Winter 1961, 66-75.

JUDITH MCDANIEL. "Wallace Stevens and the Scientific Imagination," *Contemporary Literature* 15(2), Spring 1974, 234-36.

J. HILLIS MILLER. "Stevens' Rock and Criticism as Cure," *Georgia Review* 30(1), Spring 1976, 5-31.

RALPH J. MILLS, JR. "Wallace Stevens: The Image of the Rock," *Accent* 18(2), Spring 1958, 85-89.

ROY HARVEY PEARCE. *The Continuity of American Poetry*, pp. 409-11.

ROY HARVEY PEARCE. "Wallace Stevens: The Last Lesson of the Master," *ELH* 31(1), March 1964, 66-67. Reprinted in: Roy Harvey Pearce, *Historicism Once More*, pp. 268-70.

HYATT H. WAGGONER. *American Poets*, pp. 440-41.

"The Role of the Idea in Poetry"

JOY M. SEMEL. "Pennsylvania Dutch Country: Stevens' World as Meditation," *Contemporary Literature* 14(3), Summer 1973, 315.

"Sad Strains of a Gay Waltz"

F. O. Matthiessen. *The Responsibilities of the Critic*, pp. 15-16.

"Sailing after Lunch"

John F. Lynen. "Forms of Time in Modern Poetry," *Queen's Quarterly* 82(3), Autumn 1975, 344-64.

"St. Armorer's Church from the Outside"

Isabel G. MacCaffrey. "A Point of Central Arrival: Stevens' *The Rock*," *ELH* 40(4), Winter 1973, 624-26.

Joseph N. Riddel. "Wallace Stevens' 'Visibility of Thought,'" *PMLA* 77(4), September 1962, 489.

"St. John and the Back-Ache"

J. Hillis Miller. *Poets of Reality*, pp. 257-58.

"Saturday Night at the Chiropodist's"

Kathleen A. Dale. "Extensions: Beyond Resemblance and the Pleasure Principle in Wallace Stevens' Supreme Fiction," *Boundary 2* 4(1), Fall 1975, 260-61.

"Sea Surface Full of Clouds"

Harold C. Ackerman, Jr. "Notes Toward an Explication of Stevens' 'Sea Surface Full of Clouds,'" *Concerning Poetry* 2(1), Spring 1969, 73-77.

Richard P. Adams. "Pure Poetry: Wallace Stevens' 'Sea Surface Full of Clouds,'" *Tulane Studies in English* 21 (1974), 91-122.

Michel Benamou. "Displacements of Parental Space: American Poetry and French Symbolism," *Boundary 2* 5(2), Winter 1977, 478-79.

R. P. Blackmur. "Examples of Wallace Stevens," *Hound and Horn* 5(2), January-March 1932, 233-35. Reprinted in: R. P. Blackmur. *The Double Agent*, pp. 79-80. Also: R. P. Blackmur. *Language as Gesture*, pp. 230-32.

R. P. Blackmur. *Form and Value in Modern Poetry*, pp. 192-94.

David R. Ferry. *Explicator* 6(8), June 1948, Item 56.

Stevens Foster. "The *Gestalt* Configurations of Wallace Stevens," *Modern Language Quarterly* 28(1), March 1967, 70-71.

Albert William Levi. "A Note on Wallace Stevens and the Poem of Perspective," *Perspective* 7(3), Autumn 1954, 139-42.

J. Hillis Miller. *Poets of Reality*, pp. 239-40.

Sister M. Bernetta Quinn. *The Metamorphic Tradition*, pp. 52-53.

John Crowe Ransom. "The Rugged Way of Genius — A Tribute to Randall Jarrell," *Southern Review*, n.s., 3(2), Spring 1967, 268-69.

John Crowe Ransom. *The World's Body*, pp. 58-59.

Joseph N. Riddel. "'Disguised Pronunciamento': Wallace Stevens' *Sea Surface Full of Clouds*," *Texas University Studies in English* 37 (1958), 177-86.

M. L. Rosenthal. *Explicator* 19(6), March 1961, Item 38.

M. L. Rosenthal. *The Modern Poets*, pp. 130-31.

William York Tindall. "Wallace Stevens," in *Seven Modern American Poets*, pp. 59-60.

"The Sense of the Sleight-of-Hand Man"

Harry Brown and John Milstead. *What the Poem Means*, pp. 226-27.

Laurence Perrine. *100 American Poems of the Twentieth Century*, pp. 70-71.

"Six Significant Landscapes"

L. S. Dembo. *Conceptions of Reality in Modern American Poetry*, pp. 85-86.

Albert William Levi. "A Note on Wallace Stevens and the Poem of Perspective," *Perspective* 7(3), Autumn 1954, 142-44.

Charles Moorman. *Explicator* 17(1), October 1958, Item 1.

"Six Significant Landscapes," VI

John William Corrington. "Wallace Stevens and the Problem of Order: A Study of Three Poems," *Arlington Quarterly* 1(4), Summer 1968, 54-56.

"The Snow Man"

Gémino H. Abad. *A Formal Approach to Lyric Poetry*, pp. 144-45.

Richard P. Adams. "Wallace Stevens and Schopenhauer's *The World as Will and Idea*," *Tulane Studies in English* 20 (1972), 137-39.

William Bevis. "Stevens' Toneless Poetry," *ELH* 41(2), Summer 1974, 257-69.

R. P. Blackmur. "Examples of Wallace Stevens," *Hound and Horn* 5(2), January-March 1932, 242-43. Reprinted in: R. P. Blackmur. *The Double Agent*, pp. 87-89. Also: R. P. Blackmur. *Language as Gesture*, pp. 237-38.

Richard Blessing. "Wallace Stevens and the Necessary Reader: A Technique of Dynamism," *Twentieth Century Literature* 18(4), October 1972, 252-53.

Harold Bloom. *Poetry and Repression*, pp. 269-71.

Sharon Cameron. "'The Sense Against Calamity': Ideas of a Self in Three Poems by Wallace Stevens," *ELH* 43(4), Winter 1976, 584-87.

Kenneth Fields. "Postures of the Nerves: Reflections of the Nineteenth Century in the Poems of Wallace Stevens," *Southern Review*, n.s., 7(3), Summer 1971, 807-9.

Geoffrey H. Hartman. *Beyond Formalism*, pp. 256-57.

Graham Hough. "The Poetry of Wallace Stevens," *Critical Quarterly* 2(3), Autumn 1960, 205-6.

Robert Kern. "Toward a New Nature Poetry," *Centennial Review* 19(3), Summer 1975, 210-12.

Samuel Jay Keyser. "Wallace Stevens: Form and Meaning in Four Poems," *College English* 37(6), February 1976, 589-97.

George Lensing. "Wallace Stevens and the State of Winter Simplicity," *Southern Review*, n.s., 7(3), Summer 1971, 766-69.

Frank Lentricchia, Jr. "Wallace Stevens: The Ironic Eye," *Yale Review* 56(3), March 1967, 342-43.

James McMichael. "The Wallace Stevens Vulgates," *Southern Review*, n.s., 7(3), Summer 1971, 713-15.

Robert Pinsky. *The Situation of Poetry*, pp. 71-74.

James Rother. "The Tempering of *Harmonium*: The Last Years of Wallace Stevens's Apprenticeship, 1908-1914," *Arizona Quarterly* 33(4), Winter 1977, 336-38.

William York Tindall. "Wallace Stevens," in *Seven Modern American Poets*, pp. 61-62.

C. Roland Wagner. "The Idea of Nothingness in Wallace Stevens," *Accent* 12(2), Spring 1952, 118.

"So-and-So Reclining on Her Couch"

L. S. Dembo. *Conceptions of Reality in Modern American Poetry*, pp. 106-7.

Robert M. Farnsworth. *Explicator* 10(8), June 1952, Item 60.

Philip Furia and Martin Roth. "Stevens' Fusky Alphabet," *PMLA* 93(1), January 1978, 71-72.

STEVENS, WALLACE *(Cont.)*

"So-and-So Reclining on Her Couch" *(cont.)*

RICHARD GUSTAFSON. "The Practick of the Maker in Wallace Stevens," *Twentieth Century Literature* 9(2), July 1963, 83-85.

"Sombre Figuration"

FRANK DOGGETT. "Stevens on the Genesis of a Poem," *Contemporary Literature* 16(4), Autumn 1975, 469.

"Some Friends from Pascagoula"

JAMES L. KUGEL. *The Techniques of Strangeness in Symbolist Poetry*, pp. 71-72.

J. M. LINEBARGER. *Explicator* 35(2), Winter 1976, 12-13.

JAN PINKERTON. "Wallace Stevens in the Tropics: A Conservative Protest," *Yale Review* 60(2), December 1970, 225-26.

"Someone Puts a Pineapple Together"

C. D. CECIL. "An Audience for Wallace Stevens," *Essays in Criticism* 15(2), April 1965, 203-4.

STEVEN FOSTER. "The *Gestalt* Configurations of Wallace Stevens," *Modern Language Quarterly* 28(1), March 1967, 67-70.

J. HILLIS MILLER. *Poets of Reality*, pp. 242-44.

WILLIAM YORK TINDALL. "Wallace Stevens," in *Seven Modern American Poets*, pp. 74-75.

"Somnambulisma"

JANET MCCANN. *Explicator* 35(2), Winter 1976, 7-8.

"Sonatina to Hans Christian"

FRANK DOGGETT. "Wallace Stevens and the World We Know," *English Journal* 48(7), October 1959, 367.

"Stars at Tallapoosa"

FRANK DOGGETT. "Our Number is Her Nature," in *The Twenties,* edited by Richard E. Langford and William E. Taylor, p. 37.

KENNETH FIELDS. "Postures of the Nerves: Reflections of the Nineteenth Century in the Poems of Wallace Stevens," *Southern Review,* n.s., 7(3), Summer 1971, 781-82.

GEORGE LENSING. "Wallace Stevens and the State of Winter Simplicity," *Southern Review,* n.s., 7(3), Summer 1971, 769-70.

"Street Songs"

ROBERT BUTTEL. "Wallace Stevens at Harvard: Some Origins of His Theme and Style," *ELH* 29(1), March 1962, 108-13.

"Study of Images I"

WARREN CARRIER. "Wallace Stevens' Pagan Vantage," *Accent* 13(3), Summer 1953, 165-68. Reprinted in: *Reading Modern Poetry*, pp. 361-64; revised ed., pp. 360-63.

"Study of Two Pears"

RICHARD BLESSING. "Wallace Stevens and the Necessary Reader: A Technique of Dynamism," *Twentieth Century Literature* 18(4), October 1972, 253-54.

EMILIE BUCHWALD. "Wallace Stevens: The Delicatest Eye of the Mind," *American Quarterly* 14(2), Summer 1962, 189.

JOSEPH R. BURKE and M. S. GUSSENHOVEN. "Tides and the Affairs of Men: Reflection on Art and Science," *Antioch Review* 33(2), Summer 1975, 74-76.

KATHLEEN A. DALE. "Extensions: Beyond Resemblance and the Pleasure Principle in Wallace Stevens' Supreme Fiction," *Boundary 2* 4(1), Fall 1975, 267-68.

J. HILLIS MILLER. *Poets of Reality*, pp. 250-51.

WALTER SUTTON. *American Free Verse*, pp. 41-42.

HYATT H. WAGGONER. *American Poets*, pp. 437-38.

JOHN WHEATCROFT. "Hey, Any Work for Poetry?" *College English* 28(6), March 1967, 429-30.

"Sunday Morning"

HARRY BROWN and JOHN MILSTEAD. *What the Poem Means*, p. 224.

J. V. CUNNINGHAM. "The Poetry of Wallace Stevens," *Poetry* 75(3), December 1949, 159-64. Reprinted in: *Modern Literary Criticism*, pp. 360-64.

BABETTE DEUTSCH. *Poetry in Our Time*, pp. 250-51; second ed., pp. 280-81.

FRANK DOGGETT. "Our Number is Her Nature," in *The Twenties,* edited by Richard E. Langford and William E. Taylor, pp. 40-41.

DENIS DONOGHUE. *Connoisseurs of Chaos*, pp. 191-92.

ELIZABETH DREW. *Poetry*, pp. 217-21.

DWIGHT EDDINS. "Wallace Stevens: America the Primordial," *Modern Language Quarterly* 32(1), March 1971, 75-77.

RICHARD ELLMANN. "Wallace Stevens' Ice-Cream," *Kenyon Review* 19(1), Winter 1957, 95-97. Reprinted in: *Aspects of American Poetry*, pp. 210-12.

BERNARD F. ENGEL. "A Democratic Vista of Religion," *Georgia Review* 20(1), Spring 1966, 88.

LLOYD FRANKENBERG. *Pleasure Dome*, pp. 215-17.

RALPH FREEDMAN. "Wallace Stevens and Rainer Maria Rilke: Two Versions of a Poetic," in *The Poet as Critic*, pp. 66-67.

DON GEIGER. "Wallace Stevens' Wealth," *Perspective* 7(3), Autumn 1954, 164-65.

RICHARD GUSTAFSON. "The Practick of the Maker in Wallace Stevens," *Twentieth Century Literature* 9(2), July 1963, 85-86.

JAMES L. HILL. "The Frame for the Mind: Landscape in 'Lines Composed a Few Miles Above Tintern Abbey,' 'Dover Beach,' and 'Sunday Morning,'" *Centennial Review* 18(1), Winter 1974, 43-47.

GRAHAM HOUGH. "The Poetry of Wallace Stevens," *Critical Quarterly* 2(3), Autumn 1960, 201-4.

ROBERT LANGBAUM. "The New Nature Poetry," in *The Modern Spirit*, pp. 124-26.

FRANK LENTRICCHIA, JR. "Wallace Stevens: The Ironic Eye," *Yale Review* 56(3), March 1967, 339-42.

ELIZABETH LUNZ. "Robert Lowell and Wallace Stevens On Sunday Morning," *University Review* 37(4), Summer 1971, 268-72.

JAMES MCMICHAEL. "The Wallace Stevens Vulgates," *Southern Review,* n.s., 7(3), Summer 1971, 715-17.

J. HILLIS MILLER. *Poets of Reality*, p. 222.

LINDA MIZEJEWSKI. "Images of Woman in Wallace Stevens," *Thoth* 14(1), Winter 1973-74, 14-16.

FRANCIS MURPHY. "Going It Alone: Estrangement in American Poetry," *Yale Review* 56(1), October 1966, 19-20.

EUGENE PAUL NASSAR. *The Rape of Cinderella*, pp. 46-57.

ROBERT PACK. "Wallace Stevens: The Secular Mystery and the Comic Spirit," *Western Review* 20(1), Autumn 1955, 53-55.

ROY HARVEY PEARCE. *The Continuity of American Poetry*, pp. 385-87.

MARGARET PETERSON. "*Harmonium* and William James," *Southern Review,* n.s., 7(3), Summer 1971, 660-61.

ROBERT PINSKY. *The Situation of Poetry,* pp. 145-46, 149.

JOHN CROWE RANSOM. "Stevens: Sunday Morning," in *Master Poems of the English Language,* pp. 893-97.

JOSEPH N. RIDDEL. "Walt Whitman and Wallace Stevens: Functions of a 'Literatus,'" *South Atlantic Quarterly* 61(4), Autumn 1962, 512-13.

M. L. ROSENTHAL. *Poetry and the Common Life,* pp. 13-19.

JAY SEMEL. "Stevens' Journal and 'Sunday Morning,'" *Wallace Stevens Journal* 1(2), Summer 1977, 69-70.

JOHN N. SERIO. "'The Comedian' as the Idea of Order in *Harmonium,*" *Papers on Language and Literature* 12(2), Spring 1976, 96-97.

WILLIAM BYSSHE STEIN. "Stevens' 'Sunday Morning': Harlequin the Equilibrist," *Wallace Stevens Journal* 2(3-4), Fall 1978, 35-44.

WILLIAM YORK TINDALL. "Wallace Stevens," in *Seven Modern American Poets,* pp. 77-78.

HYATT H. WAGGONER. *American Poets,* p. 433.

CAROL KYROS WALKER. "The Subject as Speaker in 'Sunday Morning,'" *Concerning Poetry* 10(1), Spring 1977, 25-31.

YVOR WINTERS. *The Anatomy of Nonsense,* pp. 88-91, 105-8. Reprinted in: Yvor Winters. *In Defense of Reason,* pp. 431-34, 447-56. Also: *Readings for Liberal Education,* II: 530-33; revised ed., II: 206-9; third ed., II: 193-96; fourth ed., II: 194-97; fifth ed., II: 174-77. Also: *Four Poets on Poetry,* pp. 72-75.

MICHAEL ZIMMERMAN. "The Pursuit of Pleasure and the Uses of Death: Wallace Stevens' 'Sunday Morning,'" *University Review* 33(2), Winter 1966, 113-23.

"Tattoo"

ARTHUR C. MCGILL. *The Celebration of Flesh,* pp. 148-49.

"Tea at the Palaz of Hoon"

SAMUEL FRENCH MORSE. "Wallace Stevens, Bergson, Pater," *ELH* 31(1), March 1964, 13-15.

MARGARET PETERSON. "*Harmonium* and William James," *Southern Review,* n.s., 7(3), Summer 1971, 681-82.

JOHN N. SERIO. "'The Comedian' as the Idea of Order in *Harmonium,*" *Papers on Language and Literature* 12(2), Spring 1976, 93.

"That Which Cannot Be Fixed"

MARIUS BEWLEY. "The Poetry of Wallace Stevens," *Partisan Review* 16(9), September 1949, 910-11.

"Theory"

JOHN GRUBE. *Explicator* 25(3), November 1966, Item 26.

"Things of August"

ALAN D. PERLIS. "Yeats' Byzantium and Stevens' Rome: A Comparison of Two Poems," *Wallace Stevens Journal* 2(1-2), Spring 1978, 18-19.

"Thinking of a Relation between the Images of Metaphor"

DWIGHT EDDINS. "Wallace Stevens: America the Primordial," *Modern Language Quarterly* 32(1), March 1971, 80.

AGNES STEIN. *The Uses of Poetry,* pp. 146-47.

"Thirteen Ways of Looking at a Blackbird"

PRICE CALDWELL. "Metaphoric Structures in Wallace Stevens' 'Thirteen Ways of Looking at a Blackbird,'" *Journal of English and Germanic Philology* 71(3), July 1972, 321-35.

FRANK DOGGETT. "Wallace Stevens and the World We Know," *English Journal* 48(7), October 1959, 368. (P)

JOHN H. HAFNER. "One Way of Looking at 'Thirteen Ways of Looking at a Blackbird,'" *Concerning Poetry* 3(1), Spring 1970, 61-66.

ALBERT WILLIAM LEVI. "A Note on Wallace Stevens and the Poem of Perspective," *Perspective* 7(3), Autumn 1954, 144-46.

PETER L. MCNAMARA. "The Multi-Faceted Blackbird and Wallace Stevens' Poetic Vision," *College English* 25(6), March 1964, 446-48.

M. L. ROSENTHAL. *The Modern Poets,* pp. 128-29.

WILLIAM YORK TINDALL. "Wallace Stevens," in *Seven Modern American Poets,* pp. 80-81.

LEONARD UNGER and WILLIAM VAN O'CONNOR. *Poems for Study,* pp. 608-16.

HELEN HENNESSY VENDLER. "Stevens' 'Like Decorations in a Nigger Cemetery,'" *Massachusetts Review* 7(1), Winter 1966, 144-46. Reprinted in: *Modern Poetry,* pp. 481-84.

"This Solitude of Cataracts"

KENNETH FIELDS. "Postures of the Nerves: Reflections of the Nineteenth Century In the Poems of Wallace Stevens," *Southern Review,* n.s., 7(3), Summer 1971, 783-84.

"A Thought Revolved"

ROBERT MOLLINGER. *Explicator* 33(1), September 1974, Item 1.

"To an Old Philosopher in Rome"

BERNARD DUFFEY. *Poetry in America,* p. 221.

LAURENCE LERNER. *An Introduction to English Poetry,* pp. 186-98.

ISABEL G. MACCAFFREY. "A Point of Central Arrival: Stevens' *The Rock,*" *ELH* 40(4), Winter 1973, 617-23.

ARTHUR C. MCGILL. *The Celebration of Flesh,* pp. 172-73.

ALAN D. PERLIS. "Yeats' Byzantium and Stevens' Rome: A Comparison of Two Poems," *Wallace Stevens Journal* 2(1-2), Spring 1978, 18-25.

JOSEPH N. RIDDEL. "Wallace Stevens' 'Visibility of Thought,'" *PMLA* 77(4), September 1962, 492-93.

"To the One of Fictive Music"

RICHARD E. AMACHER. *Explicator* 11(6), April 1953, Item 43.

JOSEPH N. RIDDEL. "Walt Whitman and Wallace Stevens: Functions of a 'Literatus,'" *South Atlantic Quarterly* 61(4), Autumn 1962, 518-19.

JOHN N. SERIO. "'The Comedian' as the Idea of Order in *Harmonium,*" *Papers on Language and Literature* 12(2), Spring 1976, 98-99.

"To the Roaring Wind"

GÉMINO H. ABAD. *A Formal Approach to Lyric Poetry,* pp. 40-41.

"Two Figures in Dense Violet Light"

HAROLD BLOOM. *Figures of Capable Imagination,* pp. 105-7.

ROBERT W. BUTTEL. *Explicator* 9(7), May 1951, Item 45.

GRAHAM HOUGH. "The Poetry of Wallace Stevens," *Critical Quarterly* 2(3), Autumn 1960, 214-15.

"Two Illustrations That the World Is What You Make of It"

MARJORIE PERLOFF. "Irony in Wallace Stevens' *The Rock,*" *American Literature* 36(3), November 1964, 337.

STEVENS, WALLACE (*Cont.*)

"Two or Three Ideas"

HAROLD E. TOLIVER. *Pastoral Forms and Attitudes*, pp. 308-9.

"Two Tales of Liadoff"

LLOYD FRANKENBERG. *Pleasure Dome*, pp. 254-56.

"Two Versions of the Same Poem"

FRED MILLER ROBINSON. "Poems That Took the Place of Mountains: Realization in Stevens and Cézanne," *Centennial Review* 22(3), Summer 1978, 284-85.

JOY M. SEMEL. "Pennsylvania Dutch Country: Stevens' World as Meditation," *Contemporary Literature* 14(3), Summer 1973, 317.

"United Dames of America"

ROBERT N. MOLLINGER. "Wallace Stevens' Search for the Central Man," *Tennessee Studies in Literature* 21 (1976), 66-67. (P)

"Vacancy in the Park"

ARTHUR C. MCGILL. *The Celebration of Flesh*, pp. 154-55.

"Variations on a Summer Day"

EDWARD BUTSCHER. "Wallace Stevens' Neglected Fugue: 'Variations on a Summer Day,'" *Twentieth Century Literature* 19(3), July 1973, 153-64.

"The Virgin Carrying a Lantern"

HOWARD BAKER. "Wallace Stevens and Other Poets," *Southern Review* 1(2), Autumn 1935, 374-75.

L. B. KENNELLY. "Stevens' 'The Virgin Carrying a Lantern,'" *Wallace Stevens Journal* 2(1-2), Spring 1978, 49.

"The Weeping Burgher"

SAMUEL FRENCH MORSE. "Wallace Stevens, Bergson, Pater," *ELH* 31(1), March 1964, 4-5.

"The Well Dressed Man with a Beard"

FRANK LENTRICCHIA, JR. "Wallace Stevens: The Ironic Eye," *Yale Review* 56(3), March 1967, 338.

"What We See Is What We Think"

ROBERT N. MOLLINGER. "An Analysis of Wallace Stevens' 'What We See Is What We Think,'" *Notes on Contemporary Literature* 4(5), November 1974, 5-7.

"Who Lies Dead?"

ROBERT BUTTEL. "Wallace Stevens at Harvard: Some Origins of His Theme and Style," *ELH* 29(1), March 1962, 97-98.

"Windy Nights"

JAMES ROTHER. "The Tempering of *Harmonium*: The Last Years of Wallace Stevens's Apprenticeship, 1908-1914," *Arizona Quarterly* 33(4), Winter 1977, 327-28.

"Winter Bells"

JAN PINKERTON. "Wallace Stevens in the Tropics: A Conservative Protest," *Yale Review* 60(2), December 1970, 221-22.

"The Woman in Sunshine"

RICHARD BLESSING. "Wallace Stevens and the Necessary Reader: A Technique of Dynamism," *Twentieth Century Literature* 18(4), October 1972, 254-55.

BABETTE DEUTSCH. *Poetry in Our Time*, second ed., pp. 276-77.

ROBERT PACK. "Wallace Stevens' Sufficient Muse," *Southern Review*, n.s., 11(4), Autumn 1975, 776-77.

"Woman Looking at a Vase of Flowers"

FRANK DOGGETT. *Explicator* 19(2), November 1960, Item 7.

"A Word with José Rodriguez-Feo"

FRANK DOGGETT. "Stevens on the Genesis of a Poem," *Contemporary Literature* 16(4), Autumn 1975, 471.

"The World as Meditation"

SHARON CAMERON. "'The Sense Against Calamity': Ideas of a Self in Three Poems by Wallace Stevens," *ELH* 43(4), Winter 1976, 587-92.

ISABEL G. MACCAFFREY. "A Point of Central Arrival: Stevens' *The Rock*," *ELH* 40(4), Winter 1973, 611-14.

LOUIS L. MARTZ. "Wallace Stevens: The World as Meditation," *Yale Review* 47(4), Summer 1958, 517-18, 533-34. Reprinted in: *Modern American Poetry*, edited by Guy Owen, pp. 37-39, 53-55.

MARJORIE PERLOFF. "Irony in Wallace Stevens' *The Rock*," *American Literature* 36(3), November 1964, 330-31.

JON ROSENBLATT. "On Wallace Stevens' 'The World as Meditation,'" *Notes on Modern American Literature* 3(1), Winter 1978, Item 2.

"World Without Peculiarity"

SISTER M. BERNETTA QUINN. *The Metamorphic Tradition*, pp. 78-79.

STICKNEY, TRUMBULL

"Emperor Julian"

AMBERYS R. WHITTLE. "The Dust of Seasons: Time in the Poetry of Trumbull Stickney," *Sewanee Review* 74(4), Autumn 1966, 908.

"Eride"

AMBERYS R. WHITTLE. "The Dust of Seasons: Time in the Poetry of Trumbull Stickney," *Sewanee Review* 74(4), Autumn 1966, 902.

"Fidelity"

BERNARD DUFFEY. *Poetry in America*, pp. 148-49.

"In a City Garden"

AMBERYS R. WHITTLE. "The Dust of Seasons: Time in the Poetry of Trumbull Stickney," *Sewanee Review* 74(4), Autumn 1966, 903-4.

"In Ampezzo"

ROSS C. MURFIN. "The Poetry of Trumbull Stickney: A Centennial Rediscovery," *New England Quarterly* 48(4), December 1975, 543-46, 553-54.

AMBERYS R. WHITTLE. "The Dust of Seasons: Time in the Poetry of Trumbull Stickney," *Sewanee Review* 74(4), Autumn 1966, 904-5.

"In Summer"

AMBERYS R. WHITTLE. "The Dust of Seasons: Time in the Poetry of Trumbull Stickney," *Sewanee Review* 74(4), Autumn 1966, 906.

"Lakeward"

ROSS C. MURFIN. "The Poetry of Trumbull Stickney: A Centennial Rediscovery," *New England Quarterly* 48(4), December 1975, 547-50.

"Mnemosyne"

ROSS C. MURFIN. "The Poetry of Trumbull Stickney: A Centennial Rediscovery," *New England Quarterly* 48(4), December 1975, 546-47, 552-53.

"Mt. Lykaion"

BERNARD DUFFEY. *Poetry in America*, p. 149.

"On Some Shells Found Inland"
>   JAMES REEVES and MARTIN SEYMOUR-SMITH. *Inside Poetry*, pp. 78-79.

"Once"
>   AMBERYS R. WHITTLE. "The Dust of Seasons: Time in the Poetry of Trumbull Stickney," *Sewanee Review* 74(4), Autumn 1966, 901.

"Oneiropolos"
>   AMBERYS R. WHITTLE. "The Dust of Seasons: Time in the Poetry of Trumbull Stickney," *Sewanee Review* 74(4), Autumn 1966, 908.

"Pity"
>   AMBERYS R. WHITTLE. "The Dust of Seasons: Time in the Poetry of Trumbull Stickney," *Sewanee Review* 74(4), Autumn 1966, 901.

STONE, RUTH

"Liberation"
>   HARVEY GROSS. "On the Poetry of Ruth Stone: Selections and Commentary," *Iowa Review* 3(2), Spring 1972, 102.

"Metamorphosis"
>   HARVEY GROSS. "On the Poetry of Ruth Stone: Selections and Commentary," *Iowa Review* 3(2), Spring 1972, 101-2.

"Seat Belt Fastened?"
>   HARVEY GROSS. "On the Poetry of Ruth Stone: Selections and Commentary," *Iowa Review* 3(2), Spring 1972, 102-3.

STRAND, MARK

"Eating Poetry"
>   WILLIAM SLAUGHTER. "Eating Poetry," *Chicago Review* 25(4), 1974, 125-27.

"Elegy for My Father"
>   LAURENCE LIEBERMAN. *Unassigned Frequencies*, pp. 142-44.

"The Man in the Mirror"
>   HAROLD BLOOM. "Dark and Radiant Peripheries: Mark Strand and A. R. Ammons," *Southern Review*, n.s., 8(1), Winter 1972, 136-37.
>   HAROLD BLOOM. *Figures of Capable Imagination*, pp. 153-54.

"The Remains"
>   HAROLD BLOOM. "Dark and Radiant Peripheries: Mark Strand and A. R. Ammons," *Southern Review*, n.s., 8(1), Winter 1972, 138-39.
>   HAROLD BLOOM. *Figures of Capable Imagination*, p. 156.

"The Room"
>   LAURENCE LIEBERMAN. *Unassigned Frequencies*, p. 145.

"To Begin"
>   LAURENCE LIEBERMAN. *Unassigned Frequencies*, pp. 146-47.

"The Untelling"
>   LAURENCE LIEBERMAN. *Unassigned Frequencies*, pp. 147-51.

SUCKLING, JOHN

"Against Absence"
>   EARL MINER. *The Cavalier Mode from Jonson to Cotton*, pp. 243-44.

"Against Fruition (II)"
>   MICHAEL H. MARKEL. "John Suckling's Semi-Serious Love Poetry," *Essays in Literature* 4(2), Fall 1977, 156-57.

"A Ballad Upon a Wedding"
>   RAYMOND A. ANSELMENT. " 'Men Most of All Enjoy, When Least They Do': The Love Poetry of John Suckling," *Texas Studies in Literature and Language* 14(1), Spring 1972, 29-32.

"The Constant Lover"
>   RAYMOND A. ANSELMENT. " 'Men Most of All Enjoy, When Least They Do': The Love Poetry of John Suckling," *Texas Studies in Literature and Language* 14(1), Spring 1972, 17-19.
>   STANLEY E. CLAYES and JOHN GERRIETTS. *Ways to Poetry*, pp. 3-5.

"Do'st see how unregarded now?"
>   RAYMOND A. ANSELMENT. " 'Men Most of All Enjoy, When Least They Do': The Love Poetry of John Suckling," *Texas Studies in Literature and Language* 14(1), Spring 1972, 20-21.

"Farewell to Love"
>   RAYMOND A. ANSELMENT. " 'Men Most of All Enjoy, When Least They Do': The Love Poetry of John Suckling," *Texas Studies in Literature and Language* 14(1), Spring 1972, 27-28.
>   MICHAEL H. MARKEL. "John Suckling's Semi-Serious Love Poetry," *Essays in Literature* 4(2), Fall 1977, 153-55.

"Loves Siege"
>   RAYMOND A. ANSELMENT. " 'Men Most of All Enjoy, When Least They Do': The Love Poetry of John Suckling," *Texas Studies in Literature and Language* 14(1), Spring 1972, 28-29.
>   MICHAEL H. MARKEL. "John Suckling's Semi-Serious Love Poetry," *Essays in Literature* 4(2), Fall 1977, 153.

"Loving and Beloved"
>   MICHAEL H. MARKEL. "John Suckling's Semi-Serious Love Poetry," *Essays in Literature* 4(2), Fall 1977, 155-56.

"Out upon it! I have loved"
>   see "The Constant Lover"

"A Sessions of the Poets"
>   JOSEPH H. SUMMERS. *The Heirs of Donne and Jonson*, pp. 42-44.

" 'Tis now, since I sate down before"
>   see "Loves Siege"

"Upon My Lady Carlisle's Walking in Hampton Court Garden"
>   DAVID FARLEY-HILLS. *The Benevolence of Laughter*, pp. 37-39.

"Why So Pale and Wan Fond Lover?"
>   L. A. BEAURLINE. " 'Why So Pale and Wan': An Essay in Critical Method," *Texas Studies in Literature and Language* 4(4), Winter 1963, 553-63. Reprinted in: *Seventeenth Century English Poetry*, revised ed., pp. 300-11.

SURREY, HENRY HOWARD, EARL OF

"Th' Assyrians' king, in peace with foul desire"
>   WALTER R. DAVIS. "Contexts in Surrey's Poetry," *English Literary Renaissance* 4(1), Winter 1974, 45-46.

SURREY, HENRY HOWARD, EARL OF *(Cont.)*

"Complaint of a Lover Rebuked"

  see "Love that doth reign and live within my thought"

"Complaint of the Absence of Her Lover, Being upon the Sea"

  see "O Happy dames, that may embrace"

"Description and Praise of His Love Geraldine"

  see "From Tuscan came my lady's worthy race"

"Description of Spring, Wherein Each Thing Renews Save Only Love"

  see "The soote season that bud and bloom forth brings"

"Divers thy death do diversely bemoan"

  C. W. JENTOFT. "Surrey's Five Elegies: Rhetoric, Structure, and the Poetry of Praise," *PMLA* 91(1), January 1976, 27-28.

  DOUGLAS L. PETERSON. *The English Lyric from Wyatt to Donne,* p. 69.

"An Epitaph on Thomas Clere"

  see "Norfolk sprang thee, Lambeth holds thee dead"

"From Tuscan came my lady's worthy race"

  WALTER R. DAVIS. "Contexts in Surrey's Poetry," *English Literary Renaissance* 4(1), Winter 1974, 49-51.

"Give place, ye lovers here before"

  C. W. JENTOFT. "Surrey's Four 'Orations' and the Influence of Rhetoric on Dramatic Effect," *Papers on Language and Literature* 9(3), Summer 1973, 250-57.

"Good ladies, you that have your pleasure in exile"

  C. W. JENTOFT. "Surrey's Four 'Orations' and the Influence of Rhetoric on Dramatic Effect," *Papers on Language and Literature* 9(3), Summer 1973, 250-55.

"In the rude age when science was not so rife"

  EDGAR F. DANIELS. *Explicator* 36(4), Summer 1978, 14-15. (P)

  C. W. JENTOFT. "Surrey's Five Elegies: Rhetoric, Structure, and the Poetry of Praise," *PMLA* 91(1), January 1976, 28-30.

"The Lady Again Complains"

  see "Good ladies, you that have your pleasure in exile"

"Laid in my quiet bed, in study as I were"

  WALTER R. DAVIS. "Contexts in Surrey's Poetry," *English Literary Renaissance* 4(1), Winter 1974, 47-48.

"London, hast thou accused me"

  C. W. JENTOFT. "Surrey's Four 'Orations' and the Influence of Rhetoric on Dramatic Effect," *Papers on Language and Literature* 9(3), Summer 1973, 250-62.

"Love that doth reign and live within my thought"

  WILLIAM O. HARRIS. "'Love That Doth Raine': Surrey's Creative Imitation," *Modern Philology* 66(4), May 1969, 298-305.

  JOSEPHINE MILES. *Major Adjectives in English Poetry,* pp. 326-27.

  HALLETT SMITH. "The Art of Sir Thomas Wyatt," *Huntington Library Quarterly* 9(4), August 1946, 334-37.

"Norfolk sprang thee, Lambeth holds thee dead"

  ALISTAIR FOWLER. *Conceitful Thought,* pp. 31-37.

  C. W. JENTOFT. "Surrey's Five Elegies: Rhetoric, Structure, and the Poetry of Praise," *PMLA* 91(1), January 1976, 24-25.

  JAMES REEVES and MARTIN SEYMOUR-SMITH. *Inside Poetry,* pp. 37-39.

"O Happy dames, that may embrace"

  WALTER R. DAVIS. "Contexts in Surrey's Poetry," *English Literary Renaissance* 4(1), Winter 1974, 49.

  C. W. JENTOFT. "Surrey's Four 'Orations' and the Influence of Rhetoric on Dramatic Effect," *Papers on Language and Literature* 9(3), Summer 1973, 250-55.

"Prisoned in Windsor, He Recounteth His Pleasure There Passed"

  see "So cruel prison how could betide, alas"

"So cruel prison how could betide, alas"

  DAVID DAICHES and WILLIAM CHARVAT. *Poems in English,* pp. 644-45.

  WALTER R. DAVIS. "Contexts in Surrey's Poetry," *English Literary Renaissance* 4(1), Winter 1974, 51-53.

  C. W. JENTOFT. "Surrey's Five Elegies: Rhetoric, Structure, and the Poetry of Praise," *PMLA* 91(1), January 1976, 30-32.

  DOUGLAS L. PETERSON. *The English Lyric from Wyatt to Donne,* pp. 69-72.

"The soote season that bud and bloom forth brings"

  WALTER R. DAVIS. "Contexts in Surrey's Poetry," *English Literary Renaissance* 4(1), Winter 1974, 40-41.

  ALISTAIR FOWLER. *Conceitful Thought,* pp. 22-25.

"The storms are past, these clouds are overblown"

  DOUGLAS L. PETERSON. *The English Lyric from Wyatt to Donne,* pp. 77-78.

"The sun hath twice brought forth the tender green"

  WALTER R. DAVIS. "Contexts in Surrey's Poetry," *English Literary Renaissance* 4(1), Winter 1974, 42.

"When raging love with extreme pain"

  WALTER R. DAVIS. "Contexts in Surrey's Poetry," *English Literary Renaissance* 4(1), Winter 1974, 46-47.

  RAYMOND B. WADDINGTON. "Shakespeare's Sonnet 15 and the Art of Memory," in *The Rhetoric of Renaissance Poetry,* p. 100.

"When youth had led me half the race"

  RAYMOND B. WADDINGTON. "Shakespeare's Sonnet 15 and the Art of Memory," in *The Rhetoric of Renaissance Poetry,* pp. 99-100.

"Wyatt resteth here, that quick could never rest"

  WALTER R. DAVIS. "Contexts in Surrey's Poetry," *English Literary Renaissance* 4(1), Winter 1974, 53-55.

  ALISTAIR FOWLER. *Conceitful Thought,* pp. 25-30.

  C. W. JENTOFT. "Surrey's Five Elegies: Rhetoric, Structure, and the Poetry of Praise," *PMLA* 91(1), January 1976, 24-27.

  DOUGLAS L. PETERSON. *The English Lyric from Wyatt to Donne,* pp. 66-68.

SWAN, JON

"The Magpie"

  JAMES M. REID. *100 American Poems of the Twentieth Century,* pp. 285-87.

SWARD, ROBERT

"Hello Poem"

  LAURENCE LIEBERMAN. "Robert Sward: A Mysticism of Objects," *Carleton Miscellany* 8(2), Spring 1967, 34-35.

"Mothers-in-Law"

  LAURENCE LIEBERMAN. "Robert Sward: A Mysticism of Objects," *Carleton Miscellany* 8(2), Spring 1967, 28-29.

"Nightgown, Wife's Gown"

LAURENCE LIEBERMAN. "Robert Sward: A Mysticism of Objects," *Carleton Miscellany* 8(2), Spring 1967, 30.

"Owl"

LAURENCE LIEBERMAN. "Robert Sward: A Mysticism of Objects," *Carleton Miscellany* 8(2), Spring 1967, 32-33.

"Turnpike"

LAURENCE LIEBERMAN. "Robert Sward: A Mysticism of Objects," *Carleton Miscellany* 8(2), Spring 1967, 20-28.

SWENSON, MAY

"Cat & the weather"

DOROTHY PETTIT. "Poem, Students, & the Teacher," *English Journal* 55(2), February 1966, 222-24.

"Lion"

LAURENCE PERRINE. *100 American Poems of the Twentieth Century*, pp. 249-51.

SWIFT, JONATHAN

"The Author Upon Himself"

RONALD PAULSON. "Swift, Stella, and Permanence," *ELH* 27(4), December 1960, 305.

"A Beautiful Young Nymph Going to Bed"

JOHN M. ADEN. "Corinna and the Sterner Muse of Swift," *English Language Notes* 4(1), September 1966, 23-31.

THOMAS B. GILMORE, JR. "The Comedy of Swift's Scatological Poems," *PMLA* 91(1), January 1976, 34-35.

JOHN L. IDOL, JR. "Thomas Wolfe and Jonathan Swift," *South Carolina Review* 8(1), November 1975, 44-46.

MURRAY KRIEGER. *The Classic Vision*, pp. 264-68.

FELICITY NUSSBAUM. "Juvenal, Swift, and *The Folly of Love*," *Eighteenth Century Studies* 9(4), Summer 1976, 540-52.

CHRISTINE REES. "Gay, Swift, and the Nymphs of Drury-Lane," *Essays in Criticism* 23(1), January 1973, 16-18.

RICHARD H. RODINO. "Blasphemy or Blessing? Swift's 'Scatological' Poems," *Papers on Language and Literature* 14(2), Spring 1978, 161-64.

PETER J. SCHAKEL. "Swift's Remedy for Love: The 'Scatological' Poems," *Papers on Language and Literature* 14(2), Spring 1978, 141-43.

JOHN F. SENA. "Swift as Moral Physician: Scatology and the Tradition of Love Melancholy," *Journal of English and Germanic Philology* 76(3), July 1977, 346-62.

ROBERT W. UPHAUS. "Swift's Poetry: The Making of Meaning," *Eighteenth Century Studies* 5(4), Summer 1972, 578-81.

"Cadenus and Vanessa"

A. B. ENGLAND. "Rhetorical Order and Emotional Turbulence in *Cadenus and Vanessa*," *Papers on Language and Literature* 14(2), Spring 1978, 116-23.

GARETH JONES. "Swift's *Cadenus and Vanessa*: A question of 'Positives,'" *Essays in Criticism* 20(4), October 1970, 424-40.

PETER OHLIN. "'Cadenus and Vanessa': Reason and Passion," *Studies in English Literature 1500-1900* 4(3), Summer 1964, 485-96.

RONALD PAULSON. "Swift, Stella, and Permanence," *ELH* 27(4), December 1960, 312-13.

RICHARD HODGE RODINO. "The Private Sense of *Cadenus and Vanessa*," *Concerning Poetry* 11(2), Fall 1978, 41-47.

JAMES L. TYNE. "Vanessa and the Houyhnhnms: A Reading of 'Cadenus and Vanessa,'" *Studies in English Literature 1500-1900* 11(3), Summer 1971, 517-34.

T. G. WILSON. "Swift's Personality," *Review of English Literature* 3(3), July 1962, 47-49.

"Cassinus and Peter"

JEFFREY R. FOX. "Swift's 'Scatalogical' Poems: The Hidden Norm," *Thoth* 15(3), Fall 1975, 3-13.

THOMAS B. GILMORE, JR. "The Comedy of Swift's Scatological Poems," *PMLA* 91(1), January 1976, 38-39.

DONALD GREENE. "On Swift's 'Scatological' Poems," *Sewanee Review* 75(4), Autumn 1967, 674-76.

RICHARD H. RODINO. "Blasphemy or Blessing? Swift's 'Scatological' Poems," *Papers on Language and Literature* 14(2), Spring 1978, 167-70.

"A Character, Panegyric, and Description of the Legion Club"

HERBERT DAVIS. "Alecto's Whip," *Review of English Literature* 3(3), July 1962, 12-16.

PETER J. SCHAKEL. "Virgil and the Dean: Christian and Classical Allusion in *The Legion Club*," *Studies in Philology* 70(4), October 1973, 427-38.

"The Day of Judgement"

W. R. IRWIN. "Swift the Verse Man," *Philological Quarterly* 54(1), Winter 1975, 234-36.

T. HENRY SMITH. *Explicator* 22(1), September 1963, Item 6.

"The Dean's Reasons for Not Building at Drapier's Hill"

CAROLE FABRICANT. "The Garden as City: Swift's Landscape of Alienation," *ELH* 42(4), Winter 1975, 546-50.

"Death and Daphne"

NORA CROW JAFFE. "Swift and the Agreeable Young Lady, but Extremely Lean," *Papers on Language and Literature* 14(2), Spring 1978, 129-37.

"A Description of a City Shower"

GÉMINO H. ABAD. *A Formal Approach to Lyric Poetry*, pp. 256-57.

A. B. ENGLAND. "World Without Order: Some Thoughts on the Poetry of Swift," *Essays in Criticism* 16(1), January 1966, 43.

JOHN I. FISCHER. "Apparent Contraries: A Reading of Swift's 'A Description of a City Shower,'" *Tennessee Studies in Literature* 19 (1974), 21-34.

BRENDAN O. HEHIR. "Meaning of Swift's 'Description of a City Shower,'" *ELH* 27(3), September 1960, 194-207.

OSWALD JOHNSTON. "Swift and the Common Reader," in *In Defense of Reading*, ppp. 175-78.

JAMES REEVES and MARTIN SEYMOUR-SMITH. *Inside Poetry*, pp. 26-29.

"The Description of a Salamander"

A. B. ENGLAND. "The Subversion of Logic in Some Poems by Swift," *Studies in English Literature 1500-1900* 15(3), Summer 1975, 410-12.

ALAN S. FISHER. "Swift's Verse Portraits: A Study of His Originality as an Augustan Satirist," *Studies in English Literature 1500-1900* 14(3), Summer 1974, 344-45.

ROBERT W. UPHAUS. "Swift's Poetry: The Making of Meaning," *Eighteenth Century Studies* 5(4), Summer 1972, 572-73.

SWIFT, JONATHAN *(Cont.)*

"A Description of the Morning"

    F. W. BATESON. *English Poetry*, pp. 175-78.

    MARIUS BEWLEY. *Masks & Mirrors*, pp. 98-100.

    A. B. ENGLAND. "World Without Order: Some Thoughts on the Poetry of Swift," *Essays in Criticism* 16(1), January 1966, 40-41.

    MURRAY KRIEGER. *The Classic Vision*, pp. 258-59.

    AGNES STEIN. *The Uses of Poetry*, pp. 218-19.

    DAVID M. VIETH. "*Fiat Lux*: Logos versus Chaos in Swift's 'A Description of the Morning,'" *Papers on Language and Literature* 8(3), Summer 1972, 302-7.

"Directions for a Birth-day Song"

    ALAN S. FISHER. "Swift's Verse Portraits: A Study of His Originality as an Augustan Satirist," *Studies in English Literature 1500-1900* 14(3), Summer 1974, 347-48.

"An Epistle to a Lady"

    JAY ARNOLD LEVINE. "The Status of the Verse Epistle Before Pope," *Studies in Philology* 59(4), October 1962, 679-80.

"An Epistle upon an Epistle"

    ROBERT W. UPHAUS. "Swift's 'Whole Character': The Delany Poems and 'Verses on the Death of Dr. Swift,'" *Modern Language Quarterly* 34(4), December 1973, 408. (P)

"The Fable of Midas"

    A. B. ENGLAND. "The Subversion of Logic in Some Poems by Swift," *Studies in English Literature 1500-1900* 15(3), Summer 1975, 412-13.

"The Lady's Dressing Room"

    LOUISE K. BARNETT. "The Mysterious Narrator: Another Look at 'The Lady's Dressing Room,'" *Concerning Poetry* 9(2), Fall 1976, 29-32.

    A. B. ENGLAND. "World Without Order: Some Thoughts on the Poetry of Swift," *Essays in Criticism* 16(1), January 1966, 32-36.

    JEFFREY R. FOX. "Swift's 'Scatological' Poems: The Hidden Norm," *Thoth* 15(3), Fall 1975, 3-13.

    THOMAS B. GILMORE, JR. "The Comedy of Swift's Scatological Poems," *PMLA* 91(1), January 1976, 35-37.

    DONALD GREENE. "On Swift's 'Scatological' Poems," *Sewanee Review* 75(4), Autumn 1967, 676-80.

    MURRAY KRIEGER. *The Classic Vision*, pp. 260-64.

    RICHARD H. RODINO. "Blasphemy or Blessing? Swift's 'Scatological' Poems," *Papers on Language and Literature* 14(2), Spring 1978, 158-61.

    PETER J. SCHAKEL. "Swift's Remedy for Love: The 'Scatological' Poems," *Papers on Language and Literature* 14(2), Spring 1978, 137-41.

    JOHN F. SENA. "Swift as Moral Physician: Scatology and the Tradition of Love Melancholy," *Journal of English and Germanic Philology* 76(3), July 1977, 346-62.

"A Libel on Dr. Delany and a Certain Great Lord"

    ROBERT W. UPHAUS. "Swift's 'Whole Character': The Delany Poems and 'Verses on the Death of Dr. Swift,'" *Modern Language Quarterly* 34(4), December 1973, 409.

"The Life and Genuine Character of Doctor Swift"

    ARTHUR H. SCOUTEN and ROBERT D. HUME. "Pope and Swift: Text and Interpretation of Swift's Verses on His Death," *Philological Quarterly* 52(2), April 1973, 211-15.

"Mrs. Harris's Petition"

    A. B. ENGLAND. "World Without Order: Some Thoughts on the Poetry of Swift," *Essays in Criticism* 16(1), January 1966, 41-42.

    RICHARD REYNOLDS. "Swift's 'Humble Petition' from a Pregnant Frances Harris?" *Scriblerian* 5(1), Autumn 1972, 38-39. (P)

"My Lady's Lamentation and Complaint against the Dean"

    CAROLE FABRICANT. "The Garden as City: Swift's Landscape of Alienation," *ELH* 42(4), Winter 1975, 543-45.

"Occasioned by Sir William Temple's Late Illness and Recovery"

    KATHRYN MONTGOMERY HARRIS. "'Occasions So Few': Satire as a Strategy in Swift's Early Odes," *Modern Language Quarterly* 31(1), March 1970, 30-31.

"Ode to Dr. William Sancroft"

    DAVID P. FRENCH. "Swift, the Non-Jurors, and Jacobitism," *Modern Language Notes* 72(4), April 1957, 258-64.

    KATHRYN MONTGOMERY HARRIS. "'Occasions So Few': Satire as a Strategy in Swift's Early Odes," *Modern Language Quarterly* 31(1), March 1970, 28-29.

    EDWARD W. ROSENHEIM, JR. "Swift's *Ode to Sancroft*: Another Look," *Modern Philology* 73(4, pt. 2), May 1976, S24-S39.

"Ode to Sir William Temple"

    KATHRYN MONTGOMERY HARRIS. "'Occasions So Few': Satire as a Strategy in Swift's Early Odes," *Modern Language Quarterly* 31(1), March 1970, 27-28.

    ROBERT W. UPHAUS. "From Panegyric to Satire: Swift's Early Odes and *A Tale of a Tub*," *Texas Studies in Literature and Language* 13(1), Spring 1971, 59-60.

"Ode to the Athenian Society"

    KATHRYN MONTGOMERY HARRIS. "'Occasions So Few': Satire as a Strategy in Swift's Early Odes," *Modern Language Quarterly* 31(1), March 1970, 26-27.

    ROBERT W. UPHAUS. "From Panegyric to Satire: Swift's Early Odes and *A Tale of a Tub*," *Texas Studies in Literature and Language* 13(1), Spring 1971, 58-59.

"Ode to the King on his *Irish* Expedition"

    KATHRYN MONTGOMERY HARRIS. "'Occasions So Few': Satire as a Strategy in Swift's Early Odes," *Modern Language Quarterly* 31(1), March 1970, 25-26.

"On Cutting Down the Old Thorn at Market Hill"

    CAROLE FABRICANT. "The Garden as City: Swift's Landscape of Alienation," *ELH* 42(4), Winter 1975, 541-42.

"On Poetry: A Rapsody"

    C. J. RAWSON. "'Tis only infinite below': Speculations on Swift, Wallace Stevens, R. D. Laing and others," *Essays in Criticism* 22(2), April 1972, 163-66.

    JAMES L. TYNE. "Swift's Mock Panegyrics in 'On Poetry: A Rapsody,'" *Papers on Language and Literature* 10(3), Summer 1974, 279-86.

    ROBERT W. UPHAUS. "Swift's Poetry: The Making of Meaning," *Eighteenth Century Studies* 5(4), Summer 1972, 582-86.

"On Stella's Birthday (1719)"

RALPH COHEN. "The Augustan Mode in English Poetry," *Eighteenth Century Studies* 1(1), Fall 1967, 7-8.

JOHN IRWIN FISCHER. "Faith, Hope, and Charity in Swift's Poems to Stella," *Papers on Language and Literature* 14(2), Spring 1978, 126-27.

OSWALD JOHNSTON. "Swift and the Common Reader," in *In Defense of Reading,* pp. 186-88.

DAVID SHEEHAN. "Swift, Voiture, and the Spectrum of Raillery," *Papers on Language and Literature* 14(2), Spring 1978, 182-84.

"A Panegyric on the Reverend Dean Swift"

ROBERT W. UPHAUS. "Swift's 'Whole Character': The Delany Poems and 'Verses on the Death of Dr. Swift,'" *Modern Language Quarterly* 34(4), December 1973, 409-11.

"Part of the Seventh Epistle of the First Book of Horace Imitated"

LEONARD A. MOSKOVIT. "Pope and the Tradition of the Neoclassical Imitation," *Studies in English Literature 1500-1900* 8(3), Summer 1968, 449-51.

"*Pethox* the Great"

W. R. IRWIN. "Swift and the Verse Man," *Philological Quarterly* 54(1), Winter 1975, 232-34.

"The Progress of Beauty"

OSWALD JOHNSTON. "Swift and the Common Reader," in *In Defense of Reading,* pp. 182-86.

RICHARD H. RODINO. "Blasphemy or Blessing? Swift's 'Scatological' Poems," *Papers on Language and Literature* 14(2), Spring 1978, 157-58.

"A Receipt to Restore Stella's Youth"

DAVID SHEEHAN. "Swift, Voiture, and the Spectrum of Raillery," *Papers on Language and Literature* 14(2), Spring 1978, 184-85.

JAMES E. TYNE. "Swift and Stella: The Love Poems," *Tennessee Studies in Literature* 19 (1974), 40-41.

"The Revolution at Market-Hill"

CAROLE FABRICANT. "The Garden as City: Swift's Landscape of Alienation," *ELH* 42(4), Winter 1975, 542-43.

"A Satirical Elegy on the Death of a Late Famous General"

ALAN S. FISHER. "Swift's Verse Portraits: A Study of His Originality as an Augustan Satirist," *Studies in English Literature 1500-1900* 14(3), Summer 1974, 348-50.

CHARLES PEAKE. "Swift's 'Satirical Elegy on a Late Famous General,'" *Review of English Literature* 3(3), July 1962, 80-89.

ROBERT W. UPHAUS. "Swift's Poetry: The Making of Meaning," *Eighteenth Century Studies* 5(4), Summer 1972, 574-76.

"A Serious Poem upon William Wood"

A. B. ENGLAND. "The Subversion of Logic in Some Poems by Swift," *Studies in English Literature 1500-1900* 15(3), Summer 1975, 417-18.

"Stella at Wood-Park"

DAVID SHEEHAN. "Swift, Voiture, and the Spectrum of Raillery," *Papers on Language and Literature* 14(2), Spring 1978, 180-82.

JAMES E. TYNE. "Swift and Stella: The Love Poems," *Tennessee Studies in Literature* 19 (1974), 41-42.

"Stella's Birth-day (1721)"

JEFFREY R. FOX. "Swift's 'Scatological' Poems: The Hidden Norm," *Thoth* 15(3), Fall 1975, 12-13.

"Stella's Birthday (1727)"

JAMES E. TYNE. "Swift and Stella: The Love Poems," *Tennessee Studies in Literature* 19 (1974), 44-46.

ROBERT W. UPHAUS. "Swift's Poetry: The Making of a Meaning," *Eighteenth Century Studies* 5(4), Summer 1972, 576-78.

"Strephon and Chloe"

JEFFREY R. FOX. "Swift's 'Scatological' Poems: The Hidden Norm," *Thoth* 15(3), Fall 1975, 3-13.

THOMAS B. GILMORE, JR. "The Comedy of Swift's Scatological Poems," *PMLA* 91(1), January 1976, 37-38.

THOMAS B. GILMORE, JR. "Freud and Swift: A Psychological Reading of *Strephon and Chloe,*" *Papers on Language and Literature* 14(2), Spring 1978, 147-51.

DONALD GREENE. "On Swift's 'Scatological' Poems," *Sewanee Review* 75(4), Autumn 1967, 680-86.

RICHARD H. RODINO. "Blasphemy or Blessing? Swift's 'Scatological' Poems," *Papers on Language and Literature* 14(2), Spring 1978, 164-67.

PETER J. SCHAKEL. "Swift's Remedy for Love: The 'Scatological' Poems," *Papers on Language and Literature* 14(2), Spring 1978, 143-47.

"To Mr. Congreve"

KATHRYN MONTGOMERY HARRIS. "'Occasions So Few': Satire as a Strategy in Swift's Early Odes," *Modern Language Quarterly* 31(1), March 1970, 29-30.

ROBERT W. UPHAUS. "From Panegyric to Satire: Swift's Early Odes and *A Tale of a Tub,*" *Texas Studies in Literature and Language* 13(1), Spring 1971, 61-64.

"To Stella, March 13, 1724"

RONALD PAULSON. "Swift, Stella, and Permanence," *ELH* 27(4), December 1960, 311.

"To Stella, Who Collected and Transcribed his Poems"

JOHN IRWIN FISCHER. "Faith, Hope, and Charity in Swift's Poems to Stella," *Papers on Language and Literature* 14(2), Spring 1978, 127.

DAVID SHEEHAN. "Swift, Voiture, and the Spectrum of Raillery," *Papers on Language and Literature* 14(2), Spring 1978, 185-88.

JAMES E. TYNE. "Swift and Stella: The Love Poems," *Tennessee Studies in Literature* 19 (1974), 43-44.

"Toland's Invitation to Dismal"

LEONARD A. MOSKOVIT. "Pope and the Tradition of the Neoclassical Imitation," *Studies in English Literature 1500-1900* 8(3), Summer 1968, 453-54.

"Verses on the Death of Dr. Swift"

JACQUES BARZUN. "Swift: Verses on the Death of Dr. Swift, D.S.P.D.," in *Master Poems of the English Language,* pp. 262-64.

JOHN IRWIN FISCHER. "How to Die: *Verses on the Death of Dr. Swift,*" *Review of English Studies,* n.s., 21(84), November 1970, 422-41.

DONALD C. MILL. "Elegiac Design and Satiric Intention in 'Verses on the Death of Dr. Swift,'" *Concerning Poetry* 6(2), Fall 1973, 15-24.

RONALD PAULSON. "Swift, Stella, and Permanence," *ELH* 27(4), December 1960, 298-302.

HUGO M. REICHARD. "The Self-Praise Abounding in Swift's *Verses,*" *Tennessee Studies in Literature* 18 (1973), 105-12.

EDWARD W. SAID. "Swift's Tory Anarchy," *Eighteenth Century Studies* 3(1), Fall 1969, 61-66.

SWIFT, JONATHAN *(Cont.)*

"Verses on the Death of Dr. Swift" *(cont.)*

PETER J. SCHAKEL. "The Politics of Opposition in 'Verses on the Death of Dr. Swift,'" *Modern Language Quarterly* 35(3), September 1974, 246-56.

ARTHUR H. SCOUTEN and ROBERT D. HUME. "Pope and Swift: Text and Interpretation of Swift's Verses on His Death," *Philological Quarterly* 52(2), April 1973, 205-31.

BARRY SLEPIAN. "The Ironic Intention of Swift's Verses on His Own Death," *Review of English Studies*, n.s., 14(55), August 1963, 249-56.

ROBERT W. UPHAUS. "Swift's 'Whole Character': The Delany Poems and 'Verses on the Death of Dr. Swift,'" *Modern Language Quarterly* 34(4), December 1973, 411-14.

MARSHALL WAINGROW. *"Verses on the Death of Dr. Swift,"* *Studies in English Literature 1500-1900* 5(3), Summer 1965, 513-18.

"Verses spoken extempore by Dean Swift on his Curate's Complaint of hard Duty"

GÉMINO H. ABAD. *A Formal Approach to Lyric Poetry*, p. 243.

"Verses Wrote in a Lady's Ivory Table Book"

A. B. ENGLAND. "World Without Order: Some Thoughts on the Poetry of Swift," *Essays in Criticism* 16(1), January 1966, 36-38.

PETER J. SCHAKEL. *Explicator* 28(9), May 1970, Item 83.

ROBERT W. UPHAUS. "Swift's Poetry: The Making of a Meaning," *Eighteenth Century Studies* 5(4), Summer 1972, 570-71.

"The Virtues of Sid Hamet the Magician's Rod"

A. B. ENGLAND. "The Subversion of Logic in Some Poems by Swift," *Studies in English Literature 1500-1900* 15(3), Summer 1975, 413-16.

SWINBURNE, ALGERNON C.

"Anactoria"

DAVID A. COOK. "The Content and Meaning of Swinburne's 'Anactoria,'" *Victorian Poetry* 9(1-2), Spring-Summer 1971, 77-93.

KERRY MCSWEENEY. "Swinburne's *Poems and Ballads* (1866)," *Studies in English Literature 1500-1900* 11(4), Autumn 1971, 679-82.

"At a Month's End"

JOHN D. ROSENBERG. "Swinburne," *Victorian Studies* 11(2), December 1967, 147-48.

"Autumn in Cornwall"

J. P. KIRBY. *Explicator* 1(7), May 1943, Item 56. (P)

"Ave atque Vale"

GERALD LEVIN. "Swinburne's 'End of the World' Fantasy," *Literature and Psychology* 24(3), 1974, 111.

JEROME J. MCGANN. "'Ave atque Vale': An Introduction to Swinburne," *Victorian Poetry* 9(1-2), Spring-Summer 1971, 145-63.

GEORGE M. RIDENOUR. "Time and Eternity in Swinburne: Minute Particulars in Five Poems," *ELH* 45(1), Spring 1978, 113-16.

JOHN D. ROSENBERG. "Swinburne," *Victorian Studies* 11(3), December 1967, 150-51.

"Before a Crucifix"

ROBERT A. GREENBURG. "Swinburne and the Redefinition of Classical Myth," *Victorian Poetry* 14(3), Autumn 1976, 186-87.

"Before the Beginning of Years"

BONAMY DOBRÉE. "Swinburne: Two Choruses from Atalanta in Calydon," in *Master Poems of The English Language*, pp. 782-85.

"Before the Mirror"

JENNIFER BREEN. "Wilfred Owen: 'Greater Love' and Late Romanticism," *English Literature in Transition* 16(3), 1974, 177-81.

JEFFREY R. PRINCE. "The Iconic Poem and the Aesthetic Tradition," *ELH* 43(4), Winter 1976, 571-74.

"A Cameo"

BROOKS WRIGHT. *Explicator* 12(2), November 1953, Item 13.

"Eurydice"

ROBERT A. GREENBURG. "Swinburne and the Redefinition of Classical Myth," *Victorian Poetry* 14(3), Autumn 1976, 183-85.

"Faustine"

JEFFREY R. PRINCE. "The Iconic Poem and the Aesthetic Tradition," *ELH* 43(4), Winter 1976, 578-80.

"A Forsaken Garden"

CURTIS DAHL. "The Victorian Wasteland," in *Victorian Literature*, pp. 37-39.

JOHN D. ROSENBERG. "Swinburne," *Victorian Studies* 11(2), December 1967, 145-47.

"The Garden of Proserpine"

WILLIAM EMPSON. "Basic English and Wordsworth (A Radio Talk)," *Kenyon Review* 2(4), Autumn 1940, 450-52. (P)

WILLIAM FROST. *English Masterpieces*, edited by William Frost, Maynard Mack, and Leonard Dean, vol. 6: *Romantic and Victorian Poetry*, pp. 19-20.

WRIGHT THOMAS and STUART GERRY BROWN. *Reading Poems: An Introduction to Critical Study*, pp. 640-41.

"Hermaphroditus"

ANTONY H. HARRISON. "The Aesthetics of Androgyny in Swinburne's Early Poetry," *Tennessee Studies in Literature* 23 (1978), 94-97.

"Hertha"

HARRY BROWN and JOHN MILSTEAD. *What the Poem Means*, p. 229.

C. C. CUNNINGHAM. *Literature as a Fine Art: Analysis and Interpretation*, pp. 101-6.

R. KEITH MILLER. "Swinburne: The Will to Believe," *Ariel* 8(4), October 1977, 70-71.

E. M. W. TILLYARD. *Five Poems, 1470-1870*, pp. 87-103.

F. A. C. WILSON. "Indian and Mithraic Influences on Swinburne's Pantheism: 'Hertha' and 'A Nypholept,'" *Papers on Language and Literature* 8(Suppl.), Fall 1972, 57-60.

"The Higher Pantheism in a Nutshell"

KERRY MCSWEENEY. "Swinburne's Tennyson," *Victorian Studies* 22(1), Autumn 1978, 25-26.

"The Hounds of Spring"

F. R. LEAVIS. *Revaluation*, pp. 238-40. Reprinted in: *Critiques and Essays in Criticism*, pp. 179-80.

LEONARD UNGER and WILLIAM VAN O'CONNOR. *Poems for Study*, pp. 555-56.

"Hymn to Proserpine"

HARRY BROWN and JOHN MILSTEAD. *What the Poem Means*, p. 229.

CURTIS DAHL. "A Double Frame for Tennyson's Demeter?" *Victorian Studies* 1(4), June 1958, 360-61.

KERRY McSWEENEY. "Swinburne's *Poems and Ballads* (1866)," *Studies in English Literature 1500-1900* 11(4), Autumn 1971, 676-79.

"Ilicet"

ANTONY H. HARRISON. "Swinburne's Craft of Pure Expression," *Victorian Newsletter* 51 (Spring 1977), 19.

"In Memory of John William Inchbold"

GEORGE M. RIDENOUR. "Time and Eternity in Swinburne: Minute Particulars in Five Poems," *ELH* 45(1), Spring 1978, 118-21.

"In the Orchard"

F. A. C. WILSON. "Swinburne, Racine, and the Permissive Morality," *English Language Notes* 10(3), March 1973, 215-16.

"Itylus"

KERRY McSWEENEY. "Swinburne's *Poems and Ballads* (1866)," *Studies in English Literature 1500-1900* 11(4), Autumn 1971, 675-76.

"The Lake of Gaube"

KERRY McSWEENEY. "Swinburne's 'A Nympholept' and 'The Lake of Gaube,'" *Victorian Poetry* 9(1-2), Spring-Summer 1971, 212-15.

MEREDITH B. RAYMOND. "'The Lake of Gaube': Swinburne's Dive in the Dark and the 'Indeterminate Moment,'" *Victorian Poetry* 9(1-2), Spring-Summer 1971, 185-99.

"The Last Oracle"

GEORGE M. RIDENOUR. "Time and Eternity in Swinburne: Minute Particulars in Five Poems," *ELH* 45(1), Spring 1978, 108-13.

"Laus Veneris"

JULIAN BAIRD. "Swinburne, Sade, and Blake: The Pleasure-Pain Paradox," *Victorian Poetry* 9(1-2), Spring-Summer 1971, 49-75.

WILLIAM EMPSON. *Seven Types of Ambiguity,* pp. 205-7; second and third eds., pp. 163-65.

GERALD LEVIN. "Swinburne's 'End of the World' Fantasy," *Literature and Psychology* 24(3), 1974, 110-11.

KERRY McSWEENEY. "Swinburne's *Poems and Ballads* (1866)," *Studies in English Literature 1500-1900* 11(4), Autumn 1971, 682-85.

"Memorial Verses on the Death of Theophile Gautier"

GEORGE M. RIDENOUR. "Time and Eternity in Swinburne: Minute Particulars in Five Poems," *ELH* 45(1), Spring 1978, 116-18.

"Nephelidia"

JOHN CIARDI. *How Does a Poem Mean?* pp. 934-36; second ed., pp. 313-14. (P)

"A Nympholept"

PAULL F. BAUM. "Swinburne's 'A Nympholept,'" *South Atlantic Quarterly* 57(1), Winter 1958, 58-68.

KERRY McSWEENEY. "Swinburne's 'A Nympholept' and 'The Lake of Gaube,'" *Victorian Poetry* 9(1-2), Spring-Summer 1971, 203-12.

PATRICIA MERIVALE. "The Pan Figure in Victorian Poetry: Landor to Meredith," *Philological Quarterly* 44(2), April 1965, 271-74.

F. A. C. WILSON. "Indian and Mithraic Influences on Swinburne's Pantheism: 'Hertha' and 'A Nympholept,'" *Papers on Language and Literature* 8(Suppl.), Fall 1972, 63-66.

"On the Cliffs"

MEREDITH B. RAYMOND. "Swinburne Among the Nightingales," *Victorian Poetry* 6(2), Summer 1968, 125-41.

GEORGE M. RIDENOUR. "Time and Eternity in Swinburne: Minute Particulars in Five Poems," *ELH* 45(1), Spring 1978, 121-26.

DAVID G. RIEDE. "Swinburne's 'On the Cliffs': The Evolution of a Romantic Myth," *Victorian Poetry* 16(3), Autumn 1978, 189-203.

"Phaedra"

F. A. C. WILSON. "Swinburne, Racine, and the Permissive Morality," *English Language Notes* 10(3), March 1973, 212-16.

"Prelude"

KERRY McSWEENEY. "Swinburne's Tennyson," *Victorian Studies* 22(1), Autumn 1978, 14-17.

"A Solitude"

EDWARD A. BLOOM, CHARLES H. PHILBRICK, and ELMER M. BLISTEIN. *The Order of Poetry,* pp. 126-29.

"The Sundew"

DOUGLAS C. FRICKE. "The Idea of Love in Swinburne's 'The Sundew,'" *English Language Notes* 13(3), March 1976, 194-201.

KERRY McSWEENEY. "Swinburne's *Poems and Ballads* (1866)," *Studies in English Literature 1500-1900* 11(4), Autumn 1971, 675.

"Thalassius"

ROBERT A. GREENBURG. "Swinburne and the Redefinition of Classical Myth," *Victorian Poetry* 14(3), Autumn 1976, 192-95.

RICHARD D. McGHEE. "'Thalassius': Swinburne's Poetic Myth," *Victorian Poetry* 5(2), Summer 1967, 127-36.

DONALD C. STUART. "Swinburne: The Composition of a Self-Portrait," *Victorian Poetry* 9(1-2), Spring-Summer 1971, 118-28.

"Tiresias"

ROBERT A. GREENBURG. "Swinburne and the Redefinition of Classical Myth," *Victorian Poetry* 14(3), Autumn 1976, 185-86.

"The Triumph of Time"

EBEN BASS. "Swinburne, Greene, and 'The Triumph of Time,'" *Victorian Poetry* 4(1), Winter 1966, 56-61.

GERALD LEVIN. "Swinburne's 'End of the World' Fantasy," *Literature and Psychology* 24(3), 1974, 112-13.

KERRY McSWEENEY. "Swinburne's *Poems and Ballads* (1866)," *Studies in English Literature 1500-1900* 11(4), Autumn 1971, 673-74.

JOHN D. ROSENBERG. "Swinburne," *Victorian Studies* 11(2), December 1967, 143-45.

DONALD C. STUART. "Swinburne: The Composition of a Self-Portrait," *Victorian Poetry* 9(1-2), Spring-Summer 1971, 112-18.

"When the Hounds of Spring"

BONAMY DOBRÉE. "Swinburne: Two Choruses from Atalanta in Calydon," in *Master Poems of the English Language,* pp. 782-85.

SYLVESTER, JOSHUA

"The Woodman's Bear"

FRANKLIN B. WILLIAMS, JR. "The Bear Facts About Joshua Sylvester, the Woodman," *English Language Notes* 9(2), December 1971, 90-98.

SYMONS, ARTHUR

"Alla Dogana"

    ED BLOCK, JR. "Lyric Voice and Reader Response: One View of the Transition to Modern Poetics," *Twentieth Century Literature* 24(2), Summer 1978, 158-61.

"A Fancy of Ferishtah"

    WILLIAM S. PETERSON. "Arthur Symons as a Browningite," *Review of English Studies,* n.s., 19(74), May 1968, 156.

"La Mélinite: Moulin-Rouge"

    KERRY POWELL. "Arthur Symons, Symbolism, and the Aesthetics of Escape," *Renascence* 29(3), Spring 1977, 161-64.

"Studies in Strange Sins"

    ROBERT L. PETERS. "The Salome of Arthur Symons and Aubrey Beardsley," *Criticism* 2(2), Spring 1960, 150-63.

SYNGE, JOHN M.

"The Passing of the Shee"

    DONALD DAVIE. *The Poet in the Imaginary Museum,* pp. 7-8.

T

TABB, JOHN BANNISTER

"The Life-Tide"

ROBIN SKELTON. *The Poetic Pattern*, pp. 96-97.

TAFT, ROBERT W.

"Attack on Barbados at Sandy Point"

ROLFE HUMPHRIES. *Explicator* 18(7), April 1960, Item 44.

TAGGARD, GENEVIEVE

"The Four Songs"

DONALD A. STAUFFER. "Genesis, or the Poet as Maker," in *Poets at Work*, pp. 63-70.

TARN, NATHANIEL

"After the Roaring Forties"

STANLEY CORNGOLD. "Where Babylon Ends: Nathaniel Tarn's Poetic Development," *Boundary 2* 4(1), Fall 1975, 71.

"The Delivery"

STANLEY CORNGOLD. "Where Babylon Ends: Nathaniel Tarn's Poetic Development," *Boundary 2* 4(1), Fall 1975, 59, 61-63.

"Ely Cathedral"

STANLEY CORNGOLD. "Where Babylon Ends: Nathaniel Tarn's Poetic Development," *Boundary 2* 4(1), Fall 1975, 67-68.

"A Rabbi's Dream"

STANLEY CORNGOLD. "Where Babylon Ends: Nathaniel Tarn's Poetic Development," *Boundary 2* 4(1), Fall 1975, 68-69.

TATE, ALLEN

"Aeneas at Washington"

CLEANTH BROOKS. *Modern Poetry and the Tradition*, pp. 98-99. Reprinted in: *Modern Poetry*, pp. 129-30.

LILLIAN FEDER. "Allen Tate's Use of Classical Literature," *Centennial Review* 4(1), Winter 1960, 94-98.

LILLIAN FEDER. *Ancient Myth in Modern Poetry*, pp. 398-400.

"Again the Native Hour"

AUGUST H. MASON. *Explicator* 7(3), December 1948, Item 23. Reprinted in: *Readings for Liberal Education*, revised ed., II: 252-54.

SAMUEL HOLT MONK. *Explicator* 6(8), June 1948, Item 58. Reprinted in: *Readings for Liberal Education*, revised ed., II: 251-52.

"The Buried Lake"

RADCLIFFE SQUIRES. "Will and Vision: Allen Tate's *Terza Rima* Poems," *Sewanee Review* 78(4), Autumn 1970, 554-59.

ALAN WILLIAMSON. "Allen Tate and the Personal Epic," *Southern Review*, n.s., 12(4), Autumn 1976, 727-32.

"Causerie"

CLEANTH BROOKS. *Modern Poetry and the Tradition*, pp. 100-1. Reprinted in: *Modern Poetry*, pp. 131-32.

VIVIENNE KOCH. "The Poetry of Allen Tate," *Kenyon Review* 11(3), Summer 1949, 366-67. Reprinted in: *Modern American Poetry*, edited by B. Rajan, pp. 20-21. Also: *The Kenyon Critics*, pp. 174-75.

"The Cross"

SISTER MARY BERNETTA. "Allen Tate's Inferno," *Renascence* 3(2), Spring 1951, 118.

ROBERT DUPREE. "The Mirrors of Analogy: Three Poems of Allen Tate," *Southern Review*, n.s., 8(4), Autumn 1972, 778-85.

RICHARD J. O'DEA. "Allen Tate's 'The Cross,'" *Renascence* 18(3), Spring 1966, 156-60.

CHARLES C. WALCUTT. *Explicator* 6(6), April 1948, Item 41.

"Death of Little Boys"

MORRIS GREENHUT. "Sources of Obscurity in Modern Poetry: The Examples of Eliot, Stevens, and Tate," *Centennial Review* 7(2), Spring 1963, 181-82.

DAVID V. HARRINGTON and CAROLE SCHNEIDER. *Explicator* 26(2), October 1967, Item 16.

VIVIENNE KOCH. "The Poetry of Allen Tate," *Kenyon Review* 11(3), Summer 1949, 358-60. Reprinted in: *Modern American Poetry*, edited by B. Rajan, pp. 12-14. Also: *The Kenyon Critics*, pp. 172-74.

DELMORE SCHWARTZ. *Selected Essays of Delmore Schwartz*, pp. 164-65.

JAMES G. SOUTHWORTH. *More Modern American Poets*, p. 97.

RADCLIFFE SQUIRES. "Mr. Tate: Whose Wreath Should Be a Moral," in *Aspects of American Poetry*, pp. 265-66.

THOMPSON UHLMAN. *Explicator* 28(7), March 1970, Item 58.

TATE, ALLEN (*Cont.*)

"Death of Little Boys" (*cont.*)

> YVOR WINTERS. *The Anatomy of Nonsense*, pp. 198-202. Reprinted in: Yvor Winters. *In Defense of Reason*, pp. 529-30.

"The Eye"

> LILLIAN FEDER. "Allen Tate's Use of Classical Literature," *Centennial Review* 4(1), Winter 1960, 107-8.

"Fragment of a Meditation"

> VIVIENNE KOCH. "The Poetry of Allen Tate," *Kenyon Review* 11(3), Summer 1949, 363-64. Reprinted in: *Modern American Poetry*, edited by B. Rajan, pp. 17-18.

"Homily"

> GEORGE HEMPHILL. "Allen Tate," in *Seven Modern American Poets*, pp. 230-31.

"Last Days of Alice"

> CLEANTH BROOKS. *Modern Poetry and the Tradition*, p. 104. Reprinted in: *Modern Poetry*, p. 134.

> ROBERT DUPREE. "The Mirrors of Analogy: Three Poems of Allen Tate," *Southern Review*, n.s., 8(4), Autumn 1972, 774-78.

> DELMORE SCHWARTZ. "The Poetry of Allen Tate," *Southern Review* 5(3), Winter 1940, 427-30. Reprinted in: Delmore Schwartz, *Selected Essays of Delmore Schwartz*, pp. 161-63.

"The Maimed Man"

> RADCLIFFE SQUIRES. "Will and Vision: Allen Tate's *Terza Rima* Poems," *Sewanee Review* 78(4), Autumn 1970, 549-53.

> ALAN WILLIAMSON. "Allen Tate and the Personal Epic," *Southern Review*, n.s., 12(4), Autumn 1976, 726-27.

"The Meaning of Death"

> CLEANTH BROOKS. *Modern Poetry and the Tradition*, pp. 106-8. Reprinted in: *Modern Poetry*, pp. 134-38.

> HOWARD NEMEROV. "The Current of the Frozen Stream: An Essay on the Poetry of Allen Tate," *Furioso* 3(4), Fall 1948, 55-60. Reprinted in: *Sewanee Review* 67(4), Autumn 1959, 590-92.

"The Meaning of Life"

> CLEANTH BROOKS. *Modern Poetry and the Tradition*, pp. 105-6. Reprinted in: *Modern Poetry*, pp. 134-36.

> R. K. MEINERS. *Explicator* 19(9), June 1961, Item 62.

> HOWARD NEMEROV. "The Current of the Frozen Stream: An Essay on the Poetry of Allen Tate," *Furioso* 3(4), Fall 1948, 54-60. Reprinted in: *Sewanee Review* 67(4), Autumn 1959, 589-92. Also: Howard Nemerov. *Poetry and Fiction*, 104-7.

"The Mediterranean"

> ROBERT DUPREE. "The Mirrors of Analogy: Three Poems of Allen Tate," *Southern Review*, n.s., 8(4), Autumn 1972, 785-91.

> LILLIAN FEDER. "Allen Tate's Use of Classical Literature," *Centennial Review* 4(1), Winter 1960, 93-94.

> LILLIAN FEDER. *Ancient Myth in Modern Poetry*, p. 398.

> R. K. MEINERS. "The Art of Allen Tate: A Reading of 'The Mediterranean,' " *University of Kansas City Review* 27(2), Winter 1960, 155-59.

> MARTIN NEWITZ. "Tradition, Time, and Allen Tate," *Mississippi Quarterly* 21(1), Winter 1967-68, 41-42.

> LOUIS D. RUBIN, JR. "The Concept of Nature in Modern Southern Poetry," *American Quarterly* 9(1), Spring 1957, 63, 64-65. (P)

RADCLIFFE SQUIRES. "Mr. Tate: Whose Wreath Should Be a Moral," in *Aspects of American Poetry*, ed. by Richard M. Ludwig, pp. 266-69.

"Message from Abroad"

> CLEANTH BROOKS. *Modern Poetry and the Tradition*, pp. 99-100. Reprinted in: *Modern Poetry*, pp. 130-31.

> VIVIENNE KOCH. "The Poetry of Allen Tate," *Kenyon Review* 11(3), Summer 1949, 364-65. Reprinted in: *Modern American Poetry*, edited by B. Rajan, pp. 18-20. Also: *The Kenyon Critics*, p. 174.

"Mr. Pope"

> MARGARET MORTON BLUM. "Allen Tate's 'Mr. Pope': A Reading," *Modern Language Notes* 74(8), 706-9.

> EARL DANIELS. *The Art of Reading Poetry*, pp. 312-14.

> JAMES EDWARD TOBIN. *Explicator* 15(6), March 1957, Item 35. (P)

"Mother and Son"

> DENIS DONOGHUE. "Nuances of a Theme by Allen Tate," *Southern Review*, n.s., 12(4), Autumn 1976, 711-13.

> JAMES G. SOUTHWORTH. *More Modern American Poets*, p. 99.

"The Oath"

> CLEANTH BROOKS. *Modern Poetry and the Tradition*, pp. 108-9. Reprinted in: *Modern Poetry*, p. 138.

"Ode to Our Young Pro-Consuls of the Air"

> M. E. BRADFORD. "Angels at Forty Thousand Feet: 'Ode to Our Young Pro-consuls of the Air' and the Practice of Poetic Responsibility," *Georgia Review* 22(1), Spring 1968, 42-57.

> BABETTE DEUTSCH. *Poetry in Our Time*, p. 370; second ed., pp. 412-13.

> FREDERICK J. HOFFMAN. *The Twenties*, pp. 385-88; revised ed., pp. 431-33.

"Ode to the Confederate Dead"

> CLEANTH BROOKS. *Modern Poetry and the Tradition*, pp. 102-3. Reprinted in: *Modern Poetry*, p. 133.

> CHRISTOPHER CLAUSEN. "Grecian Thoughts in the Home Fields: Reflections on Southern Poetry," *Georgia Review* 32(2), Summer 1978, 293-95.

> LILLIAN FEDER. "Allen Tate's Use of Classical Literature," *Centennial Review* 4(1), Winter 1960, 98-103.

> LILLIAN FEDER. *Ancient Myth in Modern Poetry*, p. 400.

> MORRIS GREENHUT. "Sources of Obscurity in Modern Poetry: The Examples of Eliot, Stevens, and Tate," *Centennial Review* 7(2), Spring 1963, 185-89.

> E. T. HELMICK. "The Civil War Odes of Lowell and Tate," *Georgia Review* 25(1), Spring 1971, 51-55.

> FREDERICK J. HOFFMAN. *The Twenties*, pp. 151-53; revised ed., pp. 178-81.

> VIVIENNE KOCH. "The Poetry of Allen Tate," *Kenyon Review* 11(3), Summer 1949, 370-72. Reprinted in: *Modern American Poetry*, edited by B. Rajan, pp. 24-26.

> LOUIS D. RUBIN, JR. "The Serpent in the Mulberry Bush Again," *Southern Review*, n.s., 12(4), Autumn 1976, 744-57.

> MARGARET SCHLAUCH. *Modern English and American Poetry*, pp. 97-98.

> JAMES G. SOUTHWORTH. *More Modern American Poets*, pp. 100-1.

ALLEN TATE. "Narcissus as Narcissus," *Virginia Quarterly Review* 14(1), January 1938, 108-22. Reprinted in: *Reading Modern Poetry*, pp. 207-19; revised ed., pp. 190-202. Also: Allen Tate. *Reason in Madness*, pp. 132-51. Also: Allen Tate. *On the Limits of Poetry*, pp. 248-62. Also: Allen Tate. *Essays of Four Decades*, pp. 595-607. Partially reprinted in: Kimon Friar and John Malcolm Brinnin. *Modern Poetry*, pp. 538-39.

HYATT H. WAGGONER. *American Poets*, pp. 541-42.

ALAN WILLIAMSON. "Allen Tate and the Personal Epic," *Southern Review*, n.s., 12(4), Autumn 1976, 717-20.

"Records"

RADCLIFFE SQUIRES. "Allen Tate's 'The Fathers,'" *Virginia Quarterly Review* 46(4), Autumn 1970, 646-47.

"Retroduction to American History"

CLEANTH BROOKS. *Modern Poetry and the Tradition*, p. 102.

VIVIENNE KOCH. "The Poetry of Allen Tate," in *Modern American Poetry*, edited by B. Rajan, pp. 15-17.

JAMES G. SOUTHWORTH. *More Modern American Poets*, pp. 99-100.

"Seasons of the Soul"

RICHMOND C. BEATTY. "Allen Tate as Man of Letters," *South Atlantic Quarterly* 47(2), April 1948, 233-34.

ALWYN BERLAND. "Violence in the Poetry of Allen Tate," *Accent* 11(3), Summer 1951, 165-71.

BABETTE DEUTSCH. *Poetry in Our Time*, pp. 199-202; second ed., pp. 216-19.

LILLIAN FEDER. "Allen Tate's Use of Classical Literature," *Centennial Review* 4(1), Winter 1960, 110-13.

GEORGE HEMPHILL. "Allen Tate," in *Seven Modern American Poets*, pp. 254-62.

VIVIENNE KOCH. "The Poetry of Allen Tate," *Kenyon Review* 11(3), Summer 1949, 374-78. Reprinted in: *Modern American Poetry*, edited by B. Rajan, pp. 28-32. Also: *The Kenyon Critics*, pp. 177-81.

R. K. MEINERS. "The End of History: Allen Tate's *Seasons of the Soul*," *Sewanee Review* 70(1), Winter 1962, 34-80.

ALLEN TATE. "Speculations," *Southern Review*, n.s., 14(2), Spring 1978, 230-31.

ALAN WILLIAMSON. "Allen Tate and the Personal Epic," *Southern Review*, n.s., 12(4), Autumn 1976, 721-25.

"Shadow and Shade"

JAMES G. SOUTHWORTH. *More Modern American Poets*, pp. 97-98.

"Sonnet at Christmas"

VIVIENNE KOCH. "The Poetry of Allen Tate," in *Modern American Poetry*, edited by B. Rajan, pp. 23-24.

DELMORE SCHWARTZ. *Selected Essays of Delmore Schwartz*, pp. 159-60.

"The Subway"

BABETTE DEUTSCH. *Poetry in Our Time*, pp. 198-99; second ed., pp. 214-16.

JOE HORRELL. "Some Notes on Conversion in Poetry," *Southern Review* 7(1), Summer 1941, 119-22.

JOHN CROWE RANSOM. *The New Criticism*, pp. 222-25.

LOUIS D. RUBIN, JR. "The Concept of Nature in Modern Southern Poetry," *American Quarterly* 9(1), Spring 1957, 66-67.

YVOR WINTERS. *Primitivism and Decadence*, pp. 4-5. Reprinted in: *The Critic's Notebook*, pp. 251-52. Also: Yvor Winters. *In Defense of Reason*, pp. 19-20.

"The Swimmers"

JAMES M. REID. *100 American Poems of the Twentieth Century*, pp. 180-84.

RADCLIFFE SQUIRES. "Will and Vision: Allen Tate's *Terza Rima* Poems," *Sewanee Review* 78(4), Autumn 1970, 553-54.

ALAN WILLIAMSON. "Allen Tate and the Personal Epic," *Southern Review*, n.s., 12(4), Autumn 1976, 727.

"To a Romantic"

HYATT H. WAGGONER. *American Poets*, pp. 540-41.

"To the Lacedemonians"

DONALD DAVIDSON. "The Meaning of War: A Note on Allen Tate's 'To the Lacedemonians,'" *Southern Review*, n.s., 1(3), Summer 1965, 720-30.

LILLIAN FEDER. "Allen Tate's Use of Classical Literature," *Centennial Review* 4(1), Winter 1960, 103-5.

"To the Romantic Traditionalist"

MARTIN NEWITZ. "Tradition, Time, and Allen Tate," *Mississippi Quarterly* 21(1), Winter 1967-68, 41.

"Unnatural Love"

DENIS DONOGHUE. "Nuances of a Theme by Allen Tate," *Southern Review*, n.s., 12(4), Autumn 1976, 705-7.

LILLIAN FEDER. "Allen Tate's Use of Classical Literature," *Centennial Review* 4(1), Winter 1960, 106-7.

"The Wolves"

RICHARD J. O'DEA. "Allen Tate's Vestigial Morality," *Personalist* 49(2), Spring 1968, 256-62.

TATE, JAMES

"Absences"

LOUIS GALLO. "James Tate's 'Absences': A Reading," *Concerning Poetry* 11(1), Spring 1978, 47-52.

"Cruisin' Even"

THOMAS LUX. "James Tate and Thor Heyerdahl on Their Way to Work," *Iowa Review* 4(4), Fall 1973, 105.

JAMES TATE. "James Tate's Response," *Iowa Review* 4(4), Fall 1973, 106-7.

"Eavesdropper Without a Port, Becoming Small"

THOMAS LUX. "James Tate and Thor Heyerdahl on Their Way to Work," *Iowa Review* 4(4), Fall 1973, 105-6.

TAYLOR, EDWARD

"The Accusation of the Inward Man"

SIDNEY E. LIND. "Edward Taylor: A Revaluation," *New England Quarterly* 21(4), December 1948, 525-27. (P)

"An Address to the Soul Occasioned by a Rain"

WILLIE T. WEATHERS. "Edward Taylor, Hellenistic Puritan," *American Literature* 18(1), March 1946, 24-25.

"Another answer wherein is recited everie verse of the Pamphlet and answered particularly, by E. T."

DAVID SOWD. "Edward Taylor's Answer to a 'Popish Pamphlet,'" *Early American Literature* 9(3), Winter 1975, 307-14.

TAYLOR, EDWARD *(Cont.)*

"Another Meditation at the Same Time"

WILLIAM K. BOTTORFF. "Edward Taylor, an Explication: 'Another Meditation at the Same Time,'" *Early American Literature* 3(1), Spring 1968, 17-21.

"Christs Reply"

GERHARD T. ALEXIS. "A Keen Nose for Taylor's Syntax," *Early American Literature* 4(3), 1969, 97-101. (P)

"A Dialogue between Justice and Mercy"

JOHN GATTA, JR. "The Comic Design of *Gods Determinations touching his Elect*," *Early American Literature* 10(2), Fall 1975, 128-30.

"The Ebb and Flow"

RAYMOND J. JORDAN. *Explicator* 20(8), April 1962, Item 67.

"An Elegy upon the Death of that Holy and Reverend Man of God, Mr. Samuel Hooker"

DONALD E. STANFORD. *"Edward Taylor Versus the 'Young Cockerill' Benjamin Ruggles:* A Hitherto Unpublished Episode from the Annals of Early New England Church History," *New England Quarterly* 44(3), September 1971, 466-68. (P)

"The Experience"

WALLACE CABLE BROWN. "Edward Taylor: An American 'Metaphysical,'" *American Literature* 16(3), November 1944, 191, 196-97.

"A Fig for thee Oh! Death"

ROBERT DALY. *God's Altar,* pp. 170-71.

"The Glory of and Grace in the Church Set Out"

G. GIOVANNINI. *Explicator* 6(4), February 1948, Item 26.

EVAN PROSSER. "Edward Taylor's Poetry," *New England Quarterly* 40(3), September 1967, 395-96.

"The Great Bones of Claverack"

LAWRENCE LAN SLUDER. "God in the Background: Edward Taylor As Naturalist," *Early American Literature* 7(3), Winter 1973, 265-71.

"Huswifery"

HARRY BROWN and JOHN MILSTEAD. *What the Poem Means,* p. 231.

NORMAN S. GRABO. "Edward Taylor's Spiritual Huswifery," *PMLA* 79(5), December 1964, 554-60.

CLARK GRIFFITH. "Edward Taylor and the Momentum of Metaphor," *ELH* 33(4), December 1966, 453-55.

"More Than Enough There: The Recognition of American Literature in England," *Times Literary Supplement,* special number, 6 November 1959, p. xiv.

"Meditation I.1"

WALLACE CABLE BROWN. "Edward Taylor: An American 'Metaphysical,'" *American Literature* 16(3), November 1944, 194-95.

ALBERT GELPI. *The Tenth Muse,* pp. 33-34.

KARL KELLER. "The Rev. Mr. Edward Taylor's Bawdry," *New England Quarterly* 43(3), September 1970, 401.

ALLEN RICHARD PENNER. "Edward Taylor's Meditation One," *American Literature* 39(2), May 1967, 193-99.

"Meditation I.3"

JOEL R. KEHLER. "Physiology and Metaphor in Edward Taylor's 'Meditation. Can. 1. 3,'" *Early American Literature* 9(3), Winter 1975, 315-20.

"Meditation I.6"

E. F. CARLISLE. "The Puritan Structure of Edward Taylor's Poetry," *American Quarterly* 20(2), Summer 1968, 156-57.

ANNE MARIE MCNAMARA. *Explicator* 17(1), October 1958, Item 3.

ROY HARVEY PEARCE. *The Continuity of American Poetry,* pp. 47-48.

ROY HARVEY PEARCE. "Edward Taylor: The Poet as Puritan," *New England Quarterly* 23(1), March 1950, 34-35.

"Meditation I.8"

CLARK GRIFFITH. "Edward Taylor and the Momentum of Metaphor," *ELH* 33(4), December 1966, 448-51.

GEORGE MONTEIRO. *Explicator* 27(6), February 1969, Item 45.

ROY HARVEY PEARCE. "Edward Taylor: The Poet as Puritan," *New England Quarterly* 23(1), March 1950, 44-45.

AUSTIN WARREN. "Edward Taylor's Poetry: Colonial Baroque," *Kenyon Review* 3(3), Summer 1941, 365-68.

AUSTIN WARREN. *Rage for Order,* pp. 12-16. Reprinted in: *Readings for Liberal Education,* revised ed., II: 65-66.

"Meditation I.19"

JAMES T. CALLOW. "Edward Taylor Obeys Saint Paul," *Early American Literature* 4(3), 1969, 89-96.

"Meditation I.20"

JAMES T. CALLOW. "Edward Taylor Obeys Saint Paul," *Early American Literature* 4(4), 1969, 89-96.

"Meditation I.21"

JAMES T. CALLOW. "Edward Taylor Obeys Saint Paul," *Early American Literature* 4(4), 1969, 89-96.

"Meditation I.22"

JAMES T. CALLOW. "Edward Taylor Obeys Saint Paul," *Early American Literature* 4(3), 1969, 89-96.

"Meditation I.28"

WALLACE CABLE BROWN. "Edward Taylor: An American 'Metaphysical,'" *American Literature* 16(3), November 1944, 192-93.

"Meditation I.29"

CECELIA L. HALBERT. "Tree of Life Imagery in the Poetry of Edward Taylor," *American Literature* 38(1), March 1966, 25-27.

LOUIS L. MARTZ. *The Poem of the Mind,* pp. 75-77.

"Meditation I.30"

CECELIA L. HALBERT. "Tree of Life Imagery in the Poetry of Edward Taylor," *American Literature* 38(1), March 1966, 30-32.

"Meditation I.32"

LOUIS L. MARTZ. *The Poem of the Mind,* pp. 60-63.

"Meditation I.33"

WALLACE CABLE BROWN. "Edward Taylor: An American 'Metaphysical,'" *American Literature* 16(3), November 1944, 193. (P)

DONALD E. STANFORD. "Two Notes on Edward Taylor," *Early American Literature* 6(1), Spring 1971, 90.

HYATT H. WAGGONER. *American Poets,* pp. 17-19.

"Meditation I.34"

EVAN PROSSER. "Edward Taylor's Poetry," *New England Quarterly* 40(3), September 1967, 387-88.

"Meditation I.38"

ALBERT GELPI. *The Tenth Muse,* pp. 25-26.

CAROLINE ZILBOORG. *Explicator* 37(1), Fall 1978, 3.

"Meditation I.39"

DAVID L. PARKER. "Edward Taylor's Preparationism: A New Perspective on the Taylor-Stoddard Controversy," *Early American Literature* 11(3), Winter 1976/77, 267-68.

WILLIAM J. SCHEICK. " 'The Inward Tacles and the Outward Traces': Edward Taylor's Elusive Transitions," *Early American Literature* 12(2), Fall 1977, 164-69.

"Meditation I.40"

ROBERT D. ARNER. "Edward Taylor's Gaming Imagery: 'Meditation I.40,' " *Early American Literature* 4(1), 1969, 38-40. (P)

"Meditation I.49"

PETER THORPE. "Edward Taylor as Poet," *New England Quarterly* 39(3), September 1966, 369-71.

"Meditation II.1"

ROBERT E. REITER. "Poetry and Typology: Edward Taylor's *Preparatory Meditations,* Second Series, Numbers 1-30," *Early American Literature* 5(1), Spring 1970, 113-14.

PETER WHITE. "An Analysis of Edward Taylor's *Preparatory Meditation 2.1,*" *Concerning Poetry* 11(2), Fall 1978, 19-23.

"Meditation II.3"

ROBERT E. REITER. "Poetry and Typology: Edward Taylor's *Preparatory Meditations,* Second Series, Numbers 1-30," *Early American Literature* 5(1), Part 1, Spring 1970, 115-16.

WILLIAM J. SCHEICK. " 'The Inward Tacles and the Outward Traces': Edward Taylor's Elusive Transitions," *Early American Literature* 12(2), Fall 1977, 169-73.

"Meditation II.7"

ROBERT E. REITER. "Poetry and Typology: Edward Taylor's *Preparatory Meditations,* Second Series, Numbers 1-30," *Early American Literature* 5(1), Part 1, Spring 1970, 116-18.

"Meditation II.9"

THOMAS M. DAVIS. "Edward Taylor and the Traditions of Puritan Typology," *Early American Literature* 4(3), 1969, 36-38.

"Meditation II.16"

JAMES BRAY. "John Fiske: Puritan Precursor of Edward Taylor," *Early American Literature* 9(1), Spring 1974, 33-35.

"Meditation II.23"

WILLIAM J. SCHEICK. "Typology and Allegory: A Comparative Study of George Herbert and Edward Taylor," *Essays in Literature* 2(1), Spring 1975, 78-82.

"Meditation II.26"

ROBERT E. REITER. "Poetry and Typology: Edward Taylor's *Preparatory Meditations,* Second Series, Numbers 1-30," *Early American Literature* 5(1), Part 1, Spring 1970, 119-22.

"Meditation II.27"

KAREN E. ROWE. "A Biblical Illumination of Taylorian Art," *American Literature* 40(3), November 1968, 370-74.

"Meditation II.29"

WILLIAM J. SCHEICK. "Typology and Allegory: A Comparative Study of George Herbert and Edward Taylor," *Essays in Literature* 2(1), Spring 1975, 82-83.

ROGER B. STEIN. "Seascape and the American Imagination: The Puritan Seventeenth Century," *Early American Literature* 7(1), Spring 1972, 28-30.

"Meditation II.43"

ROBERT M. BENTON. "Edward Taylor's Use of His Text," *American Literature* 39(1), March 1967, 39-40.

CHARLES WILLIAM MIGNON. "A Principle of Order in Edward Taylor's *Preparatory Meditations,*" *Early American Literature* 4(3), 1969, 111-15.

"Meditation II.46"

E. F. CARLISLE. "The Puritan Structure of Edward Taylor's Poetry," *American Quarterly* 20(2), Summer 1968, 157-60.

"Meditation II.56"

ROBERT R. HODGES. "Edward Taylor's 'Artificial Man,' " *American Literature* 31(1), March 1959, 76-77.

"Meditation II.60"

THOMAS M. DAVIS. "Edward Taylor and the Traditions of Puritan Typology," *Early American Literature* 4(3), 1969, 39-41.

"Meditation II.62"

SISTER M. THERESA CLARE. *Explicator* 19(3), December 1960, Item 16.

"Meditation II.63"

DONALD DAVIE. "Edward Taylor and Isaac Watts," *Yale Review* 65(4), Summer 1976, 509-10.

"Meditation II.78"

MICHAEL D. REED. "Edward Taylor's Poetry: Puritan Structure and Form," *American Literature* 46(3), November 1974, 307-8. (P)

"Meditation II.82"

WILLIAM J. SCHEICK. "Typology and Allegory: A Comparative Study of George Herbert and Edward Taylor," *Essays in Literature* 2(1), Spring 1975, 83-84.

"Meditation II.103"

JAMES W. BARBOUR. "The Prose Context of Edward Taylor's Anti-Stoddard Meditations," *Early American Literature* 10(2), Fall 1975, 149-51.

"Meditation II.106"

JAMES W. BARBOUR. "The Prose Context of Edward Taylor's Anti-Stoddard Meditations," *Early American Literature* 10(2), Fall 1975, 151-55.

"Meditation II.108"

JAMES W. BARBOUR. "The Prose Context of Edward Taylor's Anti-Stoddard Meditations," *Early American Literature* 10(2), Fall 1975, 144-48.

"Meditation II.109"

JAMES W. BARBOUR. "The Prose Context of Edward Taylor's Anti-Stoddard Meditations," *Early American Literature* 10(2), Fall 1975, 148-49.

"Meditation II.112"

EDWARD M. GRIFFIN. "The Structure and Language of Taylor's Meditation 2.112," *Early American Literature* 3(3), Winter 1968-69, 205-8.

"Meditation II.115"

KAREN E. ROWE. "Sacred or Profane? Edward Taylor's Meditations of Canticles," *Modern Philology* 72(2), November 1974, 136-37.

"Meditation II.138"

ROBERT N. BOLL and THOMAS M. DAVIS. "Saint Augustine and Edward Taylor's Meditation 138 (2)," *English Language Notes* 8(3), March 1971, 183-85.

TAYLOR, EDWARD *(Cont.)*

"Meditation II.138" *(cont.)*

> KAREN E. ROWE. "Sacred or Profane? Edward Taylor's Meditations on Canticles," *Modern Philology* 72(2), November 1974, 134-36.

"Meditation II.149"

> KAREN E. ROWE. "Sacred or Profane? Edward Taylor's Meditations on Canticles," *Modern Philology* 72(2), November 1974, 132-34.

"Preface" *(Gods Determinations touching his Elect)*

> WALLACE CABLE BROWN. "Edward Taylor: An American 'Metaphysical,'" *American Literature* 16(3), November 1944, 195-96.
>
> DALE DOEPKE. "A Suggestion for Reading Edward Taylor's 'The Preface,'" *Early American Literature* 5(3), Winter 1970-71, 80-82.
>
> JOHN GATTA, JR. "The Comic Design of *Gods Determinations touching his Elect*," *Early American Literature* 10(2), Fall 1975, 124-27.
>
> CLARK GRIFFITH. "Edward Taylor and the Momentum of Metaphor," *ELH* 33(4), December 1966, 455-58.

"The Reflexion"

> HARRY BROWN and JOHN MILSTEAD. *What the Poem Means*, p. 232.
>
> JOHN CLENDENNING. "Piety and Imagery in Edward Taylor's 'The Reflexion,'" *American Quarterly* 16(2), Summer 1964, 203-10.
>
> THOMAS M. DAVIS. "Edward Taylor's 'Occasional Meditations,'" *Early American Literature* 5(3), Winter 1970-71, 24-25.
>
> JOSEPH M. GARRISON, JR. "Teaching Early American Literature: Some Suggestions," *College English* 31(5), February 1970, 492-94.
>
> KARL KELLER. "The Rev. Mr. Edward Taylor's Bawdry," *New England Quarterly* 43(3), September 1970, 401.
>
> AUSTIN WARREN. "Edward Taylor's Poetry: Colonial Baroque," *Kenyon Review* 3(3), Summer 1941, 368-70.
>
> AUSTIN WARREN. *Rage for Order*, pp. 16-17.

"Upon a Spider Catching a Fly"

> JUDSON BOYCE ALLEN. "Edward Taylor's Catholic Wasp: Exegetical Convention in 'Upon a Spider Catching a Fly,'" *English Language Notes* 7(4), June 1970, 257-60.
>
> ROBERT SECOR. *Explicator* 26(5), January 1968, Item 42.

"Upon a Wasp Child with Cold"

> ALBERT GELPI. *The Tenth Muse*, pp. 50-51.

"Upon the Death of my ever Endeared, and Tender Wife"

> ROBERT DALY. *God's Altar*, pp. 166-69.

"Upon the Sweeping Flood"

> THOMAS M. DAVIS. "Edward Taylor's 'Occasional Meditations,'" *Early American Literature* 5(3), Winter 1970-71, 23.
>
> ROY HARVEY PEARCE. *The Continuity of American Poetry*, pp. 48-49.
>
> SANFORD PINSKER. "Carnal Love/Excremental Skies: A Reading of Edward Taylor's 'Upon the Sweeping Flood,'" *Concerning Poetry* 8(1), Spring 1975, 53-54.

"Upon Wedlock, and Death of Children"

> C. R. B. COMBELLACK. *Explicator* 29(2), October 1970, Item 12.
>
> ROBERT DALY. *God's Altar*, pp. 163-65.

> THOMAS M. DAVIS. "Edward Taylor's 'Occasional Meditations,'" *Early American Literature* 5(3), Winter 1970-71, 22-23.
>
> CECELIA L. HALBERT. "Tree of Life Imagery in the Poetry of Edward Taylor," *American Literature* 38(1), March 1966, 22-25.
>
> GENE RUSSELL. *Explicator* 27(9), May 1969, Item 71.

"Valediction to all the World preparatory to Death"

> ROBERT DALY. *God's Altar*, pp. 171-76.

TAYLOR, ELEANOR ROSS

"Woman as Artist"

> MARY C. WILLIAMS. "The Poetic Knife: Poetry by Recent Southern Women Poets," *South Carolina Review* 11(1), November 1978, 52-53.

TEASDALE, SARA

"Barter"

> LAURENCE PERRINE. *Sound and Sense*, p. 117; second ed., pp. 126-27; third ed., pp. 151-52; fourth ed., pp. 142-43.

"The Net"

> LAURENCE PERRINE. "The Untranslatable Language," *English Journal* 60(1), January 1971, 61.

TENNYSON, ALFRED

"The Ancient Sage"

> E. D. H. JOHNSON. *The Alien Vision of Victorian Poetry*, pp. 64-65.
>
> W. DAVID SHAW. "The Transcendentalist Problem in Tennyson's Poetry of Debate," *Philological Quarterly* 46(1), January 1967, 84-89.
>
> ELIZABETH HILLMAN WATERSTON. "Symbolism in Tennyson's Minor Poems," *University of Toronto Quarterly* 20(4), July 1951, 378-79.

"Armageddon"

> see also "Timbuctoo"
>
> ANDREW FICHTER. "Ode and Elegy: Idea and Form in Tennyson's Early Poetry," *ELH* 40(3), Fall 1973, 404-6.
>
> SIR CHARLES TENNYSON. "The Dream in Tennyson's Poetry," *Virginia Quarterly Review* 40(2), Spring 1964, 233-34.

"Ask me no more"

> THOMAS J. ASSAD. "Tennyson's Use of the Tripartite View of Man in Three Songs from *The Princess*," *Tulane Studies in English* 15 (1967), 31-35, 45-52.

"Aylmer's Field"

> THOMAS J. ASSAD. "On the Major Poems of Tennyson's 'Enoch Arden' Volume," *Tulane Studies in English* 14 (1965), 40-44.

"Balin and Balan"

> DAVID F. GOSLEE. "The Stages in Tennyson's Composition of 'Balin and Balan,'" *Huntington Library Quarterly* 38(3), May 1975, 247-68.
>
> E. D. H. JOHNSON. *The Alien Vision of Victorian Poetry*, pp. 49-50.
>
> WENDELL STACY JOHNSON. *Sex and Marriage in Victorian Poetry*, pp. 156-59.
>
> KERRY MCSWEENEY. "Tennyson's Quarrel with Himself: The Tristram Group of *Idylls*," *Victorian Poetry* 15(1), Spring 1977, 51-54.

"The Bandit's Death"

MICHAEL TIMKO. " 'The Central Wish': Human Passion and Cosmic Love in Tennyson's Idyls," *Victorian Poetry* 16(1-2), Spring-Summer 1978, 6.

"Break, Break, Break"

GÉMINO H. ABAD. *A Formal Approach to Lyric Poetry,* pp. 320-22.

THOMAS J. ASSAD. "Tennyson's 'Break, Break, Break,' " *Tulane Studies in English* 12 (1962), 71-80.

CLEANTH BROOKS. *The Well Wrought Urn,* pp. 175-77; revised ed., pp. 142-44. Reprinted in: *Poems and Critics,* pp. 198-99.

DAVID DAICHES and WILLIAM CHARVAT. *Poems in English,* pp. 712-13.

EARL DANIELS. *The Art of Reading Poetry,* p. 272.

BERT G. HORNBACK. "Tennyson's 'Break, Break, Break' Again," *Victorian Newsletter* 33 (Spring 1968), 47-48.

JAMES KISSANE. "Tennyson: The Passion of the Past and the Curse of Time," *ELH* 32(1), March 1965, 91-93.

JAMES R. KREUZER. *Elements of Poetry,* pp. 40-43.

WILLIAM VAN O'CONNOR. *Sense and Sensibility in Modern Poetry,* pp. 151-52.

PHYLLIS RACKIN. "Recent Misreadings of 'Break, Break, Break' and Their Implications for Poetic Theory," *Journal of English and Germanic Philology* 65(2), April 1966, 217-28.

"The Bugle Song"

THOMAS J. ASSAD. "Tennyson's Use of the Tripartite View of Man in Three Songs from *The Princess,*" *Tulane Studies in English* 15 (1967), 31-45.

CLEANTH BROOKS, JOHN THIBAUT PURSER, and ROBERT PENN WARREN. *An Approach to Literature,* pp. 458-59; second ed., pp. 458-59; third ed., pp. 311-12; fourth ed., pp. 307-8; fifth ed., p. 368.

CLEANTH BROOKS and ROBERT PENN WARREN. *Understanding Poetry,* fourth ed., pp. 94-95.

DAVID DAICHES and WILLIAM CHARVAT. *Poems in English,* p. 713.

"Cambridge"

FRANCIS GOLFFING. "Tennyson's Last Phase: The Poet as Seer," *Southern Review,* n.s., 2(2), Spring 1966, 278.

"The Charge of the Light Brigade"

ISAAC ASIMOV. *Familiar Poems, Annotated,* pp. 195-201.

DEREK COLVILLE. *Victorian Poetry and the Romantic Religion,* pp. 197-98. (P)

"Claribel"

THOMAS J. ASSAD. "The Touch of Genius in Tennyson's Earliest Lyrics," *Tulane Studies in English* 16(1968), 40-42.

KATHERINE DUNCAN-JONES. "A Note on Tennyson's 'Claribel,' " *Victorian Poetry* 9(3), Autumn 1971, 348-50.

"Columbus"

LINDA K. HUGHES. "Tennyson's 'Columbus': 'Sense at War with Soul' Again," *Victorian Poetry* 15(2), Summer 1977, 171-76.

ROGER B. WILKENFELD. " 'Columbus' and 'Ulysses': Notes on the Development of a Tennysonian Theme," *Victorian Poetry* 12(2), Summer 1974, 170-74.

"Courage, Poor Heart of Stone"

THOMAS J. ASSAD. "Tennyson's 'Courage, Poor Heart of Stone,' " *Tulane Studies in English* 18 (1970), 73-80.

"Crossing the Bar"

THOMAS J. ASSAD. "Analogy in Tennyson's 'Crossing the Bar,' " *Tulane Studies in English* 8 (1958), 153-63.

PAULL F. BAUM. "Crossing the Bar," *English Language Notes* 1(2), December 1963, 115-16.

LORD DUNSANY. "The Food of Imagination," *Poetry Review* 41(4), July-August 1950, 197-98.

FREDERICK L. JONES. *Explicator* 10(3), December 1951, Item 19.

DALE KRAMER. "Metaphor and Meaning in 'Crossing the Bar,' " *Ball State University Forum* 10(3), Summer 1969, 44-47.

G. GEOFFREY LANGSAM. *Explicator* 10(6), April 1952, Item 40.

MILTON MILLHAUSER. "Structure and Symbol in 'Crossing the Bar,' " *Victorian Poetry* 4(1), Winter 1966, 34-39.

LAURENCE PERRINE. "When Does Hope Mean Doubt? The Tone of 'Crossing the Bar,' " *Victorian Poetry* 4(2), Spring 1966, 127-31.

DANIEL RUTENBERG. "Crisscrossing the Bar: Tennyson and Lionel Johnson on Death," *Victorian Poetry* 10(2), Summer 1972, 179-80.

W. DAVID SHAW. "Tennyson's Late Elegies," *Victorian Poetry* 12(1), Spring 1974, 9-11.

DAVID SONSTROEM. " 'Crossing the Bar' as Last Word," *Victorian Poetry* 8(1), Spring 1970, 55-60.

"De Profundis"

WINSTON COLLINS. "Tennyson and Hopkins," *University of Toronto Quarterly* 38(1), October 1968, 87.

DEREK COLVILLE. *Victorian Poetry and the Romantic Religion,* pp. 204-5.

"The Death of Oenone"

MARTIN DODSWORTH. "Patterns of Morbidity: Repetition in Tennyson's Poetry," in *The Major Victorian Poets,* p. 33.

"Demeter and Persephone"

DOUGLAS BUSH. *Pagan Myth and Christian Tradition in English Poetry,* p. 54.

CURTIS DAHL. "A Double Frame for Tennyson's Demeter?" *Victorian Studies* 1(4), June 1958, 356-62.

MARTIN DODSWORTH. "Patterns of Morbidity: Repetition in Tennyson's Poetry," in *The Major Victorian Poets,* pp. 29-30.

CHRISTINE GALLANT. "Tennyson's Use of the Nature Goddess in 'The Hesperides,' 'Tithonus,' and 'Demeter and Persephone,' " *Victorian Poetry* 14(2), Summer 1976, 155-60.

E. D. H. JOHNSON. *The Alien Vision of Victorian Poetry,* p. 66.

PRISCILLA JOHNSTON. "Tennyson's Demeter and Persephone Theme: Memory and the 'Good Solid' Past," *Texas Studies in Literature and Language* 20(1), Spring 1978, 68-92.

GERHARD JOSEPH. "The Idea of Mortality in Tennyson's Classical and Arthurian Poems: 'Honor Comes With Mystery,' " *Modern Philology* 66(2), November 1968, 144-45.

GERHARD JOSEPH. "Tennyson's Death in Life in Lyric and Myth: 'Tears, Idle Tears' and 'Demeter and Persephone,' " *Victorian Newsletter* 34 (Fall 1968), 15-18.

TENNYSON, ALFRED *(Cont.)*

"Demeter and Persephone" *(cont.)*

    G. ROBERT STANGE. "Tennyson's Mythology: A Study of *Demeter and Persephone*," *Journal of English Literary History* 21(1), March 1954, 67-80.

"Despair"

    KERRY MCSWEENEY. "Swinburne's Tennyson," *Victorian Studies* 22(1), Autumn 1978, 22-23.

"A Dream of Fair Women"

    ARTHUR J. CARR. "Tennyson as a Modern Poet," *University of Toronto Quarterly* 19(4), July 1950, 368-69. Reprinted in: *Victorian Literature*, pp. 318-19.

    CLYDE DE L. RYALS. "The 'Fatal Woman' Symbol in Tennyson," *PMLA* 74(4), September 1959, 441.

"The Dying Swan"

    JOHN HOLLANDER. "Tennyson's Melody," *Georgia Review* 29(3), Fall 1975, 684-85.

"The Eagle"

    CLEANTH BROOKS, JOHN THIBAUT PURSER, and ROBERT PENN WARREN. *An Approach to Literature*, pp. 447-48; second ed., pp. 447-48; third ed., pp. 302-3; fourth ed., pp. 301-3; fifth ed., pp. 361-62.

    RAYMOND CARTER SUTHERLAND. "The 'St. John Sense' Underlying 'The Eagle: A Fragment' by Tennyson — 'To Whom the Vision Came,'" *Studies in the Literature Imagination* 1(1), April 1968, 23-25.

"Eleänore"

    CLYDE DE L. RYALS. "The 'Fatal Woman' Symbol in Tennyson," *PMLA* 74(4), September 1959, 439.

"Enoch Arden"

    THOMAS J. ASSAD. "On the Major Poems of Tennyson's 'Enoch Arden' Volume," *Tulane Studies in English* 14 (1965), 44-53.

    WINSTON COLLINS. "Enoch Arden, Tennyson's Heroic Fisherman," *Victorian Poetry* 14(1), Spring 1976, 47-53.

    DOUGLAS C. FRICKE. "A Study of Myth and Archetype in 'Enoch Arden,'" *Tennyson Research Bulletin* 2(3), November 1974, 106-15.

    WENDELL STACY JOHNSON. *Sex and Marriage in Victorian Poetry*, p. 182.

"The Epic"

    J. S. LAWRY. "Tennyson's 'The Epic': A Gesture of Recovered Faith," *Modern Language Notes* 74(5), May 1959, 400-4.

"A Farewell"

    THOMAS J. ASSAD. "Time and Eternity: Tennyson's 'A Farewell' and 'In the Valley of Cauteretz,'" *Tulane Studies in English* 17 (1969), 96-102.

"The First Quarrel"

    MICHAEL TIMKO. "'The Central Wish': Human Passion and Cosmic Love in Tennyson's Idyls," *Victorian Poetry* 16(1-2), Spring-Summer 1978, 8.

"The Flight"

    MICHAEL TIMKO. "'The Central Wish': Human Passion and Cosmic Love in Tennyson's Idyls," *Victorian Poetry* 16(1-2), Spring-Summer 1978, 7.

"Forlorn"

    MICHAEL TIMKO. "'The Central Wish': Human Passion and Cosmic Love in Tennyson's Idyls," *Victorian Poetry* 16(1-2), Spring-Summer 1978, 7-8.

"The Gardener's Daughter"

    MICHAEL TIMKO. "'The Central Wish': Human Passion and Cosmic Love in Tennyson's Idyls," *Victorian Poetry* 16(1-2), Spring-Summer 1978, 12-15.

"The Grandmother"

    THOMAS J. ASSAD. "On the Major Poems of Tennyson's 'Enoch Arden' Volume," *Tulane Studies in English* 14 (1965), 34-36.

"Guinevere"

    E. D. H. JOHNSON. *The Alien Vision of Victorian Poetry*, pp. 57-58.

    WENDELL STACY JOHNSON. *Sex and Marriage in Victorian Poetry*, pp. 176-78.

"The Hesperides"

    HAROLD BLOOM. *Poetry and Repression*, pp. 155-57.

    ERNEST FONTANA. "Virginal Hysteria in Tennyson's *The Hesperides*," *Concerning Poetry* 8(2), Fall 1975, 17-20.

    DONNA G. FRICKE. "Tennyson's *The Hesperides*: East of Eden and Variations on the Theme," *Tennyson Research Bulletin* 1(4), November 1970, 99-103.

    CHRISTINE GALLANT. "Tennyson's Use of the Nature Goddess in 'The Hesperides,' 'Tithonus,' and 'Demeter and Persephone,'" *Victorian Poetry* 14(2), Summer 1976, 155-58.

    GERHARD JOSEPH. "The Idea of Mortality in Tennyson's Classical and Arthurian Poems: 'Honor Comes With Mystery,'" *Modern Philology* 66(2), November 1968, 136-39.

    JAMES D. MERRIMAN. "The Poet as Heroic Thief: Tennyson's 'The Hesperides' Reexamined," *Victorian Newsletter* 35 (Spring 1969), 1-5.

    G. ROBERT STANGE. "Tennyson's Garden of Art: A Study of *The Hesperides*," *PMLA* 67(5), September 1952, 732-43.

    R. B. WILKENFELD. "The Shape of Two Voices," *Victorian Poetry* 4(3), Summer 1966, 166-67.

"The Holy Grail"

    HAROLD BLOOM. *Poetry and Repression*, pp. 168-74.

    KATHRYN CRABBE. "Tennyson, Faith, and the Fantastic," *Tennyson Research Bulletin* 3(2), November 1978, 55-63.

    JOHN DIXON HUNT and DAVID PALMER. "Tennyson," in *English Poetry*, edited by Alan Sinfield, pp. 144-47.

    E. D. H. JOHNSON. *The Alien Vision of Victorian Poetry*, pp. 53-55.

    WENDELL STACY JOHNSON. *Sex and Marriage in Victorian Poetry*, pp. 165-69.

    DONALD KAY. "'The Holy Grail' and Tennyson's Quest for Poetic Identity," *Arlington Quarterly* 2(1), Summer 1969, 58-70.

    JOSEPH SOLIMINE. "The Burkean Idea of the State in Tennyson's Poetry: The Vision in Crisis," *Huntington Library Quarterly* 30(2), February 1967, 162.

    DAVID STAINES. "Tennyson's 'The Holy Grail': The Tragedy of Percivale," *Modern Language Review* 69(4), October 1974, 745-56.

"I stood on a tower in the wet"

    FRANCIS GOLFFING. "Tennyson's Last Phase: The Poet as Seer," *Southern Review*, n.s., 2(2), Spring 1966, 276-77.

"In Memoriam III" ("O sorrow, cruel fellowship")

    LIONEL ADEY. "Tennyson's Sorrow and Her Lying Up," *Victorian Poetry* 8(3), Autumn 1970, 261-63.

"In Memoriam, VI" ("One writes that 'Other friends remain' ")

    PATRICIA M. BALL. *The Heart's Events*, pp. 89-90.

"In Memoriam, VII" ("Dark house, by which once more I stand")

    CHARLES ALTIERI. "Arnold and Tennyson: The Plight of Victorian Lyricism as Context of Modernism," *Criticism* 20(3), Summer 1978, 301.

    FRANCIS P. DEVLIN. "Dramatic Irony in the Early Sections of Tennyson's *In Memoriam*," *Papers on Language and Literature* 8(2), Spring 1972, 178-79.

    COLIN RADFORD and SALLY MINOGUE. "The Complexity of Criticism: Its Logic and Rhetoric," *Journal of Aesthetics and Art Criticism* 34(4), Summer 1976, 411-29.

    CHRISTOPHER RICKS. "Introduction," in *Poems and Critics*, pp. 23-28.

"In Memoriam, IX" ("Fair ship, that from the Italian shore")

    FRANCIS P. DEVLIN. "Dramatic Irony in the Early Sections of Tennyson's *In Memoriam*," *Papers on Language and Literature* 8(2), Spring 1972, 175-76.

"In Memoriam, XI" ("Calm is the morn without a sound")

    REUBEN ARTHUR BROWER. *The Fields of Light*, pp. 34-35.

    BEN W. FUSON. *Explicator* 4(5), March 1946, Item 34.

"In Memoriam, XII" ("Lo, as the dove when up she springs")

    FRANCIS P. DEVLIN. "Dramatic Irony in the Early Sections of Tennyson's *In Memoriam*," *Papers on Language and Literature* 8(2), Spring 1972, 177-78.

"In Memoriam, XV" ("To-night the winds begin to rise")

    JEROME BEATY and WILLIAM H. MATCHETT. *Poetry From Statement to Meaning*, pp. 294-95.

    RAYMOND G. MALBONE. *Explicator* 35(3), Spring 1977, 6-8.

"In Memoriam, XVII" ("Thou comest, much wept for: such a breeze")

    PATRICIA M. BALL. *The Heart's Events*, p. 93.

"In Memoriam, XVIII" ("'Tis well; 'tis something; we may stand")

    FRANCIS P. DEVLIN. "Dramatic Irony in the Early Sections of Tennyson's *In Memoriam*," *Papers on Language and Literature* 8(2), Spring 1972, 173-75.

"In Memoriam, XIX" ("The Danube to the Severn gave")

    FRANCIS P. DEVLIN. "Dramatic Irony in the Early Sections of Tennyson's *In Memoriam*," *Papers on Language and Literature* 8(2), Spring 1972, 176-77.

"In Memoriam, XX" ("The lesser griefs that may be said")

    JOHN DIXON HUNT. "The Symbolist Vision of *In Memoriam*," *Victorian Poetry* 8(3), Autumn 1970, 192.

"In Memoriam, XXII" ("The path by which we twain did go")

    HARRY BROWN and JOHN MILSTEAD. *What the Poem Means*, p. 238.

"In Memoriam, XXIII" ("Now, sometimes in my sorrow shut")

    HARRY BROWN and JOHN MILSTEAD. *What the Poem Means*, p. 239.

"In Memoriam, XXXIV" ("My own dim life should teach me this")

    HARRY PUCKETT. "Subjunctive Imagination in *In Memoriam*," *Victorian Poetry* 12(2), Summer 1974, 101-3.

"In Memoriam, XXXV" ("Yet if some voice that man could trust")

    HARRY PUCKETT. "Subjunctive Imagination in *In Memoriam*," *Victorian Poetry* 12(2), Summer 1974, 103.

"In Memoriam, XXXVI" ("Tho' truths in manhood darkly join")

    HARRY PUCKETT. "Subjunctive Imagination in *In Memoriam*," *Victorian Poetry* 12(2), Summer 1974, 104-7, *passim*.

"In Memoriam, XLIII" ("If sleep and death be truly one")

    CLYDE S. KILBY. *Poetry and Life*, pp. 149-50.

"In Memoriam, XLVII" ("That each, who seems a separate whole")

    HARRY PUCKETT. "Subjunctive Imagination in *In Memoriam*," *Victorian Poetry* 12(2), Summer 1974, 110.

"In Memoriam, XLVIII" ("If these brief lays, of sorrow born")

    HARRY BROWN and JOHN MILSTEAD. *What the Poem Means*, p. 244.

    HARRY PUCKETT. "Subjunctive Imagination in *In Memoriam*," *Victorian Poetry* 12(2), Summer 1974, 110-11.

"In Memoriam, L" ("Be near me when my light is low")

    SUSAN GLISERMAN. "Early Victorian Science Writers and Tennyson's *In Memoriam*: A Study in Cultural Exchange," *Victorian Studies* 18(4), June 1975, 450-51.

"In Memoriam, LIV" ("Oh yet we trust that somehow good")

    CHARLES ALTIERI. "Arnold and Tennyson: The Plight of Victorian Lyricism as Context of Modernism," *Criticism* 20(3), Summer 1978, 297-98.

    JAMES KILROY. "The Chiastic Structure of *In Memoriam, A. H. H.*," *Philological Quarterly* 56(3), Summer 1977, 370.

"In Memoriam, LV" ("The wish, that of the living whole")

    WALKER GIBSON. "Behind the Veil: A Distinction Between Poetic and Scientific Language in Tennyson, Lyell, and Darwin," *Victorian Studies* 2(1), September 1958, 66.

    JAMES KILROY. "The Chiastic Structure of *In Memoriam, A. H. H.*," *Philological Quarterly* 56(3), Summer 1977, 370-71.

"In Memoriam, LVI" (" 'So careful of the type'? But no")

    HARRY BROWN and JOHN MILSTEAD. *What the Poem Means*, pp. 245-46.

    WALKER GIBSON. "Behind the Veil: A Distinction Between Poetic and Scientific Language in Tennyson, Lyell, and Darwin," *Victorian Studies* 2(1), September 1958, 66-67.

    LAURENCE PERRINE. *Explicator* 12(5), March 1954, Item 29.

    W. DAVID SHAW. "Consolation and Catharsis in *In Memoriam*," *Modern Language Quarterly* 37(1), March 1976, 60-61.

"In Memoriam, LXVII" ("When on my bed the moonlight falls")

    JAMES R. KREUZER. *Elements of Poetry*, pp. 122-24.

    W. DAVID SHAW. "Consolation and Catharsis in *In Memoriam*," *Modern Language Quarterly* 37(1), March 1976, 56-57.

    W. DAVID SHAW. "*In Memoriam* and the Rhetoric of Confession," *ELH* 38(1), March 1971, 93.

TENNYSON, ALFRED (Cont.)

"In Memoriam, LIX" ("O sorrow, wilt thou live with me")
> HARRY BROWN and JOHN MILSTEAD. *What the Poem Means*, p. 246.

"In Memoriam, LXXI" ("Sleep, kinsman thou to death and trance")
> E. D. H. JOHNSON. *The Alien Vision of Victorian Poetry*, p. 26.

"In Memoriam, LXXII" ("Risest thou thus, dim dawn, again")
> CLYDE DE L. RYALS. "The 'Heavenly Friend': The 'New Mythus' of *In Memoriam*," *Personalist* 43(3), Summer 1962, 388.

"In Memoriam, LXXXIV" ("When I contemplate all alone")
> HARRY PUCKETT. "Subjunctive Imagination in *In Memoriam*," *Victorian Poetry* 12(2), Summer 1974, 112-13.

"In Memoriam, LXXXV" ("This truth came borne with bier and pall")
> PATRICIA M. BALL. *The Heart's Events*, pp. 96-97.
> HARRY BROWN and JOHN MILSTEAD. *What the Poem Means*, p. 251.
> HARRY PUCKETT. "Subjunctive Imagination in *In Memoriam*," *Victorian Poetry* 12(2), Summer 1974, 113.

"In Memoriam, LXXXVI" ("Sweet after showers, ambrosial air")
> JAMES BENZIGER. *Images of Eternity*, pp. 145-46.

"In Memoriam, LXXXVII" ("I past beside the reverend walls")
> HARRY BROWN and JOHN MILSTEAD. *What the Poem Means*, p. 251.

"In Memoriam, LLXXXVIII" ("Wild bird, whose warble, liquid sweet")
> JOHN HOLLANDER. "Tennyson's Melody," *Georgia Review* 29(3), Fall 1975, 693-94.

"In Memoriam, XCV" ("By night we linger'd on the lawn")
> HARRY BROWN and JOHN MILSTEAD. *What the Poem Means*, p. 253.
> DEREK COLVILLE. *Victorian Poetry and the Romantic Religion*, pp. 228-30.
> E. D. H. JOHNSON. *The Alien Vision of Victorian Poetry*, pp. 36-37.
> ROBERT LANGBAUM. "The Dynamic Unity in *In Memoriam*," in *The Modern Spirit*, pp. 66-68.
> KERRY MCSWEENEY. "The Pattern of Natural Consolation in *In Memoriam*," *Victorian Poetry* 11(2), Summer 1973, 94-98.
> CARLISLE MOORE. "Faith, Doubt, and Mystical Experience in *In Memoriam*," *Victorian Studies* 7(2), December 1963, 164-66.
> HARRY PUCKETT. "Subjunctive Imagination in *In Memoriam*," *Victorian Poetry* 12(2), Summer 1974, 114-15.
> CLYDE DE L. RYALS. "The 'Heavenly Friends': The 'New Mythus' of *In Memoriam*," *Personalist* 43(3), Summer 1962, 389-90.
> EDGAR F. SHANNON, JR. "Alfred Tennyson as a Poet for Our Time," *Virginia Quarterly Review* 53(4), Autumn 1977, 701-2.
> W. DAVID SHAW. "Consolation and Catharsis in *In Memoriam*," *Modern Language Quarterly* 37(1), March 1976, 57-58.

> W. DAVID SHAW. "*In Memoriam* and the Rhetoric of Confession," *ELH* 38(1), March 1971, 89-90.
> ALAN SINFIELD. "Matter-Moulded Forms of Speech: Tennyson's Use of Language in *In Memoriam*," in *The Major Victorian Poets*, pp. 58-67.
> ALAN SINFIELD. " 'That Which Is': The Platonic Indicative in *In Memoriam* XCV," *Victorian Poetry* 14(3), Autumn 1976, 247-52.

"In Memoriam, CIII" ("On that last night before we went")
> HARRY BROWN and JOHN MILSTEAD. *What the Poem Means*, pp. 255-56.
> E. D. H. JOHNSON. *The Alien Vision of Victorian Poetry*, pp. 19-20.
> CLYDE DE L. RYALS. "The 'Heavenly Friend': The 'New Mythus' of *In Memoriam*," *Personalist* 43(3), Summer 1962, 390.
> W. DAVID SHAW. "*In Memoriam* and the Rhetoric of Confession," *ELH* 38(1), March 1971, 87-88.

"In Memoriam, CXV" ("Now fades the last long streak of snow")
> KERRY MCSWEENEY. "The Pattern of Natural Consolation in *In Memoriam*," *Victorian Poetry* 11(2), Summer 1973, 92-93.

"In Memoriam, CXVIII" ("Contemplate all this work of time")
> PATRICIA M. BALL. *The Heart's Events*, p. 103.
> JOHN D. BOYD. "The Principle of Analogy and the Immortality Question in Tennyson's *In Memoriam*," *University of Toronto Quarterly* 45(2), Winter 1976, 132-33.
> WALKER GIBSON. "Behind the Veil: A Distinction Between Poetic and Scientific Language in Tennyson, Lyell, and Darwin," *Victorian Studies* 2(1), September 1958, 64-66.

"In Memoriam, CXX" ("I trust I have not wasted breath")
> MILTON MILLHAUSER. " 'Magnetic Mockeries': The Background of a Phrase," *English Language Notes* 5(2), December 1967, 108-13.

"In Memoriam, CXIX" ("Doors, where my heart was used to beat")
> CHARLES ALTIERI. "Arnold and Tennyson: The Plight of Victorian Lyricism as Context of Modernism," *Criticism* 20(3), Summer 1978, 301-2.

"In Memoriam, CXXI" ("Sad hesper o'er the buried sun")
> JOHN D. BOYD. "*In Memoriam*, Section CXXI," *Victorian Poetry* 14(2), Summer 1976, 161-64.
> HARRY BROWN and JOHN MILSTEAD. *What the Poem Means*, p. 259.
> FRANCIS P. DEVLIN. "Dramatic Irony in the Early Sections of Tennyson's *In Memoriam*," *Papers on Language and Literature* 8(2), Spring 1972, 182-83.
> KERRY MCSWEENEY. "The Pattern of Natural Consolation in *In Memoriam*," *Victorian Poetry* 11(2), Summer 1973, 93-94.

"In Memoriam, CXXII" ("Oh, wast thou with me, dearest, then")
> WALKER GIBSON. "Behind the Veil: A Distinction Between Poetic and Scientific Language in Tennyson, Lyell, and Darwin," *Victorian Studies* 2(1), September 1958, 61-64.
> SUSAN GLISERMAN. "Early Victorian Science Writers and Tennyson's *In Memoriam*: A Study in Cultural Exchange; Part II," *Victorian Studies* 18(4), June 1975, 448-49.

HARRY PUCKETT. "Subjunctive Imagination in *In Memoriam*," *Victorian Poetry* 12(2), Summer 1974, 116-17.

"In Memoriam, CXXIII" ("There rolls the deep where grew the tree")

W. DAVID SHAW. "Consolation and Catharsis in *In Memoriam*," *Modern Language Quarterly* 37(1), March 1976, 61-63.

"In Memoriam, CXXIV" ("That which we dare invoke to bless")

JAMES KILROY. "The Chiastic Structure of *In Memoriam, A. H. H.*," *Philological Quarterly* 56(3), Summer 1977, 363-64.

HARRY PUCKETT. "Subjunctive Imagination in *In Memoriam*," *Victorian Poetry* 12(2), Summer 1974, 121-22.

"In Memoriam, CXXVII" ("And all is well, tho' faith and form")

GERALD L. BRUNS. " 'The Lesser Faith'; Hope and Reversal in Tennyson's *In Memoriam*," *Journal of English and Germanic Philology* 77(2), April 1978, 252-56.

"In Memoriam, CXXVIII" ("The love that rose on stronger wings")

HARRY BROWN and JOHN MILSTEAD. *What the Poem Means*, p. 261.

GERALD L. BRUNS. " 'The Lesser Faith'; Hope and Reversal in Tennyson's *In Memoriam*," *Journal of English and Germanic Philology* 77(2), April 1978, 261-62.

"In Memoriam, CXXX" ("Thy voice is on the rolling air")

HARRY PUCKETT. "Subjunctive Imagination in *In Memoriam*," *Victorian Poetry* 12(2), Summer 1974, 118.

"In Memoriam, CXXXI" ("O living will that shalt endure")

ROBERT LANGBAUM. "The Dynamic Unity in *In Memoriam*," in *The Modern Spirit*, pp. 74-75.

HARRY PUCKETT. "Subjunctive Imagination in *In Memoriam*," *Victorian Poetry* 12(2), Summer 1974, 119-20.

CHARLES TENNYSON. "Tennyson: Mind and Method," *Tennyson Research Bulletin* 1(5), November 1971, 131-32.

"In the Garden at Swainston"

W. DAVID SHAW. "Tennyson's Late Elegies," *Victorian Poetry* 12(1), Spring 1974, 6-7.

L. G. WHITBREAD. "Tennyson's 'In the Garden at Swainston,' " *Victorian Poetry* 13(1), Spring 1975, 61-69.

"In the Valley of Cauteretz"

THOMAS J. ASSAD. "Time and Eternity: Tennyson's 'A Farewell' and 'In the Valley of Cauteretz,' " *Tulane Studies in English* 17 (1969), 105-11.

"The Islet"

NANCY R. COMLEY. "Marvell, Tennyson, and 'The Islet': An Inversion of Pastoral," *Victorian Poetry* 16(3), Autumn 1978, 270-74.

"The Kraken"

JAMES DONALD WELCH. "Tennyson's Landscapes of Time and a Reading of 'The Kraken,' " *Victorian Poetry* 14(3), Autumn 1976, 201-4.

"Lady Clara Vere de Vere"

CLYDE DE L. RYALS. "The 'Fatal Woman' Symbol in Tennyson," *PMLA* 74(4), September 1959, 440.

"The Lady of Shallot"

HARRY BROWN and JOHN MILSTEAD. *What the Poem Means*, pp. 264-65.

DEREK COLVILLE. *Victorian Poetry and the Romantic Religion*, pp. 171-72, 202-3.

DAVID DAICHES and WILLIAM CHARVAT. *Poems in English*, p. 710.

NIGEL FOXELL. *Ten Poems Analyzed*, pp. 165-83.

JAMES L. HILL. "Tennyson's 'The Lady of Shalott': The Ambiguity of Commitment," *Centennial Review* 12(4), Fall 1968, 415-29.

JOHN DIXON HUNT and DAVID PALMER. "Tennyson," in *English Poetry*, edited by Alan Sinfield, pp. 134-35.

E. D. H. JOHNSON. *The Alien Vision of Victorian Poetry*, p. 9.

WENDELL STACY JOHNSON. *Sex and Marriage in Victorian Poetry*, pp. 114-16.

GERHARD JOSEPH. "Victorian Frames: The Windows and Mirrors of Browning, Arnold, and Tennyson," *Victorian Poetry* 16(1-2), Spring-Summer 1978, 85-86.

LONA MOSK PACKER. "Sun and Shadow: The Nature of Experience in Tennyson's 'The Lady of Shallott,' " *Victorian Newsletter* 25 (Spring 1964), 4-8.

LIONEL STEVENSON. "Tennyson, Browning, and a Romantic Fallacy," *University of Toronto Quarterly* 13(2), January 1944, 184.

RICHARD C. TOBIAS. "Tennyson's Painted Shell," *Victorian Newsletter* 39 (Spring 1971), 7-10.

R. B. WILKENFELD. "The Shape of Two Voices," *Victorian Poetry* 4(3), Summer 1966, 171-73.

"The Last Tournament"

ROY GRIDLEY. "Confusion of the Seasons in Tennyson's 'The Last Tournament,' " *Victorian Newsletter* 22 (Fall 1962), 14-16.

E. D. H. JOHNSON. *The Alien Vision of Victorian Poetry*, pp. 55-57.

WENDELL STACY JOHNSON. *Sex and Marriage in Victorian Poetry*, pp. 173-76.

BOYD LITZINGER. "The Structure of Tennyson's 'The Last Tournament,' " *Victorian Poetry* 1(1), January 1963, 53-60.

KERRY MCSWEENEY. "Tennyson's Quarrel with Himself: The Tristram Group of *Idylls*," *Victorian Poetry* 15(1), Spring 1977, 55-59.

MASAO MIYOSHI. "Narrative Sequence and the Moral System: Three Tristram Poems," *Victorian Newsletter* 35 (Spring 1969), 6-7.

"Locksley Hall"

HARRY BROWN and JOHN MILSTEAD. *What the Poem Means*, p. 262.

E. C. BUFKIN. "Imagery in 'Locksley Hall,' " *Victorian Poetry* 2(1), Winter 1964, 21-28.

JUNE STEFFENSEN HAGEN. "The 'Crescent Promise' of 'Locksley Hall': A Crisis in Poetic Creativity," *Victorian Poetry* 11(2), Summer 1973, 169-71.

FRED KAPLAN. *Miracles of Rare Device*, pp. 62-77.

F. E. L. PRIESTLEY. "Locksley Hall Revisited," *Queen's Quarterly* 81(4), Winter 1974, 512-25.

JOSEPH SOLIMINE. "The Burkean Idea of the State in Tennyson's Poetry: The Vision in Crisis," *Huntington Library Quarterly* 30(2), February 1967, 154-55.

"Locksley Hall, Sixty Years After"

HARRY BROWN and JOHN MILSTEAD. *What the Poem Means*, p. 263.

DEREK COLVILLE. *Victorian Poetry and the Romantic Religion*, p. 217.

TENNYSON, ALFRED *(Cont.)*

"Locksley Hall, Sixty Years After" *(cont.)*

F. E. L. PRIESTLEY. "Locksley Hall Revisited," *Queen's Quarterly* 81(4), Winter 1974, 525-32.

JOSEPH SOLIMINE. "The Burkean Idea of the State in Tennyson's Poetry: The Vision in Crisis," *Huntington Library Quarterly* 30(2), February 1967, 164-65.

"The Lotos-Eaters"

CLEANTH BROOKS, JOHN THIBAUT PURSER, and ROBERT PENN WARREN. *An Approach to Literature,* fifth ed., pp. 357-58. (P)

DEREK COLVILLE. *Victorian Poetry and the Romantic Religion,* pp. 172-73.

ALAN GROB. "Tennyson's *The Lotos-Eaters*: Two Versions of Art," *Modern Philology* 62(2), November 1964, 118-29.

E. D. H. JOHNSON. *The Alien Vision of Victorian Poetry,* pp. 9-10.

JAMES R. KINCAID. "Rhetorical Irony, the Dramatic Monologue, and Tennyson's Poems (1842)," *Philological Quarterly* 53(2), Spring 1974, 224-27.

JAMES R. KINCAID. "Tennyson's Mariners and Spenser's Despair: The Argument of 'The Lotos-Eaters,'" *Papers on Language and Literature* 5(3), Summer 1969, 273-81.

JAMES KISSANE. "Tennyson: The Passion of the Past and the Curse of Time," *ELH* 32(1), March 1965, 107-9.

R. B. WILKENFELD. "The Shape of Two Voices," *Victorian Poetry* 4(3), Summer 1966, 168-70.

"Love and Duty"

PRISCILLA JOHNSTON. "Tennyson's Demeter and Persephone Theme: Memory and the 'Good Solid' Past," *Texas Studies in Literature and Language* 20(1), Spring 1978, 77-78.

"The Lover's Tale"

DEREK COLVILLE. *Victorian Poetry and the Romantic Religion,* pp. 177-82.

SIR CHARLES TENNYSON. "The Dream in Tennyson's Poetry," *Virginia Quarterly Review* 40(2), Spring 1964, 230-32.

"Lucretius"

CHARLES ALTIERI. "Arnold and Tennyson: The Plight of Victorian Lyricism as Context of Modernism," *Criticism* 20(3), Summer 1978, 295-96.

ALLAN DANZIG. "The Contraries: A Central Concept in Tennyson's Poetry," *PMLA* 77(5), December 1962, 579-82. Reprinted in: *British Victorian Literature,* pp. 118-25.

E. D. H. JOHNSON. *The Alien Vision of Victorian Poetry,* pp. 31-34.

SHARON MAYER LIBERA. "John Tyndall and Tennyson's 'Lucretius,'" *Victorian Newsletter* 45 (Spring 1974), 19-22.

W. DAVID SHAW. "Imagination and Intellect in Tennyson's 'Lucretius,'" *Modern Language Quarterly* 33(2), June 1972, 130-39.

"The Making of Man"

FRANCIS GOLFFING. "Tennyson's Last Phase: Poet as Seer," *Southern Review,* n.s., 2(2), Spring 1966, 282.

"Mariana"

HAROLD BLOOM. *Poetry and Repression,* pp. 147-55.

CLEANTH BROOKS and ROBERT PENN WARREN. *Understanding Poetry,* third ed., pp. 312-15; fourth ed., pp. 197-99.

W. J. FOX. "Tennyson — Poems, Chiefly Lyrical — 1830," in *Victorian Scrutinies,* pp. 79-80.

JOHN HOLLANDER. "Tennyson's Melody," *Georgia Review* 29(3), Fall 1975, 682-83.

JOHN STUART MILL. *Essays on Poetry,* pp. 49-52.

"Mechanophilus"

FRANCIS GOLFFING. "Tennyson's Last Phase: The Poet as Seer," *Southern Review,* n.s., 2(2), Spring 1966, 281.

"Merlin and the Gleam"

GORDON S. HAIGHT. "Tennyson's Merlin," *Studies in Philology* 44(3), July 1947, 560-66.

"The Miller's Daughter"

MICHAEL TIMKO. " 'The Central Wish': Human Passion and Cosmic Love in Tennyson's Idyls," *Victorian Poetry* 16(1-2), Spring-Summer 1978, 11-12.

"Northern Farmer"

THOMAS J. ASSAD. "On the Major Poems of Tennyson's 'Enoch Arden' Volume," *Tulane Studies in English* 14 (1965), 31-34.

"Now Sleeps the Crimson Petal"

THOMAS J. ASSAD. "Tennyson's Use of the Tripartite View of Man in Three Songs from *The Princess,*" *Tulane Studies in English* 15 (1967), 31-35, 52-58.

R. B. SMITH. "Sexual Ambivalence in Tennyson," *CEA Critic* 27(9), June 1965, 8-9. Reprinted in: *CEA Critic* 28(1), October 1965, 12.

"Ode: O Bosky Brook"

ANDREW FICHTER. "Ode and Elegy: Idea and Form in Tennyson's Early Poetry," *ELH* 40(3), Fall 1973, 408-10.

"Ode on the Death of the Duke of Wellington"

MARGERY STICKER DURHAM. "Tennyson's Wellington Ode and the Cosmology of Love," *Victorian Poetry* 14(4), Winter 1976, 277-92.

"Ode to Memory"

ANDREW FICHTER. "Ode and Elegy: Idea and Form in Tennyson's Early Poetry," *ELH* 40(3), Fall 1973, 406-8.

"Oenone"

ARTHUR J. CARR. "Tennyson as a Modern Poet," *University of Toronto Quarterly* 19(4), July 1950, 371. Reprinted in: *Victorian Literature,* p. 321.

DEREK COLVILLE. *Victorian Poetry and the Romantic Religion,* p. 172.

MARTIN DODSWORTH. "Patterns of Morbidity: Repetition in Tennyson's Poetry," in *The Major Victorian Poets,* pp. 30-33.

WENDELL STACY JOHNSON. *Sex and Marriage in Victorian Poetry,* pp. 116-17.

GERHARD JOSEPH. "Tennyson's Concepts of Knowledge, Wisdom, and Pallas Athene," *Modern Philology* 69(4), May 1972, 317-18.

JAMES R. KINCAID. "Rhetorical Irony, the Dramatic Monologue, and Tennyson's *Poems* (1842)," *Philological Quarterly* 53(2), Spring 1974, 222-24.

EDGAR F. SHANNON, JR. "Alfred Tennyson as a Poet for Our Time," *Virginia Quarterly Review* 53(4), Autumn 1977, 697-98.

PAUL TURNER. "Some Ancient Light on Tennyson's *Oenone,*" *Journal of English and Germanic Philology* 61(1), January 1962, 57-72.

ELIZABETH HILLMAN WATERSTON. "Symbolism in Tennyson's Minor Poems," *University of Toronto Quarterly* 20(4), July 1951, 376.

"On a Mourner"

SIR CHARLES TENNYSON. "The Dream in Tennyson's Poetry," *Virginia Quarterly Review* 40(2), Spring 1964, 244-46.

"The Palace of Art"

ANDY P. ANTIPPAS. "Tennyson, Hallam, and *The Palace of Art*," *Victorian Poetry* 5(4), Winter 1967, 294-96.

ANDY P. ANTIPPAS. "Tennyson's Sinful Soul: Poetic Tradition and 'Keats Turned Imbecile,'" *Tulane Studies in English* 17 (1969), 113-34.

PATRICIA M. BALL. *The Central Self*, pp. 173-74.

PATRICIA M. BALL. "Tennyson and the Romantics," *Victorian Poetry* 1(1), January 1963, 13-16.

CLEANTH BROOKS. *Modern Poetry and the Tradition*, p. 240.

WILLIAM CADBURY. "Tennyson's 'The Palace of Art' and the Rhetoric of Structures," *Criticism* 7(1), Winter 1965, 23-44.

DEREK COLVILLE. *Victorian Poetry and the Romantic Religion*, p. 174.

A. C. HOWELL. "Tennyson's 'Palace of Art' — An Interpretation," *Studies in Philology* 33(3), July 1936, 507-22.

E. D. H. JOHNSON. *The Alien Vision of Victorian Poetry*, pp. 11-12.

G. WILSON KNIGHT. *Neglected Powers*, pp. 244-45.

CLYDE DE L. RYALS. "The 'Fatal Woman' Symbol in Tennyson," *PMLA* 74(4), September 1959, 440-41.

JOSEPH SENDRY. "'The Palace of Art' Revisited," *Victorian Poetry* 4(3), Summer 1966, 149-62.

GEORGE H. SOULE, JR. "Walt Whitman's 'Pictures': An Alternative to Tennyson's 'Palace of Art,'" *ESQ* 22(1), First Quarter 1976, 39-47.

LIONEL STEVENSON. "Tennyson, Browning, and a Romantic Fallacy," *University of Toronto Quarterly* 13(2), January 1944, 182-84.

ELIZABETH HILLMAN WATERSTON. "Symbolism in Tennyson's Minor Poems," *University of Toronto Quarterly* 20(4), July 1951, 376-77.

"The Passing of Arthur"

JAMES R. KINKAID. "Tennyson's Ironic Camelot: Arthur Breathes His Last," *Philological Quarterly* 56(2), Spring 1977, 243-45.

"Pelleas and Ettarre"

RUSSELL M. GOLDFARB. *Sexual Repression and Victorian Literature*, pp. 92-102.

WENDELL STACY JOHNSON. *Sex and Marriage in Victorian Poetry*, pp. 169-72.

KERRY MCSWEENEY. "Tennyson's Quarrel with Himself: The Tristram Group of *Idylls*," *Victorian Poetry* 15(1), Spring 1977, 54-55.

LAWRENCE POSTON, III. "'Pelleas and Ettarre': Tennyson's 'Troilus,'" *Victorian Poetry* 4(3), Summer 1966, 199-204.

"The Poet"

T. O. MABBOTT. *Explicator* 3(1), October 1944, Item 9. (P)

W. D. PADEN. *Explicator* 2(8), June 1944, Item 56.

B. N. PIPES, JR. "A Slight Meteorological Disturbance: The Last Two Stanzas of Tennyson's 'The Poet,'" *Victorian Poetry* 1(1), January 1963, 74-76. (P)

"The Poet's Song"

THOMAS J. ASSAD. "Time and Eternity: Tennyson's 'A Farewell' and 'In the Valley of Cautretz,'" *Tulane Studies in English* 17 (1969), 93-95.

"The Progress of Spring"

ANDREW FICHTER. "Ode and Elegy: Idea and Form in Tennyson's Early Poetry," *ELH* 40(3), Fall 1973, 410-12.

"Recollections of the Arabian Nights"

JOHN HOLLANDER. "Tennyson's Melody," *Georgia Review* 29(3), Fall 1975, 680-82.

BRIAN JOHN. "Tennyson's 'Recollections of the Arabian Nights' and the Individuation Process," *Victorian Poetry* 4(4), Autumn 1966, 275-79.

"The 'Revenge'"

ISAAC ASIMOV. *Familiar Poems, Annotated*, pp. 102-13.

"The Ring"

MICHAEL TIMKO. "'The Central Wish': Human Passion and Cosmic Love in Tennyson's Idyls," *Victorian Poetry* 16(1-2), Spring-Summer 1978, 10-11.

"Rizpah"

JOSHUA ADLER. "Tennyson's 'Mother of Sorrows': 'Rizpah,'" *Victorian Poetry* 12(4), Winter 1974, 363-69.

"St. Simeon Stylites"

MARTIN DODSWORTH. "Patterns of Morbidity: Repetition in Tennyson's Poetry," in *The Major Victorian Poets*, pp. 15-17.

WILLIAM E. FREDEMAN. "'A Sign Betwixt the Meadow and the Cloud': The Ironic Apotheosis of Tennyson's *St. Simeon Stylites*," *University of Toronto Quarterly* 38(1), October 1968, 69-83.

JAMES R. KINCAID. "Rhetorical Irony, the Dramatic Monologue, and Tennyson's Poems (1842)," *Philological Quarterly* 53(2), Spring 1974, 234-36.

"Sea Dreams"

THOMAS J. ASSAD. "On the Major Poems of Tennyson's 'Enoch Arden' Volume," *Tulane Studies in English* 14 (1965), 36-40.

E. D. H. JOHNSON. *The Alien Vision of Victorian Poetry*, pp. 28-29.

"Sir Galahad"

GEORGE ARMS. "'Childe Roland' and 'Sir Galahad,'" *College English* 6(5), February 1945, 258-62.

"The Sisters"

MICHAEL TIMKO. "'The Central Wish': Human Passion and Cosmic Love in Tennyson's Idyls," *Victorian Poetry* 16(1-2), Spring-Summer 1978, 8-10.

"Song" ("It is the solemn even-time")

THOMAS J. ASSAD. "The Touch of Genius in Tennyson's Earliest Lyrics," *Tulane Studies in English* 16 (1968), 45-47.

"A Spirit Haunts the Year's Last Hours"

R. B. WILKENFELD. "The Shape of Two Voices," *Victorian Poetry* 4(3), Summer 1966, 163-65.

"Strong Son of God, immortal Love" (*In Memoriam*)

HARRY BROWN and JOHN MILSTEAD. *What the Poem Means*, pp. 233-34.

"Supposed Confessions of a Second-Rate Sensitive Mind"

PATRICIA M. BALL. *The Central Self*, pp. 169-70.

WILLIAM CADBURY. "The Utility of the Poetic Mask in Tennyson's 'Supposed Confessions,'" *Modern Language Quarterly* 24(4), December 1963, 374-85.

JOHN R. REED. "The Design of Tennyson's 'The Two Voices,'" *University of Toronto Quarterly* 37(2), January 1968, 186-88.

TENNYSON, ALFRED *(Cont.)*

"Tears, Idle Tears"

F. W. BATESON. *English Poetry*, pp. 225-33.

HAROLD BLOOM. *Poetry and Repression*, pp. 161-63.

CLEANTH BROOKS. "The New Criticism: A Brief for the Defense," *American Scholar* 13(3), Summer 1944, 286-93.

CLEANTH BROOKS. *The Well Wrought Urn*, pp. 167-75; revised ed., pp. 136-44. Reprinted in: *Readings for Liberal Education*, II: 122-26; revised ed., II: 131-35; third ed., II: 125-29; fourth ed., II: 124-28. Also: *Victorian Literature*, pp. 334-41. Also: *Master Poems of the English Language*, pp. 659-64. Abridged in: *The Case for Poetry*, p. 355; second ed., pp. 288-89.

ALLEN BARRY CAMERON. "The Extemporaneity of 'Tears, Idle Tears,'" *CEA Critic* 30(8), May 1968, 16.

DEREK COLVILLE. *Victorian Poetry and the Romantic Religion*, pp. 201-2.

GERHARD JOSEPH. "Tennyson's Death in Life in Lyric and Myth: 'Tears, Idle Tears' and 'Demeter and Persephone,'" *Victorian Newsletter,* 34 (Fall 1968), 13-15.

JAMES KISSANE. "Tennyson: The Passion of the Past and the Curse of Time," *ELH* 32(1), March 1965, 93-97.

JOHN CROWE RANSOM. "The Tense of Poetry," *Southern Review* 1(2), Autumn 1935, 221-22.

JOHN CROWE RANSOM. *The World's Body*, pp. 233-34.

LEO SPITZER. *Essays on English and American Literature*, pp. 37-50.

FRED H. STOCKING. *Explicator* 5(8), June 1947, Item 54. Abridged in: *The Case for Poetry*, p. 355; second ed., p. 288.

EDWARD P. VANDIVER, JR. *Explicator* 21(7), March 1963, Item 53.

W. K. WIMSATT, JR. and M. C. BEARDSLEY. "The Affective Fallacy," *Sewanee Review* 57(1), Winter 1949, 46-47.

"Timbuctoo"

see also "Armageddon"

ANDREW FICHTER. "Ode and Elegy: Idea and Form in Tennyson's Early Poetry," *ELH* 40(3), Fall 1973, 404-6.

JOHN HOLLANDER. "Tennyson's Melody," *Georgia Review* 29(3), Fall 1975, 679-80.

WILLIAM B. THESING. "Tennyson and the City: Historical Tremours and Hysterical Tremblings," *Tennyson Research Bulletin* 3(1), November 1977, 14-16.

"Time: an Ode"

ANDREW FICHTER. "Ode and Elegy: Idea and Form in Tennyson's Early Poetry," *ELH* 40(3), Fall 1973, 403-4.

"Tiresias"

DAVID F. GOSLEE. "Three Stages of Tennyson's 'Tiresias,'" *Journal of English and Germanic Philology* 75(1-2), January-April 1976, 154-67.

E. D. H. JOHNSON. *The Alien Vision of Victorian Poetry*, pp. 66-68.

GERHARD JOSEPH. "Tennyson's Concepts of Knowledge, Wisdom, and Pallas Athene," *Modern Philology* 69(4), May 1972, 316-17, 319-21.

"Tithonus"

HAROLD BLOOM. *Poetry and Repression*, pp. 160-68.

DOUGLAS BUSH. *Pagan Myth and Christian Tradition in English Poetry*, p. 53.

DEREK COLVILLE. *Victorian Poetry and the Romantic Religion*, pp. 173-74.

MARY JOAN DONAHUE. "Tennyson's *Hail, Briton!* and *Tithon* in the Heath Manuscript," *PMLA* 54(3), June 1949, 400-15.

WALLACE DOUGLAS, ROY LAMSON, and HALLETT SMITH. *The Critical Reader*, pp. 96-100.

CHRISTINE GALLANT. "Tennyson's Use of the Nature Goddess in 'The Hesperides,' 'Tithonus,' and 'Demeter and Persephone,'" *Victorian Poetry* 14(2), Summer 1976, 158.

E. D. H. JOHNSON. *The Alien Vision of Victorian Poetry*, pp. 13-14.

GERHARD JOSEPH. "The Idea of Mortality in Tennyson's Classical and Arthurian Poems: 'Honor Comes With Mystery,'" *Modern Philology* 66(2), November 1968, 140-41.

JAMES R. KINCAID. "Rhetorical Irony, the Dramatic Monologue, and Tennyson's Poems (1842)," *Philological Quarterly* 53(2), Spring 1974, 232-34.

PHYLLIS RACKIN. "Tennyson's Art That Conceals Itself," *CEA Critic* 28(4), January 1966, 9-10.

W. DAVID SHAW. "Tennyson's 'Tithonus' and the Problem of Mortality," *Philological Quarterly* 52(2), April 1973, 274-85.

ARTHUR L. SIMPSON, JR. "Aurora as Artist: A Reinterpretation of Tennyson's *Tithonus*," *Philological Quarterly* 51(4), October 1972, 905-21.

CARL ROBINSON SONN. "Poetic Vision and Religious Certainty in Tennyson's Earlier Poetry," *Modern Philology* 57(2), November 1959, 88-90.

WRIGHT THOMAS and STUART GERRY BROWN. *Reading Poems: An Introduction to Critical Study*, p. 675.

ARTHUR D. WARD. "'Ulysses' and 'Tithonus': Tunnel-Vision and Idle Tears," *Victorian Poetry* 12(4), Winter 1974, 311-19.

"To the Marquis of Dufferin and Ava"

W. DAVID SHAW. "Tennyson's Late Elegies," *Victorian Poetry* 12(1), Spring 1974, 7-9.

"The Two Voices"

PATRICIA M. BALL. *The Central Self*, pp. 171-73.

GEORGE BARKER. "Tennyson: The Two Voices," in *Master Poems of the English Language*, pp. 654-57.

WILLIAM R. BRASHEAR. "Tennyson's Third Voice: A Note," *Victorian Poetry* 2(4), Autumn 1964, 283-86.

HARRY BROWN and JOHN MILSTEAD. *What the Poem Means*, p. 266.

DEREK COLVILLE. *Victorian Poetry and the Romantic Religion*, pp. 174-75.

E. D. H. JOHNSON. *The Alien Vision of Victorian Poetry*, p. 39.

WENDELL STACY JOHNSON. *Sex and Marriage in Victorian Poetry*, pp. 119-24.

WENDELL STACY JOHNSON. "Some Functions of Poetic Form," *Journal of Aesthetics and Art Criticism* 13(4), June 1955, 504.

GERHARD JOSEPH. "Victorian Frames: The Windows and Mirrors of Browning, Arnold, and Tennyson," *Victorian Poetry* 16(1-2), Spring-Summer 1978, 83-84.

JOHN R. REED. "The Design of Tennyson's 'The Two Voices,'" *University of Toronto Quarterly* 37(2), January 1968, 186-96.

W. DAVID SHAW. "The Transcendentalist Problem In Tennyson's Poetry of Debate," *Philological Quarterly* 46(1), January 1967, 80-84.

CARL ROBINSON SONN. "Poetic Vision and Religious Certainty in Tennyson's Earlier Poetry," *Modern Philology* 57(2), November 1959, 86-87.

"Ulysses"

ROY P. BASLER. *Explicator* 4(7), May 1945, Item 48.

HAROLD BLOOM. *A Map of Misreading*, pp. 156-59.

HAROLD BLOOM. *Poetry and Repression*, pp. 157-60.

DOUGLAS BUSH. *Pagan Myth and Christian Tradition in English Poetry*, p. 52.

E. J. CHIASSON. "Tennyson's 'Ulysses' — A Re-Interpretation," *University of Toronto Quarterly* 23(4), July 1954, 402-9.

DEREK COLVILLE. *Victorian Poetry and the Romantic Religion*, p. 174.

WILLIAM FROST. *Explicator* 4(7), May 1945, Item 48.

ROYAL A. GETTMANN and JOHN ROBERT MOORE. *Explicator* 1(4), February 1943, Item 33.

JOHN E. GURKA. "The Voices of Ulysses and Prufrock," *English Journal* 55(2), February 1966, 205-7.

JAY L. HALIO. " 'Prothalamion,' 'Ulysses,' and Intention in Poetry," *College English* 22(6), March 1961, 392-94.

E. D. H. JOHNSON. *The Alien Vision of Victorian Poetry*, pp. 40-41.

JAMES R. KINCAID. "Rhetorical Irony, the Dramatic Monologue, and Tennyson's Poems (1842)," *Philological Quarterly* 53(2), Spring 1974, 227-32.

ROBERT LANGBAUM. *The Poetry of Experience*, pp. 90-92. Reprinted in: *Poems and Critics*, pp. 196-98.

B. J. LEGGETT. "Dante, Byron, and Tennyson's Ulysses," *Tennessee Studies in Literature* 15(1970), 143-59.

CHARLES MITCHELL. "The Undying Will of Tennyson's Ulysses," *Victorian Poetry* 2(2), Spring 1964, 87-95.

LAURENCE PERRINE. *Sound and Sense*, pp. 172-74; second ed., pp. 184-85; third ed., pp. 220-22; fourth ed., pp. 207-9.

JOHN OLIVER PERRY. "The Relationships of Disparate Voices in Poems," *Essays in Criticism* 15(1), January 1965, 55-56.

JOHN PETTIGREW. "Tennyson's 'Ulysses': A Reconciliation of Opposites," *Victorian Poetry* 1(1), January 1963, 27-45.

TONY ROBBINS. "Tennyson's 'Ulysses': The Significance of the Homeric and Dantesque Backgrounds," *Victorian Poetry* 11(3), Autumn 1973, 177-93.

GEORG ROPPEN. " 'Ulysses' and Tennyson's Seaquest," *English Studies* 40(2), April 1959, 77-90.

GEORG ROPPEN and RICHARD SOMMER. *Strangers and Pilgrims*, pp. 284-303.

EDGAR F. SHANNON, JR. "Alfred Tennyson as a Poet for Our Time," *Virginia Quarterly Review* 53(4), Autumn 1977, 698-99.

JOSEPH SOLIMINE. "The Burkean Idea of the State in Tennyson's Poetry: The Vision in Crisis," *Huntington Library Quarterly* 30(2), February 1967, 153-54.

CARL ROBINSON SONN. "Poetic Vision and Religious Certainty in Tennyson's Earlier Poetry," *Modern Philology* 57(2), November 1959, 87-88.

R. F. STORCH. "The Fugitive from the Ancestral Hearth: Tennyson's 'Ulysses,'" *Texas Studies in Literature and Language* 13(2), Summer 1971, 281-97.

WRIGHT THOMAS and STUART GERRY BROWN. *Reading Poems: An Introduction to Critical Study*, pp. 674-75.

CHARLES C. WALCUTT. *Explicator* 4(4), February 1946, Item 28.

ARTHUR D. WARD. " 'Ulysses' and 'Tithonus': Tunnel-Vision and Idle Tears," *Victorian Poetry* 12(4), Winter 1974, 311-19.

"Vastness"

WINSTON COLLINS. "Tennyson and Hopkins," *University of Toronto Quarterly* 38(1), October 1968, 84-87.

"A Voice Spake out of the Skies"

FRANCIS GOLFFING. "Tennyson's Last Phase: The Poet as Seer," *Southern Review*, n.s., 2(2), Spring 1966, 277.

"The Voyage"

E. D. H. JOHNSON. *The Alien Vision of Victorian Poetry*, pp. 41-42.

THOMAS OF HALES

"A Mayde cristes me bit yorne"

STEPHEN MANNING. *Wisdom and Number*, pp. 122-24.

THOMAS, DYLAN

"After the Funeral"

HARRY BROWN and JOHN MILSTEAD. *What the Poem Means*, p. 269.

DAVID DAICHES and WILLIAM CHARVAT. *Poems in English*, pp. 744-45.

C. DAY LEWIS. *The Poetic Image*, pp. 123-25.

BABETTE DEUTSCH. *Poetry in Our Time*, p. 342; second ed., pp. 381-82.

KIMON FRIAR and JOHN MALCOLM BRINNIN. *Modern Poetry*, p. 541.

BARBARA HARDY. *The Advantage of Lyric*, pp. 112-13.

DAVID HOLBROOK. *Llareggub Revisited*, pp. 98-100.

ROBERT H. MEYER. "Dylan Thomas: The Experience, the Picture, and the Message," *English Journal* 60(2), February 1971, 202-3.

MARSHALL W. STERNS. *Explicator* 3(7), May 1945, Item 52. Reprinted in: *Reading Modern Poetry*, pp. 313-14; revised ed., pp. 311-12.

"All All and All the Dry Worlds Lever"

JACOB KORG. "Imagery and Universe in Dylan Thomas's '18 Poems,'" *Accent* 17(4), Winter 1957, 12-14.

"Altarwise by Owl-light"

see also first lines of individual sonnets in the sequence

NAOMI CHRISTENSEN. "Dylan Thomas and the Doublecross of Death," *Ball State Teachers College Forum* 4(2), Autumn 1963, 50-53.

ERHARDT H. ESSIG. *Explicator* 16(9), June 1958, Item 53.

G. S. FRASER. *Vision and Rhetoric* pp. 223-24. Reprinted in: George Fraser. *Essays on Twentieth-Century Poets*, pp. 190-91.

DAVID HOLBROOK. *Llareggub Revisited*, pp. 134-35.

BERNARD KNIEGER. "Dylan Thomas: The Christianity of the 'Altarwise by Owl-light' Sequence," *College English* 23(8), May 1962, 623-28.

D. F. McKAY. "Aspects of Energy in the Poetry of Dylan Thomas and Sylvia Plath," *Critical Quarterly* 16(1), Spring 1974, 58-60.

M. L. ROSENTHAL. *The Modern Poets*, pp. 217-18.

MARGARET SCHLAUCH. *Modern English and American Poetry*, pp. 84-85.

THOMAS, DYLAN *(Cont.)*

"Altarwise by Owl-light" *(cont.)*

WILLIAM YORK TINDALL. "Thomas: Altarwise by Owl-light," in *Master Poems of the English Language,* pp. 1047-54.

"Altarwise by owl-light in the half-way house" ("Altarwise by Owl-light," 1)

BERNARD KNIEGER. *Explicator* 15(3), December 1956, Item 18.

RALPH N. MAUD. *Explicator* 14(3), December 1955, Item 16.

"Among Those Killed in the Dawn Raid Was a Man Aged a Hundred"

PHYLLIS BARTLETT. *Explicator* 12(3), December 1953, Item 21.

ELMER L. BROOKS. *Explicator* 12(8), June 1954, Item 49.

DAVID HOLBROOK. *Llareggub Revisited,* pp. 175-78.

"And Death Shall Have No Dominion"

THOMAS E. CONNOLLY. *Explicator* 14(5), February 1956, Item 33.

M. L. ROSENTHAL. *The Modern Poets,* pp. 210-11.

HOWARD SERGEANT. "The Religious Development of Dylan Thomas," *Review of English Literature* 3(2), April 1962, 61-63.

"Ballad of the Long-Legged Bait"

RICHARD A. CONDON. *Explicator* 16(6), March 1958, Item 37.

SUZANNE FERGUSON. "Fishing the Deep Sea: Archetypal Patterns in Thomas' 'Ballad of the Long-legged Bait,'" *Modern Poetry Studies* 6(2), Autumn 1975, 102-14.

G. S. FRASER. *Vision and Rhetoric,* pp. 237-38. Reprinted in: George Fraser. *Essays on Twentieth Century Poets,* pp. 200-1.

ELSIE LEACH. "Dylan Thomas' 'Ballad of the Long-Legged Bait,'" *Modern Language Notes* 76(8), December 1961, 724-28.

WILLIAM T. MOYNIHAN. "Dylan Thomas and the 'Biblical Rhythm,'" *PMLA* 79(5), December 1964, 641-2.

A. RICHMOND NEUVILLE, JR. *Explicator* 23(6), February 1965, Item 43.

ELDER OLSON. "The Poetry of Dylan Thomas," *Poetry* 83(4), January 1954, 214-15.

LEE J. RICHMOND. *Explicator* 23(6), February 1965, Item 43.

"Because the Pleasure-Bird Whistles"

GENE MONTAGUE. *Explicator* 34(4), December 1975, Item 30.

ELDER OLSON. "The Poetry of Dylan Thomas," *Poetry* 83(4), January 1954, 218. (P)

"Before I Knocked"

DAVID HOLBROOK. *Llareggub Revisited,* pp. 130-31.

"Ceremony After a Fire Raid"

DAVID HOLBROOK. *Llareggub Revisited,* p. 137.

ROBERT H. MEYER. "Dylan Thomas: The Experience, the Picture, and the Message," *English Journal* 60(2), February 1971, 201-2.

MYRON OCHSHORN. "The Love Song of Dylan Thomas," *New Mexico Quarterly Review* 24(1), Spring 1954, 60-64.

WILLIAM YORK TINDALL. "The Poetry of Dylan Thomas," in *On Contemporary Literature,* pp. 613-14.

"The Conversation of Prayer"

G. S. FRASER. *Vision and Rhetoric,* pp. 234-35. Reprinted in: George Fraser. *Essays on Twentieth-Century Poets,* pp. 198-99.

BARBARA HARDY. *The Advantage of Lyric,* p. 119.

ROBERT C. JONES. *Explicator* 17(7), April 1959, Item 49.

WILLIAM T. MOYNIHAN. "Dylan Thomas' 'Hewn Voice,'" *Texas Studies in Literature and Language* 1(3), Autumn 1959, 324-25.

MARY ELLEN RICKEY. *Explicator* 16(3), December 1957, Item 15.

DIANA SAUTTER. "Dylan Thomas and Archetypal Domination," *American Imago* 31(4), Winter 1974, 355-56.

"Death is all metaphors, shape in one history"
see also "Altarwise by Owl-light"

"Death is all metaphors, shape in one history" ("Altarwise by Owl-light," 2)

BERNARD KNIEGER. *Explicator* 18(2), November 1959, Item 14.

"Do Not Go Gentle into That Good Night"

OLIVER EVANS. "The Making of a Poem: Dylan Thomas' 'Do Not Go Gentle into That Good Night,'" in *The Dimensions of Poetry,* pp. 716-20.

BARBARA HARDY. *The Advantage of Lyric,* pp. 116-17.

DAVID HOLBROOK. *Llareggub Revisited,* pp. 100-1.

MICHAEL W. MURPHY. *Explicator* 28(6), February 1970, Item 55.

"Ears in the Turrets Hear"

J. HILLIS MILLER. *Poets of Reality,* p. 210.

"The Empty Purse"

JULIAN SYMONS. "Obscurity and Dylan Thomas," *Kenyon Review* 2(1), Winter 1940, 64-65.

"Especially When the October Wind"

GERALD L. BRUNS. "Daedalus, Orpheus, and Dylan Thomas's Portrait of the Artist," *Renascence* 25(3), Spring 1973, 154-55.

LAURENCE PERRINE. *Explicator* 21(1), September 1962, Item 1.

"Fern Hill"

WILLIAM BLISSETT. "Dylan Thomas — A Reader in Search of a Poet," *Queens Quarterly* 63(1), Spring 1956, 52-54.

HARRY BROWN and JOHN MILSTEAD. *What the Poem Means,* pp. 268-69.

C. B. COX. "Dylan Thomas's 'Fern Hill,'" *Critical Quarterly* 1(2), Summer 1959, 134-38.

C. B. COX and A. E. DYSON. *Modern Poetry,* pp. 122-27.

MARY C. DAVIDOW. "Journey from Apple Orchard to Swallow Thronged Loft: 'Fern Hill,'" *English Journal* 58(1), January 1969, 78-81.

ROBERT G. HAVARD. "The Symbolic Ambivalence of 'Green' in Garcia Lorca and Dylan Thomas," *Modern Language Review* 67(4), October 1972, 812-14.

DAVID HOLBROOK. *Llareggub Revisited,* pp. 154-56, 159-62.

SISTER M. JOSELYN. "'Green and Dying': The Drama of 'Fern Hill,'" *Renascence* 16(4), Summer 1964, 219-21.

JAMES G. KENNEDY. "The Two European Cultures and the Necessary New Sense of Literature," *College English* 31(6), March 1970, 585-86.

SISTER M. LAURENTIA. *Explicator* 14(1), October 1955, Item 1.

MYRON OCHSHORN. "The Love Song of Dylan Thomas," *New Mexico Quarterly Review* 24(1), Spring 1954, 56-60.

DEREK STANFORD. "Motifs in Dylan Thomas' 'Fern Hill,' " in *The Dimensions of Poetry*, pp. 714-16.

DEREK STANFORD. "Thomas: Fern Hill," in *Master Poems of the English Language*, pp. 1061-63.

"First there was the lamb on knocking knees"
see also "Altarwise by Owl-light"

"First there was the lamb on knocking knees" ("Altarwise by Owl-light," 3)

BERNARD KNIEGER. *Explicator* 18(4), January 1960, Item 25.

"The Force That Through the Green Fuse Drives the Flower"

EDWARD A. BLOOM, CHARLES H. PHILBRICK, and ELMER M. BLISTEIN. *The Order of Poetry*, pp. 59-62.

DAVID DAICHES and WILLIAM CHARVAT. *Poems in English*, p. 744.

ELIZABETH DREW. *Poetry*, pp. 181-83.

LLOYD FRANKENBERG. *Pleasure Dome*, pp. 318-19.

G. S. FRASER. *Vision and Rhetoric*, p. 218.

G. GIOVANNINI. *Explicator* 8(8), June 1950, Item 59. Reprinted in: *Readings for Liberal Education*, revised ed., II: 273-74; third ed., II: 260-62; fourth ed., II: 253-54. Reprinted in: *The Creative Reader*, second ed., pp. 947-48.

BARBARA HARDY. *The Advantage of Lyric*, pp. 115-16.

DAVID HOLBROOK. *Llareggub Revisited*, pp. 163-66.

S. F. JOHNSON. *Explicator* 8(8), June 1950, Item 60. Reprinted in: *Readings for Liberal Education*, revised ed., II: 275-76; third ed., II: 262-63; fourth ed., II: 254-56.

S. F. JOHNSON. *Explicator* 10(4), February 1952, Item 26.

S. F. JOHNSON. "Three Interpretations of Dylan Thomas' 'The Force That Through the Green Fuse Drives,' " in *The Creative Reader*, 2d edition, pp. 948-50.

D. F. MCKAY. "Aspects of Energy in the Poetry of Dylan Thomas and Sylvia Plath," *Critical Quarterly* 16(1), Spring 1974, 56-57.

ROBERT H. MEYER. "Dylan Thomas: The Experience, the Picture, and the Message," *English Journal* 60(2), February 1971, 203-4.

MYRON OCHSHORN. "The Love Song of Dylan Thomas," *New Mexico Quarterly Review* 24(1), Spring 1954, 51-54.

PETER F. PARSHALL. *Explicator* 29(8), April 1971, Item 65.

M. L. ROSENTHAL. *The Modern Poets*, pp. 209-10.

M. L. ROSENTHAL and A. J. M. SMITH. *Exploring Poetry*, second ed., pp. 286-87.

"Foster the Light"

W. E. YEOMANS. "Dylan Thomas: The Literal Vision," *Bucknell Review* 14(1), March 1966, 108-9.

"From Love's First Fever to Her Plague"

DAVID HOLBROOK. *Llareggub Revisited*, pp. 166-68.

SAM HYNES. *Explicator* 9(3), December 1950, Item 18.

DIANA SAUTTER. "Dylan Thomas and Archetypal Domination," *American Imago* 31(4), Winter 1974, 345-50.

"Grief Thief of Time"

DAVID HOLBROOK. *Llareggub Revisited*, p. 135.

"Hold Hard, These Ancient Minutes in the Cuckoo's Month"

HOWARD NEMEROV. "The Generation of Violence," *Kenyon Review* 15(3), Summer 1953, 478-80. Reprinted in: Howard Nemerov. *Poetry and Fiction*, pp. 161-63.

"How Shall My Animal"

GENE MONTAGUE. "Dylan Thomas and *Nightwood*," *Sewanee Review* 76(3), Summer 1968, 420-34.

"How Soon the Servant Sun"

MAX HALPEREN. *Explicator* 23(8), April 1965, Item 65.

"The Hunchback in the Park"

SISTER HELENA BRAND. "Structure Signals in 'The Hunchback in the Park,' " *English Journal* 59(2), February 1970, 195-200.

BABETTE DEUTSCH. *Poetry in Our Time*, p. 341; second ed., pp. 380-81.

G. S. FRASER. *Vision and Rhetoric*, pp. 236-37. Reprinted in: George Fraser. *Essays on Twentieth-Century Poets*, pp. 199-200.

BARBARA HARDY. *The Advantage of Lyric*, pp. 119-20.

S. F. JOHNSON. *Explicator* 10(4), February 1952, Item 27.

LAURENCE PERRINE. *Explicator* 20(5), January 1962, Item 45.

"I Fellowed Sleep"

DAVID HOLBROOK. *Llareggub Revisited*, p. 133.

"I Have Longed to Move Away"

NAOMI CHRISTENSEN. "Dylan Thomas and the Doublecross of Death," *Ball State Teachers College Forum* 4(2), Autumn 1963, 49-50.

G. S. FRASER. *Vision and Rhetoric*, pp. 221-23. Reprinted in: George Fraser. *Essays on Twentieth Century Poets*, pp. 189-90.

DAVID HOLBROOK. *Llareggub Revisited*, pp. 182-84.

"I, in My Intricate Image"

DAVID HOLBROOK. *Llareggub Revisited*, pp. 133-34.

"I Make This in a Warring Absence"

DAVID HOLBROOK. *Llareggub Revisited*, pp. 135-36.

W. E. YEOMANS. "Dylan Thomas: The Literal Vision," *Bucknell Review* 14(1), March 1966, 105-7.

"I See the Boys of Summer"

G. S. FRASER. *Vision and Rhetoric*, p. 219. Reprinted in: George Fraser. *Essays on Twentieth Century Poets*, pp. 187-88.

BREWSTER GHISELIN. "The Extravagant Energy of Genius," *Western Review* 18(3), Spring 1954, 246.

ROB JACKAMAN. "Man and Mandala: Symbol as Structure in a Poem by Dylan Thomas," *Ariel* 7(4), October 1976, 22-33.

MYRON OCHSHORN. "The Love Song of Dylan Thomas," *New Mexico Quarterly Review* 24(1), Spring 1954, 47-49.

WILLIAM YORK TINDALL. "The Poetry of Dylan Thomas," in *On Contemporary Literature*, pp. 609-11.

"If I Were Tickled by the Rub of Love"

MAX HALPEREN. *Explicator* 21(3), November 1962, Item 25.

"If My Head Hurt a Hair's Foot"

BARBARA HARDY. *The Advantage of Lyric*, p. 115.

THOMAS, DYLAN *(Cont.)*

"If My Head Hurt a Hair's Foot" *(cont.)*
DAVID HOLBROOK. *Llareggub Revisited*, pp. 168-70.

"In Country Heaven"
BABETTE DEUTSCH. *Poetry in Our Time*, second ed., pp. 387-88.

"In Country Sleep"
WALFORD DAVIES. "An Allusion to Hardy's 'A Broken Appointment' in Dylan Thomas's 'In Country Sleep,'" *Notes & Queries*, n.s., 15(2), February 1968, 61-62.
MARTIN E. GINGERICH. "The Timeless Narrators of Dylan Thomas' 'In Country Heaven,'" *Modern Poetry Studies* 7(2), Autumn 1976, 116-21.
DAVID HOLBROOK. *Llareggub Revisited*, pp. 146-53.
WILLIAM T. MOYNIHAN. "Dylan Thomas and the 'Biblical Rhythm,'" *PMLA* 79(5), December 1964, 645.

"In My Craft or Sullen Art"
LLOYD FRANKENBERG. *Invitation to Poetry*, pp. 99-101.
D. R. HOWARD. *Explicator* 12(4), February 1954, Item 22.
M. L. ROSENTHAL. *The Modern Poets*, pp. 203-4.
PATRICIA MEYER SPACKS. *Explicator* 18(3), December 1959, Item 21. (P)

"In the Beginning"
DAVID HOLBROOK. *Llareggub Revisited*, pp. 132-33. (P)
J. HILLIS MILLER. *Poets of Reality*, p. 194.
DIANA SAUTTER. "Dylan Thomas and Archetypal Domination," *American Imago* 31(4), Winter 1974, 344, 346-47.

"In the White Giant's Thigh"
MARLENE CHAMBERS. *Explicator* 19(1), October 1960, Item 1.
MARTIN E. GINGERICH. "The Timeless Narrators of Dylan Thomas' 'In Country Heaven,'" *Modern Poetry Studies* 7(2), Autumn 1976, 113-16.
WILLIAM T. MOYNIHAN. "Dylan Thomas and the 'Biblical Rhythm,'" *PMLA* 79(5), December 1965, 646.
WILLIAM T. MOYNIHAN. *Explicator* 17(8), May 1959, Item 59.

"Lament"
CONSTANTINE FITZGIBBON. "Thomas: Lament," in *Master Poems of the English Language*, pp. 1066-68.
DAVID HOLBROOK. *Llareggub Revisited*, pp. 178-80.

"Lie Still, Sleep Becalmed"
DAVID HOLBROOK. *Llareggub Revisited*, pp. 138-39.

"Light Breaks Where No Sun Shines"
BERNARD KNIEGER. *Explicator* 15(5), February 1957, Item 32.
J. HILLIS MILLER. *Poets of Reality*, p. 194.
WILLIAM T. MOYNIHAN. *Explicator* 16(5), February 1958, Item 28.
LOUIS SIMPSON. *A Revolution in Taste*, pp. 25-26.
MARSHALL W. STERNS. "Unsex the Skeleton: Notes on the Poetry of Dylan Thomas," *Sewanee Review* 52(3), Summer 1944, 435-40.

"Love in the Asylum"
BREWSTER GHISELIN. "Use of a Mango," *Rocky Mountain Review* 8(3), Spring 1944, 112.
BERNARD KNIEGER. *Explicator* 20(2), October 1961, Item 13.

DIANA SAUTTER. "Dylan Thomas and Archetypal Domination," *American Imago* 31(4), Winter 1974, 350-52.

"Not From This Anger"
JOHN CLARK PRATT. *The Meaning of Modern Poetry*, pp. 342, 336, 354, 356, 355, 360, 358-59, 368, 372.
W. E. YEOMANS. "Dylan Thomas: The Literal Vision," *Bucknell Review* 14(1), March 1966, 107-8.

"O Make Me a Mask"
OLGA DEHART HARVILL. *Explicator* 26(2), October 1967, Item 12.
DAVID HOLBROOK. *Llareggub Revisited*, pp. 191-93.

"On the Marriage of a Virgin"
DAVID DAICHES and WILLIAM CHARVAT. *Poems in English*, p. 745.
BREWSTER GHISELIN. "The Extravagant Energy of Genius," *Western Review* 18(3), Spring 1954, 249. (P)
S. F. JOHNSON. *Explicator* 10(4), February 1952, Item 27.
BERNARD KNIEGER. *Explicator* 19(8), May 1961, Item 61.
DIANA SAUTTER. "Dylan Thomas and Archetypal Domination," *American Imago* 31(4), Winter 1974, 352-53.

"Once Below a Time"
DAVID HOLBROOK. *Llareggub Revisited*, pp. 174-75.

"Our Eunuch Dreams"
DAVID HOLBROOK. *Llareggub Revisited*, pp. 185-87.
A. J. SMITH. "Ambiguity as Poetic Shift," *Critical Quarterly* 4(1), Spring 1962, 68-74.

"Out of the Sighs"
DAVID HOLBROOK. *Llareggub Revisited*, pp. 187-90.
DIANA SAUTTER. "Dylan Thomas and Archetypal Domination," *American Imago* 31(4), Winter 1974, 353-55.

"Over Sir John's Hill"
MARTIN E. GINGERICH. "The Timeless Narrators of Dylan Thomas' 'In Country Heaven,'" *Modern Poetry Studies* 7(2), Autumn 1976, 111-13.
BARBARA HARDY. *The Advantage of Lyric*, p. 114.
WILLIAM T. MOYNIHAN. "Dylan Thomas and the 'Biblical Rhythm,'" *PMLA* 79(5), December 1964, 646.
CARROLL F. TERRELL. *Explicator* 36(1), Fall 1977, 24-26.

"Poem in October"
HARRY BROWN and JOHN MILSTEAD. *What the Poem Means*, p. 270.
DAVID DAICHES. "The Poetry of Dylan Thomas," *College English* 16(1), October 1954, 7. Reprinted in: *English Journal* 43(7), October 1954, 355. Also: *College English* 22(2), November 1960, 127-28.
BABETTE DEUTSCH. *Poetry in Our Time*, pp. 332-33; second ed., pp. 371-72.
DAVID HOLBROOK. *Llareggub Revisited*, pp. 172-74.
SISTER M. ROBERTA JONES. "The Wellspring of Dylan," *English Journal* 55(1), January 1966, 78-79.

"A Poem in Three Parts"
ALAN YOUNG. "Image as Structure: Dylan Thomas and Poetic Meaning," *Critical Quarterly* 17(4), Winter 1975, 333-45.

"Poem on His Birthday"
HARRY BROWN and JOHN MILSTEAD. *What the Poem Means*, pp. 270-71.

DEREK STANFORD. "Dylan Thomas: A Literary Post-Mortem," *Queen's Quarterly* 71(3), Autumn 1964, 412-17.

"Prologue"

WILLIAM T. MOYNIHAN. "Dylan Thomas and the 'Biblical Rhythm,'" *PMLA* 79(5), December 1964, 646-47.

"A Refusal to Mourn the Death, by Fire, of a Child in London"

CLEANTH BROOKS, JOHN THIBAUT PURSER, and ROBERT PENN WARREN. *An Approach to Literature,* fifth ed., pp. 386-87.

HARRY BROWN and JOHN MILSTEAD. *What the Poem Means,* p. 267.

JOHN A. CLAIR. *Explicator* 17(3), December 1958, Item 25.

DAVID DAICHES. "The Poetry of Dylan Thomas," *College English* 16(1), October 1954, 3-5. Reprinted in: *English Journal* 43(7), October 1954, 351-52. Also: *College English* 22(2), November 1960, 125-26.

WILLIAM VIRGIL DAVIS. "Several Comments on 'A Refusal to Mourn the Death, by Fire, of a Child in London,'" *Concerning Poetry* 2(2), Fall 1969, 45-48.

BABETTE DEUTSCH. *Poetry in Our Time,* pp. 335-37; second ed., pp. 373-76.

WILLIAM EMPSON. "How to Read a Modern Poem," in *Modern Poetry,* pp. 243-48.

HENRY GIBSON. "A Comment," *The Critic* 1 (Autumn 1947), 19-20.

MARTIN E. GINGERICH. "Rhetoric and Meaning in 'A Refusal to Mourn,'" *Notes on Contemporary Literature* 1(1), January 1971, 5-6.

DAVID HOLBROOK. *Llareggub Revisited,* pp. 170-72.

EDWIN HONIG. "Thomas: A Refusal to Mourn the Death, by Fire, of a Child in London," in *Master Poems of the English Language,* pp. 1056-58.

BROTHER BENILDE MONTGOMERY. "The Function of Ambiguity in 'A Refusal to Mourn the Death by Fire of a Child in London,'" *Concerning Poetry* 8(2), Fall 1975, 77-81.

M. L. ROSENTHAL. *The Modern Poets,* pp. 215-16.

EDITH SITWELL. "Dylan Thomas," *Atlantic* 193(2), February 1954, 45.

GEOFFREY THURLEY. *The Ironic Harvest,* pp. 123-24.

JOHN WAIN. "Dylan Thomas," in *English Poetry,* edited by Alan Sinfield, pp. 224-25.

"A Saint About to Fall"

W. E. YEOMANS. "Dylan Thomas: The Literal Vision," *Bucknell Review* 14(1), March 1966, 110-11.

"Should Lanterns Shine"

DAVID HOLBROOK. *Llareggub Revisited,* pp. 184-85.

"The Spire Cranes"

GEORGE P. WEICK. *Explicator* 37(1), Fall 1978, 21-22.

"There Was a Saviour"

DAVID HOLBROOK. *Llareggub Revisited,* pp. 116-27.

WINIFRED NOWOTTNY. *The Language Poets Use,* pp. 187-219.

"This Bread I Break"

GEOFFREY LEECH. "'This bread I break' — Language and Interpretation," *Review of English Literature* 6(2), April 1965, 66-75.

"This was the crucifixion on the mountain"
see also "Altarwise by Owl-light"

"This was the crucifixion on the mountain" ("Altarwise by Owl-light," 8)

MARSHALL W. STEARNS. "Unsex the Skeleton: Notes on the Poetry of Dylan Thomas," *Sewanee Review* 52(3), Summer 1944, 430-33.

"Today, This Insect"

BILL CASEY. *Explicator* 17(6), March 1959, Item 43.

NAOMI CHRISTENSEN. "Dylan Thomas and the Doublecross of Death," *Ball State Teachers College Forum* 4(2), Autumn 1963, 50.

GENE MONTAGUE. *Explicator* 19(3), December 1960, Item 15. (P)

WILLIAM YORK TINDALL. "The Poetry of Dylan Thomas," in *On Contemporary Literature,* p. 612.

"The Tombstone Told When She Died"

IHAB H. HASSAN. *Explicator* 15(2), November 1956, Item 11.

"Twenty-Four Years"

BERNARD KNIEGER. *Explicator* 20(1), September 1961, Item 4.

DAVID ORMEROD. *Explicator* 22(9), May 1964, Item 76.

M. L. ROSENTHAL. *The Modern Poets,* pp. 204-6.

ANDREWS WANNING. "Criticism and Principles: Poetry of the Quarter," *Southern Review* 6(4), Spring 1941, 806-9.

"Unluckily for a Death"

LYNA LEE MONTGOMERY. "The Phoenix: Its Use as a Literary Device in English From the Seventeenth Century to the Twentieth Century," *D. H. Lawrence Review* 5(3), Fall 1972, 313-14.

"Vision and Prayer"

DAVID DAICHES. "The Poetry of Dylan Thomas," *College English* 16(1), October 1954, 6-7. Reprinted in: *English Journal* 43(7), October 1954, 354-55. Reprinted in: *College English* 22(2), November 1960, 127.

KIMON FRIAR and JOHN MALCOLM BRINNIN. *Modern Poetry,* pp. 540-41.

DAVID HOLBROOK. *Llareggub Revisited,* pp. 101-3.

SISTER M. ROBERTA JONES. "The Wellspring of Dylan," *English Journal* 55(1), January 1966, 81-82.

JOHN NIST. "Dylan Thomas: 'Perfection of the Work,'" *Arizona Quarterly* 17(2), Summer 1961, 104-6.

"We Lying By Seasand"

HENRY GIBSON. "A Comment," *The Critic* 1 (Autumn 1947), 20.

EDITH SITWELL. "Dylan Thomas," *Atlantic* 193(2), February 1954, 44-45.

EDITH SITWELL. "The Love of Man, the Praise of God," *New York Herald Tribune Book Review* 29(39), 10 May 1953, pp. 1, 14.

"When All My Five and Country Senses See"

HARRY BROWN and JOHN MILSTEAD. *What the Poem Means,* p. 272.

BABETTE DEUTSCH. *Poetry in Our Time,* p. 334; second ed., p. 373.

JAMES ZIGERELL. *Explicator* 19(2), November 1960, Item 11.

"When Once the Twilight Locks No Longer"

LINDA BERMAN HAMALIAN. "Richard Wright's Use of Epigraphs in *The Long Dream,*" *Black American Literature Forum* 10(4), Winter 1976, 120-21.

DAVID HOLBROOK. *Llareggub Revisited,* p. 130.

THOMAS, DYLAN *(Cont.)*

"Where Once the Waters of Your Face"

DAVID HOLBROOK. *Llareggub Revisited*, p. 131.

"A Winter's Tale"

LLOYD FRANKENBERG. *Pleasure Dome*, pp. 321-23.

LOUIS K. GREIFF. "Image and Theme in Dylan Thomas' 'A Winter's Tale,' " *Thoth* 6(1), Winter 1965, 35-41.

SISTER M. ROBERTA JONES. "The Wellspring of Dylan," *English Journal* 55(1), January 1966, 79-81.

R. N. MAUD. "Dylan Thomas's Poetry," *Essays in Criticism* 4(4), October 1954, 418-19.

WILLIAM T. MOYNIHAN. "Dylan Thomas and the 'Biblical Rhythm,' " *PMLA* 79(5), December 1964, 643-44.

M. L. ROSENTHAL. *The Modern Poets*, pp. 212-13.

W. E. YEOMANS. "Dylan Thomas: The Literal Vision," *Bucknell Review* 14(1), March 1966, 109.

THOMAS, EDWARD

"As the Team's Head-Brass"

LOUIS COXE. *Enabling Acts*, p. 91.

JONATHAN DOLLIMORE. "The Poetry of Hardy and Edward Thomas," *Critical Quarterly* 17(3), Autumn 1975, 205.

JON SILKIN. *Out of Battle*, pp. 99-101.

"The Bridge"

MAIRE A. QUINN. "The Personal Past in the Poetry of Thomas Hardy and Edward Thomas," *Critical Quarterly* 16(1), Spring 1974, 24.

"The Chalk-Pit"

HUGH UNDERHILL. "The 'Poetical Character' of Edward Thomas," *Essays in Criticism* 23(3), July 1973, 250-52.

"Cock-Crow"

F. R. LEAVIS. "Imagery and Movement: Notes in the Analysis of Poetry," *Scrutiny* 13(2), September 1945, 133-34.

"February Afternoon"

JON SILKIN. *Out of Battle*, p. 98.

"Fifty Faggots"

JON SILKIN. *Out of Battle*, pp. 98-99.

"The Gypsy"

STAN SMITH. "A public house and not a hermitage: nature, property and self in the work of Edward Thomas," *Critical Quarterly* 19(1), Spring 1977, 31-33.

" 'Home' "

STAN SMITH. "A public house and not a hermitage: nature, property and self in the work of Edward Thomas," *Critical Quarterly* 19(1), Spring 1977, 26-28.

"I love roads"

JOHN WAIN. *Professing Poetry*, pp. 357-60.

"If I should ever by chance grow rich"

STAN SMITH. "A public house and not a hermitage: nature, property and self in the work of Edward Thomas," *Critical Quarterly* 19(1), Spring 1977, 33-34.

"If I were to own this countryside"

STAN SMITH. "A public house and not a hermitage: nature, property and self in the work of Edward Thomas," *Critical Quarterly* 19(1), Spring 1977, 35-36.

"In Memoriam (Easter 1915)"

JON SILKIN. *Out of Battle*, p. 97.

"Interval"

JONATHAN DOLLIMORE. "The Poetry of Hardy and Edward Thomas," *Critical Quarterly* 17(3), Autumn 1975, 206-7.

"It Rains"

JOHN BURROW. "Keats and Edward Thomas," *Essays in Criticism* 7(4), October 1957, 407-8.

MAIRE A. QUINN. "The Personal Past in the Poetry of Thomas Hardy and Edward Thomas," *Critical Quarterly* 16(1), Spring 1974, 17-20.

"Liberty"

JOHN F. DANBY. "Edward Thomas," *Critical Quarterly* 1(4), Winter 1959, 310-11.

"Lights Out"

JONATHAN DOLLIMORE. "The Poetry of Hardy and Edward Thomas," *Critical Quarterly* 17(3), Autumn 1975, 211.

"Loss"

HUGH UNDERHILL. "The 'Poetical Character' of Edward Thomas," *Essays in Criticism* 23(3), July 1973, 242.

"Manor Farm"

JOHN F. DANBY. "Edward Thomas," *Critical Quarterly* 1(4), Winter 1959, 311-12.

"March"

H. COOMBES. "Edward Thomas," in *Criticism in Action*, pp. 64-69.

"Melancholy"

HUGH UNDERHILL. "The 'Poetical Character' of Edward Thomas," *Essays in Criticism* 23(3), July 1973, 246-47.

"October"

JOHN BURROW. "Keats and Edward Thomas," *Essays in Criticism* 7(4), October 1957, 405-6, 411-12.

"Old Man"

H. COOMBES. "Edward Thomas," in *Criticism in Action*, pp. 69-73.

JOHN F. DANBY. "Edward Thomas," *Critical Quarterly* 1(4), Winter 1959, 313-15.

MAIRE A. QUINN. "The Personal Past in the Poetry of Thomas Hardy and Edward Thomas," *Critical Quarterly* 16(1), Spring 1974, 21-23.

"The Other"

MICHAEL KIRKHAM. "Edward Thomas's Other Self," *Ariel* 6(3), July 1975, 65-77.

"Over the Hills"

MAIRE A. QUINN. "The Personal Past in the Poetry of Thomas Hardy and Edward Thomas," *Critical Quarterly* 16(1), Spring 1974, 23-24.

"The Owl"

T. R. BARNES. *English Verse*, p. 273.

JON SILKIN. *Out of Battle*, pp. 96-97.

"Parting"

MAIRE A. QUINN. "The Personal Past in the Poetry of Thomas Hardy and Edward Thomas," *Critical Quarterly* 16(1), Spring 1974, 24-25.

"A Private"

JON SILKIN. *Out of Battle*, pp. 97-98.

"Rain"

> JONATHAN DOLLIMORE. "The Poetry of Hardy and Edward Thomas," *Critical Quarterly* 17(3), Autumn 1975, 212-14.
>
> JON SILKIN. *Out of Battle*, pp. 91-95.

"The Sign-Post"

> C. B. COX and A. E. DYSON. *Modern Poetry*, pp. 48-51.
>
> JOHN F. DANBY. "Edward Thomas," *Critical Quarterly* 1(4), Winter 1959, 308-9.
>
> RODERICK A. JACOBS. "Regrets and Wishes," *English Journal* 54(6), September 1965, 569-70.

"Thaw"

> JOHN WAIN. *Professing Poetry*, pp. 354-55.

"This is no Case of Petty Right or Wrong"

> JON SILKIN. *Out of Battle*, pp. 87-88.

"Two Pewits"

> JOHN F. DANBY. "Edward Thomas," *Critical Quarterly* 1(4), Winter 1959, 309-10.

"Under the Woods"

> GEOFFREY THURLEY. *The Ironic Harvest*, p. 32.

"Up in the wind"

> STAN SMITH. "A public house and not a hermitage: nature, property and self in the work of Edward Thomas," *Critical Quarterly* 19(1), Spring 1977, 36-39.

"The Watchers"

> MACDONALD EMSLIE. "Spectatorial Attitudes," *Review of English Literature* 5(1), January 1964, 66-68.

"What Shall I Give?"

> STAN SMITH. "A public house and not a hermitage: nature, property and self in the work of Edward Thomas," *Critical Quarterly* 19(1), Spring 1977, 34-35.

"Wind and Mist"

> STAN SMITH. "A public house and not a hermitage: nature, property and self in the work of Edward Thomas," *Critical Quarterly* 19(1), Spring 1977, 28-31.
>
> HUGH UNDERHILL. "The 'Poetical Character' of Edward Thomas," *Essays in Criticism* 23(3), July 1973, 248.

"Word"

> JOHN F. DANBY. "Edward Thomas," *Critical Quarterly* 1(4), Winter 1959, 315-16.

THOMAS, R. S.

"After the Lecture"

> VIMALA HERMAN. "Negativity and Language in the Religious Poetry of R. S. Thomas," *ELH* 45(4), Winter 1978, 722-23.

"Age"

> JAMES F. KNAPP. "The Poetry of R. S. Thomas," *Twentieth Century Literature* 17(1), January 1971, 6.

"Amen"

> A. E. DYSON. "The Poetry of R. S. Thomas," *Critical Quarterly* 20(2), Summer 1978, 28-30.

"Because"

> VIMALA HERMAN. "Negativity and Language in the Religious Poetry of R. S. Thomas," *ELH* 45(4), Winter 1978, 715-16.

"A Blackbird Singing"

> C. B. COX and A. E. DYSON. *Modern Poetry*, pp. 133-36.

"Country Child"

> A. E. DYSON. "The Poetry of R. S. Thomas," *Critical Quarterly* 20(2), Summer 1978, 8-10.

"Cynddylan On a Tractor"

> JAMES F. KNAPP. "The Poetry of R. S. Thomas," *Twentieth Century Literature* 17(1), January 1971, 3.

"The Dark Well"

> A. E. DYSON. "The Poetry of R. S. Thomas," *Critical Quarterly* 20(2), Summer 1978, 10-11.

"Enigma"

> JAMES F. KNAPP. "The Poetry of R. S. Thomas," *Twentieth Century Literature* 17(1), January 1971, 5-6.

"The Evacuee"

> GEOFFREY THURLEY. *The Ironic Harvest*, pp. 166-67.

"The Garden"

> JAMES F. KNAPP. "The Poetry of R. S. Thomas," *Twentieth Century Literature* 17(1), January 1971, 6-7.

"Gifts"

> A. E. DYSON. "The Poetry of R. S. Thomas," *Critical Quarterly* 20(2), Summer 1978, 18-19.

"Here"

> C. B. COX and A. E. DYSON. *The Practical Criticism of Poetry*, pp. 35-45.
>
> A. E. DYSON. "The Poetry of R. S. Thomas," *Critical Quarterly* 20(2), Summer 1978, 20-22.

"H'm"

> VIMALA HERMAN. "Negativity and Language in the Religious Poetry of R. S. Thomas," *ELH* 45(4), Winter 1978, 710-11.

"Iago Prytherch"

> A. E. DYSON. "The Poetry of R. S. Thomas," *Critical Quarterly* 20(2), Summer 1978, 11-12.

"Judgment Day"

> A. E. DYSON. "The Poetry of R. S. Thomas," *Critical Quarterly* 20(2), Summer 1978, 16-18.

"The Labourer"

> LAURENCE LERNER. "An Essay on Pastoral," *Essays in Criticism* 20(3), July 1970, 277-79. Reprinted in: Laurence Lerner. *The Uses of Nostalgia*, pp. 13-15.

"Look"

> VIMALA HERMAN. "Negativity and Language in the Religious Poetry of R. S. Thomas," *ELH* 45(4), Winter 1978, 723-24.

"Meet the family"

> A. E. DYSON. "The Poetry of R. S. Thomas," *Critical Quarterly* 20(2), Summer 1978, 19-20.

"The Musician"

> VIMALA HERMAN. "Negativity and Language in the Religious Poetry of R. S. Thomas," *ELH* 45(4), Winter 1978, 725-26.

"Ninetieth Birthday"

> CALVIN BEDIENT. "On R. S. Thomas," *Critical Quarterly* 14(3), Autumn 1972, 256.

"On the farm"

> A. E. DYSON. "The Poetry of R. S. Thomas," *Critical Quarterly* 20(2), Summer 1978, 19-20.

THOMAS, R. S. *(Cont.)*

"Out of the Hills"

> R. GEORGE THOMAS. "The Poetry of R. S. Thomas," *Review of English Literature* 3(4), October 1962, 86.

"Pieta"

> A. E. DYSON. "The Poetry of R. S. Thomas," *Critical Quarterly* 20(2), Summer 1978, 5-8.

"Rough"

> A. E. DYSON. "The Poetry of R. S. Thomas," *Critical Quarterly* 20(2), Summer 1978, 25-27.

"Taliesin 1952"

> JAMES F. KNAPP. "The Poetry of R. S. Thomas," *Twentieth Century Literature* 17(1), January 1971, 8-9.

"Too Late"

> JAMES F. KNAPP. "The Poetry of R. S. Thomas," *Twentieth Century Literature* 17(1), January 1971, 3-4.

"Tramp"

> JAMES F. KNAPP. "The Poetry of R. S. Thomas," *Twentieth Century Literature* 17(1), January 1971, 4-5.

"Walter Llywarch"

> CALVIN BEDIENT. *Eight Contemporary Poets,* pp. 62-63.
>
> WILLIAM HEILIG. "Interactions of Attitude, Image, and Sound in R. S. Thomas' 'Walter Llywarch,' " in: Stanley E. Clayes and John Gerrietts, *Ways to Poetry,* pp. 357-59.

THOMAS, RICHARD W.

"The Worker"

> FRANCES FREEMAN PADEN. "Theatre Games and the Teaching of English," *English Journal* 67(2), February 1978, 46-50.

THOMPSON, FRANCIS

"Daisy"

> JAMES D. BROPHY, JR. "Francis Thompson and Contemporary Readers: A Centennial Appraisal," *Renascence* 14(4), Summer 1962, 173-74.

"Grace of the Way"

> TERENCE L. CONNOLLY. *Explicator* 9(8), June 1951, Item 56.
>
> GEORGE G. WILLIAMS. *Explicator* 9(2), November 1950, Item 16.

"The Hound of Heaven"

> CLEANTH BROOKS and ROBERT PENN WARREN. *Understanding Poetry,* revised ed., pp. 283-85.
>
> JAMES D. BROPHY, JR. "Francis Thompson and Contemporary Readers: A Centennial Appraisal," *Renascence* 14(4), Summer 1962, 174-75.
>
> HARRY BROWN and JOHN MILSTEAD. *What the Poem Means,* pp. 272-73.
>
> C. C. CUNNINGHAM. *Literature as a Fine Art,* pp. 243-49.
>
> JAMES DICKEY. *Babel to Byzantium,* pp. 241-44.
>
> JAMES DICKEY. "Thompson: The Hound of Heaven," in *Master Poems of the English Language,* pp. 817-19.

"New Year's Chimes"

> W. G. WILSON. "Francis Thompson's Outlook on Science," *Contemporary Review* 192(1103), November 1957, 266.

"The Poppy"

> JAMES D. BROPHY, JR. "Francis Thompson and Contemporary Readers: A Centennial Appraisal," *Renascence* 14(4), Summer 1962, 174.

"Sad Semele"

> MYRTLE PIHLMAN POPE. *Explicator* 17(5), February 1959, Item 35.

"To the English Martyrs"

> JAMES D. BROPHY, JR. "Francis Thompson and Contemporary Readers: A Centennial Appraisal," *Renascence* 14(4), Summer 1962, 175-76.

THOMSON, JAMES

"The Doom of a City"

> R. A. FORSYTH. "Evolutionism and the Pessimism of James Thomson (B. V.)," *Essays in Criticism* 12(2), April 1962, 152-53.

"A Hymn"

> A. S. P. WOODHOUSE. *The Poet and His Faith,* pp. 149-51.

"Proem: Lo, thus, as prostrate, 'In the dust I write' "

> JEROME J. MCGANN. "James Thomson (B. V.): The Woven Hymns of Night and Day," *Studies in English Literature 1500-1900* 3(4), Autumn 1963, 494.

"Suggested by Matthew Arnold's 'Stanzas from the Grand Chartreuse' "

> R. A. FORSYTH. "Evolutionism and the Pessimism of James Thompson (B. V.)," *Essays in Criticism* 12(2), April 1962, 151.

"The Vine"

> ALLEN TATE. "Tension in Poetry," *Southern Review* 4(1), Summer 1938, 104-8. Reprinted in: *Critiques and Essays in Criticism,* pp. 57-60. Also: *Essays in Modern Literary Criticism,* pp. 269-72. Also: Allen Tate. *Reason in Madness,* pp. 66-71. Also: Allen Tate. *On the Limits of Poetry,* pp. 78-81. Also: Allen Tate. *Essays of Four Decades,* pp. 59-63. Also: *The Modern Critical Spectrum,* pp. 85-87.

THOREAU, HENRY DAVID

"The Atlantides"

> GAIL BAKER. "Friendship in Thoreau's *Week,*" *Thoreau Journal Quarterly* 7(2), April 1975, 6-8.

"The Cliffs & Springs"

> RICHARD TUERK. "The One World of Thoreau's Verse," *Thoreau Journal Quarterly* 6(4), October 1974, 10-11.

"Fog"

> WILLARD H. BONNER. "Mariners and Terreners: Some Aspects of Nautical Imagery in Thoreau," *American Literature* 34(4), January 1963, 518-19.

"I Am the Autumnal Sun"

> MARY I. KAISER. " 'Conversing With The Sky': The Imagery of Celestial Bodies In Thoreau's Poetry," *Thoreau Journal Quarterly* 9(3), July 1977, 17.

"I Saw a Delicate Flower Had Grown up 2 Feet High"

> RICHARD TUERK. "The One World of Thoreau's Verse," *Thoreau Journal Quarterly* 6(4), October 1974, 13-14.

"Inspiration"

> BETSY FEAGAN COLQUITT. "Thoreau's Poetics," *American Transcendental Quarterly* 11(2), Summer 1971, 76.
>
> CARLA MAZZINI. "Epiphany in Two Poems by Thoreau," *Thoreau Journal Quarterly* 5(2), April 1973, 24-25.

HYATT H. WAGGONER. *American Poets,* p. 120.

"The Inward Morning"

BETSY FEAGAN COLQUITT. "Thoreau's Poetics," *American Transcendental Quarterly* 11(2), Summer 1971, 78.

CARLA MAZZINI. "Epiphany in Two Poems by Thoreau," *Thoreau Journal Quarterly* 5(2), April 1973, 23-24.

"It is No Dream of Mine"

PAUL O. WILLIAMS. "Thoreau's 'It is no dream of mine': A New Proposal," *Thoreau Society Bulletin* 86 (Winter 1964), 3-4.

"The Just Made Perfect"

KENNETH SILVERMAN. "The Sluggard Knight in Thoreau's Poetry," *Thoreau Journal Quarterly* 5(2), April 1973, 7-8.

"Life"

KARL KELLER. " 'A Cheerful Elastic Wit': The Metaphysical Strain in Thoreau," *Thoreau Journal Quarterly* 1(2), April 15, 1969, 12-13.

"Love"

MARY I. KAISER. " 'Conversing With The Sky': The Imagery of Celestial Bodies In Thoreau's Poetry," *Thoreau Journal Quarterly* 9(3), July 1977, 17-18.

"May Morning"

DOUGLAS V. NOVERR. "Thoreau's 'May Morning': Nature, Poetic Vision, and the Poet's Publication of His Truth," *Thoreau Journal Quarterly* 2(3), July 15, 1970, 7-10.

RICHARD TUERK. "The One World of Thoreau's Verse," *Thoreau Journal Quarterly* 6(4), October 1974, 8-9.

"The Moon Now Rises to Her Absolute Rule"

MARY I. KAISER. " 'Conversing With The Sky': The Imagery of Celestial Bodies In Thoreau's Poetry," *Thoreau Journal Quarterly* 9(3), July 1977, 21-22.

"My Books I'd Fain Cast Off"

BETSY FEAGAN COLQUITT. "Thoreau's Poetics," *American Transcendental Quarterly* 11(2), Summer 1971, 77-78.

"My Friends, Why Should We Live"

KENNETH SILVERMAN. "The Sluggard Knight in Thoreau's Poetry," *Thoreau Journal Quarterly* 5(2), April 1973, 8.

"Noon"

RICHARD TUERK. "The One World of Thoreau's Verse," *Thoreau Journal Quarterly* 6(4), October 1974, 10.

"The Peal of Bells"

KENNETH SILVERMAN. "The Sluggard Knight in Thoreau's Poetry," *Thoreau Journal Quarterly* 5(2), April 1973, 6-7.

"Sic Vita"

HYATT H. WAGGONER. *American Poets,* pp. 119-20.

"Smoke"

BARBARA HARRELL CARSON. "An Orphic Hymn in Walden," *ESQ* 20(2), Second Quarter 1974, 125-30.

LEONARD GILLEY. "Transcendentalism in *Walden,*" *Prairie Schooner* 42(3), Fall 1968, 207.

F. O. MATTHIESSEN. *The American Renaissance,* pp. 165-66.

DELMER RODABAUGH. *Explicator* 17(7), April 1959, Item 47.

HYATT H. WAGGONER. *American Poets,* pp. 116-17.

"Stanzas"

GAIL BAKER. "Friendship in Thoreau's *Week,*" *Thoreau Journal Quarterly* 7(2), April 1975, 12-13.

"That Phaeton of Our Day"

MARY I. KAISER. " 'Conversing With The Sky': The Imagery of Celestial Bodies In Thoreau's Poetry," *Thoreau Journal Quarterly* 9(3), July 1977, 26.

"That Thaw"

KARL KELLER. " 'A Cheerful Elastic Wit': The Metaphysical Strain in Thoreau," *Thoreau Journal Quarterly* 1(2), April 15, 1969, 12.

"To the Comet"

MARY I. KAISER. " 'Conversing With The Sky': The Imagery of Celestial Bodies In Thoreau's Poetry," *Thoreau Journal Quarterly* 9(3), July 1977, 19-20.

"Upon the Bank at Early Dawn"

KENNETH SILVERMAN. "The Sluggard Knight in Thoreau's Poetry," *Thoreau Journal Quarterly* 5(2), April 1973, 8-9.

RICHARD TUERK. "The One World of Thoreau's Verse," *Thoreau Journal Quarterly* 6(4), October 1974, 12.

"Wait Not Till Slaves Pronounce the Word"

A. G. ULLYATT. " 'Wait Not Till Slaves Pronounce the Word': Thoreau's only anti-slavery poem in the context of Civil War poetry," *Thoreau Society Bulletin* 132 (Summer 1975), 1-2.

"Walden"

BETSY FEAGAN COLQUITT. "Thoreau's Poetics," *American Transcendental Quarterly* 11(2), Summer 1971, 80.

MARY I. KAISER. " 'Conversing With The Sky': The Imagery of Celestial Bodies In Thoreau's Poetry," *Thoreau Journal Quarterly* 9(3), July 1977, 15-16.

"Winter Memories"

RICHARD TUERK. "The One World of Thoreau's Verse," *Thoreau Journal Quarterly* 6(4), October 1974, 9-10.

HYATT H. WAGGONER. *American Poets,* pp. 121-22.

"With Frontier Strength Ye Stand Your Ground"

DOUGLAS GREENWOOD. "A Prospect of the Mountains West of Concord: Thoreau's Poetic Vision," *Thoreau Journal Quarterly* 6(2), April 1974, 16-27.

"Woof of the Sun, Ethereal Gauze"

MARY I. KAISER. " 'Conversing With The Sky': The Imagery of Celestial Bodies In Thoreau's Poetry," *Thoreau Journal Quarterly* 9(3), July 1977, 23-24.

"Ethnogenesis"

ROY HARVEY PEARCE. *The Continuity of American Poetry,* pp. 235-36.

TIMROD, HENRY

"Magnolia Cemetery Ode"

CLAUD B. GREEN. "Henry Timrod and the South," *South Carolina Review* 2(2), May 1970, 32-33.

"The Unknown Dead"

BERNARD DUFFEY. *Poetry in America,* pp. 96-97.

TOLSON, M. B.

"The Harlem Gallery"

ROY P. BASLER. "The Heart of Blackness — M. B. Tolson's Poetry," *New Letters* 39(3), March 1973, 71-76.

TOMLINSON, CHARLES

"Antecedents"
> DONALD DAVIE. *The Poet in the Imaginary Museum,* pp. 67-69.

"Appearance"
> RUTH A. GROGAN. "Charles Tomlinson: The Way of His World," *Contemporary Literature* 19(4), Autumn 1978, 484-85.

"Ariadne and the minotaur"
> RUTH A. GROGAN. "Charles Tomlinson: Poet as painter," *Critical Quarterly* 19(4), Winter 1977, 75.

"The Compact: At Volterra"
> RUTH A. GROGAN. "Charles Tomlinson: The Way of His World," *Contemporary Literature* 19(4), Autumn 1978, 491.

"The Dream"
> RUTH A. GROGAN. "Charles Tomlinson: The Way of His World," *Contemporary Literature* 19(4), Autumn 1978, 495-96.

"A Given Grace"
> CALVIN BEDIENT. "Calvin Bedient on Charles Tomlinson," *Iowa Review* 1(2), Spring 1970, 95-96.
> CALVIN BEDIENT. *Eight Contemporary Poets,* pp. 17-18.

"The Gossamers"
> CALVIN BEDIENT. "Calvin Bedient on Charles Tomlinson," *Iowa Review* 1(2), Spring 1970, 84-85. Reprinted in: *British Poetry Since 1960,* pp. 173-74.
> CALVIN BEDIENT. *Eight Contemporary Poets,* pp. 2-3.

"The Hill"
> CALVIN BEDIENT. *Eight Contemporary Poets,* pp. 18-19.

"In the Fullness of Time"
> JED RASULA and MIKE ERWIN. "An Interview with Charles Tomlinson," *Contemporary Literature* 16(4), Autumn 1975, 408-9.

"Paring the Apple"
> BRIAN SWANN. "English Opposites: Charles Tomlinson & Christopher Middleton," *Modern Poetry Studies* 5(3), Winter 1974, 226.

"Poem" (*Seeing is Believing*)
> JED RASULA and MIKE ERWIN. "An Interview with Charles Tomlinson," *Contemporary Literature* 16(4), Autumn 1975, 413.

"Reflections"
> ROBERT PINSKY. *The Situation of Poetry,* pp. 90-95.

"Swimming Chenango Lake"
> RUTH A. GROGAN. "Charles Tomlinson: The Way of His World," *Contemporary Literature* 19(4), Autumn 1978, 479-84.
> EDWARD HIRSCH. "The Meditative Eye of Charles Tomlinson," *Hollins Critic* 15(2), April 1978, 8-9.

"The Way of a World"
> RUTH A. GROGAN. "Charles Tomlinson: The Way of His World," *Contemporary Literature* 19(4), Autumn 1978, 476-77.

TOMPSON, BENJAMIN

"Address to Lord Bellamont"
> NEIL T. ECKSTEIN. "The Pastoral and the Primitive in Benjamin Tompson's 'Address to Lord Bellamont,'" *Early American Literature* 8(2), Fall 1973, 111-16.

"The Grammarian's Funeral"
> ROY HARVEY PEARCE. *The Continuity of American Poetry,* p. 28.

TOOMER, JEAN

"Beehive"
> LOUISE BLACKWELL. "Jean Toomer's *Cane* and Biblical Myth," *CLA Journal* 17(4), June 1974, 540.

"Blue Meridian"
> MABEL M. DILLARD. "Jean Toomer — The Veil Replaced," *CLA Journal* 17(4), June 1974, 468-73.

"Cotton Song"
> UDO JUNG. "'Spirit-Torsos of Exquisite Strength': The Theme of Individual Weakness vs. Collective Strength in Two of Toomer's Poems," *CLA Journal* 19(2), December 1975, 261-64.

"Harvest Song"
> CHARLES T. DAVIS. "Jean Toomer and the South: Region and Race as Elements within a Literary Imagination," *Studies in the Literary Imagination* 7(2), Fall 1974, 33-34.
> CHARLES W. SCRUGGS. "The Mark of Cain and the Redemption of Art: A Study in Theme and Structure of Jean Toomer's *Cane,*" *American Literature* 44(2), May 1972, 289.

"Prayer"
> UDO JUNG. "'Spirit-Torsos of Exquisite Strength': The Theme of Individual Weakness vs. Collective Strength in Two of Toomer's Poems," *CLA Journal* 19(2), December 1975, 264-67.

"Reapers"
> DOLLY WITHROW. "Cutting Through Shade," *CLA Journal* 21(1), September 1977, 98-99.

"Song of the Son"
> BERNARD BELL. "A Key to the Poems in *Cane,*" *CLA Journal* 14(3), March 1971, 254-55.
> LOUISE BLACKWELL. "Jean Toomer's *Cane* and Biblical Myth," *CLA Journal* 17(4), June 1974, 540.
> CHARLES T. DAVIS. "Jean Toomer and the South: Region and Race as Elements Within a Literary Imagination," *Studies in the Literary Imagination* 7(2), Fall 1974, 30-31.
> TODD LIEBER. "Design and Movement in *Cane,*" *CLA Journal* 13(1), September 1969, 37.

TORREY, SAMUEL

"Upon the Death of Mr. William Tompson . . ."
> ROY HARVEY PEARCE. *The Continuity of American Poetry,* pp. 25-28.

TOULMIN, GEORGE HOGGART

"Illustrations of Affection"
> ROY S. PORTER. "Philosophy and Politics of a Geologist: G. H. Toulmin (1754-1817)," *Journal of the History of Ideas* 39(3), July-September 1978, 447-50.

TOWNSHEND, AURELIAN

"A Dialogue Betwixt Time and a Pilgrime"
> STANLEY STEWART. *The Enclosed Garden,* pp. 101-2.

TRAHERNE, THOMAS

"The Estate"
> DONALD M. KORTE. "Thomas Traherne's 'The Estate,'" *Thoth* 6(1), Winter 1965, 13-19.

"Goodnesse"
ANTHONY LOW. *Love's Architecture*, pp. 288-90.

"An Infant-Ey"
HAROLD G. RIDLON. "The Function of the 'Infant-Ey' in Traherne's Poetry," *Studies in Philology* 61(4), October 1964, 627-29.

"Love"
ANTHONY LOW. *Love's Architecture*, pp. 285-86.

"My Spirit"
MALCOLM M. DAY. " 'Naked Truth' and the Language of Thomas Traherne," *Studies in Philology* 68(3), July 1971, 314-24.

"Poverty"
ANTHONY LOW. *Love's Architecture*, pp. 269-73.

"The Preparative"
A. L. CLEMENTS. "On the Mode and Meaning of Traherne's Mystical Poetry: 'The Preparative,' " *Studies in Philology* 61(3), July 1964, 500-21.
BEN DRAKE. "Thomas Traherne's Songs of Innocence," *Modern Language Quarterly* 31(4), December 1970, 495-96.

"Shadows in the Water"
BEN DRAKE. "Thomas Traherne's Songs of Innocence," *Modern Language Quarterly* 31(4), December 1970, 499-500.

"Thanksgivings for the Body"
ANTHONY LOW. *Love's Architecture*, pp. 287-88.

"Thoughts"
ANTHONY LOW. *Love's Architecture*, pp. 286-87.

"Thoughts I"
JOHN E. TRIMPEY. "An Analysis of Traherne's 'Thoughts I,' " *Studies in Philology* 68(1), January 1971, 88-104.

"The Vision"
CARL M. SELKIN. "The Language of Vision: Traherne's Cataloguing Style," *English Literary Renaissance* 6(1), Winter 1976, 92-104.

"Wonder"
ANTHONY LOW. *Love's Architecture*, pp. 263-69.

TRUESDALE, C. W.

"Triptych"
ROY ARTHUR SWANSON. "The Still Sad Music: A Comment on the Poetry of C. W. Truesdale," *Minnesota Review* 8(3), 1968, 286.

TUCKERMAN, FREDERICK GODDARD

"The Cricket"
DENIS DONOGHUE. *Connoisseurs of Chaos*, pp. 69-74.
N. SCOTT MOMADAY. "The Heretical Cricket," *Southern Review*, n.s., 3(1), Winter 1967, 43-50.

"Nor strange it is to us who walk in bonds"
DENIS DONOGHUE. *Connoisseurs of Chaos*, pp. 67-69.

"An Upper Chamber in a Darkened House"
EUGENE ENGLAND. "Tuckerman's Sonnet I: 10: The First Post-Symbolist Poem," *Southern Review*, n.s., 12(2), Spring 1976, 323-47.

"Yet wear we on, the deep light disallowed"
DENIS DONOGHUE. *Connoisseurs of Chaos*, pp. 60-61.

TURBERVILLE, GEORGE

"A Retraction"
DOUGLAS L. PETERSON. *The English Lyric from Wyatt to Donne*, pp. 122-25.

"To His Friend Riding to Londonward"
WILLIAM E. SHEIDLEY. "George Turberville and the Problem of Passion," *Journal of English and Germanic Philology* 69(4), October 1970, 639.

TURCO, LEWIS

"The Playroom"
WILLIAM HEYEN. "The Progress of Lewis Turco," *Modern Poetry Studies* 2(3), 1971, 119-20.

"The Portrait of a Clown"
WILLIAM HEYEN. "The Progress of Lewis Turco," *Modern Poetry Studies* 2(3), 1971, 120-21.

TURNER, W. J.

"Nature and Mind"
RAYMOND TSCHUMI. *Thought in Twentieth-Century English Poetry*, p. 268.

"The Seven Days"
RAYMOND TSCHUMI. *Thought in Twentieth-Century English Poetry*, pp. 260-65.

U

UPDIKE, JOHN

"Ex-Basketball Player"
Virginia Busha. "Poetry in the Classroom: 'Ex-Basketball Player,'" *English Journal* 59(5), May 1970, 643-45.

"Shillington"
Edward R. Ducharme. "Close Reading and Teaching," *English Journal* 59(7), October 1970, 938-42.

"Vacuum Cleaner"
Patrick Bowles. *Explicator* 37(1), Fall 1978, 42-43.

V

VAN DOREN, MARK

"Big Mare"

> BABETTE DEUTSCH. *Poetry in Our Time*, pp. 66-67; second ed., pp. 71-72.

"January Chance"

> BABETTE DEUTSCH. *Poetry in Our Time*, first ed., pp. 68-69.

"Return to Ritual"

> JOHN CLARK PRATT. *The Meaning of Modern Poetry*, pp. 287, 257, 264, 259, 277, 281-82, 270, 292.

"A Winter Diary"

> BABETTE DEUTSCH. *Poetry in Our Time*, pp. 67-68; second ed., pp. 72-73.

VAN DUYN, MONA

"Economics"

> CLAIRE HEALEY. "An Interview with Dianne Wakoski," *Contemporary Literature* 18(1), Winter 1977, 3-4.

VAUGHAN, HENRY

"And do they so? have they a sense"
see "Rom. Cap. 8. ver. 19."

"Ascension-day"

> BARBARA K. LEWALSKI. "Typology and Poetry: A Consideration of Herbert, Vaughan, and Marvell," in *Illustrious Evidence*, p. 62.
>
> LOUIS L. MARTZ. "The Action of the Self: Devotional Poetry in the Seventeenth Century," in *Metaphysical Poetry*, edited by Malcolm Bradbury and David Palmer, pp. 115-17.

"Ascension-Hymn"

> ANTHONY LOW. *Love's Architecture*, pp. 168-69.

"The Ass"

> LEAH SINANGLOU MARCUS. "Vaughan, Wordsworth, Coleridge and the *Encomium Asini*," *ELH* 42(2), Summer 1975, 228-31.

"The Bird"

> GEORGIA B. CHRISTOPHER. "In Arcadia, Calvin . . .: A Study of Nature in Henry Vaughan," *Studies in Philology* 70(4), October 1973, 424-25.

"Christs Nativity"

> ANTHONY LOW. *Love's Architecture*, pp. 172-73.
>
> A. S. P. WOODHOUSE. *The Poet and His Faith*, pp. 79-81.

"Cock-Crowing"

> DON CAMERON ALLEN. "Vaughan's 'Cock-Crowing' and the Tradition," *Journal of English Literary History* 21(2), June 1954, 94-106. Reprinted in: Don Cameron Allen. *Image and Meaning*, pp. 154-69; revised ed., pp. 226-41.
>
> FRANK KERMODE. "Introduction," in *The Metaphysical Poets*, p. 28.
>
> GEORGE WILLIAMSON. *Six Metaphysical Poets*, pp. 193-94.

"Come, come, what doe I here?"

> PATRICIA BEER. *An Introduction to the Metaphysical Poets*, pp. 77-80.

"The Constellation"

> R. A. DURR. "Vaughan's Spring on the Hill," *Modern Language Notes* 76(8), December 1961, 707. (P)

"Corruption"

> LAURENCE LERNER. *The Uses of Nostalgia*, pp. 187-88.
>
> LOUIS MARTZ. "Henry Vaughan: The Man Within," in *Seventeenth Century English Poetry*, revised ed., pp. 406-7.
>
> MELISSA CYNTHIA WANAMAKER. "*Discordia Concors*: The Metaphysical Wit of Henry Vaughan's *Silex Scintillans*," *Texas Studies in Literature and Language* 16(3), Fall 1974, 470-71.

"Daphnis: An Elegiac Eclogue"

> ROBERT WILCHER. " 'Daphnis: An Elegiac Eclogue' by Henry Vaughan," *Durham University Journal*, n.s., 36(1), December 1974, 25-40.

"The Dawning"

> JOHN J. POLLOCK. *Explicator* 36(2), Winter 1978, 30-31.

"Day of Judgement"

> ANTHONY LOW. *Love's Architecture*, pp. 181-82.

"Death. A Dialogue"

> JAMES REEVES and MARTIN SEYMOUR-SMITH. *Inside Poetry*, pp. 114-15.

"Disorder *and* frailty"

> ALAN RUDRUM. "The Influence of Alchemy in the Poems of Henry Vaughan," *Philological Quarterly* 49(4), October 1970, 475-77.

"Distraction"

> GEORGE WILLIAMSON. *Six Metaphysical Poets*, pp. 190-91.

VAUGHAN, HENRY *(Cont.)*

"The Dwelling-place"

GEORGE WILLIAMSON. *Six Metaphysical Poets*, pp. 194-95.

"A Hymn to the Name and Honor of the Admirable Sainte Teresa"

AUSTIN WARREN. "Crashaw's Themes and Images," in *The Metaphysical Poets*, pp. 260-63.

"I Walked the Other Day (to Spend My Hour)"

LOUIS L. MARTZ. *The Poetry of Meditation*, pp. 64-67.

"The Incarnation, and Passion"

GEORGE WILLIAMSON. *Milton & Others*, pp. 168-69.

GEORGE WILLIAMSON. *Six Metaphysical Poets*, pp. 191-92.

"*Isaacs* Marriage"

FRANCES M. MALPEZZI. "An Approach to Vaughan's '*Isaacs* Marriage,'" *English Language Notes* 14(2), December 1976, 112-17.

"Man"

KESTER SVENDSON. *Explicator* 2(8), June 1944, Item 54. (P)

GEORGE WILLIAMSON. *Milton & Others*, pp. 171-73.

GEORGE WILLIAMSON. *Six Metaphysical Poets*, pp. 201-3.

"The Morning-watch"

CONRAD HILBERRY. *Explicator* 14(7), April 1956, Item 44.

ANTHONY LOW. *Love's Architecture*, pp. 175-77.

GEORGE WILLIAMSON. *Six Metaphysical Poets*, p. 195.

"The Night"

MELVIN E. A. BRADFORD. "Henry Vaughan's 'The Night': A Consideration of Metaphor and Meditation," *Arlington Quarterly* 1(3), Spring 1968, 209-22.

LELAND H. CHAMBERS. "Henry Vaughan's Allusive Technique: Biblical Allusions in 'The Night,'" *Modern Language Quarterly* 27(4), December 1966, 371-87.

R. A. DURR. "Vaughan's 'The Night,'" *Journal of English and Germanic Philology* 59(1), January 1960, 34-40.

FERN FARNHAM. "The Imagery of Henry Vaughan's 'The Night,'" *Philological Quarterly* 38(4), October 1959, 425-35.

BARBARA K. LEWALSKI. "Typology and Poetry: A Consideration of Herbert, Vaughan, and Marvell," in *Illustrious Evidence*, p. 61.

ANTHONY LOW. *Love's Architecture*, pp. 201-5.

A. W. RUDRUM. "Vaughan's 'The Night': Some Hermetic Notes," *Modern Language Review* 64(1), January 1969, 11-19.

BAIN TATE STEWART. "Hermetic Symbolism in Henry Vaughan's 'The Night,'" *Philological Quarterly* 29(4), October 1950, 417-22.

MELISSA CYNTHIA WANAMAKER. "*Discordia Concors*: The Metaphysical Wit of Henry Vaughan's *Silex Scintillans*," *Texas Studies in Literature and Language* 16(3), Fall 1974, 463-77.

GEORGE WILLIAMSON. *Milton & Others*, pp. 173-74.

GEORGE WILLIAMSON. *Six Metaphysical Poets*, pp. 204-6.

"Peace"

L. G. LOCKE. *Explicator* 1(6), April 1943, Item 43.

GEORGE WILLIAMSON. *Six Metaphysical Poets*, p. 197.

"The Proffer"

R. A. DURR. "Vaughan's Pilgrim and the Birds of Night: 'The Proffer,'" *Modern Language Quarterly* 21(1), March 1960, 45-58.

"Palm-Sunday"

ANTHONY LOW. *Love's Architecture*, pp. 165-66.

"The Pursuite"

JONATHAN GEORGE. *Explicator* 35(3), Spring 1977, 2-3.

"The Queer"

MACDONALD EMSLIE. *Explicator* 13(5), March 1955, Item 29.

LAURENCE PERRINE. *Explicator* 13(5), March 1955, Item 29.

CELESTE TURNER WRIGHT. *Explicator* 13(5), March 1955, Item 29.

"Quickness"

PATRICIA BEER. *An Introduction to the Metaphysical Poets*, pp. 80-83.

ELIZABETH DREW. *Poetry*, pp. 244-45.

E. C. PETTET. "A Simile in Vaughan," *Times Literary Supplement*, 27 January 1956, p. 53. (P)

GEORGE WILLIAMSON. *Milton & Others*, p. 176.

GEORGE WILLIAMSON. *Six Metaphysical Poets*, pp. 208-9.

"Regeneration"

GEORGIA B. CHRISTOPHER. "In Arcadia, Calvin . . .: A Study of Nature in Henry Vaughan," *Studies in Philology* 70(4), October 1973, 413-16.

EDGAR F. DANIELS. "Vaughan's 'Regeneration': An Emendation," *American Notes & Queries*, n.s., 9(2), October 1970, 19-20.

ROBERT ALLEN DURR. "Vaughan's Theme and Its Pattern: 'Regeneration,'" *Studies in Philology* 54(1), January 1957, 14-28.

WILLIAM H. HALEWOOD. *The Poetry of Grace*, pp. 127-33.

BARBARA K. LEWALSKI. "Typology and Poetry: A Consideration of Herbert, Vaughan, and Marvell," in *Illustrious Evidence*, pp. 59-61.

ANTHONY LOW. *Love's Architecture*, pp. 191-97.

LOUIS MARTZ. "Henry Vaughan: The Man Within," in *Seventeenth Century English Poetry*, revised ed., pp. 392-95.

STANLEY STEWART. *The Enclosed Garden*, pp. 107-11.

CLAUDE J. SUMMERS and TED-LARRY PEBWORTH. "Vaughan's Temple in Nature and the Context of 'Regeneration,'" *Journal of English and Germanic Philology* 74(3), July 1975, 351-60.

JOSEPH H. SUMMERS. *The Heirs of Donne and Jonson*, pp. 123-24.

GEORGE WILLIAMSON. *Milton & Others*, pp. 176-79.

GEORGE WILLIAMSON. *Six Metaphysical Poets*, pp. 186-90.

THOMAS J. WYLY. "Vaughan's 'Regeneration' Reconsidered," *Philological Quarterly* 55(3), Summer 1976, 340-53.

"Religion"

BARBARA K. LEWALSKI. "Typology and Poetry: A Consideration of Herbert, Vaughan, and Marvell," in *Illustrious Evidence*, pp. 55-56.

LOUIS MARTZ. "Henry Vaughan: The Man Within," in *Seventeenth Century English Poetry*, revised ed., p. 397.

"The Resolve"

LOUIS L. MARTZ. "The Action of the Self: Devotional Poetry in the Seventeenth Century," in *Metaphysical Poetry*, edited by Malcolm Bradbury and David Palmer, pp. 113-15.

"Resurrection and Immortality"

LYNA LEE MONTGOMERY. "The Phoenix: Its Use as a Literary Device in English From the Seventeenth Century to the Twentieth Century," *D. H. Lawrence Review* 5(3), Fall 1972, 270-71.

"The Retreat"

HARRY BROWN and JOHN MILSTEAD. *What the Poem Means*, p. 273.

MERRITT Y. HUGHES. "The Theme of Pre-Existence and Infancy in *The Retreate*," *Philological Quarterly* 20(3), July 1941, 484-500.

JAMES R. KREUZER. *Elements of Poetry*, pp. 159-61.

M. M. MAHOOD. "Henry Vaughan: The Symphony of Nature," in *The Metaphysical Poets*, p. 300.

LOUIS MARTZ. "Henry Vaughan: The Man Within," in *Seventeenth Century English Poetry*, revised ed., pp. 408-10.

GEORGE WILLIAMSON. *Milton & Others*, pp. 169-70.

GEORGE WILLIAMSON. *Six Metaphysical Poets*, pp. 196-97.

"Rom. Cap. 8. Ver. 19"

GEORGIA B. CHRISTOPHER. "In Arcadia, Calvin . . .: A Study of Nature in Henry Vaughan," *Studies in Philology* 70(4), October 1973, 421-23.

ALAN RUDRUM. "An Aspect of Vaughan's Hermeticism: The Doctrine of Cosmic Sympathy," *Studies in English Literature 1500-1900* 14(1), Winter 1974, 131-32.

"Rules and Lessons"

LOUIS MARTZ. "Henry Vaughan: The Man Within," in *Seventeenth Century English Poetry*, revised ed., pp. 396-97.

"The Sap"

LOUIS MARTZ. "Henry Vaughan: The Man Within," in *Seventeenth Century English Poetry*, revised ed., pp. 398-99.

"The Search"

ANTHONY LOW. *Love's Architecture*, pp. 183-88.

LOUIS L. MARTZ. *The Poetry of Meditation*, pp. 86-90.

"The Showre"

PATRICIA BEER. *An Introduction to the Metaphysical Poets*, pp. 74-77.

GEORGE WILLIAMSON. *Six Metaphysical Poets*, p. 190.

"Silence, and stealth of dayes!"

LOUIS MARTZ. "Henry Vaughan: The Man Within," in *Seventeenth Century English Poetry*, revised ed., pp. 407-8.

GEORGE WILLIAMSON. *Milton & Others*, pp. 170-71.

GEORGE WILLIAMSON. *Six Metaphysical Poets*, pp. 197-98.

"The Starre"

ALAN RUDRUM. "An Aspect of Vaughan's Hermeticism: The Doctrine of Cosmic Sympathy," *Studies in English Literature 1500-1900* 14(1), Winter 1974, 135-36.

"Sure, there's a tye of Bodyes!"

ALAN RUDRUM. "An Aspect of Vaughan's Hermeticism: The Doctrine of Cosmic Sympathy," *Studies in English Literature 1500-1900* 14(1), Winter 1974, 133-35.

GEORGE WILLIAMSON. *Six Metaphysical Poets*, pp. 198-99.

"They are all gone into the world of light"

DAVID DAICHES and WILLIAM CHARVAT. *Poems in English*, p. 662.

JOSEPH H. SUMMERS. *The Heirs of Donne and Jonson*, pp. 126-28.

GEORGE WILLIAMSON. *Milton & Others*, pp. 167-68.

GEORGE WILLIAMSON. *Six Metaphysical Poets*, pp. 203-4.

"The Timber"

A. ALVAREZ. *The School of Donne*, English ed., pp. 86-87; American ed., pp. 94-95.

"To Amoret Gone from Him"

GEORGE WILLIAMSON. *Six Metaphysical Poets*, pp. 177-78.

"To Amoret: of the Difference 'twixt him and other Lovers, and What True Love is"

GEORGE WILLIAMSON. *Six Metaphysical Poets*, pp. 178-80.

"To his Retired Friend, an Invitation to Breaknock"

GEORGE WILLIAMSON. *Six Metaphysical Poets*, pp. 182-83.

"To my Ingenuous Friend, R. W."

EARL MINER. *The Cavalier Mode from Jonson to Cotton*, pp. 254-56.

"To the pious memorie of C. W. Esquire"

EARL MINER. *The Cavalier Mode from Jonson to Cotton*, pp. 180-82.

"Trinity-Sunday"

ANTHONY LOW. *Love's Architecture*, pp. 170-71.

"Upon the Priory Grove, his Usual Retirement"

GEORGE WILLIAMSON. *Six Metaphysical Poets*, pp. 180-81.

"Vanity of Spirit"

ANTHONY LOW. *Love's Architecture*, pp. 188-90.

LOUIS MARTZ. "Henry Vaughan: The Man Within," in *Seventeenth Century English Poetry*, revised ed., pp. 400-1.

LOUIS MARTZ. *The Poetry of Meditation*, pp. 150-52.

"The Waterfall"

DAVID DAICHES and WILLIAM CHARVAT. *Poems in English*, pp. 661-62.

W. NELSON FRANCIS. *Explicator* 14(9), June 1956, Item 57.

GEORGE WILLIAMSON. *Milton & Others*, pp. 174-75.

GEORGE WILLIAMSON. *Six Metaphysical Poets*, pp. 206-8.

"White Sunday"

ANTHONY LOW. *Love's Architecture*, pp. 169-70.

"The World"

LELAND H. CHAMBERS. "Vaughan's 'The World': The Limits of Extrinsic Criticism," *Studies in English Literature 1500-1900* 8(1), Winter 1968, 137-50.

R. A. DURR. "Vaughan: The World," in *Master Poems of the English Language*, pp. 226-28.

ANTHONY LOW. *Love's Architecture*, pp. 177-79.

PAUL A. OLSON. "Vaughan's *The World*: The Pattern of Meaning And the Tradition," *Comparative Literature* 13(1), Winter 1961, 26-32.

MARIE-SOFIE RØSTVIG. "Syncretistic Imagery and the Unity of Vaughan's 'The World,'" *Papers on Language and Literature* 5(4), Fall 1969, 415-22.

VAUGHAN, HENRY *(Cont.)*

"The World" *(cont.)*

　　JAMES D. SIMMONDS. "Vaughn's Masterpiece and It's Critics: 'The World' Revaluated," *Studies in English Literature 1500-1900* 2(1), Winter 1962, 77-93.

　　GEORGE WILLIAMSON. *Milton & Others,* pp. 165-67.

　　GEORGE WILLIAMSON. *Six Metaphysical Poets,* pp. 199-201.

VAUX, THOMAS

"The aged louer renounceth loue"

　　LEONARD NATHAN. "Gascoigne's 'Lullabie' and Structures in the Tudor Lyric," in *The Rhetoric of Renaissance Poetry,* pp. 62-65.

"On the Instability of Youth"

　　RAYMOND B. WADDINGTON. "Shakespeare's Sonnet 15 and the Art of Memory," in *The Rhetoric of Renaissance Poetry,* p. 99.

VEITCH, TOM

"Improved 4-Way"

　　PAULA JOHNSON. "Getting Acquainted with a Poem," *College English* 37(4), December 1975, 360-62.

VERY, JONES

"The Baker's Island Lights"

　　CARL DENNIS. "Correspondence in Very's Nature Poetry," *New England Quarterly* 43(2), June 1970, 265-66.

"The Columbine"

　　CARL DENNIS. "Correspondence in Very's Nature Poetry," *New England Quarterly* 43(2), June 1970, 263-65.

　　JAMES A. LEVERNIER. "Calvinism and Transcendentalism in the Poetry of Jones Very," *ESQ* 24(1), First Quarter 1978, 36.

　　HYATT H. WAGGONER. *American Poets,* p. 127.

"The Dead"

　　DAVID ROBINSON. "The Exemplary Self and the Transcendent Self in the Poetry of Jones Very," *ESQ* 24(4), Fourth Quarter 1978, 209.

"The Grave-Yard"

　　JAMES A. LEVERNIER. "Calvinism and Transcendentalism in the Poetry of Jones Very," *ESQ* 24(1), First Quarter 1978, 32.

"The Hand and Foot"

　　YVOR WINTERS. "Jones Very: A New England Mystic," *American Review* 7(2), May 1936, 161-63.

　　YVOR WINTERS. *Maule's Curse,* pp. 127-29. Reprinted in: Yvor Winters. *In Defense of Reason,* pp. 264-66.

"The Houstonia"

　　JAMES A. LEVERNIER. "Calvinism and Transcendentalism in the Poetry of Jones Very," *ESQ* 24(1), First Quarter 1978, 35.

"The Kingdom of Truth"

　　JAMES A. LEVERNIER. "Calvinism and Transcendentalism in the Poetry of Jones Very," *ESQ* 24(1), First Quarter 1978, 37.

"The Lost"

　　CARL DENNIS. "Correspondence in Very's Nature Poetry," *New England Quarterly* 43(2), June 1970, 268-70.

　　YVOR WINTERS. *Maule's Curse,* pp. 138-39. Reprinted in: Yvor Winters. *In Defense of Reason,* pp. 274-76.

"Man in Harmony with Nature"

　　CARL DENNIS. "Correspondence in Very's Nature Poetry," *New England Quarterly* 43(2), June 1970, 257-58.

"The Mind the Greatest Mystery"

　　HYATT H. WAGGONER. *American Poets,* p. 128.

"Nature Intelligible"

　　CARL DENNIS. "Correspondence in Very's Nature Poetry," *New England Quarterly* 43(2), June 1970, 260.

"The New Birth"

　　CARL DENNIS. "Correspondence in Very's Nature Poetry," *New England Quarterly* 43(2), June 1970, 259.

"The Revelation of the Spirit Through the Material World"

　　CARL DENNIS. "Correspondence in Very's Nature Poetry," *New England Quarterly* 43(2), June 1970, 259-60.

"The Son"

　　DAVID ROBINSON. "The Exemplary Self and the Transcendent Self in the Poetry of Jones Very," *ESQ* 24(4), Fourth Quarter 1978, 208-9.

"The Soul's Questioning of the Universe, and Its Beginning"

　　JAMES A. LEVERNIER. "Calvinism and Transcendentalism in the Poetry of Jones Very," *ESQ* 24(1), First Quarter 1978, 37.

"Thy Neighbor"

　　LAWRENCE BUELL. *Literary Transcendentalism,* pp. 321-22.

"To the Canary Bird"

　　CARL DENNIS. "Correspondence in Very's Nature Poetry," *New England Quarterly* 43(2), June 1970, 261-62.

"The Tree" ("I love thee when thy swelling buds appear")

　　CARL DENNIS. "Correspondence in Very's Nature Poetry," *New England Quarterly* 43(2), June 1970, 262-63.

"The Tree" ("I too will wait with thee returning spring")

　　CARL DENNIS. "Correspondence in Very's Nature Poetry," *New England Quarterly* 43(2), June 1970, 267-68.

"The True Light"

　　CARL DENNIS. "Correspondence in Very's Nature Poetry," *New England Quarterly* 43(2), June 1970, 258-59.

"Yourself"

　　DAVID ROBINSON. "The Exemplary Self and the Transcendent Self in the Poetry of Jones Very," *ESQ* 24(4), Fourth Quarter 1978, 210.

VIERECK, PETER

"Better Come Quietly"

　　PETER VIERECK. "My Kind of Poetry," in *Mid-Century American Poets,* pp. 25-26.

"Crass Times Redeemed by Dignity of Souls"

　　JOHN CIARDI. *How Does a Poem Mean?* pp. 952-53; second ed., pp. 331-32.

"Don't Look Now But Mary Is Everybody"

　　RICHARD P. BENTON. *Explicator* 20(4), December 1961, Item 30.

"A Hospital Named 'Hotel Universe'"

　　JOSEPH WARREN BEACH. *Obsessive Images,* p. 300.

"Like a Sitting Breeze"

　　PETER VIERECK. "Correspondence Relating to 'Like a Sitting Breeze' by Peter Viereck," *American Scholar* 20(2), Spring 1951, 216-17.

"Poet"
JOHN CIARDI. *Dialogue with an Audience*, pp. 109-10.

"Progress: a Dialogue"
JOSEPH WARREN BEACH. *Obsessive Images*, p. 275.

"River"
LAURENCE LIEBERMAN. *Unassigned Frequencies*, pp. 237-38.

"Some Lines in Three Parts"
PETER VIERECK. "My Kind of Poetry," in *Mid-Century American Poets*, pp. 26-27.

"Vale from Carthage (Spring 1944)"
JAMES R. KREUZER. *Elements of Poetry*, pp. 93-96.
JAMES M. REID. *100 American Poems of the Twentieth Century*, pp. 240-41.

W

W. W.

"An Elegy. In Memory of Mr. *John Cleveland*"

AVON JACK MURPHY. "The Critical Elegy of Earlier Seventeenth-Century England," *Genre* 5(1), March 1972, 84-85.

WAGGONER, DAVID

"Being Shot"

LAURENCE LIEBERMAN. *Unassigned Frequencies*, pp. 163-65.

"Breaking Camp"

LAURENCE LIEBERMAN. *Unassigned Frequencies*, pp. 155-56.

"The Fisherman's Wife"

SANFORD PINSKER. "On David Waggoner," *Salmagundi* 22-23 (Spring-Summer 1973), 308-9. Reprinted in: *Contemporary Poetry in America*, pp. 362-63.

"From Here to There"

LAURENCE LIEBERMAN. *Unassigned Frequencies*, pp. 166-69.

"Missing the Trail"

LAURENCE LIEBERMAN. *Unassigned Frequencies*, pp. 165-66.

"Tracking"

LAURENCE LIEBERMAN. *Unassigned Frequencies*, pp. 160-64.

"Travelling Light"

LAURENCE LIEBERMAN. *Unassigned Frequencies*, pp. 174-81.

"Waiting in a Rain Forest"

LAURENCE LIEBERMAN. *Unassigned Frequencies*, pp. 170-74.

"Walking in the Swamp"

LAURENCE LIEBERMAN. *Unassigned Frequencies*, pp. 157-60.

WAIN, JOHN

"A Boisterous Poem about Poetry"

LAWRENCE R. RIES. *Wolf Masks*, pp. 141-42.

"Green Fingers"

LAWRENCE R. RIES. *Wolf Masks*, pp. 143-44.

"On the Death of a Murderer"

C. B. COX and A. E. DYSON. *Modern Poetry*, pp. 153-60.

LAWRENCE R. RIES. *Wolf Masks*, pp. 139-41.

"Patriotic Poem"

LAWRENCE R. RIES. *Wolf Masks*, pp. 133-34.

"A Song About Major Eatherly"

LAWRENCE R. RIES. *Wolf Masks*, pp. 137-39.

"This above All Is Precious and Remarkable"

LAWRENCE R. RIES. *Wolf Masks*, p. 135.

"To a Friend in Trouble"

LAWRENCE R. RIES. *Wolf Masks*, pp. 134-35.

"When It Comes"

LAWRENCE R. RIES. *Wolf Masks*, p. 133.

WAINWRIGHT, JEFFREY

"Thomas Müntzer"

EDWARD BRUNNER. "Uncomely Relations," *Iowa Review* 6(3-4), Summer-Fall 1975, 239-41.

RODNEY PYBUS. "Rodney Pybus on Jeffrey Wainwright," *Iowa Review* 6(3-4), Summer-Fall 1975, 203-6.

JEFFREY WAINWRIGHT. "Jeffrey Wainwright Replies," *Iowa Review* 6(3-4), Summer-Fall 1975, 206-7.

WAKOSKI, DIANE

"I Lay Next to You All Night Trying to Understand the Watering Places of the Moon"

DIANNE F. SADOFF. "Mythopoeia, The Moon, and Contemporary Women's Poetry," *Massachusetts Review* 19(1), Spring 1978, 108.

"The Lament of the Lady Bank Dick"

DIANNE F. SADOFF. "Mythopoeia, The Moon, and Contemporary Women's Poetry," *Massachusetts Review* 19(1), Spring 1978, 106-7.

"My Hell's Angel"

DIANNE F. SADOFF. "Mythopoeia, The Moon, and Contemporary Women's Poetry," *Massachusetts Review* 19(1), Spring 1978, 107-8.

"The Story of Richard Maxfield"

CLAIRE HEALEY. "An Interview with Dianne Wakoski," *Contemporary Literature* 18(1), Winter 1977, 18.

WALKER, TED

"Easter Poem"

> TED WALKER. "Writing Poetry," in *English Poetry*, edited by Alan Sinfield, pp. 234-38.

"Founder"

> TED WALKER. "Writing Poetry," in *English Poetry*, edited by Alan Sinfield, pp. 232-34.

WALLER, EDMUND

"An Apologie for Having Loved Before"

> KARL JOSEF HÖLTGEN. "Why Was Man Created in the Evening? On Waller's 'An Apologie for Having Loved Before,'" *Modern Language Review* 69(1), January 1974, 23-28.

"At Penshurst" ("While in the park I sing, the listning deer")

> EARL MINER. *The Cavalier Mode from Jonson to Cotton*, pp. 17-23.

"The Fall"

> DAVID FARLEY-HILLS. *The Benevolence of Laughter*, p. 144.

"Go, Lovely Rose"

> CLEANTH BROOKS, JOHN THIBAUT PURSER, and ROBERT PENN WARREN. *An Approach to Literature*, fifth ed., pp. 394-96.
> CLEANTH BROOKS and ROBERT PENN WARREN. *Understanding Poetry*, fourth ed., pp. 213-15.
> JAMES R. KREUZER. *Elements of Poetry*, pp. 156-58.
> EARL MINER. *The Cavalier Mode from Jonson to Cotton*, pp. 39-41.
> M. L. ROSENTHAL and A. J. M. SMITH. *Exploring Poetry*, pp. 605-6; second ed., pp. 408-9.

"Instructions to a Painter"

> WARREN L. CHERNAIK. "The Heroic Occasional Poem: Panegyric and Satire in the Restoration," *Modern Language Quarterly* 26(4), December 1965, 529-35.

"Of a Fair Lady Playing with a Snake"

> EARL MINER. *The Cavalier Mode from Jonson to Cotton*, pp. 115-17.

"Of a War with Spain, and a Fight at Sea"

> WARREN L. CHERNAIK. "Waller's *Panegyric to My Lord Protector* and the Poetry of Praise," *Studies in English Literature 1500-1900* 4(1), Winter 1964, 111-13.
> RUTH NEVO. *The Dial of Virtue*, pp. 115-17.

"Of Silvia"

> H. M. RICHMOND. "The Fate of Edmund Waller," *South Atlantic Quarterly* 60(2), Spring 1961, 236-37. Reprinted in: *Seventeenth Century English Poetry*, revised ed., pp. 297-98.

"On a Girdle"

> L. G. LOCKE. *Explicator* 1(7), May 1943, Item 52.

"On St. James's Park, as Lately Improved by His Majesty"

> EARL MINER. *The Cavalier Mode from Jonson to Cotton*, pp. 24-37.

"A Panegyrick to My Lord Protector"

> WARREN L. CHERNAIK. "Waller's *Panegyric to My Lord Protector* and the Poetry of Praise," *Studies in English Literature 1500-1900* 4(1), Winter 1964, 109-24.
> CHARLES S. HENSLEY. "Wither, Waller and Marvell: Panegyrists for the Protector," *Ariel* 3(1), January 1972, 9-10.

"The Story of Phoebus and Daphne Applied"

> F. W. BATESON. *English Poetry*, pp. 168-70.

"Upon Her Majesty's New Buildings at Somerset House"

> CHARLES LARSON. "The Somerset House Poems of Cowley and Waller," *Papers on Language and Literature* 10(2), Spring 1974, 131-33.

"Verses to Dr. George Rogers, On His Taking the Degree of Doctor of Physic at Padua, in the Year 1646"

> GARY P. STORHOFF. *Explicator* 36(2), Winter 1978, 10-11.

WALSH, CHAD

"Ode to the Finnish Dead"

> CHAD WALSH. *Doors into Poetry*, pp. 137-39.

WARREN, ROBERT PENN

"Aged Man Surveys the Past Time"

> CLEANTH BROOKS. *Modern Poetry and the Tradition*, pp. 78-79. Reprinted in: *Modern Poetry*, pp. 112-13.
> SISTER M. BERNETTA QUINN. "Robert Penn Warren's Promised Land," *Southern Review*, n.s., 8(2), Spring 1972, 347.
> W. P. SOUTHARD. "Speculation: I. The Religious Poetry of Robert Penn Warren," *Kenyon Review* 7(1), Autumn 1945, 666-67.

"Audubon"

> JASCHA KESSLER. "Keys to Ourselves," *Saturday Review* 53(18), 2 May 1970, 35-36.
> ALLEN SHEPHERD. "Warren's *Audubon*: 'Issues in Purer Form' and 'The Ground Rules of Fact,'" *Mississippi Quarterly* 24(1), Winter 1970-71, 47-56.
> PETER STITT. "Robert Penn Warren, The Poet," *Southern Review*, n.s., 12(2), Spring 1976, 267-71.

"The Ballad of Billie Potts"

> WILLIAM BEDFORD CLARK. "A Meditation on Folk-History: The Dramatic Structure of Robert Penn Warren's *The Ballad of Billie Potts*," *American Literature* 49(4), January 1978, 635-45.
> CHRISTOPHER CLAUSEN. "Grecian Thoughts in the Home Fields: Reflections on Southern Poetry," *Georgia Review* 32(2), Summer 1978, 289-93.
> BABETTE DEUTSCH. *Poetry in Our Time*, pp. 202-3; second ed., pp. 219-20.
> SAM HYNES. "Robert Penn Warren: The Symbolic Journey," *University of Kansas City Review* 17(4), Summer 1951, 280-81.
> JOHN REES MOORE. "Robert Penn Warren: You Must Go Home Again," *Southern Review*, n.s., 4(2), Spring 1968, 324-25.
> M. L. ROSENTHAL. "Robert Penn Warren's Poetry," *South Atlantic Quarterly* 62(4), Autumn 1963, 501-3.
> W. P. SOUTHARD. "Speculation: I. The Religious Poetry of Robert Penn Warren," *Kenyon Review* 7(1), Autumn 1945, 670-73.
> JOHN L. STEWART. "The Achievement of Robert Penn Warren," *South Atlantic Quarterly* 47(4), October 1948, 570-74.
> HYATT H. WAGGONER. *American Poets*, pp. 546-50.

"Bearded Oaks"

> JOSEPH WARREN BEACH. *Obsessive Images*, pp. 324-25.
> CLEANTH BROOKS. *Modern Poetry and the Tradition*, pp. 81-82. Reprinted in: *Reading Modern Poetry*, pp. 106-8; revised ed., pp. 80-82. Also: *Modern Poetry*, pp. 114-16.

WARREN, ROBERT PENN *(Cont.)*

"Bearded Oaks" *(cont.)*

> WILLIAM VAN O'CONNOR. *Sense and Sensibility in Modern Poetry*, pp. 154-55.

"Birth of Love"

> DAVID M. WYATT. "Robert Penn Warren: The Critic as Artist," *Virginia Quarterly Review* 53(3), Summer 1977, 482-87.

"Blow, West Wind, Blow"

> SISTER M. BERNETTA QUINN. "Robert Penn Warren's Promised Land," *Southern Review*, n.s., 8(2), Spring 1972, 337-39.

"Boy's Will, Joyful Labor without Pay, the Harvest Home"

> SISTER M. BERNETTA QUINN. "Robert Penn Warren's Promised Land," *Southern Review*, n.s., 8(2), Spring 1972, 332-33. (P)

"The Child Next Door"

> JAMES WRIGHT. "The Stiff Smile of Mr. Warren," *Kenyon Review* 20(4), Autumn 1958, 648-55.

"Composition in Red and Gold"

> SISTER M. BERNETTA QUINN. "Robert Penn Warren's Promised Land," *Southern Review*, n.s., 8(2), Spring 1972, 335-36.

"Courtmartial"

> JOHN REES MOORE. "Robert Penn Warren: You Must Go Home Again," *Southern Review*, n.s., 4(2), Spring 1968, 329-30.

"Crime"

> W. P. SOUTHARD. "Speculation: I. The Religious Poetry of Robert Penn Warren," *Kenyon Review* 7(1), Autumn 1945, 661-62.

"Dragon Country"

> CLEANTH BROOKS. *The Hidden God*, pp. 109-11.

> CLEANTH BROOKS. "Southern Literature; The Wellsprings of Its Vitality," *Georgia Review* 16(3), Fall 1962, 247-49.

> JAMES M. REID. *100 American Poems of the Twentieth Century*, pp. 200-4.

"The Enclave"

> GUY ROTELLA. " 'One Flesh': Robert Penn Warren's *Incarnations*," *Renascence* 31(1), Autumn 1978, 40.

"End of Season"

> JOSEPH WARREN BEACH. *Obsessive Images*, p. 328.

"Fall Comes in Back-Country Vermont"

> HELEN VENDLER. "Recent American Poetry," *Massachusetts Review* 8(3), Summer 1967, 554-55.

"The Faring"

> GUY ROTELLA. " 'One Flesh': Robert Penn Warren's *Incarnations*," *Renascence* 31(1), Autumn 1978, 39-40.

"Fog"

> GUY ROTELLA. " 'One Flesh': Robert Penn Warren's *Incarnations*," *Renascence* 31(1), Autumn 1978, 41-42.

"The Garden"

> SISTER M. BERNETTA QUINN. "Robert Penn Warren's Promised Land," *Southern Review*, n.s., 8(2), Spring 1972, 344-45.

> W. P. SOUTHARD. "Speculation: I. The Religious Poetry of Robert Penn Warren," *Kenyon Review* 7(1), Autumn 1945, 668.

"Garden Waters"

> SISTER M. BERNETTA QUINN. "Robert Penn Warren's Promised Land," *Southern Review*, n.s., 8(2), Spring 1972, 347-48.

"Gold Glade"

> SISTER M. BERNETTA QUINN. "Robert Penn Warren's Promised Land," *Southern Review*, n.s., 8(2), Spring 1972, 354-56.

"Hands are Paid"

> CLEANTH BROOKS. "Southern Literature; The Wellsprings of Its Vitality," *Georgia Review* 16(3), Fall 1962, 252-53.

"Harvard '61: Battle Fatigue"

> CLEANTH BROOKS. *The Hidden God*, pp. 118-20.

"History"

> CLEANTH BROOKS. *Modern Poetry and the Tradition*, pp. 85-87. Reprinted in: *Modern Poetry*, pp. 118-20.

"History among the Ruins"

> CLEANTH BROOKS. *Modern Poetry and the Tradition*, pp. 77-78. Reprinted in: *Modern Poetry*, pp. 111-12.

"In the Mountains"

> GUY ROTELLA. " 'One Flesh': Robert Penn Warren's *Incarnations*," *Renascence* 31(1), Autumn 1978, 40-41.

"Internal Injuries"

> GUY ROTELLA. " 'One Flesh': Robert Penn Warren's *Incarnations*," *Renascence* 31(1), Autumn 1978, 38-39.

"The Last Metaphor"

> SISTER M. BERNETTA QUINN. "Robert Penn Warren's Promised Land," *Southern Review*, n.s., 8(2), Spring 1972, 351-52.

"The Leaf"

> GUY ROTELLA. " 'One Flesh': Robert Penn Warren's *Incarnations*," *Renascence* 31(1), Autumn 1978, 34-35.

"The Letter about Money, Love, or Other Comfort, if Any"

> JOHN REES MOORE. "Robert Penn Warren: You Must Go Home Again," *Southern Review*, n.s., 4(2), Spring 1968, 330-31.

> SISTER M. BERNETTA QUINN. "Robert Penn Warren's Promised Land," *Southern Review*, n.s., 8(2), Spring 1972, 353-54.

"Letter from a Coward to a Hero"

> JOSEPH WARREN BEACH. *Obsessive Images*, p. 215.

> CLEANTH BROOKS. *Modern Poetry and the Tradition*, pp. 82-85. Reprinted in: *Modern Poetry*, pp. 116-18.

> W. P. SOUTHARD. "Speculation: I. The Religious Poetry of Robert Penn Warren," *Kenyon Review* 7(1), Autumn 1945, 659-61.

"Love's Parable"

> HOWARD NEMEROV. "The Phoenix in the World," *Furioso* 3(3), Spring 1948, 36-46.

> HYATT H. WAGGONER. *American Poets*, pp. 543-44.

"Man Coming of Age"

> W. P. SOUTHARD. "Speculation: I. The Religious Poetry of Robert Penn Warren," *Kenyon Review* 7(1), Autumn 1945, 657-58.

"The Mango on the Mango Tree"

> FREDERICK BRANTLEY. "The Achievement of Robert Penn Warren," in *Modern American Poetry*, edited by B. Rajan, pp. 78-79.

"Masts at Dawn"
GUY ROTELLA. "'One Flesh': Robert Penn Warren's *Incarnations*," *Renascence* 31(1), Autumn 1978, 32-34.

"Mexico Is a Foreign Country"
W. P. SOUTHARD. "Speculation: I. The Religious Poetry of Robert Penn Warren," *Kenyon Review* 7(1), Autumn 1945, 668-70.

"Monologue at Midnight"
JOSEPH WARREN BEACH. *Obsessive Images*, pp. 315-16.
FREDERICK BRANTLEY. "The Achievement of Robert Penn Warren," in *Modern American Poetry*, edited by B. Rajan, pp. 76-77.

"Myth on Mediterranean Beach: Aphrodite as Logos"
GUY ROTELLA. "'One Flesh': Robert Penn Warren's *Incarnations*," *Renascence* 31(1), Autumn 1978, 30-31.

"Natural History"
GUY ROTELLA. "'One Flesh': Robert Penn Warren's *Incarnations*," *Renascence* 31(1), Autumn 1978, 27-29.

"Original Sin: A Short Story"
RICHARD E. AMACHER. *Explicator* 8(7), May 1950, Item 52.
FREDERICK BRANTLEY. "The Achievement of Robert Penn Warren," in *Modern American Poetry*, edited by B. Rajan, pp. 77-78.
CLEANTH BROOKS. *The Hidden God*, pp. 111-18.
CLIFFORD M. GORDON. *Explicator* 9(3), December 1950, Item 21.
HYATT H. WAGGONER. *American Poets*, pp. 544-46.

"Penological Study: Southern Exposure"
GUY ROTELLA. "'One Flesh': Robert Penn Warren's *Incarnations*," *Renascence* 31(1), Autumn 1978, 36-38.

"A Place Where Nothing Is"
GUY ROTELLA. "'One Flesh': Robert Penn Warren's *Incarnations*," *Renascence* 31(1), Autumn 1978, 32.

"Pondy Woods"
M. L. ROSENTHAL. "Robert Penn Warren's Poetry," *South Atlantic Quarterly* 62(4), Autumn 1963, 500-1.

"A Problem in Spatial Composition"
PETER STITT. "Robert Penn Warren, The Poet," *Southern Review*, n.s., 12(2), Spring 1976, 275-76.

"Pursuit"
JOSEPH WARREN BEACH. *Obsessive Images*, pp. 296-97, 327-28.
KIMON FRIAR and JOHN MALCOLM BRINNIN. *Modern Poetry*, p. 542. (Quoting Robert Penn Warren.)
WILLIAM FROST. *Explicator* 11(4), February 1953, Item 22.
W. P. SOUTHARD. "Speculation: I. The Religious Poetry of Robert Penn Warren," *Kenyon Review* 7(1), Autumn 1945, 662-65.

"The Return: An Elegy"
FREDERICK BRANTLEY. "The Achievement of Robert Penn Warren," in *Modern American Poetry*, edited by B. Rajan, pp. 75-76.
CLEANTH BROOKS. *Modern Poetry and the Tradition*, pp. 79-80. Reprinted in: *Modern Poetry*, pp. 113-14.

"Revelation"
JOSEPH WARREN BEACH. *Obsessive Images*, pp. 89-90.
KIMON FRIAR and JOHN MALCOLM BRINNIN. *Modern Poetry*, pp. 541-42. (Quoting Robert Penn Warren.)

"Riddle in the Garden"
GUY ROTELLA. "'One Flesh': Robert Penn Warren's *Incarnations*," *Renascence* 31(1), Autumn 1978, 29.

"Small White House"
SISTER M. BERNETTA QUINN. "Robert Penn Warren's Promised Land," *Southern Review*, n.s., 8(2), Spring 1972, 333-34.

"Sunset Walk in Thaw-Time in Vermont"
HAROLD BLOOM. *A Map of Misreading*, pp. 193-98.

"Terror"
JOSEPH WARREN BEACH. *Obsessive Images*, pp. 93-95, 216.
KIMON FRIAR and JOHN MALCOLM BRINNIN. *Modern Poetry*, pp. 542-43. (Quoting Robert Penn Warren.)

"Time as Hypnosis"
PETER STITT. "Robert Penn Warren, The Poet," *Southern Review*, n.s., 12(2), Spring 1976, 273-74.

"To a Face in the Crowd"
SISTER M. BERNETTA QUINN. "Robert Penn Warren's Promised Land," *Southern Review*, n.s., 8(2), Spring 1972, 349-50.

"Variation: Ode to Fear"
JOSEPH WARREN BEACH. *Obsessive Images*, pp. 216-17.

"Walk by Moonlight in a Small Town"
CLEANTH BROOKS. *The Hidden God*, pp. 126-27.
CLEANTH BROOKS. "Southern Literature; The Wellsprings of Its Vitality," *Georgia Review* 16(3), Fall 1962, 251-52.

"What Day Is"
GUY ROTELLA. "'One Flesh': Robert Penn Warren's *Incarnations*," *Renascence* 31(1), Autumn 1978, 26-27.

"Where the Slow Fig's Purple Sloth"
GUY ROTELLA. "'One Flesh': Robert Penn Warren's *Incarnations*," *Renascence* 31(1), Autumn 1978, 27.

WARTON, JOSEPH

"The Enthusiast"
DAVID B. MORRIS. "Joseph Warton's Figure of Virtue: Poetic Indirection in 'The Enthusiast,'" *Philological Quarterly* 50(4), October 1971, 678-83.
A. S. P. WOODHOUSE. "The Poetry of Collins Reconsidered," in *From Sensibility to Romanticism*, pp. 95-97.

"Ode to Fancy"
A. S. P. WOODHOUSE. "The Poetry of Collins Reconsidered," in *From Sensibility to Romanticism*, pp. 106-7.

WATERMAN, ANDREW

"The Mountains"
EDWARD BRUNNER. "Uncomely Relations," *Iowa Review* 6(3-4), Summer-Fall 1975, 226-28.
ANDREW WATERMAN. "Andrew Waterman on Himself," *Iowa Review* 6(3-4), Summer-Fall 1975, 220-21.

"The Old, Cast up on Lawns"
ANDREW WATERMAN. "Andrew Waterman on Himself," *Iowa Review* 6(3-4), Summer-Fall 1975, 221.

WATKINS, VERNON

"Ballad of the Mari Lwyd"

ROBERT GORHAM DAVIS. "Eucharist and Roasting Pheasant," *Poetry* 73(3), December 1948, 171.

"The Butterflies"

KATHLEEN RAINE. *Defending Ancient Springs*, p. 29.

"The Death Bell"

KATHLEEN RAINE. *Defending Ancient Springs*, pp. 31-33.

"The Lace-Maker"

KATHLEEN RAINE. *Defending Ancient Springs*, p. 28.

WATTS, ISAAC

"Against Idleness and Mischief"

LEONARD UNGER and WILLIAM VAN O'CONNOR. *Poems for Study*, pp. 18-19.

"Come, Holy Spirit, Heavenly Dove"

EARL DANIELS. *The Art of Reading Poetry*, pp. 207-8.

HELEN S. and J. D. THOMAS. *Explicator* 10(6), April 1952, Item 39.

WAUGH, EDWIN

"Come, Mary, Link thi Arm i' Mine"

MARTHA VICINUS. "The Study of Nineteenth Century British Working Poetry," *College English* 32(5), February 1971, 552-55.

WEBB, MARY

"Sunset"

W. EUGENE DAVIS. "The Poetry of Mary Webb: An Invitation," *English Literature in Transition* 11(2), 1968, 98.

"Swallows"

W. EUGENE DAVIS. "The Poetry of Mary Webb: An Invitation," *English Literature in Transition* 11(2), 1968, 96-97.

WEBSTER, JOHN

"Hark, now everything is still"

IRA GRUSHOW. "Bosola's Dirge in *The Duchess of Malfi*," *Concerning Poetry* 6(2), Fall 1973, 61-62.

WEISS, THEODORE

"Caliban Remembers"

RICHARD HOWARD. "Theodore Weiss: 'No Shore Beyond Our Own,'" *Perspective* 16(1), Winter-Spring 1969, 63-65.

"An Egyptian Passage"

RICHARD HOWARD. "Theodore Weiss: 'No Shore Beyond Our Own,'" *Perspective* 16(1), Winter-Spring 1969, 50-52.

"The Generations"

LAURENCE LIEBERMAN. *Unassigned Frequencies*, pp. 241-42.

"In Defense of Dull Times"

REGINALD GIBBONS. "The Cure: Theodore Weiss's Poetry," *Modern Poetry Studies* 9(1), Spring 1978, 23-24.

"The Medium"

LAURENCE LIEBERMAN. *Unassigned Frequencies*, pp. 240-41.

"The Polish Question"

REGINALD GIBBONS. "The Cure: Theodore Weiss's Poetry," *Modern Poetry Studies* 9(1), Spring 1978, 31-33.

"The Storeroom"

REGINALD GIBBONS. "The Cure: Theodore Weiss's Poetry," *Modern Poetry Studies* 9(1), Spring 1978, 30-31.

"A Trip through Yucatan"

REGINALD GIBBONS. "The Cure: Theodore Weiss's Poetry," *Modern Poetry Studies* 9(1), Spring 1978, 21-23.

"Wunsch-settel"

LAURENCE LIEBERMAN. *Unassigned Frequencies*, pp. 242-43.

WELCH, JAMES

"Birthday in Saronis"

JAMES TATE. "On James Welch's Poems," *Iowa Review* 4(4), Fall 1973, 110.

WELCH, LEW

"Chicago Poem"

SAMUEL CHARTERS. *Some Poems/Poets*, pp. 65-69.

WELLS, NIGEL

"A Green Man"

ROBIN MUNRO. "Robin Munro on Nigel Wells," *Iowa Review* 6(3-4), Summer-Fall 1975, 170-71.

"Saturnalia"

ROBIN MUNRO. "Robin Munro on Nigel Wells," *Iowa Review* 6(3-4), Summer-Fall 1975, 170-71.

WESLEY, CHARLES

"Wrestling Jacob"

JEAN WILKINSON. "Three Sets of Religious Poems," *Huntington Library Quarterly* 36(3), May 1973, 213.

WESTON, ADELAIDE

"Feathered in Sun"

GEORGE ABBE. *You and Contemporary Poetry*, pp. 13-15; second ed., pp. 14-16.

WHEATLEY, PHILLIS

"On Being Brought from Africa to America"

TERENCE COLLINS. "Phillis Wheatley: The Dark Side of the Poetry," *Phylon* 36(1), March 1975, 83.

"To Maecenas"

TERENCE COLLINS. "Phillis Wheatley: The Dark Side of the Poetry," *Phylon* 36(1), March 1975, 81-82.

"To S.M., a young African Painter, on Seeing His Works"

R. LYNN MATSON. "Phillis Wheatley — Soul Sister?" *Phylon* 33(3), Fall 1972, 230.

"To the Right Honorable William, Earl of Dartmouth, His Majesty's Principle Secretary of State for North America"

TERENCE COLLINS. "Phillis Wheatley: The Dark Side of the Poetry," *Phylon* 36(1), March 1975, 83-85.

"To the University of Cambridge in New England"

TERENCE COLLINS. "Phillis Wheatley: The Dark Side of the Poetry," *Phylon* 36(1), March 1975, 82-83.

WHEELOCK, JOHN

"By Daylight and In Dream"

HENRY TAYLOR. "Letting The Darkness In: The Poetic Achievement of John Hall Wheelock," *Hollins Critic* 7(5), December 1970, 13-14.

"The Timid Future"

JOHN CLARK PRATT. *The Meaning of Modern Poetry*, pp. 185, 182-83, 193, 196-97, 194.

WHEELWRIGHT, JOHN

"Father"

AUSTIN WARREN. *New England Saints*, pp. 174-75.

"Obituary to Hart Crane"

BABETTE DEUTSCH. *Poetry in Our Time*, pp. 329-30; second ed., pp. 367-68.

WHITE, KENNETH

"Precentor seagull"

LYNN NOVAK. "Celtic Affinities in the Earlier Poems of Kenneth White," *Studies in Scottish Literature* 12(3), January 1975, 195-96.

WHITMAN, WALT

"Aboard at a Ship's Helm"

ROBERT LaRUE. "Whitman's Sea: Large Enough for Moby Dick," *Walt Whitman Review* 12(3), September 1966, 57.

DOUGLAS A. NOVERR. " 'Aboard at a Ship's Helm': A Minor Sea Drama, the Poet, and the Soul," *Walt Whitman Review* 17(1), March 1971, 23-25.

"After the Sea-Ship"

ROBERT LaRUE. "Whitman's Sea: Large Enough for Moby Dick," *Walt Whitman Review* 12(3), September 1966, 58-59.

"As Adam Early in the Morning"
see also "Children of Adam"

EDMUND REISS. "Whitman's Poetic Grammar: Style and Meaning in 'Children of Adam,' " *American Transcendental Quarterly* 12(1), Fall 1971, 39-40.

"As I Ebb'd with the Ocean of Life"

MELVIN W. ASKEW. "Whitman's 'As I Ebb'd With the Ocean of Life,' " *Walt Whitman Review* 10(4), December 1964, 87-92.

STEPHEN A. BLACK. "Radical Utterances from the Soul's Abysms: Toward a New Sense of Whitman," *PMLA* 88(1), January 1973, 103-5.

HAROLD BLOOM. "The Central Man: Emerson, Whitman, Wallace Stevens," *Massachusetts Review* 7(1), Winter 1966, 35-36.

HAROLD BLOOM. *A Map of Misreading*, pp. 177-84.

E. F. CARLISLE. "Walt Whitman: The Drama of Identity," *Criticism* 10(4), Fall 1968, 265.

ROHN S. FRIEDMAN. "A Whitman Primer: Solipsism and Identity," *American Quarterly* 27(4), October 1975, 456-60.

EDWIN FUSSELL. *Lucifer in Harness*, pp. 127-30.

ROBERT LaRUE. "Whitman's Sea: Large Enough for Moby Dick," *Walt Whitman Review* 12(3), September 1966, 52-54.

MARY ANN TURNER. "Reconciliation of Love and Death in 'Out of the Cradle' and Other Poems," *Walt Whitman Review* 18(4), December 1972, 126-27.

STEPHEN E. WHICHER. "Whitman's Awakening to Death: Toward a Biographical Reading of 'Out of the Cradle Endlessly Rocking,' " *Studies in Romanticism* 1(1), Autumn 1961, 18-19.

"The Base of All Metaphysics"
see also "Calamus"

R. GALEN HANSON. "A Critical Reflection on 'The Base of All Metaphysics,' " *Walt Whitman Review* 18(2), June 1972, 67-70.

"Bivouac on a Mountain Side"

VAUGHAN HUDSON. "Melville's *Battle-Pieces* and Whitman's *Drum-Taps*: A Comparison," *Walt Whitman Review* 19(3), September 1973, 88.

"A Boston Ballad"

STEPHEN D. MALIN. " 'A Boston Ballad' and the Boston Riot," *Walt Whitman Review* 9(3), September 1963, 51-57.

EDWARD A. MARTIN. "Whitman's 'A Boston Ballad (1854),' " *Walt Whitman Review* 11(3), September 1965, 61-69.

"A Broadway Pageant"

RICHARD P. SUGG. "Whitman's Symbolic Circle and 'A Broadway Pageant,' " *Walt Whitman Review* 16(2), June 1970, 35-40.

"By Blue Ontario's Shores"

WILLIE T. WEATHERS. "Whitman's Poetic Translations of His 1855 Preface," *American Literature* 19(1), March 1947, 24-27.

"By the Bivouac's Fitful Flame"

JAMES L. LIVINGSTON. "With Whitman and Hegel Around the Campfire," *Walt Whitman Review* 15(2), June 1969, 120-22.

"Calamus"
see also titles of poems in this sequence

ROBIN P. HOOPLE. "Walt Whitman and the City of Friends," *American Transcendental Quarterly* 18(1-2), Spring 1973, 48-50.

LELAND KRAUTH. "Whitman and His Readers: The Comradeship Theme," *Walt Whitman Review* 20(4), December 1974, 147-51.

JAMES E. MILLER, JR. "The Dance of Rapture," in *Start with the Sun*, pp. 108-9.

JAMES E. MILLER. "Walt Whitman and the Secret of History," in *Start with the Sun*, pp. 26-27.

JAMES E. MILLER. "Whitman's 'Calamus': The Leaf and the Root," *PMLA* 72(1), March 1957, 249-71.

ELIZABETH WELLS. "The Structure of Whitman's 1860 *Leaves of Grass*," *Walt Whitman Review* 15(3), September 1969, 157-59.

"Cavalry Crossing a Ford"

CLEANTH BROOKS and ROBERT PENN WARREN. *Understanding Poetry*, fourth ed., p. 81.

RICHARD ALLAN DAVISON. "Mixed Tone in 'Cavalry Crossing a Ford,' " *Walt Whitman Review* 16(4), December 1970, 114-17.

DALE DOEPKE. "Whitman's Theme in 'Cavalry Crossing a Ford,' " *Walt Whitman Review* 18(4), December 1972, 132-36.

WALTER SUTTON. *American Free Verse*, p. 20.

"Chanting the Square Deific"

ALBERT GELPI. *The Tenth Muse*, pp. 188-90.

STEVEN KAGLE. "Time as a Dimension in Whitman," *American Transcendental Quarterly* 12(2), Fall 1971, 57-58.

WHITMAN, WALT *(Cont.)*

"Chanting the Square Deific" *(cont.)*

ALFRED H. MARKS. "Whitman's Triadic Imagery," *American Literature* 23(1), March 1951, 112-18.

ROY HARVEY PEARCE. *The Continuity of American Poetry*, pp. 172-73.

GEORGE L. SIXBEY. " 'Chanting the Square Deific' — A Study in Whitman's Religion," *American Literature* 9(2), May 1937, 171-95.

"Chants Democratic"

ELIZABETH WELLS. "The Structure of Whitman's 1860 *Leaves of Grass*," *Walt Whitman Review* 15(3), September 1969, 138-44.

"Children of Adam"

see also titles of individual poems in this sequence

ROBIN F. HOOPLE. "Walt Whitman and the City of Friends," *American Transcendental Quarterly* 18(1-2), Spring 1973, 46-48.

ROSEMARY STEPHENS. "Elemental Imagery in 'Children of Adam,' " *Walt Whitman Review* 14(1), March 1968, 26-28.

ELIZABETH WELLS. "The Structure of Whitman's 1860 *Leaves of Grass*," *Walt Whitman Review* 15(3), September 1969, 155-57.

"A Child's Reminiscence"

CLARK GRIFFITH. "Sex and Death: The Significance of Whitman's *Calamus* Themes," *Philological Quarterly* 39(1), January 1960, 31-37.

"Clef Poem"

STEPHEN A. BLACK. "Radical Utterances from the Soul's Abysms: Toward a New Sense of Whitman," *PMLA* 88(1), January 1973, 101-2.

"Come Up from the Fields, Father"

CLEANTH BROOKS and ROBERT PENN WARREN. *Understanding Poetry*, fourth ed., pp. 126-28.

AGNES DICKEN CANNON. "Fervid Atmosphere and Typical Events: Autobiography in *Drum-Taps*," *Walt Whitman Review* 20(3), September 1974, 90-92.

"Crossing Brooklyn Ferry"

RICHARD P. ADAMS. "Whitman: A Brief Revaluation," *Tulane Studies in English* 5 (1955), 135-38.

QUENTIN ANDERSON. *The Imperial Self*, pp. 119-65.

HARRY BROWN and JOHN MILSTEAD. *What the Poem Means*, p. 275.

E. F. CARLISLE. "Walt Whitman: The Drama of Identity," *Criticism* 10(3), Summer 1968, 268-70.

V. K. CHARI. "The Limits of Whitman's Symbolism," *Journal of American Studies* 5(2), August 1971, 180-81.

V. K. CHARI. "Structure of Whitman's Catalogue Poems," *Walt Whitman Review* 18(1), March 1972, 13-14.

JAMES M. COX. "Walt Whitman, Mark Twain, and the Civil War," *Sewanee Review* 69(2), Spring 1961, 189.

MARVIN FELHEIM. "The Problem of Structure in Some Poems of Whitman," in *Aspects of American Poetry*, pp. 91-94.

EDWIN FUSSELL. *Lucifer in Harness*, pp. 61-65.

JAMES W. GARGANO. "Technique in 'Crossing Brooklyn Ferry': The Everlasting Moment," *Journal of English and Germanic Philology* 62(2), April 1963, 262-69.

EUGENE R. KANJO. "Time and Eternity in 'Crossing Brooklyn Ferry,' " *Walt Whitman Review* 18(3), September 1972, 82-90.

BRUCE R. MCELDERRY, JR. "Personae in Whitman (1855-1860)," *American Transcendental Quarterly* 12(1), Fall 1971, 30.

JOHN D. MAGEE. " 'Crossing Brooklyn Ferry': A Hundred Years Hence," *Walt Whitman Review* 15(1), March 1969, 38-43.

JAMES E. MILLER, JR. "The Mysticism of Whitman," in *The Dimensions of Poetry*, pp. 586-87.

JAMES E. MILLER, JR. *Quests Surd and Absurd*, pp. 105-6.

BARTON L. ST. ARMAND. "Transcendence through Technique: Whitman's 'Crossing Brooklyn Ferry' and Impressionist Painting," *Bucknell Review* 24(2), Fall 1978, 56-74.

WILLIAM BYSSHE STEIN. "Whitman: The Divine Ferryman," *Walt Whitman Review* 8(2), June 1962, 27-33.

WALTER SUTTON. *American Free Verse*, pp. 15-16.

GRACE D. YERBURY. "Of a City Beside a River: Whitman, Eliot, Thomas, Miller," *Walt Whitman Review* 10(3), September 1964, 67-68.

"The Dalliance of the Eagles"

ROBERTS W. FRENCH. "Symbolic Values in 'The Dalliance of the Eagles,' " *Walt Whitman Review* 24(3), September 1978, 124-28.

"Darest Thou Now O Soul"

B. CHRISTIAN MEGNA. "Sociality and Seclusion in the Poetry of Walt Whitman," *Walt Whitman Review* 17(2), June 1971, 55-56.

"Dirge for Two Veterans"

MARY ANN TURNER. "Reconciliation of Love and Death in 'Out of the Cradle' and Other Poems," *Walt Whitman Review* 18(4), December 1972, 128.

"The Dismantled Ship"

WALTER SUTTON. *American Free Verse*, pp. 22-23.

"Eidólons"

LOIS A. CUDDY. "Exploration of Whitman's 'Eidólons,' " *Walt Whitman Review* 19(4), December 1973, 153-57.

PHILLIPA P. HARRISON. " 'Eidólons': An Entrance-Song," *Walt Whitman Review* 17(2), June 1971, 35-45.

"Elemental Drifts"

ELIZABETH WELLS. "The Structure of Whitman's 1860 *Leaves of Grass*," *Walt Whitman Review* 15(3), September 1969, 145-50.

"Enfans d'Adam"

see "Children of Adam"

"Ethiopia Saluting the Colors"

J. R. LE MASTER. "Some Traditional Poems from *Leaves of Grass*," *Walt Whitman Review* 13(2), June 1967, 45-49.

"Excelsior"

THOMAS W. FORD. "Whitman's 'Excelsior': The Poem as Microcosm," *Texas Studies in Literature and Language* 17(4), Winter 1976, 777-85.

"Faces"

HAROLD ASPIZ. "A Reading of Whitman's 'Faces,' " *Walt Whitman Review* 19(2), June 1973, 37-48.

"First O Songs for a Prelude"

AGNES DICKEN CANNON. "Fervid Atmosphere and Typical Events: Autobiography in *Drum-Taps*," *Walt Whitman Review* 20(3), September 1974, 79-81.

"Hours Continuing Long"
 R. GALEN HANSON. "Anxiety as Human Predicament: Whitman's 'Calamus' No. 9," *Walt Whitman Review* 21(2), June 1975, 73-75.

"I Hear America Singing"
 CHARLES T. DAVIS. "Walt Whitman and the Problem of an American Tradition," *CLA Journal* 5(1), September 1961, 1-3.

"I Sing the Body Electric"
 see also "Children of Adam"
 ROBERT COSKREN. "A Reading of Whitman's 'I Sing the Body Electric,'" *Walt Whitman Review* 22(3), September 1976, 125-32.
 JOHN H. MATLE. "The Body Acclaimed," *Walt Whitman Review* 16(4), December 1970, 110-14.
 MARK STRAND. "Whitman: I Sing the Body Electric," in *Master Poems of the English Language*, pp. 707-9.
 STUART C. WOODRUFF. "Whitman: Poet or Prophet?" *Walt Whitman Review* 14(2), June 1968, 35-38.

"In Cabin'd Ships at Sea"
 WILLIAM J. SABO. "The Ship and Its Related Imagery in 'Inscriptions' and 'Song of Myself,'" *Walt Whitman Review* 24(3), September 1978, 119-20.

"In Paths Untrodden"
 see also "Calamus"
 RUSSELL A. HUNT. "Whitman's Poetics and the Unity of 'Calamus,'" *American Literature* 46(4), January 1975, 485-86.

"Lingering Last Drops"
 ROSE CHERIE REISSMAN. "Recurrent Motifs in *Goodbye My Fancy*," *Walt Whitman Review* 21(1), March 1975, 32-33.

"A March in the Ranks Hard-Prest"
 AGNES DICKEN CANNON. "Fervid Atmosphere and Typical Events: Autobiography in *Drum-Taps*," *Walt Whitman Review* 20(3), September 1974, 92-94.
 DOMINICK A. LABIANCA. "'A March in the Ranks Hard-Prest, and the Road Unknown': A Chemical Analysis," *American Notes & Queries*, n.s., 15(8), April 1977, 110-11.

"The Mystic Trumpeter"
 W. L. WERNER. "Whitman's 'The Mystic Trumpeter' as Autobiography," *American Literature* 7(4), January 1936, 455-58.

"A Noiseless Patient Spider"
 EDWARD BUTSCHER. "Whitman's Attitudes Toward Death: The Essential Paradox," *Walt Whitman Review* 17(1), March 1971, 17.
 WILTON ECKLEY. *Explicator* 22(3), November 1963, Item 20.
 ARNOLD MERSCH. "Teilhard de Chardin and Whitman's 'A Noiseless Patient Spider,'" *Walt Whitman Review* 17(3), September 1971, 99-100.
 VICTOR STRANDBERG. "The Crisis of Belief in Modern Literature," *English Journal* 53(7), October 1964, 479.
 MARK VAN DOREN. *Introduction to Poetry*, pp. 42-45.
 FRED D. WHITE. "Whitman's Cosmic Spider," *Walt Whitman Review* 23(2), June 1977, 85-88.

"O! Captain My Captain!"
 ISAAC ASIMOV. *Familiar Poems, Annotated*, pp. 224-28.

"On Journeys Through the States"
 B. J. LEGGETT. "The Structure of Whitman's 'On Journeys Through the States,'" *Walt Whitman Review* 14(2), June 1968, 58-59.

"On the Beach at Night"
 ROBERT LARUE. "Whitman's Sea: Large Enough for Moby Dick," *Walt Whitman Review* 12(3), September 1966, 57-58. (P)
 F. O. MATTHIESSEN. *American Renaissance*, pp. 575-77.

"Our Old Feuillage"
 V. K. CHARI. "Structure of Whitman's Catalogue Poems," *Walt Whitman Review* 18(1), March 1972, 8.
 ROBERT J. GRIFFIN. "The Interconnectedness of 'Our Old Feuillage,'" *Walt Whitman Review* 8(1), March 1962, 8-12.
 DOUGLAS A. NOVERR. "Poetic Vision and Locus in Whitman's 'Our Old Feuillage,'" *Walt Whitman Review* 22(3), September 1976, 118-22.

"Out of the Cradle Endlessly Rocking"
 see also earlier version: "A Word Out of the Sea"
 RICHARD P. ADAMS. "Whitman: A Brief Revaluation," *Tulane Studies in English* 5(1955), 138-40.
 ROY P. BASLER. *Explicator* 5(8), June 1947, Item 59.
 ROBERT J. BERTHOLF. "Poetic Epistemology of Whitman's 'Out of the Cradle,'" *Walt Whitman Review* 10(3), September 1964, 73-77.
 STEPHEN A. BLACK. "Journeys into Chaos: A Psychoanalytic Study of Whitman, His Literary Processes and His Poems," *Literature and Psychology* 24(2), 1974, 50.
 STEPHEN A. BLACK. "Radical Utterances from the Soul's Abysms," *PMLA* 88(1), January 1973, 106-10.
 HARRY BROWN and JOHN MILSTEAD. *What the Poem Means*, p. 276.
 V. K. CHARI. "The Limits of Whitman's Symbolism," *Journal of American Studies* 5(2), August 1971, 178-79.
 JAMES M. COX. "Walt Whitman, Mark Twain, and the Civil War," *Sewanee Review* 69(2), Spring 1961, 189-90.
 C. C. CUNNINGHAM. *Literature as a Fine Art: Analysis and Interpretation*, pp. 176-85.
 NED J. DAVISON. "'The Raven' and 'Out of the Cradle Endlessly Rocking,'" *Poe Newsletter* 1(1), April 1968, 5-6.
 SUSAN G. FEINBERG. *Explicator* 37(1), Fall 1978, 35-36.
 MELVIN FELHEIM. "The Problem of Structure in Some Poems of Whitman," in *Aspects of American Poetry*, pp. 85-87.
 EDWIN FUSSELL. *Lucifer in Harness*, pp. 70-72.
 THEODORE L. GROSS. *The Heroic Ideal in American Literature*, pp. 60-61.
 C. W. M. JOHNSON. *Explicator* 5(7), May 1947, Item 52.
 ERNA EMMIGHAUSEN KELLY. "Whitman and Wordsworth: Childhood Experiences and the Future Poet," *Walt Whitman Review* 23(2), June 1977, 59-68.
 ROBERT LARUE. "Whitman's Sea: Large Enough for Moby Dick," *Walt Whitman Review* 12(3), September 1966, 54-56.
 BRUCE R. MCELDERRY, JR. "Personae in Whitman (1855-1860)," *American Transcendental Quarterly* 12(1), Fall 1971, 30.
 ALFRED H. MARKS. "Whitman's Triadic Imagery," *American Literature* 23(1), March 1951, 120-26.

WHITMAN, WALT *(Cont.)*

"Out of the Cradle Endlessly Rocking" *(cont.)*

> JAMES E. MILLER, JR. "The Mysticism of Whitman," in *The Dimensions of Poetry,* pp. 587-88.

> JAMES E. MILLER, JR. *Quests Surd and Absurd,* pp. 106-7.

> TRACEY R. MILLER. "The Boy, the Bird and the Sea: An Archetypal Reading of 'Out of the Cradle,'" *Walt Whitman Review* 19(3), September 1973, 93-103.

> ROY HARVEY PEARCE. *The Continuity of American Poetry,* pp. 170-71.

> LOUISE POUND. "Note on Walt Whitman and Bird Poetry," *English Journal* 19(1), January 1930, 34-36.

> JOSEPH N. RIDDEL. "Walt Whitman and Wallace Stevens: Functions of a 'Literatus,'" *South Atlantic Quarterly* 61(4), Autumn 1962, 515-17.

> M. L. ROSENTHAL and A. J. M. SMITH. *Exploring Poetry,* pp. 695-96; second ed., pp. 489-90.

> LEO SPITZER. "*Explication de Texte* Applied to Whitman's 'Out of the Cradle Endlessly Rocking,'" *English Literary History* 16(3), September 1949, 229-49. Reprinted in: Leo Spitzer. *Essays on English and American Literature,* pp. 14-36.

> FLOYD STOVALL. "Main Drifts in Whitman's Poetry," *American Literature* 4(1), March 1932, 8-10.

> BEVERLY LUZIETTI STROHL. "An Interpretation of 'Out of the Cradle,'" *Walt Whitman Review* 10(4), December 1964, 83-87.

> LARRY SUTTON. "Structural Music in Whitman's 'Out of the Cradle,'" *Walt Whitman Review* 15(1), March 1969, 57-59.

> WALTER SUTTON. *American Free Verse,* pp. 16-19.

> MARY ANN TURNER. "Reconciliation of Love and Death in 'Out of the Cradle' and Other Poems," *Walt Whitman Review* 18(4), December 1972, 123-26.

> CHARLES C. WALCUTT. "Whitman's 'Out of the Cradle Endlessly Rocking,'" *College English* 10(5), February 1949, 277-79.

> S. E. WHICHER. *Explicator* 5(4), February 1947, Item 28.

> STEPHEN E. WHICHER. "Whitman's Awakening to Death: Toward a Biographical Reading of 'Out of the Cradle Endlessly Rocking,'" *Studies in Romanticism* 1(1), Autumn 1961, 9-28.

"Out of the Rolling Ocean the Crowd"

see also "Children of Adam"

> MARY ANN TURNER. "Reconciliation of Love and Death in 'Out of the Cradle' and Other Poems," *Walt Whitman Review* 18(4), December 1972, 130-31.

"A Pact"

> SHOLOM J. KAHN. "Whitman's 'New Wood,'" *Walt Whitman Review* 15(4), December 1969, 201-2. (P)

"Passage to India"

> RICHARD P. ADAMS. "Whitman: A Brief Revaluation," *Tulane Studies in English* 5 (1955), 141-43.

> RAYMOND BENOIT. *Single Nature's Double Name,* pp. 67-71.

> WALTER BLAIR. *The Literature of the United States,* II: 217. (Quoting Randall Stewart)

> GEORGE BOWERING. "The Solitary Everything," *Walt Whitman Review* 15(1), March 1969, 20-22.

> HARRY BROWN and JOHN MILSTEAD. *What the Poem Means,* pp. 276-77.

> V. K. CHARI. "The Limits of Whitman's Symbolism," *Journal of American Studies* 5(2), August 1971, 179-80.

> STANLEY K. COFFMAN, JR. "Form and Meaning in Whitman's 'Passage to India,'" *PMLA* 70(3), June 1955, 337-49.

> BERNARD DUFFEY. *Poetry in America,* pp. 83-86.

> MARVIN FELHEIM. "The Problem of Structure in Some Poems of Whitman," in *Aspects of American Poetry,* pp. 94-97.

> CLARE R. GOLDFARB. "The Poet's Role in 'Passage to India,'" *Walt Whitman Review* 8(4), December 1962, 75-79.

> HAROLD M. HURWITZ. "Whitman, Tagore, and 'Passage to India,'" *Walt Whitman Review* 13(2), June 1967, 56-60.

> JAMES E. MILLER, JR. "The Mysticism of Whitman," in *The Dimensions of Poetry,* 589.

> JAMES E. MILLER, JR. *Quests Surd and Absurd,* pp. 108-9.

> KARL SHAPIRO. "The First White Aboriginal," in *Start with the Sun,* p. 64.

> KARL SHAPIRO. *In Defense of Ignorance,* pp. 195-96.

> JOEL R. KEHLER. "A Typological Reading of 'Passage to India,'" *ESQ* 23(2), Second Quarter 1977, 123-29.

> JOHN LOVELL, JR. "Appreciating Whitman: 'Passage to India,'" *Modern Language Quarterly* 21(2), June 1960, 131-41.

> SOM R. SHARMA. "Self, Soul, and God in 'Passage to India,'" *College English* 27(5), February 1966, 394-99.

> FLOYD STOVALL. "Main Drifts in Whitman's Poetry," *American Literature* 4(1), March 1932, 18-21.

> CHARLES STUBBLEFIELD. "The Great Circle: Whitman's 'Passage to India,'" *Prairie Schooner* 49(1), Spring 1975, 19-30.

> ALAN TRACHTENBERG. "Brooklyn Bridge and the Mastery of Nature," *Massachusetts Review* 4(4), Summer 1963, 737-39.

> A. D. VAN NOSTRAND. *Everyman His Own Poet,* pp. 59-61.

> HYATT H. WAGGONER. *American Poets,* p. 503.

"Pictures"

> GEORGE H. SOULE, JR. "Walt Whitman's 'Pictures': An Alternative to Tennyson's 'Palace of Art,'" *ESQ* 22(1), First Quarter 1976, 39-47.

"Proto-Leaf"

> ELIZABETH WELLS. "The Structure of Whitman's 1860 *Leaves of Grass,*" *Walt Whitman Review* 15(3), September 1969, 134-37.

"Proud Music of the Storm"

> SYDNEY J. KRAUSE. "Whitman, Music, and *Proud Music of the Storm,*" *PMLA* 72(4), September 1957, 707-16.

> JAMES C. McCULLAGH. "'Proud Music of the Storm': A Study in Dynamics," *Walt Whitman Review* 21(2), June 1975, 66-73.

"A Riddle Song"

> C. SCOTT PUGH. "The End as Means in 'A Riddle Song,'" *Walt Whitman Review* 23(2), June 1977, 82-85.

"Rise O Days From Your Fathomless Deeps"

> STEVE CARTER. "The Metaphor of Assimilation and 'Rise O Days from Your Fathomless Deeps,'" *Walt Whitman Review* 24(4), December 1978, 158-61.

"Roots and Leaves"

LAWRENCE BUELL. "Transcendentalist Catalogue Rhetoric: Vision Versus Form," *American Literature* 40(3), November 1968, 326-30.

"Salut Au Monde!"

ALVIN ROSENFELD. "The Poem as Dialogical Process: A New Reading of 'Salut Au Monde!'" *Walt Whitman Review* 10(2), June 1964, 34-40.

"Scented Herbage of My Breast"

see also "Calamus"

V. K. CHARI. "Structure of Whitman's Catalogue Poems," *Walt Whitman Review* 18(1), March 1972, 15.

ROBERTS W. FRENCH. "Whitman in Crisis: A Reading of 'Scented Herbage of My Breast,'" *Walt Whitman Review* 24(1), March 1978, 29-32.

RUSSELL A. HUNT. "Whitman's Poetics and the Unity of 'Calamus,'" *American Literature* 46(4), January 1975, 486-88.

STEPHEN E. WHICHER. "Whitman's Awakening to Death: Toward a Biographical Reading of 'Out of the Cradle Endlessly Rocking,'" *Studies in Romanticism* 1(1), Autumn 1961, 19-20.

"The Ship Starting"

WILLIAM J. SABO. "The Ship and Its Related Imagery in 'Inscriptions' and 'Song of Myself,'" *Walt Whitman Review* 24(3), September 1978, 120.

"A Sight in Camp in the Daybreak Gray and Dim"

AGNES DICKEN CANNON. "Fervid Atmosphere and Typical Events: Autobiography in *Drum-Taps*," *Walt Whitman Review* 20(3), September 1974, 87-88.

WALTER SUTTON. *American Free Verse*, pp. 21-22.

ROBERT B. SWEET. "A Writer Looks at Whitman's 'A Sight in Camp in the Daybreak Gray and Dim,'" *Walt Whitman Review* 17(2), June 1971, 58-62.

HYATT H. WAGGONER. *American Poets*, pp. 176-78.

WILLIAM A. WORTMAN. "Spiritual Progression in 'A Sight in Camp,'" *Walt Whitman Review* 14(1), March 1968, 24-26.

"The Singer in the Prison"

J. R. LE MASTER. "Some Traditional Poems from *Leaves of Grass*," *Walt Whitman Review* 13(2), June 1967, 49-51.

"The Sleepers"

MUTLU BLASING. "'The Sleepers': The Problem of the Self in Whitman," *Walt Whitman Review* 21(3), September 1975, 111-19.

V. K. CHARI. "The Limits of Whitman's Symbolism," *Journal of American Studies* 5(2), August 1971, 180-81.

V. K. CHARI. "Structure of Whitman's Catalogue Poems," *Walt Whitman Review* 18(1), March 1972, 12-13.

HARRY JAMES COOK. "The Individuation of a Poet: The Process of Becoming in Whitman's 'The Sleepers,'" *Walt Whitman Review* 21(3), September 1975, 101-10.

BERNARD DUFFEY. *Poetry in America*, pp. 85-86.

JOYCE KORNBLATT. "Whitman's Vision of the Past in 'The Sleepers,'" *Walt Whitman Review* 16(3), September 1970, 86-89.

SISTER EVA MARY. "Shades of Darkness in 'The Sleepers,'" *Walt Whitman Review* 15(3), September 1969, 187-90.

F. O. MATTHIESSEN. *American Renaissance*, pp. 572-74.

ROY HARVEY PEARCE. *The Continuity of American Poetry*, pp. 168-70.

BERNICE SLOTE and JAMES E. MILLER, JR. "Of Monkeys, Nudes, and the Good Gray Poet," in *Start with the Sun*, p. 188.

R. W. VINCE. "A Reading of 'The Sleepers,'" *Walt Whitman Review* 18(1), March 1972, 17-28.

HYATT H. WAGGONER. *American Poets*, p. 174.

STEPHEN E. WHICHER. "Whitman's Awakening to Death: Toward a Biographical Reading of 'Out of the Cradle Endlessly Rocking,'" *Studies in Romanticism* 1(1), Autumn 1961, 14-16.

"A Song for Occupations"

G. THOMAS COUSER. "An Emerson-Whitman Parallel: 'The American Scholar' and 'A Song for Occupations,'" *Walt Whitman Review* 22(3), September 1976, 115-18.

"Song of the Banner at Daybreak"

EDWIN FUSSELL. *Lucifer in Harness*, pp. 72-75.

"Song of the Broad-Axe"

STANLEY K. COFFMAN, JR. *Explicator* 12(6), April 1954, Item 39. (P)

ALVIN H. ROSENFELD. "The Eagle and the Axe: A Study of Whitman's 'Song of the Broad-Axe,'" *American Imago* 25(4), Winter 1968, 354-70.

"Song of the Exposition"

ROY HARVEY PEARCE. "Whitman and Our Hope for Poetry," in *The Poetic Tradition*, pp. 134-39. Reprinted in: Roy Harvey Pearce. *Historicism Once More*, pp. 342-48.

"Song of the Open Road"

V. K. CHARI. "The Limits of Whitman's Symbolism," *Journal of American Studies* 5(2), August 1971, 179-80.

ROBIN HOOPLE. "Walt Whitman and the City of Friends," *American Transcendental Quarterly* 18(1-2), Spring 1973, 47.

ALVIN ROSENFELD. "Whitman's Open Road Philosophy," *Walt Whitman Review* 14(1), March 1968, 5-13.

MARIAN L. STEIN. "Affirmations and Negations: Lawrence's 'Whitman' and Whitman's Open Road," *Walt Whitman Review* 18(2), June 1972, 64-65.

C. W. TRUESDALE. "Theodore Roethke and the Landscape of American Poetry," *Minnesota Review* 8(4), 1968, 347-48.

A. D. VAN NOSTRAND. *Everyman His Own Poet*, pp. 52-53.

"Song of the Redwood Tree"

E. H. EBY. "Walt Whitman and the Tree of Life," *Walt Whitman Review* 7(3), September 1961, 48-49.

"A Song of the Rolling Earth"

EUGENE CHESNICK. "Whitman and the Poetry of the Trillions," *Walt Whitman Review* 22(1), March 1976, 18-22.

SUZANNE POIRIER. "'A Song of the Rolling Earth' as Transcendental and Poetic Theory," *Walt Whitman Review* 22(2), June 1976, 67-74.

"Spirit That Form'd This Scene"

HAROLD ASPIZ. *Explicator* 28(3), November 1969, Item 25.

"Spontaneous Me"

see also "Children of Adam"

V. K. CHARI. "Structure of Whitman's Catalogue Poems," *Walt Whitman Review* 18(1), March 1972, 8-10.

WHITMAN, WALT *(Cont.)*

"Spontaneous Me" *(cont.)*

> HARRY R. WARFEL. "Whitman's Structural Principles in 'Spontaneous Me,' " *College English* 18(4), January 1957, 190-95.

"Starting from Paumanok"

> FRANCES H. BENNETT. " 'Starting From Paumanok' as Functional Poetry," *Walt Whitman Review* 15(2), June 1969, 117-20.
>
> V. K. CHARI. "Structure of Whitman's Catalogue Poems," *Walt Whitman Review* 18(1), March 1972, 6-8.

"Tears"

> ROBERT LaRUE. "Whitman's Sea: Large Enough for Moby Dick," *Walt Whitman Review* 12(3), September 1966, 56.

"There Was a Child Went Forth"

> STEPHEN A. BLACK. "Radical Utterances from the Soul's Abysms: Toward a New Sense of Whitman," *PMLA* 88(1), January 1973, 105-6.
>
> LAWRENCE BUELL. *Literary Transcendentalism,* pp. 172-73.
>
> M. L. ROSENTHAL. *Poetry and the Common Life,* pp. 61-63.
>
> SISTER MARGARET PATRICE SLATTERY. "Patterns of Imagery in Whitman's 'There Was a Child Went Forth,' " *Walt Whitman Review* 15(2), June 1969, 112-14.
>
> HYATT H. WAGGONER. *American Poets,* pp. 170-74.

"This Compost"

> ROBERT J. GRIFFIN. *Explicator* 21(8), April 1963, Item 68.

"Thou Mother with Thy Equal Brood"

> ALFRED H. MARKS. "Whitman's Triadic Imagery," *American Literature* 23(1), March 1951, 106-7.

"To a Common Prostitute"

> MARIAN L. STEIN. "Affirmations and Negations: Lawrence's 'Whitman' and Whitman's Open Road," *Walt Whitman Review* 18(2), June 1972, 66-67.

"To A Locomotive in Winter"

> GEORGE ARMS. *Explicator* 5(2), November 1946, Item 14. Reprinted in: Norman C. Stageberg and Wallace L. Anderson. *Poetry as Experience,* p. 491.
>
> RONALD CHRIST. "Walt Whitman: Image and Credo," *American Quarterly* 17(1), Spring 1965, 92-103.
>
> FREDERICK J. HOFFMAN. "The Technological Fallacy in Contemporary Poetry: Hart Crane and MacKnight Black," *American Literature* 21(1), March 1949, 98. Reprinted in: Norman C. Stageberg and Wallace L. Anderson. *Poetry as Experience,* p. 491.

"To the Garden the World"

> EDMUND REISS. "Whitman's Poetic Grammar: Style and Meaning in 'Children of Adam,' " *American Transcendental Quarterly* 12(1), Fall 1971, 36-39.

"To the Sunset Breeze"

> DWIGHT KALITA. "Whitman and the Correspondent Breeze," *Walt Whitman Review* 21(3), September 1975, 125-30.
>
> DONALD BARLOW STAUFFER. "Walt Whitman and Old Age," *Walt Whitman Review* 24(4), December 1978, 147.

"To Think of Time"

> STEVEN KAGLE. "Time as a Dimension in Whitman," *American Transcendental Quarterly* 12(2), Fall 1971, 58.
>
> RICHARD D. McGHEE. "Concepts of Time in Whitman's Poetry," *Walt Whitman Review* 15(2), June 1969, 82-83.
>
> F. O. MATTHIESSEN. *American Renaissance,* pp. 610-12.
>
> ESTELLE W. TAYLOR. "Analysis and Comparison of the 1855 and 1891 Versions of Whitman's 'To Think of Time,' " *Walt Whitman Review* 13(4), December 1967, 107-22.
>
> HYATT H. WAGGONER. *American Poets,* pp. 166-69.

"To You"

> ALVIN ROSENFELD. "Whitman's Open Road Philosophy," *Walt Whitman Review* 14(1), March 1968, 5-6.

"Two Rivulets"

> ALFRED H. MARKS. "Whitman's Triadic Imagery," *American Literature* 23(1), March 1951, 105-6.

"Unfolded Out of the Folds"

> HAROLD ASPIZ. "Unfolding the Folds," *Walt Whitman Review* 12(4), December 1966, 81-87.

"Unseen Buds"

> ROSE CHERIE REISSMAN. "Recurrent Motifs in *Goodbye My Fancy," Walt Whitman Review* 21(1), March 1975, 30-31.

"Vigil Strange I Kept on the Field One Night"

> AGNES DICKEN CANNON. "Fervid Atmosphere and Typical Events: Autobiography in *Drum-Taps," Walt Whitman Review* 20(3), September 1974, 88-89.
>
> MARY ANN TURNER. "Reconciliation of Love and Death in 'Out of the Cradle' and Other Poems," *Walt Whitman Review* 18(4), December 1972, 131.

"Virginia — the West"

> JOHN P. McWILLIAMS, JR. " 'Drum Taps' and *Battle-Pieces:* The Blossom of War," *American Quarterly* 23(2), May 1971, 193-94.

"A Voice From Death"

> ROSE CHERIE REISSMAN. "Recurrent Motifs in *Goodbye My Fancy," Walt Whitman Review* 21(1), March 1975, 32.

"Walt Whitman"

> ELIZABETH WELLS. "The Structure of Whitman's 1860 *Leaves of Grass," Walt Whitman Review* 15(3), September 1969, 138-44.

"When I Heard the Learn'd Astronomer"

> WALTER BLAIR and JOHN C. GERBER. *Better Reading 2: Literature,* p. 114.
>
> BERNTH LINDFORS. "Whitman's 'When I Heard the Learn'd Astronomer,' " *Walt Whitman Review* 10(1), March 1964, 19-21.

"When Lilacs Last in the Dooryard Bloom'd"

> RICHARD P. ADAMS. "Whitman's 'Lilacs' and the Tradition of Pastoral Elegy," *PMLA* 72(3), June 1957, 479-87.
>
> HARSHARAN SINGH AHLUWALIA. "The Private Self and the Public Self in Whitman's 'Lilacs,' " *Walt Whitman Review* 23(4), December 1977, 166-75.
>
> STEPHEN A. BLACK. "Journeys into Chaos: A Psychoanalytic Study of Whitman, His Literary Processes and His Poems," *Literature and Psychology* 24(2), 1974, 50-51.

CALVIN S. BROWN. *Music and Literature* pp. 178-94. Reprinted in: Charles Feidelson, Jr. and Paul Brodtkorb. *Interpretations of American Literature*, pp. 187-96.

EDWARD BUTSCHER. "Whitman's Attitudes Toward Death: The Essential Paradox," *Walt Whitman Review* 17(1), March 1971, 17-19.

ROBERT EMERSON CARLILE. "Leitmotif and Whitman's 'When Lilacs Last in the Dooryard Bloom'd,'" *Criticism* 13(4), Fall 1971, 329-39.

V. K. CHARI. "The Limits of Whitman's Symbolism," *Journal of American Studies* 5(2), August 1971, 178-79.

MALCOLM COWLEY. *A Many-Windowed House*, pp. 70-72.

DAVID DAICHES and WILLIAM CHARVAT. *Poems in English*, p. 725.

CHARLES CLAY DOYLE. "Poetry and Pastoral: A Dimension of Whitman's 'Lilacs,'" *Walt Whitman Review* 15(4), December 1969, 242-45.

BERNARD DUFFEY. *Poetry in America*, pp. 99-100.

W. P. ELLEDGE. "Whitman's 'Lilacs' as Romantic Narrative," *Walt Whitman Review* 12(3), September 1966, 59-67.

MARVIN FELHEIM. "The Problem of Structure in Some Poems of Whitman," in *Aspects of American Poetry*, pp. 88-91.

THOMAS W. FORD. "Invitation from a Thrush: Frost Versus Whitman," *Walt Whitman Review* 22(4), December 1976, 166-67.

EDWIN FUSSELL. *Lucifer in Harness*, pp. 77-79.

GEOFFREY GRIGSON. "Whitman: Memories of President Lincoln: When Lilacs Last in the Dooryard Bloom'd," in *Master Poems of the English Language*, pp. 696-98.

THEODORE L. GROSS. *The Heroic Ideal in American Literature*, pp. 61-62.

EVELYN J. HINZ. "Whitman's 'Lilacs': The Power of Elegy," *Bucknell Review* 20(2), Fall 1972, 35-54.

OSWALD LeWINTER. "Whitman's 'Lilacs,'" *Walt Whitman Review* 10(1), March 1964, 10-14.

F. O. MATTHIESSEN. *American Renaissance*, pp. 618-23. Reprinted in: *Readings for Liberal Education*, II: 543-47; revised ed., II: 149-53.

JAMES E. MILLER, JR. "The Mysticism of Whitman," in *The Dimensions of Poetry*, pp. 588-89.

JAMES E. MILLER, JR. *Quests Surd and Absurd*, pp. 107-8.

JANE A. NELSON. "Ecstasy and Transformation in Whitman's 'Lilacs,'" *Walt Whitman Review* 18(4), December 1972, 113-23.

FERNER NUHN. "*Leaves of Grass* Viewed as an Epic," *Arizona Quarterly* 7(4), Winter 1951, 335-36.

THOMAS PARKINSON. "The Art of Loneliness," *Ohio Review* 18(2), Spring/Summer 1977, 15-16.

MARGARET C. PATTERSON. "'Lilacs,' a Sonata," *Walt Whitman Review* 14(2), June 1968, 46-50.

JOHN OLIVER PERRY. *The Experience of Poems*, p. 274.

JOSEPH N. RIDDEL. "Walt Whitman and Wallace Stevens: Functions of a 'Literatus,'" *South Atlantic Quarterly* 61(4), Autumn 1962, 511.

M. L. ROSENTHAL and A. J. M. SMITH. *Exploring Poetry*, second ed., pp. 357-58.

FLOYD STOVALL. "Main Drifts in Whitman's Poetry," *American Literature* 4(1), March 1932, 13-15.

MARY ANN TURNER. "Reconciliation of Love and Death in 'Out of the Cradle' and Other Poems," *Walt Whitman Review* 18(4), December 1972, 128-30.

HYATT H. WAGGONER. *American Poets*, pp. 178-79.

ARTHUR E. WATERMAN. "A Criticism of 'When Lilacs Last in the Dooryard Bloom'd,'" *Walt Whitman Review* 8(3), September 1962, 64-68.

STUART C. WOODRUFF. "Whitman: Poet or Prophet?" *Walt Whitman Review* 14(2), June 1968, 38-40.

"Whispers of Heavenly Death"
J. T. LEDBETTER. "Whitman's Power in the Short Poem: A Discussion of 'Whispers of Heavenly Death,'" *Walt Whitman Review* 21(4), December 1975, 155-58.

B. CHRISTIAN MEGNA. "Sociality and Seclusion in the Poetry of Walt Whitman," *Walt Whitman Review* 17(2), June 1971, 55-57.

"Whoever You Are Holding Me Now in Hand"
see also "Calamus"
LLOYD FRANKENBERG. *Invitation to Poetry*, pp. 95-99.

RUSSELL A. HUNT. "Whitman's Poetics and the Unity of 'Calamus,'" *American Literature* 46(4), January 1975, 488-90.

"A Word Out of the Sea"
EDWIN FUSSELL. *Lucifer in Harness*, pp. 130-34.

ROY HARVEY PEARCE. *Historicism Once More*, pp. 228-30.

ELIZABETH WELLS. "The Structure of Whitman's 1860 *Leaves of Grass*," *Walt Whitman Review* 15(3), September 1969, 150-55.

"The World Below the Brine"
DAVID DAICHES and WILLIAM CHARVAT. *Poems in English*, p. 724.

IDA FASEL. *Explicator* 25(1), September 1966, Item 7.

WILLIAM A. FREEDMAN. *Explicator* 23(5), January 1965, Item 39.

"The Wound-Dresser"
AGNES DICKEN CANNON. "Fervid Atmosphere and Typical Events: Autobiography in *Drum-Taps*," *Walt Whitman Review* 20(3), September 1974, 85-87.

MARIAN L. STEIN. "Affirmations and Negations: Lawrence's 'Whitman' and Whitman's Open Road," *Walt Whitman Review* 18(2), June 1972, 65-66.

"Year of the Meteors"
JERRY A. HERNDON. "Parallels in Melville and Whitman," *Walt Whitman Review* 24(3), September 1978, 98-108.

WHITTEMORE, REED
"A Day with the Foreign Legion"
HOWARD NEMEROV. *Poetry and Fiction*, pp. 170-72.

"Lines, Composed Upon Reading an Announcement by Civil Defense Authorities Recommending that I Build a Bombshelter in My Backyard"
HOWARD NEMEROV. *Poetry and Fiction*, pp. 177-78.

WHITTIER, JOHN GREENLEAF
"Amy Wentworth"
MERRILL LEWIS. "In Praise of Whittier's 'Pictures,'" *ESQ* 23(4), Fourth Quarter 1977, 245-46.

"Barbara Frietchie"
ISAAC ASIMOV. *Familiar Poems, Annotated*, pp. 216-23.

HARRY OSTER. "Whittier's Use of the *Sage* in His Ballads," in *Studies in American Literature*, pp. 73-76.

WHITTIER, JOHN GREENLEAF *(Cont.)*

"The Barefoot Boy"

> WILLIAM E. BRIDGES. "Warm Hearth, Cold World: Social Perspectives on the Household Poets," *American Quarterly* 21(4), Winter 1969, 769-71.

"Birchbrook Mill"

> GEORGE ARMS. *The Fields Were Green*, pp. 37-38.

"Brown of Ossawatomie"

> CECIL D. EBY, JR. "Whittier's 'Brown of Ossawatomie,'" *New England Quarterly* 33(4), December 1960, 452-61.

"The Countess"

> MERRILL LEWIS. "In Praise of Whittier's 'Pictures,'" *ESQ* 23(4), Fourth Quarter 1977, 245-46.

"Ichabod"

> GEORGE ARMS. *The Fields Were Green*, pp. 39-40.
> WAYNE R. KIME. *Explicator* 28(7), March 1970, Item 59.
> ROBERT PENN WARREN. "Whittier," *Sewanee Review* 79(1), Winter 1971, 100-4.

"Letter from a Missionary of the Methodist Episcopal Church South, in Kansas, to a Distinguished Politician"

> ROBERT PENN WARREN. "Whittier," *Sewanee Review* 79(1), Winter 1971, 104-7.

"Massachusetts to Virginia"

> HARRY BROWN and JOHN MILSTEAD. *What the Poem Means*, p. 279.

"Maud Muller"

> GEORGE ARMS. *The Fields Were Green*, pp. 41-43.

"Mountain Picture"

> HYATT H. WAGGONER. *American Poets*, pp. 73-76.

"The Pennsylvania Pilgrim"

> GEORGE ARMS. *The Fields Were Green*, pp. 38-39.

"Pictures"

> MERRILL LEWIS. "In Praise of Whittier's 'Pictures,'" *ESQ* 23(4), Fourth Quarter 1977, 244-51.

"The Pipes of Lucknow: An Incident of the Sepoy Mutiny"

> ROBERT PENN WARREN. "Whittier," *Sewanee Review* 79(1), Winter 1971, 114-15.

"Skipper Ireson's Ride"

> GEORGE ARMS. *The Fields Were Green*, pp. 40-41.
> MERRILL LEWIS. "In Praise of Whittier's 'Pictures,'" *ESQ* 23(4), Fourth Quarter 1977, 246.
> HARRY OSTER. "Whittier's Use of the *Sage* in His Ballads," in *Studies in American Literature*, pp. 70-73.

"Snow-Bound"

> GEORGE ARMS. *The Fields Were Green*, pp. 44-47.
> WILLIAM E. BRIDGES. "Warm Hearth, Cold World: Social Perspectives on the Household Poets," *American Quarterly* 21(4), Winter 1969, 776-77.
> BERNARD DUFFEY. *Poetry in America*, pp. 54-57.
> ROY HARVEY PEARCE. *The Continuity of American Poetry*, pp. 230-31.
> SIDNEY POGER. "'Snow-Bound' and Social Responsibility," *American Transcendental Quarterly* 1(2), First Quarter 1969, 85-87.
> DONALD A. RINGE. "Sound Imagery in Whittier's Snow-Bound," *Papers on Language and Literature* 5(2), Spring 1969, 139-44.
> LEONARD M. TRAWICK. "Whittier's *Snow-Bound*: A Poem about the Imagination," *Essays in Literature* 1(1), Spring 1974, 46-53.

HYATT H. WAGGONER. *American Poets*, pp. 76-83.
ROBERT PENN WARREN. "Whittier," *Sewanee Review* 79(1), Winter 1971, 118-30.

"Song of the Slaves in the Desert"

> ROBERT PENN WARREN. "Whittier," *Sewanee Review* 79(1), Winter 1971, 111-14.

"To J. P."

> ABE C. RAVITZ. *Explicator* 13(4), February 1955, Item 22.

"The Wreck of the Rivermouth"

> HARRY OSTER. "Whittier's Use of the *Sage* in His Ballads," in *Studies in American Literature*, pp. 63-64.

WIGGLESWORTH, MICHAEL

"The Day of Doom"

> RICHARD CROWDER. "'The Day of Doom' as Chronomorph," *Journal of Popular Culture* 9(4), Spring 1976, 948-59.

"I Walk'd and Did a Little Mole-Hill View"

> ROBERT DALY. *God's Altar*, pp. 134-36.

"Vanity of Vanities: A Song of Emptiness"

> ROBERT DALY. *God's Altar*, pp. 133-34.

WILBUR, RICHARD

"Advice to a Prophet"

> MARY S. MATTFIELD. "Some Poems of Richard Wilbur," *Ball State University Forum* 11(3), Summer 1970, 17-18.
> RALPH J. MILLS, JR. *Contemporary American Poetry*, pp. 174-75.
> JOHN P. FARRELL. "The Beautiful Changes in Richard Wilbur's Poetry," *Contemporary Literature* 12(1), Winter 1971, 77-79.
> JOSEPH SITTLER. "The care of the earth and the future of man," *Colorado Quarterly* 14(3), Winter 1966, 199-202.

"After the Last Bulletins"

> GERARD REEDY. "The Senses of Richard Wilbur," *Renascence* 21(3), Spring 1969, 147-48.

"Altitudes"

> ARTHUR E. McGUINNESS. "A Question of Consciousness: Richard Wilbur's *Things of This World*," *Arizona Quarterly* 23(4), Winter 1967, 314-15.

"The Aspen and the Stream"

> JOHN P. FARRELL. "The Beautiful Changes in Richard Wilbur's Poetry," *Contemporary Literature* 12(1), Winter 1971, 83.

"Attention Makes Infinity"

> HYATT H. WAGGONER. *American Poets*, pp. 599-600.

"Attitudes"

> ALLEN GUTTMANN. "Images of Value and the Sense of the Past," *New England Quarterly* 35(1), March 1962, 24-26.

"Ballade for the Duke of Orleans"

> PAUL CUMMINS. "Richard Wilbur's 'Ballade for the Duke of Orleans,'" *Concerning Poetry* 1(2), Fall 1968, 42-45.

"A Baroque Wall-Fountain in the Villa Sciarra"

> HARRY BROWN and JOHN MILSTEAD. *What the Poem Means*, pp. 279-80.

ARTHUR E. McGUINNESS. "A Question of Consciousness: Richard Wilbur's *Things of This World*," *Arizona Quarterly* 23(4), Winter 1967, 315-16.

LAURENCE PERRINE. *100 American Poems of the Twentieth Century*, pp. 253-57.

"The Beacon"

ARTHUR E. McGUINNESS. "A Question of Consciousness: Richard Wilbur's *Things of This World*," *Arizona Quarterly* 23(4), Winter 1967, 322-24.

"Beasts"

ARTHUR E. McGUINNESS. "A Question of Consciousness: Richard Wilbur's *Things of This World*," *Arizona Quarterly* 23(4), Winter 1967, 324-25.

ALLAN RODWAY. "Richard Wilbur," in *Criticism in Action*, pp. 16-19.

CHARLES R. WOODARD. *Explicator* 36(3), Spring 1978, 6-7.

"The Beautiful Changes"

HYATT H. WAGGONER. *American Poets*, pp. 600-1.

"Beowulf"

BRUCE F. MICHELSON. "Richard Wilbur: The Quarrel with Poe," *Southern Review*, n.s., 14(2), Spring 1978, 258-61.

"Boy at the Window"

JOHN P. FARRELL. "The Beautiful Changes in Richard Wilbur's Poetry," *Contemporary Literature* 12(1), Winter 1971, 86-87.

"Castles and Distances"

THOMAS COLE. "Wilbur's Second Volume," *Poetry* 82(1), April 1953, 38-39.

"Ceremony"

MARY S. MATTFIELD. "Some Poems of Richard Wilbur," *Ball State University Forum* 11(3), Summer 1970, 12.

"The Death of a Toad"

GEORGE ABBE. *You and Contemporary Poetry*, pp. 73-76; second ed., pp. 98-101.

"Digging for China"

GEORGE MONTEIRO. "Redemption Through Nature: A Recurring Theme in Thoreau, Frost and Richard Wilbur," *American Quarterly* 20(4), Winter 1968, 808.

LAURENCE PERRINE. "Dream, Desire, or Dizziness? — Digging in 'Digging for China,'" *Notes on Contemporary Literature* 1(3), May 1971, 13-14.

"Driftwood"

JOHN P. FARRELL. "The Beautiful Changes in Richard Wilbur's Poetry," *Contemporary Literature* 12(1), Winter 1971, 84-85.

"A Dubious Night"

MARY S. MATTFIELD. "Some Poems of Richard Wilbur," *Ball State University Forum* 11(3), Summer 1970, 13.

"A Dutch Courtyard"

CHARLES F. DUFFY. "'Intricate Neural Grace' The Esthetic of Richard Wilbur," *Concerning Poetry* 4(1), Spring 1971, 41-44.

"Epistemology"

R. H. MILLER. *Explicator* 34(5), January 1976, Item 37.

"Epistemology" Epigram 1

GERARD REEDY. "The Senses of Richard Wilbur," *Renascence* 21(3), Spring 1969, 146.

"Epistemology" Epigram 2

GERARD REEDY. "The Senses of Richard Wilbur," *Renascence* 21(3), Spring 1969, 146-47.

"Exeunt"

PHILIP C. KOLIN. "The Subtle Drama of Richard Wilbur's 'Exeunt,'" *Notes on Contemporary Literature* 5(1), January 1975, 11-13.

"Flumen Tenebrarum"

MARY S. MATTFIELD. "Some Poems of Richard Wilbur," *Ball State University Forum* 11(3), Summer 1970, 15.

"For the New Railway Station in Rome"

ARTHUR E. McGUINNESS. "A Question of Consciousness: Richard Wilbur's *Things of This World*," *Arizona Quarterly* 23(4), Winter 1967, 325-26.

LAURENCE PERRINE. *100 American Poems of the Twentieth Century*, pp. 257-59.

"Giacometti"

CHARLES F. DUFFY. "'Intricate Neural Grace': The Esthetic of Richard Wilbur," *Concerning Poetry* 4(1), Spring 1971, 47-49.

"Grasse: The Olive Trees"

THOMAS COLE. "Wilbur's Second Volume," *Poetry* 82(1), April 1953, 37-38.

"The Grasshopper"

FREDERIC E. FAVERTY. "The Poetry of Richard Wilbur," in *Modern American Poetry*, ed. by Guy Owen, pp. 230-31.

FREDERIC E. FAVERTY. "'Well-Open Eyes': or, The Poetry of Richard Wilbur," in *Poets in Progress*, p. 63.

"A Hole in the Floor"

A. K. WEATHERHEAD. "Richard Wilbur: Poetry of Things," *ELH* 35(4), December 1968, 615-16.

CHARLES R. WOODARD. "'Happiest Intellection': The Mind of Richard Wilbur," *Notes on Modern American Literature* 2(1), Winter 1977, Item 7.

"In the Elegy Season"

ALLAN RODWAY. "Richard Wilbur," in *Criticism in Action*, pp. 19-22.

"In the Field"

MARY S. MATTFIELD. "Some Poems of Richard Wilbur," *Ball State University Forum* 11(3), Summer 1970, 23.

HENRY TAYLOR. "Two Worlds Taken As They Come: Richard Wilbur's 'Walking To Sleep,'" *Hollins Critic* 6 (Special Issue), July 1969, 4-6.

"The Juggler"

SISTER MARY HESTER. "'The Juggler' by Richard Wilbur," *English Journal* 54(9), December 1965, 880-81.

"Junk"

RALPH J. MILLS, JR. *Contemporary American Poetry*, pp. 163-66.

GEORGE MONTEIRO. "Redemption Through Nature: A Recurring Theme in Thoreau, Frost, and Richard Wilbur," *American Quarterly* 20(4), Winter 1968, 804-5.

"Looking into History"

JOHN P. FARRELL. "The Beautiful Changes in Richard Wilbur's Poetry," *Contemporary Literature* 12(1), Winter 1971, 79-83.

WILBUR, RICHARD *(Cont.)*

"Love Calls Us to the Things of This World"

RICHARD EBERHART, ROBERT HORAN, MAY SWENSEN and RICHARD WILBUR. "On Richard Wilbur's 'Love Calls Us to the Things of This World,'" in *The Contemporary Poet as Artist and Critic*, pp. 2-21.

ARTHUR E. McGUINNESS. "A Question of Consciousness: Richard Wilbur's *Things of This World*," *Arizona Quarterly* 23(4), Winter 1967, 319-20.

GERARD REEDY. "The Senses of Richard Wilbur," *Renascence* 21(3), Spring 1969, 145-46.

A. K. WEATHERHEAD. "Richard Wilbur: Poetry of Things," *ELH* 35(4), December 1968, 616-17.

"Marginalia"

ARTHUR E. McGUINNESS. "A Question of Consciousness: Richard Wilbur's *Things of This World*," *Arizona Quarterly* 23(4), Winter 1967, 323.

"Merlin Enthralled"

JOHN P. FARRELL. "The Beautiful Changes in Richard Wilbur's Poetry," *Contemporary Literature* 12(1), Winter 1971, 79.

RONALD B. HERZMAN. "A Yeatsian Parallel in Richard Wilbur's 'Merlin Enthralled,'" *Notes on Contemporary Literature* 2(5), November 1972, 10-11.

ARTHUR E. McGUINNESS. "A Question of Consciousness: Richard Wilbur's *Things of This World*," *Arizona Quarterly* 23(4), Winter 1967, 321-22.

BRUCE F. MICHELSON. "Richard Wilbur: The Quarrel with Poe," *Southern Review*, n.s., 14(2), Spring 1978, 256-57.

"The Mill"

LAURENCE PERRINE. *100 American Poems of the Twentieth Century*, pp. 259-61.

"A Miltonic Sonnet for Mr. Johnson on His Refusal of Peter Hurd's Official Portrait"

JOSEPH SUMMERS. "Milton and Celebration," *Milton Quarterly* 5(1), March 1971, 7.

"Mind"

JEROME BEATY and WILLIAM H. MATCHETT. *Poetry From Statement to Meaning*, pp. 208-9, 239-40.

CHARLES R. WOODARD. "'Happiest Intellection': The Mind of Richard Wilbur," *Notes on Modern American Literature* 2(1), Winter 1977, Item 7.

"Mined Country"

VERNON SCANNELL. *Not Without Glory*, pp. 229-30.

"Objects"

CHARLES F. DUFFY. "'Intricate Neural Grace': The Esthetic of Richard Wilbur," *Concerning Poetry* 4(1), Spring 1971, 41-44.

"October Maples, Portland"

HYATT H. WAGGONER. *American Poets*, p. 604.

"On the Marginal Way"

MARY S. MATTFIELD. "Some Poems of Richard Wilbur," *Ball State University Forum* 11(3), Summer 1970, 22-23.

"A Plain Song for Camadre"

ARTHUR E. McGUINNESS. "A Question of Consciousness: Richard Wilbur's *Things of This World*," *Arizona Quarterly* 23(4), Winter 1967, 320-21.

"Poplar, Sycamore"

RALPH J. MILLS, JR. *Contemporary American Poetry*, pp. 161-62.

"The Puritans"

MARY S. MATTFIELD. *Explicator* 28(6), February 1970, Item 53.

MARY S. MATTFIELD. "Some Poems of Richard Wilbur," *Ball State University Forum* 11(3), Summer 1970, 14.

"Running"

HENRY TAYLOR. "Two Worlds Taken As They Come: Richard Wilbur's 'Walking To Sleep,'" *Hollins Critic* 6 (Special Issue), July 1969, 10.

"Sonnet"

ARTHUR E. McGUINNESS. "A Question of Consciousness: Richard Wilbur's *Things of This World*," *Arizona Quarterly* 23(4), Winter 1967, 322.

"Speech for the Repeal of the McCarran Act"

JOHN P. FARRELL. "The Beautiful Changes in Richard Wilbur's Poetry," *Contemporary Literature* 12(1), Winter 1971, 77-78.

"Statues"

JOHN P. FARRELL. "The Beautiful Changes in Richard Wilbur's Poetry," *Contemporary Literature* 12(1), Winter 1971, 85-86.

ARTHUR E. McGUINNESS. "A Question of Consciousness: Richard Wilbur's *Things of This World*," *Arizona Quarterly* 23(4), Winter 1967, 316-17.

"Still, Citizen Sparrow"

JOHN CIARDI. *How Does a Poem Mean?*, second ed., p. 149.

CHARLES R. WOODARD. *Explicator* 34(6), February 1976, Item 46.

"Stop"

RALPH J. MILLS, JR. *Contemporary American Poetry*, pp. 162-63.

"The Terrace"

MARY S. MATTFIELD. "Some Poems of Richard Wilbur," *Ball State University Forum* 11(3), Summer 1970, 15.

"To an American Poet Just Dead"

JOHN A. MYERS, JR. "Death in the Suburbs," *English Journal* 52(5), May 1963, 377-79.

"Two Voices in a Meadow"

GÉMINO H. ABAD. *A Formal Approach to Lyric Poetry*, pp. 302-4.

"Two Voices in a Meadow: A Milkweed"

ROSETTE C. LAMONT. "Joseph Brodsky: A Poet's Classroom," *Massachusetts Review* 15(4), Autumn 1974, 561-62.

"Tywater"

MARY S. MATTFIELD. "Some Poems of Richard Wilbur," *Ball State University Forum* 11(3), Summer 1970, 12.

"The Undead"

BRUCE F. MICHELSON. "Richard Wilbur: The Quarrel with Poe," *Southern Review*, n.s., 14(2), Spring 1978, 255-56.

"A Voice From Under the Table"

ARTHUR E. McGUINNESS. "A Question of Consciousness: Richard Wilbur's *Things of This World*," *Arizona Quarterly* 23(4), Winter 1967, 317-18.

"Walking to Sleep"

DANIEL HUGHES. "American Poetry 1969: From B to Z," *Massachusetts Review* 11(4), Autumn 1970, 655-56.

MARY S. MATTFIELD. "Some Poems of Richard Wilbur," *Ball State University Forum* 11(3), Summer 1970, 23-24.

HENRY TAYLOR. "Two Worlds Taken As They Come: Richard Wilbur's 'Walking To Sleep,'" *Hollins Critic* 6 (Special Issue), July 1969, 10-11.

"Water Walker"

GLAUCO CAMBON. *Recent American Poetry*, pp. 11-12.

MARY S. MATTFIELD. "Some Poems of Richard Wilbur," *Ball State University Forum* 11(3), Summer 1970, 14.

"A World Without Objects Is a Sensible Emptiness"

RAYMOND BENOIT. *Single Nature's Double Name*, pp. 127-29.

HARRY BROWN and JOHN MILSTEAD. *What the Poem Means*, p. 280.

MARY S. MATTFIELD. "Some Poems of Richard Wilbur," *Ball State University Forum* 11(3), Summer 1970, 15-16.

RALPH J. MILLS, JR. *Contemporary American Poetry*, pp. 166-68.

GERARD REEDY. "The Senses of Richard Wilbur," *Renascence* 21(3), Spring 1969, 146.

"The Writer"

LOUIS UNTERMEYER. *50 Modern American & British Poets*, p. 310.

"Year's End"

WALTON BEACHAM. *The Meaning of Poetry*, pp. 10-17, 55-57.

GLAUCO CAMBON. *Recent American Poetry*, pp. 14-15.

JOHN W. METZGER. "Imagery in 'Year's End' by Richard Wilbur," in Walton Beacham, *The Meaning of Poetry*, pp. 58-59.

GERARD REEDY. "The Senses of Richard Wilbur," *Renascence* 21(3), Spring 1969, 148-49.

WILCOX, ELLA WHEELER

"Friendship after Love"

MALCOLM PITTOCK. "In Defence of Ella Wheeler Wilcox," *Durham University Journal*, n.s., 34(1), December 1972, 86-89.

WILD, ROBERT

"An Epitaph for a Godly Man's Tomb"

GUSTAV GROSS and R. P. DRAPER. *Explicator* 15(8), May 1957, Item 50.

WILLIAM BYSSHE STEIN. *Explicator* 17(3), December 1958, Item 23.

"A Poem upon the Imprisonment of Mr. Calamy in Newgate"

P. J. C. FIELD. "Authoritative Echo in Dryden," *Durham University Journal*, n.s., 31(3), June 1970, 140-41.

WILDE, OSCAR

"The Ballad of Reading Gaol"

GEORGE ARMS and J. P. KIRBY. *Explicator* 1(5), March 1943, Item 41.

"Helas!"

RICHARD ELLMANN. "The Critic as Artist as Wilde," in *The Poet as Critic*, pp. 48-50.

"Requiescat"

DAVID RIDGLEY CLARK. *Lyric Resonance*, pp. 57-65.

WILLARD, NANCY

"In Praise of ABC"

FRANCINE DAVIS. "Nancy Willard's Domestic Psalms," *Modern Poetry Studies* 9(2), Autumn 1978, 127-29.

"The Poet Tracks Down the Moon"

DIANNE F. SADOFF. "Mythopoeia, The Moon, and Contemporary Women's Poetry," *Massachusetts Review* 19(1), Spring 1978, 103.

"Skin of Grace"

FRANCINE DAVIS. "Nancy Willard's Domestic Psalms," *Modern Poetry Studies* 9(2), Autumn 1978, 132.

WILLIAM OF SHOREHAM

"Marye, mayde mylde and fre"

STEPHEN MANNING. *Wisdom and Number*, pp. 65-72.

WILLIAMS, OSCAR

"The Leg in the Subway"

ROBERT RUSSELL. *Explicator* 19(3), December 1960, Item 18.

"The Praying Mantis Visits a Penthouse"

CHARLES W. COOPER and JOHN HOLMES. *Preface to Poetry*, pp. 163-65.

WILLIAMS, WILLIAM CARLOS

"Adam"

NORMA PROCOPIOW. "William Carlos Williams and the Origins of the Confessional Poem," *Ariel* 7(2), April 1976, 67-70.

"Address"

PAUL MARIANI. "Tomlinson's Use of the Williams Triad," *Contemporary Literature* 18(3), Summer 1977, 409-11.

"The Agonized Spires"

NEIL MYERS. "William Carlos Williams' *Spring And All*," *Modern Language Quarterly* 26(2), June 1965, 295-96.

"Arrival"

WALTON BEACHAM. *The Meaning of Poetry*, pp. 44-46.

"Asphodel, That Greeny Flower"

PAUL L. MARIANI. "The Satyr's Defense: Williams' 'Asphodel,'" *Contemporary Literature* 14(1), Winter 1973, 1-18.

J. HILLIS MILLER. *Poets of Reality*, pp. 356-58.

ROY HARVEY PEARCE. *The Continuity of American Poetry*, p. 346.

LINDA WILSHIMER WAGNER. "The Last Poems of William Carlos Williams," *Criticism* 6(4), Fall 1964, 362-65.

CHAD and EVA T. WALSH. *Twice Ten*, p. 203.

"The Attic Which Is Desire"

WILLIS D. JACOBS. *Explicator* 25(7), March 1967, Item 61.

"Between Walls"

WILLIS D. JACOBS. *Explicator* 28(8), April 1970, Item 68.

J. HILLIS MILLER. *Poets of Reality*, pp. 345-47.

ALFRED F. ROSA. *Explicator* 30(3), November 1971, Item 21.

JOHN L. SIMONS. "The Lying Cinders: Patterns of Linguistic Unity in W. C. Williams' 'Between Walls,'" *Concerning Poetry* 10(1), Spring 1977, 63-70.

WILLIAMS, WILLIAM CARLOS *(Cont.)*

"Between Walls" *(cont.)*

ROBERT VON HALLBERG. "The Politics of Description: W. C. Williams in the 'Thirties,' " *ELH* 45(1), Spring 1978, 137-38.

"Birdsong"

CHAD and EVA T. WALSH. *Twice Ten,* pp. 197-98.

"The Black Winds"

L. S. DEMBO. *Conceptions of Reality in Modern American Poetry,* pp. 52-53.

"The Botticellian Trees"

ANTHONY LIBBY. " 'Claritas': William Carlos Williams' Epiphanies," *Criticism* 14(1), Winter 1972, 29-31.

WALTER SUTTON. *American Free Verse,* pp. 126-28.

"Burning the Christmas Greens"

JAMES K. GUIMOND. "William Carlos Williams and the Past: Some Clarifications," *Journal of Modern Literature* 1(4), May 1971, 496-98.

ROY HARVEY PEARCE. *The Continuity of American Poetry,* pp. 342-43.

CHAD and EVA T. WALSH. *Twice Ten,* pp. 199-202.

"By the Road to the Contagious Hospital"

CHARLES V. HARTUNG. "A Poetry of Experience," *University of Kansas City Review* 25(1), Autumn 1958, 67-68.

ROY HARVEY PEARCE. *The Continuity of American Poetry,* pp. 340-41.

HYATT H. WAGGONER. *American Poets,* p. 381.

YVOR WINTERS. *Primitivism and Decadence,* pp. 67-70. Reprinted in: Yvor Winters. *In Defense of Reason,* pp. 78-82.

"Catastrophic Birth"

JAMES K. GUIMOND. "William Carlos Williams and the Past: Some Clarifications," *Journal of Modern Literature* 1(4), May 1971, 496.

"Choral: The Pink Church"

MICHAEL PAYNE. "William C. Williams Without Livery," *University Review* 32(2), Winter 1965, 158-60.

ROY HARVEY PEARCE. *The Continuity of American Poetry,* pp. 342-43.

WALTER SUTTON. *American Free Verse,* pp. 147-49.

"Classic Scene"

GÉMINO H. ABAD. *A Formal Approach to Lyric Poetry,* pp. 271-72.

"The Clouds"

WALTER SUTTON. *American Free Verse,* pp. 149-50.

"The Cold Night"

CHARLES V. HARTUNG. "The Poetry of Experience," *University of Kansas City Review* 25(1), Autumn 1958, 66-67.

"Complete Destruction"

CHAD and EVA T. WALSH. *Twice Ten,* pp. 198-99.

"A Coronal"

WILLIS D. JACOBS. *Explicator* 29(8), April 1971, Item 64.

JEROME MAZZARO. "Dimensionality in Dr. Williams' 'Paterson,' " *Modern Poetry Studies* 1(3), 1970, 105-6.

"The Crimson Cyclamen"

NANCY WILLARD. *Testimony of the Invisible Man,* pp. 27-31.

"The Death of See"

JOSEPH EVANS SLATE. "From the Front Page: A Note on Williams' 'The Death of See,' " *William Carlos Williams Newsletter* 3(1), Spring 1977, 16-18.

"Death the Barber"

NEIL MYERS. "William Carlos Williams' *Spring And All,*" *Modern Language Quarterly* 26(2), June 1965, 291.

"The Descent"

NEIL MYERS. "Decreation in Williams' 'The Descent,' " *Criticism* 14(4), Fall 1972, 315-27.

"The Desert Music"

L. S. DEMBO. *Conceptions of Reality in Modern American Poetry,* pp. 56-57.

L. S. DEMBO. "Williams' Imitation of Nature in 'The Desert Music,' " *Criticism* 12(1), Winter 1970, 38-50.

A KINGSLEY WEATHERHEAD. "William Carlos Williams: Poetic Invention and the World Beyond," *ELH* 32(1), March 1962, 126-38.

"An Early Martyr"

ROBERT VON HALLBERG. "The Politics of Description: W. C. Williams in the 'Thirties,' " *ELH* 45(1), Spring 1978, 132-34.

"Elaine"

LINDA WELSHIMER WAGNER. "The Last Poems of William Carlos Williams," *Criticism* 6(4), Fall 1964, 368-70.

"Eve"

NORMA PROCOPIOW. "William Carlos Williams and the Origins of the Confessional Poem," *Ariel* 7(2), April 1976, 70-72.

"Fine Work with Pitch and Copper"

HYATT H. WAGGONER. *American Poets,* p. 381.

"La Flor"

GEOFFREY H. MOVIUS. "Caviar and Bread: Ezra Pound and William Carlos Williams, 1902-1914," *Journal of Modern Literature* 5(3), September 1976, 401-2.

"Flowers by the Sea"

M. L. ROSENTHAL and A. J. M. SMITH. *Exploring Poetry,* pp. 51-53; second ed., pp. 70-72.

A. J. M. SMITH. "Refining Fire: The Meaning and Use of Poetry," *Queens Quarterly* 61(3), Autumn 1954, 355-56.

ROBERT VON HALLBERG. "The Politics of Description: W. C. Williams in the 'Thirties,' " *ELH* 45(1), Spring 1978, 134-36.

"The Gift"

JAMES M. REID. *100 American Poems of the Twentieth Century,* pp. 76-79.

"The Great Figure"

JAMES E. BRESLIN. "William Carlos Williams and Charles Demuth: Cross-Fertilization in the Arts," *Journal of Modern Literature* 6(2), April 1977, 258-61.

JOHN MALCOLM BRINNIN. "William Carlos Williams," in *Seven Modern American Poets,* p. 103.

"Great Mullen"

WILLIS D. JACOBS. *Explicator* 28(7), March 1970, Item 63.

"History"

JEROME MAZZARO. "Dimensionality in Dr. Williams' 'Paterson,' " *Modern Poetry Studies* 1(3), 1970, 105-6.

"El Hombre"

M. L. ROSENTHAL. *The Modern Poets*, p. 121.

"The Horse Show"

JAMES M. REID. *100 American Poems of the Twentieth Century*, pp. 79-81.

"The Hunter"

WILLIS D. JACOBS. *Explicator* 29(7), March 1971, Item 60.

"Late for Summer Weather"

ROBERT VON HALLBERG. "The Politics of Description: W. C. Williams in the 'Thirties,' " *ELH* 45(1), Spring 1978, 145.

"The Lesson"

CARY NELSON. "Suffused-Encircling Shapes of Mind: Inhabited Space in Williams," *Journal of Modern Literature* 1(4), May 1971, 551-52.

"The Locust Tree in Flower"

LINUS L. PHILLIPS and MRS. WILLIAM W. DEATON. *Explicator* 26(3), November 1967, Item 26.

"Love Song"

M. L. ROSENTHAL. *Poetry and the Common Life*, pp. 73-76.

"The Mental Hospital Garden"

A. KINGSLEY WEATHERHEAD. "William Carlos Williams: Prose, Form, and Measure," *ELH* 33(1), March 1966, 126.

"The Mind Hesitant"

NANCY WILLARD. *Testimony of the Invisible Man*, pp. 36-38.

"A Morning Imagination of Russia"

J. HILLIS MILLER. *Poets of Reality*, pp. 327-28.

"Nantucket"

GÉMINO H. ABAD. *A Formal Approach to Lyric Poetry*, p. 271.

CHARLES V. HARTUNG. "A Poetry of Experience," *University of Kansas City Review* 25(1), Autumn 1958, 67.

"The Orchestra"

LINDA WELSHIMER WAGNER. "The Last Poems of William Carlos Williams," *Criticism* 6(4), Fall 1964, 365-67.

"Pastoral"

ROY HARVEY PEARCE. *The Continuity of American Poetry*, pp. 337-39.

"Philomena Andronico"

KARL SHAPIRO. "The Meaning of the Discarded Poem," in *Poets at Work*, pp. 105-11.

"Pictures from Brueghel"

JOEL CONARROE. "The Measured Dance: Williams' 'Pictures from Brueghel,' " *Journal of Modern Literature* 1(4), May 1971, 565-77.

JEROME MAZZARO. "The Descent Once More: 'Paterson V' and 'Pictures from Brueghel,' " *Modern Poetry Studies* 1(6), 1970, 287-97.

"A Poem for Norman McLeod"

ROBERT VON HALLBERG. "The Politics of Description: W. C. Williams in the 'Thirties,' " *ELH* 45(1), Spring 1978, 146-47.

"Portrait of a Lady"

MORDECAI MARCUS. "Dialogue and Allusion in William Carlos Williams' 'Portrait of a Lady,' " *Concerning Poetry* 10(2), Fall 1977, 71-72.

HYATT H. WAGGONER. *American Poets*, p. 419.

"Portrait of a Woman in Bed"

NEIL MYERS. "Sentimentalism in the Early Poetry of William Carlos Williams," *American Literature* 37(4), January 1966, 465.

"Portrait of a Woman at Her Bath"

LINDA WELSHIMER WAGNER. "The Last Poems of William Carlos Williams," *Criticism* 6(4), Fall 1964, 372-73.

"The Pot of Flowers"

JAMES E. BRESLIN. "William Carlos Williams and Charles Demuth: Cross-Fertilization in the Arts," *Journal of Modern Literature* 6(2), April 1977, 254-58.

"Proletarian Portrait"

ROBERT VON HALLBERG. "The Politics of Description: W. C. Williams in the 'Thirties,' " *ELH* 45(1), Spring 1978, 137.

"Promenade"

CHAD and EVA T. WALSH. *Twice Ten*, pp. 196-97. (P)

"Queen-Ann's Lace"

WILLIAM VAN O'CONNOR. *Sense and Sensibility in Modern Poetry*, pp. 119-20.

WILLIAM VAN O'CONNOR. "Symbolism and the Study of Poetry," *College English* 7(7), April 1946, 378-79.

"Raleigh Was Right"

DEL IVAN JANIK. "Poetry in the Ecosphere," *Centennial Review* 20(4), Fall 1976, 398-99.

"The Raper from Passenack"

J. E. SLATE. "William Carlos Williams and the Modern Short Story," *Southern Review*, n.s., 4(3), Summer 1968, 655-56.

"The Red Wheelbarrow"

STANLEY ARCHER. "*Glazed* in Williams' 'The Red Wheelbarrow,' " *Concerning Poetry* 9(2), Fall 1976, 27.

JEROME BEATY and WILLIAM L. MATCHETT. *Poetry From Statement to Meaning*, pp. 181-82.

JOHN MALCOLM BRINNIN. "William Carlos Williams," in *Seven Modern American Poets*, pp. 99-100.

CLEANTH BROOKS, JOHN THIBAUT PURSER, and ROBERT PENN WARREN. *An Approach to Literature*, fifth ed., pp. 364-65.

ROBERT KERN. "Williams, Brautigan, and the Poetics of Primitivism," *Chicago Review* 27(1), Summer 1975, 51-52.

WINIFRED NOWOTTNY. *The Language Poets Use*, pp. 119-20.

ROY HARVEY PEARCE. *The Continuity of American Poetry*, p. 339.

M. L. ROSENTHAL. *The Modern Poets*, pp. 113-14.

AGNES STEIN. *The Uses of Poetry*, pp. 222-24.

WALTER SUTTON. *American Free Verse*, pp. 120-21.

HYATT H. WAGGONER. *American Poets*, pp. 342-43.

"The Right of Way"

NEIL MYERS. "William Carlos Williams' *Spring And All*," *Modern Language Quarterly* 26(2), June 1965, 293-94.

WILLIAMS, WILLIAM CARLOS *(Cont.)*

"The Rose"

ROB FURE. "The Design of Experience: William Carlos Williams and Juan Gris," *William Carlos Williams Newsletter* 4(2), Fall 1978, 11-14.

NEIL MYERS. "William Carlos Williams' *Spring And All*," *Modern Language Quarterly* 26(2), June 1965, 297-99.

"St. Francis Einstein of the Daffodils"

JOHN MALCOLM BRINNIN. "William Carlos Williams," in *Seven Modern American Poets*, pp. 95-98.

CAROL C. DONLEY. " 'A little touch of/Einstein in the night — ': Williams' Early Exposure to the Theories of Relativity," *William Carlos Williams Newsletter* 4(1), Spring 1978, 10-13.

"Struggle of Wings"

LAURA RIDING and ROBERT GRAVES. *A Survey of Modernist Poetry*, pp. 201-4.

"Sunday in the Park"

JEFFREY YOUDELMAN. "Pictures for a Sunday Afternoon: The Camera Eye in *Paterson*," *Concerning Poetry* 2(2), Fall 1969, 37-42.

"The Term"

WILLIS D. JACOBS. *Explicator* 25(9), May 1967, Item 73.

ROBERT PINSKY. *The Situation of Poetry*, pp. 62-65.

"This Florida"

JACK HARDIE. "Hibiscus and the Spaniard of the Rose: Williams' Dialogue with Wallace Stevens," *William Carlos Williams Newsletter* 4(2), Fall 1978, 20-24.

"This is Just to Say"

JONATHAN CULLER. "Structuralism and Literature," in *Contemporary Approaches to English Studies*, pp. 69-72.

"To a Dog Injured in the Street"

GEORGE ABBE. *You and Contemporary Poetry*, pp. 35-38; second ed., pp. 48-53.

"To a Poor Old Woman"

WILLIS D. JACOBS. "Williams' 'To a Poor Old Woman,' " *Concerning Poetry* 1(2), Fall 1968, 16.

ROBERT VON HALLBERG. "The Politics of Description: W. C. Williams in the 'Thirties,' " *ELH* 45(1), Spring 1978, 144.

"To a Solitary Disciple"

RICHARD J. CALHOUN. " 'No Ideas but in Things': William Carlos Williams in the Twenties," in *The Twenties*, edited by Richard E. Langford and William E. Taylor, pp. 31-32.

ROB FURE. "The Design of Experience: William Carlos Williams and Juan Gris," *William Carlos Williams Newsletter* 4(2), Fall 1978, 10-11.

SUZY B. MICHEL. "The Identity of William Carlos Williams's 'Solitary Disciple,' " *Modern Language Review* 73(4), October 1978, 741-47.

J. HILLIS MILLER. *Poets of Reality*, pp. 320-21.

"To a Wood Thrush"

DEL IVAN JANIK. "Poetry in the Ecosphere," *Centennial Review* 20(4), Fall 1976, 397-98.

"To an Old Jaundiced Woman"

NANCY WILLARD. *Testimony of the Invisible Man*, p. 23.

"To Be Recited to Flossie on Her Birthday"

SEAMUS COONEY. *Explicator* 32(3), November 1973, Item 24.

"To Elsie"

HENRY M. SAYRE. "William Carlos Williams and Robert McAlmon: Two Versions of '*Elsie*,' " *Notes on Modern American Literature* 1(2), Spring 1977, Item 8.

WALTER SUTTON. *American Free Verse*, pp. 130-31.

"To Have Done Nothing"

NEIL MYERS. "William Carlos Williams' *Spring And All*," *Modern Language Quarterly* 26(2), June 1965, 291-93.

"To make a start"

JOEL O. CONARROE. "The 'Preface' to Paterson," *Contemporary Literature* 10(1), Winter 1969, 39-53.

"To Mark Anthony In Heaven"

JOHN G. HAMMOND. *Explicator* 36(4), Summer 1978, 26-29.

"To Waken an Old Lady"

BABETTE DEUTSCH. *Poetry in Our Time*, p. 101; second ed., pp. 109-10.

NAT HENRY. *Explicator* 30(9), May 1972, Item 80.

WILLIS D. JACOBS. *Explicator* 29(1), September 1970, Item 6.

NEIL MYERS. "Sentimentalism in the Early Poetry of William Carlos Williams," *American Literature* 37(4), January 1966, 462-63.

"Tract"

HARRY BROWN and JOHN MILSTEAD. *What the Poem Means*, p. 282.

WALTER GIERASCH. *Explicator* 3(5), March 1945, Item 35.

EUGENE McNAMARA. "The Rhetoric of 'Tract,' " *CEA Critic* 28(9), June 1966, 9-10.

WALTER SUTTON. *American Free Verse*, pp. 122-23.

"The Trees"

WALTER SUTTON. *American Free Verse*, pp. 125-26.

"Two Pendants: for the Ears"

NEIL MYERS. "Williams' 'Two Pendants: for the Ears,' " *Journal of Modern Literature* 1(4), May 1971, 477-92.

"Two Pendants: for the Ears, II; Elena"

NANCY WILLARD. *Testimony of the Invisible Man*, pp. 32-36.

"A Unison"

HYATT H. WAGGONER. *American Poets*, pp. 382-83.

"View of a Lake"

ROBERT VON HALLBERG. "The Politics of Description: W. C. Williams in the 'Thirties,' " *ELH* 45(1), Spring 1978, 138-40.

"The Wanderer"

JESSE D. GREEN. "Whitman's Voice in 'The Wanderer,' " *William Carlos Williams Newsletter* 3(2), Fall 1977, 17-22.

JOHN UNTERECKER. "The Architecture of *The Bridge*," *Wisconsin Studies in Contemporary Literature* 3(2), Spring-Summer 1962, 9-10.

"The Well Disciplined Bargeman"

JACK HARDIE. *Explicator* 33(3), November 1974, Item 20.

"The Widow's Lament in Springtime"

LINDA WELSHIMER WAGNER. "Metaphor and William Carlos Williams," *University Review* 31(1), Autumn 1964, 46.

NANCY WILLARD. *Testimony of the Invisible Man*, pp. 24-25.

"Without Invention Nothing is Well Spaced"

JOEL A. CONARROE. *Explicator* 27(4), December 1968, Item 26.

"The World Contracted to a Recognizable Image"

WILLIAM V. DAVIS. *Explicator* 32(2), October 1973, Item 13.

MYRTLE P. POPE. *Explicator* 33(6), February 1975, Item 50.

EDMOND SCHRAEPEN. *Explicator* 35(1), Fall 1976, 6-7.

"The Yachts"

EMILY K. DALGARNO. "De Quincey and Williams' 'The Yachts,' " *American Notes & Queries*, n.s., 14(8), April 1976, 119-21.

BABETTE DEUTSCH. *Poetry in Our Time*, pp. 102-4; second ed., pp. 111-13.

JAMES DICKEY. *Babel to Byzantium*, pp. 244-46.

JAMES DICKEY. "The Symbolism in Williams' 'The Yachts,' " in *Ways to Poetry*, pp. 359-60.

JAMES DICKEY. "Williams: The Yachts," in *Master Poems of the English Language*, pp. 901-2.

RICHARD S. DONNELL. *Explicator* 17(8), May 1959, Item 52.

JAMES M. REID. *100 American Poems of the Twentieth Century*, pp. 73-76.

WALTER SUTTON. *American Free Verse*, pp. 123-24.

LEONARD UNGER and WILLIAM VAN O'CONNOR. *Poems for Study*, pp. 9-10.

ROBERT VON HALLBERG. "The Politics of Description: W. C. Williams in the 'Thirties,' " *ELH* 45(1), Spring 1978, 141-43.

"The Yellow Chimney"

MARSHALL W. STEARNS. "Syntax, Sense, Sound, and Dr. Williams," *Poetry* 66(1), April 1945, 38-39.

"The Young Housewife"

WILLIS D. JACOBS. *Explicator* 28(9), May 1970, Item 81.

"Young Sycamore"

WALTER SUTTON. *American Free Verse*, pp. 124-25.

WILMOT, JOHN

see ROCHESTER, JOHN WILMOT, EARL OF

WINCHILSEA, LADY ANNE

"An Invocation to Sleep"

REUBEN A. BROWER. "Lady Winchilsea and the Poetic Tradition of the Seventeenth Century," *Studies in Philology* 42(1), January 1945, 64-65.

"On Affliction"

REUBEN A. BROWER. "Lady Winchilsea and the Poetic Tradition of the Seventeenth Century," *Studies in Philology* 42(1), January 1945, 65-66.

WINTERS, YVOR

"Alcmena"

GROSVENOR E. POWELL. "Yvor Winters' Greek Allegories," *Southern Review*, n.s., 14(2), Spring 1978, 269-71.

"Before Disaster"

JOHN CIARDI. *How Does a Poem Mean?* p. 1007; second ed., p. 371.

"Chiron"

GROSVENOR E. POWELL. "Yvor Winters' Greek Allegories," *Southern Review*, n.s., 14(2), Spring 1978, 264-65.

"Heracles"

GROSVENOR E. POWELL. "Yvor Winters' Greek Allegories," *Southern Review*, n.s., 14(2), Spring 1978, 266-69.

ALAN STEPHENS. "The *Collected Poems* of Yvor Winters," *Twentieth Century Literature* 9(3), October 1963, 133-34.

"The Invaders"

DONALD F. DRUMMOND. "Yvor Winters: Reason and Moral Judgment," *Arizona Quarterly* 5(1), Spring 1949, 15-16.

ALAN STEPHENS. "The *Collected Poems* of Yvor Winters," *Twentieth Century Literature* 9(3), October 1963, 129-30.

"John Sutter"

ALAN STEPHENS. "The *Collected Poems* of Yvor Winters," *Twentieth Century Literature* 9(3), October 1963, 134-35.

"Midas"

HOWARD KAYE. "The Post-Symbolist Poetry of Yvor Winters," *Southern Review*, n.s., 7(1), Winter 1970, 191-93.

"The Moralists"

ALAN STEPHENS. "The *Collected Poems* of Yvor Winters," *Twentieth Century Literature* 9(3), October 1963, 129.

"The Old Age of Theseus"

DONALD F. DRUMMOND. "Yvor Winters: Reason and Moral Judgment," *Arizona Quarterly* 5(1), Spring 1949, 11-14.

"On the Death of Senator Thomas J. Walsh"

GABRIEL PEARSON. "Yvor Winters," in *The Modern Poet*, edited by Ian Hamilton, pp. 64-66.

"Orpheus"

HOWARD KAYE. "The Post-Symbolist Poetry of Yvor Winters," *Southern Review*, n.s., 7(1), Winter 1970, 188-89. (P)

"Quod Tegit Omnia"

ALAN STEPHENS. "The *Collected Poems* of Yvor Winters," *Twentieth Century Literature* 9(3), October 1963, 128-29.

"The Rows of Cold Trees"

ALAN STEPHENS. "The *Collected Poems* of Yvor Winters," *Twentieth Century Literature* 9(3), October 1963, 129.

"Sir Gawaine and the Greene Knight"

PAUL RAMSEY. "Yvor Winters: Some Abstractions Against Abstraction," *Sewanee Review* 73(3), Summer 1965, 458-59.

ALAN STEPHENS. "The *Collected Poems* of Yvor Winters," *Twentieth Century Literature* 9(3), October 1963, 135.

"The Slow Pacific Swell"

HOWARD KAYE. "The Post-Symbolist Poetry of Yvor Winters," *Southern Review*, n.s., 7(1), Winter 1970, 185-88.

ALAN STEPHENS. "The *Collected Poems* of Yvor Winters," *Twentieth Century Literature* 9(3), October 1963, 132.

WINTERS, YVOR *(Cont.)*

"The Slow Pacific Swell" *(cont.)*

YVOR WINTERS. "By Way of Clarification," *Twentieth Century Literature* 10(3), October 1964, 132.

"A Spring Serpent"

HOWARD KAYE. "The Post-Symbolist Poetry of Yvor Winters," *Southern Review*, n.s., 7(1), Winter 1970, 182-85.

ALAN STEPHENS. "The *Collected Poems* of Yvor Winters," *Twentieth Century Literature* 9(3), October 1963, 137-38.

YVOR WINTERS. "By Way of Clarification," *Twentieth Century Literature* 10(3), October 1964, 132-34.

"The Streets"

GROSVENOR E. POWELL. "Mythical and Smoky Soils: Imagism and the Aboriginal in the Early Poetry of Yvor Winters," *Southern Review*, n.s., 11(2), Spring 1975, 308-9.

"A Summer Commentary"

HOWARD KAYE. "The Post-Symbolist Poetry of Yvor Winters," *Southern Review*, n.s., 7(1), Winter 1970, 189-91.

PAUL RAMSEY. "Yvor Winters: Some Abstractions Against Abstraction," *Sewanee Review* 73(3), Summer 1965, 459-60.

ALAN SWALLOW. *Explicator* 9(5), March 1951, Item 35.

"A View of Pasadena From The Hills"

GABRIEL PEARSON. "Yvor Winters," in *The Modern Poet*, edited by Ian Hamilton, p. 68.

WITHER, GEORGE

"The Protector"

CHARLES S. HENSLEY. "Wither, Waller and Marvell: Panegyrists for the Protector," *Ariel* 3(1), January 1972, 7-8.

"A Suddain Flash"

CHARLES S. HENSLEY. "Wither, Waller and Marvell: Panegyrists for the Protector," *Ariel* 3(1), January 1972, 10-11.

WORDSWORTH, WILLIAM

"The Affliction of Margaret — "

EDWIN MUIR. *The Estate of Poetry*, pp. 31-33.

"After-Thought"

GEOFFREY H. HARTMAN. "The Romance of Nature and the Negative Way," in *Romanticism and Consciousness*, pp. 302-3.

STEWART C. WILCOX. "Wordsworth's River Duddon Sonnets," *PMLA* 69(1), March 1954, 139-41.

"Anecdote for Fathers"

JONATHAN RAMSEY. "Wordsworth and the Childhood of Language," *Criticism* 18(3), Summer 1976, 244-49.

GAYLE S. SMITH. "Wordsworth's Socratic Irony," *Personalist* 44(1), Winter 1963, 53-54.

JUNE STURROCK. "Heaven Lies," *Essays in Criticism* 28(1), January 1978, 92.

SUSAN J. WOLFSON. "The Speaker as Questioner in *Lyrical Ballads*," *Journal of English and Germanic Philology* 77(4), October 1978, 550-53.

"Anticipation. October, 1803"

THOMAS R. EDWARDS. *Imagination and Power*, pp. 170-73.

"Apology for the Foregoing Poems" (*Yarrow Revisited*)

JILL RUBENSTEIN. "Wordsworth and 'Localised Romance': The Scottish Poems of 1831," *Studies in English Literature 1500-1900* 16(4), Autumn 1976, 588-90.

"The Armenian Lady's Love"

FREDERICK L. BEATY. *Light from Heaven*, pp. 79-80.

"The Barberry Tree"

FORD SWETNAM. "The Controversial Uses of Wordsworth's Comedy," *Wordsworth Circle* 3(1), Winter 1972, 36-37.

"Bothwell Castle"

JILL RUBENSTEIN. "Wordsworth and 'Localised Romance': The Scottish Poems of 1831," *Studies in English Literature 1500-1900* 16(4), Autumn 1976, 585-86.

"The Brothers"

STEPHEN MAXFIELD PARRISH. "Dramatic Technique in the *Lyrical Ballads*," *PMLA* 74(1), March 1959, 96-97.

FRED V. RANDEL. "Wordsworth's Homecoming," *Studies in English Literature 1500-1900* 17(4), Autumn 1977, 587-88.

"Calais Beach"

GERALD SOLOMON. "Wordsworth and 'the Art of Lying,'" *Essays in Criticism* 27(2), April 1977, 147-49.

"Character of the Happy Warrior"

F. S. BOAS. "Wordsworth's Patriotic Poems and their Significance To-day," in *Perspectives of Poetry*, pp. 12-13.

"The Childless Father"

ROBERT R. HARSON. "Wordsworth's Narrator in 'The Childless Father,'" *American Notes & Queries*, n.s., 13(9), May 1975, 138-40.

"A Complaint"

CLEANTH BROOKS, JOHN THIBAUT PURSER, and ROBERT PENN WARREN. *An Approach to Literature*, fourth ed., pp. 304-5.

"Composed Among the Ruins of a Castle in North Wales"

LEONE VIVANTE. *English Poetry*, p. 118. (P)

"Composed by the Side of Grasmere Lake"

LESLIE BRISMAN. *Romantic Origins*, pp. 338-39.

PAUL DE MAN. "Symbolic Landscape in Wordsworth and Yeats," in *In Defense of Reading*, pp. 23-28.

"Composed upon Westminster Bridge"

JOSEPH WARREN BEACH. *A Romantic View of Poetry*, pp. 64-71.

MARIUS BEWLEY. *Masks & Mirrors*, pp. 89-93.

CLEANTH BROOKS. *The Well Wrought Urn*, pp. 5-7; revised ed., pp. 2-4. Reprinted in: *American Literary Criticism*, pp. 518-20. Also: *Criticism*, p. 359. Also: *Critiques and Essays in Criticism*, pp. 67-68. Also: *The Language of Poetry*, pp. 39-41. Also: *The Study of Literature*, pp. 174-76.

DAVID DAICHES and WILLIAM CHARVAT. *Poems in English*, pp. 697-98.

JUDITH DUNDAS. "Illusion and the Poetic Image," *Journal of Aesthetics and Art Criticism* 32(2), Winter 1973, 198.

CHARLES V. HARTUNG. "Wordsworth on Westminster Bridge: Paradox or Harmony?" *College English* 13(4), January 1952, 201-3.

G. M. HARVEY. "The Design of Wordsworth's Sonnets," *Ariel* 6(3), July 1975, 80-83.

ARCHIBALD A. HILL. *Constituent and Pattern in Poetry*, pp. 50-52.

PATRICK HOLLAND. "The Two Contrasts of Wordsworth's 'Westminster Bridge' Sonnet," *Wordsworth Circle* 8(1), Winter 1977, 32-34.

F. R. LEAVIS. "Imagery and Movement: Notes in the Analysis of Poetry," *Scrutiny* 13(2), September 1945, 127-30.

FRED B. MILLET. *Reading Poetry*, pp. 19-20; second ed., pp. 16-18.

CHARLES MOLESWORTH. "Wordsworth's 'Westminster Bridge' Sonnet: The Republican Structure of Time and Perception," *Clio* 6(3), Spring 1977, 261-73.

ALLAN RODWAY. *The Romantic Conflict*, p. 158.

MARK VAN DOREN. *Introduction to Poetry*, pp. 55-58.

"The Daffodils"
see "I wandered lonely as a cloud"

"Departure"

JEFFREY C. ROBINSON. "The Structure of Wordsworth's *Memorials of a Tour in Scotland, 1803*," *Papers on Language and Literature* 13(1), Winter 1977, 59-61.

"Descriptive Sketches"

GEOFFREY H. HARTMAN. "Wordsworth's *Descriptive Sketches* and the Growth of a Poet's Mind," *PMLA* 76(5), December 1961, 519-27.

FRED V. RANDEL. "Wordsworth's Homecoming," *Studies in English Literature 1500-1900* 17(4), Autumn 1977, 577-79.

J. F. TURNER. " 'Various Journey, Sad and Slow': Wordsworth's *Descriptive Sketches* (1791-2) and the Lure of Pastoral," *Durham University Journal*, n.s., 38(1), December 1976, 38-51.

"Elegiac Stanzas"

CARLOS BAKER. "Sensation and Vision in Wordsworth," in *English Romantic Poets*, p. 108.

ERNEST BERNHARDT-KABISCH. *Explicator* 23(9), May 1965, Item 71.

HAROLD BLOOM. *The Visionary Company*, pp. 179-82.

EDWARD E. BOSTETTER. *The Romantic Ventriloquists*, pp. 40-41.

HARRY BROWN and JOHN MILSTEAD. *What the Poem Means*, p. 283.

JOSEPH M. GRISKA, JR. "Wordsworth's Mood Disturbance: A Psychoanalytic Approach to Three Poems," *Literature and Psychology* 24(4), 1974, 151.

JAMES A. W. HEFFERNAN. "Reflections on Reflections in English Romantic Poetry and Painting," *Bucknell Review* 24(2), Fall 1978, 26-27.

MURRAY KRIEGER. *The Classic Vision*, pp. 191-95.

KARL KROEBER. *The Artifice of Reality*, pp. 112-14.

LAURENCE LERNER. *An Introduction to English Poetry*, pp. 130-44.

J. D. O'HARA. "Ambiguity and Assertion in Wordsworth's 'Elegiac Stanzas,' " *Philological Quarterly* 47(1), January 1968, 69-82.

CHARLES I. PATTERSON. "The Meaning and Significance of Wordsworth's *Peele Castle*," *Journal of English and Germanic Philology* 56(1), January 1957, 1-9.

CHARLES J. SMITH. "The Contrarieties: Wordsworth's Dualistic Imagery," *PMLA* 69(5), December 1954, 1188-89.

GEOFFREY TILLOTSON. "Wordsworth," *Sewanee Review* 74(2), Spring 1966, 426-28.

"An Evening Walk"

FREDERICK A. POTTLE. *The Idiom of Poetry*, pp. 105-12; second ed., pp. 111-21.

JONATHAN RAMSEY. "Seeing and Perceiving in Wordsworth's *An Evening Walk*," *Modern Language Quarterly* 36(4), December 1975, 376-89.

FRED V. RANDEL. "Wordsworth's Homecoming," *Studies in English Literature 1500-1900* 17(4), Autumn 1977, 576-77.

"Expostulation and Reply"

T. R. BARNES. *English Verse*, pp. 169-70.

ERNEST BERNHARDT-KABISCH. "Wordsworth's Expostulator: Taylor or Hazlitt?" *English Language Notes* 2(2), December 1964, 102-5.

"Extempore Effusion upon the Death of James Hogg"

HAROLD BLOOM. *The Visionary Company*, pp. 191-93.

JAMES REEVES and MARTIN SEYMOUR-SMITH. *Inside Poetry*, pp. 20-22.

"The Farmer of Tilsbury Vale"

FORD SWETNAM. "The Controversial Uses of Wordsworth's Comedy," *Wordsworth Circle* 3(1), Winter 1972, 32-33.

"The Fountain"

ANNE KOSTELANETZ. "Wordsworth's 'Conversations': A Reading of 'Two April Mornings' and 'The Fountain,' " *ELH* 33(1), March 1966, 43-52.

RICHARD E. MATLAK. "The Men in Wordsworth's Life," *Wordsworth Circle* 9(4), Autumn 1978, 392-93.

HAROLD E. TOLIVER. *Pastoral Forms and Attitudes*, pp. 250-51.

"Gipsies"

GENE W. RUOFF. "Religious Implications of Wordsworth's Imagination," *Studies in Romanticism* 12(3), Summer 1973, 680-81.

"Glen Allmain"

JEFFREY C. ROBINSON. "The Structure of Wordsworth's *Memorials of a Tour in Scotland, 1803*," *Papers on Language and Literature* 13(1), Winter 1977, 65-66.

"Goody Blake and Harry Gill"

JOHN E. JORDAN. "Wordsworth's Humor," *PMLA* 73(1), March 1958, 89.

"Great men have been among us"

ROBERT GRAVES. *Food for Centaurs*, pp. 141-45.

"Guilt and Sorrow"

FREDERICK L. BEATY. *Light from Heaven*, pp. 223-24.

STEPHEN C. GILL. " 'Adventures on Salisbury Plain' and Wordsworth's Poetry of Protest 1795-97," *Studies in Romanticism* 11(1), Winter 1972, 48-65.

"The Happy Warrior"

HAROLD E. TOLIVER. *Pastoral Forms and Attitudes*, pp. 257-58.

"Hart-Leap Well"

GEOFFREY H. HARTMAN. "False Themes and Gentle Minds," *Philological Quarterly* 47(1), January 1968, 65-67. Reprinted in: Geoffrey H. Hartman. *Beyond Formalism*, pp. 294-96.

JAMES B. TWITCHELL. " 'Hart-Leap Well': Wordsworth's Crucifixion Poem," *Tennessee Studies in Literature* 20 (1975), 11-16.

WORDSWORTH, WILLIAM (*Cont.*)

"Home at Grasmere"

JAMES BENZIGER. *Images of Eternity*, pp. 42-48.

HAROLD BLOOM. *The Visionary Company*, pp. 120-24.

STEPHEN C. GILL. "Wordsworth's 'Never Failing Principle of Joy,'" *ELH* 34(2), June 1967, 218-24.

LAURENCE GOLDSTEIN. "The Auburn Syndrome: Change and Loss in 'The Deserted Village' and Wordsworth's Grasmere," *ELH* 40(3), Fall 1973, 359-64.

KENNETH R. JOHNSTON. "'Home at Grasmere': Reclusive Song," *Studies in Romanticism* 14(1), Winter 1975, 1-28.

KARL KROEBER. "'Home at Grasmere': Ecological Holiness," *PMLA* 89(1), January 1974, 132-41.

MURIEL J. MELLOWN. "The Development of Imagery in 'Home at Grasmere,'" *Wordsworth Circle* 5(1), Winter 1974, 23-27.

FRED V. RANDEL. "Wordsworth's Homecoming," *Studies in English Literature 1500-1900* 17(4), Autumn 1977, 586-87.

STEPHEN J. SPECTOR. "Wordsworth's Mirror Imagery and the Picturesque Tradition," *ELH* 44(1), Spring 1977, 97-99.

"I travelled among unknown men"

PATRICIA M. BALL. *The Heart's Events*, pp. 14-15.

FRANCES C. FERGUSON. "The Lucy Poems: Wordsworth's Quest for a Poetic Object," *ELH* 40(4), Winter 1973, 541-43.

WALTER GIERASCH. *Explicator* 1(7), June 1943, Item 65.

SPENCER HALL. "Wordsworth's 'Lucy' Poems: Context and Meaning," *Studies in Romanticism* 10(3), Summer 1971, 174.

RICHARD E. MATLAK. "Wordsworth's Lucy Poems in Psychobiological Context," *PMLA* 93(1), January 1978, 61-62.

JOHN PETER. "Symbol and Implication: Notes Apropos of a Dictum of Coleridge's," *Essays in Criticism* 4(2), April 1954, 160-62.

JAMES G. TAAFFE. "Poet and Lover in Wordsworth's 'Lucy' Poems," *Modern Language Review* 61(2), April 1966, 178.

J. R. WATSON. "Lucy and the Earth-Mother," *Essays in Criticism* 27(3), July 1977, 198-99.

"I wandered lonely as a cloud"

LOUIS COXE. "Wordsworth: I Wandered Lonely as a Cloud," in *Master Poems of the English Language*, pp. 416-19.

ELIZABETH DREW. *Poetry*, pp. 87-92.

FREDERICK GARBER. "Wordsworth at the Universal Dance," *Studies in Romanticism* 8(3), Spring 1969, 168-82.

THEODORE MEYER GREENE. *The Arts and the Art of Criticism*, pp. 114-15.

MURRAY KRIEGER. *The Classic Vision*, pp. 160-61.

FREDERICK A. POTTLE. "The Eye and the Object in the Poetry of Wordsworth," *Yale Review* 40(1), September 1950, 29-40. Reprinted in: *Readings for Liberal Education*, revised ed., II: 96-100; third ed., II; 88-92; fourth ed., II: 79-83. Partial reprint in: *Romanticism and Consciousness*, p. 285.

EDWARD W. ROSENHEIM, JR. *What Happens in Literature*, pp. 140-45.

A. F. SCOTT. *The Poet's Craft*, pp. 60-63.

NORMAN C. STAGEBERG and WALLACE L. ANDERSON. *Poetry as Experience*, pp. 193-95.

JOHN E. STOLL. "Wordsworth for Modern Students," *Ball State University Forum* 11(3), Summer 1970, 52-53.

"I watch, and long have watched, with calm regret"

G. M. HARVEY. "The Design of Wordsworth's Sonnets," *Ariel* 6(3), July 1975, 83-85.

"The Idiot Boy"

PATRICIA M. BALL. *The Central Self*, pp. 67-69.

FREDERICK L. BEATY. *Light from Heaven*, pp. 229-30.

JOHN E. JORDAN. "Wordsworth's Humor," *PMLA* 73(1), March 1958, 88-89.

ROGER MURRAY. "Betty Foy: An Early Mental Traveler," *Journal of English and Germanic Philology* 70(1), January 1971, 51-61.

JONATHAN RAMSEY. "Wordsworth and the Childhood of Language," *Criticism* 18(3), Summer 1976, 249-55.

R. F. STORCH. "Wordsworth's Experimental Ballads: The Radical Uses of Intelligence and Comedy," *Studies in English Literature 1500-1900* 11(4), Autumn 1971, 628-31.

"Imitation of Juvenal's Eighth Satire"

STEPHEN C. GILL. "'Adventures on Salisbury Plain' and Wordsworth's Poetry of Protest 1795-97," *Studies in Romanticism* 11(1), Winter 1972, 51-52.

"Indignation of a high-minded Spaniard"

F. S. BOAS. "Wordsworth's Patriotic Poems and their Significance To-day," in *Perspectives of Poetry*, pp. 14-15.

"Invocation to the Earth"

LESLIE BRISMAN. *Romantic Origins*, pp. 290-91.

"It is a beauteous evening, calm and free"

CLEANTH BROOKS. *The Well Wrought Urn*, pp. 4-5; revised ed., pp. 1-2. Reprinted in: *American Literary Criticism*, pp. 518, 522. Also: *Criticism*, pp. 358-59. Also: *Critiques and Essays in Criticism*, pp. 66-67. Also: *The Language of Poetry*, pp. 38-39. Also: *The Study of Literature*, pp. 173-74.

DAVID DAICHES and WILLIAM CHARVAT. *Poems in English*, p. 698.

DONALD E. HAYDEN. *Literary Studies*, pp. 6-9.

F. R. LEAVIS. "Imagery and Movement: Notes in the Analysis of Poetry," *Scrutiny* 13(2), September 1945, 125-26.

NORMAN F. MACLEAN. "An Analysis of a Lyric Poem," *University Review* 8(3), Spring 1942, 202-9.

GERALD SOLOMON. "Heaven Lies," *Essays in Criticism* 28(4), October 1978, 351-52.

JUNE STURROCK. "Heaven Lies," *Essays in Criticism* 28(1), January 1978, 92-93.

HAROLD E. TOLIVER. *Pastoral Forms and Attitudes*, p. 255.

"Laodamia"

FREDERICK L. BEATY. *Light from Heaven*, pp. 76-78.

HAROLD BLOOM. *The Visionary Company*, pp. 183-88.

MURRAY KRIEGER. *The Classic Vision*, pp. 188-91.

RICHARD D. MCGHEE. "'Conversant with Infinity': Form and Meaning in Wordsworth's 'Laodamia,'" *Studies in Philology* 68(3), July 1971, 357-69.

ARTHUR WORMHOUNDT. *The Demon Lover*, pp. 63-67.

"The Leech Gatherer"

see "Resolution and Independence"

"Lines Composed a Few Miles Above Tintern Abbey"

JAMES BENZIGER. *Images of Eternity*, pp. 38-40.

JAMES BENZIGER. "*Tintern Abbey* Revisited," *PMLA* 55(2), March 1950, 154-62.

HAROLD BLOOM. *Poetry and Repression*, pp. 52-82.

HAROLD BLOOM. *The Visionary Company*, pp. 127-36.

JULIAN BOYD and ZELDA BOYD. "The Perfect of Experience," *Studies in Romanticism* 16(1), Winter 1977, 9-10.

PETER A. BRIER. "Reflections on Tintern Abbey," *Wordsworth Circle* 5(1), Winter 1974, 5-6.

LESLIE BRISMAN. *Romantic Origins*, pp. 296-98.

HARRY BROWN and JOHN MILSTEAD. *What the Poem Means*, p. 284.

MICHAEL G. COOKE. *The Romantic Will*, pp. 47-50.

RICHARD EBERHART. "Wordsworth: Tintern Abbey," in *Master Poems of the English Language*, pp. 424-27.

WILLIAM EMPSON. *Seven Types of Ambiguity*, pp. 192-94; second and third eds., pp. 151-54. (P)

RICHARD FADEM. "Dorothy Wordsworth: A View from 'Tintern Abbey,'" *Wordsworth Circle* 9(1), Winter 1978, 27-29.

NIGEL FOXELL. *Ten Poems Analyzed*, pp. 123-42.

ALBERT S. GERARD. "Dark Passages: Exploring *Tintern Abbey*," *Studies in Romanticism* 3(1), Autumn 1963, 10-23.

GEOFFREY H. HARTMAN. *The Unmediated Vision*, pp. 3-12, 23-26.

GEOFFREY H. HARTMAN. "Wordsworth, Inscriptions, and Romantic Nature Poetry," in *From Sensibility to Romanticism*, pp. 402-3. Reprinted in: Geoffrey H. Hartman. *Beyond Formalism*, pp. 224-26.

JAMES L. HILL. "The Frame for the Mind: Landscape in 'Lines Composed a Few Miles Above Tintern Abbey,' 'Dover Beach,' and 'Sunday Morning,'" *Centennial Review* 18(1), Winter 1974, 33-38.

JOHN A. HODGSON. "Wordsworth's Dialectical Transcendentalism, 1798: 'Tintern Abbey,'" *Criticism* 18(4), Fall 1976, 367-80.

FRED KAPLAN. *Miracles of Rare Device*, pp. 29-43.

MURRAY KRIEGER. *The Classic Vision*, pp. 170-73.

KARL KROEBER. *The Artifice of Reality*, pp. 87-96.

KARL KROEBER. "'Tintern Abbey' and *The Cornfield*: Serendipity as a Method of Intermedia Criticism," *Journal of Aesthetics and Art Criticism* 31(1), Fall 1972, 67-77.

ROBERT LANGBAUM. *The Poetry of Experience*, pp. 43-45, 48.

ROBERT M. MANIQUIS. "Comparison, Intensity, and Time in 'Tintern Abbey,'" *Criticism* 11(4), Fall 1969, 358-82.

JOHN R. NABHOLTZ. "The Integrity of Wordsworth's 'Tintern Abbey,'" *Journal of English and Germanic Philology* 73(2), April 1974, 227-38.

FREDERICK A. POTTLE. *Explicator* 16(6), March 1958, Item 36.

JOHN CROWE RANSOM. *The New Criticism*, pp. 115-19.

BERNICE SLOTE. "The Case of The Missing Abbey: Wordsworth's 'Lines,'" in *The Dimensions of Poetry*, pp. 387-94.

CHARLES J. SMITH. "The Contrarieties: Wordsworth's Dualistic Imagery," *PMLA* 69(5), December 1954, 1184-85.

STUART M. SPERRY, JR. "From 'Tintern Abbey' to the 'Intimations Ode': Wordsworth and the Function of Memory," *Wordsworth Circle* 1(2), Spring 1970, 40-42.

WILLIAM I. THOMPSON. "Collapsed Universe and Structured Poem: An Essay in Whiteheadian Criticism," *College English* 28(1), October 1966, 29-32.

DONALD WESLING. "The Inevitable Ear: Freedom and Necessity in Lyric Form, Wordsworth and After," in *Forms of Lyric*, pp. 115-20.

SUSAN J. WOLFSON. "The Speaker as Questioner in *Lyrical Ballads*," *Journal of English and Germanic Philology* 77(4), October 1978, 559-68.

A. S. P. WOODHOUSE. *The Poet and His Faith*, pp. 170-71.

ARTHUR WORMHOUDT. *The Demon Lover*, pp. 52-55.

"Lines left upon a Seat in a Yew Tree"

IRVING H. BUCHEN. "Wordsworth's Gothic Ballads," *Genre* 3(1), March 1970, 89-90.

GEOFFREY H. HARTMAN. *Beyond Formalism*, pp. 206-22.

"Lines Written in Early Spring"

T. R. BARNES. *English Verse*, pp. 172-73.

RICHARD RAY KIRK and ROGER PHILIP MCCUTCHEON. *An Introduction to the Study of Poetry*, pp. 76-79.

MURRAY KRIEGER. *The Classic Vision*, pp. 150-53.

"London, 1802"

CLEANTH BROOKS, JOHN THIBAUT PURSER, and ROBERT PENN WARREN. *An Approach to Literature*, pp. 496-98; second ed., pp. 496-98; third ed., pp. 487-90; fourth ed., pp. 383-85; fifth ed., pp. 377-78.

WALTER GIERASCH. *Explicator* 2(6), April 1944, Item 42.

"Lucy Gray, or Solitude"

SPENCER HALL. "Wordsworth's 'Lucy' Poems: Context and Meaning," *Studies in Romanticism* 10(3), Summer 1971, 170-71.

HAROLD E. TOLIVER. *Pastoral Forms and Attitudes*, pp. 248-49.

LEONARD UNGER and WILLIAM VAN O'CONNOR. *Poems for Study*, pp. 362-65.

"The Mad Mother"

STEPHEN MAXFIELD PARRISH. "Dramatic Technique in the *Lyrical Ballads*," *PMLA* 74(1), March 1959, 92.

"The Matron of Jedborough and Her Husband"

JEFFREY C. ROBINSON. "The Structure of Wordsworth's *Memorials of a Tour in Scotland, 1803*," *Papers on Language and Literature* 13(1), Winter 1977, 67-68.

"Matthew"

HAROLD E. TOLIVER. *Pastoral Forms and Attitudes*, p. 249.

"Michael"

HAROLD BLOOM. *The Visionary Company*, pp. 178-79.

CLEANTH BROOKS and ROBERT PENN WARREN. *Understanding Poetry*, pp. 83-85; revised ed., pp. 36-38.

HARRY BROWN and JOHN MILSTEAD. *What the Poem Means*, p. 285.

GEOFFREY H. HARTMAN. "Wordsworth, Inscriptions, and Romantic Nature Poetry," in *From Sensibility to Romanticism*, pp. 401-2. Reprinted in: Goeffrey H. Hartman. *Beyond Formalism*, pp. 223-24.

MURRAY KRIEGER. *The Classic Vision*, pp. 179-86.

KARL KROEBER. *Romantic Narrative Art*, pp. 80-83.

SYDNEY LEA. "Wordsworth and His 'Michael': The Pastor Passes," *ELH* 45(1), Spring 1978, 55-68.

PETER J. MANNING. "'Michael,' Luke, and Wordsworth," *Criticism* 19(3), Summer 1977, 195-211.

WORDSWORTH, WILLIAM *(Cont.)*

"Michael" *(cont.)*

LORE METZGER. "Wordsworth's Pastoral Covenant," *Modern Language Quarterly* 37(4), December 1976, 307-23.

ROGER N. MURRAY. "Synecdoche in Wordsworth's 'Michael,'" *ELH* 32(4), December 1965, 502-10.

FRED V. RANDEL. "Wordsworth's Homecoming," *Studies in English Literature 1500-1900* 17(4), Autumn 1977, 589-91.

JAMES SMITH. *Shakespearian and Other Essays*, pp. 297-98.

JAMES SMITH. "Wordsworth: A Preliminary Survey," *Scrutiny* 7(1), June 1938, 52-54.

ARTHUR WORMHOUDT. *The Demon Lover*, pp. 55-58.

" 'Miserrimus!' and neither name nor date"

BURTON R. POLLIN. "Wordsworth's 'Miserrimus' Sonnet: Several Errors Corrected," *Wordsworth Circle* 1(1), Winter 1970, 22-24.

"Mutability"

JOHN WAIN. "The Liberation of Wordsworth," *Twentieth Century* 157(935), January 1955, 72-73.

"My heart leaps up when I behold"

RICHARD GREENLEAF. "Emerson and Wordsworth," *Science and Society* 22(3), Summer 1958, 228-29.

KENNETH R. LINCOLN. "Wordsworth's Mortality Ode," *Journal of English and Germanic Philology* 71(2), April 1972, 214.

ABBIE FINDLAY POTTS. "The Spenserian and Miltonic Influence in Wordsworth's *Ode* and *Rainbow*," *Studies in Philology* 29(4), October 1932, 607-16, *passim*.

JOHN CROWE RANSOM. "William Wordsworth: Notes Toward an Understanding of Poetry," *Kenyon Review* 12(3), Summer 1950, 516.

HAROLD E. TOLIVER. *Pastoral Forms and Attitudes*, pp. 242-43.

"A Night on Salisbury Plain"

STEPHEN C. GILL. "Wordsworth's Breeches Pocket: Attitudes to the Didactic Poet," *Essays in Criticism* 19(4), October 1969, 393-400.

"A Night-Piece"

NEIL H. HERTZ. "Wordsworth and the Tears of Adam," *Studies in Romanticism* 7(1), Autumn 1967, 17-20.

JAMES KISSANE. " 'A Night-Piece': Wordsworth's Emblem of the Mind," *Modern Language Notes* 71(3), March 1956, 183-86.

KARL KROEBER. *Romantic Narrative Art*, pp. 51-53.

"Not in the lucid intervals of life" *(Evening Voluntaries,* IV)

NEWTON P. STALLKNECHT. "The Tragic Flaw in Wordsworth's Philosophy," in *British Romantic Poets*, pp. 79-80.

"Nutting"

FREDERICK L. BEATY. *Light from Heaven*, p. 232.

HAROLD BLOOM. *The Visionary Company*, pp. 124-27.

LESLIE BRISMAN. *Romantic Origins*, pp. 298-300.

ROBERTS W. FRENCH. "Wordsworth's *Paradise Lost*: A Note on 'Nutting,' " *Studies in the Humanities* 5(1), January 1976, 42-45.

ALAN GROB. "Wordsworth's *Nutting*," *Journal of English and Germanic Philology* 61(4), October 1962, 826-32.

"October, 1803"

THOMAS R. EDWARDS. *Imagination and Power*, pp. 173-76.

LEWIS B. HORNE. *Explicator* 24(1), September 1965, Item 10.

RENÉ RAPIN. *Explicator* 24(1), September 1965, Item 10.

"Ode: Intimations of Immortality"

CARLOS BAKER. "Sensation and Vision in Wordsworth," in *English Romantic Poets*, pp. 107-8.

F. W. BATESON. *English Poetry*, pp. 196-205.

HAROLD BLOOM. *A Map of Misreading*, pp. 144-49.

HAROLD BLOOM. *The Visionary Company*, pp. 166-73.

EDWARD E. BOSTETTER. *The Romantic Ventriloquists*, pp. 36-39.

C. M. BOWRA. *The Romantic Imagination*, pp. 76-102.

CLEANTH BROOKS. "The Intimations of the Ode (Reconsiderations V)," *Kenyon Review* 8(1), Winter 1946, 80-102.

CLEANTH BROOKS. *The Well Wrought Urn*, pp. 124-50; revised ed., pp. 101-23.

CLEANTH BROOKS and ROBERT PENN WARREN. *Understanding Poetry*, revised ed., pp. 639-45.

HARRY BROWN and JOHN MILSTEAD. *What the Poem Means*, pp. 285-86.

MERLE E. BROWN. "Interpretation or Poetry," *Genre* 1(3), July 1968, 237-41.

DEREK COLVILLE. *Victorian Poetry and the Romantic Religion*, pp. 23-24.

ROGER L. COX. *Explicator* 19(6), March 1961, Item 34.

WALLACE W. DOUGLAS. "The Professor and the Ode," *Western Review* 13(1), Autumn 1948, 4-14.

JOSEPH M. GRISKA, JR. "Wordsworth's Mood Disturbance: A Psychoanalytic Approach to Three Poems," *Literature and Psychology* 24(4), 1974, 150-51.

ALAN GROB. "Wordsworth's *Immortality Ode* and the Search for Identity," *ELH* 32(1), March 1965, 32-61.

GEOFFREY H. HARTMAN. *The Unmediated Vision*, pp. 40-44.

GILBERT HIGHET. *The Powers of Poetry*, pp. 228-35.

KENNETH R. JOHNSTON. "Recollecting Forgetting: Forcing Paradox to the Limit in the 'Intimations Ode,' " *Wordsworth Circle* 2(2), Spring 1971, 59-64.

WALLACE KAUFMAN. "Revolution, Environment, and Poetry," *South Atlantic Quarterly* 71(2), Spring 1972, 144-47.

G. WILSON KNIGHT. *The Starlit Dome*, pp. 37-49.

KARL KROEBER. *The Artifice of Reality*, pp. 168-74.

ROBERT LANGBAUM. "The Evolution of the Soul in Wordsworth's Poetry," in *The Modern Spirit*, pp. 22-23.

KENNETH R. LINCOLN. "Wordsworth's Mortality Ode," *Journal of English and Germanic Philology* 71(2), April 1972, 211-25.

FLORENCE G. MARSH. "Wordsworth's *Ode*: Obstinate Questionings," *Studies in Romanticism* 5(4), Summer 1966, 219-30.

JOHN K. MATHISON. "Wordsworth's *Ode: Intimations of Immortality from Recollections of Early Childhood*," *Studies in Philology* 46(3), July 1949, 419-39.

GEORGE W. MEYER. "A Note on the Sources and Symbolism of the *Intimations Ode*," *Tulane Studies in English* 3(1952), 33-45.

JAMES W. PIPKIN. "Wordsworth's 'Immortality Ode' and the Myth of the Fall," *Renascence* 30(2), Winter 1978, 91-98.

ABBIE FINDLAY POTTS. "The Spenserian and Miltonic Influence in Wordsworth's *Ode* and *Rainbow*," *Studies in Philology* 29(4), October 1932, 607-16.

C. E. PULOS. "The Unity of Wordsworth's Immortality Ode," *Studies in Romanticism* 13(3), Summer 1974, 179-88.

JOHN CROWE RANSOM. "William Wordsworth: Notes Toward an Understanding of Poetry," *Kenyon Review* 12(3), Summer 1950, 514-18.

THOMAS M. RAYSOR. "The Themes of Immortality and Natural Piety in Wordsworth's Immortality Ode," *PMLA* 69(4), September 1954, 861-75. Reprinted in: *British Romantic Poets*, pp. 45-62.

DAVID ROGERS. "God and Pre-existence in Wordsworth's *Immortality Ode*," *Durham University Journal*, n.s., 30(3), June 1969, 143-46.

ROBERT L. SCHNEIDER. "The Failure of Solitude: Wordsworth's Immortality Ode," *Journal of English and Germanic Philology* 54(4), October 1955, 625-33.

CHARLES J. SMITH. "The Contrarieties: Wordsworth's Dualistic Imagery," *PMLA* 69(5), December 1954, 1186-88.

STUART M. SPERRY, JR. "From 'Tintern Abbey' to the 'Intimations Ode': Wordsworth and the Function of Memory," *Wordsworth Circle* 1(2), Spring 1970, 40-49.

DONALD A. STAUFFER. "Cooperative Criticism: A Letter from the Critical Front," *Kenyon Review* 4(1), Winter 1942, 133-44.

JOHN E. STOLL. "Wordsworth for Modern Students," *Ball State University Forum* 11(3), Summer 1970, 54-56.

WRIGHT THOMAS and STUART GERRY BROWN. *Reading Poems: An Introduction to Critical Study*, pp. 660-61.

HAROLD E. TOLIVER. *Pastoral Forms and Attitudes*, pp. 255-57.

LIONEL TRILLING. "Wordsworth's 'Ode: Intimations of Immortality,'" *English Institute Essays*, 1941, pp. 1-28. Reprinted in: *English Romantic Poets*, pp. 123-43. Also: *Explication as Criticism*, pp. 175-202. Also: Lionel Trilling. *The Liberal Imagination*, pp. 125-54. Also: *The Proper Study*, pp. 484-502. Also: *Master Poems of the English Language*, pp. 395-414.

J. P. WARD. "Wordsworth and The Sociological Idea," *Critical Quarterly* 16(4), Winter 1974, 341-45.

GEORGE WHALLEY. "Literary Romanticism," *Queen's Quarterly* 72(2), Summer 1965, 243-45.

A. S. P. WOODHOUSE. *The Poet and His Faith*, pp. 174-76.

ARTHUR WORMHOUDT. *The Demon Lover*, pp. 58-62.

"Ode to Childhood"

FRANKLIN BENJAMIN SANBORN. *Lectures on Literature and Philosophy* Reprinted in: *American Transcendental Quarterly* 34(1), Spring 1977, 35-36.

"Ode to Duty"

HAROLD BLOOM. *The Visionary Company*, pp. 182-83.

EDWARD E. BOSTETTER. *The Romantic Ventriloquists*, p. 39.

MURRAY KRIEGER. *The Classic Vision*, pp. 187-88.

NEWTON P. STALLKNECHT. "The Tragic Flaw in Wordsworth's Philosophy," in *British Romantic Poets*, pp. 75-78.

A. S. P. WOODHOUSE. *The Poet and His Faith*, pp. 185-86.

"Ode to Lycoris"

ALEX ZWERDLING. "Wordsworth and Greek Myth," *University of Toronto Quarterly* 33(4), July 1964, 346-47.

"The Old Cumberland Beggar"

FREDERICK L. BEATY. *Light from Heaven*, pp. 228-29.

HAROLD BLOOM. *The Visionary Company*, pp. 173-78.

EDWARD E. BOSTETTER. *The Romantic Ventriloquists*, pp. 55-56.

STEPHEN C. GILL. "Wordsworth's Breeches Pocket: Attitudes to the Didactic Poet," *Essays in Criticism* 19(4), October 1969, 388-93.

KARL KROEBER. *The Artifice of Reality*, pp. 127-30.

"Old Man Travelling"

GEOFFREY H. HARTMAN. *Beyond Formalism*, pp. 252-54.

"On the Extinction of the Venetian Republic"

ISAAC ASIMOV. *Familiar Poems, Annotated*, pp. 152-57.

Z. S. FINK. "Wordsworth and the English Republican Tradition," *Journal of English and Germanic Philology* 47(2), April 1948, 118-19.

"On the Power of Sound"

G. WILSON KNIGHT. *The Starlit Dome*, pp. 78-81.

SEYMOUR LAINOFF. "Wordsworth's Final Phase: Glimpses of Eternity," *Studies in English Literature* 1(4), Autumn 1961, 71-73.

"The Pedlar"

FRED V. RANDEL. "Wordsworth's Homecoming," *Studies in English Literature 1500-1900* 17(4), Autumn 1977, 582-85.

"A Poet's Epitaph"

CLEANTH BROOKS and ROBERT PENN WARREN. *Understanding Poetry*, pp. 579-82; revised ed., pp. 423-27, 632.

ABBIE FINDLAY POTTS. *The Elegiac Mode*, pp. 114-18.

JONATHAN RAMSEY. "Wordsworth's Silent Poet," *Modern Language Quarterly* 37(3), September 1976, 263-65.

"A Poet! — he hath put his heart to school"

PAUL FUSSELL, JR. "Some Observations on Wordsworth's 'A POET! — He hath put his heart to school,'" *Philological Quarterly* 37(4), October 1958, 454-64.

"Processions. Suggested on a Sabbath Morning in the Vale of Chamouny"

GEOFFREY H. HARTMAN. "The Romance of Nature and the Negative Way," in *Romanticism and Consciousness*, p. 299.

"The Rainbow"

see "My heart leaps up when I behold"

"The Recluse"

see "Home at Grasmere"

"The Redbreast Chasing the Butterfly"

LAURENCE LERNER. "What did Wordsworth mean by 'Nature'?" *Critical Quarterly* 17(4), Winter 1975, 306-8.

"Resolution and Independence"

SHYMAL BAGCHEE. "Anxiety of Influence: 'Resolution and Independence' and Yeats's 'The Fisherman,'" *Yeats Eliot Review* 5(1), 1978, 51-57.

GORMAN BEAUCHAMP. "Wordsworth's Archetypal Resolution," *Concerning Poetry* 7(2), Fall 1974, 13-19.

WORDSWORTH, WILLIAM *(Cont.)*

"Resolution and Independence" *(cont.)*

HAROLD BLOOM. *The Visionary Company,* pp. 160-66.

ANTHONY E. M. CONRAN. "The Dialectic of Experience: A Study of Wordsworth's *Resolution and Independence,*" *PMLA* 75(1), March 1960, 66-74.

MICHAEL G. COOKE. *The Romantic Will,* pp. 210-14.

GEOFFREY GRIGSON. "Wordsworth: Resolution and Independence," in *Master Poems of the English Language,* pp. 432-34.

JOSEPH M. GRISKA, JR. "Wordsworth's Mood Disturbance: A Psychoanalytic Approach to Three Poems," *Literature and Psychology* 24(4), 1974, 148-50.

ALAN GROB. "Process and Permanence in *Resolution and Independence,*" *ELH* 28(1), March 1961, 89-100.

SHELDON HALPERN. "The Imagery of Perception in Two Poems by Wordsworth," *Journal of Popular Culture* 4(2), Fall 1970, 435-41.

JAMES L. HILL. "The Function of the Poem in Keats's 'Ode to a Grecian Urn' and Wordsworth's 'Resolution and Independence,'" *Centennial Review* 22(4), Fall 1978, 437-44.

STANLEY EDGAR HYMAN. "A Poem of Resolution," *Centennial Review* 5(2), Spring 1961, 195-205.

MURRAY KRIEGER. *The Classic Vision,* pp. 176-79.

ROBERT LANGBAUM. *The Poetry of Experience,* pp. 54-55.

VINCENT NEWEY. "Wordsworth, Bunyan, and the Puritan Mind," *ELH* 41(2), Summer 1974, 219-24.

W. W. ROBSON. "William Wordsworth: Resolution and Independence," in *Interpretations,* pp. 117-28.

CHARLES J. SMITH. "The Contrarieties: Wordsworth's Dualistic Imagery," *PMLA* 69(5), December 1954, 1185-86.

MILTON TEICHMAN. "Wordsworth's Two Replies to Coleridge's 'Dejection: An Ode,'" *PMLA* 86(5), October 1971, 983-96.

CHARLES WILLIAMS. "Wordsworth," in *English Romantic Poets,* pp. 114-16.

"The Reverie of Poor Susan"

JULIAN BOYD and ZELDA BOYD. "The Perfect of Experience," *Studies in Romanticism* 16(1), Winter 1977, 6-7.

"The River Duddon"

G. WILSON KNIGHT. *The Starlit Dome,* pp. 62-63.

"Roman Antiquities"

DAVID ROGERS. "Wordsworth's *Roman Antiquities,*" *Durham University Journal,* n.s., 33(3), June 1972, 248-50.

"The Ruined Cottage"

JAMES H. AVERILL. "Suffering and Calm in Wordsworth's Early Poetry," *PMLA* 91(2), March 1976, 223-34.

FREDERICK L. BEATY. *Light from Heaven,* pp. 72-73.

HAROLD BLOOM. "Visionary Cinema," *Partisan Review* 35(4), Fall 1968, 563-66.

STEPHEN C. GILL. "Wordsworth's 'Never Failing Principle of Joy,'" *ELH* 34(2), June 1967, 214-18.

NEIL H. HERTZ. "Wordsworth and the Tears of Adam," *Studies in Romanticism* 7(1), Autumn 1967, 30-32.

PETER J. MANNING. "Wordsworth, Margaret, and The Pedlar," *Studies in Romanticism* 15(2), Spring 1976, 195-220.

MARY MOORMAN. "The Ruined Cottage," *Ariel* 1(2), April 1970, 39-41.

PHILIP DARRAUGH ORTEGO. "Wordsworth's 'The Wanderer' and the Pastoral Tradition," *CEA Critic* 31(3), December 1968, 8-9.

REEVE PARKER. "'Finer Distance': The Narrative Art of Wordsworth's 'The Wanderer,'" *ELH* 39(1), March 1972, 87-111.

FRED V. RANDEL. "Wordsworth's Homecoming," *Studies in English Literature 1500-1900* 17(4), Autumn 1977, 582-85.

LUCIO P. RUOTOLO. "Wordsworth's Religious Hope: A Study of the Margaret Story," *Renascence* 24(2), Winter 1972, 96-101.

"The Sailor's Mother"

GENE W. RUOFF. "Wordsworth on Language: Toward a Radical Poetics for English Romanticism," *Wordsworth Circle* 3(4), Autumn 1972, 205-7.

"Salisbury Plain"

STEPHEN C. GILL. "'Adventures on Salisbury Plain' and Wordsworth's Poetry of Protest 1795-97," *Studies in Romanticism* 11(1), Winter 1972, 48-51.

"The sea was laughing at a distance, all"

WILLIAM EMPSON. "Basic English and Wordsworth (A Radio Talk)," *Kenyon Review* 2(4), Autumn 1940, 450-57.

"She dwelt among the untrodden ways"

GÉMINO H. ABAD. *In Another Light,* p. 252.

PATRICIA M. BALL. *The Heart's Events,* pp. 13-14.

CLEANTH BROOKS. "Literary Criticism: Poet, Poem, and the Reader," in *Varieties of Literary Experience,* pp. 100-2.

CLEANTH BROOKS and ROBERT PENN WARREN. *Understanding Poetry,* fourth ed., pp. 220-21.

EDWIN BERRY BURGUM. "The Cult of the Complex in Poetry," *Science and Society* 15(1), Winter 1951, 37-41.

MICHAEL G. COOKE. "The Mode of Argument in Wordsworth's Poetry," in *Romantic and Victorian,* pp. 105-6.

C. B. COX and A. E. DYSON. *The Practical Criticism of Poetry,* pp. 30-35.

EARL DANIELS. *The Art of Reading Poetry,* pp. 222-24.

FRANCES C. FERGUSON. "The Lucy Poems: Wordsworth's Quest for a Poetic Object," *ELH* 40(4), Winter 1973, 540-41.

RICHARD RAY KIRK and ROGER PHILIP McCUTCHEON. *An Introduction to the Study of Poetry,* pp. 90-92.

RICHARD E. MATLAK. "Wordsworth's Lucy Poems in Psychobiological Context," *PMLA* 93(1), January 1978, 54-55.

ROGER L. SLAKEY. "At Zero: A Reading of Wordsworth's 'She Dwelt Among the Untrodden Ways,'" *Studies in English Literature 1500-1900* 12(4), Autumn 1972, 629-38.

JAMES G. TAAFFE. "Poet and Lover in Wordsworth's 'Lucy' Poems," *Modern Language Review* 61(2), April 1966, 176-78.

J. R. WATSON. "Lucy and the Earth-Mother," *Essays in Criticism* 27(3), July 1977, 189-91.

"She was a Phantom of delight"

FREDERICK L. BEATY. *Light from Heaven,* pp. 73-74.

JEROME BEATY AND WILLIAM H. MATCHETT. *Poetry From Statement to Meaning,* pp. 113-15.

WALTER HOUGHTON. *Explicator* 3(3), December 1944, Item 20.

J. E. WHITESELL. *Explicator* 1(6), April 1943, Item 46.

"Simon Lee"

ANDREW L. GRIFFIN. "Wordsworth and the Problem of Imaginative Story: The Case of 'Simon Lee,'" *PMLA* 92(3), May 1977, 392-409.

R. F. STORCH. "Wordsworth's Experimental Ballads: The Radical Uses of Intelligence and Comedy," *Studies in English Literature 1500-1900* 11(4), Autumn 1971, 621-28.

"The Simplon Pass"

VINCENT BUCKLEY. *Poetry and the Sacred*, pp. 45-47.

"A slumber did my spirit seal"

PATRICIA M. BALL. *The Heart's Events*, pp. 17-18.

F. W. BATESON. *English Poetry*, pp. 32-34. Reprinted in: *Poems and Critics*, pp. 135-37. Also: Cleanth Brooks and Robert Penn Warren. *Understanding Poetry*, third ed., p. 379.

JOHN BEER. "Coleridge, the Wordsworths, and the State of Trance," *Wordsworth Circle* 8(2), Spring 1977, 136-37.

WALTER BLAIR and W. K. CHANDLER. *Approaches to Poetry*, first ed., p. 262.

CLEANTH BROOKS. "Iron and 'Ironic' Poetry," *College English* 9(5), February 1948, 235-37. Reprinted in: *English Journal* 37(2), February 1948, 61-63. Also: *Literary Opinion in America*, second and third eds., pp. 735-37. Also: Cleanth Brooks and Robert Penn Warren. *Understanding Poetry*, pp. 379-80. Also: Cleanth Brooks, John Thibaut Purser, and Robert Penn Warren. *An Approach to Literature*, fifth ed., pp. 404-5.

HUGH SYKES DAVIES. "Another New Poem by Wordsworth," *Essays in Criticism* 15(2), April 1965, 135-61.

C. DAY-LEWIS. *The Lyric Impulse*, p. 16.

ELIZABETH DREW. *Poetry*, pp. 132-33.

FRANCES C. FERGUSON. "The Lucy Poems: Wordsworth's Quest for a Poetic Object," *ELH* 40(4), Winter 1973, 546-47.

SPENCER HALL. "Wordsworth's 'Lucy' Poems: Context and Meaning," *Studies in Romanticism* 10(3), Summer 1971, 168-74.

T. R. HENN. *The Apple and the Spectroscope*, pp. 33-37.

JAMES R. KREUZER. *Elements of Poetry*, pp. 200-4.

MURRAY KRIEGER. *The Classic Vision*, pp. 169-70.

F. R. LEAVIS. "'Thought' and Emotional Quality: Notes in the Analysis of Poetry," *Scrutiny* 13(1), Spring 1945, 53-55. Reprinted in: *The Creative Reader*, p. 851; second ed., pp. 904-5.

FLORENCE MARSH. *Wordsworth's Imagery*, pp. 55-56. Reprinted in: Cleanth Brooks and Robert Penn Warren. *Understanding Poetry*, third ed., p. 378.

RICHARD E. MATLAK. "Wordsworth's Lucy Poems in Psychobiological Context," *PMLA* 93(1), January 1978, 55-56.

JOHN OLIVER PERRY. *The Experience of Poems*, pp. 9-10.

M. L. ROSENTHAL and A. J. M. SMITH. *Exploring Poetry*, pp. 89-90; second ed., pp. 111-12.

ROBIN SKELTON. *The Poetic Pattern*, pp. 182-85.

WARREN STEVENSON. "Cosmic Irony in Wordsworth's 'A Slumber Did My Spirit Seal,'" *Wordsworth Circle* 7(2), Spring 1976, 92-94.

WRIGHT THOMAS and STUART GERRY BROWN. *Reading Poems: An Introduction to Critical Study*, pp. 642-43.

HAROLD E. TOLIVER. *Pastoral Forms and Attitudes*, p. 246.

J. R. WATSON. "Lucy and the Earth-Mother," *Essays in Criticism* 27(3), July 1977, 199-201.

"Sole listener, Duddon! to the breeze that played" (River Duddon, V)

I. A. RICHARDS. *Principles of Literary Criticism*, pp. 207-8.

"The Solitary Reaper"

MELVIN W. ASKEW. "Form and Process in Lyric Poetry," *Sewanee Review* 72(2), Spring 1964, 291.

CLEANTH BROOKS. "Literary Criticism: Poet, Poem, and the Reader," in *Varieties of Literary Experience*, pp. 99-100.

MICHAEL G. COOKE. *The Romantic Will*, pp. 41-48.

C. DAY LEWIS. "The Poet's Way of Knowledge," *Essays by Divers Hands*, 3rd Series, 33 (1965), 5-7.

C. DAY LEWIS. "The Poet's Way of Knowledge," in *The Study of Literature*, pp. 73-75.

BABETTE DEUTSCH. *Poetry in Our Time*, first ed., pp. 248-49.

GEOFFREY J. FINCH. "Wordsworth's Solitary Song: The Substance of 'true art' in 'The Solitary Reaper,'" *Ariel* 6(3), July 1975, 91-100.

FREDERICK GARBER. "Wordsworth and the Romantic Synecdoche," *Bucknell Review* 14(1), March 1966, 34.

JOHN EDWARD HARDY. *The Curious Frame*, pp. 61-81.

G. INGLI JAMES. "Wordsworth's *Solitary Reaper*," *Essays in Criticism* 15(1), January 1965, 65-76.

MURRAY KRIEGER. *The Classic Vision*, pp. 174-76.

MALCOLM PITTOCK. "*The Solitary Reaper*," *Essays in Criticism* 15(2), April 1965, 243-45.

FREDERICK A. POTTLE. "The Eye and the Object in the Poetry of Wordsworth," *Yale Review* 40(1), September 1950, 40-42. Reprinted in: *Romanticism and Consciousness*, pp. 285-86.

JOHN PRESTON. "'The Moral Properties and Scope of Things': The Structure of *The Solitary Reaper*," *Essays in Criticism* 19(1), January 1969, 60-66.

JEFFREY C. ROBINSON. "The Structure of Wordsworth's *Memorials of a Tour in Scotland, 1803*," *Papers on Language and Literature* 13(1), Winter 1977, 65.

DONALD JEROME RYAN. "Scansion Scanned," *College English* 2(4), January 1941, 390-92.

MARK VAN DOREN. *Introduction to Poetry*, pp. 50-55.

GEORGE WHALLEY. "Literary Romanticism," *Queen's Quarterly* 72(2), Summer 1965, 245-47.

W. K. WIMSATT, JR. "The Structure of the 'Concrete Universal' in Literature," *PMLA* 62(1), March 1947, 274-75. Reprinted in: *Criticism*, pp. 399-400.

W. K. WIMSATT. *The Verbal Icon*, p. 80. Reprinted in: *Readings for Liberal Education*, third ed., II: 86-87; fourth and fifth eds., II: 77-78.

"Stanzas Written in My Pocket-Copy of Thomson's 'Castle of Indolence'"

MILTON TEICHMAN. "Wordsworth's Two Replies to Coleridge's 'Dejection: An Ode,'" *PMLA* 86(5), October 1971, 986-88.

"Stepping Westward"

JOSEPH WARREN BEACH. *A Romantic View of Poetry*, pp. 74-75.

FREDERICK GARBER. "Wordsworth and the Romantic Synecdoche," *Bucknell Review* 14(1), March 1966, 37-38.

WORDSWORTH, WILLIAM *(Cont.)*

"Strange fits of passion have I known"

PATRICIA M. BALL. *The Heart's Events,* pp. 10-13.

KENT BEYETTE. "Wordsworth's Medical Muse: Erasmus Darwin and Psychology in 'Strange Fits of Passion Have I Know,' " *Literature and Psychology* 23(3), 1973, 93-101.

FRANCES C. FERGUSON. "The Lucy Poems: Wordsworth's Quest for a Poetic Object," *ELH* 40(4), Winter 1973, 538-40.

FREDERICK GARBER. "Wordsworth and the Romantic Synecdoche," *Bucknell Review* 14(1), March 1966, 38-39.

SPENCER HALL. "Wordsworth's 'Lucy' Poems: Context and Meaning," *Studies in Romanticism* 10(3), Summer 1971, 163-66.

F. R. LEAVIS. *Revaluation,* pp. 199-202.

RICHARD E. MATLAK. "Wordsworth's Lucy Poems in Psychobiological Context," *PMLA* 93(1), January 1978, 51-54.

JOHN PRICE. "Wordsworth's *Lucy,*" *American Imago* 31(4), Winter 1974, 360-77.

JAMES G. TAAFFE. "Poet and Lover in Wordsworth's 'Lucy' Poems," *Modern Language Review* 61(2), April 1966, 176-77.

"Surprised by Joy"

REUBEN ARTHUR BROWER. *The Fields of Light,* pp. 88-92.

ELIZABETH DREW. *Poetry,* pp. 123-24.

F. R. LEAVIS. "Imagery and Movement: Notes in the Analysis of Poetry," 13(2), September 1945, 125-27.

"The Tables Turned"

T. R. BARNES. *English Verse,* pp. 170-71.

ERNEST BERNHARDT-KABISCH. "Wordsworth's Expostulator: Taylor or Hazlitt?" *English Language Notes* 2(2), December 1964, 102-5.

"There Was a Boy"

STEPHEN J. SPECTOR. "Wordsworth's Mirror Imagery and the Picturesque Tradition," *ELH* 44(1), Spring 1977, 86-92, 102-4.

"These chairs they have no words to utter"

FORD SWETNAM. "The Controversial Uses of Wordsworth's Comedy," *Wordsworth Circle* 3(1), Winter 1972, 37-39.

"The Thorn"

THOMAS L. ASHTON. "*The Thorn*: Wordsworth's Insensitive Plant," *Huntington Library Quarterly* 35(2), February 1972, 171-87.

FREDERICK L. BEATY. *Light from Heaven,* pp. 71-72.

ALBERT S. GÉRARD. "Of Trees and Men: The Unity of Wordsworth's *The Thorn,*" *Essays in Criticism* 14(3), July 1964, 237-55.

MICHAEL KIRKHAM. "Innocence and Experience In Wordsworth's 'The Thorn,' " *Ariel* 5(1), January 1974, 66-80.

W. J. B. OWEN. " 'The Thorn' and the Poet's Intention," *Wordsworth Circle* 8(1), Winter 1977, 3-17.

STEPHEN MAXFIELD PARRISH. " 'The Thorn': Wordsworth's Dramatic Monologue," *Journal of English Literary History* 24(2), June 1957, 153-63.

GENE W. RUOFF. "Religious Implications of Wordsworth's Imagination," *Studies in Romanticism* 12(3), Summer 1973, 673-74.

GORDON K. THOMAS. "Coleridge Stuck on 'The Thorn,' " *Wordsworth Circle* 9(4), Autumn 1978, 379-81.

SUSAN J. WOLFSON. "The Speaker as Questioner in *Lyrical Ballads,*" *Journal of English and Germanic Philology* 77(4), October 1978, 553-59.

"Three years she grew in sun and shower"

PATRICIA M. BALL. *The Heart's Events,* pp. 15-17.

FRANCIS CHRISTENSEN. *Explicator* 4(3), December 1945, Item 18.

FRED A. DUDLEY. *Explicator* 2(4), February 1944, Q19.

FRANCES C. FERGUSON. " 'The Lucy Poems': Wordsworth's Quest for a Poetic Object," *ELH* 40(4), Winter 1973, 543-46.

SPENCER HALL. "Wordsworth's 'Lucy' Poems: Context and Meaning," *Studies in Romanticism* 10(3), Summer 1971, 166-68.

MURRAY KRIEGER. *The Classic Vision,* pp. 167-69.

RICHARD E. MATLAK. "Wordsworth's Lucy Poems in Psychobiological Context," *PMLA* 93(1), January 1978, 57-58.

CHARLES J. SMITH. "The Contrarieties: Wordsworth's Dualistic Imagery," *PMLA* 69(5), December 1954, 1185.

JAMES G. TAAFFE. "Poet and Lover in Wordsworth's 'Lucy' Poems," *Modern Language Review* 61(2), April 1966, 178.

HAROLD E. TOLIVER. *Pastoral Forms and Attitudes,* pp. 247-48.

J. R. WATSON. "Lucy and the Earth-Mother," *Essays in Criticism* 27(3), July 1977, 191-93.

"Thy Art be Nature"

MAX F. SCHULZ. "The Perseverance of Romanticism: From Organism to Artifact," *Clio* 3(2), February 1974, 165-66.

"To Joanna"

JOHN A. HODGSON. "Wordsworth Teaching: 'To Joanna,' " *Wordsworth Cirle* 9(4), Autumn 1978, 362-64.

"To my Sister"

T. R. BARNES. *English Verse,* pp. 173-75.

MURRAY KRIEGER. *The Classic Vision,* pp. 165-67.

"To the Cuckoo"

JEROME BEATY and WILLIAM H. MATCHETT. *Poetry From Statement to Meaning,* pp. 250-54.

MURRAY KRIEGER. *The Classic Vision,* pp. 161-65.

HAROLD E. TOLIVER. *Pastoral Forms and Attitudes,* pp. 220-21.

"To the Torrent at the Devil's Bridge, North Wales, 1824"

GEOFFREY H. HARTMAN. "Blessing the Torrent: On Wordsworth's Later Style," *PMLA* 93(2), March 1978, 196-204.

"The Tuft of Primroses"

JAMES A. BUTLER. "Wordsworth's *Tuft of Primroses*: 'An Unrelenting Doom,' " *Studies in Romanticism* 14(3), Summer 1975, 237-48.

LAURENCE GOLDSTEIN. "The Auburn Syndrome: Change and Loss in 'The Deserted Village' and Wordsworth's Grasmere," *ELH* 40(3), Fall 1973, 364-71.

KENNETH R. JOHNSTON. "Wordsworth's Last Beginning: *The Recluse* in 1808," *ELH* 43(3), Fall 1976, 316-41.

"The Two April Mornings"

ANNE KOSTELANETZ. "Wordsworth's Conversations: A Reading of 'Two April Mornings' and 'The Fountain,' " *ELH* 33(1), March 1966, 43-52.

RICHARD E. MATLAK. "The Men in Wordsworth's Life," *Wordsworth Circle* 9(4), Autumn 1978, 392-93.

HAROLD E. TOLIVER. *Pastoral Forms and Attitudes*, pp. 252-54.

"Vaudracour and Julia"

FREDERICK L. BEATY. *Light from Heaven*, pp. 67-70.

"Vernal Ode"

RICHARD D. McGHEE. " 'And Earth and Stars Composed a Universal Heaven': A View of Wordsworth's Later Poetry," *Studies in English Literature 1500-1900* 11(4), Autumn 1971, 641-57.

"The Wanderer"

see "The Ruined Cottage"

"We Are Seven"

MARCEL KESSEL. *Explicator* 2(6), April 1944, Item 43.

ARTHUR K. MOORE. "A Folk Attitude in Wordsworth's 'We Are Seven,' " *Review of English Studies* 23(91), July 1947, 260-62. (P)

GAYLE S. SMITH. "Wordsworth's Socratic Irony," *Personalist* 44(1), Winter 1963, 55.

GERALD SOLOMON. "Heaven Lies," *Essays in Criticism* 28(4), October 1978, 350-51.

JUNE STURROCK. "Heaven Lies," *Essays in Criticism* 28(1), January 1978, 91-92.

SUSAN J. WOLFSON. "The Speaker as Questioner in *Lyrical Ballads*," *Journal of English and Germanic Philology* 77(4), October 1978, 549-50.

"When, to the attractions of the busy world"

JONATHAN RAMSEY. "Wordsworth's Silent Poet," *Modern Language Quarterly* 37(3), September 1976, 275-78.

FRED V. RANDEL. "Wordsworth's Homecoming," *Studies in English Literature 1500-1900* 17(4), Autumn 1977, 588-89.

"The world is too much with us"

ARNOLD B. FOX and MARTIN KALLICH. "Wordsworth's Sentimental Naturalism: Theme and Image in 'The World Is Too Much With Us,' " *Wordsworth Circle* 8(4), Autumn 1977, 327-32.

G. M. HARVEY. "The Design of Wordsworth's Sonnets," *Ariel* 6(3), July 1975, 85-89.

GILBERT HIGHET. *The Powers of Poetry* pp. 193-94.

KARL KROEBER. "A New Reading of 'The World Is Too Much With Us,' " *Studies in Romanticism* 2(3), Spring 1963, 183-88.

ALEX ZWERDLING. "Wordsworth and Greek Myth," *University of Toronto Quarterly* 33(4), July 1964, 348-49.

"Written in March"

CLEANTH BROOKS and ROBERT PENN WARREN. *Understanding Poetry*, fourth ed., pp. 74-75.

"Written in Very Early Youth"

MICHAEL G. COOKE. *The Romantic Will*, pp. 208-10.

"Yarrow Revisited"

JILL RUBENSTEIN. "Wordsworth and 'Localised Romance': The Scottish Poems of 1831," *Studies in English Literature 1500-1900* 16(4), Autumn 1976, 580-82.

RONALD SCHLEIFER. "Wordsworth's Yarrow and the Poetics of Repetition," *Modern Language Quarterly* 38(4), December 1977, 363-66.

"Yarrow Unvisited"

JEFFREY C. ROBINSON. "The Structure of Wordsworth's *Memorials of a Tour in Scotland, 1803*," *Papers on Language and Literature* 13(1), Winter 1977, 66-67.

RONALD SCHLEIFER. "Wordsworth's Yarrow and the Poetics of Repetition," *Modern Language Quarterly* 38(4), December 1977, 349-60.

"Yarrow Visited"

RONALD SCHLEIFER. "Wordsworth's Yarrow and the Poetics of Repetition," *Modern Language Quarterly* 38(4), December 1977, 360-63.

"Yes! thou art fair, yet be not moved"

HERBERT READ. "Apology for E. S.," *Sewanee Review* 76(2), Spring 1968, 206-7.

"Yew-Trees"

CLEANTH BROOKS and ROBERT PENN WARREN. *Understanding Poetry*, third ed., pp. 273-78.

GENE W. RUOFF. "Wordsworth's 'Yew-Trees' and Romantic Perception," *Modern Language Quarterly* 34(2), June 1973, 146-60.

GEORGE RYLANDS. "English Poets and the Abstract Word," *Essays and Studies* 16 (1930), 64-65. (P)

WOTTON, HENRY

"A Hymn to My God in a Night of My Late Sickness"

EARL DANIELS. *The Art of Reading Poetry*, pp. 438-42.

WRIGHT, JAMES

"Ars Poetica: Some Recent Criticism"

LAURENCE LIEBERMAN. *Unassigned Frequencies*, pp. 184-85.

"As I Step Over a Puddle at the End of Winter, I Think of an Ancient Chinese Governor"

PAUL CARROLL. *The Poem In Its Skin*, pp. 190-98.

"At the Executed Murderer's Grave"

PAUL A. LACEY. *The Inner War*, pp. 63-64.

RALPH J. MILLS. JR. *Contemporary American Poetry*, p. 207.

RALPH J. MILLS. JR. "James Wright's Poetry: Introductory Notes," *Chicago Review* 17(2-3), 1964, 136.

PETER A. STITT. "The Poetry of James Wright," *Minnesota Review* 11(2), Spring 1972, 15-16.

"At the Slackening of the Tide"

CLEANTH BROOKS, JOHN THIBAUT PURSER, and ROBERT PENN WARREN. *An Approach to Literature*, fifth ed., pp. 387-88.

WILLIAM B. TOOLE, III. *Explicator* 22(4), December 1963, Item 29.

"Autumn Begins in Martin's Ferry, Ohio"

ADRIAN BIRNEY. "Cursing America: The Tradition of the 'Anti-Whitman,' " *Genre* 2(4), December 1969, 311-12.

GEORGE S. LENSING and RONALD MORAN. *Four Poets and the Emotive Imagination*, pp. 115-16.

"Beginning"

PAUL A. LACEY. *The Inner War*, pp. 65-66.

"A Blessing"

GEORGE S. LENSING. "The Neo-Romanticism of James Dickey," *South Carolina Review* 10(2), April 1978, 26.

WRIGHT, JAMES (Cont.)

"A Blessing" (cont.)
GEORGE S. LENSING and RONALD MORAN. Four Poets and the Emotive Imagination, pp. 111-12.

"Blue Teal's Mother"
PAUL A. LACEY. The Inner War, pp. 74-75.

"Bologna: A Poem about Gold"
LAURENCE LIEBERMAN. Unassigned Frequencies, pp. 188-89.

"A Christmas Greeting"
PETER A. STITT. "The Poetry of James Wright," Minnesota Review 11(2), Spring 1972, 23.

"The Cold Divinities"
JAMES SEAY. "A World Immeasurably Alive and Good: A Look at James Wright's Collected Poems," Georgia Review 27(1), Spring 1973, 74.

"A Dream of Burial"
RALPH J. MILLS, JR. Contemporary American Poetry, pp. 216-17.

"Eisenhower's Visit to Franco, 1959"
PAUL BRESLIN. "How to Read the New Contemporary Poem," American Scholar 47(3), Summer 1978, 368-69.
PAUL A. LACEY. The Inner War, p. 64.
RALPH J. MILLS, JR. Contemporary American Poetry, pp. 214-15.
RALPH J. MILLS, JR. "James Wright's Poetry: Introductory Notes," Chicago Review 17(2-3), 1964, 141-42.

"Fear Is What Quickens Me"
NORMAN FRIEDMAN. "The Wesleyan Poets — III," Chicago Review 19(2), 1967, 71.
PAUL A. LACEY. The Inner War, p. 65.
RALPH J. MILLS, JR. Contemporary American Poetry, pp. 213-14.
RALPH J. MILLS, JR. "James Wright's Poetry: Introductory Notes," Chicago Review 17(2-3), 1964, 140.

"A Fit against the Country"
MADELINE DEFREES. "James Wright's Early Poems: A Study in 'Convulsive' Form," Modern Poetry Studies 2(6), 1972, 242-49.

"A Girl in the Window"
RALPH J. MILLS, JR. Contemporary American Poetry, pp. 198-200.
RALPH J. MILLS, JR. "James Wright's Poetry: Introductory Notes," Chicago Review 17(2-3), 1964, 129-30.

"Goodbye to the Poetry of Calcium"
GEORGE S. LENSING and RONALD MORAN. Four Poets and the Emotive Imagination, pp. 55-56.

"I Am a Sioux Brave, He Said in Minneapolis"
PETER A. STITT. "The Poetry of James Wright," Minnesota Review 11(2), Spring 1972, 24-25.

"I Was Afraid of Dying"
PAUL A. LACEY. The Inner War, p. 66.

"The Idea of the Good"
PAUL A. LACEY. The Inner War, pp. 73-74.

"In Shame and Humiliation"
PAUL A. LACEY. The Inner War, p. 62.

"The Jewel"
PAUL BRESLIN. "How to Read the New Contemporary Poem," American Scholar 47(3), Summer 1978, 360.

"Living by the Red River"
PAUL A. LACEY. The Inner War, p. 69.

"Lying in a Hammock at William Duffy's Farm in Pine Island, Minnesota"
NORMAN FRIEDMAN. "The Wesleyan Poets — III," Chicago Review 19(2), 1967, 71.
BRUCE HENRICKSEN. Explicator 32(5), January 1974, Item 40.
PAUL A. LACEY. The Inner War, pp. 66-67.
GEORGE S. LENSING and RONALD MORAN. Four Poets and the Emotive Imagination, pp. 107-10.
R. J. SPENDAL. Explicator 34(9), May 1976, Item 64.
PETER A. STITT. "The Poetry of James Wright," Minnesota Review 11(2), Spring 1972, 18.

"Many of our Waters: Variations on a Poem by a Black Child"
PAUL A. LACEY. The Inner War, pp. 78-80.
CHARLES MOLESWORTH. "James Wright and The Dissolving Self," Salmagundi 22-23 (Spring-Summer 1973), 231-32. Reprinted in: Contemporary Poetry in America, pp. 276-77.

"A Message Hidden in an Empty Wine Bottle"
RALPH J. MILLS, JR. Contemporary American Poetry, pp. 203-4.

"Milkweed"
PAUL A. LACEY. The Inner War, pp. 67-68.

"Miners"
PETER A. STITT. "The Poetry of James Wright," Minnesota Review 11(2), Spring 1972, 20-21.

"The Morality of Poetry"
PAUL A. LACEY. The Inner War, pp. 60-62.
RALPH J. MILLS, JR. Contemporary American Poetry, pp. 204-6.
RALPH J. MILLS, JR. "James Wright's Poetry: Introductory Notes," Chicago Review 17(2-3), 1964, 133-35.
CHARLES MOLESWORTH. "James Wright and The Dissolving Self," Salmagundi 22-23 (Spring-Summer 1973), 226-27. Reprinted in: Contemporary Poetry in America, pp. 271-72.

"Morning Hymn to a Dark Girl"
GEORGE S. LENSING and RONALD MORAN. Four Poets and the Emotive Imagination, pp. 93-95.

"Names Scarred at the Entrance to Chartres"
LAURENCE LIEBERMAN. Unassigned Frequencies, pp. 187-88.

"Northern Pike"
PETER A. STITT. "The Poetry of James Wright," Minnesota Review 11(2), Spring 1972, 132.

"The Old WPA Swimming Pool in Martins Ferry, Ohio"
GEORGE S. LENSING and RONALD MORAN. Four Poets and the Emotive Imagination, pp. 129-30.

"On the Skeleton of a Hound"
RALPH J. MILLS, JR. Contemporary American Poetry, pp. 202-3.
RALPH J. MILLS, JR. "James Wright's Poetry: Introductory Notes," Chicago Review 17(2-3), 1964, 131-32.

"Outside Fargo, North Dakota"
CHARLES MOLESWORTH. "James Wright and The Dissolving Self," Salmagundi 22-23 (Spring-Summer 1973), 228-29. Reprinted in: Contemporary Poetry in America, pp. 273-74.

"Prayer to the Good Poet"
LAURENCE LIEBERMAN. *Unassigned Frequencies,* pp. 185-87.

"The Quest"
PETER A. STITT. "The Poetry of James Wright," *Minnesota Review* 11(2), Spring 1972, 31-32.

"Saint Judas"
PETER A. STITT. "The Poetry of James Wright," *Minnesota Review* 11(2), Spring 1972, 16-17.

"A Secret Gratitude"
PAUL A. LACEY. *The Inner War,* pp. 75-76.
PETER A. STITT. "The Poetry of James Wright," *Minnesota Review* 11(2), Spring 1972, 29-31.

"Small Frogs Killed on a Highway"
PAUL A. LACEY. *The Inner War,* p. 77.
GEORGE S. LENSING and RONALD MORAN. *Four Poets and the Emotive Imagination,* p. 124.

"Speak"
EDWARD BUTSCHER. "The Rise and Fall of James Wright," *Georgia Review* 28(2), Summer 1974, 264-65.
PAUL A. LACEY. *The Inner War,* pp. 70-72.
PETER A. STITT. "The Poetry of James Wright," *Minnesota Review* 11(2), Spring 1972, 25.

"Spring Images"
MORRIS DICKSTEIN. "Allen Ginsberg and the 60's," *Commentary* 49(1), January 1970, 69.

"Three Sentences for a Dead Swan"
PETER A. STITT. "The Poetry of James Wright," *Minnesota Review* 11(2), Spring 1972, 27.

"To a Fugitive"
RALPH J. MILLS, JR. *Contemporary American Poetry,* p. 201.
RALPH J. MILLS, JR. "James Wright's Poetry: Introductory Notes," *Chicago Review* 17(2-3), 1964, 131.

"To Harvey, Who Traced the Circulation"
PAUL A. LACEY. *The Inner War,* pp. 77-78.

"To the Ghost of a Kite"
GEORGE S. LENSING and RONALD MORAN. *Four Poets and the Emotive Imagination,* pp. 102-5.

"To the Muse"
PETER A. STITT. "The Poetry of James Wright," *Minnesota Review* 11(2), Spring 1972, 28.

"Trying to Pray"
JAMES SEAY. "A World Immeasurably Alive and Good: A Look at James Wright's *Collected Poems,*" *Georgia Review* 27(1), Spring 1973, 73-74.

"Two Hangovers"
EDWARD BUTSCHER. "The Rise and Fall of James Wright," *Georgia Review* 28(2), Summer 1974, 259-63.

"Two Poems about President Harding: His Death"
ROBERT PINSKY. *The Situation of Poetry,* pp. 166-67.

WRIGHT, RICHARD

"Between the World and Me"
DAVID P. DEMAREST, JR. "Richard Wright: The Meaning of Violence," *Negro American Literature Forum* 8(3), Fall 1974, 236-37.
KENETH KINNAMON. "Richard Wright: Proletarian Poet," *Concerning Poetry* 2(1), Spring 1969, 44-45.

"Everywhere Burning Waters Rise"
KENETH KINNAMON. "Richard Wright: Proletarian Poet," *Concerning Poetry* 2(1), Spring 1969, 42-43.

"I Have Seen Black Hands"
KENETH KINNAMON. "Richard Wright: Proletarian Poet," *Concerning Poetry* 2(1), Spring 1969, 39-41.

WYATT, THOMAS

"Behold, Love, thy power how she despiseth"
JOSEPHINE MILES. *Major Adjectives in English Poetry,* pp. 322-25.

"Caesar when that the traitor of Egypt"
JONATHAN Z. KAMHOLTZ. "Thomas Wyatt's Poetry: The Politics of Love," *Criticism* 20(4), Fall 1978, 355-56.

"Desire, alas, my master and my foe"
HALLETT SMITH. "The Art of Sir Thomas Wyatt," *Huntington Library Quarterly* 9(4), August 1946, 329-31.

"Disdain me not without desert"
JOHN T. SHAWCROSS. "The Poet as Orator: One Phase of His Judicial Pose," in *The Rhetoric of Renaissance Poetry,* pp. 8-11.

"Divers doth use, as I have heard and know"
DONALD M. FRIEDMAN. "Wyatt's *Amoris Personae,*" *Modern Language Quarterly* 27(2), June 1966, 144-46.
MURRAY KRIEGER. *The Classic Vision,* pp. 62-66.
MURRAY KRIEGER. "The Continuing Need for Criticism," *Concerning Poetry* 1(1), Spring 1968, 14-16.
DOUGLAS L. PETERSON. *The English Lyric from Wyatt to Donne,* p. 105.

"Each man me telleth I change most my devise"
DONALD M. FRIEDMAN. "Wyatt's *Amoris Personae,*" *Modern Language Quarterly* 27(2), June 1966, 140-41.

"Farewell Love, and all thy laws forever"
DONALD M. FRIEDMAN. "The 'Thing' in Wyatt's Mind," *Essays in Criticism* 16(4), October 1966, 376.

"Forget not yet the tried intent"
DAVID DAICHES and WILLIAM CHARVAT. *Poems in English,* p. 642.
JOHN T. SHAWCROSS. "The Poet as Orator: One Phase of His Judicial Pose," in *The Rhetoric of Renaissance Poetry,* pp. 11-12.

"The furious gun in his raging fire"
JONATHAN Z. KAMHOLTZ. "Thomas Wyatt's Poetry: The Politics of Love," *Criticism* 20(4), Fall 1978, 357.

"Go, burning sighs, unto the frozen heart"
DONALD L. GUSS. "Wyatt's Petrarchism: An Instance of Creative Imagination in the Renaissance," *Huntington Library Quarterly* 29(1), November 1965, 12-13.

"Grudge on who liste"
RICHARD LEIGHTON GREENE. "A Carol of Anne Boleyn by Wyatt," *Review of English Studies,* n.s., 25(100), November 1974, 437-39.

"Hate whom ye list"
NANCY S. LEONARD. "The Speaker in Wyatt's Lyric Poetry," *Huntington Library Quarterly* 41(1), November 1977, 16-17.

"He is not dead that sometime hath a fall"
JONATHAN Z. KAMHOLTZ. "Thomas Wyatt's Poetry: The Politics of Love," *Criticism* 20(4), Fall 1978, 349-52.

WYATT, THOMAS *(Cont.)*

"Heaven and earth, and that hear me pain"

> HALLETT SMITH. "The Art of Sir Thomas Wyatt," *Huntington Library Quarterly* 9(4), August 1946, 342-44.

"If chance assigned"

> JOOST DAALDER. "Wyatt and 'Liberty,' " *Essays in Criticism* 23(1), January 1973, 64-65.

"If fancy would favor"

> DONALD M. FRIEDMAN. "Wyatt and the Ambiguities of Fancy," *Journal of English and Germanic Philology* 67(1), January 1968, 36-45.

"If thou wilt mighty be"

> DOUGLAS L. PETERSON. *The English Lyric from Wyatt to Donne,* pp. 110-11.

"In eternum I was once determed"

> NANCY S. LEONARD. "The Speaker in Wyatt's Lyric Poetry," *Huntington Library Quarterly* 41(1), November 1977, 11-13.

"Is it possible"

> THOMAS A. HANNEN. "The Humanism of Sir Thomas Wyatt," in *The Rhetoric of Renaissance Poetry,* pp. 45-51.
>
> DOUGLAS L. PETERSON. *The English Lyric from Wyatt to Donne,* pp. 114-15.

"It may be good, like it who list"

> JOOST DAALDER. "Wyatt and 'Liberty,' " *Essays in Criticism* 23(1), January 1973, 63-64.
>
> DONALD M. FRIEDMAN. "Wyatt's *Amoris Personae,*" *Modern Language Quarterly* 27(2), June 1966, 141-42.
>
> THOMAS A. HANNEN. "The Humanism of Sir Thomas Wyatt," in *The Rhetoric of Renaissance Poetry,* pp. 51-55.
>
> DOUGLAS A. PETERSON. *The English Lyric from Wyatt to Donne,* pp. 111-12.
>
> RONALD A. REBHOLZ. "Love's Newfangleness: A Comparison of Greville and Wyatt," *Studies in the Literary Imagination* 11(1), Spring 1978, 26-28.
>
> RAYMOND SOUTHALL. "The Personality of Sir Thomas Wyatt," *Essays in Criticism* 14(1), January 1964, 50-52.

"It was my choice, it was no chance"

> DONALD M. FRIEDMAN. "Wyatt and the Ambiguities of Fancy," *Journal of English and Germanic Philology* 67(1), January 1968, 47-48.
>
> DOUGLAS L. PETERSON. *The English Lyric from Wyatt to Donne,* pp. 106-9.

"Like as the bird in the cage enclosed"

> LEIGH WINSER. "The Question of Love Tradition in Wyatt's 'They Flee From Me,' " *Essays in Literature* 2(1), Spring 1975, 6-7.

"The long love that in my thought doth harbor"

> JOSEPHINE MILES. *Major Adjectives in English Poetry,* pp. 325-26.
>
> HALLETT SMITH. "The Art of Sir Thomas Wyatt," *Huntington Library Quarterly* 9(4), August 1946, 333-37.
>
> RAYMOND SOUTHALL. "The Personality of Sir Thomas Wyatt," *Essays in Criticism* 14(1), January 1964, 55-57.

"The Lover Compareth His State to a Ship in a Perilous Storm Tossed on the Sea"

> see "My galy charged with forgetfulness"

"The Lover for Shamefacedness Hideth His Desire within His Faithful Heart"

> see "The long love that in my thought doth harbor"

"The Lover Sendeth Sighs to Move His Suit"

> see "Go, burning sighs, unto the frozen heart"

"Mine own John Poyntz, since ye delight to know"

> JERRY MERMEL. "Sir Thomas Wyatt's Satires and the Humanist Debate Over Court Service," *Studies in the Literary Imagination* 11(1), Spring 1978, 69-73.
>
> DOUGLAS L. PETERSON. *The English Lyric from Wyatt to Donne,* pp. 88-90.

"My galy charged with forgetfulness"

> T. R. BARNES. *English Verse,* pp. 2-3.
>
> NANCY S. LEONARD. "The Speaker in Wyatt's Lyric Poetry," *Huntington Library Quarterly* 41(1), November 1977, 6-8.
>
> MAXWELL S. LURIA. "Wyatt's 'The Lover Compareth His State' and the Petrarchan Commentators," *Texas Studies in Literature and Language* 12(4), Winter 1971, 531-35.
>
> JOHN OLIVER PERRY. *The Experience of Poems,* pp. 180-81.
>
> DOUGLAS L. PETERSON. *The English Lyric from Wyatt to Donne,* pp. 99-100.
>
> RAYMOND SOUTHALL. "The Personality of Sir Thomas Wyatt," *Essays in Criticism* 14(1), January 1964, 57.

"My Lute awake!"

> T. R. BARNES. *English Verse,* pp. 6-7.
>
> DAVID DAICHES and WILLIAM CHARVAT. *Poems in English,* p. 644.
>
> WINIFRED MAYNARD. "The Lyrics of Wyatt: Poems or Songs?" *Review of English Studies,* n.s., 16(63), August 1965, 250-51.
>
> HALLETT SMITH. "The Art of Sir Thomas Wyatt," *Huntington Library Quarterly* 9(4), August 1946, 344-45.

"My mother's maids, when they did sew and spin"

> JERRY MERMEL. "Sir Thomas Wyatt's Satires and the Humanist Debate Over Court Service," *Studies in the Literary Imagination* 11(1), Spring 1978, 73-77.

"Once as me thought fortune me kissed"

> MICHAEL BATH. "Wyatt and 'Liberty,' " *Essays in Criticism* 23(3), July 1973, 322-28.

"Patience: though I have not"

> JOHN T. SHAWCROSS. "The Poet as Orator: One Phase in His Judicial Pose," in *The Rhetoric of Renaissance Poetry,* pp. 14-16.

"Perdie, I said it not"

> DONALD L. GUSS. "Wyatt's Petrarchism: An Instance of Creative Imitation in the Renaissance," *Huntington Library Quarterly* 29(1), November 1965, 9-10.
>
> ANTHONY LABRANCHE. "Imitation: Getting in Touch," *Modern Language Quarterly* 31(3), September 1970, 312-15.

"The pillar perished is whereto I leant"

> THOMAS A. HANNEN. "The Humanism of Sir Thomas Wyatt," in *The Rhetoric of Renaissance Poetry,* p. 55.
>
> JONATHAN Z. KAMHOLTZ. "Thomas Wyatt's Poetry: The Politics of Love," *Criticism* 20(4), Fall 1978, 357-58.

"Process of time worketh such wonder"

NANCY S. LEONARD. "The Speaker in Wyatt's Lyric Poetry," *Huntington Library Quarterly* 41(1), November 1977, 5-6.

"Psalm 38" ("O Lord, as I thee have both prayed and pray")

DONALD M. FRIEDMAN. "The 'Thing' in Wyatt's Mind," *Essays in Criticism* 16(4), October 1966, 378.

"Psalm 102" ("Lord, hear my prayer, and let my cry pass")

DONALD M. FRIEDMAN. "The 'Thing' in Wyatt's Mind," *Essays in Criticism* 16(4), October 1966, 379-80.

"Resound my voice, ye woods that hear me plain"

DOUGLAS L. PETERSON. *The English Lyric from Wyatt to Donne*, pp. 96-97.

RAYMOND SOUTHALL. "The Personality of Sir Thomas Wyatt," *Essays in Criticism* 14(1), January 1964, 53-54.

"Satire I"

see "Mine own John Poyntz, since ye delight to know"

"Satire II"

see "My mother's maids, when they did sew and spin"

"Satire III"

see "A spending hand that alway poureth out"

"Since love is such that as ye wot"

MICHAEL MCCANLES. "Love and Power in the Poetry of Sir Thomas Wyatt," *Modern Language Quarterly* 29(2), June 1968, 158-60.

"Some fowls there be that have so perfect sight"

DOUGLAS L. PETERSON. *The English Lyric from Waytt to Donne*, pp. 97-99.

"A spending hand that alway poureth out"

JERRY MERMEL. "Sir Thomas Wyatt's Satires and the Humanist Debate Over Court Service," *Studies in the Literary Imagination* 11(1), Spring 1978, 77-79.

"Stand whoso list upon the slipper top"

VINCENT BUCKLEY. *Poetry and the Sacred*, pp. 83-85.

THOMAS A. HANNEN. "The Humanism of Sir Thomas Wyatt," in *The Rhetoric of Renaissance Poetry*, pp. 38-39.

"There was never nothing more me pained"

JOHN DOUGLAS BOYD. "Literary Interpretation and the *Subjective* Correlative: An Illustration from Wyatt," *Essays in Criticism* 21(4), October 1971, 327-46.

JAMES REEVES and MARTIN SEYMOUR-SMITH. *Inside Poetry*, pp. 40-42.

"They flee from me, that sometime did me seek"

F. W. BATESON. *English Poetry*, pp. 142-48.

F. W. BATESON. *English Poetry and the English Language*, pp. 59-60.

ANN BERTHOFF. "The Falconer's Dream of Trust: Wyatt's 'They Fle From Me,'" *Sewanee Review* 71(3), Summer 1963, 477-94.

VINCENT BUCKLEY. *Poetry and the Sacred*, pp. 95-98.

FREDERICK M. COMBELLACK. *Explicator* 17(5), February 1959, Item 36.

DAVID DAICHES and WILLIAM CHARVAT. *Poems in English*, pp. 642-44.

C. DAY-LEWIS. *The Lyric Impulse*, pp. 6-7.

LEONARD DEAN. *English Masterpieces*, edited by William Frost, Maynard Mack, and Leonard Dean, vol. 3: *Renaissance Poetry*, pp. 2-3.

E. E. DUNCAN-JONES. *Explicator* 12(2), November 1953, Item 9.

ALISTAIR FOWLER. *Conceitful Thought*, pp. 11-18.

DONALD M. FRIEDMAN. "The Mind in the Poem: Wyatt's 'They Fle From Me,'" *Studies in English Literature 1500-1900* 7(1), Winter 1967, 1-13.

ALBERT S. GERARD. "Wyatt's 'They Fle From Me,'" *Essays in Criticism* 11(3), July 1961, 359-65.

RICHARD LEIGHTON GREENE. "Wyatt's 'They Fle From Me' and the Busily Seeking Critics," *Bucknell Review* 12(3), December 1964, 17-30.

J. D. HAINSWORTH. "Sir Thomas Wyatt's Use of the Love Convention," *Essays in Criticism* 7(1), January 1957, 90-95.

RICHARD HOWARD. "Wyatt: They Flee From Me," in *Master Poems of the English Language*, pp. 3-5.

S. F. JOHNSON. *Explicator* 5(6), April 1947, Item 40.

S. F. JOHNSON. *Explicator* 11(6), April 1953, Item 39.

STANLEY J. KOZISKOWSKI. "Wyatt's 'They Flee From Me' and Churchyard's Complaint of Jane Shore," *Notes and Queries*, n.s., 25(5), October 1978, 416-17.

MICHAEL MCCANLES. "Love and Power in the Poetry of Sir Thomas Wyatt," *Modern Language Quarterly* 29(2), June 1968, 152-57.

ARTHUR K. MOORE. "The Design of Wyatt's *They Fle From Me*," *Anglia* 71(1), 1952, 102-11.

LEONARD E. NATHAN. "Tradition and Newfangleness in Wyatt's 'They Flee From Me,'" *ELH* 32(1), March 1965, 1-16.

WILLIAM R. ORWEN. *Explicator* 5(6), April 1947, Item 40.

M. L. ROSENTHAL. *Poetry and the Common Life*, pp. 125-29.

AGNES STEIN. *The Uses of Poetry*, pp. 99-100.

ARNOLD STEIN. "Wyatt's 'They Flee From Me,'" *Sewanee Review* 67(1), Winter 1959, 28-44.

ROBERT G. TWOMBLY. "Beauty and the (Subverted) Beast; Wyatt's 'They fle from me,'" *Texas Studies in Literature and Language* 10(4), Winter 1969, 489-503.

MARK VAN DOREN. *Introduction to Poetry*, pp. 33-39.

LEIGH WINSER. "The Question of Love Tradition in Wyatt's 'They Flee From Me,'" *Essays in Literature* 2(1), Spring 1975, 3-9.

"Though I cannot your cruelty constrain"

NANCY S. LEONARD. "The Speaker in Wyatt's Lyric Poetry," *Huntington Library Quarterly* 41(1), November 1977, 8-10.

"To rail or jest ye know I use it not"

DONALD M. FRIEDMAN. "Wyatt's *Amoris Personae*," *Modern Language Quarterly* 27(2), June 1966, 143-44.

"To wish and want and not obtain"

NANCY S. LEONARD. "The Speaker in Wyatt's Lyric Poetry," *Huntington Library Quarterly* 41(1), November 1977, 3-5.

"Unstable dream, according to the place"

RAYMOND SOUTHALL. "The Personality of Sir Thomas Wyatt," *Essays in Criticism* 14(1), January 1964, 58-59.

"What meaneth this? When I lie alone"

NANCY S. LEONARD. "The Speaker in Wyatt's Lyric Poetry," *Huntington Library Quarterly* 41(1), November 1977, 10-11.

WYATT, THOMAS *(Cont.)*

"What 'vaileth truth? Or by it to take pain"

> THOMAS A. HANNEN. "The Humanism of Sir Thomas Wyatt," in *The Rhetoric of Renaissance Poetry*, pp. 42-43.

"What word is that, that changeth not"

> JONATHAN Z. KAMHOLTZ. "Thomas Wyatt's Poetry: The Politics of Love," *Criticism* 20(4), Fall 1978, 360-62.
>
> ANTHONY LOW. "Wyatt's 'What Word Is That,' " *English Language Notes* 10(2), December 1972, 89-90.

"Whoso list to hunt: I know where is an hind"

> F. W. BATESON. *English Poetry*, pp. 141-48.
>
> HARRY BROWN and JOHN MILSTEAD. *What the Poem Means*, pp. 294-95.
>
> VINCENT BUCKLEY. *Poetry and the Sacred*, pp. 87-89.
>
> ALISTAIR FOWLER. *Conceitful Thought*, pp. 2-6.
>
> JEAN OVERTON FULLER. "Wyatt and Petrarch," *Essays in Criticism* 14(3), July 1964, 324-26.
>
> DONALD L. GUSS. "Wyatt's Petrarchism: An Instance of Creative Imitation in the Renaissance," *Huntington Library Quarterly* 29(1), November 1965, 10-11.
>
> JONATHAN Z. KAMHOLTZ. "Thomas Wyatt's Poetry: The Politics of Love," *Criticism* 20(4), Fall 1978, 362-65.
>
> NANCY S. LEONARD. "The Speaker in Wyatt's Lyric Poetry," *Huntington Library Quarterly* 41(1), November 1977, 13-16.
>
> DOUGLAS L. PETERSON. *The English Lyric from Wyatt to Donne*, pp. 100-2.
>
> RAYMOND SOUTHALL. "The Personality of Sir Thomas Wyatt," *Essays in Criticism* 14(1), January 1964, 60-62.
>
> ROBERT G. TWOMBLY. "Beauty and the (Subverted) Beast; Wyatt's 'They fle from me,' " *Texas Studies in Literature and Language* 10(4), Winter 1969, 493-95.

"Ye old mule, that think yourself so fair"

> RAYMOND SOUTHALL. "Wyatt's 'Ye Old Mule,' " *English Language Notes* 5(1), September 1967, 5-11.
>
> ROBERT G. TWOMBLY. "Beauty and the (Subverted) Beast; Wyatt's 'They fle from me,' " *Texas Studies in Literature and Language* 10(4), Winter 1969, 501-3.

WYCHERLEY, WILLIAM

"I love variety, 'tis true"

> JOHN HAYMAN. "Raillery in Restoration Satire," *Huntington Library Quarterly* 31(2), February 1968, 116-17.

WYLIE, ELINOR

"August"

> THOMAS A. GRAY. "Elinor Wylie: The Puritan Marrow and the Silver Filigree," *Arizona Quarterly* 19(4), Winter 1963, 354-55.

"Castilian"

> RICHARD E. AMACHER. *Explicator* 7(2), November 1948, Item 16.

"Chimaera Sleeping"

> CELESTE TURNER WRIGHT. "Elinor Wylie: The Glass Chimaera and the Minotaur," *Twentieth Century Literature* 12(1), April 1966, 24-25.

"Cold-Blooded Creatures"

> CHARLES CHILD WALCUTT. "Critic's Taste or Artist's Intention," *University of Kansas City Review* 12(4), Summer 1946, 279-82.

"Death and the Maiden"

> THOMAS A. GRAY. "Elinor Wylie: The Puritan Marrow and the Silver Filigree," *Arizona Quarterly* 19(4), Winter 1963, 346-47.

"Fable"

> THOMAS A. GRAY. "Elinor Wylie: The Puritan Marrow and the Silver Filigree," *Arizona Quarterly* 19(4), Winter 1963, 345-46.

"Hymn to Earth"

> W. NELSON FRANCIS. *Explicator* 17(6), March 1959, Item 40.

"Let No Charitable Hope"

> HARRY BROWN and JOHN MILSTEAD. *What the Poem Means*, p. 295.

"Let us leave talking of angelic hosts" *(One Person*, XVIII)

> THOMAS A. GRAY. "Elinor Wylie: The Puritan Marrow and the Silver Filigree," *Arizona Quarterly* 19(4), Winter 1963, 347-50.

"Minotaur"

> CELESTE TURNER WRIGHT. "Elinor Wylie: The Glass Chimaera and the Minotaur," *Twentieth Century Literature* 12(1), April 1966, 25-26.

"Puritan Sonnet"

> LAURENCE PERRINE. *100 American Poems of the Twentieth Century*, pp. 86-87.

"Sanctuary"

> JAMES R. KREUZER. *Elements of Poetry*, pp. 165-66.

"This Corruptible"

> BABETTE DEUTSCH. *Poetry in Our Time*, p. 231; second ed., p. 254.

"The Tortoise in Eternity"

> RICHARD E. AMACHER. *Explicator* 6(5), March 1948, Item 33.

"Velvet Shoes"

> LAURENCE PERRINE. *Explicator* 13(3), December 1954, Item 17.
>
> MACKLIN THOMAS. "Analysis of the Experience in Lyric Poetry," *College English* 9(6), March 1948, 319-20.
>
> THOMAS J. WERTENBAKER, JR. "Into the Poet's Shoes," *English Journal* 53(5), May 1964, 370-72.

"Would I might make subliminal my flesh" *(One Person*, Sonnet VII)

> THOMAS A. GRAY. "Elinor Wylie: The Puritan Marrow and the Silver Filigree," *Arizona Quarterly* 19(4), Winter 1963, 347.

Y

YEATS, W. B.

"An Acre of Grass"

ELIZABETH DREW. *Poetry*, pp. 116-18.

LAURENCE PERRINE. *Explicator* 22(8), April 1964, Item 64.

WILLIAM V. SPANOS. "The Sexual Imagination in Yeat's Late Poetry: A Reading of 'An Acre of Grass,' " *CEA Critic* 32(1), October 1969, 16-18.

RAYMOND TSCHUMI. *Thought in Twentieth-Century English Poetry*, pp. 41-42.

"Adam's Curse"

JOHN CIARDI. *Dialogue with an Audience*, pp. 107-8.

GEORGE FRASER. *Essays on Twentieth-Century English Poets*, pp. 63-64.

ARNOLD GOLDMAN. "The Oeuvre Takes Shape: Yeats's Early Poetry," in *Victorian Poetry*, pp. 219-20.

M. L. ROSENTHAL. *Sailing into the Unknown*, pp. 139-40.

STEPHEN SPENDER. "W. B. Yeats as a Realist," *Criterion* 14(54), October 1934, 18-19.

CHAD and EVA T. WALSH. *Twice Ten*, pp. 139-42.

"After Long Silence"

CLEANTH BROOKS and ROBERT PENN WARREN. *Understanding Poetry*, pp. 224-30; revised ed., pp. 116-17; third ed., pp. 164-65; fourth ed., pp. 515-16.

WALLACE CABLE BROWN. " 'A Poem Should Not Mean But Be,' " *University of Kansas City Review* 15(1), Autumn 1948, 63.

F. O. MATTHIESSEN. "The Crooked Road," *Southern Review* 7(3), Winter 1942, 462-63. Reprinted in: F. O. Matthiessen. *The Responsibilities of the Critic*, pp. 32-33.

FRED B. MILLETT. *The Rebirth of Liberal Education*, pp. 166-68.

JOHN E. PARISH. "The Tone of Yeats' *After Long Silence*," *Western Humanities Review* 16(4), Autumn 1962, 377-79.

THOMAS PARKINSON. "Vestiges of Creation," *Sewanee Review* 69(1), Winter 1961, 86-92.

LAURENCE PERRINE. "Yeats's 'Supreme Theme,' " *Concerning Poetry* 10(1), Spring 1977, 13-15.

JOHN CROWE RANSOM. "The Irish, The Gaelic, the Byzantine," *Southern Review* 7(3), Winter 1942, 530-31.

ROBERT SCHRAMM. "The Line Unit: Studies in the Later Poetry of W. B. Yeats," *Ohio University Review* 3 (1961), 35-37.

"All Souls' Night"

CLEANTH BROOKS. *Modern Poetry and the Tradition*, pp. 29-30.

DENIS DONOGHUE. *The Ordinary Universe*, p. 117.

STUART HIRSCHBERG. " 'All Souls' Night': A Prototype for 'Byzantium,' " *Yeats Eliot Review* 5(1), 1978, 44-50.

JAMES H. O'BRIEN. "Yeats' Dark Night of Self and *The Tower*," *Bucknell Review* 15(2), May 1967, 24-25.

M. L. ROSENTHAL. *Sailing into the Unknown*, pp. 150-53.

J. I. M. STEWART. *Eight Modern Writers*, pp. 375-77.

RAYMOND TSCHUMI. *Thought in Twentieth-Century English Poetry*, pp. 63-67.

"Among School Children"

T. R. BARNES. *English Verse*, pp. 310-14.

C. M. BOWRA. *The Heritage of Symbolism*, pp. 211-12.

CLEANTH BROOKS. *The Well Wrought Urn*, pp. 178-91; revised ed., pp. 145-56.

CLEANTH BROOKS and ROBERT PENN WARREN. *Understanding Poetry*, revised ed., pp. 359-60; third ed., pp. 337-38.

HARRY BROWN and JOHN MILSTEAD. *What the Poem Means*, pp. 297-98.

RICHARD CHASE. "Myth as Literature," *English Institute Essays*, 1947, pp. 18-20. (P)

LEVEN MAGRUDER DAWSON. " 'Among School Children': 'Labour' and 'Play,' " *Philological Quarterly* 52(2), April 1973, 286-95.

BABETTE DEUTSCH. *Poetry in Our Time*, p. 269; second ed., pp. 302-3.

VIVIAN DE SOLA PINTO. *Crisis in English Poetry*, pp. 107-9; fifth ed., pp. 95-97.

STEPHEN FEINBERG. *Explicator* 33(6), February 1975, Item 45.

G. S. FRASER. *Vision and Rhetoric*, pp. 73-81.

MICHAEL P. GALLAGHER. "Yeats, Syntax, and the Self," *Arizona Quarterly* 26(1), Spring 1970, 9-16.

CHRISTOPHER GILLIE. *Movements in English Literature*, pp. 151-53.

DAVID HOLBROOK. *Lost Bearings in English Poetry*, pp. 194-203.

YEATS, W. B. *(Cont.)*
"Among School Children" *(cont.)*

WALLACE G. KAY. "'As Recollection or the Drug Decide': Images and Imaginings in 'Among School Children' and *Blowup*," *Southern Quarterly* 12(3), April 1974, 225-32.

FRANK KERMODE. *Romantic Image,* pp. 83-84.

L. C. KNIGHTS. *Explorations,* pp. 200-2.

L. C. KNIGHTS. "W. B. Yeats: The Assertion of Values," *Southern Review* 7(3), Winter 1942, 436-38.

ROBERT LANGBAUM. "The Mysteries of Identity: A Theme in Modern Literature," *American Scholar* 34(4), Autumn 1965, 581-83. Reprinted in: *The Modern Spirit,* pp. 178-80.

JOHN F. LYNEN. "Forms of Time in Modern Poetry," *Queen's Quarterly* 82(3), Autumn 1975, 362.

JAMES H. O'BRIEN. "Yeats' Dark Night of Self and *The Tower*," *Bucknell Review* 15(2), May 1967, 21-23.

JAMES OLNEY. "W. B. Yeats's Daimonic Memory," *Sewanee Review* 85(4), Fall 1977, 602-3.

THOMAS PARKINSON. "The Individuality of Yeats," *Pacific Spectator* 6(Autumn 1952), 492-93, 496.

THOMAS PARKINSON. "Vestiges of Creation," *Sewanee Review* 69(1), Winter 1961, 92-111.

JOHN OLIVER PERRY. *The Experience of Poems,* pp. 303-5.

CHARLES A. RAINES. "Yeats' Metaphors of Permanence," *Twentieth Century Literature* 5(1), April 1959, 18-19.

JOHN CROWE RANSOM. "The Irish, the Gaelic, the Byzantine," *Southern Review* 7(3), Winter 1942, 536-38.

M. L. ROSENTHAL. *Poetry and the Common Life,* pp. 25-27, 30-32.

M. L. ROSENTHAL. *Sailing into the Unknown,* pp. 149-50.

ROBERT S. RYF. "Yeats's Major Metaphysical Poems," *Journal of Modern Literature* 4(3), February 1975, 617-20.

J. I. M. STEWART. *Eight Modern Writers,* pp. 373-75.

WILLIAM I. THOMPSON. "Collapsed Universe and Structured Poem: An Essay in Whiteheadian Criticism," *College English* 28(1), October 1966, 35-39.

HELEN VENDLER. "Sacred and Profane Perfection in Yeats," *Southern Review,* n.s., 9(1), Winter 1973, 110-12.

JOHN WAIN. "W. B. Yeats: Among School Children," in *Interpretations,* pp. 196-210.

CHARLES C. WALCUTT. *Explicator* 8(6), April 1950, Item 42.

"Ancestral Houses"
see also "Meditations in Time of Civil War"

GRAHAM MARTIN. "Fine Manners, Liberal Speech: A Note on the Public Poetry of W. B. Yeats," *Essays in Criticism* 11(1), January 1961, 54-55.

"The Apparitions"

R. P. BLACKMUR. "Between Myth and Philosophy: Fragments of W. B. Yeats," *Southern Review* 7(3), Winter 1942, 412-13. Reprinted in: R. P. Blackmur. *Language as Gesture,* pp. 110-12. Also: R. P. Blackmur. *Form and Value in Modern Poetry,* pp. 64-66.

"At Algeciras — A Meditation upon Death"

BABETTE DEUTSCH. *Poetry in Our Time,* p. 267; second ed., p. 300.

"Baile and Aillinn"

T. K. DUNSEATH. "Yeats and the Genesis of Supernatural Song," *ELH* 28(4), December 1961, 400-4.

"The Ballad of Father Gilligan"

MARK VAN DOREN. *Introduction to Poetry,* pp. 130-33.

"Before the World Was Made"

T. R. HENN. *The Apple and the Spectroscope,* pp. 54-56.

"Beggar to Beggar Cried"

DANIEL HOFFMAN. *Barbarous Knowledge,* pp. 43-44.

"The Black Tower"

JAMES BENZIGER. *Images of Eternity,* pp. 234-35.

W. J. KEITH. "Yeats's Arthurian Black Tower," *Modern Language Notes* 75(2), February 1960, 119-23.

T. R. HENN. "The Accent of Yeats' *Last Poems*," *Essays and Studies,* n.s., 9 (1956), 67-69.

SUSAN MATTHEWS. "Defiance and Defeat in W. B. Yeats' 'The Black Tower,'" *Concerning Poetry* 5(2), Fall 1972, 22-26.

"Blood and the Moon"

CLEANTH BROOKS, JR. "The Vision of William Butler Yeats," *Southern Review* 4(1), Summer 1938, 121-23. (P)

DENIS DONOGHUE. "Notes Towards a Critical Method: Language as Order," *Studies* 44(174), Summer 1955, 186-87. (P)

LILLIAN FEDER. *Ancient Myth in Modern Poetry,* pp. 286-88.

JEFFREY MEYERS. *Explicator* 30(6), February 1972, Item 50.

THOMAS R. WHITAKER. "Poet of Anglo-Ireland," in *Modern Poetry,* pp. 433-37.

"A Bronze Head"

ROBERT D. DENHAM. *Explicator* 29(2), October 1970, Item 14.

BARBARA HARDY. *The Advantage of Lyric,* p. 77.

MARJORIE G. PERLOFF. "'Heart Mysteries': The Later Love Lyrics of W. B. Yeats," *Contemporary Literature* 10(2), Spring 1969, 280-81.

F. A. C. WILSON. "Yeats's 'A Bronze Head': A Freudian Investigation," *Literature and Psychology* 22(1), 1972, 9-12.

"Byzantium"

ROBERT MARTIN ADAMS. "Now That My Ladder's Gone — Yeats Without Myth," *Accent* 13(3), Summer 1953, 143-48.

T. R. BARNES. *English Verse,* pp. 306-10.

MICHAEL BELL. "The Assimilation of Doubt in Yeats's Visionary Poems," *Queen's Quarterly* 80(3), Autumn 1973, 393-94.

HARRY BERGER. "Biography as Interpretation, Interpretation as Biography," *College English* 28(2), November 1966, 124.

R. P. BLACKMUR. *The Expense of Greatness,* p. 98. Reprinted in: *Critiques and Essays in Criticism,* pp. 372-73. Also: R. P. Blackmur. *Form and Value in Modern Poetry,* pp. 52-53. Also: R. P. Blackmur. *Language as Gesture,* pp. 98-99.

HAROLD BLOOM. *Poetry and Repression,* pp. 222-28.

CLEANTH BROOKS. *Modern Poetry and the Tradition,* pp. 192-200.

CLEANTH BROOKS, JR. "The Vision of William Butler Yeats," *Southern Review* 4(1), Summer 1938, 133-40.

HARRY BROWN and JOHN MILSTEAD. *What the Poem Means*, p. 299.

DAVID DAICHES. *Poetry and the Modern World*, pp. 181-85.

DAVID DAICHES and WILLIAM CHARVAT. *Poems in English*, pp. 733-35.

A. DAVENPORT. "W. B. Yeats and the Upanishads," *Review of English Studies*, n.s., 3(9), January 1952, 59-60.

DENIS DONOGHUE. *The Ordinary Universe*, pp. 143-44.

ELIZABETH DREW and JOHN L. SWEENEY. *Directions in Modern Poetry*, pp. 166-71.

RICHARD ELLMANN. "The Art of Yeats: Affirmative Capability," *Kenyon Review* 15(2), Summer 1953, 360-63.

RICHARD ELLMANN. *The Identity of Yeats*, pp. 219-22. Reprinted in: *Readings for Liberal Education*, third ed., II: 168-70; fourth ed., II: 173-75; fifth ed., II: 155-57.

WILLIAM EMPSON. "Donne and the Rhetorical Tradition," *Kenyon Review* 11(4), Autumn 1949, 576-77.

WILLIAM EMPSON. "Mr. Wilson on the Byzantium Poems," *Review of English Literature* 1(3), July 1960, 53-56.

LILLIAN FEDER. *Ancient Myth in Modern Poetry*, pp. 84-86, 190.

G. S. FRASER. "Yeats' Byzantium," *Critical Quarterly* 2(3), Autumn 1960, 253-61.

GEORGE FRASER. *Essays on Twentieth-Century Poets*, pp. 34-37.

KIMON FRIAR and JOHN MALCOLM BRINNIN. *Modern Poetry*, pp. 552-54.

HARVEY GROSS. *The Contrived Corridor*, pp. 87-88.

FREDERICK L. GWYNN. "Yeats's Byzantium and Its Sources," *Philological Quarterly* 32(1), January 1953, 9-21.

ELIZABETH HUBERMAN. "To Byzantium Once More: A Study of the Structure of Yeats's 'Byzantium,' " *Essays in Literature* 1(2), Fall 1974, 193-205.

A. NORMAN JEFFARES. "The Byzantine Poems of W. B. Yeats," *Review of English Studies* 22(85), January 1946, 49-52.

FRANK KERMODE. *Romantic Image*, pp. 87-89.

G. WILSON KNIGHT. *Neglected Powers*, pp. 256-59.

ANNE KOSTELANETZ. "Irony in Yeat's Byzantium Poems," *Tennessee Studies in Literature* 9 (1964), 134-41.

JOAN TOWEY MITCHELL. " 'Byzantium': Vision as Drama," *Concerning Poetry* 6(2), Fall 1973, 66-71.

ALAN D. PERLIS. "Yeats' Byzantium and Stevens' Rome: A Comparison of Two Poems," *Wallace Stevens Journal* 2(1-2), Spring 1978, 18-25.

CHARLES A. RAINES. "Yeats' Metaphors of Permanence," *Twentieth Century Literature* 5(1), April 1959, 18-19.

GEORG ROPPEN and RICHARD SOMMER. *Strangers and Pilgrims*, pp. 337-52.

ROBERT S. RYF. "Yeats's Major Metaphysical Poems," *Journal of Modern Literature* 4(3), February 1975, 620-23.

VILAS SARANG. "The Byzantium Poems: Yeats at the Limits of Symbolism," *Concerning Poetry* 11(2), Fall 1978, 51-54.

AGNES STEIN. *The Uses of Poetry*, pp. 302-4.

J. I. M. STEWART. *Eight Modern Writers*, pp. 377-80.

WRIGHT THOMAS and STUART GERRY BROWN. *Reading Poems: An Introduction to Critical Study*, pp. 714-15.

RAYMOND TSCHUMI. *Thought in Twentieth-Century English Poetry*, pp. 69-73.

HELEN VENDLER. "Sacred and Profane Perfection in Yeats," *Southern Review*, n.s., 9(1), Winter 1973, 113.

YVOR WINTERS. "The Poetry of W. B. Yeats," *Twentieth Century Literature* 6(1), April 1960, 11-12.

"The Cap and Bells"

C. M. BOWRA. *The Heritage of Symbolism*, pp. 192-93.

HARRY BROWN and JOHN MILSTEAD. *What the Poem Means*, p. 301.

GEORGE FRASER. *Essays on Twentieth-Century Poets*, pp. 71-75.

FRED L. MILNE. "Yeats's 'The Cap and Bells': A Probable Indebtedness to Tennyson's 'Maud,' " *Ariel* 3(3), July 1972, 69-79.

J. H. NATTERSTAD. *Explicator* 25(9), May 1967, Item 75.

MORTON IRVING SEIDEN. "A Psychoanalytical Essay on William Butler Yeats," *Accent* 6(3), Spring 1946, 179-80.

"The Cat and the Moon"

GROVER SMITH. "Yeats, Minnaloushe, and the Moon," *Western Review* 11(4), Summer 1947, 241-44.

MARK VAN DOREN. *Introduction to Poetry*, pp. 85-89.

"Certain Noble Plays of Japan"

HAZARD ADAMS. "Yeatsian Art and Mathematic Form," *Centennial Review* 4(1), Winter 1960, 82-86.

"The Choice"

WALLACE CABLE BROWN. " 'A Poem Should Not Mean But Be,' " *University of Kansas City Review* 15(1), Autumn 1948, 59-60.

"Church and State"

M. L. ROSENTHAL. *The Modern Poets*, pp. 29-30.

"The Circus Animals' Desertion"

JEAN ALEXANDER. "Yeats and the Rhetoric of Defilement," *Review of English Literature* 6(3), July 1965, 53-54.

T. R. BARNES. *English Verse*, pp. 317-19.

HARRY BERGER. "Biography as Interpretation, Interpretation as Biography," *College English* 28(2), November 1966, 124-25.

RICHARD ELLMANN. "Yeats Without Analogue," in *Modern Poetry*, pp. 401-2.

LILLIAN FEDER. *Ancient Myth in Modern Poetry*, pp. 89-90.

FRANK KERMODE. *Romantic Image*, pp. 89-90.

JOYCE CAROL OATES. "Yeats: Violence, Tragedy, Mutability," *Bucknell Review* 17(3), December 1969, 10.

M. L. ROSENTHAL. "On Yeats and the Cultural Symbolism of Modern Poetry," *Yale Review* 49(4), Summer 1960, 579-81.

HELEN VENDLER. "Sacred and Profane Perfection in Yeats," *Southern Review*, n.s., 9(1), Winter 1973, 114.

"The Cloak, the Boat and the Shoes"

ARNOLD GOLDMAN. "The Oeuvre Takes Shape: Yeats's Early Poetry," in *Victorian Poetry*, p. 203.

"A Coat"

LILLIAN FEDER. *Ancient Myth in Modern Poetry*, pp. 74-75.

YEATS, W. B. *(Cont.)*

"The Cold Heaven"

BARBARA HARDY. *The Advantage of Lyric,* pp. 77-78.

GARY and LINDA STORHOFF. "'A Mind of Winter': Yeats's Early Vision of Old Age," *CLA Journal* 21(1), September 1977, 94-97.

"The Collar-Bone of a Hare"

HUGH KENNER. "The Sacred Book of the Arts," *Sewanee Review* 64(4), Autumn 1956, 580-81.

MARION WITT. *Explicator* 7(3), December 1948, Item 21.

"Coole Park, 1929"

DENIS DONOGHUE. *The Ordinary Universe,* pp. 139-41.

GRAHAM MARTIN. "Fine Manners, Liberal Speech: A Note on the Public Poetry of W. B. Yeats," *Essays in Criticism* 11(1), January 1961, 47-51.

YVOR WINTERS. "The Poetry of W. B. Yeats," *Twentieth Century Literature* 6(1), April 1960, 16-17.

"Coole Park and Ballylee"

CHARLES ALTIERI. "From a Comic to a Tragic Sense of Language in Yeats's Mature Poetry," *Modern Language Quarterly* 33(2), June 1972, 166-68.

T. R. BARNES. *English Verse,* pp. 315-17.

D. S. CARNE-ROSS. "A Commentary on Yeats' 'Coole and Ballylee, 1931,'" *Nine* 1 (Autumn 1949), 21-24.

PAUL DE MAN. "Symbolic Landscape in Wordsworth and Yeats," in *In Defense of Reading,* pp. 29-37.

MARJORIE PERLOFF. "'Another Emblem There': Theme and Convention in Yeats's 'Coole Park and Ballylee, 1931,'" *Journal of English and Germanic Philology* 69(2), April 1970, 223-41.

DONALD A. STAUFFER. "The Reading of a Lyric Poem," *Kenyon Review* 11(3), Summer 1949, 437-38. (P)

GEORGE WHALLEY. "Literary Romanticism," *Queen's Quarterly* 72(2), Summer 1965, 248-49.

THOMAS R. WHITAKER. "Poet of Anglo-Ireland," in *Modern Poetry,* pp. 439-42.

"Cradle Song"

MARGARET B. MCDOWELL. "Folk lullabies: Songs of anger, love, and fear," *Women's Studies* 5(2), 1977, 216-17.

"Crazy Jane and Jack the Journeyman"

LUCAS CARPENTER. "Yeats' Crazy Jane Poems," *Concerning Poetry* 11(2), Fall 1978, 55-56, 60-61.

LAURENCE PERRINE. "Yeats's 'Crazy Jane and Jack the Journeyman,'" *CEA Critic* 34(3), March 1972, 22.

"Crazy Jane and the Bishop"

LUCAS CARPENTER. "Yeats' Crazy Jane Poems," *Concerning Poetry* 11(2), Fall 1978, 55-57.

"Crazy Jane Grown Old Looks at the Dancers"

LUCAS CARPENTER. "Yeats' Crazy Jane Poems," *Concerning Poetry* 11(2), Fall 1978, 55-56, 63.

LILLIAN FEDER. *Ancient Myth in Modern Poetry,* pp. 191-92.

"Crazy Jane on God"

LUCAS CARPENTER. "Yeats' Crazy Jane Poems," *Concerning Poetry* 11(2), Fall 1978, 55-56, 61.

WALTER E. HOUGHTON. "Yeats and Crazy Jane: The Hero in Old Age," *Modern Philology* 40(4), May 1943, 326-27.

"Crazy Jane on the Day of Judgment"

LUCAS CARPENTER. "Yeats' Crazy Jane Poems," *Concerning Poetry* 11(2), Fall 1978, 55-56, 59-60.

DENIS DONOGHUE. *The Ordinary Universe,* pp. 112-13.

"Crazy Jane on the Mountain"

JEAN ALEXANDER. "Yeats and the Rhetoric of Defilement," *Review of English Literature* 6(3), July 1965, 54-55.

LUCAS CARPENTER. "Yeats' Crazy Jane Poems," *Concerning Poetry* 11(2), Fall 1978, 55-56, 63-64.

BARBARA L. ESTRIN. "Alternating Personae in Yeats' 'Lapiz Lazuli' and 'Crazy Jane on the Mountain,'" *Criticism* 16(1), Winter 1974, 13-22.

"Crazy Jane Reproved"

LUCAS CARPENTER. "Yeats' Crazy Jane Poems," *Concerning Poetry* 11(2), Fall 1978, 55-58.

"Crazy Jane Talks With the Bishop"

ANSELM ATKINS. "The Vedantic Logic of Yeats' 'Crazy Jane,'" *Renascence* 19(1), Autumn 1966, 37-40.

R. P. BLACKMUR. "Between Myth and Philosophy: Fragments of W. B. Yeats," *Southern Review* 7(3), Winter 1942, 423-24. Reprinted in: R. P. Blackmur. *Language as Gesture,* pp. 121-22.

LUCAS CARPENTER. "Yeats' Crazy Jane Poems," *Concerning Poetry* 11(2), Fall 1978, 55-56, 62.

ELIZABETH DREW. *Poetry,* pp. 210-11.

RICHARD ELLMANN with PETER WILSON. "W. B. Yeats," in *English Poetry,* edited by Alan Sinfield, pp. 181-82.

CHAD and EVA T. WALSH. *Twice Ten,* pp. 144-45.

"Cuchulain Comforted"

HAROLD BLOOM. *Figures of Capable Imagination,* pp. 95-99.

HAROLD BLOOM. *Poetry and Repression,* pp. 228-31.

KATHLEEN RAINE. "Life in Death and Death in Life: Yeats's 'Cuchulain Comforted' and 'News for the Delphic Oracle,'" *Southern Review,* n.s., 9(3), Summer 1973, 562-73.

"Cuchulain's Fight with the Sea"

JON STALLWORTHY. "W. B. Yeats and Wilfred Owen," *Critical Quarterly* 11(3), Autumn 1969, 209-11.

"Death"

R. P. BLACKMUR. "Between Myth and Philosophy: Fragments of W. B. Yeats," *Southern Review* 7(3), Winter 1942, 418. Reprinted in: R. P. Blackmur. *Language as Gesture,* p.116.

CLEANTH BROOKS. *The Hidden God,* pp. 62-67.

"A Deep-Sworn Vow"

CLEANTH BROOKS and ROBERT PENN WARREN. *Understanding Poetry,* pp. 274-77; revised ed., pp. 148-52; third ed., pp. 160-63; fourth ed., p. 519.

ROBERT SCHRAMM. "The Line Unit: Studies in the Later Poetry of W. B. Yeats," *Ohio University Review* 3 (1961), 34-35.

"The Delphic Oracle upon Plotinus"

DONALD PEARCE. "Yeats's 'The Delphic Oracle upon Plotinus,'" *Notes and Queries,* n.s., 1(4), April 1954, 175-76.

"Demon and Beast"

CLEANTH BROOKS. *Modern Poetry and the Tradition,* pp. 188-89.

CLEANTH BROOKS, JR. "The Vision of William Butler Yeats," *Southern Review* 4(1), Summer 1938, 129.

M. L. ROSENTHAL. *Poetry and the Common Life*, pp. 32-37.

M. L. ROSENTHAL. *Sailing into the Unknown*, pp. 142-43.

"A Dialogue of Self and Soul"

HARRY BROWN and JOHN MILSTEAD. *What the Poem Means*, pp. 296-97.

BABETTE DEUTSCH. *Poetry in Our Time*, pp. 267-68; second ed., p. 301.

NORMAN FRIEDMAN. "Permanence and Change: What Happens in Yeats's 'Dialogue of Self and Soul'?" *Yeats Eliot Review* 5(2), 1978, 21-30.

STELLA REVARD. "Verlaine and Yeats's 'A Dialogue of Self and Soul,'" *Papers on Language and Literature* 7(3), Summer 1971, 272-78.

M. L. ROSENTHAL. *The Modern Poets*, pp. 10-12.

M. L. ROSENTHAL and A. J. M. SMITH. *Exploring Poetry*, pp. 702-3; second ed., pp. 490-92.

J. I. M. STEWART. *Eight Modern Writers*, pp. 380-82.

RAYMOND TSCHUMI. *Thought in Twentieth-Century English Poetry*, p. 40.

REED WHITTEMORE. "Yeats: A Dialogue of Self and Soul," in *Master Poems of the English Language*, pp. 861-63.

"The Dolls"

DELMORE SCHWARTZ. "The Poet as Poet," in *Selected Essays of Delmore Schwartz*, p. 79.

CHAD and EVA T. WALSH. *Twice Ten*, pp. 142-44.

"The Double Vision of Michael Robartes"

C. M. BOWRA. *The Heritage of Symbolism*, p. 207.

LILLIAN FEDER. *Ancient Myth in Modern Poetry*, pp. 77-78, 188-89.

FRANK KERMODE. *The Romantic Image*, pp. 59-60.

RAYMOND TSCHUMI. *Thought in Twentieth-Century English Poetry*, pp. 45-47.

THOMAS R. WHITAKER. "The Dialectic of Yeats's Vision of History," *Modern Philology* 57(2), November 1959, 109-10.

"Easter, 1916"

CHARLES ALTIERI. "From a Comic to a Tragic Sense of Language in Yeats's Mature Poetry," *Modern Language Quarterly* 33(2), June 1972, 162-63.

C. M. BOWRA. *The Heritage of Symbolism*, pp. 202-3.

VINCENT BUCKLEY. *Poetry and the Sacred*, pp. 186-87.

C. B. COX and A. E. DYSON. *Modern Poetry*, pp. 57-65.

TERRY EAGLETON. "History and Myth in Yeats's 'Easter 1916,'" *Essays in Criticism* 21(3), July 1971, 248-60.

THOMAS R. EDWARDS. *Imagination and Power*, pp. 185-97.

GEORGE FRASER. *Essays on Twentieth-Century Poets*, pp. 31-34.

ROB JACKAMAN. "Black and White: The Balanced View in Yeats's Poetry," *Ariel* 9(4), October 1978, 79-91.

ARCHIBALD MACLEISH. *Poetry and Experience*, pp. 141-44.

EDWARD MALINS. "Yeats and the Easter Rising," *Massachusetts Review* 7(2), Spring 1966, 279-80.

GEORGE MAYHEW. "A Corrected Typescript of Yeats's 'Easter 1916,'" *Huntington Library Quarterly* 27(1), November 1963, 53-71.

JOHN R. MOORE. "Yeats as a Last Romantic," *Virginia Quarterly Review* 37(3), Summer 1961, 438-40.

WILLARD PATE, ED. "Interview with Richard Wilbur," *South Carolina Review* 3(1), November 1970, 9.

MARJORIE PERLOFF. "Yeats and the Occasional Poem: 'Easter 1916,'" *Papers on Language and Literature* 4(3), Summer 1968, 318-27.

CHARLES A. RAINES. "Yeats' Metaphors of Permanence," *Twentieth Century Literature* 5(1), April 1959, 13-14.

JOHN CROWE RANSOM. "The Irish, the Gaelic, the Byzantine," *Southern Review* 7(3), Winter 1942, 535-36.

M. L. ROSENTHAL. *The Modern Poets*, pp. 30-32.

M. L. ROSENTHAL. "On Yeats and the Cultural Symbolism of Modern Poetry," *Yale Review* 49(4), Summer 1960, 582.

M. L. ROSENTHAL. *Sailing into the Unknown*, pp. 140-41.

ARNOLD STEIN. "Yeats: A Study in Recklessness," *Sewanee Review* 57(4), Autumn 1949, 623-26.

"Ego Dominus Tuus"

LILLIAN FEDER. *Ancient Myth in Modern Poetry*, pp. 75-76.

HERBERT J. LEVINE. "Yeats at the Crossroads: The Debate of Self and Anti-Self in 'Ego Dominus Tuus,'" *Modern Language Quarterly* 39(2), June 1978, 132-53.

J. I. M. STEWART. *Eight Modern Writers*, pp. 354-55.

RAYMOND TSCHUMI. *Thought in Twentieth-Century English Poetry*, pp. 38-40.

MARION WITT. "William Butler Yeats," *English Institute Essays*, 1946, pp. 92-99.

"The Empty Cup"

W. J. KEITH. "Yeats's 'The Empty Cup,'" *English Language Notes* 4(3), March 1967, 206-10.

"Epitaph" ("Cast a cold eye . . .")

JAMES LOVIC ALLEN. "'Horseman, Pass By!': Metaphor and Meaning in Yeats's Epitaph," *Concerning Poetry* 10(1), Spring 1977, 17-22.

"Father and Child"

JEFFREY P. NEILL. "The Study of Literature: An Introductory Method," *College English* 31(5), February 1970, 456-58.

DELMORE SCHWARTZ. "An Unwritten Book," *Southern Review* 7(3), Winter 1942, 484-85.

"Father O'Hart"

LENNOX ROBINSON. "Yeats: The Early Poems," *Review of English Literature* 6(3), July 1965, 26-27.

"Fergus and the Druid"

ARNOLD GOLDMAN. "The Oeuvre Takes Shape: Yeats's Early Poetry," in *Victorian Poetry*, pp. 210-11.

SISTER M. BERNETTA QUINN. *The Metamorphic Tradition*, p. 228.

"The Fish"

ED BLOCK, JR. "Lyric Voice and Reader Response: One View of the Transition to Modern Poetics," *Twentieth Century Literature* 24(2), Summer 1978, 162-64.

"The Fisherman"

SHYMAL BAGCHEE. "Anxiety of Influence: 'Resolution and Independence' and Yeats's 'The Fisherman,'" *Yeats Eliot Review* 5(1), 1978, 51-57.

BABETTE DEUTSCH. *Poetry in Our Time*, pp. 259-60; second ed., pp. 292-93.

BABETTE DEUTSCH. *This Modern Poetry*, pp. 201-3.

YEATS, W. B. *(Cont.)*

"The Folly of Being Comforted"

SAMUEL HYNES. "All the Wild Witches: The Women in Yeats's Poems," *Sewanee Review* 85(4), Fall 1977, 573-74.

PAUL R. MAIXNER. *Explicator* 13(1), October 1954, Item 1.

PETER J. SENG. *Explicator* 17(7), April 1959, Item 48.

"The Four Ages of Man"

VILAS SARANG. "W. B. Yeats: 'The Four Ages of Man,' " *Notes and Queries*, n.s., 25(4), August 1978, 327.

"Fragment I" (*The Tower*)

HOWARD NEMEROV. "Poetry and History," *Virginia Quarterly Review* 51(2), Spring 1975, 313-18.

"Fragment II" (*The Tower*)

HOWARD NEMEROV. "Poetry and History," *Virginia Quarterly Review* 51(2), Spring 1975, 314-18.

"Friends"

SAMUEL HYNES. "All the Wild Witches: The Women in Yeats's Poems," *Sewanee Review* 85(4) Fall 1977, 566-68.

"A Friend's Illness"

WILLIAM M. CARPENTER. "The *Green Helmet* Poems and Yeats's Myth of the Renaissance," *Modern Philology* 67(1), August 1969, 58.

ELSIE LEACH. "Yeats's 'A Friend's Illness' and Herbert's 'Vertue,' " *Notes & Queries*, n.s., 9(6), June 1962, 215.

"The Gift of Harun Al-Rashid"

JAMES H. O'BRIEN. "Yeats' Dark Night of Self and *The Tower*," *Bucknell Review* 15(2), May 1967, 23-24.

F. A. C. WILSON. "Yeats's 'A Bronze Head': A Freudian Investigation," *Literature and Psychology* 22(1), 1972, 7-8.

"The Grey Rock"

ARCHIBALD MACLEISH. *Poetry and Experience*, pp. 133-40.

"The Gyres"

MICHAEL BELL. "The Assimilation of Doubt in Yeats's Visionary Poems," *Queen's Quarterly* 80(3), Autumn 1973, 392-93.

ROBERT BIERMAN. *Explicator* 19(7), April 1961, Item 44.

LILLIAN FEDER. *Ancient Myth in Modern Poetry*, pp. 289-91.

ARRA M. GARAB. "Yeats's 'Dark Betwixt the Polecat and the Owl,' " *English Language Notes* 2(3), March 1965, 218-20. (P)

HARVEY GROSS. "W. B. Yeats," in *The Contrived Corridor*, pp. 89-91.

A. NORMAN JEFFARES. "Yeats's 'The Gyres': Sources and Symbolism," *Huntington Library Quarterly* 15(1), November 1951, 87-97.

DONALD A. STAUFFER. "W. B. Yeats and the Medium of Poetry," *English Literary History* 15(3), September 1948, 244-45.

RAYMOND TSCHUMI. *Thought in Twentieth-Century English Poetry*, pp. 53-55.

"The Happy Townland"

C. M. BOWRA. *The Heritage of Symbolism*, p. 190.

"He and She"

SHAMSUL ISLAM. "The Influence of Eastern Philosophy on Yeats's Later Poetry," *Twentieth Century Literature* 19(4), October 1973, 289.

"He bids his Beloved be at Peace"

DAVID RIDGLEY CLARK. *Lyric Resonance*, pp. 31-38.

"He Thinks Evil of Those Who Have Spoken Evil of His Beloved"

BABETTE DEUTSCH. *This Modern Poetry*, pp. 201-3.

"He Thinks of His Past Greatness When a Part of the Constellations of Heaven"

SISTER M. BERNETTA QUINN. *The Metamorphic Tradition*, p. 229.

"Her Vision in the Wood"

JAMES L. ALLEN, JR. *Explicator* 18(8), May 1960, Item 45.

LILLIAN FEDER. *Ancient Myth in Modern Poetry*, pp. 86-87, 198-99.

BARBARA HARDY. *The Advantage of Lyric*, pp. 78-79.

MICHAEL RAGUSSIS. *The Subterfuge of Art*, pp. 109-32.

"High Talk"

BRIAN JOHN. *Explicator* 29(3), November 1970, Item 22.

B. L. REID. "The House of Yeats," *Hudson Review* 18(3), Autumn 1965, 348-50.

"His Bargain"

SHAMSUL ISLAM. "The Influence of Eastern Philosophy on Yeats's Later Poetry," *Twentieth Century Literature* 19(4), October 1973, 285.

"His Dream"

GEORGE FRASER. *Essays on Twentieth-Century Poets*, pp. 75-78.

ROBERT M. SCHULER. "W. B. Yeats: Artist or Alchemist?" *Review of English Studies*, n.s., 22(85), February 1971, 48.

"His Memories"

SAMUEL HYNES. "All the Wild Witches: The Women in Yeats's Poems," *Sewanee Review* 85(4), Fall 1977, 577-78.

"His Phoenix"

LYNA LEE MONTGOMERY. "The Phoenix: Its Use as a Literary Device in English From the Seventeenth Century to the Twentieth Century," *D. H. Lawrence Review* 5(3), Fall 1972, 310.

"The Hosting of the Sidhe"

FRANK KERMODE. *Romantic Image*, pp. 74-76.

"I Am of Ireland"

G. S. FRASER. *Vision and Rhetoric*, pp. 66-73.

MARTHA GROSS. *Explicator* 17(2), November 1958, Item 15.

F. O. MATTHIESSEN. "The Crooked Road," *Southern Review* 7(3), Winter 1942, 460-62. Reprinted in: F. O. Matthiessen. *The Responsibilities of the Critic*, pp. 30-32.

ELEANOR M. SICKELS. *Explicator* 15(2), November 1956, Item 10.

"I See Phantoms of Hatred and of the Heart's Fullness and of the Coming Emptiness"

LILLIAN FEDER. *Ancient Myth in Modern Poetry*, pp. 283-85.

"An Image from a Past Life"

BARBARA HARDY. *The Advantage of Lyric*, pp. 76-77.

M. L. ROSENTHAL. *Sailing into the Unknown*, pp. 122-24.

"In Memory of Eva Gore-Booth and Con Markiewicz"

MARJORIE PERLOFF. "Spatial Form in the Poetry of Yeats: The Two Lissadell Poems," *PMLA* 82(5), October 1967, 446-47, 449-53.

"In Memory of Major Robert Gregory"

GEORGE FRASER. *Essays on Twentieth-Century Poets*, pp. 38-39.

FRANK KERMODE. *Romantic Image*, pp. 30-42.

MARJORIE PERLOFF. "The Consolation Theme in Yeats's 'In Memory of Major Robert Gregory,'" *Modern Language Quarterly* 27(3), September 1966, 306-22.

YVOR WINTERS. "The Poetry of W. B. Yeats," *Twentieth Century Literature* 6(1), April 1960, 15-16.

MARION WITT. "The Making of an Elegy: Yeats's 'In Memory of Major Robert Gregory,'" *Modern Philology* 48(2), November 1950, 112-21. Reprinted in: *Readings for Liberal Education*, revised ed., II: 183-90.

"The Indian to His Love"

NANDINI PILLAI KUEHN. *Explicator* 33(3), November 1974, Item 23.

"An Irish Airman Foresees His Death"

MURRAY BAUMGARTEN. "Lyric as Performance: Lorca and Yeats," *Comparative Literature* 29(4), Fall 1977, 344-45.

CHRISTOPHER GILLIE. *Movements in English Literature*, pp. 75-76.

GEORGE NEWTOWN. "Explication of 'An Irish Airman'," in: Walton Beacham, *The Meaning of Poetry*, pp. 250-53.

"King and No King"

RICHARD WILBUR. "Round About a Poem of Housman's," in *The Moment of Poetry*, pp. 92-94. Reprinted in: Richard Wilbur. *Responses*, pp. 33-35.

"The Lake Isle of Innisfree"

RICHARD ELLMANN WITH PETER WILSON. "W. B. Yeats," in *English Poetry*, edited by Alan Sinfield, pp. 176-78.

JAMES R. KREUZER. *Elements of Poetry*, pp. 117-19.

JOHN CROWE RANSOM. "The Irish, the Gaelic, the Byzantine," *Southern Review* 7(3), Winter 1942, 526-30.

M. L. ROSENTHAL. *The Modern Poets*, p. 37.

GARY SLOAN. "Yeats, Tennyson, and 'Innisfree,'" *Victorian Newsletter* 54 (Fall 1978), 29-31.

AGNES STEIN. *The Uses of Poetry*, pp. 262-63.

"Lapis Lazuli"

JEROME BEATY and WILLIAM H. MATCHETT. *Poetry From Statement to Meaning*, pp. 255-62.

MICHAEL BELL. "The Assimilation of Doubt in Yeats's Visionary Poems," *Queen's Quarterly* 80(3), Autumn 1973, 385-90.

BARBARA L. ESTRIN. "Alternating Personae in Yeats' 'Lapiz Lazuli' and 'Crazy Jane on the Mountain,'" *Criticism* 16(1), Winter 1974, 13-22.

GEORGE FRASER. *Essays on Twentieth-Century Poets*, pp. 53-55.

KIMON FRIAR and JOHN MALCOLM BRINNIN. *Modern Poetry*, pp. 551-52.

A. NORMAN JEFFARES. "Notes on Yeats's 'Lapis Lazuli,'" *Modern Language Notes* 65(7), November 1950, 488-91.

ROBERT LANGBAUM. "The Mysteries of Identity: A Theme in Modern Literature," *American Scholar* 34(4), Autumn 1965, 583-85. Reprinted in: *The Modern Spirit*, pp. 180-82.

LAURENCE LERNER. "Reading Modern Poetry," in *English Poetry*, edited by Alan Sinfield, 160-64.

DERICK MARSH. "The Artist and the Tragic Vision: Themes in the Late Poetry of W. B. Yeats," *Queen's Quarterly* 74(1), Spring 1967, 112-18.

SYDNEY MENDEL. *Explicator* 19(9), June 1961, Item 64.

JOHN R. MOORE. "Yeats as a Last Romantic," *Virginia Quarterly Review* 37(3), Summer 1961, 446-47.

FRANK O'CONNOR. "W. B. Yeats," *Critic* 25(3), December 1966-January 1967, 56.

DAVID PARKER. "Yeats's Lapis Lazuli," *Notes & Queries*, n.s., 24(5), October 1977, 452-54.

CHARLES A. RAINES. "Yeats' Metaphors of Permanence," *Twentieth Century Literature* 5(1), April 1959, 15-16.

M. L. ROSENTHAL. *The Modern Poets*, pp. 33-35.

KATHERINE SNIPES. "The Artistic Imagination in Action: Yeats's 'Lapis Lazuli,'" *CEA Critic* 39(1), November 1976, 15-16.

RAYMOND TSCHUMI. *Thought in Twentieth-Century English Poetry*, pp. 64-65.

JOHN M. WARNER. "'Lapis Lazuli': Structure Through Analogy," *Concerning Poetry* 3(2), Fall 1970, 41-48.

"Leda and the Swan"

JOHN F. ADAMS. "'Leda and the Swan': The Aesthetics of Rape," *Bucknell Review* 12(3), December 1964, 47-58.

JAMES L. ALLEN, JR. "William Butler Yeats's One Myth," *Personalist* 45(4), Autumn 1964, 528-30.

R. P. BLACKMUR. "The Later Poetry of W. B. Yeats," *Southern Review* 2(2), Autumn 1936, 360-62. Reprinted in: R. P. Blackmur. *Expense of Greatness*, pp. 102-4. Also: *Critiques and Essays in Criticism*, pp. 375-76. Also: R. P. Blackmur. *Language as Gesture*, pp. 101-3.

KENNETH BURKE. "On Motivation in Yeats," *Southern Review* 7(3), Winter 1942, 554-55.

DOUGLAS BUSH. *Pagan Myth and Christian Tradition in English Poetry*, pp. 76-79.

E. R. COLE. "Three Cycle Poems of Yeats and His Mystico-Historical Thought," *Personalist* 46(1), Winter 1965, 74-76.

BABETTE DEUTSCH. *Poetry in Our Time*, pp. 260-62; second ed., pp. 293-95.

ELIZABETH DREW. *Poetry*, pp. 65-67.

ELIZABETH DREW and JOHN L. SWEENEY. *Directions in Modern Poetry*, pp. 164-66.

RICHARD ELLMANN. "Yeats Without Analogue," in *Modern Poetry*, pp. 396-98.

LILLIAN FEDER. *Ancient Myth in Modern Poetry*, pp. 193-94.

BERNARD LEVINE. "A Psychopoetic Analysis of Yeats's 'Leda and the Swan,'" *Bucknell Review* 17(1), March 1969, 85-111.

JOSEPH MARGOLIS. *Explicator* 13(6), April 1955, Item 34.

J. HILLIS MILLER. *Poets of Reality*, p. 89.

JOHN CLARK PRATT. *The Meaning of Modern Poetry*, pp. 375-76, 369, 382-83, 378, 391.

YEATS, W. B. *(Cont.)*

"Leda and the Swan" *(cont.)*

SISTER M. BERNETTA QUINN. *The Metamorphic Tradition*, pp. 233-35.

CHARLES A. RAINES. "Yeats' Metaphors of Permanence," *Twentieth Century Literature* 5(1), April 1959, 16-17.

JANE DAVIDSON REID. "Leda, Twice Assaulted," *Journal of Aesthetics and Art Criticism* 11(4), June 1953, 378-82.

M. L. ROSENTHAL. *The Modern Poets*, pp. 41-42.

M. L. ROSENTHAL. *Sailing into the Unknown*, pp. 120-21, 148-49.

M. L. ROSENTHAL and A. J. M. SMITH. *Exploring Poetry*, pp. 576-77; second ed., pp. 385-86.

ROBIN SKELTON. *Poetry*, pp. 137-38.

LEO SPITZER. "On Yeats's Poem 'Leda and the Swan,'" *Modern Philology* 51(4), May 1954, 271-76. Reprinted in: Leo Spitzer. *Essays on English and American Literature*, pp. 3-13.

ARNOLD STEIN. "Yeats: A Study in Recklessness," *Sewanee Review* 57(4), Autumn 1949, 617-20.

HOYT TROWBRIDGE. "'Leda and the Swan': A Longinian Analysis," *Modern Philology* 51(2), November 1953, 118-29.

YVOR WINTERS. "The Poetry of W. B. Yeats," *Twentieth Century Literature* 6(1), April 1960, 7-8.

"Lines Written in Dejection"

LILLIAN FEDER. *Ancient Myth in Modern Poetry*, p. 75.

THOMAS PARKINSON. "The Sun and the Moon in Yeats's Early Poetry," *Modern Philology* 50(1), August 1952, 50-55.

"The Living Beauty"

FRANK KERMODE. *Romantic Image*, pp. 84-85.

GARY and LINDA STORHOFF. "'A Mind of Winter': Yeats's Early Vision of Old Age," *CLA Journal* 21(1), September 1977, 91-94.

"Long-Legged Fly"

JAMES L. ALLEN, JR. *Explicator* 21(6), February 1963, Item 51.

DAVID DAICHES and WILLIAM CHARVAT. *Poems in English*, pp. 735-36.

MARIO L. D'AVANZO. *Explicator* 34(3), November 1975, Item 23.

ROBERT R. HODGES. "The Irony of Yeats's 'Long-Legged Fly,'" *Twentieth Century Literature* 12(1), April 1966, 27-30.

DERICK MARSH. "The Artist and the Tragic Vision: Themes in the Late Poetry of W. B. Yeats," *Queen's Quarterly* 74(1), Spring 1967, 105-12.

WILLIAM ELFORD ROGERS. "Yeats's 'Long-legged Fly' and Coleridge's *Biographia Literaria*," *Concerning Poetry* 8(1), Spring 1975, 11-21.

B. C. SOUTHAM. "Yeats: Life and the Creator in 'The Long Legged Fly,'" *Twentieth Century Literature* 6(4), January 1961, 175-79.

JON STALLWORTHY. "Two of Yeats's Last Poems," *Review of English Literature* 4(3), July 1963, 48-55.

RAYMOND TSCHUMI. *Thought in Twentieth-Century English Poetry*, pp. 61-63.

CHAD and EVA T. WALSH. *Twice Ten*, pp. 145-47.

YVOR WINTERS. "The Poetry of W. B. Yeats," *Twentieth Century Literature* 6(1), April 1960, 21.

"The Lover Asks Forgiveness because of His Many Moods"

LYNA LEE MONTGOMERY. "The Phoenix: Its Use as a Literary Device in English From the Seventeenth Century to the Twentieth Century," *D. H. Lawrence Review* 5(3), Fall 1972, 307-9.

"The Lover Mourns for the Change That Has Come upon Him and His Beloved and Longs for the End of the World"

DONALD STAUFFER. *The Nature of Poetry*, pp. 170-71.

"The Lover Mourns for the Loss of Love"

BARBARA HARDY. *The Advantage of Lyric*, p. 70.

"The Lover Tells of the Rose in His Heart"

BARBARA HARDY. *The Advantage of Lyric*, pp. 67-69.

"The Magi"

E. R. COLE. "Three Cycle Poems of Yeats and His Mystico-Historical Thought," *Personalist* 46(1), Winter 1965, 79-80.

HARVEY GROSS. *The Contrived Corridor*, pp. 78-79.

PAUL SANDERS. *Explicator* 25(7), March 1967, Item 53.

HELEN VENDLER. "Sacred and Profane Perfection in Yeats," *Southern Review*, n.s., 9(1), Winter 1973, 107.

THOMAS R. WHITAKER. "The Dialectic of Yeats's Vision of History," *Modern Philology* 57(2), November 1959, 108.

"The Man and the Echo"

VINCENT BUCKLEY. *Poetry and the Sacred*, pp. 178-84.

LILLIAN FEDER. *Ancient Myth in Modern Poetry*, pp. 291-93.

JOYCE CAROL OATES. "Yeats: Violence, Tragedy, Mutability," *Bucknell Review* 17(3), December 1969, 8-9.

CHARLES A. RAINES. "Yeats' Metaphors of Permanence," *Twentieth Century Literature* 5(1), April 1959, 14-15.

"The Man Who Dreamed of Faeryland"

ARNOLD GOLDMAN. "The Oeuvre Takes Shape: Yeats's Early Poetry," in *Victorian Poetry*, p. 213.

M. L. ROSENTHAL. *The Modern Poets*, pp. 36-37.

ROBERT M. SCHULER. "W. B. Yeats: Artist or Alchemist?" *Review of English Studies*, n.s., 22(85), February 1971, 45-46. (P)

"A Man Young and Old"

BARBARA HARDY. *The Advantage of Lyric*, p. 82.

M. L. ROSENTHAL. *Sailing into the Unknown*, pp. 127-28.

JOHN SOMER. "Unageing Monuments: A Study of W. B. Yeats' Poetry Sequence, 'A Man Young and Old,'" *Ball State University Forum* 12(4), Autumn 1971, 28-36.

"The Mask"

RICHARD J. WALL and ROGER FITZGERALD. "Yeats and Jung: An Ideological Comparison," *Literature and Psychology* 13(2), Spring 1963, 47-49.

"Meditations in Time of Civil War"

CLEANTH BROOKS. *Modern Poetry and the Tradition*, pp. 179-82.

MICHAEL NORTH. "Symbolism and obscurity in *Meditations in time of civil war*," *Critical Quarterly* 19(1), Spring 1977, 5-18.

JAMES H. O'BRIEN. "Yeats' Dark Night of Self and *The Tower*," *Bucknell Review* 15(2), May 1967, 14-18.

M. L. ROSENTHAL. *Sailing into the Unknown*, pp. 26-41.

SARAH YOUNGBLOOD. "The Structure of Yeats's Long Poems," *Criticism* 5(4), Fall 1963, 328-35.

"Memory"

DWIGHT H. PURDY. "Singing Amid Uncertainty: Image and Idea in Yeats's 'Memory,'" *English Language Notes* 15(4), June 1978, 295-302.

M. L. ROSENTHAL. *Sailing into the Unknown*, pp. 116-20.

"A Memory of Youth"

BARBARA HARDY. *The Advantage of Lyric*, p. 77.

"Men Improve with the Years"

HUGH KENNER. "The Sacred Book of the Arts," *Sewanee Review* 64(4), Autumn 1956, 578-80.

"Meru"

JAMES D. BOULGER. "Moral and Structural Aspects in W. B. Yeats's *Supernatural Songs*," *Renascence* 27(2), Winter 1975, 64.

RICHARD ELLMANN. "The Art of Yeats: Affirmative Capability," *Kenyon Review* 15(3), Summer 1953, 373-76.

LILLIAN FEDER. *Ancient Myth in Modern Poetry*, pp. 87-88.

HARVEY GROSS. *The Contrived Corridor*, pp. 95-96.

"Michael Robartes and the Dancer"

FRANK KERMODE. *Romantic Image*, pp. 52-55.

"Mohini Chatterjee"

MARION WITT. *Explicator* 4(8), June 1946, Item 60.

"The Moods"

MARION WITT. *Explicator* 6(3), December 1947, Item 15.

"The Mother of God"

JAMES L. ALLEN, JR. "William Butler Yeats's One Myth," *Personalist* 45(4), Autumn 1964, 528-30.

PETER ALLT. "Yeats, Religion, and History," *Sewanee Review* 60(4), Autumn 1952, 647-51.

CLEANTH BROOKS. "Religion and Literature," *Sewanee Review* 82(1), Winter 1974, 98-99.

E. R. COLE. "Three Cycle Poems of Yeats and His Mystico-Historical Thought," *Personalist* 46(1), Winter 1965, 76-78.

ROBERT SCHRAMM. "The Line Unit: Studies in the Later Poetry of W. B. Yeats," *Ohio University Review* 3(1961), 37-40.

MELVIN G. WILLIAMS. "Yeats and Christ: A Study in Symbolism," *Renascence* 20(4), Summer 1968, 175-76.

"The Municipal Gallery Revisited"

GEORGE FRASER. *Essays on Twentieth-Century Poets*, pp. 39-40.

B. L. REID. "The House of Yeats," *Hudson Review* 18(3), Autumn 1965, 343-45.

"A Nativity"

MELVIN G. WILLIAMS. "Yeats and Christ: A Study in Symbolism," *Renascence* 20(4), Summer 1968, 175.

"The New Faces"

A. NORMAN JEFFARES. "'The New Faces': A New Explanation," *Review of English Studies* 23(92), October 1947, 349-53.

"News for the Delphic Oracle"

JEAN ALEXANDER. "Yeats and the Rhetoric of Defilement," *Review of English Literature* 6(3), July 1965, 55-57.

DAVID RIDGLEY CLARK. *Lyric Resonance*, pp. 39-54.

LILLIAN FEDER. *Ancient Myth in Modern Poetry*, pp. 88-89.

KIMON FRIAR and JOHN MALCOLM BRINNIN. *Modern Poetry*, pp. 550-51.

HARVEY GROSS. *The Contrived Corridor*, p. 89.

J. HILLIS MILLER. *Poets of Reality*, p. 130.

JOYCE CAROL OATES. "Yeats: Violence, Tragedy, Mutability," *Bucknell Review* 17(3), December 1969, 6-7.

JOHN OWER. *Explicator* 28(1), September 1969, Item 7.

KATHLEEN RAINE. "Life in Death and Death in Life: Yeats's 'Cuchulain Comforted' and 'News for the Delphic Oracle,'" *Southern Review*, n.s., 9(3), Summer 1973, 573-78.

CHARLES A. RAINES. "Yeats' Metaphors of Permanence," *Twentieth Century Literature* 5(1), April 1959, 12-13.

"Nineteen Hundred and Nineteen"

KIMON FRIAR and JOHN MALCOLM BRINNIN. *Modern Poetry*, pp. 559-60.

ROB JACKAMAN. "Black and White: The Balanced View in Yeats's Poetry," *Ariel* 9(4), October 1978, 79-91.

J. HILLIS MILLER. *Poets of Reality*, pp. 129-30.

HOWARD NEMEROV. "Poetry and History," *Virginia Quarterly Review* 51(2), Spring 1975, 320-23.

JAMES H. O'BRIEN. "Yeats' Dark Night of Self and *The Tower*," *Bucknell Review* 15(2), May 1967, 18-20.

MARJORIE PERLOFF. "Spatial Form in the Poetry of Yeats: The Two Lissadell Poems," *PMLA* 82(5), October 1967, 453-54.

MICHAEL RAGUSSIS. *The Subterfuge of Art*, pp. 91-107.

M. L. ROSENTHAL. *Sailing into the Unknown*, pp. 26-29, 41-44.

ROBIN SKELTON. "Yeats: Nineteen Hundred and Nineteen," in *Master Poems of the English Language*, pp. 855-58.

DONALD A. STAUFFER. "The Reading of a Lyric Poem," *Kenyon Review* 11(3), Summer 1949, 435-36. (P)

J. I. M. STEWART. *Eight Modern Writers*, pp. 371-72.

RAYMOND TSCHUMI. *Thought in Twentieth-Century English Poetry*, pp. 55-56.

"No Second Troy"

LILLIAN FEDER. *Ancient Myth in Modern Poetry*, pp. 281-82.

"The Old Foxhunter"

LENNOX ROBINSON. "Yeats: The Early Poems," *Review of English Literature* 6(3), July 1965, 27.

"Old Tom Again"

DONALD A. STAUFFER. "W. B. Yeats and the Medium of Poetry," *English Literary History* 15(3), September 1948, 241-42.

"On a Picture of a Black Centaur by Edmund Dulac"

LILLIAN FEDER. *Ancient Myth in Modern Poetry*, pp. 80-81.

JOHN CROWE RANSOM. "The Irish, the Gaelic, the Byzantine," *Southern Review* 7(3), Winter 1942, 522-23.

MARGARET E. NIELSEN. "A Reading of W. B. Yeats's Poem 'On a Picture of a Black Centaur by Edmund Dulac,'" *Thoth* 4(2), Spring 1963, 67-73.

YEATS, W. B. *(Cont.)*

"On a Political Prisoner"

DAVID DAICHES and WILLIAM CHARVAT. *Poems in English*, p. 732.

GEORGE FRASER. *Essays on Twentieth-Century Poets*, pp. 55-56.

MARJORIE PERLOFF. "Spatial Form in the Poetry of Yeats: The Two Lissadell Poems," *PMLA* 82(5), October 1967, 446-49.

"On Woman"

SAMUEL HYNES. "All the Wild Witches: The Women in Yeats's Poems," *Sewanee Review* 85(4), Fall 1977, 569-71.

"Pardon, old fathers, if you still remain"

B. L. REID. "The House of Yeats," *Hudson Review* 18(3), Autumn 1965, 332-34.

"Parnell's Funeral"

LILLIAN FEDER. *Ancient Myth in Modern Poetry*, pp. 199-200, 288-89.

"Parting"

R. P. BLACKMUR. *Form and Value in Modern Poetry*, pp. 74-75.

"The Peacock"

ROBERT M. SCHULER. "W. B. Yeats: Artist or Alchemist?" *Review of English Studies*, n.s., 22(85), February 1971, 48-49.

"The People"

DENIS DONOGHUE. *The Ordinary Universe*, p. 121.

LYNA LEE MONTGOMERY. "The Phoenix: Its Use as a Literary Device in English From the Seventeenth Century to the Twentieth Century," *D. H. Lawrence Review* 5(3), Fall 1972, 309-10.

"The Phases of the Moon"

MURRAY BAUMGARTEN. "Lyric as Performance: Lorca and Yeats," *Comparative Literature* 29(4), Fall 1977, 345-47.

LILLIAN FEDER. *Ancient Myth in Modern Poetry*, pp. 76-77.

GEORGE FRASER. *Poets of Reality*, pp. 93-94.

STEVEN HELMLING. "Yeats's Esoteric Comedy," *Hudson Review* 30(2), Summer 1977, 242-43.

M. L. ROSENTHAL. *Sailing into the Unknown*, pp. 129-38.

J. I. M. STEWART. *Eight Modern Writers*, pp. 355-56.

RAYMOND TSCHUMI. *Thought in Twentieth-Century English Poetry*, pp. 42-45.

"Politics"

M. L. ROSENTHAL. *The Modern Poets*, pp. 32-33.

M. L. ROSENTHAL. "On Yeats and the Cultural Symbolism of Modern Poetry," *Yale Review* 49(4), Summer 1960, 574.

"A Prayer for My Daughter"

CHARLES ALTIERI. "From A Comic to a Tragic Sense of Language in Yeats's Mature Poetry," *Modern Language Quarterly* 33(2), June 1972, 159-65.

WARREN BECK. "Boundaries of Poetry," *College English* 4(6), March 1943, 349-50.

CLEANTH BROOKS, JOHN THIBAUT PURSER, and ROBERT PENN WARREN. *An Approach to Literature*, third ed., pp. 368-71; fourth ed., pp. 359-63; fifth ed., pp. 411-14.

HARRY BROWN and JOHN MILSTEAD. *What the Poem Means*, p. 297.

JOHN EDWARD HARDY. *The Curious Frame*, pp. 116-50.

GRAHAM MARTIN. "Fine Manners, Liberal Speech: A Note on the Public Poetry of W. B. Yeats," *Essays in Criticism* 11(1), January 1961, 42-43.

MARJORIE PERLOFF. "'The Tradition of Myself': The Autobiographical Mode of Yeats," *Journal of Modern Literature* 4(3), February 1975, 552-53.

SARAH YOUNGBLOOD. "Yeats: A Prayer for my Daughter," in *Master Poems of the English Language*, pp. 842-45.

"A Prayer for My Son"

R. P. BLACKMUR. *Expense of Greatness*, pp. 101-2. Reprinted in R. P. Blackmur. *Form and Value in Modern Poetry*, p. 55.

CLEANTH BROOKS. "Religion and Literature," *Sewanee Review* 82(1), Winter 1974, 100-1.

"Quarrel in Old Age"

MARJORIE G. PERLOFF. "'Heart Mysteries': The Later Love Lyrics of W. B. Yeats," *Contemporary Literature* 10(2), Spring 1969, 272-78.

"The Ragged Wood"

ROBERT M. SCHULER. "W. B. Yeats: Artist or Alchemist?" *Review of English Studies*, n.s., 22(85), February 1971, 47.

"The Realists"

LILLIAN FEDER. *Ancient Myth in Modern Poetry*, pp. 73-74.

"Reconciliation"

SAMUEL HYNES. "All the Wild Witches: The Women in Yeats's Poems," *Sewanee Review* 85(4), Fall 1977, 575-76.

"Red Hanrahan's Song About Ireland"

SISTER M. BERNETTA QUINN. "Yeats and Ireland," *English Journal* 54(5), May 1965, 449-50.

"The Results of Thought"

RICHARD ELLMANN. "The Art of Yeats: Affirmative Capability," *Kenyon Review* 15(3), Summer 1953, 368-69.

SISTER M. BERNETTA QUINN. *The Metamorphic Tradition*, p. 236.

"Ribh at the Tomb of Baile and Aillinn"

T. K. DUNSEATH. "Yeats and the Genesis of Supernatural Song," *ELH* 28(4), December 1961, 404-16.

SHAMSUL ISLAM. "The Influence of Eastern Philosophy on Yeats's Later Poetry," *Twentieth Century Literature* 19(4), October 1973, 287.

J. I. M. STEWART. *Eight Modern Writers*, pp. 410-11.

PETER URE. "Yeats's Supernatural Songs," *Review of English Studies*, n.s., 7(25), January 1956, 39-46.

"Ribh denounces Patrick"

SHAMSUL ISLAM. "The Influence of Eastern Philosophy on Yeats's Later Poetry," *Twentieth Century Literature* 19(4), October 1973, 287-88.

PETER URE. "Yeats's Supernatural Songs," *Review of English Studies*, n.s., 7(25), January 1956, 46-48.

"Ribh in Ecstasy"

SHAMSUL ISLAM. "The Influence of Eastern Philosophy on Yeats's Later Poetry," *Twentieth Century Literature* 19(4), October 1973, 288.

PETER URE. "Yeats's Supernatural Songs," *Review of English Studies*, n.s., 7(25), January 1956, 38-50.

"Roger Casement"

JOHN R. HARRISON. *The Reactionaries*, p. 45.

"The Rose"

> HIRAM HAYDN. "The Last of the Romantics: An Introduction to the Symbolism of William Butler Yeats," *Sewanee Review* 55(2), Spring 1947, 308-9.
>
> ARCHIBALD MACLEISH. *Poetry and Experience*, pp. 131-33.

"The Rose of Battle"

> ARNOLD GOLDMAN. "The Oeuvre Takes Shape: Yeats's Early Poetry," in *Victorian Poetry*, pp. 211-12.

"The Rose Tree"

> C. M. BOWRA. *The Heritage of Symbolism*, p. 204.

"Running to Paradise"

> DANIEL HOFFMAN. *Barbarous Knowledge*, pp. 44-46.

"The Sad Shepherd"

> ARNOLD GOLDMAN. "The Oeuvre Takes Shape: Yeats's Early Poetry," in *Victorian Poetry*, pp. 202-3.
>
> MICHAEL RAGUSSIS. *The Subterfuge of Art*, pp. 89-90.
>
> MARION WITT. "The Making of an Elegy: Yeats's 'In Memory of Major Robert Gregory,'" *Modern Philology* 48(2), November 1950, 113-14.

"Sailing to Byzantium"

> GÉMINO H. ABAD. *A Formal Approach to Lyric Poetry*, pp. 48-50, 53.
>
> T. R. BARNES. *English Verse*, pp. 303-6.
>
> R. P. BLACKMUR. *Expense of Greatness*, pp. 98-99. Reprinted in: R. P. Blackmur. *Language as Gesture*, pp. 98-99.
>
> PAUL A. BOVE. "Cleanth Brooks and Modern Irony: A Kierkegaardian Critique," *Boundary 2* 4(3), Spring 1976, 745-47.
>
> CLEANTH BROOKS. *Modern Poetry and the Tradition*, pp. 62-64, 190-92. Abridged in: *The Case for Poetry*, p. 401; second ed., p. 329.
>
> CLEANTH BROOKS. "A Note on Symbol and Conceit," *American Review* 3(2), May 1934, 209-11.
>
> CLEANTH BROOKS, JR. "The Vision of William Butler Yeats," *Southern Review* 4(1), Summer 1938, 131-33.
>
> HARRY BROWN and JOHN MILSTEAD. *What the Poems Means*, p. 301.
>
> VINCENT BUCKLEY. *Poetry and the Sacred*, pp. 197-204.
>
> HARRY MODEAN CAMPBELL. "Yeats's 'Sailing to Byzantium,'" *Modern Language Notes* 70(8), December 1955, 585-89.
>
> DENIS DONOGHUE. *The Ordinary Universe*, pp. 142-43.
>
> WALLACE DOUGLAS, ROY LAMSON, and HALLETT SMITH. *The Critical Reader*, pp. 115-18.
>
> ELIZABETH DREW. *Poetry*, pp. 262-67.
>
> DAVID EGGENSCHWILER. "Nightingales and Byzantine Birds, Something Less Than Kind," *English Language Notes* 8(3), March 1971, 186-91.
>
> RICHARD ELLMANN WITH PETER WILSON. "W. B. Yeats," in *English Poetry*, edited by Alan Sinfield, pp. 178-81.
>
> WILLIAM EMPSON. "Mr. Wilson on the Byzantium Poems," *Review of English Literature* 1(3), July 1960, 51-53.
>
> LILLIAN FEDER. *Ancient Myth in Modern Poetry*, pp. 82-84.
>
> LLOYD FRANKENBERG. *Invitation to Poetry*, p. 383.
>
> KIMON FRIAR and JOHN MALCOLM BRINNIN. *Modern Poetry*, pp. 554-55.
>
> FREDERICK L. GWYNN. "Yeats's Byzantium and Its Sources," *Philological Quarterly* 32(1), January 1953, 9-21.

STANLEY M. HOLBERG. "'Sailing to Byzantium': A New Source and a New Reading," *English Language Notes* 12(2), December 1974, 111-16.

A. NORMAN JEFFARES. "The Byzantine Poems of W. B. Yeats," *Review of English Studies* 22(85), January 1946, 44-49.

G. WILSON KNIGHT. *Neglected Powers*, pp. 255-56.

G. WILSON KNIGHT. *The Starlit Dome*, pp. 310-11.

L. C. KNIGHTS. *Explorations*, pp. 202-4.

L. C. KNIGHTS. "W. B. Yeats: The Assertion of Values," *Southern Review* 7(3), Winter 1942, 438-39.

ANNE KOSTELANETZ. "Irony in Yeat's Byzantium Poems," *Tennessee Studies in Literature* 9 (1964), 129-34.

SIMON O. LESSER. "'Sailing to Byzantium' — Another Voyage, Another Reading," *College English* 28(4), January 1967, 291-310.

SIMON O. LESSER. *The Whispered Meanings*, pp. 128-48.

MALCOLM MAGAW. "Yeats and Keats: The Poetics of Romanticism," *Bucknell Review* 13(3), December 1965, 87-96.

CLARE M. MURPHY. "Reply," *Literature and Psychology* 17(1), 1967, 38-40.

JOYCE CAROL OATES. "Yeats: Violence, Tragedy, Mutability," *Bucknell Review* 17(3), December 1969, 7.

JAMES H. O'BRIEN. "Yeats' Dark Night of Self and *The Tower*," *Bucknell Review* 15(2), May 1967, 11-12.

ELDER OLSON. "An Interpretation of W. B. Yeats' 'Sailing to Byzantium,'" in *The Creative Reader*, second ed., pp. 925-31.

ELDER OLSON. "'Sailing to Byzantium': Prolegomena to a Poetics of the Lyric," *University of Kansas City Review* 8(3), Spring 1942, 209-19. Reprinted in: *Critiques and Essays in Criticism*, pp. 284-88. Also: *Reading Modern Poetry*, pp. 139-49. Also: *The Dimensions of Poetry*, pp. 642-48. Also: *Five Approaches of Literary Criticism*, pp. 215-30. Also: *Master Poems of the English Language*, pp. 833-38. Abridged in: *The Case for Poetry*, p. 401; second ed., pp. 328-29.

CHARLES A. RAINES. "Yeats' Metaphors of Permanence," *Twentieth Century Literature* 75(1), April 1959, 18.

JOHN CROWE RANSOM. "The Irish, the Gaelic, the Byzantine," *Southern Review* 7(3), Winter 1942, 518-22.

JOHN CROWE RANSOM. "Yeats and His Symbols," *Kenyon Review* 1(3), Summer 1939, 318-20.

WILLIAM O. RAYMOND. "'The Mind's Internal Heaven' in Poetry," *University of Toronto Quarterly* 20(3), April 1951, 231-32.

GEORG ROPPEN and RICHARD SOMMER. *Strangers and Pilgrims*, pp. 337-52.

M. L. ROSENTHAL. *The Modern Poets*, p. 40.

M. L. ROSENTHAL. *Sailing to the Unknown*, pp. 118-20.

M. L. ROSENTHAL and A. J. M. SMITH. *Exploring Poetry*, pp. 577-82; second ed., pp. 386-90.

ROBERT S. RYF. "Yeats's Major Metaphysical Poems," *Journal of Modern Literature* 4(3), February 1975, 613-15.

VILAS SARANG. "The Byzantium Poems: Yeats at the Limits of Symbolism," *Concerning Poetry* 11(2), Fall 1978, 49-51.

DONALD STAUFFER. *The Nature of Poetry*, pp. 243-46. Abridged in: *The Case for Poetry*, pp. 401-3; second ed., pp. 329-30.

YEATS, W. B. *(Cont.)*

"Sailing to Byzantium" *(cont.)*

J. I. M. STEWART. *Eight Modern Writers*, pp. 368-69.

RUTH ELIZABETH SULLIVAN. "Backward to Byzantium," *Literature and Psychology* 17(1), 1967, 13-18.

WRIGHT THOMAS and STUART GERRY BROWN. *Reading Poems: An Introduction to Critical Study*, pp. 712-14.

RAYMOND TSCHUMI. *Thought in Twentieth-Century English Poetry*, pp. 67-69.

FRANCIS LEE UTLEY. "Stylistic Ambivalence In Chaucer, Yeats and Lucretius — The Cresting Wave and Its Undertow," *University Review* 37(3), Spring 1971, 192-98.

HELEN VENDLER. "Sacred and Profane Perfection in Yeats," *Southern Review*, n.s., 9(1), Winter 1973, 109-10.

CHAD WALSH. *Doors into Poetry*, pp. 30-32.

AILEEN WARD. "The Psychoanalytic Theory of Poetic Form: A Comment," *Literature and Psychology* 17(1), 1967, 31-33.

YVOR WINTERS. "The Poetry of W. B. Yeats," *Twentieth Century Literature* 6(1), April 1960, 10-11.

"The Scholars"

DELMORE SCHWARTZ. "An Unwritten Book," in *Selected Essays of Delmore Schwartz*, pp. 93-94.

"The Second Coming"

MICHAEL BELL. "The Assimilation of Doubt in Yeats's Visionary Poems," *Queen's Quarterly* 80(3), Autumn 1973, 390-91.

EDWARD A. BLOOM. "Yeats' 'Second Coming': An Experiment in Analysis," *University of Kansas City Review* 21(2), Winter 1954, 103-10.

EDWARD A. BLOOM, CHARLES H. PHILBRICK, and ELMER M. BLISTEIN. *The Order of Poetry*, pp. 43-52.

HAROLD BLOOM. *Poetry and Repression*, pp. 216-22.

C. M. BOWRA. *The Heritage of Symbolism*, pp. 208-9.

CLEANTH BROOKS and ROBERT PENN WARREN. *Understanding Poetry*, fourth ed., pp. 295-96.

DAVID DAICHES and WILLIAM CHARVAT. *Poems in English*, pp. 732-33.

BABETTE DEUTSCH. *Poetry in Our Time*, pp. 272-74; second ed., pp. 306-8.

LILLIAN FEDER. *Ancient Myth in Modern Poetry*, pp. 79-80.

GEORGE FRASER. *Essays on Twentieth-Century Poets*, pp. 40-42.

HARVEY GROSS. *The Contrived Corridor*, pp. 80-82.

JOE HORRELL. "Some Notes on Conversion in Poetry," *Southern Review* 7(1), Summer 1941, 123-26.

JOHN OLIVER PERRY. *The Experience of Poems*, p. 324.

M. L. ROSENTHAL. *The Modern Poets*, pp. 42-44.

D. S. SAVAGE. "Two Prophetic Poems," *Western Review* 13(2), Winter 1949, 67-78.

J. I. M. STEWART. *Eight Modern Writers*, pp. 365-67.

WRIGHT THOMAS and STUART GERRY BROWN. *Reading Poems: An Introduction to Critical Study*, pp. 715-16.

RAYMOND TSCHUMI. *Thought in Twentieth-Century English Poetry*, pp. 56-57.

LEONARD UNGER and WILLIAM VAN O'CONNOR. *Poems for Study*, pp. 582-84.

MARK VAN DOREN. *Introduction to Poetry*, pp. 80-85.

DONALD WEEKS. "Image and Idea in Yeats' *The Second Coming*," *PMLA* 63(1), March 1948, 281-92.

RICHARD P. WHEELER. "Yeats' 'Second Coming': What Rough Beast?" *American Imago* 31(3), Fall 1974, 233-51.

THOMAS R. WHITAKER. "The Dialectic of Yeats's Vision of History," *Modern Philology* 57(2), November 1959, 111-12.

MELVIN G. WILLIAMS. "Yeats and Christ: A Study in Symbolism," *Renascence* 20(4), Summer 1968, 178.

YVOR WINTERS. "The Poetry of W. B. Yeats," *Twentieth Century Literature* 6(1), April 1960, 9-10.

"The Secret Rose"

C. M. BOWRA. *The Heritage of Symbolism*, p. 191.

"September 1913"

VINCENT BUCKLEY. *Poetry and the Sacred*, pp. 186-87.

BABETTE DEUTSCH. *Poetry in Our Time*, p. 258; second ed., p. 291.

"The Seven Sages"

THOMAS R. WHITAKER. "Poet of Anglo-Ireland," in *Modern Poetry*, pp. 432-33.

"Solomon and the Witch"

BARBARA HARDY. *The Advantage of Lyric*, p. 83.

"The Song of the Happy Shepherd"

ARNOLD GOLDMAN. "The Oeuvre Takes Shape: Yeats's Early Poetry," in *Victorian Poetry*, p. 202.

MICHAEL RAGUSSIS. *The Subterfuge of Art*, pp. 86-88.

"The Song of Wandering Aengus"

C. M. BOWRA. *The Heritage of Symbolism*, pp. 189-90.

THOMAS PARKINSON. "The Sun and the Moon in Yeats's Early Poetry," *Modern Philology* 50(1), August 1952, 55.

SISTER M. BERNETTA QUINN. *The Metamorphic Tradition*, pp. 210-11.

BRUCE A. ROSENBERG. "Irish Folklore and 'The Song of Wandering Aengus,' " *Philological Quarterly* 46(4), October 1967, 527-35.

"The Sorrow of Love"

PHYLLIS BARTLETT. *Poems in Process*, pp. 193-95.

ARNOLD GOLDMAN. "The Oeuvre Takes Shape: Yeats's Early Poetry," in *Victorian Poetry*, pp. 212-13.

"The Stare's Nest by My Window"

T. R. HENN. *The Apple and the Spectroscope*, pp. 49-52.

HOWARD NEMEROV. "Poetry and History," *Virginia Quarterly Review* 51(2), Spring 1975, 327-28.

"The Statues"

HAZARD ADAMS. "Yeatsian Art and Mathematic Form," *Centennial Review* 4(1), Winter 1960, 78-80.

ARCHIBALD MACLEISH. *Poetry and Experience*, pp. 145-46.

JOHN FREDERICK NIMS. *Western Wind*, pp. 350-51.

JOYCE CAROL OATES. "Yeats: Violence, Tragedy, Mutability," *Bucknell Review* 17(3), December 1969, 5-6.

JON STALLWORTHY. "Two of Yeats's Last Poems," *Review of English Literature* 4(3), July 1963, 55-69.

HELEN VENDLER. "Sacred and Profane Perfection in Yeats," *Southern Review*, n.s., 9(1), Winter 1973, 114-16.

SARAH YOUNGBLOOD. "The Structure of Yeats's Long Poems," *Criticism* 5(4), Fall 1963, 324-27.

"A Stick of Incense"

MELVIN G. WILLIAMS. "Yeats and Christ: A Study in Symbolism," *Renascence* 20(4), Summer 1968, 174-75.

"The Stolen Child"

ROBERT W. CASWELL. *Explicator* 25(8), April 1967, Item 64.

M. L. ROSENTHAL. *The Modern Poets,* pp. 35-36.

CHAD and EVA T. WALSH. *Twice Ten,* pp. 137-39.

"That the Night Come"

CLEANTH BROOKS, JOHN THIBAUT PURSER, and ROBERT PENN WARREN. *An Approach to Literature,* pp. 469-71; second ed., pp. 469-71; third ed., pp. 319-21; fourth ed., pp. 317-19.

H. L. DEAN. *Explicator* 31(6), February 1973, Item 44.

LEONARD UNGER. "Yeats and *Hamlet,*" *Southern Review,* n.s., 6(3), Summer 1970, 698-709.

"There"

ROBERT M. SCHULER. "W. B. Yeats: Artist or Alchemist?" *Review of English Studies,* n.s., 22(85), February 1971, 49-50.

PETER URE. "Yeats's Supernatural Songs," *Review of English Studies,* n.s., 7(25), January 1956, 50-51.

RICHARD J. WALL and ROGER FITZGERALD. "Yeats and Jung: An Ideological Comparison," *Literature and Psychology* 13(2), Spring 1963, 46-47. (P)

"These Are the Clouds"

WILLIAM M. CARPENTER. "The *Green Helmet* Poems and Yeats's Myth of the Renaissance," *Modern Philology* 67(1), August 1969, 56-58.

"The Three Bushes"

ARRA M. GARAB. "Fabulous Artifice: Yeats's 'Three Bushes' Sequence," *Criticism* 7(3), Summer 1965, 235-49.

DANIEL HOFFMAN. *Barbarous Knowledge,* pp. 52-53.

EDWARD B. PARTRIDGE. "Yeats's 'The Three Bushes' — Genesis and Structure," *Accent* 17(2), Spring 1957, 67-80.

ALAN SPIEGEL. "From Divided to Shared Love in the Art of Yeats," *Renascence* 26(2), Winter 1974, 66-68.

LEONARD UNGER. "The New Collected Verse," *Poetry* 80(1), April 1952, 48-49.

"The Three Hermits"

BABETTE DEUTSCH. *Poetry in Our Time,* pp. 269-70; second ed., pp. 303-4.

"Three Things"

NAT HENRY. *Explicator* 33(5), January 1975, Item 38.

LAURENCE PERRINE. *Explicator* 32(1), September 1973, Item 4.

THOMAS J. WERTENBAKER, JR. *Explicator* 34(9), May 1976, Item 67.

"To a Friend Whose Work Has Come to Nothing"

MALCOLM BROWN. "The Sweet Crystalline Cry," *Western Review* 16(4), Summer 1952, 265.

ARCHIBALD MACLEISH. *Poetry and Experience,* pp. 125-26.

"To a Shade"

DAVID DAICHES. "On Yeats's 'To a Shade,'" in *Introduction to Literature,* fifth ed., pp. 148-51.

DAVID DAICHES and WILLIAM CHARVAT. *Poems in English,* pp. 731-32.

ARCHIBALD MACLEISH. *Poetry and Experience,* pp. 126-28.

"To Be Carved on a Stone at Thoor Ballylee"

CHARLES ALTIERI. "From a Comic to a Tragic Sense of Language in Yeats's Mature Poetry," *Modern Language Quarterly* 33(2), June 1972, 165.

"To His Heart Bidding It Have No Fear"

MARION WITT. *Explicator* 9(5), March 1951, Item 32.

"To the Rose Upon the Rood of Time"

ARNOLD GOLDMAN. "The Oeuvre Takes Shape: Yeats's Early Poetry," in *Victorian Poetry,* pp. 209-10.

"Towards Break of Day"

BARBARA HARDY. *The Advantage of Lyric,* pp. 75-76.

W. J. KEITH. "Yeats's Double Dream," *Modern Language Notes* 76(8), December 1961, 710-15.

M. L. ROSENTHAL. *Sailing into the Unknown,* pp. 124-27.

"The Tower"

LILLIAN FEDER. *Ancient Myth in Modern Poetry,* pp. 81-82.

KIMON FRIAR and JOHN MALCOLM BRINNIN. *Modern Poetry,* pp. 557-59.

DANIEL HOFFMAN. *Barbarous Knowledge,* pp. 62-83.

PHILLIP L. MARCUS. "'I declare my faith': Eliot's 'Gerontion' and Yeats's 'The Tower,'" *Papers on Language and Literature* 14(1), Winter 1978, 74-82.

MARJORIE PERLOFF. "'The Tradition of Myself': The Autobiographical Mode of Yeats," *Journal of Modern Literature* 4(3), February 1975, 566-73.

JOHN CROWE RANSOM. "The Irish, the Gaelic, the Byzantine," *Southern Review* 7(3), Winter 1942, 542-43.

M. L. ROSENTHAL. *Sailing into the Unknown,* pp. 143-48.

ROBERT S. RYF. "Yeats's Major Metaphysical Poems," *Journal of Modern Literature* 4(3), February 1975, 615-16.

J. I. M. STEWART. *Eight Modern Writers,* pp. 369-71.

RAYMOND TSCHUMI. *Thought in Twentieth-Century English Poetry,* pp. 47-49.

ROSEMOND TUVE. *Elizabethan and Metaphysical Imagery,* pp. 269-71.

THOMAS R. WHITAKER. "Poet of Anglo-Ireland," in *Modern Poetry,* pp. 417-25.

SARAH YOUNGBLOOD. "A Reading of 'The Tower,'" *Twentieth Century Literature* 5(2), July 1959, 74-84.

"The Travail of Passion"

ROBERT M. SCHULER. "W. B. Yeats: Artist or Alchemist?" *Review of English Studies,* n.s., 22(85), February 1971, 46-47.

"Two Songs from a Play"

CLEANTH BROOKS. *The Hidden God,* pp. 54-55.

CLEANTH BROOKS. *Modern Poetry and the Tradition,* pp. 182-83.

CLEANTH BROOKS, JR. "The Vision of William Butler Yeats," *Southern Review* 4(1), Summer 1938, 123-24.

CLEANTH BROOKS and ROBERT PENN WARREN. *Understanding Poetry,* pp. 615-21; revised ed., pp. 458-64; third ed., pp. 404-9.

REUBEN ARTHUR BROWER. *The Fields of Light,* pp. 83-88.

DOUGLAS BUSH. *Pagan Myth and Christian Tradition in English Poetry,* pp. 71-76.

LILLIAN FEDER. *Ancient Myth in Modern Poetry,* pp. 195-96.

YEATS, W. B. *(Cont.)*

"Two Songs from a Play" *(cont.)*

> GEORGE FRASER. *Essays on Twentieth-Century Poets,* pp. 42-44.
>
> KIMON FRIAR and JOHN MALCOLM BRINNIN. *Modern Poetry,* pp. 555-57.
>
> JOHN F. LYNEN. "Forms of Time in Modern Poetry," *Queen's Quarterly* 82(3), Autumn 1975, 359-61.
>
> ROBERT S. RYF. "Yeats's Major Metaphysical Poems," *Journal of Modern Literature* 4(3), February 1975, 616-17.
>
> YVOR WINTERS. "The Poetry of W. B. Yeats," *Twentieth Century Literature* 6(1), April 1960, 8-9.

"The Two Trees"

> FRANK KERMODE. *Romantic Image,* pp. 96-103.

"Under Ben Bulben"

> R. P. BLACKMUR. "Between Myth and Philosophy: Fragments of W. B. Yeats," *Southern Review* 7(3), Winter 1942, 415-17. Reprinted in: R. P. Blackmur. *Language as Gesture,* pp. 113-15.
>
> CURTIS B. BRADFORD. "Journeys to Byzantium," *Virginia Quarterly Review* 25(2), Spring 1949, 212-14.
>
> JOSEPH J. COMPRONE. "Unity of Being and W. B. Yeats' 'Under Ben Bulben,'" *Ball State University Forum* 11(3), Summer 1970, 41-49.
>
> JOYCE CAROL OATES. "Yeats: Violence, Tragedy, Mutability," *Bucknell Review* 17(3), December 1969, 13.
>
> RAYMOND TSCHUMI. *Thought in Twentieth-Century English Poetry,* pp. 59-61.

"Under the Moon"

> THOMAS PARKINSON. "The Sun and the Moon in Yeats's Early Poetry," *Modern Philology* 50(1), August 1952, 56.

"Under the Round Tower"

> THOMAS PARKINSON. "The Sun and the Moon in Yeats's Early Poetry," *Modern Philology* 50(1), August 1952, 55-56.

"Vacillation"

> CLEANTH BROOKS. *The Hidden God,* pp. 58-60.
>
> LILLIAN FEDER. *Ancient Myth in Modern Poetry,* pp. 196-98.
>
> J. I. M. STEWART. *Eight Modern Writers,* pp. 389-90.
>
> RAYMOND TSCHUMI. *Thought in Twentieth-Century English Poetry,* pp. 40-41.

"The Valley of the Black Pig"

> THOMAS R. WHITAKER. "The Dialectic of Yeats's Vision of History," *Modern Philology* 57(2), November 1959, 101-2.

"Veronica's Napkin"

> MELVIN G. WILLIAMS. "Yeats and Christ: A Study in Symbolism," *Renascence* 20(4), Summer 1968, 176.

"The Wanderings of Oisin"

> RUSSELL K. ALSPACH. "Some Sources of Yeats's *The Wanderings of Oisin,*" *PMLA* 58(3), September 1943, 849-66.
>
> MADELEINE PELNER COSMAN. "Mannered Passion: W. B. Yeats and the Ossianic Myths," *Western Humanities Review* 14(2), Spring 1960, 163-71.
>
> ARNOLD GOLDMAN. "The Oeuvre Takes Shape: Yeats's Early Poetry," in *Victorian Poetry,* pp. 200-202.
>
> MORTON IRVING SEIDEN. "A Psychoanalytical Essay on William Butler Yeats," *Accent* 6(3), Winter 1946, 180-89.

"What Magic Drum?"

> JAMES D. BOULGER. "Moral and Structural Aspects in W. B. Yeats's *Supernatural Songs,*" *Renascence* 27(2), Winter 1975, 68.
>
> DENNIS E. SMITH and F. A. C. WILSON. "The Source of Yeats's 'What Magic Drum?'" *Papers on Language and Literature* 9(2), Spring 1973, 197-201.

"What Then?"

> ROBIN SKELTON. "The Workshop of W. B. Yeats," *Concerning Poetry* 1(2), Fall 1968, 21.
>
> RAYMOND TSCHUMI. *Thought in Twentieth-Century English Poetry,* p. 63.

"The Wheel"

> NICHOLAS A. SALERNO. "A Note on Yeats and Leonardo Da Vinci," *Twentieth Century Literature* 5(4), January 1960, 197-98.

"When You Are Old"

> ARTHUR MINTON. *Explicator* 5(7), May 1947, Item 49.
>
> ELISABETH SCHNEIDER. *Explicator* 6(7), May 1948, Item 50.
>
> MARION WITT. *Explicator* 6(1), October 1947, Item 6.

"The White Birds"

> DAVID DAICHES. *The Place of Meaning in Poetry,* pp. 42-43.
>
> ROBERT M. SCHULER. "W. B. Yeats: Artist or Alchemist?" *Review of English Studies,* n.s., 22(85), February 1971, 44-45.

"Who Goes With Fergus?"

> WILLIAM EMPSON. *Seven Types of Ambiguity,* pp. 238-40; second and third eds., pp. 187-90.
>
> CHRISTOPHER GILLIE. *Movements in English Literature,* p. 75.
>
> M. L. ROSENTHAL. *The Modern Poets,* pp. 37-38.
>
> ANDREW RUTHERFORD. *Explicator* 13(7), May 1955, Item 41.

"The Wild Swans at Coole"

> CLEANTH BROOKS, JOHN THIBAUT PURSER, and ROBERT PENN WARREN. *An Approach to Literature,* pp. 456-57; second ed., pp. 456-57; third ed., pp. 314-15; fourth ed., pp. 311-12; fifth ed., pp. 358-60.
>
> GEORGE FRASER. *Essays on Twentieth-Century Poets,* pp. 29-31.
>
> SISTER M. NORMA HAHN. "Yeats's 'The Wild Swans at Coole': Meaning and Structure," *College English* 22(6), March 1961, 419-21.
>
> HUGH KENNER. "The Sacred Book of the Arts," *Sewanee Review* 64(4), Autumn 1956, 582-83.
>
> MARJORIE PERLOFF. "'The Tradition of Myself': The Autobiographical Mode of Yeats," *Journal of Modern Literature* 4(3), February 1975, 530-32.
>
> DONALD A. STAUFFER. "The Reading of a Lyric Poem," *Kenyon Review* 11(3), Summer 1949, 428-40.

"Wisdom"

> CLEANTH BROOKS. "Religion and Literature," *Sewanee Review* 82(1), Winter 1974, 99-100.

"The Withering of the Boughs"

> DONALD A. STAUFFER. "The Reading of a Lyric Poem," *Kenyon Review* 11(3), Summer 1949, 432-34.

"A Woman Young and Old"

> J. I. M. STEWART. *Eight Modern Writers,* pp. 383-85.

YERBY, FRANK

"Wisdom"

> ALAN C. LUPACK. "Frank Yerby's 'Wisdom,' " *Notes on Contemporary Literature* 7(4), September 1977, 8.

YOUNG, DAVID

"Occupational Hazards"

> ALBERTA T. TURNER. "The Smaller Camels and the Needle's Eye: Poet and Magazine Editor in 1976," *College English* 38(6), February 1977, 597-99.

Z

ZUKOFSKY, LOUIS

"Anew"

L. S. DEMBO. "Louis Zukofsky: Objectivist Poetics and the Quest for Form," *American Literature* 44(1), March 1972, 85.

"At eventide, cool hour" (*A*,3)

BARRY AHEARN. "Origins of 'A': Zukofsky's Materials for Collage," *ELH* 45(1), Spring 1978, 171.

"Bottom"

L. S. DEMBO. "The 'Objectivist' Poet: Four Interviews," *Contemporary Literature* 10(2), Spring 1969, 214-16.

"Clear music" (*A*,2)

BARRY AHEARN. "Origins of 'A': Zukofsky's Materials for Collage," *ELH* 45(1), Spring 1978, 169-70.

"Glad they were there"

L. S. DEMBO. "Louis Zukofsky: Objectivist Poetics and the Quest for Form," *American Literature* 44(1), March 1972, 84-85.

"Horses: who will do it? out of manes? Words" (*A*,7)

BARRY AHEARN. "Origins of 'A': Zukofsky's Materials for Collage," *ELH* 45(1), Spring 1978, 172-73. (P)

"Immature Pebbles"

L. S. DEMBO. "Louis Zukofsky: Objectivist Poetics and the Quest for Form," *American Literature* 44(1), March 1972, 94.

L. S. DEMBO. "The 'Objectivist' Poet: Four Interviews," *Contemporary Literature* 10(2), Spring 1969, 212-13.

"Mantis"

L. S. DEMBO. "Louis Zukofsky: Objectivist Poetics and the Quest for Form," *American Literature* 44(1), March 1972, 87-91.

"Not much more than being"

L. S. DEMBO. "The 'Objectivist' Poet: Four Interviews," *Contemporary Literature* 10(2), Spring 1969, 210-11.

"The old poet moves to a new apartment 14 times"

L. S. DEMBO. "The 'Objectivist' Poet: Four Interviews," *Contemporary Literature* 10(2), Spring 1969, 206-9.

"Poem Beginning 'The' "

BARRY AHEARN. "Origins of 'A': Zukofsky's Materials for Collage," *ELH* 45(1), Spring 1978, 161-64.

L. S. DEMBO. "Louis Zukofsky: Objectivist Poetics and the Quest for Form," *American Literature* 44(1), March 1972, 91-94.

"A/Round of fiddles playing Bach" (*A*,1)

BARRY AHEARN. "Origins of 'A': Zukofsky's Materials for Collage," *ELH* 45(1), Spring 1978, 165-69.

SOURCES

BOOKS

Abad, Gémino H. *A Formal Approach to Lyric Poetry.* Quezon City: University of the Philippines Press, 1978.

———. *In Another Light: Poems and Essays.* Quezon City: University of the Philippines Press, 1976.

Abbe, George. *You and Contemporary Poetry: An aid-to-appreciation.* North Guilford, Conn.: Author-Audience Publications, 1957.

———. Noone House, Peterborough, N. H.: William L. Bauhan, 1968.

Abrams, M. H., ed. *English Romantic Poets: Modern Essays in Criticism.* New York: Oxford University Press, 1960.

Adams, Robert M. *Strains of Discord: Studies in Literary Openness.* Ithaca, N.Y.: Cornell University Press, 1958.

The Age of Johnson: Essays Presented to Chauncey Brewster Tinker. F. W. Hilles, ed. New Haven: Yale University Press, 1949.

Allen, Don Cameron. *Image and Meaning: Metaphoric Traditions in Renaissance Poetry.* Baltimore: Johns Hopkins Press, 1960.

———. New enlarged ed. Baltimore: Johns Hopkins Press, 1968.

Alvarez, Alfred. *The School of Donne.* New York: Pantheon Books, 1961.

———. London: Chatto & Windus, 1961.

American Literary Criticism, 1900-1950. Charles I. Glicksberg, ed. New York: Hendricks House, 1951.

Anderson, Quentin. *The Imperial Self: An Essay in American Literary and Cultural History.* New York: Alfred A. Knopf, 1971.

Anderson, Wallace L. *see* Stageberg, Norman C.

Anglo-Saxon Poetry: Essays in Appreciation for John C. McGalliard. Lewis E. Nicholson and Dolores Warwick Frese, eds. Notre Dame: University of Notre Dame Press, 1975.

Anniversary Lectures 1959: Robert Burns, 1759, by Robert Hillyer; *Edgar Allan Poe, 1809,* by Richard Wilbur; *Alfred Edward Housman, 1859,* by Cleanth Brooks. Lectures Presented Under the Auspices of the Gertrude Clarke Whittall Poetry and Literature Fund. Washington: Reference Dept., Library of Congress, 1959.

Arms, George. *The Fields Were Green: A New View of Bryant, Whittier, Holmes, Lowell, and Longfellow, with a Selection of Their Poems.* Stanford, Calif.: Stanford University Press, 1953.

Asimov, Issac. *Familiar Poems, Annotated.* Garden City, N.Y.: Doubleday & Company, 1977.

Aspects of American Poetry: Essays Presented to Howard Mumford Jones. Richard M. Ludwig, ed. Columbus: Ohio State University Press, 1962.

Auden, W. H., and Norman Holmes Pearson. *Poets of the English Language.* 5 vols. New York: Viking Press, 1950.

Ball, Patricia M. *The Central Self: A Study in Romantic and Victorian Imagination.* London: Athlone Press, 1968.

———. *The Heart's Events: The Victorian Poetry of Relationships.* London: Athlone Press, 1976.

Barnes, T. R. *English Verse: Voice and Movement from Wyatt to Yeats.* Cambridge: The University Press, 1967.

Barnet, Sylvan, Morton Berman and William Burto. *The Study of Literature: A Handbook of Critical Essays and Terms.* Boston: Little, Brown, 1960.

Bartlett, Phyllis. *Poems in Process.* New York: Oxford University Press, 1951.

Basler, Roy P. *Sex, Symbolism, and Psychology in Literature.* New York: Octogon Books, 1967. Reprint of 1948 edition.

Bateson, F. W. *English Poetry: A Critical Introduction.* London: Longmans, 1950.

———. 2nd ed. London: Longmans, 1968.

———. *English Poetry and the English Language: An Experiment in Literary History.* Oxford: Clarendon Press, 1934.

———. 2nd ed. New York: Russell & Russell, 1961.

———. 3rd ed. Oxford: Clarendon Press, 1973.

Beach, Joseph Warren. *Obsessive Images: Symbolism in Poetry of the 1930's and 1940's.* Ed. by William Van O'Connor. Minneapolis: University of Minnesota Press, 1960.

———. *A Romantic View of Poetry: Being Lectures Given at the Johns Hopkins University on the Percy Turnbull Memorial Foundation in November 1941.* Minneapolis: University of Minnesota Press, 1944.

Beacham, Walton. *The Meaning of Poetry: A Guide to Explication.* Boston: Allyn and Bacon, 1974.

Beaty, Frederick L. *Light from Heaven: Love in British Romantic Literature.* DeKalb: Northern Illinois University Press, 1971.

Beaty, Jerome, and William H. Matchett. *Poetry From Statement to Meaning.* New York: Oxford University Press, 1965.

Bedient, Calvin. *Eight Contemporary Poets: Charles Tomlinson, Donald Davie, R. S. Thomas, Philip Larkin, Ted Hughes, Thomas Kinsella, Stevie Smith, W. S. Graham.* London: Oxford University Press, 1974.

Beer, Patricia. *An Introduction to the Metaphysical Poets.* Totowa, N.J.: Rowman and Littlefield, 1972.

Benoit, Raymond. *Single Nature's Double Name: The Collectedness of the Conflicting in British and American Romanticism.* The Hague: Mouton, 1973.

Benziger, James G. *Images of Eternity: Studies in the Poetry of Religious Vision from Wordsworth to T. S. Eliot.* Carbondale: Southern Illinois University Press, 1962.

Bergonzi, Bernard. *Heroes' Twilight: a Study of the Literature of the Great War.* New York: Coward-McCann, 1965.

Berryman, John. *The Freedom of the Poet.* New York: Farrar, Straus & Giroux, 1976.

Bewley, Marius. *Masks & Mirrors: Essays in Criticism.* New York: Atheneum, 1970.

The Black American Writer: Volume II: Poetry and Drama. C. W. E. Bigsby, ed. Deland, Fla.: Everett/Edwards, Inc., 1969.

Blackmur, R. P. *The Double Agent: Essays in Craft and Elucidation.* Gloucester, Mass.: Peter Smith, 1962. Reprint of 1935 edition.

———. *The Expense of Greatness.* Gloucester, Mass.: Peter Smith, 1958. Reprint of 1940 ed.

———. *Form and Value in Modern Poetry.* Garden City, N.Y.: Doubleday & Company, 1957. Reprint of 1946 ed.

———. *Language as Gesture: Essays in Poetry.* New York: Harcourt, Brace and Company, 1952.

Blair, Walter. *The Literature of the United States: An Anthology and History.* 2 vols. Ed. by Walter Blair, Theodore Hornberger, and Randall Stewart. Chicago: Scott, Foresman and Co., 1946–47.

_____. *Manual of Reading: A Text on Methods, with an Anthology of Varied Writings from Revolutionary Times to World War II*. Chicago: Scott, Foresman and Co., 1943.

Blair, Walter, and John C. Gerber. *Better Reading*. Vol. 2: *Literature*. Chicago: Scott, Foresman and Co., 1948.

Blair, Walter, and W. K. Chandler. *Approaches to Poetry*. New York: D. Appleton-Century Co., 1935.

_____. 2nd ed. New York: Appleton-Century-Crofts, 1953.

Bloom, Edward A., Charles H. Philbrick and Elmer M. Blistein. *The Order of Poetry: An Introduction*. New York: Odyssey Press, 1961.

Bloom, Harold. *The Anxiety of Influence*. New York: Oxford University Press, 1973.

_____. *Figures of Capable Imagination*. New York: The Seabury Press, 1976.

_____. *A Map of Misreading*. New York: Oxford University Press, 1975.

_____. *Poetry and Repression: Revisionism from Blake to Stevens*. New Haven: Yale University Press, 1976.

_____. *The Visionary Company: A Reading of English Romantic Poetry*. Garden City, N.Y.: Doubleday & Co., 1961.

Bodkin, Maud. *Archetypal Patterns in Poetry: Psychological Studies of Imagination*. London: Oxford University Press, 1934.

Bostetter, Edward E. *The Romantic Ventriloquists: Wordsworth, Coleridge, Keats, Shelley, Byron*. Seattle: University of Washington Press, 1963.

Boulton, Marjorie. *The Anatomy of Poetry*. London: Oxford University Press, 1934.

Bowra, C. M. *The Creative Experiment*. London: Macmillan, 1949.

_____. *The Heritage of Symbolism*. London: Macmillan & Co. Ltd., 1943.

_____. *In General and Particular*. Cleveland: World Publishing Co., 1964.

_____. *The Romantic Imagination*. London: Oxford University Press, 1969. Reprint of 1949 ed.

Boyers, Robert. *Excursions: Selected Literary Essays*. Port Washington, N.Y.: Kennikat Press, 1977.

Brett, R. L. *Reason & Imagination: A Study of Form and Meaning in Four Poems*. London: Oxford University Press, 1960.

Brisman, Leslie. *Romantic Origins*. Ithaca: Cornell University Press, 1978.

British Poetry Since 1960: A Critical Survey. Michael Schmidt and Grevel Lindop, eds. Pin Farm, South Hinskey, Oxford: Carcanet Press, 1972.

British Romantic Poets: Recent Revaluations. Shiv K. Kumar, ed. New York: New York University Press, 1966.

British Victorian Literature: Recent Revaluations. Shiv K. Kumar, ed. New York: New York University Press, 1969.

Brooks, Cleanth. *The Hidden God: Studies in Hemingway, Faulkner, Yeats, Elliot, and Warren*. New Haven: Yale University Press, 1963.

_____. *Modern Poetry and the Tradition*. Chapel Hill: University of North Carolina Press, 1939.

_____. *The Well Wrought Urn: Studies in the Structure of Poetry*. New York: Harcourt, Brace & World, 1947.

_____. Rev. ed. London: Dennis Dobson, 1968.

Brooks, Cleanth, and Robert B. Heilman. *Understanding Drama*. New York: Henry Holt and Company, 1945.

Brooks, Cleanth, John Thibaut Puser, and Robert Penn Warren. *An Approach to Literature: A Collection of Prose and Verse with Analyses and Discussions*. Baton Rouge: Louisiana State University Press, 1936.

_____. Rev. ed. New York: F. S. Crofts & Co., 1946.

_____. 3rd ed. New York: Appleton-Century-Crofts, Inc., 1952.

_____. 4th ed. New York: Meredith Publishing Company, 1964.

_____. 5th ed. Englewood Cliffs: Prentice-Hall, 1975.

Brooks, Cleanth, and Robert Penn Warren. *Understanding Poetry: An Anthology for College Students*. New York: Henry Holt and Co., 1938.

_____. Rev. ed. New York: Henry Holt and Co., 1950.

_____. 3rd ed. New York: Holt, Rinehart and Winston, 1960.

_____. 4th ed. New York: Holt, Rinehart and Winston, 1976.

Brower, Reuben Arthur. *The Fields of Light: An Experiment in Critical Reading*. New York: Oxford University Press, 1951.

Brown, Calvin S. *Music and Literature: A Comparison of the Arts*. Athens: University of Georgia Press, 1948.

Brown, Harry, and John Milstead. *What the Poem Means: Summaries of 1000 Poems*. Glenview, Ill.: Scott, Foresman and Company, 1970.

Buckley, Vincent. *Poetry and the Sacred*. London: Chatto & Windus, 1968.

Budick, Sanford. *Poetry of Civilization: Mythopoeic Displacement in the Verse of Milton, Dryden, Pope, and Johnson*. New Haven: Yale University Press, 1974.

Buell, Lawrence. *Literary Transcendentalism: Style and Vision in the American Renaissance*. Ithaca, N.Y.: Cornell University Press, 1973.

Burke, Kenneth. *A Grammar of Motives*. New York: Prentice-Hall, 1945.

_____. *The Philosophy of Literary Form: Studies in Symbolic Action*. Baton Rouge: Louisiana State University Press, 1941.

_____. 2nd ed. Baton Rouge: Louisiana State University Press, 1967.

Burton, S. H. *The Criticism of Poetry*. London: Longmans, Green, 1950.

Bush, Douglas. *Pagan Myth and Christian Tradition in English Poetry*. Memoirs of the American Philosophical Society, v. 72. Philadelphia: American Philosophical Society, 1968.

Cambon, Glauco. *The Inclusive Flame: Studies in American Poetry*. Bloomington: Indiana University Press, 1963.

_____. *Recent American Poetry*. University of Minnesota Pamphlets on American Writers, No. 16. Minneapolis: University of Minnesota Press, 1962.

Cargas, Harry J. *Daniel Berrigan and Contemporary Protest Poetry*. New Haven, Conn.: College & University Press, 1972.

Carroll, Paul. *The Poem In Its Skin*. Chicago: Follett Publishing Co., 1968.

The Case for Poetry: A New Anthology. Frederick L. Gwynn, Ralph W. Condee and Arthur O. Lewis, Jr., eds. New York: Prentice-Hall, 1954.

The Case for Poetry: A Critical Anthology, 2nd ed. Frederick L. Gwynn, Ralph W. Condee, Arthur O. Lewis, Jr., eds. Englewood Cliffs, N.J.: Prentice-Hall, 1965.

Charters, Samuel. *Some Poems/Poets: Studies in American Underground Poetry Since 1945*. Berkeley: Oyez, 1971.

Chase, Richard. *Emily Dickinson*. New York: Sloane, 1951.

Chaucer and Middle English Studies in Honour of Rossell Hope Robbins. Beryl Rowland, ed. London: George Allen & Unwin Ltd., 1974.

Ciardi, John. *Dialogue with an Audience*. Philadelphia: J.

B. Lippincott, 1963.

_____. *How Does a Poem Mean?* Boston: Houghton Mifflin, 1959.

_____. 2nd ed. Boston: Houghton Mifflin, 1975.

Clark, David R. *Lyric Resonance: Glosses on Some Poems of Yeats, Frost, Crane, Cummings & Others.* Amherst: University of Massachusetts Press, 1972.

Clayes, Stanley A., and John Gerrietts. *Ways to Poetry.* New York: Harcourt Brace Jovanovich, 1975.

Collingwood, R. G. *The Principles of Art.* Oxford: The Clarendon Press, 1938.

Colville, Derek. *Victorian Poetry and the Romantic Religion.* Albany: State University of New York, 1970.

Contemporary American-Jewish Literature: Critical Essays. Irving Malin, ed. Bloomington: Indiana University Press, 1973.

Contemporary Approaches to English Studies. Hilda Schiff, ed. London: Heinemann Educational Books, 1977.

The Contemporary Poet as Artist and Critic: Eight Symposia. Anthony Ostroff, ed. Boston: Little, Brown, 1964.

Contemporary Poetry in America: Essays and Interviews. Robert Boyers, ed. New York: Schocken Books, 1974.

Cooke, Michael G. *The Romantic Will.* New Haven: Yale University Press, 1976.

Cooper, Charles W., and John Holmes. *Preface to Poetry.* New York: Harcourt, Brace and Co., 1946.

Cowley, Malcolm. *A Many-Windowed House: Collected Essays on American Writers and American Writing.* Ed. by Henry Dan Piper. Carbondale: Southern Illinois University Press, 1970.

Cox, C. B., and A. E. Dyson. *Modern Poetry: Studies in Practical Criticism.* London: Edward Arnold, 1963.

_____. *The Practical Criticism of Poetry.* London: Edward Arnold, 1965.

Coxe, Louis. *Enabling Acts: Selected Essays in Criticism.* Columbia: University of Missouri Press, 1976.

The Creative Reader: An Anthology of Fiction, Drama, Poetry. R. W. Stallman and R. E. Watters, eds. New York: Ronald Press, 1954.

_____. 2nd ed. New York: Ronald Press, 1962.

Criticism: The Foundations of Modern Literary Judgment. Mark Schorer, Josephine Miles, and Gordon McKenzie, eds. New York: Harcourt Brace & Co., 1948.

_____. Rev. ed. New York: Harcourt Brace & Co., 1958.

Criticism in Action: A Critical Symposium on Modern Poems. Maurice Hussey, ed. London: Longmans, Green & Co., 1969.

The Critic's Notebook. Robert Wooster Stallman, ed. Minneapolis: University of Minnesota Press, 1950.

Critiques and Essays in Criticism: 1920-1948. Robert Wooster Stallman, ed. New York: Ronald Press, 1949.

Cruttwell, Patrick. *The Shakespearean Moment: And its Place in the Poetry of the 17th Century.* New York: Columbia University Press, 1955.

Cunningham, C. C. *Literature as a Fine Art: Analysis and Interpretation.* Ann Arbor, Mich.: University Microfilms, 1969. Reprint of 1941 ed.

Daiches, David. *The Place of Meaning in Poetry.* Folcroft, Pa.: Folcroft Press, 1969. Reprint of 1935 ed.

_____. *Poetry and the Modern World: A Study of Poetry in England between 1900 and 1939.* New York: Biblio and Tannen, 1969. Reprint of 1940 ed.

_____. *A Study of Literature for Readers and Critics.* New York: W. W. Norton, 1964.

Daiches, David, and William Charvat. *Poems in English, 1530-1940.* New York: Ronald Press, 1950.

Daly, Robert. *God's Altar: The World and the Flesh in Puritan Poetry.* Berkeley: University of California Press, 1978.

Daniels, Earl. *The Art of Reading Poetry.* Freeport, N.Y.: Books for Libraries Press, 1969. Reprint of 1941 ed.

Davie, Donald. *The Poet in the Imaginary Museum: Essays of Two Decades.* Ed. by Barry Alpert. New York: Persea Books, 1977.

Day Lewis, C. *The Lyric Impulse.* Cambridge: Harvard University Press, 1965.

_____. *The Poetic Image.* New York: Oxford University Press, 1947.

Dembo, L. S. *Conceptions of Reality in Modern American Poetry.* Berkeley: University of California Press, 1966.

Determinations: Critical Essays. F. R. Leavis, ed. Folcroft, Pa.: Folcroft Press, 1969. Reprint of 1934 ed.

Deutsch, Babette. *Poetry in Our Time.* New York: Columbia University Press, 1952.

_____. *Poetry in Our Time: A Critical Survey of Poetry in the English-speaking World 1900 to 1960.* 2nd ed. Garden City, N.Y.: Doubleday & Co., 1967.

_____. *This Modern Poetry.* New York: W. W. Norton, 1935.

Dickey, James. *Babel to Byzantium: Poets & Poetry Now.* New York: Farrar, Straus and Giroux, 1968.

The Dimensions of Poetry: A Critical Anthology. James E. Miller, Jr. and Bernice Slote, eds. New York: Dodd, Mead & Co., 1967.

Donoghue, Denis. *Connoisseurs of Chaos: Ideas of Order in Modern American Poetry.* New York: Macmillan, 1968.

_____. *The Ordinary Universe: Soundings in Modern Literature.* New York: Macmillan, 1968.

Douglas, Wallace, Roy Lamson and Hallett Smith. *The Critical Reader: Poems, Stories, Essays.* New York: W. W. Norton, 1949.

Drew, Elizabeth. *Discovering Poetry.* New York: W. W. Norton, 1933.

_____. *Poetry: A Modern Guide to Its Understanding and Enjoyment.* New York: W. W. Norton, 1959.

_____. *T. S. Eliot: The Design of His Poetry.* New York: Charles Scribner's Sons, 1949.

Drew, Elizabeth, and John L. Sweeney. *Directions in Modern Poetry.* New York: W. W. Norton, 1940.

Dronke, Peter. *The Medieval Lyric.* London: Hutchinson, 1968.

_____. 2nd ed. New York: Cambridge University Press, 1977.

Duffey, Bernard. *Poetry in America: Expression and Its Values in the Times of Bryant, Whitman, and Pound.* Durham, N.C.: Duke University Press, 1978.

Dyson, A. E. *Between Two Worlds: Aspects of Literary Form.* New York: St. Martin's Press, 1972.

Dyson, A. E., and Julian Lovelock. *Masterful Images: English Poetry from Metaphysicals to Milton.* London: Macmillan Press Ltd., 1976.

Eastman, Max. *The Literary Mind: Its Place in an Age of Science.* New York: Octagon Press, 1969. Reprint of 1931 ed.

Edwards, Thomas R. *Imagination and Power: A Study of Poetry on Public Themes.* New York: Oxford University Press, 1971.

Elizabethan Lyrical Poets. Ed. by Patricia Thomson. London: Routledge & Kegan Paul, 1967.

Elizabethan Poetry: Modern Essays in Criticism. Paul J. Alpers, ed. New York: Oxford University Press, 1967.

Ellmann, Richard. *The Identity of Yeats.* New York: Oxford University Press, 1954.

———. 2nd ed. New York: Oxford University Press, 1964.

Empson, William. *English Pastoral Poetry.* New York: W. W. Norton, 1938.

———. *The Gathering Storm.* London: Faber and Faber, 1940.

———. *Seven Types of Ambiguity.* London: Chatto & Windus, 1930.

———. Rev. ed. New York: New Directions, 1947.

———. 3rd ed. Norfolk, Conn.: New Directions, 1953.

———. *The Structure of Complex Words.* New York: New Directions, 1951.

English Masterpieces: An Anthology of Imaginative Literature from Chaucer to T. S. Eliot. 7 vols. Maynard Mack, Leonard Dean and William Frost, eds. New York: Prentice-Hall, 1950.

———. 2nd ed. Englewood Cliffs, N.J.: Prentice-Hall, 1961.

English Poetry. Alan Sinfield, ed. London: Sussex Publications, Ltd., 1976.

English Poetry and Prose: 1540-1674. Christopher Ricks, ed. History of Literature in the English Language, v. 2. London: Barrie & Jenkins, 1970.

English Romantic Poets: Modern Essays in Criticism. M. H. Abrams, ed. New York: Oxford University Press, 1960.

English Studies in Honor of James Southall Wilson. Fredson Bowers, ed. University of Virginia Studies, v. 4. Charlottesville: University of Virginia Press, 1951.

Enright, D. J. *Conspirators and Poets.* Chester Springs, Pa.: Dufour, 1966.

Essays and Studies in Language and Literature. Herbert H. Petit, ed. Duquesne Studies, Philological Series, no. 5. Pittsburgh: Duquesne University Press, 1964.

Essays in Modern Literary Criticism. Ray B. West, ed. New York: Holt, Rinehart and Winston, 1952.

Explication as Criticism: Selected Papers from the English Institute, 1941-1952. W. K. Wimsatt, Jr., ed. New York: Columbia University Press, 1963.

Fair Forms: Essays in English Literature from Spenser to Jane Austen. Maren-Sofie Röstvig, ed. Cambridge: D. S. Brewer, 1975.

Farley-Hills, David. *The Benevolence of Laughter: Comic Poetry of the Commonwealth and Restoration.* London: Macmillan Ltd., 1974.

Feder, Lillian. *Ancient Myth in Modern Poetry.* Princeton, N.J.: Princeton University Press, 1971.

Ferry, Anne. *All in War with Time: Love Poetry of Shakespeare, Donne, Jonson, Marvell.* Cambridge, Mass.: Harvard University Press, 1975.

The Fifties: Fiction, Poetry, Drama. Warren French, ed. Deland, Fla.: Everett/Edwards, 1970.

Five Approaches of Literary Criticism: An Arrangement of Contemporary Critical Essays. Wilbur S. Scott, ed. New York: Macmillan, 1962.

Forms of Lyric: Selected Papers from the English Institute. Rueben A. Brower, ed. New York: Columbia University Press, 1970.

The Forties: Fiction, Poetry, Drama. Warren G. French, ed. Deland, Fla.: Everett/Edwards, 1969.

Four Poets on Poetry. Don Cameron Allen, ed. Baltimore: Johns Hopkins Press, 1959.

Fowler, Alistair. *Conceitful Thought: The Interpretation of English Renaissance Poems.* Edinburgh: University Press, 1975.

Foxell, Nigel. *Ten Poems Analysed.* Oxford: Pergamon Press, 1966.

Frankenberg, Lloyd. *Invitation to Poetry: A Round of Poems from John Skelton to Dylan Thomas, Arranged with Comments.* Garden City, N.Y.: Doubleday, 1956.

———. *Pleasure Dome: On Reading Modern Poetry.* Boston: Houghton Mifflin, 1949.

Fraser, G. S. *Vision and Rhetoric: Studies in Modern Poetry.* New York: Barnes & Noble, 1960.

Fraser, George. *Essays on Twentieth Century Poets.* Totowa, N.J.: Rowman and Littlefield, 1977.

Friar, Kimon, and John Malcolm Brinnin. *Modern Poetry: American and British.* New York: Appleton-Century-Crofts, 1951.

From Sensibility to Romanticism: Essays Presented to Frederick A. Pottle. Frederick A. Hilles and Harold Bloom, eds. New York: Oxford University Press, 1965.

Frye, Northrop. *Fables of Identity: Studies in Poetic Mythology.* New York: Harcourt, Brace & World, 1963.

Fussell, Edwin. *Lucifer in Harness: American Meter, Metaphor, and Diction.* Princeton: Princeton University Press, 1973.

Gardner, Helen. *The Business of Criticism.* Oxford: Clarendon Press, 1959.

Gelpi, Albert. *The Tenth Muse: The Psyche of the American Poet.* Cambridge, Mass.: Harvard University Press, 1975.

Georgian Poetry: 1911-1922: The Critical Heritage. Timothy Rogers, ed. London: Routledge & Kegan Paul, 1977.

Gibson, Walker. *Poems in the Making.* Boston: Houghton Mifflin, 1963.

Gillie, Christopher. *Movements in English Literature, 1900-1940.* Cambridge: Cambridge University Press, 1975.

Goldfarb, Russell M. *Sexual Repression and Victorian Literature.* Lewisburg: Bucknell University Press, 1970.

Goodman, Paul. *The Structure of Literature.* Chicago: University of Chicago Press, 1954.

Graves, Robert. *Food for Centaurs: Stories, Talks, Critical Studies, Poems.* Garden City, N.Y.: Doubleday, 1960.

Greene, Theodore Meyer. *The Arts and the Art of Criticism.* Princeton: Princeton University Press, 1947.

Grigson, Geoffrey. *The Harp of Aeolus, and Other Essays on Art, Literature & Nature.* London: Routledge, 1947.

Gross, Harvey. *The Contrived Corridor: History and Fatality in Modern Literature.* Ann Arbor: University of Michigan Press, 1971.

Gross, Theodore L. *The Heroic Ideal in American Literature.* New York: Free Press, 1971.

Grundy, Joan. *The Spenserian Poets: A Study in Elizabethan and Jacobean Poetry.* London: Edward Arnold, 1969.

Halewood, William H. *The Poetry of Grace: Reformation Themes and Structures in English Seventeenth-Century Poetry.* New Haven: Yale University Press, 1970.

Hamilton, Ian. *A Poetry Chronicle: Essays and Reviews.* London: Faber and Faber, 1973.

Harding, D. W. *Experience Into Words: Essays on Poetry.* London: Chatto and Windus, 1963.

Hardy, Barbara. *The Advantage of Lyric: Essays on Feeling in Poetry.* London: Athlone Press, 1977.

Hardy, J. P. *Reinterpretations: Essays on Poems by Milton, Pope and Johnson.* London: Routledge & Kegan Paul, 1971.

Hardy, John Edward. *The Curious Frame: Seven Poems in Text and Context.* Notre Dame, Ind.: University of Notre Dame Press, 1962.

The Harlem Renaissance Remembered: Essays. Arna Bontemps, ed. New York: Dodd, Mead, 1972.

Harrison, John R. *The Reactionaries: A Study of the Anti-Democratic Intelligentsia.* New York: Schocken Books, 1966.

Hartman, Geoffrey H. *Beyond Formalism: Literary Essays, 1958-1970.* New Haven: Yale University Press, 1970.

———. *The Unmediated Vision: An Interpretation of Wordsworth, Hopkins, Rilke, and Valéry.* New Haven: Yale University Press, 1954.

Hawkins, Robert. *Preface to Poetry.* New York: Basic Books, 1965.

Hayden, Donald E. *Literary Studies: The Poetic Process.* University of Tulsa Monograph Series, no. 15. Tulsa: University of Tulsa, 1978.

Henn, T. R. *The Apple and the Spectroscope: Lectures on Poetry designed (in the main) for Science Students.* New York: W. W. Norton, 1966.

Highet, Gilbert. *The Classical Tradition: Greek and Roman Influences on Western Literature.* Oxford: Clarendon Press, 1949.

———. *The Powers of Poetry.* New York: Oxford University Press, 1960.

Hill, Archibald A. *Constituent and Pattern in Poetry.* Austin: University of Texas Press, 1976.

Hoffman, Michael J. *The Subversive Vision: American Romanticism in Literature.* Port Washington, N.Y.: Kennikat Press, 1972.

Hoffmann, Daniel. *Barbarous Knowledge: Myth in the Poetry of Yeats, Graves, and Muir.* New York: Oxford University Press, 1967.

Hoffmann, Frederick J. *The Twenties: American Writing in the Postwar Decade.* New York: Viking Press, 1955.

———. Rev. ed. New York: The Free Press, 1962.

Holbrook, David. *Llareggub Revisited: Dylan Thomas and the State of Modern Poetry.* London: Bowes and Bowes, 1962.

———. *Lost Bearings in English Poetry.* London: Vision Press Ltd., 1977.

Holmes, John. *Writing Poetry.* Boston: Writer, Inc., 1970.

Hungerford, Edward B. *Shores of Darkness.* Cleveland: World Publishing Co., 1963. Reprint of 1941 ed.

I. A. Richards: Essays in His Honor. Ruben Brower, Helen Vendler and John Hollander, eds. New York: Oxford University Press, 1973.

Illustrious Evidence: Approaches to English Literature of the Early Seventeenth Century. Earl Miner, ed. Berkeley: University of California Press, 1975.

The Importance of Scrutiny: Selections from Scrutiny, a Quarterly Review, 1932-1948. Eric Bentley, ed. New York: New York University Press, 1964. Reprint of 1948 ed.

In Defense of Reading: A Reader's Approach to Literary Criticism. Reuben A. Brower and Richard Poirier, eds. New York: E. P. Dutton & Co., 1962.

Interpretations: Essays on Twelve English Poems. John Wain, ed. London: Routledge & Kegan Paul, 1955.

———. 2nd ed. London: Routledge & Kegan Paul, 1972.

Interpretations of American Literature. Charles Feidelson, Jr. and Paul Brodtkorb, Jr., eds. New York: Oxford University Press, 1959.

Jack, Ian. *Augustan Satire: Intention and Idiom in English Poetry, 1660-1750.* Oxford: Clarendon Press, 1952.

Jacobus, Lee A., and William T. Moynihan. *Poems in Context.* New York: Harcourt Brace Jovanovich, 1974.

Johnson, E. D. H. *The Alien Vision of Victorian Poetry: Sources of Poetic Imagination in Tennyson, Browning, and Arnold.* Hamden, Conn.: Archon Books, 1963. Reprint of 1952 ed.

Johnson, Wendell Stacy. *Sex and Marriage in Victorian Poetry.* Ithaca: Cornell University Press, 1975.

Juhasz, Suzanne. *Naked & Fiery Forms: Modern American Poetry by Women, A New Tradition.* New York: Harper & Row, 1976.

Kalstone, David. *Five Temperaments: Elizabeth Bishop, Robert Lowell, James Merrill, Adrienne Rich, John Ashbery.* New York: Oxford University Press, 1977.

Kaplan, Fred. *Miracles of Rare Device: The Poet's Sense of Self in Nineteenth-Century Poetry.* Detroit: Wayne State University Press, 1972.

The Kenyon Critics: Studies in Modern Literature from the 'Kenyon Review.' John Crowe Ransom, ed. Cleveland: World Publishing Co., 1951.

Kermode, Frank. *Romantic Image.* New York: Macmillan Co., 1957.

———. *Shakespeare, Spenser, Donne: Renaissance Essays.* London: Routledge & Kegan Paul, 1971.

Kilby, Clyde S. *Poetry and Life: An Introduction to Poetry.* New York: Odyssey Press, 1953.

Kirk, Richard Ray, and Rogert Philip McCutcheon. *An Introduction to the Study of Poetry.* New York: American Book Co., 1934.

Knickerbocker, William S. *Twentieth Century English.* New York: The Philosophical Library, 1946.

Knight, G. Wilson. *The Burning Oracle: Studies in the Poetry of Action.* London: Oxford University Press, 1939.

———. *Neglected Powers: Essays on Nineteenth and Twentieth Century Literature.* New York: Barnes & Noble, 1971.

———. *Poets of Action: Incorporating Essays from the Burning Oracle.* London: Methuen, 1967.

———. *The Starlit Dome: Studies in the Poetry of Vision.* London: Oxford University Press, 1941.

Knights, L. C. *Explorations: Essays in Criticism, Mainly on the Literature of the Seventeenth Century.* New York: New York University Press, 1964. Reprint of 1947 ed.

Kreuzer, James R. *Elements of Poetry.* New York: Macmillan, 1955.

Krieger, Murray. *The Classic Vision: The Retreat from Extremity in Modern Literature.* Baltimore: Johns Hopkins Press, 1971.

———. *The New Apologists for Poetry.* Minneapolis: University of Minnesota Press, 1956.

Kroeber, Karl. *The Artifice of Reality: Poetic Style in Wordsworth, Foscolo, Keats, and Leopardi.* Madison: University of Wisconsin Press, 1964.

———. *Romantic Narrative Art.* Madison: University of Wisconsin Press, 1960.

Kugel, James L. *The Techniques of Strangeness in Symbolist Poetry.* New Haven: Yale University Press, 1971.

Lacey, Paul A. *The Inner War: Forms and Themes in Recent American Poetry.* Philadelphia: Fortress Press, 1972.

Langbaum, Robert. *The Poetry of Experience: The Dramatic Monologue in Modern Literary Tradition.* London: Chatto & Windus, 1957.

The Language of Poetry. Allen Tate, ed. New York: Russell & Russell, 1960.

Lawler, J. G. *The Christian Image: Studies in Religious Art and Poetry.* Pittsburgh: Duquesne University Press, 1965.

Le Comte, Edward. *Poets' Riddles: Essays in Seventeenth-Century Explication.* Port Washington, N. Y.: Kennikat Press, 1975.

Leavis, F. R. *Education & the University: A Sketch for an 'English School.'* London: Chatto & Windus, 1943.

──────. New ed. London: Chatto & Windus, 1948.

──────. *English Poetry: A Critical Introduction.* London: Longmans, 1950.

──────. 2nd ed. London: Longmans, 1966.

──────. *New Bearings in English Poetry: A Study of the Contemporary Situation.* 2nd ed. New York: George W. Stewart, 1950.

──────. *Revaluation: Tradition & Development in English Poetry.* New York: George W. Stewart, 1947.

Legouis, Pierre. *Donne the Craftsman: An Essay upon the Structure of the Songs and Sonnets.* New York: Russell & Russell, 1962. Reprint of 1928 ed.

Leishman, J. B. *The Metaphysical Poets: Donne, Herbert, Vaughan, Traherne.* Oxford: Clarendon Press, 1934.

Lensing, George S., and Ronald Moran. *Four Poets and the Emotive Imagination: Robert Bly, James Wright, Louis Simpson, and William Stafford.* Baton Rouge: Louisiana State University Press, 1976.

Lerner, Laurence. *An Introduction to English Poetry: Fifteen Poems Discussed by Laurence Lerner.* London: Edward Arnold, 1975.

──────. *The Uses of Nostalgia: Studies in Pastoral Poetry.* London: Chatto and Windus, 1972.

Lesser, Simon O. *The Whispered Meanings: Selected Essays of Simon O. Lesser.* Ed. by Robert Sprich and Richard W. Noland. Amherst: University of Massachusetts Press, 1977.

Lieberman, Laurence. *Unassigned Frequencies: American Poetry in Review, 1964-77.* Urbana: University of Illinois Press, 1977.

Literary Opinion in America: Essays in Illustrating the Status, Methods, and Problems of Criticism in the United States Since the War. Morton Dauwen Zabel, ed. New York: Harper & Brothers, 1939.

──────. Rev. ed. New York: Harper, 1951.

──────. 3rd ed. New York: Harper & Row, 1962.

Literature and Ideas in America: Essays in Memory of Harry Hayden Clark. Robert Falk, ed. Athens: Ohio University Press, 1975.

Literature in Revolution. George Abbot White and Charles Newman, eds. New York: Holt, Rinehart and Winston, 1972.

Locke, Louis G., William M. Gibson, and George Arms. *Readings for Liberal Education.* New York: Rinehart, 1948.

──────. Rev. ed. New York: Rinehart, 1952.

──────. 3rd ed. New York: Rinehart & Co., 1957.

──────. 4th ed. New York: Rinehart & Co., 1963.

──────. 5th ed. New York: Holt, Rinehart & Winston, 1967.

Low, Anthony. *Love's Architecture: Devotional Modes in Seventeenth-Century English Poetry.* New York: New York University Press, 1978.

Lutyens, David. *The Creative Encounter.* London: Secker & Warburg, 1960.

McCanles, Michael. *Dialectical Criticism and Renaissance Literature.* Berkeley: University of California Press, 1975.

McGill, Arthur C. *The Celebration of Flesh: Poetry in Christian Life.* New York: Association Press, 1964.

MacLeish, Archibald. *Poetry and Experience.* Cambridge: Riverside Press, 1961.

Madden, David. *The Poetic Image in 6 Genres.* Carbondale: Southern Illinois University Press, 1969.

The Major Victorian Poets: Reconsiderations. Isobel Armstrong, ed. Lincoln: University of Nebraska Press, 1969.

Manlove, C. N. *Literature and Reality: 1600-1800.* New York: St. Martin's Press, 1978.

Manning, Stephen. *Wisdom and Number: Toward a Critical Appraisal of the Middle English Religious Lyric.* Lincoln: University of Nebraska Press, 1962.

Martz, Louis L. *The Poem of the Mind: Essays on Poetry/ English and American.* New York: Oxford University Press, 1966.

──────. *The Poetry of Meditation: A Study in English Religious Literature of the Seventeenth Century.* Yale Studies in English, vol. 125. New Haven: Yale University Press, 1954.

──────. Rev. ed. New Haven: Yale University Press, 1962.

──────. *The Wit of Love: Donne, Carew, Crashaw, Marvell.* University of Notre Dame Ward-Phillips Lectures in English Language and Literature, vol. 3. Notre Dame: University of Notre Dame Press, 1969.

Master Poems of the English Language: Over One Hundred Poems Together with Introductions by Leading Poets and Critics of the English-Speaking World. Oscar Williams, ed. New York: Trident Press, 1966.

Matthiessen, F. O. *American Renaissance: Art and Expression in the Age of Emerson and Whitman.* London: Oxford University Press, 1941.

──────. *The Responsibilities of the Critic: Essays and Reviews.* Ed. by John Rackliffe. New York: Oxford University Press, 1952.

Maxwell, D. E. S. *Poets of The Thirties.* New York: Barnes & Noble, 1969.

Metaphysical Poetry. Malcolm Bradbury and David Palmer, eds. New York: St. Martin's Press, 1970.

Mid-Century American Poets. John Ciardi, ed. Twayne Library of Modern Poetry, vol. 7. New York: Twayne, 1950.

Miles, Josephine. *Major Adjectives in English Poetry from Wyatt to Auden.* Berkeley: University of California Press, 1946.

──────. *Poetry and Change: Donne, Milton, Wordsworth, and the Equilibrium of the Present.* Berkeley: University of California Press, 1974.

──────. *The Primary Language of Poetry in the 1640s.* University of California Publications in English, v. 19, no. 1. Berkeley: University of California Press, 1974.

Mill, John Stuart. *Essays on Poetry.* Ed. by F. Parvin Sharpless. Columbia: University of South Carolina Press, 1976.

Miller, J. Hillis. *Poets of Reality: Six Twentieth-Century Writers.* Cambridge, Mass.: Belknap Press of the Harvard University Press, 1965.

Miller, James E. *Quests Surd and Absurd: Essays in American Literature.* Chicago: University of Chicago Press, 1967.

Millet, Fred B. *Reading Poetry: A Method of Analysis with Selections for Study.* New York: Harper & Bro., 1950.

──────. *The Rebirth of Liberal Education.* New York: Harcourt Brace, 1945.

Millet, Fred B., Arthur W. Hoffman, and David R. Clark. *Reading Poetry.* 2nd ed. New York: Harper & Row, 1968.

Mills, Ralph J. *Contemporary American Poetry.* New York: Random House, 1965.

──────. *Creation's Very Self: On the Personal Element in Recent American Poetry.* Fort Worth: Texas Christian University Press, 1969.

──────. *Cry of the Human: Essays on Contemporary American Poetry.* Urbana: University of Illinois Press, 1975.

Miner, Earl. *The Cavalier Mode from Jonson to Cotton.* Princeton, N.J.: Princeton University Press, 1971.

_____. *The Metaphysical Mode from Donne to Cowley.* Princeton: Princeton University Press, 1969.

_____. *The Restoration Mode from Milton to Dryden.* Princeton: Princeton University Press, 1974.

Modern American Poetry. B. Rajan, ed. New York: Roy Publishers, 1950.

Modern American Poetry: Essays in Criticism. Jerome Mazzaro, ed. New York: David McKay, 1970.

Modern American Poetry: Essays in Criticism. Guy Owen, ed. Deland, Fla.: Everett/Edwards, Inc., 1972.

Modern Black Poets: A Collection of Critical Essays. Twentieth Century Views. Donald B. Gibson, ed. Englewood Cliffs, N.J.: Prentice-Hall, 1973.

The Modern Critical Spectrum. Gerald Jay Goldberg and Nancy Marmer Goldberg, eds. Englewood Cliffs, N.J.: Prentice-Hall, 1962.

Modern Literary Criticism: An Anthology. Irving Howe, ed. Boston: Beacon Press, 1958.

The Modern Poet. Ian Hamilton, ed. New York: Horizon Press, 1968.

Modern Poetry: Essays in Criticism. John Hollander, ed. London: Oxford University Press, 1968.

The Modern Spirit: Essays on the Continuity of Nineteenth- and Twentieth-Century Literature. Robert Langbaum, ed. New York: Oxford University Press, 1970.

The Moment of Poetry. Don Cameron Allen, ed. Baltimore: Johns Hopkins Press, 1962.

Moore, Arthur K. *The Secular Lyric in Middle English.* Lexington: University of Kentucky Press, 1951.

Mourgues, Odette de. *Metaphysical, Baroque & Précieux Poetry.* Folcroft, Pa.: Folcroft Press, 1969. Reprint of 1953 ed.

Muir, Edwin. *The Estate of Poetry.* Cambridge: Harvard University Press, 1962.

Myth and Symbol: Critical Approaches and Applications. Bernice Slote, ed. Lincoln: University of Nebraska Press, 1963.

Nassar, Eugene Paul. *The Rape of Cinderella: Essays in Literary Continuity.* Bloomington: Indiana University Press, 1970.

Nelson, Lowry. *Baroque Lyric Poetry.* New Haven: Yale University Press, 1961.

Nemerov, Howard. *Poetry and Fiction: Essays.* New Brunswick, N.J.: Rutgers University Press, 1963.

_____. *Reflexions on Poetry & Poetics.* New Brunswick, N.J.: Rutgers University Press, 1972.

Nevo, Ruth. *The Dial of Virtue: A Study of Poems on Affairs of State in the Seventeenth Century.* Princeton, N.J.: Princeton University Press, 1963.

The New Orpheus: Essays toward a Christian Poetic. Nathan A. Scott, ed. New York: Sheed and Ward, 1964.

Nicholson, Marjorie Hope. *The Breaking of the Circle: Studies in the Effect of the "New Science" Upon Seventeenth Century Poetry.* Evanston, Ill.: Northwestern University Press, 1950.

_____. Rev. ed. New York: Columbia University Press, 1960.

Nims, John Frederick. *Western Wind: An Introduction to Poetry.* New York: Random House, 1974.

Nowottny, Winifred. *The Language Poets Use.* London: Athlone Press, 1962.

Oberg, Arthur. *Modern American Lyric: Lowell, Berryman, Creeley, and Plath.* New Brunswick, N.J.: Rutgers University Press, 1978.

O'Connor, William Van. *Sense and Sensibility in Modern Poetry.* New York: Barnes & Noble, 1948.

Old English Literature: Twenty-Two Analytical Essays. Martin Stevens and Jerome Mandel, eds. Lincoln: University of Nebraska Press, 1968.

On Contemporary Literature: An Anthology of Critical Essays on the Major Movements and Writers of Contemporary Literature. Richard Kostelanetz, ed. New York: Avon Books, 1964.

Palmer, Herbert. *Post-Victorian Poetry.* London: J. M. Dent & Sons, 1938.

Pearce, Roy Harvey. *The Continuity of American Poetry.* Princeton, N.J.: Princeton University Press, 1961.

_____. *Historicism Once More: Problems & Occasions for the American Scholar.* Princeton, N.J.: Princeton University Press, 1969.

Pepper, Stephen C. *The Basis of Criticism in the Arts.* Cambridge, Mass.: Harvard University Press, 1945.

Perrine, Laurence. *Sound and Sense: An Introduction to Poetry.* New York: Harcourt Brace, 1956.

_____. 2nd ed. New York: Harcourt Brace & World, 1963.

_____. 3rd ed. New York: Harcourt Brace & World, 1969.

_____. 4th ed. New York: Harcourt Brace Jovanovich, 1973.

Perrine, Laurence, and James M. Reid. *100 American Poems of the Twentieth Century.* New York: Harcourt Brace & World, 1966.

Perry, John Oliver. *The Experience of Poems: A Text and Anthology.* New York: Macmillan Co., 1972.

Perspectives of Poetry: Some Notable Discourses on 'A Many Splendoured Thing.' The English Association Pamphlets. London: Dawsons of Pall Mall, 1968.

Perspectives on Poetry. James L. Calderwood and Harold E. Toliver, eds. New York: Oxford University Press, 1968.

Peterson, Douglas L. *The English Lyric from Wyatt to Donne: A History of the Plain and Eloquent Styles.* Princeton: Princeton University Press, 1967.

Phillips, Robert. *The Confessional Poets.* Crosscurrents/Modern Critiques. Ed. by Harry T. Moore. Carbondale: Southern Illinois University Press, 1973.

Pinsky, Robert. *The Situation of Poetry: Contemporary Poetry and Its Traditions.* Princeton, N.J.: Princeton University Press, 1976.

Pinto, Vivian de Sola. *Crisis in English Poetry 1880-1940.* London: Hutchinson's University Library, 1951.

_____. 2nd ed. London: Hutchinson University Library, 1955.

_____. 3rd ed. London: Hutchinson University Library, 1958.

_____. 4th ed. London: Hutchinson University Library, 1961.

_____. 5th ed. London: Hutchinson University Library, 1967.

Poems and Critics: An Anthology of Poetry and Criticism from Shakespeare to Hardy. Christopher Ricks, ed. New York: Harper & Row, 1972.

The Poet as Critic. Frederick P. W. McDowell, ed. Evanston: Northwestern University Press, 1967.

The Poet Speaks: Interviews with Contemporary Poets. Peter Orr, ed. New York: Barnes & Noble, 1966.

The Poetic Tradition: Essays on Greek, Latin, and English Poetry. Don Cameron Allen and Henry T. Rowell, eds. Baltimore: Johns Hopkins Press, 1968.

Poets at Work: Essays Based on the Modern Poetry Collection at the Lockwood Memorial Library, University of Buffalo. New York: Harcourt Brace, 1948.

Poets in Progress: Critical Prefaces to Ten Contemporary

Americans. Edward B. Hungerford, ed. Evanston, Ill.: Northwestern University Press, 1962.

Poets in Progress: Critical Prefaces to Thirteen Modern American Poets. Edward B. Hungerford, ed. Evanston, Ill.: Northwestern University Press, 1967.

Poets on Poetry. Charles Norman, ed. New York: Free Press, 1962.

Pottle, Frederick A. *The Idiom of Poetry.* Cornell University Messenger Lectures on the Evolution of Civilization. Ithaca, N.Y.: Cornell University Press, 1941.

———. Rev. ed. Bloomington: Indiana University Press, 1963.

Potts, Abbie Findlay. *The Elegiac Mode: Poetic Form in Wordsworth and Other Elegists.* Ithaca, N.Y.: Cornell University Press, 1967.

Pratt, John Clark. *The Meaning of Modern Poetry.* Garden City, N.Y.: Doubleday, 1962.

The Proper Study: Essays on Western Classics. Quentin Anderson and Joseph A. Mazzeo, eds. New York: St. Martin's Press, 1962.

Prose Keys to Modern Poetry. Karl Shapiro, ed. New York: Harper & Row, 1962.

Quinn, Bernetta. *The Metamorphic Tradition in Modern Poetry: Essays on The Work of Ezra Pound, Wallace Stevens, William Carlos Williams, T. S. Eliot, Hart Crane, Randall Jarrell, and William Butler Yeats.* New Brunswick, N.J.: Rutgers University Press, 1955.

Ragussis, Michael. *The Subterfuge of Art: Language and the Romantic Tradition.* Baltimore: Johns Hopkins University Press, 1978.

Raines, Kathleen. *Defending Ancient Springs.* London: Oxford University Press, 1967.

Ransom, John Crowe. *The New Criticism.* Norfolk, Conn.: New Directions, 1941.

———. *The World's Body.* New York: Charles Scribner's Sons, 1938.

Reading Modern Poetry: A Critical Anthology. Paul Engle and Warren Carrier, eds. Chicago: Scott, Foresman, 1955.

———. Rev. ed. Glenview, Ill.: Scott, Foresman and Company, 1968.

Readings from the Americas: An Introduction to Democratic Thought. Guy A. Cardwell, ed. New York: Ronald Press, 1947.

Reeves, James. *Commitment to Poetry.* London: Heinemann, 1969.

Reeves, James, and Martin Seymour-Smith. *Inside Poetry.* New York: Barnes & Noble, 1970.

Reid, James M. *see* Perrine, Laurence

Reiss, Edmund. *The Art of the Middle English Lyric: Essays in Criticism.* Athens: University of Georgia Press, 1972.

Restoration and Eighteenth-Century Literature: Essays in Honor of Alan Dugald McKillop. Chicago: University of Chicago Press, 1963.

The Rhetoric of Renaissance Poetry: From Wyatt to Milton. Thomas O. Sloan and Raymond B. Waddington, eds. Berkeley: University of California Press, 1974.

Richards, I. A. *Poetries: Their Media and Ends.* Ed. by Trevor Eaton. The Hague: Mouton, 1974.

———. *Practical Criticism: A Study of Literary Judgement.* London: Routledge & Kegan Paul, 1929.

———. *Principles of Literary Criticism.* New York: Harcourt Brace & World, 1926.

———. 2nd ed. New York: Harcourt Brace & World, 1949.

Riding, Laura, and Robert Graves. *A Survey of Modernist Poetry.* London: W. Heinemann Ltd., 1927.

Ries, Lawrence R. *Wolf Masks: Violence in Contemporary Poetry.* Port Washington, N.Y.: Kennikat Press, 1977.

Rodway, Allan. *The Romantic Conflict.* London: Chatto & Windus, 1963.

Romantic and Victorian: Studies in Memory of William M. Marshall. W. Paul Elledge and Richard L. Hoffman, eds. Rutherford: Fairleigh Dickinson University Press, 1971.

Romanticism and Consciousness: Essays in Criticism. Harold Bloom, ed. New York: W. W. Norton, 1970.

Roppen, Georg, and Richard Sommer. *Strangers and Pilgrims: An Essay on the Metaphor of Journey.* Norwegian Studies in English, no. 11. New York: Humanities Press, 1964.

Rosenheim, Edward W. *What Happens in Literature: A Student's Guide to Poetry, Drama, and Fiction.* Chicago: University of Chicago Press, 1960.

Rosenthal, M. L. *The Modern Poets: A Critical Introduction.* New York: Oxford University Press, 1960.

———. *Poetry and the Common Life.* New York: Oxford University Press, 1974.

———. *Sailing into the Unknown: Yeats, Pound, and Eliot.* New York: Oxford University Press, 1978.

Rosenthal, M. L., and A. J. M. Smith. *Exploring Poetry.* New York: Macmillan, 1955.

———. 2nd ed. New York: Macmillan Co., 1973.

Rosenthal, M. L., W. C. Hummel, and V. E. Leichty. *Effective Reading: Methods and Models.* Boston: Houghton Mifflin Co., 1944.

Rukeyser, Muriel. *The Life of Poetry.* New York: A. A. Wyn, 1949.

Savage, Derek S. *The Personal Principle: Studies in Modern Poetry.* Folcroft, Pa.: Folcroft Press, 1969. Reprint of 1944 ed.

Scannell, Vernon. *Not Without Glory: Poets of the Second World War.* London: The Woburn Press, 1976.

Schlauch, Margaret. *Modern English and American Poetry: Techniques and Ideologies.* London: C. H. Watts & Co., 1956.

Schneider, Elisabeth. *Aesthetic Motive.* New York: Macmillan, 1939.

Schwartz, Delmore. *Selected Essays of Delmore Schwartz.* Ed. by Donald A. Dike and David H. Zucker. Chicago: University of Chicago Press, 1970.

Scott, A. F. *The Poet's Craft: A Course in the Critical Appreciation of Poetry Based on the Study of Holograph Manuscripts, Earlier and Later Versions of Printed Poems, Transpositions of Prose into Verse, and Contrasted Translations.* Cambridge: Cambridge University Press, 1957.

Scott, Nathan A. *Rehearsals of Discomposure: Alienation and Reconciliation in Modern Literature: Franz Kafka, Ignazio Silone, D. H. Lawrence, T. S. Eliot.* New York: King's Crown Press, 1952.

Scottish Poetry: A Critical Survey. James Kingley, ed. London: Cassell & Co., 1955.

Scrutinies, Volume II, By Various Writers. Compiled by Edgell Rickword. Folcroft, Pa.: Folcroft Press, 1969. Reprint of 1928 ed.

Seven American Poets from MacLeish to Nemerov: An Introduction. Denis Donoghue, ed. Minneapolis: University of Minnesota Press, 1975.

Seven Modern American Poets: An Introduction. Leonard Unger, ed. Minneapolis: University of Minnesota Press, 1967.

Seventeenth-Century English Poetry: Modern Essays in Crit-

icism. William R. Keast, ed. New York: Oxford University Press, 1962.

――――. Rev. ed. London: Oxford University Press, 1971.

Seventeenth-Century Imagery: Essays on Uses of Figurative Language from Donne to Farquhar. Earl Miner, ed. Berkeley: University of California Press, 1971.

Sewell, Elizabeth. *The Human Metaphor*. Notre Dame, Ind.: University of Notre Dame Press, 1964.

――――. *The Structure of Poetry*. London: Routledge & Kegan Paul, 1951.

Shapiro, Karl. *In Defense of Ignorance*. New York: Random House, 1960.

Silent Poetry: Essays in Numerological Analysis. Alistair Fowler, ed. London: Routledge & Kegan Paul, 1970.

Silkin, Jon. *Out of Battle: The Poetry of the Great War*. London: Oxford University Press, 1972.

Simpson, Louis. *A Revolution in Taste*. New York: Macmillan, 1978.

Six American Poets from Emily Dickinson to the Present: An Introduction. Allen Tate, ed. Minneapolis: University of Minnesota Press, 1969.

Skelton, Robin. *The Poetic Pattern*. Berkeley: University of California Press, 1956.

――――. *Poetry*. London: English Universities Press, 1963.

Smith, Elton Edward. *The Angry Young Men of the Thirties*. Crosscurrents/Modern Critiques. Ed. by Harry T. Moore. Carbondale: Southern Illinois University Press, 1975.

Smith, Hallett. *Elizabethan Poetry: A Study in Conventions, Meaning, and Expression*. Cambridge, Mass.: Harvard University Press, 1952.

Smith, James. *Shakespearean and Other Essays*. London: Cambridge University Press, 1974.

Southworth, James G. *More Modern American Poets*. Oxford: Basil Blackwell, 1954.

――――. *Some Modern American Poets*. Oxford: Basil Blackwell, 1950.

Spacks, Patricia Meyer. *The Poetry of Vision: Five Eighteenth-Century Poets*. Cambridge, Mass.: Harvard University Press, 1967.

Spearing, A. C. *Criticism and Medieval Poetry*. New York: Barnes & Noble, 1964.

――――. 2nd ed. London: Edward Arnold, 1972.

――――. *Medieval Dream-Poetry*. Cambridge: Cambridge University Press, 1976.

Spears, Monroe K. *Space Against Time in Modern Poetry*. Fort Worth: Texas Christian University Press, 1972.

Spencer, Jeffry B. *Heroic Nature: Ideal Landscape in English Poetry from Marvell to Thomson*. Evanston, Ill.: Northwestern University Press, 1973.

Spitzer, Leo. *Essays on English and American Literature*. Ed. by Anna Hatcher. Princeton, N.J.: Princeton University Press, 1962.

――――. *A Method of Interpreting Literature*. Northampton, Mass.: Smith College, 1949.

Stageberg, Norman C., and Wallace L. Anderson. *Poetry as Experience*. New York: American Book Co., 1952.

Start with the Sun: Studies in Cosmic Poetry. By James E. Miller, Karl Shapiro and Bernice Slote. Lincoln: University of Nebraska Press, 1960.

Stauffer, Donald A. *The Nature of Poetry*. New York: W. W. Norton & Co., 1946.

Stein, Agnes. *The Uses of Poetry*. New York: Holt, Rinehart and Winston, 1975.

Stevens, Wallace. *The Necessary Angel: Essays on Reality and the Imagination*. New York: Alfred A. Knopf, 1951.

Stewart, J. I. M. *Eight Modern Writers*. Oxford: Clarendon Press, 1963.

Stewart, Stanley. *The Enclosed Garden: The Tradition and the Image in Seventeenth-Century Poetry*. Madison: University of Wisconsin Press, 1966.

Studies in American Literature. Waldo McNeir and Leo B. Levy, eds. Louisiana State University Studies, Humanities Series, no. 8. Baton Rouge: Louisiana State University Press, 1960.

Summers, Joseph H. *The Heirs of Donne and Jonson*. New York: Oxford University Press, 1970.

The Survival of Poetry: A Contemporary Survey. Martin Dodsworth, ed. London: Faber & Faber, 1970.

Sutton, Walter. *American Free Verse: The Modern Revolution in Poetry*. New York: New Directions, 1973.

Swardson, H. R. *Poetry and the Fountain of Light: Observations on the Conflict between Christian and Classical Tradition in Seventeenth-Century Poetry*. Columbia: University of Missouri Press, 1962.

Tate, Allen. *Essays of Four Decades*. Chicago: Swallow Press, 1968.

――――. *On the Limits of Poetry: Selected Essays, 1928-1948*. Freeport, N.Y.: Books for Libraries Press, 1969. Reprint of 1948 ed.

――――. *Reactionary Essays on Poetry and Ideas*. New York: Charles Scribner's Sons, 1936.

――――. *Reason in Madness: Critical Essays*. New York: G. P. Putnam's Sons, 1941.

The Thirties: Fiction, Poetry, Drama. Warren G. French, ed. Deland, Fla.: Everett/Edwards, Inc., 1967.

Thomas, Wright and Stuart Gerry Brown. *Reading Poems: An Introduction to Critical Study*. New York: Oxford University Press, 1941.

Thompson, Denys. *The Uses of Poetry*. Cambridge: Cambridge University Press, 1978.

Three Studies in the Renaissance: Sidney, Jonson, Milton. Benjamin Christe Nangle, ed. Yale Studies in English, v. 138. New Haven: Yale University Press, 1958.

Thurley, Geoffrey. *The Ironic Harvest: English Poetry in the Twentieth Century*. London: Edward Arnold, 1974.

Tillyard, E. M. W. *Essays, Literary & Educational*. New York: Barnes & Noble, 1962.

――――. *Five Poems: 1470-1870: An Elementary Essay on the Background of English Literature*. London: Chatto & Windus, 1948.

――――. *The Metaphysicals and Milton*. London: Chatto & Windus, 1956.

――――. *Poetry Direct and Oblique*. London: Chatto & Windus, 1934.

――――. Rev. ed. London: Chatto & Windus, 1948.

Toliver, Harold. *50 Modern American & British Poets, 1920-1970*. Ed. by Louis Untermeyer. New York: McKay, 1973.

――――. *Pastoral Forms and Attitudes*. Berkeley: University of California Press, 1971.

Trial Balances. Ann Winslow, ed. New York: Macmillan Company, 1935.

Tschumi, Raymond. *Thought in Twentieth-Century English Poetry*. London: Routledge and Kegan Paul, 1951.

Tuve, Rosemond. *Elizabethan and Metaphysical Imagery: Renaissance Poetic and Twentieth-Century Critics*. Chicago: University of Chicago Press, 1947.

The Twenties: Fiction, Poetry, Drama. Warren French, ed. Deland, Fla.: Everett/Edwards, Inc., 1975.

The Twenties: Poetry and Prose. Richard E. Langford and William E. Taylor, eds. Deland, Fla.: Everett Edwards

Press, 1966.

Unger, Leonard. *Donne's Poetry and Modern Criticism.* Chicago: Regnery Company, 1950.

_____. *The Man in the Name: Essays on the Experience of Poetry.* Minneapolis: University of Minnesota Press, 1956.

Unger, Leonard, and William Van O'Connor. *Poems for Study: A Critical and Historical Introduction.* New York: Rinehart & Co., 1953.

The Uses of Poetry. By Agnes Stein. New York: Holt, Rinehart, Winston, 1975.

Van Doren, Mark. *Introduction to Poetry.* New York: Dryden Press, 1951.

Van Nostrand, A. D. *Everyman His Own Poet: Romantic Gospels in American Literature.* New York: McGraw-Hill, 1968.

Varieties of Literary Experience: Eighteen Essays in World Literature. Stanley Burshaw, ed. New York: New York University Press, 1962.

Vernon, John. *The Garden and the Map: Schizophrenia in Twentieth-Century Literature and Culture.* Urbana: University of Illinois Press, 1973.

Victorian Literature: Modern Essays in Criticism. Austin Wright, ed. New York: Oxford University Press, 1961.

Victorian Poetry. Stratford-upon-Avon Studies, no. 15. Malcolm Bradbury and David Palmer, eds. London: Edward Arnold, 1972.

Victorian Scrutinies: Reviews of Poetry 1830-1870. Compiled by Isobel Armstrong. London: Athlone Press, 1972.

Vivante, Leone. *English Poetry and Its Contribution to the Knowledge of a Creative Principle.* London: Faber and Faber, 1950.

Waggoner, Hyatt H. *American Poets: From the Puritans to the Present.* Boston: Houghton Mifflin Co., 1968.

_____. *The Heel of Elohim: Science and Values in Modern American Poetry.* Norman: University of Oklahoma Press, 1950.

Wain, John. *Professing Poetry.* London: Macmillan, 1977.

Walsh, Chad. *Doors Into Poetry.* Englewood Cliffs, N.J.: Prentice-Hall, 1962.

_____. 2nd ed. Englewood Cliffs, N.J.: Prentice-Hall, 1970.

Walsh, Chad, and Eva T. Walsh. *Twice Ten: An Introduction to Poetry.* New York: John Wiley & Sons, 1976.

Warren, Austin. *New England Saints.* Ann Arbor: University of Michigan Press, 1956.

_____. *Rage for Order: Essays in Criticism.* Chicago: University of Chicago Press, 1948.

Wasserman, Earl R. *The Subtler Language: Critical Reading of Neoclassic and Romantic Poems.* Baltimore: Johns Hopkins Press, 1959.

Watts, H. H. *Hound and Quarry.* London: Routledge and Kegan Paul, 1953.

Weber, Brom. *Hart Crane: A Biographical and Critical Study.* New York: Bodley Press, 1948.

Weber, Sarah Appleton. *Theology and Poetry in the Middle English Lyric: A Study of Sacred History and Aesthetic Form.* Columbus: Ohio State University Press, 1969.

Weitz, Morris. *Philosophy of the Arts.* New York: Russell & Russell, 1964. Reprint of the 1950 ed.

Wells, E. K. *The Ballad Tree.* New York: Ronald Press, 1950.

Wells, Henry W. *New Poets from Old: A Study in Literary Genetics.* New York: Columbia University Press, 1964. Reprint of the 1940 ed.

West, Ray B. *Writing in the Rocky Mountains.* Lincoln: University of Nebraska Press, 1947.

Wheelwright, Philip. *The Burning Fountain: A Study in the Language of Symbolism.* Bloomington: Indiana University Press, 1954.

Whicher, George Frisbie. *This Was a Poet: A Critical Biography of Emily Dickinson.* Ann Arbor: University of Michigan Press, 1957. Reprint of the 1938 ed.

Wilbur, Richard. *Responses: Prose Pieces, 1953-1976.* New York: Harcourt Brace Jovanovich, 1976.

Willard, Nancy. *Testimony of the Invisible Man: William Carlos Williams, Francis Ponge, Rainer Maria Rilke, Pablo Neruda.* Columbia: University of Missouri Press, 1970.

Williamson, George. *Milton & Others.* Chicago: University of Chicago Press, 1965.

_____. *A Reader's Guide to T. S. Eliot: A Poem-by-Poem Analysis.* New York: Farrar, Straus & Giroux, 1953.

_____. *Seventeenth Century Contexts.* London: Farber and Farber, 1960.

_____. Rev. ed. Chicago: University of Chicago Press, 1969.

_____. *Six Metaphysical Poets: A Reader's Guide.* New York: Farrar, Straus & Giroux, 1967.

Wilson, Edmund. *Axel's Castle: A Study in the Imaginative Literature of 1870-1930.* New York: Charles Scribner's Sons, 1948.

Wimsatt, W. K. *Day of the Leopards: Essays in Defense of Poems.* New Haven: Yale University Press, 1976.

_____. *The Verbal Icon: Studies in the Meaning of Poetry.* Lexington: University of Kentucky Press, 1954.

_____. *What to Say About a Poem.* CEA Chap Book. (CEA Critic, v. 26, no. 3, December 1963 Suppl.) Saratoga Springs, N.Y.: College English Association, 1963.

Winters, Yvor. *The Anatomy of Nonsense.* Norfolk, Conn.: New Directions, 1943.

_____. *The Function of Criticism: Problems and Exercises.* Denver: Alan Swallow, 1957.

_____. *In Defense of Reason.* New York: Swallow Press & William Morrow & Co., 1947.

_____. 3rd ed. Denver: Alan Swallow, 1957.

_____. *Maule's Curse: Seven Studies in the History of American Obscurantism: Hawthorne, Cooper, Melville, Poe, Emerson, Jones Very, Emily Dickinson, Henry James.* Norfolk, Conn.: New Directions, 1938.

_____. *Primitivism and Decadence: A Study of American Experimental Poetry.* New York: Arrow Editions, 1937.

Woodhouse, A. S. P. *The Poet and His Faith: Religion and Poetry in England from Spenser to Eliot and Auden.* Chicago: University of Chicago Press, 1965.

Wormhoudt, Arthur. *The Demon Lover: A Psychoanalytical Approach to Literature.* New York: Exposition Press, 1949.

Yeats, W. B. *Essays.* New York: Macmillan, 1924.

JOURNALS

Accent, vol. 20(1960).
American Imago, vols. 17(1960)–35(1978).
American Literary Realism, vols. 1(1967/8)–11(1978).
American Literature, vols. 31(1959/60)–50(1978/9).
American Notes & Queries, n.s., vols. 1(1962/3)–
  17(1978/9).
American Quarterly, vols. 12(1960)–30(1978).
American Scholar, vols. 39(1959/60)–48(1978/9).
American Transcendental Quarterly, no. 1(1969)–40(1978).
Anglo-Saxon England, vols. 1(1972)–6(1978).
Antioch Review, vols. 19(1959/60)–36(1978).
Ariel: a Review of International Literature, vols. 1(1970)–
  9(1978).
Arizona Quarterly, vols. 16(1960)–34(1978).
Arlington Quarterly, vols. 1(1967/8)–2(1969/70).
Atlantic Monthly, vols. 205(1960)–244(1978).

Ball State Teachers College Forum, vols. 1(1960)–6(1965).
Ball State University Forum, vols. 6(1965)–19(1978).
Black American Literature Forum, vols. 10(1976)–12(1978).
Blake: An Illustrated Quarterly, vols. 11(1977/8)–
  12(1978/9).
Blake Newsletter, vols. 1(1967)–10(1976/7).
Boundary 2, vols. 1(1972/3)–7(1978/9).
Browning Newsletter, no. 1(1968)–8/9(1972).
Browning Society Notes, vols. 1(1970/1)–8(1978).
Bucknell Review, vols. 9(1960/1)–24(1978).
Bulletin of Research in the Humanities, vol. 81(1978).

CEA Critic, vols. 22(1960)–41(1978/9).
CLA Journal, vols. 3(1959/60)–22(1978/9).
Carleton Miscellany, vols. 1(1960)–19(1978).
Catholic World, vols. 190(1960)–213(1971).
Centennial Review, vols. 4(1960)–22(1978).
Chaucer Review, vols. 1(1966/7)–13(1978/9).
Chicago Review, vols. 13(1959/60)–30(1978/9).
Clio, vols. 1(1971/2)–8(1978/9).
College English, vols. 21(1959/60)–40(1978/9).
Colorado Quarterly, vols. 8(1959/60)–27(1978/9).
Commentary, vols. 29(1960)–65(1978).
Comparative Literature, vols. 12(1960)–30(1978).
Concerning Poetry, vols. 1(1968)–10(1978).
Contemporary Literature, vols. 9(1968)–19(1978).
Critic, vols. 18(1959/60)–37(1978/9).
Critical Quarterly, vols. 1(1959)–20(1978).
Criticism, vols. 1(1959)–20(1978).

D. H. Lawrence Review, vols. 1(1968)–11(1978).
Dalhousie Review, vols. 40(1960/61)–58(1978/9).
Dickinson Studies, vol. 34(1978).
Durham University Journal, n.s., vols. 26(1964/5)–
  40(1978/9).

ELH, vols. 27(1960)–45(1978).
ESQ, vols. 18(1972)–24(1978).
Eighteenth Century Studies, nos. 1(1967/8)–12(1978/9).
Emerson Society Quarterly, nos. 18(1960)–65(1971).
Emily Dickinson Bulletin, nos. 1(1968)–33(1978).
Encounter, vols. 14(1960)–51(1978).
English Journal, vols. 49(1960)–67(1978).
English Language Notes, vols. 1(1963/4)–16(1978/9).
English Literary Renaissance, vols. 1(1971)–8(1978).
English Literature in Transition, vols. 3(1960)–21(1978).

Essays and Studies, vols. 13(1960)–31(1978).
Essays by Divers Hands, vols. 30(1960)–39(1977).
Essays in Criticism, vols. 10(1960)–28(1978).
Essays in Literature, vols. 1(1974)–5(1978).
Explicator, vols. 18(1959/60)–37(1978/9).

Focus on Robert Graves, vols. 1(1972)–5(1976).

Genre, vols. 1(1968)–11(1978).
Georgia Review, vols. 14(1960)–32(1978).

Hibbert Journal, vols. 58(1959/60)–66(1967/8).
Hollins Critic, vols. 1(1964)–15(1977).
Hopkins Quarterly, vols. 1(1974/5)–5(1978/9).
Hudson Review, vols. 12(1959/60)–31(1978/9).
Huntington Library Quarterly, vols 23(1959/60)–42(1978/9).

Iowa Review, vols. 1(1970)–9(1978).

John Berryman Studies, vols. 1(1975)–4(1978).
Journal of Aesthetics and Art Criticism, vols. 18(1959/60)–
  37(1978/9).
Journal of American Studies, vols. 1(1967)–12(1978).
Journal of English and Germanic Philology, vols. 59
  (1960)–77(1978).
Journal of Modern Literature, vols. 1(1970/1)–6(1977).
Journal of the History of Ideas, vols. 21(1960)–39(1978).

Keats-Shelley Journal, vols. 9(1960)–27(1978).
Kenyon Review, vols. 22(1960)–32(1970).

Literature & Psychology, vols. 10(1960)–28(1978).
Literature East and West, vols. 4(1960)–22(1978).
London Quarterly and Holborn Review, vols. 29(1960)–
  37(1968).

MLN, vols. 77(1962)–93(1978).
Massachusetts Review, vols. 1(1959/60)–19(1978).
Michigan Quarterly Review, vols. 1(1962)–17(1978).
Midwest Quarterly, vols. 1(1959/60)–20(1978/9).
Milton Quarterly, vols. 1(1967)–12(1978).
Milton Studies, vols. 1(1969)–9(1978).
Minnesota Review, vols. 1(1960/1)–11(1973); n.s., nos.
  1(1973)–11(1978).
Mississippi Quarterly, vols. 13(1959/60)–32(1978/9).
Modern Language Notes, vols. 75(1960)–76(1961).
Modern Language Quarterly, vols. 21(1960)–39(1978).
Modern Language Review, vols. 55(1960)–73(1978).
Modern Philology, vols. 57(1959/60)–76(1978/9).
Modern Poetry Studies, vols. 1(1970/1)–9(1978/9).

Negro American Literature Forum, vols. 1(1967)–10(1976).
New Catholic World, vols. 214(1971)–221(1978).
New England Quarterly, vols. 33(1960)–51(1978).
New Letters, vols. 38(1971/2)–45(1978/9).
New York Public Library Bulletin, vols. 64(1960)–
  80(1976/7).
Notes & Queries, n.s., vols. 7(1960)–25(1978).
Notes on Contemporary Literature, vols. 1(1971)–8(1978).
Notes on Modern American Literature, vols. 1(1976/7)–
  3(1978/9).

Ohio Review, vols. 13(1971/2)–19(1978).
Ohio University Review, vols. 1(1959)–12(1970).

PMLA, vols. 75(1960)–93(1978).

Papers on Language and Literature, vols. 1(1965)–14(1978).
Partisan Review, vols. 27(1960)–45(1978).
Personalist, vols. 41(1960)–59(1978).
Perspective, vols. 12(1960/2)–18(1976/78).
Philological Quarterly, vols. 39(1960)–57(1978).
Phylon, vols. 21(1960)–39(1978).
Prairie Schooner, vols. 34(1960)–52(1978/9).
Psychoanalytic Review, vols. 46(1959/60)–65(1978/9).

Queen's Quarterly, vols. 66(1959/60)–85(1978/9).

Renaissance Quarterly, vols. 13(1960)–31(1978).
Renascence, vols. 12(1959/60)–31(1978/9).
Review of English Literature, vols. 1(1960)–8(1967).
Review of English Studies, vols. 11(1960)–n.s., vol. 29(1978).

Saturday Review, vols. 43(1960)–55(1972); vols. 3(1975/6)- -6(1978/9).
Saturday Review World, vols. 1(1963/4)–2(1974/5).
Scrutiny, vols. 17(1960)–20(1963).
Sewanee Review, vols. 68(1960)–86(1978).
Shakespeare Newsletter, vols. 10(1960)–28(1978).
Shakespeare Quarterly, vols. 11(1960)–29(1978).
Shakespeare Studies, vols. 1(1965)–14(1978).
Shakespeare Survey, vols. 13(1960)–31(1978).
South Atlantic Quarterly, vols. 54(1960)–77(1978).
South Carolina Review, vols. 1(1968/9)–11(1978/9).
South Dakota Review, vols. 1(1964)–15(1978).
Southern Quarterly, vols. 1(1960/1)–17(1978/9).
Southern Review, n.s., vols. 1(1965)–14(1978).
Studies in Browning and His Circle, vols. 1(1973)–6(1978).
Studies in English Literature, 1500-1900, vols. 1(1961)–18(1978).
Studies in Philology, vols. 57(1960)–75(1978).
Studies in Romanticism, vols. 1(1961/2)–17(1978).
Studies in Scottish Literature, vols. 1(1963/4)–13(1978).

Studies in the Humanities, vols. 1(1969/70)–7(1978/9).
Studies in the Literary Imagination, vols. 1(1968)–11(1978).
Studies in the Renaissance, vols. 7(1960)–21(1974).

T. S. Eliot Newsletter, vol. 1(1974).
T. S. Eliot Review, vols. 2(1975)–4(1977).
Tennessee Studies in Literature, vols. 5(1960)–23(1978).
Texas Studies in Literature and Language, vols. 1 (1959/60) –20(1978).
Thoreau Journal Quarterly, vols. 1(1969)–10(1978).
Thoreau Society Newsletter, nos. 12(1960)–145(1978).
Thoth, vols. 1(1959/60)–16(1975/6).
Tulane Studies in English, vols. 12(1960)–30(1978).
Twentieth Century Literature, vols. 5(1959/60)–24(1978).

University of Kansas City Review, vols. 27(1959/60)–29(1962/3).
University of Toronto Quarterly, vols. 29(1959/60)–48(1978/9).
University Review, vols. 30(1963/4)–37(1970/1).

Victorian Newsletter, nos. 17(1960)–55(1978).
Victorian Poetry, vols. 1(1963)–16(1978).
Victorian Studies, vols. 3(1959/60)–22(1978/9).
Virginia Quarterly Review, vols. 36(1960)–54(1978).

Wallace Stevens Journal, vols. 1(1977)–2(1978).
Walt Whitman Review, vols. 6(1960)–24(1978).
Western Humanities Review, vols. 14(1960)–32(1978).
Wisconsin Studies in Contemporary Literature, vols. 1(1960)–8(1967).
Women and Literature, vols. 3(1975)–6(1978).
Wordsworth Circle, vols. 1(1970)–8(1978).

Yale Review, vols. 49(1959/60)–68(1978/9).
Yeats/Eliot Review, vol. 5(1978).